ERNEST BEVIN
FOREIGN SECRETARY
1945–1951

ERNEST BEVIN

FOREIGN SECRETARY

1945–1951

Alan Bullock

W. W. NORTON & COMPANY
NEW YORK   LONDON

ISBN 0-393-01825-3

Photoset in Great Britain by
Rowland Phototypesetting Ltd, Bury St Edmunds, Suffolk
and printed by St Edmundsbury Press
Bury St Edmunds, Suffolk

Contents

List of Illustrations

Acknowledgements

I wish to thank: Lady Dixon and Mr Piers Dixon, MP, for permission to quote from the diaries of the late Sir Pierson Dixon; Miss Ivy Saunders for permission to quote from letters from Mr Bevin in her possession; Lady Younger for permission to quote from the diaries of the late Sir Kenneth Younger, and Professor Geoffrey Warner for making available to me a transcript of them.

Grateful acknowledgement is made for permission to quote the following copyright material: George Weidenfeld & Nicolson Ltd (*Attlee* by Kenneth Harris and *The Memoirs of Lord Gladwyn*); Victor Gollancz Ltd and John Farquharson Ltd (*In My Way* by Lord George-Brown); William Collins Sons & Co Ltd and Doubleday & Co Ltd (*Memoirs* by Jean Monnet); Hamish Hamilton Ltd (*Sketches from Life of Men I have Known* by Dean Acheson); Hughes Massie Ltd and W. W. Norton Inc (*Present at the Creation* by Dean Acheson); Faber & Faber Ltd and Alfred A. Knopf Inc (*Modern British Politics* (American edition: *British Politics in the Collectivist Age*) by Samuel H. Beer); William Heinemann Ltd and Consolidated Publishing Corporation (*A Prime Minister Remembers* by Francis Williams); Frederick Muller Ltd (*High Tide and After* by Hugh Dalton); Victor Gollancz Ltd and Harold Matson Co (*The Private Papers of Senator Vandenberg* ed. by Arthur H. Vandenberg Jr); Sir Roderick Barclay (*Ernest Bevin and the Foreign Office 1932–69*).

Abbreviations

AAC:	Anglo-American Committee of Inquiry into the Problems of European Jewry and Palestine
ACC:	4-Power Allied Control Council for Germany
APW Committee:	Armistice and Post War Committee of the Cabinet
CDU:	German Christian Democratic Party
CFM:	Council of Foreign Ministers
CIGS:	Chief of the Imperial General Staff
CO:	Colonial Office
COS:	Chiefs of Staff
EAC:	European Advisory Commission
EAM:	Greek National Liberation Front
ECA:	Economic Cooperation Administration (US)
ELAS:	Greek National People's Liberation Army
ERP:	European Recovery Programme (US)
FO:	Foreign Office
GATT:	General Agreement on Tariffs and Trade
HC:	House of Commons
HMG:	His Majesty's Government
ILO:	International Labour Office
JA:	Jewish Agency
KKE:	Greek Communist Party
LP:	Labour Party
MAP:	Military Assistance Programme (US)
MRP:	Mouvement Republicain Populaire (France)
NEC:	National Executive Committee of the Labour Party
NSC:	National Security Council (US)
NUM:	National Union of Mineworkers
PCI:	Italian Communist Party

PLP:	Parliamentary Labour Party
POWs	Prisoners of War
PPS:	Principal Private Secretary
PSI:	Italian Socialist Party
SED:	German Socialist Unity Party
SPD:	German Socialist Party
SWNCC:	State War Navy (Departments) Coordinating Committee (US)
TGWU:	Transport & General Workers' Union
TUC:	Trades Union Congress
UNAEC:	UN Atomic Energy Commission
UNSCOB:	United Nations Special Committee on the Balkans
UNSCOP:	United Nations Special Committee on Palestine
WEU:	Western European Union
WFTU:	World Federation of Trade Unions

A note on abbreviations used in the footnotes (for fuller details see the section on Sources & Bibliography, pp. 858–69).

CM 34 (46):	Cabinet Minutes, 34th meeting in the year 1946.
CP (46) 34:	Cabinet Papers, 34th in the series for the year 1946.
DO (46):	Defence Committee minutes and papers for the year 1946.
FO 371:	The general political files of the Foreign Office.
FO 800:	The Bevin Papers.
FRUS:	*Foreign Relations of the United States*, the multi-volume series of US government papers.
HC:	House of Commons, Hansard.
RIIA:	Royal Institute of International Affairs (Chatham House).
Dalton:	Where quotations are taken from those parts of Hugh Dalton's diaries and papers used in his *Memoirs*, a page reference is given. Where quotations are taken from the unpublished parts of his diaries and papers, they are cited as Dalton's diaries, with the date of the entry or paper.
Dixon:	The diaries of Sir Pierson Dixon. Where quotations are taken from those parts of the diaries used in Piers Dixon's life of his father, *Double Diploma*, the reference is given as Piers Dixon, with the page number. Where they are taken from the unpublished parts of the diaries, they are cited as Dixon's diary, with the date of the entry.
Vol. I:	Volume I of *The Life and Times of Ernest Bevin, Trade Union Leader 1881–1940*.
Vol. II:	Volume II of *The Life and Times of Ernest Bevin, Minister of Labour 1940–1945*.

Preface

This book is the last volume of a political biography of Ernest Bevin and at the same time a free-standing study of British foreign policy from 1945 to 1951. Obviously an account of the final phase of Bevin's career, when he held the office of Foreign Secretary, must be largely concerned with foreign policy, but I have gone beyond the biographical to take a wider historical approach and I have written this volume on a larger scale than the other two. I have chosen to do this for several reasons.

The first is the wealth of the original material on which I have been able to draw. The heart of it is the collection, now in the Public Record Office, known as the Bevin papers, here used for the first time. These are in fact the working files kept by Bevin's Principal Private Secretary in his Private Office, and they contain not only private papers in the form, for example, of personal notes exchanged between Bevin and Attlee, but a large number of official papers selected over his five and a half years in office as those most important to keep easily available for reference and the conduct of business.

In addition, then, to their intrinsic interest, the Bevin papers provide an invaluable guide into the intimidating mass of material deposited in the Public Record Office from the Cabinet offices (including the records of Cabinet Committees such as the Defence Committee, as well as of the Cabinet itself) and from the Foreign Office. Use has already been made of this material for a number of studies dealing with particular aspects of British foreign relations; now, with the help of the Bevin papers, it has been possible to draw on this larger collection of British government records to provide the first over-all study, based on original sources, of British policy after the war.

The British records have in turn made it possible for me to make extensive use of the great collection of American state papers published in the massive volumes of the *Foreign Relations of the United States*, an invaluable additional source for Anglo–US relations but one only marginally exploited so far for the view it provides of British policy.

Rich source material would not by itself justify a volume of this length, if the transactions on which the evidence throws light were not of major importance. It would be hard to deny that description to the events of 1945–51, a period in which the framework of international relations was entirely re-made and which includes the first phase of the Cold War, the Marshall Plan, the North Atlantic Alliance, the division of Germany, the Schuman Plan, the creation of Israel, the independence of India and Pakistan, and the Korean War. Britain was deeply involved in all of these events and in the controversies which arose from them. But the material has not hitherto been available to make possible a clearer understanding of British policy, or indeed of the importance of the role the United Kingdom played—hardly less important, I suggest, in relation to the post-war settlement than that which she had played during the War itself.

The same is true of Bevin personally. He was hardly ever able to speak freely of the reasons for his decisions and neither by temperament nor by experience was he well equipped to explain his policy. As the *Manchester Guardian* wrily remarked, it was often when he was most interesting that he became most obscure.

It does not necessarily follow that the fresh light shed by the documents on British policy, or on Bevin's own attitude in particular cases, will silence criticism. I hope, however, while not disguising my own views, that I have provided the material on which a more fully-informed judgement can be made, whether it emerges as favourable or unfavourable. With this in mind I have frequently preferred to quote directly from, rather than to paraphrase, documents, even although this has meant adding to the length of the book.

The fact that close on twenty-five years separate the publication of the first from the last volume of this work is due to the fact that I have had to wait until thirty years after Bevin's death before his papers became available for use. The disadvantage is obvious: I have had to disappoint many people who admired Bevin and were naturally impatient to see me reach the final and most striking phase of his career.

On the other hand there have been advantages, certainly for the author, and I hope for the reader as well. One is that, knowing more than twenty years in advance that I should one day be writing about Ernie Bevin as Foreign Secretary as well as trade union leader, I was able to talk to many who were involved closely with him after the War, and whose recollections of him were still vivid, but many of the most valuable witnesses amongst whom have since died. These names, including those of Lord Attlee, Dean Acheson, Lewis Douglas, to mention only three, will be found in the note on sources at the end of the book.

The other advantage has been that of watching a period and a series of events of which I was myself a witness (I was thirty when Bevin became Foreign Secretary) slowly change and display new facets as the historical perspective has lengthened under my eyes. This is an instructive as well as a fascinating experience, and I hope that my account has gained from the fact that, although I have thought about the subject of my book for more than thirty years, it is only in the last two and a half that I have written the greater part of it.

In writing this book I have received much help for which I am deeply grateful.

In the Note on Sources I give a list of those who were good enough to let me put questions to them and to recall their experiences of Ernest Bevin. I offer my thanks to all of them for the trouble they went to in order to help me. I must express particular thanks for the continued interest they have taken in my book to Lord Franks; Miss Ivy Saunders; the late Lord Attlee; the late Dean Acheson, and the late Lord Strang.

It would be hard to exaggerate the debt I owe to two old friends and colleagues, R. R. A. Wheatley and W. F. Knapp. To my great benefit Miss Elizabeth Monroe invited me, years ago, to join her in interviewing those who had been most closely involved with Ernest Bevin over the question of Palestine. Irwin Herrmann over a long period has kept me informed of publications on the same controversial issue.

It is a particular pleasure to record the assistance I have received from Israeli scholars working in this field. I wish particularly to thank Dr Shabtai Teveth, the biographer of Ben Gurion; Mr Gaby Cohen, of Tel Aviv University; Dr Amikam Nachmani, of the Hebrew University of Jerusalem, and Mr Ilan Pappe, of St Antony's College, Oxford. Without their help I could not have made use of the material now becoming available from Israeli and Zionist sources. That help does not, of course, mean that they necessarily agree with my conclusions; but it has been gratifying to discover that it is possible for British and Israeli historians to engage in friendly discussion of this troubled period in Anglo-Jewish relations.

When I was working on the final draft of the sections of my book dealing with the Middle East, Professor Roger Louis, of the University of Texas, and Michael Cohen, of Bar-Ilan University, were good enough to make available to me in advance their own versions of the same events – Professor Louis in his *The British Empire in the Middle East*, to be published by the Oxford University Press in the spring of 1984, and Dr Cohen in his *Palestine and the Great Powers 1945–48*, published by the Princeton University Press in 1983. I have benefited greatly from their willingness to share the results of their researches with me.

I wish to express my thanks to the staff of the libraries and archives where I have worked: the Royal Institute of International Affairs (Chatham House); the Commonwealth Office Library and Research Department; the Public Record Office at Kew; the Bodleian Library, and the Rhodes House Library at Oxford.

When I gave up office as Master to devote my time to historical research and writing, the Fellows of St Catherine's generously elected me to a Fellowship which has enabled me to continue to work as a member of the College. For this privilege I am more grateful than I can say. To Joseph Slater, President of the Aspen Institute, I owe, besides much else, the opportunity to spend time as a scholar in residence at Aspen, Colorado, as I do to the Rockefeller Foundation for earlier visits to the Villa Serbelloni on Lake Como.

I have carried out the original research and reading for this book myself, but I was greatly helped at an early stage by Mrs Betsy Morgan who read extensively for me in Hansard and the press. At a later stage Miss R. Malyn, Mrs Jenny Surrey, Robert Hoveman, Peter Mandelson and Colin Greenstreet have given me assistance in filling gaps in my coverage of the same material. I am indebted to the Leverhulme Trust and to the Aspen Institute as well as to St Catherine's College for their help in meeting my research and secretarial expenses. Without the skill and patience of Mrs Pamela Thomas and Mrs Betty Willbery in deciphering and typing a confusing succession of barely legible drafts, there would have been no book to publish, and I am most grateful for their help.

I was fortunate to find in A. S. Frere a publisher who had spent much time in Ernest Bevin's company during the War as his Director of Public Relations at the Ministry of Labour. As Chairman of Heinemann's after the War he was eager to see Bevin's life written and was able to provide some fascinating reminiscences. I have been equally fortunate to find in Roland Gant a publisher who has never lost interest in the long-delayed completion of the work and who has himself acted as the editor of this final volume, bringing to it a wealth of experience from which I have greatly benefited. To my literary agent and friend, Andrew Best, of Curtis Brown, I owe the agility in negotiating contracts which enabled me to continue as an author and editor while occupied with administration and committees.

My greatest debt of all remains all that I owe to my wife Nibby to whom I renew the dedication of the earlier volumes as the dearest of companions and the most perceptive of critics.

St Catherine's College   Alan Bullock
Oxford
6 April 1983

NOTE

Inflation since 1945–50 means that the figures quoted in the text can easily give a misleading impression of values in terms of today's prices. As a rough guide for a comparison with today (1983), figures in the text should be multiplied by a factor of between 8 and 10.

PART I

Where Bevin Came In

CHAPTER 1

The World in the Summer of 1945

I

On the afternoon of Saturday 28 July 1945, Clement Attlee and Ernie Bevin set out from Northolt Aerodrome for Berlin. After an electoral victory which had ousted Churchill and astonished the world they had become respectively Prime Minister and Foreign Secretary of the first Labour Government ever to command a majority in the House of Commons. Now they were on their way to Potsdam to take the place of Churchill and Eden in the last of the "Big Three" conferences.

At the age of 64 Bevin was making his first journey out of the United Kingdom since the beginning of the War. After a lifetime's experience in dealing with industrial and economic problems, he was on his way to take part for the first time in an international conference which was to settle the pattern of post-war relations between the Great Powers. There was no sign that the prospect disturbed him although less than twenty-four hours before he drove out to Northolt Bevin had believed he was going to the Treasury, and the Foreign Office had expected that Dalton would succeed Eden as Foreign Secretary. It was only the previous afternoon that Attlee had finally decided to switch them and not until 9 p.m. that Bevin had called at the Foreign Office for an hour's briefing on the Conference. Pierson Dixon, his new private secretary, wrote in his diary that he "absorbed it all and said very little except, on parting, that he liked regular hours and found work better done and better decisions taken by work at day and not, like Winston, at night."[1]

Five years before, explaining his decision to accept the Ministry of Labour in Churchill's government, Bevin had told the Executive Committee of his union that this would give him "the chance to lay down the conditions on which we shall start again. . . . The Ministry of Labour can have the biggest say, next to the Foreign Office, in the Peace Treaties and the new economic arrangements

---

[1] Piers Dixon: *Double Diploma, The Life of Sir Pierson Dixon* (London 1968) p. 168.

3

that have got to be made."[1] Now, after more than fulfilling the role he had claimed for the Ministry of Labour, so far as domestic affairs were concerned, he had an unexpected chance to take over the Foreign Office. In a career which had taken him from a carter's round in Bristol to a seat in Churchill's war cabinet, no one had ever found Ernie Bevin lacking in confidence. He was to need it all in the five years that lay ahead.

The Labour Ministers came to power at a time which marked not only the end of the most destructive war in history, but the end of the international system within which, for more than four centuries, relations between European states had been contained. This system had been constantly threatened by the ambition of successive Powers to establish a dominant position, but no less constantly restored by the combination of the others to set limits to the threat. It had never been confined to Europe, since its origins coincided with the European powers' expansion overseas in the late fifteenth and sixteenth centuries; but the issue had always been the struggle for mastery in Europe itself. The renewal of imperial expansion overseas in the late 19th century, although it put an additional strain on it, did not destroy the system. What proved fatal was the rise of a European state, the German Empire, whose industrial and military power made possible a bid for hegemony on such a scale that it could no longer be contained by any purely European combination. Germany's victory, and with it the German domination of Europe after the defeat of Russia in 1917–18, were only prevented by the entry of the United States into the war.

Germany's defeat in 1918, however, and the peace settlement which followed were not decisive. Without American support, withdrawn in 1920, Britain and France proved unable to maintain the European balance of power which the peace treaties had been designed to restore, and Germany's second attempt to win the mastery of Europe required an even greater effort, from Russia, the USA and Britain combined, to frustrate it.

This time the German defeat was final: Germany was not just weakened, as in 1919, but destroyed as a state. The result, however, was not to restore a balance of power in Europe but to leave a vacuum, with no agreement at all between the victorious allies about how it was to be filled.

No other state in modern times had been so closely identified with the principle of maintaining a balance of power in Europe as Britain. With no ambition to dominate the continent themselves, the British had fought a succession of wars to prevent anyone else from doing so—the Hapsburgs, Louis XIV, Napoleon and finally, twice, the Germans. If Germany's defeat was not followed by the restoration of a stable balance of power in Europe; if some other Power such as Russia now succeeded in establishing the dominant position which, after six years of bitter fighting had been denied to Germany, then it could be argued that the British would have failed to secure the most

[1] Vol. I, p. 653.

4

important objective—after their own survival as an independent nation—for which they had fought the war.

This was not, however, the way in which the case for fighting, even in 1914–18, still less in 1939–45, had been presented to the British or the American people. Their support for the war had been sought and secured as a struggle between the forces of good and the forces of evil, with the latter of which Hitler's Nazi regime could be very convincingly identified. The "aggressor nations", to use the phraseology of the time, were confronted by the "peace-loving nations", who had been reluctantly persuaded to take up arms as a moral crusade to defend freedom against despotism. The calculations of power politics were seen as part of the evil against which the war was being fought in order to replace them by the alternative of an international organization based on justice and fair-dealing between states. This was true not only of American opinion but of majority opinion in the UK as well, certainly of opinion in the Labour Party which had now taken over the responsibilities of government. After five years in the War Cabinet, Bevin and Attlee did not need to be told that the calculations of power politics were not got rid of as easily as party conference resolutions might suggest, and that the alternative in practice to creating a new balance of power might well be having to live with an unbalance. But they had also to take account of the strength of Labour feeling in favour of breaking with such traditional concepts of foreign policy as national interests, balance of power and spheres of influence, and of using the opportunity of the peace settlement to put into practice a distinctive socialist view of international relations.

The danger of a split in the Labour Party over foreign policy was compounded by the care which the Coalition Government had taken during the War to play down disagreements between the Allies. The result was a widespread popular expectation that, with victory in Europe, the dangers which had clouded people's lives for so long would be removed and the nation could forget about foreign affairs, leaving to the "Big Three", the British, American and Soviet Governments, the much easier task of arranging the peace settlement now that the really difficult job of winning the war had been brought to a successful end.

The prospect of Allied disagreements was of more consequence to Britain than either of her Allies since it was already clear—to the Americans and Russians as well as to her own leaders—that she would have the greatest difficulty in pursuing a policy of her own, without the support of at least one of the other two. An independent policy was an option open to the Americans and, as events were to show, to the Russians as well; but it was not open to the British, whose military strength by the end of the war was no longer equal to that of either of her allies with their much larger populations and territories. This consideration had borne heavily on Churchill in the last year of the war when he had frequently found himself at odds with either Stalin or the Americans, sometimes with both, and had to swallow his doubts or be satisfied with a protest rather than run the risk of pushing disagreement to a confrontation. Once the fighting stopped, the decline in Britain's power became more obvious and with it the need to avoid becoming isolated, particularly if it was at the expense of seeing the two Super-Powers (a newly-coined term) reach agreement without her.

The attitude of *both* their allies presented difficult problems to the British, and these need to be considered separately.

2

Bevin and Attlee, like Churchill, recognized in principle that Russia would now claim, and could not be denied, the place in European and world politics from which she had been excluded between the wars; that her claim to greater security on her western frontiers could not be resisted either in equity or in fact; and that it was essential to reach agreement with her if there was to be any satisfactory settlement of the future of Germany and if they were to avoid the division of Europe into hostile camps with the threat of a third war.

This was all very well in principle but in practice when Bevin and Attlee met Stalin at Potsdam, they were again stepping into a historical situation in which attitudes were powerfully charged by what had gone before.

The history of the Russian state from the time of Ivan the Great[1] has been one of steady and continuing expansion. Unlike the overseas expansion of the Western European powers (which also began at the same time) Russia's was overland and had much more of a defensive character, the search for defensible frontiers—or at least the protection of space—in the vast featureless plains stretching from the Baltic to the Caspian and the Aral Sea. The other side of the picture, providing the justification both for her expansion and for the suspicion with which Russia's rulers viewed the outside world, was Russia's vulnerability to attack and the number of times she had been invaded. The burning of Moscow in the face of Napoleon's invasion and the defeat of the French at Borodino was one of the greatest events of Russian history (its memory kept alive by Tolstoy's *War and Peace*), and it was followed by the German attack in World War I, leading to the collapse of the Russian state and the loss of virtually all the territory acquired since the reign of Peter the Great (1689–1725). This in turn had been followed by a second attack in 1941 which brought German tanks within sight of Moscow and held Leningrad under siege for seventeen months.

The expansion, however, which the Russians saw as a natural search for greater security appeared to their European neighbours as aggrandisement. Thus the Tsar's renewal of the partitions of Poland, which nineteenth-century liberals branded as a crime, was the natural sequel in Russian eyes to the

[1] Ivan reigned from 1462 to 1505, the same epoch in which the earliest version of the classical European state system began to take shape.

6

defeat of Napoleon's invasion. In the same way, the Nazi–Soviet Pact, which the West denounced as cynical power politics, was regarded by Stalin as his greatest diplomatic coup, not only guaranteeing Russia against a German invasion but securing the recovery of a large part of the territory lost to the Poles and others in 1917–21. Stalin's minimum terms in 1945 were the recognition by his allies of Russia's right to retain the gains which he had made as a result of the Nazi–Soviet Pact and which the Red Army had since recovered.

A second obstacle to better relations between Russia and the West between the wars had been the fact that the Bolsheviks had not only revolutionized Russian society but made Moscow the headquarters of an international revolutionary movement. It was hard to know how far this would still be important after the war. It could be argued that Stalin's willingness to sign a pact with the Devil in the form of Hitler showed that, when there was a conflict between Russia's national interests and those of world revolution, Stalin would not hesitate to subordinate the second to the first, a logical enough extension of the policy of "Socialism in one country". And there were many in Britain (and not only in the Labour Party, as the attitude of *The Times* demonstrated) who believed, or at least hoped, that the dissolution of the Comintern in 1943 and the playing up of nationalism in wartime propaganda meant that diplomatic relations with the Soviet Government would no longer be complicated by clandestine relations between Moscow and Communist parties in other countries.

While these hopes proved to be illusory, looking back from the safe distance of the 1980s it is possible to recognize that Stalin avoided anything like the indiscriminate appeal for revolution which Moscow made after the First World War, and that far from encouraging, he intervened to restrain those in the Communist parties of France and Italy who argued in favour of seizing power. Instead, he urged them to enter national coalitions with the bourgeois parties and build up Communist strength in the administration where they could obstruct any anti-Soviet line of policy such as the creation of a Western European bloc.

From his own point of view, Stalin's reasons were sound enough. A Communist attempt to take power in France or Italy while large British and American forces were still stationed there would not only invite immediate suppression, but would provoke a reaction which might well compromise the Russian take-over of Eastern Europe (under cover of National Fronts and anti-Fascist coalitions) and increase Western resistance to Russia's claim to reparations from Germany. Nor was Stalin at all eager to see Communist regimes set up outside the range of his control, as the Yugoslavs discovered, to their dismay and the West's astonishment.

But it was not at all easy to recognize this at the time, as the Russians occupied one country after another and the Red Army pushed forward to a line two thirds of the way from the Russian frontier to the English Channel.

Conditions in Europe appeared to favour the chances of a revolutionary seizure of power as much in the early years after the Second World War as they had after the First. With the Resistance emerging into the open; with much talk of a swing to the Left in Europe, and widespread expectation of a possible attempt to seize power in half a dozen countries from Belgium to Greece, the historical myth of Revolutionary Russia was more powerful than ever, strengthened by the victories of the Red Army and the advance into Europe. Stalin might never hesitate in practice to subordinate the interests of "the Revolution" to Russia's national interests or those of his own position, but he was careful to do nothing overtly to repudiate the identification of the Soviet Union with the revolutionary hopes of the Left, an identification which added greatly to the length of the shadow Russia cast on the international scene. As a result, even those in the West who suspected that Stalin was neither a revolutionary idealist nor a doctrinaire Marxist but a hardened and cynical politician, could not afford to ignore the advantages which he derived from Russia's revolutionary image: a "Russian" party in every country—in France and Italy a mass party attracting millions of votes—providing a receptive audience for Soviet propaganda and a potential fifth column weakening and confusing resistance to Soviet pressure.

Nor should one underestimate the extent to which the view of the world shared by Stalin and the ruling group in Russia was coloured by the assumptions of Marxist-Leninist thought, in particular the belief that conflict between the Soviet Union and the capitalist world was in the long run inevitable. Such a conflict was not seen as the result of the policies pursued by either side but as determined by the historical pattern of economic and social development, which guaranteed victory to the Soviet Union in the long run through the self-destructive contradictions of capitalism. This was a set of beliefs which left plenty of room for tactical manoeuvring on the Russian side but presented a formidable obstacle to anyone seeking to find some basis for the accommodation of conflicting power interests which would give the long-suffering peoples of Europe and Asia a chance of peace.

A third obstacle to such an accommodation with Russia was presented by a further characteristic of the Soviet regime, besides its identification with the Communist movement and its Marxist-Leninist ideology: the fact that it was a dictatorship. The urbanity and confidence with which Stalin conducted his relations with Churchill and Roosevelt at Teheran and Yalta were misleading. The basis of his power was very different from theirs, the result of a naked struggle in which Stalin's opponents and even potential rivals had been eliminated and in most cases put to death. The system had been consolidated by the establishment of a police state, the built-in principles of which were universal distrust and systematic repression. Stalin's first concern in all his actions, never absent from his mind, was the preservation of his own position and the system of totalitarian rule with which he had buttressed it.

The personal characteristics of the dictator were as important as "the sinister dynamics"[1] of the system he had created. Stalin was a very different man from Hitler; he was not a gambler nor did he share Hitler's fanatical belief in intuition, his special mission and the power of the will to carry it out. But he was every bit as ruthless as Hitler and he shared with him the same Hobbesian view of human history as a war of all against all. His daughter wrote of him that "he sees enemies everywhere", and Krushchev said that, after the War, "Stalin became even more capricious, irritable and brutal; in particular his suspicion grew. His persecution mania reached unbelievable dimensions." Stalin's distrust was absolute and applied as much to foreign as to domestic affairs. No foreign statesman any more than his own associates could penetrate it. Stalin did not make a distinction between Britain, the USA and Hitler's Germany. Any foreign power was to be regarded as an enemy, and the object of Stalin's diplomacy was to keep them divided, in 1939 by an alliance with Hitler (for which Stalin had been eager), later by accepting (with suspicion) the alliance which the British and Americans offered him.

Such an attitude made highly improbable, if it did not rule out altogether, any "normalization" of international relations as much as the "liberalization" of relations between government and people. Such concepts and the idea that it might be possible to modify or overcome the Soviet Government's distrust by offers of friendship or gestures of goodwill belonged to a different world. The same difference is illustrated by the elaborate measures taken to prevent any contact, however innocent, between the Russian people and the world outside, measures which included sending to labour camps millions of returning soldiers, prisoners of war, and workers conscripted by the Germans whose sole offence was that they had spent time abroad and were therefore automatically regarded with suspicion by the security police. It could hardly be made plainer that a policy which involved even the most limited relations with the people of any other country was regarded as a danger to the Soviet regime.

Stalin had justified the brutal measures taken to strengthen his hold on power in the 1930s by the dangers pressing upon the Soviet Union from the hostile world outside its borders. These dangers, it was soon made clear to the Russian people, had not been removed by the defeat of Hitler. The image of a beleaguered camp surrounded by hostile powers, was refurbished after the war to meet the needs of a regime that depended upon a permanent state of crisis to maintain its powers and justify the new demands it had to make upon the Russian people. Even if Stalin had not seen an obvious advantage in exploiting the situation at the end of the war to expand Soviet power to the maximum extent compatible with avoiding the risk of open confrontation with the USA, his freedom to choose alternative courses of policy, in particular the alternative of collaboration with the West, was limited by the logic of the system of government on which he relied to rule Russia.

[1] Arthur Schlesinger's phrase: "The Origins of the Cold War", *Foreign Affairs* Vol. 46, No. 1, October 1967, p. 49.

The strongest support for the opposite view, even if at times it appears to be inadvertent, has come from American revisionist historians whose primary thesis has been that it was the US Government which attempted to impose on its Allies as well as a defeated Germany its own plans for the post-war world and so was responsible for turning the wartime alliance with the USSR into the Cold War. In place of the orthodox American version that it was only with reluctance that the USA reacted to the aggressive attitude of Communist Russia, the revisionists substitute its mirror-image, that of a Soviet Union, exhausted by the War and driven to defend its national interests in reaction to the aggressive attitude of a United States which had emerged as the strongest state in the world and which was determined to use that strength to enforce a post-war settlement that would suit the interests of a liberal-capitalist America.

The revisionists, however, having exploded the idea that American policy was simply a reaction to the threat of Communism—which no one outside the United States ever thought—have fallen into the same trap themselves in treating Russian policy as simply a reaction to American imperialism. It is possible to argue that it would have been in the United States' own interests to make a reconstruction loan to the Soviet Union after the War; not to oppose the Russian claim to reparations from Germany, and even to share the secrets of the atomic bomb. But it is quite a different matter to go on and assume that, if the USA had done so, it would have changed the course of Soviet policy. It is at least as plausible to argue that Stalin would have continued to pursue the same objectives and not have allowed himself to be diverted. Soviet policy had historical roots and followed a logic of its own which was not dependent on the attitude of the United States, whether hostile or friendly.

There is no need to postulate a "blueprint" or "timetable" for Soviet expansion or world revolution. What Stalin had in mind from the beginning was a minimum programme; anything beyond that would depend on the circumstances in which the war ended. The minimum, expressed to Eden in Moscow as early as 16 December, 1941, not much more than a week after the Russian counter-attack had halted the German advance, sought recognition by Russia's allies of the territorial gains of 1939–41 which had wiped out most of the losses of the Treaty of Brest-Litovsk, the Paris Peace Conference and the Treaty of Riga. Having failed to secure their agreement, Stalin did not abandon his minimum but waited until he could secure it without asking anyone's leave. His moment came in 1944. Between the summer of that year and the spring of 1945, the Russian armies not only recovered the gains of 1939–41 by force of arms, but drove on to the Elbe in the West and the borders of Greece and Turkey in the South, occupying Rumania, Bulgaria, Poland, Hungary, Czechoslovakia and substantial parts of Germany and Austria, including both capitals, Berlin and Vienna. These sensational advances, added to the price the Americans were prepared to pay—at others' expense —to secure the Soviet Union as an ally in the Far Eastern War, opened up a prospect wider than ever before in Russian history. That Stalin was well aware of the historical continuity is shown by his insistence that the price for Russia's entry into the war against Japan must include the reversal of the terms imposed on Russia after her defeat in the Russo–Japanese war of 1904–5, and his later reference to the wiping out of this humiliation in his proclamations to the Russian people. Now, with Germany crushed, Poland occupied and France out of the reckoning; with Japan on the verge of defeat and China of civil war, there remained no power on the Eurasian continent which could set limits to Russian expansion, once the American armies withdrew.

Stalin, however, did not let himself be carried away by this glittering prospect. The essential thing was to extend the area of occupation by Russian troops as far as possible while the war was still going on and the alliance still held. Thus a costly effort was put into the occupation of the Balkans when the shortest route to Berlin lay through Poland: in Hungary in particular this cost many Russian lives when there was no apparent need to storm Budapest as if it were Stalingrad or Berlin. Bulgaria, again, had never been at war with Russia—the reason given for occupying Rumania when that country switched sides—but the moment the Bulgars asked the Western Powers for an armistice, the Russians declared war and occupied the whole of Bulgaria. They were to show themselves in an even greater hurry to take what had been promised them in the Far East. Manchuria, North Korea and Sakhalin were occupied without thought of casualties and without taking any notice of the Japanese surrender on 14 August.

How far and in what direction Stalin would be able to press his advantage beyond the control of Eastern Europe, neither he nor anyone else could foresee in the summer of 1945. He was well aware that if Britain had emerged weakened from the war, the USA had become the most powerful state in the world, too powerful for the USSR, which had suffered immense losses in the war, to consider challenging in direct confrontation. Stalin never seriously thought of war with the USA: the disparity of forces was too great.

But neither was Stalin seriously afraid of an American attack, as he had certainly been afraid earlier of a German attack. The evidence for this is the fact that the period when the United States possessed a monopoly of atomic weapons, 1945–1949, coincides with the period when the Soviet Union carried out the sovietization of Eastern Europe in defiance of American protests and was prepared to run the risks of trying to force the Western powers out of Berlin by the 1948 blockade. This is a record which hardly suggests fear of an imminent attack or even of atomic blackmail, that *deus ex machina* of revisionist historians. Nor did the Russians in 1945–47 hesitate to probe and test the Western will to resist, or alternatively its willingness to make concessions, along "the Northern Tier", from the Mediterranean to Iran, as well as in Europe.

In short while American power and, more important, American willingness to use it set limits to Russian expansion after the war, limits which Stalin never lost sight of, they were not the prime cause of Soviet foreign policy which pursued an independent course on its own initiative and not simply as a reaction to Western attitudes. As another American historian, Adam Ulam, remarks: "the simplest and most banal explanation is not necessarily wrong. The Soviet Union was bent upon expanding her sphere of power and influence but without incurring the risk of war."[1] To which one may add, in what earlier century would anyone have thought of looking for any explanation other than this?

3

The question which confronted Bevin and Attlee was what the British were to do in face of this situation: a war begun to prevent Germany dominating Europe ending with the danger that Russia would take her place. Since it had been in alliance with the United States that Britain had faced the earlier threat, this question led immediately to the second, what was the American view?

There was no doubt about the closeness of the wartime relationship between Britain and the United States. With the combined Chiefs of Staff and combined commands on the military side; the Combined Boards and Lend-Lease on the economic, and the unique correspondence between Churchill and Roosevelt, it was the most successful alliance in history. Churchill wished for nothing better than to see it continued into the postwar period.

The American Administration, however, had ideas of its own and although many of its members were personally friendly to the British, was determined not to let American post-war policy be shaped by Britain. Although the alliance held firm to the end of the war, the Americans chafed at the need always to pay attention to British views, particularly after the scale of the United States' contributions to the war outstripped their partner's. They had no intention of putting themselves in the same position after the fighting ended. Once the armistice was signed, the United States, under a new president, proceeded to disengage itself from the special relationship with the United Kingdom and re-assert the independence of American policy. This change was already in process when the Labour Government came into office and, if only because it was more unexpected, was hardly less disturbing for the British than the question of how they were to come to terms with the Soviet Union, particularly when the two were taken in combination.

The disasters in which the United States later became involved in South East Asia led a new generation of Americans to call in question the whole record of US foreign policy since World War II, and to examine the American

[1] Adam B. Ulam: *Expansion and Coexistence: The History of Soviet Foreign Policy 1917-67* (NY 1968) p. 404.

role when the war ended for the origins of the course which led to defeat and humiliation in Vietnam. The revisionist debate showed an obsessive tendency to focus on American policy, as if this by itself determined the pattern of the post-war world, and the more extreme views to which it gave rise at the height of the controversy have failed to find general acceptance. Revisionism revised, however, still leaves a different view of American foreign policy from that popularly held in the USA in the late 1940s and 1950s. The biggest difference is recognition of the extent to which the US Government was not just reacting to the behaviour of other powers, especially the Russians, but had plans of its own and intended to use its unique position of strength at the end of the war to get them adopted. The British, it must be said, needed no revisionists to make this clear to them:[1] they had no difficulty in recognizing it at the time, even if the pressure which the Americans were prepared to put on their wartime allies came as a shock and took time to absorb.

American planning for the postwar world had set up two major objectives, one economic, the other political. The first, reflecting the strongly-held views of the American Secretary of State, Cordell Hull, as well as the interests of American business, was to create an international economy in which freedom of trade, of investment and of access to raw materials would no longer be impeded by trade and currency controls, and all the other protectionist devices of economic nationalism which Hull believed had powerfully contributed to the outbreak of the Second World War.

America's economic strength at the end of the war—when other nations would be clamouring for American aid—was seen as offering a unique opportunity to enforce such a policy. In doing so, the United States would be creating the best possible conditions both for economic recovery in the world at large and for the expansion of American trade on which—and on the avoidance of another Depression—depended the survival of the United States' own combination of capitalism and democracy at home. The belief in the natural coincidence of these objectives was as sincerely held by Americans as that between the welfare of the impoverished masses, revolution and the interests of the Soviet regime in Russia was by the Communists.

The economic planning had gone further but, in Roosevelt's eyes certainly, the political objective was more important. Unlike economic policy, which no one thought of extending to the Soviet Union and which could therefore largely be settled in talks between the Americans and British, Roosevelt's political objective was an international organization covering the whole world and therefore including the Soviet Union and the crucial issue of relations between the Russians and the Western Powers. On this new organization Americans focused their hopes of avoiding a repetition of the two world wars by providing a way of settling disputes between nations by peaceful means and mobilizing

---

[1] "Others, we find", writes the American A. W. de Porte, "have not seen us as we have seen ourselves, and at last neither do we." *Europe between the Super Powers* (New Haven 1979) p. 74.

overwhelming force against any state which threatened to resort to war. Roosevelt and Hull saw themselves completing the work which President Wilson had begun with the foundation of the League of Nations but which, partly through America's own default, he had failed to carry through to success. As Walter Rostow put it, the sort of world the USA looked forward to after World War II was essentially the one which would have been possible if everyone had acted more intelligently after World War I.[1]

The difference this time was that, behind the idealistic, moralistic and legal façade of the new United Nations Organization which corresponded to the strength of American liberal internationalist sentiment, Roosevelt built in a power structure firmly based on the realistic recognition that the wartime allies ("the four policemen", as Roosevelt called them, including China) had to take the responsibility for dealing with future threats to peace. If they were agreed, then the UNO would be effective and peace would be assured; if not, not. The same powers alone were to be given permanent seats on the Security Council, and to be armed with a veto which would allow them to coerce others but not to be coerced themselves.

Although in principle both were objectives which the British Government was prepared to endorse, Roosevelt and the other leading members of his Administration were convinced that in practice Britain, not Russia, would be the principal obstacle to the economic and might well fatally compromise the political.

British power at its zenith had been identified with free trade, but in the Depression of the 1930s the world's greatest trading nation had protected itself through a system of imperial preference set up by the Ottawa Agreements. When war came a few years later, and the British were obliged to sell the greater part of their foreign investments, they maintained the level of their economic war effort by the device of blocked sterling balances, the closed system of the sterling bloc, and by a whole range of other wartime controls limiting the volume and freedom of trade.

It was essential to American ideas of post-war economic policy to get the British to dismantle this system of economic defences and, in the wartime negotiations between the two countries, the Americans persistently sought to secure a British commitment to do so: for example, in Article 7 of the 1943 Lend-Lease Agreement, and in the Bretton Woods negotiations to set up an International Monetary Fund and an International Bank, institutions which were designed to the American (not the alternative British) specifications and located in the United States with American chairmen.[2]

The British did not give in easily. No nation stood to gain more from a multilateral trading system, but they knew that their economic situation at the end of the war was going to be difficult, if not desperate, and that controls

---

[1] W. W. Rostow: *The United States in the World Arena* (NY 1960) p. 139.
[2] See the account given in Richard N. Gardner: *Sterling-Dollar Diplomacy* (2nd edn. NY 1969).

would be essential for a time if they were to avoid economic collapse. They suspected that American devotion to free trade did not extend (as it had in the case of Britain before 1914) to applying it to their own domestic markets. American business, without waiting for the end of the war, was already seeking to take advantage of Britain's economic weakness to capture her prewar markets (for example in Latin America) and such sources of supply as the Middle East oilfields where a vigorous fight for post-war concessions, with no holds barred, was already being waged between American and British oil interests.

In the summer of 1945 the British were still holding out. No Labour Minister was more aware of what was at stake than Ernest Bevin whose own choice of office, left to himself, would have been the Treasury, not the Foreign Office, and whose long experience as leader of the British dockers (and seamen) had made him particularly aware of Britain's dependence on recovering her overseas trade. On the other side of the Atlantic, the end of the war in Europe and the return of a Labour Government in Britain committed to a socialist programme made the US Administration more determined to use America's economic strength to put pressure on the British and bring them into line with America's objective in economic and financial policy.

A similar divergence of views, again reflecting the difference between the circumstances of the two countries, had already appeared in their political objectives. True to the Wilsonian tradition, Roosevelt and Hull saw the international organization they sought to create as a substitute for power politics. In words Hull used when speaking to Congress in 1943, there would be no longer any need

"For spheres of influence, for alliances, for balance of power or any other of the special arrangements through which in the unhappy past, the nations strove to safeguard their security or promote their interests."[1]

Such a proposal made a strong appeal to the idealist and moralizing strain in American politics, and Roosevelt believed that the creation of an international organization was the only foreign policy for which popular support in America could be won. The alternative was for the USA to relapse into isolationism.

The Wilsonian tradition, however, also encouraged the separation of planning for a world organization from the concrete issues of power in the post-war world. Practical reasons reinforced this. The success of the UN Organization turned on preserving the unity of the Great Powers. Nothing would more surely divide them than disputes over frontiers, the recognition of governments, spheres of influence and all the other questions to be dealt with in the post-war settlement, and nothing would more rapidly disillusion American opinion if the establishment of the UN became embroiled with the quarrels and the power politics to which such disputes were likely to lead.

---

[1] 18 November 1943, *Documents on American Foreign Relations, 1943-44*, p. 14.

Roosevelt, then, had every reason to put off coming to grips with his allies over such matters as the future of Poland, to gloss over any conflict of interest with the Russians in Eastern Europe and defer decisions until the UN was established. The US military too were in favour of such a policy since it would enable them to avoid complicating the operations of war with political calculations. As Raymond Aron puts it, "military pragmatism first, utopian vision later," adding, "Utopia did not rule out a new 'manifest destiny for the American republic'."[1]

This was all very well, so long as decisions could be postponed and everyone else agreed. In many cases they could not and so were taken on an *ad hoc*, piecemeal basis as military expediency suggested without thought of the political consequences. (Examples are the decision not to drive on to Berlin and get there before the Russians, and the decision not to send American troops to liberate Prague, both taken without consideration of the political implications.) If the US Government continued to stand aloof and refuse to commit itself on such matters as frontiers and the recognition of governments in the liberated countries until the UN Organization was set up, there was a real danger that these would be decided by the course of events, that the provisional would become permanent and that the most powerful state in the world would have excluded itself from an effective voice in the European settlement.

Churchill saw the danger clearly enough but could neither persuade the Americans nor find ways of forestalling it on his own. His efforts to bring about a Russo–Polish agreement before the Red Army occupied Polish territory failed, as did the notorious attempt to express the division of interests in crude terms of percentages (Moscow, October, 1944). The only practical result was to secure a free hand for the British in Greece, but not to limit the occupation of the rest of Eastern Europe by the Russians.

The US Administration gave little support to Churchill's efforts which were seen as a return to the traditional practice of power politics in an attempt to restore a British sphere of influence in Europe (e.g. in Greece) parallel to the recovery of the colonial empire. Roosevelt was after something bigger, a world not a European settlement, to be achieved through the new international organization and guaranteed by continuing cooperation, a condominium between the two Great Powers of the future, the USA and the USSR. This was the prize on which he set his hopes when he made his last journey, to Yalta, to establish relations of confidence with Stalin and secure Russia's agreement to take part in the UN Organization. If he could achieve that and Allied unity could be preserved after the war, then Roosevelt was confident that the details of the European, as of the Far Eastern, settlement would fall into place.

The President's confidence that he had succeeded (less in private than he displayed in public) did not survive more than a few weeks. With the end of the

[1] Raymond Aron: *The Imperial Republic* (Paris 1973. Eng. tr. London 1975) p. 18.

war in sight, the Russians moved rapidly into Central Europe and made plain by their actions, in Poland in particular,[1] and also in Rumania, that they did not regard anything they had agreed to at Yalta as preventing them from establishing their control over the countries they now occupied in Eastern Europe. Recriminations flew between the Western capitals and Moscow, including Soviet charges that the Western allies were negotiating a separate peace. At the time of Roosevelt's death (12 April 1945) the alliance was under severe strain.

The question whether Truman departed from Roosevelt's policy towards the Soviet Union has been much debated by American historians. What is clear is that the new President was not ready to accept Churchill's advice to press for a summit conference with Stalin at the earliest possible moment and to meet first by themselves to agree on a common front. The Prime Minister had already criticized Eisenhower's decision not to try and take Berlin before the Russians, but to hold his troops on the Elbe. This was still well within the occupation zone assigned to the Soviet Union, and Churchill sent a stream of messages to Washington[2] urging that no withdrawal should take place until "the old question of the future relations of the two Governments with the Soviet Government" in Europe had been resolved. This was the last moment, he argued, before dispersal of the Anglo–US forces now at their peak and standing a hundred miles inside the Soviet zone of occupation when it was possible to confront Stalin with a clear choice between a post-war settlement in Europe reached in agreement with his allies and a unilateral settlement imposed by Russia on the parts of Europe she occupied, with the risk that this would lead to the break-up of the alliance.

Amongst Truman's advisers there were certainly some—Harriman, Forrestal and Leahy—in favour of a show-down with the Russians. The President himself had begun by taking a tough line, speaking bluntly to Molotov about Russian actions in Poland and promising support to Churchill in confronting Tito in Istria. But there were others who believed, for differing reasons, that Eastern Europe and Churchill's concern for a balance of power on the continent were not worth a quarrel with the Soviet Union; that America's—and the world's—interest was above all to preserve a close working relationship between the USA and the USSR and patch over the rift which had opened between them.

It was this view which prevailed and led Truman, without consulting Churchill first, to send Harry Hopkins, one of its chief exponents, to Moscow with instructions to make it clear to Stalin "that we have no territorial ambitions or ulterior motives in Poland, Rumania, Bulgaria, Czechoslovakia, Austria, Yugoslavia, Latvia, Lithuania or elsewhere and that our only

---

[1] For example, the arrest and trial of 16 representatives of the Polish Resistance invited by the Russians to take part in talks with a Russian guarantee of personal safety.

[2] The first was sent on 18 April 1945, and the argument repeated in a variety of forms until Truman's refusal on 11 June.

interests concern world peace."[1] At the same time Joseph Davies was sent to London, amongst other things to tell the Prime Minister that the President was thinking of holding a preliminary meeting not with Churchill but with Stalin. The former American Ambassador to the Soviet Union reproached Churchill for espousing the anti-Bolshevik views of Hitler and Goebbels and provoked Eden to the comment that he was "a born appeaser and would gladly give Russia all Europe, except perhaps us, so that America might not be embroiled. All the errors and illusions of Neville C., substituting Russia for Germany."[2]

It was hardly surprising that Hopkins was welcomed in Moscow and was able to restore relations on the basis of a new deal, in effect withdrawing American objections to Russian policy in Poland in return for the Soviet Union accepting the US plan for voting procedures in the UN Security Council. Churchill, putting the Anglo-American alliance before anything else, did his best to swallow his doubts and on 5 July joined Truman in recognizing the reconstituted Polish Government. The three leaders agreed to meet at Potsdam before the end of July, although in different circumstances and with a different purpose from those Churchill had in mind when he originally proposed the meeting. In his anxiety not to give Stalin any impression that he was "ganging up" with the British against him, Truman refused Churchill's invitation to visit London first, and went direct to Berlin.

Which was the wiser policy; whether Stalin would have changed course in face of a resolute Anglo–American stand, or whether this would simply have led to a confrontation three years earlier, are controversial questions not requiring to be discussed here. All that is necessary is again to make clear the situation Bevin found on becoming Foreign Secretary. American support had been crucial to Britain and had been given ungrudgingly during the war; it was to become crucial and again be given without stint at the time of the Marshall Plan (1947) and the trial of strength over Berlin (1948). But there was a gap, coinciding with the final stages of the war and the first year and a half of the Labour Administration, when relations between the two governments became much more distant; when American support, if not cut off, was much reduced and more grudgingly given. Knowing that this was only a temporary intermission, we can easily fail to understand how it looked at the time to the Labour Ministers, who had been members of the wartime coalition and who now felt the difference in the American attitude to Britain. In time, opposition to Russian policy and fear of Soviet expansion were to re-create a common interest and restore the former alliance, but in the summer of 1945 not only was this in the future, but it represented a prospect which (as Churchill had discovered) the American Government was not yet prepared to accept and which the Labour Party angrily repudiated. In July 1945 the immediate

[1] William Hillman (ed.) *Mr President: Personal Diaries, Papers &c of Harry S. Truman* (London 1952) p. 99.
[2] *The Eden Memoirs: The Reckoning* (London 1965) p. 539.

prospect from Whitehall as Bevin took over from Eden was the disturbing combination of anxiety about Russian *and* uncertainty about American policy.

4

When the three heads of government met at Yalta in February 1945, they had been discussing a situation which was in the future, and so could still find formulas with which to paper over conflicts or postpone the most difficult decisions. At Potsdam in July the situation they met to discuss was no longer in the future, but visibly confronting them.

In the final weeks of the war, the Red Army had been ordered to push as far west as possible, eventually reaching a line running from Lübeck to the Adriatic and only being narrowly prevented (by the British under Montgomery) from moving into Denmark as well. This put Stalin in a position to exercise a controlling voice in the Eastern half of Europe, a claim staked out in advance, not just on the map, but on the ground. What did this mean for the future and what were the Western allies going to do about it?

The second and even more urgent question was what were they and the Russians going to do about Germany and Central Europe. It was already ten weeks since Hitler had committed suicide and the German Army had surrendered. The German State had ceased to exist, the whole country was under occupation and divided between the Allied armies. But there was no agreement yet on what was to become of an area and a population which had provided the power-base for a regime that it had taken the combined efforts of Britain, Russia and the USA to overthrow.

These were the two interrelated sets of questions which the Potsdam Conference met to settle, and which in part it did settle although in ways no one was prepared to recognize openly at the time.

None of the three powers had yet decided their answers to these questions. It had been a summer of tremendous events in which decisions were more often the product of improvisation than of a calculated plan. This was true both of Stalin and the Americans, and Professor Mastny's description of Russian policy after Yalta as "erratic and inconsistent rather than pre-meditated and methodical"[1] could be applied to American policy as well. Nonetheless, it was clear in which direction events were moving. Stalin may not have been following any clear-cut plan or timetable for imposing controls over the countries the Red Army had occupied, but the way he had gone about securing "friendly governments" in Rumania and Bulgaria, after the example of Poland, strongly suggested the pattern he would follow—and in fact did.

The Western Powers protested that the Rumanian and Bulgarian Governments were unrepresentative and that Russia had acted in breach of the

---

[1] Vojteck Mastny: *Russia's Road to the Cold War* (NY 1979) p. 261.

Declaration on Liberated Europe. The protests produced little result. Litvinov's private comment was to the point:

"Why did you Americans wait until now to begin opposing us in the Balkans and
Eastern Europe? . . . You should have done this three years ago. Now it's too late and
your complaints only arouse suspicion here."[1]

Promises were made to improve the facilities of the Allied Control Commissions in Rumania and Bulgaria, the situation in which, Stalin claimed, was no
different from that in Italy. Nothing was conceded which would affect Soviet
control over either country, and British complaints about Tito's aggressive
behaviour were met by a counter-attack on the iniquities of the Greek
Government for which the Russians held the British responsible.

After accepting the Curzon Line as Russia's western frontier and reluctantly
recognizing the Russian-installed Polish Government, the Western Powers
had not anticipated another major battle over Poland. The question of Polish
compensation, however, at the expense of Germany for the territory they had
ceded to the Soviet Union had been left open at Yalta. The British and
Americans were prepared to see the Oder as the new frontier between Poland
and Germany, but had not agreed whether the line further south was to
follow the Eastern or the Western Neisse. They now discovered, to their anger,
that in April the Russians had settled the matter without either consulting or
informing their allies, transferring to Polish administration at once over 21 per
cent of German territory, including the whole of the rich province of Silesia.
With the transfer of 3,500 sq. miles of East Prussia to the Soviet Union itself, a
quarter of German territory as it had been in 1937 before the annexation of
Austria had been unilaterally redistributed. This materially affected the basis
for any German settlement by making a major reduction in the resources from
which reparations would have to be met and a major increase in the number of
refugees for which the parts of Germany under British and American occupation would have to provide.

Meanwhile, in their own zone of Germany, the Russians had started at once
on stripping everything that could be moved without waiting for any agreement on reparations and without making any attempt to account for what they
took. By the time the British and Americans got to Potsdam, these were *faits
accomplis*; and Stalin must have felt a fair confidence that, while they would
protest, as they had before, they would eventually accept what they had no
power to alter. If that had been all Stalin was interested in, recognition of
Russian control over Eastern Europe including the Soviet zone of Germany,
the facts would have been enough in the end to settle the matter. But Stalin was
also very much interested in the rest of Germany, and here the Russians were
not in a position to decide unilaterally what was to happen; here the Americans
and the British for once were in a position to exert counter pressure.

[1] Edgar Snow: *Journey to the Beginning* (London 1959) quoted by Mastny, op. cit., p. 283.

As late as the Yalta Conference, six months before, the three Allied leaders had been seriously discussing the dismemberment of Germany. They had since come, independently, to the opposite conclusion, that Germany should not be split up; but they still had to decide what they meant by the principle of treating Germany as a unit, and how this was to be done in practice.

So far as there was agreement on arrangements for the occupation it had been arrived at in the European Advisory Commission. This was a body which Eden had persuaded the two other powers to set up at the beginning of 1944[1] in the hope that it would provide a focus for the discussion of European problems. This hope had not been realized. The Commission met in London and that was enough to make the Americans regard it with suspicion as a device to enable the British to exercise an undue influence on the post-war settlement. In practice, its scope was restricted to German questions and it was only after many delays that any agreements were signed, the most important of which fixed the division of Germany into zones of occupation.

The delays from which the Commission suffered reflected the difficulty each of the three governments found in deciding its own policy towards the future of Germany. On the British side, as early as July 1943, Attlee had circulated to the Cabinet a paper dealing with policy towards Germany, and in April 1944 a Cabinet Armistice and Post-War (A.P.W.) Committee was set up with terms of reference which included not only the conditions of a German armistice and the administration of occupied territories but "general political and military questions in the post-war period". The A.P.W. had a regular membership of seven ministers including Bevin. Attlee, not Churchill or Eden, acted as chairman, and the Committee became the focus for the discussion of post-war questions and a clearing house for proposals from the Foreign Office, from the Chiefs of Staff, from William Strang as British representative on the European Advisory Committee, and from the various official committees. It met 23 times between April and the end of 1944 and considered no fewer than 127 papers and reports. No better apprenticeship for a future Prime Minister and Foreign Secretary could have been devised.

A great deal of the A.P.W. Committee's time was spent discussing the future of Germany. There were wide differences of opinion, with Attlee and Bevin strongly opposed to a centralized German government and Eden preferring this to the Allies undertaking responsibility for administering Germany themselves. Bevin at one meeting (ironically on 20 July 1944, the day of the unsuccessful German attempt to overthrow Hitler) argued in favour of breaking up Germany into German states and "returning to the Germany of Bismarck". The argument was revived by a Chiefs of Staff paper in September which set out the pros and cons for dismemberment, taking account at the same time of a possible need to re-insure against a hostile Russia. Eden and the

---

[1] Eden made his proposal at the Moscow conference of Foreign Ministers in October 1943 and the Commission met for the first time on 14 January 1944. The French (as a result of British pressure on the other two powers) were invited to join the Commission in November 1944.

Foreign Office protested strongly that any suggestion of a combination with part of Germany against Russia would make co-operation with the Soviet Union impossible. Discussion continued in the A.P.W. Committee up to Yalta (February 1945) with two other Labour ministers, A. V. Alexander and Dalton, joining in and the argument extending to the level of German industry and reparations. After Yalta discussion was resumed in the Cabinet itself and on 22 March 1945 Sir John Anderson presented a Treasury paper (dated 9 March) which put a powerful case for treating Germany as a unit on economic grounds and, if that failed, incorporating Western Germany into the West European economy.

The Treasury memorandum effectively ended any thought the Coalition Government may have had of partitioning Germany by spelling out the economic and social consequences of breaking up the German economy, quite apart from the stimulus which (it was argued) partition would give to German nationalism. It would have the effect of putting off Europe's as well as Germany's recovery and for a long time keeping Central Europe in an impoverished condition which would be a threat to any hopes of political and social stability in post-war Europe.

The experience of the British (and American) Military Governments once they began to take over their zones in Germany reinforced these arguments. Instead of holding down a hostile people, rooting out Nazism and destroying Germany's military-industrial power, they found themselves struggling to bring some sort of order out of the chaos of defeat, and feed and house a demoralized population swollen by the arrival of millions of refugees from the East. The British Government began to realize what they had taken on in insisting that they should have the north-western zone of occupation which contained the largest concentrations of heavy industry, urban population and damaged cities. The Ruhr, the Rhineland, Westphalia and Hamburg could not be made self-supporting unless two conditions were satisfied—unless German industry could be started up again to provide employment and manufactured goods with which to pay for bringing in supplies, and unless trade could be restored with those parts of Eastern and Central Germany now under Soviet occupation from which Western Germany had traditionally drawn an important part of its food supplies and raw materials. The only alternative, if the Military Government was not to see the German population for which they were now responsible die of hunger and cold, was to ask the British people, already short of everything themselves, to provide supplies and pay for them, a result of fighting the Germans for six years which was unlikely to be popular.

The British therefore (and the Americans) went to Potsdam determined to insist that taking reparations from Germany had got to take second place to enabling the population of their own zones to feed and support themselves. For the same reason they wanted east–west trade revived and the unified pattern of the German economy restored.

The Russians, not surprisingly, saw the situation differently. Unlike the British and the Americans they had experienced a brutal invasion of their own country, had suffered far greater losses than either of their allies in lives and material destruction and felt that they had contributed more than any other nation to the defeat of Germany. If there was one thing on which the Russian people were united it was in their belief that justice required that the Germans should be made to pay for the damage and suffering they had inflicted. At Yalta Stalin had put the total of reparations to be exacted from the Germans at 20,000 million dollars, half of which should go to the USSR. The Western Powers might argue that this was an arbitrary figure which bore no relation to Germany's capacity to pay, but this was an argument which made no impression on the Russians: it represented the scale of reparation which they felt the Germans should be forced to make for the crimes they had committed. How a defeated country with its economy at a standstill was to provide such a sum was not a problem which worried the Russians: if it meant that the Germans would starve, so much the worse for the Germans; they had not worried if others starved.

It was for this reason that the Russians had already begun to take what they wanted from their own zone of occupation, but that did not mean that they were prepared to forgo their claim to reparations from the rest of Germany, in particular from the Ruhr. Although for different reasons, they too had an interest in insisting that Germany—less, of course, the territories transferred to the Poles—should be treated as an economic unit. This would enable them not only to draw on the Western zones as well as their own for reparations, but also to claim a voice in future arrangements for the whole of Germany—for example the proposal, which Stalin pressed, for the internationalization of the Ruhr.

Despite their different approach, therefore, both sides wanted an agreement. But little sign of one had appeared by the time (25 July) Churchill and Eden left Potsdam to learn the result of the British General Election. By then the conference, which had opened on the 16th, had seen nine plenary sessions of the heads of governments and nine meetings of the three foreign ministers without settling more than a modest list of topics. A Council of Foreign Ministers to prepare the peace treaties, bringing in France and China as well as the three powers represented at Potsdam; final arrangements for the occupation of Austria and Vienna, including the Western Powers' recognition of the Renner Government set up by the Russians; the annexation of Königsberg by the Soviet Union; the political principles on which the Allied Control Council was to supervise the joint occupation of Germany: this was as far as the three delegations had got in reaching even provisional agreements.

No ground at all had been made on the chief stumbling block for the West, the Russians' transfer of the Oder–Neisse territories to the Poles. Stalin defended his action as the logical consequence of the restoration to Russia of the Polish territories in the East to which the Western powers had already

23

agreed, no more than just compensation to the Poles for their sufferings at German hands and a loss which the Germans must accept as part of the consequences of first starting and then losing the war. If this meant that more had to be found from the rest of Germany that too was part of the same consequences: it was no reason why the Russians should receive less reparations or the Poles less territory. In support of his case he brought in the leaders of the Polish Government which the West had now recognized—including their own nominee Mikolajczyk—to impress on the Americans and the British how impossible it was for Poland to forgo a square kilometre of the territory they had been given.

Since Stalin was unwilling to give way (he was to some extent the prisoner of his own Polish policy), the Western Powers had the choice of two alternatives. The first was to take up an equally uncompromising position and tell Stalin that if he would make no concessions then the conference would end with no agreement. Churchill said as much in the last session he attended before leaving to hear the result of the British election, and he later declared that if he had returned to Potsdam he would never have accepted the Polish–German frontier. But Churchill did not return, and what he said later is not relevant. While he was away Byrnes, the new American Secretary of State, proceeded to sound out the second of the two alternatives, a deal. The Americans were irritated by the Russians, but Truman (his confidence increased by news of the successful test of the A-bomb and the prospect of an early end to the Japanese war) was more interested in finding a quick way to resolve the difficulty and get back to Washington than in a confrontation. Neither Truman nor Byrnes yet saw the national interests of the USA as affected by the territorial settlement in Europe; they repeated that they had no intention of becoming involved in any commitment to a new balance of power in Europe and, provided they were not called upon to subsidize German reparations, they were more interested in getting agreement with the Russians on the best terms available than in the details of the European settlement.

Byrnes might be ignorant of foreign affairs but had not won his reputation as a political fixer for nothing. On 23 July Byrnes met twice with Molotov (the second time with the British present as well), and put to him the outline of a compromise which would combine a "Russian" solution on the issue on which the Russians had the obvious advantage, the Polish–German frontier, with a "Western" solution on reparations, where the Russians were asking for something the Americans and the British had the power to refuse. By the time Attlee and Bevin reached Potsdam on the evening of the 28th, Byrnes believed he had the makings of a deal.[1]

---

[1] The minutes of the meetings on 23 July are to be found in FRUS *The Conference of Berlin 1945*. A further meeting followed on 27 July, ibid.

5

It was a bad time to arrive. The conference had now lasted thirteen days; the general feeling among the Western delegations, strongly shared by Truman, was one of impatience to reach a settlement and get away. The last thing anyone wanted was for the late arrivals to make difficulties just when the negotiations were coming to the point of decision, and when the Americans had already made up their minds what they were prepared to settle for.

Attlee, at Churchill's invitation, had been present during the earlier part of the conference but had said nothing. Stalin asked who would take Churchill's place if he did not return and was told it would be Attlee. He remarked: "He does not look a greedy man."[1] The unknown quantity was Bevin, and at the airport he told General Ismay, who had come to meet them, "I'm not going to have Britain barged about". But although he might put a bold face on it, Bevin was as much aware as Attlee that the British had few cards in their hand, even when it had been played by Churchill, and that there would be uproar at home if, after turning the experienced Churchill and Eden out of office, they came back without a settlement.

They were given no time to get their bearings. A plenary session was scheduled for ten o'clock that evening and the new Prime Minister and Foreign Secretary could only pay a brief visit first to the American President. There was enough time, however, for Truman to outline on the map the line which the Russians proposed for the German–Polish frontier. This can hardly have been news to the British ministers, but Bevin, Byrnes recalls, "immediately and forcefully presented his strong opposition to those boundaries. His manner was so aggressive that both the President and I wondered how we would get along with this new Foreign Minister."[2]

The plenary session which followed gave Bevin his first sight of Stalin, a man whose shadow was to lie heavily over the rest of his career. Attlee had already formed a clear impression of the Russian leader which it would be hard to better: "Reminded me of the Renaissance despots—no principles, any methods, but no flowery language—always Yes or No, though you could only count on him if it was No."[3] Unlike Churchill, however, who had talked at length and always held the centre of the stage, Attlee left Bevin to speak for Britain, most of the time contenting himself with an occasional nod or laconic comment. On this occasion Stalin skilfully used Truman's desire to secure relief from the armistice terms for Italy, to reopen the question of recognition for the new regimes in Eastern Europe. Bevin was prepared for the Americans

---

[1] I owe this to Lord Bridges, the Secretary to the Cabinet, who was present and pointed Attlee out to Stalin. The British records of the Potsdam conference are to be found in CAB 99/38 (Plenary sessions and meetings of Foreign Secretaries); 99/39 (Chiefs of Staff meetings and papers); 99/40 (Staff conferences of Prime Minister, Foreign Secretary and FO officials). The U.S. records are printed in FRUS *The Conference of Berlin 1945*.
[2] James F. Byrnes, *Speaking Frankly* (NY 1947) p. 79.
[3] Quoted in Kenneth Harris: *Attlee* (London 1982) p. 267.

to make the running but he left no doubt that the British had their own views on Italian questions, and did so with sufficient force to make Stalin as well as the Americans stare at this newcomer who showed no trace of being abashed by the company in which he found himself.

When Stalin objected to the distinction drawn between the Italian and the other ex-satellite governments, saying "I cannot understand the difference", Bevin retorted: "We know about the Italian government, but we don't know about the others." Why were they being asked to commit themselves in advance? "I must be perfectly straight with the House of Commons. I do not quote things in words of doubtful meaning. I will take the last suggestion of the American delegation and leave the whole matter to later consideration."

When they turned to discuss Russian reparations from Italy, Bevin pressed Stalin for a more precise statement of Russian intentions. Would the supplies furnished by the USA and UK be protected? Would they be "once for all" removals? When Stalin spoke of reparations in military equipment did he mean military equipment with peacetime use? "It is so difficult to define what you can take away without affecting the economic life of a nation."

Plenary sessions, however, especially with Churchill no longer there to spark them off, had lost their interest for the other two leaders. The real business had now to be done behind the scenes, and the next morning Bevin sat down with his advisers to discuss the position.[1] They were a strong team, some of whom—Edward Bridges, the Secretary to the Cabinet, Norman Brook and William Strang—were well known to him. Others, including Cadogan, the permanent head of the Foreign Office, and Clark Kerr, the British Ambassador in Moscow, were seeing Bevin in command of a committee for the first time. After the temperamental performance of Churchill, they were impressed by the business-like way in which Bevin conducted the meeting. They were equally impressed by the grasp he showed, without any prompting, of the central issue in the conference.

Like Byrnes, Bevin was looking for the basis of a deal. Despite his outburst the previous evening, he had little doubt that they would have to accept the Oder–Neisse line. He wanted to keep open a choice between the Eastern and Western Neisse but he also wanted to find out what they might get in return for accepting the full Russian claim. He proposed to explore in two directions: in talks with Molotov and Byrnes on reparations and in talks with the Polish Ministers on guarantees of free elections and other freedoms in the new Polish state.

Bevin would have liked to go on and promise early elections in Greece and Italy in return for similar elections in the other East European countries, without singling out any particular one for special mention. And if such a general settlement could be reached, he was prepared to consider a bigger concession on reparations, offering Russia more than 10 per cent—up to 20

---

[1] Staff Conference with the Prime Minister and Foreign Minister, 29 July.

per cent—of "once for all" deliveries from the Ruhr, which was in the British zone.

A proposal of 10 per cent from all three Western zones was finally drafted for Bevin to put to the meeting of Foreign Ministers. By the time they met, however, Byrnes' own approach to Molotov had borne fruit and the Russian Foreign Minister soon made it clear that he preferred to take the American rather than the British proposal as the basis for discussion. Both began from the same position: since the Russians had chosen to start taking reparations out of their own zone they should look to this as their main source, and the other occupying powers would follow suit. The Western Powers, however, would offer the Russians in addition, not a fixed amount from the Western zones (as the Russians wanted), but a percentage of "such industrial equipment as we determine is not necessary for a peace economy". Part of this would be handed over to the Russians in return for equivalent supplies of food, coal and other raw materials from Eastern Germany; part would be transferred free.

The American draft was undoubtedly simpler than the British, but Molotov's principal reason for preferring it was the higher percentage figure for deliveries than the British offered, and Byrnes' agreement in a private talk immediately before the meeting to accept the Western instead of the Eastern Neisse as the Polish–German frontier.

Once the Americans had tabled a better offer, Bevin could see it was a waste of time to argue for the British proposal, but he insisted that the British were not yet committed to the line of the Western Neisse and before the plenary session at which the package deal was to be completed exerted all the pressure he could to secure guarantees from the Warsaw Government. In private meetings with the Polish delegation, he confronted the Polish President with a list of written questions and when Bierut resorted to generalizations, demanded a date—he suggested February 1946—for the Polish elections. Bierut finally committed himself to one not later than the early part of 1946 and under further pressure promised that the Western Powers should be given facilities to report the elections.[1] He also agreed to a public statement aimed at removing doubts about the rights of Poles returning from abroad.

When the plenary session re-assembled in the afternoon of the 30th, it was clear that Stalin had made up his mind to accept the American offer, but still hoped to improve the figures for reparation deliveries. A horse-trading session followed in which Truman and Byrnes agreed to raise the figure to 15 per cent in return for an equivalent value in supplies from the Soviet zone plus 10 per cent free of any return. Bevin objected to this as too liberal. Why, Stalin asked, if the USA was willing to agree, should the British stand out? Because, Bevin retorted, most of the reparations from the Western zones would have to come

[1] Record of a meeting at the Prime Minister's Residence, Potsdam at 3 p.m. on 29 July 1945. In all there were three meetings. The Polish Government was represented by Bierut, Grabski, Mikolajczyk, Stanczyk, Mink and Modzelewski and at the final meeting on the 30th by Gomulka as well.

from the British zone, and Britain, although she wanted little in the way of reparations for herself, had to think of the claims of her other allies. He refused to discuss a Russian proposal to internationalize the Ruhr on the grounds that this concerned all the occupying powers, and the French were not present.

The American and Russian delegations were now ready to conclude, and that, as Bevin well knew, settled the matter. But, ignoring the angry looks he attracted, he proceeded to ask a string of awkward questions about the Polish frontier settlement. His instructions, he said, had been to stand to the Eastern Neisse, and he wanted to know what was involved in the new proposal. Would the area of Germany to be taken over by the Poles remain under allied military control, or was it in effect a transfer of territory in advance of the peace conference? Could the British too (he asked) give away pieces of their zone without the approval of the other occupying powers?

After Byrnes had poured oil on the troubled waters with the assurance that all understood that the cession of territory was left to the peace conference, Bevin said he would not press the matter although the British Government thought the decision unwise. Still he would like to ask what would now happen in this Polish "zone". Would the Poles take over and the Soviet troops be withdrawn? Yes, Stalin replied, adding that most of the Russian troops in Poland had already been brought home. At this point Truman took advantage of a momentary pause to say that all were then agreed on the Polish question and the others nodded.

The meeting on 31 July effectively marked the end of the Potsdam Conference. Two more days and two more plenary sessions were needed to put the agreements into order but the bargain had been struck and everyone was in a hurry to get away. By 2 August Bevin and Attlee were free to fly back to England and to reflect on the experience of their first international conference.

The communiqué issued after the conference was long, impressive and misleading. The 37 paragraphs dealing with Germany suggested a measure of agreement which bore little relation to the bargain which had been struck. The detailed provisions for the occupation were taken over from the European Advisory Commission and incorporated *en bloc* in the communiqué. They depended, however, on the occupying powers treating Germany as a single administrative and economic unit, and this principle, explicitly stated in the communiqué, was constantly appealed to in the polemics of the next few years in order to prove that, if it had not been for the perfidy of the Russians (or, in the Russian version, of the Americans and British) the Americans (or in the rival version, the Russians) would have adhered to their proclaimed policy and Germany have remained united. But the one specific agreement reached at Potsdam, on reparations, assumed the opposite, the continued division of Germany, and it was this, not the high-flown sentiments of the proclamation, which proved to be decisive. Attempts were made subsequently to overcome the division, but with less and less conviction that either side to the dispute would accept the conditions which the other side regarded as essential.

So the Potsdam Conference, while proclaiming the principle of German unity in fact settled the German problem by dividing the country, and thereby (it can be argued) laid the foundation of a stable and peaceful Europe.[1] It took time for this to become clear, and longer still before it could be said publicly. The reparations agreement was not made in order to divide Germany, and Byrnes, who promoted it, may not have realized its implications; but others, including the British team, certainly did even if they hoped that the contradiction could in some way be overcome.

The Potsdam communiqué was misleading in another way. Its bland sentences perpetuated, in the public if not in the official mind, the belief that the three wartime allies would continue to work together after the war was over. The point had not yet been reached at which the Western Powers and the Soviet Union had begun to work systematically against each other across the board; there was still a desire to reach agreement and on specific issues accommodation had proved possible. But the differences which separated British and American views of the post-war world from the Russian, although not explicitly stated, had become clear to both sides. Everyone who had taken part in the discussion went away wondering (if not convinced) whether these differences could be contained or must lead to open conflict. It is easy to see why the British and American leaders refrained from stating their doubts or suspicions in public, but their reluctance to do so added to their difficulties with public opinion in their own countries and may have encouraged Stalin's belief that he had to deal with men who would protest but in the end acquiesce.

From a personal point of view, Bevin could feel he had come through his first diplomatic engagement as creditably as circumstances allowed. Arriving too late to influence the outcome, he had at most given nothing away. If the Americans and Russians assumed that, once they decided on a settlement, the British would have to go along, Bevin had done his best to prevent this being taken for granted. His attitude had not endeared him to either of the other two delegations, but it had done as much as anything to establish him in the eyes of his own. Cadogan, who could be a harsh judge of politicians and had not looked forward to the change, wrote in his diary:

"Bevin will, I think, do well. He knows a good deal, is prepared to read any amount, seems to take in what he does read, and is capable of making up his own mind and sticking up for his (or our) point of view against anyone. I think he's the best we could have had."[2]

The greatest value of his visit to Potsdam, however, was that, while the Labour Party was still celebrating its electoral triumph full of hope for the future, Bevin was brought up sharp against the realities of the post-war world, even before he had had time to get used to the idea of being Foreign Secretary.

---

[1] See the discussion in Chapter 8 of de Porte: *Europe.*
[2] *The Diaries of Sir Alexander Cadogan*, ed. by David Dilks (London 1971) p. 778.

Sitting at the conference table with the Russians and Americans, the first in occupation of half Europe, with every indication that they meant to stay, the second with unequalled economic and now atomic power, had made clear the gap that separated the two super-powers from Britain, and the difficulty any Foreign Secretary would have in getting either to pay serious attention to independent British views.

"In politics," Stalin had said during the conference, "one should be guided by the calculation of power." The sight of Red Army troops milling about in the ruins of Hitler's Chancellery brought home to Bevin the fact that there was now no continental state, or combination of states, which could provide a balance to Soviet power once the US forces had withdrawn. What use would Stalin make of this situation?

The other major anxiety of the British, US policy, had been relieved but not removed by Potsdam. Truman too had learned from his first encounter with the Russians: though it remained the object of US policy to reach a settlement with the Soviet Union, the illusions of Yalta were dead. This made it easier to establish a working relationship with the Americans during the conference. On the other hand, Byrnes had left the impression of being devious and quite prepared to do a deal with the Russians, without taking the British into consultation, if the opportunity offered. For the present the policies of the two countries, at least as far as a European settlement was concerned, were not far apart, but the British were left uneasily wondering whether, if a settlement proved hard to reach, the Americans might lose patience, and pull out as they had after 1918, leaving the British to make the best terms they could with the Russians.

6

When the Labour Government took office, Britain was still committed to continuing the war with Japan. Four days after Bevin got back from Potsdam, however, the first atomic bomb was dropped on Hiroshima and a week later the Japanese surrendered. To the immense relief of the Labour leaders, they did not have to face adding another year or more to a war which the British had already been fighting for close on six years. The Second World War was over at last. But as the impression of what had taken place at Hiroshima and Nagasaki sank in, the relief was overlaid by alarm at a development which was felt to mark the start of a new and even more perilous era of history. One war ending gave birth to the fear of a third fought with nuclear weapons, and added a new contentious item, how to ban the bomb, to the Foreign Ministers' agenda.

The end of the war also uncovered a formidable set of problems outside Europe in the broad arc of territory which constitutes the southern rim of the Eurasian land mass all the way from the Straits of Gibraltar and the Mediterranean to the Straits of Formosa and the East China Sea.

The Americans regarded the Pacific as their war, tolerating—but not much more—the British as allies.[1] They left no doubt that they intended to treat East Asia (China, Japan and Korea) and its Pacific approaches as their sphere of influence now that the war was over. The British insisted on reoccupying Hong Kong, in spite of American disapproval, but they exercised no influence on the course of events in mainland China during the years which saw the defeat of Chiang Kai-Shek and the triumph of Mao Tse-tung. Considering how little effect the Americans had in practice, for all their efforts, this was hardly a loss to the British.

There was no doubt of the influence General MacArthur and his occupying forces exercised in Japan. So powerful was MacArthur's position that the US Government, leave alone the governments of its Allies, found it difficult to get attention paid to its own views. This was an irritating situation, not only to the British but to the Australians who protested vigorously in Washington and London.

American demands for a whole string of island bases in the Pacific (as well as in Iceland and the Portuguese Atlantic Islands) produced a similar impression of high-handedness, not least because of the Americans' obvious hurry to forestall decisions by the United Nations, which they had promoted as the alternative to the British practice of "power politics".

Once formulas had been found to settle these immediate difficulties and give the Americans their way, Britain made no attempt (she had not got the resources, apart from anything else) to resume the role she had once played in the Far East. It was only in his last two years of office, with his recognition of Communist China and the Korean War (1950) that Bevin became closely involved with a part of the world with which his predecessors at the Foreign Office had been very much occupied.

Southern and South East Asia were a different story. Here was the real heart of the European colonial empires, the British in Malaya, Singapore, Burma, Ceylon and above all the Indian sub-continent; the French in Indo-China; the Dutch in Indonesia. Nowhere had the Japanese war, the failure of the colonial powers to defend South East Asia and its occupation by the Japanese produced a greater impact. The effect had been to stimulate nationalism and the demand for independence, and nowhere was it more open to question whether the European colonial powers would be able to recover their former possessions and powers.

The Indian Empire, an empire in its own right with its own Government, its own Secretary of State in the British Cabinet and the Indian Army of a quarter of a million men as a central strategic reserve was the foundation of Britain's imperial role. It was also a great commercial asset, ranking in 1913 and again in 1946 as Britain's best customer.[2] Defence of the route to India had been

---

[1] See Christopher Thorne: *Allies of a Kind* (Oxford 1978).
[2] 11.2% of British exports went to India in 1913; 8.3% in 1946.

second only to the defence of the United Kingdom in Britain's strategic priorities. Per contra, the Indian movement for independence led by Gandhi and Nehru was by far the most serious indigenous challenge to British colonial rule. In principle this had already been conceded and the advent of a Labour Government in London was widely expected to lead to it in practice.

India was a country in which Bevin felt a strong interest as his wartime scheme for training Indian trade unions shows.[1] But he took no direct part in the Indian negotiations other than as a senior member of the Cabinet; these were not the responsibility of the Foreign Secretary but of the Secretary of State for India and the Prime Minister. On the other hand the Labour Government's unexpected success in keeping India, Pakistan and Ceylon, after independence, as members of the Commonwealth made a great impression on Bevin as well as Attlee. It strengthened their belief in a continuing world role for Britain as the leader of a multi-racial Commonwealth of self-governing nations, with major consequences for British foreign policy *vis-à-vis* Europe and the USA.

The return of the British to Singapore and Malaya; the creation of a Malaysian Federation; the recognition of Burma's independence, and her right to secede from the Commonwealth—all these, like the negotiations with India, lay outside Bevin's responsibility as Foreign Secretary. But in other parts of South East Asia which had never been under British rule, he was involved both as Foreign Secretary and as Chairman of the Cabinet's Overseas Reconstruction Committee.

The British, who were in command in the South East Asia theatre, were faced with the job of accepting the surrender of three-quarters of a million Japanese troops and releasing 123,000 Allied prisoners of war and internees scattered over a vast area of one and a half million square miles with rudimentary communications and a population of 160 million people. Only at the last moment, at Potsdam, had the Joint Chiefs of Staff transferred responsibility for the liberation of the Netherlands East Indies from the Americans and of Southern Indo-China from the Chinese, to the British South East Asia Command which had no time to prepare itself for the task. With little more than token forces at their disposal, British commanders were called on to undertake the occupation not only of the former British colonies of Burma, Singapore, Malaya and Borneo, but Siam, Java, Sumatra and the rest of the Dutch East Indies as well as of Indo-China south of 16°N. In both countries native governments claiming independence had established themselves on the surrender of the Japanese—in Indonesia, with Japanese connivance—and were preparing to contest the return of the former colonial powers. The British found themselves caught in the crossfire and denounced by both sides and their sympathizers. In Indo-China this was only for a limited time and the British handed over with relief to the French in the spring of 1946. But Britain

---

[1] See Vol. II, pp. 205–207.

was involved with Indonesian affairs, and Bevin in controversy about them, for almost the whole of his period at the Foreign Office, partly because of Britain's close relations with her Dutch ally in Western Europe.

Not only was South East Asia in political turmoil, in several countries verging on civil war, but like the rest of the world it faced economic breakdown and was short of food. The British were saddled with the responsibility for establishing order and for re-starting production and distribution in the three principal rice exporters, Burma, Siam and Indo-China, on supplies from which (on average six million tons a year before the war) many parts of Asia, including India and Malaya, depended for avoiding famine. These emergency measures were organized by the Overseas Reconstruction Committee of which Bevin was chairman.[1] Rice was as essential to the reconstruction of Asia as coal and wheat to that of Europe, and when the military handed over the responsibility for supplies it was taken on by the British Special Commissioner for S.E. Asia (Lord Killearn) appointed on Bevin's recommendation in March 1946.

The one course that was not discussed was for Britain to withdraw from Asia altogether, and make no effort to reoccupy the countries she had previously ruled. The Labour Government, as it was to demonstrate, was ready to grant independence but not to abandon any British role in Asia in advance. Was this a real possibility? Could the British have simply left these countries, at least those from which they had been driven out by the Japanese, to settle their own future; and refused to become involved in anything beyond recovering the prisoners of war in the Dutch East Indies and French Indo-China? Given the slowness with which people adjust to new situations, and the strong pressure on the British as the only power with forces available to restore some sort of order and avert famine, the answer is probably "No".

Two consequences followed. The first was to confirm the suspicion and hostility with which Asian opinion regarded the British as bent upon opposing the claims of Asian nationalists and restoring their own and other European nations' colonial rule. This was to expose Bevin and the Labour Government to a great deal of criticism in 1945–6 from all quarters, not only from Asian countries but from the Soviet bloc as well as the Americans and the Australians, and not only in the press and broadcasts but at meetings of the United Nations. The second consequence was a heavy addition in financial and manpower costs to an overburdened British budget, helping to bring on the financial and economic crisis of early 1947. Even after that and the cuts which it made necessary, it was not until 1968 (more than twenty years later and four years after Harold Wilson had repeated: "We are a world power and a world influence, or we are *nothing*"[2]) that a successor Labour Government

---

[1] At the beginning of December 1945 the Far Eastern Ministerial Committee, of which Bevin was also chairman, was merged into the ORC which then had two panels, one for Europe, the other for the Far East.

[2] Quoted in Thorne, p. 687.

announced that no British forces would be stationed in the Far East or east of Suez after 1971. So long did it take to complete a process beginning, as Christopher Thorne points out, with the Anglo–Japanese treaty of 1902 and the withdrawal of British battleships from the China station three years later and taking almost 70 years (and two world wars) to carry through before Britain gave up any pretence to be a Far Eastern Power.

It was the need to safeguard the route to her Eastern possessions—above all to India, the greatest of them—at first overland, then (after 1869) through the Suez Canal which involved the British in the Middle East as well. Several generations of Britons had been brought up to regard the Mediterranean, the Red Sea, the Persian Gulf and the adjoining territories as falling as naturally under British control as the English Channel. Cyprus, Egypt and the Sudan had been occupied before the end of the 19th century and the break-up of the Ottoman Empire added mandates for Iraq, Jordan and Palestine, making Britain between the wars the paramount power in the Middle East. The Second World War underlined the strategic importance of an area which was the main theatre of operations for the British until the expulsion of the Germans and Italians from North Africa carried the war back into continental Europe. So important was it held to be that on 5 September 1940, only three months after Dunkirk, when the German forces were massing for the invasion of the United Kingdom, Churchill ordered strong reinforcements to be sent from the British Isles to hold Egypt and the Suez Canal. The German attack on Russia opened up the possibility that German troops driving through the Caucasus might meet Rommel's forces driving across the Suez isthmus, converge on the oilfields of Iraq and Iran and threaten India overland—a dream which Napoleon had shared, and Nelson had shattered at the Battle of the Nile in 1798. When that threat was removed, the Allied Powers were able in their turn to use the geographical position of the Middle East to their own advantage. It became the main route, through Iran, for American and British supplies to reach Russia; the reopened short route to India and the Pacific theatre; a base for the attack on Europe from the south; a short-haul source of oil for fronts as widely separated as the Mediterranean and South East Asia; and a central staging post in air communications round the globe.

The strategic importance of the area was not reduced when, in the latter days of the Second World War, the threat from Germany and Italy was replaced by fears of Soviet expansion with the object of creating a buffer zone of satellite states in the Middle East, to the south, as well as to the west, in Europe. These were fears with much more substance historically and geopolitically than those projected by Hitler and Mussolini.

The immediate need was to support the countries directly threatened, Iran and Turkey, in resisting Russian demands. But, forced to consider this revival of an old threat, the British Chiefs of Staff argued that the only way in which they could strike at targets on Russian soil was from airfields such as those the RAF had created in Iraq and insisted that they must retain the use of the huge wartime base in the Canal Zone, or find a substitute for it in Palestine. India could no longer be expected to provide, in the Indian Army, the strategic reserve of a quarter of a million men on which, with the Royal Navy's capacity to move them east or west as need arose, British world power had largely depended for a hundred years. But the prospective loss of India made the Chiefs of Staff all the more anxious to retain a base in the Middle East. The traditional argument of the need to defend the route to India was now generalized into the importance of the Middle East for the main lines of communication (by air as well as sea) between the two chief concentrations of power in the non-Communist world, Europe and the Atlantic seaboard of North America on one side, India, South East Asia and the Far East on the other. And to this was now added recognition during the war of the importance of the Middle Eastern oilfields and the need to guarantee Western access to them.

British interest in Middle Eastern oil, of course, went back to the early years of the century. The Anglo-Persian Oil Co was founded in 1909 and, thanks to Churchill's advocacy, the British Government acquired a controlling share in it, thus safeguarding the Royal Navy's oil supplies, six days before war broke out in 1914. As well as Iranian oil production—9½ million long tons in 1939—the Iraq Petroleum Co produced another 4 million, but Middle Eastern oil that year amounted to less than 6 per cent of the world's total, and even Britain only imported 22 per cent of its oil from the Middle East compared with 57 per cent from the Americas. Two wartime developments, however, changed the position. The first was that the American oil companies, with support from a US Government worried about the exhaustion of America's own resources, challenged the British in a part of the world which the latter had come to regard as their preserve, acquiring large concessions in Arabia and the Persian Gulf. The aggressive American attitude towards Middle East oil resources, and the resentment this aroused on the British side, produced a good deal of friction in the field, the repercussions of which reached back to London and Washington. "There is apprehension . . . here", Churchill wrote to Roosevelt in the spring of 1944, "that the USA has a desire to deprive us of our oil assets in the Middle East, on which, among other things, the whole supply of our Navy depends." "On the other hand," Roosevelt replied, "I am disturbed about the rumor that the British wish to horn in on our Saudi Arabian oil reserves."[1] The result of this exchange at the top was negotiations which produced a draft Anglo–US Petroleum Agreement in August 1944. However, the American oil companies' suspicion of government interference was too strong for this to be ratified, and Anglo–American commercial rivalry in the field continued, extending from oil concessions to post-war markets in the Middle East and competition for civil airline

---

1 Quoted in Bruce R. Kuniholm: *The Origins of the Cold War in the Near East* (Princeton 1980) p. 184.

facilities.[1] The other development was a gradual realization that the reserves of oil in the Middle East were greater than in any other part of the world. In 1945 the US Government was told that they were equal to three quarters of the American proved reserves; by 1965 the figure was to be upgraded to 61 per cent of the whole world's reserves, with Kuwait, Saudi Arabia and Iran each outstripping the figures for the USA and for the Soviet bloc. Saudi production (a wholly American operation) multiplied twofold between 1945 and 1950 (26 million tons); and Kuwait (fifty-fifty Anglo–American), which did not come on stream until 1946, was producing 37 million tons in 1952, 6 per cent of a greatly increased world production. All this gave the Middle East a new importance for Britain just as the old importance of the route to India was reduced with Indian independence. It was to be highlighted by the shortage of dollars in Western Europe to buy oil from the USA and the adoption of the Marshall Plan which depended on a lavish and continuous supply of Middle Eastern oil. By 1955 80 per cent of Western Europe's oil consumption was to be supplied from the Middle East compared with 19 per cent in 1938. It did not escape the attention of either Western or Russian military planners that the Soviet Union was closer than any other Great Power to the sources on which the West was increasingly dependent for its energy supplies, or that Russia's own oilfields round Grozny and Baku were open to attack by British or American planes from Middle Eastern airfields.

7

In the Middle East, the problems Bevin inherited in the northern line of states, Iran, Turkey and Greece, were very different from those he encountered in the Arab countries of the Fertile Crescent. For more than a century the British had met Russian pressure southwards, towards the Straits and into Central Asia by a policy of treating the states which lay between the Russians and the route to India as a buffer zone which they themselves did not want to occupy but were unwilling to see occupied by anyone else. The continuity of policy was not affected by the disappearance of the Tsarist and Ottoman Empires and reappeared, after Bevin's death, in the Baghdad Pact[2] of 1955 for the defence of what had then come to be called the states of the "Northern Tier".

Continuity was equally clear on the other side. In 1921 Stalin personally negotiated the Soviet Union's frontier with Turkey and, against Lenin's

---

[1] In 1944 the US War Department decided to build a large air base at Dhahran, the headquarters of Aramco; the British believed that the reason was not military need but preparations to challenge the pre-war connections built up by Imperial Airways. In January 1946 Aramco (jointly owned by Standard Oil of California and the Texas Oil Company) secured a concession to construct a pipeline from the Persian Gulf across Arabia. Saudi Arabia became a virtual American protectorate.
[2] This included Iran, Iraq, Turkey and Pakistan (but not Greece) together with Britain.

wishes, gave armed support to the Soviet Republic of Gilan in northern Iran. As Bruce Kuniholm writes:

"If after 1943, the Soviets carved out a sphere of influence in the Balkans, supported Bulgarian irredentism in Macedonia and Thrace, asked for a port on the Aegean and sought to control the Straits; if they attempted to acquire Turkey's eastern provinces, attempted to carve out a sphere of influence in Iran or contemplated a port on the Persian Gulf, every action had a precedent in Tsarist policies."[1]

The interest in Soviet expansion southwards was the same whether Stalin was dealing with Hitler or the British and Americans. One of the main factors in the breakdown of negotiations for a new Soviet–Nazi Pact in November 1940 was Hitler's reaction to Molotov's statement of Stalin's conditions as including "the establishment of a base for land and naval forces of the USSR within the range of the Bosporus and Dardanelles" and recognition of the Soviet Union's centre of aspirations as lying in "the area south of Batum and Baku in the general direction of the Persian Gulf".[2]

In 1907 the British and Russians had agreed on a definition of their spheres of influence in Persia. This suited the British well. A neutral zone was left between them in which the British succeeded in acquiring the right to develop the rich oil fields around Abadan. The Anglo-Russian Treaty lapsed after the Russian Revolution but the Anglo-Persian (later Anglo-Iranian) Oil Company remained, producing 10 million long tons a year by the outbreak of war in 1939 and representing by its end one of Britain's largest remaining assets overseas.

When Britain and Russia became allies in 1941 they made a new agreement to occupy Iran jointly and use it as the main channel of wartime supplies to the Soviet Union from the West. An undertaking was given to the Iranians that their troops would be withdrawn not later than six months after the end of the war. When the war began to go in their favour, Americans, British and Russians all started to press for oil concessions. The Iranians were reluctant to grant any, and in the end deferred a decision until after the war was over. The behaviour of the Russians, however, suggested that they were interested in more than oil. They had taken advantage of their occupation to establish control over the province of Azerbaijan (adjoining the Soviet Republic of Azerbaijan) and to use this as a base for the economic penetration of Iran and political pressure on the government in Teheran.

In September 1944 the Soviet Vice-Commissar of Foreign Affairs, Kavtaradze, brought a large delegation to Teheran to negotiate for oil concessions and a political agreement. When put off by the Iranians, he openly criticized the Prime Minister at a press conference and expressed the hope that Iranian

---

[1] Kuniholm, p. 4.
[2] Molotov's statement of the Soviet conditions for a 4-power pact with Germany, Italy and Japan, 26 Nov. 1940. *Documents on German Foreign Policy 1918-45*. Series D, vol. xi, pp. 714–15.

public opinion would force a resolution of Irano–Soviet differences. Employing the same tactics as in Eastern Europe, the Russians used the Soviet-controlled Tudeh (Masses) Party, the Central Council of Trade Unions and the Freedom Front to organize demonstrations and a press campaign against the government. Russian troops prevented the Iranian police from restoring order and disarmed them; the American Chargé d'affaires in Moscow delivered a note which spoke of "undue interference in the internal affairs of Iran". On 8 November 1944 the Soviet Union and the Tudeh Party forced the resignation of the Prime Minister. Both the British and US Governments regarded the crisis as a test case for Soviet intentions towards Iran and other countries adjacent to the Soviet Union. A stiffening of Iranian resistance[1] resolved the matter for the moment, but the Russians rejected British and American attempts to get Iran discussed at Yalta.[2] When Eden proposed a staged withdrawal from Iran at the Potsdam conference, Stalin only agreed to the first stage, withdrawal from Teheran, deferring a decision on the remainder and securing deletion of even this from the published communiqué.[3]

Between Iran and and the Balkans lay Turkey and Greece, to both of which the British had given guarantees in 1939 against attack by the Axis powers. The experience of the two peoples in the war which followed differed sharply and this difference was reflected in the problems they were faced with, and faced the British with, at its end.

The Turks had managed, despite strong pressure from the British, to stay out of the war and avoid occupation either by the Germans or by the Russians, the fate of Poland which the Turks regarded as their touchstone. Once the war turned against the Germans and the Russians started to advance into Eastern Europe, their neutrality exposed the Turks to the Russian argument that they had forfeited any claim to special consideration when the war was over. This argument formed the basis of a propaganda campaign which the Soviet press and radio kept up against the Turks from 1943 onwards. The Turks found themselves exchanging the threat of demands under pressure from the Germans for a similar threat from Russia.

Turkish familiarity with the fear of Russian expansion—whatever the regime, Ottoman Empire or Turkish republic on one side, Tsarist or Stalinist autocracy on the other—was grounded in a long history of thirteen wars fought to block a Russian advance towards the Mediterranean. For most of the time it had been British policy to support the Turks. When they found themselves on opposite sides of the 1914–18 war, the British had to swallow,

---

[1] The Majlis passed a law on 2 December prohibiting oil negotiations between the Iranian government and foreigners and requiring the consent of the Majlis to any future concessions.

[2] According to Eden, Stalin laughed when he brought up the matter: "You should not talk to Molotov about Iran. Didn't you realize that he had a resounding diplomatic defeat there? He is very sore with Iran." When Eden suggested a joint plan for the withdrawal of allied forces after hostilities ceased, Stalin said he would think about it, and the discussion ended. Eden, *The Reckoning*, p. 515.

[3] Eden, pp. 595–6.

with great reluctance, a Russian claim to Constantinople and the Straits. Russia's withdrawal from the war relieved her allies of any obligation to enforce the claim; but Russian interest in control of the Straits re-appeared in the conditions Molotov laid down in November 1940 for a pact with the Axis powers, a Soviet base within reach of the Bosporus and the Dardanelles.

Once the Russians had turned back the Germans at Stalingrad, they employed a war of nerves as well as diplomacy to build up pressure on the Turks in anticipation of post-war claims. In March 1945 they denounced the Soviet–Turkish Treaty of 1925 saying that it no longer fitted the circumstances. The Turks were told by Molotov in June that the price of a new treaty would be Turkish consent to Soviet bases in the Straits; Turkish agreement with the Russians on the revision of the 1936 Montreux Convention governing the Straits before it was taken up by an international conference; and the cession of the Kars and Ardahan districts in north eastern Turkey, adjoining the Soviet Republics of Georgia and Armenia.

There was a long history behind the latter claim as well as that for control of the Straits. Four times in the 19th century the Russians had invaded the two provinces of Kars and Ardahan and three times had been forced to restore them to the Turks. They had succeeded in occupying them from 1878 to 1921 but returned them to the Turks under the Soviet–Turkish Treaty of 1921. On that occasion, Stalin had been involved in settling the frontier lines. According to Krushchev,[1] in 1945 Stalin's fellow-Georgian Beria teased and goaded Stalin about recovering territory which the Turks had seized from Russia, persuading Stalin that the Turks had been too much weakened by the effects of the war to be able to resist.

The British were sufficiently impressed by Soviet demands on Turkey to press for these to be discussed at Potsdam. The discussion settled nothing. Both British and Americans were ready to consider revising the Montreux Convention but were opposed to Russian bases or fortifications of any kind at the Straits. As a second best, Stalin sounded out the proposal of a base at Dedeagatch on the Aegean coast of Greece,[2] but preferred to defer a decision, removing any mention of the Straits from the final communiqué. He kept up the pressure on the Turks with press and radio attacks and a crop of rumours, while taking almost a year to send them formal proposals (August 1946).

The impression left on the British by Russian behaviour—and on the Iranians and the Turks—was that Stalin saw the situation left by the war as offering opportunities to realize old Russian ambitions in the Middle East no less than in Europe and the Far East. The opportunities were different in each case. In Europe they were provided by the retreat of the Germans and occupation by the Red Army; in the Far East by the concessions the Americans were willing to make in order to bring the Soviet Union into the war against

---

[1] Krushchev's memoirs, *Krushchev Remembers* (Boston 1974) pp. 295–6.
[2] Churchill *Triumph and Tragedy*, p. 669.

Japan. In the Middle East it was the wartime occupation of Iran, the disadvantage at which the Turks found themselves as a result of their equivocal role during the war and the decline of British power which offered openings to Russian rulers whose confidence had been inflated by the defeat of Germany and the occupation of half Europe. How far they could pursue these opportunities was still uncertain in the summer of 1945: it had still to be seen whether the British would be able to maintain their position in the Middle East or be forced to withdraw; and what interest the Americans would take in the area. At Potsdam therefore Stalin preferred to have nothing decided; thereby he kept his options open and left the uncertainty about Russian interests to do its work.

Greece represented the link between the states of the Northern Tier and the Balkans, and had to be seen in both contexts. Including the Aegean islands and Crete, as well as mainland Greece, it was of strategic importance in British eyes for defence of the route to India, control of the passage into and out of the Straits and the Black Sea, and for the Royal Navy's command of the Eastern Mediterranean. The British had long been concerned to see that there was a friendly government in Athens, while on their side the Greeks had received British support against external threats and in their efforts to enlarge their frontiers to include the Greek-speaking population of the former Ottoman empire. The British made good their 1939 guarantee to Greece in 1941. At a time when the United Kingdom itself faced the prospect of invasion, 74,000 British and Commonwealth troops who could ill be spared from the defence of the Suez Canal, were sent to support the Greeks who had beaten off the Italians but were now faced with a German invasion. The German victory and the consequent loss of the Greek mainland and the Aegean was a severe handicap throughout the war. It was accepted by both the Americans and the Russians that Greece fell within the British sphere of operations and that when the Germans began to withdraw British forces would carry out its liberation.

As the Soviet armies advanced into Eastern Europe in 1944, occupying not only Rumania but Greece's neighbour Bulgaria, Churchill became alarmed at the possibility that the whole of the Balkans, including Greece, might become part of a Soviet bloc after the war. If this were to happen and the Russians were able to use Greek ports and airfields, Turkey's flank would be turned and Britain's command of the Eastern Mediterranean which she had fought hard to recover, would again be challenged. To avert this Churchill made his "percentages agreement" with Stalin in October, recognizing Russia's right to "the first say" in Rumania in return for Stalin's recognition of a similar right for the British in Greece. Stalin, who appears to have had no interest in occupying Greece, made no difficulties and is believed to have already told the Greek Communists that they could expect no material help from the Russians. As Churchill acknowledged at Yalta, the Russian leader kept his agreement and neither intervened nor protested during the events which followed the German withdrawal.

This was not, however, the end of British anxieties. For the real danger in Greece was not external in the form of a Russian invasion, but internal, the capture of power by the Greek Communists acting through some form of united front which they would effectively control. The Greek Communist Party (KKE) had come into its own with the wartime occupation for which its experience of operating underground during the pre-war Metaxas dictatorship had prepared it better than the other parties. In 1941 the Communists took the lead in forming the National Liberation Front (EAM) and in 1942 the National People's Liberation Army (ELAS), taking care to make them representative of a wide spectrum of republican and patriotic opinion and concealing their power over both organizations. Subsequent recriminations among the Communist leaders about the mistakes made in exercising it provide the evidence, but the fact only became widely known later.

EAM/ELAS was not the only resistance group in Greece, but it was the largest and the most effective; this led the KKE to conceive the possibility of monopolizing the Resistance and so gaining control of Greece as the Germans withdrew. The "first round" in the KKE's plan was an unsuccessful attempt to eliminate rival organizations, especially EDES (the National Republican Greek League) under General Zervas, in a civil war in the mountains which lasted for four months of 1943–4. The "second round" was the confrontation after liberation between EAM/ELAS and the Government of National Unity formed by Papandreou in which EAM was represented. If ELAS, with 70,000 men under arms, had seized control of Athens as the Germans left nothing could have stopped them; but there were divided counsels on their side as well as on the side of the Government, and it was only seven weeks after British forces landed that a trial of strength took place. So seriously was this taken by the British that Churchill himself flew to Athens at Christmas 1944 and reinforcements were hastily landed, leading to the defeat of ELAS, and the Varkiza Agreement in mid-February 1945. ELAS, however, although beaten in Athens, still controlled three quarters of Greece, and both sides anticipated that there would be a "third round". If there was, and if the KKE won it, it was hard to believe that Stalin would continue to show lack of interest and not accept whatever advantages offered themselves.

By the time Bevin took office in July the situation had already deteriorated further. Greece was a poor country at the best of times and her economy had been wrecked by the sequence of invasion, occupation, resistance, reprisals and civil war. Eight per cent of the population of seven million had been killed or had died, ten times the death rate for the UK during the war. The Germans stripped the country of livestock and everything else that could be moved; railways, roads, bridges, ports, had been destroyed. When UNRRA brought in supplies, a huge proportion disappeared on to the black market, and the Athens Government proved incapable of mastering the chaos or making a start on reconstruction.

The Greek people were too bitterly divided by the experience to recognize

41

the other side, whichever it was, as belonging to the same nation. Left and Right, as in the Spanish Civil War, denounced the atrocities committed by the others while remaining silent about those they committed themselves. The execution of hostages and reprisals were commonplace and the Government was unable to establish order or guarantee protection.

The political focus for the divisions in Greek society had long been the question, "monarchy or republic". The Varkiza Agreement promised a plebiscite as well as elections: until then the King remained in London. The Communists were allowed to conduct their activities and propaganda as a legal party. They ignored the efforts which the British made to exercise a moderating influence, promote reconciliation and help Greece's economic recovery. Whatever the British might do or say, their policy was represented as intent upon imposing "a reactionary monarcho-fascist regime" by force on the Greek people, and allowing a "right-wing reign of terror" to continue unchecked. These charges had a considerable impact on British liberal and left-wing opinion which was sympathetic to EAM's claim to represent the democratic and progressive elements in Greece and had been critical of Churchill's orders to use British troops to put down an indigenous resistance movement. Greece was one of the countries where Bevin's policy came in for most criticism during the first two years in office; though there were few where his refusal to give way to the criticism had a more directly attributable effect on the outcome of events.

Greece's Balkan context and what was happening in neighbouring Yugoslavia were much in the minds of both the Greeks and the British. In Yugoslavia, a native Partisan movement, in effect a peasant army led by Communist organizers who were professional revolutionaries, had not only defeated every effort by the Germans to suppress them, but in 1944 liberated half their country before the Red Army reached Belgrade. Committees of National Liberation, controlled by the Communists, took over the administration of the liberated areas and, through the partisan assembly (A.V.N.O.J.)[1] elected a provisional government with Tito as premier. Although the British had transferred support from Mihailović to Tito and had sent in large supplies from the spring of 1944, liberation was carried out from within the country without any British or American force landing as happened in Greece. All that the British were able to secure was an agreement (Dec. 1944) between Tito and Subasič (acting for King Peter) which set up a united government with Subasič as Foreign Minister, but required the king to transfer his prerogatives to a regency of three until the question of monarchy or republic could be decided. The politicians who joined the new government (March 1945) soon found that behind the façade of the People's Front all power was in the hands of the Communists. They themselves were isolated, not consulted, and not

[1] Meeting at Jajce in Bosnia in Nov. 1943, declaring itself the "supreme executive and legislative body of the Yugoslav State" and denying the right of the exiled government in London to represent Yugoslavia.

allowed to create any party organizations. When Churchill complained at Potsdam Stalin replied that such serious charges should not be made without the Yugoslavs being brought to Potsdam to answer them, and Truman effectively put an end to discussion by asking whether the matter was serious enough for that, adding that he would find it inconvenient. One by one the non-Communist ministers were forced out or resigned; elections in November 1945, with no opposition candidates, produced a majority of 96 per cent for the Government. Yugoslavia was then proclaimed a republic, and in 1947 the ministers who had left the Government were put on trial for treasonable contacts with the British and Americans and given heavy sentences. Tito and his fellow Communists had made themselves masters of Yugoslavia after a revolution which alone among the Eastern European regimes had its origin inside the country, was not imposed by the Russians and commanded sufficient support to survive every effort by Stalin to subvert it after the open breach of 1948.

In 1945, however, nothing appeared less probable than such a breach. What impressed the world in the regime's first two years was the intense hostility the Yugoslav leaders showed towards the Western powers, not only over Trieste, but during the Paris Peace Conference of 1946, and the impression they left of being even more intransigent than the Russians.

The Yugoslav attitude faced Bevin with a number of problems, notably over Trieste and Yugoslav–Italian relations, but apart from these, it also suggested what might happen in Greece if the EAM ever came to power under Communist leadership. Those on the Left who admired Tito's Yugoslavia might applaud such a development; what continued to impress Bevin was that because of Greece's strategic importance in the Mediterranean it would have greater consequences for the West than a Communist takeover in any other part of Eastern Europe.

8

South of the Northern Tier lay the countries of the Fertile Crescent. Only a small part of it was under direct British rule. Britain's paramount position depended far more upon a network of treaties, protectorates and concessions, and the military force which had been built up during the war and had successfully defended it, capturing Mussolini's African empire in the process. In July 1945 there was hardly a country of the Middle East, from Iran to Libya in the west and Eritrea in the south, which did not have British troops in occupation. There were never less than 150–200,000 in Egypt alone.

Despite their victory, however, the British position was less strong than it appeared. The war had powerfully stimulated nationalism in the Middle East as much as in Asia and well before the fighting in Europe was over this found expression in the demand that the British should get out and leave the Arabs to govern themselves. The election of a Labour Government in Britain, committed by many past pronouncements to ending British rule over other peoples, encouraged the expectation that these demands would be met.

In the case of Syria and the Lebanon it was obvious to the British, even before Attlee and Bevin succeeded Churchill and Eden, that de Gaulle's attempt to put the clock back and restore the special position of France was certain to fail. When fighting broke out between the French and the nationalists in May 1945, the British Army forced the French to desist and to withdraw their troops from the Syrian capital. Refusing to see the changes the war had produced, the French blamed everything on the British, convincing themselves that it was the latter who had encouraged the nationalists and then used the danger of civil war as a pretext for ejecting their traditional rival, France, from her historic position in the Levant in order to replace her. Relations between Paris and London were stretched to breaking point and de Gaulle told the British Ambassador: "We are not, I recognize, in a state to wage war on you now. But you have outraged France and betrayed the West. That can never be forgotten."[1]

But the British themselves were just as firmly convinced that, if they avoided the heavy-handed mistakes the French had made, there was no reason at all why they should not retain their own position. They underrated the resentment of a younger generation of Arab nationalists smarting at the contrast between the condition of their own peoples and the privileges of the occupying power. Preoccupied with the aftermath of war, they did not take sufficiently seriously the absorption of both Egyptian and Iraqi political opinion, now that the war had ended, with achieving independence in fact as well as fiction; seeing all foreign troops withdraw from their soil and, in the case of Egypt, securing recognition of her claim to the Sudan. Even if the British had been quicker to understand the changes they had to deal with, the chances cannot be rated high of their finding such a way of coming to terms with Arab nationalism short of withdrawal. But whatever chances there may have been were reduced to nothing by the complication of Palestine and the impact this had not only on Anglo–Jewish but also on Anglo–Arab relations.

The theme of this introductory chapter, that Bevin did not start with a clean slate but stepped into a highly charged world situation is nowhere more clearly and tragically illustrated than in the case of Palestine. The Palestine Mandate had been bedevilled from the beginning by the double undertaking of irreconcilable commitments to the Jews and Arabs. To the Jews it repeated the promise of the Balfour Declaration to establish a national home in Palestine for the Jewish people. This was to be done, however, without prejudice to "the civil and religious rights of existing non-Jewish communities". But these at the time the Mandate was granted to Britain (1920) made up 90 per cent of the population of Palestine, the overriding majority of them Palestinian Arabs

---

[1] De Gaulle: *Mémoires de Guerre*, vol. 3, *Le Salut 1944-46*, p. 194. (4 June 1945).

who took the terms of the Mandate[1] to be a recognition that they would in time become a self-governing and independent nation in the same way as the other Arab peoples under mandate in Iraq, Syria, Lebanon and Jordan were eventually to do.

There was no possibility of the Zionists realizing their objective of a Jewish state—whether as an immediate or an ultimate objective—unless the balance of population in Palestine could be altered by immigration. This is why immigration became the key issue and was always seen by those opposed to the Zionist programme in political, not humanitarian, terms. The figures for immigration in the 1920s were small—eight thousand a year in the early 1920s—and even began to show a fall in 1929 to a figure of 4,075 in 1931. In 1933, however, the year Hitler came to power, the total rose to over 30,000; in 1934 to over 42,000, and in 1935 (the year of the Nuremberg Laws) to just under 62,000. Exiles from Germany made up a little less than one-eighth of the total between 1932 and 1935, compared with 43 per cent from Poland. Nonetheless, it was the publicity given to Hitler's openly anti-Semitic policy which aroused the European Jews to the danger which threatened them and gave to the Zionist dream of a National Home in Palestine a hold on Jewish imaginations and a desperate urgency which it was never to lose. The consequence was immediate. In 1936 the Palestinian Arabs, seeing themselves faced with what they regarded as a bid to take over their country, rose in rebellion. Between the two irreconcilable forces, the British pursued for another ten years the search for a compromise which would satisfy neither Jews nor Arabs but could be regarded as fair because it would deny to both alike their hope of seeing Palestine become either a Jewish or an Arab state.

Both Arabs and Jews complained of the unfairness of British policy before the war, but there were two reasons why the British Administration leaned more towards the Arab than the Jewish side. In their eyes the Jews were the aggressors who could only secure their objectives by challenging the *status quo* in Palestine, which the British administrators saw themselves as there to defend. Secondly, with the approach of war, the British Government took the view that, while the Jews would have no option as to which side they supported, it was essential to secure Arab goodwill, not just in Palestine but throughout the Middle East, if Britain was to defend her position there successfully. The Palestine White Paper of 1939 and its reception illustrate the difference. It did not satisfy the Arabs because it still allowed a limited Jewish immigration, but it outraged the Zionists because this was to be restricted to 75,000 over the next five years, after which no further Jewish immigration would be allowed "unless the Arabs of Palestine are prepared to acquiesce in it".

[1] The "A class" mandates applied to "certain communities belonging to the Turkish Empire" which had "reached a stage of development where their existence as independent nations could be provisionally recognised". The Palestinian Arabs took this to refer to themselves in the same way as the Arab populations of the other mandated territories.

The war was won and Britain's position in the Middle East successfully defended; and it can be argued that the White Paper, by taking the edge off Arab anger with the British over Palestine, helped to contribute to this. But in every other way the war increased the difficulties of the British in Palestine, and exposed the inadequacy of the White Paper as a policy.

For the war had brought with it increased persecution of the European Jews culminating in Hitler's deliberate attempt to destroy them, the horrific "Final Solution" which transformed the situation in Palestine. The refusal of the Palestine Administration and the Colonial Office to recognize this and to admit more than the quota of refugees fixed in the White Paper was seen by the Jews as making the British Hitler's accomplices in the extermination of their people. The consequences which followed from these two facts defined the Palestine problem as it confronted the Labour Government immediately on taking office.

The first was the conviction among a growing number of Jews throughout the world that the Zionists were right and that the only way to save the Jewish people was to establish a state of their own which could be nowhere else than in Palestine.

The second was the determination of the Zionists to defy the British ban on "illegal" immigration and run the blockade maintained by the Royal Navy, at whatever risk to the refugees. The blowing up of the *Patria* by the Jewish Haganah in November 1940 with the loss of 250 lives, and the sinking of the *Struma* off Istanbul in February 1942, with the loss of nearly 800, were blamed without question on the British by the great majority of Jews in Palestine and helped to induce their total alienation from the Administration, turning in many cases to passionate hatred.

Even before news of the Final Solution reached the outside world, a Zionist conference of 600 delegates was held in the Biltmore Hotel, New York, in May 1942. It adopted a programme calling for the abrogation of the White Paper; opening Palestine to Jewish immigration under control of the Jewish Agency; the creation of a Jewish Army and the establishment of a Jewish Commonwealth.

Once the details of the Nazi extermination camps became known the Zionists were seized with a single-minded determination, which subordinated all other considerations, to provide a refuge for the survivors of the Holocaust. As Christopher Sykes says, only a great people could wrest political advantage from such a tragedy; but it removed still further any possibility of a peaceful solution to the Palestine problem.[1]

No less important was the initiative now taken by American Zionists to lobby the US Government with the object of securing American pressure on the British Government to abandon their opposition to the creation of a Jewish state. This campaign was pursued with unremitting purpose and brilliant

[1] Christopher Sykes: *Cross Roads to Israel* (London 1965) p. 170.

organization until it culminated six years later in American recognition of the State of Israel.

In Palestine itself the Jewish community, the Yishuv, organized a shadow government and the acquisition of arms. These preparations could provide for self-defence, or be employed against the British once the war was over. The extremists refused to wait, carrying out acts of terrorism which culminated in the murder of Lord Moyne, the British Resident Minister in the Middle East on 6 November 1944.

The Arabs, on the other hand, their nationalism and demands for independence stimulated by their wartime experience, saw no reason at all why an Arab land, as they regarded Palestine, should be required to accept a flood of refugees for whose misfortunes they bore no responsibility, while the rest of the world, including the Americans and the British, passed resolutions of protest but were adamant that they could offer no places. Their leadership warned the British that they expected them to keep the undertaking of the White Paper that further Jewish immigration would depend upon the acquiescence of Palestine Arabs.

In the midst of these conflicts and mounting passions, relations between the Palestine Administration and the Jewish community had come to resemble those between an occupying army and the actively hostile population of an occupied country. Beneath strained official relations, each regarded the other as the enemy. Not even Churchill, a lifelong supporter of Zionism, with the exceptional powers of a wartime Prime Minister, had been able to reverse the conviction of successive British Governments and their advisers that British interests in the Middle East (including the increased importance of access to Middle Eastern oil) and the large Muslim population of India (90 millions) made it necessary to give priority to not alienating Arab and Muslim opinion rather than to re-settling the survivors of European Jewry in a Jewish state in Palestine. In face of opposition from the Foreign and Colonial Offices, Churchill had insisted on reviving the idea of partition recommended by the Peel Commission in 1937, only to let it drop again after Moyne's murder.

Would the election of a Labour Government produce a change? In April 1944 the National Executive of the Labour Party had published a paragraph in its annual report which declared:

"There is surely neither hope nor meaning in a 'Jewish National Home' unless we are prepared to let Jews, if they wish, enter this land in such numbers as to become a majority. There was a strong case for this before the War. There is an irresistible case now, after the unspeakable atrocities of the . . . Nazi plan to kill all Jews in Europe."

The Executive Report actually advocated a generously subsidized transfer of the Arab population elsewhere, a proposal from which Ben Gurion was at pains to dissociate the Zionist Labour Movement.[1] What remained to be seen

---

[1] Text of the NEC Report and of Ben Gurion's comment (11 May 1944) in George Kirk: *The Middle East in the War* (London 1952) p. 317.

was whether the Labour Party, in office, would make good the commitment which it had consistently undertaken to Zionism while in Opposition; or, once in power again, would repeat the reversal represented by Sidney Webb's White Paper of October 1930, a White Paper which Bevin's intervention, at the request of the Zionists, had helped to modify.[1]

The question was soon put. A fortnight after VE Day, before the British election, Weizmann sent Churchill a memorandum demanding the full and immediate implementation of the Biltmore Programme. Abdul Rahman Azzam, Secretary General of the Arab League, declared that Western support of Zionism could cause "a new Crusaders' War", while President Truman, who had been pressed by the Governors out of 38 of the 48 States of the Union to declare unequivocal American backing for the Zionists, wrote urging Attlee to issue the 100,000 certificates as soon as possible. The Jewish demands and the Arab reaction were predictable; direct intervention by the American President was not. This was a move which Roosevelt had carefully avoided making. It represented the first fruits of the Zionist change of tactics after the Biltmore conference and a new factor which none of Bevin's predecessors had had to contend with.

---

[1] See Vol. I, pp. 456–7.

CHAPTER 2

The Labour Government of 1945–50

I

Taken together this was as formidable a list of problems as any British Foreign Secretary had ever been called upon to face. Even so, it was only half the story. The unique difference between Bevin and his predecessors, for the first time since Britain began to play a leading part in world affairs in the 18th century, was the lack of the power with which to sustain such a rôle. The British had frequently been caught unprepared for war: that was nothing new in their history and had happened again at the beginning of the Second World War. But they had never, before the end of that war, lacked the industrial, economic and financial power to make good their deficiencies and support their diplomacy.

The change was due to a combination of two factors. One was the full emergence as world powers of the USA and the USSR, each of which could draw upon continental resources on a scale which automatically pushed other nations down into the second rank. No European state could henceforward compete with them on equal terms, and if Europe remained the focus of world politics for another decade, it was as the object of Russo–American rivalry, no longer as an independent centre of power.

This development coincided with another, a weakening in Britain's position by comparison not simply with the new standards set by the two continental powers, but with her own strength at earlier periods in her history. After the extraordinary exertions she had made during the war, Britain was insolvent for the first time in her history, could not pay her debts or even pay her way without further borrowing from the United States and Canada. According to the figures presented in the negotiations for an American loan, the war had cost Britain a quarter of her national wealth, or some £7,300M. A large part of this was accounted for by the destruction of physical assets such as housing and shipping, but the most important item in the calculation was the sale of foreign assets valued at £4,200M to pay for supplies bought abroad during the war. The earnings on these foreign assets had played a big part in paying for

British imports before the war. Now, simply to pay for the pre-war level of imports, which included much of her food and raw materials for industry, Britain would have to increase her exports by 50 to 75 per cent over the pre-war figure,[1] and this at a time when the pent-up demand at home was quite capable of absorbing everything that a rundown British industry, still turning back from war production, could hope to supply.

At the same time Britain had increased her debts to other countries from £476M. in August 1939 to £3,355M. in June 1945. Thanks to Lend-Lease, she was not burdened with a further load of war debts to the USA, but Lend-Lease was very soon to be ended abruptly, and Great Britain, not so many years before the world's leading financial and industrial power, could only hope to buy what she needed to keep her people fed and employed, if the United States could come to her aid again with a loan of at least £1,500M.

From the day they came into office, Labour ministers were confronted with the hard fact that the country's economic and financial weakness was going to set limits to all their plans. This applied as much to foreign policy as to domestic, perhaps even more. Britain no longer had the spare resources to put into the reconstruction of Europe, to undertake the development of the Middle East or to smoothe the transition from empire to Commonwealth by grants-in-aid to India and other colonies moving towards independence. On the contrary—largely, as the Americans thought, through an improvident imperial pride—she had burdened herself with a series of debts to her partners in the Sterling Area which she was to find it beyond her power to liquidate. Egypt, in place of her former dependency, had become a creditor to whom Britain owed £400M. in blocked sterling balances, India £1,116M. Before long it became a question whether, even with the American loan, Britain could afford to import sufficient supplies to maintain a reduced standard of living for her own people, and nothing so heavily underlined her loss of power as her forced abandonment, less than two years after the war ended, of the unilateral commitments she had accepted in occupying the British zone in Germany and promising military and economic aid to Greece and Turkey.

The Americans and the Russians had realized well before the end of the war that Britain's resources were no longer adequate to support the place Churchill claimed for her as their equal among the Great Powers. The Americans welcomed this as likely to force the British to accept the American lead in the post-war settlement, to adopt economic policies they had hitherto resisted and grant independence to their colonial empire. On the other hand they took it for granted that Britain would continue to play a world role —modified to accommodate American interests—and had not yet faced the question, what would be the consequences if the British were no longer able to do that and what changes this might bring in the USA's own role. The Russians were very much aware of both questions and kept open their options

[1] From 150 to 175 where 100 = 1938.

until they could see how long the British would be able to maintain their position in the Middle East and Europe, what opportunities a British withdrawal would open up for them, and whether the Americans would take the British place.

Once the war was over and Britain's economic weaknesses were no longer disguised by her military efforts, other foreign powers—and her own dependent territories—were not slow to read the signs and also treat Britain as a once great empire in decline. It fell to Bevin (and this was one of the reasons why Attlee had put him at the Foreign Office) to make clear to those who presumed too far that while Britain might no longer be as powerful as she had been, she was still a nation to be reckoned with and had no intention of being pushed around or left out of account.

The British, of course, were not the only people to come down in the world. The same thing had happened even more drastically to the Germans, the Japanese, the Italians and the French, all of whom had suffered defeat and occupation. But this was where the difference lay. The British had not been defeated, they had won the war and felt that proportionately they had made as great a contribution to winning it as any of their allies. Most British people, without thinking much about it, assumed that when the war was over—a war in which they alone of the victorious coalition had fought from the first day to the last—the efforts they had made would entitle them to resume their old place in the world. Few yet realized that it was a question not of entitlement but of power. Their first reaction to the economic difficulties in which they found themselves was to treat them as a bad patch due to the war from which the country would recover. Only gradually was it borne in on them that, even with the economic recovery which eventually bore fruit in the 1950s, there had been a permanent change in Britain's position and that she would never again dispose of the resources to play the role of an independent Great Power.

The process of adjustment on the part of the British—involved at the same time in the abdication of their imperial position—was long and painful. It was not complete until long after Bevin's death, not even when the British joined the European Economic Community more than twenty years later.[1] Bevin, however, was the first Foreign Secretary to have to face Britain's changed position and the need for adjustment both in relations with foreign states and in attitudes at home. Frustration and resentment at the limitations on Britain's freedom of action, as much among the disappointed idealists of the Left as among indignant traditionalists on the Right, easily found expression in belabouring the Foreign Minister who could be denounced, according to point of view, for betraying the cause of socialism or failing to defend British

---

[1] I was present at a dinner in Bonn in 1976 given by the German Chancellor, Helmut Schmidt, at which James Callaghan, the British Prime Minister, and Tony Crosland, the Foreign Minister, were the principal guests. Replying to Helmut Schmidt, James Callaghan remarked: "The mistake we made was to think we won the war." The Germans and British present agreed that this was a comment which went to the heart of the matter.

interests. His own party in particular showed itself divided on the role Britain should seek to play in the post-war world and Bevin's sharpest critics were to be found on the benches behind him, an uncomfortable situation for any minister.

Attlee and Bevin came back from Potsdam to find the Labour Party still elated by its victory and largely unaware of the diplomatic tensions abroad or of the true economic and financial situation of the country. The war was over, a new world was there to be made and at precisely this moment the Party had captured power for the first time since it had been established in 1900. The two previous Labour governments had lacked a majority in the House of Commons and held office on sufferance: in 1945 Labour had captured 393 out of the 640 seats against the Tories' 213, with an unassailable majority over all parties of 146. There were many who believed that the election of 1945 marked an irreversible alteration in the political balance; that Labour had acquired a permanent advantage over the Tories and that it was in office, if not for ever, at least for a long time, with the power to make far-reaching changes. For those who had spent their lives working for the Labour Movement the Promised Land seemed at last in sight and the establishment of a "socialist commonwealth" only a matter of time.

Later, a disillusioned Left was to see 1945 as a lost opportunity for making a break in the continuity of British history, without which (they argued) it was impossible to establish a socialist society. But little, if any, of this was heard in the Labour Party at the time. The Government's foreign and defence policy came in for plenty of criticism from the Left, especially in 1946 and 1947, and the antecedents of Bevanism and the disputes which shook the Party in the 1950s can now be seen to lie in the amendment criticizing Bevin's foreign policy in November 1946 and the publication of *Keep Left* in 1947 which provided a focus for left-wing disenchantment. But on domestic policy, Labour's primary interest, the Party succeeded in preserving a remarkable degree of unity for almost the whole of the time it was in office, indeed up to the resignation of Aneurin Bevan, Harold Wilson and John Freeman in April 1951.

There were good reasons for this. No previous British government in modern times ever carried through such a series of reforms and no parliament faced such a crowded timetable of legislation. In the first nine months, Attlee told the party conference in 1946, 75 bills had been introduced and 55 had received the Royal Assent. In all, the Parliament elected in 1945 put 347 Acts on the Statute Book. The implementation of the Beveridge Report (which has been described as the real "social gospel" of the 1940s); the creation of the National Health Service and the welfare state; the commitment to full employment and economic planning; the nationalization of coal, steel, transport and the power industries; the transformation of the Empire by the grant of independence to India, Burma and Ceylon; the retention of controls, rationing and food subsidies (the wartime policy of "fair shares") to regulate the transition from war to peace—all these could be viewed by the Left as the first stage in the introduction of socialism and by the majority of the Parliamentary Party and Labour voters as carrying out Labour's election programme pretty well to the letter. There were dark suspicions that the nationalization of steel, regarded by many in the Labour Party as well as by the Tories as the touchstone of the Government's socialist purpose, would not be put into effect, but it was. Not until 1949, when the Government was coming to the end of the original programme to which the Labour Party had committed itself in 1918, did the question, What next? begin to raise the differences about future policy which were to divide the Party so sharply in the 1950s.[1]

In the elections of 1950 and 1951 the Labour Party lost the massive majority of seats it had won in 1945, but it added to the aggregate number of votes cast for it in the country, raising this from 11.9 million in 1945 to 13.2 in 1950 and 13.9 in 1951.[2] In both 1950 and 1951 Labour still polled a higher percentage of the total vote than the Conservatives.[3] In other words, there is no evidence of disillusionment on the part of Labour voters—certainly not of Labour's working class supporters—with the Attlee Government's performance. This suggests that the programme which the Labour Government carried out between 1945 and 1950, however much it might later disappoint the Left, was pretty much what Labour supporters had voted for in 1945.

The result was not a social revolution in any Marxist sense or a socialist society, but when added to the changes which had already occurred during the war—in which Bevin and other Labour ministers had played a leading part and which they were now able to make permanent—it left Britain in 1950 a very different country, with its welfare state and mixed economy, from the Britain of the 1930s, and for Labour's working class supporters at least a better one. This was achieved in face of external conditions far worse, and a loss of economic and financial power far greater, than anyone had foreseen.

The abrupt ending of Lend-Lease in 1945 was followed by a world food crisis leading to the introduction of bread rationing in 1946; by devaluation in 1949; and finally by the economic crisis which followed the outbreak of the Korean War. It was a cruel irony for the Labour Government that when they had at last come to power with a clear mandate to carry out their programme, when

---

[1] See the *New Statesman's* comment in its issue of 15 May 1949: "The plain fact is that the Labour Party is reaching the end of the road it first set itself to traverse in 1918 . . . What next?" For the disputes of the 1950s, see Stephen Haseler, *The Gaitskellites* (London 1969); Philip Williams, *Hugh Gaitskell* (London 1979); and Michael Foot: *Aneurin Bevan*, vol. 2. (London 1973).

[2] The Conservatives raised theirs from 9.9 million in 1945 to 12.5 in 1950 and 13.7 in 1951. The difference is accounted for by a higher turn-out of the electorate in 1950 (84%) and 1951 (82.5%) in comparison with 1945 (72.7%) and by the drop in the Liberal vote from 2.2 million in 1945, 2.6 million in 1950 to 0.7 in 1951.

[3] Figures:

	Labour	Conservatives	Nos. voting
1945	11,995,000 (50.4%)	9,988,000 (39.8%)	25,085,000 (72.7%)
1950	13,266,000 (46.7%)	12,502,000 (43.5%)	28,772,000 (84%)
1951	13,948,000 (49.2%)	13,717,000 (48.6%)	28,595,000 (82.5%)

the expectations of their supporters were at their highest, they should be forced to bend so much of their energies to preventing the economy from breaking down and to put a far higher proportion of their limited resources than they would have wished, if they had been free to choose, into meeting the requirements of foreign policy and defence.

It is to the credit of the Labour leaders that they did not let this succession of emergencies divert them from their long term domestic programme and still managed to achieve a surprising degree of economic recovery: in 1950, on the eve of the Korean War, the British balance of payments was better than at any time since the 1920s. If this was due more than anything else to American aid (the dollar loan followed by the Marshall Plan), it is also true that in 1951 British exports came within one point of the target figure of 175 per cent compared with the level of 1938.

2

If circumstances had given him the chance, Bevin would have made as big a contribution to solving the economic and industrial problems of the transition from war to peace as any man in the Labour Movement. These were problems he had thought about for years, and by 1945 he had acquired the experience of government and the mastery of the administrative process to put his ideas into effect with a drive and resourcefulness which, judging by his wartime performance, none of his colleagues could have matched. If he had been given the chance, for example, to take on housing instead of Nye Bevan, he was one of the few men who might have succeeded in getting on top of a problem which has defeated one administration after another in 20th-century Britain. Nor was there anyone better fitted by temperament and native ability to cope with the emergencies, such as the 1947 fuel crisis, which threatened to swamp the Government's programme. As it was, his contribution could only be made indirectly, or at any rate behind the scenes.

Instead of being given the opportunity to add to the reputation he had won in wartime and earn the gratitude of the Labour Movement, he was called on to accept the most thankless task in the Government and one which was virtually certain to bring anyone who undertook it into conflict with his party. It would be a serious mistake, however, to let his departmental responsibilities as Foreign Secretary obscure the central rôle which he played in the Labour Cabinet, a rôle which extended to much more than foreign affairs. Once again, as in the wartime coalition, he was one of a small group of senior ministers —Attlee, Morrison, Dalton (until 1947), Cripps—who effectively ran the government of the country, and within that small group he held a special place, not only by virtue of his personal qualities but because of his relationship with Attlee on the one hand and his unique position, not so much as the representative but as the embodiment of the trade union movement, on the other.

Although he was the head of an administration which must be counted amongst the strongest in modern British history, Attlee showed himself the most elusive of Prime Ministers. No doubt anyone succeeding Churchill at the height of his renown would have found it hard to avoid the impression of anti-climax: Attlee seemed to go out of his way to create it. No politician ever made less effort to project his personality or court popularity; in place of Churchill's heroic style, his speeches were dry, matter of fact and often banal. He preferred understatement to rhetoric, and his most effective weapon in debate was a gift for deflation which more than once took the wind out of Churchill's sails.

For the leader of a party, particularly a party of movement, Attlee was remarkably lacking in any charismatic quality and showed little interest in ideas. In Cabinet he behaved more like the impartial chairman of a committee than the leader of a government. He rarely expressed an opinion of his own, let others do most of the talking, contenting himself with collecting views round the table and then crystallizing the consensus. "He doodled when he should have led", Morrison complained, and every one of his colleagues at one time or another, including Bevin, expressed exasperation with his detachment, his lack of emotion and refusal to give a lead. Nye Bevan would entertain his friends by quoting Hazlitt on Pitt—"With few talents and fewer virtues, he acquired and preserved in one of the most trying situations and in spite of all opposition, the highest reputation for the possession of every moral excellence"—and go on to describe Attlee as "Labour's Lord Liverpool", the Arch-Mediocrity delineated by Disraeli: "He was peremptory on small questions and the great ones he left open".[1]

Attlee's unassuming manner and laconic habit of speech, however, were deceptive: they concealed both a determination to stay Prime Minister and a confidence in his ability to do so. There were half-a-dozen men in the Government with more obvious talents than his own; it was Attlee's strength as a Prime Minister that he turned this to his advantage. Unaffected by vanity and with a shrewd eye for the strengths and weaknesses of his colleagues, he left them a free hand in carrying out their different jobs and made little or no attempt to impose his own views on departmental policy. He was, as Henry Pelling puts it, a master of the *coup de repos*.[2] It was not a way of running a government to satisfy the more assertive characters who sat in Cabinet with him, but by refusing to commit himself to one side or the other, Attlee established not only his impartiality but his indispensability: he was the one man under whom all the others could agree to serve, the man best suited to hold together a party which contained very different, and at times conflicting, views.

There could hardly have been a greater contrast in appearance and manner

---

[1] Foot, *Bevan*, 2, pp. 28–9.
[2] Henry Pelling: *A Short History of the Labour Party* (London 1961) p. 125.

than that between Attlee and Bevin: one spare, dry, and undemonstrative, the other a heavyweight in personality as well as physique, temperamental, passionate and egocentric. But from their very different backgrounds, the one as impeccably English middle class as the other was English working class, they found it natural to take the same pragmatic view of politics. Bevin was a suspicious man, especially where politicians were concerned, but he had slowly come to regard Attlee as being one of the few men in politics whose word could be relied on, and once he made his mind up his loyalty was unshakeable. With greater historical insight than Bevan, he compared Attlee to Campbell-Bannerman, another political leader patronized and under-estimated by abler men on both sides of the House who had proved his indispensability as Prime Minister. For his part Attlee was as much aware of Bevin's weaknesses as of those of his other colleagues, but he looked on them as unimportant by comparison with his strength of character and steadiness of judgement. More than that: "he had", Attlee declared, "the most capacious mind of any man I ever knew."[1]

In a Government which had its full share of jealousies, quarrels and ambitions, it was a major source of strength to the Prime Minister (as Attlee was the first to recognize) to be able to count, from first to last, on the support of the most powerful member of his administration. No move to replace him as Prime Minister could succeed without Bevin's agreement and, as 1947 as well as 1945 showed, Bevin would have nothing to do with any such manoeuvre.[2] Like so many men who worked closely with Bevin, Attlee held him in affection as well as respect.

"My relationship with Ernest Bevin was the deepest of my political life", he told his biographer. "I was very fond of him and I understand he was very fond of me. Loyalty is a great virtue in private life and an even greater one in the stormy sea of politics—second only to courage. . . . Ernest was the living symbol of loyalty . . . once he gave his trust to you he was like a rock."[3]

The benefits Bevin derived in return were equally important. Apart from their personal relationship it was the Prime Minister alone who could give him the scope in which to play the role he did as Foreign Secretary and their five and a half years' co-operation, which was undisturbed by any serious disagreement until Bevin as a dying man gave up the Foreign Office in 1951, constitutes one of the most successful political partnerships in English history. "In fact," Michael Foot remarks, "often enough Bevin *was* Attlee. It would be folly to overlook the powerful authority of this composite figure."[4]

There was no danger that anyone would overlook it at the time. At the end of

---

[1] In conversation with the author.
[2] For 1947, see below, pp. 441–2 and 455–6; for 1945, see vol. II, pp. 391–5.
[3] Harris, *Attlee*, p. 294.
[4] Foot, *Bevan*, 2, p. 32.

Cabinet meetings it was Attlee's habit to keep Bevin behind when the other ministers left and settle in private with him what was to be done. As Attlee cheerfully admitted, there was no record of these talks, but the constant exchange of notes between the two men shows that it extended to the whole range of Government business, and bears out Attlee's statement that he was as careful as Bevin was not to take any important decision without first making sure that he had the other's agreement.[1]

Bevin's responsibilities as Foreign Secretary were regarded by Attlee as extending to a general supervision of the country's external relations and not stopping short at Commonwealth or colonial affairs, economic policy or defence. Thus immediately after the war he was chairman of the Overseas Reconstruction Committee and of the Far East ministerial committee which dealt with colonial reconstruction and food supply as well as foreign policy. Bevin took over the responsibility for finding a solution in Palestine and in 1946 for the administration of the British Zones in Germany and Austria. He was hardly less involved than the Chancellor, in the crucial economic relations with other countries playing the leading part in taking up Marshall's offer of June 1947, in creating the Organization for European Economic Co-operation and launching the Colombo Plan. His role on the Defence Committee was second only to that of the Prime Minister; he was a member of the secret *ad hoc* committee, General 75, which made the decisions on Britain's atomic programme and the manufacture of atomic weapons, and he took the lead in creating the Western European Union and NATO, the framework of Britain's post-war defence policy.

On the domestic side, besides being chairman of the Cabinet's Manpower Committee, Bevin was a member (sometimes acting as chairman) of the Economic Policy Committee and of the Socialization of Industries Committee. George Isaacs at the Ministry of Labour soon found that Bevin had no intention of letting his old Ministry out of his sight for long. Even when he was not directly involved, no minister was more frequently consulted by his colleagues: thus, Dalton discussed both his 1945 and 1946 budgets in detail with Bevin, and most other Ministers at one time or another as well as successive Chiefs of Staff (Alanbrooke, Montgomery and Slim) found occasion to talk over their problems with him and get his support. The Secretary of the Cabinet, Sir Edward Bridges, thought there was no member of the Labour Cabinet more prepared to take trouble in helping his colleagues in this way, adding that he was also "immensely helpful" in pushing on the business of government.

There were of course other trade unionists in the Cabinet besides Ernie Bevin, but none who ever questioned Bevin's right to speak for the trade unions. More important still, although he had severed his formal links with the Movement, no Labour Cabinet has ever had a minister who could talk with

[1] In conversation with the author.

Bevin's authority to the union leaders or who retained until his death so great a hold on the loyalty of the active members serving on union committees and delegations.

It would be hard to exaggerate the importance for the Attlee Government of a close and dependable relationship with the trade union leadership. In face of the economic problems which beset them from the start of 1947 union support was essential if industrial troubles were to be contained and if Cripps' policy of increased productivity and wage restraint was to have a chance of succeeding. But the importance of union support extended beyond the industrial and economic sphere: it was an essential element in enabling Bevin to carry out his foreign policy and the key to holding steady behind the Government the political support of a Party which, as its later history shows, was liable to ideological division. How important that was can be seen from the swing to the Left in the 1960s of the leadership of the TGWU and the miners, and the change which this produced in the Labour Party. In the 1940s these two unions together with the Municipal and General Workers formed the solid base on which the Attlee Government was able to pursue its policies without much fear that it might have to face effective opposition from within its own party.

Although trade unionists were not so strongly represented in the Parliamentary Labour Party after the war as they had been before, in 1945 there were still 188 out of 393 Labour MPs who had held trade union office and altogether 120 who were sponsored by unions. Outside the parliamentary party, the two possible alternative centres of power (apart from the TUC itself) were the Labour Party's National Executive and its annual conference. Election to two-thirds of the seats on the Executive was effectively controlled by trade union votes and as Laski, its chairman in 1945–6, discovered to his chagrin, unless the unions so wished, it could not be used as a base from which to exert pressure on the Government. At the Party's annual conference the affiliated membership (and therefore the voting strength) of the unions heavily outnumbered that of the constituency parties: the unions' block votes added up to 80% of the total.[1]

No one understood the power of the trade unions within the Labour Party better than Ernie Bevin. The affiliated membership of the TGWU which he had created accounted for one million or 13 to 15 per cent of the votes at every Conference between 1945 and 1958 and it has been calculated that on the 56 card votes taken in the same period the way the TGWU delegation voted was decisive in thirteen, nearly one in four. Not that the trade unions' votes were all cast one way. That is a myth. There was always a minority which, on occasion, could muster a substantial number of votes, and the majority had to be worked, and sometimes fought, for.[2] Throughout his ten years of office as a

---

[1] See Martin Harrison: *Trade Unions and the Labour Party since 1945* (London 1960).
[2] See below, pp. 551.

minister Bevin kept in constant and close touch with Arthur Deakin, his successor as the TGWU's General Secretary,[1] with Will Lawther, Sam Watson, Tom Williamson and other members of the TUC's General Council. These were not men of straw—they could not have carried their unions with them if they had been—but they were prepared to listen to Bevin not only on foreign affairs, but on economic, industrial and political issues, as they would have done to no other minister because they regarded him as still one of themselves. In return, Bevin's position in the Government gave them access to the Cabinet, inside knowledge of what was happening and a guarantee that their point of view would never go unrepresented. Only a man as completely trusted as Bevin by the Prime Minister and the Cabinet on the one hand and by the union leaders on the other could have maintained such a link without disaster. Bevin managed to do it until his death without either side feeling that its long-term interests were being sacrificed to the other's, a feat in which he has had no successor and one of the keys to understanding the history of the 1940s.

3

Bevin's relations with the Labour Party, particularly with the Parliamentary Labour Party, were more equivocal and had always been so. Unlike some of the other union leaders, he had never doubted the need to support the political activities of the Labour Party, and the Party's Secretary, Morgan Phillips —like his predecessor Jim Middleton—regarded him as one of the first men to go to whenever the Party was in financial difficulties. On the other hand Bevin made it very clear in the 1930s that he looked on the Party not as an autonomous body but as the political wing of the Labour Movement the real trustees of which were the trade unions. The block vote and the 80 per cent of the Party's funds provided by the unions[2] reinforced his view, but Bevin's heavy-handed intervention at Party conferences to remind the delegates of the limits to their freedom of action was bitterly resented by the more politically-minded, especially on the Left.

All this was years before and Bevin was no longer the General Secretary of the TGWU but had himself become one of the leaders of the Labour Party. None the less, this earlier history was not forgotten and it was underlined by the circumstances in which he had joined the Parliamentary party. He was nearly 60 when he entered the House of Commons for the first time and he took

---

[1] Sir Roderick Barclay, one of Bevin's Principal Private Secretaries, writes: "When, as sometimes happened, he failed to appear at the F.O. at the expected time after lunch, we usually discovered that he had gone off to Transport House for a gossip." Sir Roderick Barclay: *Ernest Bevin and the Foreign Office* (London 1975) p. 80.

[2] This is the average figure for the unions' contributions to central Party funds between 1944 and 1950 (inclusive). It does not take account of union contributions to regional and constituency Labour Party funds.

his seat (which had been found for him) as a minister from the start. This meant that he missed the years of apprenticeship on the back benches, by way of which almost every other minister had reached the Cabinet, and never served on the Executive Committee of the PLP or the National Executive of the Labour Party. Even more to the point he had never experienced the long years in opposition which left so deep a mark on the Labour Party. His own political experience was limited to the Government front bench and was reflected in his remark that the Labour Party had to get rid of its opposition mentality and instead of a party of protest become a party of power.

This was true enough but Bevin's irritation with the difficulties that the Party had in making the adjustment, his anger with what he regarded as its "factionalism", put him at a disadvantage by comparison with old party hands like Attlee or Morrison who took it as a matter of course and were far more skilled in managing potential opposition within the Party's ranks. It was a disadvantage from which Arthur Henderson, Bevin's predecessor as Foreign Secretary in the 1929 Labour Government, had not suffered either. For although he too had begun his career as a trade union official, he had served a long parliamentary apprenticeship, entering the House in 1903, 26 years before he became Foreign Secretary. Even more important, Henderson was Secretary of the Labour Party from 1910, and so in control of the party organization as well as co-author with Sidney Webb of the 1918 Constitution which established it as a national party and committed it to a socialist policy. Bevin's attitude, by contrast, even after he became a minister, continued to be coloured by his experience in the trade union movement where opposition to the majority view meant disloyalty, a threat to the solidarity on which any negotiation or industrial action depended and the gravest crime in the trade unionist's calendar. As Attlee said:

"There was no place for the rebel in Ernest's organization (the TGWU) not, at any rate, in its formative years or at any other time when it might be in danger. He was a 'majorities' man and was impatient of minorities. In this respect he ran counter to one of the most important traditions in the Labour Party."[1]

The large number of new Labour Members of Parliament—253 out of 393—who entered the House of Commons for the first time in 1945, many of them young and straight out of war service with little knowledge of the Party they had joined, set the Labour leadership a difficult problem. All the places in the Cabinet and a good many outside went to the Old Guard who had served the Party loyally before it came to power in 1945; only a limited number of junior offices could be found for the ablest of the newcomers and the average age of the Cabinet was over 60, a good deal older than that of the parliamentary party it now led. The new recruits were not only younger, they included a much higher proportion than before the war of men and women of middle-

---

[1] In a review of volume I of this work, published in *The Observer*, 13 March 1960.

class origins. Where elementary schooling had been the common experience before, over a hundred of the PLP in 1945 had been educated at universities and more than a third followed professional occupations—lawyers, teachers, university lecturers, journalists—not to mention a group of twenty or thirty classified by Professor Guttsmann[1] as entrepreneurs or managers. The Labour Party was changing in composition and nothing showed this more plainly than the fact that teachers now outnumbered miners as the largest occupational group on the Labour side of the new House of Commons.

In these circumstances, with more than three hundred of its 383 members condemned to serve on the back benches and little, if any, hope of office for the majority, there was bound to be frustration at the inability of the rank and file to influence leaders from whom they were separated by the gap of a generation. There was little opportunity for this frustration to find expression on domestic issues: the Government was carrying out a legislative programme on which the Party was agreed. Herbert Morrison who was in charge of it was a skilful Leader of the House, and in fact on only eight occasions in the years 1945–50 was there even the threat of a revolt, and none of major importance. Foreign policy and defence were different matters. Foreign affairs in particular was a subject in which a number of the newcomers were deeply interested, felt themselves to be knowledgeable and whether acting out of conviction, frustration or ambition were more prepared to criticize their leaders than on issues directly affecting the traditional working-class interests of the Party.

Dissent is news, and the Press as well as the Opposition (which largely agreed with the Government's handling of foreign policy) were eager to magnify the differences in the Labour Party. The galaxy of talent which the Left inside and outside Parliament disposed of as journalists and pamphleteers (Crossman, Michael Foot, Kingsley Martin, Harold Laski, to name only four) provided them with plenty of copy. To keep the scale of opposition within the Parliamentary Labour Party in perspective, it is important to remember that the number of MPs classified as "persistent offenders"[2] amounted to no more than twenty-four (all but two of whom had entered the House in 1945 or later); that the largest body of support they were able to attract was some 70 (out of 393 Labour MPs) who abstained on the decision to join NATO in 1949; and that the one issue on which the Government retreated in face of a back-bench revolt was the traditionally sensitive question of conscription (March 1947).

None the less it is also true that dissent within the Labour Party between 1945 and 1950 was concentrated on issues of foreign affairs and defence; that a minority on the Left of the Party kept up a persistent criticism of the Government's foreign policy both inside and outside the House and that the principal target of this guerrilla warfare from first to last was Ernest Bevin.

[1] W. L. Guttsmann: *The British Political Elite* (London 1963) p. 270 and generally c. 9.
[2] Defined by Guttsmann (p. 268) as those who opposed the Government on four, five or at most seven different occasions.

Granted that Bevin was never deterred from doing what he wanted to do by this opposition from his own back benches, his way of handling it added to his difficulties. His attitude to the External Affairs Group illustrates this well. As a means of improving communication, Morrison instituted a number of such groups which would enable back benchers interested in a particular subject to meet regularly with the minister concerned. Dalton at once set out to collect a hand-picked group of the ablest younger members he could find, invited them to meet in the Chancellor's private room and turned a potential source of trouble to real advantage.

"Bevin in sharp contrast," Dalton wrote in his memoirs, "had a terrible group on Foreign Affairs. He did not pick it, as I did. He let it pick itself. And in came all the pacifists, and fellow-travellers, pro-Russians and anti-Americans, and every sort of freak harboured in our majority. . . . The group as a whole was hopeless. Bevin seldom met them . . . They met, not in the Foreign Secretary's room, but in Committee Rooms upstairs. And there they drafted critical resolutions and prepared argumentative papers which, if he ever read them, merely infuriated him. One difference between Bevin and myself in 1945 was that I knew a majority of the Labour MPs and made it my business to get to know them all, whereas Bevin knew very few of them and made no serious efforts to extend his knowledge."[1]

This is fair criticism: Bevin was no more prepared to try and win over his critics, or even meet them, than he had been when faced with a break-away group in the TGWU. He scorned such tactics as politicians' tricks, preferring to fight his critics—and win—rather than sit down and talk. The difference was less one of tactics than of personality and experience. But it would be a mistake to let the personal feeling which was involved between Bevin and his critics—on both sides—obscure the fact that there was a real conflict of views which went back to the 1930s, and during the 1950s became part of the fight between fundamentalists and revisionists in the Labour Party to which it can be seen as a prelude.

In an often quoted passage published in 1937, eight years before he became Prime Minister, Attlee wrote:

"There is a deep difference of opinion between the Labour Party and the capitalist parties on foreign as well as on home policy, because the two cannot be separated. The foreign policy of a Government is the reflection of its internal policy . . . Particular instances of action which can be approved by Socialists do not affect the proposition that there is no agreement on foreign policy between a Labour Opposition and a capitalist government."[2]

---

[1] Hugh Dalton: *High Tide and After. Memoirs 1945-60* (London 1962), pp. 22–3.
[2] C. R. Attlee: *The Labour Party in Perspective* (London 1937) pp. 226–7.

This quotation sums up the Labour Party's attitude to foreign policy in the 1930s, an amalgam of views derived from pre-1914 radicalism, pacifism and Marxism. It rejected the pursuit of national interests and power politics as the traditional ruling class's conception of foreign policy, in favour of friendship and co-operation between peoples whose "real" interests, it was argued, were the same in all countries. It rejected (in theory at least) loyalty to the nation state in favour of loyalty to the world community, and it rejected imperialism in favour of equality between peoples and the end of economic exploitation. Capitalism and war, indissolubly linked, were seen as the twin evils which Labour was committed to eradicate. From this followed strong suspicion of the foreign policy of any capitalist government, particularly that of a leading imperialist power like Britain: the task of the Labour Party was not only to fight capitalism at home but its natural expression abroad, imperialism, power politics and war. From this in turn followed the rejection of force in settling international disputes; resistance to any increase in armaments or preparation for war; international solidarity with other working class movements, support for Left-wing parties and governments in other countries and strong sympathy for the Soviet Union as the only socialist state in existence.

These views, although held in different individual versions, were hardly questioned at all in the Labour Party until the mid-Thirties and were as much part of orthodox belief, particularly on the Left, as Clause 4 of the 1918 Constitution committing the Party to nationalization. They were first challenged in 1934–5—and the challenge came from the trade union leadership. Bevin and Citrine were quicker than most politicians in Britain to grasp the threat represented by the Dictators, and to ask how Mussolini and Hitler were to be stopped. Bevin took the lead in a campaign to bring the Labour Movement to face the issue of the use of force in support of collective security, the turning point in which was his attack on Lansbury at the Brighton Conference of 1935. He went on, as Chairman of the TUC, in combination with Dalton and Citrine, to get the Labour Movement to end its opposition to rearmament under a capitalist government as a necessary condition of organizing resistance to the Dictators. It was, in fact, in the discussion of foreign rather than domestic policy that Bevin played his most important role in Labour Party politics before 1940.[1]

The Labour Party remained divided on foreign policy up to and indeed after the outbreak of war. The debate, however, was not only bitter (Bevin was never forgiven for his attack on Lansbury and on the other side Cripps as well as Nye Bevan was expelled from the Party) but confused, not least by the Conservatives' policy of avoiding war by appeasement. It was also inconclusive; it did not lead to any agreement on the lessons to be drawn from the experience of the Thirties or to a fundamental re-thinking of the principles of a socialist foreign policy before it was overtaken by the events of 1940.

---

[1] See vol. I, pp. 546–51; 560–71 and 590–95.

The decisive experience in bringing the Labour leaders to take a different view of foreign policy was their five years in office as members of the wartime coalition. This affected not only Bevin (who had already gone a long way in questioning the orthodox socialist view before the war) but Attlee, Morrison, Dalton and, most surprising of all, Stafford Cripps.[1] To exercise power and share in real decisions had a profound effect on men whose abilities had hitherto been cramped by lack of scope and by membership of a party which was more at home in opposition than in office. The circumstances of wartime, the concentration of issues, the narrowness of the margin by which Britain scraped through, heightened the impression.

This was an experience of government at its peak, uncomplicated by parliamentary manoeuvring or party rivalry which were suspended during the war. With it went the experience of working successfully for five years in the closest co-operation with men who were their political opponents and, in the view of many in the pre-war Labour Party, their class enemies. Attlee and Bevin, Morrison and Dalton were not so naive as to suppose that, once the war was over, there would not be a return to party politics on domestic issues where there were clear conflicts of interest as well as opinion which had been put on one side during the war but were already re-appearing whenever the Cabinet discussed post-war reconstruction. They no longer, however, took the view which Attlee had expressed in 1937, that differences between the parties in domestic politics were bound to express themselves in foreign policy as well.

By joining the coalition the Labour leaders had recognized that for them, as much as for Churchill and the Tories, there was an overriding national interest, a concept which many in the Labour Party had traditionally rejected in theory at least as incompatible with loyalty to internationalism and irreconcilable with the class war. The same was true of Labour's traditional rejection of armaments and the use of force. In the minds of Bevin and Attlee, this could hardly survive their experience of the risks run by an ill-prepared country in a war of national survival, any more than Labour's refusal as a matter of principle to recognize power politics, when this was the environment under pressure of which all the coalition's wartime decisions had to be made.

Nor did Labour ministers any longer see the Commonwealth and Empire in terms of the imperialism denounced by radicals and Marxists, but instead as a powerful support to Britain in the war and the guarantee of her continued influence as a world power afterwards. A Labour Government's policy for the development of self-government in India and the colonies would still be very different from Churchill's, but no more than Churchill did Attlee intend to preside over the dissolution of the British Empire. In a Cabinet paper circulated in June 1943, he wrote:

[1] Cripps had been a leader of the Left before the War and had been expelled from the Labour Party. After the War and particularly after he became Chancellor of the Exchequer, he bore an equal responsibility for the Labour Government's foreign policy with Bevin and Attlee and defended it vigorously against left-wing criticism.

"I take it to be a fundamental assumption that whatever post-war international organisation is established, it will be our aim to maintain the British Commonwealth as an international entity, recognised as such by foreign countries, . . . If we are to carry our full weight in the post-war world with the US and the USSR it can only be as a united British Commonwealth."[1]

The mention of the USA and the Soviet Union in Attlee's paper points to another lasting impression, that of the limited resources of a nation of less than 50 million people which had to be stretched to the utmost during the war to match the much greater national resources of her two allies and which would not allow Britain to maintain her position in the post-war world by her own exertions. Although it still came as a shock to them when they resumed office on their own, Labour Ministers were already aware during the war that the country would be in a much weaker position than anyone outside the closed circle of Whitehall yet realized.

These general impressions were reinforced by the part which Labour Ministers took in the discussion of post-war international policy in the War Cabinet and its committees. Besides Germany, other post-war questions which the War Cabinet and the Armistice and Post-War Committee considered were the future world organization (the United Nations); the prospects of agreement with the Russians and Americans on a European settlement; Soviet attitudes towards the West, both before and after Yalta; Russo–Polish relations; France and a Western Union; South East Europe and the importance for British communications of retaining control of the Eastern Mediterranean.

The range of topics and the part played in these discussions by Labour Ministers, especially Attlee and Bevin, is of capital importance in understanding the policies that the Labour Government was to adopt after the war. Left-wing critics like Laski were mistaken in their belief that the coalition foreign policy which they wanted to see ended was a Churchillian policy imposed on the Labour members of the coalition. It was a mistake which the subsequent publication of Churchill's war memoirs did nothing to correct. To judge by Churchill's account, which for many years was the principal source for the history of the war on the British side, post-war policy was something which he largely settled in personal communication with Roosevelt and Stalin, with Eden acting as his faithful lieutenant and the rest of the War Cabinet little more than cyphers. But this is an over-simplified picture. Now that the official British records are available, it is possible for the first time to see how much preparation and discussion lay behind Churchill's personal diplomacy and how much others—Eden and the Foreign Office, the Chiefs of Staff, Labour Ministers, in particular Attlee and Bevin—contributed to what was a genuine coalition policy. It was this joint contribution which made it natural for the

---

[1] PREM 4, 30/3, W.P. (43), June 1943. "The Relations of the British Commonwealth to the Post-War International Political Organisation" by C. R. Attlee.

Labour leaders to insist on continuity of foreign policy, even after they accepted their Party's desire to break up the coalition and fight the Tories on domestic issues. And it was this experience of two years' preparatory discussion of the post-war international settlement, discussions conducted in office not in opposition, as members of a coalition not a party administration, with all the resources of government, including a mass of secret information, and with their minds focused on the national interest in a world dominated by power politics, not on hopes of a European revolution or the principles of a socialist foreign policy, which shaped the Labour leaders' and particularly Bevin's and Attlee's views when they came to formulate the policy of a Labour Government after the election.

4

This experience, however, was limited at most to the twenty or thirty members of the Labour Party who held office during the war. Because they were members of a coalition not a party government, and because wartime conditions cut them off behind a screen of secrecy, ministers' responsibilities were not shared in the normal way with other members of the PLP, still less with the rank and file in the constituencies. The leaders, busy with their official duties, found little time to argue the case for the change which had taken place in their own views and were in any case reluctant, in time of war, to raise issues which could only prove divisive.

The result was to leave the Left free, with little or no competition within the Labour Party, to expound their version of the lessons of the Thirties and to argue that the war must be followed by a revolutionary peace if its cost was ever to be justified and if the defeat of Nazism was to be completed by removing the conditions which in the Left's view had produced it, namely capitalism. Despite their differences, this was a theme common to the *New Statesman* and *Tribune*, to left-wing politicians in the House like Nye Bevan and Konni Zilliacus, and to intellectuals like Kingsley Martin, Harold Laski and G. D. H. Cole outside it.

There was a widespread belief, extending far beyond the Labour Party, that Europe after the War would go left, that this was the general trend of Resistance politics and that it would be supported by the Soviet Union. The war, Laski argued, was part of a European revolution, a European civil war, and he went on to draw a parallel between Churchill and Pitt fighting to preserve the *ancien régime* against the revolutionary idea symbolized by Napoleon. That was the danger: intervention by the Anglo–American alliance which Churchill had made the basis of his foreign policy, an Unholy Alliance of the leading imperialist and the leading capitalist power to check the tide of revolution, as they had sought to do in Russia (with Churchill in the lead) after the First World War. "The State Department and Foreign Office," *Tribune* declared in January 1945, "are set on trying to prevent the peoples of Europe from making any revolutionary changes in their political and social organisation." For confirmation they pointed to the deal with Badoglio in Italy, and at the end of 1944 to Churchill's forceful intervention in Greece which had drawn protests even from the Americans.

This was a difficult argument for Labour Ministers to answer as long as they remained members of the coalition government. For any defence they might make of the coalition's policies—as Bevin did in the case of Greece—invited the retort either that they had been duped by Churchill or that they had sold out to the Tories, as MacDonald, Snowden and Thomas had done when they took part in a National Government in 1931. The matter was not settled when the coalition was dissolved after victory in Europe. It was known that three of the Labour Ministers at least, Attlee, Bevin and Dalton, had thought there would be advantage in continuing the coalition into the post-war period and that one of the reasons for this was their anxiety about the international situation. The Left was suspicious that Labour's leaders had not yet purged themselves of the heresy of continuity or accepted the need for Labour to carry out a socialist foreign policy. This explains Laski's reaction, as Chairman of the Labour Party, when he protested at Churchill's invitation to Attlee (his successor as Prime Minister if Labour won the election), to accompany himself and Eden to the Potsdam Conference. If Attlee accepted, Laski declared, it was essential that he should only go in the role of an observer. The Labour Party could not be committed to any decisions arrived at by the Conference, as the Party had a foreign policy which in many respects would not be continuous with that of a "Tory-dominated coalition".[1]

Laski's statement provoked an exchange of letters between Churchill and Attlee in which both made it clear that there was no question of Attlee going as a mere observer. Ignoring Laski, Attlee agreed with Churchill that "there seemed to be a great public advantage in preserving and presenting to the world at this time the unity on foreign policy which we maintained through the last five years". He added that he did not anticipate differing from Churchill on the main lines of policy which they had so often discussed together.[2]

It was not a hastily considered reply. In the debate on Yalta in March 1945, Attlee had spoken of the vote of confidence for which the Government was asking as a step towards "the achievement of a unity of policy in foreign affairs and defence"[3]—the exact opposite of the view which he had expressed in 1937. Bevin took the same line. In a speech at Leeds in April 1945, an occasion which he used to underline the difference between the parties in the coalition on domestic questions Bevin went on to draw a clear distinction between these and questions of defence and foreign policy on which "there is an imperative necessity for the will of the nation as a whole to be expressed, for

[1] *The Times*, 13 June 1945.
[2] *Ibid.*, 16 June 1945.
[3] HC 1 March 1945.

a combined effort to be made."[1] But neither Attlee, Bevin nor any other Labour leader elaborated the reasons which had brought them to a conclusion so different from traditional socialist views.

It is easy enough now to see why ministers were reluctant to speak out. While the British people, and not just those who were supporters of the Labour Party, were still looking forward to a post-war world in which freedom from conflict would be secured by the continued co-operation of the wartime allies, in the inner circle of government the hopes raised by Yalta were replaced in the spring of 1945 by alarm at the evidence that the Russians meant to act on their own, without worrying about British and American agreement or protests, and see how far they might be able to extend their power beyond their pre-war frontiers. It was still true that no country had more to gain from a genuine three-power agreement on Europe than Britain, but a genuine agreement not a sham. As Bevin told the Labour Party Conference at Blackpool in May: "Round the table we must get, but do not present us with *faits accomplis* when we get there." The reference to Poland which he made immediately afterwards leaves no doubt to whom he was referring.[2] It was under the impression of these anxieties that Attlee and Bevin insisted on the need for continuity in foreign policy. When Bevin addressed the Party Conference at Blackpool he warned the delegates that foreign affairs would face a Labour Government with "its most vexed and difficult problems". Nobody had any doubt that the security for peace rested with the three Great Powers, but it was not going to be easy to remove the differences and prejudices between them.

"You will not do it, comrades, by slogans . . . by saying that one country is all angels and the other all devils. You have got to do it by patience." Bevin went on to remind the conference that "Collective security involves commitments and I do beg Labour not to bury its head. . . . I do not know how the World Organisation will turn out, whether it will be effective . . . but we must introduce another National Service Act for a limited period until we know exactly what is going to happen. . . . With the experience I have gained, I will not be a party to misleading the country or the conference."

This was as far as Bevin ventured to go. Even Churchill, who was more depressed by the prospect in Europe than anyone and was moved to make some of his most eloquent pleas to the Americans and Russians, hesitated to say anything in public that would make agreement more difficult. Attlee, always pre-occupied with party unity, had an additional reason for not revealing his anxieties: he would have run the risk of dividing his Party and discouraging it on the eve of an election which it was crucial for Labour to win if it wanted to carry out the reconstruction programme on which its members

[1] Vol. II, pp. 349–50 and pp. 368–70.
[2] See Vol. II, pp. 382–5 for further extracts from Bevin's speech. At the time he made the speech, Bevin had no idea that he would become Foreign Secretary and no particular wish to do so. His real wish was to become Chancellor of the Exchequer.

had set their hearts. The cursory treatment of international relations in the election manifesto did nothing to enlighten them.

It is true that Bevin's speech at Blackpool received a standing ovation and he now began to be spoken of as a possible Labour Foreign Minister, but his hint of trouble ahead made little impact on a conference excited by the defeat of Hitler, the feeling that the tide of history was flowing in Labour's favour and the recovery of its political freedom to fight the first general election for ten years. How little impact is shown by the curious fact that the one remark in Bevin's speech which was quoted again and again in subsequent months was taken out of context and misrepresented what he had said. This was the phrase "Left understands Left, but the Right does not". Bevin had applied the phrase to France, referring to the leftward trend in French politics at the time of the Popular Front and the lack of sympathy with which it met in Britain. But it was universally quoted as if he meant it to apply to Russia and was claiming that a Labour Government would find it easier than a Conservative to reach agreement with the Soviet Union—a claim the conference would have loved to hear Bevin make and been happy to endorse but not at all what he said or thought.

The Left was as aware of the latent conflict as the leaders of the Party but no more than Attlee wanted to run the risk of a split on the eve of the poll. So Labour fought and won the election with the majority of the Party unaware of the anxiety with which its leaders regarded the international situation or how far they were from agreeing with those who believed that, with a Labour victory coinciding with the end of the war in Europe, the time had at last come to put into effect "socialist principles" in foreign no less than in domestic policy. This unresolved conflict added an extra dimension to the long list of international problems which confronted Bevin when he took over the Foreign Office.

5

The radical change in foreign policy for which the Left-wing of the Labour Party hoped could only have come about as part of a much wider and radical break with that tradition of continuity in government which was the essential characteristic of the British political system. In retrospect it is clear that the Labour Government did not make such a break and that in practice (whether they realized its implications or not) men like Attlee and Morrison accepted, and were indeed attached to, the complex and interlocking structure of Parliament, Cabinet and Civil Service which they had inherited. The only thing that might have driven them into revolutionary courses would have been a refusal by the Opposition or, more serious, by the permanent servants of the State, the Civil Service as the guardians of continuity, to accept their authority as a constitutionally elected government. This did not happen: as a result the changes introduced, though real enough, were absorbed, the structure of Government adapted and continuity preserved. Socialism remained the myth which kept the Party actively reformist.

In retrospect one can reasonably ask whether the continuity in foreign policy to which Bevin committed himself was all that different from the rest of the policy of the Labour Government, but at the time there is no doubt that to many in the Labour Party it seemed so. This was partly because there was a genuine ambiguity about Labour's domestic programme, which kept alive the enthusiasts' hope that it was only the first instalment of a real break with the past; but also because, while Opposition and Labour leaders vied with each other in crying up the revolutionary effect of the Government's legislative proposals, Bevin made no attempt to dress up his foreign policy in partisan, still less in revolutionary, colours.

While he never explicitly repudiated the aspirations of socialism in foreign policy—any more than he had in economic policy while negotiating as a trade unionist—he made it clear enough during the course of his first year of office that he did not regard these aspirations as capable of providing him with any basis for an operational programme in the very difficult world with which he had to deal after the war. In Bevin's view not only were they irrelevant to the real world in the middle of the 20th century: he also regarded them as misleading in the illusions, both idealist ("an end to power politics") and ideological ("Left understands Left"), which they perpetuated.

It took time for the full implications of Bevin's attitude to sink in and longer still for him to find the framework in which he could develop a positive policy with a real chance of rallying support in the Labour Party. But from the very first day he appeared in the House as Foreign Secretary he made no attempt to conceal where he stood on the issue of continuity.

Although foreign affairs played little part in the election campaign, the moment Labour's victory was announced, speculation started up, both in the British Press and abroad, whether the change of government[1] would be followed by a reversal of the coalition's foreign policy. Harold Laski, the Chairman of the Labour Party National Executive argued that the new Government had been elected with as clear an expectation of radical change in foreign as in domestic policy and repeated the claim when he attended the French Socialist Party conference as a fraternal delegate. Laski was neither a member of the Government nor even of Parliament, but people abroad did not understand the position he held in the Labour Party (no more, it appears, did Laski) and were likely to take what he said as authoritative.

Laski's statements in Paris brought him a sharp rebuke from Attlee:

"You have no right whatever to speak on behalf of the Government. Foreign Affairs are in the capable hands of Ernest Bevin. His task is quite sufficiently difficult without the

---

[1] Between the break-up of the Coalition Government and the result of the general election, Churchill held office with a caretaker Conservative administration from 25 May to 26 July 1945.

embarrassment of irresponsible statements of the kind which you are making. . . . I can assure you there is widespread resentment in the Party at your activities and a period of silence on your part would be welcome."[1]

Characteristically, however, Attlee's rebuke was delivered in private: he left it to Bevin to make the Government's position clear in public, and the expectation of this added to the interest in Bevin's first speech as Foreign Secretary in the course of the debate on the King's Speech.

For anyone less sure of himself it would have been an ordeal. Never at home in the House, he had now to leave the ground on which he was acknowledged master and move on to the unfamiliar territory of foreign affairs, in Tory eyes the preserve of the traditional governing class, and in the eyes of many of the newcomers, on the Labour benches a subject more properly reserved for one of the intellectuals of the Party than for a trade unionist. Such thoughts did not trouble Bevin, any more than the knowledge that he would be speaking after Churchill and would be followed by Eden.

A day or two before he was due to speak, he summoned one of his Private Secretaries (Valentine Lawford, who has described the scene) and a secretary to his room.

"'Come in, Missy,' said Bevin 'and sit down here beside me.' He was puffing with defiant satisfaction at a forbidden cigar. Then, gazing quizzically up at the gilded girders on the ceiling, the Foreign Secretary slipped, as it were, *con sordino* into a rambling after-luncheon monologue, uninhibited by considerations of grammar or syntax, and punctuated less by any recognisable vocal equivalent of commas or semi-colons or full stops than by the occasional pauses required for blowing smoke, coughing, removing tobacco leaf from his tongue, or dusting the ash from the lapels of his coat. . . . And then, at the fifth or sixth page of her shorthand notes, the soliloquy ceased as softly, almost imperceptibly, as it had begun. 'All over, Missy,' said the new Secretary of State with a wink . . . 'and Lawford here,' he added, looking still at her and not at me, 'will just turn that into English if he can.'"[2]

In opening the debate, Churchill was friendly enough to the new Secretary of State, but did not conceal his dislike of what was happening in the Russian-occupied half of Europe or his foreboding of what this meant for the future. When his turn came to reply, Bevin did not evade the issue of "continuity" but showed skill in steering a middle course. On the one hand, he was forthright in declaring that the governments which had been set up in Rumania and Bulgaria did not represent the majority of the people and in pressing the Polish Government to fulfil its assurances of free elections. He refused to accept Left-wing views on the situation in Greece or to embark on a policy of intervention in Spain. On both these questions, which the Left regarded as tests of the Government's intentions, Bevin's answer was in favour

---

[1] Attlee to Laski, 20 August 1945, quoted in Francis Williams: *A Prime Minister Remembers* (London 1961) p. 169.

[2] From an article "Three Ministers" by Valentine Lawford in *The Cornhill Magazine* No. 1010 (Winter 1956–7) comparing three Secretaries of State he had worked for: Halifax, Eden, Bevin.

of "continuity", and he did not draw back when Eden, his Conservative predecessor at the Foreign Office, speaking later in the debate, underlined this.

"What the Foreign Secretary has said," Eden declared, "represents a foreign policy on behalf of which he can speak for all parties in this country".[1] Earlier, referring to their close collaboration in the War Cabinet, Eden said:

"During that period there were many discussions on foreign affairs but I cannot recall one single occasion when there was a difference between us. I hope I do not embarrass the Foreign Secretary by saying that."
"*Mr Bevin:* 'No.'"

On the other hand, although he found time to say something about Iran, the future of Hong Kong and relations with Siam, Bevin refused to be drawn on Potsdam. Only at the end of his speech did he refer—and then perfunctorily—to the most important question of all, Britain's relations with Russia and the United States.

Bevin's first appearance as Foreign Secretary got a remarkably good press both in Britain and abroad. *The New York Times* praised his steadiness of judgement,[2] the *Manchester Guardian* called him "a Foreign Secretary in the big mould"[3] and *The Observer* a great one.[4] Although his speech was well received by Tories and Liberals, however, there was a noticeable lack of enthusiasm on the Labour benches. Bevin had appeared, as he meant to, in the role of a man appealing for national, all-party support, and this was a role which had little attraction as yet for the bulk of Labour members who would have cheered him to the echo if he had made a partisan speech aimed at Churchill and the Opposition.

In the next few months Bevin did nothing to add to his popularity in the Party by his refusal to carry out a purge in the Foreign Office. The Foreign Office was a powerful symbol for many members of the Labour Party of all that they most objected to in traditional foreign policy. Its unrepresentative, class character and that of the Diplomatic Service had been a target for Radical criticism since the days of Tom Paine and William Cobbett. Zara Steiner, in her study of the Foreign Office in the period 1898–1914, writes:

"All the clichés were true: it was indeed the stronghold of the aristocracy and everything was done to preserve its class character and clannish structure."[5]

Between the wars some changes had been made: it would not otherwise have been possible for a man like William Strang, a farmer's son from a

[1] HC 20 August 1945.
[2] *New York Times*, 26 August 1945. See also the same paper's leading article of 22 August, the *Christian Science Monitor* and the *Chicago Daily News* of 22 August.
[3] *Manchester Guardian*, 21 August 1945. See also *The Times, News Chronicle, Daily Telegraph, Daily Mail* of the same date.
[4] *The Observer*, 26 August 1945.
[5] Zara S. Steiner: *The Foreign Office & Foreign Policy 1898-1914* (Cambridge 1969) p. 16.

country grammar school, to enter the Foreign Office and eventually become Bevin's Permanent Under-Secretary. Other changes were discussed between Bevin and Eden during the war and were incorporated in the *Proposals for the Reform of the Foreign Service*, published as a White Paper in January 1943 and implemented by Bevin as the foundation of the post-war foreign service. Bevin's starting point in his discussions with Halifax and Eden, as early as the autumn of 1940[1], had been the neglect of economic and social questions in foreign policy. His own tenure of office made certain that this was remedied. Apart from such major measures as the Marshall Plan, by the end of the 1950s Labour Attachés were serving at British Embassies in eighteen countries and regularly reporting on social and economic conditions. Finally, for the crucial negotiations on the Marshall Plan and NATO, Bevin did not hesitate to bring in Sir Oliver Franks from outside the Foreign Service and persuade him to continue in the key post of Ambassador in Washington. Nonetheless, at the time when Bevin became Secretary of State, the Foreign Office was still something of a world apart in Whitehall and nothing would have made Bevin more popular with his own Party than the clearing out of the "Old Gang" which Dalton (a product of Eton and King's himself) was certain he would have carried out.

Sir Alexander Cadogan (the son of one earl who had served in Salisbury's Cabinet and been Viceroy of Ireland, the grandson of another) had been Permanent Under-Secretary and head of the Foreign Office since 1938, a longer term of office than usual. He expected to be retired and Bevin's initial request to him to stay on could be interpreted as a desire not to make changes until the task of handing over had been accomplished. Questions were soon being asked in the House as well as in the Press: "Are the present diplomats with their present outlook" (a Labour back-bencher, Dr Morgan, demanded) "to carry on the policy in Europe, or are we to have diplomats with a Labour and Socialist outlook?"

By the end of the year Bevin's answer was uncompromisingly clear. No one was dismissed and in every case where he might have justified a political appointment he chose a career diplomat instead: Cadogan himself as Britain's first Permanent Representative at the UN; Sir Archibald Clark-Kerr to replace Halifax in Washington (a post for which Laski had made a bid and for which a trade unionist, Jack Tanner, had been tipped as a favourite); Sir Maurice Peterson to replace Clark-Kerr in Moscow. As Cadogan's successor at the Foreign Office, Bevin appointed his Deputy, Sir Orme Sargent, and in Paris allowed a former Tory minister, Duff Cooper, to remain as the British Ambassador until 1947, a decision which could be justified on the grounds of his exceptional standing with the French but one which certainly aroused criticism in the Party. Bevin's only concession to party feeling was his agreement to Attlee's choice of the high-minded and respected Philip Noel-Baker as

---

[1] For the memorandum drawn up by Bevin at that time, see Vol. II, pp. 199–202.

Minister of State at the Foreign Office, where he had little, if any, influence on policy and in October 1946 was replaced by the more congenial Hector McNeil.

Criticism of Bevin's action was expressed in a formal resolution at the Party's Conference in 1946 calling on him to replace officials who were unsympathetic with socialist principles by others with more progressive views. He was unrepentant, defending himself with gusto[1], and making much of the reforms which he had helped to introduce during the Coalition Government, amongst them the appointment of Labour Attachés, the merger of the Diplomatic, Colonial and Consular Services, the widening of recruitment, and equality between men and women.[2] In time, he declared, these changes would transform the newly combined Foreign Service but "I am not going sacking right and left. Before I make a change I want to know I can . . . carry on successfully."

On one point he was adamant: he would not make political appointments to the top posts in the Foreign Service. This would only have a depressing effect on the prospects of young men entering the Service as a career.

"You can keep on prodding me every year. I do not mind. But I want to work out a clear, well-defined, organised method to make this service worth while for the Labour Governments that you will elect as time goes on. It is said that these men do not carry out my policies. I deny that. I beg of you not to try to introduce the wrong principle into the Civil Service. I have had a good experience now for six years. What the Civil Service likes is a Minister who knows his mind and tells the officials what to do. They will then do it. If it is wrong, the Minister must take responsibility and not blame the Civil Service (applause). That I am prepared to do."[3]

Instead of appeasing his critics, Bevin challenged them to stop sniping and come into the open. His defence was successful not only in winning him an easy victory at the Conference but in moving the debate to the real issue between them.

6

After Bevin's declaration that anyone who wanted to criticize the Government's foreign policy had better hold him responsible, less was heard of reactionary officials in the Foreign Office, and left-wing criticism in the

[1] "I am not one of those who decry Eton and Harrow. I was very glad of them in the Battle of Britain—by God! I was—those fellows paid the price in the RAF in those fatal days."
[2] Although he defended the Foreign Office against external attack, Bevin himself was critical of its administration. In a letter to Sargent (13 May 1946), his principal private secretary Dixon wrote: "He is frankly dissatisfied both with the position regarding the recruitment of new personnel and with the administration of the Office." Improvements followed but not of a sort to satisfy the politically-minded critics of the FO.
[3] Speech at the Labour Party Conference, Bournemouth, 12 June 1946.

autumn of 1946 focused on Bevin himself as the man responsible for the "betrayal" of Socialist hopes.[1]

By then, anxiety over Bevin's handling of relations with Russia and the USA was coming to a head and the campaign against him reached its height with the tabling of an Amendment to the Address signed by 57 Labour MPs in November 1946 (in effect, a vote of censure on the Labour Government's foreign policy) and the publication of *Keep Left* in April 1947.[2] After that the tide of opinion in the Party and in the country generally turned in Bevin's favour, but for most of 1946 and part of 1947 he had the uncomfortable experience of being singled out as the main target of criticism not by the Opposition but from within his own Party. The fact that he not only survived but did so without making any concessions to his critics and emerged to achieve his greatest successes as Foreign Secretary, underlines the strength of the position he held in the Government.

Professor Donald Watt distinguishes between two different interpretations of the role of the Secretary of State for Foreign Affairs.[3] One requires him to be the representative of the Cabinet, acting in its name, and the channel by which the professional advisers can make their advice known to the Cabinet. The Foreign Office and Diplomatic Service play the part of counsellors and executives but the responsibility for deciding policy lies with the Cabinet. Professor Watt thinks this is the proper view, but as he points out there is a second, and historically more prominent, version which makes the Foreign Secretary the originator of policy and the principal spokesman on foreign affairs in both Cabinet and Parliament. There is no doubt that this was the case with Bevin, and he stands as the last of the line of foreign secretaries in the tradition created by Castlereagh, Canning and Palmerston in the first half of the 19th century, with Salisbury, Grey and Austen Chamberlain as his predecessors in the 20th century and (thanks to the reduction in British power) with no successors.[4]

Bevin was able to play this role, because Attlee, reversing the practice of the two previous prime ministers, Churchill and Chamberlain, took the line that "foreign affairs are the province of the Foreign Secretary. It is in my view a mistake for the Prime Minister to intervene personally except in exceptional circumstances."[5] Or, as he put it to Kenneth Harris, "You don't keep a dog and bark yourself—and Ernie was a very good dog."[6]

Attlee of course may well have taken the view that as foreign policy was the

---

[1] Examples are the four articles "Reorientations" published by the *New Statesman* on 31 August 1946 and successive weeks in September. See below, p. 313.
[2] See below, pp. 327–9.
[3] D. C. Watt: *Personalities and Policies* (London 1965) Essay 9.
[4] Sir Orme Sargent who served under every British foreign minister in the 20th century from Salisbury onwards and ended up as Bevin's Permanent Under-Secretary, went out of his way to tell the author that by comparison with any of his predecessors he considered Bevin a great foreign secretary.
[5] Francis Williams, *Prime Minister*, p. 149.
[6] Harris, p. 268.

main source of contention in the Party, there was advantage to his own position as well as to the unity of the Party if someone other than its Leader fought the necessary battles. Such an arrangement suited Bevin's masterful temperament, and made it difficult for other members of the Cabinet to question Bevin's policy. Attlee not only allowed Bevin the room in which to develop a policy of his own but protected his back against his critics in the Party. The two men's own discussions of foreign and defence policy were searching and taken very seriously by Bevin. But it is noticeable that although Attlee was the first prime minister to set up a permanent structure of Cabinet committees in peacetime covering most of the other important areas of government, he did not create one for foreign affairs.[1] Every Monday when he was in London, Bevin gave a report to the Cabinet and this was placed at the head of the agenda, but it was primarily intended for information, and neither Bevin's nor Attlee's attitude encouraged extended discussion. "What Ernie wanted," one of his colleagues said, "was support, not criticism: he got enough of that outside."

In fact, most of the other members of the Cabinet, a majority of whom[2] had served in the wartime coalition, were ready enough to give Bevin their support and leave him to get on with the job. Although he was accustomed, when speaking to his officials, to refer to the Cabinet as "they" he played a pivotal role in its proceedings whenever he was present and took a leading part in its discussions, whatever the subject. Bevin had never failed to impress any committee of which he was a member by his resourcefulness and judgement, and the Cabinet was no exception.

Of his senior colleagues, Morrison was still the object of Bevin's undisguised distrust. The feud was far more of Bevin's than Morrison's making, but the latter's efforts to end it[3] had been harshly rebuffed and ministers, long familiar with it, accepted it as one of the facts of political life. Attlee had his own reasons for distrusting Morrison[4] (a distrust which, in the end, did far more damage to Morrison's prospects than Bevin's more open hostility), but he recognized his indispensability as Party manager and the driving force behind Labour's domestic programme. His plan to keep the two men as far apart as possible worked sufficiently well to prevent the feud from weakening the Government. Morrison had too much to do to take an interest in foreign policy.

Dalton was certainly interested and eager to give his views on the international situation; his diary shows that he never got over the feeling that he would have made a much better Foreign Secretary. As Chancellor of the Exchequer, Bevin had to listen to him and was on friendly enough terms with "'ugh'", but held him at arm's length and did not trust his judgement (any more than Attlee

---

[1] Cf. P. C. Gordon Walker: *The Cabinet* (London 1970) pb. edit. p. 41.
[2] Thirteen out of twenty including Bevin. There were another thirteen ministers outside the Cabinet, five of whom had held office in the Coalition.
[3] See for examples Vol. II, pp. 337–8.
[4] See Vol. II, pp. 391–2.

did), believing him to be "clever but wrong" about most things. "Close co-operation and complete distrust", was his private secretary's version. Cripps was different. Although Bevin started with doubts about his political stability (hardly surprising in view of Cripps' past record), he soon came to respect him for the quality of his mind and above all for his disinterestedness: he was straight, not a political careerist. From the time Cripps succeeded Dalton as Chancellor (in 1947) the two men worked closely together. A. V. Alexander, who took over from Attlee as Minister of Defence in 1946, was an old crony (they both came from Bristol), but Bevin had never taken "Albert" very seriously and did not hesitate to deal direct with the Chiefs of Staff or, as a member of the Cabinet's Defence Committee and a former Minister of National Service, to express his own views on defence policy.

The one man who might have challenged Bevin was Nye Bevan, the coalition's (and Bevin's) sharpest critic during the War. Bevan was not a man to be stopped from talking in Cabinet about any subject that interested him. In private he was highly critical of the Government's foreign policy and as contemptuous of Bevin as of his other colleagues: "He's a big bumble bee caught in a web and he thinks he's the spider", a remark Dalton recounted with pleasure.[1] But Attlee's move in including Bevan in the Cabinet was a shrewd one: it pinned him down with responsibilities of his own of which he had to make a success if he was ever to prove himself more than a brilliant debater. He remained the most restless member of the Cabinet and always the potential leader of a left wing revolt, but for that very reason he was isolated and could make his opposition effective only by resigning, a step which could cost him his political future as the man who split the Party. This was not a risk to be run lightly,[2] as Attlee well understood, and it was not until after Bevin's death that Nye Bevan made up his mind to take it. During the five years they served together in the Cabinet, there were rows between them but Bevan never pressed home his disagreement and Bevin, although angered by Nye's jibes, had enough political sense not to force an open rupture. Ernie's retort, when he heard Nye Bevan described as "his own worst enemy" was among those Attlee remembered and repeated with most enjoyment. "Not while I'm alive, he ain't."

Most Labour Ministers came to discuss their problems with Bevin, finding him easier to talk to and more helpful with advice than Attlee. He was on friendly terms with Chuter Ede (Leader of the House as well as Home Secretary) and Jim Griffiths, a trade unionist and Minister of National Insurance, whom Bevin would have liked to see succeed him. He had no opinion of Shinwell while he was at the Ministry of Fuel and Power, but got on well with him as Minister of Defence, where he thought he did a good job. He

---

[1] Dalton, p. 129.

[2] Sir Edward Bridges, who kept the Minutes of the Cabinet, remarked on one occasion that among those "Also Present" should be included "The ghost of 1931", so palpable was its influence whenever the Cabinet threatened to become divided.

thought well too of the youngest Cabinet Minister, Harold Wilson, until he began to move closer to Nye Bevan and lost Ernie Bevin's trust. In that famous quarrel Bevin's sympathies were all with Hugh Gaitskell whom he liked and encouraged. He took trouble to try out and bring on other young men, most of them (with the notable exception of Crossman, "that wicked man") with success.

The Foreign Secretary's frequent absences abroad meant that his junior ministers had the often difficult task of answering questions in Parliament and deputising for him at meetings. Hector McNeil was close to Bevin personally and understood his mind. He had been Parliamentary Private Secretary to Philip Noel-Baker and succeeded him as Minister of State at the FO to Bevin's relief, when Noel-Baker became Secretary of State for Air in October 1946. McNeil was a powerful debater who scored a particular success in his speeches in the UN General Assembly. Bevin thought he would go far in the Labour Party and, although sad to lose him, was pleased to see him made Secretary of State for Scotland in 1950.[1] Kenneth Younger succeeded at a difficult time when Bevin was absent for long periods through illness and never established the close relationship which McNeil had enjoyed. Christopher Mayhew had been President of the Oxford Union, served throughout the war and came into the House in the 1945 election at the age of thirty. He carried much of the burden in the House of Commons where he acted as Bevin's Parliamentary Under-Secretary from 1946 to 1950.

When Bevin assumed over-all responsibility for British policy towards Germany, Frank Pakenham was appointed in April 1947 to act as minister responsible for the British zone. Pakenham's views on the Germans, much influenced by his Christian beliefs,[2] were very different from Bevin's, and since he was outspoken in expressing them, the relationship was not easy for either man. Pakenham was more than once on the verge of resignation and both men were relieved when he was appointed Minister for Civil Aviation in June 1948. Pakenham however (now Lord Longford) came through the experience with a high regard for Bevin and the tolerance he had shown to a younger man's enthusiasm. He was succeeded in his German responsibilities by Lord Henderson, Arthur Henderson's son Will, who was not given an independent ministerial position (Pakenham had been Chancellor of the Duchy of Lancaster) but served as an additional Parliamentary Under-Secretary in the House of Lords.

As long as he retained Attlee's confidence, Bevin had little reason to worry about opposition in the Cabinet. He took no step without first making sure that he had the Prime Minister's support and if he did not hear from him regularly when he was abroad, became restive and disturbed. Attlee was the only one of his colleagues with whom he thrashed out the broad lines of policy and whose

[1] McNeil died in 1955 while still under the age of 50.
[2] Lord Pakenham: *Born to Believe* (London 1953) cc. 19–22.

objections he took up and answered immediately. Bevin's complaint was not that Attlee occasionally disagreed with him, but that, when consulted, he would sometimes give no more than a laconic "Yes", or leave Bevin to reach his own decision. What Bevin wanted was not a decision from Attlee—he was quite capable of reaching that for himself—but reassurance. Attlee, who understood Bevin's more intense and emotional temperament, was generally willing to provide this but—having his own problems as Prime Minister —would sometimes withdraw into his shell and could be very curt when his patience was tried. These were no more than the rubs to be expected when men are under the pressures Bevin and Attlee had to withstand. They did not affect the basic understanding between them and, although Attlee was always reluctant to take sides in disputes within the Party, at one of the blackest moments of Bevin's career, the amendment tabled in November 1946 while he was out of the country, Attlee laid his authority as Prime Minister on the line and personally defended his Foreign Secretary's policy.

Much of Bevin's difficulty with the Parliamentary Labour Party was due to poor communication. He was never "a good House of Commons man", lacking the politician's arts and not much given to chatting with back benchers in the smoking-room. For one thing, he was too busy, and often away or unwell. He appointed Percy Wells as his Parliamentary Private Secretary with a special brief to keep in touch with the trade union members of the House, but for the younger generation of MPs who had no trade union, and often not much Party, background, he was a remote and formidable figure whom it required courage to approach. Every week they could read his critics in the *New Statesman* or *Tribune*, to which official hand-outs and speeches read from a Foreign Office brief were no reply. Bevin did not lack admirers in Fleet Street—A. P. Wadsworth, the editor of the *Manchester Guardian*, for example, and W. N. Ewer, the diplomatic correspondent of the *Daily Herald*—but he was too suspicious of journalists (T.V. interviews had still to be invented) to make use of the Press in the way that other ministers did. Not until Denis Healey took up the cudgels on his behalf in *Cards on the Table*, published in May 1947, was there a really effective defence of his policy.

The Conservatives in opposition found it easier to accept a bi-partisan foreign policy than the Labour Party did initially and saw the advantage in a Labour Foreign Secretary rather than a Tory like Eden standing up to the Russians.[1] On the other hand, in the first year and a half, Opposition speakers, well aware of the divided feelings on the other side of the House, took pleasure in creating embarrassment for the Government and anger among its supporters by heaping praise on Bevin and contrasting the enthusiasm with which some of his statements about Russia or Spain were greeted on the Opposition side with the glum faces on the Labour back benches. Bevin had to put up with

[1] The same point was neatly made at the time by using the title of Oscar Wilde's play *The Importance of Being Earnest*, to underline the importance of the Foreign Secretary "being Ernest".

the innuendo, on which his Left-wing critics seized, that he was following a Tory not a socialist policy.

All this was part of the parliamentary battle, for which Bevin had little taste but which was waged with great vigour by the more partisan members on both sides, including Churchill who could change from the role of world statesman to party leader without a trace of awkwardness. Bevin admired Churchill, but regarded him as too much rooted in the past and out of touch with the post-war world. The temperamental difference between them comes out in the way each looked on the Anglo–American alliance. Churchill romanticized it as "the partnership of the two great English-speaking peoples"; Bevin looked on it as a necessity and worked hard to make it a success but without losing sight of the differences in interest and outlook between the two nations. It was Eden not Churchill with whom he felt most in common on the Tory side of the House. He had told Smuts in 1944 that on certain conditions he would be willing to serve under Eden in a post-war coalition, and when he became Foreign Secretary it was with Eden not Churchill that he kept in touch on questions of foreign policy.

From time to time there was a flare-up between the two front benches (over Egypt, for example, in 1946, and over the Council of Europe later[1]), but for most of the time the Opposition accepted Bevin's plea to lift foreign policy out of the arena of party politics, rarely pressed differences of opinion to a vote and gave him solid support in moments of crisis. At a time when party feeling on other issues often ran high, this was a considerable addition to the strength of Bevin's position.

No position in democratic politics, however, is invulnerable or independent of the ability and will to hold it. Neither the Prime Minister's friendship, the trade union block vote nor the Opposition's support in the House would have saved Ernie Bevin—or been available to him—if he had not been able to convince the men whom he met daily face-to-face in the Cabinet, in the House of Commons and across the conference table that he possessed the qualities of character and judgement to measure up to the position he occupied in post-war Britain. It is time, therefore, to turn from politics and look more closely at the man himself.

[1] See below, pp. 251–2 (Egypt); pp. 553–4 (Council of Europe).

CHAPTER 3

Bevin as Foreign Secretary

I

In a leading article at the time of Bevin's death, *The Times* wrote that, like Churchill, he seemed a visitor from the 18th century. Neither conformed to the conventional pattern, largely created by the public schools in the second half of the 19th century, of the Englishman in public life, with marked habits of understatement and self-control. Although very different men, one in the plebeian, the other in the aristocratic mode, both struck their contemporaries as fiercer and less inhibited in expressing their feelings, enjoying the possession of personalities which seemed larger than life and full (to use Attlee's phrase) of "an exuberant and unselfconscious egoism" which they were at no pains to conceal.

Peter Ustinov, whom Bevin liked and sometimes asked to official parties to relieve the tedium, saw him as a character Shakespeare would have delighted to create and compared him to the great French actor Raimu playing one of his powerful peasant roles, shrewd, cunning and earthy. This was one side of Bevin and the first to catch the eye. He belonged to a generation (he was born in 1881) who still bore visible traces of their class origins, perhaps as a result of differences in nutrition as well as upbringing. Anyone who saw Bevin in the company of his predecessor, Lord Halifax, would not have had much difficulty in guessing that one came from the labouring, the other from the landowning class. Although his body had grown thick and heavy, Bevin still had the broad shoulders and powerful hands of a man who had once earned his living by manual labour. His massive head and features possessed an almost geological irregularity. It was only when he removed his horn-rim glasses that his brown eyes, with their shrewd and amused smile, would light up a face the most prominent feature of which otherwise was an unusually flat nose above full lips.

Both Halifax and Eden, his predecessors at the Foreign Office, had upper-class voices which proclaimed their origins as plainly as Bevin's; his was lower and grittier with a harsh but impressive quality of firmness when raised in a big hall and a touch of West country burr in conversation. His voice was very much a part of Bevin's personality: "his remarks," one of his private secretaries wrote, "even the most serious, owed a part of their strange vigour to the kind of voice that gave them utterance." Equally individual was his use of the English language. His grammar was improvised. "He never bothered," Attlee remarked, "about the difference between the singular and the plural. He seemed not to care. Aitches were of no consequence." "He was not unconscious," wrote the same private secretary, Valentine Lawford, "of the advantages enjoyed by those who combine an invincible native accent with a vividly personal vocabulary."[1] He had a noticeable difficulty with proper names, especially if they were foreign—Bidault was rendered in a variety of ways from Biddle to Bidet and the Italian Foreign Secretary Count Sforza (whom he disliked) became "that man Storzer"—but he was unperturbed and took them as they came. In one particular case he could not be acquitted of a certain degree of wilfulness. He habitually addressed the Soviet Foreign Minister as Mowlotov. When the latter corrected him, Bevin would nod his agreement, "That's right, Mowlotov," a re-iteration that rarely failed to irritate the precise Russian. Undeniably, as Valentine Lawford says, Bevin's treatment of foreign names (like Churchill's pronunciation of "Nazis") was one of the characteristics that most endeared him to his countrymen, including the staff of the Foreign Office.

Yet, as the author of an *Observer* Profile remarked in 1948, the caricaturist's picture of Bevin as a working-class John Bull missed more than it told about a man who on closer viewing appeared complicated and even mysterious. It was an easy mistake to make. It is arguable that Ernest Bevin owed less to formal education than any Englishman to hold so high an office under the Crown in modern times. It was not simply that he left elementary school with little more than the rudiments of reading, writing and numbering, for like other Labour leaders he went on to serve an intellectual apprenticeship of sorts in the Chapel, adult education and the socialist movement.[2] But from his early years it was from what he saw and reflected on, from the people he met and the events he took part in, rather than from books that Bevin formed his views. Far from being impressed by the advantages of those who went on to complete their education at the secondary level and university, he regarded them as poor creatures whose natural capacity to learn directly from experience had been overlaid and weakened by accepting at second-hand knowledge and ideas which they all too rarely put to any test for themselves.

This sounds like the familiar contempt for ideas of the practical man, but Bevin had a powerful natural intelligence and it was his use of this that marked him out early from the ruck of trade union leaders. A highly educated Board of Trade official noticed to his surprise that in any discussion it was the uneducated Minister who was seeking all the time to find the general principle

[1] Valentine Lawford, "Three Ministers".
[2] See Vol. I, pp. 10–15.

behind the mass of detail, and Keynes, who used the meetings of the Macmillan Committee on Finance and Industry to give a trial run to the ideas expressed in his *Treatise on Money*, regarded Bevin as the quickest among the members of the committee in grasping the practical implications of what he was trying to say when many of the other members and expert witnesses shut their minds to such unorthodox ideas.

Kingsley Martin, exasperated by Bevin's scorn for intellectuals, retorted that Bevin was an intellectual himself, although he would never admit it. This is unconvincing. Bevin certainly had as good an intelligence as most intellectuals, but he reached conclusions in a different way. It was characteristic that what impressed him about Keynes' ideas was not—as it was for many intellectuals—their originality and logical coherence, but the fact that they corresponded with his own experience.

It was of course a limitation, as Kirkpatrick noted, that "he could only look at events through the spectacles of his own experience ... Most of our transactions [in the Foreign Office] were equated to some experience in his trade union or Ministry of Labour days."[1] Another consequence, as Oliver Franks realized, was that the experience on which he relied in place of education almost always had a personal context and associations which continued to colour and personalize his views, a frequent criticism of Bevin by those with whom he disagreed. He found it hard to conceptualize his thinking and lacked the intellectual shorthand to communicate his ideas without referring to the experience from which they sprang, often in the form of an anecdote.

For this reason he was not at home in the sort of wide-ranging discussion of general ideas which delighted Nye Bevan or Cripps. Oliver Franks discovered that it was not easy to exchange ideas with Bevin but that he could interrupt him, put a different point of view and ask if he really meant what he said or whether the evidence supported it. Bevin would sit back and listen, and could be persuaded to modify his own views. Acheson's experience was the same: "His mind was not closed. It was tough and often stubborn, but always open to arguments strongly and honestly presented."[2] But what was possible for familiars like Oliver Franks or Hector McNeil whom Bevin trusted and felt to be in sympathy with what he was trying to do, was a risky operation for anyone else. He was a hard man to argue with, and very positive in expressing disagreement. Once the initial difficulty was overcome, he was a good listener and learned much in this way. But even Franks found there were days when, like Churchill, Bevin would pull the shutters down and communication became impossible. He had never taken easily to criticism from those he thought were trying to make difficulties. Although he had mellowed since his trade union days, his suspicions were still easily aroused and his instinctive reaction to opposition had always been to flatten it.

[1] Sir Ivone Kirkpatrick, later Permanent Under-Secretary of the Foreign Office.
[2] Dean Acheson: *Sketches from Life* (London 1961) p. 35.

On the other side must be set the value of having in the Foreign Office a man whose experience of life was so radically different from that of his staff and who had the confidence to draw on it in questioning their views. By the time he became Foreign Secretary his own experience of five years working with the ablest men in government and the civil service had taught him to recognize the contribution which his officials' training could make to solving a problem. The sorrow which he affected for those who had never had a chance because of their sheltered upbringing and education was more than half banter. He had also learned the advantage to a minister of briefing himself well and was admired by his staff for the diligence with which even when he was hard pressed and unwell, he would master the papers which they crammed into his boxes every evening when he left the office. But it was still on the knowledge that he had gathered for himself, as he told King George, "from the 'edgerows of experience" that he relied for his judgement of men and situations, an experience frequently recalled by fishing up from a capacious memory unexpected pieces of information. One example which Attlee remembered him producing in the middle of a Cabinet meeting was the Danube route by which the Greek currant exports reached British ports before the war and how much the trade was worth. Another is the fascinating advice which he gave to Sir Ivone Kirkpatrick, if he should ever find himself addressing a difficult meeting of boilermakers, to pitch his voice low, since boilermakers were occupationally deaf and the effort to hear kept them quiet.

What most impressed those who worked with Bevin, however, was that he not only stored up what he observed and heard in his memory but continually turned it over in his mind. While he was very quick to take a point or grasp an idea, he refused to be hurried into reaching a conclusion. "He never," Kirkpatrick says, "allowed himself to be bounced into anything against his better judgement. Indeed it was misguided to try. . . . 'I will not be rushed', was his reply, and if anyone tried to he would blow his top. He required time to read the files and subject his experts to a penetrating cross examination."[1] Above all he required time to let a considered judgement precipitate from a mixture of reasoning, intuition and experience which he neither fully understood nor could explain ("visceral" is Lord Franks' word) but which he trusted far more than any powers of logical argument. "He was like an elephant which never really sleeps but grunts, twitches and paws the ground during the night." Once the process was complete and he had made up his mind he was impervious to warnings that his policy might be unpopular in Parliament, in the Press or the trade unions. "I'll speak to them," he would growl, "you go ahead."

Attlee saw Bevin's role in the Labour Party before the war as that of a stabilizer rather than a rudder or propeller: by constantly stating the trade unions' point of view (which had to be realistic) he "kept the Party's feet on the

---

[1] Sir Ivone Kirkpatrick: *The Inner Circle* (London 1959) p. 203.

ground". On the other hand, Attlee went on, although Bevin looked the embodiment of common sense, "I have never met a man in politics with as much imagination as he had, with the exception of Winston." Perhaps the best example of this in his time as Foreign Secretary was the speed with which he seized upon General Marshall's speech in June 1947, and took the lead in turning it into a plan for the economic reconstruction of Europe. Another is the trouble he took in 1950, when he knew the journey might cost him his life, in going to Ceylon to launch the Colombo Plan.

His staff at the Foreign Office, as earlier in the Union and the Ministry of Labour, learned to recognize the portents of Bevin returning from a weekend and calling them in for a discussion with the words, "I've been thinking". What he had been thinking about had often little to do with immediate problems.[1] It was his habit to absorb an idea or experience and ruminate on it, intermittently, for months or even years, until he could see a way of using it. On other occasions, when his staff or one of his colleagues confronted him with a problem, he would nod and send them away with the assurance: "I'll think of something." Almost invariably he did, but not on the spur of the moment. Sometimes his proposals would be impracticable and his officials would have the delicate task of weaning him away from them. But they learned to listen carefully to what he was driving at, often in a clumsy half-formed fashion (the same lack of an intellectual shorthand), and in a surprising number of cases (the outstanding one is his proposal for a Western Union) his ideas proved to be the starting point of new initiatives.

Although in retrospect Bevin's rise to power in the trade union movement appeared inevitable, his fight to establish the amalgamated TGWU and his own position had left their mark on him. His insistence on loyalty as the supreme political virtue reflected the disloyalty, jealousy and petty treachery which he had encountered on his way up. So did the suspiciousness which was one of his least attractive characteristics. In his trade union days, he had learnt to proceed on the principle that anyone not on his side was against him and once his suspicions were aroused he could still relapse into what Frank Owen called his "Corsican concept of public business"—the vendetta.[2] The difference was that he did not employ Corsican methods. As George Brown said, Bevin might trample on you but he did not stick a knife in your back. Unreserved in his loyalty to those he trusted, he scorned intrigue, made no attempt to wrap up his hostility towards those who aroused his distrust, and was forthright in expressing it.

When he encountered opposition—and he had, all his life—he squared up to it and hit back hard, if possible getting his blow in first. "He was", to quote

---

[1] Donald MacLachlan, later editor of *The Economist*, recalled being summoned along with other diplomatic correspondents to meet Bevin at the height of the Berlin crisis in 1948, only to find that he wanted to talk to them about the future of Africa, another session which he introduced with the words "I've been thinking".

[2] Frank Owen in the *Daily Express*, 10 March 1951.

Lord Franks again, "prepared to wound rather than receive hurt." Nor did he allow criticism to divert him from a course of action. After his trade union experience he found it hard to believe in the disinterestedness of those who disagreed with him, and (surprisingly for a man who had always been remarkable for his self-confidence) it was an old complaint against him that he was too sensitive to attacks and took both opposition and criticism too personally.

The truth was that underneath the toughness, which he had had to acquire in order to survive, lay a naturally emotional rather than a cold nature. He cared deeply about what he was trying to do, was anything but detached about it and looked with anger on those whom he saw as trying to thwart him. From time to time he would be overcome with a wave of indignation at the thought of the baseness and treachery of particular groups or individuals in the Party and would then complain bitterly, in tones of self-pity, of how much he had to put up with and how little support he got from "Clem" or any of his other colleagues. There had always been a vein of the dramatic in Bevin's make-up which he had exploited, for example, with great success in the Shaw Inquiry[1] and which enabled him to dramatize his leadership to the members of his Union. His reaction to these dark suspicions of conspiracy and stabs-in-the-back was pure Grand Guignol and once his outburst had relieved the tension under which he worked, his mood would clear as suddenly as it had formed.

The same was true of his occasional outbursts of anger. "What the hell did you do that for?" he would shout at an official, or thump the desk and utter dire threats against those who obstructed him: "I'll swing that fellow Dalton round my head." Those who did not know him could be put off by such displays of temper, failing to realize that they were the way in which he relieved his feelings rather than a guide to what he would do. As was the case with Arthur Henderson, who had got red in the face and shouted, Bevin's anger did not last. After such an exhibition of "getting wild" he would be contrite, apologize to those he might have offended (if they were still around) and rebuke himself for his language. "I oughtn't to have said that."

After Eden, whose touchiness was notorious, those who worked for him found him patient as long as he was not rushed, and considerate of the demands he made on them. He had a rich, if broad sense of humour, with an inexhaustible repertoire of what used to be called smoking-room stories (another relic of trade union days); liked to tease his staff (a side his Party colleagues rarely saw) and at once noticed if anyone was in distress. He kept a list on his desk of everyone in the Foreign Office who was reported sick and if they were away for more than a day or two sent them messages of encouragement. Relations with his officials in the Union had not been happy: they felt themselves overshadowed, complained that he "hogged the credit" and were jealous of his reputation. The change came when he entered the

[1] Cf. Vol. I, c. 6.

Government in 1940: civil servants and secretaries alike thought him one of the best ministers to work for, human, approachable and entirely without pomposity or self-importance.

Many who did not know Bevin at all well were put off by the egocentricity of a man who habitually spoke of "my" foreign policy, and declared "I won't stand for that". Almost without exception, however, those who did know him well discounted his vanity and thought it harmless or childlike. Lord Bridges, whose years as Secretary of the Cabinet gave him much experience of politicians and their failings, did not regard him as vain. "He knew his powers and took pleasure and pride in them. It was his self-confidence which gave offence." Lew Douglas, the American Ambassador in London, took a different view: "Of course he was vain, but he was too big a man to be swayed by it. He had no need, like Eden, to show that he was in the top class: he was, and knew it. He also knew he was vain. I teased him about it and he would laugh at himself over it." Attlee, one of the least egocentric of prime ministers, distinguished between egotism and vanity—defining egotism as a fascination with abilities you actually have, vanity as an overvaluation of yourself. Attlee regarded Ramsay MacDonald as vain, but thought Bevin and Churchill were "tremendous egotists". He went on to describe Cripps, whom he looked on as the other big man in his Cabinet, as an egotist too—"Ernest having the egoism of the artist, Stafford the egoism of the altruist", a tribute, in Bevin's case, to the imaginative quality of his mind which Attlee valued so highly. Arthur Deakin, his successor as General Secretary of the TGWU and well-placed to see Bevin's weaknesses at close quarters, once summed up with the remark that "Ernie had no more ego than he needed to get where he did". This was a reminder that if he had not had a strong belief in his own abilities he would still have been working on the land or driving a mineral-water wagon round the Somerset lanes. To which those who saw at close quarters the contribution he made to the recovery of Europe, the Marshall Plan and NATO would add that he claimed not too much but too little credit, and that when he spoke of "my foreign policy" he was not far off the mark. If Bevin had not been at the Foreign Office, who can say what difference this might not have made to the foreign policy followed by the Labour Government at a critical period in history?

Bevin was certainly fascinated by his own career and loved to relax by talking about it, an autobiographical exercise which his private secretaries learned to endure philosophically. For there is no doubt either that he inspired an exceptional degree of affection as well as loyalty among those who worked with him. One reason for this was the total absence of any snobbery: he had, in fact, one of his Private Secretaries remarks, considerable difficulty in "placing" anyone socially. Untroubled by any sense of class distinction he treated everyone he met, from the King to the office doorkeeper (both equally admirers of Bevin), in exactly the same way and always as human beings. He had no ambition to become middle class and although he had a proper sense of the dignity of his office and conformed to what was expected of him so far as external appearances went—for example in his clothes—he remained, without a trace of self-consciousness, still as much identified in his own mind with the class from which he had sprung as when he had been a trade union leader.[1] He was never more at home than when he returned each Spring for the Bristol Festival of the TGWU, delighting in seeing old friends and talking to them about the job he was doing, not as a high political mystery but as essentially concerned with decent standards of living and security for ordinary working people not only in Britain but in all countries. Whatever might be his difficulties in the House of Commons, Bevin never lost his ability to communicate with a working class audience and some of his best expositions of his foreign policy are to be found in his speeches to the Bristol Festival. For their part, his union members, far from being put off by the display of "ego" which offended middle-class taste found it entirely natural and took great pride in seeing "Ernie" as the nation's representative to the outside world.

2

Bevin himself not only took pride but a great interest in his famous predecessors as Foreign Secretaries. Dean Acheson, with whom he established closer relations than have ever existed between any other British Foreign Secretary and American Secretary of State, wrote later that he believed Bevin, sitting at the familiar desk under the portrait of George III, communed with their shades.

"He read their papers; he talked of them as slightly older people whom he knew with affectionate respect. In listening to him, one felt strongly the continuity and integrity of English history. He conferred a single title on each of them. It was 'old'. 'Last night', he said to me, 'I was reading some papers of Old Salisbury. Y'know 'e had a lot of sense.' 'Old Palmerston', too, came in for frequent and sometimes wistful mention . . . With George III he was very companionable. When sherry was brought in, he would twist around to look at the portrait. 'Let's drink to him', he would say. 'If 'e 'adn't been so stoopid, you wouldn't 'ave been strong enough to come to our rescue in the war, and after it with Marshall aid.'"[2]

When he learned of the motion of censure on him by Left-wing members of his own party while he was out of the country in November 1946, Bevin expressed his indignation with the phrase: "Ain't nothing like this been heard of since the days of Castlereagh."[3] Kirkpatrick, on the other hand, noted how often for some inexplicable reason, Bevin would ask "I wonder what Lord

[1] Averell Harriman returning to London from a visit to Rumania in January 1946, sent a box of *pâté de foie gras* to Bevin. Writing to thank him, Bevin said that he and Mrs Bevin wanted to know what it was. Harriman recorded the incident as an illustration of Bevin's "complete lack of any false pride". W. Averell Harriman and Elie Abel: *Special Envoy* (NY 1975) p. 530.
[2] Dean Acheson, *Sketches*, p. 24.
[3] Recounted by Percy Wells MP, his Parliamentary Private Secretary who claimed to have persuaded him not to resign at once, but to sleep on it.

Curzon would do if he were in my shoes?" Although little more than twenty years separated them as Foreign Secretaries it would be hard to think of the two men who made more of a contrast as representatives of their country.

By no means all the advantages were on Curzon's side. Bevin had none of his aristocratic pride of family but enjoyed a self-confidence which was positively imperial. "There was a great deal of the Emperor in Mr Bevin's outlook", Sir Ivone Kirkpatrick wrote. Wherever he was, in the Kremlin, the United Nations, the Quai d'Orsay as much as in Buckingham Palace, he was entirely himself: the thought of behaving any differently never crossed his mind. This could be criticized as provincialism—"When in Rome do as Taunton does" (Peter Ustinov's phrase)—but it had the advantage of making him free of any inhibitions in meeting foreigners. He was as indifferent to nationality or race as to social distinctions, placing everyone he met on the footing of a common humanity, whatever their origins or the colour of their skin, and speaking to them with the same directness and frankness as to a fellow member of the Labour Party. Some were offended by what they took to be undue familiarity —Stalin complained that he was no gentleman and Molotov that he did not treat the Soviet representatives with proper respect—but many warmed to a man who cut through the barriers in the way of human contact and who was without any trace of that assumption of superiority or aloofness of which Englishmen (no one more than Curzon) had so often been suspected abroad.

While he was still a trade unionist, Bevin had shown that his ignorance of languages other than his own was no barrier to his making an impact on any international gathering or group of which he was a member. This remained true when he became Foreign Secretary and it was as well that it did, for Britain's right to be consulted in international decisions could no longer be taken for granted as it could in Curzon's day. To put it in language which would have come naturally to him, Bevin found himself the representative of a union with reduced assets and a falling membership, whose ability to resist amalgamation and retain its independence would largely depend on its secretary's ability to put on a bold front at the negotiating table. This was a role for which Bevin was cast by nature. The force of his personality needed no translation to be understood: he was an immediate centre of attention at any international conference and there was no danger that Britain's case would go by default or her interests be overlooked as long as he was there to represent them.

But the familiar picture of a truculent Bevin angrily declaring "I won't 'ave it", Palmerston in a cloth cap, although true to life is misleading unless it is completed by other and more important sides of the role he played as Foreign Secretary. He was, for example, a patient and resourceful negotiator who frequently suggested a way out of a diplomatic or procedural impasse; most important of all, he never made the mistake of thinking that Britain could go it alone. This was the crucial difference from Palmerston's and even Curzon's day, and one of which Bevin never lost sight, that Britain had to persuade other powers to work with her if she was to retain any of her former influence in world affairs. To do that meant winning the confidence of other governments and their representatives and finding a common basis on which they could co-operate, a task that called for very different qualities in a Foreign Secretary from the ability to stand up for British rights. If Bevin had not possessed such qualities, if he had not been able to convince the Americans and Europeans with whom he worked that he was a man to whom they could look for leadership and on whom they could rely, he would never have been able to play the part he did as one of the principal architects of the Western alliance.

It was equally characteristic of the man that the good judgement and breadth of view which constantly impressed those who had to deal with him should have been combined with a number of prejudices which, once aroused, closed his mind to further argument and clouded it with suspicion or anger. Some were personal prejudices: the mere mention of Herbert Morrison, Beaverbook ("Rasputin" was Bevin's name for him) or Dick Crossman was enough to set him off. He persisted in regarding Molotov (though not apparently Vyshinsky or even Stalin) as responsible for the murder of millions. He had no use for Communists or fellow travellers—nor they, it must be said, for him. Priests of any denomination he regarded with horror and thought it unlucky even to see one—"black crows"—in the street. His relations with the Zionists became coloured with personal feeling (on both sides) and brought down on him the charge of anti-Semitism.[1] The Germans he could never forgive for the war and because he felt they had betrayed the efforts which he and other trade unionists had made to re-establish relations of trust after 1918. "I tries 'ard, Brian", he told General Robertson, the British Military Governor, "but I 'ates them", and he showed reluctance to visit Germany or meet German politicians.

Robertson went on, however, to say that he did not believe Bevin allowed his feelings to influence his policy towards Germany, a view shared by his successor as High Commissioner, Sir Ivone Kirkpatrick, and borne out by the consistency with which Bevin argued that European recovery was impossible without the recovery of Germany. His critics were equally sure that British policy towards the Soviet Union and towards the Zionists and Israel was affected by Bevin's personal prejudices. These are charges to be examined in more detail later, although it is arguable that what attracted attention and gave offence was not prejudices deeper than other people held but the freedom with which Bevin gave expression to them.

Whether it is to be described as a prejudice or not, there was no doubt of his hostile attitude towards intellectuals. In part this was due to his own reliance on experience and intuition and his distrust of those who talked about society, economics and politics in terms of abstract ideas. Kingsley Martin, who

---

[1] See below, pp. 163–83 for a discussion of this.

personified most of the characteristics he disliked in the left-wing intellectual, wrote:

"He saw in them the type he most despised—the man who talks in generalities without experience and criticizes without inside knowledge; who proposes action without responsibility for the consequences."[1]

George Brown put the difference another way when he drew a contrast between Ernie Bevin and Nye Bevan.

"The latter," he wrote, "loved discussion and except on one or two matters, I don't think he really much minded which way the vote at the end went. Ernie always wanted to do things, he wasn't much interested in discussion, he wanted to get things done. . . . But he had certain broad principles about people, how they should live and how they should be treated, and he stuck to them . . . What he didn't have was dogma: he accepted that there could be more than one way of accomplishing a purpose. I think this mainly explains why the Left hated him; they wanted everything decided according to their ideological touchstone."[2]

He was particularly scornful of those with a middle or upper class upbringing and a university education who joined the Labour Party out of Socialist conviction. He regarded them as interlopers in the Labour Movement, incapable of sharing the working-class experience on which it was based and politically unreliable. At one time or another most of the leading intellectuals of the Party—G. D. H. Cole, Harold Laski, Kingsley Martin—had tried to get on terms with Bevin, recognizing his natural ability and intelligence. All such attempts ended in disaster.

"The fact that Bevin himself was an Intellectual" Kingsley Martin wrote, "though he would not admit it, only increased his contempt for those who carried the label. . . . He was the most difficult man I ever met in controversy. If you attempted to make an argumentative point he would at once turn on you with a personal denunciation which had nothing to do with the subject. At times he was a bulldozer rather than a colleague."[3]

The real difficulty which the *New Statesman* and Hampstead intellectuals had was in believing that a man so unlike themselves, without their education, their familiarity with economics, social philosophy or history—not to mention foreign languages—their fluency in handling ideas, could ever understand anything other than the world of industrial relations of which he had had direct experience. Bevin was aware of this and had always resented it. Nor was he at all impressed by the claim of the intellectuals in the Labour Party to have a superior understanding of politics and economics or of foreign policy. The T.U.C. in his day seemed to him to have had a better record of judgement than the Labour Party, and it may be left to the reader to decide for himself whether

[1] Kingsley Martin: *Editor* (London, pb. edn. 1968) p. 62.
[2] Lord George-Brown: *In My Way* (London, pb. edn. 1972) p. 45.
[3] Kingsley Martin: *Editor*, pp. 62–4.

Bevin or his intellectual critics, such as Crossman, showed the surer grasp in understanding what Communism and the Soviet Union represented under Stalin's leadership or Nazism and Germany under Hitler's. Bevin's view of the *New Statesman* and its editor is summed up in the remark he made at the Party's celebration of its 1945 election triumph. When Bevin came in, as C. H. Rolph recounts it, "he glared round like a basilisk and spotted Kingsley. "'Ullo, gloomy," he said very loudly. "I give you about three weeks before you stab us all in the back."[1]

The other side of the coin to Bevin's hostility towards intellectuals was the sense, not of sympathy, but of identification which he felt with ordinary men and women. This had been the most consistent principle in his career, underlying and legitimizing the earlier ambition, assertiveness and struggles for power—in a word, the "ego" Arthur Deakin spoke of—and it did not lose its force when he became Foreign Secretary. Here was the root of Bevin's socialism and of much of his distrust and disagreement with the Left, especially the intellectual Left. He suspected that what they were really interested in was a fundamental remodelling of society on abstract principles and that their interest in the working class was simply as the agent by which this great historical purpose was to be carried out. Bevin looked at socialism the other way round, as a general framework of ideas about society within which the real content was the task of improving the conditions of working people and creating a greater measure of social justice and security for them here and now.

It would be a mistake, however, to suppose that because he rarely spoke about them—any more than Attlee did—he did not have strong political beliefs. Talking to American correspondents in London at the end of 1947, Bevin put them in a couple of sentences:

"We believe as good Social Democrats, that it is possible to have public ownership, great advance and social development, and with it maintain what I think is the most vital thing of all, liberty. I don't believe the two things are inconsistent, and never have. If I believed the development of socialism meant the absolute crushing of liberty, then I should plump for liberty, because the advance of human development depends entirely on the right to think, to speak and to use reason, and allow what I call the upsurge to come from the bottom to reach the top."[2]

As *The Times* said when he died, "he drew politics from the radical roots of the Labour Movement rather than from the Marxist graft on it".[3] Both points of view could be defended and the conflict between them runs right through the history of European socialism and of the working class movement. Where

---

[1] C. H. Rolph, *Kingsley, The Life, Letters and Diaries of Kingsley Martin* (London 1973) p. 310.
[2] Speech at the lunch of the Association of American Correspondents, London, 22 December 1947. This was just after the fifth session of the Council of Foreign Ministers which effectively marked an open breach between the Western Powers and the Soviet Union.
[3] *The Times* leading article, 16 April 1951.

Bevin was at fault, and Kingsley Martin justly complained, was in constantly personalizing what was at bottom an intellectual and political issue.

Bevin's uninhibited personality, never subdued to conventional tones, threw his faults into sharper relief than in most men. To those who disliked or were critical of him they were the source of much which they thought wrong in British foreign policy and which they attributed to Bevin's egotism, ignorance, vanity, prejudice and susceptibility to Foreign Office flattery. There are two things, however, to be said about Bevin's enemies. For the most part their quarrels with him dated from his trade union days. He made few new enemies after 1940, when he moved into Government, the most important exceptions being the Zionists and Crossman. One reason for this no doubt was that power and success mellowed Bevin, making him a less difficult man to deal with; another was that many of those he came across after 1940 he was meeting for the first time. As Lord Franks said of himself, he had no previous "history" and so did not arouse Bevin's suspicions or revive old grudges on either side. Sir Ben Smith, on the other hand, the original Minister of Food in Attlee's Government, nursed grievances against Bevin which went back to the days of the Amalgamation and still spoke of him with rancour after Bevin's death as "a carter all his life, with no manners and no ideas".

The other point is that most of the criticism of Bevin on personal grounds comes from those who disagreed with him politically. He was more hated by the Left than any man in post-war British politics except Churchill. Unlike Attlee, who largely shared his views but could disappear into a neutral background, Bevin's personality had always provoked controversy and, as George Brown (who admired him) says, made you want to disagree with him. He had never been one to disarm or conciliate his critics and they retaliated by leaving a portrait of him which has too easily been accepted as a part of Labour history.

Yet his critics, although vociferous, were never more than a minority in the Party and barely that after the first year or two of the Labour Government. Against the view of Bevin perpetuated by Laski, Crossman and Kingsley Martin (not perhaps the most impressive judges of character) can be set that taken by three such men as Attlee, Morgan Phillips (the Party's Secretary) and Labour's Home Secretary Chuter Ede, the last named of whom summed it up in his reply to the question, "Was he the biggest man I met in the Labour Movement? He was the biggest man I met in any movement." To this may be added another view, that of George Brown, who had often felt the rough side of Bevin's tongue and rowed with him ("You had to have a taste for strong meat to like Ernie") but who wrote in his memoirs:

"There can be no doubt that Ernest Bevin stands out among all the people I have met. He is in a place by himself. He was a man with little or no taught advantages, who relied wholly upon his own brain, his own imagination and his capacity for envisaging things and people. In this capacity he was not surpassed and I think not even matched by anyone else I have ever met. The Churchills, the Attlees and most other leaders, political and industrial, had all the advantages which their social position and long formal education could bestow. Bevin had none of these advantages, but I have seen him in every kind of situation—trade union negotiations round a table, trade union meetings facing often hostile critics, meetings with industrialists, with statesmen—and on every occasion it was quite clear that he was master of the situation. He said that he hated politics, yet in making politics or in running a political department few could match him. He had a natural dignity that offset his endowment of determination and ruthlessness . . .

"His work as Minister of Labour during the war contributed as much to victory as that of any of the generals and, as Foreign Secretary, there were times when he seemed to hold the Western world itself on his great shoulders."[1]

This other Labour view of Bevin needs to be recalled and put alongside that of his critics. Those who worked most closely with him saw his faults as no more than surface blemishes, due as much as anything to the hard way in which he had come to the top, and not as reducing the stature of a man who stood out as plainly on the Labour side of the House of Commons as Churchill on the other.

Some of the qualities which they appreciated in him have already been mentioned: his imagination, as well as his sense of what was practicable, his resourcefulness, his steadiness of judgement. To these should be added three or four other traits, mention of which recurs in talking with those who knew him well. The first was his sincerity, the belief that he spoke and acted from conviction not calculation, and that he was not a trimmer who would bend to what was popular or appease opposition, but a man much more likely to speak his mind and come out with the truth as he saw it, whether it was palatable or not.

The second was his reliability, the quality which had won him the reputation as a trade union leader, of a man of integrity whose word was his bond, who did not run away from his commitments or back down when the going got rough. Byrnes and Bevin were far from seeing eye to eye on foreign affairs, but at a time when there was still considerable suspicion of British policy in Washington (February 1946), Byrnes paid tribute to Bevin's qualities at a private meeting of Truman's chief officers. (The quotation is from Forrestal's diary):

8 February 1946

". . . Byrnes gave it as his opinion that we could not be in the position of doubting the good faith of Britain. He said he was confident that so long as Bevin was in his post as Foreign Minister there would be no possibility of such a break. He said that he could conceive of a case where such a promise might not be lived up to completely through no fault of the Foreign Office, but as long as Mr. Bevin was in the Foreign Office, he didn't believe this could happen. He said that Bevin had lived up completely and wholeheartedly to his agreements—he had debated vigorously and sometimes harshly

---

[1] George-Brown, pp. 235 and 237.

before entering into them, but having once committed himself he would carry out his contracts to the full."[1]

Lord Strang made the shrewd observation that Bevin took more easily to diplomacy than he did to the House of Commons. *The Observer* called him "the happy negotiator as Churchill is the happy warrior", and he was more at home in negotiations—whether industrial or diplomatic—than in politics. He never showed in the House of Commons the mastery he could display at a trade union or even a Labour Party conference; he was awkward in handling a departmental brief, was not easy to follow when he improvised (though frequently impressive) and never mastered parliamentary procedure.

Part of his difficulty in the ordinary give and take of politics was his strength of will and character. He did not easily give way, had no belief in compromise simply for the sake of avoiding conflict, and, once he had made his mind up that a course was right, was not to be deterred from following it either by threats and opposition or the fears of the faint-hearted. But these were not qualities which were lost on the House. Sir David Maxwell Fyfe, a former Conservative minister and future Lord Chancellor, wrote in his memoirs:

"His transparent integrity and dogged determination were so manifest that he never lost the attention of the House. As Lord Rosebery once wrote of Chatham's oratory, it was 'character breathing through the sentences' which counted."[2]

These qualities appeared to their true advantage during the Cold War, when Bevin refused to let Russian threats frighten him into abandoning Berlin or the policy of building up the strength of Western Europe. He was never troubled by indecisiveness, was a determined man at any time and in a crisis showed a strength and self-confidence which calmed other people's fears. Far from being worried by responsibility, he did not (as Attlee said) so much enjoy power as embrace it.

But it was the power to get something done, not power for its own sake or to improve his own position, that attracted Bevin. This was an attitude which he shared with Cripps and which marked him off from Morrison, Dalton, Bevan, all of whom were intensely interested in their political careers and the chances of becoming Prime Minister. Bevin was not and was scornful of those who were. Both as Minister of Labour and Foreign Secretary, he saw himself in a national not a party role, such as Churchill played during the war and Cripps was to play in relation to the economy. By 1940, certainly by 1945, Bevin had no further ambitions for himself, and this combination of disinterestedness, so

---

[1] *The Forrestal Diaries*, p. 139.
[2] Lord Kilmuir: *Political Adventure* (London 1964) p. 146. He made the same impression on a young Labour member, Jack Diamond, who told Philip Williams that he put Bevin amongst the best parliamentary performers on the Labour side of the House "for a major impact on Parliament by his seen and unseen presence, only added to by the aitches arbitrarily dropped or inserted. He always kept your attention and when he made speeches on things he was interested in, the place vibrated."

far as personal advancement was concerned, with a natural aptitude for accumulating and exercising power put him at an advantage in a Cabinet where more than one man was measuring himself—and known to be—for Prime Minister, Foreign Secretary or Chancellor. He was equally uninterested in the rewards of office—honours, status, salary or official position—and if he had ever thought about them would have said, truly enough, that, in his case, these would add nothing to being Ernie Bevin.

3

Short of a revolution powerful enough to break the Civil Service's hold on the machinery of government, every minister has to come to terms with his Department. The Permanent Under-Secretary of the Foreign Office, Sir Alec Cadogan, waiting for the new ministers to reach Potsdam, wrote in his diary:

"I think we may do better with Bevin than with any other of the Labourites. I think he's broad-minded and sensible, honest and courageous." (Surprising praise from a man who regarded politicians with marked scepticism.) "But whether he's an inspired Foreign Minister or not I don't know. He's the heavyweight of the Cabinet and will get his own way with them, so if he can be put on the right line, that may be all right."[1]

The experience of seeing Bevin in action during the conference confirmed Cadogan's good opinion. There was in fact very little difference on the broad outlines of policy between Bevin and his officials when he took over from Eden. Both sides accepted as their starting point the Coalition's decisions and discussions on post-war policy, to which Bevin and Attlee as well as the Foreign Office officials had contributed, and took these up where they had left off two months before. Bevin, however, still held some residual radical suspicions of the Foreign Office. One of the earliest papers he had produced on joining the War Cabinet in 1940 was a memorandum urging reform of the Foreign Service,[2] which he criticized as drawn from too narrow a circle, and the wartime proposals for reform had been the subject of lengthy discussions between Eden and Bevin before they were published.[3] Certainly for his first three months in his new office, Bevin showed considerable reserve towards his senior officials. Instead of working through Cadogan or his deputy, Sir Orme Sargent, he would call in his Principal Private Secretary, Pierson Dixon, and say "The way I want the Middle East handled is this", leaving Dixon to get his views on to paper and pass them on. It was only in the autumn of 1945, after the London meeting of the Council of Foreign Ministers, that Bevin's suspicions were overcome. The change came when he discovered that the officials of

---

[1] Cadogan: *Diaries* p. 776 (28 July 1945).
[2] See Vol. II, pp. 199–202.
[3] Published as a White Paper, Cmd. 6420 in January 1943: they became the basis of the post-war Foreign Service.

the Foreign Office were as hard-working and efficient as those in the Ministry of Labour or the Cabinet offices with whom he had "the good experience" he spoke of during the war. Most of them might be drawn from a restricted social group, but they lacked neither skill nor professional pride in their work. As Bevin learned to appreciate, no foreign minister at an international conference was better briefed or served by his staff, hardly any (as Acheson recognized) as well.

Bevin's initial behaviour reflected a feeling of awkwardness at finding himself in a job he had never wanted and surrounded by people with whom (although he would never have admitted it) he was not at first at ease. Gladwyn Jebb, summoned to the Secretary of State's room to report on the preparations to set up the United Nations Organization, found his reception formidable.

"In fact he said nothing for a few moments and simply looked me over in my chair. Finally he observed 'Must be kinda queer for a chap like you to see a chap like me sitting in a chair like this?' Slightly nonplussed, I thought it better not to take up the challenge. So I just shrugged my shoulders and smiled. Bevin was rather nettled. 'Ain't never 'appened before in 'istory,' he remarked, scowling ferociously. I thought I couldn't let that one go by. 'Secretary of State,' I said, on the spur of the moment, 'I am sorry that the first time I open my mouth in your presence is to contradict you. But you're wrong. It has.'"

Jebb then reminded him that in the 16th century Thomas Wolsey, a butcher's son from Ipswich, had become Henry VIII's "Foreign Secretary" and a Cardinal as well—"and incidentally, he was not unlike you physically." Whether historically accurate or not, the comparison visibly impressed Bevin and secured Jebb a permanent place in his good books.[1]

With his interest in human beings, it did not take long for Bevin to appreciate the individual qualities of his officials or even the merits of a public school education. They were clever but did not behave like intellectuals. His views were listened to with respect, even when they horrified his hearers, and opposition was always aimed at diversion not confrontation. The young men who acted as his private secretaries saw that he was looked after, and his wife as well: it was like riding in a Rolls Royce, and he liked this, especially when he was feeling tired or ill.

Bevin did not succumb to "the aristocratic embrace"; he was as free of social ambitions as he was of snobbery and never ceased to congratulate himself on the very different experience of life from which he had drawn his own education. But he enjoyed the piquancy of the contrast.

"You know, Gladwyn" he remarked to Jebb on another occasion, "I don't *mind* the upper class. As a matter of fact, I even rather like the upper class. They may be an abuse but they're often, as like as not, intelligent and amusing. Of course I love the lower class

---

[1] *The Memoirs of Lord Gladwyn* (London 1972) pp. 175–6.

and it's the backbone of this country. But Gladwyn, what I frankly can't abide is the middle class. For I find them self-righteous and narrow-minded.'[1]

In fact, during his five years at the Foreign Office, Bevin brought together as strong a team as any British Foreign Secretary has ever led, several of them of middle-class rather than upper-class origins. Amongst them were Head of the German Section of the Foreign Office and then Permanent Under-Secretary; Ivone Kirkpatrick who succeeded General Robertson (another of Bevin's men) as British High Commissioner in Germany and later follow Strang as head of the Foreign Office; Oliver Franks, brought in by Bevin from Oxford to carry out the crucial negotiations setting up the OEEC and NATO; the two senior Deputy Under-Secretaries, Roger Makins, later to succeed Franks in Washington, and Gladwyn Jebb, later UK Permanent Representative to the United Nations; Frank Roberts, who became British Ambassador to Germany and Edmund Hall-Patch, seconded to the FO from the Treasury, who went on from being a Deputy Under-Secretary to take over the position of UK Representative to the OEEC.[2] Five of those listed were created life peers and Franks and Makins were among the half dozen or so ablest men of their generation in British official life. Bevin soon called them all by their Christian names (to the scandal of his successor, Herbert Morrison), treating them "as a benevolent uncle might treat some promising nephew who had talent but still a good deal to learn about the ways of the world."[3]

From the officials' point of view, as Cadogan had been quick to see, there were great advantages in having Bevin as Foreign Secretary. The first was the strength of his position in the Cabinet and with the Prime Minister, which brought the Foreign Office right back to the centre of policy-making in a way which had not been true of Chamberlain or Churchill. Bevin was now well acquainted with the machinery of government, a veteran of Whitehall battles and well able to defend against other departments the claims of the Foreign Office to have a general oversight of the country's external relations not confined to diplomacy. Thanks to his wartime experience he spoke with more authority than other Foreign Secretaries on economic and manpower questions, was on good terms with the Chiefs of Staff and was the minister whom Attlee most frequently consulted over the whole range of government business.

The second was Bevin's bi-partisan approach to foreign policy. He kept in close touch with Eden, using Dixon as his intermediary and seeing that all important information on foreign affairs was made available to his opposite number in the Conservative Party. His insistence that foreign policy had to be seen in national not party terms was naturally congenial to men brought up in

---

[1] Gladwyn, pp. 176–7. I put this in quotation marks with hesitation. Although the views expressed sound authentic, the language does not.
[2] It was of Hall-Patch that the story is told that when Bevin heard that a member of his staff was optimistic about finding a solution for a particular problem he snorted: "Optimistic, is he? Send for 'all-Patch. 'E'll chill 'is bones."
[3] Barclay, pp. 81–2.

the tradition of "continuity", and the fact that there was usually broad agreement between the two front benches on foreign policy made their task easier.

The third advantage was Bevin's method of working. The bane of every Foreign Secretary's life is his "boxes", crammed with the never-ending flow of telegrams, papers and drafts, which he has to take home to read every evening. Although he hardly ever looked at a book, Bevin was a thorough and interested reader of documents with ability to take in a whole page at a time. And this extended not only to the mass of memoranda, reports and telegrams which every 24 hours produced at the Foreign Office, but to the rest of the papers circulated to the Cabinet on other subjects. Bevin read them all, and this gave weight to his interventions in Cabinet discussions on domestic as well as foreign affairs. He did it by getting up at 5 a.m. or earlier (he was a poor sleeper), putting on a dressing gown, making himself a cup of tea, and settling down to three hours' uninterrupted reading and reflection. His annotations were brief, often no more than "Speak", "See me", "Yes", "No", and it was the job of his Principal Private Secretary to follow up these clues when the boxes were brought back to the office. By the time Bevin arrived, at 9.30 or 10 a.m., he had a clear idea of what he wanted to do in a day that was sure to be filled with meetings. If he had finished his boxes, he was content; but if for some reason he had not he would be irritable. Overnight more telegrams would have come in, and these he had to look through before his first appointment.

Apart from calls by ambassadors or foreign visitors to London about which Bevin was punctilious; meetings of the Cabinet or Cabinet committees, particularly the Defence and Chiefs of Staff Committees; attending a debate in the House, or making a speech at some conference or official lunch, whatever time was left when he was in London was taken up with departmental conferences. The officials dealing with a particular problem, sometimes from the Treasury or the Board of Trade as well as from the Foreign Office, up to six or eight all told, would be summoned and expected to discuss it fully in front of him. Kirkpatrick recalls him letting his eye rove round the room at such meetings and saying: "Are none of you going to argue with me?" He liked the less senior members present to speak up and if they did not do so spontaneously he would turn to Gladwyn Jebb to ask "And what does Mr Minority think?"

Dean Acheson remarked of Bevin that "he could lead and learn at the same time".[1] His role in these office discussions was to provoke thought by asking unexpected questions and approaching a problem from an unfamiliar angle. To begin with, he took nothing for granted, questioning traditional assumptions and practices and wanting to know the reasons for them. "We never knew where he would start," Strang says, "because he had a way of going round and round a subject, getting gradually closer and closer to the centre, and closer

[1] Dean Acheson: *Present at the Creation* (London 1970) p. 270.

and closer to the point at which he was going to take a decision." Before that was reached, he would always ask whether he had given any undertaking to another government or was under a treaty obligation which might clash with what was proposed. Having made sure of that, he would then sum up the discussion and say what should be done. One of the officials, usually the Principal Private Secretary, would draft a dispatch or reply and show it to the Secretary of State for approval. This was by no means a formality and might not be given until there had been considerable revision. Although a quick reader, Bevin found writing laborious and seldom wrote anything. When he did it was in a barely legible scrawl, for which he used an outsize silver fountain-pen christened by Roger Makins "the Caber", and held between his first and second fingers.

Bevin was as clear as he had been at the Ministry of Labour on the respective roles of minister and officials. His job was to weigh up the arguments, give a decision, get agreement from the Prime Minister, other ministers or the Cabinet and, when necessary, defend it in parliament. Theirs was to see that he was fully briefed not only on the background and the latest information about any problem but on the alternative courses of action. He expected them to criticize and oppose him in discussion, stating their views without fear or favour. In Bevin's eyes this was quite a different matter from criticism and opposition in Cabinet or in the House of Commons. To quote Lord Strang again, "He regarded us as part of himself and it was no worse for us to criticise him than for him to criticise himself." Once the discussion was ended, it was the officials' job to see that decisions were properly recorded and put into effect. He had the great virtue, from the officials' point of view, of being business-like in reaching decisions; not running away from them afterwards, and of not interfering in their part of the operation, that is to see that they were carried out.

Finally, they enjoyed his engaging habit of looking on the members of the Foreign Service as his "union", whose interests he defended against the outside world with all the tenacity of the former General Secretary of the Transport and General Workers. Lord Inverchapel (Sir Archibald Clark Kerr) was fond of telling the story of his nomination to the post of Ambassador in Washington. When Bevin told him that he was going to propose his name, Inverchapel could not conceal a smile of satisfaction, since this had been his ambition ever since he had served in Washington as a young Secretary. The smile did not escape Bevin who leaned back in his chair with a chuckle and remarked: "Ah, Archie, I know you want the job, but you needn't think you're the best man for it. What you are is a member of the Union and I'm the General Secretary. So you're going to get it." For the first time the Foreign Service had a political chief who took an interest in pay, allowances and conditions of service, and set about correcting anomalies and removing grievances which (as a result of their failure to set up a trade union, he told them) had been causing friction and irritation for years. Bevin had the gift of creating a sense of common effort which drew the best out of the people who worked for him. "He made you feel you were in a big boat." The mutual confidence which he established with his staff (as in the case of the Ministry of Labour) survived five very exacting years and left a lasting impression on those who worked with him of having lived through an outstanding period in the history of the Foreign Office.

What Bevin did, just as he had at the Minstry of Labour, was to accept and make the best possible use of the organization he found to his hand. In time he introduced changes and carried out the reforms agreed on during the war. These left the Foreign Office and Foreign Service different in many ways from the institutions he had found on taking office, but they were adaptations designed to make them work more efficiently rather than to change them. The question that has been asked is whether Bevin (and the country) did not pay too high a price for his institutional conservatism, whether it did not lead him to accept too easily the traditional assumptions of British foreign policy, to identify himself too readily with the views of the Foreign Office, derived from a world which no longer existed, and so fail to carry out the radical reassessment which was called for at the end of the war.

If he had, it is urged, he would not necessarily have adopted a socialist foreign policy in Laski's sense—that is not at all the direction in which this criticism is pointed—but he would have realized that Britain's resources were no longer adequate to play the part of a major Power and so have avoided the mistakes and painful experiences which followed (the failure to join Europe in 1956, for example; Suez; the prolonged defence of sterling) and not left it for the Heath government to accept the logic of Britain's reduced circumstances, twenty-five years later than need have been the case. This is a question which can best be answered when the time comes to set Bevin's period as Foreign Secretary in an historical perspective in the Epilogue (Part VI). But it leads naturally to a second question. What did Bevin himself contribute to the foreign policy associated with his name? Was he more than the authoritative spokesman of Foreign Office views?

It can be argued that such a question looks back to the 19th century when policy was made by the Foreign Secretary or Cabinet without regard to a Foreign Office which was primarily concerned with sending and receiving dispatches. Those days, however, were past: the Foreign Office had grown in size and acquired the other characteristics of bureaucracy.[1] No Foreign Secretary could ignore it or its views. This did not worry Bevin. He had more experience than most ministers in running big organizations—the TGWU and the wartime Ministry of Labour—and had never had any difficulty in impressing his views on them. He had always had enough ideas of his own not

---

[1] In 1914 the FO staff numbered 176, including 40 doorkeepers and cleaners, and the Diplomatic and Consular staff abroad numbered 446, of whom less than 150 were career diplomats. By 1955 the combined staff of the Foreign Service at home and abroad (where 80 missions were maintained) numbered 10,000.

to mind picking up others from a staff which he expected to argue the case for alternative courses of action. The view popular amongst left-wing members of the Labour Party that either a minister dictated policy or was mere wax in the hands of his permanent officials was naive. For there were a score of examples (among them Bevin himself at the Ministry of Labour) to show that the most successful ministers were those who worked closely with their officials and profited from the interaction with them without allowing any confusion about the different roles they had to play.

In Bevin's case this was made easier by the fact that there was little disagreement between them on the main issues of policy relations with Britain's major allies and the European settlement, although a good deal on timing. It is true, as Lord Strang says, that there were none of "the long and carefully drafted minutes by which a Curzon or Austen Chamberlain would convey their instructions to their subordinates". But this is easily explained: thanks to his lack of formal education and difficulty in writing, Bevin had to rely far more on oral communication and on others turning his thoughts into written form. Such memoranda as he did dictate himself lack the lucidity and balance of the great state papers produced by some of his predecessors. On the other hand it is usually easy enough to spot Bevin's own phrases embedded in an official document.

But, granted this, the evidence of those who worked most closely with him, ministers as well as officials, is unanimous. In their view there was no doubt at all that, allowing for the more restricted scope open to a British Foreign Secretary after the war, he played as decisive a part in shaping policy as any Foreign Minister in modern times, and more than most because of the Prime Minister's abstention from interfering.

This is hardly surprising. Ernie Bevin had never been a man to let other people make decisions for him or to take his opinions ready made from those around him. All the descriptions of his way of working at the Foreign Office lay stress on the questioning to which he subjected his officials; the care which he took to look at the implications of action in one area on policy in another (Strang's "sense of international relationships", Pierson Dixon's "ability to connect detail with a world view of politics"); the importance he attached to a sense of timing and to waiting until the time for action was ripe—for example, over Germany and the abandonment of the Potsdam principle of economic unity. When he judged it urgent to act quickly, Bevin could move with great decisiveness, without looking over his shoulder or worrying to provide an alibi in case of failure. But *when* to act was his decision, and for the most part he took time to weigh the consequences and let his conclusions form in that curious form of self-communion which he never found it easy to explain.

In reaching a conclusion, of course, Bevin had to rely on the information and the appreciation of that information supplied by the Foreign Office. This is true of all Foreign Ministers but it is natural to ask whether the degree of dependence was not much greater in the case of a man like Bevin who had never been to secondary school, leave alone university, and who must therefore be ignorant of so much that a Curzon or an Eden could be assumed to know in dealing with other nations. Was this true? If so, did it matter?

4

Bevin had the great advantage of having been on the inside of government for the past five years, of having served as a member of the Cabinet's Armistice and Post War Committee, and of having read a great deal on international questions that came his way as a Cabinet minister. As a result Bevin had a better idea than any commentator, diplomatic correspondent or back bencher, of what had been going on in the later years of the war and presented the post-war world with its most difficult problems.

Moreover, although Bevin arrived at the Foreign Office without any experience of diplomacy, the experience he brought with him, although unusual, was far from irrelevant to his new office. Thirty years spent in organizing the dockers and other transport workers had made him acutely aware of the extent to which employment and wages in Britain were affected by the level of international trade and economic conditions abroad. Proof of this is to be found, for example, in his opposition to the restoration of the gold standard by Churchill as Chancellor of the Exchequer in 1925 and the views which he expressed in the Macmillan Committee on Finance and Industry in 1930–31[1]. Drawing conclusions from a visit to the USA which were to become commonplace twenty years later, he shocked the Left at the Edinburgh conference of the TUC in 1927 by arguing the case for a European customs union which would remove all barriers to trade and the mobility of labour and create the same size of common market as American industry enjoyed.[2] He had followed the Bretton Woods negotiations closely and one of the reasons why he wanted to go to the Treasury in 1945 was his recognition of how important international financial and economic policies were going to prove for Britain's recovery of her trade and the prospects of full employment.

Bevin's experience of working and reaching agreement with Europeans went back to the 1919 meeting of the International Transport Workers Federation, and when the completion of Transport House was held up by lack of funds and the General Strike, he put his credit to a practical test by raising, at short notice, a large interest-free loan from trade unions in nine different European countries, including Germany.[3] He was equally prominent in the work of the International Labour Office whose director-general he might well

---

[1] For the first, see Vol. I, pp. 267–70, and for the second, *ibid.*, pp. 425–434.
[2] Vol. I, pp. 387–8.
[3] *Ibid.*, p. 356. When Sir Brian Robertson was asked to illustrate what he meant by saying Bevin was a Socialist, he replied: "Well, 'Workers of the world, unite' was a phrase that meant something real to him."

have become in 1945, if Labour had not won the election, and in 1936 he scored
a personal triumph in carrying through, after several weeks of negotiation with
employers and government representatives, an international charter for seamen for which their organizations had campaigned, without success, since
1920[1]. He had first become interested in Africa and the problems of the
under-developed parts of the world when he served on the Colonial Development Advisory Committee set up by the Second Labour Government. In 1938
he made a tour round the world to join an unofficial Commonwealth Conference in Australia, returning to deliver a striking speech at the 1939 Labour
Party conference at Southport in favour of extending the Commonwealth idea
to form an international group which would provide an economic version of
collective security.[2]

The Foreign Office had been criticized (by Bevin, among others) for its
neglect of economic factors in international relations. After the war when these
became more important than ever, particularly for Britain, it was of great
value to have at the head of the Foreign Office a man who could supplement his
officials' expertise with practical experience of international trade and labour
and the ways in which these could be affected by Governments' policies. One
of his characteristic beliefs was that, if people were left to get on with earning
their living and governments did not neglect their economic and social
well-being, there would be little risk of war. Give them economic security and
they would find no cause to quarrel with each other.

"My experience of 30 years of international trade", he told the House of Commons in
his first speech as Foreign Secretary, "is that if you get men talking together about the
same occupation, the same trade, the same machines, nationalism ceases, and occupation and life interest takes its place."[3]

He referred to:

"The vicious circle whereby between the wars trade could not flourish because of lack
of security, while security was endangered through lack of trade. Now, at last, we have
found our way to what is, for the time being, security. Therefore this is the moment to
break the vicious circle.

"It is with this in mind," he concluded, "that H.M. Government regard the
economic reconstruction of the world as a primary object of their foreign policy."

Nothing was more frustrating to Bevin than Britain's lack after the war of
the resources with which to take the lead in the economic reconstruction and
development—not only in Europe, but in the Middle East and the Commonwealth—which he would have liked to make the basis of his policy. Circum-

[1] *Ibid.*, p. 578. Bevin, who was described by one witness as "Minister Plenipotentiary" for the
world's seamen, had been invited by the National Union of Seamen to present the men's case,
although they were not members of his own union.
[2] *Ibid.*, pp. 627–34.
[3] HC, 23 August 1945.

stances beyond his control denied him the chance of working out a Labour version of foreign policy which, with its emphasis on international co-operation in economic development, would have had a strong attraction for many members of the Labour Party. He did not, however, abandon his ideas, and they found at least partial expression in the eagerness with which he seized the opportunity presented by the Marshall Plan, in the creation of the Organization for European Economic Co-operation and at the end of his life in the Colombo Plan.

One of the fruits, then, of Bevin's experience in the trade union movement was a belief in practical international action which found expression in the importance he attached to the ILO and such bodies as the International Transport Workers' Federation.

Another was a distrust of Communists and of the Soviet Union which went back to the early 1920s. It did not spring from any attachment to the capitalist system of "free enterprise": although never sharing the conventional enthu-siasm of many in the Labour Party for the "Soviet experiment", in 1920 Bevin had taken the lead in stopping the shipment of arms and setting up a Council of Action, with the threat of widespread strikes, if Lloyd George intervened on the side of Poland against Russia. The trade unions, he told Lloyd George in an interview at Downing Street, would not stand by and see British and Allied forces used to put down a workers' government or stamp out revolution.[1] Twelve years later, at the Prague Conference of the International Transport Workers' Federation in 1932, he attacked the Council's refusal to send a delegation to the USSR to study conditions and establish relations with Russian transport workers, describing the decision as an "ostrich policy of self delusion".

"The map of the world is being re-drawn", he told the delegates. "I can quite understand the Russians fighting for the world revolution, I can understand their difficulties, for they believe it to be incumbent upon them to defend their new economic system . . . We are here dealing with an actual living instance of superhuman efforts to rebuild a state on socialistic lines. Whether this is being done in a satisfactory manner is a matter about which the international labour movement should be well-informed."[2]

Well before the war, however, Bevin and the majority of the Labour Party leaders had come to their own conclusions about the regime which Stalin had established: it was a dictatorship of the Left as inimical to freedom as any dictatorship of the Right. The TUC led by Bevin and Citrine denounced both with equal impartiality, refusing to be taken in by the sophistical argument that in the capitalist states of the West there was no freedom worth defending.

"The State has not yet the authority to shoot citizens without trial. Nor do people disappear at the hands of a secret police; nor is criticism of the Government a crime . . .

---

[1] See Vol. I, pp. 133–40.
[2] *Ibid.*, p. 508.

The institutions of free citizenship and the organisations of democracy are our strongest safeguards."

Bevin's views were not changed by the tremendous resistance of the Russian people to the German invasion. This did not alter the fact that, as the Russians were to discover to their own disillusionment at the end of the war, they still lived under a dictatorship, indifferent to human rights, ruthless in suppressing any shadow of dissent and concerned first and foremost with the defence and extension of its own power. Far from regarding the Soviet Union as close to the ideals of the British Labour Movement, because it called itself socialist, Bevin thought it was a denial of everything Labour stood for and a travesty of socialism.

In coming to this conclusion Bevin had certainly been influenced (as had other Labour leaders, for example Morrison in the London Labour Party) by long experience of the persistent attempts of the Communist Party, faithfully following the Moscow line on tactics, to penetrate and capture the British Labour Movement. This was a bitter fight which Bevin fought in his own union, and in the national and international trade union organizations. It was accompanied by systematic propaganda to smear Labour leaders like Bevin as "lackeys of capitalism" who were engaged in betraying the working class. The attempt failed miserably in Britain. The Communist "tactics" were self-defeating: as Bevin remarked in 1925, "Working class men in this country want people to be straight with them". But the attempt was never abandoned and it left an indelible impression on the Labour leaders of Bevin's generation.

"By God," he told his Union biennial conference in 1925, "I wish Russia could have seen that if she had never supported the Communist Party in England but allowed the British trade union movement to help Russia she would have been in a much better position than today "[2]

Bevin had seen the same process at work on the Continent, where it had much graver consequences in weakening the resistance of the working class movement to the Nazis and other Fascist movements. As early as 1922 he attended a conference in Berlin of the 2nd and 3rd Internationals with the Vienna Union of Socialist Parties (the so-called "Two and a Half" International). This was intended to restore working-class unity and the Communists were represented by Bukharin, Radek and Clara Zetkin. On his return, he told the first biennial conference of the TGWU:

"Up to the time I attended the Berlin conference, I did not understand the Russian position as well as I did when I came away. . . . It is contrary absolutely to our conception of democracy and the curious thing is that the supporters of the Red International are ultra democrats one moment and ultra dictators the next. You can't

---

[1] TUC Report, 1933, *ibid.*, pp. 527–8.
[2] Vol. I, p. 559.

reconcile the two. . . . You must carry democracy with you and change stage by stage by democratic consent."[1]

Those who accused Bevin of "hysterical anti-Communism" failed to take account of the long experience he had of Communists and their tactics. He was already familiar with the device of the non-political "front organisation", the anti-Fascist and United Fronts, "spontaneous" resolutions and demonstrations, appeals to working class unity and the rest of the Agitprop repertoire. This did not affect Bevin's view of the need to try and reach a settlement of differences with the Soviet Union which went further than the 25-year Anglo–Soviet Treaty; but it meant that he approached the negotiations without any of the sentiment about friendship between fellow socialists or the illusions about the character of Stalin's regime which were still to be found in the Labour Party.

A third principle which Bevin drew from his experience was a belief in democratic institutions: free elections, the right to choose one's own government, free speech, freedom of the press, and not least freedom to organize independent trade unions.

It was the suppression of these freedoms and of the trade unions in Germany and Austria which had first alerted him to the danger from the Dictators and taken him into the fight over foreign policy in the Labour Movement in the 1930s. He had not forgotten the lesson when he became Foreign Secretary.

"There are two kinds of hunger in Europe today," he said in a speech of October 1945. "One is physical hunger, but I sometimes think . . . that the awful blackout over Europe is creating a spiritual hunger which is more devastating even than physical hunger. If every country could get free parliaments and free expression without dictatorship or orders, and if people could express themselves freely on these problems, we might make a better world for the future than we have experienced in the last 25 years."

Bevin was particularly impressed with the effect that living under a dictatorship had produced in Germany. A nation which had gone through this experience, he told the House, "almost entirely loses the use of its reason".

"They have no sense of judgment because so long as there is a dictator at the top giving all decisions, the power of decision is lost lower down. I think that one of the greatest tributes to democracy is that it retains the power of responsibility and decision."[2]

It was for this reason that he attached importance to securing assurances for these democratic rights from the Polish Government at Potsdam and that he criticized the regimes set up in the rest of Soviet-occupied Europe as the replacement of one form of totalitarianism by another.

[1] *Ibid.*, pp. 231–2.
[2] HC, 26 October 1945.

Whether he had to deal with the Russians or anyone else, Bevin needed no instruction in the art of negotiation. His reputation as a trade union leader had been built on his skill as a negotiator, and he had learned in a hard school. The setting and the issues in diplomatic negotiations were different, the stakes larger, but the game was the same and Bevin was familiar with every move in it. This was not the first time he had found himself with few cards in his hand and the need to rely on bluff and adroitness to make the most of them. He may have lacked the finesse of his predecessors, he certainly lacked the power with which they were able to support their diplomacy, but in shrewdness and resourcefulness as a negotiator he could stand comparison with any of them.

Bevin took advantage whenever he could of opportunities to supplement and check the official sources of information available to him through the Foreign Service and the British Intelligence agencies. Sir Orme Sargent, his Permanent Under-Secretary from 1946 to 1949, believed that he had a wider range of contacts in Europe and the USA than any Foreign Secretary he had served under since Salisbury. He owed these largely to the international trade union movement. He never, for example, visited New York as Foreign Secretary without arranging to meet the leaders of the American trade unions privately (George Meaney, Sidney Hillman, Dave Dubinsky, William Green and Matt Woll) to get their assessment of the world situation and American opinion. Another source of information was the World Federation of Trade Unions of which Arthur Deakin became president in 1946 and in which a bitter struggle was waged with the Communists. Yet a third was the international socialist movement, with which he kept in touch through Morgan Phillips, its president, and Denis Healey, the Labour Party's international secretary.

Bevin was rarely at a loss for other ways of supplementing official advice. In the spring of 1946, dissatisfied with the estimates he received of German food stocks, he arranged for Sir Norman Vernon, of Spillers, a friend from the days when they had both served on the Joint Industrial Council for the Flour Milling Industry, to go to Germany in company with an official of the Co-operative Wholesale Society and visit every granary, barn and warehouse they could see and talk to the millers in order to give him an independent assessment. On another occasion when he was discussing the currency allowance for foreign travel after the war he surprised his officials by demanding that "Joe" should be brought across to the Foreign Office. "Joe", when he appeared, turned out to be J. J. Taylor, the secretary of the Workers' Travel Association which Bevin had helped to found in the 1920s. "How much, Joe," Bevin asked him "would a couple need to spend a fortnight in Paris?" When Joe answered £40, this was the figure Bevin went for, finally getting the Treasury to agree to £35. He took a similar childlike delight in mystifying his officials when, to their disbelief, he forecast the resignation of de Gaulle in 1946 two or three weeks before it occurred, and continued for months afterwards to chaff them on the inadequacy of their own intelligence service.

The many anecdotes about Bevin are testimony to the impression his personality made on his contemporaries. But they can be misleading if they obscure the fact, in Oliver Franks's words, that "he was a big man doing a big job which he took with great seriousness and thought about all the time." The anecdotes belong to the moments of relaxation. But when he concentrated his energies on carrying through a policy on the scale of the Marshall Plan or the North Atlantic Pact, the quirks of character, of temperament and vanity, the differences of experience ceased to matter and he communicated to everyone involved the sense of being part of a design bigger than themselves, to the achievement of which everything else was subordinated without question. The 1940s continued to be a decade of decisions right until their end and those who worked with Bevin knew that they were close to the decision-making and part of the action.

There was never any doubt in Bevin's mind that his prime responsibility as Foreign Secretary was to maintain the national interests of his own country. What did he mean by that? In general terms, the security of the United Kingdom and its overseas possessions against external attack; the continued financial and economic as well as political independence of Britain; the right of its people to trade freely with the rest of the world, their right to maintain a policy of full employment and a decent standard of living. Unmoved by the argument that (apart from the last two) this amounted to no more than taking over the traditional principles of British foreign policy, he saw the crucial difference in the fact that the Labour Party was no longer a party of protest but accepted as the constitutional government of the country, and the working class and trade union movement which he represented were no longer excluded from the concept of the national interest but entrusted with the responsibility for its maintenance. His anger and resentment at this exclusion and the unfitness for responsibility which it implied had been one of the most powerful springs of his political activity and had led him to attack the Baldwin and Chamberlain administrations as class governments. Once the exclusion was removed, he found it natural to take a national rather than a class view of his responsibilities.

He was equally unmoved by the accusation that, in safeguarding his own country's national interests, he was turning his back on Labour's traditional internationalism. Nobody who ever heard him address a trade union audience on foreign policy could doubt that he was sincere when he said that it must be possible to find a more satisfactory and juster way of conducting international relations. This belief represented something as real and important to him as his commitments to the ILO and the international trade union movement before the war. On the other hand, as he had already shown in the Labour Party debates of the 1930s, even before his experience of the war, Bevin never supposed that power could be left out of account in international any more than in industrial relations; nor did he believe that governments in practice would (or should) make a unilateral sacrifice of national interests to uphold some international principle. Bevin's internationalism was pragmatic, concerned not with the universal principles proclaimed in the UN Charter, but taking the world as it was, as unregenerate and divided as it had ever been, with seeing how far it was possible to discover common interests between nations and bring together those of them prepared to act in common for self-protection and self-help. Such an approach was strongly reinforced by the argument that in 1945 Britain was no longer in a position to provide for her national interests by herself but could only secure them by practical international action.

Many people in the Labour Party, however, and in the Liberal Party too, believed that the right way to do this was through a new international organization, the UN, embracing all nations and overriding national interests, not by the pursuit of a separate British foreign policy through the traditional machinery of Foreign Office, diplomacy and national armed forces, even when this was aimed at a combination of like-minded nations.

Bevin attached importance to the United Nations, which he saw undertaking the continuing task, once the peace settlement was made, of regulating international disputes. In his speech of 7 November 1945, he told the House of Commons:

"If I may say so with almost religious conviction, when I have been asked to table a decision on policy . . . I have remembered all the time the implied obligations that this House and this Government have entered into a connexion with the United Nations."[1]

His approach, however, was again a pragmatic one. During his visits to Geneva for ILO Conferences, he had taken the chance to look in at the proceedings of the League of Nations. While critical of what he saw, Bevin was not one of those who regarded the League as a complete failure and now thought they could advance to world government at a single step.

"It was a beginning and a trial . . . The advance represented by the present charter would have been impossible had it not been for the Covenant of the League."

It was consistent with this view that he should refuse to attach too much importance to the constitutional shortcomings of the UN Charter. In his first speech as Foreign Secretary, he urged the House not to worry overmuch about "vetoes and votes":

"If the Great Powers cannot be reasonably true to the promises which they have made in the charter, no promise to inflict sanctions upon each other will save the world . . . If they refuse to carry out their responsibilities, it is not a change in the system of voting that will make them do so."[2]

---

[1] HC, 7 November, 1945.
[2] HC, 23 August 1945.

He argued with conviction that no nation stood to gain as much from the creation of a strong international authority as Britain, a Power with world-wide commitments which she no longer had the strength to meet by herself and which it would be a great relief to transform into collective responsibilities shared with other Powers. But he did not share the idealist view, which coloured much Labour and Liberal sentiment about the UN, that campaigning and passing resolutions in favour of a world organization would make its authority effective or remove the need, in the meantime, for Britain to develop a foreign and defence policy of her own—any more than he had accepted in the 1930s the argument that the slogan of collective security removed the need for Britain to rearm. To put it another way, he was not willing, pending the establishment of *the* international community as conceived by the idealists, which would bring all nations under the rule of law, to renounce the advantages to Britain of *an* international community, limited to the Atlantic nations, or the Commonwealth, but providing an opportunity for action collectively which Britain could no longer secure on her own.

This was the crux of Bevin's disagreement with those who "put their faith in the UN." The UNO had not yet been brought into existence and it was wholly unrealistic to suppose that it would at once take over responsibility for a distracted world in the aftermath of the most destructive war in history. That had to rest with the major powers which defeated Germany and Japan and who alone had the resources and experience to deal with such a situation. Once they had agreed on a settlement, then it might be left to the UN to police it. If the major powers could not agree, however, as the very first session of the Security Council in January 1946 showed, the UN would be in constant danger of becoming no more than a sounding board for their disputes.

A more substantial criticism of Bevin from a later vantage point is that he continued to identify Britain's national interests with the maintenance of the world role which the UK no longer had the resources to sustain. Instead of straining to keep up the part she had played as a leading power since the 18th century, so the argument runs, Labour should have taken the opportunity to withdraw from all overseas commitments in the shortest possible time and concentrate the country's energies on rebuilding her economy and foreign trade.

In common, perhaps with most of the British, he regarded the difficulties as temporary, rather than as part of a long term pattern of declining power, the result of Britain's efforts during the war, which—with time and some help from the USA and the Commonwealth—were capable of being mastered.

The economic pressures the Labour Government met on taking office however, forced Bevin to recognize that a reduction in the country's overseas commitments could not be resisted indefinitely, and that these would have to be scaled down to a more realistic relationship with the resources Britain could provide from her limited base. But he was opposed to an abrupt withdrawal from any British possession or sphere of influence, at least until satisfactory alternative arrangements could be made which would prevent a vacuum being filled by some other Power hostile or indifferent to British interests. The problem was how to make such arrangements, within what framework, and, increasingly important, whether this could be done in time before Britain's capacity to act by herself became exhausted.

This time the British Government had no territorial claims of its own to make as they had in 1815, and indeed in 1918 when they took over a large part of the former German and Turkish empires. There were, however, five areas in which Bevin believed that the British, having fought the war, could not give up their claim to have their interests considered, and their views listened to:

The Commonwealth and Empire.

The international economic system to be established after the war.

An international security system with particular regard to controlling the development of atomic weapons.

The post-war settlement in the Mediterranean and Middle East.

The peace settlement in Europe and in particular what was to be done with Germany.

So far as the first of these was concerned, the framework existed already. The Labour Government's policy was to see that it was not broken up under external pressure but that self-government should be extended to convert the dependent territories of the Empire, beginning with India, into the voluntary and free association of the Commonwealth. This in turn affected British foreign policy in three ways. It powerfully reinforced the argument that, despite her reduced power, Britain should not abandon her world role; it meant that Bevin and the Foreign Office, in any course they decided on, had always to remember that Britain was the centre of a group of nations whose governments had to be kept informed and, where necessary, consulted if conflicts of interest were to be avoided; and it added another strong argument to the list of reasons why Bevin and Attlee were opposed to merging Britain in some form of Western European union.

In the second case, the post-war international economic system, a framework had been proposed by the USA at Bretton Woods which the British had accepted in principle but which the Labour Government had considerable doubts about ratifying. This question soon became entangled with the British request for an American loan. The answer which the Americans sought to impose on the British was a sharp reminder, both of the extent to which Britain's ability to follow an independent economic policy had been reduced and of the need to defend it.

The third issue, security and particularly the control of atomic weapons, again involved Britain heavily with the Americans with whom they had developed the joint research effort to produce the A-bomb. Whether the Americans would be willing to continue this now that the war was over and how, if at all, it could be adapted to bring in the Russians, were questions with which Attlee and Bevin were more concerned than any other ministers and had a powerful effect on foreign policy.

In one of his earliest speeches in the House of Commons, Bevin wrily complained that there was hardly any part of the world which the Foreign Secretary could regard as lying outside the scope of his office. In practice, although the British moved quickly to reoccupy Malaya and Hong-Kong, they accepted that the USA would now replace them as the leading non-Asian power in the Far East and the Pacific. But the Mediterranean and the Middle East were a different matter. Britain's role in that part of the world was of such a long standing that it was taken for granted by most Englishmen as part of the natural order, a belief confirmed by the effort the British had put into its defence during the war as the main theatre of British operations up to the invasion of Europe.

The question Bevin found himself having to answer from the sceptics in his own Party, including the Prime Minister and other Cabinet colleagues, was why the British should remain in the Middle East at a cost they could no longer afford when the war was over and everyone wanted them out. There is no doubt of Bevin's answer. As late as August 1949 after many setbacks and disappointments in his Middle Eastern policy he was still prepared to say in a paper circulated to the Cabinet:

"In peace and war, the Middle East is an area of cardinal importance to the U.K., second only to the UK itself. Strategically the Middle East is a focal point of communications, a source of oil, a shield to Africa and the Indian Ocean, and an irreplaceable offensive base. Economically it is, owing to oil and cotton, essential to United Kingdom recovery."[1]

Both strands of thought have to be taken into account in understanding what Dalton called Bevin's "fascination" with the Middle East. The strategic arguments were exhaustively discussed in 1946–7.[2] All that needs to be added at this point to what has already been said is that, while Bevin and the Chiefs of Staff agreed on the importance of maintaining British control over the area, Bevin differed from the generals on how this could best be done. He did not share their belief that there was no substitute for Suez as the main British base and he was prepared to consider a wide variety of alternatives. He was equally interested in finding a different footing for Britain's position from the existing

---

[1] C.P. (49) 188. 25 August 1949. A point sometimes forgotten is that further British investment in oil production in Iran, Iraq and Kuwait after the war both accounted for a rapidly rising percentage of the UK's needs, at low cost and without having to pay dollars (the AIOC's refinery at Abadan was the largest in the world), and enabled Britain to maintain her position as second only to the USA in the international oil trade. This in turn brought benefits for her balance of payments and her bargaining power in international negotiations. That was what Bevin had in mind when he told the Cabinet Defence Committee in 1946: "Without the Middle East and its oil . . . he saw no hope of our being able to achieve the standard of living at which we are aiming in Great Britain." DO (46) 45. CAB 131/2.

[2] See below, pp. 239–44; 348–54; 359; 363; 470–75.

treaties and bases imposed on the local peoples, which he regarded as outmoded and indefensible. He was eager to replace these with some form of regional defence system or at least with arrangements under joint defence boards to train the armed forces of Britain's allies such as Egypt and Iraq "up to a standard capable of meeting the needs of modern warfare."[1]

This same notion of replacing the old relationship of domination with one of partnership, and treating the Arabs as "genuine partners" is equally important in understanding Bevin's views on the economic importance of the Middle East. From the time when he served on the Colonial Development Advisory Committee set up by the Second Labour Government in 1929, Bevin's imagination had been fired by what might be done to open up the resources and raise the living standards of the under-developed world. The continuity of his interest can be followed through the speech he made to the Labour Party Conference in 1939, urging that the Commonwealth should be made the basis for "a real pooling of the whole of the colonial empires and their resources" to form an economic equivalent to collective security; his welcome for the Colonial Development and Welfare Acts of 1940 and 1945; to his proposal for Western Union in January 1948 which was to include the African and other colonial territories of the Western powers; and finally to the Colombo Plan of 1950 in which he sought to create, on the same basis of mutual help as the Marshall Plan, a Commonwealth version in South East Asia of Truman's Point 4 proposals for aid to the under-developed world.

Far from seeing such schemes as incompatible with the development of self-government in the colonies, Bevin regarded them as essential to it, the necessary economic ground on which to create democratic political institutions. Bevin shared the Labour view that the colonial relationship on which the British Empire had been built must be changed; but this was to be accomplished not by breaking up the Empire but by converting it into a voluntary association of self-governing peoples, a concept to which the decision of India, Pakistan and Ceylon to remain within the Commonwealth appeared to give substance and validity. Bevin extended the concept from the formal to the "informal empire" in the Middle East, "a common basis of partnership between the Middle East and ourselves" (as he described it in a speech of 1 November 1945) involving joint cooperation not only in defence but in economic development and technical co-operation as well.

"In that way I can see the mutual interest, the mutual character, the great design of that area contributing not only to its own security and its own prosperity, but contributing a great example to wider regions of the world by its mutual understanding and common efforts."[2]

Bevin was trying to find a basis of common interest which would represent a

[1] Bevin at the Cabinet Defence Committee's meeting of 5 April 1946, Minutes DO (46) 10.
[2] Speech to the Anglo–Egyptian Chamber of Commerce, London, 1 November 1945.

more acceptable and advantageous relationship to both partners than economic exploitation on the one hand or economic nationalism on the other. The core of it was his belief (developed over many years in the ILO) that raising the standard of living in the less developed countries would lead to an increase in trade and the joint opening up of resources which was in the interests of both the peoples who lived there and of the developed countries as well.

In this way Bevin hoped to adapt positions which Britain no longer had the power or will to maintain by herself without abandoning them. It was a grandiose plan, certainly, and one which—apart from nationalist suspicion and resistance—Britain proved not to have the resources to carry out. But it was a view which reflected Labour thinking about the colonies in the 1940s as this was developed by the Fabian Colonial Bureau under the chairmanship of Arthur Creech-Jones,[1] and it is an essential clue to understanding the framework in which Bevin tried to work out a policy for the Middle East.

Finally, Europe. Britain's interest there was of a different kind from that in the Middle East. Europe was the one continent on the mainland of which she held no territory of her own since the loss of Calais in 1558; but in the politics and wars of which she had repreatedly intervened whenever any European powers looked like establishing a preponderance which might threaten her own security and independence. The war the British had just fought was the most striking example of this policy, especially as it followed immediately on the period of appeasement in which it had been abandoned with near-disastrous consequences. With Hitler's defeat, was the threat from Germany to be replaced by one from Russia?

6

The question was easy to pose, but not easy to answer. Even with access to the Soviet archives it might still be difficult to answer with certainty. In the summer of 1945 before the first meeting of the Council of Foreign Ministers in September, Stalin had achieved far more than his minimum programme, both in Europe and the Far East. Beyond that lay not a maximum programme of further expansion, but a series of possibilities—in Germany and the rest of Europe, the Mediterranean, the Middle East—which the Russians obviously considered and continued to probe without ever committing themselves. If circumstances were favourable; if, for example, the British withdrew, the Russians might go further—or they might not. When Bevin tried to get Stalin or Molotov to say what it was they wanted, to put down a line on the map between Soviet and British spheres of influence which could provide a basis for negotiation, they evaded him, preferring to keep their options open. Why not?

---

[1] See David Goldsworthy, *Colonial Issues in British Politics 1945-61* (Oxford 1971), c. 4 "Labour and Colonies: the Fabian Years".

They were well aware that Britain was over-stretched and would have to abandon some of her commitments. It was in Britain's interest as a power in decline to try and define the situation, and in theirs to leave it undefined, not to forgo opportunities which might arise, particularly if (as the Russians firmly believed) the Americans faced a severe slump which might lead them to show less interest in Europe and the Middle East.

Bevin had the strongest possible motive for reaching agreement with the Russians as well as the Americans, both in Europe and in the Middle East: if he had been able to bring it off, nothing would have won him more applause, particularly from his own party. The question, however, was not just on what terms a settlement could be obtained, but whether the Russians were interested at all in an Anglo-Russian agreement as distinct from one with the United States which the British would have to accept in any case.

Some of his critics took the view at the time that Bevin's object from the first was to create an anti-Soviet coalition based on American power—the policy Churchill spelled out in his Fulton speech of February 1946—and that his repeated declarations of his wish to reach a settlement with the Russians were no more than camouflage to conceal his true purpose from the Labour Party. After the wartime experience of partnership, it was natural for any British Government to look on its relations with the United States in a different light from those with any other country outside the Commonwealth, and to seek backing from the Americans in any difficulties it might have with the Russians. Bevin's greatest achievement as Foreign Secretary was his part in securing American support for Europe's recovery through the Marshall Plan and for her security through NATO, and it had been accepted in the coalition's discussions well before the end of the war that American participation, in some form or other, was essential for both purposes.

Nevertheless, an Atlantic alliance such as Bevin took a leading part in creating between 1947 and 1951 in order to defend Western Europe against the Soviet Union—although a possibility which he always had in mind—was not his primary objective when he came into office in 1945, although it gradually came to play a more and more important part in his thinking. The evidence for this view will be examined in the chapters that follow, but at least three reasons may be given in advance for accepting it as a working hypothesis.

The first is that in 1945 neither the US Government nor the majority of Americans were prepared to accept the role which the United States undertook in 1947 and which was the key to any idea of an Atlantic alliance. American post-war policy, like British, evolved in stages. In December 1945 Bevin's greatest anxiety was that Byrnes might conclude a deal with the Soviet Union over his head and well into 1946 Anglo–American relations were still marked by disagreement in a number of areas.

The second is that British opinion, alarmed at the prospect of another war, was not prepared to see the attempt to reach agreement with the Russians abandoned or, so far as the Labour Party was concerned, to accept the idea of an alliance with a capitalist America against a socialist Russia.

The third, and most important, was that neither Attlee nor Bevin had given up hope of making a satisfactory peace settlement in agreement with the Russians as well as the Americans. The advantages for the British of such an agreement were so obvious that every Foreign Office planning paper for the past two years and every editorial for the next two returned to it again and again. Bevin certainly had no illusions about the character of Stalin's regime, or the difficulty of negotiating with the Russians, but it was so obviously in Britain's interest and, he believed, in Russia's too, to avoid the alternative of a division of Europe, and particularly a division of Germany, into hostile blocs that he regarded it as worth a great deal of effort to try and get such a settlement. In August 1945 Smuts wrote to Attlee to express his concern at the "commanding world position" the Russians were acquiring in Europe. After consulting Bevin, Attlee replied:

"I do not disagree with your diagnosis of the threatening situation in Europe, more particularly in the Eastern countries. The growth of Anglo–Russian antagonism on the Continent, and the creation of spheres of influence, would be disastrous to Europe and would stultify all the ideals for which we have fought. But I think we must at all costs avoid trying to seek a cure by building up Germany or by forming blocs aimed at Russia. It is of course true that to depress the level of Germany's industry and standard of living below a certain point would do harm to Europe and to ourselves. We shall do everything in our power to prevent this, but any suspicion—and the Russians are not slow to form suspicions—that we were trying to deal softly with Germany, or to build her up, would be such an obvious threat to Russia that we should thereby harden the Soviet Government's present attitude in Eastern Europe and help to give actual shape to our fears."[1]

Attlee's letter illustrates a general point which must strike anyone who reads through the documents, the press and parliamentary debates of the second half of 1945: that is the extent to which everyone who wrote and spoke about foreign affairs was struggling to adjust to an unfamiliar world in which no one had yet got his bearings. This was true of ministers too. Bevin and Attlee were better prepared for the difficulties they encountered and better informed, but both were still learning in 1945, still feeling their way in foreign policy. "Continuity" was a principle they accepted but the coalition had not been able to foresee how the post-war situation would develop and did not pass on to the Labour Government a ready-made policy. Indeed it was only in the course of his first year of office that the size and multiplicity of the problems he had to cope with, and the extent to which Britain was in danger of being left on her own without the resources to solve any of them by herself, really became clear to Bevin.

[1] Copies of Smuts' letter (10 August 1945) and of Attlee's reply (31 August) are in FO 800/443/COM/45/1 & 10.

It needed great strength of character on his part to absorb all this and not to lose his nerve, not to retract Britain's claim to take a full part in the post-war settlement and not to settle for something less than he believed essential. Later, he was to show that besides toughness he possessed other and more creative gifts as a Foreign Secretary, but if it had not been for the resolution with which he faced the difficulties of his first year he would have had little chance to use them. Up to the spring of 1946 it was against Britain that the Soviet Government concentrated its hostility, avoiding a confrontation with the United States and doing its best to drive a wedge between the Western Powers. The initial uncertainty of American policy not only encouraged the Russian tactics, but made it more difficult for Bevin to resist Soviet pressure when he could not be sure of American support. Nonetheless, Bevin held his ground and refused to let himself be rushed into hasty decisions by the clamour for economies, demobilization and a quick settlement. Apart from anything else, this gave time for opinion in the Party and in the country at large to come to terms with a situation very different from the expectations fostered by the victory over the Axis Powers.

Bevin's determination was also of value to the Americans. In retrospect it may seem inevitable that the United States could not have allowed a Russian attempt to establish a dominant position in Europe and the Mediterranean to pass without challenge, but it looked anything but certain at the time, and even if it was, it can be argued that Bevin's stubborn refusal to acquiesce in Russian manoeuvres to extend and strengthen their power position during 1945 and 1946 helped to secure the time needed for the Americans to make up their minds without anything irrevocable being lost before they were ready to commit themselves.

No doubt historians will long continue to dispute how real was the threat of Russia extending her power in the Middle East and dominating Europe after the Second World War just as they continue to debate the inevitability of war breaking out in 1914 and 1939. In both the latter cases, the hesitations and uncertainty of British policy have been regarded as a contribution to the failure to avoid war. This is not a criticism that can be made of Bevin's foreign policy. However great the lack of material resources to support it, British policy was not inhibited by any lack of political will or resolution. Bevin failed to achieve his original objective, to secure an agreed settlement with the Russians as well as the Americans, but he had given nothing away and had defended with vigour the interests not only of his own country but of the rest of Europe not occupied by the Russians. By the time he had to admit failure and the exhaustion of British resources, in 1947, he was able to fall back on his second line of policy, the partnership with the United States and Western Europe, which his stand between 1945 and 1947 had given time to develop. And despite all the fears and forebodings, his policy of firmness did not lead to the outbreak of a third world war.

PART II

Frustration, 1945–1946

CHAPTER 4

First Encounters

I

The first crisis of the new Administration started with President Truman's announcement on 21 August that Lend-Lease was to end immediately, an announcement which fell on Whitehall like a V2, without warning. This was a possibility for which the coalition had made no provision and which took Churchill as much as Attlee by surprise. The new Prime Minister did not attempt to conceal the shock: the abrupt decision in Washington, he told the House, had put Britain "in a very serious financial position".[1] Keynes described it as "without exaggeration a financial Dunkirk".

In 1945 there was a gap in the balance of payments between overseas expenditure (excluding munitions) of £2000 M. and overseas earnings of £350 M., a gap which could not be closed before 1949, even by the most drastic policy of withdrawal from commitments, cuts in imports and rationing. Even then there would be an accumulated deficit of the order of £1,500 to £2,000 million which could only be met by borrowing. There was only one country which could provide such a loan, the United States.

Immediately plans were made to send Keynes to Washington and in talks with ministers before he left Keynes was confident that he would be able to secure £1,500 million as a gift or at least as an interest-free loan. Bevin was more doubtful. "When I listen to Lord Keynes talking", he is reported to have said, "I seem to hear the coins jingling in my pocket; but I cannot see that they are really there."[2]

More surprising than anything else is the fact that such a situation had not been foreseen. Not only British public but British official opinion had been reluctant to admit that Britain would need to ask for a loan at the end of the war. American opinion was equally unprepared for such a request, and there

---

[1] HC, 29 August 1945.
[2] Roy Harrod: *Life of J. M. Keynes* (London 1951) p. 596.

was a good deal of impatience with the British when they protested at the abrupt decision to end Lend-Lease. The practice of the Press—on both sides of the Atlantic—of picking up and magnifying the more extreme comments from the other side did nothing to reduce the mutual irritation.

The autumn of 1945 was as bad a time as there could have been for such a negotiation. With the end of the war there was a revulsion in American public opinion against international affairs and even more against assuming further international obligations.[1] Americans were impatient to see the boys back home, controls ended, taxes cut and a return to normalcy. The standing of the new Democratic Administration was unusually low, with a hostile Congress and a president still too unsure of himself to challenge popular views, as Roosevelt might have done, with a strong display of leadership. In a Gallup poll, 60% of those interviewed opposed any loan to Britain; only 27% were in favour, and the majority view was endorsed by "elder statesmen" like Hoover and Baruch.

The line initially taken by the British press, justifying a request for aid on the grounds of disproportionate sacrifices and a greater relative contribution to the war, only made Americans angry. Nor was Keynes' task made easier by the dismissal of Churchill and the election of a Labour (translated into American headlines as a Socialist) Government bent on a policy of nationalization. Early in November Bernard Baruch in a powerful warning to Congress, urged it not to aid foreign countries "to nationalize their industries against us".[2]

A grant in aid was clearly out of the question; even a loan would have to bear interest and would only be made on conditions. To a convinced multilateralist like Will Clayton, Vice-Chairman of the American negotiating team, the British request for aid was a Heaven-sent opportunity to commit the UK to Bretton Woods and the multilateral policies for international trade which he believed to be in Britain's and the world's best interest. He undertook to load the loan negotiations "with all the conditions the traffic would bear". To others, more concerned with their own interests, it was a chance to force the British to give up the sterling area, abandon imperial preference and eliminate quotas and exchange controls, all of which were seen as obstacles to American trade. As the Chairman of Sears, Roebuck wrote to Clayton, "If you succeed in doing away with the Empire preference and opening up the Empire to United States commerce, it may well be that we can afford to pay a couple of billion dollars for the privilege".[3]

It was the American attempt to tie such conditions to the loan that aroused the most resentment in Britain where they were variously seen as an encroach-

---

[1] See the table quoted from Gabriel Almond's study, on p. 192 of Gardner. The public opinion polls cited by Almond show that the percentage of Americans who considered foreign problems more vital than domestic was lower in October 1945 than at any other time between 1935 and 1950: only 7% by comparison with an average of 33% between October 1945 and October 1949 and a peak of 73% in April 1948 (after Prague).

[2] Gardner, p. 194.

[3] Gardner, p. 197.

ment on Britain's economic sovereignty, an attempt to break up the Common-wealth and Empire and a first step towards "enslaving" a socialist Britain to capitalist America.

The Washington negotiations lasted from 13 September to 6 December and proved so difficult that more than once it appeared they would break down. The difficulties were not all on the American side. Constant recourse had to be made back home for agreement or instructions, and Bevin was one of the committee of three (the other two being Dalton and Cripps) which bore the responsibility at the London end and secured the reluctant consent of the Cabinet. This was far from easy. Several ministers not only found it hard to follow the course of the negotiations but harder still to adjust to the facts of the country's post-war situation. "Most of the objections", Dalton noted in his diary, "consisted of wistful moralizing *in vacuo*."

This was written after a hard fought battle in the Cabinet on 6 November, when agreement was finally obtained to a fresh proposal from the British side. After a discussion in the morning the Cabinet met again from half past four to seven in the evening.

"Bevin, Cripps and I" Dalton recorded, "were in firm coalition. We took on the assault in successive waves and effectively backed each other up. In the end it was agreed that we should instruct our delegates as proposed, with no modification whatsoever. Alexander, Bevan and Shinwell were most unhappy and apprehensive about the future, although none of them pressed their objections so hard as to threaten to resign."[1]

Bevin told the Cabinet:

"He himself felt the most profound reluctance to agree to any settlement which would leave us subject to economic direction from the US . . . He would much have preferred a straightforward loan without conditions." But struggling on without American assist-ance meant "asking the British people to endure for perhaps another three years standards of living even lower than those to which they had been reduced at the end of six years of war. . . . That in his view was the real issue . . . Were we to reject these terms and demand further sacrifices from the British people?"[2]

On the 29th, ministers were again summoned to consider the state of negotiations. In the face of further objections by Bevan and Shinwell, Bevin insisted that they had to take a decision without delay. He too had looked at the possibility of a loan free of conditions in return for a higher rate of interest, but it was unrealistic. Even if the Americans were prepared to make such a loan—and there was evidence that they were not—the financial burden would be beyond Britain's capacity.[3] With Morrison, Dalton and Cripps taking the same view, the Cabinet agreed to the amount proposed for the loan, the rate of interest and period of repayment (2% per annum over 50 years). Reluctantly,

[1] Dalton, *Memoirs*, p. 79.
[2] CM, 6 Nov. (45) 50.
[3] CM, 29 Nov. (45) 57.

they accepted a commitment to "liberalise" the Sterling Area and British commercial policy (no quantitative restrictions on US exports to the UK after the end of 1946), and undertook to recommend ratification of the Bretton Woods Agreement to Parliament. Convertibility of sterling into dollars was to come into force one year after the US loan began. Beyond that they refused to go, and Dalton, cabling the result to Keynes, added that they could not stand much more of the American attitude.[1]

After another week of haggling[2], agreement was finally reached on 6 December, leaving the Labour Government with no more than three weeks in which to secure the approval of Parliament before the deadline for British ratification of Bretton Woods[3] by the 31st. The weakness of the British bargaining position was underlined by the fact that they had to commit themselves to the American conditions without any guarantee that Congress would be willing, even then, to approve the loan.

The implications of these negotiations were as serious for Bevin as for the Chancellor of the Exchequer, for two reasons.

The first was the light in which Anglo–American relations had now to be seen. The alliance with the United States had been the foundation of British policy during the war. In the coalition discussions it had been assumed that the "special relationship" with the United States would continue after the war, at least for a transitional period. This assumption was now called in question, and not only by the abrupt ending of Lend Lease and the difficulties encountered in securing an American loan. Thus on 25 September, Truman approved a statement calling for the early abolition of the Anglo–US Combined Boards responsible for the joint planning of the countries' economic resources during the war. The Combined Chiefs of Staff Committee was reprieved until the peace treaties had been signed (an event which was thought to be not far in the future), but lost its wartime importance largely because of a growing reserve on the American side which was most marked in anything to do with atomic weapons. The British had now to recognize that their view of the importance of the special relationship was not shared across the Atlantic, where the value of the connection with Great Britain appeared to be regarded with a mixture of impatience and septicism. Most Americans saw no reason at all why the USA should bind itself to a special relationship with Britain in which all the benefits (in American eyes) would be on the British side.

[1] Dalton to Keynes, 24 November 1945. FO 800/512/US/45/12.
[2] The Cabinet's final decision was taken on 5 December. CM (45) 49.
[3] Bretton Woods is a shorthand phrase to refer to the meetings held in 1944 at Bretton Woods in Maine, USA, at which the Americans, British and Canadians agreed to set up the International Monetary Fund (IMF) and the International Bank for Reconstruction and Development (generally known as the World Bank). These were seen as the key institutions for the international economic system in the post-war period, and by 1973 almost all non-Communist countries belonged to both organizations. For a detailed account of the meetings at Bretton Woods (in which Keynes played a leading part) and of the issues on which the Americans and British differed, see the book by Richard Gardner already cited: *Sterling Dollar Diplomacy* (rev. edn. N.Y. 1969).

If there was to be a loan at all, it was clearly going to be without favours, and the Americans could be expected to try to impose conditions in other matters than commercial policy. In October 1945, the US Secretary of State, Byrnes, presented Bevin with a list of bases which the Americans would like to operate around the world, from Iceland to the Pacific Islands, and pressed for British support in securing them.[1] At the same time, strong pressure was brought on London to accede to Zionist demands in Palestine, an issue on which the White House and Congressional leaders were under heavy pressure themselves.[2] At the very least the Labour Government must expect to encounter a tough attitude in Washington and little disposition to recognize a greater common interest with the United Kingdom than with other countries.

In a letter to Stafford Cripps in September 1945, Bevin wrote:

"There does seem to be an assumption that Britain is down and out because of what she has done in this war. When the P.M. made his statement in the House on Lend Lease, we were met with headlines in the U.S. calling us 'Cry Babies' . . . I cannot help feeling that Britain has got to stand up for herself . . . and the world must realise that though we have paid such a terrible price in this war we are not down and out. We shall survive . . ."[3]

These were brave words, but the fact was that Britain was very close to being down and out, and that the only obvious way out of her difficulties was to cut her overseas commitments—the second reason why the situation revealed by the end of Lease Lend had direct implications for the Foreign Secretary. These commitments were of very different kinds: the occupation of the British zones in Germany and Austria; the occupation of the former Italian colonies; British troops in Egypt and in Palestine, where civil war was threatening; the re-occupation of British possessions, Burma, Malaya, Hong-Kong, after the Japanese surrender; British troops in Trieste, Greece and soon Indonesia —not to mention the considerable British contribution to UNRRA and other relief operations, or the large debts which the United Kingdom had contracted abroad in the sterling area (a total of £2143 M.) in payment of wartime supplies. It was this heavy weight of unproductive overseas expenditure and debt on top of the cost of the imports of food and raw materials (without which the population of the United Kingdom could not survive) that constituted the heart of Britain's economic problem. Something could of course be done by such devices as funding the sterling balances, but the real question which Bevin had to face, was whether, even with an American loan, Britain could any longer afford to support the cost of being a Great Power.

Put as crudely as this and as early as the autumn of 1945, there could be no doubt of the answer. However much their former allies might regard their

---

[1] See below, pp. 151; 200–201.
[2] See below, pp. 164–83.
[3] Bevin to Cripps, 20 Sept. 1945. FO 800/512/US/45/25.

pretensions as exaggerated, the British were not going voluntarily to abdicate a position they had held for so long. This was as true of the Labour Party as of the Conservatives and of the Left-wing of the Labour Party as of its leaders. The Left was to become increasingly critical of the substance of Bevin's foreign policy, but it did not disagree with the view that Britain ought to continue to play a leading role in the world. "Britain stands today", Michael Foot declared in the debate on the King's speech, "at the summit of her power and glory and we hold that position because today, following the election, we have something unique to offer."

Nor was it national pride alone which led the British to take this view. There was an immense and urgent job to be done. There were millions of displaced persons and refugees and desperate problems of food supply and health in Europe, Asia and the Middle East. In a score of countries there was a need to re-establish some sort of government and order, to make a start on reconstruction, plant crops, and open up the channels of trade. And almost the only countries which could do anything to help besides the USA were the United Kingdom and the British Dominions.

As the centre of the Commonwealth and Empire, Britain commanded the communications (including the all-important shipping), the skilled manpower and the experience, and she had in her Armed Forces some five million men and women deployed, all the way from the Atlantic seaboard to the Indian Ocean and the Pacific, who could be drawn on at once to help. For the British to have withdrawn at this time from the responsibilities they had hitherto exercised as a World Power would have been unthinkable. On the other hand, as Dalton kept insisting, and as Bevin and Attlee well knew, even if they got the American loan, the Government was going to be hard pressed to pay for the essential imports and start on the reconstruction of their own country.

The immediate form the issue took—apart from argument about the terms of the American loan—was the question, how quickly and how far demobilization should be carried and how large were the forces Britain could afford—or needed—to maintain abroad. This was a question which obviously concerned Bevin as Foreign Secretary and chairman of the Overseas Reconstruction Committee; but he was also, by virtue of his wartime experience as Minister of Labour and National Service, chairman of the Cabinet's Manpower Committee and so at the centre of the controversy which developed about the speed of release from the Forces.

In a Cabinet discussion at the end of August, Nye Bevan declared there would have to be radical revision of the scheme Bevin had drawn up for the demobilization if he and other ministers were to get the labour they needed for housing and reconstruction. Besides early release for men with experience in mining, farming and the building trades, there was also pressure for deferring the call-up of men in these trades. Bevin refused to give way. He was determined to see no change in the principle which based a man's priority in demobilization on age plus length of service (Class A) and he insisted that the number of those given early release in Class B because of special qualifications (it was these that Bevan and the other ministers wanted) should not be allowed to rise above ten per cent of the general release.[1]

In October, the Opposition took a hand, Churchill himself appearing in the House (22 October) to criticize the Government's mishandling of demobilization as "the fountainhead of all other domestic difficulties". The dispute rumbled round the Manpower Committee and the Cabinet until, after a meeting of the Committee on 14 November which all the ministers with claims for labour were asked to attend, Bevin decided he had had enough and wrote to the Prime Minister to say that the demands now being made threatened to call in question the pledges which he and Attlee had made during the election that there would be no tampering with either the general release scheme or the continued call-up of younger men. If there was any suggestion of this, he wrote, "I should have great difficulty in being associated with an administration that would go back on its word".[2] He also said that he believed there was no need for the numbers of skilled men called for in the housing programme and that employers had got to get used to the fact that labour was not going to be as easily available as it had been before the war or had been made by government action during the war.

The stubbornness with which Bevin defended the principles of his demobilization scheme reflected his strong sense of a personal commitment to the men and women serving in the forces overseas and his determination to avoid the bitterness and mutinies which had marked the end of the First World War. But he recognized the force of the critics' practical objections and he sought a way of meeting them by pressing the Service Ministries and the Ministry of War Transport to speed up the rate of release. As a result, the figure for men and women to be demobilized by the end of 1945 was raised to 1.5 million and the same rate fixed for the first half of 1946 so that by the end of April over three million would be out of the Forces. The key was shipping and at the end of September 1945 the Cabinet gave Bevin authority to decide priorities between the use of transport for demobilization and for other schemes. With the rate of general release speeded up, Bevin was then ready to agree to increase the percentage of men released under the special Class B scheme and put the ceiling at 15 instead of 10 per cent.[3] He was also prepared in the New Year of 1946, to take drastic steps to cut back the manpower employed in munitions work.

---

[1] For these discussions see the Cabinet minutes for 16 & 30 August; 4, 18 and 28 Sept., 1 and 20 Nov. 1945, and the reports of the Manpower Committee printed in Cabinet Papers CP (45) 113; 141; 191; 311 and (46) 35. See also Bevin's papers on manpower in the following files: for 1945, FO 800/473/MAN/45; for 1946, FO 800/474/MAN/46. The minutes and papers of the Cabinet's Manpower Committee are in CAB 134/509.

[2] Bevin to Attlee 15 November 1945. FO 800/473/MAN/45/42A.

[3] CP (45) 311. Report of the Manpower Committee approved by the Cabinet on 3 December, CM 58 (45). See also FO 800/473/MAN/45/54.

All these were surprising issues for a Foreign Secretary to concern himself with, but it was fortunate for the Administration to have a man who combined responsibility for Britain's overseas commitments with the experience to form an independent judgement of the demands of the Services and the supply ministries.

The crucial issue was the size of Britain's armed forces in the future.[1] This was a question which early attracted Bevin's attention, the more so as his new office gave him a seat on the Cabinet's Defence Committee. He wrote to the PM on 3 September 1945[2] to set out some of his ideas, beginning with the question, What can we afford? The coalition, he reminded Attlee, had thought of £500 m. out of a total national income of £8,000 m. as the maximum to be spent on defence. Could the country now afford to spend so much, and with nuclear weapons was such expenditure needed? By relying more on air power, it should be possible to reduce the commitments of the other Services. Had the Navy any need of more than its pre-war total of 90,000 men, in view of the existence of the United Nations and the strength of the US Navy? Why not drop naval shipbuilding for five years and concentrate on re-equipping the merchant marine? The Army had 20 divisions: why not cut to ten in two years (fewer, if India took over the responsibilities of the Indian Army) and reduce the size of a division to 10 or 11,000 men? By pooling research and organizing a joint intelligence service it would be possible to save money. For this and for other reasons, it was important, Bevin argued,[3] to retain the office of Minister of Defence and a single co-ordinated budget for all the Services. The Dominions should be encouraged to follow the same pattern and to divide the responsibility of defending the Empire into regional zones, an old idea of Bevin's.

Between September 1945 and the beginning of 1946 Bevin took a leading part in the discussions on the Defence White Paper which went on parallel with those in his Manpower Committee and produced the figures in time for the Government's Economic Survey. His proposals, finally approved by the Cabinet on 14 February 1946[4], cut the total figure of trained men and women in the three services to 1.1 million (with a further 100,000 in training) by the end of 1946, and set a ceiling of 650,000 (Bevin hoped to get it down to 500,000) for manpower in the munitions industries (including aircraft and shipbuilding) by the same date. With this reduced strength, which it would still require conscription to maintain, Bevin believed Britain could meet all her commitments on the assumption, which he accepted, that a considerable number of these would be liquidated in the course of 1946. Even so, by the time the end of

---

[1] At the peak of mobilization during the war, Britain had 5.1 M. men and women serving in the Armed Forces and another 4 M. in the munitions industries.

[2] Bevin to Attlee, 3 September 1945. FO 800/451/DEF/45/1.

[3] In a second note to Attlee, three days later, 6 September 1945. FO 800/454/DEF/45/3.

[4] The proposals are set out in Bevin's report from the Manpower Committee, 1 February 1946, CP (46) 35. It was discussed by the Cabinet on 7 February, CM 13 (46) and agreed on the 18th, CM 16 (46).

the year was reached, the programme was to prove too ambitious and beyond the country's economic strength.

2

While the Labour Government was still trying to adjust to the shock of the American decision to cut off Lend-Lease, Bevin was brought up sharp against the difficulties of reaching agreement with the Russians. On 11 September the Council of Foreign Ministers set up at Potsdam met for the first time, in Lancaster House, London, with Bevin acting as host. Its business was to prepare the peace settlements with Italy, Rumania, Bulgaria, Hungary and Finland. After three weeks' wrangling, the Council broke up unable to agree on anything, even the text of a final communiqué.[1]

The conference opened with a proposal by Bevin which raised no difficulty at the time but was later to provide Molotov with a pretext for bringing it to an inconclusive end. At Potsdam the Americans had pressed for all five permanent members of the Security Council, i.e. China and France in addition to the three wartime allies, to be members of the Council. Stalin would have preferred to keep the membership to three, but eventually agreed to a compromise: all five states were to be formally included in the Council but in drawing up the peace treaties only those who had signed the terms of surrender were to take part. If strictly interpreted, this meant excluding China and France, except in the case of Italy where it was agreed that France should be regarded as a signatory. When the Council met in London, Bevin proposed that, while no power should have the right to take part in *decisions* of the Council unless it had been a signatory, all five powers should be free to take part in the *discussions*. After standing out for the stricter view of what was intended at Potsdam,[2] Molotov fell in with Bevin's suggestion and all five Foreign Ministers took part in the first sixteen sessions spread over the next ten days.

Nothing had been done to work out a common Western position and on most of the matters discussed the British and Americans, and even more the French, held different views. But once Molotov began to table the Russian demands—and they were put forward precisely as demands—these generated a common resistance. Thus each of the three Western powers had its own version of the future boundary between Italy and Yugoslavia, but all were agreed in opposing Molotov's proposal to transfer the whole of Venezia Giulia, including Trieste, to Yugoslavia. Similarly, each had different plans for the disposal of the Italian colonies, but all opposed Molotov's claim for the Soviet

---

[1] The British record of the CFM meeting is in CAB 133/15; the US record is in FRUS 1945(2) pp. 112–555.
[2] This would have excluded France from any part in the discussion of the East European Treaties, the United States from discussing the Finnish Treaty, and China from any part at all.

Union to be given the UN trusteeship of one of them, preferably Tripolitania, Molotov's bid was at once seen by Bevin (and by Smuts) as a bid to replace Britain in the Mediterranean, and put in the context of Russian pressure on Turkey and Iran and the Communist propaganda campaign to get the British troops out of Greece. Commenting on Molotov's remark that Russia wanted a colony somewhere in Africa and "If you won't give us one of the Italian colonies, we should be quite content to have the Belgian Congo", Dalton wrote in his diary: "E.B. is convinced that what the Russians really wanted was uranium."[1]

Bevin's response was unequivocal. After consulting the Cabinet,[2] he told the Council that he would never agree and would support instead the American proposal for a United Nations trusteeship for Italy's Mediterranean colonies. Blocked in his demands on Italy (he also proposed heavy reparations of $600 M.), Molotov retaliated by withholding Soviet agreement to the return of the Dodecanese to Greece.

From the Mediterranean, the Council turned to see if it could get nearer agreement in the Balkans. It is unlikely that Stalin had ever regarded the Yalta Declaration on Liberated Europe as more than another device to save appearances while leaving the Russians free to take such steps as they thought necessary to provide for their control of Eastern Europe. At Potsdam, however, Truman and Byrnes had made it clear that they took the promise of free elections in the Declaration seriously, and if it was too late to do much about Poland, Byrnes came to London determined to dig in his heels over Rumania and Bulgaria and refuse recognition of the governments the Russians had set up until some concessions were made over their representative character, free access for the world press and the promise of free elections. He was confident that, with the power of the A-bomb now demonstrated, American diplomacy would have the backing to get its own way.[3]

Molotov was equally determined not to make concessions and gave no sign at all that the Russians were impressed by America's possession of atomic weapons. The continued interest of the Americans and British in Eastern Europe and the presence of Allied Control Commissions in Bucharest and Sofia encouraged local opposition to the efforts of the Soviet occupying power to establish control, and he had evidently come to London with instructions to put an end to this situation, secure Western recognition of the existing regime in both countries, get rid of the Allied Control Commissions and so obtain a free hand for the Soviet representatives to enforce their will. He met Byrnes' arguments with the counter charge that the Americans were supporting

---

[1] Dalton, *Memoirs*, p. 56.
[2] At a meeting specially summoned on Saturday 15 September to discuss a paper from Bevin, CP (45) 162. CM 32 (45). There had been earlier discussions of the colonies in the Cabinet on 3 and 11 Sept. 1950.
[3] Cf. Byrnes' remarks to Joseph Davies, J. J. McCloy and Stimson before leaving for London, F. L. Gaddis: *The US and the Origins of the Cold War 1941–47* (NY 1972) p. 264.

anti-Russian elements and asserted that the regimes in Rumania and Bulgaria were more representative than the British-sponsored government in Greece. Unless the Americans and British accepted Russian terms for peace treaties in Eastern Europe he would not accept the Anglo–American draft to end hostilities with Italy.

If the decision had been theirs, it is probable that Bevin and the Foreign Office would have been readier than the Americans to seek a compromise from the beginning. They had little faith that reiteration of the principles of the Yalta Declaration would alter the fact that the Russians were in physical occupation of these countries. There was no feeling of obligation as in the case of Poland; instead, considerably scepticism about the chances for democratic régimes in the Balkans. But the real question was whether the Western Powers would acquiesce in the Soviet claim to close off Eastern Europe, and the American answer on Rumania and Bulgaria—whether Byrnes understood its full implications or not—at once made this the central issue of the conference, without either side being willing to say so openly. The official debates were reduced to by-play, but behind the scenes the principals tried to grapple more realistically with their differences. On 19 September, for example, Molotov asked Byrnes privately what it was America wanted, what "lay behind" the insistence on free elections. Byrnes, on his side, thought that Russian suspicion might spring from fear of renewed German aggression and offered a 25-year treaty, to which the USA would be a party, guaranteeing the demilitarization of Germany. Molotov accepted it as an interesting idea, but promptly returned to Rumania. Bevin had now come out in support of the American stand and Molotov declared that the other Foreign Ministers were conducting an offensive against him based on hostility towards the Soviet Union.

Social occasions did little to reduce the growing tension in the conference room. On the 18th, the British Government gave a State dinner for the delegates at St James's Palace. On the way in, Dalton asked Bevin how things were going and got the reply: "Like the strike leader said: 'Thank God, there's no chance of a settlement.'"[1] During the course of an after-dinner speech Molotov remarked that everyone had to listen to Mr Byrnes because America had the atomic bomb. In an effort to liven up the latter part of the proceedings, Bevin began to sing "Cockles and Mussels". According to Byrnes, this saved the evening: even Molotov joined in singing "Roll out the Barrel". But the next morning the dispute on Rumania was resumed with no change in positions.

On Sunday the 23rd, primed with new instructions from Moscow, Molotov told Bevin and Byrnes that he must insist on rescinding the initial agreement on procedure and ask for the exclusion of France and China from their discussions. Bevin was angry at this obvious device to apply pressure and did not try to conceal it, insisting that France could not be excluded from the discussion of Balkan questions. After further argument, he declared that it was

[1] Dalton, *Memoirs*, p. 56.

not the French problem which was holding them up, it was the "whole philosophy and attitude behind the Conference". The argument over procedure was evading the real issue. "I am anxious", he added, "to avoid the division of Europe". In an effort to break the deadlock, President Truman and Attlee agreed to send messages to Stalin, asking him to accept French and Chinese participation and urging that this was too small an issue on which to disrupt the conference.

While they waited for an answer Bevin took the opportunity to call on Molotov at the Soviet Embassy on the evening of the 23rd. While he was ready enough to give as good as he got over the conference table, he was frustrated as well as angered by an exchange of recriminations which bore no resemblance to negotiation as he understood it and he was resolved to try and get at the root of the difficulties. He was accompanied only by the British Ambassador to Moscow (Clark-Kerr) who described in his report how Bevin began the interview:

"It seemed to him that our relations with the Russians about the whole European problem were drifting into the same condition as that in which we had found ourselves with Hitler. . . . He wanted to get into a position in which there was not the slightest room for suspicion about each other's motives. . . . He wanted to hear precisely what was the Soviet policy in Europe so that any move made by HMG need not provoke suspicion. If we made a treaty with France as a neighbour we did not want to be accused of creating a Western bloc against Russia. . . . He was not willing to go on with a conference in which it was impossible to deal frankly and in a friendly way with each other. If M. Molotov would tell him frankly what was in his mind, what we were expected to agree to, the Secretary of State would lay all his cards on the table with equal frankness."

Molotov took up the reference to Hitler, but Bevin at once interrupted him:

"He did not wish the talk to start with a misunderstanding. He had not wanted to suggest that the USSR in any way resembled Hitler. All he had wished to suggest was that the absence of frankness led to situations which became irretrievable."

Molotov took Bevin at his word. The Russians, he declared, were not going to be treated as inferiors but as equals. During the war there had been differences, but they had got along; this was because the Russians were needed. Now there was a change: was this because they were no longer needed? Why, Molotov asked, did Britain refuse to grant the Soviet Union bases in the Straits which she had been willing to offer the Tsar's government? Britain could not maintain a monopoly in the Mediterranean, as her attitude to Russian interest in Tripolitania suggested. She was conducting an offensive to rouse antagonism to Russia in the Balkans and doing all she could to prevent Russia getting reparations.

Bevin retorted that if anyone was being treated as an inferior power, it was Britain—by both the Russians and the Americans. He had no views about the Straits, but he was concerned about the British lifeline through the Mediterranean. He would prefer to give the trusteeship in Tripolitania to Italy, but would then claim the trusteeship in Cyrenaica for Britain because of her interest in Egypt. "Let us agree," Molotov interrupted, adding that he would support a British proposal to this effect.

From North Africa, the two Foreign Ministers proceeded to go over their other differences: the Dodecanese (which Bevin wanted to give to Greece); European waterways, and Rumania. None of these caused much difficulty until they came to the question of "Soviet citizens" created by changes in the Russo–Polish frontier. *Were* these Soviet citizens, Bevin asked, a question to which Molotov replied sharply that Britain was obliged to recognize them as such because of the Yalta agreement.

After a further exchange on German reparations, in which Molotov declared that there was a deliberate delay and Bevin retorted that the agreement would be kept, the Russian suddenly brought up the occupation of Japan. Was Bevin satisfied that the USA should be left in control of Japan? Bevin was cautious: Had Molotov talked to Byrnes? When it became clear that he had not, Bevin contented himself with promising to think the matter over.

Finally, Bevin announced his intention of seeking a treaty with France, adding that he was not trying to create a "Western bloc" and that the treaty would not be aimed at the USSR. Molotov was sympathetic: the Russians understood, he said, and he expected no objection from Moscow. All the same, he pointed out, they had consulted the United Kingdom first before signing their own treaty with France, a point which Bevin turned with the remark that there had been no negotiations yet between London and Paris.

The talk ended in a friendly enough fashion, but can hardly be said to have broken through the barrier of suspicion. Bob Dixon, Bevin's Principal Private Secretary, who had been present at the Yalta and Potsdam Conferences, summed up his (and no doubt Bevin's) impressions in a note dated 24 September.

"The main objective of the Russians is access to and a base in the Mediterranean. The Mediterranean is, therefore, the real Russian challenge at this conference. . . .

"The Russians see that the war has left us financially and economically weak and dependent on the US. They also know the American phobia about the British Empire and calculate that we cannot count fully on American support when defending our imperial interests. The present Conference is therefore a good forum and the present a good time, to press their demands."[1]

Bevin was almost certainly wrong in thinking that the Mediterranean was the principal issue for the Russians at the London conference. Molotov was far more concerned immediately to get recognition of the Rumanian and Bulgarian governments. But it was the Mediterranean rather than the Balkans or the Far East which concerned Bevin and the impression he derived from his talk with Molotov reflected this.

[1] Pierson Dixon, pp. 248–9. Pierson Dixon was more commonly known as Bob.

Until Stalin's reply to Truman's and Attlee's appeal arrived no further progress could be made. When it came, it did no more than confirm Molotov's position and the last week of the conference was spent in further wrangles about procedure. On the 30th, Dixon noted, the participants became emotional and even abusive. The Russians did their best to make Bevin lose his temper: amongst Molotov's comments which the interpreter translated for the conference was the remark: "Eden is a gentleman, Bevin is not." The final outburst came over Molotov's insistence that there must be four separate protocols to record the proceedings of the conference instead of the usual one, and his refusal to sign any of them unless the decision on procedure taken at the beginning of the conference, was stricken from the record.

"This prompted E.B. to retort that agreements freely entered into could only be annulled by the agreement of all the parties, and that Molotov's attitude was reminiscent of Hitler.[1] As this was being translated, Molotov went pale and blotchy and got up and walked towards the door saying that he had been insulted. E.B. apologised, and Molotov resumed his place, but after this incident it was clearer than ever that no agreement was possible."[2]

In fact, Bevin spent the next day trying to save the Conference by getting Byrnes and Molotov to agree to a British compromise proposal. From this it is evident that Bevin did not attach the same importance as Byrnes to the question of recognizing the Rumanian and Bulgarian governments. As he told the American Secretary of State, "In these countries we must be prepared to exchange one set of crooks for another." If he could find a formula, such as a guarantee of elections to be held on the same lines as in Finland, he was prepared to agree to recognition and get on to drawing up the peace treaties. These could then be submitted to the wider peace conference for which the Americans were pressing. His way round the procedural difficulty was to make France a full voting member of the Council of Foreign Ministers, so avoiding any need either to uphold or to withdraw the original decision to admit her to the conference. As a further contribution to breaking the deadlock he offered to follow the Americans in recognizing the Hungarian government, and the Austrian as soon as the Allied Commission sent a recommendation.[3] Byrnes was willing to agree but told Bevin he thought there was little chance of getting Molotov to accept his proposals. Bevin was at least resolved to try and went round to see the Soviet Foreign Minister at the Russian Embassy on the

---

[1] Byrnes' version of Bevin's remark was "the nearest thing to the Hitler theory I have ever heard". This sounds more like Bevin's way of speaking than Dixon's summarized version. Byrnes, p. 105.
[2] Dixon, p. 192. A passage in Harriman's memoirs sheds an interesting light on Bevin's reaction to the incident. Meeting him in the corridor after the meeting Harriman reports: "He appeared ashamed to have shown his ignorance of diplomatic manners. I urged him to be himself, not to deviate from his blunt-spoken ways and assured him that in the long run he would get along better with the Russians that way. But he walked on to luncheon, depressed and humiliated." Harriman and Abel, p. 507.
[3] The British proposals were settled at a meeting of Bevin and his advisers on 1 October and drawn up, under ten headings, by Clark-Kerr.

afternoon of 1 October. The exchange between the two men again brings out the obstacles to an understanding on the Russian side which both frustrated and exasperated Bevin.

After listening to the British proposals, Molotov remarked that the procedural question was due to a misunderstanding and was of trivial importance. The main difficulty was over Rumania and Bulgaria, but Russia was not in a hurry, and if Britain and the USA were not yet ready to recognize their governments he was willing to wait.

When Bevin asked Molotov if he would join in recommending the admission of France to the Council of Foreign Ministers, urging him strongly to co-operate and assuring him that this would dispel all suspicions, the Russian blandly replied that the Soviet Union made no claim to interfere in British actions—despite strong pressure on her to do so over Greece and Italy. Russia, he continued, was favourable to France and had been the first to sign a treaty with de Gaulle. But France would take time to recover: it was wise to wait and see what happened. Sooner or later she would have to be admitted, but patience was required. It would be difficult for him to recommend reconsideration of the Potsdam decision on procedure.

Bevin then pressed Molotov to agree that they should say something about a wider peace conference. Molotov replied that they must not be in a hurry. This was a new suggestion which would have to be reported back to Moscow: it might be possible to reach agreement in one or two months. Bevin asked if it would not be possible at least to mention it in the protocol. Molotov's response was to ask what sort of conference was possible until Britain and America recognized the Rumanian and Bulgarian governments. It would be better to wait.

"Bevin: What about the Dodecanese?
Molotov: The question was both simple and complex. If we agreed to Russia getting a corner in Tripolitania and if Britain were given Cyrenaica, the question of the Italian colonies could be settled very quickly. Why did the British need Tripolitania which did not belong to them?
Bevin: What did the Russians want it for?
Molotov: Russia had no place in the Mediterranean for her merchant ships and the expansion of her trade."

When Molotov pressed Bevin, the latter suggested that an international trusteeship would be better.

"Molotov: So you don't want to give us even a corner of the Mediterranean?
Bevin: It was not a question of power politics, but it would cause a great uproar if any new military power were to come across the lifeline of the British Empire. He was being quite honest about this. In his position Molotov would feel the same.
Molotov: It was clear that the Secretary of State did not want to come to terms with anybody about anything. He was claiming everything, even Somaliland.

Bevin: He would welcome an international trusteeship for Tripolitania and Somaliland."

Molotov asked if it was not possible for the Secretary of State to meet him in something.

"Bevin: Molotov had met the British in nothing. They did not want an inch of territory."

Molotov then switched to the German fleet and complained that the British were not carrying out their obligations. Russia met such breaches at every step. How was it possible to have good relations on this basis?

"Bevin: That was all very well, but one nation seemed to want to make itself the sole judge.
Molotov: His country wanted to be treated on an equal footing and did not like to see the British ignoring agreements."

Bevin was no match for the much more adroit Russian in verbal fencing and had let himself be provoked into an angry and futile tit-for-tat. What discouraged him most, however, was Molotov's refusal to give any indication of the terms on which the Russians might be willing to reach a settlement, trading gains on one point for concessions on another. The real reason, no doubt, was that Molotov had no power to act as a foreign minister, and could only carry out his instructions from the Kremlin to the letter with no room for manoeuvre. But the impression it left on Bevin was that the Russians were not interested in a settlement, only in re-iterating their demands and scoring propaganda points.

A late-night meeting of the three delegations which went on to 3.15 a.m. failed to break the impasse. The next morning, quite unembarrassed by his admission to Bevin the previous afternoon (and to Byrnes) that the procedural difficulty was of trivial importance, Molotov returned to his demand that the original decision to invite France and China to attend should not only be revoked but expunged from the minutes. Otherwise, he declared, he could not sign the protocol. Despite renewed and angry argument, Molotov refused to budge and after three weeks of discussion the conference petered out without a final communiqué.

Both Byrnes and Molotov held press conferences after the breakdown, for which each side blamed the other. Bevin, however, decided to hold his hand. He took the same line with Parliament. The Opposition agreed not to press for a debate and, although Bevin was tempted to tell the House that "the real reason for the breakdown was our refusal to meet Russian ambitions in the Mediterranean", he was easily persuaded to keep to a low-keyed and factual account of the conference proceedings. Leaving others to draw their own conclusions, his own comment was limited to the remark: "Perhaps we were a little too close to two great victories for us to be able to reach immediate agreement."[1]

3

When he had had time to recover from the Conference,[2] Bevin came back convinced that the Russians, although responsible for its breakdown, must have been surprised by the result of their tactics. He thought it probable that Stalin and Molotov had been misled by their experience over Poland into believing that the Western Powers would always give way if they were pressed hard enough, and had overplayed their hand. He concluded that the right course was not to show anxiety and run after them, but to sit tight, leaving it to the Russians to take the initiative in starting up talks again.

The London meeting had one advantage for Bevin. The fact that it was being held in their own capital attracted a lot of attention from the British press and radio, and although the Council met behind closed doors, enough was known of the way things had gone to impress on many people for the first time the difficulties of reaching agreement with the Russians. Comment was restrained but realistic. The view most commonly expressed was well put by the *Manchester Guardian*:

"Though no nation has much to be proud of in this affair, it is arguable that Russia has suffered the most. During his stay in London Mr. Molotov has recklessly squandered the vast credit of goodwill towards Russia which had accumulated in this country during the war. . . . Many would still gladly give to Russia the benefit of the doubt—if only there were a doubt. But Mr. Molotov has done his best to make it difficult. . . . Russia must realise that by her attitude she is working far harder than any French or British statesman to create the 'Western bloc' she fears with so much anguish and so little cause."[3]

There was disagreement over the wisdom of trying to interfere in Eastern Europe, and the *New Statesman*, which thought Bevin and Brynes had done much to confirm Russian suspicions, argued that "they could have chosen no worse ground to stand on than the lack of 'democracy' in Hungary, Rumania and Bulgaria". The *New Statesman*, however, represented only a minority view when it declared "the first object of Soviet policy is to preserve the peace. To believe otherwise is to display either ignorance or prejudice."[4] Far more common were references to Russian imperialism, including, as Bertrand Russell pointed out in the *Guardian*, the revival of "ancient designs against Turkey and Persia". Russell concluded that appeasement of Russia would

---

[1] HC, 9 Oct. 1945.
[2] He took a week off at Brighton and made his statement in the House of Commons on his return.
[3] *Manchester Guardian*, 4 October 1945.
[4] *New Statesman*, 6 October, 1945.

only make matters worse. It was possible to hope that the Russian regime might in time become more liberal and co-operative. "But this will not happen unless the limits of Russian power are made plain to the Soviet Government while at the same time it is unmistakably shown that within these limits Russia has nothing to fear."[1] *The Economist* came to the same conclusion: Russia was not so much pursuing a deliberate policy of aggression as suffering from suspicion on the one hand and over-confidence on the other, "kicking at every door on the off-chance that some of them will be unlocked". The right comparison, *The Economist* added, was not with Hitler, but with the Kaiser's diplomacy between 1890 and 1912.[2]

If the Press is anything to go by, majority opinion in Britain was not very far from Bevin's own assessment of the situation. The generous illusions of wartime were over. There was going to be no Brave New World. The peace settlement in Europe was going to be as much the product of tough negotiation and power politics as after every other war, with the Russians ready to take any opportunity which offered to strengthen their control over and extend the sphere of influence which Hitler's defeat had put in their hands. On the other hand, there was no sign of panic or of an anti-Communist crusade. It was assumed, and this was Bevin's assumption too, that with a mixture of firmness and patience a settlement could be made. Nor was this assumption to be proved altogether wrong: most of the issues raised at the London conference (they did not, of course, include Germany) were settled and peace treaties signed before the end of 1946.

This is a point which needs underlining. One of the dangers in writing about the immediate post-war period is that of associating it too closely to the international situation in 1947–8, when the positions on both sides had hardened, and the conflict between east and west reached a crisis in the Berlin blockade. The clash which then came to a head goes back, of course, to the wartime differences over Poland which were not resolved by the Yalta Agreement and, historically viewed, it is only one more phase in the long history of hostility and distrust between the Soviet Union and Britain and the other Western Powers from the time of the Bolshevik Revolution and wars of intervention. But in making clear the continuity of the conflict, it is important not to overlook the differences between the successive periods of its development. Thus in 1945–46 relations between Russia and the Western Powers were full of difficulties and distrust, gradually building up to a crisis, but still different, even in 1947, from 1948 when the lines were drawn tight and each side prepared for a trial of strength. In the earlier period the international situation was more fluid, not yet finally set in a pattern. Neither side had yet made up its mind how far it could afford or wanted to push disagreement.

So far as Eastern Europe was concerned, the West's difficulty was to find a

---

[1] "Britain & Russia", by Bertrand Russell reprinted from *Forward* by the *Manchester Guardian*, 2 October 1945.
[2] *The Economist*, 26 September.

line of policy between two logical alternatives neither of which was acceptable to Western opinion. The first course was to recognize that Eastern Europe now constituted a Russian sphere of influence and to turn a blind eye to what went on there in return for Russia recognizing a Western sphere of influence on the same terms. However realistic this may appear now with the advantage of hindsight, it would probably have been too cynical a deal for either the British or the American Government to advocate so soon after the end of the war. On the other hand, the alternative, to force the Russians to withdraw from or at least relax their hold on Eastern Europe, was certainly more than either British or American opinion was prepared to accept and was in any case impracticable. The Russians held their positions in strength, while the British and particularly the American forces were being demobilized. Whatever hope Byrnes and other Americans may have had that possession of the atomic bomb would be a trump card in negotiations with Stalin, it soon became clear that the Russians were not going to be bluffed into giving up control of the territories they had occupied and that (as Stalin evidently guessed) neither Britain nor America would back their protests by action which might involve the threat of war. The best Bevin and the Foreign Office could do was to try to discriminate between the case of one country and another in the hope of retaining some voice in the face of the 100 million people living in Eastern Europe.

Britain accepted without protest the largest group of changes, Russian annexation of territory in Eastern Europe amounting in all to 180,000 square miles and bringing some eighteen and a half million people forcibly under Soviet rule.[1] In Yugoslavia, the British made no attempt to intervene and did not withdraw their recognition when Tito violated the Agreement with Subasič which Churchill had sponsored, got rid of the monarchy, proclaimed a Yugoslav republic (29 November 1945) and established complete Communist control. They would not, it is true, agree to Yugoslav claims to annex Trieste or the Carinthian districts of Austria. British troops were the main obstacle to the Yugoslavs making good these claims by force and this in itself was enough to earn the London government violent abuse from Belgrade, but the British limited themselves to holding the ring: they accepted the result of the Yugoslav elections (11 November) as a vote in favour of a republic and the Communist government. The same month they extended recognition to the Communist government of Albania, at that time a satellite of the Yugoslavs and a base for Communist guerilla activity in Greece.

In Yugoslavia there was at least a native Communist movement which could claim that it had proved its right to lead the nation by its wartime record in fighting the Germans. Rumania and Bulgaria were different. In Rumania anything like free elections would have swept out of office the Groza govern-

---

[1] This was quite apart from the countries under Soviet occupation and control, comprising another 425,000 square miles and over 84 million people.

ment which the Russians had imposed on King Michael. In Bulgaria, unlike Rumania, there was a tradition of friendship with Russia, but Communist attempts to manipulate the Fatherland Front and "fix" the elections led to the British and US protest and the postponement of the vote from August to November. By the time they were held (13 November), the legendary Dimitrov had arrived in Sofia to reinforce the shaky prestige of the Fatherland Front, but neither Bevin nor Byrnes was prepared to recognize the government which emerged.

There was much to be said for the original British view that such protests, which they had no means of making effective other than by delaying recognition, were not worth the disputes to which they led. But the line taken in regard to these two countries was not characteristic of British policy towards the rest of Soviet-occupied Europe. Where there still seemed a chance that the coalition governments which had been set up might retain some independence of action, Bevin was prepared to be more accommodating and helpful. The easiest case was Czechoslovakia where full relations were established from the start and where the British showed understanding of Benes' and Masaryk's need to come to terms with the Russians and with their own Communists. In Austria the Renner Government installed by the Russians in the summer, was recognized by Britain and the other three occupying powers on 20 October and justified the confidence that it would stand up to undue Soviet pressure.

The most interesting cases are Hungary and Poland. In the August debate in the House, Bevin had included the Hungarian with the Rumanian and Bulgarian as governments which Britain should refuse to recognize as unrepresentative. The Smallholders Party, however, succeeded in exercising sufficent independence of the Communist embrace in the coalition to win a majority of 51 per cent in the Budapest municipal elections (2 October 1945) and an even more striking majority of nearly 60 per cent in the national elections a month later. This was encouraging, the more so since the results were accepted by the Russian Control Commission and the Communists agreed to continue in the coalition under the Smallholders' leadership. The Americans had recognized the Hungarian government on the eve of the poll; Bevin waited until the middle of November, but then followed suit when he had satisfied himself about the composition of the new Cabinet.

In Poland, which had been the touchstone of British relations with the USSR, Bevin decided after the assurances he had received from the Polish leaders at Potsdam to give the new coalition the benefit of the doubt. He attached great importance to the fact that Mikolajczyk was still optimistic about his chances.[1] The Polish leader was sent on a mission to North America

---

[1] Mikolajczyk, who had spent the war as a member of the Polish government in exile, was well known to the British who had urged him to return to Poland in 1945 and as the leader of the largest non-Communist party (the Polish Peasant Party) to join the Communist-dominated government set up by the Russians. Mikolajczyk followed this course and became a Deputy Prime Minister. He resisted the pressure for a complete Communist takeover of Poland until 1947, but had then to flee for his life.

to secure additional relief for Poland and on his way back stopped in London for a private talk with Bevin (15 November). He defended the Polish occupation of the Oder–Neisse territories, as any patriotic Pole might be expected to do, and went on to say that Poland was settling down, that the withdrawal of Russian troops was going well and that the battle for political freedom was being won. Mikolajczyk laid great stress on increasing trade with the West, in order to avoid Poland becoming isolated, and he asked Bevin if the British could not follow the French example and release to the Warsaw government the £7 million in gold still blocked in London.

It was no doubt under the impression left by his talk with Mikolajczyk that Bevin spoke more positively about Poland in the debate on foreign affairs a week later.

"I see signs," he declared, "in spite of the difficulties, of Polish independence asserting itself vigorously but in friendly relation with Soviet Russia. There are signs that the recovery from the stunning effect of the war is beginning to show itself. . . . I ask the House not to be too impatient. I know that the Polish state creates very great difficulties, but I like to see the plant growing, and I am not going to pull it up every moment to make sure that it is growing."[1]

The greatest difficulty in Anglo–Polish relations was the existence of large Polish forces outside of Poland who had fought alongside the British with great bravery, towards whom there was a strong sense of obligation in Britain and who refused to go back or conceal the implacable hostility which many of them (especially the officers) felt towards the new regime. Bevin made it clear that there was going to be no question of compulsion, but he took trouble to find shipping for the 23,000 (out of 67,000) in the United Kingdom who elected to return and he put continued pressure on the Polish Government to produce a detailed statement of the conditions anyone choosing to go back could expect to find. In his talks with the Polish representatives he left no doubt of the strong feelings in Britain about the interference by the government and especially by the secret police with political and private freedom in Poland; nor would he take steps to curb the activities of Polish refugees in London—they were not recognized by the British Government and they had no access to it, but he refused point blank to tamper with the right of asylum or subject them to censorship, and he protested vigorously about anti-British propaganda in Poland.

None the less in the case of Poland, it is fair to say that Bevin tried hard to reach a *modus vivendi*, without sacrificing principles on the one hand or failing to make allowance on the other for the difficulties any government would have to face in a country which had been through the appalling experiences of the Poles in the past six years. Privately he told the Poles he thought they were trying to take more territory than they could digest and

[1] HC, 23 November 1945.

storing up trouble with Germany in the same way they had with Russia after the 1914–18 war, but he refused to join in public in condemning them, or the Czechs, for the expulsion of the German population[1] without considering the circumstances.

"I do not think," he told the House of Commons, "we need be too hard on Poland or Czechoslovakia. I am never tired of reminding this House and the country how long it has taken to build this state of ours. It has not been done in a minute.

"Poland was under bondage for 150 years, divided and cut up, and yet she preserved her nationality and culture in an amazing manner. Czechoslovakia had only 21 years to build a state, and no one can examine that 21 years without being filled with admiration at what they achieved. Then Hitler came along and used his minority crowd for ulterior motives. He destroyed their work, invaded their country. . . . If somebody did that to me, if I had helped to create an organisation of that character and my life's work was broken up, I could not feel very affectionate when the victory turned the other way. We really want to keep a sense of proportion in dealing with this terrible problem. . . . I would ask hon. members to imagine what this country would be like if it had been invaded by two armies and the whole machinery of government entirely destroyed. Could we expect a new and improvised organisation brought into being in six months to handle the situation to perfection? Really, it is asking the impossible."

Bevin said this during a Commons debate (26 October) on a motion expressing concern at the number of people in Europe threatened with death from cold and starvation in the coming winter. He did not gloss over the seriousness of the situation and spoke particularly of the danger of epidemics. Not only had Europe been ravaged by war, but since the fighting stopped he estimated that between 20 and 25 million people had been on the move under primitive conditions.

"When I was going to the airport to leave Berlin, I saw as many refugees coming out of Berlin as were going in. It was a pathetic sight—the stream of perambulators and small vehicles of one kind or another, the people were nearly all women and children, with very few men. One could not help saying, 'My God, this is the price of stupidity and war.' It is a problem which it is almost beyond human capacity to solve quickly."[2]

As Chairman of the Cabinet's Overseas Reconstruction Committee[3] he was responsible for the British part in the emergency measures and he told the House what they were trying to do to raise more coal, clear the waterways, start a new European Transport Organization and get more food from the countries like USA and Argentina which had surpluses. What frustrated him

---

[1] These expulsions aroused considerable criticism in Britain. Two debates were moved on the adjournment by a Labour member (Stokes) in order to protest against them, 10 October and 2 November 1945. A debate on the adjournment to protest against conditions in Poland was moved by Conservative members on 7 December.
[1] HC, 26 October 1945.
[2] The minutes and papers of the Overseas Reconstruction Committee are in CAB 134/594 (1945); 595–6 (1946); 597–9 (1947); 600 (1948); 601 (1950–51).

was the obstacles placed in the way by politics, frontiers, and the fears created by insecurity.

"I believe we can very quickly rehabilitate Europe on peaceful lines . . . if only the statesmen can be left free, without fear of one another, to devote their energy to creative work."

Bevin spoke up strongly for the UN Relief and Rehabilitation Agency (UNRRA). He believed that many more would have died of starvation and disease if it had not been for its operations; he defended the Agency against its critics and used his influence to secure the funds it needed. Many of its troubles, he thought, sprang from too great expectations being formed of it in advance. It could not—and it had never been intended that it should—solve the economic problems of liberation and reconstruction.

"The hopes were placed too high and the demands. . . . When the difficulties that beset it in that role were realised, people then began to think that UNRRA was no use at all. This danger always arises from the Press and the public attempting to ride a thing too high and beyond what its promoters intended it to accomplish . . ."[1]

Bevin believed that UNRRA did a good job in meeting the emergency needs of relief, and he urged its officials to keep clear of political controversy so that those they helped should look on them as they looked on the Quakers, concerned only with the relief of suffering and poverty.[2]

Ninety-four per cent of UNRRA's funds and supplies came from the USA, Great Britain and Canada, each of which contributed 1% of its national income. In three years supplies worth 2,332 million dollars were shipped to Europe, two-thirds of which went to countries in Eastern and Central Europe, including the Soviet Ukraine and Byelorussia, Poland, Yugoslavia and Greece, without political discrimination. This was at a time when the British Government for the first time had to introduce bread rationing in their own country, something that had never been done during the war. No one however gave Britain or the other Western powers any credit for their contribution; on the contrary, they were continually abused, but the fact is that in many parts of Europe UNRRA's operations were decisive in averting disaster.

4

In Western Europe too a series of elections by the end of the year created national coalitions, with the Communists sharing power and for the present, at least, containing their ambitions within the framework of constitutional

[1] HC, 26 October 1945.
[2] Speech to UNRRA Council on 7 August 1945.

activities. Bevin's biggest problem—apart from Germany—was France. (The French would not allow the two problems to be separated). The trouble did not come from the Communists, but from de Gaulle. Back in Paris as head of the Provisional French Government, he proved as difficult to deal with as in exile—and for the same reason, his determination to make France a Great Power again. In the hope of securing more independence from the "Anglo–Saxon powers", the General visited Moscow in December 1944 and persuaded Stalin to sign a Franco–Russian Treaty of alliance against any revival of German power. The French press claimed this as recognition of France's restored status amongst the Great Powers, but it was nothing of the sort. Stalin showed no sympathy with de Gaulle's ambitions: France was not invited to Yalta or Potsdam, despite great efforts on de Gaulle's part to secure an invitation, nor was she given any choice in framing the principles for the occupation of Germany.

The Americans were as opposed to recognizing French claims as the Russians. They had their own difficulties with de Gaulle, and twice in 1945 threatened to cut off supplies from the French Army unless it abandoned the attempt to occupy Stuttgart on the first occasion and to annex the Val d'Aosta on Italy's north-western frontier on the second. The British alone of France's major allies had put up a fight for her representation, wresting agreement to a French zone in Germany from a hostile Stalin and a reluctant Roosevelt and later attempting, unsuccessfully, to secure a place for France on the Reparations Commission. The British had their own reasons for this: they were as impressed as Stalin (though in the opposite sense) with Roosevelt's remark at Yalta that two years was the most that American troops could be expected to remain in occupation of Germany and they were eager to see France take a share in the responsibility for preventing any revival of German power. But British interest in the restoration of France to a leading role was not limited to the occupation of Germany. Both Churchill and Eden, despite their irritation with de Gaulle, had a strong feeling for the historical greatness of France and this—to some people's surprise—was shared by Bevin.[1] All three saw clearly that there was no other nation in Western Europe which could provide a counter-balance to German power, if this should ever revive—or to Russian —and that the burden would otherwise fall solely on Britain, particularly if the United States, as Roosevelt had foretold, were to withdraw from Europe.

De Gaulle was not impressed by British efforts on France's behalf, for several reasons. France's historic role was, in his eyes, so obvious that he felt no gratitude when it was recognized, only anger when it was ignored. He had quarrelled bitterly with the British during the war and never more so than in the summer of 1945 when French efforts to retain a special position in Syria and Lebanon, against the wishes of the local population, had led the British to intervene with the object, as de Gaulle and most Frenchmen firmly believed, of

See e.g. his speech of 23 November 1945 in the House of Commons, quoted below, p. 147.

using the risk of civil war in the Levant as a pretext for ejecting a traditional rival from her historic position in the Middle East.

The General and the Quai d'Orsay could make the same calculations as the Foreign Office, but they arrived at a different conclusion, that the British needed France and that the longer France waited, the more the British would see that they had to accept French policies and pay the French price. So de Gaulle visited Moscow and Washington—at his own request—but did not visit London. When he failed however to get any response to his approaches to the Russians and the Americans, he opened communications with London, but did so not by a visit or diplomatic talks but by a press interview, the timing of which (10 September, the day the Council of Foreign Ministers was assembling in London) hardly appeared accidental. In a special interview with *The Times*, he declared that there was a community of interest between Britain and France—West European, imperial and democratic—which made it expedient, even necessary, for them to concert their actions. But a true alliance must involve laying down a common policy in advance. "This has been lacking to date and this lack would have made the signature of a treaty a meaningless and unwholesome gesture because it would have been belied by every diplomatic vicissitude." The prerequisite to improved relations between Paris and London was agreement on Syria and above all on Germany.

"That Britain should have consented to a settlement of the German problem without France is not only galling for France, but an absurdity with regard to Europe. For Britain to declare that she desired a treaty with France and at the same time to leave France out of these discussions was a contradiction in terms."

The General then went on to sketch the possibilities opened up by Western cooperation. Western Europe, he pointed out, was a natural complex, an "economic aggregate" which, though not self-sufficient, "would have the same sort of completeness that is possessed by the other economic masses of the world in face of which it would not be in a position of inferiority." Holland, Belgium, Italy, West Germany and (normally) the Iberian Peninsula were drawn to co-operation with Britain and France, which had also a world role to play. The link with Germany was obvious: "if the Ruhr and the river Rhine are internationalized they become the focus of European co-operation."

De Gaulle's interview elicited a striking response from the London press over a wide spectrum of political opinion.

"We can see how right Gladstone was in 1860," the *Manchester Guardian* wrote in an editorial, "when he said that alliance between Britain and France was the true basis of peace in Europe. . . . Today it is plain to everybody that the two nations need each other and that the interests of the Western democracies who look to them as leaders demand their closest co-operation."[1]

---

[1] *Manchester Guardian*, 11 Sept. 1945.

Similar views were expressed not only by *The Times* and *The Economist*, but by the left-wing *New Statesman* and *Tribune* as well.

This promising opening, however, had no sequel, at least in 1945. The London Conference, with an eye to which de Gaulle's interview had been published, proved the worst humiliation yet for French diplomacy. Having received admission for the first time since 1940 to a meeting of the major powers, the French found that their exclusion was made a condition of continuing the conference at all by the one power with which they had concluded a treaty of alliance, the Soviet Union. Britain and America stood by the French and preferred to let the conference break up rather than accept the Russian terms, but the delegations had hardly left London when reports began to circulate that both the Russians and the Americans were seeking means to break the impasse created at London and revert to the old policy of the three wartime allies meeting on their own. These reports proved to be true and when the Foreign Ministers met in Moscow in December, neither France nor China was invited. While the British neither wanted this result nor were blamed by the French for what had happened, the fact that France continued to be excluded from the triumvirate of Great Powers while Britain continued to belong to it did not make it any the easier to take up the ideas de Gaulle had developed, particularly when, as he himself pointed out, the necessary agreement on policy between London and Paris was lacking.

The suggestion of a "Western bloc" aroused immediate suspicion and open hostility from Russia and from the French Communists. It was denounced as a plot against the Soviet Union and it is possible that Russian anger at de Gaulle's proposal may have contributed to their decision to make the exclusion of France and China a breaking point in the London conference. The Russians kept up their propaganda campaign against the "Western bloc", but it could hardly be said that it was this which deterred either the British or the French from taking the idea further. In the political crisis which followed the first French elections in October,[1] the Communists tried to make an issue of "No participation in a Western bloc", but failed to carry with them either of the other two big parties, the Socialists or the MRP (both of whom favoured closer relations with Britain), or to supplant de Gaulle.

Expressing pleasure that the French had overcome the crisis and welcoming de Gaulle on his return to office, Bevin took the opportunity of the Commons' November debate on foreign affairs to rebut Soviet suspicions of the "alleged Western bloc" with indignation:

"Suspicion or no suspicion", he declared, "they have no right to accuse us and I am not going to accept it. But HM Government must go on with the task of building up friendships with our immediate neighbours . . . We shall not, in any arrangements that

---

[1] In the Constituent Assembly with 571 members the Communists emerged as the largest single party with 151 seats; the Christian Democratic MRP won 150 and the Socialists 139. The Assembly re-elected de Gaulle as head of the Provisional Government on 13 November.

we make commit any unfriendly act towards any other nation . . . I cannot accept the view that all my policy and the policy of HM Government must be based entirely on the 'Big Three'.

"Neither can we be influenced", he added, "by the fact that, owing to the aggression of other nations—temporarily, I hope—some nations have been knocked down. We must have regard to their history, their culture, their contribution and their civilising influence—and I would say that civilising influence is not determined by the volume of armaments you have got but by the cultural development you possess.

"In the case of France there is a great history and I am convinced that there is a great future."[1]

Bevin tried hard to clear up the quarrel in the Levant which had aroused so much feeling in Paris and in December he and Bidault, the MRP Foreign Minister in de Gaulle's government, exchanged letters on the evacuation of British and French troops. The French high command however found pretexts for delaying their withdrawal and in the New Year Syria and Lebanon took their dispute with France to the UN Security Council.

But the principal obstacle to that agreement on policy which de Gaulle had made the pre-requisite of any alliance, remained the difficulty of reaching agreement between British and French views on Germany.

Looking back, it is easy to see that the Potsdam conference, by accepting the practical separation of the Russian- and Polish-occupied parts from the rest of Germany, effectively ended any chance of treating Germany as a single economic unit. In the autumn of 1945, however, the British still hoped that the Potsdam promise that common economic polices would be pursued and a number of central administrative departments set up would be carried out and would provide a counter-poise in the centre to prevent Germany falling apart and each of the occupying powers treating its own zone as if it were a separate state.

None of the occupying powers stood to lose as much by this *de facto* partition of Germany as the British. If hope of getting Germany treated as an economic unit had to be abandoned, the British would be left with an over-crowded zone less capable of supporting itself than any of the others and with no alternatives but to see its population starve or keep them going at British expense.

At this stage Bevin was not responsible—other than as a member of the Cabinet—for the administration of the British Zone. The Control Office for Germany and Austria was transferred from the War Office in October 1945 and placed under the supervision of John Hynd, one of the Labour MPs for Sheffield and Chancellor of the Duchy of Lancaster. But Bevin was responsible for the four-power framework within which the British control commission was supposed to work. It was here that British and French polices clashed. The French, not surprisingly, had strong views on the treatment of Germany and in order to prevent the re-creation of Germany's industrial-military power and a fourth invasion of their country in less than a hundred years, they put forward

---

[1] HC, 23 November 1945.

a series of demands designed to end for good German control of the resources of the Rhenish–Westphalian region. These called for the immediate separation from Germany of the territory on the left bank of the Rhine which would become a state or states under permanent military occupation; the separation from Germany of the Ruhr industrial district with its 5 million inhabitants to form an independent territory under an international commission, again with a permanent garrison; the transfer of the Saar mines to France and the incorporation of the Saarland into the French customs and currency system.

The French submitted their proposals to the London Council of Foreign Ministers and although they were not discussed in the conference, Bidault (the French Foreign Minister) and Massigli (the French Ambassador) had an opportunity to talk them over with Bevin at Chequers.[1]

Bevin was not unsympathetic with French feelings: after 1918 he had been eager to resume relations with the German trade unionists and to listen indignantly to the wrongs suffered by Germany, but not this time. He did not feel vindictive himself, but he could understand those who did, like the Poles and Czechs, and even more those, like the French, who wanted something more than paper guarantees that Germany would never invade her neighbours again. And he was attracted to the idea of some form of international control of the Ruhr. He suggested therefore that experts from the two countries should meet to discuss the proposals in more detail, and these meetings took place between 12 and 26 October in London.[2]

The French justified their proposals on the grounds of security not economics. Deprived of the Ruhr as well as Silesia, there would be no risk of a German state ever again dominating Europe. The British drew back from the cost to the British zone of disrupting the main resource for its economic recovery, the *Ruhrgebeit*, and were sceptical whether such a solution could ever be made to last. On 13 September the Cabinet had discussed and in the end approved a statement of policy on Germany's industrial disarmament which Bevin had brought forward as chairman of the ORC.[3] It started from a set of assumptions opposed to those of the French plan. Germany would be prohibited from maintaining armed forces or an armaments industry for an indefinite period. But this was based on the assumption that the Rhenish–Westphalian industrial district would not be withdrawn from the German economy; that the occupation of Germany would not last for more than ten years and that whatever was proposed for the disarmament of Germany must

---

[1] 16 September 1945. FO 800/464/FR/45/7.

[2] A report on the meetings with British and French comments was sent to the British Ambassador in Paris on 16 November and re-printed as Annex B to Bevin's paper on "The Future of Germany & the Ruhr" originally prepared for the Committee on German Industry as Gen. 121/1 (11 March 1946) and circulated to the Cabinet as CP(46) 156 on 15 April 1946. See below p. 266.

[3] Overseas Reconstruction Committee CP (45) 160. The draft statement of policy for British representatives on the Control Commission for Germany and on the Reparations Commission is contained in the annexe to the covering memorandum signed by Bevin and dated 10 Sept. 1945. CM, 31 (45) 13 Sept.

command sufficient support for the democracies to be ready to enforce the settlement with sanctions for a generation ahead, and not be so oppressive to the Germans as to encourage them to seize the first opportunity to overthrow the settlement once the occupation ended.

Bevin thought that such a scheme offered a more realistic chance of security in practice than the much more drastic measures proposed by the French. He did not push the differences between them to an issue, but the talks led to nothing, and the French could read the British doubts without needing to have them spelt out. They were content to put pressure on the British and their other allies by following the policy indicated by de Gaulle: since France had not been invited to Potsdam, she would refuse to accept agreements to which she had not been a party. As the four-power Allied Control Council, to which the British looked to carry out the Potsdam recommendations, required a unanimous vote for anything to be done, this gave the French a power of veto, and they did not hesitate to use it.

In October, concrete proposals to create five German central administrative departments according to the Potsdam Agreement, were at last placed before the Allied Control Council. General Koeltz at once declared that he was instructed by his Government in Paris to oppose them and this brought the attempt to set up a unified economic administration for Germany to a dead stop. The link with the inconclusive Anglo–French talks was made clear by a strong hint in *Le Monde*: "If the Ruhr should come out from under the control of Berlin, the question of a central administration for the rest of Germany would lose much of its importance"[1] Thus the immediate aim of British policy in Germany was frustrated by a French veto, and at the same time de Gaulle's prerequisite for an Anglo–French alliance, agreement on policy especially in regard to Germany, was made more difficult of attainment than ever. The impasse on the Allied Control Council continued into the New Year and British hopes of starting up the German economy again by getting trade going across the zonal boundaries became more and more remote.

The British had no better luck with their second objective, to get the level of German industrial output placed sufficiently high to allow the economy to bear the cost of essential imports, especially food, as well as to meet the demand for reparations. This again particularly affected the British zone which not only had a deficiency in food supplies, but because of its industrial character would have to provide the greater part of the reparations from the Western zones not only for the Russians but for the other allies as well, including the French who were heavily dependent on coal from the Ruhr. Here the British found themselves at odds with the Russians and the Americans as well as the French.

The crucial question was the level of steel production and the British consistently argued for a realistic figure. The original figure proposed in the

---

[1] *Le Monde*, 30 October 1945, quoted by A. W. de Porte: *De Gaulle's Foreign Policy 1944–46* (Cambridge, Mass. 1968) p. 261.

ORC recommendations to the Cabinet was half the pre-war capacity of 23 million tons, i.e. 11.5 million a year. This was scaled down to 9 million tons a year, still well above that proposed by the other three powers.[1] The argument continued all winter and well into the spring of 1946: until it was settled nothing could be done to bring relief to an end and make a start on reconstruction. The Germans, with millions unemployed, starved and despaired; the Russians and French continued to take what they wanted from their zones to make good their own shortages, and the British, like the Americans, found themselves forced to import supplies at heavy expense in order to keep the population of their zones alive. Between June 1945 and April 1946, the British Government—at a time when they were hard pressed to provide rationed supplies in the United Kingdom—had to import a million tons of food into the British zone in addition to the supplies needed to prevent the British forces from having to live off the country. Even this provided less than the minimum necessary for subsistence.[2]

Bevin needed no convincing that a four-power agreement on Germany was the only satisfactory solution to the problems of the British zone. The question that bothered him was, how much longer the British could afford to wait in the fading hope of getting such an agreement. British opinion would not tolerate for many more months the sort of conditions which were daily reported from the zone for which the British Government was responsible, and British finances could not bear much longer a subsidy of £80 million a year (much of it paid out in scarce dollars), inadequate though that sum was to do more than stave off disaster.

The stalemate could not be allowed to continue and some alternative would have to be found well before the next winter (1946–7) came in sight. Bevin could not yet see what would be the best alternative to a four-power agreement, only that one would have to be found and that the consequences would be far-reaching. Germany, defeated and divided, was still the central problem of any European settlement, and from the way in which it was solved—or, more likely, from the way in which they failed to solve it—the rest of the pattern would follow.

5

The other area of the world besides Europe left in turmoil by the war was Asia and the Far East. What was to be done with Japan was second only in

---

[1] The Russians' opening bid was 4.6 million tons, raised to just under 5. The French figure was 7 millions; the Americans finally came down in favour of 5.5 million. Even in the last year of the war, according to *The Economist* (6 April 1946), 9.6 million tons of steel had been used for civilian purposes.
[2] The ration of 1,500 calories a day, instead of the minimum figure of 2,000, was cut to 1,015 in March 1946.

importance to what was to be done with Germany, but it soon became clear that it was not a question in which the British or any of the USA's allies were going to have much of a voice. There were complaints from the Far Eastern Department of the Foreign Office that, while it was reasonable for the Americans to take the lead, General MacArthur was behaving as if Britain had acquiesced in his exercising the powers of a dictator. When Bevin tackled Byrnes at the London Council of Foreign Ministers, the American Secretary of State explained that the American object was to make sure, at all costs, that the Russians did not obtain a zone of occupation in Japan. This was an argument Bevin could appreciate but he was not at all satisfied—the Australians were even less so—with the arrangements for representing British views on the future of Japan. As in the case of Germany, Bevin was not in favour of reducing the level of Japanese industry below what was justified by the needs of security, or of trying to restrict Japanese competition with British industry.[1] When the Chinese foreign minister, T. V. Soong, spoke of China taking Japanese industrial equipment as reparations and making the Japanese economy largely agricultural, Bevin told him this was impracticable for a nation of 80–90 million.[2]

There was friction with the Americans over other matters. When the British presented their peace terms to the Siamese Government, the Americans encouraged the latter to resist and secure revision on the grounds that the British were trying to establish a dominant position in Bangkok. When Byrnes pressed Bevin in November for support in securing US sovereignty or long-term leases for a long list of island bases not only in the Pacific (where twenty five of them were in dispute with Britain and New Zealand from before the war) but in other parts of the world as well, it was the turn of the British to call the kettle black.

Bevin's greatest difficulty was in Indonesia. Both here and in Indo-China, the task of the British forces sent by South East Asia Command was to accept the surrender of the Japanese and to release their prisoners. It was not their job to intervene in local politics; but there was no way in which they could avoid doing so. The French and the Dutch expected the British to restore their colonies to them, and the British had strong incentives for doing so: the fact that they were anxious to recover their own colonies in South East Asia; the common interest all three colonial powers had in supporting each other when faced with American hostility to all forms of imperialism except their own, and the importance the British attached to good relations with France and Holland as their neighbours in Western Europe. On the other hand, the British commanders on the spot had to take account of the fact that in both Indonesia and Indo–China nationalist governments had installed themselves with a

---

[1] Bevin's views are spelled out in the memorandum "Policy towards Japanese industry" which he wrote for the Cabinet, as Chairman of the Overseas Reconstruction Committee. CP (46) 78 (CAB 129/7/HN/01393) 23 Feb. 1946.
[2] Talk with T. V. Soong, London 17 Sept. 1945. FO 800/461/FE/45/49.

programme of independence before they arrived. In Indo-China General Gracey was forced to intervene in support of the French; but on 15 October a French armoured division arrived and with General Leclerc in command of operations the French were able to take over increasing responsibility for restoring their control.

In Indonesia, however, the Dutch were not in a position to follow the French example. The Netherlands had been liberated long after France, with much greater devastation; the greater part of their colonial empire had been lost, the greater part of the French empire had been retained intact, and Dutch shipping was being used by the Allies for other purposes. The result was that the Dutch took much longer than the French to get adequate forces out to Indonesia and the British forces under General Christison (which did not begin their occupation of Java until October) had to take the military and political responsibility for much longer than in Indo-China, and with it a great deal of criticism. There was widespread disorder, including the massacre of a convoy of Dutch women and children making their way to the docks in Soerabaja, of the British Indian troops escorting them and of their CO Brigadier Mallaby. It took 10 days' hard fighting for the British to bring the city under control and similar operations were needed in other towns. At one time the British forces were reinforced to a strength of 92,000 and the last of them were not withdrawn until a year later, 30 November, 1946.

Meanwhile the Soekarno government which had proclaimed Indonesian independence broadcast to the world daily descriptions of the "crimes" committed by the British imperialists. This aroused anger in the USA where the American press began to see signs of a conspiracy between the European colonial powers in S.E. Asia, and the US military began to restrict American support. The bulk of the British forces were Indian troops and their use to suppress an Asian nationalist movement produced a strong reaction from the Congress Party, while the Australians, with designs of their own on the former British colonies were loud in their criticism of British willingness to re-impose Dutch rule. The irony was that the Dutch, in whose interest the British incurred so much unpopularity, were equally critical—for the opposite reason. Many Dutchmen believed that if the British had only acted with greater decisiveness they could have crushed the nationalist movement—news of which came as a great shock to the Dutch—and criticized Christison and Mountbatten for their willingness to deal with "rebels".

The British in Indonesia were exasperated by what they saw as the inability of the Dutch to recognize the impossibility of imposing a military solution and the need for them to come to terms with the nationalists. Dening, Mountbatten's political adviser, as well as his chief shared in his exasperation but Bevin reminded him that:

"From the political angle, the arguments in favour of non-intervention . . . must be balanced against the very harmful effect of Anglo–Dutch relations which may be produced . . . Our action must be conditioned by the power available. But I feel that no recognition should be given to any authorities not approved by the Netherlands Government."

That was written at the beginning of October[1] and the worst of the fighting was still to come. A month later Attlee was still prepared to tell the Australian Prime Minister that further concessions would encourage the extremists and that their "need for good relations with a neighbour in Europe" must restrict their intervention.[2] But liberal and left-wing opinion in Britain was also becoming restive. The *Manchester Guardian* which in mid-October had declared: "Order must be restored in Java and the Dutch must go back", reflected the change when it wrote on 22 November.

"We cannot go on reinforcing troops and allow ourselves to be dragged into a minor war to overcome rebels . . . And we get no support, indeed something perilously like abuse, from our American and Russian friends, to whom this miserable involvement is only fresh evidence of our 'Imperialist' habits."[3]

Although talks between the Dutch and the Republican Government under General Christison's auspices broke down in November, discussions with Dutch Ministers visiting London in December produced agreement that they would have to be resumed, with the British undertaking to establish conditions in which negotiations could be carried on. In early 1946 Bevin sent out Sir Archibald Clark-Kerr (with whom he had stayed during the Moscow Conference of December 1945) to push on the search for a settlement.

By far the biggest question for the British in Asia was the handling of the demand for independence, not in Dutch or French colonies, but in their own—above all in India—and the bold attempt to transform an Empire into a Commonwealth. But although Bevin was deeply interested, relations with the Commonwealth, the Dominions and the colonies did not fall within his terms of reference as Foreign Secretary. The responsibility for these was divided between the Secretary of State for India and Burma, the Colonial Secretary and the Secretary for Commonwealth Relations, with the Prime Minister taking a special interest in India. The questions he had to deal with in Southern Asia were peripheral. Thus the British role in Indonesia, which produced such an outcry at the time, was fortuitous, the result not of an

---

[1] FO 371, F 7649/6398/61.
[2] FO 371/1, F 9294/6398/61. Both quoted in Thorne, p. 682.
[3] Quoted in Thorne's article: "Britain, Australia and the NEI. 1941–45", published in Dutch in *International Spectator* (The Hague) August 1975. I am indebted to Professor Thorne for letting me see an English version of this article.

"imperialist" initiative on Britain's part but of a last minute change of plan by the Combined Chiefs of Staff at Potsdam. There was nothing peripheral or fortuitous, however, about Bevin's involvement in the Middle East.

At the end of August he summoned home the British representatives in that part of the world for a conference which lasted from the 5th to the 17th September, overlapping with the Council of Foreign Ministers. Bevin took the chair himself and focussed attention on two questions. The first was

"Whether we are to continue to assert our political predominance in the Middle East and our overriding responsibility for its defence, or whether . . . it is thought to be essential on financial and manpower grounds that we should seek the extensive assistance of other Powers in the defence of the Middle East."[1]

The second question was how to promote schemes for economic development, in partnership with Britain, which would benefit the peoples of the area and so put Britain's relationship with them on a different footing.

The first question did not take long for the conference to answer.[2] Of the possible partners with whom the British might have shared responsibility for their Middle Eastern policy, the French were ruled out because of the "impossible position" they had got themselves into in Syria and the Lebanon, which could only end in their withdrawal from the Middle East; and the Russians because they were engaged in the political and economic penetration of the region and were seen as the principal threat to its stability. This left the Americans. Bevin himself saw great advantages in involving them in the Middle East, including Palestine. This was not a view shared by the Foreign Office, still less by British representatives in the field who saw them as commercial rivals bent on pushing into markets and sources of supply, especially oil, which the British had long regarded as their preserve. What defeated Bevin was that the Americans themselves took much the same view, preaching the virtues of free trade but suspicious of political entanglements. They were ready to criticize British policy but not to accept any part in what they saw as propping up an out-moded imperialist position, and were still divided over the question whether their own national interests were affected by what might happen in the Middle East.

If Bevin had any doubts about the answer to his first question, they were removed by the Soviet Union's claim to the trusteeship of Tripolitania. When he secured authority from the Cabinet to reject such a proposal, he argued that control of the route through the Mediterranean and the Red Sea was vital to the British Empire; that primary responsibility for the area must be retained

---

[1] Bevin's proposal to call the conference, CP (45) 130, was approved by the Cabinet on 30 August 1945.
[2] The conference's report was circulated as CP (45) 174 and discussed by the Cabinet on 4 October 1945.

by the British and that they should refuse to share this with the Russians or allow them a foothold anywhere along the route.[1]

The conference's other recommendation to the Cabinet equally clearly reflected Bevin's own views, that the most effective counter to Russian advances lay in a combined effort by Britain and the Middle Eastern countries to attack the poverty of the region and raise the living standards of its peoples. In a letter to Halifax in Washington, he wrote:

"The benefits of partnership between Great Britain and the countries of the Middle East have never reached the ordinary people, and so our foreign policy has rested on too narrow a footing, mainly on the personalities of kings, princes or pashas. There is thus no vested interest among the people to remain with us because of benefits obtained. Hence it is easy for Great Britain to be blamed when difficulties arise."[2]

This was unusual language for a British foreign secretary to use, and it can be argued that Bevin had hit upon the idea of economic aid before Truman formulated it in his famous Point IV.

But could the old relationship of empire be converted into the new one of partnership? After years of the British lording it as masters, neither the Arabs—nor the British residents in the Middle East—were going to find either partnership or equality easy to believe in. The mistake Bevin made was both to over-estimate Britain's capacity to play the role he cast her for and to under-estimate the strength of nationalist feeling among the Arab peoples he cast in the role of partners. Post-war Britain had no resources to spare with which to support development programmes on a scale sufficient to make any impression on the political situation. She could not even release the sterling balances which Egypt and Iraq had piled up in London during the war. And what the Egyptians and Iraqis wanted was not partnership but evacuation, the British out of their countries, their bases dismantled and their clubs and barracks closed.

There is no reason to doubt that Bevin was sincere when he spoke of a partnership aimed at raising the standard of living of the Middle Eastern peoples, but he believed it was also essential that it should make provision for the security of the area.

"We do not want to dominate Egypt", he told the Anglo-Egyptian Chamber of Commerce. "It is the thing farthest from the mind of H.M. Government. But until we have got security, there is one matter of great importance to both of us in a vital region of this character, and that is mutual defence. . . . I would like to see that defence built up not on a basis of our protecting you, but on joint co-operation, a partnership, paid for and manned by both of us on a common basis of partnership between the Middle East and ourselves."[3]

---

[1] Bevin's proposals in CP (45) 162, dated 10 September, discussed and approved by the Cabinet on the 11th. See above, pp. 129–30.
[2] Bevin to Halifax, 12 October 1945 FO 800/484/PA/45/13. Another copy in FO 371/45381/E 7757/G. For the remainder of the dispatch dealing with Palestine, see below, pp. 176–7.
[3] 1 November, 1945.

A few days before, the Chief of the Imperial General Staff had been sent off, with a brief from Bevin, to sound out the Arab rulers about

"Some form of Confederation of Defence in the Middle East, namely a partnership between all those Powers who had an interest in its defence, each Power providing its quota either of troops, aerodromes, bases, facilities for transit or locations for troops."[1]

Summing up his impressions of his tour, Alanbrooke wrote in his diary:

"There was no doubt that the nearer you got to Russia, the greater was the desire for some sort of co-operation in defence. Both Transjordania and Iraq were all for some such plan; it was only Egypt that was so intent on the removal of Occupation Forces that she refused to look at the advantages to be derived from a Federation."[2]

Unfortunately for Bevin's hopes of putting Britain's relations with the Arabs on a new footing, it was the exception that counted and reflected nationalist feelings not only in Egypt but throughout the Middle East. Whatever chances of success his proposal of partnership had—and they cannot be rated high in view of Britain's lack of economic resources to give it substance—they were fatally compromised in nationalist eyes when it turned out that this involved what they saw as all the old apparatus of occupation —foreign troops, bases, facilities, etc.,—under a new name.

Withdrawal would have been popular with the Labour Party, and not only with the rank and file. Attlee was sceptical about the need or the value of bases maintained in face of nationalist opposition; Dalton, as Chancellor, argued that they represented expenditure Britain could no longer afford, and Bevin would have been as relieved as the rest of the Cabinet if the Chiefs of Staff had been able to convince themselves that West Africa would do as well for a base as the Canal Zone.[3] With hindsight it can certainly be argued that the best way for the British to have kept what they wanted—access to oil supplies, access to markets and security of communications—would have been to act promptly to break the connection between these and the attempt to perpetuate a predominant position backed by force which it proved to be beyond their capacity to sustain.

What this argument ignores, however, is the fact that the Russians were probing the limits of possible Soviet expansion not only to the west, in Europe, but to the south as well. The counter-argument which Bevin had to take into account was that a British withdrawal from the Middle East in 1945–6 would leave a "power vacuum" which the local states would not be able to fill and which would tempt Stalin to believe that he could expand the Soviet sphere of influence there with the same impunity as he had in Eastern Europe and the

[1] Alanbrooke's Diary, quoted in Arthur Bryant: *Triumph in the West 1943-46* (London 1959) p. 496.
[2] *Ibid.*, p. 500. Cf. Beeley's minute of a talk with the Iraqi leader Nuri Pasha, 26 August 1945: "Nuri . . . talked for half an hour continuously about Russian expansion. He was particularly insistent on the importance of a firm British policy in Greece, Turkey and Persia." FO 371/48773/411226/G.
[3] See below pp. 239–44.

Far East. The fact that this did not happen when the British were driven to reduce their commitment drastically in 1947 does not prove the fears of 1945–6 to have been exaggerated or groundless. By then, the firmness of British and even more of American reaction to Soviet pressure in the countries of the Northern Tier had convinced Stalin that expansion to the south could not be carried out without risk of a confrontation, and the American attitude had hardened to the point where the US Government was now prepared not only to take over Britain's responsibilities in Turkey and Greece (the Truman Doctrine) but to commit itself to play an increasingly interventionist role in Europe as well (the Marshall Plan).

Although he did not always make this clear in public, Bevin thought of the Middle East as including not only the Arab countries of the Fertile Crescent and Palestine, but the Northern Tier as well: Iran and Greece in which British troops were stationed and Turkey to which (as well as Greece) Britain was bound by a treaty of alliance dating from before the war. He saw all three countries as threatened by Soviet pressure for expansion towards the Mediterranean and the Persian Gulf; and this threat in turn provided the key to his insistence that the new form of partnership which he sought with the Arab countries must include defence as well as development. As Alanbrooke reported, it was only as one got nearer to the Soviet Union that the force of Bevin's argument was recognized; but Bevin never wavered in his belief that the whole of the area from the Mediterranean in the west and the Black Sea in the north to the Indian Ocean in the east and the Horn of Africa in the south had to be considered as a single region, the same view that was expressed in his strong reaction to the Soviet claim to Tripolitania.

The Russian war of nerves against the Turks was maintained throughout 1945. Rumours of preparations for war with Turkey were denied by Moscow (another way of giving them circulation). So were reports of troop concentrations and movements in the Balkans. Declarations of support for the restitution of Kars and Ardahan were secured from the Armenian diaspora; expatriate Armenians were invited to return to Soviet Armenia from all over the world to be present at the installation of a Catholicos (Patriarch) of Etchmiadzin, an office which had lapsed under the Soviet regime. The new Catholicos at once called for the return of the lands forcibly seized by Turkey and their union with Soviet Armenia. Georgian as well as Armenian irredentism was patronized by Moscow and a Georgian claim to a further block of territory west of Kars and Ardahan given wide publicity in the Soviet press and radio. All this in addition to daily attacks in both media put a heavy strain on the Turks and on their economy which had to bear the costs of keeping substantial forces mobilized. The US Ambassador in Ankara, Edwin Wilson, was not the only observer to be reminded of Hitler's war of nerves against his intended victims, and to predict a major crisis in the Middle East by the spring of 1946. The American and British Governments as well as the Turks informed the Russians that they were willing to discuss the revision of the Montreux

Convention on control of the Straits;[1] but the Russians remained silent and made no reply for a further nine months, preferring to wait and see what results their pressure on the Turks would produce. In the meantime the Turkish Government reaffirmed that their alliance with Britain remained the basis of their foreign policy and the British gave such financial, economic and technical aid as they could.

Soviet tactics towards Turkey could not be separated from Soviet behaviour in Turkey's neighbour, Iran. On Soviet instructions, a new Democratic Party was formed in Azerbaijan at the end of August and with open Soviet support mobilized the well-founded Kurdish and Azeri resentment against the central government in Teheran. It remained an open question whether the Russians would use this control of north-western Iran to separate it from the rest of the country or to secure ascendancy over the Iranian Government. The best answer, Bevin believed, was to get all foreign troops out of the country, British and American as well as Russian, and at the London Council of Foreign Ministers he called on Molotov to agree to 15 December as the date for withdrawal and 2 March 1946 as the latest date for completing the evacuation of troops from Azerbaijan and the British oil area. Molotov affected to see no reason for discussion: the Anglo-Soviet–Iranian Treaty of 1942 had stated the terms for withdrawal. When Bevin tried to pin him down to the March date, Molotov sanctimoniously reminded him that "the Soviet Government attach exceptional importance to the strict fulfilment of obligations undertaken." With this Bevin had to be content and the question of troop withdrawals was removed from the Council's agenda.

The reason for Soviet evasiveness became clear in November 1945. After the Red Army had distributed arms to the local populace in key areas of Azerbaijan, on the 19th of the month news reached the outside world of large-scale uprisings. All roads were closed and a force of 1500 Iranian troops ordered into the province was turned back at Qazvin under threat from the Soviet commander that he would open fire if his order was disobeyed. Protests by the British and Americans were rejected by the Russians. When the Americans announced that their troops would be out of Iran by 1 January 1946 and called on Britain and Russia to do the same, the Russians retorted that the length of stay of Soviet troops was determined not only by the Tripartite Treaty but also by the Soviet–Iranian Treaty of 1921.[2] In the light of

---

[1] An American note with fresh proposals for the Straits which made substantial concessions to the Black Sea Powers was delivered on 2 November 1945, followed by one from the British supporting the US proposals on 21 November, and a public statement by the Turkish Prime Minister that Turkey would accept them as a basis for discussion. No Soviet reply was received until 8 August 1946, and this insisted that control of the Straits was a matter for Turkey and the Soviet Union to settle by themselves.

[2] The reference to the 1921 Treaty which applied only to situations in which there were preparations for armed attack on the Soviet Union and had not previously been mentioned, suggests that Molotov had such a use of the Treaty in mind when he evaded Bevin's enquiry with an ambiguous reply at the London Council of Foreign Ministers in September 1945. See footnotes 183 and 198 on p. 277 and p. 281 of Kuniholm.

"incidents" which had occurred, the Soviet Government saw no grounds for removing its forces by 1 January.

The Democratic Party went on to capture Tabriz (10 December) and to proclaim it the capital of an autonomous Republic of Azerbaijan. This was immediately followed (15 December) by the proclamation in the presence of Soviet officers of a Kurdish People's Government in Mahabad, claiming independence for a Kurdish Republic in the strip of Iranian territory adjoining the Armenian Soviet Republic on the north and separating Azerbaijan on the west from Turkey and Iraq. The timing can hardly have been fortuitous. The next day (16 December) Bevin and Byrnes sat down with Molotov for the first session of the meeting of Foreign Ministers in Moscow, confronted as the British and Americans had been at Potsdam, with a *fait accompli*, in July in Poland, in December in Iran.

6

What gave substance to distrust of Russian interest in any particular case —the Straits, Kars and Ardahan, or Azerbaijan—was the appearance of a pattern repeating itself not only in the Middle East, but in Eastern Europe as well, and even in the Far East. It was a pattern which those such as the Turks and the Poles with long experience of the Russians as neighbours found entirely familiar, and not at all surprising given the opportunities offered by the destruction of the old international balance of power at the end of the war. Bevin's anxieties about leaving a power vacuum in the Middle East could be supported by putting together an accumulation of evidence that Stalin was following a policy of applying pressure at any point round Russia's borders where the weakness of the resistance might open the way to extending Russian power.

This was not an argument, however, which Bevin felt able to use publicly in 1945–6, not because he doubted its validity, but because in the climate of opinion after the war it opened up a prospect of conflict, in place of the hoped for agreement between the wartime allies, which many, perhaps a majority, of people in Britain, certainly in the Labour and Liberal parties, were unwilling to accept. Instead he had to deal with each issue separately, not letting his anxieties appear too plainly and taking care not to emphasize an overall pattern. When he departed from this practice and spoke out—for example, in the foreign affairs debate in the House of Commons on 7 November[1]—the sharpness of the reaction both in the House and in the press showed the limits of what could be said by a Foreign Secretary in public, particularly a Labour Foreign Secretary. This put a heavy strain on the patience of a man who had never found it easy to disguise his feelings.

[1] See below, pp. 190–2.

Greece provides a further illustration of Bevin's difficulties in this phase of his policy. These had their origin in December 1944 when Churchill ordered British troops to prevent a Communist seizure of power in Athens, to the scandal of liberal opinion in Britain and the USA which refused to believe either that such a threat existed or that it was necessarily to be resisted if it did—two very different propositions between which many of those who protested did not clearly distinguish. The British action created a crisis in the Labour Party and led to demands from the Left that it should withdraw from the coalition. It was Bevin, then Minister of Labour, not Attlee, the leader of the Party, who took on the job of facing an angry Party conference and securing the trade union block vote in support of a policy which he insisted was as much his and the rest of the Cabinet's as Churchill's.[1]

Although the Varkiza Agreement (February 1945) ended the fighting it did not allay the political passions which had been aroused in Greece—and in Britain. The moment the Labour Government took office, the demand for the withdrawal of British troops was revived in force. Bevin refused. In a paper circulated to the Cabinet he gave as "the most overpowering reason" his belief that

"We must maintain our position in Greece as a part of our Middle East policy, and [that] unless it is asserted and settled it may have a bad effect on the whole of our Middle East position."[2]

He was not concerned whether Greece became a monarchy or a republic, or who formed the government, except in so far as these questions affected Britain's interest in seeing that Greece did not become part of the expanding Soviet sphere of influence, thereby turning the flank of the Turks and providing the Russians with bases in the Mediterranean. As soon as the British were sure there was no more danger of this and the Greeks could defend their own independence, they should withdraw, but not before.

However, if Bevin had said as much as this in public, it would have led to an almighty row, provoking all Labour's traditional dislike of power politics and spheres of influence, to the advantage of those who wanted to see the British out.

Moreover, although true enough, such a statement would have failed to do justice to the complexity of the problem. While the result which concerned Bevin might be the effect on the international balance of power of Greece joining the Communist camp, the key to preventing this lay in the domestic struggle for power inside Greece. So Bevin conformed to the usage of the time, played down—as in Eastern Europe—the balance of power and laid stress on the British responsibility to help the Greeks recover from the effects of the German occupation and decide their own future for themselves.

[1] See Volume II, pp. 340–47.
[2] CP (45) 107, dated 11 August 1945.

Neither argument was a sham. In 1947 the ILO was to confirm that Greece had suffered more heavily in the war than any other allied country except the Soviet Union. The British were on the spot, and without the food and supplies they brought in and the help they gave in restoring communications, there could not even have been a start on the job of reconstruction. Nor was Bevin's concern with elections a piece of window-dressing. If there was a threat to Greece's independence it would come not from without—as it had in 1941 —but from within, from the capture of power by the Communist-controlled EAM (National Liberation Front), leading with the help of Greece's Communist-controlled neighbours to the establishment of a People's Democracy on the pattern emerging in Eastern Europe, and the alignment of Greece with the Soviet bloc. As long as British troops were in occupation they could stop a renewed attempt to seize power by force as they had the winter before, but this was no answer in the long run. A Greek government had got to be established with sufficient authority to take the responsibility for restoring Greece as an independent state and eventually allowing the British to withdraw.

This was a programme Bevin could defend with conviction but it bore little relation to the actual situation in Greece in 1945 and he had great difficulty in finding anyone to carry it out. The civil war had polarized Greek politics into a bitter conflict between Right and Left. While the non-party government of Admiral Voulgaris struggled helplessly to cope with the country's economic problems, the Right (particularly Grivas's "Khi" bands) took advantage of the government's weakness to repay the Left's earlier acts of terrorism in kind. Hundreds were arrested and held without trial, or sent into exile; political murders were commonplace; corruption widespread. Huge profits were made on the black market to which an alarming proportion of UNRRA supplies were diverted, and inflation continued unchecked. For all this the British, as the occupying power, and the British Foreign Secretary were held responsible.

Bevin took a number of practical measures. He got a police mission and a trade union mission sent out to reorganize the Greek gendarmerie and the Greek trade unions. Later, a British legal mission secured the grant of an amnesty and the release of many of those held in gaol without trial. British military missions undertook the training and supply of each of the fighting services. Financial and economic experts were seconded to the Athens government and a loan of £24 million made available for reconstruction. This was the priority to which all British efforts were directed, urging moderation and discouraging the pursuit of recrimination and revenge. But the political problem was central to Greek recovery and Bevin could see only one way out: to hold elections at the earliest possible date and form a government with sufficient popular support to assert its authority.

This was easier said than done. Greek politicians of all parties, instead of concentrating on the reconstruction of their country, were obsessed with the question whether the King should return to Athens or Greece become a republic, and which party would gain most if a plebiscite on this issue were held first (as the Varkiza Agreement laid down) before elections or vice versa.

When he addressed the House of Commons in August,[1] Bevin refused to express an opinion publicly on this burning question: the Greeks must settle it for themselves, but they must make a decision soon, for until elections were held no government would have authority. The Left, however, were now convinced that they would lose any election, and they and their sympathizers in Britain sought by any means they could to postpone a vote. Bevin soon found himself accused of planning to restore the Greek monarchy, while on the other hand the monarchists and their sympathisers denounced the delay in holding a plebiscite and demanded the return of the King—who continued to live in Claridge's and play an active role in party politics.

In the end the decision was taken by the three Western powers who announced (19 September) that the elections would be held first and British, American and French observers sent to see that they were conducted fairly. Bevin's view was that if the elections produced (as the British hoped) a government of the Centre, the question of the monarchy or a republic could be decided in a calmer atmosphere; if the plebiscite were taken first, it would be turned into a straight contest between the two extremist parties, the monarchists and the Communists. The Soviet Union dissented, refusing to send observers, and when the Voulgaris government tried to fix a date for the elections, it was forced to resign in face of general opposition.

For three weeks no one was able to form a government; this was followed by one which lasted for no more than another three weeks. Despite his wish to keep out of Greek politics, Bevin felt obliged to intervene. In an effort to knock some sense into the Greek politicians, he sent out his Parliamentary Under-Secretary, Hector McNeil, a tough Clydesider who was closer to him than any other member of the Parliamentary Labour Party. Apart from the question of elections, he was worried by the marked deterioration of the economic and financial situation in Greece despite large shipments of supplies from UNRRA. More or less by main force, McNeil pushed the Liberal leader Sofoulis into forming a government and secured a promise to hold elections, under international supervision, by 31 March 1946.

Although it was widely believed at the time that the Greek Communists were acting on Russian instructions, no firm evidence of this has subsequently come to light. On the contrary, to the disappointment of the Greek Communist leaders, Stalin appears to have discouraged any idea of counting on Soviet support,[2] if the civil war were renewed in the so-called "third round". The support came not from the Soviet Union but from the Communist-controlled regimes in Yugoslavia, Albania and Bulgaria and there was at least a strong possibility that if the Greek Communists had been successful (with help from their neighbours) in securing power, Stalin would not have turned down the

---

[1] HC 20 August 1945.
[2] See the discussion in C. M. Woodhouse: *The Struggle For Greece 1941-49* (London 1976) pp. 154–65.

opportunities offered to him. In the meantime the Soviet propaganda agencies took full advantage of the awkward situation in which the British found themselves in Greece to make the continued presence of British troops in support of a "fascist" government and the wrongs suffered by the "democratic forces" a major item in their indictment of the "reactionary, imperialist" foreign policy of the Labour Government. Whenever Russian actions in Eastern Europe were questioned, Molotov's stock retort was to demand the withdrawal of British troops from Greece, and he arrived at the London Council of Foreign Ministers with a long memorandum denouncing British "crimes" in Greece which he tried unsuccessfully to place on the agenda.

Even apart from the fellow travellers who echoed the Communist line, liberal opinion in England was uneasy over the continued British intervention, and the Left saw in Bevin's policy further confirmation of his betrayal of socialist principles. Many of the Left wing of the Labour Party found it hard to give up their wartime hopes of a democratic, socialist revolution in Europe, based upon wartime resistance movements, which it should be the first task of a socialist foreign policy to support. In their eyes EAM represented just such a movement and Bevin (whose support of Churchill in December 1944 had not been forgotten) was held to blame for committing the Labour Government to the wrong side in what was seen as part of a European civil war.

The same charge was brought against him for his policy, at the other end of the Mediterranean, towards Spain, where his crime was not intervention (as in Greece) but his refusal to intervene. The Spanish Civil War had been a burning issue in the Labour Party before the war and the *New Statesman* accurately represented left-wing opinion when it declared (18 August 1945): "British Labour is committed to the restoration of Spanish democracy". The same day the *Daily Herald* reported that Harold Laski, the Chairman of the Party's National Executive, in a signed article in a French weekly[1] had announced that the Labour Government would, if necessary, bring economic pressure to bear on Spain to allow a Republican coalition to organize the election of a parliament.

Bevin had no love for Franco, and he told the House of Commons: "It is obvious from what I have said that we shall take a favourable view if steps are taken by the Spanish people to change their regime."[2] But, he went on, "H.M. Government is not prepared to take any steps which would promote or encourage civil war in that country." Without a change of regime, Spain would not be accepted "into the club", but it was for the Spanish people, and them alone, to decide whether they would make such a change. For foreign powers to intervene would have the opposite effect to that desired and would probably strengthen Franco's position. He pointed to the long history of unsuccessful intervention in Spain to support his case.

Bevin did not accept either of the Left's assumptions. He did not believe as a

[1] *La Tribune économique.*
[2] HC 20 August, 1945.

matter of fact that at the end of the war either Spain, Greece or the rest of Europe was on the verge of a popularly supported socialist revolution; and as a matter of principle he held that British foreign policy should be determined not by ideological sympathies or socialist solidarity, but by national interests which did not change with a change of government. It was in British interests (and in those of the Greek people as well, he believed) to prevent the Communists from seizing power in Greece; it was not in British interests (nor in those of the Spanish people, be believed) for any outside power to intervene in Spain and take the risk of intervention by rival powers. In Bevin's mind there was no contradiction between a policy of intervention in the one case, and of non-intervention in the other: both derived from the same view of British interests being best served by avoiding any further disturbance of the international balance of power in the Mediterranean. There were many questions of fact in dispute between Bevin and his critics, but the real issue in both cases was the assumptions on which the foreign policy of a Labour Government should be based and Spain soon joined Greece in the Left's litany of complaints against the Foreign Secretary and became the subject of questions in the House and resolutions at the Party conference.

7

While Bevin was at the Potsdam conference he had been handed Truman's note, originally delivered to Churchill, expressing the "great interest" of Americans in the Palestine problem and their "passionate protest" against the restrictions imposed on Jewish immigration by the British White Paper of 1939. It was his first encounter as Foreign Secretary with a question which was to cause him more angry frustration and bring down more bitter criticism on his head than any other issue in his whole career.

The Jews were more than disappointed, they felt betrayed, by the failure of the Labour Government to implement its pledge of support for the Jewish National Home, a pledge made in December 1917 and renewed at ten other party conferences, the last in May 1945. The fact was that these resolutions were almost invariably put forward at the end of a long week and accepted because nobody objected[1]; but to the Zionists they were a binding commitment to which they attached great and—as it turned out—mistaken importance. They soon came to believe and to give widespread currency to their belief, that this reversal of policy was due to Bevin and that he was moved by a personal hatred of the Jews. From this sprang the stereotype of him as the latest in the long series of persecutors of the Jews beginning with Titus and Haman and continuing down to Hitler and Himmler.

---

[1] Evidence to the Anglo-American Committee by T. Reid, a Labour MP who had served on the 1938 Woodhead Commission, London, 29 January 1946.

Until the summer of 1945 it had never entered anyone's head to regard Bevin as anti-Semitic. Considering that he had then reached his sixty-fifth year and that he was widely known as a man with strong likes and dislikes which he made no effort to conceal, this is evidence not to be ignored, and is supported by the fact that no one has since come forward with instances which would contradict it.

In 1930 Bevin had intervened with Ramsay MacDonald at the request of the Jewish trade unionist Dov Hos to secure modification of Passfield's White Paper in the Jews' favour. In 1937, in his presidential address to the TUC he went out of his way to speak warmly of the Jewish settlers' achievement in Palestine, and the admiration it had won. In the same speech Bevin made clear that he was not convinced of the wisdom of the Peel Commission's proposal to partition Palestine and create a Jewish as well as an Arab state, saying that the test would have to be

"Whether it will contribute towards the ending for all time of the persecution of the Jewish race. Will the fact that they are a State with Ambassadors at various Chancelleries of the world assist them to a greater extent than the mandate granted by the League?"

But he was not committed to opposing the Zionist programme and in 1940–41, there is conclusive evidence from Jewish sources (Moshe Shertok and Ben Gurion, as well as Dov Hos) that the Zionists regarded him as one of their friends in the British War Cabinet.[1] Indeed in a minute of December 1940 Weizmann described him as the one man who understood the Jewish Agency's wartime problems and was willing to listen to them and take action. Weizmann repeated this favourable verdict in January 1941 when he wrote that he had a great belief in Bevin who was open-minded and energetic. Another note of the same period records that Bevin had secured the cancellation of the deportation order against the refugees in the S.S. *Patria*. In October 1941 Ben Gurion wrote, after earlier references to Bevin's helpful attitude towards raising a Jewish Army,

"Our failure (so far) to achieve a Jewish Army should not, as Mr Bevin seems to think, move us to seek an immediate final settlement in Palestine. For friendly British Ministers like Mr Bevin and Mr Amery it is easier to talk—without of course committing the Government or themselves to any real degree—of the necessity of establishing a Jewish state in Palestine. . . . Mr Bevin's suggestion (to drop the idea of a Jewish Army and get instead some form of Jewish State or autonomy in Palestine at once) indicates more lofty sentiment than sound judgment or sufficient knowledge.'[2]

---

[1] Moshe Shertok to Mapai's Political Committee 14 May 1940. Dov Hos to Mapai's Central Committee 7 August 1940. Ben Gurion to Mapai's Central Committee 19 February 1941. I am indebted for these references to Mr Shabtai Teveth, Ben Gurion's biographer.
[2] I am indebted for this quotation to Mr Teveth. The earlier reference to Bevin and the Jewish Army is in a report to Mapai's Central Committee 19 February 1941.

It is true that later in the war Bevin's attitude was more reserved. In April 1943 Shertok no longer found him helpful about the Labour laws in Palestine[1] and in March 1944 Weizmann reported him as saying that Britain had had more than enough trouble in Palestine and that he was not going to allow British blood to be shed for either Jew or Arab. At this time he appears to have favoured the transfer of the Mandate to the USA, but Weizmann's note ends with Bevin saying that he thought Zionism was a good thing because it gave the Jews status.[2] Certainly at the Cabinet Meeting of 25 January 1944 at which Churchill's efforts led to the revival of plans for partition, Bevin made no objection, although both Eden as Foreign Secretary and Richard Law as his Minister of State stated their reservations.

The truth is that until he became Foreign Secretary himself Bevin had never taken an interest in Palestine or the Middle East comparable with that which he had long had in Europe and that he was nothing like so well-informed about the issues. He recognized this when he noted at Potsdam:

"I consider the matter of Palestine urgent and when I return to London I propose to examine the whole question, bearing in mind the repercussions on the Middle East and the U.S.A."

The key to the change which took place in Bevin's—and the Labour Government's—attitude is to be found, I believe, in two things: the direct responsibility which he and other Labour ministers had for the first time to take for British policy in Palestine and the Middle East, and the much greater difficulties which Palestine presented in 1945 than it had for any of Bevin's predecessors.

As a result of the unparalleled suffering inflicted on Jews in Europe during the war, the Jewish people were now more united than ever before in their concentration on a single purpose, the creation of a Jewish state in Palestine which they were ready to fight for with the energy and passion born of desperation. "To fight" meant what it said, preparation for armed rebellion against the British authorities in Palestine if they tried to prevent—as they had during the war—the arrival of "illegal" immigrants outside the official quota. For this the Jewish Agency had organized a force of 50,000 men in the Haganah (to which should be added another 6,000 in the Irgun and the Stern group) trained to pursue urban guerilla tactics which put the regular British forces (facing a war of liberation for the first time) at a great disadvantage. At the same time the Zionist leadership in the USA in particular, but also in other countries, showed unequalled skill in propaganda and in mobilizing support in favour of their claims to a Jewish state and against the British "imperialists" as the enemy who alone prevented its realization.

---

[1] Moshe Shertok to Mapai's Secretariat, 27 April 1943, another quotation which I owe to Mr Teveth.
[2] I owe this reference to Mr Gaby Cohen.

One of the greatest handicaps from which the British suffered was the difficulty they had in grasping this transformation of Zionism and the seriousness of the challenge with which they were now faced by comparison with the ineffective Jewish protests of the 1930s. They continued to regard Weizmann with his belief in gradualism and diplomacy as the representative of Zionism when he was already losing the effective leadership to the hard-liners, Ben Gurion and Rabbi Silver. A new generation of Zionists for whom the Holocaust was the decisive experience discounted the goodwill of the British on which Weizmann had pinned his hopes and cast them in the role of the hated occupying power with themselves in the role of a Jewish Resistance Movement. When Bevin and the British criticized the Zionists for making political capital out of the sufferings of the Jews, they missed the point. This was the strength, not the weakness, of the post-war Zionist movement which was no longer pleading for compassion on humanitarian grounds—an appeal which had opened no doors in the United States, Britain or anywhere else—but asserting the political will of a nation in the making. Brought up in his Baptist days to regard Jews as members of another religious group with whose special customs—the keeping of the Sabbath and kosher food—he became familiar as a trade union organizer, Bevin could not see them as a separate nationality. When a delegation from the American League for a Free Palestine came to see him in November 1945 he told them that the fundamental decision Jews had to make was whether Judaism was a matter of race or religion, adding that if they were prepared to regard Judaism as a religion, there would be no trouble about their place in Europe. It is easy to put this down to Bevin's ignorance of the question; but the Refugee Department of the Foreign Office took the same view:

"We insistently deny" runs a minute of 2 October 1945 "that it is right to segregate persons of Jewish race as such . . . It has been a cardinal policy hitherto that we regard the nationality factor as the determining one as regards people of Jewish race just as in the case of other racial or religious groups. Once abandon that and the door is open for discrimination in favour of Jews as such, which will ultimately become discrimination against Jews as such."[1]

This was an argument repeated by both Attlee and Bevin, as if the Nazi persecution of the Jews "as such", ignoring their claim to be German nationals, had never taken place, or could be erased from men's minds. It wholly failed to meet the force of the Zionist argument. For it was not only that the European Jews—reduced by Hitler's Final Solution from just under 10 million before the war to four and a quarter million in 1946—"do not wish", as the British Embassy in Warsaw reported, "to continue residence in what is for them one huge cemetery"[2]; it was precisely the risk Bevin pointed to of

[1] FO 371/54380X/MO3655, a quotation I owe to Dr Nachmani.
[2] Warsaw to FO, 20 February 1946. 371/57688/WR 736, quoted by Nachmani.

being discriminated against which supported the Zionist thesis that only when there was a Jewish state to act as a refuge and protecting power would Jews ever be released from this threat.

A year later, Churchill was still prepared to argue that it was ridiculous to suppose that the Jewish problem could be solved or even helped by "a vast dumping of the Jews of Europe into Palestine . . . I am not absolutely sure that we should be in too great a hurry to give up the idea that European Jews may live in the countries where they belong."[1] In 1945 British officials had no difficulty in convincing themselves and the incoming Foreign Secretary and Prime Minister that there was no necessary connection between the plight of the Jews in the DP camps and Palestine. If it were not for the pressure exercised by Zionist agents, they maintained, the Jewish refugees would prefer to remain in Europe or go to other countries, preferably the USA.

There was no doubt that Zionists were active in urging Jews to demand entry to Palestine and accept no alternative. With the funds provided by the American–Jewish charitable organization (the Joint Distribution Committee) the Haganah's Committee for Illegal Immigration created an effective underground route (the Bricha) for transporting Jewish immigrants from Central and Eastern Europe to Palestine. But the belief that if it had not been for the Zionist activists the agitation would have died down was not plausible. The idea of the Promised Land and the gathering-in of the exiles to their ancestral home, where they could establish their own community without fear of persecution, had seized the imagination of outcast people and was supported by the practical argument that there was no other country in the world willing to admit them, neither the USA nor Britain nor anywhere else. Those who insisted that no more Jews should be admitted to their own countries saw Palestine as the obvious solution and could support the Zionist case with a good conscience. Russian and Polish officials, eager to rid themselves of the Jewish minorities left in their countries, urged them to move into the American and British zones of Germany and seize the chance to get to Palestine. How could Bevin and Attlee say that Jews in Poland should stay to contribute to the reconstruction of "their" country when, out of the pre-war figure of 3,351,000 Polish Jews, only 230,000 survived, 150,000 of them in Russia? Anti-Semitic feeling was still prevalent. The British Embassy in Warsaw reported that 300 Jews were killed in Poland in the seven months between the end of the war and the end of 1945. The same question could be put even more pointedly in the case of Germany. In June 1933, shortly after Hitler's rise to power, a census taken of the German Jews showed a figure of half a million. By 1939 this figure had been at least halved by emigration. In 1946 the Anglo-US Commission of Enquiry visiting group found only 20,000 Jews left, and 74,000 Jewish Displaced Persons, 85% of whom were Polish.

In Austria where the Jewish population in March 1938, at the time of the

[1] HC, 1 August 1946.

Anschluss, numbered 185,000, only 15,000 were to be found in April 1946, slightly more than half from outside Austria, many from Poland. The phrase which the British Embassy in Warsaw used of the Jews in Poland could be applied to the greater part of Central Europe: why could the British not see what seemed obvious to Americans, French, Italians, Dutch and to most people (outside the Muslim world) who took any interest in what happened to the Jewish survivors of the Holocaust—that they should be allowed to settle in Palestine?

The answer, I suggest, is not that Bevin or Attlee any more than George Hall and Arthur Creech-Jones (the two Colonial Secretaries) or Morrison (as Chairman of the Cabinet's Palestine Committee) were moved by hatred of the Jews or anti-Semitism, but that the British alone among the Western nations, because they were responsible for the government of Palestine as the Mandatory power, could not ignore the political consequences of the Zionists' demand to create a Jewish state there and the bitter opposition to it, already expressed in the Arab revolt before the war, of the majority of the population. Arab opposition, with the threat of civil war, affected not only Britain's responsibility for the peace in Palestine itself, but also her position as the paramount power in the Middle East, a position requiring the goodwill of Arab states as hostile to Zionist claims as the Palestinian Arabs.

As long as the Labour Party was in opposition it was possible for it to give full rein to its sympathies with the Jews without paying attention to the views of the Arabs which were dismissed with scorn because they were still at the stage of "feudalism" and living under "reactionary regimes". The Zionists in the Party, especially those on its Left Wing, took the same view of the Arabs as Marx and Engels did of the Slavs.[1] But once Labour formed the Government, this was no longer an adequate view. Nor was it sufficient to say that the British were only interested in the Arabs because of their own interests as the paramount power. The price for treating the Arab view-point as unimportant has continued to be paid long after the British have left the Middle East.

While the Jewish community in Palestine remained small and grew slowly, the British were able to ignore the contradiction in the double promise they had given of a National Home for the Jews and self determination for the Arabs. Once the Jewish numbers began to rise, however, the British could no longer escape the open conflict between them; it was certain that it would be renewed if the Jews pressed their demand for unlimited immigration. Even Churchill, lifelong friend of Weizmann and Zionism as he was, failed to find a way out of this conflict, and the great majority of those in government, during and after the war—whether as ministers, Labour, Liberal or Conservative; as officials or soldiers—accepted with varying degrees of uneasiness the view that arguments from humanity could not be allowed to override political

---

[1] Relics of a nation mercilessly trampled under foot in the course of history, as Hegel says, "these residual fragments of peoples always become fanatical standard-bearers of counter-revolution". Engels' article on "The Magyar Struggle" published in *Neue Rheinische Zeitung*, 13 January 1849.

considerations. This, one can argue, is the nature of states and their governments, going on to point out that when the Jews founded one themselves they
took the same view in regard to the human rights of the Palestine Arabs. But it
presented the British with a problem that no other nation had to face at a time
when the survivors of the Holocaust had a unique claim on the conscience of
the world.

This was the situation, not of his creating, in which Bevin found himself, and
I suggest that whatever prejudice the Jews believed Bevin developed towards
them was the result of the policy to which he felt committed as Foreign
Secretary, rather than the other way round. And that policy is to be seen as
neither anti-Jewish nor pro-Arab (the latter a description which, as Elizabeth
Monroe points out, no Arab ever accepted) but rooted in the view which Bevin
shared with every other Foreign Secretary, that he had to concern himself first
with the interests of the nation he represented.

What were these interests? They were, first and foremost, as Bevin had
remarked to Weizmann in March 1944, that British blood should not be shed
in enforcing a settlement in face of rebellion and civil war. Their experience in
1936–39 and the fact that the Arabs constituted the majority of the population
led the British to see the danger of this arising from a renewal of the Arab revolt
provoked by Jewish immigration. For this reason the Labour Cabinet's
Palestine Committee on 6 September—with a pro-Zionist chairman in Morrison and another in the Chancellor of the Exchequer, Hugh Dalton—decided
that there could be no question of the mass immigration for which the Zionists
were pressing, that the 1939 White Paper could not be abrogated as the
Zionists demanded and that continuation of the limited quota of 1500
immigrants a month must be dependent on Arab agreement.

The members of the Cabinet, endorsing the report when it was presented by
Morrison, reassured themselves that these were only temporary measures
until a long-term policy could be devised and that, since any course involved
risks, it was better to choose "the possibility of localised trouble with the Jews
in Palestine" than "the virtual certainty of widespread disturbance among the
Arabs throughout the Middle East and possibly among the Muslims in India
. . . a military commitment two or three times as great as the former."[1]

The phrase used in the Committee's report points to the other major British
interest, the impact of British policy and what happened in Palestine on
Britain's position in the Middle East. The report defined this wider interest as
follows:

"The Middle East is a region of vital consequence for Britain and the British Empire. It
forms the point in the system of communications, by land sea and air which links
Britain with India, Australia and the Far East; it is also the Empire's main reservoir of
mineral oil . . . The attitude of the Arab states to any decision which may be reached is a
matter of the first importance . . . Protection of our vital interests depends, therefore,

---

[1] Report of the Palestine Committee, 8 September 1945, CP (45) 156.

upon the collaboration which we can obtain from these independent states . . . Unfortunately the future of Palestine bulks large in all Arab eyes. . . . To enforce any such policy [to which they object] and especially one which lays us open to a charge of breach of faith, is bound seriously to undermine our position and may well lead not only to widespread disturbances . . . but to the withdrawal of cooperation on which our Imperial interests so largely depend."[1]

To this had to be added the uncertainty about Egypt and the continued use of the Suez base which increased the importance of Palestine as the one territory (apart from Cyprus) directly under British rule and the one alternative to Egypt acceptable to the Chiefs of Staff as the main base for British forces in the Middle East.

With hindsight it can be argued that this view of British interests was already out-of-date; that closing Palestine to Jewish immigration was not going to win Arab goodwill; that only British withdrawal from the Middle East would satisfy the Arab nationalists, and that the best course for Britain in her own interests, not out of charity, was to create a Jewish state under British auspices and base her Middle Eastern policy on an Israeli alliance, as the Americans eventually did.

Closer examination, however, strengthens the negative half of the argument, the futility of trying to appease the Arabs short of withdrawal, without making the positive half, the replacement of the Arabs by Israel as Britain's ally, more convincing. The United States was free to follow such a policy because the Americans had no prior commitment to the Arabs, and it did not involve a reversal of alliances, as it would have done in the case of the British. Even if the British had been capable of carrying out so striking an example of *realpolitik*, the lack of the USA's financial and economic resources to moderate the consequences of Arab resentment would have made it impossible to execute with success. Bevin sought to put the British position in the Middle East on a different basis, that of partnership, but even if he had succeeded, this would have made the British more dependent on Arab goodwill as their partners. The only real alternative, as Bevin finally recognized in Palestine, and his successors recognized in the rest of the Middle East, was withdrawal.

Harold Beeley, the Foreign Office official who was responsible for briefing Bevin on Palestine and the Middle East, spoke later of

"A process which can be called the 'absorption' of a minister by his department . . . He at once had access to a lot of information that he had not seen before . . . and within the first few weeks he came to the conclusion that the traditional Labour Party policy was wrong."[2]

There is no doubt that Bevin accepted the case which his officials and the Chiefs of Staff made for holding on to Palestine, for not allowing an influx of

---

[1] *Ibid.*

[2] Quoted by Nicholas Bethell: *The Palestine Triangle* (London 1979) p. 202.

Jewish refugees to provoke a civil war and for separating the problem of what to do with the Jewish survivors in Europe from the future of Palestine. The fact was, however, that Bevin did not inherit, and his officials were unable to suggest, a convincing alternative for the first or a long-term policy for the second.

Discussion by the Conservatives' short-lived "Caretaker Government" before the general election had produced no agreement. Partition had then been rejected[1] and in a despairing minute addressed to the Colonial Secretary and Chiefs of Staff (his final comment as Prime Minister) Churchill wrote:

"I don't think we should take the responsibility upon ourselves . . . while the Americans sit back and criticize. Have you ever addressed yourself to the idea that we should ask them to take it over? . . . Somebody else should have their turn now."[2]

The Labour Cabinet's Palestine Committee in its turn could do no better than postpone a decision on a long-term policy for at least six months, maintaining the White Paper policy in the meantime, and moving in additional troops to keep order. George Hall, Labour's Colonial Secretary, listed four options besides "the present system of governing without either the consent or the cooperation of the governed."[3] Bevin added a variant of his own, a scheme for federal union. This was to consist of three parts: one Jewish, the remaining Arab area of Palestine, and Transjordan, the whole to be ruled by an Arab king.[4] This did not long survive expert criticism, although Bevin continued to show an interest in a bi-national Palestine under British rule with a cantonal system on the Swiss model.

While members of the Cabinet stared at Hall's list of options without any reason to suppose they would do better in reaching a decision than their predecessors, Bevin came up with a new initiative.

On 6 September he had told the Cabinet's Palestine Committee

"It would be advantageous to postpone a decision on long-term policy for as long as possible, because the pressure for Jewish immigration into Palestine was likely to diminish . . . as the months went by and the resettlement of Europe progressed."[5]

This was good Foreign Office doctrine. But a month later (despite the process of "absorption" described by Beeley) Bevin was taking a quite different line which was disapproved of by the officials most concerned in his own and other departments and which took shape in a proposal of his own devising.

[1] On the grounds "that it would be resisted by both Jews and Arabs, would lose us the goodwill and friendship of the whole Moslem world, and would shatter British prestige in the Middle East". Memorandum on Palestine Policy, 11 June 1945 (FO 371/45378 E 4849).
[2] PM's personal minute, 6 July 1945 M/679/5–D6. For Churchill's development of this view in 1946, see below p. 299.
[3] Hall's memorandum to the Cabinet, dated 28 Sept. CP (45) 196, p. 3.
[4] The scheme was spelled out, and criticized, by the Colonial Office in a paper dated 7 Sept. 1945.
[5] CAB 95/14.

8

There were still hopes amongst Jews that the Labour victory would be followed by a reversal of policy. When a World Zionist Conference met in London on 1 August, Weizmann spoke optimistically of the prospects with Labour in power. But the hard-liners, Ben Gurion and Rabbi Silver, the leader of the American Zionists, were wary and talked in terms of resistance and struggle. To put Labour's intentions to the test, Ben Gurion led a Zionist delegation to the Colonial Office and demanded immediate admission of 100,000 Jews into Palestine and the declaration of Palestine as a Jewish state. The Colonial Secretary, Hall, was shocked by their aggressive attitude, but their demands were no more than the expectations successive Labour Party conference resolutions had created. The most Hall was able to offer, after three weeks' delay, was the 2,000 places remaining from the White Paper quota with a promise to seek Arab agreement to a further 1,500 places monthly. The Zionists indignantly rejected Hall's offer and were strengthened by Truman's unequivocal support for the figure of 100,000.

August turned into September with no further indication of British policy, no repudiation of the White Paper, and no consultation. On 21 September Weizmann sent a warning to Attlee saying that there were reports of discussions and decisions affecting the future of Palestine of which they were told nothing:

"If what we hear is true, it would mean that nothing short of tragedy faces the Jewish people, that a very serious conflict might ensue, which we would all deplore."[1]

Attlee's reply was curt and dismissive. It may have been influenced by the British interception of a message sent on 23 September to the Jewish Agency's London office by Moshe Sneh, the leader of the Haganah, proposing a "serious incident" to be carried out in cooperation with the two terrorist organizations, the Stern group and the Irgun. Knowledge of what was being planned, despite Weizmann's disavowal of violence, may also explain Bevin's outburst when he saw the Jewish leader on 5 October.

"What do you mean by refusing the White Paper certificates? Are you trying to force my hand? If you want a fight you can have it."

Weizmann deeply resented the tone in which Bevin addressed him. He had staked everything, including the trust of his own people, on his confidence in British good faith, and now, when both his policy and his own position were under attack in the Zionist movement, such a rebuff at the hands of a British Foreign Secretary was an affront he would never forgive.[2] A second meeting,

[1] FO 371/45380.
[2] Weizmann's account is in Chaim Weizmann: *Trial and Error* (NY 1949) p. 440.

on 10 October, which Weizmann does not mention, was more friendly and the two men discussed the idea of a bi-racial Palestine on the Swiss model.[1] "It had been a very good talk", Attlee reported to Truman,[2] but neither he nor Bevin gave any hint to Weizmann of the move they were now contemplating.

The man who did most to encourage Bevin to persevere was Lord Halifax, the British Ambassador in Washington and a former Foreign Secretary. In a long letter of 1 July 1945 before the election Halifax had raised the question (as Churchill did) whether it was in British interests "to continue to shoulder alone the unenviable responsibility for the future of Palestine."[3] This was an argument which the Foreign Office and the Chiefs of Staff were unwilling to accept at this time.

By the end of the summer, however, it was obvious to the British Embassy in Washington that London could not ignore the success the Zionists were having in concentrating their efforts on the American Government and Congress. At a time when the full horror of the Nazi extermination camps was becoming known to the American public through correspondents' reports, newspaper photographs and newsreels, the British found themselves put in the dock for refusing to lift the ban on immigration to Palestine which had already (the Zionists maintained) cost the lives of a million Jews who might otherwise have escaped from Europe in time.[4] The Zionist campaign chimed well with American criticism of British efforts to restore the Empire and Halifax warned that it could affect the outcome of the British negotiations on the Lend-Lease settlement and a dollar loan.[5] Officials in the Foreign Office and the Colonial Office might complain that Bevin was too ready to listen to Halifax, but the former's own experience with the Americans during September confirmed the Embassy's warnings.

For, when Byrnes arrived in London for the Council of Foreign Ministers, he brought with him a report by Earl Harrison, Dean of the University of Pennsylvania Law School, who had been asked to investigate the condition of the Jewish DPs in Germany, and an accompanying letter from Truman in which he strongly supported Harrison's recommendation of the immediate admission of 100,000 Jews into Palestine.

Looking back one is driven to ask whether it would not have been better if the Labour Government had listened to Truman's advice—or better still, acted on its own initiative—and offered up to 100,000 places as a once-for-all gesture. Despite the difficulties it would create with the Arabs, it was a course

---

[1] Zionist archives Z4/15202.
[2] PREM 8/89.
[3] Halifax to FO. FO 371/45378/E4849.
[4] Halifax reported: "There is a feeling in influential liberal quarters that, if HMG had admitted more Jews into Palestine before the War, more Jews would have escaped Nazi persecution, that more might have been done to get Jews out of Europe into Palestine during the war, and that Palestine is the natural asylum for the many Jews who, it is believed, now wish to leave Europe." FO 371/45378.
[5] See Halifax's dispatches of 3 October and 8 October. FO 371/45380/E7599.

Bevin was prepared to consider in the summer of 1946. Acted on in 1945, it would have produced a far greater impact. At that time it would have provided for all the Jewish refugees in the Displaced Persons' camps before the influx from the East. It would also have established British readiness to recognize the unique situation created by the attempt to exterminate the European Jews before Jewish violence in Palestine and the Zionist propaganda campaign in the USA had begun to stiffen British resistance. On the other hand, as the Arabs argued, would it not have encouraged the Zionists to demand more, and to believe they could get it by intensifying their pressure on the British?

What is clear is that such a course was not seriously considered and that Truman's intervention only aroused resentment in London. Alarmed at the news that Truman was proposing to make his views public, Attlee cabled urgently that "grievous harm" would be done to Anglo-US relations by putting out a figure which had been fixed without consideration of the consequences in the Middle East. He followed this with a letter (16 September) in which he elaborated his opposition (in the Jews' own interests) to putting Jewish refugees "in a special racial category at the head of the queue", and argued that the Arabs as well as the Jews had to be considered in regard to immigration.[1] Despite their representations and Truman's promise to take no action until Byrnes got back, Attlee and Bevin learned to their anger that at a White House press conference (29 September), the American press had been given a summary of the Prime Minister's correspondence with Truman and told that after more than a month the President had still had no reply to his appeal to admit 100,000. When Bevin protested, Byrnes told him frankly that the White House had broken the promise to say nothing because of pressure from the Democratic Party managers. The Democrats had their eyes on the mayoral election in New York, where a third of the votes were Jewish and the Republicans were bidding for their support.

Bevin never got over his indignation at the willingness of the President (and Congress) to let the Jewish vote and Jewish contributions to party funds influence their policy on Palestine—ignoring the complexities of the situation, not least the fact that the Arab majority of the Palestine population were strongly opposed to further Jewish immigration. This was not only naive (for politicians have to win elections, and it was the Jews, not the Arabs, who had the votes) but it clouded his judgement, leading him to see only the elements of political calculation and self-interest in American support for Zionism (no more Jews need be admitted to the USA) and to ignore the genuine sympathy which many Americans felt for the Zionist case. But if, as he wrote to Halifax, he believed the Americans had been "thoroughly dishonest in handling this problem", Bevin was enough of a realist to recognize more quickly than anyone else on the British side, in Whitehall or the Middle East, that American pressure could not be ignored, and that in the interests of good relations with

[1] Attlee's cable, PREM 8/89 & FRUS 1945(8) p. 739; Attlee's letter, FO 371/45380/E7251; FRUS *ibid.*, pp. 740–41.

the USA which were crucial for the British, they would have to come up with a new initiative.

His idea, first put informally to Halifax, was to invite the USA to join Britain at once in setting up an Anglo-American Commission of Inquiry (henceforward, AAC) to examine the position of the Jews in Europe and how it could be relieved. On 4 October the Cabinet was due to discuss Bevin's recommendations on the Middle East after his conference with British representatives. On Palestine, however, it had nothing more to go on than the Colonial Secretary's list of possible options for a long-term policy. In view of Attlee's admission that agitation was growing in the USA, this was a depressing prospect, and there was general relief when Bevin intervened with his proposal for a joint enquiry with the Americans, extended to consider how many Jews could reasonably be admitted to Palestine, and possibly presided over by Field-Marshal Smuts.

Bevin had grasped the need for urgency but his proposal had still to be given substance. In the next few days the possibility was canvassed of adding an Arab (Azzam Bey, the Secretary General of the Arab League) and a Jew (Weizmann) to the Commission, and Bevin minuted on the papers:

"What about the idea of us calling a conference of Jews and Arabs to be held concurrently with U.S. observers to discuss the future of Palestine?"

Bevin's idea was not taken further, any more than was his suggestion of Smuts as chairman—both opposed by the Foreign Office and the Colonial Office—but when the Cabinet's Palestine Committee met on 10 October, Bevin was still prepared to argue against the Colonial Secretary that even if there was a risk that such a conference might fail, they must make an attempt to bring the parties together as a step on the road to a permanent solution. It was in these terms that he was now talking, saying plainly that "we could no longer adhere to the White Paper policy, and a new approach was essential."[1]

With the support of the Palestine Committee, Bevin's scheme was put to the Cabinet on 11 October, a week after he had first launched it. Morrison presented it on behalf of the committee and Bevin established the two positions he had to reconcile: the first, that a solution to the problem of Palestine must be part of HMG's policy for the Middle East as a whole (i.e. they had to keep Arab goodwill); the second, that "the agitation in the U.S.A. was poisoning our relations with the U.S. Government in other fields" (i.e. they had to carry the Americans with them). Bevin's plan was approved without opposition and Attlee thanked him on behalf of the Cabinet for the effort he had made to produce "an entirely new approach to the problem."[2]

The same day Bevin drafted a long cable to Halifax[3] in which he set out his policy for the Middle East including Palestine. In the personal message which

[1] Minutes of the Palestine Committee meeting on 10 October 1945. CAB 95/14.
[2] Cabinet minutes CM 40 (45) 11 October 1945.
[3] Sent on 12 October, FO 371/45381/E 7757G; FO 800/484/PA/45/13.

he sent first he again referred to the need to remove anything that might poison relations between America and Britain, saying that he regarded this as vital in view of the turn of events at the London Council of Foreign Ministers.[1] How far Bevin and the official British mind were from grasping the driving force behind Zionism is shown by his comment to Halifax that he did not accept that "all the Jews or the bulk of them must leave Germany . . . They have gone through, it is true, the most terrible massacres and persecutions, but on the other hand, they have got through it and a number have survived. Now succour and help should be brought to assist them to resettle." He was not satisfied with Earl Harrison's report which looked "like a device to put pressure on England". The first thing the joint Commission must do was to find out what really were the views of the Jews in Europe. The second was to get impartial evidence on the claims made for the number of Jews Palestine could absorb if its economic potentialities were exploited.

"I do not think it is right to go on asserting that there are these great opportunities unless we can show to the Arabs that they are practicable and that the Admission of more Jews will not necessarily increase the pressure on the land."[2]

Halifax welcomed Bevin's proposals, adding that he did not expect the Zionists to like them or the American Government to be keen to accept a share of responsibility, However,

"If the U.S. Government accepts your proposal they will be committed to search for a solution. If they reject it, as is possible, although I should be inclined to think improbable, our position will none the less be greatly strengthened."[3]

British officials, whether in London or in the Middle East, showed little enthusiasm for Bevin's initiative. Their comments in minutes and memoranda range from indignation to scepticism. The Eastern Department of the FO for example, described the plan as a complete change in attitude towards the Arabs, who identified the USA with Zionism, adding tartly that British representatives in the Middle East would need to be informed immediately as they were under the impression that British policy remained as settled at the recent conference they had attended in London. Most officials were sceptical that the joint enquiry, even if the Americans accepted the invitation, could produce any basis for agreement. The only advantage they could see was in facing the Americans with the issue of responsibility and, if they took part, in confronting them with the difficulties the British had to contend with.

In the meantime the Jewish leadership in Palestine had decided to put pressure on the British. On 10 October the Haganah carried out a raid on a camp at Athlit releasing more than 200 illegal immigrants and ambushing a

[1] Bevin to Halifax, 11 October No. 10267.
[2] Bevin to Halifax, 12 October. FO 371/45381/E7757G.
[3] Halifax to Bevin, 14 October 1945. FO 371/45381.

177

police truck. When the Colonial Secretary Hall put it to Weizmann that the Haganah action began to look like rebellion, Weizmann gave him a "categorical assurance" that neither he nor his colleagues in the Jewish Agency had any responsibility for such incidents or knew of them until they had read the newspapers. "He himself saw all the messages which went out so that he was in a position to know."[1] In view of the messages they had intercepted, the British did not believe Weizmann, even less so when, on the night of 31 October, the "serious incident" took place which Moshe Sneh's intercepted message had forecast.

A series of coordinated attacks was carried out on communications and British installations throughout Palestine, including the Haifa oil refinery. Bevin summoned Weizmann and Moshe Shertok to see him. The latter's account describes Bevin as speaking with "great anger and tension, a muscle at the side of his mouth giving a warning signal". He laid stress on the cooperation between the Haganah and the terrorist organizations; saying that this amounted to a declaration of war by the Yishuv[2] on Britain. When Weizmann replied that the Jewish Agency had condemned the violence, Bevin after reading the statement dismissed it as, not a condemnation, but a condonation.[3] If they had decided on war, they should be straight about it, and say so. Then the British would give up their efforts to find a solution; they would not negotiate under the threat of violence.

Bevin's further remarks, as reported by Shertok, show how far removed was his way of looking at the situation from that of the two Jews.

"I cannot bear English Tommies being killed. They are innocent." When Weizmann referred to the millions of Jews who had been killed, and were still dying in refugee camps, Bevin replied: "I do not want any Jews killed either, but I love the British soldiers. They belong to my class. They are working people. . . . The problem is intolerably difficult. It would have been difficult if the Balfour Declaration had been worded more clearly, if they had not tried to ride two horses at once. It is a very difficult business, but we are honestly trying to find a way out."

Shertok noted that "Bevin's anger and fury against the United States are unimaginable." As an example of American dishonesty he cited Truman's claim "for electoral purposes for the immediate entry of 100,000—a course which the President and everyone else who understood the problem knew was impossible today." Shertok summed up his impression of Bevin as sincere and perturbed, but also distant from the matter and ignorant. "He gets extremely angry, of course, but he is also shocked, shocked and stunned."[4]

[1] 19 October 1945. FO 371/45419.
[2] The Jewish community in Palestine.
[3] The statement read: "The Agency repudiates recourse to violence, but finds its capacity to impose restraint severely strained by a policy which Jews regard as fatal to their future."
[4] Zionist archives, S25/7566. The FO record of the interview dated 2 November 1945 is in FO 800/484/PA/45/22. It substantiates Shertok's account but I have preferred the letter for its view of Bevin as seen through Zionist eyes.

Bevin however refused to let fear of failure deter him from the course on which he had embarked even when a month's negotiations proved necessary before agreement could be reached with the Americans on terms of reference and a timetable. The American Government to the surprise of many on the British side—though not of Bevin—proved willing to take part in the enquiry, but only on condition that the terms of reference were rewritten, a time limit for the Commission's report imposed, and the date of an announcement deferred until after the New York election. Bevin's patience was sorely tried, but if he wanted the Americans to come in he had to take what he could get.

Although Bevin's original proposal[1] had mentioned Jewish immigration into Palestine immediately after the position of the Jews in Europe, as the twin objects of the enquiry, it emerged from discussion by the Palestine Committee and Cabinet and redrafting by the officials with no mention of Palestine, which was replaced by an investigation of "immigration into other countries outside Europe including the U.S.A." The final version dictated by the Americans however not only restored Palestine but made the problem of Jewish immigration and self-government there the first, and the position of the Jews in Europe the second, term of reference. Bevin's efforts to reverse the order were unavailing: only with great difficulty was he able to keep in a reference to immigration to other countries outside Europe as well as Palestine.[2] He had also to accept a time limit of 120 days for the Commission to present its recommendations. Nonetheless, when he was at last free to reveal his plan to the House of Commons (on 13 November) he was able at the same time to announce American agreement to make it a joint enquiry.

In Bevin's mind, although he took care not to draw attention to it in his speech, this was his real achievement: to have brought the Americans off the sidelines and involved them in finding a solution to the problem. For his first preoccupation as Foreign Secretary was to prevent a quarrel over Palestine and the Jews from souring the close relationship with the USA which he believed essential to Britain's economic recovery and to her continuing to play a leading role in international affairs, not only in the Middle East but across the board. But that still left unanswered the awkward question: what reason was there to suppose that a joint enquiry involving the Americans would find a solution to the specific problem, however this was to be defined? Bevin could only convince himself that it would—and risk the personal assurance he gave in the House that "I will stake my political future on solving this problem" —because of the qualification he added: "but not in the limited sphere presented to me now." Bevin's statement to the House and many other remarks make clear that what he meant was: but not if a solution to the Jewish problem left by the Nazi persecution is limited to Palestine.

---

[1] As put to the Cabinet on 4 October. CAB 128/1 CM(45) 38.
[2] The correspondence between Bevin and Halifax during the negotiations is to be found in FO 371/45382. There is no doubt that Bevin owed a considerable debt to Halifax's advice and diplomatic skill.

"Palestine", as he said in the same speech, "while it may be able to make a contribution, does not, by itself, provide sufficient opportunity for grappling with the whole problem. . . . I must emphasise that the problem is not one which can be dealt with only in relation to Palestine: it will need a united effort by the Powers to relieve the miseries of these suffering people!"

The Zionist case was that Palestine provided the *only* opportunity, that there was no alternative, no other country, whatever Bevin might say, where the survivors of European Jewry could go, and that the Jewish problem could only be solved in the "limited sphere" of Palestine. But to accept that meant facing an outcry of betrayal from the Arabs, which the Americans could brush aside but no British Foreign Secretary could ignore. The only hope of avoiding this was to work on the opposite premise, the possibility of separating the two, and dispersing the survivors of the Holocaust, some remaining in Europe, a limited number going to Palestine, some going to other countries outside Europe, including the USA. Bevin's further hope was that if the Americans could be brought to look at the problem through British eyes, they would see how complex it was and instead of uncritically accepting the simplistic solution urged on them by the Zionists would bring the latter to take a more reasonable view of what was possible.

Bevin's statement in the Commons was well received in Britain. The announcement that the United States had agreed to join in an enquiry took the House by surprise and overshadowed everything else. When attempts were made to draw him further by both Zionist and pro-Arab sympathizers, he had the sympathy of the House in appealing to them not to pursue racial antagonisms. With hindsight Bevin's belief that it was possible to avoid such antagonisms and find a compromise solution not confined to Palestine can be seen for the illusion it was; but it was one still shared by the majority in the House and in the country, and his willingness to stake his political future on doing so (with the qualification, "but not in the limited sphere presented to me now", forgotten) impressed most people with his sincerity and was not yet made into a taunt and a reproach. Jewish spokesmen, Sidney Silverman in the Commons and Lord Samuel in the Lords, expressed appreciation of the spirit in which Bevin had spoken and Harold Laski wrote the next day:

"My dear Ernest,
    Though it is a little early to judge, I should have thought from what I have read and heard that the Palestine statement yesterday went over with great success. . . ."[1]

Attlee, writing from Ottawa after his visit to Washington, sent similar congratulations on "having amid so many difficulties made such a success with the Palestine statement", adding that "except for the extreme Zionists, the reaction over here was good."[2]

[1] Laski to Bevin, 14 November 1945. FO 800/484/PA/45/23.
[2] Attlee to Bevin, 15 November 1945, *ibid*, PA/45/26.

It was the Zionist reaction, however, which counted in the USA. The announcement of the joint enquiry came as a bombshell, and the Zionist leaders were disturbed by the fact that nothing had been said in advance in London, or leaked to them in Washington. Bevin was at once seen as a committed and unscrupulous enemy who planned to outwit them by robbing them of their chief resource, American pressure on the British to secure Zionist demands. Truman still insisted that he held to his demand for the admission of 100,000 Jews to Palestine but he was taken to be the dupe of a clever trick, who had fallen into Bevin's trap without realizing that he was acceding to the anti-Zionist thesis that the Jewish survivors in Europe should be dispersed and assimilated, not recruited to establish a Jewish state in Palestine. British attempts to explain Bevin's statement—for example, the omission of any reference to the 1939 White Paper which had been intended to please the Jews—were dismissed as deception. The Jewish Agency declared that the policy of the White Paper was still being followed in violation of the Balfour Declaration and the terms of the Mandate. The long-term intention was to liquidate Zionism; the short-term to delay any decision and spin out time.[1]

The impression left by Bevin's statement was made much worse, in Zionist eyes, by his press conference afterwards. "Elated by the reception of a very full House", Pierson Dixon noted in his diary, "E.B. charged back to the F.O. and into the press conference which he addressed with unusual gusto."[2] Believing that he would find the solution which had eluded everyone else, he was in an expansive mood. Nothing would please him more, he told the seventy correspondents who came to hear him, than for all the Jews to be gathered back into Abraham's bosom, but they should draw a distinction between Zionism and Jewry. They should not ride roughshod over Arab and Moslem opinion and they should read the Koran as well as the Bible. Such bluff remarks, repeated in cold print, showed extraordinary insensitivity to Jewish feelings. When he was asked what he thought of Zionist plans for increasing Palestine's natural resources, he replied: eighty per cent propaganda and twenty per cent fact. Worst of all, in trying to sum up his speech for the Press in plain down-to-earth language, he used the phrase which Weizmann in his memoirs described as "gratuitously brutal" and which is still held against him as proof of his anti-Semitism:

"I am very anxious", he said, "that Jews shall not in Europe over-emphasise their racial position. The keynote of the statement I made in the House is that I want the suppression of racial warfare, and therefore if the Jews, with all their sufferings, want to get too much at the head of the queue, you have the danger of another anti-Semitic reaction through it all."

---

[1] See the minutes of the Jewish Agency Executive meetings, 14 & 21 November, which were brought to my notice and translated for me by Dr Nachmani; and the statement by the Inner Zionist Council issued on 15 December 1945.
[2] Dixon, p. 198.

This was a phrase which Attlee had used two months before in writing to Truman about the DP camps in the British and US zones of Germany, where (contrary to the impression created by Zionist propaganda) Jewish refugees were only 10 per cent of the total numbers[1] and discrimination in their favour could (so the FO Refugee Department argued) produce resentment in other groups. Whether soundly based or not, neither the argument nor the phrase were Bevin's, but it was he who blurted them out in public, without making clear their context, and was at once taken to be branding the Jews as queue-jumpers.

If the argument presented here is correct, however much Bevin may be censured for the clumsiness and insensitivity he showed on this and other occasions, these failings do not supply the key to British policy. Leonard Stein, looking at the Zionist dealings with the Labour Government from the point of view of Weizmann reaches the same conclusion:

"The real reason for Weizmann's failure to make any impression on the Attlee Government was not that Bevin had started with a personal dislike for Jews (there is no evidence that he had) or that he had all along been antipathetic to Zionism (there is evidence to the contrary) but that the identity of British and Zionist interests so strongly stressed at the time of the original British commitment (1917) could no longer be shown to exist. The Zionists could justly urge that they were asking for no more than they had been encouraged to expect, but they could produce no persuasive reasons for believing that Britain could satisfy their demands, if not with positive advantage to herself, at least without involving herself in any serious embarrassment."[2]

The reaction at the time to the 13 November statement, however, crystallized the Zionist stereotype of Bevin as a "Jew-hater", "the heir to Hitler's mantle", inspired by the same anti-Semitism as the Nazis and the man personally responsible for Britain's refusal to allow Jewish refugees to find a home in Palestine.

Bevin's personalization of British policy by staking his own political future on its success, his egocentric and emotional temperament, his disposition to fight when faced with opposition and not to guard his tongue when angered all combined to make him vulnerable to such charges in a way that would not have been plausible if Attlee had been the spokesman. He shared Bevin's views and the responsibility for British policy, but said little in public, did not become emotionally involved, and so did not attract the lightning.

Bevin paid a high price for these failings. The time and effort he devoted to trying to find a compromise solution to the problem of Palestine were ignored. Henceforward he became the principal target of Zionist propaganda which progressively identified him with the Nazi image the Jews had learned to hate. And since he naturally resented being compared with Hitler and the organ-

---

[1] This estimate is the AAC's figure for June 1946; it was a lower percentage in November 1945 when the total of DPs was considerably higher.

[2] Leonard J. Stein: *Weizmann and England* (London 1964) pp. 24–25.

izers of the death camps, this in its turn had its effect on Bevin's own attitude. Prejudice was cumulative, on both sides, making it more difficult for Bevin to form a cool judgement and to disengage from a problem which had defeated and marred the reputation of every British minister who touched it. His one consolation was that their disagreement over Palestine did not poison the relationship between the UK and the USA (his original objective) or prevent them from cooperating more and more closely in other parts of the world, even at times in the Middle East.

CHAPTER 5

"All the world is in trouble and I have to deal with all the troubles at once"

I

There was still one further problem, the atomic bomb, which not only complicated all the others but was inherently the most difficult for any government to handle and particularly for a Labour government coming new into office.

The Labour Ministers were at a double disadvantage. None of them had been admitted by Churchill to knowledge of the "Tube Alloys" project, not even Attlee, the Deputy Prime Minister; nor did they know anything of the history of atomic collaboration with the USA. The Labour Party was in any case ill-equipped to deal with an issue of this sort. It had little experience of defence or foreign affairs; was inclined to judge such matters as questions of principle and traditionally regarded the exercise of power and the use of force as evils to be eradicated. This was not a promising background against which to formulate a policy while ministers were still struggling to absorb the implications of an invention which appeared to make all previous thinking about defence obsolete. "Until decisions are taken on this vital matter," Attlee wrote to Truman, "it is difficult for any of us to plan for the future."

Bevin's first decision was to fasten on the political rather than on the technical issues. In his first speech as Foreign Secretary,[1] he told the House of Commons:

"War is not caused by the invention of weapons. It is policy that makes war . . . the intention to go to war." It was no good blaming the scientist or trying to stop scientific research; "I am perfectly certain that the late Lord Rutherford had no idea of war at all. . . . It is we in the form and control of our policy, who misdirect the results of scientific research."

---

[1] HC 20 August 1945.

Certainly it was necessary to control the manufacture of such weapons, but it was equally necessary "to keep a careful watch to ensure that no one Government starts out with warlike intentions and proceeds to lead us all into war."

Bevin agreed, however, with Attlee's decision to keep discussion of atomic questions within a very limited circle. During the whole period of the Labour Government, there was not a single Commons debate devoted to atomic energy. In the same six years the subject figured less than ten times on the full Cabinet's agenda and seven of these were concerned with the Attlee–Truman meetings in November 1945 and December 1950. Expenditure on atomic research and development was concealed under other heads. Interest by Parliament or the Press was not encouraged and Emrys Hughes, one of the few Labour MPs who tried to find out what was happening, complained: "When we ask a question about it, one would almost think an A-bomb has been dropped." In the first eighteen months there was not even a standing committee on atomic energy: discussions were held and decisions were taken by an *ad hoc* committee, known from its file as General 75, to which the Prime Minister invited not more than half-a-dozen at most of his senior colleagues, all of whom had served in the coalition.[1] At the third meeting of General 75, on 3 October, Bevin insisted that the Prime Minister, like the President in the USA, must have final authority in atomic matters, adding that he would "consult from time to time with those of his colleagues principally concerned". In fact the colleague principally concerned was Bevin himself, since Attlee kept responsibility for defence in his own hands until October 1946, and although others—Cripps, for example, and Morrison—were involved, Attlee and Bevin together played a greater role than any other ministers in shaping British atomic policy after the war.

As in the case of foreign policy, the first few months, leading up in this case to Attlee's meeting with Truman on 9 November, were a period during which both men showed considerable change and indeed fluctuation in their opinions. Both were reluctant to give up the hope of an international authority in the UN, but as the discussions went on, can be seen recognizing—again, as in the case of foreign policy—that they had to deal with a world in which national interest and national power were still the predominant factors. This process of self-education can be followed in the meetings of General 75 of which there were seven between August and November 1945.

The confusion in which the discussions began is shown not only by the informal status of General 75 but also by the arrangement to which ministers agreed at their first meeting for the chairmanship of the other key committee,

---

[1] Bevin, Cripps, Morrison, Greenwood and Dalton, to whom Wilmot as Minister of Supply was added later. The records of General 75 and its successors are not publicly accessible but have been used by Professor Margaret Gowing in her official (but far from uncritical) history *Independence and Deterrence. Britain and Atomic Energy, 1945–51*, vol. 1. *Policy-Making* (London 1974) on which I have drawn for this section.

an advisory council with a membership of scientists, civil servants and representatives of the Services to advise the Government on atomic policy especially in its international aspects. Sir Edward Bridges, the Secretary of the Cabinet, recognizing both the new ministers' lack of experience in atomic matters and the importance of continuity, suggested that the chairman should be Sir John Anderson, who had been the Coalition minister in charge of atomic development on the British side during the war. There were good reasons for this suggestion: Anderson's familiarity with the problems and their past history; his outstanding ability as an administrator and the confidence in his judgement that Attlee and Bevin had acquired from working with him as chairman of the Lord President's Committee which acted for the War Cabinet in everything except the conduct of the fighting war. But Anderson, although not by temperament a party man, now sat on the Opposition front bench in the House of Commons and although accommodated in the Cabinet Offices was unable to attend ministerial meetings. As a result there was no personal link between the advisory committee which represented a remarkable concentration of talent and experience and Cabinet committees deliberating on its recommendations. This anomalous arrangement is only one example of a general confusion of responsibiliites for atomic affairs within the machinery of government which was not cleared up until 1947, by which time the most important decisions had been taken.

Attlee's starting point was the need for international control of atomic weapons and for joint action by the USA, Britain and Russia to secure this. He proposed to put the case for such action to Truman, and then jointly with Truman to Stalin. At the second meeting of the General 75 committee, however, on 29 August, Bevin said he agreed with Attlee's sentiments but not with the procedure. He argued that it was a mistake to raise the question of the A-bomb with Truman and Stalin in isolation from other subjects which had to be settled between the three Powers. As a first step he suggested they should propose to Truman a review of the world situation in the light of the A-bomb. There followed a month of drafting and re-drafting before the letter to Truman was sent on 25 September.[1] Amongst others, Churchill was shown the draft. Returning it, he asked what H.M.G. wanted the Americans to do. To hand over the secret of the bomb to the Russians? If so, he remarked, the Americans would not and, in his view, should not.

Truman did not reply for three weeks and only under British pressure agreed to a meeting on 9 November. The American President was worried about the possible effect on the Russians of talks between Britain, the USA and Canada from which the Russians were excluded. The minds of British ministers were equally divided. At the meeting of the General 75 committee on 11 October, Bevin argued that there was everything to gain by letting Russia into the secret of the bomb. This could change the whole atmosphere of the

---

[1] The text is printed in full in Gowing, pp. 78–81.

negotiations between Russia and the West which at the London Council of Foreign Ministers had been heavily prejudiced by Russian suspicion of the use to which the Americans might put the advantage which the bomb gave them. "We should take the risk of giving this information to the Russians in the interests of our foreign policy", he said. But a week later, at the next meeting of General 75, Bevin had lost confidence in his own argument. Declaring that he felt like calling a plague on both their houses, he now argued that the USA and Russia alike seemed bent on dividing the world up into spheres of influence without regard for British interests. He no longer thought that the recent difficulties with Russia could be attributed to the A-bomb: "further study had convinced him that Russian policy had shown no variation." Nor did he believe that the difficulties would be removed by an offer which the Russians were likely to receive without gratitude and regard with suspicion or at least as a sign of weakness. "It must be clear first," he said, "what we should ask for in exchange." Attlee was not prepared to go the whole way with this line of argument but before he left for Washington he had come round to the view that international control would have to be reached by stages; that better relations would have to be established with the Russians before they were offered the technical knowledge of how to make the bomb, and that there should be no pooling of strategic raw materials such as uranium except in return for substantial advantages.

Another issue on which ministers found it hard to make up their minds was what to do about the discovery of the Soviet spy-ring which had penetrated the security defences of the atomic work being carried out in Canada. The discovery was made after the defection, early in September, of Igor Gouzenko, a Russian cypher clerk employed by the Soviet Military Attaché in Ottawa, and implicated a British scientist, Dr Nunn May who was later found guilty of making secret information available to the Russians. Attlee and Mackenzie King, the Canadian Prime Minister, were anxious to postpone action for fear that the uproar over the case would prejudice any approach to Russia on a scheme for international control. Bevin on the other hand thought they should go ahead with the interrogation and prosecution: "I think we are being too tender." In the end the Americans came down in favour of delay and interrogation did not begin until February 1946.

One of the reasons which led Attlee to move from his initial position on international control of nuclear weapons was the difficulty of finding a practical way to make this effective. The best that a committee of permanent officials under Bridges' chairmanship could come up with was the threat of collective retaliation with atomic weapons against any aggressor who used them first, a proposal which roused the Prime Minister's scorn. "What British Government," he asked, "would accept an obligation to embark on atomic warfare when this might mean the destruction of London?"

These discussions in the late summer and autumn of 1945 bring out the characteristic paradox of atomic politics in which Truman as well found himself trapped. While waiting for that mutual trust to be established which would allow international control of A-weapons to be effective, every nation had to look out for itself and make itself as strong as possible in nuclear weapons (the Russians were wasting no time either), despite the fact that this was the surest way to increase mutual distrust and so reduce the chances of international control. Attlee had asked for the Washington meeting in the first place in the urgent conviction that it was necessary to establish as soon as possible some system of international control of atomic power for the good of all. Before he left, however, he and Bevin had already come to recognize that international control could only be reached a step at a time; that there was no short cut which would enable them to by-pass the lack of confidence between nations and that in the present stage it was best for the Americans to retain in their own hands the knowledge of how to make the bomb.

More than that: under pressure from the scientists and civil servants Attlee had agreed that he would do his best to secure the continuation of the wartime collaboration with the USA in atomic development now that the war was over, thereby seeking to maintain the advantage which the British enjoyed over every other nation except the United States. The American scientists no longer felt any need for the co-operation of the British, and Churchill's efforts[1] to secure a continuing role for the British team and continued access to technical information had not settled the matter. If Attlee could bring this off and return with a new agreement guaranteeing the British position, this was a prize that would carry greater weight with most of his advisers than any scheme for international control in which few of them had much real faith.

One other decision was taken before Attlee left for Washington. In October, the General 75 Ministers, on the advice of Anderson's Committee, agreed to set up an atomic research establishment in the United Kingdom: a site had been found at Harwell and a director in John Cockcroft. The question left open for the moment was whether to start on a large-scale production programme as well. Bevin was sceptical about the prospect of atomic energy rapidly becoming available for industrial purposes. "I do not believe it at all," he told the House of Commons. "It will be long, weary, hard patient work before this new form of energy is available to revolutionise the energy of the world." But the real question, and one much more difficult for a Labour Government to answer, was whether Britain should start on the manufacture of her own stock of A-bombs. At this stage neither Attlee nor the other ministers he consulted were prepared to give the directive for the production of bombs for which Bridges' committee of officials had asked. The most they were prepared to do was to leave the option open, and it remained open (at least in principle) until January 1947, fifteen months later, when the same small group of ministers finally agreed to Britain making her own A-bombs—without telling either the rest of the Cabinet or Parliament what they had decided.

[1] The Quebec Agreement of 1943 and the Hyde Park *Aide Mémoire* of 1944. See Margaret Gowing, *Britain and Atomic Energy 1939-45* (London 1964), Appendix 4 & Appendix 8.

On 8 November, the day before Attlee was due to meet Truman, the full Labour Cabinet, for the only time before December 1950, discussed the issues raised by the Bomb. Some ministers were still prepared to argue for the position from which Attlee and Bevin had started. "If it was our policy to build world peace on moral foundations, we should be prepared to apply that principle at once to the A-bomb." If the Russians were unco-operative—and they agreed they were—this was due to their suspicions of the West and their experience of the West before the war. All the more need then to remove the causes of suspicion, to offer full disclosure of the secrets of the bomb and secure Russia's co-operation in return.

Bevin intervened to suggest that Attlee should explore the possibility of putting in the hands of the UN the task of devising suitable machinery for disclosure and exchange between all its members of the results of all scientific research including that which had a bearing on the development of new weapons. This was welcomed by Attlee and ended almost the only discussion the Labour Cabinet ever had of atomic policy.[1] Despite their misgivings, ministers in the end endorsed the general line Attlee and Bevin proposed to take and left the Prime Minister a free hand in negotiating with the Americans, a formula that sums up many of the unpalatable decisions in defence and foreign policy which the Labour Cabinet—despite its misgivings—found no alternative to endorsing in the next five years.

2

After the shock of seeing the first meeting of the Council of Foreign Ministers break up in disagreement, there was a revulsion of feeling in the British press and parliament against the prospect opened up by allied disunity. The *Christian Science Monitor*,[2] highly thought of for its foreign news service, printed a dispatch from its London correspondent in which he reported a widespread view that "Mr Eden never would have made the mistakes that Mr Bevin has made and that the Conservatives would not have allowed ideological differences to create what has virtually amounted to breaking off relations with Russia for a month in so far as the discussion of major issues is concerned." On the Labour and Liberal side, if there was uneasiness about Russian intentions, there was also a strong disposition to reprove anyone who voiced it in public or drew uncomfortable conclusions out loud. Above all, there was alarm at a state of affairs in which, less than six months after the end of the Second World War, there was already talk of a third and of a nuclear arms race.

In the course of October Truman, who was in the thick of his own domestic controversy about atomic energy, felt it necessary to say unequivocally that the United States would not share the secrets of how to manufacture the A-bomb

[1] CM (45) 51, 8 Nov. 1945.
[2] 5 November 1945.

but would treat these (in a phrase President Wilson could not have bettered) as "a sacred trust for humanity". This was not well received in Britain where there was a strong body of opinion in favour of handing over the A-bomb and the future development of nuclear energy to an international body. The reception of Truman's Navy Day speech setting out twelve principles of American foreign policy[1] was equally mixed, some taking his speech as a pledge that America would not return to isolationism but was resolved to play a leading part in world affairs, while others linked his statement on the A-bomb with his claim to strategic bases overseas and his promise to maintain America's national armaments as an alarming assertion of US power.

A few days later (31 October) Churchill met Bevin in the House for the first time since the election. According to Dixon's note of the conversation:

"The Secretary of State said what a pity it was that Mr Churchill, owing to his election tactics, had become a party man and had thus imperilled his position as a great national figure above party. He reminded Mr Churchill that he had advised him against holding an election immediately after the end of the European war since he foresaw a possible early end to the Japanese war and regarded a slide to the Left as inevitable whenever the election was held. Mr Churchill would have done better to accept the Labour Party's offer to maintain the coalition until November when he could have thought again."[2]

The occasion seems to have been a sentimental one. They talked of the trials and anxieties they had shared and Bevin pleased Churchill by saying that he had no objection to his visiting the United States and urged him to go. They agreed to hold a non-partisan debate on atomic energy just before Attlee left for Washington with the object of showing that, however divided they might be on domestic issues, on foreign policy there was a large measure of agreement between the parties. So far as the front benches went this was true. The split was between both of the front benches and the Labour back benchers who felt that the hopes of ordinary people everywhere were being betrayed by the return to power politics.

Churchill's opening speech did nothing to reassure them: on the contrary, he appeared to go further than moderate opinion in his own party was prepared to follow.[3] He welcomed Truman's declaration that America would continue to play a world role, a declaration which (he said) if made before 1914 or before 1939 might have prevented either war. He saw in this resolve and in American strength the one new hope, now that "those same deep uncontrollable anxieties which some of us felt in the years before the war recur". He rejoiced that the secret of the A-bomb was in American hands, hoped it would remain there, repudiated any suggestion of giving it to Russia, said bluntly he hoped Britain would make her own atomic bombs and finally appeared to look

[1] Text in Harry S. Truman: *Year of Decisions 1945*. Eng. ed. of Truman's Memoirs, vol. 1 (London 1955) pp. 476–7.
[2] FO 800/491/PLT/45/24.
[3] HC, 7 November 1945.

on a renewed Anglo-American alliance as the best safeguard of peace for Britain and the world. The *Manchester Guardian* and the *News Chronicle* the next day repudiated Churchill's argument as "a counsel of despair". *The Times* was equally critical, reminding the former Prime Minister that, if friendship with the USA was one main pillar of British foreign policy, the Anglo-Soviet alliance formed the other, while Clement Davies, the Leader of the Liberal Party, speaking immediately after Churchill in the debate, expressed the dismay which so many people felt at hearing talk of another war: "Let there be talk only of permanent peace, mutual understanding and mutual aid."

The speech Labour members wanted to hear from their own Party's spokesman on foreign affairs was a repudiation of Churchill's views as an obsolete form of power politics and a reassurance that, in some way or other, a means would be found to create a new system of international relations to match the needs of "the atomic era" and their own deeply felt idealism. They did not get it from Bevin who had arrived at the opposite conclusion, that it was time to break his silence and speak more frankly than he had yet done about relations with Russia and the obstacles to agreement between the Powers, even if this brought him into conflict with the prevalent mood in his Party.

He prefaced his reply to the debate with a warning to scientists who claimed to set their own judgement on atomic policy above the interests of the State: the responsibility for such policy was the Government's and they would not hesitate to enforce that responsibility, a warning which grated on the expectations of the Left at the very beginning of his speech.[1] It was possible, Bevin argued, to hope that in time the UN Organization could provide an effective international authority, but that time had not yet come. They were living in a difficult period in which there was a conflict between the desire for co-operation and the desire for power. "Sometimes in these negotiations, I make the confession that power politics seem to me to be naked and unashamed; the next moment you are searching and striving for the other ideal." What was it that the Great Powers wanted? He appealed to them, "Put the cards on the table face upwards. We are ready to do it."

It is evident from all the debates on foreign policy in 1945 that there was still a strong feeling in the Labour Party that a better case could be made for Russia's attitude of suspicion towards the West than the Government was prepared to admit, that Labour ministers (as one MP put it) were "too coalition-minded", too inclined to follow Churchill in regarding the USA as a friendly and the Soviet Union as a hostile power, despite the fact that one was a capitalist and the other a socialist state. It was this feeling, going back to the Revolution of 1917, which Bevin now affronted by going on to speak as if by "power politics" he had only Soviet policies in mind and letting his indignation at these appear too openly for many on the Labour benches behind him.

[1] Bevin was speaking in the knowledge, not yet public, of the part which Dr Nunn May, a British scientist, had played in passing secret information to the Russians.

"We will take no steps, we will do nothing nor allow any of our agents or diplomats to do anything which will stir up hatred or provoke or create a situation detrimental to Russia in the Eastern countries . . .

But, taking up the Russian propaganda campaign against a Western European bloc, he declared that he was not prepared

"To accept the contention, so often blared from Moscow radio, that Russia claims the right to have friendly relations with her near neighbours; but that I am to be regarded as a criminal if I ask to be on good relations with nations bordering on the British frontier . . . What HM Government are willing to give, they claim the right to have, for their part, with France, with Holland, Belgium, Scandinavia or other countries —not a Western bloc for war purposes. They are our cultural friends; they are our historical associates; they acknowledge the same democracy as we do and therefore I say that I am entitled, on behalf of HM Government, to have good neighbours in my street just as any other country is . . . I am perhaps a little energetic about this, but I am a little resentful and I think the House will agree that I am entitled to be."

One side of the House, the Opposition, clearly did think he was entitled, and roared its approval, but Bevin's own side sat in disapproving silence. Nor were Labour members better pleased when the Foreign Secretary told the House that, like Churchill, he welcomed Truman's declaration of America's intention to play a world role, adding that he assumed the President meant what he said and that "our planning, our arrangements in economics and defence must be such that we are ready to stop aggression should the occasion arise".

Here was the same assumption as Churchill had made that war was a possibility not to be washed away by words or exorcized by appeals for disarmament. The need for conventional armaments, Bevin told those who wanted an end to conscription, had not been removed by the A-bomb.

"I hope that, as the UN Organisation grows, we shall succeed in cutting down military expenditure to a minimum, but not to such a point that it will make the UNO ineffective, in itself, to stop aggression . . ."

At the end of his speech Bevin came back to Russia and her interest in the Mediterranean and the Middle East.

"At Moscow, at Yalta and the rest of those conferences, no-one dreamt there would be further territorial demands. . . . I must say that having conceded all this and not having taken one inch of territory or asked for it, one cannot help being a little suspicious if a Great Power wants to come right across, shall I say, the throat of the British Commonwealth which has done no harm to anybody, but has fought this war. One is driven to ask oneself the motive; that is not unreasonable, and I think that we next get down to stopping this demand for transfer of territory and, within reason, make adjustments here and there."[1]

"It is not," the *Manchester Guardian*'s Political Correspondent reported, "the speech that many Labour members would have liked to hear" and the same paper's Parliamentary Correspondent added that they "felt chilled" by it.

[1] HC, 7 November, 1945.

"No one questions Mr Bevin's integrity but the education process which he seems to have begun would be more palatable but for 'those Tory cheers'."[1]

The "education process" was also a process of self-education. The day after the debate (8 November) Bevin drafted a memorandum to his Cabinet colleagues which bears every sign of having been dictated by Bevin himself and shows how far his ideas on the international situation had advanced since July and how far they had still to go. It is worth quoting as a fuller and more balanced expression of what he thought at this time than his speech in the Commons.[2]

"I should be willing," he wrote, "to pursue the policy of working in with the U.N. Organisation on the ground that it gives the best hope for the world, if the facts of the situation allowed us to do it. But my colleagues must be made aware of the situation that has arisen . . . Instead of world co-operation we are rapidly drifting into spheres of influence or what can be better described as three great Monroes."

What did he mean by this?

"The United States have long held, with our support, to the Monroe doctrine for the Western hemisphere, and there is no doubt now that, notwithstanding all the protestations, they are attempting to extend this principle financially and economically to the Far East to include China and Japan, while the Russians seem to me to have made up their minds that their sphere is going to be from Lübeck to the Adriatic in the west and to Port Arthur in the east. Britain therefore stands between the two with the Western world all divided up."

Admitting that the position of Franco was embarrassing, Bevin went on:

"If Spain was settled, the western area would be improved, and I do not believe that it is entirely love of democracy that causes Russia to want to keep the Spanish pot boiling. If this sphere of influence business does develop, it will leave us and France on the outer circle of Europe with our friends, such as Italy, Greece, Turkey, the Middle East, the Dominions, India and our colonial empire in Africa: a tremendous area to defend and a responsibility that, if it does develop, would make our position extremely difficult . . . The Continental side of this western empire would also be influenced and to a very large extent dominated by the colossal military power of Russia and by her political power which she can bring to bear through the Communist parties in the various countries. . . . The future too of the German people is going to be a constant source of insecurity and every sort of political trick will be resorted to in order to control or eliminate this eventual reservoir of power . . ."

Bevin pointed out that under the original Monroe doctrine both economic and political institutions afforded freedom of intercourse with the rest of the world, but under the new there was an attempt to incorporate the whole life of

---

[1] *Manchester Guardian*, 9 November 1945.
[2] Bevin's paper entitled "The Foreign Situation", did not appear on the Cabinet agenda and does not appear to have been given general circulation. It is to be found in Bevin's Papers, FO 800/478/MIS/45/14.

the communities concerned into the Russian economy. While the USA adhered to multilateralism in principle, they appeared to him, in practice, to be using their financial and economic power to establish similar preserves in the Far East and South America.

". . . It seems vital to me not to deceive the people of the world by leading them to believe that we are creating a United Nations Organisation which is to protect them from future wars, in which we share . . . our secrets . . ., while we know, in fact, that nothing of the kind is happening.

"There are at least two mighty countries in the world which, by the very nature of things, are following the present policy which is certain to see them line up against each other, while we in Great Britain who have had the brunt of two great wars will be left to take sides either with one or the other."

There are at least two points to make about this memorandum. First, it provides support for the hypothesis already advanced that Bevin's views on foreign policy were not something fixed, a set of prejudices which he brought with him into office or accepted ready-made from the Foreign Office, but that they developed over a period of time in response to his own experience as Foreign Secretary. The language in which the paper is written suggests that it was only reluctantly and with a mixture of frustration and indignation that he accepted the postponement of the hopes of the UN Organization and of the economic approach to international relations with which he had accepted office, and faced the consequences of a world divided between rival power blocs. The reason why, despite the criticism which he had to put up with from his own party, Bevin in the end rallied the great majority of Labour members to support of his policy was that this was arrived at by a process of self-education which, although it was, in Bevin's case, for a long time in advance of it, proceeded along parallel lines with that of the Party itself.

Second, it seems plain that Bevin in November 1945 had no clear idea of where to find an answer to the external problems with which he now realized the Government was faced. The United Nations (which had not yet been set up) plus the Commonwealth plus a vague reference to near neighbours did not add up to an answer: it only stated the scope of the problem. There were in fact only "two Monroes", the Russian and American spheres of influence. The third, the rim of the Eurasian land mass, stretching from Western Europe through the Mediterranean and the Middle East to India and S.E. Asia, might with difficulty be organized and defended, but hardly by Britain alone with her depleted resources. The missing piece, Churchill argued, was the United States. But, while Bevin and Churchill did not differ much in their view of Russian intentions, Bevin saw American policy in a less favourable light than Churchill. Lord Halifax, reading Bevin's paper in Washington, felt he was mis-judging the American attitude and wrote to say so.[1] Bevin's scepticism,

---

[1] Halifax to Bevin, 12 December 1945. FO 800/478/MIS/45/28.

however, was not easily dispelled. Apart from the harsh line the Americans had taken in the loan negotiations and the demand that Britain should accept the US view on trade policy, Bevin came out of the London Council of Foreign Ministers very distrustful of Byrnes. Circumstances had brought them together in common opposition to Molotov, but Bevin felt little confidence in Byrnes' grasp of policy or his reliability, regarding him as capable of reaching an agreement with the Russians on his own without taking others' interests into account and leaving the British to make the best of it. Nor did he take kindly to the pressure Byrnes had put on him over American bases.[1] Indeed "a plague on both their houses" aptly summed up his mood in the autumn of 1945 but left him still with no better answer to Britain's own problems than holding on in the hope that something would turn up before British resources ran out.

3

In fact, Attlee found a surprising measure of agreement with Truman during his visit to Washington. They agreed to give a lead in setting up a UN Commission on Atomic Energy—this was published—and they also agreed in principle on a working relationship between the two countries in further atomic development. This was not published, but Sir John Anderson and General Groves[2] drew up a joint directive to guide the Combined Anglo-US Policy Committee in preparing a new agreement. The British party returned believing that they had succeeded in reconciling their two objectives, securing Anglo-American (and Canadian) collaboration on equal terms in developing nuclear energy and at the same time making a start on its control by the United Nations. Only in the course of the next few months did it become clear that the hopes based upon both agreements were illusory.

The Press, knowing only of the agreement on the UN Commission, received the communiqué, as *The Economist* said, "with respect and some hope, but not with very much enthusiasm."[3] When the debate was resumed in the Commons, however, although the division of opinion over Russia was still evident, the mood of the House was different.[4] Clement Davies declared that, with agreement to take the initiative in handing over atomic power to an international body, even if by stages, a new era had begun. And R. A. Butler, winding up for the Opposition, summed up the general feeling when he said: "This has been a notable Debate and a great House of Commons occasion."

If so, it was certainly not the opening statement by Attlee which managed to make even the official communiqué sound more informative and inspiring. It

[1] See below, pp. 200–201.
[2] General Groves had been director of the Manhattan Project which produced the Atomic Bomb and continued after the war as director of the Los Alamos nuclear research centre.
[3] *The Economist*, 24 November 1945.
[4] For the debate see HC 23 November 1945.

was Eden who brought the debate to life, winning as much applause from the Labour side as Bevin a fortnight before had from the Tories.[1] Eden welcomed "the new departure" in the Washington talks: since the proposed UN Commission would have to proceed by stages, there was all the more reason to make a start immediately and call a special meeting of UNO and set up the Commission. In a striking passage, he went on to say:

"For the life of me, I am still unable to see any final solution which will make the world safe for atomic power, save that we all abate our present ideas of sovereignty. . . . We should make up our minds where we want to go. I know where I want to go. I want to get a world in which the relations between the nations can be transformed in a given period of time as the relations between this country and Scotland and Wales have been transformed."

As a first step to reducing the power of nationalism, Eden suggested that the charter of the United Nations, which was drawn up before the world knew about nuclear power, should be revised to exclude the "anachronism" of the veto.

The former Foreign Secretary was far more successful than Bevin had been on the 7th in hitting on the right tone to carry moderate opinion with him in discussing Britain's relations with the Soviet Union. He did not disguise the difficulties, but he spoke about them as if they could be removed and he appealed persuasively to Bevin, despite his disappointment at the failure of the London CFM to persevere in his efforts to bring about another meeting.

When his turn came to reply to the debate, Bevin began by repeating the phrase "cards on the table" but made it clear that his purpose was to remove suspicion, and promised that he would "not in any way decline to have anything Britain does or wants or seeks to promote, discussed in open assembly, at the United Nations if necessary". He dealt one after another with the matters in dispute. "I am sorry to be so long," he remarked half-way through, "I cannot help it. All the world is in trouble and I have to deal with all the troubles at once." When he came to Greece he announced the formation of the new government as a result of Hector McNeil's efforts and energetically rebutted Churchill's accusation of bad faith in the postponement of the plebiscite on the return of the King. An altercation with Churchill always improved Bevin's standing with his own Party. Labour members were delighted when he overrode the interruptions and named the King and the monarchist politicians as the source of much of the trouble, calling on them to stop putting spokes in the wheel and instead help Greece to achieve sufficient stability for a vote to be taken on the basis of "judgement and not prejudice and starvation". He was equally forthright in rejecting attacks on Britain's

---

[1] Cf. *The Economist*, 1 December: "It seems that the foreign policy of the Opposition as represented by Mr. Eden, is more acceptable to Labour back benchers than the foreign policy of the Government which, as represented by Mr. Bevin, pleases the Conservatives."

intentions in Indonesia, where British troops, he pointed out, had been sent by the Allied command to disarm the Japanese and release their prisoners. If they had become involved in political disputes, it was through no fault of theirs. The sooner they could get the Dutch and the Indonesians to reach agreement and let them withdraw, the better the British Government would be pleased.

All this, however, would hardly be worth recalling if it were not that in a long final passage of his speech Bevin took up the lead on "the abatement of sovereignty" that Eden had given the day before. No longer speaking to an official brief, and so becoming both more interesting and more obscure, the Foreign Secretary argued, from a number of historical examples of federation, that "no-one ever surrenders sovereignty; they merge it into a greater sovereignty". He recalled that in 1927 he had persuaded the TUC to pass a resolution in favour of a United States of Europe, a great free trade area which, if it had been established, might have saved the Weimar Republic by removing tariff barriers and allowing trade to flow freely throughout Europe. Welcoming the revival of such "regional" ideas, probably on a wider scale than could be visualized in 1927, he added: "I cannot see a single frontier in Europe today that is economically sound."

Bevin, however, wanted to go a great deal further:

"I feel we are driven relentlessly along this road: we need a new study for the purpose of creating a world assembly elected directly from the peoples of the world, as a whole, to whom the Goverments who form the United Nations are responsible and who, in fact, make the world law which they, the people, will then accept and be morally bound and willing to carry out."

Two sentences later there is a further passage that suggests what Bevin had in mind when he made this surprising (and far from clear) statement.

"You may invent all sorts of devices," he said, "to decide who is the aggressor but the only repository of faith I have been able to find to determine that is the common people. There has never been a war yet which, if the facts had been put calmly before the ordinary folk, could not have been prevented."

As his final word, Bevin told the House with great earnestness:

"I am willing to sit with anybody, of any party, of any nation, to try to devise a franchise or a constitution for a world assembly, with a limited objective, the objective of peace." From that moment international law would be replaced by world law. "It would be a world law with a world judiciary to interpret it, with a world police to enforce it, with the decision of the people with their own ideas resting in their own hands, irrespective of race or creed, as the great world-sovereign elected authority."

There was no doubt of Bevin's success. When he sat down, it was for the first time to loud applause from his own side of the House as well as from the Tories. "We regard him," Butler said, "as a diamond lying on a vast heap of coke. He sparkles and brightens in front of his contemporaries. He has never been brighter or more sparkling than today." For once, however, Tory praise did not prevent Labour members from saying that Bevin had at last given promise of the Government "applying a socialist mind" to foreign policy. The fact that both Eden and Bevin, neither of them a visionary, should have spoken seriously of the abatement of sovereignty and a world assembly going much further than the San Francisco charter of the UN illustrates the anguished atmosphere of the time in which experienced politicians felt that the A-bomb faced them with problems to which nothing in the conventional wisdom could provide an answer. Bevin had appeared to ignore this feeling in his earlier speech; his recognition of it now, coming on top of the Washington agreement, restored Labour confidence in the Government's policy.

It would be a mistake, however, to treat Bevin's references to world government as simply trimming his sails to the party wind. He refused to be discouraged by the cold water which the more sceptical commentators poured on his remarks. The week after he had spoken in the House of Commons, he told the Delegates to the UN Preparatory Commission,[1] "Science has developed to such a point that it has made boundaries look silly." Quoting Tennyson's phrase "the parliament of man and Federation of the world", he declared:

"I have faith enough to believe that, if I live a reasonable length of time, I shall see it. I have a profound faith in the common man of the world. Somehow, I have always felt that he has more sense than I have and more judgement."

He went on to make the best known and most endearing of his remarks as Foreign Secretary, an echo of the days when he had been one of the founders of the Workers' Travel Association:

"His common interest is to live, to have a good standard of life, to be free to travel, free to exchange and to know the other peoples of the world. That is the great future of the common man. Somebody once asked me when I became Foreign Secretary, what my policy really was. I said I have only one: it is to go down to Victora Station here, take a ticket and go where the hell I like without anybody pulling me up with a passport."

To dismiss this side of Bevin and to treat his views on foreign policy, as both the Tories and the Left (for very different reasons) were eager to do, as no more than a working class copy of Churchill's is to ignore the strands in his thinking which bound him to the Labour Movement and which enabled him in the end to bring round the majority in the Party to accept his views as their own.

Whatever their opinions on world government, there was one practical step on which everyone agreed, the need for another meeting with the Russians,

[1] 29 November, 1945.

and there was general approval when it was announced that Bevin and Byrnes would meet Molotov in Moscow before Christmas. Approval from everyone except the Foreign Secretary himself, who was furious.

The proposal had started with Byrnes who, by his own account, acted impulsively in telegraphing immediately to Moscow. The first Bevin heard of it was in a message sent back by the British Ambassador in Russia on 24 November.[1] Harriman, the US Ambassador, had shown him the text of Byrnes' message sent to Molotov the day before. Molotov, the American added, "beamed with pleasure" when he learned what it contained.

The failure to consult, whether it was deliberate or an oversight, strongly suggested that the American Secretary of State did not attach much importance to British agreement. There was no opportunity for preparation in advance of the meeting, or for discussion between the Americans and the British of where they stood on the main issues left over in dispute from the London Council of Foreign Ministers. Byrnes seemed to think that reaching agreement with the Russians could be handled in the same informal way as fixing up a deal in the Senate.

Bevin's view was that the Russians had over-reached themselves at London, had been taken aback by the break up of the conference and were looking for a way to re-start negotiations. The right tactics, he believed, were to leave the Russians alone and wait until they realized that they would have to retreat from the position they had adopted if they wanted the Council of Foreign Ministers to meet again. Now, in a single ill-considered gesture, Byrnes had thrown away all the tactical advantage and put the Russians back in the game on favourable terms: no wonder Molotov had "beamed with pleasure".

Despite the maladroit way in which Byrnes had behaved, the advice of the British Ambassadors in both Washington and Moscow was in favour of Bevin agreeing to join Byrnes and Molotov.[2] If he refused to attend, this would only strengthen the impression that it was the British, and Bevin in particular, who were dragging their feet. Both agreed with the American view that the first meeting of the UN in January was unlikely to be a success without preliminary discussion; Clark-Kerr was even doubtful whether Molotov would come at all if he was disappointed by the Moscow meeting on which he had set "his malevolent heart".[3] On 3 December Clark-Kerr sent another long and eloquent telegram from Moscow in which he set out the Russian point of view, their obsession with security ever since the Revolution; their belief that the rest of the world was against them; the immense relief they felt when the Germans were driven back; the shock of discovering that the old nightmare of insecurity was still there with the West's invention of the A-bomb; the disappointment of

---

[1] Clark-Kerr to Bevin. FO 800/446/CONF/45/4.
[2] The correspondence between Halifax, Clark-Kerr and Bevin is to be found in FO 800/446/CONF/45/4; 9; 12; 21; 22; 50 and FO 800/501/SU/45/39A; 40; 41C; 64; 74.
[3] Clark-Kerr to Bevin, 29 November 1945. FO 800/446/45/12.

their hopes that the secret would be shared with them; the humiliation to their pride and the revival of all their distrust of the West when it was not.[1]

Molotov had already agreed to Byrnes' proposal and on 5 December Byrnes told the British Ambassador that he could not go on waiting for a reply from Bevin. He wanted the British to come to Moscow, but if necessary he would go alone. The same day Bevin discussed with Sir Orme Sargent the possibility of letting Byrnes go ahead on his own. They recognized that the British would be under strong pressure to agree to whatever was decided at Moscow, whether they were present or not. Nor could they ignore the strong desire in Britain to see contact with Moscow renewed and the Russians brought into discussion of the control of atomic energy. However reluctantly, Bevin concluded that he would have to go.

On 8 December Clark-Kerr reported that Molotov was already proposing to alter the agenda, asking that the Americans' first item, control of atomic energy, should be put at the end of the business and that the withdrawl of US troops from China and of British troops from Greece should be added. This was enough to confirm all Bevin's suspicions, but he left it to Byrnes to settle the agenda with Molotov. The announcement of the visit was welcomed in the House by Churchill, and by all sections of political opinion which in the general mood of anxiety continued to believe that, if only discussions were resumed, some good must come of them.

4

There was another issue on which Byrnes continued to press Bevin, that of overseas bases. Bevin had refused to discuss the matter until he could see a full list of what the USA wanted and this Byrnes sent him in a letter of 7 November 1945.

Apart from bases in Iceland and the Portuguese Azores and Cape Verde Islands, Byrnes' memorandum[2] contained two lists: one of some twenty-five Pacific islands or island groups, sovereignty over which had long been disputed between the USA and the UK[3], and the other a list of ten island bases wholly or jointly under British control on which the USA had spent considerable sums and which they wished to retain.[4] The British were asked to cede the

---

[1] FO 800/501/SU/45/41C. From a reference in an earlier telegram (24 Nov, FO 800/446/CONF/45/4) to a talk with Litvinov, it is possible that Clark-Kerr was repeating the views which the former Russian Foreign Minister had expressed.

[2] Byrnes' memorandum, dated 7 November, was forwarded by Halifax on 8 November 1945. FO 800/512/US/45/98. A further letter from Byrnes, dated 19 November, dealt with the bases in the Azores and Cape Verde Islands. FO 800/512/US/45/19.

[3] Amongst these were the Caroline Islands, Christmas Island and the Phoenix group.

[4] These included Ascension Island; Espiritu Santo, a naval and air base on which the USA had already spent 61M. dollars; Guadalcanal-Tulagi: and Manus, Australian mandated territory where the USA claimed to have spent nearly 150M. dollars. Two islands, Christmas Island and Funafuti appeared in both lists.

territories in the first list and either to give or use their good offices to obtain permission for the USA to go on using the bases on the second.

Halifax had already reported on the good effect which an agreement on bases would have on American opinion and on the negotiations for the loan. He wrote to Bevin that he would have liked an overall Anglo-American agreement covering the loan, commercial agreements, bases, civil aviation, oil and telecommunications.[1] This was not an argument that made any appeal to Bevin. He was particularly suspicious of the American airlines which were putting pressure on the US Government to extract commercial concessions from the British in return for the loan, and he looked at any request for an air base as much with an eye to the advantages for the Americans in developing civil aviation as to defence. He sent Byrnes' memorandum to Churchill and Eden as well as Attlee and asked for their comments.

Churchill's were illuminating. Addressing Bevin as "Dear Ernest", he wrote that the great object of policy should be to intertwine the affairs of the Commonwealth and the USA to such an extent that any idea of conflict between them was unthinkable. The more strategic points held in joint occupation, the better: joint occupation was the key and could help to strengthen the case for retaining the Combined Chiefs of Staff and the close association between the British and American Services. Uninterested in the United Nations, he put everything on creating a special relationship between the United Kingdom and the USA, arguing a little ingenuously that this was the best way to strengthen the UNO and to get friendship with the Soviet Union.[2]

Bevin did not turn down the American proposals, but in his reply to Byrnes argued that they could not ignore the UN Organization they were setting up or the views of the Dominions. He was attracted by Churchill's idea of *joint* bases but urged that it was essential to frame the proposals in such a way that they could be brought under the operation of Article 48 of the UN Charter, and the two Governments not be accused of sharp practice towards the UN and confronting it with a *fait accompli*. Australia and New Zealand would have to be brought into a discussion so far as the Pacific was concerned and Bevin added two further questions: Was the USA asking anything similar from the Dutch and the French? And how much were air bases wanted for civil aviation, how much for military purposes?[3]

In May 1946 Byrnes and Bevin were still discussing their differences, news of which had by then leaked out, fortunately without creating a crisis. Very different was the explosion which followed publication of the American Loan Agreement. The terms to which the British Government had finally agreed were published immediately after signature of the agreement on 6 December.

---

[1] Halifax to Bevin, 10 October 1945. FO 800/512/US/45/43.
[2] Churchill to Bevin, 13 November 1945, *ibid.*, US/45/110.
[3] Bevin to Halifax, 15 November 1945, *ibid.*, US/45/114.

They fell into two parts. The first, the Financial Agreement proper, provided for a generous settlement of the Lend-Lease Agreement, on payment of $620M. by the British, and a dollar loan of $3,750 million to be repaid over fifty years at 2 per cent. The second and much more controversial part was a commitment to establishing a multilateral system of international trade, by ratifying the Bretton Woods Agreement on an international bank and monetary fund and by the adoption of joint proposals for an international trade conference including negotiations for the elimination of preferences and the reduction of tariffs. Publication at once let loose a storm of criticism showing the wide gap which separated opinion in the two countries.[1]

In the United States, public opinion pools recorded less interest in foreign problems in the autumn of 1945 than at any other time in the past ten years[2] and a pre-occupation with domestic issues hostile to any proposal for further loans abroad. The war was over and Americans recognized no continuing obligation to help the British get back on their feet again. To traditional American dislike of the Empire and the hostility of American business to the barriers represented by imperial preference and the sterling area, were now added strong disapproval of a socialist government and of that government's refusal to admit more Jews to Palestine. Why should Americans provide a loan that, as one leading member of the House of Representatives put it, would be used to "promote too damned much Socialism at home and too much damned Imperialism abroad"?[3] Those who were more internationally-minded put their faith in the United Nations which they regarded as likely to be compromised by too close an association between the USA and a Britain still clearly suspected of practising power politics.

On the British side there was resentment, on the morrow of victory, at having to go cap in hand to the Americans for a loan at all. "In the country there is a feeling," The *Sunday Times* wrote, "that as victors we are being asked to pay reparations."[4] Convinced that the Americans had fought the war at much less cost than themselves, the British took the settlement of Lend-Lease, which the Americans regarded as an act of unprecedented generoisity, as the least that equality of sacrifice required. To begin with, the British government had thought the same principle justified their expectation of an outright grant and not a loan at all. When this had to be abandoned, there was still hope that the money would be made available without any charge other than simple repayment and Keynes, defending the agreement in the House of Lords, was moved to declare: "I shall never, so long as I live, cease to regret that this is not an interest-free loan." *The Economist*, hardly extremist in its views, wrote that "it would be hard to find an Englishman who did not think that advantage had been taken of his country's honourable extremity to drive a very bad

---

[1] For a full discussion of the background to the Loan and the debate, see Gardner, Part III.
[2] Or in the five succeeding years. See the table printed in Gardner, p. 192.
[3] Emmanuel Celler, quoted in the *Daily Mail*, 7 December 1945. (Gardner, p. 237).
[4] 16 December, 1945.

bargain,"[1] and a week later in an article headed "Second Thoughts" concluded:

"It is aggravating to find that our reward for losing a quarter of our national wealth in the common cause is to pay tribute for half a century to those who have been enriched by the war . . . Beggars cannot be choosers. But they can by long tradition, put a curse on the ambitions of the rich."[2]

These were views expressed by newspapers and politicians of all shades of opinion from Robert Boothby, who called the Agreement "an economic Munich", to Jennie Lee, Aneurin Bevan's wife, who told the House of Commons: "There is no wisdom in this loan, and there is no kindness in it", and went on to describe the settlement as "niggardly, barbaric and antediluvian".[3] The terms of the loan in effect touched off an outburst of anti-American feeling, accumulating but held in check during the war, and now reinforced by British resentment at finding themselves forced to take second place to the United States as the leading power of the Western world.[4]

Those who could follow the technicalities, however, were much less concerned with the terms of repayment than with the conditions the American negotiators had sought to impose—in general the commitment to a system of multilateral trading premised upon the removal, as soon as possible, of such "obstacles to trade" as the sterling area and imperial preferences,[5] and in particular the requirement to make sterling convertible within a year of the Loan Agreement being signed.

The Americans saw British acceptance of these commitments as essential to their hopes of re-making the international economy on an American pattern and took advantage of the situation in which the British found themselves to pin them down in advance of Congress's decision whether to endorse the loan or not. Resentment at these tactics brought together on the British side both Conservatives, who saw in it a threat to British industry in face of American competition and to the system of imperial preferences, and the Left, who saw in it a threat to full employment, the welfare state and the power of a Labour government to manage the country's economy on socialist lines. Moderate

---

[1] *The Economist*, 8 December 1945.

[2] *Ibid.* 15 December 1945.

[3] Quoted by Gardner, p. 226.

[4] See Leon D. Epstein: *Britain, Uneasy Ally* (Chicago, 1954) for an analysis of the different elements in British criticism of the USA, ranging from dislike of American materialism ("money talks") the "vulgarity" of American mass culture and the "immaturity" and "irresponsibility" of American politics to an ill-concealed envy of American power and prosperity, the Left's hostility to the United States as the bastion of capitalism and fears of an American recession producing another world depression.

[5] L. S. Amery, a former Conservative Minister, wrote: "The British Empire is the oyster which this loan is to prise open . . . to become a field for American industrial exploitation, a tributary of American finance and in the end an American dependency." *The Washington Loan Agreements* (London 1946) quoted by Gardner, p. 279.

opinion did not object to multilateralism in principle, but it did object strongly to the way in which the Americans deliberately exploited Britain's need to enforce their own version of it, complete with time limits which took too little account of Britain's post-war difficulties. These were conditions which as the Oxford economist, Sir Hubert Henderson, wrote to *The Times* (12 Dec.) were "calculated to ensure default", a view which *The Economist* endorsed with the remark that "it is very difficult to understand how any man in his senses can think that the obligations now to be assumed can possibly be assumed".[1] This view was to be fully borne out by events. The *Manchester Guardian* protested at the American attempt to dictate how Britain was to conduct her economic relations with the Empire and the world at large; Churchill described the obligation to make sterling convertible within a year of the Agreement being signed as "too base to be true" and Lord Woolton, another Conservative leader, spoke of "dollar blackmail".

The debate in the House (12–13 December) came on less than a week after the Tories had made an ill-judged attempt to carry a vote of censure on the Government's domestic programme of nationalization. The Government defeated this without difficulty but they were much less at ease in presenting the financial agreement with America, with no more than three weeks to go before the time limit for British ratification of Bretton Woods ran out. The most Dalton and Cripps could find to say was that the country had no choice; it could not manage without the loan and had no alternative but to accept the conditions. The Conservatives were even more divided than the Labour Party. Churchill, who maintained without much conviction that he would have got better terms, urged his party to abstain but could not prevent a substantial minority voting against. No front bench speaker on either side came within a mile of Keynes' defence of the agreement in the Lords and it was left to back benchers (and the Liberals) to point out the genuine opportunities for expansion offered by Bretton Woods.

Bevin wound up for the Government on the second day and did his best to put some life into his defence by provoking party feeling. Nobody ever liked going to a moneylender, he told the Tory front bench, but it was twice as hard when you had been a moneylender yourself for so long.

"I know the feeling when you cannot feel that you are top dog any longer. . . . For 20 years you were on top and the blow which you received must have been terrific. But I feel myself tonight more in the position that I have been in so many times in my career. . . . I had to face thousands of members of this country with cuts in wages and I had to do it because of the action of the Rt. Hon. gentleman [Churchill] and his friends. Circumstances were too much for me. I say that when national circumstances are too great for the Government to avoid facing this issue . . . there must be no failure to take a decision. The decision is the thing."

---

[1] *The Economist*, 15 December 1945.

Bevin would have nothing to do with the argument that the effect of accepting the Bretton Woods Agreement would be the same as a return to the gold standard. He pointed out with relish that it had been Churchill who restored the gold standard in 1925, with disastrous results for the wages of "my members". Robert Boothby interrupted: "And now you are going back to it."

"No," Bevin retorted, "not even half-way. If this thing is used as the gold standard was used, then both America and ourselves will land ourselves into a revolutionary position. I am satisfied that under the rules which have been laid down, the situation in which we found ourselves then need never recur. . . . I feel that this is not the gold standard."

Bevin argued that to have cleared up Lend-Lease, war debts and all the arguments these could have led to, for the price of $650 million, was a great gain. The cost of the loan was negligible; what mattered was the willingness or not of the Americans to put their own belief in free trade into practice by allowing their debtors to work off their debts by selling goods freely in the American market. "It has been said that, inevitably, this will lead to another repudiation. That is in the hands of the US and nobody else."

With the aid of a three-line whip to keep its rebels in line, the Government got a majority of 343 to 200, with 169 abstaining. It was enough, and Keynes' speech in the Lords a few days later not only ended talk of a Tory revolt but helped to swing informed opinion to a more favourable view of the American terms.[1] None the less, as Bevin set out on the long journey to Moscow his feelings about the United States were mixed. He had no doubt that Britain needed American support to get through the period of post-war recovery, but no-one could say it was proving an easy relationship. After the abrupt end of Lend-Lease had come the shock of the American conditions for a new loan; after the pressure to accept Zionist demands in Palestine, Byrnes's unilateral approach to Molotov which was now taking him against his better judgement to the Russian capital. The American attitude was summed up by the remarks of the US Ambassador, Harriman, to his Embassy staff in Moscow after returning from London. The Labour Government, he told them, "could ill afford an independent foreign policy in spite of Bevin's distaste for Byrnes and his high-handed measures." Having mortgaged her future to pay for the war, Britain was on the edge of bankruptcy. "England is so weak she must follow our leadership. She will do anything that we insist upon and she won't go out on a limb alone."[2]

---

[1] Cf. the results of the Gallup poll (February 1946) quoted in Gardner, p. 235 footnote 5. This showed that, out of 72% who said they had been following the debate, 50% approved acceptance, 17% opposed and 5% were undecided.
[2] Harriman and Abel, p. 531.

Despite his misgivings, the result of the Loan debate—and particularly his own exchanges with Churchill—put Bevin in better spirits which survived a two-days' wintry journey by air. His chief anxiety was that Byrnes had so far engaged his reputation that he could not return home without some sort of agreement and that in practice this would mean, as Dixon put it in his journal, that "The Russians will gain, we shall gain nothing and the Americans will give away our interests to the Russians for the sake of a settlement."[1] When he met Byrnes, therefore (17 December), Bevin went out of his way to lay stress on the importance of the area south of Russia (Greece, Turkey, Persia) where the British were most worried about Russian intentions and where the Americans seemed least ready to give their support.[2] Byrnes was unresponsive. George Kennan, then Minister-Counsellor at the US Embassy, saw the Secretary of State's main purpose as reaching an agreement with the Russians.

"He doesn't much care what. The realities behind this agreement, since they concern only such problems as Koreans, Rumanians, and Iranians, about whom he knows nothing, do not concern him."[3]

Byrnes saw the evacuation of Russian troops from Iran as an issue which might hold up agreement and so proposed that it be dropped from the agenda and discussed informally. He raised it at both his meetings with Stalin, but did not press the matter and left Bevin to make the best he could of it on his own.

Kennan had no doubt that the Russians were aware of the awkward position in which Bevin found himself "and were squeezing the last drop of profit out of it". Describing the session which he attended, Kennan wrote in his journal the same evening:

"Molotov, conducting the meeting, sat leaning forwards at the table, a Russian cigarette dangling from his mouth, his eyes flashing with satisfaction and confidence as he glanced from one to the other of the other foreign ministers, obviously keenly aware of their mutual differences and their common uncertainty. . . . He had the look of a passionate poker player who knows that he has a royal flush and is about to call the last of his opponents."[4]

Bevin's objective was different from Byrnes'. He too wanted an agreement, but only if it was based on a frank discussion with the Russians of the differences between the two countries and if it provided a firm basis for their relationship, something more than a package deal put together by a process of piecemeal bargaining. At this first attempt, in an informal meeting with

---

[1] Piers Dixon, p. 199. His father, Pierson Dixon, was secretary of the British delegation and the phrase is taken from the latter's diary, 7 December 1945.
[2] British record of the Moscow conference, CAB 133/82; US record FRUS 1945 (2) pp. 610–808.
[3] George F. Kennan: *Memoirs 1925–50* (London 1968) p. 287.
[4] *Ibid.*, pp. 286–7, 19 December 1945.

Molotov on the 18th, he was no more successful than he had been in London.[1] Why, he asked Molotov, had he insisted on raising the question of Greece which at London had been left to the British? The answer, both the British and Americans privately believed, was because they had raised the question of the Russian troops in Iran; but this sort of "tit for tat" seemed childish to Bevin. Why could they not get down to a discussion of the real issue, the general withdrawal of occupation forces by both the British and the Russians, instead of a repetition of formal accusations which led nowhere? Molotov refused to depart from the Russian official line. The Russian position in the countries they occupied was wholly different from that of the British in Greece or Indonesia; the Russians had every justification for maintaining forces of occupation, the British none; the Red Army in no way hampered the free expression of popular opinion, the British Army was preventing it. The only reply Molotov gave to Bevin's request for frankness was the remark that the British did not take Soviet interests into account, for instance in states bordering on the Soviet Union such as Rumania—a return to the diplomatic trading from which Bevin was trying to break away.

If Molotov was bound by his instructions, Bevin hoped he might have better luck with Stalin when he visited him in the Kremlin on the evening of the 19th.[2] He decided that the best way was to start straightaway with the most recent cause of friction, the delay in Russia's withdrawal from Iran. Stalin's claim that Russia was afraid of an Iranian threat of sabotage to her Baku oilfields seemed to Bevin no more to be taken seriously than it had to Byrnes. So he went on to say that there was a feeling in Britain that the Soviet Government was thinking of the incorporation of Azerbaijan into Russia. Nothing could be further from his mind, Stalin replied, "but he must safeguard the oil of Baku against diversionary activities". Bevin had more success when he turned to Turkey. At least Stalin was quite ready to avow his desire to secure a permanent base in the Straits to prevent the Turks from being able to cut off Russian access to and from the Mediterranean, and to secure the return of those Turkish territories (Kars and Ardahan) inhabited by Georgians and Armenians.

"It was agreed," Bevin reported to Attlee, "that the question could not be settled at the present conference, but I expressed the hope that Turkey need not continue her present state of mobilisation, which was due to her fear of the Soviet Union. Stalin said she had no need to be frightened."[3]

---

[1] British record, pp. 44–51.

[2] British record, pp. 116–19. Bevin sent a personal report in a letter to Attlee dated 21 December 1945. FO/800/507/SU/45/7.

[3] In fact, the Soviet press campaign against Turkey was stepped up the next day when *Pravda*, *Izvestia* and *Red Star* all reprinted an article by two members of the Georgian Science Academy in which they demanded a strip of northeastern Turkey, 180 by 75 miles in extent.

After discussing the inclusion of India in any peace conference (the Russians had objected that she was not a sovereign state and wanted compensation in the form of an invitation to the Baltic States), Bevin reported the conclusion of his talk:

"I would always do my best to remove every difficulty arising between the two Governments and if Stalin thought we were taking a line that might cause difficulty I hoped he would let me know at once. Stalin said that that followed the terms of the Anglo-Soviet Treaty to which I replied that I wanted to go beyond its terms and to implement it in the spirit. I personally should be quite ready to extend its duration for 20 to 50 years. If the three Governments could keep the spirit of Treaties it would be a long time before another war occurred. . . .

"Before leaving I said that I wished to raise one other question, namely the Western Bloc. I explained that we must have some arrangement with France and other neighbouring countries like that which Russia had with her neighbours. But I would do nothing against the Soviet Government and would always keep the Generalissimo informed. Stalin said 'I believe you'."[1]

Dixon reported that Bevin returned from the Kremlin "in high fettle" and even the Foreign Office professionals felt that the Conference was making some progress in a better atmosphere than had prevailed in London. But in the formal sessions it was still progress on a US–Soviet agenda, which failed to cover many of the points to which the British attached most importance, and Molotov's attitude very clearly distinguished between a willingness, admittedly after a prolonged process of bargaining, to reach a settlement with the Americans and a desire to miss no opportunity of scoring off Bevin. An example was a Russian memorandum on Germany which Molotov tabled without notice and which led off with a bitter attack on the British for maintaining powerful German military units in their zone of occupation.[2] When Bevin had had time to read it, he reacted angrily:

"It was ridiculous to assume that Great Britain, which had fought two bloody wars against Germany for its national existence, would have any ulterior desire to retain intact any German military units. . . . Great Britain was beginning to get the feeling that they were constantly being put in the dock by other nations and the people of England were beginning to resent it."

If the Russians were serious in their accusations (which he plainly doubted) then he proposed the appointment of a joint commission with power to investigate the situation in all the zones, the Russian included.[3] The next day, Molotov blandly announced that he had received a further report from Marshal Zhukov which made it plain that there was no substance in the reports: there was consequently no need to set up a joint commission. This did not prevent him from making similar accusations against the British in Austria

---

[1] Bevin to Attlee, 21 December. FO 800/507/SU/45/7.
[2] Plenary Session, 20 December 1945. British record, pp. 57–62. US record FRUS pp. 692–705.
[3] Informal session 21 December. British record, pp. 62–9. US record FRUS pp. 710–19.

which Bevin angrily refuted, again with the offer of a joint commission, and the remark that he was tired of having unfounded charges thrown against the British Government which did nothing to help good relations.[1]

The conference lasted eleven days in all, with meetings every day including Christmas Day and often late into the evening. Even when the foreign ministers attended the Bolshoi Ballet, it was an official occasion and they took their seats in a box with Molotov. At the end of the performance, they applauded, only to find that when the curtain went up, the dancers came forward to applaud them. This went on for some time. "I could see no future in it", Bevin told Peter Ustinov, "I didn't know who was applauding who." (The story lost nothing when retold by Ustinov). "So I got up and behind Molotov's back I gave them the clenched fist salute. That brought the house down, but I got a rocket from Clem when I got back."

Bevin's only break came on the afternoon of the 23rd when he slipped off to see the aged Alexandra Kollontai, one of the Old Bolsheviks of Lenin's generation now living in retirement. He recounted his visit in a letter to Margaret Bondfield describing her as "very old and ill and a wonderful woman. All the old conferences and figures of the Socialist Movement came under review and our talk was tremendously interesting.".[2] When he got back to the Embassy after a diplomatic reception by the French he was still in a reminiscent mood, put on his slippers and dressing gown and was still telling music-hall stories when Pierson Dixon slipped away to bed.[3]

The next day (24th) he had his second talk with Stalin before the ceremonial dinner at the Kremlin.[4] Bevin was in a determined mood and wasted no time on preliminaries. He told Stalin bluntly that, while the British government recognized the Soviet Union's right to defend Baku, they felt the situation did not justify the Russians maintaining so large a force in Northern Iran. British troops had been reduced to no more than a thousand and were held at some distance from the capital. It would be unfortunate if the Iranians took the question to the United Nations at its first meeting, and the British Government did not wish it to interfere with Anglo-Soviet relations. He had therefore submitted a proposal for a three-power commission to go to Iran and assist the Iranians in setting up provincial councils under their 1921 Constitution. This would help to meet whatever claims the people of Azerbaijan might have to a greater measure of autonomy and lead to closer co-operation between the Powers in dealing with Iranian affairs. Bevin had already made this suggestion at their earlier meeting on the 20th, but Stalin would only say that the proposal might serve as a basis for agreement. He would communicate any amendments he might wish to make and hoped they could find common ground.

[1] Plenary Session, 22 December. British record, pp. 69–74; FRUS pp. 727–34.
[2] Ernest Bevin to Margaret Bondfield, 24 December 1945. FO 800/501/SU/45/78.
[3] Dixon, p. 202.
[4] British record, pp. 124–7. Bevin again made a personal report to Attlee, dated 26 December. FO 800/489/PER/45/2.

Bevin then turned to the Balkans: the British would like to see the restoration of the Danube Commission. Stalin said he would look into the question. The Bulgarian reparations to Greece? All they had done so far, Bevin said, was to hand over a number of old horses and he hoped that Stalin would see the Bulgarians met their obligations. Certainly, Stalin replied, Bulgaria was under an obligation and the Three Powers must see they carried it out. Then Rumania: the negotiations agreed to at Potsdam on the pre-war British oil installations had come to a standstill. Stalin promised they would be resumed now that a new Russian representative had been appointed. Still pressing, Bevin asked why a direct air link could not be established between London and Moscow served by both countries' aircraft: it was a rule that only Soviet planes could fly over Russian territory and this was a matter of principle.

Evidently irritated by Bevin's direct tactics, Stalin began to ask questions in his turn. The first caused Bevin no embarrassment. When the Russians asked whether the Skagerrak and the entrance to the Baltic were open and Soviet shipping entitled to free passage, he answered without hesitation, "Absolutely". But the second touched on a more sensitive area. The Soviet Government, Stalin remarked, had been offended by the attitude of the British and Americans on Tripolitania. The United States and the United Kingdom had bases all over the world. Why should not the interests of the Soviet Union be taken into account?

Bevin turned the question by saying that the British had been ready to put Tripolitania under Italian trusteeship, but when this raised difficulties, they had been prepared to agree to a Four-Power arrangement. International arrangements of this sort were best for peace in the Mediterranean.

Stalin was not to be put off. He noted, he said, that the British were not prepared to trust the Soviets in Tripolitania.

Bevin: It was not lack of trust, but a desire to avoid competition.
Stalin: The United Kingdom had India and the Indian Ocean in her sphere of interest; the United States, China and Japan; the U.S.S.R. had nothing.

Bevin retorted that the Soviet sphere of influence extended from Lübeck to Port Arthur. In any case, he added, British troops were already due to leave Indo-China and, if the Dutch and Indonesians could agree, would withdraw from Indonesia too. British intentions were not so reprehensible as Stalin might think.

Stalin adroitly brought the conversation to a more friendly end by saying that he was not particularly anxious to see the British leave certain territories: it might be to the disadvantage of everyone. It had been a great advantage to have them in Egypt during the war.

While Stalin and Bevin were finishing their talk, the other guests were

already gathering in the Kremlin. It was an unusual way to spend Christmas
Eve. The banquet was held in an 18th-century salon, with green malachite
columns, white walls and gilt decoration. Stalin, in his Marshal's uniform, and
looking restored after a holiday in the Crimea, had Bevin on his left and Byrnes
on his right. The ceremonial, Dixon noted,[1] was impressive and entirely
Imperial in character. After dinner, Stalin took his guests into his private
cinema for the showing of a Russian film about the war with Japan. In true
patriotic style this showed the Russians playing the decisive part in Japan's
defeat, with the Americans in a secondary role and the British nowhere. It was
Byrnes' turn to be offended and he left rather stiffly at midnight, refusing
Stalin's invitation to see another film. Bevin was amused. "You know,
Jimmy," he said to Byrnes as they walked to their cars, "it reminds me of your
American film about the war in Burma: all the fighting was done by Errol
Flynn and the US Army, without an Englishman in sight."

Bevin had left Stalin in good hopes that his Iranian proposal would go
through. On the afternoon of the 25th Molotov told Byrnes that it was
acceptable; then 24 hours later abruptly reversed his position, insisting that
Iran had been removed from the agenda at Byrnes' suggestion and that
Bevin's proposal could not be considered.[2] Byrnes said nothing. Molotov
made no attempt to meet Bevin's argument that, if they did not do something,
there was bound to be trouble for all of them over Iran, and when Bevin in a
private conversation pressed him for an explanation of the Soviet change of
front, the supercilious tone of his replies leaves the impression that he was not
interested in what Bevin had to say or prepared to discuss the question
seriously.[3] Bevin's only consolation was to see himself proved right within less
than a month.

By contrast the Russians came a considerable way, at least on paper, to meet
the Americans. They agreed to support the American proposal for a UN
Atomic Energy Commission and finally accepted the way out of the impasse
over Rumania and Bulgaria which they had refused at the London meeting,
agreeing to send a three-power Commission to Bucharest which would advise
the government to take in two additional ministers, and to make a similar
proposal themselves to the Bulgarians. These concessions were likely to
change the reality of Soviet control as little as the token broadening of the
Polish government that Stalin had conceded in answer to Hopkins' pleas in
May, but it saved face all round and enabled Byrnes to claim that he had
removed the chief obstacle to starting work on the peace treaties with Italy and
Germany's other allies. A list of states to be invited to the peace conference was
settled and the date fixed for 1 May 1946. In return the Secretary of State
agreed to establish a Far Eastern Commission of eleven powers in Washington

[1] Dixon, pp. 203–4.
[2] Informal sessions, 25 December, British record, pp. 90–96 and 26 December, pp. 97–103. US
record 25 December, FRUS 1945 (2) pp. 781–98; 26 December, *ibid.*, pp. 801–808.
[2] 26 December 1945. British record, pp. 127–9.

and a four-power Allied Council with purely advisory powers in Tokyo,[1] token concessions with little more substance than that which Stalin had made in the case of Rumania and Bulgaria. A further compromise in China to suit the USA was traded for a compromise in Korea to suit the Russians.

The final session to settle the communiqué lasted longer than any of the others, with Molotov fighting hard to whittle down the concessions on making the Rumanian and Bulgarian governments more representative and at the same time to commit the Americans and British to recognition in advance. At the very last moment, when after hours of argument the text of the communiqué had been agreed, Molotov announced that "by mistake" the Russian typist had incorporated the Soviet version on Bulgaria and inquired "whether something along these lines could not be included in the Protocol after all". Both Byrnes and Bevin refused and even Molotov found it difficult to persevere with so bare-faced a move. It was half past three in the morning when the Foreign Ministers at last signed the communiqué and left.[2]

At first sight the results of the Moscow conference were encouraging. Byrnes had abandoned the tough line he had taken at London and any further practice of "atomic diplomacy" in order to secure the same sort of package deal for which he had worked at Potsdam. The immediate reaction was one of general relief in both Britain and America that negotiations had been resumed with the Russians and a strong disposition to believe that the results, particularly the opening of the way to a peace conference, had been worthwhile. They were certainly better than the results of the London Council of Foreign Ministers, and Byrnes could claim—and was quick to do so—that his initiative had borne fruit. The Russians were equally satisfied: without conceding anything that mattered they had gone a long way to securing recognition of their control over Rumania and Bulgaria as well as Poland and had recovered from the mistake of over-playing their hand in London. But the compromise, as *The Economist* soon pointed out, was almost entirely between Russian and American interests.

"What has Mr. Bevin received in return for abandoning his objections to the regimes in Rumania and Bulgaria and for permitting the drafting of the Peace Treaties to be handed back from the Big 5 to the Big 3?

"Far from receiving a suitable compensation for his compliance the two questions over which British diplomacy is most particularly exercised—Persia and Germany —were passed over at the Conference."[3]

The obvious omission from the communiqué was anything about Iran or Turkey and the reason was equally obvious. Byrnes was interested in Eastern

---

[1] Bevin secured a place for India on the Commission and for Australia, as the representative of the Commonwealth, on the Allied Council.
[2] 26 December. British record, pp. 97–103; US record, FRUS pp. 801–8.
[3] *The Economist*, 5 January 1946.

Europe and the Far East, not in the Middle East, and let the Russians see that
Bevin had little support from the USA. It did not take much diplomatic skill on
the Russian part to separate the two Western Powers and leave the British
isolated.

The result, *The Observer* commented, was not simply a Russo-American
compromise in which Russia got the better of the bargain and from which
Britain was left out, but

"The first open sign of a narrowing down of the circle of real Great Powers from the Big
Three to the Big Two. Britain is still . . . just strong enough to hang on permanently,
unlike France, to the exclusive innermost circle of the biggest Powers; she no longer
seems to carry sufficient weight to get her way or even to make others meet her half-way
on any fundamental question."[1]

6

A month after the conference ended, the British Ambassador called on Stalin
for a farewell talk before moving to Washington and reported to Bevin that the
Russians had not been at all pleased with his attitude while in Moscow. Far
from ill-will being dissipated,

"The impression had not been good. Stalin did not understand why it had not been
possible to arrive at a good official and personal relationship with yourself. He had
achieved it with the late government. On further pressure from me, he said that when
you had seen him at the Kremlin, you had not been 'natural' about Turkey. Your
approach to him on that matter had offended him. But he had been 'patient' and had let
it pass. Nevertheless he had not liked it and I could tell you so if I liked."

Stalin went on to show that he knew of Bevin's visit to Kollontai.

"She had taken a great fancy to you. But there were those at the Kremlin who could not
forget that you were a man of the 'Old International' which had been against the
Bolsheviks in 1917."

Since his return Bevin had spoken of Russia's territorial ambitions.

"What you said had been rough and given offence to him and public opinion in
Russia. . . . All he wanted was to be trusted and treated as an ally. He was not getting
such treatment."[2]

The picture of Stalin, one of the most ruthless men in modern history, being
offended by the rough manners of an English trade unionist is more affecting
than convincing. But the word had gone forth and was diligently spread by the

[1] 30 December 1945.
[2] Sir A. Clark-Kerr to Bevin, 29 January 1946. FO 800/501/SU/46/2.

Russians and their friends: it soon became common talk in London that Bevin's aggressive attitude was one of the obstacles to good relations between the two countries.[1]

Bevin himself said nothing publicly when he got back from Moscow, but on New Year's Day he met the diplomatic correspondents of the British Press for an off-the-record talk which provides the best evidence for the way in which he saw relations with the Soviet Union at the turn of the year. It is worth quoting verbatim, at least in part, for the flavour which it gives of Bevin talking at large about foreign affairs in a way often described by those who worked with him, but rarely documented.

Bevin began by saying that the British people wanted to see power politics replaced by the United Nations, but that this could not be done by passing a resolution or waving a magic wand.

"On the one hand you have Russia, who was defeated in the last war and who in foreign policy is quite clearly as imperialistic as the greatest of the Czars, Peter the Great or anybody else, and who is seeking to put around herself for security purposes whole groups of satellites in the south, east and west with the view of controlling every kind of place which is likely to come in contact with her. I think she has an inherent fear, quite unnecessarily, that the big Powers like us and America may some day or other attack her . . . Therefore she adopts methods which are very much out of date."

Bevin illustrated what he meant with the example of Turkey:

"Russia is seeking, as far as I can see, to get one paw down the back of Turkey with those provinces [Kars-Ardahan] and Azerbaijan, and the other paw through the Straits so that there would be a grip on Turkey, and Turkey would become virtually a satellite state with her foreign policy controlled by Russia."

The same kind of policy, pushing away danger as far as possible, was being followed in China and the Far East, and in the Balkans. The object was "a Russian Monroe from Lübeck and the Adriatic right through to Port Arthur".

"In all these explanations and talks they do not say this, but in every motion they move, in every step they take, that is obviously the design. The method adopted of course is to provoke revolt or disturbance, or grievances as in Azerbaijan (where no doubt the people should have had a provincial council), and with an army there Russian supporters have been able to carry this thing off.

"On the other hand, the United States policy is a mixture of idealism, with the United Nations, at the same time making secure as many bases as she can in case the United Nations don't work, and it is a little difficult to mould these two things together."

Bevin spoke vividly of the destruction caused by the war in Russia: 1,700 towns and 60,000 villages destroyed.

---

[1] One of the first to report this was Randolph Churchill, in a dispatch from Mocow to the *Evening Standard*.

"As for the conditions under which her people are living, due to this terrific invasion, I am quite certain we have no measure of it at all. Therefore you have her great fear from attack outside and need for immense reconstruction inside. It seems to me that with all that Russia has achieved in the last 25 years she has been put back in effect nearly 100 years by the invasion."

This was one of the reasons why Bevin did not think that Russian pressure in the Middle East would lead to war. When one of the correspondents asked him why, if Russia had been so much weakened, Britain and the USA did not resist her claims against Turkey and Iran, Bevin replied that they were being resisted but not by physical force. "I think diplomatic moves will be sufficient."

Daily Telegraph correspondent: "Then we are not prepared to fight Russia?"

Bevin: "Good God, no."

Bevin reiterated his view that the real problems of Europe and of the rest of the world were economic, the destruction caused by the war, a world shortage of food threatening famine, the despair created by the delays in starting on reconstruction. If only the peace treaties could be got out of the way, then it would be possible to make a start, in Europe at least, with re-creating the economic conditions in which people could live normal lives again.

He made a particular point of the war of nerves which the Soviet Union was waging against its southern neighbours, arguing that next to physical warfare, this form of aggression (practised by Hitler against the Czechs and the Poles) was the greatest danger to peace and ought to be outlawed.

"Turkey has had to be mobilised for over six months owing to this constant war of nerves which has upset all her economy not knowing whether she is going to be attacked or not. . . . I do not say that this behaviour is limited to Russia. If the war of nerves is not dropped, it will get worse and it will make the settlement of atomic energy impossible. If public opinion is roused, it will be dropped. Otherwise, it will keep the countries in fear, first the fear of the little Power being overrun, and secondly, the fear of the big Power that they might be involved and it will be ruinous to the U.N. and everybody else, if this technique is not dropped."

Bevin again used the Middle East as an illustration of a general point, the particular importance of avoiding friction where the Great Powers' spheres of influence touched each other, "and that needs very plain discussion of points where you think friction is likely to arise".

"It is likely to arise in Persia, in Turkey or anywhere in the Middle East, and if we are not careful, in the Baltic, or it may come in the Pacific. There, everybody has to walk with very great care and it depends entirely on what we do in the next three or four years whether you are going to have peace for a couple of hundred years or for ever. That is why I said in Moscow you can only regard this conference as a stage which leads you on to the next stage and try to consolidate as you go along."

Two features of Bevin's talk are noticeable. The first is the extent to which his attention in relations with Russia was focussed on the Northern Tier of states. In an hour's talk, neither Germany nor Western Europe was mentioned and Europe as a whole came a poor third after the Middle East and Far East. The only exception was Greece. After recalling the number of wars in which the Greeks had been involved in this century, and the cost of these—so that "she has no civil service, no army, no proper police force, not anything" —Bevin continued:

"I don't know whether I have said this to you before. I have got very irritable over Greece, as one naturally would, and I might easily have succumbed to the policy Russia adopted in Rumania. But I felt that Greece was like a man who had not used his legs through illness for many years. . . . And I decided to proceed, with all the irritation it meant and all the criticism that went on throughout the world about Greece, difficult as it was, to let governments rise and fall and not interfere with them, in order that they should get their political legs again. . . . But things reached a stage when it was quite clear that to make it work we had to tackle the whole economy and that is why I sent Hector McNeil out, not to interfere with the political side but to get their production, roads and railways . . . put on solid lines. I am trying my damnedest to build a sound economy in Greece upon which the political structure of the country will ultimately rest. . . . The standard of life is far too low and things far too unsettled. . . . I regard success in Greece as absolutely vital, not only to help herself, but to be a stabilising factor in the Mediterranean."

As Bevin's final sentence makes clear, he saw Greece in a Mediterranean and Middle Eastern as much as a European context, and the time he devoted to it does not invalidate the general point that on 1 January 1946 he could talk for an hour or more about foreign affairs without paying more than passing attention to European problems. The other surprising feature of Bevin's talk is the absence of virtually any reference to United States' policy, an omission which cannot have been accidental. For he had returned from Moscow with the impression that Byrnes still thought of bringing off a settlement with the Soviet Union which would allow the Americans to withdraw from Europe and in effect leave the British to get on with the Russians as best they could. He had found Byrnes even less prepared to co-operate over Middle Eastern than European issues.

The Russians, delighted at Byrnes' initiative in offering to come to Moscow, had evidently formed the same impression and were acting accordingly. While Bevin could make no progress with those items which primarily concerned Anglo-Soviet relations, Byrnes was able to report to the American people that he and the Russians had reached agreement on all the items on the US–Soviet agenda.[1] *The New York Times* greeted Byrnes' report with the banner headline: "UNITY IN WIDE ACCORD".[2] Soviet propaganda directives clearly dis-

---

[1] Byrnes' broadcast, 27 December 1945.
[2] *New York Times*, 28 December 1945.

tinguished between Britain—with its "reactionary" social democratic government and Bevin as the chief villain, now represented as the principal obstacle
to "peace"—and the United States. It was British imperialism, not American
capitalism, which was made the target of a concerted attack through the
Communist-controlled radio and press: British troops occupying Greece and
Indonesia, British intrigues in Iran and other parts of the Middle East, the
British denial of freedom to the Indians and other subject populations, Britain
trying to create an anti-Soviet "Western bloc". This same month of January,
Soviet diplomacy was to launch a parallel campaign to indict Britain before
world opinion at the first meeting of the UN Security Council. The United
States would not be mentioned in the indictment.

As long as there was any chance of driving a wedge between the two Western
Powers, Soviet tactics were obviously aimed at avoiding any issue (Germany,
for example) which might bring them together again in common opposition to
the USSR and concentrating on areas (Greece and the Middle East) where
Britain could most easily be isolated.

The American administration was still divided in its views of Soviet policy
and was slower to recognize a possible threat to its own interests from Soviet
actions in the Middle East than in Eastern Europe and the Far East. The
majority view was still that the Middle East was a traditional British sphere of
influence in which Americans had no wish, and saw no need, to become
involved. This was quite compatible with determination to break down the
British economic and commercial monopoly in that part of the world and open
it up to American business; but the British were still expected to take
responsibility for its defence and stability. It took time for opinion in the
Administration to accept the view of Loy Henderson, the influential head of
the Near Eastern and African Division of the State Department, that Russian
interest in expanding its control towards the Persian Gulf at the expense of
Iran and through the Straits to the Mediterranean at the expense of Turkey
had a long history; that the British no longer had the means to resist this on
their own and that the American Government had to consider whether its own
interest did not require that it act to set limits to Soviet expansion in the
Middle East as much as in Europe and the Far East.

Judging by Byrnes' attitude in Moscow the answer was that it did not. But
the omission of any mention of Iran and Turkey did not pass unnoticed in
Congress or the White House. *The New York Times* reported that one of the
questions members of Congress wanted answered was: "Why was nothing
settled about Russia's activities in Iran and its demands on Turkey?"[1]
Truman did not wait to get his question answered. Byrnes had not consulted
him about the communiqué or his proposal to broadcast to the nation on his
return.

"I did not like what I read", Truman wrote in his memoirs. "There was not

---

[1] 30 December 1945, quoted in Kuniholm, p. 294.

a word about Iran or any other place where the Soviets were on the march. . . . Byrnes had taken it upon himself to move the United States in a direction to which I could not and would not agree."

Truman was angry at the independent way in which Byrnes had conducted the negotiations in Moscow, without referring or even reporting to him as President. Having made his dissatisfaction clear, he had a further interview with the Secretary of State (5 January 1946) in which he relied on a letter he had written out in longhand to question the substance of the policy Byrnes was pursuing, as well as the manner. He drew a parallel between the Soviet *fait accompli* in Poland with which they were faced at Potsdam and the *fait accompli* in Iran with which Byrnes was faced at Moscow.[1]

"There isn't a doubt in my mind that Russia intends an invasion of Turkey and the seizure of the Black Sea Straits . . . Unless Russia is faced with an iron fist and strong language another war is in the making. . . . I do not think we shall play compromise any longer. . . . I'm tired of babying the Soviets."[2]

Bevin did not know what Truman said to Byrnes. Although Byrnes' refusal to consult with the British and the ambiguity of American policy gave him little less cause for anxiety than the Soviet attitude, this was not a question to be discussed in public even in an "off the record" talk: he had to be silent as well as patient, leaving the Americans to make up their own minds. Fortunately it was later to become clear that Truman's (and other Americans') criticism of the line Byrnes had followed in Moscow represented an important stage—Truman called it a new departure—in the development of American policy. The next stage was not long in following as a consequence of the Iranian complaint to the UN Security Council.

[1] The proclamation of autonomous republics in Azerbaijan and Kurdistan immediately before the conference and the Soviet refusal to withdraw Russian troops from Iran.
[2] Truman, vol. 1, pp. 492–3. Byrnes subsequently denied that Truman ever read the letter to him; Acheson suggests that the President may have used it as an *aide-mémoire* in making clear his position to Byrnes.

CHAPTER 6

The Northern Tier, the Middle East and Palestine

I

The New Year opened with an event which Bevin took very seriously, the first meeting of the United Nations General Assembly, held at Church House in London.[1] Despite the disillusioning experience which he had been through since becoming Foreign Secretary he still put his hopes for the long-term improvement of international relations on the success of the UN.

Bevin's appearance among the assembled Foreign Ministers and diplomats at once attracted attention. As he approached the rostrum with his rolling sailor's walk, one foreign observer remarked, "The British working man".[2] In his speech he listed the different international organizations grouped under the United Nations from the FAO and the ILO to UNESCO, the Economic and Social Council, the Military Staff Committee and now the proposed Atomic Commission. "By a natural process, the functional instruments of the world state are coming into existence. All that was needed was the final coping stone on the arch, an organization to guarantee security." An international audience already inclined to be sceptical about the prospects of the United Nations, was impressed by the earnestness with which he spoke.

Trouble began on 19 January, when the Iranian Government lodged a complaint against the interference of the Soviet Union in the internal affairs of its country. It was to avoid this confrontation that Bevin had tried to get the Russians to agree to his proposal for a commission of inquiry and he had no hand in the Iranian move, if only because he was anxious not to put too heavy a strain at the outset on the Security Council. Nonetheless, once the matter had come into the open, the British as well as the Americans would not allow it to be brushed aside.

[1] FO papers relating to the 1st UN General Assembly, Jan.–Feb. 1946, are in FO 371/57025–57060.
[2] Peterborough in the *Daily Telegraph*, 18 January 1946.

The Russians, put on the defensive by the Iranian action, retorted by making a formal complaint (1 February) against British troops in Greece, where they were alleged to be a threat to peace, and in Indonesia. Although the Russians were careful to distinguish between the British and the Americans (against whom they made no complaint) their move proved a serious tactical mistake. Vyshinsky saw Bevin several times over the weekend of 26–28 January and hinted at the possibility of a package deal over the Balkans and Iran. But Bevin would have nothing of the sort. When Vyshinsky, having failed to get the Iranian complaint turned down on procedural grounds, argued that the Soviet Union should be left to settle the matter with the Iranians by negotiation, Bevin demanded to be told what there was to negotiate about and insisted that the results of any negotiations should be reported to the Council and the dispute remain on its agenda. This was carried unanimously.

Having in this way out-manoeuvred Vyshinsky over Iran, Bevin proceeded to rout him over Greece, relishing the chance the Russians had given him to reply to the constant sniping he had to put up with. Undeterred by the fact that the encounter would take place in the full blaze of publicity, Bevin rose to the occasion and delivered what Dixon described with enthusiasm in his diary as "the frankest and most forthright speech any Foreign Secretary has made since Palmerston".

It was significant, Bevin pointed out, that "whenever the problem of Greece has arisen in any negotiations with the Soviet Union it has always come about when we have been discussing Rumania or Bulgaria or Poland". When the British explained their policy in Greece, the Russians either said they were satisfied or let the matter drop; but renewed their attack whenever it suited their purposes. "Indeed, I know when I displease the Soviet Government because all the shop stewards who are Communists send me resolutions in the exact same language . . . one of those strange coincidences that occur."

The civil war had started in Greece because of a determined attempt on the part of the Communists to seize power and establish a minority Government. The British Army by its intervention had put down the civil war: the object of the Communist campaign was to get the British troops out, then renew their attempt to capture power. Bevin quoted from a *Manchester Guardian* interview with Zakhariades, the Greek Communist leader (who had been allowed to return to Greece) that the civil war would last two months "and then everything will be all right".

If the Russians were really concerned about Greece, Bevin asked, why had no use been made of the Treaty of Friendship between Russia and Britain to raise the matter through diplomatic channels before launching these charges in the Security Council? Not a word had been said to him. If there was anxiety about the Greek elections, why had the Soviet Union refused to join the USA, France and Britain in the international commission which he had set up to supervise them? If there was anxiety about the situation on Greece's frontiers, why had Russia made no response to his proposal of a four-power commission to go and investigate on the spot?

Vyshinsky had spoken of the danger of an attack by Greece on her neighbours. In the countries to the north of her there were 700–800,000 Russian, Yugoslav and Bulgarian troops. Could anyone seriously imagine that the Greek army, which was still being rebuilt, even with the aid of the 80,000 British troops, would declare war on or attack these countries?

"I have great difficulty in believing that this is brought forward because of what we are doing in Greece. . . . I am going to ask the Security Council for a straight declaration, no question of compromise in this: Is the British Government, in lending some of its forces to help get order and economic reconstruction in that country, endangering peace? I am entitled to an answer, Yes or No. . . .

"The danger to the peace of the world has been the incessant propaganda from Moscow against the British Commonwealth as a means to attack the British . . . as if no friendship existed between us. That is the danger to the peace of the world which sets us one against another."[1]

The debate continued for another ten days, the Ukrainian delegate bringing the occupation by British troops of Indonesia as well as Greece before the Council (9 February). But the Russian case lacked the conviction which Bevin put into its rebuttal, and he remained master of the situation. At the end the Security Council took note of the different views expressed on Greece and declared the matter closed, refusing at the same time to send out an investigating commission to Indonesia as the Ukrainian delegate had proposed. Bevin did not get the "Yes" or "No" he had demanded, but there was no question but that he had got the better of the argument and that the Russians' manoeuvre had rebounded on them.

This was the more striking since the Russians had carefully avoided including the USA in their indictment and the Americans had responded by giving no support to the British. Byrnes left for Washington before the Security Council met and the US representative, Stettinius, played the role of an impartial mediator both between Russia and Iran and between Russia and Britain. Bevin, however, had not let the lack of US support inhibit him and the popular verdict was summed up by the *Manchester Guardian*: "In the language of the common man, Mr Vyshinsky asked for it and he got it."[2]

The impact on British opinion was all the greater because the exchanges took place in Church House, and were reported at greater length than if it had all happened abroad. Soviet hostility to Britain was no longer in question: there was general relief that the dispute was now in the open and this was a real gain for Bevin. Nor was he taken to task for rejecting the charges made by the Russians. Even the radical weekly *Tribune*, normally critical of Bevin's performance as Foreign Secretary, wrote that, if the Russian attitude stemmed

[1] Bevin's speech to the Security Council, 1 February 1946.
[2] *Manchester Guardian*, 4 February 1946.

from a belief in the decay of the British Empire and Labour's inability to hold it together, "then the very ardour and determination of Ernest Bevin's fighting speeches will have done a world of good".[1] But the bluntness and force with which he had spoken worried many people. Compared with later displays in the United Nations like Krushchev's shoe-banging episode, Bevin's manner had been a model of restraint, but as the *Manchester Guardian* remarked, in a leader headed "The Plain Dealer": "The people of this country and the United States have long called for open diplomacy and plain speaking. Now they have got it, and they are not quite sure whether they like it."[2] *The Economist* as well as the *Guardian* chided Bevin with letting his indignation carry him too far.

"Mr Bevin has won a notable victory this week. He will receive many congratulations on the forthrightness and success of his action. But what will they be worth, if his very forcefulness prevents the achievement of his wider objectives? The operation of defending British policy has been successful. But is the patient still alive?"[3]

For once, criticism was openly expressed in the Cabinet as well as the Press. After Bevin had reported on the UN debate on Indonesia and voiced his suspicions of Soviet objectives in South East Asia and the Mediterranean, Nye Bevan is recorded as saying that "he doubted whether the prospects were quite so black as the Foreign Secretary suggested." After a tactful tribute to Bevin's handling of the proceedings in the Security Council, the Minister of Health expressed the view that the Communist wave in Europe might be about to recede. "We must not therefore allow Russian intransigence to drive us into an untenable position in foreign policy."[4]

Bevin evidently took notice of what was being said, for when the House next discussed British relations with Russia, later in the month, he took the unusual course of waiting to speak until the end of the Debate after he had heard what his critics had to say. The debate still makes fascinating reading for the light it throws on the evolution of British opinion. Although it was accepted that the hopes of close collaboration after the war had largely disappeared, and that Russia's hold on Eastern Europe was not likely to be shaken, there was an almost unanimous refusal, on both sides of the House, to believe that the conflict with the Soviet Union had gone beyond the point where conciliation was still possible.

When he finally rose to reply Bevin could see that he had still to reassure a House reluctant to accept the division of the world into spheres of influence and harried by the fear of another war. He told them that, in his talks with Stalin, he had offered to extend the Anglo-Soviet Treaty from twenty to fifty years and amend it too, if the Russians wished to.

[1] *Tribune*, 8 February 1946.
[2] *Manchester Guardian*, 4 February 1946.
[3] *The Economist*, 9 February 1946.
[4] CM(46) 14: Confidential Annex, attached to the minutes but not circulated.

"It is said that we are drifting into war with Russia. I cannot conceive any circumstances in which Britain and the Soviet Union should go to war. . . . It never enters my mind and I am certain it does not any of my colleagues."

On the other hand he was still determined to be firm. He refused to yield to the pressure from the friends of EAM to postpone the Greek elections or the demand that he should disband the Polish army of General Anders without worrying about the future of its officers and men. Nor did he conceal his view that Russia was waging a war of nerves on Turkey.

"I really must be frank and say I do not want Turkey converted into a satellite State. What I want her to be is really independent and I should like to see the treaty of friendship renewed between Soviet Russia and Turkey."

Much of Bevin's speech was taken up with the Mediterranean and the Northern Tier, but he also had something to say about the country which was to become the focus of the conflict between Russia and the West—Germany. Asked by Eden if the Government would accept the internationalization of the Ruhr, Bevin confessed that he had not yet made up his mind. His "industrial instinct" was in favour of putting the Ruhr under public international control so that its production could help to raise the standard of life throughout Europe; but there was also security to take into account, the Ruhr's role as an arsenal, and that—although Bevin did not elaborate on it—might lead to a different conclusion.[1]

But the theme to which he returned constantly was his favourite one of reconstruction, the conflict in peace-making between nationalist demands and economic facts. "After all, what do the people want? They want homes, food, light, markets and they want to enjoy the decencies of life. The mere drawing of an ethnic boundary ought not to mean poverty to them, and the raw materials ought to flow, whichever way it is." He came back to it again in his peroration:

"I am more concerned with the economic rehabilitation of Europe than with geography. When I see millions suffering in the world, I would like to be sitting down considering how . . . I could conquer hunger and misery. I would rather do that than be arguing back about 19th century imperialism . . . Indeed nothing would give me greater joy if it were possible not to have one plan for one country, but with all the devastation in the world . . . to see an international pool and effort for the rehabilitation of the world".[2]

This was the authentic Bevin and the House believed him. Although his speech was rambling—a consequence of trying to answer rather than lead the debate—he had reassured many of those who feared that he had become so absorbed in the quarrel with Russia as to neglect the more positive side of

[1] See index under Ruhr.
[2] HC, 21 February 1946.

Britain's international policy. Even the *New Statesman* admitted that, when he spoke like this, the Foreign Secretary "wins every Socialist heart".[1]

No sooner had the controversy over relations with Russia calmed down, however, than it was revived in full force by the Fulton speech (5 February). Churchill had not been present for the February debate as he had left for a much publicized visit to the USA. Now, when everyone else had had their say, the most powerful voice of all was heard, with perfect timing and maximum effect. Making use of the phrase "the Iron Curtain", he pointed to the fact that the greater part of Eastern and Central Europe lay "in what I must call the Soviet sphere and all are subject in one form or another, not only to Soviet influence but to a very high, and in many cases, increasing measure of control from Moscow. . . .

"Turkey and Persia are both profoundly alarmed and disturbed at the claims which are being made upon them and at the pressure being exerted by the Moscow Government. . . . I do not believe that Soviet Russia desires war. What they desire is the fruits of war and the indefinite expansion of their power and doctrines. . . . Our difficulties and dangers will not be removed by . . . a policy of appeasement. . . . I am convinced that there is nothing they admire so much as strength, and there is nothing for which they have less respect than for weakness."

Churchill ended his speech, which recalled his warnings against appeasing Germany in the 1930s, by urging the United States and the British Commonwealth to co-operate, with the assurance that then "there will be no quivering, precarious balance of power to offer its temptation to ambition or security".

Churchill had not told Bevin or Attlee what he intended to say at Fulton and the first reaction in Whitehall was one of consternation, not so much because of the views Churchill had expressed as because of the impact his speech might have on American opinion at a time when the loan to Britain was still under discussion in Congress. First reports from New York and Washington bore this out. Many Americans welcomed the frankness with which he had spoken about Russia, but his proposal for an alliance between the USA and the British Empire aroused all the old suspicions and received little support.

While Attlee and Bevin were wondering what to do or say, a telegram from Churchill himself (7 March) reassured them. He reported that the President had read his speech in advance, and had "seemed equally pleased before and after". So had Byrnes. The telegram contained other important news. Truman had told Churchill that he proposed to send the remains of the Turkish Ambassador, who had died more than a year before, back to Istanbul on board the U.S.S. *Missouri* and that the American battleship, accompanied by a strong task force, would remain in the Sea of Marmara for an unspecified period.

[1] *New Statesman*, 2 March 1946.

"This strikes me," Churchill telegraphed, "as a very important act of State and one calculated to make Russia understand that she must come to reasonable terms of discussion with the Western democracies." It would reassure Turkey and Greece and place "a demurrer on what Bevin called cutting our line through the Mediterranean by the establishment of a Russian naval base at Tripoli". As to his speech, Churchill maintained that "some show of strength and resistance is necessary to a good settlement with Russia. I predict that this will be the prevailing opinion in the United States in the near future."[1]

Churchill's message confirmed Bevin's view that the Government should say nothing. It was impossible for him as Foreign Secretary, or for anyone else, to be as forthright as Churchill in addressing the Americans; he was certainly not going to repudiate him or do anything to weaken the impact of his words.

The Russian reaction was predictable. *Pravda* published an interview with Stalin in which he compared Churchill with Hitler and the Fulton speech with the *Führer's* racial theories: "The English-speaking nations are the only nations of full value and must rule over the remaining nations of the world." Churchill was issuing "an ultimatum saying 'recognise willingly our domination, then everything will be all right!' . . . There is no doubt that the set-up of Mr. Churchill is a set-up for war, a call for war against the Soviet Union."[2]

Opinion in Britain was as divided as in the USA, though for different reasons. The *Manchester Guardian*, which took Churchill's part, concluded that

"Perhaps neither country is at the moment ready to be as logical as Mr. Churchill. Emotionalism wells up. We are to become 'the 49th State', the tool of American capitalism; the United States is to bolster up a crumbling British 'Imperialism' and underwrite colonial oppression. . . . And the fearful ask: What will Russia think about it?"[3]

The Economist,[4] which like the *Guardian* was much warmer in support for Churchill than, for example, *The Times*, wrote:

"The very pointed anti-Communist, if not plain anti-Soviet, purpose of it will cause much heart-searching over here. In spite of the fact that Russia is openly anti-British, there still seems to be an astonishing amount of charity in this country towards Russian motives. . . . The majority of the British people still cling to the belief that there is a limit to the Russians' expansionist aims, and that in their own queer way they are as peace-loving and willing to be co-operative as anyone else. It begins to look very much like wishful thinking."

More serious for the Government was the unanimous condemnation of Churchill in the Labour press from the *Daily Herald* to the *New Statesman* and

[1] Churchill to Attlee and Bevin, 7 March 1946. FO 800/513/US/46/37, published in Francis Williams, *Prime Minister*, pp. 162–4.
[2] The complete text of the interview is to be found in the *Information Bulletin* put out by the Soviet Embassy in Washington, 19 March 1946.
[3] Reported in the *Manchester Guardian*, 11 March 1946.
[4] 9 March.

the demand from the Left-wing of the Labour Party that the Government should openly repudiate his views. Attlee however refused to give an opinion either way, on the grounds that Churchill was free to express his opinions and had not consulted him as Prime Minister in advance: the Government's own policy had been expounded "very plainly" by Bevin in his recent speech to the House.

William Warbey, the left-wing MP for Luton claimed 105 members' signatures (a third of the Parliamentary Labour Party) for a motion deploring Churchill's proposal of an alliance as inimical to peace but this made no impression on Bevin—or Churchill. The Left then resolved to challenge Bevin's Greek policy in the External Affairs Group of the Parliamentary Labour Party. This was one of the few occasions (27 March 1946) when Bevin agreed to meet the Group and he attracted an audience of three hundred Labour MPs.

In January he had announced to the Commons an agreement with the Greek Government to provide a credit of £10M. for the stabilization of the Greek currency; to waive repayment of £46M. lent to Greece in 1940–41; and to give economic, industrial and financial assistance through the newly formed British mission.[1] Bevin had forced the agreement through against Treasury opposition and he was in no mood to give an inch to his critics. He turned down flat any suggestion that the Greek elections should be postponed beyond 31 March. They had already been postponed once and further delay would mean keeping British troops in Greece longer. He insisted that the Greeks must settle their own affairs; he was not prepared to take sides, beyond seeing that fair elections were held and helping with economic reco. `truction. Outflanking his critics who wanted only to discuss Greece, Bevin declared that British foreign policy had to be considered as a whole. Thus the continued presence of Allied troops was a great element of disturbance wherever it occurred, not just in Greece, and he reminded his audience that the Soviet Union had still over a million troops in Austria and the Balkans.

By the time Bevin had finished talking, an hour had passed and, after answering questions, he turned the tables on his critics by calling for a vote of confidence which he got with only six voting against and 30 abstaining out of 300.[2] *The Times* quite rightly described this meeting as something of a personal triumph for Bevin, and for the moment it silenced those who claimed that he did not have the support of his own Party. A Gallup Poll organized by the *News Chronicle* earlier the same month showed how much support he had won in the country at large since December. In the last month of 1945 47% of those questioned had thought he was doing a good job as Foreign Secretary, 18% that he was not, and 35% did not know. By March 1946 the figure for approval had risen to 73% and for disapproval had fallen to 12%; only 15% no longer

---

[1] HC, 25 January 1946.
[2] Bevin's statement to the External Affairs Group of the PLP, circulated to all missions, 4 April 1946. FO 800/492/PLT/46/20.

had an opinion, a figure which no doubt reflected the impact made by the United Nations' sessions in London. Of Labour Party supporters who were questioned 82% approved, only 7% disapproved; of Conservatives questioned 65% and of Liberals 75% thought that he was doing the job well. In the first three months of 1946 Bevin could feel that public opinion was coming round to a better understanding of his attitude without any attempt on his part to court popularity.

2

The Labour Government was now well into its stride: Dalton called 1946 its *annus mirabilis*. The second reading of the Coal Nationalization Bill took place at the end of January; of the National Insurance Bill early in February and of the National Health Service Bill at the end of April. Bevin never allowed his interests to be confined to foreign policy and he took part in the Cabinet discussion of all three bills. Unlike Morrison, who did his best to delay action, Bevin was in favour of nationalizing steel and Dalton noted in his diary: "Bevin was very good, as usual, on this subject which he thoroughly understands."[1] In Cabinet Bevin urged the need, if nationalization had to be postponed, to set up a strong Control Board which would see that the industry was not run down and a bold programme of development carried out pending the transfer of ownership to the State. The Cabinet agreed and put Bevin on the ministerial committee to draft a scheme for his proposed Board. He brought the other ministers together and had a draft ready to circulate to the Cabinet within a week; it was approved four days later without change.[2] Dalton was appreciative of Bevin's help on another topic, his second Budget for which Bevin proposed an increase in earned income relief. The Treasury was opposed, but Dalton was impressed by Bevin's argument on incentives and put it in.[3]

It is important not to lose sight of these domestic issues since these were the real stuff of politics for politicians and the electorate most of the time. While foreign policy divided Labour and blurred the distinction between parties, the Government's domestic policies united the Party—and united Bevin with it—marking a clear and welcome division between Labour and the Opposition.

Bevin's views carried great weight in the Cabinet on the sort of questions with which he had been concerned as Minister of Labour and a trade union leader. Manpower[4] was an obvious one, but only one. National insurance was another, and after hearing the points Bevin had to make the Cabinet twice

[1] Dalton, *Memoirs*, p. 138.
[2] CM (45) 30, 4 April and (46) 35, 11 April. The scheme was circulated as CP (46) 152.
[3] Dalton, pp. 106 and 122.
[4] See index under Manpower.

asked the ministers responsible for the new legislation to consult with him and produce a redraft.[1] In any matters affecting the trade unions he was the first to be consulted. Two examples taken from the Cabinet minutes for March 1946 show why Bevin was listened to. When the Home Secretary put up proposals for the use of emergency powers, if needed, Bevin (who had taken over the organization of the General Strike twenty years before) advised against consulting the unions:

"They would expect the Government to be ready to maintain essential services in an emergency; but if they were asked in advance to collaborate . . ., they might regard this as an invitation to assist in building up a strike-breaking organisation."[2]

The following week the Cabinet discussed wages policy. Bevin, as might be expected, was in favour of allowing collective bargaining to continue without Government interference; but the basis of his argument was not the right of the unions to get the best deal they could for their members, but the danger to a Labour Government of taking a hand in fixing wages, thereby becoming a party to every industrial dispute and exposing itself to political pressures to raise wages. He thought it easy to exaggerate the danger of an upward spiral of wages even if steps were taken to improve the pay and conditions of the million lowest paid workers. What was gained from intervening to hold down wages could be more than offset by prejudicing the development of industrial efficiency.[3]

Ironically, the first industrial challenge to the Labour Government's authority came from the group of workers with whom Bevin had been more closely identified than any other, the dockers. A dispute on Merseyside at the end of September 1945 produced a national strike in sympathy, bringing out 40,000 men in all and halting work at the ports for six weeks. The strike was led by an unofficial strike committee acting against union advice and is described by V. L. Allen as "a strike which defies analogies, an excellent example of the inscrutability of dockers' behaviour."[4] It was finally ended by a ballot on Merseyside which established that over 7,000 of the 10,000 dockers favoured a return to work, a result which even the unofficial committee had to accept. The other dockers who had struck in support of their mates on Merseyside at once went back.

Bevin kept in the background, leaving it to George Isaacs as Minister of

[1] The first occasion was in December 1945 when a meeting of ministers in Bevin's room produced a redraft (8 December and 12 December. FO 800/491/PLT/45/37 &39); the second was on 17 January 1946, CM (46) 6.
[2] CM (46) 22, 8 March 1946. For Bevin's role in the General Strike see vol. I, pp. 318–20.
[3] CM (45) 24, 14 March 1946. Manual workers' wage rates in 1946 were 172 over the base rate of 100 in 1936 and 195.9 in 1950, a percentage rise of 14%. The comparable figures for wage earnings were 196 in 1946 and 262.9 in 1950, a rise of 26%.
[4] V. L. Allen: *Trade Union Leadership, based on a study of Arthur Deakin* (London 1957), p. 195, footnote 3. Allen's chapters 11 & 12 are the best account of the labour difficulties in the docks during and after the war.

Labour and Arthur Deakin, his successor as General Secretary of the TGWU, to get the men back to work. But he was active behind the scenes in looking for a long-term solution to the labour problems of the docks. He was still convinced that decasualization offered the only chance of improvement, although he had no illusions that the habits of casual labour would easily be overcome. He had prepared a bill which he planned to introduce in July 1945, only to see it lost with the break-up of the coalition. His advice to George Isaacs, however, was to take more time than he himself had allowed to bring in a permanent scheme and in the meantime to prolong the wartime arrangements which he had made in 1940.[1] This proved good advice. For the employers rejected the scheme put up by Isaacs and three separate and independent inquiries failed to remove their objections. It was only in July 1947 that the new regulations could be introduced, but thanks to Bevin's foresight the delay did not produce a crisis in the docks. Bevin was too experienced to suppose that the election of a Labour Government would bring the millennium in industrial relations. If productivity was to be raised and conflict avoided, every gain would have to be worked for, and this put an extra burden on the man who had the double task of explaining Government policies to the unions and union difficulties to the Government.

Bevin's interests, however, extended a good deal further than strikes and wages—as they had when he was a General Secretary. He strongly supported Labour's nationalization proposals—not only for steel, but for coal, gas, electricity, the railways and canals. When Morrison brought the nationalization programme to the Cabinet for approval (13 November 1945) Bevin asked for and secured the inclusion in the list of the dock and harbour undertakings.[2] The proposals for the future of the cotton industry and for the nationalization of the Bank of England provide two other examples of Bevin's intervention leading to changes accepted by the Cabinet.[3] He was equally interested in housing, and when Nye Bevan outlined his proposals to the Cabinet, had a number of ideas to offer, among them giving powers to the Ministry of Works to build houses and so bring down building costs.[4]

Bevin was the first Minister to urge the Cabinet to see the development of tourism as another way, besides the drive for exports, to earn the dollars needed to pay for imports. In a paper which he circulated in November 1945 he asked if it was possible to promote visits by Americans in the summer of 1946.[4] The difficulty was the shortage of accommodation and food which was brought home to Bevin when the London hotels refused to take in delegates at the time of the first session of the United Nations in January 1946. He solved that one by threatening to use compulsory powers if the hotels would not cooperate. But he

[1] Bevin to Isaacs, 12 Nov. 1945 and Isaacs' reply sending his proposal for Bevin's approval, 30 November. FO 800/491/PLT/45/28 and 33.
[2] CM (45) 52.
[3] CM (45) 18, 7 July; (45) 31, 13 September 1945.
[4] CM (45) 39, 9 October.
[5] CP (45) 284.

took the point and pressed for Government departments to release requisitioned accommodation in time for it to be re-furbished. In a letter to Dalton and Attlee, he said that tourism had been one of the reasons for setting up the Catering Wages Commission[1], and putting the hotel trade on a proper footing, and he asked why they should not try to get the Olympic Games for London in 1948. "The more people we can get to Britain, the more it helps the F.O. and the Board of Trade."[2]

Bevin had to accept that it was impossible to bring in tourists in 1946, only to ask that steps be taken at once to do so in 1947.[3] Dissatisfied with Treasury scepticism, he wrote to Attlee in the middle of the Paris Peace Conference, to press for a strong Cabinet committee which would take the Catering Commission's suggestions seriously. The French and the Swiss, he added, were already getting ahead, and he urged the Prime Minister to take a personal interest in the matter.[4] A Foreign Secretary who concerned himself with tourism (at a time when its importance had still to be generally recognized) was as much of a surprise in Whitehall as one who thought it part of his job to promote exports. But his advice was heeded and an interdepartmental committee set up under the Secretary for Overseas Trade, Hilary Marquand, with a promise that if this did not work a committee of senior ministers would take over.

Bevin's part in the Government's domestic programme was played in Cabinet and committees, only occasionally in public. Attending debates was difficult with the demands of the Foreign Office on his time, especially with the United Nations meeting in London, and after losing his Christmas holidays he was forced by fatigue to take ten days' rest in Cornwall at the end of February. Before then, however, he had treated the House of Commons to a display of the forcefulness and passion which had made him a great trade union leader.

The occasion was the repeal of the Trade Disputes and Trade Unions Act of 1927, which he had always regarded as the Tory Government's revenge for the General Strike of 1926. Without consulting anyone or worrying whether his intervention was consistent with his new role as Foreign Secretary or with a bi-partisan foreign policy, Bevin came straight from addressing the United Nations General Assembly and charged into the debate.[5]

The discussion until Bevin's appearance had been calm and the Chamber thinly attended. When word went round that "Ernie" was up, members came flocking in and he spoke to a crowded and very soon a noisy House. He had waited, he said, twenty years to make this speech, and plainly no one was going to stop him. Objections by the Opposition that he was breaking the rules of the House by addressing members opposite as "you" were brushed aside like gnat stings. *The Times*, describing the scene, reported that "he stirred the whole

---

[1] For the controversy over the Catering Wages Bill in 1943 and Bevin's part in it, see vol. II, pp. 221–4; 235–7.
[2] Bevin to Dalton, copy to Attlee, 7 January 1946. FO 800/492/PLT/46/4.
[3] CM (46) 23, 11 March 1946.
[4] Bevin to Attlee, 27 April 1946. FO 800/479/MIS/46/55.
[5] HC, 13 February 1946.

House, the Opposition into protest and the ranks behind him to almost ecstatic cheering as he delivered his rhetorical blows, sometimes accompanied by physical blows on the dispatch box in front of him". At one point he made the Tories so angry that even his powerful voice could not be heard above the uproar, although "he continued to try to make himself heard and to gesticulate with great energy". "The dispatch box," the *Guardian* parliamentary correspondent reported, "had not had such a knocking about in one's recollection of the House. In striking it once the impact of his fist sent his spectacles flying." At last the Deputy Speaker gently suggested to Mr Bevin that he should observe the rules and order was restored.

From beginning to end of an hour-long speech, Bevin hardly mentioned the Bill which was now before the House. What he had come to do was to set straight the record of Britain's industrial history in the 1920s, and in particular to argue that the trade unions throughout the 1920s had been acting on the defensive in face of a deliberate attempt by the Tory Government to push down wages and create unemployment in order to maintain a sound currency. The strike of 1926, he maintained, never need have taken place.

"On Sunday, the 2nd May, we were within five minutes of a settlement. . . . Suddenly a message came to us that the negotiations were off. We did not know what had happened. We were told 'It is the *Daily Mail* incident'. I have a copy of that night's paper in my pocket now. . . . There was not one word of a general strike in the whole dispute. What happened? I am sorry the Rt. Hon. Member for Woodford [Churchill] is not in his place. He dashed up to Downing Street, . . . rushed Baldwin off his feet—if he was awake—and in a few minutes the ultimatum was given to us and the country was thrown into this terrible turmoil when within the same few minutes it might have been saved.". . .

The heart of Bevin's case was that the unions had not sought a confrontation but had had one forced on them.

"If there is a strike against the State, it is obviously illegal, but this was not a strike against the State. It was a strike in support of people whose wages were at the lowest possible level at which they could live and from which certain powers in this country sought, unjustly, to drive them lower. . . .
"They cast the trade unions for the role of enemies of the State. . . . I have never been an enemy of the State. I have been as big a constitutionalist as any member on the other side of the House, and I am fighting to remove the stigma which the Tory Party in 1927 put upon me as the leader of a trade union. . . . Just as I have a clear card in my union, I want this Act off the Statute Book so that we may have a clear card before the law. . . . If ever there was a class Act, this was one."

The Labour members behind cheered him as never before or perhaps again. But Bevin was not courting popularity with his own party—"I am never afraid of opposition", he remarked, "whether it comes from that side or this." Conservatives continued to protest that Bevin's outburst was "unworthy of himself and his high office".[1] But there were more who, knowing their

---

[1] Harold Macmillan, opening the foreign affairs debate, HC, 20 February 1946.

"Ernie", did not take it too seriously. For once he had overcome the lack of ease which sometimes inhibited his parliamentary performance and been himself. The *Manchester Guardian* called his speech "gloriously irrelevant" and *The Economist* added: "No one enjoyed the afternoon out so much as Mr Bevin who fitted into a crowded day at UNO an hour of vitriolic thunder against the Conservative Party." The universal regret was that Churchill ("the father of all these troubles" as Bevin called him) had not been present to make it an even more exciting parliamentary occasion.

It was noticeable that Bevin, when he next appeared in the House for the foreign affairs debate, listened docilely to criticism, spoke with moderation and generally behaved himself. In the course of that debate Bevin made the remark that the first and greatest problem was food. It was a problem to which he devoted a lot of energy, working closely with Attlee to give a lead to the United Nations—and particularly to the food-producing countries, the USA, Canada, Australia—in organizing an international effort to cut consumption, grow more and prevent famine. Over Europe as a whole food production was 25% below normal, and for the world 12% below. Besides Europe, the worst hit area was South and SE Asia, particularly India. Here at last was an issue on which he could hope to get concerted action. While Attlee wrote to enlist the support of Truman and other heads of government, Bevin tried to bring home the urgency of the situation to the House of Commons, the UN General Assembly, the trade unions, the International Conference of Agricultural Producers.[1] He appointed Lord Killearn as Special Commissioner to grapple with the problem of procuring rice in South East Asia; addressed an emergency conference on Europe's cereals supply which the British Government convened in London and would have liked to attend the FAO conference in Canada, if he had not been held in Europe by the Council of Foregin Ministers.

Much the most effective lead Britain could give was by making food available herself, and Attlee and Bevin decided that this must be done even at the cost of cutting British rations still further. They agreed that 200,000 tons of wheat should be diverted from the UK quota to help Asia, especially India, and a total of 400,000 tons of food exported to the British zone in Germany.[2] The cut in rations was unpopular at home and was seized on by the Opposition as evidence of mismanagement. There was some truth in this. But the Government refused to bow to the storm and on the principle of sharing Bevin demanded to know whether the Opposition, which was loud in proclaiming its belief in the Empire, looked on the 500 million people of India and the East as British subjects, or only the people of the United Kingdom, when it came to food supplies.[3]

The party row over rationing went on well into the summer, leading to Ben

[1] For the last three, see his speeches of 13 February, 30 March (TGWU Annual Festival at Bristol) and 20 May.
[2] See Francis Williams, *Prime Minister*, c. 10.
[3] HC, 21 February 1946.

Smith's resignation as Minister of Food on 27 May (he was succeeded by John Strachey) and the introduction of bread rationing, a step never taken in wartime, a month later. In the midst of all the charges and counter charges,[1] it was easy to lose sight of the fact that, largely thanks to the initiative taken by Attlee and Bevin in the winter, and the response of President Truman, the threat of a major famine was averted.

Another issue in which Bevin was inevitably involved was the drive to raise industrial productivity and so help to close the trade gap by increasing exports. In March he spoke on successive days (6th and 7th) to a national conference of trade union executives and a national conference of employers. In April he travelled to Manchester and Birmingham for the same purpose, making great use of his gift for explaining the relationship of trade and industry with foreign and defence policy in a vivid way which everyone could understand.

"We must get rice out of Siam", he told a trade union audience in Bristol. "There's a good quantity, but there are no consumer goods. The people in Siam don't believe in money any more. What the poor peasant wants is something to wear, some goods. To get the goods cotton must be got out of Lancashire, spinners must go in, miners must produce coal. If consumer goods can then be sent to Siam, you get the rice, the rice comes to Malaya and instead of the Malay being on half rations, he gets his full ration and produces the tin and the rubber to keep the industries going here.[2]

Production was linked directly with manpower. There was still discontent over the rate of demobilization, especially when compared with the Americans, and demands to know why Britain had to maintain such large forces abroad. The 1946 White Paper on Defence showed how large these were.[3] By 30 June there would still be 1,900,000 in the three Services (there had been 5.1M. at the time of Germany's defeat) and 1.1M. at the end of 1946. A big debate on defence policy in March turned almost entirely into an argument about demobilization, with a characteristic attack by Zilliacus on Bevin's foreign policy as the cause of inflated defence expenditure:

"We seem to be blindingly impelled by the momentum of Imperial inertia. We are not blazing new trails to world peace. We have sunk into ancient ruts running back to the 19th century and punctuated by two world wars."[4]

---

[1] There were some inside the Labour Party. Sir Ben Smith's resignation followed a disagreement with Bevin over sending food to Germany. Smith had been an official in the TGWU and in the 1920s had known Bevin well.

[2] TGWU Annual Bristol Festival, 30 March 1946.

[3] The principal commitments were: three major bases in the UK, Middle East and India; the occupation of Germany and Austria, and a token force in Japan; Trieste, Greece, Palestine, S.E. Asia (including the Netherlands East Indies); garrisons at Gibraltar, Malta, Aden and in the colonial empire; mine sweeping.

[4] HC, 4 March 1946. A few weeks earlier Zilliacus had written to Attlee sending him a long memorandum highly critical of the Government's foreign policy. Attlee replied: "My dear Zilly, Thank you for sending me your memorandum which seems to me to be based on an astonishing lack of understanding of the facts. Yours sincerely, C. R. Attlee." (17 February 1946, Attlee Papers, Bodleian Library, Oxford.)

The same month that Zilliacus accused the Government of "Imperial inertia", a Cabinet mission left for India with instructions to bring matters to a head and get over, or round, the obstacle to Indian independence presented by the quarrel between Congress and the Muslim League. It was an essential part of Bevin's concern for the defence of the Empire that he believed it could be transformed into a Commonwealth of self-governing peoples.

"When I say I am not prepared to sacrifice the British Empire," he asked the House of Commons, "what do I mean? I know that if the British Empire fell, the greatest collection of free nations would go into the limbo of the past, or it would be a disaster."[1]

When Attlee, speaking in the Commons, gave India the clear choice between remaining in the Commonwealth or going out, Bevin was deeply moved:

"As I thought of the great men who had helped to build this Commonwealth, I felt that Mr. Attlee was filling a similar role. I thought of Durham who saved us Canada and united the French- and the English-speaking peoples in the great Dominion. I thought of Campbell Bannerman who created the Union of South Africa. . . . I am glad that it was a Labour Government that had the courage, the wisdom, to take this step regarding India. For in that Eastern territory" (and he spoke of China and South East Asia as well as India) "a great new area is being born."[2]

3

While the Cabinet Mission in India wrestled with the problems of creating a new Commonwealth, the Prime Ministers of the old Commonwealth met in London during April and May.[3] High on the agenda was the British Government's assessment of what the Russians were up to, and in anticipation of this Bevin sent Attlee a note on 10 April in which he gave his own view of the answer.

"The Russians," he wrote," have decided upon an aggressive policy based upon militant Communism and Russian chauvinism . . . and seem determined to stick at nothing, short of war, to obtain her objectives. At the present time [Russia's] aggressive policy is clearly directed to challenging this country everywhere, partly because H.M.G. are the leaders of the Social Democracy in Europe and partly, no doubt, because we appear the less formidable of Russia's only two rivals as Great Powers."

Bevin expressed the view that this campaign was not a reaction to any measures the British had taken but the opening phase in Russia's strategy for the future. They had therefore, he argued, to defend themselves by exposing

[1] HC, 21 February 1946.
[2] Speech to the Bristol Festival of the TGWU, 30 March 1946.
[3] CAB 133/86 contains the record of their meetings and the papers prepared for them.

Soviet myths; give support to the social democrats, liberals and progressives who were fighting Communism, especially in France, Germany and Austria, where it was vital to prevent the Communists coming to power, and fight them in such sham international organizations as the World Federation of Trade Unions.[1] When the Prime Ministers discussed the situation Bevin said that he did not think Stalin wanted war, but he feared that

"the Soviet policy of expansion has engendered its own dynamic which may prove too strong for him [Stalin] in spite of all his shrewdness and power. I don't think he's planning for war but he may be unable to control the forces he's started. We've always got to be prepared for that."[2]

The Foreign Office preparation for the Prime Ministers' conference and Bevin's own memorandum laid particular stress on keeping Russia away from the Mediterranean. "If we went out," Oliver Harvey minuted, "the Russians would go in", and this would have incalculable effects on Italy and Southern Europe and on Africa. "These are far weightier reasons than the route to India argument for our making heavy sacrifices to hold on to the Mediterranean."[3] Smuts had already expressed his own mistrust of Russian intentions in the Mediterranean and Middle East, strongly opposing any move—such as a trusteeship for one of the ex-Italian colonies—that would allow the Soviet Union to acquire a foothold in Africa.[4] The Commonwealth Prime Ministers had differing views on what should be done with the Italian colonies, but on the central point all were agreed: Russia should be excluded from Africa at whatever cost.[5]

There was no doubt that since the beginning of the year tension between Russia and the West had increased sharply as a result of the continued Russian war of nerves against the northern tier of states, Iran, Turkey and Greece, which separated her from the Middle East and the Mediterranean.

When Senator Vandenberg and John Foster Dulles had dined with him in January, Bevin had shown them on the map how Russian intrigues in Iran were also directed against the Turks and how a Soviet-controlled province of Azerbaijan would enable the Russians to penetrate and put further pressure on Turkey. Bevin urged on his American visitors the importance of standing up to Russia over Iran. It was the same technique as Hitler's, one at a time: if they checked Russia over Iran, they could also save Turkey. The USA, he maintained, could not and must not stand aloof.[6]

---

[1] Bevin to Attlee, 10 April, 1946. FO 800/501/SU/46/15.
[2] Francis Williams, *Prime Minister*, p. 170. Williams was Attlee's press adviser at the time and close to both Attlee and Bevin.
[3] Minute by Harvey, 11 March 1946. FO 371/57173. See also the minute dated 12 March by Orme Sargent in the same file.
[4] Smuts to S. African High Commissioner. London, 26 Jan. 1946, DO 116/90/27; Smuts' other letters and telegrams in FO 371/57173.
[5] Transcript of the Prime Ministers' meeting on 28 April 1948. FO 371/57178.
[6] Pierson Dixon's note (dated 26 January) of a talk on 24 January. FO 800/513/US/46/20.

All American troops, however, had now been withdrawn from Iran and on 2 March the last 600 British soldiers were due to leave. It was at this point that a situation suddenly turned into a crisis, the first major crisis after World War II. On 1 March Moscow Radio announced that the Iranian Prime Minister, Qavam (who had been in the Russian capital since 18 February), had been informed that while the evacuation of Russian troops from Eastern Iran would begin on the date originally agreed they would remain in the rest of the country "pending further clarification". "Further clarification", Stalin made clear to the Prime Minister, meant among other things Iranian agreement to recognize the "autonomy" of Azerbaijan.

It was in the middle of this crisis that Churchill spoke at Fulton on the 5th. While Byrnes hesitated, Bevin had already sent a strong protest of his own to Moscow on 3 March. Dalton, meeting him by chance, "found him in a great state, saying that the Russians were advancing in full force on Teheran, that 'this meant war' and that the US were going to send a battle fleet to the Mediterranean". Attlee as well as Dalton thought Bevin was "strung up".[1] But the impression that war was a possibility was equally strong on the other side of the Atlantic. Truman, persuading Harriman to go as ambassador to London, told him: "It is important. We may be at war with the Soviet Union over Iran."[2]

What had startled both the Foreign Office and the State Department were the reports they received from Tabriz, the chief town of Azerbaijan, of heavy Soviet troop movements in the direction of the Iranian capital, Teheran, and the Turkish frontier. On 5 and 6 March Rossow, the US Vice-Consul in Tabriz, reported that reinforcements, including armour, were coming in from Russia and that General Bagramian, a Soviet officer with a spectacular combat record, had arrived to take over command. On the 6th he radioed to Byrnes: "All observations and reports indicate inescapably that Soviets are preparing for major military operations", and on the following day, "I cannot overstress the seriousness and magnitude of current Soviet troop movements here. This is no ordinary reshuffling of troops but a full-scale combat deployment."[3]

Byrnes had sent an urgent telegram to Moscow on the 5th, making clear that the US would not acquiesce in the Soviet decision to keep troops in Iran. No reply was received and on the 8th, after a session with a map, Byrnes and his advisers agreed that it looked as if the USSR was about to confront the world with a *fait accompli*. The battleship *Missouri* had already been ordered to sail for

---

[1] Entry in Dalton's unpublished diary, 27 March 1946, referring to a talk with Bevin a fortnight before. Dalton, it must be said, is never an unprejudiced witness when noting Bevin's shortcomings as Foreign Minister—whether it was lack of judgement or shortness of breath. His diaries show, perhaps unconsciously, how frequently he reflected on the improvement it would have been if he had been Foreign Secretary, not Bevin.

[2] H. Feis: *From Trust to Terror* (London, 1970), pp. 82–3, quoting Truman's papers.

[3] FRUS 1946 (7), pp. 343–4. See Robert Rossow: "The Battle of Azerbaijan 1946", *Middle East Journal* 10 (1956) and Kuniholm, pp. 303–42.

the Eastern Mediterranean and Byrnes now sent a further telegram asking the Soviet Government whether, instead of withdrawing, it was moving further troops into Iran and, if so, why?

There is no need to follow the development of the crisis in detail. Whatever the original Russian plans may have been, no coup took place, although rumours that one would continued to circulate in Teheran until the end of the month. By then the focus of interest had moved from Iran to the Security Council meeting in New York. The Russians had done everything they could to stop the "dispute" between Iran and the Soviet Union coming to the Council; when this failed, the Soviet representative, Gromyko, asked (19th March) that the question be postponed on the grounds that negotiations were in progress. Bevin strongly urged Byrnes to insist on taking the Iranian complaint without postponement even if Gromyko walked out.[1] The Americans needed no prompting. When the Council met on the 26th, Byrnes himself unexpectedly appeared to represent the United States and successfully opposed Gromyko's demand for postponement, even when the Russian carried out his threat to withdraw. Despite repeated claims from Moscow that agreement had been reached with the Iranian Government, the Americans and the British insisted on retaining the dispute on the Council's agenda until 6 May, the date by which the Russians had now announced they would complete evacuation of their troops. When 6 May came round and there was still no satisfactory report that the Russians had left Azerbaijan, they refused to let the question be removed from the Council's jurisdiction until there was.

The crisis in fact was over; in the course of May Iran dropped out of the news, Tass announcing on the 23rd that all Soviet troops had finally been withdrawn. But the consequences of the crisis remained important, for two reasons.

One is that it confirmed Bevin, Churchill, and those who thought like them, in their view that Stalin was not interested in pacification but in expanding Soviet power; that he was unlikely, however, to press this to the point where there was risk of war and that the way to avoid this was not by appeasement but by making clear where the limits lay and above all by the USA and Britain acting in agreement. All these lessons could be drawn from this first major crisis with the Soviet Union since the war, not least the lesson that, although there had been a real fear of the Russians using force or at least threatening to, the Western Powers were able, by reacting firmly but not over-reacting, to avert this by diplomacy, leaving the Russians (as Acheson stressed that they should) with a way out if they wanted to avoid a showdown.[2]

The other reason is that the Iranian crisis marked the point at which, after two and a half years[3] of indecision, acquiescence, or ineffectual opposition in

---

[1] Bevin to Byrnes, 21 March 1946, FRUS 1946 (7) pp. 368–9.
[2] Acheson at the meeting with Byrnes on 8 March, FRUS 1946 (7) p. 347.
[3] Calculated from the Teheran conference of November 1943 when Roosevelt first agreed to the Russian claims to Poland.

the face of Soviet probing and *faits accomplis*, the United States at last said "No" unequivocally. After that nothing was the same again.

The change was not as sudden as it appeared. There had been a good deal of criticism in Washington of Byrnes' initiative in going to Moscow in December 1945 to try and re-open the way to an agreement with Russia. It was repeated on his return and echoed by the President. Truman himself, however, had so far failed to give a lead publicly in defining American objectives or interests in a way that would guide the conduct of foreign policy: at the beginning of 1946 the most powerful state in the world appeared not only to have rushed into demobilization but to be incapable of translating its strength into effective influence. This impression and the sense of frustration which it created helped to produce the change which first became evident in the spring of 1946. It was, for example, exasperation not only with the attitude of the Soviet government but with the confusion and indecision of his own which led George Kennan, the US *chargé d'affaires* in Moscow, to send his famous 5,000-word dispatch in late February analysing the character of Soviet policy and the implications for America.

"Six months earlier," Kennan remarks in his *Memoirs*, "this message would probably have been received in the Department of State with raised eyebrows and lips pursed in disapproval. Six months later, it would probably have sounded redundant, a sort of preaching to the converted."[1]

But in February 1946 it chimed with and reinforced the change of mood in Washington. Kennan's argument that the Soviet leaders saw the world as divided into capitalist and socialist camps between which there could be no co-existence and that this view derived from the need to justify their own autocratic rule at home, gave added weight to the impression made by Stalin's speech of 9 February in which he re-asserted the Marxist view of the inevitability of conflict between communism and capitalism. Its practical implications were underlined by the news (16 February) of the arrest in Canada of a spy ring engaged in passing information about the atomic bomb to the Soviet Union.

By the end of February the shift of opinion in the Administration was sufficiently clear for Byrnes to feel the need to remove any doubt about his own position. He chose the occasion of a speech to the Overseas Press Club on 28 February to give the first public expression to the American Government's changed attitude towards the Soviet Union.

"Only an inexcusable tragedy of errors could cause serious conflict between us. . . ." But, he continued, "We will not and we cannot stand aloof if force or the threat of force is used contrary to the purposes and principles of the UN Charter. . . . If we are to be a great power we must act as a great power, not only in order to ensure our own security but in order to preserve the peace of the world."[2]

---

[1] Kennan, *Memoirs*, p. 295. The text of the despatch is in Appendix C.
[2] *Department of State Bulletin XIV* (10 March 1946) pp. 355–8.

Byrnes still hesitated when he first received the news that the Russians were going to keep troops in Iran, but from the time that he sent (and published) his two notes to Moscow (5 and 8 March) even his critics admitted that he never wavered in the firm line he took. The week that followed was described by *Newsweek* as reminiscent of the height of the Munich crisis, with the all-important difference that this time there was no weakening in the resolution of the Western Powers. When the dispute came before the Security Council Byrnes stepped in to take the lead and after that no more was heard of his following a policy of appeasement. Talking with Bidault in Paris at the beginning of May, Byrnes acknowledged that he had been criticized for yielding too much to the Russians and added: "This period had passed and American opinion was no longer disposed to make concessions on important questions."[1]

There was no one to whom this change mattered more than Ernest Bevin. Only a few weeks before, during the Security Council debate on Greece —arising out of the original Iranian complaint—he had had to face the Soviet charges on his own and (to the indignation of Senator Vandenberg) had been given no support by the USA in rebutting them. Bevin had not allowed this to weaken his stand, but if the USA were to continue to take no interest in what happened in the Middle East and Mediterranean (apart from Palestine), the British could have little hope of maintaining the balance of power in that part of the world from their own resources. This was equally true of Europe, where the consequences of the Americans disengaging themselves would have been even graver.

The American Government, and even more American opinion, had a long way to go before it was prepared for a Marshall Plan or a North Atlantic alliance. Churchill's warning of the threat from Russia was one thing, his call for a renewal of the wartime partnership between the "Anglo-Saxon peoples" quite another. It was only in July that the loan for Britain was passed by Congress, after six months' debate in which distrust of the British and dislike of the costs of foreign policy were strongly expressed. Nonetheless a watershed had been passed. The worst of Bevin's fears, a settlement between the USA and the USSR which Britain would be left to accept and the consequent withdrawal of American interest from Europe and the Mediterranean, was removed. US and British policies towards the USSR were now beginning to move on parallel lines and by the winter of 1946–47 began to converge.

4

The argument over demobilization which had occupied much of Bevin's time in the autumn of 1945 had now turned into one on the future size of the Forces

---

[1] FRUS 1946 (2), p. 204. Bohlen's note of Byrnes–Bidault conversation, 1 May 1946. The best short account I have come across of the change in American attitudes and policy is in Gaddis, c. 9.

and the overseas commitments which Britain could afford to maintain. These were vigorously debated several times during 1946 in the Cabinet's Defence Committee of which the important members were Attlee, Bevin and Dalton (representing the Treasury's point of view) and the Chiefs of Staff, led by Alanbrooke (CIGS until June) and then by Montgomery. As chairman, Attlee played a more active role than in Cabinet and from the first meeting in the New Year showed himself a radical and persistent critic of the Services' plans. A Labour Government was not likely to take the Chiefs' of Staff case for granted; the key figure was Bevin, who enjoyed the confidence both of the Prime Minister and—thanks to his wartime achievement as Minister of National Service—of the Chiefs of Staff as well. His experience of manpower problems was unrivalled (he was still chairman of the Manpower Committee) and as Secretary of State he was responsible for the foreign policy which set the scale of the military commitments the Forces had to meet.

At the Committee's meeting on 21 January the Prime Minister, supported by Morrison and Dalton, said bluntly that the nation could not afford either the manpower or the money asked for by the Chiefs of Staff. Bevin did not disagree, if they were talking about the size of the Forces in peacetime; but they had not yet reached peacetime and he made a strong plea not to reduce British strength in the Mediterranean until the peace treaties with Italy and Germany's other allies, as well as the negotiations for a new treaty with Egypt, had been completed. The Prime Minister accepted his argument, fixing a ceiling of 1.9 million for all three Services up to 30 June 1946, but he insisted on more drastic cuts in the following six months to bring the total down to 1.1 million by the end of the year.[1]

Bevin himself was sceptical of the figure of 650,000 accepted by the Defence Committee for the workforce needed to produce arms and supplies. He reported to the Cabinet on 7 February that the Manpower Committee recommended a reduction to that figure to be achieved in the first six months of the year; then went on to say that, on further reflection, he now thought it should be cut to half a million. He stood his ground however on the size of the Forces when Attlee re-opened the discussion in the Defence Committee a week later. The Chiefs of Staff had now produced a paper on the implication of the cuts needed to meet Attlee's figure for the end of 1946. Attlee was prepared for this and, before the Chiefs could elaborate on their foreboding, laid down three assumptions:

That there was no risk of war in the next 2–3 years; that there was no possibility of war with the USA; that there would be no fleet capable of being a menace in the next few years.

For good measure, he forestalled the most likely line of reply by calling for a re-examination of the assumption that it was vital to keep open the Mediterra-

---

[1] Defence Committee minutes, DO (46) 3rd meeting.

nean, adding that he did not see how it was possible to do so under modern conditions.

Once Attlee's own assumptions were accepted—and no one questioned them—the Chiefs' of Staff warning that the cuts would leave the country without reserves and make it impossible for the Services to meet a major emergency over the next two years produced little effect. Bevin had too much experience of manpower budgets to follow this line of argument. 31 December 1946 was a long way off and he concentrated on avoiding cuts in the next three months when British forces—in Venezia Giulia and Greece, for example, or Egypt—were wanted as a backing for British foreign policy in a delicate period of negotiation. He disarmed objections by promising that, if the negotiations in Paris went well and made it possible to reduce British commitments, he would support reductions in the second half of the year.[1] On this basis he got the agreement of the Cabinet as well as the Defence Committee, Alanbrooke noting in his journal:

"Cabinet from 11 to 12.30 to discuss Estimates and White Paper. . . . Thanks to Bevin we finally got it all through."[2]

Alanbrooke had served as CIGS with Churchill, and after the great days of the war might have been expected to take a critical view of a trade unionist as Foreign Secretary. He wrote in his diary however, at the beginning of 1946 (4 January) "The more I see of Bevin, the more impressed I am by him and his great qualities." Two months later he wrote again:

"He is a most wonderfully helpful individual always full of ideas. It is astonishing the ease with which he absorbs international situations and the soundness of his judgement."[2]

By then the Defence Committee was into another searching discussion, prompted by Attlee's scepticism about the strategic importance for Britain, of the Mediterranean and the Middle East. Dalton who as Chancellor was on the look-out for any measures that would reduce overseas expenditure, wrote in his journal in February:

"Attlee is fresh-minded on Defence. It was no good, he thought, pretending any more that we could keep open the Mediterranean route in time of war. That meant we could pull troops out of Egypt and the rest of the Middle East as well as Greece. Nor could we hope, he thought, to defend Turkey, Iraq or Persia against a steady pressure of the Russian land masses. And if India goes her own way before long, as she must, there will be still less sense in thinking of lines of imperial communications through the Suez Canal. We should be prepared to work round the Cape to Australia and New Zealand."[3]

---

[1] Defence Committee minutes, DO (46) 3rd and 5th meetings, 21 January and 15 February.
[2] 18 February. This and the two other quotations are from Bryant, p. 531 and footnote.
[3] Dalton, *Memoirs*, p. 101.

The discussion in the Defence Committee started on 8 March when Bevin said that the treaty negotiations with Egypt were adversely affected by the large number of British troops in Cairo and urged that they should be removed, unostentatiously, as soon as possible. His objective as he said at the next meeting on the 18th was "to clear right out of Cairo as soon as practicable". The Chiefs' of Staff reply was that the evacuation of Cairo and Alexandria could be completed in a year's time, and it was agreed that, if necessary, the principle of withdrawal could be conceded in the negotiations with Egypt.[1]

The Committee then started on a discussion of a paper circulated by Attlee on 2 March,[2] which must be amongst the most radical produced by a British Prime Minister in office. Attlee's case was that the British Empire had been built up in the era of sea power which had now become vulnerable to air power in land-locked seas like the Mediterranean. After setting out the arguments he had rehearsed to Dalton, Attlee concluded:

"We must not for sentimental reasons based on the past give hostages to fortune. It may be we shall have to consider the British Isles as an easterly extension of a strategic area the centre of which is the American continent rather than as a power looking eastwards through the Mediterranean to India and the East."

He added that he had not taken account of the changes resulting from atomic warfare.

Bevin had already circulated his own comments on Attlee's paper.[3] He was less concerned with the closing of the Mediterranean in wartime (which had not proved fatal in the recent war) than with its importance in peacetime; his argument was that the British presence in the Mediterranean served a political as well as a military purpose.

"The Mediterranean is the area through which we bring influence to bear on Southern Europe, the soft underbelly of France, Italy, Yugoslavia, Greece and Turkey. Without our physical presence in the Mediterranean, we should cut little ice with these states which would fall, like Eastern Europe, under the totalitarian yoke. . . . If we move out of the Mediterranean, Russia will move in, and the Mediterranean countries, from the point of view of commerce and trade, economy and democracy, will be finished."

The same argument applied to Spain, where Bevin saw Franco's regime as a passing phase but feared that the Iberian peninsula would be lost to the West if the British withdrew from the southern flank of Europe. The UK was "the last bastion of social democracy" in Europe between American capitalism and the Communist dictatorship of Russia.

"We talk a lot of a 'Western group' but shall we be able to bring it into existence or maintain it once we abandon our position as a Mediterranean power? I doubt it."

---

[1] Minutes of Defence Committee, 8 and 18 March, DO (46), 7th and 8th meetings.
[2] DO (46) 27.
[3] DO (46) 40.

Bevin then went on to develop his ideas about Britain's strategic position. He was concerned that the vital centre of communications and command for the whole Empire and Commonwealth (not just the Middle East, as the Chiefs of Staff had stressed) was in Egypt. He thought it would be much less vulnerable if it were placed in British territory. This would then open the way to a partnership agreement on defence with Egypt, allowing the use of bases and facilities in the Canal Zone in time of war. "It is a far better position to be asked to defend the Canal than to have to ask others for privileges."

Bevin thought Palestine, with its uncertain political future, too great a risk to spend millions on developing a major base and headquarters there. Cyprus would encourage the Russians to ask for a base in the Aegean and he thought the island should be demilitarized. His preference was for Kenya, making use of Mombasa as a port, and at the same time providing an alternative for the defence of the Indian Ocean, once facilities in India were withdrawn.

He ended his paper by recalling that during the war he had argued in favour of employing Italian prisoners of war to create a big port on the West African coast at Lagos and building a road right across Africa. He revived the idea with the double purpose of opening a great expanse of territory (including the uranium deposits in the Congo) to trade and development as well as providing a route of great strategic value if the route through the Mediterranean was closed. The whole scheme would require a large capital outlay and take years to accomplish, but he argued that it was worth beginning at once.

Attlee and Dalton were in favour of such a scheme which, as Dalton put it, "would put a wide glacis of desert and Arabs between ourselves and the Russians", and Liddell Hart who had similar ideas wrote to put them to Bevin.[1] But the Chiefs' of Staff reply gave little encouragement. East Africa might be useful as a reserve base, but it was as far from Port Said (2000 miles) as the UK and completely lacked the infrastructure of communications and facilities as well as the labour needed for a big base.[2] They were even more strongly opposed (as was Bevin) to Attlee's idea of abandoning the Mediterranean and the Middle East altogether,[3] arguing that, with Russia as the only power with which Britain might become involved in war, it was essential to deny her the use of these areas and to retain bases in the Middle East from which alone it would be possible to attack Russian territory. The best place to defend the United Kingdom and the communications on which it depended was as far east as possible both in Europe and the Mediterranean.

The discussion was continued through several meetings of the Defence Committee without reaching any clear conclusion. At the 9th meeting, on 27 March, it was extended to Greece, Dalton reporting that the removal of British

---

[1] Liddell Hart to Bevin, 5 June 1946, enclosing the memoranda dated 11 and 20 May 1946. Bevin wrote on the top of Liddell Hart's letter: "This is largely in keeping with the same defence schemes I put to the Defence Committtee. E.B." FO 800/513/US/46/62.
[2] COS Report, Location of Middle East Forces. DO (46) 48, 2 April 1946.
[3] COS Report, Strategic Position of the British Commonwealth. DO (46) 47 2 April 1946.

troops would save £15 million per annum and asking for this to be done by 1 September. Bevin succeeded in deferring a decision on this too and, despite Attlee's scepticism—"Our strategic position in Greece was weak and the only defence against aggression lay in an agreement with Russia"—prevented any weakening of British financial support in building up a Greek Army of 100,000.[1] In late May Bevin wrote in a paper circulated to the Cabinet:

"I do not anticipate a direct Russian attack on Greece, but I cannot put out of my mind the possibility of encouragement being given by Russia to these other [Balkan] powers to create trouble with Greece. . . .

"It would be unwise to commit ourselves to withdrawing British forces from Greece until the international situation is clearer and at least until we know what we can obtain about the withdrawal of Russian troops from South East Europe, and until the Greek Army is strong enough to defend its frontier against Yugoslav and Bulgarian aggression."[2]

How far Attlee would have pressed withdrawal from the Middle East in face of the opposition of the Chiefs of Staff is uncertain. In July they restated their objectives in a revised paper underlining the importance of the Middle East for Britain's oil supplies, and as the focus of a worldwide network of communications. Attlee remained sceptical but as negotiations were in progress about the three countries most affected—Egypt, Palestine and Cyrenaica—he agreed that further examination would have to be deferred.[3]

What could not be deferred was a decision about the size of the Forces and the call-up in 1947. On 15 April Bevin had put before the Defence Committee three alternative schemes for the continuation of military service, if this was to be extended beyond the end of 1946. Attlee's response was that he could not see how the country could possibly afford Armed Forces of over a million.[4] They must get them down to something like their pre-war strength. Bevin did not disagree if they were talking of peacetime; the argument with which he carried the Committee was that they were still living in an unsettled postwar transitional period.[5] The scheme he favoured did not go as far as the Services wanted but it would require men called up in 1947 and the first half of 1948 to serve for two years, reducing it to one-and-a-half in the latter part of 1948, and allowing deferment for coalminers, agricultural and building workers. This was the proposal Bevin put to the Cabinet on 20 May and defended against those who thought the country could not afford more than a million men in the Forces at the end of 1947. Bevin was prepared to make the same tactical concessions as before—this was a maximum which could be reduced if tension eased—but not to compromise on the main issue. His justification was not the danger of war, but the need for sufficient military power to make British foreign policy credible:

[1] DC minutes, 27 March. DO (46) 9th meeting.
[2] CP (46) 213, 30 May 1946.
[3] DC minutes, 19 July. DO (46) 22nd meeting.
[4] Defence expenditure in 1946, at £1,736 million, represented a fifth of the GNP.
[5] DC Minutes, 15 April 1946. DO (46) 12th meeting.

"Any precipitate reduction in the size of the Forces would be damaging to our position at the present critical stage of international affairs. Experience after the 1914–18 war had shown the disastrous effect on our foreign policy of the failure to back it up with adequate Armed Forces."[1]

Nobody was prepared to challenge this outright and, as the Cabinet minute drily records, "Discussion then turned to the question how far it would be possible to defer the call-up of apprentices."

The manpower debate was to be renewed even more sharply in the winter of 1946–7; before then the delay in concluding the Italian and other peace treaties made it necessary to keep British troops in Venezia Giulia, Italy and Greece and so exceed the ceiling set for the end of 1946.[2] Far more important, however, was a development in the summer of 1946 which, although known only to a handful of men at the time, was powerfully to affect British defence and foreign policy in the future and in which Bevin was deeply involved.

Attlee had returned from his meeting with Truman in November 1945 believing that he had secured the continuation of the wartime co-operation between the USA and Britain on atomic energy, including the manufacture of atomic bombs. There was no doubt, however, by the spring of 1946 that the Americans were not prepared to implement the November Agreement and were strongly opposed to the British building an atomic production plan of their own in the UK on the grounds of security.[3]

The President justified his attitude by referring to the American plan for the international control of atomic energy (the so-called Baruch plan) which was under consideration by the United Nations Atomic Energy Commission. Neither the American nor the Soviet governments, however, saw anything inconsistent in promoting schemes for international action to control the bomb and, in the meantime, taking good care that they should not be put at a disadvantage—the Americans by refusing to share the technological lead they already had and by continuing tests, the Russians by devoting all their energies to catching up with their own bomb. The British faced the same dilemma: they took part in the meetings of the UN Commission and tried hard to find a practical method of international control which both Americans and Russians would accept, but like the other two governments Attlee and Bevin believed they had also to look to the national interest and no more than the Russians were going to be inhibited by American disapproval.

Attlee made a further appeal to Truman in June, but this remained unanswered and the McMahon Act passed by Congress (1 August) categorically forbade the exchange of atomic information with foreign countries. The

---

[1] CM 50 (46) 20 May 1946.
[2] DC minutes 19 and 22 July. DO (46), 22nd and 23rd meetings.
[3] Professor M. M. Gowing gives an account of the unsuccessful negotiations leading up to this conclusion in *Independence and Deterrence, Britain and Atomic Energy 1945–52*, vol. 1. *Policy Making*, c.4. The exchange of telegrams between Attlee and Truman is printed in Francis Williams, *Prime Minister*, c. 8.

one consolation for the British was that, before the McMahon Act brought down the shutters, they were able to secure a share of the uranium supplies from the Belgian Congo which the Americans would otherwise have monopolized and without which any independent British project would have been impossible.

No one on the British side, certainly not Bevin, seems to have had any doubt about continuing with the project. The scientists and engineers were confident that they could build a plant without American aid, and none of the small number of ministers who knew of the proposal questioned the need for Britain to have atomic energy. The Cabinet was not consulted and the nearest the General 75 Committee came to a general discussion was on 25 October 1946 when they had to decide whether to extend the programme by adding a second pile that might well cost an additional £30–40 million. They recognized that the country might be faced with an economic crisis in two–three years' time, but argued that Britain could not afford to be left behind in a field of such revolutionary importance for industrial as well as military purposes. Bevin was absent from the meeting but fully shared the view of the other ministers who included Dalton and Cripps as well as Attlee.[1]

The other point which comes out clearly from Professor Gowing's history is that, although no formal decision was taken until January 1947, everyone concerned with the British atomic programme assumed that they were going to manufacture bombs. It would be perhaps five years before the material became available but the Chiefs of Staff had already told the Prime Minister[2] that the only reliable defence against atomic attack was likely to be the threat of retaliation, and that it was essential that the British should control their own deterrent in the form of their own stock of A-bombs. This too was not challenged, except by the lonely voice of Professor Blackett, and the result of the Americans cutting off co-operation was not to discourage, but if anything to stimulate the British to try and perpetuate their role as a major power into the atomic age.

5

Bevin could only make good the stand he had taken on overseas commitments if he could devise alternative arrangements to the British maintaining them on their own. The only practical alternative was to bring in American resources in some form or other and during 1946 the American administration was coming round to the idea that the United States would have to take over at least a part of Britain's commitments in Europe and the Northern Tier. The critical question was how long it would take the Americans to reach a decision in principle and even then to translate that into action in terms of budgets, the

[1] Gowing, c. 6.
[2] Memorandum of 1 January 1946, quoted in Gowing, pp. 169–71.

mobilization of support in Congress, and the provision of men and material on the ground; and at the same time, how long Bevin could hold out before the strain of an over-strained economy forced him to make concessions. What made 1946 so anxious a year for Bevin was that he could not be sure that the answers to the two questions would coincide; he might be driven to turn to the Americans in an emergency before they were ready to respond. He was particularly anxious about the Northern Tier where all three states continued to suffer from insecurity fanned by Communist propaganda.

Russian troops had been withdrawn from Iran, but the Russians retained their political influence and used it without inhibitions to keep up their pressure on the Teheran government. Azerbaijan and Kurdistan still enjoyed Soviet support for their claims to autonomy; the Tudeh-controlled Workers' Union organized a general strike in the British oilfields in the South, and the Iranian Prime Minister, Qavam, found it politic to take three Tudeh ministers into his cabinet. Many Iranians saw this as a first step to a "popular front" government on familiar lines and Iran's largest tribe, the Qashqu'i, staged a revolt in September against the growing influence of the Tudeh Party and Soviet penetration.

To ensure the safety of British personnel and the operatives in the oilfields, Bevin asked Cabinet approval for moving an Indian brigade to Basra and a cruiser to Abadan.[1] The investment in the Iranian oilfield and the Abadan field and the proportion of her oil supplies which Britain drew from it were too important for any British Government to consider giving it up, but at the same meeting Bevin said that he was convinced more could be done to make the operations of the Anglo-Iranian Company more acceptable to the Iranians.

In the course of July he circulated his proposals to the Cabinet. By Iranian standards, he conceded, the Company was a reasonable employer, but it ought to do much more to set an example and raise the standard of industrial relations in the country. What argument, Bevin asked, had he got against anyone who claimed to nationalize Iranian oil? The Labour Government was following a programme of nationalization in the UK, why shouldn't the Iranians do the same? He asked why the British should not take a leaf out of the Russians' book and offer the Iranian Government a 50% share in the operations. A joint Anglo-Iranian company would put relations between the Iranian Government and Abadan on mutually advantageous terms and win a more secure basis for British oil supplies by giving the Iranians a stake in developing and protecting their own property.[2] Unfortunately, as Attlee told Francis Williams, the oil people were

"Very difficult. They'd been a kind of imperial power and they couldn't get out of the habit. Ernie Bevin tried hard to get them to change and they did make some

---

[1] CM 68 (46) 15 July. Bevin's proposals were circulated as CP (46) 269.
[2] See the minute by Bevin, 20 July 1946 after talking to the chairman of AIOC, Sir William Fraser, FO 371/52735.

improvements, but they . . . clung on, wouldn't relax their hold and move with the times. They brought a lot of trouble on themselves and us as a result."[1]

The Abadan crisis, which broke over Morrison's hapless head five years later and ended with the expropriation of the company, is the proof of Bevin's foresight.

In Greece the elections, on which Bevin had placed his hopes, provided no answer to the country's problems. The Populist Party (despite its name, pro-royalist and right-wing) having won a majority, soon showed itself as inept and irresponsible as its predecessors in office, more interested in staging a plebiscite on the return of the King than in tackling Greece's economic problems and the inflation. There were still divided counsels as well as personal rivalries among the Greek Communist leadership, and mixed motives in any help they could expect from the Yugoslavs and the Bulgarians, both of whom had their eyes on Greek Macedonia. Communist broadcasts and press comment sharply condemned British intervention in Greece but Stalin gave no sign of wanting to intervene himself. Whenever the decision was taken to renew the civil war in Greece, there is no evidence that it was as the result of any directive from Moscow. None the less, a pattern became clearer in the course of 1946. The plebiscite on the return of the King was held on 1 September, again under international supervision and, with the Communists this time taking part in the vote, ended Communist hopes of coming to power by the ballot box. The arguments in favour of another attempt at seizing power by force ("the third round", in Greek reckoning) were correspondingly increased. As the scale of guerilla activities expanded, the fear they created and the support the guerillas were able to draw across the frontiers from Yugoslavia and Albania, later Bulgaria as well, added weight to these. The Greek Army made a poor showing and but for the continued presence of British troops resistance might have collapsed. The forces involved on both sides were small, but the stakes high. For if the British could only be got out, a Communist government—or a Communist-dominated coalition—might well take over in Athens, thereby completing Communist control of the Balkans, outflanking Turkey and providing the Soviet Union with a Mediterranean base, before the Americans could make up their minds or organize themselves to intervene. The day the British withdrew, the Turkish Ambassador in Athens forecast, the Yugoslavs would occupy Salonika and the Bulgarians Western Thrace. As part of an intensified propaganda campaign organized by the Communists around the world, the Ukrainian delegate in August 1946 again brought the situation before the Security Council, claiming that the Greek Government was endangering peace by threatening its neighbours and that the principal factor in encouraging it to do so was the continued presence of British troops.

In June 1946 the Russians renewed their propaganda offensive against the

[1] Francis Williams, *Prime Minister*, pp. 178–9.

Turks and called for bilateral talks between the two countries on the future of the Straits. A Soviet note delivered to the Turks on 7 August proposed that the arrangements controlling access through the Dardanelles and the Bosporus should henceforward be under the exclusive control of the Black Sea states and that the Soviet Union should join Turkey in organizing the joint defence of the Straits. The first would exclude the other powers which had been signatories of the Montreux Convention and leave the Turks to settle matters alone with the Russians and their two satellites, Rumania and Bulgaria; the second pointed to the admission of Soviet forces to Turkish territory where, once established, they could be used for other purposes than defending the international waterways. The British and Americans were ready to accept other Soviet proposals for the revision of the Montreux Convention, but not at all that this was a matter from which they should be excluded, leaving Turkey to come to terms with the Russians on their own. The episode underlined the extent to which the US Government now accepted the Turkish and Foreign Office view that the Russian objective was to reduce Turkey to the status of a satellite and that, if they succeeded, this would open the way to "the Near and Middle East, including the Eastern Mediterranean, falling under Soviet control . . . and being cut off from the Western world."[1] But it remained to be seen what the Western powers would do if the Russians increased their pressure. Unlike the Iranians and the Greeks, the Turks were united in their distrust of the Russians and had no Tudeh Party or EAM to divide them, but the cost to a poor country of maintaining 600,000 men under arms was widespread discontent and 38% of the 1946 budget. The British were committed to support the Turks as allies but had increasing worries about the strain on their own budget.

On the farther shore of the Mediterranean, Bevin had better luck in settling another problem which had been taken to the Security Council, the continued presence of French and British troops in the Levant States. When this came before the Council in January, Vyshinsky had a field day supporting the Syrians and Lebanese and refusing to allow the Western powers to smother the debate and settle the dispute privately. Bevin, who was only too anxious to get both British and French troops out, had every incentive to end a situation which was an embarrassment to Britain (although for different reasons) in both the Middle East and France. With de Gaulle's resignation (20 January 1946), the chances of the British and French acting together were improved and talks in Paris at the beginning of March at last produced agreement,

---

[1] The quotation is from the joint memorandum prepared by the US State, War and Navy Departments and approved by the President on 15 August 1946. FRUS 1946 (7) pp. 840–42. In mid-May, Walter Lippmann, the most influential columnist in the USA, wrote an article in the *Washington Post* (16 May 1946) in which he argued that the Russians were aiming at the break-up of the British Empire, beginning with a bid to dominate the Eastern Mediterranean which would separate the UK from the Middle East, Africa and S.E. Asia. "This is a blatantly crude plan to transform the Mediterranean from a British into a Russian lake." I owe this reference to Professor Roger Louis.

however reluctant, on the French side. On 17 April the Syrians held a national holiday to celebrate the withdrawal of all foreign troops from their country and the evacuation of the Lebanon was completed during the summer.

The French withdrawal from the Levant States, however—on Britain's insistence—only increased the Egyptian demand that the British should follow their example and evacuate Egypt. Bevin was still talking in terms of partnership and at the end of 1945 succeeded in establishing a Middle East Office in Cairo which carried on the advisory and technical services of the war-time Middle East Supply Centre. But Britain's inability to provide any large-scale financial support for development schemes meant that the most promising and original element in this concept of partnership never achieved more than a marginal effect. Bevin never gave up hope that he would be able to do something. In May he took up the idea again in the House of Commons and, when the British Ambassador in Cairo expressed his doubts, sent him a friendly but spirited reproof:

"I can well believe that the Rulers and Pashas of Egypt are made to feel uncomfortable when the rotten conditions of the working people of their country are published to the world. I doubt, however, whether the people themselves feel similar resentment. . . . Nor can I forget what has happened in Persia where the Russians have managed to use the bad social condition of the people as an instrument in founding their Tudeh Party."[1]

But Bevin continued to feel that, until the question of defence could be settled, there was no possibility of putting Britain's relations with the Middle East on a new footing. Meeting Byrnes in Paris, Bevin reproached him with thwarting his attempt to get the trusteeship over Cyrenaica for Britain at the first meeting of the CFM in September 1945. If the Americans had not proposed a collective UN trusteeship, the British, who were in occupation of Cyrenaica and on good terms with the Senussi, would have been able to establish a base there and carry out the evacuation of Egypt without difficulty.[2] Bevin renewed his attempt at the Paris meeting of the CFM in May,[3] and undeterred by American opposition,[4] put up a scheme to the Cabinet in September for a trusteeship which could combine the military facilities Britain needed immediately with independence after ten years.[5] But the negotiations over the Italian colonies dragged on without agreement and the only alternative available when the evacuation from Egypt started was Palestine—still further complicating the problems the British faced there.

The negotiations on the revision of the 1936 Treaty with Egypt (which still

[1] Bevin to Sir R. Campbell, 21 June 1946. FO 800/457/EG/46/32.
[2] British record of Bevin's talk with Byrnes, Paris, 26 April 1946. FO 800/446/CONF/46/1.
[3] Bevin to Attlee, 11 May 1946. FO 800/501/SU/46/15.
[4] Bevin's talk with Harriman in London, 24 May, FO 800/457/EG/46/23.
[5] CM 46 (83) 26 September 1946.

had ten years to run) had got off to a bad start. It was a year after the end of the Mediterranean war before talks began in earnest. The delay was very much to the British disadvantage: the most likely explanation is that many of the officials on whom Bevin depended, whether civilian or military, on the spot or in London, were lukewarm or opposed to the policy he wanted to carry out and that little was done to forward it unless the Foreign Secretary constantly supplied the driving force. Unfortunately, with much else to preoccupy him, it was not until the spring of 1946 that Bevin seems to have grasped that valuable time was being lost and to have taken a much more direct part in pushing on the negotiations.

When the Egyptian Government finally took the initiative (in December 1945) the British let five weeks elapse before replying and then said that "the essential soundness" of the principles underlying the 1936 Treaty had been demonstrated by the war. Not before the end of March (by which time demonstrations and rioting had begun in favour of "national liberation") did the British announce the names of their delegation which contained no major political figure to match the Egyptian Prime Minister and his Cabinet colleagues, but consisted entirely of senior officers and Embassy officials, the last people likely to make a success of working out a new relationship in which they had no belief.

Once he recognized the blunder that had been made, Bevin did his best to retrieve it by announcing two days later that he would lead the British delegation himself and that the Secretary for Air, Lord Stansgate (who, as Wedgwood Benn, had defended the Egyptian point of view between the wars) would conduct the earlier part of the negotiations along with the British Ambassador. Then, when it became clear that the talks would get nowhere until the Egyptian insistence on evacuation was recognized, Bevin agreed with Attlee that they should publicly offer the withdrawal of all British forces from Egyptian territory before sitting down to discuss defence arrangements for the future.

The announcement of this in the Commons on 7 May roused an outraged Churchill to demand an emergency debate. Bevin returned from the Council of Foreign Ministers in Paris to take part in it. By that time (24 May) he had convinced himself that the debate had been deliberately engineered in his absence abroad as an attack on the Government's foreign policy and was a "Tory trap". He refused to listen to Pierson Dixon's argument that many people were genuinely sceptical

"Of the experts' advice that, if we offered to withdraw, the Egyptians would be so pleased, and so frightened of Russia, that they would invite us in. Ernest Bevin is determined to go for Winston and is rolling vituperative phrases round his mouth (swollen from the extraction of three teeth, making him almost indistinguishable from a bloodhound.)"[1]

---

[1] Pierson Dixon's diary, 22 May 1946, quoted in Dixon, p. 214.

Some of the heat was taken out of the debate by Attlee's assurance that, if the talks broke down, the 1936 Treaty would remain in force and would guarantee Britain's right to maintain troops in Egypt. But both Churchill and Bevin were still spoiling for a fight. After listening to an attack full of Churchillian invective, Dixon recorded in his diary that, no sooner was Bevin on his feet, than he

"Launched into personal insults on Winston, which soon had both sides of the House in an uproar. At one moment Winston and Ernie were on their feet on either side of the mace shaking their fists at one another, and supporters making a pandemonium all round. . . ."[1]

These exchanges over, Bevin proceeded to make a successful defence of his efforts to find a middle way between those who called for immediate evacuation and those who wanted to make no concessions but stand on the existing Treaty. The row in the House served to discharge the tensions which had built up in the Paris talks[2] and two days later Dixon found his chief at No. 10 restored, buoyant and unrepentant. But the problem of getting agreement with the Egyptians remained.

Throughout the summer, much of which he had to spend in Paris in the Council of Foreign Ministers and the subsequent Peace Conference, Bevin did his best to keep in touch with the negotiations. He saw Harriman and pressed for American support, arguing that the right to re-enter the Suez base in an emergency and the maintenance of the installations there were as much an American as a British—or Egyptian—interest.[3]

"There must not be a vacuum", he told the House of Commons. "If the Egyptian Government try to force a situation in which there is a vacuum—meaning that we have gone and that there is nothing there for security instead, regional defence or other organisation—to that I can never agree. But I have offered . . . a new basis of approach, in which I believe. Perhaps partnership is the wrong term, but it is a joint effort for mutual defence."[4]

Bevin continued to have difficulty with the British as well as the Egyptians. On 25 May and again on 19 June he wrote to the Prime Minister urging him to impress on the Chiefs of Staff the need to speed up the evacuation of Cairo and

[1] *Ibid.*, 24 May, p. 215.
[2] See below, c.7.
[3] Bevin to Washington Embassy, 24 May, following a talk with Harriman in HC. FO 800/457/EG/46/23. After a report by Harriman, Byrnes instructed the US Minister in Cairo to make clear to the Egyptian Prime Minister and the King American interest in seeing an agreement reached which would provide both for Egypt's independence and the effective defence of the Middle East. Following Harriman's recommendation, Byrnes added that, whatever mistakes the British had made in the past, the US Government was convinced of Bevin's sincerity in trying to combine the two.
[4] HC 24 May 1946.

Alexandria. ("It needs a warlike operation to get them to move.")[1] As Attlee said later: "Wonderful capacity to play for time some of the military had."[2]

Attlee and Bevin had only got the reluctant agreement of the Chiefs of Staff to the evacuation of Egypt on condition that the main British base moved no further than Palestine, and that the Army should have the right to keep a maintenance staff in the Canal Zone base and move back in if trouble threatened. The Egyptians, Bevin reported to the Cabinet on 7 June, were quite unwilling to agree to any such proposals which they regarded as leaving them as much under foreign occupation as before. In an effort to meet the Egyptian objections, Bevin got Cabinet agreement to replacing the formal provision in the Treaty for the maintenance of installations in peace-time and re-entry in time of war with arrangements for cooperation between the two military staffs on the model of the Joint Defence Board between the USA and Canada.[3] He also proposed to complete the evacuation by March 1947. Bevin consulted the Cabinet again on 1 August and drew up fresh instructions which he told Stansgate and the Egyptian Ambassador in London must be regarded as the limit of concessions. To the former, he wrote that he should present the new draft with confidence as he was sure the Egyptians wanted to avoid a breakdown; to the latter, he said that if it was not acceptable, then the only alternative was to revert to the 1936 Treaty.[4] When the Ambassador asked if the British could not make some gesture to acknowledge the Egyptian claim over the Sudan, Bevin replied: "No, not till after the Treaty is signed."

In writing to the Prime Minister, Bevin insisted that they must be able to use Egyptian territory if British interests were threatened, say, in Iraq or Southern Iran ("I am thinking five or ten years hence") and that, with talks on Palestine about to start, it was important to avoid appearing to give in to the Arabs. He added that Stansgate was ready to make concessions when the Arabs, as in the market place, piled their demands high and expected the other side to bargain.[5] Bevin still underestimated the strength of anti-British feeling in Egypt; when the Egyptians refused to accept the new draft, however, he did not break off negotiations, but sat tight and waited until the Prime Minister Sidqi Pasha offered to come to London and renew the talks in the autumn.

6

Although Bevin talked of treating the Middle East as a whole, his greatest difficulty was exactly the opposite: inability to isolate the problems he had to deal with and prevent them complicating each other. The Sudan is a good

---

[1] FO 800/457/EG/46/24 and 26.
[2] Francis Williams, *Prime Minister*, p. 178.
[3] CP (46) 219 discussed by the Cabinet on 6 & 7 June 1946. CM (46) Nos. 57 & 58.
[4] Bevin's account of his talk with the Ambassador in a dispatch of 8 August 1946 to Stansgate. FO 800/457/EG/46/41.
[5] Bevin to Attlee, 4 August 1946, FO 800/457, EG/46/40.

example of this. In March 1946 Bevin gave a promise in the House of Commons that the Sudanese would be consulted before any change was made in their country's status, adding that Sudanese self-government should be seen "as a first step towards eventual independence". This sounded well in London and Khartoum, and was said with complete sincerity, but it cut clean across the Egyptians' insistence that the Sudan was permanently linked to Egypt in a union under the Egyptian crown and prejudiced any chance of agreement in the Anglo-Egyptian talks.

The most important example, however, was Palestine. Palestine was to provide the substitute for the Suez base which was vital if there was to be any hope of agreement with Egypt. But the Government had not even time to announce their offer to evacuate Egypt before the Report of the Anglo-American Committee of Inquiry was published and set the whole Palestine issue ablaze again.

Between the announcement of the AAC and its report at the end of April 1946, relations between the Yishuv, the Jewish community in Palestine, and the British administration grew steadily worse. There were several incidents involving loss of Jewish and British lives. The Haganah not only cooperated with the extremist groups in raids on police and army installations but resumed illegal immigration on an increased scale: both were intended as a challenge to the British authorities and a provocation to take action which could then be blazoned to the world as persecution in a Nazi-style British police state. The equivocal attitude of the Jewish leaders to the activities of the Irgun and the Stern Gang was one of the chief reasons for the anger and distrust Bevin displayed in meetings with them.

The British were given a preview of the problem they were to be confronted with, time and again, in the next two years. A convoy of 1200 young Jewish men (in British Army trucks) was stopped on its way to the Italian port of La Spezia, where two schooners were to take them to Palestine. The Italians were sympathetic to the plight of the refugees which received world-wide coverage, reinforced by a hunger strike of the whole Jewish community in Palestine. Harold Laski visited La Spezia and had to listen to charges that the British were responsible for the death of four million Jews. He retorted that if it had not been for the British probably none of them would have been alive. But he agreed to plead their case with Bevin, and Bevin intervened with the Palestine Administration to secure their admission "in driblets, say 100 at a time" over and above the fixed quota. By the end of May they were all in Palestine and the Yishuv leaders were jubilant.

For six months, however (November 1945–April 1946) policy discussions of what to do were suspended until the Anglo-American Committee produced its report. When its members visited London, Bevin invited them to lunch and promised that if they submitted a unanimous report he would do his best to get it implemented. Crossman (who had been appointed as one of the British members of the Committee) wrote that this "made an enormous impression on all of us, especially on my American colleagues".

Although Bevin would have liked to have Smuts as chairman of the Committee, the members finally chosen included no leading political figures. The fact that its chairmen were two judges—who found it impossible to get along with each other—and that the most forceful member of the Committee the Texan Judge Hutcheson, interpreted the terms of reference as excluding political considerations, gave the proceedings a judicial character, concentrating (in Hutcheson's words) on the attempt "to discover objectively what were the rights and wrongs of the conflict", instead of on a possible solution to it.

Nonetheless, the evidence presented to the Committee, and especially the public hearings which it conducted in New York, the DP centres in Germany and Austria and in the Middle East, left its members in no doubt of the passions aroused, amongst both Jews and Arabs, by the Zionist plan to create a Jewish state in Palestine. Neither government brought pressure to bear on the Committee about the conclusions it should reach, but Bevin's remarks about unanimity had an influence in persuading its members that they should subordinate their differences to recommendations on which they could agree. The Report, signed by all twelve members on 19 April, was unanimous in declaring that Palestine alone could not solve the Jewish refugee problem and in rejecting the idea of making the country into either a Jewish or an Arab state; but recommended the immediate admission of 100,000 Jewish refugees and the continuation of Jewish immigration without the White Paper's requirement of Arab acquiescence. It opposed partition in favour of keeping a unitary state, but recommended the abolition of the restrictions on land purchase which the Jews regarded as discriminatory. It urged the Jewish Agency to cooperate actively in suppressing terrorism and illegal immigration but did not make disarmament of the illegal forces a prior condition of the admission of the 100,000.

Inevitably, the Report when published on the night of 30 April–1 May satisfied no one. It was at once attacked by both Jews and Arabs, and the Press in Britain as well as the USA expressed a universal sense of disappointment that it offered no clear-cut solution. "When it comes to policy", the *Daily Telegraph* commented, "the Report bases itself on the hope that the apparently irreconcilable can be reconciled."[1] But the Report offered an opportunity Bevin might be able to use to achieve his objective of involving the United States with Britain in finding a solution. As a basis he had a unanimous report signed by the six American as well as the six British members of the Committee and, even more important, a report which confronted the Zionists with the dilemma which threatened to split the Zionist movement —between choosing no immigration and rejection, or no statehood and acceptance.[2] The dilemma was sharpened by the fear, voiced by both Horo-

---

[1] 2 May 1946.
[2] So defined by Moshe Shertok in the Jewish Agency Executive meeting, 20 June 1946. Central Zionist Archives, quoted by Nachmani, p. 357.

witz and Weizmann in the JA Executive, that rejection would mean opposition to a joint Anglo-US policy. The immediate reaction of the Yishuv's moderates was in favour of acceptance, and Weizmann at the meeting of the JA Executive, argued that it would be better to go for the reality of admitting 100,000 immigrants than the dream of a Jewish state.[1] Ben Gurion was categorical in rejecting the report but feared that the Zionists would not be strong enough to prevent an Anglo-American agreement to accept it.[2]

If anything was to be made of this situation, it turned on the way in which the British Government treated the report. With hindsight, it appears clear that the wisest course for the British would have been to accept it, including the recommendation to admit 100,000 Jewish DPs and use it as a basis on which to carry the moderate Zionists and the Americans with them in working out a settlement. With all its shortcomings, none of the other plans devised during the next two years came as close as the AAC to British requirements and as Churchill wisely said, referring to another set of proposals later in the year:

"It is far more important that there should be agreement than that there should be this or that variant of the scheme. Any solution in which the U.S.A. would join us could be made to work."[3]

The blame for letting this opportunity slip has often been laid on Bevin,[4] but this is too simple a view to survive examination of the British and American evidence.

When the Report first came up for discussion at the Cabinet's Defence Committee on 24 April, Bevin expressed reservations about Arab reactions to the admission of 100,000 Jews and to the withdrawal of restrictions on land sales.

"Nevertheless (the minute continues) he felt that it would be difficult to avoid acceptance of the broad outline of the report. It was a unanimous document and, as such, he hoped that it was an augury of cooperation by the U.S. Government in solving the problems of Palestine."

He suggested that the first step, before they admitted more immigrants, was to disarm illegal organizations; he proposed to ask the US Government for troops to help in doing so.

In spite of his reservations, Bevin's was the only voice in favour of accepting the Report.

---

[1] *Ibid.*

[2] Ben Gurion's Paris diary, 22 April, quoted by Nachmani, pp. 360–61.

[3] HC, 1 August 1946.

[4] For example by James MacDonald: (*My Mission in Israel*, NY 1951 pp. 24–6) who, together with Bartley C. Crum, another American member of the AAC (*Behind the Silken Curtain* NY 1947), and Richard Crossman was prominent in spreading the view that Bevin's "pathological hatred" of the Jews was the driving force behind British policy.

"The Prime Minister said that he took a less rosy view of the report than the Foreign Secretary . . . He found little grounds for the view that we could obtain American cooperation in the solution of Palestine problems. On the contrary the report proposed a policy which would set both Arabs and Jews against us and that we should implement it alone."[1]

Attlee proposed handing the Report to a group of officials headed by Sir Norman Brook, Secretary to the Cabinet, which, in line with their dislike of the AAC operation from the beginning, found little to commend in its Report. They echoed the Chiefs' of Staff opinion that if implemented it would lead to an Arab rising in Palestine which would be supported by the Arab states and require British reinforcements. Their recommendation to the Cabinet was that Britain should decline to carry out the Report's proposals on its own, but should turn either to the UN or to the USA for support and assistance.[2] Bevin would not agree to the UN. He flew back from the CFM in Paris specially to introduce the Report to the Cabinet on the 29th and in doing so repeated that he had already had a talk with Byrnes in Paris before the Cabinet decision.

"The essence of our policy should be to retain the interest and participation of the U.S. Government in this problem. The inquiry had been made by an Anglo-U.S. Committee and the report should be considered by the two Governments jointly."

His conclusion was that, if skilfully handled the proposals could form the basis of a reasonable settlement but only if the Americans would join in implementing it. He suggested they should look to a joint body of experts to consider the problems in detail. In the meantime he urged that the Government should not rush to define its own attitude to the Report as soon as it was published, but wait to see the reaction to it—and not be unduly alarmed by some initial clamour from the Arab states.[3]

With this Bevin returned to Paris and was absent for the next eleven meetings of the Cabinet. He had already sent a note to Byrnes saying that he hoped the US Government would make no statement about the Report without consulting London first. Truman, however, received very different advice. Rabbi Silver, the leader of the American Zionist movement, was proposing to denounce the Committee's report because it did not endorse a Jewish state. The two pro-Zionist members of the Committee, however, MacDonald and Crum, persuaded him that this would only anger Truman and that the best course would be to get the President to accept the first recommendation calling for 100,000 Jews to be admitted to Palestine and put off a decision on the other recommendations. With the help of David Niles, the White House staff member who dealt with Palestine and who was deeply

---

[1] Defence Committee, 24 April 1946, DO (46) 61; FO 371/52517/E 3839/G.
[2] CP (46) 173.
[3] CM 38 (47) 29 April.

committed to the Zionist cause, a statement on these lines was put before Truman who signed it out of hand.[1]

The President's action, taken without consultation, made both Bevin and Attlee furious. If that was a natural response, it was a mistake to let resentment alter the course which the two had earlier agreed on, not to make an immediate statement of the British attitude. At a Cabinet meeting hurriedly called for noon on 1 May (at which Bevin was not present) Attlee said that in view of Truman's statement it had become necessary for him to say something too. He proposed to make clear the practical difficulties of absorbing 100,000 immigrants in a short time and to insist that the Commission's recommendation to this effect could not be accepted unless the illegal organizations in Palestine were first disbanded and disarmed.[2]

The need to do this had certainly been raised, by Bevin among others, at the Defence Committee, but nothing appears to have been said of making it a condition at the Cabinet meeting on the 29th. It was only decided to make the condition explicit and to do so in public after Truman's statement. If it was in British interests, however, as Bevin continued to believe, to involve America in finding a solution to the Palestine problem by means of the Report, Attlee's statement—which was widely taken as a retort to the President—could only make that more difficult to achieve, could only strengthen the hands of those, in the British administration as well as the Zionist Movement who for quite different reasons, wanted to keep the Americans out of Palestine.

It was not, however, a fatal mistake. On the same day that he made his statement in the House Attlee sent a message to Bevin in Paris, asking his advice on how best to make a formal approach to the US Government and a week later he wrote again to say: "The sooner we get to grips with the Americans the better.'[3] There followed a correspondence between the Prime Minister and the President[4] which makes clear that Attlee was still following Bevin's idea of a joint meeting of experts to discuss the recommendations of the Report in detail. More surprisingly it shows Truman coming round to and finally accepting the same idea. By July the meeting took place and, more surprisingly again, before the end of the month had produced an agreed report.[5]

[1] See Zvi Ganin: *Truman, American Jewry and Israel 1945-48* (NY 1979) pp. 60–64, which is based on the Silver papers.
[2] CM 39 (46).
[3] Attlee to Bevin, 1 and 8 May 1946. FO 800/485/PA/46/13 and 16.
[4] This extends from 8 May to 4 July and is to be found in FO 800/485/PA/46/16–18; 20; 24–25; 28; 31–32; 38.
[5] The account I have given can be compared with that of Melvin I. Urofsky: *We Are One! American Jewry and Israel*, published in 1978: "A furious Bevin refused to accept the [AAC] Report and in so doing profoundly affected Jewish history. By reneging on his word, he alienated an American President, wiped out the last traces of moderation within the Zionist leadership, and created a set of circumstances that made the establishment of Israel possible." (p. 112).

CHAPTER 7

Paris, Summer 1946: "Open disagreements openly arrived at"

I

Bevin had had to leave for Paris and the Council of Foreign Ministers before the Palestine Committee's report was published and Truman made his statement. The Foreign Ministers' deputies had been working in London since the Moscow conference on the peace treaties to be signed with Italy and the other ex-satellites of Germany. They had made virtually no progress. There was no longer any prospect of the peace conference meeting on the agreed date of 1 May and Byrnes proposed that the Foreign Ministers should meet again, in Paris, and try to recover some of the ground lost since Moscow.

The search for a settlement which took Bevin to France at the end of April was to last until December. On more than 80 of the 157 days he was away from London Bevin and Byrnes spent several hours, sometimes as many as eight or nine, each day in repetitive, frustrating and often angry argument with Molotov in the CFM before finally reaching agreement on the Italian and satellite treaties—and all this without doing more than skirt the main issue likely to divide them, the settlement with Germany. Even for a man who had passed as much of his life in negotiation as Bevin this was an exhausting and dispiriting experience. Apart from meetings of the Council he spent a large part of two months (mid-August to mid-October) in Paris for the Peace Conference attended by representatives of 21 nations[1], and took part in the meeting of the UN General Assembly and Security Council in New York (November–December), continuously involved in controversy under the blaze of publicity and the search for a settlement behind the scenes. Not a day passed but he was confronted with a sheaf of telegrams from the Foreign Office or Prime Minister requiring decisions on issues as difficult and urgent as Palestine, Germany, Greece, the negotiations with Egypt, Iran, Turkey,

---

[1] This was called to consider the draft treaties with Italy, Finland, Hungary, Rumania and Bulgaria.

defence policy (including the A-bomb) and the world shortage of food. Both in Paris and New York he had to find time for talks with Jewish leaders and the Americans on Palestine, with the foreign ministers and ambassadors of a score of other countries, and all the time he had to stand up to a constant stream of criticism and abuse from the communist press and radio, from Zionists and Arabs and from the Left-wing of his own Party, culminating in the November motion of "No confidence" tabled in the House of Commons.

This was an inhuman burden for any man to bear: Bevin was in his sixties, far from well and (a very important point for someone of his temperament) away from his base and unable to confront his critics and draw encouragement from his supporters. No wonder that on occasion his temper was tried beyond endurance and that his staff were anxious whether his health would not break down under the strain. Yet at the end of the year, in a Christmas broadcast to the nation, he was able to announce that "After 98 meetings . . . patience has triumphed and I am fully convinced that understanding will grow. For at last we have succeeded and the treaties are ready for signature."[1]

The first session of the Council of Foreign Ministers in Paris, lasting from 25 April to 16 May, gave Bevin a foretaste of what he was in for during the rest of the year.[2] The meeting took place under the shadow of the confrontation with the Soviet Union in the Security Council, first over Greece, then over Iran and with echoes of Churchill's Fulton speech still in everyone's mind. Writing in advance of the meeting, *The Economist* asked: "What conclusion can be drawn but that their [i.e. Russian] policy is built on invincible hostility and implacable distrust? Why should Mr. Bevin and Mr. Byrnes undertake yet another fruitless pilgrimage?" But this would not do. "If not a threat of war, at least a fever of expectation hangs over Europe", and an open breach "might very well be the signal for civil strife in more than one European country". The West had to look for areas where it could compromise without appeasement.[3] The *Manchester Guardian* was hardly more cheerful: "The choice," its leading article concluded on the day the conference opened, "is no longer between a good peace or a bad peace, but between a bad peace and no peace at all. And no peace is dangerously close to war."[4]

The Council began its meetings in a deceptive calm. The French had gone to great trouble to put on an impressive show and when the ministers met for the first time in the Luxembourg Palace not a word was said about the Russian insistence on excluding them which had led to the break up of the Council meeting in London eight months before. With a referendum due to be held on the new French Constitution followed by a general election, in both of which the Communists hoped to poll an increased vote, the Russians had no

---

[1] BBC Home Service, 22 December, 1946.
[2] The British record of the CFM meeting in Paris, both parts, April–July 1946 is in FO 371/57265–283. The US record is in FRUS 1946 (2): pp. 1–87 (the Deputies' meeting); pp. 88–440 (Part 1, April–May); pp. 441–92 (Deputies); pp. 493–940 (Part 2, June–July).
[3] *The Economist*, 20 April, 1946.
[4] *Manchester Guardian*, 25 April, 1946.

intention of spoiling their chances. But at the end of eighteen days of meetings, often with two sessions in a day, the Foreign Ministers had not advanced much further than the Deputies, save (to repeat Alistair Cooke's phrase) in open disagreements openly arrived at.

The principal topic of discussion was the Italian peace treaty: how much Italy should pay in reparations; what should happen to the Italian colonies; and who was to have Trieste and the greater part of the Venezia Giulia, the Italians or the Yugoslavs? On all three questions the Russians made demands and the Western powers, particularly the USA as the protector of Italy, refused them. They would not agree to Italy having to make reparation beyond her limited capacity to pay, since this would only mean that the USA and Britain, as in the case of Germany, would have to provide the means; they would not agree to allow the Russians a foothold in North Africa and they would not agree to let the Yugoslavs take over Trieste and the greater part of the Istrian peninsula.

Although uncompromising in the formal sessions, Molotov dropped hints in private of his willingness to make a deal which led Bidault to propose that the Foreign Ministers should meet in restricted session to see if they could make more progress that way. With the Communists as the largest party in the French coalition government, with the fear that they would increase their vote at the coming referendum and general election, and might even attempt a coup—Bidault twice referred in a talk with Byrnes to the possibility of "Cossacks on the Place de la Concorde"[1]—the French had a strong incentive to play the role of mediators and on 2 May the Council began a series of informal and restricted meetings of which nine in all were held before it adjourned.

At a private dinner with Byrnes on the 5th Molotov sketched the outlines of a deal: Trieste and as much as possible of the Istrian peninsula for Yugoslavia plus 100 million dollars in reparations for the Soviet Union in return for dropping Yugoslav (and Greek) claims to reparations from Italy and the Russian bid for the trusteeship of an Italian colony which he knew he was never going to get. The American reply was a blunt "No". This time Byrnes was not prepared, as he had been at Moscow in December, to secure the success of the meeting by falling in with the Russian tactics, and the change of attitude was deliberate policy on the Americans' part. Senator Vandenberg, who attended all the meetings as a member of the US delegation, wrote a fortnight after the Council adjourned:

"There is no doubt that Molotov was in a 'trading mood'. He constantly referred—day after day—to the fact that he had made a 'big decision' (namely Tripolitania) and what was he going to get in return? He asked that question a hundred times. . . .

"Personally I think we had to do at least one thing in Paris—namely to demonstrate that the 'appeasement' days are over. Stalin and Molotov had Roosevelt at a perpetual

---

[1] Bidault's talk with Byrnes, 1 May. FRUS 1946 (2) pp. 203–5.

disadvantage in their war conferences because we were afraid the Russians would quit the war and make a separate peace. As a result, I am sure they got the habit (with justification) of believing that they can always 'write their own ticket' in these international meetings."[1]

It was Byrnes, not Bevin, who now made the running on the Western side and for the first time in the Council of Foreign Ministers confronted the Russians with an American veto. Vandenberg noted, however, that "Molotov seems determined to bait Bevin", as he had at both the London and Moscow meetings. When the latter, at the session on 6 May, made fresh proposals about the Italian colonies in East Africa, Molotov dismissed these as simply aimed at expanding the British Empire. Bevin retorted that Britain had set an example by seeking no new territory at the end of the war.

"In fact, if he could be given credit for an honest motive, it would be seen that he was merely trying to remedy some 19th-century wrongs. . . . 19th-century imperialism in England is dead. We are no longer an expansionist country. I am driven to suspicion sometimes that our place has been taken by others. But as a social democrat I am not envious."

Bidault, who was in the chair, tried to close the meeting at this point, but Molotov would not be denied.

"19th-century imperialism may be dead in England," he declared, "but there are now 20th-century tendencies. When Mr Churchill calls for a new war . . ., he represents the worst of 20th-century imperialism, and he evidently approves Mr. Bevin's foreign policies. Of course one is free to divert attention from oneself but it won't succeed. . . . Britain has troops in Greece, Palestine, Iraq, Indo-China and elsewhere. Russia has no troops outside the security zones and their lines of communication. This is different. We have troops only where provided by treaties." Egypt and India, Molotov added, were both members of U.N.O. but were denied their rights by the British. "What kind of relationship exists, when one nation imposes its will by force on another? How long can such things go on?"

Bevin waited until Molotov had finished and then said: "Now that you have got that off your chest, Mr. Molotov, I hope you feel better."[2]

The two sides were no nearer agreement on the Balkan treaties. Byrnes pressed for equal access in trade for all the United Nations, Bevin for restoring freedom of navigation and trade on the Danube as it had existed before the war and the withdrawal of Russian troops from Bulgaria as they had agreed at London. Molotov, accusing the West of "aiming at capitalist enslavement", resisted any proposal which would infringe the monopoly of economic as well as political control which the Soviet Union was in process of imposing on Rumania and Bulgaria.

[1] *The Private Papers of Senator Vandenberg* (London 1953) pp. 285–6, giving the Senator's journal under date 28 May, 1946.
[2] Vandenberg, pp. 277–8.

After a fortnight of barren and often acrimonious argument, Byrnes determined to force the issue by proposing that they should recognize that they had got as far as they could and report to the Peace Conference of 21 nations, calling it for 15 June and asking the other powers to help in reaching agreement. There followed four more days of wrangling in which Molotov insisted that no conference should be called until agreement had been reached on the main points of the peace treaties. Bevin suggested the alternative course of adjourning the Council of Foreign Ministers until a date in June, when they could try again to reach agreement, and allowing a month after they completed their second meeting before the Peace Conference met. He refused to agree with Molotov that they must reach agreement first before calling the conference—this (he argued) would give a veto to any one member of the Council and they would never get to the conference—but he pointed out that a majority vote by the Peace Conference would not be binding on the Council and it would still be necessary for the four of them to reach agreement on the final text of the treaties.

In an effort to counter Molotov's proposal for a joint Soviet–Italian trusteeship over Libya, Bevin suggested immediate independence, no doubt with the hope that a treaty with an independent Libya would provide Britain with strategic rights in Cyrenaica which he saw as a way of relieving the position in Egypt. At this point Bevin reported to Attlee:

"Molotov took us all by surprise by definitely dropping his claim to be in the African continent and backing the French proposal that all the Italian colonies should be returned to Italy. . . .

"With the Egyptian situation and Palestine in my mind I felt it imperative that I should at once spring a claim for Cyrenaica."[1]

Bevin was worried that, once Molotov dropped the Russian claim to Tripolitania, Byrnes would lose interest in the British claim to Cyrenaica and revert to the original American idea of a UN Trusteeship. He was also worried, knowing Attlee's opposition to taking on any fresh commitments in the Arab world, that he might be going too far on his own. His instinct was right. On 12 May he flew back to England for a talk with Attlee. For once, he got little comfort from the Prime Minister, and the next day when they got back to Paris, Dixon noted in his diary: "Secretary of State railed for an hour at Attlee's coolness to him yesterday at Chequers—most unlike him."

They had at least agreed on the line Bevin was to take over the Italian colonies and the dispute between the Italians and the Yugoslavs over Trieste. On the first he insisted that the British wartime promise to the Senussi not to return them to Italian rule must be honoured, but he withdrew the proposal he had advanced earlier, on his own responsibility, to give Britain the trusteeship for Cyrenaica, in favour of turning over all the Italian colonies to the trusteeship of the United Nations. He also dropped, at least for the time being,

---

[1] Bevin to Attlee, 11 May 1946. FO 371/57179.

the Colonial Office proposal for a United Somalia.[1] On the second, Bevin withdrew the British line for the division of Venezia Giulia and accepted instead the French line which would give the Yugoslavs Pola and Fiume. These changes brought the Council no nearer agreement on either issue, but Bevin's proposal (made before his London visit) to adjourn for a month and meet again in June was finally accepted, with the addition of provisional dates in July for the Peace Conference.

2

All three of the Western Foreign Ministers, for differing reasons, were anxious to have the Council of Foreign Ministers discuss other matters besides the peace treaties. Both Bevin and Byrnes had arrived in Paris intent on getting Austria added to the agenda. The situation here was more satisfactory than in Germany: the restoration of the Austrian republic and an Austrian government whose authority extended to all four zones of occupation had been recognized by the Soviet Union as well as by the Western Powers. Free elections had been held in November 1945 resulting in the formation of a Catholic–Socialist coalition in which the Communists, despite winning no more than 5% of the votes, continued to receive representation; and all four powers had foregone their claims for reparations. Austria, however, was a small country to stand up to the strains of four power occupation, "four elephants in a rowboat" as the Austrian President, Dr Renner, described it. The costs of the armies of occupation (a total of 700,000 men at the beginning of the year) were a crippling burden on an economy which was producing less than half what it had done before the *Anschluss* of 1938. Food rations in Vienna fell to 950 calories in May 1946, and the effects of hunger were compounded by insecurity. The arbitrary way in which the Russians behaved in the eastern zone gave substance to the fear that Austria would be swallowed up into a Soviet sphere of influence as she had been earlier into Hitler's Greater Germany. The greater part of the country's resources were in the Soviet zone and, after stripping the place bare of everything that could be moved, the Russians proceeded to take over and run for their own needs some 400 enterprises—including the Zistersdorf oilfields—on the pretext that they were German assets, a major blow to Austrian hopes of recovery.

Before Bevin left for Paris he was visited by Adolf Schärf, the Austrian Vice-Chancellor. Schärf drew a picture of the difficulties under which Austria was labouring which at once captured Bevin's sympathies. He had never forgotten the courageous resistance which the Austrian Socialists had made to Dolfuss' brutal attack on their Vienna settlements in 1934 and he admired the firmness which they and their coalition partners were now showing in face of Soviet harassment. He promised Schärf that he would do everything in his power to help them.

[1] 20 June 1946. FRUS 1946 (2) p. 558.

The obvious way was by ending the occupation for which there was no longer any justification now that Austria's independent existence as a state had been restored and a responsible government elected. The Americans had already made up their minds to press for this too and Byrnes brought a draft treaty to Paris which he wanted considered along with the Italian and other treaties. With Bevin's support, he asked for the Austrian question to be placed on the agenda as soon as the conference opened.

Molotov refused. Apart from the economic benefits the Soviet Union derived from the continued occupation of Austria, withdrawal would remove the formal grounds on which the Russians maintained troops in Rumania and Hungary in order to protect their lines of communication. Molotov, however, did not attempt to justify his attitude, simply refusing to discuss the matter. At the end of their first series of meetings in Paris, when the Foreign Ministers were drawing up the agenda for their second session, all three of the Western powers again tried to get Austria included only to run into a Soviet veto for the second time. "The Soviet Union," Bevin told the House of Commons on 4 June, "argued that they were not ready to discuss Austria. I could not understand this, and I do not understand it now."

The biggest question of all was the future of Germany. The French in particular were anxious to put it on the Council's agenda in the hope that they could secure agreement to the separation of the Ruhr and the Rhineland from any future German state, as well as the annexation of the Saar. Bevin thought this the wrong way to approach the subject. The right way was to discuss the future of Germany as a whole, not piecemeal, and for this reason he opposed the French move to make their proposal part of the formal agenda. But he was willing to have informal talks after the agenda had been dealt with.

There was growing impatience in Britain with pious reiteration of the Potsdam formula of economic unity when there was no agreement between the occupying powers on how this should be implemented and nothing was done. Failure to reach agreement pressed more sharply on the British than any of the other occupying powers. The highly-industrialized, highly-urbanized, now over-crowded British zone had produced little more than half its own food even before the war; it could not live except as part of a larger economic unit. The British found themselves, as Dalton said, "paying reparations to the Germans" in the form of food supplies and subsidies which they could not afford to continue. Even so, there was not enough to do more than just keep people alive in conditions which appalled everyone who saw them, and this in an area the population of which had been famous throughout the world for its industrial skill and productivity. Bevin said nothing in public but with his long experience in industry there was nothing that interested him more than the question which was at the heart of any discussion of the future, what was to be done with German industrial power. Contrary to the common German belief that British policy was motivated by the desire to destroy a commercial rival, it was the British who were most dissatisfied with the limits placed on Germany's industrial recovery by the Level of Industry Agreement finally reached in March 1946.[1] The reason was not only the cost to Britain of a zone with the biggest concentration of heavy industry and the highest figure for unemployment, but Bevin's strongly held belief that there could be no European recovery without a major contribution from the Ruhr. The problem was how to make this compatible with security against a revival of German military power.

In the early months of 1946 Bevin tried to clear his own mind. The long paper which he circulated to the Cabinet Committee on German Industry (and subsequently to the Cabinet)[2] shows how seriously he weighed the pros and cons of the French plan to separate the Ruhr and Rhineland from the rest of Germany. His own preference was for a scheme which he asked the Economic and Industrial Planning Staff to work out for him.[3] This would leave the Ruhr territory as part of a future German state, but provide for the control of its industries through the transfer of their ownership to an international public utility corporation (comparable with the Tennessee Valley Authority), voting control of which would be retained by the participating Powers. Management would be in the hands of Germans and profits would be made available to the German people to pay for imports to meet the costs of occupation and reparations.

By the time he took the question to the Cabinet, in preparation for the Council of Foreign Ministers (17 April) Bevin had come down definitely against the French plan for a separate state west of the Rhine. Instead he recommended a variant of his own original idea for the Ruhr:

"A new German province would be formed . . . Instead of the industries being owned internationally they would be made into a socialised German corporation whose relation to the Provincial Government would be the same as that of the National Coal Board in this country to HMG. Germany's obligations in regard to the transferred industries would be laid down in such detail as was necessary in the peace treaties, and an international control organisation would be formed to supervise the programme of these obligations."

Bevin hoped that a scheme for political rather than industrial control, with provision for sanctions, would be more acceptable to the French, while German opinion would prefer to see the Ruhr industries in German socialized ownership rather than owned by an international corporation.[4] The Cabinet,

[1] See the papers circulated to the Cabinet by John Hynd and Bevin for the discussion on 18 March, CP (46) 114 & 115, CM (25) 46. Bevin reluctantly recommended acceptance only because he believed it useless to keep up the single-handed fight for a higher ceiling in face of the insistence not only of the Russians and the French but of the Americans as well at this stage on holding down German production.

[2] CAB 129/9/HN 01660: Gen 121/1 dated 11 March 1946; circulated to the Cabinet as part of CP (46) 156 on 15 April.

[3] The EIPS draft was circulated to the Committee and later to the Cabinet as Annex A of Gen. 121/1 and CP (46) 156.

[4] CP (46) 139. Bevin's memorandum on the Ruhr and Western Germany circulated to the Cabinet on 15 April and discussed on the 17th, CM 36 (46).

however, while agreeing that the French plan for the separation of the Ruhr should be opposed, was divided on the alternatives, some members still preferring Bevin's original to his revised plan. Bevin did not press for a decision, being content to try out both schemes with the other Foreign Ministers. He added, however that if there was a general preference for a scheme for international ownership he would try to combine it with the creation of a new German province, the future *Nord Rhein-Westfalen.*

But what was Bevin or anyone else thinking of when they spoke about the future of "Germany"? From time to time he reiterated that the transfer of nearly a quarter of Germany's 1937 territory to the Poles was provisional, but the internal memoranda of the Foreign Office suggest that a revision of the Oder–Neisse frontier was not regarded as a serious possibility.[1] On the other hand, the proposal to detach the Ruhr and Rhineland, in addition to the Saar, never found support outside of France. That still left unanswered the question whether Germany, whatever her external frontiers, was to be a single state or divided into two.

This was a matter already much discussed in the first half of 1946. Three separate lines of argument converged in favour of accepting the division between the Soviet zone and the Western zones as likely to be permanent and no longer delaying the reconstruction of Western Germany for the sake of a fictitious unity. One was financial: until the British zone was made economically self-sufficient, the British would have to provide a subsidy which they could not afford to go on paying. A second was humanitarian: the British could not allow the population of their zone to continue to live in conditions of hunger and hopelessness. The third, for which there was considerable support in the Foreign Office,[2] was political: if the British and the other Western Powers did not make a vigorous effort to create a Germany on their own model of democracy comparable with the effort which the Russians were making in the Soviet zone, the Germans would conclude that there was nothing to be hoped for from the West and accept the Communist argument that their future lay with the East.

Although he listened to his advisers' views, Bevin refused to be hurried into making a decision. In a paper drawn up for the Cabinet and the Commonwealth Prime Ministers, and signed on 3 May 1946, he explored his own uncertainties.

"The danger of Russia", he accepted, "has become certainly as great as, and possibly even greater than that of a revived Germany. The worst situation of all would be a revived Germany in league with or dominated by Russia."

---

[1] Eg "The cessions of territory which have already been agreed cannot be cancelled and the Polish provisional administrative boundaries in the east are likely to become the permanent frontiers." FO memorandum in preparation for the Moscow meeting of the CFM, 3 January 1947. FO 371/64504/13596.
[2] See Victor Rothwell: *Britain and the Cold War, 1941-47* (London 1982) pp. 307–17.

So far the Russians had not come down in favour of a unitary or a zonal Germany.

"They are at present hedging and making the best of both worlds. They have established themselves securely in their own zone, are making a strong bid to capture Berlin for the Communists, and are proposing to launch on a more forward policy in the West."

It might become necessary to abandon the idea of a unified Germany, but if so Bevin insisted that the responsibility for the break must be seen to rest squarely with the Russians. Nor was it tactics alone that led him to say this; he went on to list the substantive dangers he saw in openly abandoning Potsdam. Britain might then be driven to embark on creating a West German state as part of an anti-Soviet Western bloc. That would be impossible without full American support and "the Americans are not yet ready for this". If the Americans and the French backed down, the British might find themselves left out on a limb, with the Germans as their only allies.

"Meanwhile we should have lost the one factor which *might* hold us and the Russians together, viz. the existence of a single Germany which it would be in the interest of us both to hold down."[1]

Bevin's conclusion was in favour of seeking the agreement of the three other occupying powers to reconstituting Germany as a loose federation with a central administration which would only handle such matters as were necessary for economic unity. This would offer the best safeguard against the Communists extending their power if they got control of the centre and would lend itself to "the possibility of splitting Germany into two parts if, owing to Russian non-cooperation, this latter becomes inevitable."

Bevin's memorandum was accepted by both the Cabinet and the Dominion Prime Ministers, but was soon overtaken by the decision to create the Anglo–American Bi-zone. The reason for recalling it now is that it provides a base line from which to chart the development of Bevin's attitude between the spring of 1946 and the end of 1947.

During that period Bevin moved from refusing to admit the impossibility of reaching agreement with the Russians and the consequent division of Germany and now accepted this as the assumption on which British policy had to be based. His conversion was reluctant, and slower than any of his staff and a substantial section of British political opinion thought justifiable. This reluctance is explained by a combination of three instinctive feelings on Bevin's part. The first was anxiety at the prospect opened up by an open breach with the Russians and the need to satisfy himself—and the Labour Party, if he was to carry it with him—twice over that there really was no alternative. The second was uncertainty about the Americans and the reliability of their commitment to Europe. The third was the difficulty he found in accepting the Germans as

[1] The memorandum; the confidential Cabinet minutes of 7 May 1946, and the minutes of the Commonwealth Prime Ministers' meeting on the same day, at both of which it was discussed, are to be found in FO 371/55587/5181; 5223; 5822.

allies and reconciling himself to the risk of re-creating German industrial $\underline{\perp}$ military power, the destruction of which in two wars had cost British, French and Russians so dear.

The process by which Bevin's reservations were overridden by the logic of the facts was uneven. It began with his acceptance of the arguments for merging the British and American zones, but made little progress until after the Moscow meeting of the CFM in March and April 1947. This was the watershed. Three months later, with the breakdown of the Paris talks with the Russians on the Marshall offer, there was little doubt that an open breach was inevitable, and the adjournment of the Council of Foreign Ministers in London in December 1947, with no arrangements for a further meeting, formally recognized it.

Even then Bevin could remark to Bidault that "he doubted whether Russia was as great a danger as a resurgent Germany might become"[1], and his later resistance to the abandonment of dismantling and reluctance to accept German rearmament shows the residual strength of his distrust of Germany. But it was only residual: by the beginning of 1948 the diplomatic revolution had been accomplished and as a necessary consequence the creation of a West German state as part of an anti-Soviet Western bloc was accepted. When Bevin used that phrase in his memorandum of May 1946, it was to describe a possibility which he was reluctant even to contemplate; in the spring of 1948 it had become a policy from which he was resolute in refusing to be diverted either by Soviet threats or European fears.

3

All this was a long way in the future when the Council of Foreign Ministers meeting in Paris finally got round to the discussion of Germany, on 15 and 16 May 1946. Byrnes had arrived in France with the draft of a treaty to be signed by all four Powers, including the United States, which would guarantee German demilitarization for 25 years with continuous inspection to enforce it. In tabling the draft at the meeting on 29 April, Byrnes stressed that the USA was offering to underwrite European security, "a guarantee that this time the United States was not going to leave Europe after the War". As the Americans saw it, if the Russians were really concerned with security, here was a way of obtaining it without any need for spheres of influence, *cordons sanitaires* and armies of occupation. If they refused it, this would confirm the belief that under cover of security what they were really interested in was the expansion of their own power. Molotov's reply was discouraging and evasive: before they went on to discuss the future, they should deal with the present and satisfy themselves by inspecting all four zones that Germany was being disarmed now. From this Bevin as well as Byrnes concluded that the Russians did not want to discuss the American proposal seriously.

[1] Conversation between Bevin and Bidault, 17 December 1947. FO 371/67674/11010.

A further shadow was cast on the Foreign Ministers' discussion by the American announcement on 3 May that, until the other powers were prepared to treat the whole of Germany as a single economic unit, the USA would suspend any further deliveries of reparations, a measure aimed at the French as much as the Russians. Byrnes told Bevin in a private talk on the 6th, that the Americans were no longer prepared to let the situation in Germany drift, and he proposed to his colleagues on the Council (15 May) that they should appoint special deputies to prepare a draft settlement with Germany and submit it to a peace conference to be summoned for 12 November. Molotov would not agree; he wanted time to study the proposal to appoint special deputies before committing himself. Bevin too thought Byrnes in too much of a hurry, persuaded him to drop his November date and got the discussion of the special deputies deferred until the further sessions of the Council in June.

Bidault's efforts to secure agreement to the French proposals for the Ruhr and Rhineland attracted no support. But the more Bevin thought about Byrnes' proposal, the more he liked it. To anyone who remembered the American withdrawal after the First World War, this seemed an enormous step forward towards a stable peace settlement after the Second. Here was a way of providing for security without hobbling the German economy and holding down the German people to a sub-standard level of life, a course which Bevin was convinced was likely to prove fatal to the chances of European recovery and of future European peace.

Molotov, however, would have nothing to do with it: he continued to suggest that it was simply a device to divert attention from the failure to carry out the immediate disarmament of Germany and repeated the stock Soviet charge that German forces were being maintained in the Western zones. What were the British up to in the Ruhr, where there were reports that the British were nationalizing the key industries?

"The plans being made by the British and by German trusts and cartels have a great bearing on Germany's military potential. It is obvious that we should discuss Germany as a whole. But I shall not conceal the fact that the Soviet wants to know what goes on in the British Zone."[1]

This at once brought the angry retort from Bevin that Molotov could have all the information he wanted—more than could be said for the Soviet zone—but that he was not going to have the British zone singled out for attack for propaganda purposes. Thereafter the argument continued on depressingly familiar lines, the chance offered by Byrnes' initiative was lost and the deadlock on Germany remained—with this difference, that the new mood of the Americans strongly suggested that they would not be content to let the Russians and French exercise a veto indefinitely and, if they could not get the Potsdam Agreement implemented in full, would look for some other way to break the deadlock.

[1] FRUS 1946, (2) pp. 393–402 (15 May); pp. 426–33 (16 May); Vandenberg p. 283.

There was little doubt what the alternative would be. Meeting Byrnes in Paris at the beginning of the Paris talks, General Clay and his political adviser, Robert Murphy, had put forward the case for a merger of the American with the British zone which would create a viable economic unit out of the Western half of Germany at least.[1] From the British point of view this had obvious advantages, particularly if the Americans could be persuaded to share the occupation costs of the British zone. But the long-term consequences weighed heavily on Bevin's mind. When Dalton again pointed out the cost to Britain of the occupation, Bevin reminded the Cabinet that

"There were most weighty arguments against taking the measures which would be necessary to make the British zone self-supporting. . . . This would mean a complete break with Russia, and that was a major decision with most far-reaching implications. If Potsdam had to be cast aside, he would prefer that Russia should take the initiative in doing so."[2]

He got the Cabinet to defer a decision until they could see if any better result came out of the second sessions of the CFM in Paris.

On the same day, 6 June 1946, Bevin secured the Cabinet's agreement to end the forced repatriation of Soviet citizens. Anxious to win Soviet confidence, the British and American Governments had made an agreement in October 1944 to send back to the USSR all those who fell into their hands and were claimed by the Russians as Soviet citizens. Under this arrangement more than two million men, women and children were handed over, whether they wanted to return or not. When the full details were brought to light many years later[3] this extraordinary passage in the twilight zone of history between the wartime alliance with the USSR and the Cold War was justly described as horrifying in its indifference to human rights and feelings. Under the new arrangement proposed by Bevin[4] repatriation was to be limited to those Soviet citizens who were captured in German uniforms, or could be shown to have served in the German armed forces or to have aided the enemy. This was a step towards recognizing the injustice of the earlier agreement but was still open to objection; repatriation was not finally ended until 1947.

When the Council of Foreign Ministers broke up, Bevin found some relief in holding an after dinner sing-song in his hotel which delighted his Foreign Office staff and brought scandalized protests from the other residents. But the next day as he returned to London he was depressed and preoccupied. After three weeks of intense effort, they appeared to be as far as they had been eight months before in London from reaching a settlement for which millions of people in Europe were waiting in order to be able to get on and rebuild their

---

[1] Lucius D. Clay: *Decision in Germany* (London 1950) p. 165.
[2] Bevin in CM (46) 56, 6 June 1946.
[3] By Nicholas Bethell in *The Last Secret, Forcible Repatriation to Russia 1944–47* (London 1974) and Alexis Tolstoy, *Victims of Yalta* (London 1977).
[4] CP (46) 210.

lives. If these were the difficulties over a peace with Italy, what were they going to be like when the Powers tried to draw up a peace with Germany—and all this trouble, so it seemed to Bevin, because Stalin and Molotov hoped by holding up agreement to screw out a little more advantage for the Soviet Union and its satellites.

The point which impressed most of the commentators, however, was the change in the American role and the vigour with which Byrnes had combatted the Russian claims. After the anxiety which he had felt about Byrnes' attitude at Moscow this was a great relief to Bevin. But it was moderated by two other considerations.

The first, increased rather than abated by the abruptness of the change, was an instinctive feeling that American policy remained unpredictable. As long as Byrnes was Secretary of State Bevin never got rid of this feeling, and there were other issues apart from the East–West balance which continued to disturb the two countries. One was the American repudiation, as it looked from London, of earlier promises on the development of atomic power. Another was American sympathy with the Zionist campaign to bring pressure on Britain to open Palestine, the *New York Times* and other papers carrying full-page advertisements which presented the British as continuing the Nazi persecution of the Jews. A third was the long delay in confirming the American loan. In February 1946 there were serious doubts on both sides of the Atlantic whether the Loan and the accompanying Financial Agreement would get through Congress. It was nearly four months after the Agreement had been sent to the Capitol before the Senate voted on 10 May by 46 votes to 34 to approve the Loan. A public opinion poll in June showed only 38% Americans in favour, and 40% disapproving, and it was not until 15 July, after a further acrimonious debate in the House of Representatives, that the President was able to sign the legislation authorizing the Loan. The long-drawn-out discussion had done nothing to reassure the British, and the *Manchester Guardian*, on the day the President signed, declared:

"The British public, it is only honest to say, has watched the progress of the loan through Congress with something like horror. Most people must often have felt they would like to withdraw the whole thing rather than be under obligation to a legislative body containing so many ignorant and ill-natured members."[1]

Still, when all this is said, the development of American policy in the remainder of 1946 showed that the hardening of attitudes in Washington was something more than a transient change of mood. And even if the prime cause of it was a clearer perception of Russia as an adversary, it rapidly began to affect American relations with Britain as well.

This was already evident in the later stages of the debate on the Loan. When Churchill made his proposal of an Anglo–American alliance at Fulton, in March, the *Wall Street Journal* summed up the almost universal view when it

---

[1] 15 July 1946.

wrote: "This country's reaction to Mr. Churchill's Missouri speech must be convincing proof that the U.S. wants no alliance, or anything that resembles an alliance with any other nations."[1] By July, however, the decisive argument in carrying the loan through the House was the value to the USA of keeping Britain independent and not driving her into the arms of Russia. Minority leader Jesse Wolcott concluded that Congress' decision would determine for years to come "whether there shall be a coalition between the British sphere and the American sphere, or whether there shall be a coalition between the British sphere and the Soviet sphere". And Speaker Sam Rayburn reflected the rapidly changing view of the majority as the debate ended when he testified: "I do not want Western Europe, England, and all the rest pushed toward an ideology that I despise. I fear if we do not co-operate with our great natural ally that is what will happen."[2]

In the course of 1946, then, the first consideration lost much of its force. The second, however, was of a different sort. However angry he might get with Molotov and Soviet tactics, Bevin continued to accept (as Lord Gladwyn put it, speaking of the Paris Council of Foreign Ministers) "the necessity, as we still saw it, of trying to co-operate with the Russians and achieve some kind of European and German settlement which they would be disposed to take".[3] In so far as the changed American attitude meant increased pressure on the Russians to recognize that it was in their interests as much as the Western powers' to reach a settlement which was acceptable to both sides, Bevin of course welcomed it. But in so far as the changed American attitude led to impatience and an insistence on forcing the issue, this could present the British with problems of a new kind.

Liberal papers like the *Manchester Guardian* and *The Economist* had been saying for some time that the economic part of Potsdam was a dead letter, that the British were paying too high a price in their zone for reaching agreement with their allies and that they should look for a new framework of policy.[4] The same opinions were expressed in a Commons debate on Germany in May[5] and the *Guardian* summed up a general view, applauding Clay's action in suspending reparations, when it spoke of "a limit to which the farce of a four-Power unity in Germany can be carried".[6]

But was there an alternative that did not mean dividing Germany in two? Byrnes' treaty of guarantee, if it had been adopted by the Russians, might have provided one, but to Bevin's disappointment this now seemed unlikely. Joint action by the two Western Powers acting on their own to merge their zones might be the only course open if any hope of European recovery was not to be

---

[1] 19 March 1946, quoted in Gardner, note 4, p. 239.
[2] 12 July, *ibid.* p. 251.
[3] Gladwyn, p. 190.
[4] See, for example, the *Manchester Guardian* for 12 and 30 March, 13, 21 and 30 May; *The Economist* for 2 February and six articles on Germany beginning on 6 April.
[5] 10 May 1946.
[6] 30 May 1946.

postponed for years. But precisely because Britain was so much more immediately affected than the USA by what happened in Europe, Bevin wanted time before he committed himself to a course from which there might be no turning back once it was set. Hence his insistence that nothing should be decided before the Foreign Ministers returned to Paris. Before then he had to report to the House of Commons and to the Labour Party Conference on his conduct of foreign affairs; both were occasions which would allow him to sound out opinion and help him to decide what line to take when he returned to Paris.

4

One problem at least Bevin had grasped and dealt with, the problem of what to do with the large number of Polish troops serving under British command who were unwilling to return to a Communist Poland. 30,000 had agreed to go back, but this still left 60,000 in Britain and 100,000 in Italy, where their presence under the command of General Anders, who made no secret of his anti-Communist and anti-Soviet feelings, had been denounced by the Soviet bloc. Bevin turned down flat Churchill's suggestion that they should be used as part of the army of occupation in Germany. That would only increase the outcry against a "Fascist" army and make a political settlement more difficult.[1] Instead he proposed that the 2nd Polish Corps should be brought back to Britain and that the total of 160,000 men (many with families) should be formed into a Polish Resettlement Corps which would prepare them for entry into civilian life in Britain or overseas. When Bevin announced his plan to the House of Commons on 22 May, it was accepted as the best way out of the difficulty, but clearly without enthusiasm. The Government concluded that the admission of so large a number of Poles, the majority of whom settled in the UK was as much as the country could be expected to accept and ruled out offering further places to Jewish refugees in the DP camps.

A fortnight later (4 June) Bevin made his report to the House on the first session of the Council of Foreign Ministers—detailed, lengthy and, as he admitted, tedious to listen to. The pattern of disagreement, he told the House, had been the same throughout, Russia always taking one side, Britain and the USA the other. Part of the trouble, Bevin suggested, was the Soviet claim that they alone represented the workers and practised democracy:

"Their concept of certain other governments is that they are either Fascist or crypto-Fascist or something of that kind. This leads to the idea that the security of Russia can only be maintained when every country in the world has adopted the Soviet system. This, I think, is one of their greatest handicaps and a great handicap to peace. . . . I do not for a moment deny the right of Russia to pursue her own way of achieving an industrial revolution, but for us in this country, who started our industrial revolution over 150 years ago, to adopt the Russian method would really be retrogres-

---

[1] Bevin's note to Attlee, 22 May 1946. FO 800/485/POL/46/7.

sive. . . . I have the impression that the majority of the working classes of Western Europe at least feel like us."[1]

He was very careful, however, not to add to the disagreement by saying anything provocative, ploughing his way through his text and allowing himself no improvisations.

"In the settlement of the last war Russia was not a party. Personally, I have always felt that was a tragedy. . . . It is an important step forward that she is to take part again because it is only if Russia enters freely into the European settlement that there can be any guarantee of permanent peace on the Continent of Europe."

Bevin laid particular emphasis on the US draft treaty of guarantee and urged the Russians to study the text again and realize what an opportunity it presented.

"In fact, I state to the Soviet Government, if you value peace above all else, do not miss it; it may never come again. For France it is vital. For Britain it is indispensable. For the Soviet Union, who have been invaded so many times, I should have thought that a 4-Power Pact carried out with vigour and honesty between us, would have created a situation far more secure than the harnessing of a few satellite weak states as buffers between them and a possible future aggressor. I will not admit failure yet. We will try again."

Only towards the end of his speech did he mention the impossibility of acquiescing in an indefinite stalemate.

"We must regularise our relations with the ex-enemy countries. It cannot go on very much longer. There have been, in the course of these difficulties, other ideas promulgated, but I will not pronounce an opinion upon them now. I propose to make another attempt at agreement before deciding on any final or alternative form."

Although Bevin kept throughout to an unemotional tone without a touch of rhetoric, his speech made a strong impression on both the House and the Press. When he said that he would try again, the London correspondent of the *Christian Science Monitor*, Saville Davis, reported "The House seemed to sense that this was not just verbiage, but showed a man wrestling with adversity, unwilling to give in, and it listened with respect". Davis went on to make the interesting comment that "He does not relish the sudden hardness of the US point of view because Britain has no unlimited national strength to fall back upon and does not wish to become a satellite of the proudly capitalist United States."[2] The *Manchester Guardian* emphasized the other side of Bevin's dilemma, the growing impatience over the situation in Germany.

"No speeches had a good word to say for the Potsdam and level of industry agreements. Everyone realised the unwisdom of forcing down and keeping Germany in destitution

[1] HC, 4 June 1946.
[2] 5 June 1946.

and hunger. . . . If we cannot get Germany treated as an economic unit on an intelligent basis its division into two parts will be inevitable. Western opinion will not stand much longer for what Mr. Churchill well called 'the ceaseless degeneration of the heart of Europe'." [1]

Even the *New Statesman*, after listing the omissions from Bevin's speech, went on to say that "it remains true that it was the

"Russians who rejected compromise and refused to agree to peace treaties for Italy, Germany and Austria. It is also true that, dangerous though it is for the Western Powers alone to rebuild the Ruhr and Rhineland, they will have no alternative to some form of union in non-Soviet Europe if the U.S.S.R. remains uncooperative." [2]

The following week Bevin had to face a more critical audience, the Labour Party Conference at Bournemouth, the first since the general election of 1945. At the end of Labour's first ten months in office, the Conference was in good spirits, well pleased with ministers and ready to applaud them: the one exception was on the international situation. Bevin's critics, including the Chairman of the Conference, Harold Laski, were there in force and of the 46 resolutions relating to foreign and defence policy which appeared on the final agenda, 44 were critical of the Government.

In one important matter the Left had been outmanoeuvred before the Conference met. At the 1945 Conference affiliation of the Communist Party had been defeated by a bare 95,000 votes. In March 1946 the National Executive had issued a well-argued statement of the case against allowing the Communists to affiliate and held a conference of trade union representatives to line up trade union support. By June an overwhelming vote for the Executive position was assured. Bevin took no public part in this operation but, in view of his relationship with the unions, was widely believed to have inspired it.

The day before the debate on foreign policy he took his seat on the platform beside the chairman and tested the temperature of the Conference, "looking (the *Guardian* correspondent reported) as forceful and formidable as a power station". [3] He knew what to expect. In the words of the Hendon Branch resolution:

"This Conference is of the opinion that world peace can only be based on a British policy directed to ensure firm friendship and co-operation with the progressive forces throughout the world, and in particular with the U.S.S.R. . . . . The Conference therefore calls upon the Government (a) to maintain and foster an attitude of sympathy and friendship towards the Soviet Union, . . . and (b) to repudiate Mr. Churchill's defeatist proposal to make the British Commonwealth a mere satellite of American Monopoly Capitalism which will inevitably lead to our being aligned in a partnership of hostility to Russia." [4]

---

[1] 6 June 1946.
[2] 8 June 1946.
[3] *Manchester Guardian*, 12 June 1946.
[4] Labour Party Conference Report 1946, p. 157.

The new note was the resolution on the Government's Palestine policy moved by Crossman.[1] That apart, Bevin had heard it all before—much of it in the conferences of the 1930s. As he sat listening to the debate he heard himself criticized for continuing a Conservative policy of calculated hostility towards Russia, for deliberately supporting Fascist regimes in Greece and Spain, for preferring Tory-minded public school diplomats to men who shared the hopes of the British electorate, worst of all for earning Churchill's praise and allowing himself to be made (in Zilliacus' phrase) "the white hope of a Black International".

Most of those listening to the attacks on Bevin from the Left were ready enough to acquit him of the charges made against him, but there remained a feeling of anxiety about the international situation and Labour's foreign policy which it was important for him not to ignore. The majority were prepared to be re-assured and give Bevin their support, provided he did not alienate them, as he had more than once in the past at Labour conferences, by too truculent a reply. Bevin had rarely failed to impress a party conference, but he had too often left delegates with the feeling that he did not much care what they thought as long as he had the trade unions on his side and the block vote in his pocket. This time he made no such mistake. He answered his critics fully, making no concessions but—avoiding an old fault—not letting them provoke him into forgetting that the audience it was important for him to convince was the moderate majority. He did this most effectively by talking to them not as Foreign Secretary but as one of themselves, a man with a difficult job trying to find practical ways of dealing with the host of problems left by the war.

The one exception to his restraint came when he turned to Palestine. Following the same line as the Anglo-US Commission, he rejected the idea of an exclusively racial state whether Jewish or Arab. His object, he declared, was to create an independent Palestine State which would "represent the people in that State, whether Jews or Arabs, all over the world . . . so that from that State there can be a voice in the Chancelleries of the world". Bevin repeated his argument that the Jews should not be excluded from Europe. He added that quite apart from a solution of the Palestine problem, the Jews had also a role to play in raising the living standards of the Middle East. "They possess scientific, cultural and other abilities which the Middle East require."

If little of what he said was acceptable to Zionist sympathizers, it was not marked by hostility towards the Jews as a race. But the one sentence which was quoted round the world was his remark that the American campaign for 100,000 Jews to be admitted to Palestine "was proposed with the purest of motives. They did not want too many Jews in New York." What Bevin said

[1] Richard Crossman recalled twenty years later in conversation with the author that Bevin had gone out of his way to be encouraging to him personally when he met him in the bar the night before the debate. As a result Crossman moderated his attack considerably, only to find that Bevin "came down on him like a ton of bricks" when he replied. Crossman's indignation was mingled with admiration for the simple but effective device with which Bevin, an old hand at party conferences, had confused his aim.

was known to every politician and newspaperman in the United States. A year before Halifax had warned him that there was an overriding consensus, if for very different reasons, between Zionists, WASPs and Catholics that the United States was no place for Jewish refugees from Europe. But it was something no one could say in public without paying a heavy penalty. Once again Bevin had to let his tongue run away with him. His gratuitous sneer cancelled out the effort of many hours of negotiation, earning him a severe rebuke from the American Press and offering the Zionists all the confirmation they needed of his anti-Semitism.

Bevin was on much surer ground when he challenged Labour Party sentiment about Franco, arguing that a gesture like the withdrawal of Ambassadors (which the Poles had proposed to the Security Council) was valueless unless backed by a positive policy. "We broke relations with Russia, but we never changed Russia's policy. . . . In my opinion if you start trouble you will get the resentment of the Spanish people instead of their support." More than anything else they feared a renewal of the Civil War. "The Spanish people are anxious not to be thrown into turmoil again, but if left alone there are wide classes in Spain anxious to get rid of Franco."

"It has been said that I have not attempted to discuss the Treaty with Russia.[1] Why do you say these things? If you want to mellow and soften this position between Russia and Great Britain, the greatest enemies are the Russian supporters in this country. I discussed the Treaty in Moscow, I offered to extend it to fifty years. When Generalissimo Stalin said: 'I should need to amend it', I said: 'Let me know what would suit you'. . . ."

America might be a capitalist country but when she offered a 25-year treaty to keep Germany disarmed, he welcomed it with both hands.

"There are minds in America, as Laski knows, which represent the flower of liberal and progressive thought and when this finds its way through the State Department in proposals of this kind, am I going to say 'I don't like you'?"

He had been accused of setting up a Western bloc. On the contrary

"I am not going to be a party," Bevin declared, "as long as I hold this office, to any design . . . any alignment of forces . . . to attack Russia. I will be no party to it. . . . But this division of Europe, this awful business of a line from Stettin to Albania, if that solidifies—which God forbid—we shall have two camps in Europe by the very force of events and that will be the road to another struggle.

"I say to Generalissimo Stalin and M. Molotov: '*We* will not divide Europe.' I have offered that they should come into our Zone and examine what happens before they accuse us of not carrying out the Treaty of Potsdam. I have said: 'Let the 4-Power Commission go everywhere. . . . Then, when we have done it, let our deputies sit down and try to work out a settlement for Middle Europe . . . a settlement that will give to France, will give to Russia security, not dependent upon the poverty of the people, but dependent upon the mutual confidence of the great Allies who won the war. That is my purpose.'"

[1] The Anglo-Soviet Treaty signed in 1942 after the German invasion of Russia.

As Bevin finished the whole conference rose to cheer and applaud him, an occurrence not so common in the 1940s as it has since become. He had routed his critics on their own ground. "Anyone who does not recognise that the Foreign Secretary has the support of the bulk of the Labour Movement," the *News Chronicle* concluded, "is not facing political reality."[1] In the *Evening Standard*, W. J. Brown, an old enemy of Bevin's, wrote that, while ministers had in general strengthened their position, "it was essentially Bevin's conference. That great mountain of a man is pivotal, while his health lasts, to the future of the Socialist Government."[2] The left-wing *Tribune* did not dissent: "At the end of it all, Ernest Bevin retained his formidable place in the Labour Movement as surely as Big Ben was unaffected by the cascades of water from the River Thames."[3]

No one knew better than Bevin that he had not solved his problem, that if there was no change of mind on the part of the Russians when the Council of Foreign Ministers resumed he was going to find it hard to avoid moving closer towards the division of Europe which he deplored. Nonetheless, as the *Manchester Guardian* summed up, "Mr. Bevin goes to the Paris conference with his hand greatly strengthened. Last week he was assured of the backing of the House of Commons; yesterday he was assured of the backing of the rank and file of his own party."[4]

5

Although Bevin spent much of the spring and summer of 1946 in Paris, he was as far as ever from the close co-operation with the French which had been so frequently talked about. The French Ambassador, Massigli, came to see him when he was back in London between the two sessions of the Council and brought a complaint from Bidault that he had had no support from the British in the French claim to the Saar. Bevin exploded. If Bidault had followed his advice on procedure, he declared, the Saar question would have been settled in France's favour, but Bidault chose to press as well for the political separation of the Ruhr from Germany, although he knew the British could never agree to this. The British had their own complaint: without previous warning Bidault had suggested the return of Cyrenaica and Tripolitania to Italy, a solution to which (as he knew) the British were strongly opposed. The truth was, Bevin told Massigli, there was no sharing of confidences by the French; they kept close and told him little. So long as they maintained that, until the Ruhr was settled in the way they wanted, there could be no alliance, so long would there be no progress towards one.[5]

[1] 13 June 1946.
[2] 14 June.
[3] 14 June, a reference to high tides in the Thames which flooded the terrace at Westminster.
[4] 13 June 1946.
[5] Report by Bevin of his talk with Massigli, 22 May 1946. FO 800/464/FR/46/17.

After de Gaulle's resignation in January 1946, France continued to be governed by a coalition of Communists, Socialists and MRP. The Communists were the largest of the three parties, with 5 out of 19 million votes cast in their favour in October 1945[1]. Many believed the political tide was flowing in their favour and that France would be under Communist rule before the end of 1946. The Communists were irrevocably opposed to a "Western bloc" and supported Bidault on Germany. The only party in the coalition which looked favourably on moving closer to Britain was the Socialists, and at the Socialist Congress in the spring of 1946 the Prime Minister, Felix Gouin, came out in favour of a Franco–British Pact on the same lines as the Franco–Soviet.

Bevin at once took this up and sent Oliver Harvey with the British Ambassador, Duff Cooper, to ask Gouin if the French wanted an alliance first or a settlement of the Ruhr and Rhineland. Bevin was prepared to follow either path, but Gouin could only reply that he could give no answer yet as the French Cabinet was divided.[2] The next day Bidault secured a public commitment by the Cabinet to "the continuity of France's policy with regard to the Ruhr, the Rhineland and the Saar", and the Communist spokesman, Duclos, declared that, while they had no objections to an Anglo–French Pact, they were against having it "at the price of French security, of which the internationalisation of the Ruhr was an essential condition." This put an end to Gouin's initiative and Bevin told Churchill that he found the French Premier was only speaking for himself.[3]

Churchill's own advice was to wait for the French elections and see what changes these produced. So far as the threat of a Communist France went —and there is no doubt that Bevin viewed such a possibility as a threat—the results were re-assuring. Communists and Socialists combined failed to win a majority in the May referendum for the new draft constitution for which they had campaigned, and in the June general election, although the Communist vote went up a little, it was overtaken by the MRP, which now emerged as the largest party and provided the next prime minister. As this, however, was Georges Bidault, still committed to a programme of dismembering Western Germany, the June election did nothing to advance the prospects of closer Anglo–French co-operation. The way would only be opened when the French recognized that they were not going to get the settlement they wanted in Germany. That might come about as a result of the discussion of Germany to which the Council of Foreign Ministers was committed in its second session, but Bevin went back to Paris in mid-June no nearer to a working arrangement with the French than he had been in the earlier session.

---

[1] This represented 26% of a much larger electorate which now included women: their pre-war peak had been 15% in 1936.
[2] Duff Cooper (Paris) to Bevin, 4 April 1946, FO 800/464/FR/46/9.
[3] Bevin to Churchill, 11 April 1946, answering a letter from Churchill dated 5 April, *ibid.*, FR/46/13 and 10.

His first concern on reaching Paris was to call the British delegation together and work out a plan of campaign. This practice of Bevin's met with the strong approval of his staff. "Proceedings with E.B.," Dixon wrote in his journal, "are always orderly, and we start the day with a Delegation meeting at 10 a.m. This means that everybody is happy and we all have our tasks assigned for the day." On 17 June he noted "an extraordinary intellectual performance by E.B. running over 50 pages of detailed arguments on the economic clauses of the Italian treaty. I enjoyed the clash of minds between him and the experts."[1]

The first twelve days of meetings produced little more than a repetition of familiar disagreement.[2] The state of frustration to which this reduced the participants is illustrated by an exchange late on the 26th.

"Mr. Bevin remarked that they had discussed three subjects this afternoon and one this evening without decision. It appeared to him that the procedure of this conference was not to decide anything.

"Mr. Molotov remarked that Bevin should not underestimate his own services in helping to produce that result.

"Mr. Bidault said that there was a French proverb which stated that night brings counsel and another one that the handle should not be thrown after the axe-head."[3]

The next day in fact saw the log-jam begin to break as a result of a series of private meetings in which Molotov probed Byrnes' intentions and evidently reached the conclusion that Russia would have to compromise on her demand that Trieste be given to the Yugoslavs if there was to be any agreement. Byrnes' readiness to leave a settlement to the Peace Conference of 21 nations, in which the Russian bloc would be in a minority, was an argument which Molotov could appreciate. Characteristically he signalled his willingness to bargain by an oblique gesture. Minor but unexpected agreements on the Balkan treaties were followed by Molotov's surprise withdrawal of Soviet objections to the line of the Franco–Italian frontier already accepted by the other three. "When we were packing up our papers," Dixon wrote in his diary, "Byrnes jokingly said 'As we are in an agreeing mood, how about settling the Dodecanese?'" The official US record continues:

"Mr Molotov said that the Soviet Delegation had no objection to that proposal. Mr. Bevin asked whether Mr. Molotov had said he agreed that the islands should go to Greece. Mr. Molotov said that he had. Mr. Bevin asked for a minute or two to recover.

"Mr. Molotov suggested that they make some other good agreements. Mr. Byrnes said that they might settle the question of the colonies. Mr. Molotov asked whether it might be settled on the basis of the U.S. proposal of 15 May."[4]

Between 28 June and 4 July, the four Foreign Ministers at last thrashed out a compromise on the Italian peace treaty. The key was a French proposal that

[1] Dixon's diary, 27 April, 15 June, 17 June 1946.
[2] For the documentation of the CFM meetings, see footnote 2 on p. 260 above.
[3] FRUS 1946 (2) 13th informal meeting, p. 646.
[4] Dixon, 27 June; FRUS 1946, (2) p. 661.

Trieste should go neither to Yugoslavia nor Italy but be internationalized, a move for which Bevin gave full credit to Bidault. No one liked the idea in itself or thought it likely to prove practicable, but it offered a way out of the impasse and after much argument about the details it was accepted. At the same time, it was agreed to defer a decision on the future of the Italian colonies for a year and, in the meantime, to leave their administration in British hands. Finally, Molotov agreed to a date for the Peace Conference (29 July) in return for which the others agreed to the USSR receiving reparations of $100 million out of Italian assets abroad and current production (Russia supplying the raw materials).

If anyone thought—to use a favourite phrase of Bevin's—that peace had broken out, they were soon disillusioned. There followed some of the most acrimonious passages of the conference, over the Soviet refusal to agree that China should be one of the Powers sending out the invitations to the Peace Conference and, more substantially, over Molotov's attempt to fix the rules of the Conference in advance. The Americans believed that Molotov made a bad slip in failing to settle the rules before he agreed to the date of the conference and was under sharp instructions from Moscow to recover the ground he had lost. This he was unable to do but the attempt stretched everyone's nerves to snapping point. Bohlen, who acted as Byrnes' interpreter, recalls Bevin returning to a late night session after a good dinner at which he had plenty to drink, and reacting violently to another of Molotov's attacks on Britain's past sins.

"Bevin rose to his feet, his hands knotted into fists and started towards Molotov, saying 'I've had enough of this, I 'ave', and for one glorious moment it looked as if the Foreign Minister of Great Britain and the Foreign Minister of the Soviet Union were about to come to blows."[1]

Bevin, in fact, was not so easily provoked by Molotov's sarcasm as he had been at earlier conferences and, having taken the Russian's measure, was able to get the better of him in argument on several occasions. He told Molotov that he was trying to go back on his previous agreement to set a date for the Peace Conference by now making the adoption of rules of procedure a condition of sending out the invitations. Would Molotov show him in what document he had ever agreed to lay down the rules in advance? The agreement at Moscow merely said that the Council would convoke the Conference. All Molotov could find to say was that he was not obliged to answer Mr Bevin's question.

The strain told on Molotov as well as the others, Dixon noting (8 July) that after three days of acrimonious argument, "he is looking worried, yellower than usual and the bump on his right temple prominent". After sticking it out to the point where he was completely isolated and Byrnes asked bluntly whether the earlier agreement (in effect reparations from Italy in exchange for

[1] Charles E. Bohlen: *Witness to History* (London 1973) p. 255.

fixing a date for the Peace Conference) was to be abandoned, Molotov suddenly gave ground, accepted a face-saving formula invented by the French, and next morning settled everything amicably within an hour.

Molotov's retreat on the Peace Conference, however, was immediately followed by a fierce attack on American and British policy in Germany. In June Molotov had not been ready to reveal the Soviet hand; he was now, with an effect which overshadowed all the rest of the Conference.

Molotov began, on 9 July, by reading a prepared statement directed at Byrnes' proposed 25-year treaty which he dismissed as "completely inadequate" to safeguard the security of Germany's neighbours. From this he went on to accuse the British and Americans of failing to carry out the disarmament and disbandment of German armed forces and the elimination of the country's war potential, as they had promised to do at Potsdam. Byrnes' treaty was represented as a device for evading promises and concealing the abandonment of the Potsdam Agreement. The view of the British and American delegations was that Molotov's speech, with its concentration on disarmament and security, and its suggestion that the other Western powers were being "soft" with Germany, was aimed at a French audience and designed to aid the French Communists. The surprise came the following day (10 July) in a second statement by Molotov.

Bevin opened the proceedings on the 10th with a welcome for Byrnes' draft treaty which offered the best way of keeping the four Powers together and avoiding the division of Europe. He, too, was in favour of implementing the Potsdam Agreement, but it had to be the whole of that Agreement, and he went on to list the provisions for treating Germany as an economic whole which the Russians had ignored. This was true enough, but hardly carried the argument much further. The real question was what to do if Potsdam could not be made to work. The only answer on the Western side, which Bevin was still reluctant to do more than hint at, was to accept the division of Germany and organize the Western half. The Russians, however, had already given signs of moving towards a different answer. The most important was the creation of a Socialist Unity Party (SED) by a forced merger of the Socialists in the Eastern Zone with the Communists, and the new Party's adoption of a strong propaganda line in favour of a unified and centralized Germany under Communist leadership, with a revived industry orientated towards the East. As *The Economist* said, by comparison with anything the West had yet put forward, such a policy "has the attraction that it offers the Germans a reasonably clear-cut picture of the future, and of the prospects for which they can hope, provided they work hard and are politically submissive".[1]

In his statement of 10 July—circulated to the Press in advance—Molotov for the first time gave official Soviet support to the new line. While he insisted on the need for Germany to pay reparations in full and on her complete disarmament, he disclaimed any idea of revenge or identification of the

[1] *The Economist*, "The Divided Reich", 8 May 1946.

German people with Hitler. Instead he underlined their future in a united German state, continuing to play an important role in world trade and with the right to develop their civilian industries beyond the level fixed by the Allied Control Council. As a first step towards a future German Government, Molotov called for the setting up of a central German administration.

"It has of late become fashionable to talk about dismembering Germany into several 'autonomous' states, federalising her and separating the Ruhr from her. All such proposals stem from this same line of destroying and agrarianising Germany, for . . . without the Ruhr Germany cannot exist as an independent and viable state. But . . . the destruction of Germany should not be our objective."[1]

After his speech of the previous day, aimed at a French audience, that of 10 July was skilfully pitched for a German audience and given maximum publicity there. It was the first time any of the wartime Allies had offered the German people a prospect of their future in positive terms and in the absence of any alternative on the Western side other than the reiteration of a Potsdam settlement no one any longer expected to be carried out, it could have a considerable impact on the Western zones as well as the Eastern. The Americans were sufficiently impressed for Byrnes to agree with Clay and Murphy the same evening that, in view of Molotov's bid, the United States could no longer allow its policy in Germany to be hamstrung by the failure to carry out Potsdam.

The next day Bevin brought the issue to a head by asking Molotov directly if he was prepared to agree to three proposals which the British regarded as essential. The gist of these was to distribute German resources equitably without regard to zonal boundaries; to construct a joint export-import programme for Germany as a whole, and to give this priority over any removal of surplus for reparations. Bevin's questions brought out clearly the clash between Western and Russian interests in Germany and, not surprisingly, Molotov's answer was an equally blunt "No". In that case, Bevin replied, the British would be driven to organize industry in their own zone to produce for export; they could not go on borrowing dollars to pay for importing food into Germany. It was left to Byrnes to spell out the implications. He hoped, he said, that they could avoid the situation outlined by Bevin and still agree on a common programme, but "pending agreement that Germany be treated as a whole I am ready to enter into agreement with any other zone for the treatment of the two zones as an economic whole".

Byrnes' statement was received without comment and the meeting adjourned. But none of those present missed its point. As Clay wrote,

"We said in effect that we had tried for many months to pursue a common policy while the Soviet Government had pursued deliberately a policy of its own, and that we would

---

[1] Translation of Molotov's speech in *Documents on Germany under Occupation 1945–54* ed. B. R. von Oppen (London 1955) pp. 144–7.

wait no longer in the effort to reach agreement but would strive alone or with such others as joined with us for the attainment of the objectives in Germany to which we had all agreed. I think this was clearly understood by all four delegations."[1]

The next morning Bevin formally announced that HM Government would respond to Byrnes' proposal "urgently and sympathetically". Bidault, alarmed at the prospect of the French proposals being brushed aside, tried to secure something for France out of the discussion of Germany which he had initiated, but without success. However careful Byrnes and Bevin were to insist that any move towards a bi-zonal agreement was dictated by the practical need to do something about conditions in their zones, had no political implications and was not aimed at the division of Germany, it opened a new prospect.

The final day of the conference was—at last—secured for a discussion of Austria. Bevin as well as Byrnes had circulated a draft of the Treaty which the Western Powers were anxious to see signed. This would not only relieve the country of the burden of occupation but also remove the Russian pretext for keeping troops in Hungary and Rumania in order to protect their lines of communication. Molotov was fully equal to the occasion. There were, he announced, 437,000 Displaced Persons in the Western zones of Austria, many of whom had fought for Hitler; some Nazi laws were still in force and other remnants of Hitlerism had not been liquidated. The final severance with Germany had not been completed. When all these tasks had been carried out, then it would be possible to talk about restoring the independence of Austria, not before. He refused to allow the deputies to start work on the Treaty in advance and vetoed Bevin's attempt to discuss the definition of German assets in Austria, a loophole which the Russians had notoriously used to take possession of the resources of their zone—including the Zistersdorf oilfields —after renouncing all claim to reparations.

Fortunately Western hopes of doing something for the Austrians did not rest solely on getting a treaty signed. Work on revising the Four Power Control Agreement had begun before the end of 1945 and the draft of a new agreement finally came before the Allied Control Council and was signed by all four powers on 28 June 1946.[1] The evidence suggests that the Russians failed to realize the importance of the changes, which greatly increased the freedom of action of the Austrian Government; when they did, they were defeated in their efforts to whittle this freedom down by the resistance of the Western Powers. The British element on the Control Commission had put a lot of effort into drafting and then getting the new agreement accepted. Bevin was equally pleased with another initiative which the United Kingdom had strongly supported, the extension of the UNRRA programme to Austria. The first Chief of Mission was an Englishman, Brigadier Parminter, and UNRRA

[1] Clay, p. 131.

supplies which began to flow in during June 1946 played a major part in saving the Austrians from starvation in the next twelve months. [1]

On Austria, then, despite Molotov's veto, Bevin could feel that he had made some practical progress. On the settlement with Italy and the other ex-satellites, after ten months' argument, the way was now open to the Peace Conference, which was due to meet the following month, and as he returned to London, Bevin was given the news that Congress had finally approved the US loan to Britain. None the less, the Foreign Secretary came back, the *Herald Tribune* correspondent reported, "looking as tired and glum as he undoubtedly felt". [2]

The gains so laboriously secured seemed out of all proportion to the effort which had gone into their negotiation, even more to the needs of a world which, more than twelve months after the end of the European war, had barely begun on the task of reconstruction. It was this that appealed most strongly to Bevin, restoring the food supplies, rebuilding the towns, making good the destruction of war and getting people to work again so that they could begin to plan and hope for a future. Instead, day after day, they sat round the table arguing about claims and counter-claims to territory and reparations, scoring points in an elaborate diplomatic game in which the real issues were never stated. Bevin went on taking part in it because he could see no alternative, short of giving the Russians everything they wanted. But when the pressure let up, he felt a great weariness of spirit and returned home, frustrated and depressed.

6

There was another reason why Bevin returned looking tired and glum. The long hours and tension of the negotiations in Paris had over-taxed his strength. If he had been wise, he would have taken a proper holiday, but he was soon back at his desk in the Foreign Office, trying to clear off the work which had accumulated while he was abroad.

In the course of the next ten days he made three speeches, two of which happily illustrated the imagination which he brought to thinking about the future of international relations. The first was at an exhibition of designs for holiday centres organized by his old friends of the Workers' Travel Assocation. Recalling the part he had played in securing Holidays with Pay for workers in the 1930s,[3] he went on to speak of 20 million people taking a fortnight's annual holiday in four or five years' time, a social revolution which it could not be left to private enterprise to organize for profit.

---

[1] For a summary see Michael Balfour and John Mair: *Four Power Control in Germany and Austria 1945-46* (London 1956) pp. 327–8.
[2] 14 July.
[3] See Vol. I, p. 601.

"There is another side to all this. I visualise within about two or three years very great numbers of people, from east and west, and particularly from America and from the continent of Europe, exchanging with our people here. I promise you to try at the very earliest possible moment I can to get rid of all the hindrances on travel. Visas are an abomination. . . . I do not think I ought to build new buildings to issue passports and visas but ought to get rid of them. . . . What kind of accommodation and what sort of life will the young people and families from abroad come into? . . . The whole standard of catering for travellers has not hitherto been on too high a level, nor can all foreigners afford to go to first class hotels."[1]

Tourism and mass travel on the scale foreseen by Bevin have since come to be taken for granted, but in 1946 a Foreign Secretary who thought in these terms and kept on prodding away at Government and others to provide for it was something unheard of in the traditional world of diplomacy.

He struck a different note when he talked to the Anglo-Netherlands Society at a lunch in the Grocers' Hall. Well aware of the sharpness of Dutch feelings about Indonesia, he told his audience that, although the West had been dominant in the past, they had to appreciate the changes that were taking place in the world.

"They are fundamentally economic but they express themselves in a nationalistic form. It would be very unwise of the Western nations not to recognise them. . . . These wakening, stirring forces are vital among the so-called backward races of the world and they are going to be a tremendous factor. . . . This uprising is not confined to territories like India and the Netherlands East Indies. . . . Among the colonial races and the so-called black races there is the same thing going on and we have to shape our economic policies and our political outlook to reach forward to meet these advances."[2]

Two days later Bevin had to defend to a critical House of Commons the CFM's decision not to give South Tyrol to Austria and to leave the Brenner frontier with Italy unchanged. He left the Chamber immediately after his speech and collapsed with a heart attack. He was taken to his flat in Phillimore Gardens, Kensington, and arrangements made for Attlee to head the British delegation to the Paris Peace Conference which opened on 29 July. This did nothing to improve Bevin's frame of mind. He fretted at the thought of decisions being taken without him, and with good cause, since neither Attlee nor A. V. Alexander, who accompanied him, had anything like Bevin's knowledge of the relations between the Great Powers. His daughter Queenie, however, told a visitor from the Foreign Office that his nerves were absolutely in pieces and he needed a long rest.

This was not Bevin's idea at all. When his doctor Alec (later Sir Alexander) McCall came, Bevin told him "I want to get out of this", but when McCall suggested a nursing home, Bevin refused. "Where would you like to go, then?" the doctor asked. "That boat of yours." This was a small yacht, of no more

[1] Speech at the WTA exhibition, Institute of Civil Engineers, 22 July 1946.
[2] 23 July 1946.

than 20 tons and with no facilities, which McCall kept at the Hamble; but there they went, getting an exhausted Foreign Secretary down the 100 yard jetty with great difficulty and out to the boat in wind and rain. After a few days he began to feel better and to worry about what was happening in Paris. He was sure things were going wrong and insisted on going ashore to telephone. The result was further calls, a visit by one of his private secretaries to talk to him in the Red Lion at Fareham and finally his return to London on 7 August long before he had properly recovered.[1] He went straight to a Cabinet meeting and looked so poorly that Attlee asked to see his doctor and called for a second opinion. None the less, Bevin flew to Paris on 9 August and took his place as leader of the British delegation.

His remarkable powers of recuperation pulled him through this time, but henceforth his staff were never free from anxiety about his health. Part of the trouble was that Bevin had only been seriously ill once before in his life, in 1937, when his year as president of the TUC had taken him away from home on 48 out of 52 weekends and left him exhausted. After a six months trip to Australia, he returned restored and stood up to a punishing schedule during the war. Although blessed with a strong constitution and long accustomed to making excessive demands on it, at 65 his neglect of his health began to catch up with him.

When Dr McCall first examined him in 1943, he found (so he said) not a sound organ in his body, apart from his feet. He later described Bevin, comprehensively, as suffering from angina pectoris, cardiac failure, arteriosclerosis, sinusitis, enlarged liver, damaged kidneys and high blood pressure. He was overweight, smoked and drank more than was good for him, took no exercise and was a poor sleeper. McCall not only became Bevin's doctor but a close friend as well, frequently accompanying him abroad if he was going to be away for more than a few days. He described Bevin as an "unruly and undisciplined" patient. His patient retaliated by introducing him with the remark: "This is Alec. 'E treats me be'ind like a dartboard," a phrase he first used (to the King's great delight) to describe his injections when comparing notes with George VI on their sufferings at the hands of doctors.[2] In Moscow (where McCall went with him at the end of 1945 and slept in the next room with a communicating door) Bevin returned from the dinner in the Kremlin in the early hours of the morning and demanded to know if he could have another whisky. When McCall agreed, Bevin called out: "I should damn well think so; you've been watering my whisky ever since we left London." When he was under pressure, Bevin drank a lot—whisky, champagne, brandy, whatever was to hand. He used alcohol, one of his secretaries said, like a car uses petrol, to keep himself going, and he and his doctor (who certainly watered his whisky) had a running fight on the subject, not least because the effect of drink was to make him truculent. At one time he was persuaded to undergo a strict

[1] Interview with Sir Alexander McCall.
[2] Barclay, p. 48.

diet and lost three stones in weight, but the beneficial effect was slight and he soon regained what he had lost, weighing 250 pounds in all.

Uncertain health—"the old ticker" as he called it—was a particular hazard for a man required to travel more than any other member of the Government. It made it impossible for him to fly across the Atlantic and although the journeys on one of the *Queens* or the *Mauretania* gave him the opportunity to recover his strength, they also prolonged the length of time he was away. Even in London, Bevin had little time in which to relax. He was one of the members of the Labour Government whom most visitors to London wanted to see and whose absence from an official reception was at once noticed and commented on.

The Secretary of State's room where he received them in Scott's ornate Foreign Office was large, high-ceilinged and uncomfortably furnished in club style, with much red leather and highly-polished tables. It was by the tall windows with their view over St James's Park and the Horse Guards' Parade that Grey had been standing when he made his famous remark, on the evening of 3 August 1914: "The lamps are going out all over Europe: we shall not see them lit again in our life-time."[1] Bevin was very conscious—and proud—of his place in the succession of Foreign Secretaries who had occupied the room before him. It was a setting in which his personality expanded and many among the foreign ministers and ambassadors who visited him there came away impressed, and often surprised, by the man whom they now found representing His Majesty's Government.

On most weekdays Bevin had to leave the Foreign Office in time for an evening engagement, either a reception or dinner. Nothing but the most formal occasion would induce him to change into full evening dress, but he acquiesced in a dinner jacket. Social life, if it had no great attraction for him, held no terrors either. He suffered neither from false modesty nor from an inverted snobbery and could be an entertaining, if sometimes disconcerting, dinner companion. On one occasion not long after he went to the Foreign Office, he found himself sitting next to the wife of his Principal Private Secretary at dinner and, to start the conversation, asked her what town she came from. Although born in Athens herself, she told him that her father, grandfather and great-grandfather had all come from Bristol and had lived in such and such a street. "Was it a large house?" Bevin asked, and went on to describe it in some detail. "Yes," Mrs Dixon exclaimed. "But how did you know?" "I used to deliver the laundry there," was the reply, which delighted both of them equally. Bevin had the gift of making such remarks without causing embarrassment or detracting from his own dignity.

He was equally natural as a host when he had to entertain important visitors from abroad, able to pass through national as easily as social barriers as if they did not exist. Sir Roderick Barclay, the last of his Private Secretaries, recalls a grand occasion in the superb setting of the Painted Hall at Greenwich when

[1] Viscount Grey: *Twenty Five Years*, vol. 2 (London 1925) p. 20.

Bevin was host at lunch to the President of France and Madame Auriol, the King and Queen of England and the two princesses. Barclay himself was seated at the far end of the Hall, but towards the end of the meal saw that Bevin was peering down the tables and sensed he was wanted. When he slipped up to the dais and bent over, the Secretary of State said: "I don't know how we get out of here." While the mysteries of protocol were explained to him, the Queen listened and smiled her encouragement, until Bevin, suitably briefed, rose without embarrassment and led his distinguished guests from the table.[1]

Yet, official duties apart, Bevin's tastes and way of life remained unpretentious and modest. His staff found that, unlike other ministers of whom they had had experience, he neither asked for nor expected special privileges. Sir Oliver Franks, when Ambassador in Washington, thought him—unlike some other visitors—undemanding as a house guest, taking the children in his stride and not constantly expecting attention. It was noticed that when he walked into the Foreign Office in the morning, he not only spoke to the doorkeeper and the liftman, but told the latter which floor he wanted to go to as if he were any ordinary member of the staff going to his office. Another member of his private office, who admitted that he was not always efficient in seeing that the Foreign Secretary went to the right place for a meeting, recalled that on more than one occasion Bevin returned, and, without recrimination, simply announced "They weren't there", before going on into his own room to take off his coat and start work again. The few occasions when he showed anger were usually when Mrs Bevin could not secure something, such as a seat for a big debate, on which she had set her heart. Towards Mrs Bevin herself, who was sometimes given to interrupting him with a telephone call about domestic problems, he showed invariable patience. On one occasion when his Private Secretary went into the Secretary of State's room he heard Bevin saying on the telephone: "You want to beat it and then put olive oil on it." He turned round with a grin and said: "Mrs Bevin's got a tough bit of steak. You know I was once assistant to a chef in a restaurant in Bristol." He told the same Secretary on their first visit together to New York that he must be sure to tip the page boy: "I was a page boy once myself."[2]

Bevin could only cope with the demands made on him because he was able to rely on a Private Office whose staff were devoted to him. The head of it was his Principal Private Secretary, a key post, whose occupant had to act as the link between Bevin and the Foreign Office, and in addition see that all his needs were met, or better still, anticipated. The work of the Private Office was at its most hectic in the middle of conferences abroad when all hours had to be worked and feats of improvisation performed behind the scenes by the PPS, one or other of his two assistants and the five secretaries whom Sir Roderick Barclay describes as "ruled over by a diminutive redhead, Alison David",[3] the

---

[1] Barclay, p. 85.
[2] *Ibid.*, p. 45.
[3] *Ibid.*, p. 32.

most efficient of them all. In more normal circumstances the PPS had still to organize an over-crowded day and see that the Secretary of State always had the papers he needed; learn to interpret his moods; translate his thoughts into English; smooth over unexpected problems; administer first aid when he was ill and generally ease his burdens. The post was held in succession by three men, Pierson (Bob) Dixon (1945–47), Frank Roberts (1947–49) and Roderick Barclay, all of whom not surprisingly went on to successful diplomatic careers.

Bevin brought with him from the Ministry of Labour as an additional member of his Private Office, Pat Kinna, on whom he relied to look after his social engagements, including entertaining, travel plans and also (despite the fact that Kinna was a Tory) a good deal of party political work. Finally, as part of his "household" there was Ben Macey, his detective, who accompanied him everywhere and always had a box of pills (his "pellets") available if Bevin showed signs of distress.

Besides being Foreign Secretary, Bevin was also an MP for a London constituency. There was no hope—there never had been since his election in 1940—of his being able to find the time to perform the services which constituents expect of their Member. He turned to Ivy Saunders, his former secretary at Transport House, and during the eleven years he was in Parliament she devoted her remarkable gifts as an organizer and a great deal of her time to handling constituency matters for him, working closely with Pat Kinna and the local Labour agent, Herbert. To talk to any member of this group is to understand why Attlee singled out as the most striking index of Bevin's character his capacity to win loyalty and affection from those who worked most closely with him.

A search for a suitable official residence for the Foreign Secretary produced in the summer of 1946 No 1 Carlton Gardens. A flat was provided on the second floor and handsome rooms for entertaining on the floors beneath. This at once made life easier by giving him a proper home within a few hundred yards of the Foreign Office and, once installed, Bevin remained there for the rest of his life. Successive Private Secretaries, however, soon found, as others had before in Union as well as Ministry of Labour days, that, if he had no engagement, it was difficult to get Ernie Bevin to go home once he had finished work. On Saturdays in particular, although no engagements were arranged, he would come into the Foreign Office at his normal hour and it was often half-past two or half-past three before his Secretary could get away to a belated lunch, while the Foreign Minister, in the course of several whiskies, rumbled his way round a succession of topics which were on his mind.

If he had had more time for relaxation, he would not have known what to do with it. His wife remarked that he had never had any real recreation. The worlds of literature, the arts and music were largely closed to him, and talk, though he enjoyed it, centred round his experience, not ideas, and tended to be anecdotal. Apart from his contacts in the course of business or official entertainment, Bevin saw nothing of his party or even trade union associates socially. The idea of his spending a weekend with a Cabinet colleague was unthinkable, even the prospect of a visit to Chequers where Attlee liked to ask him filled him with gloom. "You don't get enough to eat," he told one of Dixon's successors, Roderick Barclay. "They give you sherry in glasses the size of thimbles and the only warm room in the house is the lavatory."[1] He would sometimes go away with his wife for the weekend, but his circle was limited to a few old friends whom he had known before the war and who (as one of his staff unkindly put it) "sat around telling him what a great man he was". No doubt that too was characteristic: the impressive side of Bevin was shown when he took advantage of a free weekend in Paris, not to go and stay in the country, but to drive out to Orleans and return refreshed from spending the whole of Sunday looking over pre-fabricated houses and talking to the workers who lived in them.

7

After the publication of the AAC Report, Jewish attacks on the British in Palestine had largely ceased while the Yishuv waited to see what would come of it. In June, however, they were resumed with the blowing up of railways and bridges and the kidnapping of British officers. Montgomery, visiting Palestine before taking up office as CIGS, found much to criticize in the Army's hesitation in face of the Jewish challenge which he traced back to lack of support in London.[2] He thought strong measures necessary to restore the troops' morale and to re-establish British authority, and he supported the High Commission's request for the breaking off of the discussions which had begun with the Americans until the kidnapped officers were returned, and for authority to take action against the Jewish Agency and the illegal organizations.

Bevin also sent a message from Paris in support of taking the action against the illegal groups which had been talked about, but constantly deferred, since the beginning of the year. He was insistent, however, that the talks with the Americans on the admission of 100,000 "should not (repeat NOT) be even partially suspended." The point he wanted brought out was that no action would follow the talks unless the attacks were stopped. He urged the Government to launch a publicity campaign in the UK and USA along the lines:

"H.M.G. accept entry of 100,000 Jews as part of a comprehensive plan to solve the two problems of Palestine and the Jews in Europe, but will not tolerate having their hand forced by terroristic methods."[3]

---

[1] Barclay, p. 44.
[2] *The Memoirs of F. M. Montgomery* (London 1958) p. 243.
[3] Bevin to Attlee, 20 June. FO 371/52530.

The Cabinet was in a dilemma. It did not break off talks with the Americans but felt it had to respond to the demand of soldiers as experienced as Alanbrooke, Montgomery and Cunningham for the Army to be allowed to take the initiative and not wait to be attacked. "We could no longer tolerate a position in which the authority of government was set at nought."[1]

On the night of 29–30 June a large force of troops and police was used to occupy the headquarters of the Jewish Agency and other Jewish offices as well as 25 settlements. Among the 2700 detained were Moshe Shertok, Bernard Joseph and other members of the Jewish Agency Executive.[2] Challenged in Parliament by pro-Zionist members of the Labour Party, Attlee defended the action on the grounds of close links between the Jewish Agency and the Haganah, and the cooperation between the Haganah and the Irgun. This was true enough, but thanks to their superior Intelligence, the leaders of the Haganah and other armed bands had secured advance warning and gone into hiding, making sure that much less incriminating evidence was found that had been expected. Attlee's retort to Montgomery in an argument in Cabinet later in the year was justified: the Army, having been given the freedom to act which it asked for, had failed to produce the result it had promised, to break the organization of the armed bands.[3] If proof of that was needed, it was provided by the blowing up of the King David Hotel a month later.

Bevin, however, though he thought the Army's action necessary, never doubted that a solution to the Palestine problem would have to be political, not military. He had not changed his view that the key was agreement with the Americans, and in June–July he was optimistic that this might be within sight.[4]

Truman had insisted that any talks between the two governments must start with the logistics of moving 100,000 Jewish DPs to Palestine; a meeting for this purpose was held in London between the 17th and 27th June. But Truman had come round to accepting that no decision should be made on the 100,000 until agreement had been reached on the other recommendations of the AAC Report. American readiness to discuss these was an important advance from Bevin's point of view and was due to the initiative of Loy Henderson, Head of the State Department's Near Eastern Division, and another *bête noire* of the Zionists. Henderson had secured the appointment of a Cabinet Committee which in turn appointed deputies, under the chairmanship of Henry F. Grady, to work out the American response. Grady was a lawyer who had acted as a special envoy for President Roosevelt in several parts of the world, and his committee produced a plan for a bi-national state in Palestine under UN Trusteeship.

[1] 20 June 1946, CM 60 (46). Bevin was not present.
[2] Ben Gurion was in Paris.
[3] DC Minutes, 20 November DO (46) 33rd meeting. Attlee was commenting with some asperity on Montgomery's démarche demanding that the Army should be allowed to take the initiative against the Jewish armed bands.
[4] See his message to Attlee of 30 June. FO 800/485/PA/46/34.

Paradoxically, as the Americans moved to accepting the AAC Report, the British were turning away from it. It was the weight of official opposition in Palestine as well as London (including that of the COS[1]) which finally sank it, primarily on the grounds that to implement it would lead to an Arab rising in Palestine (in addition to continued Jewish rebellion) and a rupture between the Arab states and Britain fatal to the latter's position in the Middle East. The Cabinet's minutes for the meeting of 11 July (at which Bevin was not present) recorded:

"General agreement that the recommendations in the AAC Report offered no practical prospect of progress towards a solution of the constitutional problem in Palestine, and discussion turned on the alternative policy."[2]

The alternative—the division of Palestine into separate and autonomous Arab and Jewish provinces under a central Trustee government—was not new. It had been revived by the Colonial Office in January 1946 but turned down by the Foreign Office as unsuitable for submission to the AAC on the grounds that it "savours of partition".[3] The Colonial Office now brought it forward—this time with FO agreement—as a better basis on which to secure American support than the AAC Report. In presenting the plan to the Cabinet, the Colonial Secretary (George Hall) argued that it would give the Jews the substance of the Jewish National Home which they had been promised, including the admission of the 100,000 immigrants, while providing safeguards for the Palestinian Arabs. It would also keep open future development, whether in the direction of a federation, if Arabs and Jews proved able to work together, or in the direction of partition if that proved impossible.[4]

Sir Norman Brook and Harold Beeley flew over to Paris to obtain Bevin's views in advance of the Cabinet discussion.[5] Bevin told them that he was anxious not to be put in a position of having to oppose the admission of the 100,000. He proposed to say so to Byrnes, making the sole condition that there must be consultation first with the Jewish and Arab representatives on all the issues raised by the Report. He thought this could be carried out at a conference in London in early September for which invitations should go out at once. He was still anxious to settle the Egyptian negotiations before making public any proposals for Palestine, believing it would be much easier to get Egyptian support if their own problems had been settled first. In the meantime, however, he was prepared to explore the scheme for provincial autonomy although doubtful whether it would produce a definitive settlement.

To Brook's and Beeley's surprise Bevin told them he was considering a different proposal which would partition Palestine by attaching a major part of

[1] Report of the COS 10 July. FO 371/52538.
[2] CAB 128/6 CM (46) 67.
[3] FO 371/52504.
[4] Hall's memorandum on "Long-Term Policy in Palestine", 8 July 1946, CP (46) 259.
[5] Sargent minuted to Bevin on 8 July to say that Brook and Beeley would be coming to Paris to see him on the 10th. FO 800/485/PA/46/40.

the proposed Arab province to Transjordan and the Arab portion of Galilee to Lebanon. This would make possible an independent Jewish state with more territory than under the scheme for a Jewish province. Jerusalem and the Holy Places would become an international area with its local administration in British hands and a Council representing all the major religious bodies including Jews and Muslims. Bevin said he was not ready to put forward his proposal yet but wanted to keep the way open for it.[1]

Having thought more about American participation, he told Brook that he believed it important to have the United States' political support in negotiations with the Jews and Arabs, and in the United Nations, but did not contemplate involving them in the administration of Palestine. He thought, however, that they should be asked for financial support not only in the settlement of the Jewish immigrants but also in raising the Arab standard of living. He saw no immediate need of American military assistance, but if it became necessary to impose a solution by force, believed the British should make it clear that they would not be willing to do this on their own but would require active American help.[2]

Bevin's views were put before the Cabinet when it met on 11 July but he himself was not present.[3] Some members would have liked to go ahead at once with his plan for partition and if Bevin had been there in person he might have come round to the same view and carried the Cabinet with him. That remains a tantalizing "might have been" but one worth pondering since the High Commissioner in Palestine, General Cunningham, also stated a clear preference for partition (which would at least be acceptable to the Jews) over the provincial autonomy scheme which would be acceptable to neither Jews nor Arabs.[4] As it was, the Cabinet accepted the argument that it would be easier to set up autonomous provinces with administrative boundaries which could be altered than to embark on exhausting wrangles about the frontiers of a Jewish and an Arab state. So it was decided that in the talks with the American delegation the British should try to move discussion as soon as possible from the AAC Report—which had stated the principle that neither Arabs nor Jews should dominate the other but made no proposal how this was to be done—to the Provincial Autonomy scheme.[5]

The Chiefs of Staff, intent as always on not alienating the Arab states, showed no enthusiasm for the new plan and tried to get the boundaries altered to the advantage of the Arab province by giving it a corridor to the sea at Jaffa which would cut the Jewish province in two, and to Britain's advantage by including an important airfield in Arab instead of Jewish territory. The

---

[1] There is a link between Bevin's plan in 1946 and that which he persuaded Bernadotte to adopt in 1948. See below, pp. 595–7.
[2] Note of conversation with Bevin in Paris, 10 July 1946. FO 800/485/PA/46/44. The identification of Brook and Beeley is provided by Sargent's letter of 8 July (footnote on p. 294).
[3] CM 67 (46).
[4] Cunningham to Hall, 9 July 1946, quoted by Nachmani, p. 369.
[5] CM 67 (46).

Cabinet, however, with Bevin now present, overruled the Chiefs of Staff, Bevin suggesting a different change which would give the Jews more territory in the area between Haifa and Tiberias. With the American delegation already in London and the talks going unexpectedly well, Bevin's hopes were high of a settlement which the Americans would support and he pressed for invitations to be sent out to both Jews and Arabs to attend a conference in August.[1]

At this moment the fatal counter-point between violence in Palestine and the attempt to reach agreement was repeated with the blowing up of the British Secretariat and Army HQ in the King David Hotel by the Irgun (leader, Menachem Begin) leaving 91 killed and 45 wounded. Many Jews were shocked by Irgun's calculated act of terrorism and the number of victims it claimed, but Zionist propaganda soon found a way of diverting attention. In his anger at the attack the British GOC General Barker issued a confidential order forbidding "fraternization" (the term borrowed from a similar British Army order in occupied Germany) between British soldiers and the Jewish population, and in the course of it used such anti-Semitic language as "punishing the Jews in a way the race dislikes—by striking at their pockets". This outburst, uttered under provocation, was seized on and blown up by well organized publicity in Palestine, the USA and Europe into an atrocity story which completely overshadowed the deaths inflicted by the Jewish terrorists.

The British reaction, as the Arabs bitterly complained, fell far short of the measures they had used to control the Arab rebellion in the 1930s. The High Commissioner's request for a fine of half a million pounds on the Yishuv and a complete end to Jewish immigration was turned down by the Cabinet.[2] The only action allowed was a full-scale search for the terrorists in Tel Aviv, the Cabinet (with Bevin present) accepting Attlee's view that it would be a mistake to rush into a widespread search for arms which would alienate all sections of Jewish opinion and might interrupt the Anglo–American discussions.[3]

Ambassador Grady, the leader of the US delegation, proved surprisingly amenable to accepting the British preference for the Provincial Autonomy scheme in place of the AAC Report and reached agreement with Brook and his team of officials on this basis within ten days (24 July). In making the change Grady does not appear to have been going beyond his instructions. Truman was not a convinced Zionist nor in 1946 committed to support of a Jewish state. Provided that room was found for 100,000 Jewish DPs in Palestine, the issue on which he never wavered, he was prepared to leave it to the British to find a solution to the problem of Palestine's future. The advantage of the Morrison–Grady plan, as it became known, was that it could be taken as a step either to partition or to a bi-national state.

[1] CM 71 (46), 22 July.
[2] In making it Cunningham had repeated his personal view that a political solution was the only remedy, and that this would probably have to be partition.
[3] CM 71 (46). Attlee wrote to Truman on 25 July saying they must not allow "this inhuman crime" to deter them from trying to bring peace to Palestine.

In July 1946, according to James MacDonald, the most pro-Zionist member of the Anglo-American Commission of Inquiry, Truman was eager to disengage himself from further involvement with the Zionists whom he felt nothing could satisfy.[1] The American Zionists' suspicions of the President, already aroused by his agreement to the London talks, appear to be confirmed by the statement of Henry Wallace, the US Secretary of Commerce, that Truman was in daily contact with the Grady delegation: "The President said he has . . . given them explicit instructions and they follow them exactly."[2]

The British Cabinet congratulated Brook on his successful negotiations.[3] Part of the agreement was the admission of the 100,000 Jews, Truman's principal condition, now accepted by the British. That had been a roughly accurate estimate of the number of Jewish DPs in the British and US zones in summer 1945, but the real figure now, a year later, was probably over 250,000 as a result of the emigration of Jews from Russia and Eastern Europe. The original figure, however, had acquired a symbolic importance, especially in the USA, and acceptance of it would have removed the most dangerous cause of friction between the British and the Jews in Palestine, the illegal immigration. In the Arab province there would be 815,000 Arabs and 15,000 Jews; in the Jewish, 451,000 Jews and 301,000 Arabs; in Jerusalem roughly equal numbers. A similar scheme had worked in India in the province of Sind and the Bombay Presidency, and it was hoped that a few successful settlement schemes in the Arab province would attract the Arabs in the Jewish province to sell their land and migrate. The Arab province would be larger, but the 1500 square miles of the Jewish' contained the best land, most of the industry, ports seaboard, railways and water supply. Both provinces would have a large measure of self-government.

As we have seen, Bevin's heart-attack led to his missing the next act in the drama and obliged Attlee to take his place at the Paris Peace Conference. Morrison acted as chairman of the Cabinet and introduced the Provincial Autonomy scheme (hence its name, the Morrison–Grady plan) in the Commons. Meanwhile, several thousand illegal immigrants had either reached Palestine or were on their way. The COS pressed urgently for a decision on what should be done with them. They left no doubt of their own view that the boats, some with 2,000 or 2,500 refugees on board, should be prevented from landing, transferred to British ships and taken to camps in Cyprus or Cyrenaica. The Cabinet thought it unacceptable to turn them back when within sight of Palestine, and agreed with the Prime Minister's advice that such action when agreement with the Americans seemed likely must be avoided. Although Attlee discussed the problem at three successive meetings

[1] Truman interview with MacDonald, 27 July 1946. President's file, Zionist Archives, New York, quoted by A. Ilan: "Messianism and Diplomacy 1945–48: The Struggle for a Jewish State", *Wiener Library Bulletin*, 1977 vol. xxx, p. 43.
[2] Quoted by Nachmani from *The Price of Vision: The Diary of Henry A. Wallace*, ed. John Blum (Boston 1971) p. 604, 26 July 1946.
[3] Brook's report was printed as CP (46) 295 and taken at the Cabinet on 25 July. CM 73 (46).

and was strongly pressed by the Chiefs of Staff and the Chief Secretary for Palestine (all of whom warned of the danger of an Arab outbreak) no decision was taken.

Reports from Washington suggested that the reaction of the US Government to the Provincial Autonomy plan was favourable. After talking to Attlee Byrnes telegraphed his support for it from Paris, and the prospect that the problem of the 100,000 immigrants would be removed had a powerful attraction for the President. The American Zionists, however, seeing their aim of a Jewish state about to be undercut made an all out effort to bring the President back into line. The co-chairmen of the American Zionist Executive, Wise and Silver, belonged respectively to the Democratic and Republican parties. Neither could afford to compromise for fear of losing Jewish votes for his party. On the other hand if they put aside their rivalry and formed a united front against Autonomy, they could hold a whip hand over Congressmen of either party anxious about re-election in the autumn. There was also strong opposition to the costs the USA would have to bear in endorsing the new plan.

The outcry against the plan became so fierce that Truman declared at his Cabinet meeting on 30 July that he was "put out" with the Jews. "Jesus Christ couldn't please them when he was here on earth, so how could anyone expect that I would have any luck?"[1] But the pressure produced its effect. At a meeting with the SWNCC committee on the morning of the 29th, opinion had been in favour of accepting the proposals and the President acquiesced. But a telegram from Byrnes reneging on his previous endorsement in view of the domestic repercussions had its effect. When a vote was taken at the full meeting of the Cabinet in the afternoon, Acheson found himself the one man voting in favour.[2]

The President decided that the only course open to him was to reject the plan, a decision which Loy Henderson, of the State Department, told the British Ambassador was solely attributable to reasons of domestic politics —there was nothing in the plan itself not acceptable to the USA.[3]

Truman's capitulation to Zionist pressure and his repudiation for the second time of a scheme worked out and agreed to by his nominees made the worst possible impression in London. Expressing his "great disappointment" Attlee cabled that the offer to assist the 100,000 refugees would fall with the Autonomy Plan if this was discarded.[4] Morrison's presentation to the House of the provincial autonomy scheme was cautiously received. During the summer the British Press was clearly moving towards partition as the one way out and this opinion was shared by members on both sides of the House. The one thing that would have kindled enthusiasm would have been an indication of support from the White House, but this was precisely what the Government spokes-

[1] Wallace's diary (*The Price of Vision*), p. 607.
[2] Bronley's summary of Acheson's account in a cable to Burrows. FO 371/68650.
[3] Inverchapel to FO, 30 July. FO 371/52546.
[4] PREM 8/627.

man could not provide. Churchill, criticizing the handling of Palestine as "a monument of incapacity", was still prepared to say, "Almost any solution in which the United States will join us could be made to work". But, he concluded:

"If the United States will not come and share the burden of the Zionist cause . . . we should now give notice that we will return our Mandate . . . and will evacuate Palestine within a specified period."[1]

At the Cabinet on 7 August (this was the meeting at which Bevin looked so poorly that Attlee asked to see his doctor) George Hall reported on talks with Weizmann—another sick man—who was said to be not unfavourable to the Autonomy plan in principle if concessions could be made to the Jews, including handing over the Negev to them at once. But having waited a week for any sign of American support, Attlee and the Cabinet reluctantly concluded that, if there was no reply to his appeal to Truman by the 12th, they could no longer refuse the authority to deal with the illegal immigrants for which the High Commissioner and Montgomery were pressing. While 3000 Jews who had arrived during July were moved from their ships to Athlit Camp in Palestine, the rest and all future arrivals were to be removed to camps in Cyprus, a move which produced an immediate and continuing escalation of the Jewish–British confrontation and, dramatically publicized by Zionist propaganda, did more than anything else to turn world opinion against the British. For this as for so much else the Zionists held Bevin personally responsible although it is quite clear from the discussions that the initiative came not from him, but from the Palestine Administration and the military, that it was resisted by ministers and that Bevin took no part in the Cabinet discussions which led to the decision.

Bevin in fact, through illness or absence abroad, missed no less than 46 out of 69 Cabinet meetings between 22 April 1946, when the AAC Report was signed, and the end of the year. He was constantly consulted while away and his views reported, but this was not the same thing as being physically present at meetings of the Cabinet and the Defence Committee and putting them in person. As a result, Attlee perforce played a much bigger role on Palestine than in 1945, no longer leaving the exchanges with the USA to Bevin and the Ambassador but conducting them direct with the President.

Of course Bevin continued to be a central figure in the discussions on Palestine, but to speak of what was decided as Bevin's policy—or Attlee's—is to ignore how many other people had to be brought into the discussions and the often sharp differences of opinion between them. Responsibility was divided between the Foreign Office and the Colonial Office, the Foreign Secretary being responsible for Palestine as an issue in international relations, but the Colonial Secretary for the Palestine Administration and conditions inside the country. The two departments frequently disagreed on the policy to

[1] HC, 31 July 1946.

be followed, the Foreign Office (but not always the Foreign Secretary) opposing partition; the Colonial Office regarding it as a lesser evil than the other options. The fact that the British officials and officers serving in Palestine found themselves in the position of an occupying power on the edge of civil war added a further layer of disagreement between Jerusalem and London, as well as producing sharp criticism from the Chiefs of Staff and the local commanders that the Forces were expected to keep order and stop illegal immigration but were constantly handicapped by the politicians' indecision and hesitations. The Chiefs of Staff are also to be found constantly reminding ministers of the threat that the loss of Arab goodwill could bring to Britain's strategic position in the Middle East, a subject on which ministers—including Bevin and Attlee—differed among themselves.

A similar conflict of views marked the discussions of the other interested parties—the American Administration, the Zionists and the Arabs. And as in their case, so too in the case of the British, not only were opinions divided, but in response to a rapidly changing situation the same people held different opinions at different times. So Bevin came round to partition and the admission of the 100,000 in the summer of 1946, but was not present to argue a case in the Cabinet for this rather than provincial autonomy, and later rejected partition. Truman's, Weizmann's, even Ben Gurion's views show similar fluctuations. None of the parties were free agents but subject to pressures to which they had to respond; but the pressures never acted on them equally. At one time or other all were prepared to make concessions and seek compromise; but the times never coincided.

8

By the time Bevin, still far from recovered, got to Paris on 9 August, the Peace Conference had established its refusal to be bound by the Russians' restrictive views on procedure.[1] The battle had been fought out in public, with Molotov and the Eastern European representatives ranged on one side, Byrnes, A. V. Alexander and Evatt (Australia) the leaders on the other. The final decision on the treaty provisions remained with the Council of Foreign Ministers, but the Conference proceedings were given substance and rescued from futility by Byrnes' declaration that the USA would accept any recommendations passed by a two-thirds majority, regardless of the position taken up by the Americans themselves, and by the British proposal that recommendations supported by a majority of less than two-thirds should go forward to be considered by the CFM. As a result, more than three hundred amendments to the five draft treaties were debated by the Conference; of these fifty-three were passed by a

---

[1] British records of the Paris Peace Conference, July–Oct. 1946 are in FO 371/57334–94; US records in FRUS 1946, (3): Proceedings, and (4): Documents, draft treaties and recommendations.

two-thirds vote and forty-one by a simple majority, almost invariably with the Soviet bloc voting in the minority.

Bevin took no part in the decisive confrontation over procedure nor in the work of the seven Commissions into which the conference broke up a few days after his arrival. It was not until 21 August that he presided at one of the plenary sessions and not until 8 October that he made his first speech, in the final discussion of the Italian treaty. In public, therefore, his role was much less prominent than that of Byrnes, Molotov or Bidault. Instead, as he told Dalton, he changed his tactics and "worked things from behind the scenes". This was much better than plunging into constant public debate with Molotov and others.[1] He said the same thing to Byrnes: "We are only playing the Russian game if we get involved in a campaign of charges and counter-charges."[2]

In his first week in Paris, Bevin was as much concerned with Palestine as with the Peace Conference. Despite the anger and frustration which he and Attlee felt at Truman's withdrawal of support for the Morrison–Grady report, they did not abandon their idea of holding a conference with Jews and Arabs in London and putting the scheme to them. The events of the summer, the Army's action on 29 June and the blowing up of the King David Hotel had shaken the confidence of the Jewish leadership, and there were signs, as Hall reported, that they might be prepared to talk. The members of the Jewish Agency Executive still at liberty, meeting in Paris, heard Ben Gurion express the fear that while Bevin would "not imitate Hitler's furnaces", short of that he would do everything to dismember the Jewish Agency and break the Haganah if they continued their attacks. The prospect of the tension in Palestine erupting into war between the Jews and the British led Nahum Goldmann to propose that they should abandon the Biltmore programme and negotiate partition. Ben Gurion abstained and a majority of the Executive voted in favour. As a first step Goldmann set off for New York in order to win American support. He proved a convincing advocate, winning over Acheson and the members of the SWNCC sub-committee on Palestine and through them reaching Truman who accepted partition as the best way out on 9 August. There then followed a series of talks involving Bevin as well as the Colonial Secretary and the Prime Minister.

The Zionists sought to use acceptance of the invitation to the Conference as a means of getting the British to agree to certain conditions in advance. Their first bid was transmitted to Bevin by the US Ambassador, Harriman,[3] and supported by the State Department. It led to a talk between Bevin and Goldmann in Paris and was elaborated at a meeting with Hall and Colonial Office officials on 15 August when Weizmann was accompanied by the

---

[1] Dalton, *Memoirs*, p. 155.

[2] Bevin's report to Attlee of a talk with Byrnes in Paris, 13 August 1946. FO 800/501/SU/46/26.

[3] Harriman's communication, with a covering letter from Bevin to Attlee, 13 August 1946. FO 800/485/PA/46/61.

American Zionist Wise as well as Goldmann. The most important point was that while the Jewish Agency rejected the Autonomy Plan, insisting that there must be a Jewish state with immediate control of immigration during the transition, they no longer claimed the whole of Palestine but were prepared to see it partitioned and an Arab state established as well, both in treaty relations with the UK. The frontiers could be discussed, but the Agency's present idea was the area allotted to them in the Peel Report plus the Negev, much the same as the territory of Israel before the Seven Days War, with the important difference that no claim was made to Jerusalem.

This was in fact, despite all the mistakes and delays which had preceded it, the best opportunity ever presented of getting an agreed settlement. A majority of the Jewish Agency Executive supported the proposal; President Truman had been shown it and given his approval. What about the British?

Hall told Weizmann that they were not finally committed to provincial autonomy and were ready for any other plan to be discussed at the Conference. What they were unwilling to do was to mention partition specifically, knowing that if they did so, the Arabs would make exclusion of it a condition of their acceptance. At this point Wise interjected that if Weizmann could not say more than that partition was to be considered amongst other things, he would not secure a majority at the next Zionist Congress. Goldmann then added a second condition: the release of members of the Jewish Agency from detention so that they could share the responsibility of attending the Conference. All invitations to Jewish representatives should go not from HMG but from the Agency.[1]

The British were not willing to accept these conditions as they stood, but talks continued, the British re-iterating that all delegations were free to put forward alternative proposals and asking the JA to produce a list of those they wanted to be invited.[2] When Bevin spoke to members of the Commonwealth delegation at the Paris Peace Conference, he told them that the Zionists had not given up the idea of a national home but were ready to see it established in a part of Palestine and within a federation which could include Transjordan. He said he was "not unhopeful" of getting a settlement, particularly if the frontiers claimed by the Jews coincided with those proposed by the Peel Commission of 1937. Smuts who was present welcomed the plan as "a great step forward".[3]

At this time (late summer 1946) partition had come to attract support among the British as well as the moderate Zionists and the US Administration. Brigadier Clayton in the Middle East Office in Cairo, one of the shrewdest observers of the Middle Eastern scene, and the High Commissioner in Jerusalem, General Cunningham—as well as Loy Henderson in the State Depart-

---

[1] British record of the talk, 15 August. FO 800/485/PA/46/63.
[2] Bevin to Attlee reporting on his talk with Goldmann, Wise and Locker, 17 August, *ibid.* PA/46/66.
[3] PREM/8/PS/10. Meeting between Bevin and British Commonwealth delegations in Paris, 23 August.

ment—agreed that if the British and Americans were determined, Arab opposition need not prove a fatal obstacle to its success. Bevin had an open mind, but was ready to accept the solution of a bi-national state with the possibility of its leading to eventual peaceful partition.

No compromise had been found by the time the Palestine Conference opened in London on 9 September,[1] and neither the Jewish nor the Arab community in Palestine was represented, the latter staying away because the British refused to receive the Mufti of Jerusalem who had led the Arab revolt in the 1930s and allied himself with Hitler. Only three Arab states sent delegates. They rejected the Autonomy plan on the grounds that it would inevitably lead to a Jewish State, and this in turn serve as a bridgehead for Jewish penetration of the whole area. Instead, they proposed a Palestinian state in which the Arabs would remain a permanent majority—no further immigration or land sales—with guarantees of minority rights for the Jews.

The British spent the rest of September trying to persuade the Arabs to discuss partition and the Zionists to send such Jewish leaders as were free. Goldmann found Bevin "as a whole rather helpful and with a certain amount of goodwill . . . but he has to overcome the hostility of his advisers. Whenever he was ready to accept a formula . . . other elements in London interfered and made it impossible."[2] He contrasted Bevin favourably with Hall saying that the latter was "much more narrow-minded and a bureaucrat who cares about his Conference more than about the solution of the Palestine problem."[3] In fact Hall was soon to be replaced as Colonial Secretary by Arthur Creech-Jones who was regarded as more sympathetic to the Zionists and whose appointment could be taken as a friendly gesture.

Bevin's conclusion was that there would be no Jewish representation until they found some way of releasing the Jewish leaders arrested on 29 June—and to that the Palestine Administration and the Army remained opposed. But he did not despair of finding a formula to bridge their differences and on 1 October had further talks with Weizmann (this time accompanied by Kaplan and Fishman, flown specially by the British from Jerusalem).

Bevin complained bitterly about the anti-British attitude of the Zionists. It was not the British "who had taken the initiative in blowing people up".

"The destruction of the King David Hotel had burned deeply into the hearts of the British people. Jews in this country had been citizens for years, had held high public office and had contributed greatly to the commercial prosperity of the country. As an old trade unionist he spoke with deep affection of the Jews he had associated with in many trades, many of whom were not Zionists. Great Britain had accepted more people as refugees in proportion to its size than any other country. The treatment we had received in return was very poor recognition of all we had done for the Jews. The feeling

---

[1] The British records of the Conference on Palestine, Sept–Oct. 1946 are in CAB 133/85.
[2] Goldmann to Judge Proskauer, President of the American Jewish Committee, 8 September 1946. AJC Archives, New York. Quoted by Nachmani.
[3] *Ibid.*, 26 August.

in Great Britain was that the Jews had declared war. Ever since he had taken office he had been trying to create an atmosphere conducive to final settlement. But his task was made very difficult by the acts of the Jews."

Palestine was important for the British but the alternative if no settlement could be reached was for the British to hand the problem back to the UN "with a confession that we could not solve it".[1] He refused to accept the view that Palestine was the only home for the Jewish people, declaring that he hoped the Jewish people would be a great force in the reconstruction of Europe. But there was the future of the great dream of Zionism. He did not know how to reconcile the vital prejudices of the Arabs with the vital demands of the Jews. The best answer seemed to be a trial transitional period on the basis of a bi-national state ensuring proper rights for every citizien.

Weizmann agreed that the Jewish Agency would never quarrel over the length of the transitional stage which might be 2, 3 or 5 years. "Statehood could not be reached in one day." The outcome of the meetings was that the Zionists would not participate in the conference until the members of the JA Executive detained in Palestine were released; but there were hopes that an agreement could be reached about law and order in Palestine which would open the way to Jewish delegates attending.[2] This was not chimerical. A month later Creech-Jones was able to report to the Cabinet that the Inner Zionist Council in Jerusalem had passed a resolution condemning terrorism and calling on the Yishuv to withhold support. On Creech-Jones' recommendation, the Cabinet thereupon agreed to release the Jewish leaders under detention.[3]

By then, however, like so many changes of attitude in the Palestine conflict, it was too late to achieve what it might have done a month earlier. With the UN Assembly opening in New York, the Arab representatives to the Palestine Conference were anxious to leave London. The British thought it best to suspend the Conference until 16 December, by which time the UN meetings would be over. This would give more time to try and get agreement with the Jews who could not in any case reach a binding decision before the Zionist Congress in the same month. The explanation for the suspension of the Conference is necessary since the delay was given as a reason by President Truman for an intervention which Bevin never ceased to believe fatally impaired the chances of reaching a settlement.

The American Zionists, alarmed at the prospect of a compromise, brought pressure to bear on Truman for presidential support, linking the question of Palestine openly to the prospects of the Democratic Party in the mid-term

---

[1] Minutes of meeting at the FO (1 October 1946). FO 371/52560/E10030/4/31; Zionist Central Archives, 525/7566.
[2] Bevin and Creech-Jones presented a report on this abortive Palestine Conference and their informal conversations (CP (46) 358) dated 5 October to the Cabinet on 5 October, CM 91 (46).
[3] CM 96 (46) 4 November 1946.

congressional elections due in November. Truman did not want to say anything publicly when the question of Jewish participation in the London Conference was still in the balance, and the State Department urged him not to. But Zionist access to the White House was again decisive and for the third time Truman came out with the pronouncement which cut the ground from under the British.[1] Attlee's plea for a few hours' delay and consideration of the effect anything the President said might have on the negotiations was turned down. For the first time Truman publicly committed the United States to support the Zionist plan for partition and called for the 100,000 Jewish refugees to be admitted at once.

Bevin was prepared to consider both as the outcome of the negotiations, perhaps on a timetable, in return for concessions from the Jews towards the Arabs. But for Truman to assure the Jews of American support and to call for the immediate admission of the 100,000 in advance of the conference relieved the Jews of any need to make concessions, and confirmed the Arabs in their resistance.

Attlee's anger was expressed in the sharp tone of the message he sent to the President:

"I have received with great regret your letter refusing even a few hours grace to the Prime Minister of the country which has the actual responsibility for the government of Palestine in order that he might acquaint you with the actual situation and the probable results of your action. These may well include frustration of the patient efforts to achieve a settlement and the loss of still more lives in Palestine.

"I am astonished that you did not wait to acquaint yourself with the reasons for the suspension of the conference with the Arabs. You do not seem to have been informed that so far from negotiations having been broken off, conversations with leading Zionists with a view to their entering the conference were proceeding with good prospects of success."[2]

Truman's excuse was that he could not wait because 5 October was the Jewish Day of Atonement and he could not leave the Jewish DPs disappointed by the suspension of the London conference without a word of hope.[3] No doubt Yom Kippur was in Truman's mind but the evidence now available confirms Acheson's remark to the British Ambassador at the time that the reason for Truman's refusal to wait was the need to forestall an attack on the Administration on 6 October, in which Tom Dewey and the Republican candidates standing for election in New York were expected to outbid the Democrats for the votes of the world's biggest Jewish electorate by calling for, not one hundred, but several hundred thousand Jews to be admitted to Palestine.[4]

Bevin's and Attlee's anger was natural. But it was Bevin who had sought to involve the United States in the Palestine problem and he could not complain

[1] See the account in Zvi Ganin: *Truman, American Jewry & Israel 1945–8* (NY 1979) c.6.
[2] FRUS 1946 (7) 704–5. 4 October 1946; PREM 8/627/5.
[2] Truman to Attlee, 10 October. FO 800/486/PA/46/94.
[3] Inverchapel to Attlee, 4 October 1946. FO 371/52560 E 9987/4/31.

if the President proceeded to take a different view from the one he would have liked. Truman could certainly claim—timing apart—that he was not misrepresenting American opinion when he said it would support the Jewish proposals for partition. Nor can anyone be certain that, even if Truman had not made his announcement when he did, Bevin's hopes of a settlement would have been realized. Both obligation and interest made it impossible for the British to dismiss the Arab case, as the Zionists and the Americans did, and concentrate solely on the Jewish. There had to be concessions by both sides, and the chances of that could not be rated high.

What I believe the evidence does establish, however, is this. If one takes the whole period from the signature of the AAC report in April to Truman's statement in October, it supports the view that Bevin consistently pursued the objective of a settlement with American participation which would be as fair as circumstances allowed to both Jews and Arabs; that failure was due neither to his inflexibility nor to a refusal to consider partition, and that British policy is not to be explained in personal terms of "an implacable hatred" of the Jews on Bevin's part which—despite his angry reproaches at Jewish hostility towards the British—there is no reason to believe he felt.

CHAPTER 8

Six Weeks in New York,
November–December 1946

I

If Bevin found the Americans as unsatisfactory as ever over Palestine, their response to the Soviet pressure on Turkey roused his hopes. The joint memorandum from the State War and Navy Coordinating Committee (SWNCC) recommending firm resistance to the Soviet "trial balloon" was sent to the White House for approval. In presenting it, Acheson said that the President should realize that if the Russians did not back down and the Americans maintained their attitude, the confrontation could lead to war. After asking a number of questions and examining the map, Truman explicitly endorsed pursuing the recommended reply "to the end".[1] The State Department took steps to make sure that the British understood how seriously the situation of the Turks was viewed in Washington, including the President's endorsement. It was this which led the British Ambassador to say to Acheson that the reports from Washington had created "quite a bit of excitement" in London.

The excitement was justified. Acting independently, the American Chiefs of Staff in a memorandum of 23 August recommended that the Turks should be allowed to buy American military equipment and be offered technical assistance, a reversal of policy which a further meeting of the SWNCC recommended should be broadened to include Greece and Iran as well as Turkey.

While the diplomatic trial of strength over Turkey was going on behind the scenes, the conflict between the Western Powers and the Communist bloc over the Balkans came out into the open. From the moment the Peace Conference met there were recurrent rumours that the Yugoslavs would seize Trieste by force if they were not given it by treaty. The truculent attitude of the Yugoslav delegates at the Conference lent colour to these rumours and so did the

[1] Dean Acheson: *Present at the Creation* (London 1970) pp. 195–6; *The Forrestal Diaries*, ed. Walter Millis (London 1952) pp. 192–3.

307

harrassment to which the Yugoslavs subjected the staff of Allied military government on the ground in Venezia Giulia. Two strong protests were made by the British on 19 August; the same day the Yugoslavs shot down an American transport plane flying from Italy to Austria, the second such incident in ten days, and Byrnes delivered an ultimatum demanding satisfaction from the Yugoslavs within 48 hours.

In May British destroyers sailing through the Corfu Strait had been fired on from the Albanian shore. Later evidence confirmed the belief that this incident and the mine-laying in the Strait which severely damaged two British destroyers in October were contrived by the Albanians with the help of the Yugoslavs and Greek Communists.[1]

In the public sessions of the Peace Conference (which lasted from 29 July to 15 October 1946) a bitter exchange between the Greeks and their traditional enemies, Bulgaria and Albania, over territorial claims and counter-claims in Northern Epirus and Thrace opened the way for Molotov to widen the debate into an indictment of the Greek Government as responsible for stirring up trouble in the Balkans and subjecting the Greek people to a reign of terror in which (he added) they were supported by the presence of British troops and American warships. Bevin and Byrnes had tried to discourage Tsaldaris, the Greek Prime Minister, from launching into Greece's frontier claims against her northern neighbours, but they could not sit by silent when the Greeks came under concentrated attack from the Soviet bloc. To intensify the pressure, Manuilsky, the Ukrainian foreign minister, left Paris for New York to present his complaint to the Security Council against the Greek Government's policy as "a threat to peace" and against the continued presence of British troops in the country. Between 28 August and 20 September the Council held 14 meetings to consider the complaint which was given widespread publicity. No decision was reached. The Soviet Union vetoed an American proposal for a UN commission to carry out an investigation on the spot. On their side, the British and Americans not only blocked Soviet moves in the Security Council and gave support to the Greeks in the Peace Conference debates, but Bevin and Byrnes began to discuss privately in Paris ways in which the Americans could supplement British aid to both Greece and Turkey.

The conflict of power between the Soviet and Western blocs in the Balkans and the Aegean, magnified by the open diplomacy of the Peace Conference and the Security Council, had now reached a point where Bevin began to fear that the conclusion of the peace treaties with Italy and the ex-satellites might have to be deferred and the preparation of those with Germany and Austria postponed indefinitely. In an effort to avoid this happening, he called the first of a series of informal meetings of the CFM on 29 August and at least got Molotov to agree that their deputies should start to sort out the amendments to the draft treaties. They did not succeed, however, in reaching agreement on the future timetable of international meetings.

[1] Woodhouse, p. 181.

While Molotov went to consult Stalin, Byrnes brought Germany back into the forefront of discussion by his speech at Stuttgart on 6 September. This was the American reply to Molotov's speech of 10 July. Byrnes spoke of the American desire to see the early establishment of a provisional German government; called for an upward revision of the level of industry if the Potsdam Agreement was not to be carried out in full; repudiated any idea of separating the Ruhr and the Rhineland from Germany and gave the promise: "We are not withdrawing. We are staying here. As long as there is an occupation army in Germany, the American armed forces will be part of it."[1]

The last was the most important point from Bevin's point of view, a further step in the re-commitment of the United States to the restoration and independence of Europe. Of more immediate interest, however, were the negotiations for the economic merger of the British and American zones. The primary motive on both sides was economic, not political, to prevent the deadlock over implementing Potsdam from holding up indefinitely the recovery of the two western zones. Bevin had not been persuaded easily to take up the American offer. At a meeting with Hynd and Robertson on 23 July he had repeated his objections to an Anglo-Saxon bloc, which would not afford "the best position for negotiating with the Russians", and his anxiety "in dealing with the Americans lest they should suddenly change their minds —and leave him in the lurch". But the practical arguments for merging the two zones were overwhelming. Conditions in the British zone during the coming winter threatened to be disastrous. The British could not face the continuing drain on their resources to pay for the imports needed to keep the German population alive. Something would have to be done to get production going again and this could be secured with a much greater chance of success if American and British resources could be pooled and a joint plan worked out. Bevin could not argue against the facts. He agreed to the plan going ahead and to halting reparations deliveries to the Russians from the British zone.[2] He wrote to Attlee saying he had been convinced and the same day (25 July 1946) the Cabinet approved the scheme in principle.[3]

The Bi-zonal agreement was, in effect, a joint three-year plan to make Western Germany self-sufficient by the end of 1949. Both the British and Americans argued that they were not abandoning but carrying out the Potsdam provision of economic unity, at least for the part of Germany they controlled, and continued to invite the Russians and the French to join them in abolishing zonal frontiers. Neither had much doubt that the logical conclusion was the establishment of a West German government, but both were careful to avoid any move which could be taken to commit them to this. Thus, despite the

---

[1] Text in B. R. von Oppen, pp. 152–60.
[2] Record of the meeting, FO/371/55589/8643; Dean's minute on 24 July FO 371/55844/8990.
[3] Bevin to Attlee, 25 July 1946. FO 371/55589/8855. Bevin's paper to the Cabinet CP (46) 292 gave a full report on the second round of discussions in Paris and recommended acceptance of the Bizone proposal. CM 73 (46).

inconvenience, each of the German executive committes set up to deal with separate aspects of the bi-zonal economy—food and agriculture, transport, communications, finance—was located in a different city to avoid the appearance of creating a West German capital.

Politics, however, could not be left out of the German picture and on 4 September Bevin sent Attlee from Paris a draft directive for the British C-in-C on the policy he was to follow in the Zone and the Allied Control Council in anticipation of the next session of the CFM which Bevin hoped would be held in November.

Patrick Dean, the Head of the FO German Department, was sent out to Berlin to work on the draft with General Robertson and his political adviser, William Strang. To guide him, Oliver Harvey, one of the Deputy Under Secretaries, produced a paper which reflects Bevin's thoughts at this stage after he had agreed to the Bizone.

The Secretary of State was eager, Harvey wrote,

"That Germany should be reconstructed as a loose federal state with a minimum of powers in the centre. Here Mr Dean must be on his guard against the arguments on efficiency which General Robertson and Sir William Strang will advance in Berlin. We do not want an efficient Germany, but one with strong local vested interests, such as will naturally develop if wisely fostered in the zones. The Dutch, Belgian and French Governments are all with us in this, and we must . . . not let our policy be dictated to us by our zone authorities, who think only in terms of manpower and output. The Soviets on the other hand are backing a highly centralised Germany and a Communist dictatorship."

Harvey's note ended:

"Last of all Mr Dean will realise that it is the policy of the Secretary of State to use our control of the Ruhr not against France or the U.S.A. but against the Soviets solely to secure the lifting of the Iron Curtain . . . [Russia] hopes to get into the Ruhr while keeping us out of the Eastern zone. But if we are firm and allow absolutely no infiltration she must in the end give way and open the Eastern zone to us."[1]

The directive Bevin laid down reflected these instructions: the object was to create a de-centralized system of government, with certain questions and powers reserved for a central German government and the Länder possessing complete powers in everything else, a federal state which (as he explained to the House of Commons in October) "would avoid the two extremes of a loose confederation (*Staatenbund*) of autonomous States and a unitary centralised State".[2] It was necessary to get ahead with settling the boundaries of the Länder in the British zone, nominating their governments and establishing their powers before the CFM met and before a central government was created; it was no less important that these measures should not be held up by disagreement at the CFM. To this sketch of a German future Bevin added

[1] Harvey's note, 13 August 1946. FO 371/55591/10014.
[2] HC, 22 October 1946.

international control, economic and military, of the Ruhr, and international occupation by the Western Powers of the area west of the Rhine, the most that he was prepared to concede to the French point of view.

If the Prime Minister agreed, he wrote in his covering letter, there was no need to consult the Cabinet before issuing the directive: he would send it out at once and circulate the paper to the Cabinet for information. (As an afterthought, he remembered that he should send a copy to John Hynd, the Minister nominally responsible for Germany). The Prime Minister agreed and the directive went off to the C-in-C, and was circulated to the Cabinet on 6 September, the day of Byrnes' Stuttgart speech.[1] In the next few months Bevin's directive at last provided a framework within which to revive the political as well as the economic life of the British zone.

On 9 September (the day the Palestine Conference began) Bevin had a long talk with Dalton, who told him he was troubled by the continual difficulties with the Russians.

"He [Bevin] said he didn't understand just why the Russians were so difficult. Molotov was like a Communist in a local Labour Party. If you treated him badly, he made the most of the grievance and, if you treated him well, he only put his price up and abused you next day."

They speculated on how far it might be the A-bomb which was the root of the trouble. "Bevin thought both the Americans and the Russians were too bomb-minded. . . . 'I won't have the bomb in the Foreign Office'." As Dalton remarked, that was a good principle, if he could carry it out—and Dalton doubted if he could.

From the bomb they turned to Greece. Dalton was worry the King had won the plebiscite (held on 1 September), and so was Bevin. He had done his best to impress George II that he must be a constitutional monarch, or he would soon come to grief. "'Kings are pretty cheap these days', he had said."[2] Meanwhile he was bringing a division of British troops out of Greece, which should help Dalton's search for economies.

The French too continued to present problems. Bevin expressed disappointment with Bidault and the unrealistic scheme which he put forward for detaching the Rhineland and the Ruhr from Germany—a scheme which none of the other major Powers would accept.

"He had said to Bidault, that he wanted an economic and financial agreement with France, but 'I shall never ask you for a military alliance, unless you propose it from your side'. He had said this, he told me, with an eye on the Communists."

---

[1] Bevin's memorandum together with the covering letter to Attlee (dated 4 September) are in FO 800/466/GER/46/29.
[2] When Bevin urged the King to get the Greek politicians to stop playing politics and concentrate on the real problems of their country, the King's reply—"Perhaps I shouldn't say it, but they are a bloody lot"—did nothing to raise his hopes. Piers Dixon, p. 228, 26 September 1946.

Now that France not only had a tripartite government but every Minister a tripartite *Cabinet*, everything discussed with the French became known to the Communists and to the Russians. Dalton's comment was:

"Full of bright ideas, as well as earthy sense, but dangerously obsessed with Communists."[1] A month later, he added: 'Some think Anglo-Russian relations can never go right until he disappears. I can't be sure that anyone else would do better, but some other line of approach might well be tried."[2]

The "open diplomacy" of the Paris Peace Conference and the bitterness of the exchanges had come as a shock to the majority of people on both sides of the Atlantic. The headlines and daily reports from Paris drove home, for the first time for millions of newspaper readers, even to a minister as well-informed as Dalton, how serious and far-reaching was the dispute between the Soviet bloc and the West. The rest of the news, from the Balkans and the Mediterranean, from Germany, from the United Nations, only confirmed the pattern.

The long-term effect was, no doubt, to harden feelings against the Russians, but immediately the shock added to the general anxiety and confusion about foreign policy and stimulated protest from a minority in both the USA and Britain who thought that much of the blame rested on their own governments for the hostility they showed towards Communism and the Soviet Union. There are indeed obvious features in common between the attack on 12 September by Henry Wallace, Truman's Secretary of Commerce, on US foreign policy while his colleague, the Secretary of State, was abroad in Paris and the attack which Crossman and other Labour back-benchers made on Bevin's foreign policy in November while the latter was abroad in New York. Both Byrnes and Bevin protested that their position as representatives of their governments engaged in negotiations with foreign states was being made impossible; both demanded and got the repudiation of their critics by their political leaders. The parallel extends to the distorting influence which Wallace ascribed to America's entanglement with British imperialism, and which in the British version later in the year was replaced by British dependence on American capitalism.

Wallace's speech got a poor press in Britain, largely because of its anti-British slant, and several papers remarked, as *The Economist* put it, "If anybody at the moment is driving anybody into hostility with Russia it is the Americans who are driving the British".[3] There was no disposition, as yet, to put the blame for this on Bevin; if anything, there was wider appreciation of the difficulties he had with the Russians after the public demonstration of their intransigence and hostility at the Paris Peace Conference which no one, this time, could attribute to Bevin's provocative attitude.

[1] Dalton, *Memoirs*, pp. 155–7.
[2] *Ibid.*, p. 158.
[3] *The Economist*, 20 September.

The exception was the *New Statesman* which in August began a sustained attack on Bevin's foreign policy which it described as

"A long series of extemporisations . . . the unarticulated judgement of a practical man who instinctively rejects the idea of basing his policy on anything so abstract as political analysis and principles, a personal rather than a Government policy based on instinct rather than reason."[1]

In subsequent articles, the author held up to scorn "the role in which he so much delights of the patient, blunt and battered Englishman defending himself and his country against the below-the-belt attacks of alien assailants", criticized the Cabinet for allowing Bevin's egoism and prejudices to determine British foreign policy, and called for a complete reorientation which would scale down British commitments to a level appropriate to her loss of power, try to extricate British interests from the Russo-American contest which lay ahead and associate with other Powers who wanted to keep out of the power struggle. "Strategically, these islands are probably defenceless and large parts of our Empire are in process of dissolution." Instead of embarking on a foolhardy attempt to defend the Empire, the Labour Government must return to its socialist principles and create a middle way independent of the rival power blocs.

How this was to be done, the *New Statesman* did not say: no-one outside the Foreign Office could provide a blueprint for foreign policy. The Prime Minister should call for proposals from the different departments to be discussed in Cabinet and lay down a Cabinet policy which would be binding. It must be a socialist policy and there must be socialists in the Foreign Service to carry it out.

The *New Statesman* articles did not attract much support at the time they were published; their historical interest lies in the preview which they provided of the line to be taken by the future "Keep Left" group when it launched its much more damaging attack on Bevin as Foreign Secretary in November 1946. What most Labour supporters hoped in September was that Bevin would return to Paris and try to pull the Peace Conference back from political warfare to diplomacy. This was exactly what Bevin hoped to do himself and the evening that he returned to Paris (21 September) he saw Byrnes, then Molotov and Bidault, and got all three to agree to hold an informal meeting of the CFM. The following day, a Sunday, he held a meeting of the British delegation in the morning, and put new heart into them. After lunch, and a siesta, he drove out to Fontainebleau with Bob Dixon and went for a "slow, damp trudge in the forest on a brilliant autumn afternoon".[2] When the Foreign Ministers met, two

---

[1] *New Statesman.* "Re-orientations I", 31 August, with subsequent instalments on 7, 21 and 28 September. See also the leading article of 24 August, calling for recognition of Russian control of the Black Sea region "which has already taken place and which we cannot reverse even if we accept the position of senior satellite of the USA".
[2] Dixon diary, 22 September 1946.

days later, Bevin produced the idea of a timetable, both for the Peace Conference and for the Council of Foreign Ministers. In this way he hoped to get the Foreign Ministers back to regular meetings in private. His proposal was that the various commissions should be given until 5 October to finish their work and the Conference until 15 October to hold the necessary plenary sessions for taking votes on the draft treaties. If this could be done then, he suggested, the CFM would meet in New York with the amended draft before them, in early November, and Bevin added the hope that talks on Germany might start at the end of that month.

The exchange at the CFM's informal session was frank but friendly, and the next day the world press greeted with undisguised relief Stalin's oracular replies to an interviewer (Alexander Werth, of the *Sunday Times*) in which the Russian leader said that he saw no real danger of a new war. After the intensive propaganda campaign of the summer, Stalin struck a whole range of reassuring notes. The USA was incapable of creating a "capitalist encirclement" of the USSR and Stalin would not say that they wanted to. The Soviet Union did not want to use Germany against the West; it believed in the possibility of friendly and lasting co-operation with the western democracies. Finally, Stalin declared that the A-bomb was not such a serious threat to peace as many believed: it could not decide the outcome of a war. America's monopolistic possession of it would not last long and its use might be prohibited.[1]

It is uncertain why Stalin should have chosen to intervene to damp down tension at this particular time, but there was no doubt of the effect his words had in lifting the fear of war. Even the sceptical *Economist* wrote: "For a brief time the spell of universal ill-will has been weakened", adding that now was the time to work for better understanding.[2] With the Foreign Ministers and their Deputies meeting again, it was possible to keep to the timetable Bevin had proposed for the Peace Conference. At another informal session of the CFM on 3 October, agreement was reached on the rules of procedure to be followed at the plenary sessions and on the 6th Bevin got these adopted when he presided over the full conference.

In the meantime, Bevin took advantage of his presence in Paris to have further talks with Byrnes and other political leaders. Although there was as yet no formal alliance, the more frequent meetings between Bevin and Byrnes reflected the increasing "parallelism" of British and US policy. Describing this parallelism as one of the most important factors in international affairs, the *New York Times* wrote:

"This is not the product of deep diplomatic scheming . . ., nor has it been imposed by one country upon the other. It results from the inevitable reaction of two democratic nations to developments since the war."[3]

---

[1] Published 25 September 1946.
[2] 28 September 1946.
[3] 24 October 1946.

When they met on 20 August, Byrnes threw out a suggestion that there should be a "common user" policy between the USA and the British Commonwealth for the reciprocal use of ports and possibly of air bases. Reporting this to Attlee, Bevin said that it could be a big thing and serve as a substitute for the earlier talks on American bases which had come to nothing. He thought the Americans had not thought through their policy, but it was moving rapidly: they were worried about the USSR and aware of the possibility of war.[1] The British Chiefs of Staff viewed the proposal favourably, so long as it was world wide and reciprocal: they were more confident about its working with naval facilities than with air bases.[2] Bevin took the matter up again with Byrnes on 2 September and urged him to put forward more precise proposals. He suspected that the reason for the American suggestion was their need of bases in the Mediterranean and he insisted that any scheme would have to be world-wide and include, for example, the Pacific as well as Gibraltar or Malta.[3]

When they came back to the subject on 25 September, both agreed that it would be best to avoid any formal written agreement,[4] and a month later the British Ambassador reported from Washington that the State Department now proposed that the wartime practice of arranging for US and British naval vessels to use each other's ports should be continued indefinitely. Where similar arrangements existed for aircraft, it was suggested that they should continue, but that no attempt should be made to extend them.[5] These proposals were accepted by both sides early in December.[6] In this way, the wartime practice of co-operation between the US and British navies was quietly resumed.

Greece and Turkey were now as much the focus of American as of British anxiety, at least for the handful of men who knew how little effective force the United States had to cope with an emergency in the Eastern Mediterranean. Beginning with the Joint Chiefs' of Staff memorandum of 23 August, a succession of state papers and despatches[7] document the US Government's recognition of an American interest in the independence and territorial integrity of Turkey and Greece and of the need to give greater support to both countries—a preliminary sketch of the Truman doctrine.

In mid-September the British CIGS, Montgomery, met the American Joint Chiefs of Staff and reached agreement to begin talks as soon as possible on a coordinated strategy in case of war. When Monty asked his opposite numbers what value they attached to Middle Eastern oil—the question Attlee had

[1] Bevin to Attlee, 23 August. FO 800/513/US/46/91.
[2] Note by General Ismay, 30 August, *ibid.*, US/46/94.
[3] Bevin to Attlee, 2 September, *ibid.*, US/46/95.
[4] Bevin to Attlee, 26 September, *ibid.*, US/46/105 and FO 800/479/MIS/46/112.
[5] Inverchapel to FO, 24 October 1946. FO 800/513/US/46/114.
[6] Inverchapel to FO, 11 December, *ibid.*, US/46/128.
[7] Printed in FRUS 1946 (7) pp. 194–256 for Greece and pp. 827–96 for Turkey.

pin-pointed in talking to Dalton—"their reply was immediate and unanimous —vital."[1]

Byrnes, reporting back to Washington on a talk with Bevin on 21 September, still hoped to leave Britain to continue supplying arms to Greece and Turkey, while the USA gave economic assistance.[2] The possibility that, if Britain could no longer afford to provide arms, the USA would have to take its place is mentioned in the documents but only as a possibility, nowhere clearly defined. This was the rub: not agreement in principle, which was now accepted, but the necessary action by the USA to implement its promises of support. The one convincing demonstration of this was Forrestal's announcement on 1 October that a US naval command was being established in the Mediterranean in support of American policy, and the assignment to it of the world's largest aircraft carrier, the *Franklin D. Roosevelt*, to which were added by the end of the year three cruisers and eight destroyers. It is probable that when the Russians pressed the Turks in a further note to take up their proposal of direct talks, it was this display of American readiness to support their diplomacy with power rather than the exchange of diplomatic notes which led the Russians not to take the matter further.

The Turkish "crisis" was over and Soviet ambitions in the Straits once again shelved; but its lasting effect was to push a stage further the development of American policy catalysed by the Iranian crisis. In the course of October, Will Clayton produced three new papers on Turkey, Greece and Iran[3] which, with the Secretary of State's approval, represented a reversal of earlier American policy and a tacit acceptance of Bevin's argument that the USA had as great an interest as Britain in seeing the buffer-zone of the Northern Tier preserved intact. The new policy was confirmed to British officials by Loy Henderson (head of the State Department's Near Eastern Division and as much responsible for the change as any man) on 30 October.

2

Bevin used his time in Paris not only to talk with the Americans but to resume discussions with the French. Since his sharp reply to Massigli in May,[4] neither Bevin nor Bidault had made any further attempt to narrow the gap between British and French policy. The French had followed an independent line in the Peace Conference without producing much effect on the outcome and by September they were more isolated than ever on Germany, the issue which mattered more than any other to them. On the 5th of that month Bidault came to see Bevin, told him that the French Government was in economic and

[1] Montgomery, p. 442.
[2] Byrnes to Clayton, 24 September. FRUS 1946 (7) pp. 223–4.
[3] On Turkey, 21 October, FRUS 1946 (7) pp. 894–7; on Greece, 21 October, *ibid.*, 240–45; on Iran, *ibid.*, pp. 529–36.
[4] See above, pp. 279–80.

financial difficulties and expressed the wish to meet and see how far their two countries could help each other. Bevin welcomed his approach, fixed a meeting of experts for 9 September and suggested there should be regular discussions, not just to deal with their immediate problems but for the closest possible long-term co-operation.[1] By the 17th Bevin was able to report that agreement had been reached not only on French debts to Britain but on regular meetings to review the balance of trade and payments between the two countries and deal with any difficulties which might arise.[2]

The next encounter was not so happy. When Bevin went to see the French Prime Minister on 24 September to discuss a timetable for the Peace Conference and the CFM, Bidault told him that he was proposing to make a unilateral declaration of a customs union with the Saar, and wanted him to know in advance. Bevin had never had a high opinion of Bidault and thought that his proposal was framed with the forthcoming elections in mind and little thought of the wider consequences. He told Bidault he was making the old mistake of dealing with Germany piecemeal, reserved his own position and in a dispatch to Attlee the following day advised him to withhold British agreement. If the French took this isolated unilateral action, he added, it would be difficult to resist similar action by the Russians and bad for any prospect of four-power agreement on Germany.[3] At the same time Bevin reported to the Foreign Office that Bidault had laid great stress on the importance of German coal deliveries for France's recovery and had complained that the British were giving the Germans priority over the French in their allocation of Ruhr coal.[4]

Fortunately these difficulties did not prove fatal to further talks and over dinner at the British Embassy on 11 October Bevin and Bidault thrashed out a number of their differences.[5] Bevin began by proposing the abolition of visas and on his side Bidault announced that he had given up the idea of unilateral action on the Saar. In return Bevin promised to say in the House of Commons that HMG thought the Saar should go to France and to press for this at the next meeting of the CFM. Coal was a stumbling block, if only for electoral reasons: the Communists, Bidault complained, were making propaganda about coal from Poland and wheat from Russia. Bevin pointed out the difficulties shortage of coal was making in the British Zone, but he promised to see that the allocation to France was not cut before the elections.[6]

When Bidault tried to draw him by remarking that he was not happy to see France and the UK being led by the USA in world affairs, Bevin was guarded

[1] Notes of meeting on 5 September, in a report to the Foreign Office dated 7 September. FO 800/464/FR/46/19.
[2] Bevin's report to the Cabinet. CM (46) 82.
[3] Bevin to Attlee, 24 September, 25 September. FO 800/464/FR/46/21–22.
[4] Bevin to FO, 25 September, *ibid.*, FR/46/23.
[5] British report of discussion, 11 October 1946, *ibid.*, FR/46/24.
[6] The British priority was to restore the economy of the British Zone to working order and so eliminate the need for subsidies. The key to this was more coal and until the productivity of the Ruhr mines was restored to a level where it could meet both German and French needs, the British dilemma and the French complaints continued.

and said they had better have a separate talk about that. Bidault was in an anxious state, pessimistic about the outlook for the New York meeting of the CFM and more than anything else worried about his election prospects. The Communists, he declared, needed only seven seats to emerge as the largest party in the Chamber and he spoke bitterly of de Gaulle whose pronouncements from retirement were losing the MRP much-needed votes. It was not a reassuring discussion but Bevin could at least feel satisfaction that at the very end of his six months of visits to Paris he had made the first step towards a better understanding with the French.

As soon as Bevin had cleared the accumulation of business awaiting him on his return from Paris, he drafted a paper for the Cabinet,[1] proposing that an examination be started in Whitehall of the possibility of a customs union or some other form of closer economic cooperation between the UK and her Western European neighbours, particularly the French. The impetus came partly from his success in reaching a commercial and financial agreement with France but also from a belief that if Germany and Europe were to be divided it might be necessary for the Western European countries to act quickly to strengthen their mutual ties. If this should mean a full customs union, Bevin argued, it would be important to have examined in advance the questions it would raise not only for the UK but for the Commonwealth. It would also be necessary to look at the relationship between such a proposal and the plans for an International Trade Organization which the USA was promoting in its efforts to remove the barriers to multilateral (and American) trade. A preparatory committee had just assembled in London to start work on a draft charter for the ITO. The British were committed by their Financial Agreement with the Americans to give it their support, but although reported by the American delegation to be "scrupulously correct" in fulfilling their obligations, they showed no zeal in the cause.[2] The possibility that the ITO proposals might only come into partial operation or fail altogether were among the alternative assumptions—as well as their success—on which Bevin wanted his own suggestion of a closer economic union with Western Europe looked at. When the paper came up for discussion on 25 October, however, Bevin had had second thoughts and told his colleagues that he thought it better to defer consideration until after the French elections.[3] It was not until January 1947 that he brought the proposal before the Cabinet again.

There remained the task of bringing the Peace Conference to a conclusion on time, and in this Bevin played a more prominent part than he had in its earlier stages. Three days of the concluding sessions were taken up with discussion of the Italian Treaty, most of the time being claimed by the Soviet bloc, led by the Yugoslavs and Russians, for a series of attacks on the Trieste settlement. Bevin

[1] CP (46) 380, 18 October 1946.
[2] Confidential Report by the Chairman of the US Delegation to the Secretary of State, 27 December 1946, with the relevant papers FRUS 1946 (1) pp. 1351–66.
[3] CM 91 (46).

admitted that he had had doubts too but defended what was proposed as a fair compromise. His speech, more than that of any other delegate, tried to lift the Conference out of its preoccupation with nationalist quarrels and see it as a part of history. But virtually all the amendments were pressed to a vote, 81 in all, which the Eastern group lost almost without exception. It was half-past three in the morning before the voting was finished, but the next day the Conference reassembled to go through the Rumanian Treaty and take another 46 votes before it broke up at 1.40 a.m.

Bevin was more combative over the Rumanian than the Italian Treaty. Molotov's and Kardelj's argument that the Western demand for equality of economic opportunity in the Balkans and the internationalization of the Danube were only another name for "imperialist exploitation" struck him as hypocritical. If any country was trying to establish a privileged position in the Balkans and close that area off from the rest of the world in order to exploit its resources it was the Soviet Union, and he spoke up strongly for freedom of navigation on the Danube.

Two more days were given to the Bulgarian and Hungarian treaties and the job was done within the limits of Bevin's timetable. This was only possible because the understanding between the four members of the CFM survived their public disagreements. On 14 October, after Bevin had mentioned the undisputed settlement with Finland and Molotov had made a final indictment of the group of nations, led by the USA, which had dictated to the Conference by its majority voting power, the CFM held the last of its informal meetings. Even Molotov showed his relief that the Conference had been brought to an end, and made a number of sly but not unfriendly digs at his colleagues. The Council had now to meet in order to settle which of the amendments carried in Paris were to be incorporated in the final text of the peace treaties, but Bevin in particular was anxious to pin it down to start discussing the German settlement at the same time. As they had all to be in New York for meetings of the United Nations, Bevin argued that this was the obvious place for the CFM to meet too. New York, Molotov declared, was no place for a meeting on Germany: "it is impossible to see Berlin even from the highest skyscraper". But he did not dissent from Bevin's suggestion that they should open their German discussion in New York and, according to the progress made, decide whether to continue there or meet again in Europe.[1]

A week later Bevin had to present his account to the House of Commons. If there was little enthusiasm in Britain for the "open diplomacy" practised at Paris, there was not much disposition (as there had been in earlier encounters with the Russians) to blame Bevin himself for the undisguised quarrel between the Eastern bloc and the West which had dominated the proceedings.[2] Bevin was careful not to revive the quarrel in his speech and claimed no more than

[1] Piers Dixon, pp. 229–30.
[2] The best contemporary assessment is by Harold Nicolson in *Foreign Affairs*, Vol. 25 No. 2, Jan. 1947, pp. 190–203: "Peace-making in Paris: Success, Failure or Farce?"

that the recommendations of the Conference represented a reasonable, if rough, balance between the conflicting claims.

He took the opportunity, however, to report on foreign affairs over a much wider spectrum, beginning with the Far East. Here at least he could report a success which everybody welcomed. Thanks to British mediation, a truce had been arranged between the Dutch and the Indonesians and long-term negotiations were about to begin: "Our troops will be out of Indonesia finally on 30 November and I have every hope that, by that date, a settlement will have been reached."

The other part of the world about which he had something new to say was Germany. Having made the required gesture towards Potsdam, he accepted that the British could not go on waiting for the economic unity of Germany to be put into practice before taking action in their own zone. He set before the House in more detail the programme he had initiated with his September directive: the three Länder to be established as part of a future federal Germany; the agreement with the Americans to set up the Bi-zone; the need to raise the level of industry (taking a steel-making capacity of 11m tons per annum, not 7.5m as a yardstick, as the British had argued from the beginning) and to get the Ruhr mines to produce more coal as the basis for the Germans' recovering their self-sufficiency and ending British subsidies. Nominated councils would take over the government of the three Länder and draw up constitutions to be submitted to elected parliaments. For the first time Bevin committed the British Government to the public ownership of German heavy industry, as a step towards which the coal and steel industries in the British zone had been taken over and vested in the C-in-C. Similar action would follow with chemicals and engineering: "Our intention is that these industries should be owned and worked by the German people subject to such international control that they cannot again be a threat to their neighbours." Bevin was firm in his opposition to the dismemberment of Western Germany but he kept his promise to Bidault by accepting the French case for incorporating the Saar into their economy without annexing it. As Byrnes had done in his Stuttgart speech, he repeated that the Western Powers had only agreed to the Russian transfer of the Oder–Neisse territories to Poland with reluctance and in return for assurances of free elections in Poland and other conditions: "We see no reason why we should finally ratify the cession of this vast territory to Poland without being satisfied that those assurances have been fully carried out."[1]

---

[1] Bevin had obtained authority to make his statement from the Cabinet the previous day, when a discussion had taken place on Bevin's recommendation for talks to be conducted between British and American teams while he was in New York. The supporting paper (CP (46) 383, dated 17 October) fills out Bevin's statement in the House. Documenting the rundown conditions of the British zone, he said it would take three years and an additional investment of £250 M. to make it self-sufficient. The comparable figure for the US zone was £125 M. The greater part of this capital investment would have to be provided by the Americans. Bevin was also very anxious to get the USA to provide more than 50% of the expenses of the combined zones. Dalton had already proposed a ratio of 4 to 1 as in the financing of UNRRA and Bevin suggested this as a starting point for the negotiations.

There were several reasons for Bevin's restraint in not saying all that was in his mind and not letting appear too plainly his anger at the consequences of the Russian attitude for a Europe which had already suffered so much.

One was the hope, to which he still held, that if the Western Powers made plain to the Soviet Union—as they had in Iran and Turkey—that there were clear limits to what they would tolerate, the Russians would in time accept these and a new balance of power would be struck. (This is of course what happened, but on a longer time scale than Bevin envisaged, at least in 1946, and not without the division of Germany and Europe). Plainly they had not yet done so or given up the hope, on their side, of wearing down and undermining the British and American will to resist. Both Governments had to put up with a constant stream of misrepresentations and calumny from the Communist propaganda agencies—"mephitic" was the word J. L. Garvin used in *The Observer* to describe the atmosphere it created. But (a second reason for his restraint) Bevin had learned, as he said in his speech, that the temptation to reply in kind was best resisted. For (the third reason) a substantial number of Labour members had not altogether rid themselves of the suspicion, fanned by the Left, that it would all have been different if Bevin had followed a different policy. Any display of aggressiveness on his part only revived this suspicion. Bevin's speech on this occasion was listened to in silence by the Labour benches, without applause, and the majority of Labour speakers in the debate that followed were critical of their Foreign Secretary.

Bevin's statement on Germany was generally approved, without much enthusiasm: he should have made it in May, not October, was the *Guardian*'s comment,[1] and not have let the Americans get in first—a remark which ignored the virtual certainty that, if he had, he would have been taken to task for dividing Germany and making agreement with the Russians more difficult. Reaction to the speech as a whole was more one of disappointment than criticism, summed up by the Liberal *News Chronicle* when it wrote:

"The policy which emerged has something of a patchwork quality. Few people at home or abroad will quarrel with most of what Mr. Bevin had to say, but the unifying thread linking British policy all over the world is still hard to find."[2]

Bevin's delivery of his speech strengthened this impression: he stuck closely to his text, reading it in a subdued and monotonous voice. This reflected not only his physical tiredness but also a reluctance to spell out, in so many words, the conclusion to be drawn from his own speech. In nearly every one of the disturbed areas Bevin mentioned, at least in Europe and the Levant, he saw the principal obstacle to pacification and recovery in the determination of the Soviet Government (as well as the Yugoslavs) to exploit the post-war situation in order to expand their own power. Yet although this was clear in relation to

[1] *Manchester Guardian*, 23 October 1946.
[2] 24 October.

the situation in each area—Austria, Germany, Poland, Venezia, the Balkans, Greece and Turkey—Bevin avoided placing the individual instances in a common pattern which would have highlighted the conflict between the Soviet Union and the Western Powers; he preferred to leave them as a catalogue.

Bevin's closely argued, largely factual, account of the situation in particular countries like Austria and Greece had a much better chance of making an impression on his audience than any appeal to emotion or controversial generalization. In the end it was facts which overcame Labour suspicions of Bevin's policy; in October 1946, however, this was still some way off and all Bevin could do was to show patience as well as firmness in his policy and wait for the facts to have their effect.

There was yet one more reason, pointed out by *The Observer*, why Bevin's speech "laid down no broad principles of policy and opened up no long-term perspectives". This was the dramatic reversal in American foreign policy in the course of 1946. The almost universal assumption that the USA would withdraw from Europe as after 1918 had been proven wrong; she had moved instead to take the lead in resisting the expansion of the Soviet Empire. Obviously this eased Britain's position but, *The Observer* argued, it was a change to which the British "have to adjust ourselves with some discretion". It was almost inevitable that Britain would side with the USA in any conflict with Russia,

"But it is equally understandable that the Government—and this is the main difference between Mr. Bevin's and Mr. Churchill's policies—are careful not to commit themselves beyond the matters actually in hand. To reserve our long-term policies and to avoid too close and too permanent an association between Britain and the USA was the more provident since American foreign policy is notoriously exposed to the unpredictable stresses of internal politics. . . . Mr. Bevin's policy of putting down his foot firmly, without deciding too far in advance where he will put it next, may not be inspiring and may not lend itself to great parliamentary orations. But it is the policy most fitted to the present situation; and the debate suggests that it is the one which divides the country least."[1]

By the time *The Observer* article was printed, Bevin was on board the *Aquitania* on his way to a seven weeks' stay in the United States. Before he left he had the satisfaction of getting Cabinet approval for the continuation of military service and of concluding a draft treaty with Egypt.

When the discussion of the call-up was resumed in the Defence Committee, Bevin spoke more bluntly than it was politic to do in the House of Commons:

"He was convinced that if we were not prepared to accept certain risks and to show by our example that we are determined to fight . . . then all Europe would fall under Russian influence. It was now clear that Russia sought by every means to bring about the dissolution of the British Empire. However by 1950 the position might have clarified and it would be possible to determine if U.N.O. would be an effective

[1] *The Observer*, 27 October.

instrument . . . Legitimate risks to safeguard our interests should be accepted until that date."[1]

Three meetings in all[2] were devoted to the size of the Forces, Bevin saying he could give no forecast of when overseas commitments could be liquidated: in Venezia Giulia British troops might be needed for 2–3 years to prevent a Yugoslav coup d'etat. Dalton pointed out that the coalition had thought £500 m. per annum was the maximum the country could afford for defence, while Labour was now proposing an expenditure of £700–750 m. Nonetheless he supported compulsory national service and so after much discussion did the Cabinet. Attlee gave a firm lead, not evading the effect this would have on production and the standard of living and accepting Bevin's argument that the country had to face the cost if it was to live up to its responsibilities. Bevin was equally forthright, saying it had always been his view that there should be a permanent scheme of compulsory national service. In the past the Forces had been in large part recruited from the unemployed; with full employment and the planned economy on which they had embarked, with its comprehensive system of social services, there should be an obligation on all citizens to undertake national service. Most of the discussion turned on the length of service, a year and a half, or a year. The longer period was finally accepted, with power to reduce it later if this became expedient.[3]

Bevin's other contribution to defence was to cut through the confused negotiations for replacing the 1936 Treaty with Egypt. His refusal to put up new proposals when these broke down in Cairo had produced the effect he had calculated. In October Sidqi proposed that he and the Egyptian Foreign Minister should come to London. Stansgate had been dropped from the Government at the beginning of October and Bevin conducted the negotiations personally. As a result of five meetings between 17 and 25 October, he and Sidqi finally reached agreement on a draft treaty for which the latter promised to seek ratification from the Egyptian parliament. The British undertook to evacuate Cairo, Alexandria and the Delta by 31 March 1947 and the rest of Egypt by 1 September 1949. In return Egypt agreed to take action in the event of aggression against countries adjacent to her territories while a Joint Defence Board would examine the repercussions of "all events which may threaten the security of the Middle East" and make recommendations to the two Governments who "will consult together in order to take in agreement such measures as may be recognised as necessary".[4]

Of the defence arrangements, Dixon wrote in his diary:

"We couldn't have done better than this. The days are past when we could treat Egypt

---

[1] DC Minutes, 16 October 1946, DO (46) 27th meeting.
[2] In addition to the 27th, the 28th and 29th meetings on 17 and 22 October.
[3] CM 90 (46), 24 October 1946.
[4] The text of the Bevin–Sidqi agreement was published in a British White Paper, Cmd. 7179 (1947).

de haut en bas, and act as a Great Power using a little Power's territory for our own purposes as and when we judged our interests required it."[1]

However reluctantly, Montgomery accepted that, by replacing specific military rights with a reliance on Egyptian goodwill, the arrangements were a model of the new basis on which Bevin would have liked to place British relations with other Middle Eastern countries as well[2]. The London talks, however, (as Dixon added) really revolved around the Sudan[3]. For reasons which had seemed convincing at the time, Bevin's predecessors (including Salisbury and Curzon) had preferred to avoid trouble, first with the Turks, later with the Egyptians, and not insist on a claim to sovereignty in addition to the occupation of the Sudan.[3] Now it was too late and while the British retained the administrative rights in the Sudan established by Cromer, they had to admit the sovereignty of the Egyptian King. A protocol on the Sudan annexed to the Treaty recognized "the framework of the unity between the Sudan and Egypt under the common Crown of Egypt". Within this framework the Sudanese were to enjoy the right to achieve independence and decide their own future; until this could be realized, "after consultation with the Sudanese", as Bevin had promised in March 1946, the Anglo-Egyptian Agreement of 1899 and British responsibility for the defence of the Sudan were to remain in force.

The British would have a problem in satisfying the Sudanese that they had not given away their rights of self-determination, but the crucial question was whether Sidqi could persuade the Egyptians to accept the Treaty he had negotiated. Bevin left for America before there could be any answer. If he hoped that at last he might have cleared the way for a new British policy in the Middle East, he was cautious enough to keep his hopes to himself. Before he had been many days in New York he was to see these, like so many other of his hopes for a Middle Eastern settlement, proved illusory.

3

The Egyptian negotiations, on top of everything else, made the last ten days before they left for New York the worst Dixon remembered in the FO. "I really thought our machine would crack under it." Bevin was unwell and collapsed as soon as he relaxed on board ship: for each of the first three days at sea he stayed in bed until tea-time. He summoned up enough energy to hold a successful press conference when the ship was invaded by a "mass rush" of journalists as soon as it docked at Pier 90. But Dixon wrote in his diary the same evening (2 November):

[1] Piers Dixon, p. 232.
[2] At the Defence Committee, 24 October, DO (46). Minutes of 30th meeting.
[3] Piers Dixon, pp. 232–3.

"S. of S., who hates this whole trip, is suffering from claustrophobia and nostalgia. A rather gloomy dinner in his room, during which we massaged him into some form of contentment."[1]

Not only was the Council of Foreign Ministers meeting in New York, but the UN was in full session, both the General Assembly and the Security Council. On the evening of his first day in New York, Bevin met the full UK delegation to the Assembly and urged them to press strongly for work to be started in defining human rights and setting up a tribunal of appeal. He also talked frankly with them about the Soviet motion to break off relations with Franco, which many in the Labour Party would have liked to support. Bevin told the delegates that it would be a major disaster if they could only oust the Spanish dictator at the price of another civil war, and maintained that the internal regime of a country could only be modified by due constitutional process. He urged them to look at the possibility of bringing near the dismissal of Franco: it was a matter that called for much patience and the acceptance of unmerited blame.[2] Bevin repeated the performance with the Commonwealth delegates and, to Dixon's surprise, carried them with him on Spain.

Bevin kept in close touch with what was going on at the UN and made an unexpected intervention in the Assembly later in the month; but his main reason for coming to New York was to try and settle finally the Italian and other peace treaties. New York was so crowded with UN delegates that it was only with difficulty that a meeting place had been found for the CFM on the 27th floor of the Waldorf Astoria Hotel, from which (as they waited through the interminable translation of their remarks) Bevin and the other Foreign Ministers could look out over the towers of New York. Bidault was missing, detained in Paris by elections and the formation of yet another French government: his place was taken by Couve de Murville who proved to be a far more impressive representative of France, especially in the chair. But all the other familiar faces were there and Bevin steeled himself for one more protracted session with Molotov and Byrnes, his sixth, this time lasting from 4 November to 12 December.[3]

Personal relations with Molotov were easier than they had been in Paris. At a Soviet reception on Red Army Day, Bevin reported finding him "both amenable and inquisitive", asking whether the US election results (a defeat for Truman and the Democratic Party[4]) would produce any change in US foreign policy. Bevin replied "with an emphatic No" and told him that no amount of "warfare across the conference table" would make any difference either. Molotov was equally inquisitive about British policy. Had the Labour Government, he asked, still got popular support, an inquiry to which Bevin had a

---

[1] Piers Dixon, p. 235.
[2] 3 November 1946. FO 800/508/UN/46/36.
[3] British records of the 3rd session of the CFM in New York, Nov.–Dec. 1946 in FO 371/57400–414; US records in FRUS 1946 (2) pp. 965–1566.
[4] See below, pp. 326–7.

convincing answer in the municipal election results.[1] Molotov expressed satisfaction: he did not want Churchill back, but why didn't Bevin repudiate Churchill, why was there continuity in foreign policy, if Bevin and his colleagues held different views? It had been a coalition government, Bevin retorted, and its foreign policy had not been that of Mr Churchill. The two men were no nearer agreement but at least they met and talked like human beings.[2]

Once sitting at the conference table, however, Molotov was as obstructive as he had ever been. The Paris Peace Conference might as well never have been held for any difference it made to the Russian attitude. With a few minor exceptions, all the recommendations of the Peace Conference, whether passed by a two-thirds majority or not, were objected to by the Russians and had to be deferred. This went on for a week; then, on 12 November, the Foreign Ministers started on the Statute for an internationalized Trieste and conducted a detailed argument about the powers of the Governor and the other provisions which lasted for 11 days, in three formal and no less than seven informal meetings. Although Couve de Murville was able to effect a few compromises, none of the three protagonists was really prepared to give ground. The British and Americans were convinced that the Russian tactics were to restrict the powers of the Governor to such a degree that, once Allied troops had been withdrawn, the Yugoslavs could carry out a *coup* and absorb the Free Territory with impunity. Bevin and Byrnes were determined not to let this happen and fought stubbornly over every line of the Statute. By the 23rd, seventeen days after its first session, the Council had not reached agreement on a single issue of importance. When the Deputies presented yet one more report recording disagreement, Byrnes remarked that, if they went on like this, Trieste would not be settled by Christmas and the Italian Treaty alone—with 28 articles outstanding and eight unsettled annexes—would keep them going until 1950. Byrnes' remarks suggested—and were intended to suggest—that he had had enough and that either the Russians changed their tactics or no treaties were going to be signed.

All the Foreign Ministers, of course, were working within a political context. If we can only guess what this meant in the case of Molotov, in the case of each of the other three, domestic events in November had a clear relationship to foreign policy.

The day after the CFM opened, Americans went to the polls for the mid-term Congressional elections. Truman's preoccupation with the results of these had already made itself felt in US foreign policy, notably in connection with Palestine, and accounted for his reluctance to part with Wallace, the leader of the liberal wing of the Democratic Party, despite his open attacks on the Administration's handling of relations with Russia. The results, when published, were as bad as Truman had feared: for the first time since 1930, the Democrats lost control of the Senate and House of Representatives. A

---

[1] See below, p. 327.
[2] Bevin's record, 6 Nov. 1946. FO 800/501/SU/46/42.

Republican congress was more likely to criticize the Administration for being "soft" than being "tough" with the Russians, and there was a good chance that the main lines of foreign policy which Truman and Byrnes had worked out with Vandenberg (now chairman of the powerful Senate Foreign Relations Committee) would continue to receive bi-partisan support. But the domestic programme of reducing taxes, cutting government expenditure and raising tariffs, on which the Republicans had been elected, threatened to undermine that foreign policy at its most vulnerable point, the unwillingness of the American people to find the money with which to give it substance by providing the armed forces, economic aid and liberal trade policies necessary to make it credible. Vandenberg needed no convincing of this but the rest of his Party, led by Senator Taft, put cutting taxes above anything else, regardless of the consequences for America's policy abroad. The impact of the change in Congress was not felt until the debate on the budget began in the New Year, but enough was known in advance of Republican attitudes to suggest that Molotov's inquiry, whether the election results would affect US foreign policy, was not to be brushed aside as easily as Bevin, with his "emphatic No", wished to admit.

The French too held elections in November (the 10th) and these gave the Communists a clear lead over any other party, 5.4 million votes (out of 25m.) and 183 seats in the Assembly (out of 618). Both the parties in Bidault's administration, the MRP and Socialists, lost ground and the Communists announced that they were ready to take the lead in forming a new government. Fears of a Communist take-over and the extension of Russian influence to Western Europe at once revived, and if these appear exaggerated now, they were not so easy to discount at the time. The weakness of France as a factor in the European balance of power was underlined: no government could be formed for five weeks (and then only lasted a month), and no French foreign minister ever appeared to take Couve de Murville's place in New York.

There was no comparable weakening in electoral support for the British Labour Government: the municipal elections held in England and Wales at the beginning of November recorded 159 gains for Labour, only four for the Tories. But support for Bevin's foreign policy, within the Labour Party, was a different story. A meeting of the PLP was held on 13 November to discuss an amendment to the King's Speech (eventually signed by 58 Labour MPs) criticizing the Government's foreign policy. Both Attlee and Hector McNeil, Bevin's Minister of State, spoke but they did not succeed in persuading the rebels to withdraw their motion of censure although an undertaking was given that it would not be pressed to a division.

This compromise only added to Bevin's anger.

"I would ask you," he telegraphed to the Prime Minister, "to appreciate my position here. Forty MPs will encourage every opponent both in the UN and in the CFM to use it [the motion of censure] against me. Am I not entitled to know where Parliament and the Cabinet stand, and is not the world entitled to know, by a vote? I think the permission to members of the Party to attack one member of the Government carrying out the difficult task that I am at this stage, leading the world to believe that I do not represent the policy of the Party, places me in an unfair position. In addition, the element of treachery in it ought to be brought to a head. I hope it is not too late to announce in the House that the vote will be taken as a vote of censure, and a decision taken as to whether or not the Cabinet's policy is endorsed. It is vital if I am to carry on here."[1]

The amendment, when finally agreed, called on HMG to recast its conduct of international affairs so as

"To afford the utmost encouragement to and collaboration with all nations and groups striving to secure full socialist planning and control of the world's resources and thus provide a democratic and constructive socialist alternative to an otherwise inevitable conflict between American capitalism and Soviet communism in which all hope of World Government would be destroyed".

As soon as he had the text, Bevin cabled his answer to the Prime Minister. It was "an over-simplification", he argued, "to suggest that this is solely an ideological conflict which could be solved or even eased by producing our own ideological solution out of a hat." The Soviet Government was using the Communist ideology as an instrument of national policy.

"It is more accurately a clash between the expansive policies of the U.S.S.R. and the resolution of post-war America to stand up to them now and prevent a situation which may lead later to a general war."

Of course he wanted to pursue an independent policy but the British were "mutually attracted to close relations with the U.S.A. by the comparative closeness of our way of thinking and more compellingly by our present dependence on them for our survival". He had tried a policy of equal frankness and friendliness towards both sides, without any response. The truth was that the Russians did not like socialist governments, regarding them as a greater threat to the advance of Communism than capitalist governments like the American.

After describing the trial of strength over Trieste and its relationship to Italian domestic policies, Bevin wrote: "It is difficult to resist the conclusion that the Soviet game in Europe is the establishment of Communist governments not only in Italy but also in France, and that in Spain their objective is the civil war which would follow active intervention." The only answer he could see was to be firm and hope that this would lead to a change in Russian policy.

"If Russia alters her ways and is genuinely ready to co-operate both in the settlement of Europe and in the work of the UN, can it be believed that there will be any real

---

[1] Bevin to Attlee, 14 November 1946. FO 800/492/PLT/46/63.

difficulty in establishing relations of confidence between the three Great Powers or in settling the peace of Europe or in using the UN as a genuine organ of international co-operation?"[1]

When the amendment was taken on the 18th, it produced a muted debate. Crossman (unlike Silverman who followed him) was frank in saying that the Soviet Union was as much to blame as the USA for the international tension; but the Labour Government had allowed itself to become identified too much with one side, with the aggressive foreign policy of a capitalist and imperialist America. He called upon it to repudiate the Fulton speech and with it any idea of an Anglo-American bloc, of staff talks and the standardization of arms. Distrust of the USA and the call for a socialist foreign policy—still undefined —were the two points, and not much else, on which all supporters of the amendment could agree.

Winding up the debate (in which George Brown spoke from the back benches in defence of Bevin's policy) Attlee used few of the arguments Bevin had put in his cable. He was more concerned to play down than highlight the differences but he left no doubt where he himself stood, insisted that Bevin was following a governmental not a personal policy, and spoke warmly of his restraint in face of "grossly unfair attacks" and misrepresentation.

Attlee, like the movers of the amendment, would have preferred it not to have been pressed to a division, but others were more persistent. No one was found to support the amendment, which was defeated by 353–0. The damaging figure, however, was that for abstentions. Some of these represented members sick or absent with good cause, but the total of 130 (against a party strength of 352 seats) made it a demonstration of disapproval which clearly extended beyond the Left-wing of the Party.

Bevin was troubled as well as hurt by the result, which was widely reported in the United States and Europe and could easily be taken as evidence that the foreign policy which he represented might not always be that of the Labour Government. Whatever his private feelings, however, he was determined to show in public that it had not affected his confidence, and on the morning of 21 November, he decided at short notice to go down to the UN General Assembly and intervene in the disarmament debate.

Since the middle of June, the UN Atomic Energy Commission had been labouring over rival American and Russian proposals for the international control of atomic power. The conflict of interest was too sharp to make agreement possible: the Americans were not going to hand over or destroy their stock of A-bombs until they could see an international authority in operation and capable of enforcing security; the Russians would agree to no proposal (e.g. international inspection) which would interfere with their all-out effort to produce their own atomic weapons. Each side began to seek political advantage in showing that the other was to blame for the failure to make progress. On 29 October, just before Bevin got to New York, Molotov

---

[1] Bevin to Attlee and McNeil, 15 November 1946, *ibid.*, PLT/46/64–65.

transferred the contest to the UN General Assembly by making a scathing attack on the American plan and taking the lead in calling for a general reduction in armaments. As part of the Russian campaign to present American (and British) foreign policy as a threat to the peace of the world and the USSR as its defender, Molotov also pressed for a report to the United Nations on the number of troops stationed abroad. Before setting out for New York, Bevin had told Byrnes that he would oppose any such demand. It was a propaganda move, he declared. "Powers with a high proportion of air and naval forces and scattered bases would have far more to lose by publicity of this sort than a land power depending mainly on an army within its own frontiers, such as the Soviet Union."[1] He now followed this up by putting the British view in person to the First Committee of the UN General Assembly.

Recalling the efforts of his predecessor, Arthur Henderson, at Geneva (a telling point with the Labour members of the British delegation), Bevin reminded the Committee that Britain's disarmament between the Wars had brought her within inches of defeat,

"And I ask this conference to consider what would have been the fate of the world if Britain had failed in 1940 and 1941. . . . I mention this because we cannot approach this problem again and afresh without taking all the lessons, from 1918 to 1939, into account and we cannot plunge without careful study into an action which would leave us open to attack . . . without being quite sure that the instrument we are creating is effective and will, in fact, work."

Picking up a remark of Molotov's—"He said that if these returns [of the number of troops serving overseas] are made, it will have a great political effect"—Bevin asked: "But is this being done for political effect or is this being done for disarmament? . . .

"It is true that this question of troops being in certain parts of the world represents one phase of this problem, and probably agitates minds. But I do remind this body that Hitler had no troops on any territory outside Germany yet that did not stop him from building an army within Germany which nearly brought down the rest of the world."

The question of overseas bases and troops could only be dealt with as part of the bigger issue of disarmament and security, not singled out by itself. This was what the General Assembly should be doing, pressing the Security Council to get on with the real job—"to build a structure of disarmament that will enable Governments to come to a conclusion whether it is of such a character that they can to a large extent surrender their sovereignty to the UN." If so, no one would welcome it more than the UK whose people "for the last 30 years have had to be mobilised longer than anybody else—one day in three—and who today are paying a frightful price in the standard of life".[2]

[1] A message from Bevin relayed by the British Embassy to the Department of State, 23 October 1946. FRUS 1946 (1) pp. 962–3.
[2] Speech to First Committee of the UN General Assembly, 21 November 1946.

The line taken by Bevin was good tactics but it also happened to be what he believed, and this combination, expressed with the directness which came naturally when he spoke extempore, made a powerful impression on the UN delegates who crowded into the committee room to hear him. By 4 o'clock, however, he had to be back in the conference room at the Waldorf Astoria and sit down to another round of argument with Molotov over Trieste. Fortunately, as Bevin had always hoped, his own and Byrnes' refusal to give in to Soviet pressure was at long last to produce a readiness to reach a compromise on the Russian part.

The turning point followed the informal meeting on the 23rd at which Byrnes gave a strong hint that he was not prepared to go on any longer trying to find agreement. Two days later Byrnes met Molotov privately and told him that he had almost come to the conclusion that it would be better to admit frankly that they could not agree on the Italian and other peace treaties and go on to discuss Germany. Molotov said that a lot had already been done for the Yugoslavs and he was not prepared to re-open the discussion. It would be better to leave them and the Italians to talk and see if they could reach agreement by themselves.

Molotov evidently realized that, if the Russians were not to lose the advantages to be gained from the Western Powers' signing the other treaties (which effectively gave the Soviet Union most of what they wanted), he would have to make concessions on the Italian. At any rate he now showed himself willing to sit down with Byrnes and sketch out the terms of a possible compromise over Trieste. The next day the Foreign Ministers, meeting alone with their interpreters, settled the most contentious issues in a session which started over lunch and went on to dinner time. This opened a way to settle the rest. Molotov did not give way without a fight, especially over reparations, and Bevin's efforts to secure more for Greece or at least some improvement of her frontier with Bulgaria, were unsuccessful. On the very last day, 6 December, Molotov again appealed to Byrnes in private to get the Yugoslavs to sign the Italian treaty by offering them some further concession on the Trieste frontier line, but the American was adamant. The Yugoslavs, he told the Russian Foreign Secretary, had done very well: they had received $25m. more in reparations than they expected and owed a great debt to Molotov personally for his advocacy. His answer was a plain unvarnished "No". Molotov was equally blunt in refusing "to do something" for the Greeks. But these last-minute exchanges did not disturb the compromises already reached and in all, 47 of the 53 recommendations of the Paris Peace Conference were incorporated in the final texts of the Treaties; Molotov even accepted 24 of the 41 which had received only a simple majority. By the time the Foreign Ministers broke off for the day on 6 December they had effectively removed the Italian and the other four peace treaties from their agenda, and by the time they left for home had agreed that they should be signed in Paris on 10 February in the New Year.

4

Bevin's long absence at the CFM in New York did not relieve him of the rest of his responsibilities for British foreign policy. There was a daily flow of telegrams and telephone calls across the Atlantic, from the Prime Minister as well as the Foreign Office; and the need for Bevin to give answers while isolated from other ministers, his senior advisers, the trade unions and all the other channels by which he kept in touch with the movement of opinion in Britain, added to the strain on him. Palestine, Iran, the Egyptian negotiations, the situation in Greece, the necessary changes in Germany following the decision to create the Anglo-American Bi-zone, all these required urgent attention.

Before leaving for America Bevin had given a full report to the Cabinet on the Palestine negotiations up to that point.[1] Despite the adverse effect of Truman's statement he said his hopes had been revived by indications that the President might allow the State Department (which was less susceptible to Zionist pressures) to resume its conduct of the negotiations on the American side, and by the conclusion of the draft treaty with Egypt which might help with the Arabs.

But if at the beginning of December there seemed to be no prospect of a negotiated settlement, Bevin told the Cabinet it would face a choice between three courses. The first would be to impose a solution acceptable to one or other of the two communities in Palestine, the COS having ruled out imposing by force a solution which would be actively resisted by both. The second was to surrender the Mandate and withdraw, with serious consequences for the strategic position and Britain's standing in the Middle East. The third was to propose partition, possibly merging the Arab part with Transjordan, an old idea of Bevin's which he had revived in July. "Several Ministers", the Cabinet minute records, "said that they were glad that the possibility of Partition was not excluded . . . and expressed the view that this would in the end be found to be the only practicable solution." Bevin, however, did not ask the Cabinet to choose between the alternatives at this stage and he asked for his thanks to be given to the Jewish members of the Party who had refrained from raising the Palestine issue in the foreign affairs debate.[2]

While Bevin was away discussion of the options continued actively in the two departments concerned, the Colonial and Foreign Offices, and between them. Creech-Jones' appointment as Colonial Secretary (5 October, the day after Truman's statement) gave added impetus to the consideration of partition of which he remained a convinced advocate, despite the warning of Brigadier Clayton that Arab opinion had hardened against it since August, and that if the British now adopted it, their position in the Middle East would

---

[1] 25 October 1946. CM 91 (46) making use of the paper which he and Creech-Jones had circulated, CP (46) 358.
[2] CM 91 (46).

be gravely weakened.[1] A possible alternative was a revised version of the provincial autonomy plan which could provide a transition to partition. The discussions show how divided the officials responsible still were on the best course for Britain to adopt. If partition was an ambiguous term, which could mean very different things when used by different people, so was the proposal to refer the Palestine question to the UN. This was the second subject of discussion: whether the reference should be made with or without a British recommendation; whether the object should be to secure a UN trusteeship or to open the way to British withdrawal from Palestine, and what calculations could be made of the voting for and against each variant.

In the meantime, Bevin, arriving in New York, had been made aware of the strength of anti-British feeling over Palestine. The dockers refused to handle his luggage and when his presence at a football game was announced over the loudspeakers, the crowd booed him. He was shocked and angered by the violent attacks he read in the New York press, particularly in the whole page advertisements inserted by the Zionists denouncing the British occupation of Palestine as a concentration camp regime run on Nazi lines. However, he controlled his temper, and sounded out Zionist as well as Administration opinion. At the end of November he sent the Cabinet a report on his discussions.[2]

The Palestine conference had now been postponed until after Christmas to allow time for the Zionist Congress meeting in Basle to reach a decision on participation, and Bevin twice saw Silver, the leader of the most militant group among the American Zionists. Silver told Bevin that if the USA and Britain agreed on a solution no troops would be required to impose it: Arab military strength was "illusory and merely a matter of propaganda". At a second meeting on 20 November, he went further and assured Bevin "that the Arabs would agree if it were known that HMG and the US Government supported partition."[3] Bevin reported that Byrnes himself was not too keen on partition and hinted that, if he were in Bevin's position, he would hand the whole problem over to the UN.[4]

But there was no doubt that partition was the solution most Americans wanted to see Britain adopt. Dean Acheson, talking to the British Ambassador, said the USA would "go along with" partition and like Silver felt no anxiety about Arab military action provided Britain and the USA were united.[5] Bevin got the same advice—to go for partition—from his trade union friends, Dave Dubinsky and Matt Woll, of the Jewish Garment Workers'

---

[1] Howe to Bevin, 23 October 1946, reporting a talk between Clayton and Beeley in London. FO 371/52562/ E 10668/4/31G.
[2] 26 November, FO 800/486/PA/46/131.
[3] Report of the two meetings with Silver on 14 and 20 November. FO 371/52565.
[4] Bevin's report on his talks in New York, 26 November. See above, footnote 2.
[5] Inverchapel's report of a talk with Acheson on 26 November. FO 800/475/ME/46/21.

Union and from the British Ambassador himself, Lord Inverchapel, who wanted him to meet Ben Gurion.

Mulling over the problem in his report, Bevin wrote:

"In the Coalition Government we did favour the idea of partition but I am quite satisfied that if we had put it forward at the end of the War, the whole of Jewry would have opposed us and demanded the whole of Palestine. We should also have been in conflict with the whole Arab world."

The Jews were now in favour of partition, but Truman's readiness to respond to Zionist pressure had made Bevin distrustful. If the British came out for partition, how could they rely on the Americans staying with it? Was it not possible, if the Jews got the British to concede partition, that they would then go further and press the Americans for the whole of Palestine? Bevin concluded that they would have to pin down both the Jews and the US Government in writing, especially in view of the competition between Truman and Dewey for the New York vote.

When Bevin's report was discussed in the Cabinet,[1] Attlee remarked that opinion in a number of quarters was moving towards partition but insisted that it was essential the Government should not commit itself in advance. If no agreed solution could be reached and they had to impose a solution, it was most important this should emerge from the Conference with the Arabs and Jews. He proposed therefore to send a message to Bevin (which he had already drafted)[2] to the effect that no assurances should be given; any talks even with the US Government, must be regarded as exploratory. Attlee's warning was to the point, for not only Goldmann but Byrnes as well was pressing Bevin for an assurance that partition would be seriously considered. In his reply Bevin said he was glad to give assurances that all proposals made by the British, Jewish or Arab delegates to the Conference would be given equal status on the agenda, and that HMG did not regard themselves as committed in advance to their own proposals or any other.[3] Anything more would have made certain Arab refusal to attend the Conference. Bevin followed this up with a secret talk with Byrnes in which the American Secretary of State promised to publish their exchange of letters and make clear to the Jewish leaders that it was the wish of the US Government they should accept the British invitation.[4]

There the matter rested until the Zionist Congress should meet. Within the limited room for manoeuvre available to him, Bevin had done his best to keep open the possibility of a negotiated settlement, and Creech-Jones believed that with the Zionist Council's repudiation of terrorism, the release of the detained Jewish Agency members, and a drop in the number of incidents in Palestine,

[1] 28 November, CM 101 (46).
[2] Draft reply from Attlee to Bevin, 27 November. FO 800/486/PA/46/134.
[3] Bevin to Byrnes, 29 November and exchange of letters between the two on 2 December, *ibid.*, PA/46/136 & 140.
[4] Bevin to Attlee, 4 December 1946. FO 800/486/PA/46/143. Note left by Byrnes after his talk with Bevin, 6 December, *ibid.*, PA/46/148.

there was a good chance that the Zionist Congress would produce a majority for attending the conference with a mandate for partition and a Jewish state in part of Palestine.

While Bevin was in New York telegrams from Teheran warned him that the struggle for power in Iran was about to come to a head. The leading role was no longer played by the British Ambassador but by the American, George Allen, who was able—with little concrete evidence to go on—to persuade the Iranian prime minister, Qavam, that American promises of support could be relied on if he defied Soviet threats and sent in troops to restore Iranian control of Azerbaijan. When the Shah's forces entered the province in December, the Azerbaijani house of cards collapsed, followed by the surrender of the Kurdistan "capital" of Mahabad, a year almost to the day after the Soviet-sponsored republics had been proclaimed. There was no resistance, the rebel leaders fled across the Soviet border and the Russians made no attempt to repeat their earlier intervention.

In Moscow at the end of 1945 Bevin had failed to impress either Byrnes or Stalin with the dangers of the situation in Iran. At the end of 1946 he could take satisfaction in seeing both his objectives achieved. The Iranian Government had stood up to Russian pressure and restored its sovereignty in the north; the Americans had moved from a position of neutrality to an explicit commitment to uphold Iranian independence and territorial integrity.[1] Within five years, it is true, the nationalization of the oilfields ended Anglo-Iranian's concession and with it the special position which Britain had enjoyed in Iran for many years. But at least the British withdrawal did not leave behind the vacuum Bevin had feared, and Iran, which might have become a Soviet satellite in 1945–6, emerged strong enough to assert its independence.

Unlike the telegrams from Teheran, the news that reached him from Cairo was far from reassuring. No sooner had Sidqi got back to Egypt after the October negotiations in London than the fragility of the compromise over the Sudan became clear. All the Egyptians were interested in was the British recognition of the Egyptian Crown's historical claim to sovereignty, ignoring the fact that the draft protocol made clear that this did not affect the *status quo* in the Sudan or the right of the Sudanese people to determine their own future, including the right to become independent if they so chose. As soon as Sidqi returned, reports began to appear in the Egyptian press that he "had brought the Sudan to Egypt." He succeeded in securing a vote of confidence from 159 of the 264 deputies who constituted the Egyptian Chamber but only (as Orme Sargent cabled Bevin) by a "policy of deliberate misrepresentation".[2] The view of the Cairo Embassy, supported by the Foreign Office, was that if the British insisted on making this clear, Sidqi would be swept out of office and the Treaty doomed.[3] The view of the Governor-General of the Sudan was that

[1] Statement by the US Ambassador, 27 November 1946.
[2] Sargent to Bevin, 29 November 1946. FO 800/457/EG/46/58.
[3] Foreign Office to Bevin, 2 December 1946, *ibid.*, EG/46/57.

silence would be taken for acquiescence and the abandonment of Bevin's promise to the Sudanese people of self-determination.

However much he wanted Egyptian agreement, Bevin was not prepared to prevaricate. He sent Sidqi a letter of interpretation which removed any doubt of what was intended. The Egyptian Prime Minister refused to accept it and after issuing a denial that he had ever recognized the Sudanese people's right to secede from the Egyptian Crown, resigned on 9 December. Bevin's view was expressed in a Foreign Office statement to the effect that "it would be manifestly impossible for any British Government to acquiesce in an interpretation of a treaty with Egypt . . . which denies one of the fundamental rights of free people—a right which Egypt has never ceased to claim for herself".[1] Any hope of agreement, however, had now to be abandoned. The new Egyptian Government was not prepared to renew negotiations but preferred instead to take its case to the Security Council and Bevin had no option but to fall back on British rights under the 1936 Treaty.

Although Bevin's personal intervention in the UN meetings was limited to his speech on disarmament, his presence in New York meant he was constantly consulted about the line the British representatives should take, and on most days talked with the delegation. The disarmament debate in the General Assembly finished inconclusively. True, the proceedings in the UN Atomic Energy Commission closed (31 December) with a clear-cut decision, a vote of 10–0 in favour of the American Baruch plan, with Russia and Poland abstaining; but it was a decision that made no difference since the plan was never put into operation and the arms race continued. It was the Security Council, the organ of the United Nations that suffered most from the divisions between the Powers, which produced an unexpected agreement between them—and this, even more surprisingly, on the subject of Greece.

Having failed to get satisfaction for Greek territorial claims from the Paris Peace Conference, the Greek Government was determined to press them on the Council of Foreign Ministers when it met in New York. The Greeks had a case and their claims both in Northern Epirus and in Thrace, were the one issue on which all parties in Greece (including EAM and the Communists[2]) agreed. But it was not a case which was ever likely to be considered on its merits. The Russians were totally opposed to anything which would work to the advantage of the Athens Government and the disadvantage of their protégé regimes in Bulgaria and Albania. The Americans were interested in getting an agreed settlement with the Russians in the Balkans and unsympathetic to any claims (whether from the Greeks or their neighbours) which would disturb the prospects of this. Their consistent advice to the Greeks was to settle for the *status quo* and put an end to frontier disputes as more in

[1] *The Times*, 10 December 1946.
[2] See, for example, the telegram which EAM and the Greek Communist Party sent to the Council of Foreign Ministers on 8 November 1946. Stephen G. Xydis: *Greece and the Great Powers 1944–47* (Thessaloniki 1963) pp. 417–18.

Greece's own national interests than keeping alive quarrels which they could have no hope of winning.

The British attitude was more equivocal. Bevin regarded the Greek claims as both exaggerated and unrealistic. His advice to the Greek Prime Minister was the same as Byrnes', not to come to New York and press the Greek claims—which could only have a counter-productive effect—but to get on with the job of reconstruction at home.[1] On the other hand, he felt committed to seeing that the case for a limited transfer of territory in Northern Epirus and possibly on the frontier with Bulgaria as well was considered by the Council of Foreign Ministers. This was the line he followed (without much conviction, it must be admitted) when the Council met,[2] but in face of Russian opposition and without support from the Americans, failed to carry through. He had no more success in his efforts to get Greece invited to the Danube Conference which Molotov finally agreed to hold or in the much fiercer fight he put up to obtain a bigger share of Italian reparations for the Greeks.[3] On 1 December Bevin cabled to the British Embassy in Athens that the Council was about to reach agreement on the peace treaties and that the Greeks must be prepared to see their hopes disappointed. He had done his best but when the cards were down he was no more prepared than the Americans to put satisfaction for the Greeks above the chances of an overall settlement of the Balkan questions, nor even convinced that this was in the Greeks' own interests.

This was the end of Greece's territorial claims, but not at all of "the Greek question". The Communist press and radio throughout the world began to give prominence to communiqués from what was described as the HQ of the "Democratic Army of Northern Greece". In Greece itself, EAM, the Greek Communist Party and its newspaper *Rizospastis*—which, despite their denunciation of a "Fascist reign of terror", continued to enjoy the freedom to organize and express their views—did everything in their power to undermine confidence in the Government and to spread the belief that the triumph of the Left, with Soviet backing, was inevitable. The guerilla war in the mountains continued throughout the winter and 10,000 men were estimated to be engaged in it. An attack on the village of Skra by guerillas operating out of Yugoslav territory in mid-November woke the Western press up to what was happening. On 20 November several London papers carried headlines and maps about the "undeclared war" in northern Greece.

For the third time in a year "the Greek question" occupied the Security Council from the 10th to the 19th of December, this time on the complaint of the Greek Government. The Greeks asked for the appointment of a commission to discover the facts about the situation on their northern borders, where (Tsaldaris declared) an attempt was being made, with the support of

[1] Bevin to the British Embassy in Athens, 14 and 16 November 1946. FO 800/466/GRE/46/32.
[2] 5th meeting on 11 November.
[3] 10th and 11th meetings of the CFM on 28 and 29 November. FRUS 1946 (2) p. 1335 and pp. 1342–50.

Yugoslavia, to seize Greek territory and make an "Aegean Macedonia". The Yugoslavs, supported by the Bulgarians and Albanians, rejected Tsaldaris' charges and called on the Security Council to investigate conditions inside Greece which (they declared) were the source of all the trouble. This time American and British support for the Greeks was unequivocal: the Security Council should appoint a commission to investigate the facts as the Greeks had requested. To the astonishment of the other members of the Security Council, the Soviet Union joined the USA and Britain in voting for the commission. There was much speculation about the reason for the Soviet volte-face. The most likely explanation (and it remains a guess) is that the Russians preferred to go along with a UN procedure in which they would have a major voice, rather than risk the alternative of unilateral American or Anglo-US intervention.

The possibility of the USA assuming a larger role in Greece, as well as Turkey and Iran, was discussed several times in the autumn of 1946. In mid-October, the Foreign Office learned secretly that the Americans were working on a new policy towards Greece.[1] This was welcome news to British officials increasingly exasperated with the Greeks' unwillingness to tackle their country's economic and financial problems. "No Greek Government," Hector McNeil minuted, "of the eight we have had in fifteen months has shown the guts for this complex and unpalatable task." This was written on 29 November.[2] The same month Montgomery visited Greece and on his return warned the Chiefs of Staff Committee that British troops faced the danger of becoming involved in a civil war.[3] In his most recent talk with Byrnes, on 25 November, Bevin had thrown out the possibility of Britain being forced, by the need for economies, to withdraw her forces in the near future. Byrnes, however, was not to be drawn: he pointed out that they had encouraged Greece to appeal to the Security Council and that any announcement of a British intention to withdraw could only have a bad effect.[4] The arrival of an American naval force off Athens on 6 December prompted Moscow Radio to declare, in a Greek broadcast, that this was further evidence of the "American imperialists" intention to turn Greece into an "American colony".[5] The truth was, however, that Byrnes and the State Department, although agreeing in principle, were very reluctant to take on additional commitments, especially if they involved asking a hostile Congress for more money. They hoped they could persuade the British to retain the principal responsibility and took two months to organize the economic mission to Greece (under Paul Porter) which Byrnes had promised in October. Until the Porter mission reported—and that

---

[1] Minutes by Selby 17 October 1946, FO 371/58710/E14984 and Warner 20 October, FO 371/58712/R 15723.
[2] FO 371/58716.
[3] COS Committee (46) 288 10 December 1946; minutes in FO 371/58718.
[4] Bevin to Foreign Office, 26 November 1946. FO 800/468/GRE/46/35.
[5] Xydis, pp. 423–4.

could not be until well into the New Year—Tsaldaris was told that no decision about further aid could be taken.

4

Bevin was as anxious to have the Americans take a greater share of responsibility for maintaining the independence of Greece as he was in Turkey, Iran and throughout the Middle East. But he had a better understanding than his colleagues in London of the difficulty Americans found—in the country, in Congress, and even in the Administration—in adjusting themselves to the world role they were now called upon to play. From this he continued to draw the same conclusion as he had throughout 1946: that it was essential to give them time, be patient and not to try to force the pace. In his judgement, the risks were too great, the American Government's new-found sense of purpose too brittle, American opinion too unsettled for Britain to surrender her own independence of action into American hands.

He was taken aback, therefore, to learn that the Prime Minister, influenced by feeling in the Party and the Cabinet and with Bevin not at hand to counter it, was again questioning the validity of a policy of which he had never been convinced. This unwelcome news came in a letter from Attlee dated 1 December 1946 which the Prime Minister took the trouble to type himself. Knowing how sensitive Bevin was likely to be to criticism after the recent parliamentary debate and more than a month's absence from Britain, Attlee was careful to begin with praise of his performance in New York. He was showing great skill in the Treaty negotiations, Attlee wrote, and it looked as if he would bring it off. The Prime Minister also assured him that there was no disagreement in the Cabinet with his policy on Germany. Then, referring to the need for a full discussion of foreign policy when Bevin got back, Attlee continued:

"I think that we have got to consider our commitments very carefully lest we try to do more than we can. In particular, I am rather worried about Greece. The C.O.S. are suggesting that we must keep our forces there for at least another year. I cannot contemplate the financial and military burden with equanimity.[1] . . . Meanwhile we have to accept a very great deal of criticism. I feel that we are backing a very lame horse.

"While I recognise the desirability of supporting the democratic elements in S.E. Europe and while I am conscious of the strategic importance of oil, I have, as you know, always considered that the strategic importance of communications is very much over-rated by our military advisors, a view that is shared by some Service authorities. I

---

[1] There had been a difficult meeting of the Defence Committee on 20 November at which the COS' figure of 1.1 million men and women in the Forces at the end of March 1947 had come in for strong criticism, Dalton declaring that it was quite impossible for the country to support such numbers.

agree wholeheartedly with you that the real line of the British Commonwealth runs through Lagos and Kenya. The Middle East position is only an outpost position. I am beginning to doubt whether the Greek game is worth the candle.

"I do not think that the countries bordering on Soviet Russia's zone, viz Greece, Turkey, Iraq and Persia, can be made strong enough to form an effective barrier. We do not command the resources to make them so. If it were possible to reach an agreement with Russia that we should disinterest ourselves as far as possible in them, so that they became a neutral zone, it would be much to our advantage. Of course it is difficult to tell how far Russian policy is dictated by expansionism and how far by fear of attack by the U.S. and ourselves. Fantastic as this is, it may very well be the real grounds of Russian policy. . . . I think, therefore, that we have got to be very careful in taking on military obligations in Greece and Turkey when the U.S.A. only gives economic assistance.

"There is a tendency in America to regard us as an outpost, but an outpost that they will not have to defend. I am disturbed by the signs of America trying to make a safety zone round herself while leaving us and Europe in No Man's Land.

"While I think that we should try to find out what the Americans are prepared to do, we should be careful not to commit ourselves.

"With all good wishes,
   Yours ever,
      Clem"[1]

On the 4th, Bevin's henchman, Hector McNeil, telegraphed that the Cabinet was to discuss the whole question of policy towards Greece and Turkey, although Attlee wanted to wait for Bevin's return first. It would be useful, McNeil added, if Bevin could get some idea of what the Americans proposed in both cases, but his personal opinion was that the whole question of policy towards Greece and Turkey was in the melting pot and there was great reluctance to continue military, financial and political commitments to Greece —or to Turkey.[2]

Bevin cabled back at once to McNeil that his telegram had come as a shock. It was useless for him to talk to Byrnes if the whole question of policy was under review. He had been acting on the assumption that Greece and Turkey were essential to Britain's political and strategic position, for example in his attitude over the Straits. "Am I to understand that we may now abandon this position? I really do not know where I stand."[3]

Dixon prepared some notes for a possible reply to Attlee,[4] but Bevin does not appear to have used them or to have sent any considered reply at this time, contenting himself with blowing off steam in his cable to Hector McNeil and reserving what he had to say until he could talk to the Prime Minister in person. The news from London, however, made him more anxious than ever for the Council of Foreign Ministers to end its proceedings and allow him to get back to England.

---

[1] Attlee to Bevin 1 December 1946. FO 800/475/ME/46/22.
[2] Minister of State to Bevin, 4 December. FO 800/468/GRE/46/39.
[3] Bevin to Minister of State, 5 December 1946, *ibid.*, GRE/46/40.
[4] These included the comment that Russia's "exaggerated sense of security, which is almost indistinguishable from an imperialist instinct, would lead her to fill a vacuum, if it was there to fill". 9 December, FO 800/475/ME/46/24.

Fortunately, before the Council broke up, it at last agreed to make a start on the German and Austrian treaties. In anticipation of this Bevin had been anxious to get the arrangements for the economic merger of the British and US Zones completed first, and agreements setting up five bi-zonal agencies were signed in the course of the autumn. In making these, the British and Americans again went out of their way to avoid any suggestion of a political union between the two zones which might stand in the way of a provisional government for all Germany. The five agencies were established in five different cities; no co-ordinating agency was created in case it might be taken for an embryonic government and no bi-zonal legislature set up; the relationship between the new agencies and the Länder governments remained ill-defined, and both parties continued to stress their wish to see the other two occupying powers join them in an economic merger of all four zones in fulfilment of Potsdam rather than divide Germany.

Bevin had had to leave for the USA before the Cabinet considered his proposals for socializing the industry of the Ruhr. McNeil cabled him that when they came up for discussion, strong exception was taken to the appointment of observers from the USA and other Western allies such as the French and Benelux countries. Some members of the Cabinet felt that there should be no observers at all and that if the idea of internationalization was to be abandoned, the responsibility for socialization should be Britain's alone; others thought the exclusion of Russia a mistake, ignoring Bevin's argument that, as long as the Russians refused to allow British observers into the Soviet zone, they should not be allowed to send their own into the British zone.[1] Bevin urged the Cabinet to reconsider its attitude. In view of the economic fusion of the two zones, it was impossible to exclude the Americans and a mistake to exclude France and the other Western allies. He added that, although internationalization was ruled out for the present, he hoped eventually to set up a form of international control in the Ruhr of which the USA and the Western allies would be full members.[2]

An attempt by Hynd, the minister nominally responsible for the British zone, to get the ownership of the Ruhr industries vested in a future central German Government at once aroused Bevin's opposition.[3] He cabled back that he would never agree to any such step: apart from the danger of a future German Government falling under Communist-Russian control, any such move would cause great alarm in France, and justifiably so. The British objective, Bevin concluded, was to decentralize, not concentrate, power in Germany, and the best solution was to vest ownership in the new *Land Nord*

---

[1] CM 92 (46) 29 October; Minister of State to Bevin on the SS *Aquitania*, 31 October 1946. FO 800/466/GER/46/45.
[2] Bevin to Minister of State from New York, 3 November, *ibid.*, GER/46/47.
[3] Hynd spoke in this sense at Cabinet meetings on 29 October and 19 November. CM 92 & 97 (46).

Rhein-Westfalen.[1] The Cabinet decided to leave the question unanswered for the present.[2]

The Cabinet discussions had brought into the open much criticism of the British Control Commission in Germany and a strong demand for a Resident Minister to be appointed. When Attlee passed these views on to Bevin, the latter replied that he was worried too, but thought the proposal of a Resident Minister a bad one. Who would answer in Parliament or report to the Cabinet? What would be his relation to the Commander-in-Chief or to the Control Commission's HQ in London? Couldn't this wait until they had settled the organization of the Bi-zone with the Americans?[3]

The question of a Resident Minister, Attlee cabled back, might be left for the moment, but not the question of what was to be done in Germany. Food and coal shortages were threatening, the economic machine was running down; the Cabinet was apprehensive and pressure for drastic action was mounting. "What brooks no delay," Bevin answered, "is a strong set-up in German industry, more devolution on the Germans to make them work out their own salvation and a drastic cut down of our overheads."[4]

The next day Bevin sent a further message to the Prime Minister. After talking to Strang (the Permanent Under-Secretary of the FO's German Section), he was more than ever sure that they ought not to appoint a Resident Minister. He suggested setting up a Cabinet committee and working party to examine the operation of the Control Commission, underlining the degree to which the Foreign Secretary was involved in, and hence responsible for, what happened in Germany.[5] This pointed to the solution which Bevin had eventually, and reluctantly, to accept: placing ministerial responsibility fairly and squarely on the Foreign Secretary.

The case for this was illustrated by the negotiations which Bevin had to conduct in New York. In a talk with Byrnes at the beginning of October, Bevin told the Secretary of State that the American proposal to split the costs of the new Bi-zone 50–50 would add £120m. to the British contribution over the three years and would have to be reconsidered.[6] On 20 November he reported to the Prime Minister and Chancellor of the Exchequer that he had taken the question up again with Byrnes, proposing 40–60 in Britain's favour, but without success. Congress (Byrnes said) would not agree to anything more than a 50–50 division, and nobody doubted that he was right. Byrnes refused to take seriously Bevin's threat to withdraw from the arrangement, pointing out that it would cost the British more to run their zone on their own.[7] In further talks, Byrnes called Bevin's bluff and offered to take over the more

---

[1] Minister of State to Bevin 4 November; EB to M/S 6 November. FO 800/466/GER/46/47 & 50.
[2] CM 98 (46) 19 November 1946.
[3] Bevin to Attlee, 17 and 20 November. FO 800/466/GER/46/58 & 63.
[4] Attlee to Bevin, 21 November; Bevin to Attlee, 23 November, *ibid.*, GER/46/65 & 69.
[5] Bevin to Attlee, 24 November, *ibid.*, GER/46/70.
[6] Note of conversation, 3 October 1946, *ibid.*, GER/46/33.
[7] Bevin to Attlee and Dalton, 20 November, *ibid.*, GER/46/63.

highly industrialized British Zone in exchange for the American: with American methods of organization they would make it a success in a short time, and in that case would be willing to go to 60–40 or even 65–35. Bevin dismissed this as politically impossible: "it would also jeopardize our own plans for the socialization of the German coal and steel industry to which I attach great importance".[1] His conclusion was that the British had to accept the equal sharing of costs and he telephoned to London the same day (22 November) pressing for agreement before the CFM started to discuss Germany.

The Cabinet showed great reluctance to accept Bevin's view but, after much huffing and puffing, finally authorized him to sign the Agreement which he did on 2 December.

The same week (6th) Byrnes proposed to the CFM that they should now appoint special deputies for the settlement with Germany; that they should ask the Allied Control Commission for a report on the form of a provisional German Government and central agencies, and that the next meeting of the Council should be ready to discuss the outlines of a peace treaty, with Austria as well as Germany, the signature of which would enable occupying forces to be reduced throughout Europe. Molotov was not to be rushed. Having got agreement to hold the next meeting of the Council in Moscow, he proposed that the first item on the agenda should be a report on the extent to which the Potsdam provisions had been carried out. Only then should the Council discuss the procedure for preparing a treaty with Germany and the appointment of special deputies.

Bevin supported Byrnes in arguing that they should appoint deputies then and there, in New York, so that the latter could get on with the job and produce a report for the Foreign Ministers when they met in Moscow. This was finally agreed, an agenda drawn up which satisfied both the Americans and the Russians, and 10 March 1947 fixed for the date, one month after the Italian and other treaties were due to be signed in Paris.

5

Before he left the USA, Bevin was invited to the White House on 8 December for a talk with President Truman. Neither man tried to avoid the subject of Palestine, but thanks to Byrnes' efforts there was a better understanding of the British difficulties and, as Truman remarked, it was easier to help now the American elections were over. Bevin was not hopeful of an accord: it would never be possible, he declared, for Jews and Arabs to agree. The trouble was that the British had given conflicting pledges (Truman—"So have we"): his object was to narrow the differences. The worst problem was immigration. The only place for the European Jews to go was Palestine; if there were somewhere else, this would reduce the tension. Any move by the US Govern-

---

[1] Bevin to same, 22 November, 1946, *ibid.*, GER/46/66 & 68. See also Byrnes, p. 196.

ment to increase the quota for entry to the USA at the time of the Palestine Conference next month would be a great help. Truman promised to take the question up with Congress.

Bevin went on to say that he thought the Morrison–Grady plan fair and practical. It would not involve any reference to the UN, which would only bring in the Russians. Truman remarked that he got nowhere with Rabbi Silver and agreed with Bevin's view that Weizmann was the most intelligent of the Jewish leaders. Bevin admitted that he found the Jews difficult. "They somehow expect me to fulfil all the prophecies of all the prophets. I tell them sometimes that I can no more fulfil all the prophecies of Ezekiel than I can those of that other great Jew, Karl Marx." He found the Arabs difficult too, but they would not be able to maintain the *status quo* in Palestine.

They talked over the prospects of a German settlement and Bevin said he found it difficult to assess Molotov's more conciliatory attitude: perhaps things were getting better. They ended with reminiscences about their early days, Truman calculating with pleasure that while Bevin had been selling mineral water in Bristol 40 years before he had been selling corn in Missouri. On this note the conversation ended.[1]

A week later Bevin was at sea, on board the *Queen Elizabeth* and at last headed for home after six long weeks away which Dixon described, in retrospect, as a nightmare. Reviewing the negotiations in which they had been involved, he wrote in his diary (18 December):

"We were at the same time handling: (1) the final stages of the C.F.M. on the Treaties; (2) the first stages of the C.F.M. on Germany . . .; (3) Anglo–American negotiations about the fusion of our zones in Germany; (4) U.N.O., with the very different nexus of disarmament, troops and the Atom; (5) the Anglo–Egypt negotiations which we continued to direct awkwardly from New York; (6) Palestine. . . . To the major problems should be added (7) Persia and (8) Greece."

To Dixon's surprise, the results had not been bad. But he concluded:

"It was a horribly uncomfortable party, really, and I was never so glad to leave a place as New York. Until the Russian change of front about two weeks before the end, the poor S. of S. was almost unmanageable."[2]

Parliament had risen by the time Bevin got back to London and he made his report in the form of a radio broadcast on 22 December. "I believe" (he declared) "we have entered the first stage of establishing concord and harmony between the Great Powers." As grounds for this belief he gave the conclusion of the five peace treaties, the shaping of the UN Organization and (as an illustration of the British role) the agreement between the Dutch and Indonesians. He ended with a reference to the charges that British policy was

[1] British note of the conversation. FO 800/513/US/46/127.
[2] Piers Dixon, pp. 244–5.

too closely identified with that of the USA, too hostile to the Soviet Union and "that this course will retard the pacification of the world and may lead to another war". His answer was that Britain considered every problem on its merits—"we have a mind and purpose of our own"—and that there was a great desire to co-operate with the Russians and see them develop their system in their own way, "but with the recognition that others equally have the right to their own way of life".

The tone of Bevin's broadcast was re-assuring, but only because he stuck to generalities. As soon as one began to consider the balance sheet of foreign affairs in detail, it was anything but reassuring. Indeed, if Ernie Bevin had died or resigned for reasons of health (as Byrnes did) at the end of 1946, the record of his eighteen months as Foreign Secretary would be regarded by all as one of failure, the same sort of verdict as that passed on Herbert Morrison when he succeeded Bevin in 1951, one more example (the Tories would have said) of how difficult it was for a man with his limited experience and lack of education to deal with foreign policy.

His hopes of initiating a new policy of partnership in the Middle East (which he did not mention in his broadcast) had come to nothing: Egypt had rejected the Bevin–Sidqi agreement and was about to take her case against the British to the UN. Palestine was sliding into civil war, Bevin's hopes of a settlement in tatters, the British denounced by both Arabs and Jews and Bevin himself vilified as an anti-Semite.

It was no fault of Weizmann's that the British invitation to attend the Palestine Conference along the lines foreseen by Creech-Jones was rejected by the Zionist Congress. He made one of his greatest speeches against terrorism and against the American Zionists, Silver and Neumann in particular, who encouraged a Jewish revolt in Palestine with the promise of the American Jews' support. But when Silver rejected partition and spoke in favour of "resistance", it was he who got the majority and defeated Golda Meir's proposal to allow the Zionist executive to attend the Conference. Although the Conference was reconvened in January, the search for an agreed solution which, despite their differences, was common ground between Bevin and Weizmann, had failed by the end of 1946.

True, Russian pressure on Iran and Turkey had been successfully resisted and the Soviet Union denied a base on the Straits or in the Mediterranean, but the decisive factor in this had been American not British policy (which did not coincide elsewhere in the Middle East) and the Russians might yet turn the trick if the Communists captured power in Greece, where Britain's ability to continue giving support and American readiness to take over her commitment were both in doubt.

The treaties with Rumania, Bulgaria and Hungary, which the British and Americans claimed as successes for patient diplomacy, in fact amounted to the legitimation of Soviet domination of Eastern Europe. The withdrawal of Soviet troops from Rumania and Hungary which Bevin and Byrnes had hoped to secure had been frustrated by the Russian refusal to consider an Austrian treaty: as long as the Soviet Union had a zone of occupation in Austria it could maintain troops in Rumania and Hungary to guard its lines of communication. The same argument did not apply to Bulgaria, but there the Communist Party was already in control and the national quarrel with Greece ensured Bulgaria's dependence on her Soviet patron. Yugoslavia and Albania were equally involved in the offensive against Greece and the Yugoslavs, particularly after their failure to secure Trieste, out-did the Russians in their hostility to the West.

As long as Russian troops were stationed in Germany, the Soviet Union claimed the same right to keep troops in Poland as in Rumania and Hungary. The guarantees of civil and political freedom which Bevin had tried to secure from the Polish Government provided little protection for Mikolajczyk and his Peasant Party. An official referendum held on 30 June 1946 demonstrated the strength of the support he still commanded in the country,[1] and taking the lesson to heart, in the remaining months of 1946, the Polish Government subjected his followers, despite British and American protests, to a ruthless campaign of intimidation, vilification and terror as a preliminary to the "free" elections postponed until the end of January 1947.

Western Europe, fortunately, retained its independence, but even with loans and other forms of aid from the USA, was still far from recovering its economic self-sufficiency or its political confidence. The post-war regimes in France and Italy were shaky, and large Communist parties, both represented in Government, kept anxieties about the future alive. Distrust of unreliable French coalitions and disagreement over Germany had so far prevented close co-operation with France to the disappointment of those who believed this should be a principal aim of British policy. Bevin had avoided becoming involved in intervention in Spain but at the cost of angering a considerable section of the Labour Party and presenting the Left with another "betrayal" to flourish against him.

Eastern Europe having become part of the Soviet sphere of influence, the decisive question was what would happen to Central Europe: Austria, Hungary, Czechoslovakia—above all, Germany. Austria's will to recover her independence owed not a little to British encouragement and was one of the pluses in Bevin's balance sheet. The merger of the two Western zones of Germany was another, but it still left unanswered, more than eighteen months after Hitler's defeat, the question whether Germany was to remain divided, with all the consequences for the rest of Europe whichever way the answer went. In the meantime conditions in Germany, and in much of the rest of Europe, were as bad as they had been in the first winter after the war. Every

---

[1] On the issue on which Mikolajczyk urged the Polish people to vote "No" (the proposal to abolish the Senate) the Government itself—of which he was still a member—admitted an adverse vote of 68%. Mikolajczyk claimed that the vote would have been far higher if it had not been for arrests and falsification.

one of these problems, each difficult enough to solve by itself, had become distorted by the disagreements and suspicion between the two Western powers and the Soviet-led Communist bloc, and the fear that these would lead to a third war, this time waged with atomic weapons.

Bevin might try to keep alive the fading hope that the United Nations would one day provide an answer but, as he well understood by now, long before that day was reached, the shape of the post-war world—including in all probability the future of the United Nations Organization—was likely to have been settled by the assertion and counter-assertion of power exercised in a score of different ways, from propaganda, the promotion of revolution and guerrilla warfare to financial aid, economic pressure and the threat of war.

There was always the possibility that Stalin might decide that the risks involved in antagonizing the West were too great, and, despite his distrust of all Communists, Bevin never gave up hope that the Russians might modify their policy—although, unlike his critics, he thought this more likely to be the result of firmness than of appeasement on the part of the Western powers. Such a change, however, was not to be relied on. Given the situation as it was and Britain's lack of the resources with which to pursue a policy independently of both the Soviet Union and the United States, Bevin saw only two alternatives: for Britain to resign any hope of influencing the post-war settlement or to persuade the Americans to provide the necessary backing of power for a joint Anglo-American policy.

Bevin believed that too much was at stake for the British to accept the first and contract out voluntarily. The second, however, was only to a limited degree in the British Government's power to decide. Without surrendering Britain's freedom of action—an essential condition—he had done everything he could since becoming Foreign Secretary to work closely with the Americans. But at the end of 1946 American foreign policy, in particular the extent of the American commitment to a world policy, was still too ill-defined, America's relationship with Britain too equivocal for Bevin to feel certain that, if the worse came to the worst in any particular case—for example in Greece—the United States would step in and take over a position the British could no longer hold on their own.

Looking at the change which had taken place in US policy since the first Moscow conference, only a year before, Bevin was opposed to forcing the issue, in favour of maintaining as long as possible the commitments the Labour Government had inherited and leaving the Americans time to reach their own conclusions—as they had in proposing the merger of the two Western zones in Germany. Such a policy involved a double gamble. The first was a gamble on the British having the resources and the will to hang on until the United States was ready to share or take over their commitments. The second was a gamble on the Americans being ready, if they were given the time, to act in the way Bevin hoped and not pull out of Europe and the Middle East, as they appeared to be pulling out of China with the withdrawal of the Marshall mission

347

(December 1946). Such a policy also called not only for time but patience since it could be neither explained nor defended in public without risk that it might be repudiated in the United States and, by a section of the Labour Party, in Britain too.

The number of abstentions in the November debate and the correspondence with Attlee since left him in no doubt that the support on which he could rely in the Labour Party had been reduced during his absence. If, to the political arguments of the Left that Britain was moving too close to the United States and too far away from the Soviet Union to maintain her independence, was added the economic argument that she was purusing a foreign policy beyond her means and endangering recovery at home, as Attlee and Dalton now appeared to believe, Bevin was going to come under pressure, which even he would have difficulty in withstanding, to abandon a policy with which an increasing number of members of his own Party were unhappy and which so far appeared to have produced few positive results.

6

1947 was to provide Bevin with the opportunity, which he seized decisively, to reverse the verdict of 1946, at least in Europe. But there was little sign of this when the New Year opened. It began with the fullest exchange between Attlee and Bevin on foreign and defence policy since the Labour Government had been formed. In a memorandum dated 5 January Attlee took as his starting point the views of the Chiefs of Staff, which he summarized as follows.

The UK, the COS argued, was vulnerable to attack by long range weapons against which there was at present no effective defence. The only way to defend the country was to deter an enemy by the threat of counter-attack. Russia was the only possible enemy and the only bases from which she could be attacked lay in the Middle East. It was therefore essential to maintain British influence and forces there, a conclusion reinforced by the need to secure Britain's oil supplies from Middle Eastern fields and her communications through the Mediterranean.

The consequences were: heavy military commitments which had to be considered in relation to Britain's manpower and economic resources; support for a large number of states in the Middle East and the maintenance of the British position in Palestine; competition for political and economic influence with the USSR. These needed careful consideration.

What the British regarded as necessary measures of defence, Attlee continued, would inevitably appear to the Russians as preparations for an offensive which, in their view, was a natural course for a non-Communist state to pursue. They might react by pressing forward in Europe to get nearer to the UK, or by increasing their penetration of the Middle East to deny us bases—or both. He understood that it was not considered possible to put sufficient forces on the Continent to give support to a Western bloc. This meant that any resistance to a Soviet thrust to the Atlantic coast could only come from the Western European states themselves, and that could only be expected after several years when economic recovery had taken place and the attractions of Communism had been reduced. A period of peace would help by reducing tension and making it less possible to continue the war mentality and war economy in the USSR.

Turning to the Middle East, the Prime Minister pointed out that the countries Britain would have to support were all weak. Turkey alone had a fighting record. All of them were undeveloped industrially and would require much capital investment. Apart from their strategic weakness, especially those bordering on Russia, their social and political composition made them very vulnerable.

"Greece appears to be hopelessly divided. In all the other countries, there is a small class of wealthy and corrupt people at the top and a mass of poverty-stricken land-workers at the bottom. Their governments are essentially reactionary. They afford excellent soil for the sowing of Communist seed. . . . We shall constantly appear to be supporting vested interests and reaction against reform and revolution in the interests of the poor. We have already that difficulty in Greece."

After examining the weaknesses of the British strategic position in the Middle East—compared with the much stronger Soviet position—Attlee described the COS' view as "a strategy of despair". The threat of air attack from Middle East airfields was not a sufficiently strong deterrent; it was very doubtful if it would work and it might well act as a provocation to the USSR. "Unless we are persuaded that the USSR is irrevocably committed to a policy of world domination and that there is no possibility of her alteration, I think that before being committed to this strategy, we should seek to come to an agreement with the USSR." If there was no longer a common fear of Germay to bring them together, there was a common fear of what another war might bring to everyone.

Attlee went on to ask what were the chances of success in such a negotiation. The answer, he admitted, depended upon imponderables: how far were the Soviet rulers in fact committed to the necessity of world revolution? Could they be convinced that we had no offensive intentions? What were the prospects of change in the Russian attitude? Did the Russians believe that war with the USA was inevitable and could they be persuaded to the contrary?

If satisfactory answers could be given to these questions, it should not be too difficult to deal with the points of friction. We had, for example, had trouble in Iran before but had overcome it. Was it not possible to get an agreement on oil rights in Iran? Ought we not to be able to settle the Dardanelles on principles applicable to all international waterways, and so on.[1]

This was the most radical criticism Bevin had to face from inside the

[1] Memorandum by Attlee, 5 January 1947. FO 800/476/ME/47/1.

Government during his five and a half years as Foreign Secretary. It came not from the Left but from the Prime Minister, who had defended him in the November debate, and it went much further than Attlee's arguments of the previous summer in favour of withdrawal from the Middle East.

After discussion with his officials,[1] Bevin sent Attlee a long reply of eight foolscap pages which Dixon appears to have drafted.[2] He left the strategic arguments to be discussed with the Chiefs of Staff,[3] concentrating on the political aspects of Attlee's thesis.

Bevin started from long-term British policy which he described as aimed at developing the Middle East into a prosperous producing area which would help the British economy and take the place of India as a market, another version of his belief in the common interest of the Middle East countries and Britain in raising the living standard of the area. Once they had settled with Egypt and Iraq, and if a settlement could be reached in Palestine, little British manpower would be needed for the defence of the Middle East which could be committed to local forces grouped round the British.

What were the arguments against such a policy? The first, that the British position in the Middle East, although defensive in character, must seem offensive to the Russians, he described as a dangerous argument to use: it could apply wherever Britain turned for a friend. The British had been in the Middle East for a lot longer than they could be supposed to be preparing to attack Russia, and were in any case reducing their forces throughout the area. If it was said that the Middle East was a weak position to defend and a poor investment as well, this was no reason for handing over its manpower and oil to the Russians. It had once been a rich area and could be built up again with good government and modern methods, providing a valuable market once it became prosperous. Attlee's criticism of the existing regimes was valid, but the same had been said about Abyssinia in 1935–6 by those opposed to sanctions, and if the situation provided fertile ground for Communism, it was all the more certain that, if the British quit, the Russians would move in.

After a year and a half's practical experience of negotiating with the Russians, Bevin was sceptical about the chances of reaching agreement on making the Middle East into a neutral zone:

"I think we must accept the fact that the present rulers of Russia are committed to the belief that there is a natural conflict between the capitalist and the communist worlds. They also believe that they have a mission to work for a communist world. But they would naturally prefer to achieve this end by infiltration without an armed conflict. If we disinterest ourselves in the Middle East, they will take it over by infiltration. . . .

---

[1] Pierson Dixon circulated a note for discussion at a meeting on 8 January, to be attended by Sir Orme Sargent, R. G. Howe, C. F. A. Warner, William Hayter and Dixon himself. FO 800/476/ME/47/2.
[2] Bevin's reply to the PM 9 January, *ibid.*, ME/47/4.
[3] See below, pp. 470–71.

There is no suggestion of a corresponding retreat by Russia from the countries she has seized since the War, such as the Balkans and Poland.

"Even if, by reducing ourselves to impotence, we convinced the Russians of our pacific intentions, they would remain suspicious of American intentions to use these islands in a war against Russia.

"There are better prospects of changes in the Russian mentality if it becomes clear to the Russians that her plans will not come to fruition of themselves. . . . A surrender of the type you suggest would only encourage the Russian leaders to believe that they could get their ends without war and would lead them into the same error that Hitler made of thinking that he could get away with anything by bluff and bullying."

Bevin added that they could probably reach an agreement with the Russians on oil rights in Iran, but there was no need to abandon the whole Middle Eastern position to do that. As for the Dardanelles, amendments to the present regime in Russia's favour had already been proposed—with no effect, because the Russians wanted exclusive control. So far as the other points of friction were concerned, what had they been doing all along but try and get economic co-operation and unity in Europe, against stiff Russian resistance? He was off again to Moscow shortly to see if it was not possible to deal with Germany on a basis of mutual interest.

Bevin thought that Attlee was exaggerating the cost of Britain's present commitments as well as the chances of negotiation. British troops were being withdrawn from Egypt and soon from Greece as well: they would then only have occupation forces in Palestine. In proportion as the USA realized the importance of the Middle East, it was reasonable to expect them to take a greater part of the burden.

He summed up his opposition to Attlee's proposals in two final paragraphs. The effect of withdrawal from the Middle East

"Would be disastrous to our position there, in the neighbouring countries, in Europe and the world. It would lead the U.S.A. to write us off. . . . Even if we do not believe that the Russians have plans for world domination, I am certain that they will not be able to resist advancing into any vacuum we may leave.

"Your proposal would involve leading from weakness. Our economic and military position is now as bad as it will ever be. When we have consolidated our economy, when the economic revival of Europe has made progress, when it has become finally clear to the Russians that they cannot drive a wedge between the Americans and ourselves, we shall be in a position to negotiate with Stalin from strength. There is no hurry. Everything suggests that the Russians are now drawing in their horns and have no immediate aggressive intentions. Let us wait until our strength is restored and let us meanwhile, with U.S. help as necessary, hold on to essential positions and concentrate on building up U.N.O."

Surprisingly, in the middle of their argument about foreign and defence policy, Bevin and Attlee, without any apparent disagreement, took a decision which they must have realized (Bevin certainly did) had far-reaching implications.

Just before he had left for New York a meeting of the atomic committee

351

General 75 had been summoned (26 October) to decide whether or not to proceed with the building of a gaseous diffusion plant for the production of uranium 235. The decision was crucial to any programme for manufacturing a British atomic bomb. Dalton and Cripps were opposed on the grounds that the country could not afford it; it was Bevin's intervention which prevented their view prevailing. Arriving late—and explaining that he had fallen asleep after a good lunch—he turned the meeting round, declaring (according to Sir Michael Perrin, who was present):

"That won't do at all, we've got to have this. . . . I don't mind for myself, but I don't want any other Foreign Secretary of this country to be talked at or by a Secretary of State in the United States as I have just had [sic] in my discussions with Mr. Byrnes. We have got to have this thing over here whatever it costs. . . . We've got to have the bloody Union Jack flying on top of it."[1]

The phrase Bevin used about a future British Foreign Secretary inevitably recalls the words Nye Bevan was to use when he shocked the Labour Party Conference of 1947 by opposing a resolution in favour of unilateral nuclear disarmament, declaring:

"If you carry this resolution and follow out all its implications and do not run away from it, you will send a Foreign Secretary, whoever he may be, naked into the conference chamber. . . . You call that statesmanship, I call it an emotional spasm."[2]

The October meeting kept open the possibility of making a British bomb; but a substantive decision had still to be made and Attlee deferred it until Bevin got back from the States. When the meeting took place on 10 January 1947, General 75 was re-convened as a new committee, General 163. Dalton, Cripps and Greenwood who had normally attended the General 75 meetings were not invited. Besides Attlee and Bevin the other ministers present were Morrison, A. V. Alexander, Addison (Dominions) and Wilmot (Supply).

Bevin was in no doubt of the answer they ought to give to the question put to them by Lord Portal, the wartime Chief of the Air Staff, who was now in charge of Britain's atomic programme. Britain should press on with the study of all aspects of atomic energy. "We could not afford to acquiesce in an American monopoly of this new development." Other countries might also develop it and unless there was an effective international system prohibiting the production and use of nuclear weapons, Britain must do the same.

Attlee took the same view both at the time and many years later when nuclear armaments had become a major issue in the Labour Party. For both

---

[1] The quotation from Sir Michael Perrin was secured by Peter Hennessy and the minutes of the General 75 meeting released for a BBC programme, *Timewatch*, on the 30th anniversary of the first explosion of a British A-bomb in 1952. See Hennessy's article in *The Times*, 30 September 1982.
[2] Foot, *Bevan*, vol. 2, pp. 574–5.

him and Bevin their experience with the Americans in 1945 and 1946 was decisive: the cancellation, without warning, of Lend-Lease; the revocation of the atomic agreements made by Roosevelt; Truman's abrupt changes of policy over Palestine. The years 1947–49 were to present a different picture, of steadily increasing reliance on a resurrected Anglo–American alliance by both sides, but nobody could foresee or be sure of this in January 1947. As Attlee said to Kenneth Harris long afterwards:

"If we had decided not to have it, we would have put ourselves entirely in the hands of the Americans. That would have been a risk a British government should not take. It's all very well to look back and to say otherwise, but at that time nobody could be sure that the Americans would not revert to isolationism—many Americans wanted it, many Americans feared it. There was no N.A.T.O. then."[1]

Even when there was it did not extend to the sharing of atomic secrets—and to quote Attlee again (this time to Francis Williams in 1960): "We had to look to our defence, and to our industrial future. We could not agree that only America should have atomic energy."[2] None of the other ministers disagreed and Portal's proposals were approved.[3] They were not reported to the Cabinet or to Parliament.

More striking than the secrecy in which the decision was taken was the fact that it was taken at a time when the country was already running into serious economic difficulties, when the Labour Party was restless and the Prime Minister himself highly critical about the Government's foreign policy and defence commitments. Bevin's attitude, at least, was all of one piece. No bomb could be produced for five years. By then, he believed, Britain would have weathered her economic difficulties and be ready to resume her role as a Great Power. As he wrote to Attlee in his reply on 9 January: "Let us wait until our strength is restored and let us meanwhile, with U.S. help as necessary, hold on to essential positions. . . ." An independent deterrent was one of the "essential positions", made all the more so by the prospect that, for a time at least, Britain was going to become more dependent on the USA. From the paper he had sent Bevin a few days before one might have expected Attlee at least to question this assumption. But there is no record that he did and only Professor Blackett amongst those involved in the discussions expressed doubts and considered seriously the logical alternative of a policy of strict neutrality.[4]

Attlee's paper of 5 January, which was free of the ideological preoccupations of the search for a "socialist foreign policy", remains perhaps the most striking sketch of an alternative foreign policy. As such it has to be brought back into the reckoning when trying to evaluate Bevin's own version.[5] But, whether

[1] Harris, *Attlee*, p. 288.
[2] Francis Williams, *Prime Minister*, p. 119.
[3] Gowing, p. 183.
[4] For Blackett's views see Gowing, pp. 115–16; 163, 172; 183–4 and App. 8, pp. 194–206.
[5] See the final chapter, c. 23 below.

Attlee was convinced by Bevin's reply or not, it had no sequel. After a talk between the two men and Alexander on the 9th, Bevin dictated a brief note to say that his general policy was to be continued and no British troops to be withdrawn beyond those already agreed.[1] The PM said he was not satisfied that Britain's defence plans required the maintenance of the present policy in the Middle East. Even that reservation, however, was not pursued further when he and Bevin met Alexander and the Chiefs of Staff on the 13th, the three ministers endorsing the soldiers' view that a firm hold in the Middle East went with the defence of the UK and the maintenance of Britain's communications as the fundamental principles of British defence policy.[2]

The following day (14 January) the Defence Committee met to consider the size of the Armed Forces and the Defence Estimates for the year 1947–8. Although there were cuts from the figures for 1946–7, these did not go nearly far enough to satisfy the Chancellor, Hugh Dalton, who warned his colleagues that the country could not possibly afford such an establishment.[3] When the Cabinet, however, discussed the Economic Survey for 1947 in three meetings on the 16th and 17th, Dalton was astonished at the opposition which he met to his proposal for economies, particularly a 10% cut in the Defence Estimates, as an essential measure for reducing the deficit on the balance of payments. Describing it as "a bad and rowdy Cabinet in which a substantial group ganged up against Cripps and myself in opposition to all our proposals", he took particular exception to the fact that the Prime Minister gave him no support, only intervening to say that he did not think they could cut expenditure on the Forces further. Experience after the 1914–18 war, Attlee added, showed the disastrous effect on British foreign policy of allowing them to become too weak.[4] In saying this, Attlee was echoing Bevin, but Dalton went on in his journal to lament the absence of Bevin who was ill and who would, he was sure, have grasped better than Alexander or the Prime Minister the strength of the Treasury case.[5] The most he was able to secure, when the discussion was renewed on 28 January (with Bevin present), was a cut of 5 instead of 10% in the Defence estimates.[6]

[1] Dixon's note, 9 January. FO 800/476/ME/47/5.
[2] Minutes of Chiefs of Staff Committee, 9th meeting, 13 January 1947.
[3] Defence Committee DO (47). Minutes of 2nd meeting, 14 January 1947.
[4] CM 9 (47), 17 January 1947.
[5] Dalton *Memoirs*, c. 23.
[6] CM 13 (47), 28 January.

PART III

Break Through, 1947

CHAPTER 9

Seven Weeks in Moscow, March–April 1947

I

Good fortune had not entirely deserted Bevin. Early in 1947 he was able to sign the Treaty of Alliance with France which had been one of his objectives from the day he took office. It was Léon Blum at the head of a stop-gap Socialist ministry without a parliamentary majority, who made the decisive move on the French side.

Although a strong supporter of the idea of a Franco–British alliance, Blum shared the common French assumption that the future of Germany, on which the two countries were divided, would have to be settled first, and that this meant nothing could be done until after the next meeting of the Council of Foreign Ministers in Moscow. Duff Cooper claims that it was he, as British Ambassador, who first suggested to Blum that he might use his few weeks in office to conclude an alliance.[1] The French socialist leader, although surprised, on further reflection took to the idea, and on New Year's Day 1947 wrote to Attlee pleading strongly for extra supplies of coal for France from the British Zone of Germany and suggesting that he should visit London to discuss relations between the two countries.

When the visit came up in Cabinet on the 6th, Cripps warned against any move towards the integration of the French and British economies under the Monnet Plan. But Bevin came out strongly in favour of inviting Blum.

"We should do anything we could to strengthen the position of his Government; for France was now at the crossroads and if his Government could survive, this would be very valuable not only for France but for the whole future of social democracy in Europe."

Bevin saw no need to get drawn into discussing the integration of the two economies, but some means might be found to help the French with their difficulties and reassure them that the British wanted to see the French economy re-established and were not thinking of integrating their own economy with the German at the expense of the French.[2]

[1] Duff Cooper: *Old Men Forget* (1953) p. 369: diary entry of 26 December 1946.
[2] CM 2(47) 6 January 1947.

The permanent officials on both sides were full of doubts,[1] but Bevin's support secured a favourable response and once Blum got to London (13 January) Bevin brushed aside objections and insisted on the official communiqué being re-written to include the specific mention of an alliance.

When the Foreign Secretary gave a lunch for Blum at the House of Commons, Duff Cooper wrote in his diary:

"Bevin was in remarkable form and despite the difficulty of the language . . . managed to keep the thing going in a wonderful way. He ragged me, telling the Frenchman that I was more French than English, that I had lost all interest in England and never stopped telling him what he ought to do to help France. He said that there was only one point on which he agreed with me, namely that the danger still came from Germany rather than from Russia. This was very satisfactory. He told a number of not very funny vulgar stories which were difficult to translate but at which Blum laughed valiantly. At 5.30 we had a meeting in the Secretary of State's room. It lasted only an hour and everything went well."[2]

Blum was as delighted with the outcome as Bevin, but three days later his caretaker Government resigned from office on the formation of a new coalition (including the Communists) in which Bidault returned to the Quai d'Orsay. Fortunately, to Bevin's relief, Bidault took what had been done in good part, and told Duff Cooper that he was prepared to conclude a Treaty of Alliance without waiting for the Moscow meeting.

At the same time Bevin revived his proposal for a study of a customs union or some other form of closer economic cooperation with France or with Western Europe as a whole including the western zone of Germany. He told the Cabinet that he saw obvious political advantage in a closer association between British and Western Europe and thought the best way to achieve this might be by creating a community of commercial interests. The economic pros and cons, however, needed to be weighed against the political advantage, and this was why—without saying anything to the French—he wanted a preliminary study made. Cripps said his departmental officials at the Board of Trade were too busy preparing for the International Trade Conference for which the Americans were pressing; but suggested he and Dalton should join Bevin in setting up a group of economists outside Government to carry out such a study.[3] The enquiry was overtaken by, and merged into the negotiations to set up the Organization for European Economic Cooperation as the response to Marshall's offer.[4]

The negotiations with the French did not take more than a month, and on 28 February agreement on the terms of an alliance was announced to a warm welcome in both capitals. The Treaty, signed at Dunkirk on 4 March, bound

[1] Bevin to Attlee, enclosing draft letter, 7 January 1947. FO 800/465/FR/47/3.
[2] Duff Cooper, pp. 370–1, quoting from his diary.
[3] CM 13 (47) 28 January 1947. Bevin's proposal was re-circulated as CP (47) 35 after being deferred from the meeting on 25 October. See above, p. 318.
[4] See FO 371/62398.

the British in the event of hostilities with Germany to come to the aid of France with "all the military and other support and assistance" in their power and committed both parties to constant consultation on economic matters. Nothing was said of a threat from any other direction than the Germans but Bevin hoped that a specific British guarantee would help to reduce the greatest obstacle to closer collaboration between the two countries, their disagreement over the treatment of Germany. But even if, as a result, relations between London and Paris became closer, this could do little to help Bevin overcome the difficulties with which he was confronted immediately and which were concerned with the Mediterranean and the Middle East rather than Western Europe and Germany.

The Prime Minister and the Foreign Secretary sat down to discuss the situation in the Eastern Mediterranean immediately after Christmas. According to the minute of the talk,[1] Attlee was in favour of withdrawing British troops from Greece and handing over the mandate for Palestine. Bevin does not appear to have contested either proposal, but to have concentrated on the circumstances in which they could be carried out with the least disadvantage. It might be possible, he thought, to strike a bargain with the Russians for the withdrawal of Soviet troops from Bulgaria in return for a British withdrawal from Greece. His other suggestion was to delay a decision on Palestine until he had the chance to sound out Stalin and see whether the Russians would be interested in a deal which would allow the British to take over the mandate for Cyrenaica. This was an old grievance of Bevin's. Reporting to the Cabinet on the Peace Treaties concluded in New York, he remarked that most of the territorial claims of the Soviet Union had been conceded before the discussion began:

"It was unfortunate that we had ourselves renounced in advance any claim to territorial advantage as a result of the war; for if we could have asserted our right to retain Cyrenaica, we could have spared ourselves our present difficulty in retaining a foothold elsewhere in the Mediterranean."[2]

On this occasion Attlee agreed that if Britain could make use of bases in Cyrenaica, the need to stay in either Palestine or Egypt would disappear, and the way be opened for a settlement with the Egyptians.

At a meeting of the Defence Committee on New Year's Day Bevin spoke of the weakening of Britain's position in the Middle East during the past month. He had the impression, he said, that we had lost the ability and the will to live up to our responsibilities. "Without the Middle East and its oil and other potential resources, he saw no hope of our being able to achieve the standard of life at which we were aiming in Great Britain."[3]

The same day, Bevin sent the Prime Minister a memorandum which,

---

[1] 27 December 1946, minute dated 28th. FO 800/475/ME/46/25.
[2] 2 January 1947. CM 1 (47).
[3] Defence Committee minutes. DO (47), 1st meeting, 1 January 1947.

although primarily concerned with India, had obvious implications for the Middle East as well. Bevin had played no part in the difficult negotiations with the Congress and Muslim leaders but was roused by the situation he found on his return to write of "the defeatist attitude adopted both by the Cabinet and by F. M. Wavell".

"I am against fixing a date," he declared. "I am willing to support a declaration, as we have done, that we are ready to hand India over as a going concern to established governments. I do not mind even using the plural in this sense, if Nehru and Jinnah are not going to agree, but the qualification should be that they can preserve law and order. I cannot get it out of my head that there must be millions of Indians who, as a result of the murder incidents in the last few months, would welcome a strong and courageous lead so as to preserve their safety. Personally I do not think it depends on the number of British troops there, but it is the complete lack of leadership in the Indian Army that I believe will cause the disaster that will overtake the British. . . . Not only is India going but Malaysia, Ceylon and the Middle East, with a tremendous repercussion on the African territories."

After throwing out the suggestion that they might use the Indian Army to run a transitional occupation regime as in Germany, so that responsibility could be handed over to the Indians "as a going concern", Bevin rounded off his memorandum:

"I would impress you with this fact. I can offer nothing to any foreign country, neither credit nor coal nor goods—I am expected to make bricks without straw. And on top of this, in the British Empire, we knuckle under at the first blow and we are expected to preserve the position. It cannot be done and I beg of you in all sincerity, even if it does involve a certain risk, to take it and I believe the world will respect us.

"We appear to be trying nothing except to scuttle out of it, without dignity or plan, and I am convinced that if you do that, our Party, as a leading party in this new world settlement, will lose irrevocably when the public become aware of the policy of the Cabinet at this moment."[1]

In his reply, dated 2 January, Attlee showed no irritation with Bevin's outburst. Addressing him as "My dear Ernie", he argued that the Cabinet's attitude was not defeatist but realist. He agreed that there were millions of Indians who did not wish for change, but the active elements were indoctrinated with nationalism. Britain, he pointed out, had always governed India through the Indians and it was impossible to continue to govern India against the opposition of the politically-minded. Was he really prepared to go back on the consistent policy of 25 years, to govern by force if necessary and put in enough troops to hold the country down?

This was hardly what Bevin had suggested, but Attlee clearly felt that there was no other alternative. He ended his letter:

"We are seeking to fulfil the pledges of this country with dignity and to avoid an ignominious scuttle. But a scuttle it will be if things are allowed to drift. . . . If you

---

[1] Bevin to Attlee, 1 January 1947. FO 800/470/IND/47/1.

disagree with what is proposed, you must offer a practical alternative. I fail to find one in your letter.

Yours ever,
Clem"[1]

Apart from its intrinsic interest in relation to India, this exchange of letters fills in an important part of the background to the two men's later decision, which they were already considering, to withdraw from Palestine as well.

2

At the time when these discussions took place, no one had yet grasped how serious or how immediate was the threat of economic disaster. Even Dalton, who argued the case for economies, was thinking of a crisis in the future rather than the present.

"What shall it profit Britain," he wrote to the Prime Minister (on 20 January), "to have even 1,500,000 men in the Forces and Supply, and to be spending nearly £1,000 millions a year on them, if we come an economic and financial cropper two years hence?"[2]

Government was about to "come a cropper" not in two years' but in two weeks' time, and the critical factor was to prove the shortage, not of dollars but of coal.

Although coal production had gone up in 1946, it still fell far short of the supplies industry needed. At the end of the year stocks had fallen dangerously low and with the colder weather in January 1947 power cuts became frequent and factories began to go on to short time. The fuel position was reported every time the Cabinet met, but the real crisis did not come until the end of the month. The night of 28–29 January was the coldest since 1929, the Thames froze at Windsor and on the 30th *The Times* headlines read: "All Britain Freezes". Even then no one foresaw either the length of time the cold spell would last or the extent to which it would cripple industry. When the Minister of Fuel and Power (Shinwell) told the Cabinet and later the House of Commons, on Friday 7 February, that a number of power stations would have to shut down completely and that from Monday electricity could no longer be supplied to industry over the greater part of the country, his statement was greeted with astonishment. For the first time in its history, British industrial production was effectively halted for three weeks—something German bombing had never been able to do. Registered unemployment rose from under 400,000 to over 2.3 million; the chances of Britain's economic recovery suddenly appeared more doubtful than ever, particularly abroad, in Washington

---

[1] Attlee to Bevin, 2 January 1947, *ibid.*, IND/47/2.

[2] Dalton, *Memoirs*, p. 197.

and Moscow; and with floods following the frost for most of March, the British people's morale was tested to the limit.

Although he refused to acknowledge it, Bevin was too ill to play much part in coping with the emergency. (A few days before, on 22 January, he had at last given up the chairmanship of the Cabinet's Manpower Committee). Morrison was in hospital and away until after Easter; Bevin persisted in carrying on but was close to exhaustion, his heart strained by walking up two flights of stairs in Great George Street when the lifts were out of action.

"How he will fare at Moscow" Dalton wrote in his diary, "is anybody's guess. It is quite on the cards, I fear, that he will collapse completely. But it is terribly difficult to know what to do, since he won't think of giving up. At any rate he has a doctor always with him."[1]

Rumours were widespread that he would have to give up the Foreign Office. Even if he did not, it seemed obvious that the position he had fought to defend in the earlier discussion with Attlee could no longer be held. The gap between policy and resources was not created by the February emergency but it was driven home with a force that could not be denied. The Economic Survey for 1947 when finally published was described by *The Times* as "the most disturbing statement ever made by a British Government.'[2] Even before the Economic Survey came out, *The Times'* Washington correspondent reported, on 12 February:

"The extent and gravity of the British fuel crisis have now become a major topic of discussion notably in the form of the question to what extent economic weakness may affect foreign policy.

"Today's article by Walter Lippman refers to the Imperial commitments of Britain and to the effect upon them of a crisis which, if allowed to run its course, 'could shake the world and make our [the U.S.] position highly vulnerable and precariously isolated'. The *New York Herald Tribune* considers a possible 'revaluation' of British commitments as something to which the U.S.A. as well as Britain must 'face up', since 'our own foreign policy will inevitably be affected'. Other Americans point out that the Labour Government seems to have been forced into a contest for priority between foreign and domestic policies."

The gloomy view taken in Washington appeared to be amply confirmed in the week that followed. Between the 14th and 20th February Bevin gave notice that Britain would refer the Palestine problem to the United Nations; the Cabinet agreed that British aid to Greece and Turkey could not be renewed after 31 March and the remaining British troops in Greece would have to be withdrawn, and Attlee announced in the House of Commons that Britain would hand over its responsibilities in India "by a date not later than June 1948". A similar announcement was expected to cover withdrawal from Ceylon

[1] Dalton, 24 February, p. 211.
[2] *The Times* first leader, 22 February 1947.

and Burma. The Egyptians had already broken off negotiations and placed their dispute with the British before the United Nations. The British Empire appeared to be in process of dissolution, and the British lacking either the resources or the will to prevent it.

This represented the low point in the Labour Government's fortunes, and of Bevin's own career. The American view quoted by *The Times* that the Government was being forced into a contest for priority between foreign and domestic policies was very much to the point. Attlee might not push home his doubts about the former, but there were others in the Labour Party who would, if it came to an open choice between cutting expenditure on overseas and defence commitments and the Party's programme of social reform. It was in these circumstances, with a Cabinet and Party deeply depressed by the setback to their hopes and with doubts about his own ability to carry on, that Bevin had to prepare for the Moscow conference on Germany and before he left make difficult decisions about Palestine, Greece and Turkey.

In the middle of this unsettling and unsettled discussion of Britain's role in the world, which called the whole of Bevin's foreign policy into question, and with ominous signs of Britain's inability to meet the cost of such a policy, Bevin was plunged back into the discussions on Palestine which had been going on while he was in the USA. Between mid-January and mid-February 1947 these were extended to the Cabinet; the Palestine Conference reopened with an Arab delegation at the end of January, and parallel informal talks with the Zionist group led by Ben Gurion took place in London at the same time.[1]

Bevin and Attlee had to take account of three factors. The first was the need to make a statement of British policies to the United Nations, which as successor to the League must accept the surrender of the Mandate and approve the terms on which any new trusteeship was to be granted. Whatever position the British took up, no one could say how the voting might go, except that the chances of partition securing the necessary two thirds majority seemed slight. The second was the strategic situation in the Middle East, with the Egyptian rejection of the Sidqi–Bevin agreement and the approaching withdrawal from India. Both made British ability to retain bases and facilities in Palestine more important. In December 1946 it had been decided to move another British division out of Egypt to Palestine, the only alternative to Egypt the military were prepared to consider. The Chiefs of Staff remained equally strongly opposed to any proposal to establish a Jewish state whether in the whole or a part of Palestine on the grounds that this would lose the British the goodwill of the Arab states and undermine the capacity to operate from the Middle East which they regarded as essential to the defence of the UK. This view was supported by the Foreign Office:

---

[1] The British records of the Conference on Palestine and the meetings with the Arabs and Jews are in CAB 133/85. See also FO 371/61746–9.

"The loss of Arab goodwill would mean the elimination of British influence from the Middle East to the great advantage of Russia. And this in turn would greatly weaken the position of the British Commonwealth in the world."[1]

The third factor, working the other way, was the support for partition in the Parliamentary Labour Party and the Cabinet. Dalton wrote in his diary (17 January):

"On Palestine a number of us have been shouting for partition—Creech-Jones is very good on this and much more decisive than his predecessor."

The Colonial Secretary advocated partition with skill as well as vigour, adding that it was "most in harmony with the trend of public opinion in this country and most likely to win US support and the endorsement of the Labour Party".[2] Dalton, Nye Bevan, Shinwell and John Strachey all spoke in support, as did the High Commissioner for Palestine, General Sir Alan Cunningham, from outside the Cabinet. Picking up a phrase of Cunningham's, Creech-Jones argued:

"This solution possesses an element of finality which is elsewhere absent. It would give to each community a maximum degree of power to manage its own affairs and a minimum degree of power to interfere in the affairs of the other."[3]

Such advice as Acheson could give pointed in the same direction:

"The American Government, for domestic and other reasons, would find it easier to support in the U.N. and elsewhere the solution of the Palestine problem calling for partition and the setting up of a viable Jewish state."[4]

Finally, the Jewish delegation in their talks at the Colonial Office, although still maintaining their claim to a Jewish state in the whole of Palestine, declared themselves ready to accept one in part of Palestine as a compromise.[5]

There were others besides Bevin opposed to partition including the Prime Minister, the Minister of Defence and the Chiefs of Staff. It is possible but by no means certain that if Bevin had thrown his weight in favour of it, partition might have been adopted—or at least, as Creech-Jones suggested, recommended by the British to the UN. What is certain is that with Bevin against it there was no chance of the Government accepting it.

[1] Memorandum by Robert Howe, 21 January 1947. FO 371/61858. The Chiefs of Staff presented their case to the Cabinet on 15 January: see CM (47) 6, Minute 3 Confidential Annex, 15 Jan. 1947. CAB 128/11.
[2] See Creech-Jones' memorandum of 16 January, CP (47) 32. "Palestine: Future Policy" and the Cabinet minutes for 15 and 22 January, CM 6 (47) and CM 11 (47).
[3] "Palestine: Future Policy", memorandum by the Secretary of State for the Colonies. CP (47) 32, 16 January 1947. Creech-Jones also circulated two earlier papers by Cunningham, CP (47) 31, in which the High Commissioner opposed provincial autonomy and Bevin's attempt to combine it with Arab proposals.
[4] 27 January FRUS 1947 (5) pp. 1014–15.
[5] Central Zionist Archives, S 25/7567. British record in CAB 133, 85: Jewish Delegation Meetings.

More important then, than pursuing the details of fruitless negotiations is to ask, why Bevin had come round to ruling out partition. The arguments against it had been put by the Foreign Office and the Chiefs of Staff in 1946; and yet Bevin was prepared in July of that year to consider partition seriously and in the late summer believed he was within sight of agreement with Weizmann and Goldmann. What had happened to change his attitude since then?

Dalton wrote in his journal that the important thing was to agree on the principle of partition and settle the details later. Bevin, however, believed this was to evade the difficulties which lay not in the principle of partition, but in its implementation. It was impossible to create two viable states in an area the size of Palestine. If the Zionists settled for something less than the whole of the country, they would claim the bulk of its economic resources, both urban and rural, leaving the Arabs with the much poorer parts, which, even if joined to Transjordan, would offer no prospect comparable with that of the Jewish state, and leaving also half a million (out of 1.2 million) Arabs under Jewish rule. The frontiers awarded later by the UN bore out this forecast. Even the partition scheme which Bevin considered the best would have left 450,000 Jews and 360,000 Arabs in the Jewish state, the minority position the Jews rejected for themselves but expected the Arabs to accept.

A second forecast was that the Jews would use partition as a springboard to take over the whole of Palestine once they had brought up their population by immigration to a majority. Belief that partition in practice would lead to annexation of the rest hardened the Palestinian Arabs' determination to rebel rather than acquiesce in such a solution. And this in turn meant reinforcing British troops in order to impose a manifestly one-sided settlement by force. Apart from the difficulty of finding additional troops and additional finance at a time when Bevin was being pressed to reduce Britain's overseas commitments, it was uncertain how far public opinion in the UK—and in the Forces—would tolerate the use of British troops to force the Arabs to knuckle under to a solution favourable to those who were directing a campaign of terrorism and vilification against British soldiers as the successors of the Nazis.

Arab resistance would not be limited to the Palestinian Arabs; it would be supported by the Arab states on whose goodwill the British depended for providing the facilities they required to maintain their position in the Middle East.

"The risk cannot be excluded", Bevin wrote, "that [partition] would contribute to the elimination of British influence from the whole of the vast Moslem area lying between Greece and India. This would have not only strategic consequences, it would also jeopardise the security of our interest in the increasingly important oil production of the Middle East."[1]

At the very least the Arab states would seek to block partition in the UN (where it would require a two-thirds majority) and would turn to the Soviet

---

[1] Bevin's memorandum for the Cabinet on Palestine, 14 January 1947. CP (47) 30.

group for support, "a diplomatic combination which it should be one of the first aims of our policy to prevent."[1]

But what tipped the scale with Bevin was his experience with the Americans. From the very beginning he had staked his hopes of success on involving the United States in finding an answer. Like Churchill he believed that any policy for which the USA could be got to share responsibility could be made to work. Per contra, if it was the case (as he now said in a joint memorandum to the Cabinet with Creech-Jones)[2] "that the U.S. Government will to the end remain an uncertain and unreliable factor in the problem", he believed there was little hope of Britain being able to work out a policy with any confidence that it would hold. He could foresee a situation in which, once the principle of partition was conceded, the Zionists would expand their demands and again put pressure on Truman to secure his support in doing so. The Americans would support partition and press it on the British, but refuse to accept the responsibility for implementing it. For the one thing Acheson felt able to say with certainty about American policy was that the USA would never allow American troops to be used in Palestine. The British could thus find themselves committed to partition, under strong American pressure to accept the most generous interpretation of this in Zionist interests—and then left to incur the odium of enforcing it on the Arabs with no help from the USA. It was Bevin's determination not to let Britain be put in this situation that governed his actions when, later in 1947, the US Government exerted all the pressure it could on the United Nations to endorse partition and on the British to stay in Palestine and carry it out.

Bevin had not intervened to prevent Creech-Jones putting the case for partition to the Cabinet, but by the meeting on 7 February the Colonial Secretary himself had come to the conclusion that it was unworkable, and this impression was confirmed by his meetings with the Arab and Jewish delegations.[3] He agreed to join Bevin in putting forward a final set of proposals (known as "the Bevin plan") for a five-year trusteeship under the UN Trusteeship Council which would be a preparation for Palestine's independence as a bi-national state. Cantons, determined by the size of Jewish or Arab majority, and not necessarily continuous, were to take the place of the Morrison–Grady autonomous provinces and would be more restricted in their powers of self-government. Jews and Arabs would share in the central government and 96,000 Jewish immigrants would be admitted within two years.[4] According to Beeley the plan was Bevin's own. He was summoned to the Secretary of State's room where Bevin told him that he had been "thinking" about Palestine, gave him an outline of his proposals, and told him

---

[1] *Ibid.* This calculation was accepted by the Zionists too down to the unexpected Soviet reversal of policy in May 1947, and accounts for their own reluctance to take the issue to the UN.
[2] CP (47) 49, 6 February 1947.
[3] See the joint report to the Cabinet by Bevin and Creech-Jones. Author's interview with Sir Harold Beeley.
[4] Appendix to CP (47) 49, 6 February 1947.

to put them into shape. The important difference from earlier plans was that Bevin put a definite term of five years to the period of trusteeship, after which Palestine would become independent. The plan was uncompromisingly rejected by both sides. The Arabs would not agree to Jewish self-government in any form or further Jewish immigration; the Jews would not agree to any scheme not based on the promise of an eventual Jewish state. On 18 February Bevin announced in the House that Britain would refer the Palestine problem to the United Nations.

The Zionists were convinced the reference was a trick. They knew that the Foreign Office calculated it would never be possible to obtain a two-thirds majority for partition and they believed that Bevin's object was to secure the return of the Mandate to Britain as a UN Trusteeship under conditions she would accept, relieved of the obligation to create a Jewish national home.

There is nothing in the British documents to confirm the Zionist suspicion. Sir Harold Beeley is surely right when he says that neither Attlee nor Bevin could realistically have expected such an outcome. "The United States was firmly committed to the Jewish national home and strong enough to block any plan that would have brought its further development to a close."[1] In the middle of all the troubles which now beset the Labour Government, there were growing attractions in the idea of getting rid of the problem altogether. In their joint paper to the Cabinet (13 February) Bevin and Creech-Jones had ruled out withdrawal as a "humiliating course",[2] and the Jews were convinced that if only for strategic reasons, the British would never give up Palestine. But in their talk on 27 December 1946, after Bevin's return from Palestine, Attlee had spoken in favour of withdrawal and Bevin (although at that time he had opposed withdrawal from India) had only suggested deferring withdrawal from Palestine until he could see whether the Russians would agree to a British trusteeship for Cyrenaica which would remove the need for bases in either Egypt or Palestine.[3]

On the day Bevin announced the Government's decision to refer the Palestine problem to the UN, the Cabinet fixed the date for British withdrawal from India, whatever happened. The adoption of a similar course of action in Palestine where the irreconcilable claims of Jews and Arabs could be taken to match those of Hindus and Moslems, could not fail to occur to Bevin and other members of the Government. Abba Eban was close to the mark when he told the American Zionists that whatever some British officials might hope, "Britain was prepared to surrender the Mandate, not necessarily determined to but prepared to."[4] Everything that happened in the next six months hardened preparedness into determination.

[1] Quoted by Bethell, p. 311.
[2] CP (47) 59.
[3] See above, p. 359.
[4] Quoted by Bethell, p. 312.

Bevin felt keenly the admission of failure in Palestine, the responsibility for which, whether justly or not, was firmly placed at his door: but he was more anxious immediately about what was going to happen in Greece. He believed that the Labour Party (including even Attlee) had never grasped what was at stake in Greece; how much difference a Communist take-over in Greece would make to the balance of power in the Eastern Mediterranean, and how a British withdrawal, if clumsily handled, could affect Anglo–American relations.

The Greek Government's appeal to the UN over the support given to the rebel forces by her neighbours in the North brought it little comfort. When the UN Commission opened its hearings in Athens at the end of January, the representatives of Yugoslavia, Albania and Bulgaria who appeared before it were able—thanks to the co-operation of the Commission's Soviet and Polish members—to secure far more time than the Greeks. They used it to give maximum publicity to their claim that all Greece's troubles were due to the repressive policy of the "monarcho-fascist" Greek Government and not at all to threats from across the frontiers. On the day the Commission began its hearing, 3 February, the British announced that they would be withdrawing half their troops, which had already been reduced from 80,000 to 16,000 men.[1] The Greek Government, re-formed in late January to include all the political leaders with one exception (Sofoulis), appeared to be no more capable of mastering the situation than its predecessors, managing (to borrow a phrase from C. M. Woodhouse) to combine complacency with defeatism.

In such a situation, the effect of an announcement that the British were withdrawing their support altogether could well be to precipitate the collapse of the Greek administration (including the Army and the police force), which was as dependent psychologically as economically upon the continued presence of an ally to prop up its confidence. For this reason Bevin proposed that a brigade of four battalions should remain in Greece until the Russians withdrew their forces from Bulgaria; and that Britain should continue to help the Greeks to build up their own forces and the Turks to re-organize and re-equip theirs.[2] But faced with the prospect of Britain's own economic collapse, he no longer felt able to resist the pressure from Dalton and the Treasury to end what appeared to Attlee and most other members of the Cabinet to be a futile expenditure of precious resources.

Bevin had only one card left to play. When he finally accepted Dalton's argument on 18 February it was agreed that nothing should be said to the Greeks—"We get no help from the Greeks"—until he had tried to persuade

---

[1] This announcement followed Bevin's proposal to the Cabinet on 30 January. C.M. 14 (47).
[2] CM 14 (47), the Cabinet meeting on 30 January at which Bevin proposed the cut in British forces announced on 3 February.

the Americans to take over the British obligations in both Greece and Turkey.[3] The idea was hardly new: it had been discussed in Whitehall for several months. An informal arrangement had been reached with the Americans to share the cost of supporting both countries, and by the beginning of 1947 both Americans and British accepted, without spelling it out, that if anything more was to be done for the Greeks, it would have to be by the USA not Britain. The American economic mission headed by Paul Porter was already in Athens, and Porter, as well as the experienced US Ambassador MacVeagh, and Byrnes' special envoy Mark Ethridge, all reported a deteriorating situation. Loy Henderson, the State Department's Near Eastern Director, prepared a paper entitled "Crisis and Imminent Possibility of Collapse", after reading which General Marshall gave instructions to get ready the necessary steps for sending economic and military aid to Greece.[2] This was on the morning of 21 February, the same day on which the British Ambassador asked to see the Secretary of State with an urgent message from London.

The ground therefore had been well prepared. Nonetheless it was a step which Bevin had hitherto refused to take and only took now with considerable misgiving, partly because it meant admitting publicly Britain's inability to go on playing an equal role with the Americans, but, even more perhaps, because he was unsure how the Americans would take it. The question of timing was all-important and Bevin could only hope he had got it right.

The British note began by recalling earlier exchanges of views in which it had been agreed that Greece and Turkey could not be allowed to fall under Soviet control. The British however were unable to offer any further assistance after 31 March, less than six weeks away, and Bevin could only appeal to the USA to take over the burden of providing both civilian and military aid which had hitherto been chiefly borne by the United Kingdom. A second brief note referred to the situation in Turkey which was not so desperate, but where Britain was no more able than in Greece to continue giving the support necessary for Turkey to defend her independence.

Although everything they said could have been and, in large part, had been foreseen, Bevin was quite right in believing that the notes would come as a shock in Washington. Added to the news of other imminent British withdrawals, from India, Burma and the Middle East, they left no doubt in the minds of those who had to deal with them that the United States was confronted with the historic decision, going far beyond the immediate crisis in Greece, whether or not to take over the world role which the British were no longer strong enough to bear by themselves. What had made Bevin hold out against Attlee's

---

[1] Note of talk between Dalton and Bevin, FO 800/466/GRE/47/2. "I agreed . . . that we should put up a strong telegram to the United States asking them what they were going to do and on the other hand telling the Greeks that we could not continue for the sole purpose of bringing matters to a head."

[2] Acheson, *Present at the Creation*, p. 217.

arguments in favour of Britain withdrawing from her overseas commitments was his anxiety that the Americans might read into this an abandonment of her role in the world which would make Britain no longer worth considering—or supporting—as an ally. The fact that American policy for the past twelve months had been moving logically towards a decision about the United States' own expanded role as a world power did not make it easy for the Americans to take that decision when the moment came. The Administration might be ready for such a drastic change in their perception of America's role in the world, but a Republican Congress and, even more, public opinion in the nation at large were certainly not.

There is no need to recount here the dramatic but familiar history of the ensuing weeks in Washington leading up to Truman's speech to both Houses of Congress on 12 March,[1] nor to enter into the historical controversy over the mixture of motives which lay behind the announcement of the "Truman Doctrine".[2]

Once he had sent the notes which precipitated these events, Bevin's part in them was peripheral. For a few days he waited anxiously to see whether his gamble had come off. A protest from General Marshall at the short notice with which he had thrust the problem on the Americans was accompanied by the inquiry whether this meant any fundamental change in British policy. Bevin at once replied that it did not, that the British view remained that the freedom of Greece and Turkey and also of Iran and Italy from Soviet domination was absolutely essential to Anglo–US and Western European security and to the Middle East's stability. But the United Kingdom could no longer carry the burden alone and the USA should now play its part. Marshall assured Bevin that the USA would accept a full share of the responsibilities but pointed out that it would take 5–6 weeks to get approval from Congress and that the earliest date by which American aid could begin to reach Greece was the latter part of April. He asked the British to find additional funds to keep the Greek army going in the meantime and, above all, not to remove the remaining British troops. This Bevin was able to do. On 5 March the British Ambassador saw Acheson and told him that while one brigade would have to leave by 31 March, the other's departure would be only "as soon as practicable". Christopher Mayhew, speaking for Bevin in the House of Commons, added "in the course of the summer", but in fact the remaining British troops stayed on in Greece until the civil war was over (the last left in 1950) and the British military mission continued its work of training the Greek Forces in co-operation with an American mission sent out under General Van Fleet. Bevin was also able to secure a relaxation of the immediate cut-off of British funds in

---

[1] Although it needs to be supplemented by subsequent publications drawing on the documentary material now available, no first-hand account equals that of Joseph Jones: *The Fifteen Weeks* (NY 1955).
[2] See bibliographical note, pp. 865–6 below.

order to tide the Greeks over the transition. An additional four million dollars was found and twice that amount made available to the Greek Army in supplies and equipment.

Reporting on foreign affairs to the House of Commons on 26 February Bevin mentioned Greece only in passing and Mayhew's statement to the House on 5 March gave little hint of the importance of what was happening. Even the Chancellor of the Exchequer, if his memoirs are to be relied on, only grasped what was involved from a broadcast by the American commentator, Joseph Harsch, on 14 March, two days after Truman's speech.[1] By the time he left for Moscow, on the 4th, however, it was clear to Bevin, to his immense relief, that his gamble had come off, that the Americans were responding to his appeal and that Greece would not be abandoned by her allies.

In the meantime, preparations for the Moscow meeting had been going ahead, with the deputies of the four Foreign Ministers meeting in London since the middle of January. Shortly before, on 11 January, Attlee and Bevin had received a report from Montgomery, the CIGS, on his return from Moscow, where he had dined and talked with Stalin. Monty was asked by the Russian leader if there was not a military alliance between the UK and the USA: how else could he explain the standardization of weapons between the two armies? The CIGS replied that standardization was a natural result of the close co-operation during the War and assured him that there was no military alliance or agreement at all. He went on to ask whether Stalin thought there should be a military alliance between the UK and Russia, to which Stalin said: "That is what I would like and I think it is essential!"

Stalin argued that Part I of the 1942 Agreement between the two countries only applied to the war against Germany, and Part II promised mutual assistance for 20 years "or until the World Organisation has been set up". With the foundation of UNO, it was not at all clear what status the Agreement now had and whether it had been superseded by UNO. This was a view which *Pravda*[2] proceeded to attribute to Bevin who was said to regard the Anglo–Soviet Treaty as "suspended in the air".

It was not at all clear to Bevin or his advisers why Stalin should have raised this particular issue just before the Moscow Conference.[3] But there was no doubt in anyone's mind that they ought to seize the opportunity Stalin had offered and Bevin sent a message to the Russian leader saying that it was not his view that the Anglo–Soviet Treaty was suspended and that the British had several times urged its extension, only to find that the Russians did not like their proposals.[4]

On the last day of January, the Defence Committee discussed what should

---

[1] Dalton, *Memoirs*, c. 25.
[2] *Pravda*, 15 January 1947.
[3] See the paper written by Hector McNeil on 21 January 1947. FO 800/502/SU/47/12.
[4] Bevin to Moscow, 18 January, *ibid.*, SU/47/11.

be done about the standardization of arms with the USA and Canada and about the Soviet proposal of a military alliance with the UK. It was agreed that the best course was to keep arrangements for the standardization of arms informal—a continuation of existing practice, no new departure—so that no statement would be necessary which might arouse Russian suspicions. As for a military alliance with the USSR, the Committee agreed that the proposal needed careful examination: the negotiations for revising the existing Anglo–Soviet Treaty would provide an opportunity for finding out more about Russian intentions. Bevin laid stress on keeping the United States informed of any discussions with the Soviet Government—otherwise they might believe "we had gone over to the Russian camp"—and for reassuring public opinion in the UK that "we are not entering into exclusive commitments on either side".[1] When Bevin reported the exchanges to the Cabinet on 3 February, he was authorized to tell Stalin that they were willing to enter into negotiations to bring the Anglo–Soviet Treaty up to date; but at the present stage he was to say nothing about the possibility of a military alliance.[2]

It is clear that Bevin did not see Stalin's action in raising the question of the Anglo–Soviet Treaty as opening the way to a real settlement of the difficulties between the two Governments, but as another move in the diplomatic game, to which (as Hector McNeil pointed out) the British had to respond if only to prevent Stalin using it against them later. There would be great advantages, McNeil added, in getting such an alliance, even in starting talks which later broke down. If the Moscow Conference was to have real value, however, it would not be in general declarations of goodwill but in getting down to the particular issues on which the British and Russians held opposing views.[3]

The most important of these was Germany, the principal item on the agenda for Moscow. At a meeting of the Cabinet on 4 February Bevin presented his proposals for the socialization of Germany's basic industries, coal, iron and steel as well as the heavy engineering and chemical industries which were concentrated in the British zone. He advocated the appointment of custodians, with German advisory committees, on behalf of the German people in each Land where the plants in question were situated, leaving until after the Moscow meeting a decision on the exact form public ownership should take. Bevin himself clearly favoured vesting ownership in the Land governments rather than in any central German government, but was willing to wait provided this option was kept open. He also urged that when the time came they should press ahead "regardless of American reactions". The Cabinet was impressed by Bevin's arguments and agreed that Germany must be enabled to export in order to pay for her imports. The minute records the Cabinet's view

[1] DC minutes, DO 4th meeting, 31 January 1947; Bevin's draft paper for the Cabinet, 27 January. FO 800/502/SU/47/14.
[2] CM 15 (47), 3 February 1947.
[3] Paper by McNeil already referred to, 21 January 1947.

that there was room for German exports as well as British and if occasionally there was some competition between them, this must be faced: Britain's major interest was in expanding the world economy.[1]

At the end of February Bevin presented another paper summarizing the position he proposed to take at Moscow on the economic and political future of Germany. Dalton and Cripps supported his proposals but Nye Bevan argued that they would prove impracticable—both the attempt to place a limit on Germany's industrial expansion and the attempt to promote decentralization and prevent the creation of a central German government. All Bevin asked for was approval of the position he was to start from; what the result would be after hearing the views of the Russians, the Americans and the French was a very different matter.[2]

Before Bevin left for Moscow, it was agreed between him and Attlee that he should take over responsibility for Germany. This meant that the separate Control Office in London was brought under the Foreign Office (with effect from April 1947); Hynd was found another job and Frank Pakenham made Chancellor of the Duchy of Lancaster with responsibility under Bevin for German affairs.[3] Both Sir Maurice Dean, the civil service head of the Control Office, and Sir Brian Robertson the head of the Military Administration in Germany welcomed the move with relief. It gave them direct access to the man who had the biggest say in determining British policy on Germany, and they were not disappointed with the result. Bevin proved, in Dean's words, "a fount of power", who would quite often settle a question by putting on his hat and walking across Downing Street to see Attlee. "If they were agreed, it was 90% sure it would go through the Cabinet: there were few papers, no fuss, no delay and clear decisions."[4]

It was widely believed in Germany during the occupation that the Labour Government favoured and had strong links with the Social Democratic Party. Whatever may have been true of other ministers, this was certainly not true of Bevin. He regarded the Christian Democrats with suspicion as reactionaries (Frank Pakenham as an ardent Catholic was naturally more sympathetic) but on the testimony of Morgan Phillips, the Secretary of the Labour Party and Chairman of the Socialist International, as well as of General Robertson, Bevin was equally critical of the SDP. Towards the Austrian Social Democrats he was friendly and helpful but he regarded the German Social Democrats as having let him and other socialists down in 1914 and after the First World War. This reproach was strengthened by the strongly nationalist line taken by the socialist leader, Kurt Schumacher, in attacking the Occupying Powers,

---

[1] Bevin's paper "Socialisation of the German Basic Industries" was circulated (1 February) as CP (47) 37. The discussion is recorded in CM 16 (47) 4 February.

[2] Bevin's paper was circulated (20 February) as CP 47(68). For the main proposals, see below, pp. 376–8; 383–4. The Cabinet discussion is recorded in CM 25 (47), 27 February.

[3] Notes of two talks between Attlee and Bevin, 24 & 28 February 1947. FO 800/463/FO/4 and 5.

[4] Interview with Sir Maurice Dean. Robertson spoke equally warmly of the change which followed Bevin's appointment.

particularly over dismantling. Bevin was more favourable to the German trade union movement and its leader, Hans Boeckler, a German version of himself, and one of the benefits, in Robertson's view, of Bevin's becoming more closely involved was the trouble he took to put the British in touch with German union leaders.

None of the new arrangements for Germany would become effective until Bevin got back from Moscow. When he left for the long journey out on 4 March, Britain was still snow-bound and industry only beginning to start up again. He broke his journey to visit Dunkirk where he and Bidault met to sign the new Anglo–French Treaty as we have seen. The *sous-Préfecture* in which the ceremony took place was one of the few undamaged buildings still standing in the town and Bevin recalled with emotion the meeting in 1940 at which Churchill warned the Cabinet that they would be fortunate if 10% of the British Army got back from Dunkirk. He spoke of his determination that Britain and France should never be divided again and afterwards, standing with Bidault on the snow-covered beaches, repeated the Frenchman's pledge: "For all time." Far from well and depressed by the position in which Britain now found herself, he needed no prompting to see another Dunkirk situation in the making. The prospect of the weeks ahead in Moscow did nothing to cheer him up.

4

Forbidden to fly because of his heart, Bevin had to make the journey by train. He boarded his special carriage in Belgium, travelling (with his private physician) in a style which, during most of his lifetime, had been reserved for monarchs and millionaires. But the train's speed was restricted and it took from Tuesday afternoon to Saturday noon before it steamed into Moscow station. It was a long dull ride across the snow-covered North European plain, with a change of trains to the Russian broad gauge at Brest-Litovsk, where, thirty years before, a victorious Germany had dictated terms to a defeated Russia. The tedium was interrupted by tea in Berlin with William Strang who, as political adviser to the British Military Governor, was to follow them to Moscow, and by a drive in the snow round Warsaw where Bevin was received by the Polish Foreign Minister.

Housing conditions in Moscow meant an uncomfortable conference for most of the visiting staffs and the journalists who accompanied them. Bevin was well lodged with Sir Maurice Peterson, the Ambassador, at the Embassy, in what he described as his "old" bedroom and sitting-room. A little ungratefully, Bevin returned later with a story which began with his asking members of his Foreign Office staff: "Do you know Brindle?" This was the name of the Petersons' elderly Scotch Terrier. After the inevitable question, How does Brindle come into the story, Bevin would continue:

"Well, it was like this. Towards the end of our little meal they gave me with the cheese what I took to be dog biscuits, so, I said by way of a joke like, and quite unsuspecting: 'Lady Peterson, these look to me like dog biscuits.' 'As a matter of fact they are, Secretary of State,' she said, 'but we like them.'

"Well, after a bit of a pause, I said, 'Lady Peterson, I 'ope I'm not depriving Brindle of his dinner?' And do you know what she replied?

" 'That's quite all right, Secretary of State, Brindle won't eat 'em.' "[1]

Snow was still falling when they reached Moscow and was followed by the spring thaw which made movement even more difficult. The amenities of Paris and New York were lacking; social life was restricted to official entertainment, and long before the end everybody was longing to get away. On the other hand, the isolation of Moscow, the fact that official papers took a long time to arrive from London, that there were no other visiting delegations as there had been in both Paris and New York to take up time and very little to do outside the conference, gave Bevin an enforced rest which was of great benefit to him. He wrote to Miss Saunders, who had been his secretary in the Union:

"It has been very cold here and my chest reacts badly in these days but on the whole I have been very well. No pains, they have gone, and what a relief, the first time really free since before New York. I have been able the first week to rest a good deal: we got no planes through so no papers hardly from home, only the conference work.

"Today is Sunday, there is no meeting, so a day to work at each problem calmly.

"It is thawing just a little but it will be some time before we shall see anything but snow and ice, feeling is pretty good and friendly, no ruffled feelings yet. Marshall is quiet and firm and very direct with a voice and manner like Ashfield was ten years ago."[2]

The sessions of the 4th meeting of the Council of Foreign Ministers, usually held in the late afternoon, took place in the Hall of Aviation Industry. The first was held on 10 March, the last—the 43rd—more than six weeks later, on 25 April.[3] With the Russians anxious to make a success of a conference at which they were the hosts, the conference got off to an easy start, there was little difficulty over the agenda and Bevin captured the headlines by proposing that the Foreign Ministers formally approve the abolition of the State of Prussia. This put him in an excellent temper.

The rest of the first week was taken up with discussion of the Allied Control Council's report on the occupation of Germany. Molotov seized the opportunity to arraign the Western Powers for their failure to carry out the four 'D's in their zones—disarmament, demilitarization, de-Nazification and democratization. Bevin, by now a veteran of these propaganda engagements, at once weighed in with a repudiation of the Russian charges and launched a series of

---

[1] Recounted in Gladwyn, p. 207.

[2] Bevin to Ivy Saunders, 16 March 1947. Lord Ashfield had been the Chairman of London Transport between the wars.

[3] British records of the 4th session of the CFM, FO 371/64183–207; US records in FRUS 1947 (2) pp. 1–491.

his own against the administration of the Soviet zone. Marshall, who was attending his first conference with the Russians and made little impact to begin with, was shocked by an exchange of accusations which he thought a waste of time. Bevin thought the same, but always found it difficult to let Molotov go unanswered. By the end of the conference, however, Marshall had not only impressed everybody by the firmness which underlay his restraint of manner, but had evolved his own way of meeting the offensive style of Soviet diplomacy.

The exchange of accusations may not in fact have been as much a waste of time as it appeared. Bevin, for example, was nettled to discover that there were 81,000 German POWs in the British Zone of Germany working under their own officers on such tasks as mine-clearing, tree-felling, etc., and he telegraphed Attlee asking for authority to undertake that these *Dienstgruppen* would be dissolved by the end of 1947, as nothing would ever persuade the Russians they were not a military formation. After some argument with the War Office, he told the CFM that it was intended to replace them with civilian labour under contract, apart from 5,000 who would be engaged on minesweeping into 1948.

Nor did the process work only one way. One of Bevin's counter-demands was to ask the Russians how many German prisoners they were keeping in the USSR and what use was being made of them. Although the Russians were only prepared to admit to 900,000 prisoners still held (claiming that a further 1 million had already been freed), Bevin succeeded in getting figures from all four powers and on almost the last day got the others to agree that the repatriation of all POWs should be completed by the end of 1948—one of the few positive results of the conference.

These were details, however. It was in the second week, when each of the four powers in turn stated the principles which it believed should govern a settlement with Germany, that the real difference of views opened up. Bevin led off on the theme of economic unity.

"We all maintain," he said, "that we wish to see this principle applied and yet Germany is still not treated as an economic whole. The reason for this is that each of us attaches certain conditions which we regard as essential to economic unity. We have our conditions too . . . If I were to single out one condition that we hold to be . . . necessary to ensure the reality of economic unity, I should say that it is . . . unrestricted freedom of movement throughout Germany. The zonal barriers must come down. In the absence of this essential condition, economic unity would be a travesty."[1]

Because they could not get unification of all four zones, the British had made the bi-zone agreement with the Americans. This was not intended to be exclusive and they would happily extend it to the other two zones, but until such an agreement for the fusion of the four zones was reached, the bi-zonal agreements would stand.

---

[1] Bevin's statement (17 March) and the corresponding statements by Molotov and Marshall are printed in Part IV of the RIIA's *Documents on International Affairs 1947–48* (London 1952), pp. 412–510.

The British had always wanted to see a higher figure set for the level of industrial recovery in Germany. They were more than ever convinced that the level fixed in March 1946 was too low.

"While we must endeavour to eliminate all risk that Germany shall retain a war potential, we must also take great care that she has an adequate peace potential. If the standard of life in Germany is reduced to too low a level, if she becomes an economic cesspool in the middle of Europe, we shall sow the seeds of war just as surely as if we were to leave her with a potential for making armaments."[1]

Nobody was satisfied about reparations and it was essential to speed up deliveries. The present scheme, however, went beyond the limits of practicable achievement within a reasonable time. There was no need to depart from the Potsdam principles, Bevin concluded, but they must make a fresh start on carrying them out: first, fix a revised level of industry for Germany, beginning with steel; then let the ACC make, by 1 July 1947, a fresh determination of how much plant and equipment it was practicable to remove from Germany and issue a final list not later than 15 August.

If Bevin's proposals on reparations went too far and too fast for the Americans, who were bent upon securing the economic unification of Germany before resuming deliveries, they fell far short of what Molotov claimed in the same sacred name of the Potsdam Agreement and the economic unity of Germany. The unilateral action of the USA and Britain in creating the bi-zone must be cancelled; the Ruhr industries must be removed from the control of the British and brought under the joint control of all four occupying powers; the Soviet Union's claim to reparations worth 10 billion dollars, already (Molotov claimed) recognized at Yalta, reinstated; the German level of industry raised to provide for the payment of reparations as well as imports; all cartels and monopolies abolished; the deliveries of plant and equipment agreed at Potsdam resumed and completed and (a new claim, which Molotov argued had also been accepted at Yalta) the balance met from current production in Germany, German assets abroad and the services of German labour.[2]

The French view was as different again. While the other three powers agreed on the need to raise the level of German industry and to set up a central German administration to apply economic unification (each on their own very different terms) the French were opposed to either proposal. The industrial recovery of France and other countries occupied by the Germans must be given priority over that of Germany: this meant stricter limits on German consumption of coal and holding down, not increasing, the level of German steel production. Nor could France agree to creating a central German administration so long as German frontiers were left undefined and the political and economic future of the Ruhr, the Rhineland and the Saar remained unsettled. The Saar, in any case, must become part of the French

[1] From a statement by Bevin on 12 March to which he referred back when speaking on the 17th.
[2] RIIA *Documents 1947–48*, pp. 427–39.

economy and the transfer of capital equipment for reparations resumed at once, with further consideration of the Russian proposal for reparations from current production as well.

In the discussion that followed, the priorities became clearer. For the Russians, it was reparations from the Western zones. For the French, coal and a prior claim for the needs of French over German industry. For the British and Americans, the restoration of the German economy to the point where the German people could provide for themselves and no longer be subsidized. "We cannot accept", Marshall declared, "a unified Germany under a procedure which in effect would mean that the American people would pay reparations to an ally." "The first concern of the Allies," Bevin reiterated, "was that the German economy should not be a charge upon them." Bevin made it equally plain that the bi-zonal arrangements would not be dismantled nor the Ruhr singled out for four-power control until the whole of Germany was treated as a single economic unit.

From economics, the Foreign Ministers passed to politics. The British, Bevin explained, were opposed to a highly centralized German state. They wanted all powers to be vested in the Länder except those expressly delegated to the central government, and the Länder to be charged with executing the central government's legislation in the territory. The Länder would also be represented in a Second Chamber with a veto on constitutional changes.[1] The Russians, Molotov announced, took the opposite view and strongly opposed the federalization of Germany; they were in favour of taking the Weimar constitution as a basis for discussion. The Americans shared the British preference for a federal constitution and like the British and Russians were ready to start on the steps necessary to create a provisional government but they regarded economic unity and the guarantee of the democratic freedoms throughout Germany as the essential basis for such a development. The French wanted to carry federalization to the point where a central German government would be left with very few powers or resources of its own, and they thought it premature to consider setting up any form of provisional government. The French apart, however, Molotov and Marshall agreed that there was enough common ground to justify a recess while the Deputies saw how far they could get with a draft report.

Early in the first week of the conference, reports had reached Moscow of President Truman's address to Congress on 12 March. The news that he had asked for authority to take over Britain's support of Greece and Turkey and to provide 400 million dollars in aid for the period up to 30 June 1948 was an immense relief to Bevin. He was surprised, however, by the open-ended

---

[1] Bevin was the first of the Foreign Ministers to unveil his proposals for the political future of Germany and extraordinary measures were taken to make sure that they were given prominence in the British Press. Dixon, who had to see to this, wrote in his diary: "Although only seven years in the House of Commons, he is as sensitive as any hard-bitten politician to his personal publicity" (21 March).

commitment represented by the Truman Doctrine, very different from the Monroe Doctrine from which it took its name. After referring to the coercion and intimidation practised in Poland, Rumania and Bulgaria, the President declared:

"At the present moment in world history nearly every nation must choose between alternative ways of life. The choice is too often not a free one. One way of life is based upon the will of the majority. . . . The second . . . is based upon the will of a minority forcibly imposed upon the majority. It relies upon terror and oppression, a controlled press and radio; fixed elections and the suppression of personal freedoms.

"I believe that it must be the policy of the U.S. to support free peoples who are resisting attempted subjection by armed minorities or by outside pressure. I believe that we must assist free peoples to work out their own destinies in their own way."[1]

Bevin was not shocked by the substance of what Truman said but, like most European politicians, questioned the wisdom of stating it publicly in such black and white terms at the very moment that the Moscow conference was opening and while there might still be a chance of effecting a compromise with the Russians.[2]

However, although *Izvestia* replied at once, denouncing "a fresh intrusion of the U.S.A. into the affairs of other states",[3] no public statement was made by any of the Soviet leaders. Stalin indeed, shortly afterwards, gave an interview to a leading American politician, Harold Stassen, in which he made no mention of Truman's speech and went out of his way to deny that he had ever said socialist and capitalist societies could not exist together and even co-operate to their mutual benefit.[4] So far as can be seen from the British and American records, no mention of the Truman Doctrine was made by the Russians in any session of the Moscow conference or even in the private talks which went on at the same time.

Bevin said in his final report on the Conference that Truman's announcement removed any chance of agreement on the general principles of a German settlement and changed the whole scene. This may have been so, but without access to the Russian sources there is no evidence to support it and there was a case for arguing the opposite, that Truman's declaration would make the Russians more anxious to reach a settlement on Germany.

Certainly the British view when the first part of the Conference came to an end was far from pessimistic. Writing in his diary on 20 March, Dixon reported:

"No real information about the Russian attitude, but the indications are that, though they have given nothing away, they want a settlement. We can afford not to be over-eager, as our zone, fused, will work, and the Russian, we suspect, is in a bad way. So a workable settlement is not impossible."

---

[1] Full text in RIIA *Documents 1947–48*, pp. 2–7.
[2] This was a general reaction in the British Foreign Office: see Gladwyn, pp. 197–202.
[3] *Documents 1947–48*, pp. 7–10.
[4] *Ibid.*, pp. 116–21.

Molotov's attitude in the conference chamber seemed to bear this out. After he had staked out the Russian position, he adopted a more conciliatory manner, speaking of common ground and the need for compromises. The same impression, that the Russian object was to secure concessions by encouraging hopes of a settlement, is left by the record of Bevin's talk with Stalin[1] on the evening of 24 March when he drove to the Kremlin for the interview which the Russian leader accorded to each of the Foreign Ministers in turn.

Bevin was as determined as he had been in December 1945 (when Stalin had complained of his rough manner) to speak bluntly and not avoid any of the difficult issues. He began by plunging straightaway into reparations. He told Stalin that Britain could only agree to reparations being paid at Germany's, not her own, expense. To this Stalin replied that Russia was not asking much, and, when Bevin interjected that it was necessary to create a balanced economy, added that it was also necessary not to allow Germany to build up a new war potential.

Moving to another sensitive issue, Bevin remarked that the German–Polish frontier had been fixed too far west, would create an explosive situation in the future and foster irredentism. Stalin was not to be drawn. There were not many Germans, he observed, left in the territories occupied and Germany could be prevented from attempting to recover them. At Teheran, Bevin went on, it had been decided to break up Germany. Now the Russians had changed their minds and wanted a centralized German administration. He thought it was a mistake to go too far with centralization, for reasons of security. The Russian proposals, Stalin returned equably, were not in conflict with the British. Power would be centralized and administration decentralized, as under Weimar.

Bevin, however, was not to be disarmed. The Ruhr, now, he persisted, would have to be treated in the same way as the rest of Germany. All German industry, not just the Ruhr's, must be brought under four-power control. If agreement was reached on that, then Britain would agree that the Ruhr's production should be dealt with by a central German administration, under Allied supervision, in the same way as that of the rest of Germany. Stalin again refused to be drawn. He would like time to think this over, he said. In any case, he would not wish to do anything harmful to Britain in the Ruhr.

Bevin then declared his support for the American proposal of a four-Power treaty to guarantee the demilitarization of Germany. Yes, said Stalin, provided the democratization of Germany, reparations and the duration of the treaty could be dealt with satisfactorily, then he was in favour in principle. He was more forthcoming when Bevin proposed a start to negotiations for the revision of the Anglo–Soviet Treaty. He was ready, he told the Englishman, and named Vyshinsky as the Soviet negotiator.

Neither man mentioned Greece, Turkey or Truman's declaration, but Bevin seized the opportunity to raise a number of Middle Eastern issues.

[1] FO 800/502/SU/47/24–30.

Egypt, for instance. His object was to make a mutual defence agreement with Egypt, an agreement which (he added disingenuously) was directed against no one. Stalin nodded. He understood, he said. If Great Britain had not been in Egypt, the Egyptian Government might well have sided with the Nazis. He had no intention of interfering with British policy in Egypt.

There was no truth, Bevin continued, in rumours that Britain was trying to prevent the Soviet Union obtaining oil concessions in northern Persia. He would advise the Persians to live up to their agreements. If Stalin wondered why Bevin volunteered this promise (which he kept), the answer was forthcoming in the next sentence. Britain, her Foreign Secretary added, had concessions in southern Persia and had no intention of interfering with Persia's independence. We hold the same position, Stalin replied.

India. Well, India, Bevin admitted, was full of difficulties. Stalin reassured him: Russia would not interfere and wished Britain success in the enterprise on which she had embarked there.

Finding so sympathetic a reception, Bevin took up other questions that had hung fire between the two countries. He was anxious, he said, to start trade talks and in particular to get timber from Russia. The Soviet Union too wanted to reach agreement was the answer. She needed railway equipment, Stalin said, and if the British could supply this, they would soon get timber. What about an air service between London and Moscow Bevin asked. With a transfer point in Berlin, was Stalin's reply. Why not a direct service? Because the same rights would then have to be given to everybody, but Stalin added that he would consider it. Only on one issue did Stalin profess inability to meet Bevin's wishes. When the latter asked if Russian wives married to Englishmen —there were only a dozen involved—could not be allowed to join their husbands in Britain, Stalin shook his head. He had already been censured by the Supreme Soviet for raising the matter: nothing could be done.

Having exhausted every topic he could think of, Bevin asked his host if he had any question he wished to put. Only one, said Stalin. Was there a real coal crisis in Britain, or was it merely a lot of noise in the Press? Bevin assured him the crisis was real enough and explained the difficulties. Stalin sympathized: We have the same difficulties here in Russia. The men do not want to work underground. But why, he asked, don't the British take more coal from Germany and get more production out of the Ruhr? Bevin's answer was that the British felt that, after satisfying German needs, any surplus from the Ruhr should go to France. Stalin was unimpressed: the Germans, he remarked, should be made to mine more coal.

The meeting ended with mutual courtesies, Bevin assuring Stalin that he was anxious to work with Russia and avoid unfriendly feelings and Stalin responding in the same vein.

5

For all his experience by now of Russian tactics in negotiations, Bevin was obviously at a loss how to deal with Stalin. He let the Georgian put him in the disadvantageous position of being the party who demanded and protested, allowing Stalin to hold the power of assent or dissent. In his anxiety to place his own cards on the table, he never noticed that Stalin put down none at all, contenting himself with picking up and fingering one or two which interested him but keeping his own hand out of sight and letting the Englishman make the running. To clumsiness, on this occasion, Bevin added a surprising naivety, taking Stalin's replies at their face value and allowing himself to be lulled into forgetting that for the Russian leaders diplomacy was a contest which never ended, a game in which the moves were governed by calculation not by such irrelevancies as goodwill or understanding, although at any particular stage of the game, as now, it might be opportune to disarm suspicions and encourage hopes of agreement. The next day Bevin wrote to Miss Saunders: "I met Stalin last night, had a good talk and understandings on many points. I was encouraged but they are very difficult." Earlier in the letter, still under the influence of the Kremlin meeting, Bevin said: "We are getting ahead. This week will see things take shape, I have a quiet confidence of success, but it is too early yet to judge."

Bevin was not the only visiting politician to be impressed by Stalin's ability to present the appearance of moderation and patience when it suited him. He did not, however—like Roosevelt, for example—base anything on his impressions in practice. Where it was possible to follow proposals without compromising the position he had taken at the conference, he acted promptly. An example is the favourable reception he received to his proposal of trade talks. He got the youthful President of the Board of Trade, Harold Wilson, out to Moscow before the conference ended and on 15 April Cripps made an announcement about the talks in the House of Commons. Nor was Bevin content simply to block Russian demands, but put forward the most complete and coherent set of proposals for Germany presented by any of the four delegations. On the central issues, however, the economic unification of Germany and priority for making Germany self-supporting, he was unwilling to bargain. The Americans, it soon became clear, were equally firm.

The break in the proceedings which Molotov had suggested lasted only two days (23–24 March) but the Foreign Ministers did not return to questions of substance until the 31st: the intervening week was taken up with discussions of procedure, how to organize the future peace conference and how to deal with the report of the Allied Control Council.

On Sunday the 30th Bevin wrote again to Miss Saunders:

"I have just had lunch and now I am going for a drive into the country. It cheers one up to see the great thaw and the trees are breaking into bud. Looking out of the Embassy windows we look across to the Kremlin with its great golden domes, hideous yet beautiful. Hideous because it represents years of repression; beautiful because in spite of that it is a great design. Round it is the great wall which is symbolic of its secrecy. Few people enter, and who does no one knows what happens within it. It is typical of policy here almost impenetrable, next week must see it unfold. . . . Last week was puzzling. I have today cleared everything, made up my mind and I shall set it forth tomorrow I hope, or Tuesday at the latest."

No doubt because the sun shone from time to time and he was feeling better, Bevin's spirits rose as the conference proceeded and he began to enjoy social occasions more. After a visit to the ballet—with a supper served in the interval—he went on to the Greek Ambassador's where he ate another meal and started to drink. Dr McCall tried to stop him taking another glass of champagne: the only answer he got was a straight look in the eye as his patient downed the glass. On the way back, McCall told Bevin there was no point in his remaining: they had a row and went into the Embassy by different doors. When McCall started to pack, Bevin came into his room and asked him what he was doing. "I'm packing to go." "Oh no, you're not," he was told, "there's no plane tomorrow." Next day Bevin was contrite and apologized. In fact, he twice had sharp attacks of pain during the April meetings of the conference and had to be helped out of the room. After that, McCall sat at the back of the conference chamber and Bevin was glad to have him there.[1]

When the substantive discussions were resumed, the American Secretary of State was the first to lead off. Marshall was sparing both of unnecessary words and emotion: the firmness with which he now spoke made all the more impression. A paper agreement on the economic and political unity of Germany, he said, was no good: they had had that at Potsdam but it had not been implemented. Nor did he believe it was possible to proceed by ultimatum, either a Russian ultimatum on reparations from current production—which the USA regarded as no part of Potsdam—or a French one on coal deliveries —which the USA also could not accept. He was not clear, he remarked, that these conflicts could be remedied. The USA wanted Germany to be treated as an economic unity: that had priority, for they wished to avoid both a divided Germany and a divided Europe. But they were not seeking an agreement for agreement's sake: "The U.S. recognises that its responsibilities in Europe will continue"—a sentence which everyone around the table weighed carefully —"and it is more concerned in building solidly than in building fast."

Marshall then left Bevin to set out in detail a British plan for restoring the economic unity of Germany and proceeding to the first stages of recreating its political unity as a federal state. A great deal of hard work had gone into this set of proposals which Bevin's staff referred to as "the new Potsdam". They were presented as a supplement to the original Potsdam agreement (no one could ever afford to admit they were not adhering to the Potsdam principles) and represented a British not an Anglo–American initiative, although most of it

[1] McCall's personal account to the author.

was common ground between the two Western Powers.[1] The need to settle the plant and equipment to be provided as reparations (by 15 August 1947) and to hasten deliveries was recognized in the plan; this was one of the reasons for raising the level of German industry, with a steel-making capacity of 10 million tons as the key figure. Nothing, however, was said of the figure of 10 billion dollars to which the Russians attached so much importance and it was clear that priority was to be given to agreement on the economic unification of Germany (including the Soviet zone) by 1 July 1947 and to the achievement of a balanced economy which would enable the Germans to pay for essential imports with the proceeds of their exports without external assistance.

To leave no doubts, Bevin introduced the British plan with a statement which listed those features of it not accepted by the Russians and the French and rejected the conditions which they sought to impose as the price of their agreement. The British, he announced, could not agree to reparations being taken from current production, since this was incompatible with using exports to make Germany self-supporting; neither would they place the Ruhr under four-power control nor give up the merger of the British and American zones, until the unification of all four zones had been effected. They would accept the French claims to the Saar but not to the separation of the Ruhr and the Rhineland; and while agreeing that France's demands for coal must be met, were opposed to making this a formal condition of a settlement with Germany.

The only point Molotov found acceptable—but not Bidault—was the proposal to raise the level of industry, but this (as Marshall pointed out) would mean a reduction in the number of plants available for reparations. Bevin was prepared not to pre-judge what might be done after an economic balance had been restored and the UK had recovered the costs of keeping Germany alive, but this had to come first. "They could then see what sort of a country they were dealing with."

Paradoxically, while the Foreign Ministers could not reach agreement on the policy to be pursued, they got some way on the machinery for implementing it if they could: a central German administration, working under the Allied Control Council, and a German advisory council. Once they tried to go beyond that and establish the constitution of a future German state, they were as deeply divided as ever. At this point—they were now at their 24th meeting on 9 April—Marshall started a new subject of discord, by proposing a boundary commission to settle the Polish–German frontier and provide compensation for the loss of Polish territory to Russia. In the American view, he added, the southern part of East Prussia and Upper Silesia should go to Poland, but the division of the remaining territory, which was largely agricultural and could help to restore the balance of the German economy, required further consideration. Molotov would not admit that the matter was open for discussion. There was no question, he declared, of compensating

[1] It was published by the Foreign Office on 31 March and is printed in RIIA *Documents 1947–48*, pp. 453–62.

Poland for the transfer of territory to Russia. The new Poland had willingly given up territory occupied by Byelorussians and Ukrainians and been glad to acquire lands in the West which were the cradle of the Polish state—an act of historical justice which gave Poland back her true frontiers. The decisions taken at Potsdam were fundamental, they could not be reversed and all the CFM had to do was formally to confirm them.

Bidault took advantage of this discussion of frontiers to put forward the French proposals for separating the Rhineland from Germany and taking ownership as well as control of the Ruhr industries out of German hands. Bidault already knew that he would get no support from the British and the Americans, but this time the Russians turned him down as well. Molotov would not even agree to a decision on the Saar (which Bevin and Marshall were prepared to make there and then) without further consideration. This was a bitter blow for Bidault, in effect marking the end of the French attempt to pursue an independent policy on Germany by balancing between the Russian and Anglo–American positions.

Although the Deputies laboured away to reduce, or at least define, the differences on the organization of the conference which was to conclude peace with Germany, it was by now clear that no draft of a treaty to submit to it was going to emerge from the Moscow meetings. However, there were drafts of two other treaties which the Americans still hoped might be accepted before the Council broke up, and the remainder of the Conference was largely devoted to their discussion.

At the session on 14 April Marshall asked for a decision on the four-power treaty to keep Germany disarmed for 25 years which Byrnes had tabled at the Council Meeting in Paris the year before. Bevin was still as strongly in favour as he had been from the beginning and announced that he was authorized to accept the US draft as a working basis and appoint plenipotentiaries to conclude a final text. Bidault wanted some changes in the draft but also welcomed Marshall's suggestion to agree in principle and put in hand negotiations on detail. Molotov, however, announced that, in the Soviet view, the Treaty did not go far enough. He therefore wished to add a number of new provisions—such as putting the Ruhr under four-power control and the establishment of a democratic state. As Marshall at once objected, these were appropriate to a peace treaty not to Byrnes' proposal, and, as Bevin pointed out, were simply the same subjects they had been arguing about for weeks without reaching agreement. Having asked Molotov plainly if he was prepared to negotiate quickly a treaty aimed solely at the demilitarization of Germany—he had had affirmative answers from Britain and France, what about Russia?—and having got in return further qualifications, but no answer, Marshall suggested they should pass on to the next item: he could draw his own conclusions.

The other Treaty was to make a peace settlement with Austria, and a detailed draft was ready for the Foreign Ministers to approve. They agreed to let the Yugoslavs come to Moscow and make their case for the cession of 2,600 square kilometres of Carinthia and Styria and $150 m. in reparations. The Austrian Foreign Minister, Gruber, put the Austrian case; to no one's surprise, the Russians supported the Yugoslavs, the three Western Powers the Austrians. Nonetheless, it was not this but the question of German assets in Austria which ended any hope of signing an Austrian treaty in Moscow. What the Russians were asking, it was pointed out to them, amounted to the right to decide for themselves what was a German asset, to assume its ownership free of all mortgages and other liabilities and to operate it entirely outside the framework of Austrian law. The greater part of Austria's industrial capacity was in the Soviet zone and Russian claims were estimated to cover 300 plants which were not to be removed but to produce entirely for the Russians, two-thirds of Austria's oil production, three-quarters of her refining capacity and three-quarters of the Danube Steamship Company's fleet of barges and tugs. The Soviet Union had agreed in the Moscow Declaration of 1943 not to seek reparations from Austria; what she now proposed would have reduced the small country to the status of a dependency with a large part of its economy owned by the Soviet Union.

In an effort to break the deadlock the Foreign Ministers appointed an Austrian Treaty Commission which met in Vienna eighty-five times between May and October.[1] Bevin's instructions to the British representative were to eschew formulas and work out a new approach, from the particular to the general, by discovering the (often complicated) facts about the ownership of the assets claimed by the Russians. The question was no nearer to a solution when the London meeting of the CFM took place in December, but at least the facts had been dug out and published—without producing any change in the Russian attitude.

Marshall had deliberately delayed his meeting with Stalin until he could see what agreements the conference was likely to reach. When he finally went to the Kremlin, on the late evening of 15 April, although he spoke as calmly as ever, he left Stalin in no doubt of what he thought.[2] He began by reviewing the deterioration of relations between the USSR and the USA, spoke of the cooling of American wartime sympathy with the Russian people and mentioned a number of Soviet actions and positions which had contributed to this. The conference, he said, had come to an impasse that very afternoon on the treaty for the demilitarization of Germany; he had reached the conclusion that the Soviet Union did not want such a treaty and would report accordingly to the President.

Leaving the conference aside, Marshall observed that the USA recognized the right of any country to live under the kind of political and economic system

---

[1] The best published record of its proceedings is in FRUS 1947 (2).

[2] See the US record in FRUS (2) pp. 337–414. The Americans gave a copy to the British which is in FO 800/502/SU/47/38. See also W. Bedell Smith: *Moscow Mission 1946–49* (London 1950) pp. 210–12.

it wanted, but the USA was determined to give all the assistance it could to countries threatened with economic collapse and—as a result—with the collapse of any hopes of preserving democracy. The American intention was to give help in so far as it could to restore the economy of those countries. They did not seek to dominate any country but he felt, he concluded, that if he spoke frankly, it might clear away suspicions and improve understanding.

Stalin, who had sat impassively while Marshall spoke, puffing at his cigarette or doodling, did not say anything, until the American had finished. Speaking in the same quiet tone as Marshall, he then reviewed and defended the main Russian positions at the conference. But, he remarked, it was wrong to give too tragic an interpretation to their present disagreements. There had been differences before, but as a rule when people had exhausted themselves in disputes, they came to recognize the need for compromise. These were "only the first skirmishes and brushes of reconnaissance forces". Compromises were possible on all the principal questions, including demilitarization, reparations, economic unity and the political structure of Germany. It was only necessary to have patience and not give way to pessimism.

As in Bevin's case, Stalin's expressions of goodwill did not affect the toughness of Molotov's tactics at the conference table. Perhaps to their own surprise the Foreign Ministers settled easily the problem of interim financing for the Trieste Free Territory, but when the Deputies presented their summary of the points on which Ministers had agreed and disagreed, the fruits of six weeks' meetings and months of preparation in advance were meagre enough. Outside the conference, the three Western Foreign Ministers reached agreement on meeting France's coal requirements. Molotov protested at this "unilateral" action, but as Marshall pointed out, was on weak ground since the Russians had hitherto refused to take part in a four-power scheme for the allocation of coal and had insisted on keeping the Soviet zone's coal production for their own use.

Ministers' final statements firmly placed the blame for the failure of the conference on the other side and at the last meeting (the 43rd) on the afternoon of 24 April, they found a new subject on which to disagree. Marshall proposed a reduction in occupation forces in order to make fewer demands on the German economy. Molotov agreed and promptly suggested cutting the American and British forces combined to the same size as the Russian (200,000) and the French from 70,000 to 50,000. All three Western ministers protested and the matter was referred to the Allied Control Council—where the generals proved no more capable of reaching agreement than their political masters. It was at least agreed to meet in London in November and (pace Bevin, who wanted to put the Austrian treaty first) to settle the agenda through diplomatic channels. The longest of all the Foreign Ministers' meetings had ended with less agreed than at any of their other conferences.

6

Before the Conference ended Bevin sent Attlee a personal letter in which he summed up his view of Soviet objectives (16 April).

"The Russians clearly want to create a situation in which everyone will forget what they have done in their Zone and we shall be forced to ignore the hundreds of millions we have put into our Zone and the Americans into their Zone, and that they shall be able to come in, disregarding all this, force the British and American taxpayer to stand it, rehabilitate their own Zone at our expense and then on top of that get reparations from current production."

The discussions, he reported, had been "cold, frank but firm". He particularly regretted the Russian rejection of the American proposal for a Four Power Treaty. "If the Russians had accepted it, a bridge could have been built and the antagonism growing so fast in the U.S.A. would have been checked." It was "sickening and saddening" to see such a great opportunity thrown away: "Russia has made a bad mistake, as bad as when she linked up with Hitler in 1939."

He had begun discussions, he told the Prime Minister, on the Anglo–Soviet Treaty, but added that he thought it would be too risky to go an inch beyond the Dunkirk treaty with France. "It looks," he concluded, "as if we are getting perilously near a position in which a line-up is taking place." Before coming to Moscow he had hoped this could be avoided, but he was no longer so confident. "There is courtesy, there are no high words being used, no tempers, but all of it is cool, calculated and between the two big boys looks to me to be pretty determined."[1]

Marshall, when he delivered a broadcast report to the nation on his return home, did nothing to conceal or soften the conflict between American and Soviet policy on Germany. He quoted Stalin's remark, that these were only "the first skirmishes and brushes of reconnaissance forces" and that "although people had exhausted themselves in dispute, they then recognised the necessity of compromise".

"I sincerely hope that the Generalissimo is correct in the view he expressed and that it implies a greater spirit of co-operation by the Soviet Delegation in future conferences. But we cannot ignore the factor of time. . . . The recovery of Europe has been far slower than had been expected. Disintegrating forces are becoming evident. The patient is sinking while the doctors deliberate. So I believe that action cannot await compromise through exhaustion. New issues arise daily. Whatever action is possible to meet these pressing problems must be taken without delay."[2]

When Bevin addressed the Commons on 15 May, he reminded the House that he had warned it not to expect too much of the Moscow meeting and

---

[1] Bevin to Attlee, 16 April 1947. FO 800/447/CONF/47/7.
[2] 18 April 1947. RIIA *Documents 1947–48*, pp. 471–481.

suggested it was only if they failed to make progress at the next Council of Foreign Ministers in November, that it would then become impossible to "prophesy the course the world will take".[1] However, while he did not rule out a change of tactics by the Russians, which would make agreement easier, Bevin was resolved not to let the hope of securing the economic unity of all Germany any longer hold up plans for making the Bi-zone economically self-sufficient, and he began to urge this on Marshall well before the end of the Moscow conference. Lunching with the Secretary of State on 5 April he came out strongly for a prompt revision of the level of industry figure and a fresh determination of what could and could not be made available for reparations. He spoke of British and Americans getting together to deal with a situation in Germany which was "urgent for correction".

The German food position in the spring of 1947 was as bad as it had ever been, and this despite imports of food into the Bi-zone in the four months January–April which cost the Americans and British 163 million dollars. In April the Ruhr miners went on strike in protest at their rations and the possibility that there might be other strikes and demonstrations while the Moscow conference was going on worried Bevin enough for him to write to Attlee and urge that something be done to distribute more food.[2] The initial plans for organizing the Bi-zone had failed; re-organization was urgent and admitted to be so, but had been put off on the chance that the Moscow conference might alter the situation. Above all, the Germans showed little sign of the energy they were later to display in helping themselves, and Bevin was convinced that so long as there was so much uncertainty about their future, they never would. He believed this to be the Russians' trump card, their ability to prolong the uncertainty as long as it suited them. The only way round the impasse was not to accept their veto but to set to work to restore life and hope to the western zones at least.

Bevin was particularly concerned to get agreement with Marshall before they left Moscow on the steps to be taken, and at a meeting on 8 April he urged that a new level of industry should be fixed for the Bi-zone with an annual figure for steel production of 10 million tons.[3] The British plan called for the bi-zonal agencies, which had been deliberately placed in different centres, to be concentrated in Frankfurt and for an advisory council to be set up with representatives of the German political parties and trade unions; it also proposed a review of the plants to be made available for reparations in the light of the new level of industry to be allowed in Germany, followed by removal and delivery as soon as possible.

The Americans felt they were being hustled and there was strong resistance to the British initiative from General Clay, the US Military Governor in Germany. Clay, who took a Roman view of his proconsular position, was

---

[1] HC, 15 May 1947.
[2] Bevin to Attlee, 29 March 1947, and Attlee's reply on the 30th. FO 800/GER/47/19–20.
[3] Note of Bevin's talk with Marshall, 8 April. FO 800/502/SU/47/35.

responsible to the War Department and had long been critical of State Department policy in Europe. He disliked the idea of decisions being taken about Germany anywhere else than in Berlin, had been very reluctant to go to Moscow for the conference and had left again as soon as he could. Reports of Clay's opposition to the Berlin plan led Bevin to write to Marshall on 14 April saying that he had heard

"That certain difficulties had arisen and that the discussions were not going perhaps as smoothly as was intended. . . . There has even been an indication given that it might be better to cancel these arrangements and work our own Zones separately. . . . In the circumstances I very much hope that on your way through Berlin you will be able to spare the time to go into the whole position."[1]

Four days later, Bevin got Marshall to agree to a memorandum which made the British proposals the basis for detailed discussions with the proviso by Marshall that any public announcements should be delayed in order to avoid the charge that the Western powers had come to Moscow with a plan to go ahead without the Russians. On his way back to the States, Marshall found time to see Clay for an hour at the Tempelhof aerodrome in Berlin and to impress on him the urgency of making the Bi-zone self-sufficient as soon as possible. Marshall's intervention, however, did not settle the matter.

Much of the trouble was a continuation of the long-standing dispute between Clay and the War Department on the one hand and the State Department on the other. The US Army was saddled with responsibility for the occupation of Germany; it did not wish to be held responsible either for a breakdown of the German economy or for exasperating Congress by continually asking for the appropriations needed to prevent this. Having failed to hand over its duties, apart from security, to a civilian agency responsible to the State Department, Clay and his staff were inclined to look at American policy towards the rest of Europe from their point of view in Berlin, a view not always acceptable to the State Department, which had other considerations to bear in mind as well and regarded for example the strengthening of France as one of the United States' prime objectives, even if this meant putting up with French obstruction of American policy in Germany.

Clay objected to the British proposals for two separate reasons. He argued, first, that the plan to which Marshall had agreed to cut US and British occupation costs, had not faced up to the difficulties. Germany was virtually bankrupt and had no funds with which to buy raw materials and start up the export-import programme on which the British were relying. It could only do this and get back on its feet economically by taking measures—such as restricting German coal exports to countries like France and charging economic prices for everything exported, including coal—which would lead to a storm of protest from the countries which had suffered from German occupa-

---

[1] Bevin to Marshall, 14 April 1947. FRUS 1947 (2) pp. 490–91.

tion, on the grounds that this was to give priority to the reconstruction of the German economy over their own.

Clay's second objection was of a quite different character. The British would expect the Americans to contribute the greater part of the funds needed to make the Bi-zone programme work, and Clay claimed that the Labour Government was planning to introduce socialist measures quite unacceptable to American opinion.[1]

According to Clay, Robertson had told him that he must have an agreement before Bevin arrived in Berlin on his way back from Moscow. Whether this was so or not, Clay had clearly convinced himself that the British were trying to exploit the situation for long term political ends. In a message to Marshall he declared:

"I am sure that these terms are not consistent with our political objectives in Germany and even more sure that they would not be acceptable to the American business men and bankers on whom we must depend in the final analysis for the success, not only of our [i.e. Germany's] export program, but for subsequent financing to enlarge the export program. I regret that the problem has to pass to governmental level but see no other recourse."[2]

Fortunately, after talking to Bevin Robertson was able to reassure Clay that no immediate decision was necessary and that there was time to make a careful study of the British proposals. American opposition was to be made unequivocally clear in the course of the summer, but for the moment was not enforced. Once Clay got down to negotiations with Robertson and their political advisers, Murphy and Strang, they were able to reach agreement on the reorganization of the Bi-zone[3] in time for Bevin to announce it at the Labour Party Conference on 29 May.

The most important innovation was the establishment of an Economic Council, and an Executive Committee, both composed of representatives of the several Länder, which would undertake the economic reconstruction of the two zones as an integrated economic area. The work of the Economic Council and the Executive Committee was subject to review and approval by an Allied Bipartite Board and everyone denied that the changes were intended as a first step towards setting up a German government. Bevin hoped, however, that they went far enough in giving the Germans responsibility to get the economic life of the Western zones going again. The other step for which he had pressed in Moscow, revision of the level of industry, was also agreed between the British and Americans by mid-July, although, as we shall see, the new figures, based on an annual steel production of 10.7 million tons, nearly

[1] FRUS 1947 (2) p. 909.
[2] FRUS 1947 (2) pp. 910–11.
[3] Bevin's report to Attlee, 14 May 1947. FO 800/466/GER/47/27.

twice the March 1946 limit,[1] had acquired a different significance by the time they were published at the end of August.

Bevin was entitled to feel, therefore, that, in taking over responsibility for the British Zone, he had broken the deadlock and had produced results by the initiative he had taken, before leaving Moscow, to press on with the reorganization of the Bi-zone and not wait to see whether the Foreign Ministers would get any nearer to four-power agreement in their November meeting. But the context in which he and Marshall had agreed on his proposals in mid-April was changed out of recognition by the beginning of June. Bevin was concerned, as Britain's economic situation forced him to be, with restoring the viability of the German economy in order to end the drain of the British Zone on Britain's dollar reserves. But once Marshall was back in Washington, as Clay had foreseen, it was the importance of Europe's, not just the Bi-zone's recovery, and the contribution German resources (above all, German coal) could make to this which came to occupy his and his advisers' minds.

In his broadcast of 28 April, the Secretary of State described the economic rehabilitation of Germany as something demanding immediate decision but put it in the context of European recovery and spoke of Germany as "the vital center of Europe". In another report to the nation, John Foster Dulles, the Republican spokesman on foreign affairs, who had been an influential member of the American delegation at Moscow, said: "As we studied the problem of Germany in its European setting, we became more and more convinced that there is no economic solution along purely national lines." The studies which the State Department now began to produce were based on the assumption that a way could be found for fitting the rehabilitation of the German economy, which Marshall had agreed to with Bevin in Moscow, into the wider context of a European recovery and overcoming the conflict between the two which Clay had foreseen. It was out of the search for such a framework that Marshall's offer of American aid to Europe emerged.

Bevin needed no convincing of the validity of the arguments which led Marshall to this conclusion, but only the Americans had the resources to give effect to it. Once they did, he showed by the vigour with which he seized upon Marshall's offer in his Harvard speech in June, how great a contribution he could make in turning it into an effective programme. In the meantime he had to wait, as he had earlier in the case of Greece, to see what the Americans would come up with, now that the Moscow conference was over.

---

[1] The March 1946 figure for steel *production* was 5.8 million tons in any single year. This has to be distinguished from the figure for steel-making *capacity* which was fixed at 7.5 million tons. The 1947 agreement simply said that sufficient capacity would be retained to give an annual production of 10.7 million tons.

CHAPTER 10

Marshall's offer, Bevin's response

I

Bevin had set out for Moscow depressed and feeling ill. He returned in good spirits and much better health, at once impressing his colleagues with the recovery of his old confidence and power of decision. For other Labour Ministers, as Dalton says, 1946 had been a year of "triumphant ease"; 1947 was much more difficult and, under its growing pressures, "our self-confidence weakened, individually and collectively".[1] With Bevin, it was the other way round: by April 1947 his worst period as Foreign Secretary was over and the rest of 1947, for all the difficulties he had to contend with, was a year in which he both felt and showed himself equal to mastering them, at least in Europe.

As a result of his experience in Moscow Bevin had made up his mind that the Western Powers could no longer allow Russia's refusal to agree to inhibit them from acting on their own, out of anxiety lest this should lead them to a divided Germany or a divided Europe. He had insisted that the prospects which he had presented at Moscow should still be based upon the assumption that the four Powers could reach agreement on the future of a single Germany, and the Foreign Office had put a lot of work into the preparation of what was described as "the new Potsdam". The only result had been to make clear once again the gap which separated the British and American from the Soviet view. This time however Bevin was prepared to draw the conclusion that they could no longer sit down under the Soviet veto. The longer they hesitated to act, the more the Russians would be confirmed in their belief that they had only to hold out long enough for the Western Powers either to capitulate to their demands, or for the Americans at least to lose interest and withdraw. Even if that did not happen, the Western Powers might well find, if they delayed much longer, that they had left it too late to prevent a mood of despair in Germany and an economic and moral collapse in Europe which could only work to Russia's advantage. Bevin

[1] Dalton, pp. 236–7.

recognized, even before he returned to London, that if this was to be avoided, the British and Americans must press ahead with the rehabilitation of Germany. Until the Council of Foreign Ministers met again in London at the end of the year, Bevin maintained, at least in public, the hope that the Russians might alter their tactics and still agree to a settlement acceptable to both sides. But he was no longer prepared to make action conditional upon keeping this possibility open, and in that sense the Moscow meeting represents the real watershed in British policy.

It is of course true that, if the Americans had not come to the same conclusion at the same time, Bevin's resolution of the conflict which had hitherto inhibited him—between fear of taking action which might close off any chance of agreement with Russia and anxiety over the consequences for Europe of not taking action in time—would have produced little if anything in the way of practical results. Nonetheless, as his initiative in pressing Marshall to start on reorganizing the Bi-zone shows, it was a resolution independently arrived at, with the great advantage that the parallel reaction of the Americans to their experience in Moscow at least opened the possibility of the resources for action, which Britain no longer commanded, being made available.

Bevin waited a long time for American policy to evolve from the position taken by Byrnes at the first Moscow conference, in December 1945, to that taken by Marshall at the second, in April 1947. From the beginning of his foreign secretaryship he had believed that, without American strength, Britain alone could neither secure a satisfactory settlement with the Russians nor face the consequences of not securing one at all. As late as March 1947 he had not been certain that the USA would take over the burden Britain could no longer sustain of supporting Greek and Turkish independence. After Moscow and the firmness with which Marshall, from a shaky start, had met the Russian manoeuvring, any doubts Bevin had left were soon to disappear. The new relationship between the two super-powers posed problems of its own for a weakened Britain which Bevin had no intention of seeing become a satellite of the United States. But the relief of feeling that he no longer had to stand up to Russian pressure on his own was immense and it was not surprising that on his return from Moscow, even before the changed American attitude took concrete shape in Marshall's offer of 5 June, he should have told Dalton that he looked forward hopefully to the next phase in foreign policy.

Relief from the strain of 1946 came in another form as well during 1947. For all the truculence with which he met the attacks of the Left, Bevin had been discouraged as well as wounded by the November amendment criticizing his foreign policy; even more perhaps by the discovery, on his return from America, that he could no longer rely on Attlee's and the Cabinet's support in holding out against withdrawal from Greece and the Eastern Mediterranean. In the winter of 1946–7, Bevin felt keenly that he was being left to face as difficult a situation abroad as any Foreign Secretary had ever had to meet, with little understanding among his ministerial colleagues of what was at stake and even less disposition to come to his support against his critics in the Labour Party.

At first sight the situation did not change much in the spring of 1947. The Government felt obliged to make concessions to Labour opponents of conscription who mustered 72 Labour votes against it (plus some 20 deliberate abstentions) when the National Service Bill was given its second reading in March. The proposed period of service was then cut from 18 months to 12, a retreat which led to much criticism of Attlee's leadership. Most of the opponents of Bevin's foreign policy took the opportunity to vote against the Government, although a number, like Crossman, were not opposed to conscription as such. Zilliacus, for example, wrote to the *New Statesman* that he opposed the Bill not on principle but because young men might be required to give their lives for bad causes, to support the Government's decisions in Greece or Palestine, or as "cannon fodder" for Wall Street's campaign against world socialism.[1] Ernest Millington expressed his fears that the real purpose of the Bill was "to put an iron glove on the fist of the Foreign Secretary which he is so fond of shaking at the leaders of the U.S.S.R."[2] Bevin was in Moscow at the time, or there might have been stronger resistance in the Cabinet to compromising with the critics. He was too familiar, however, with the history of opposition to conscription in the Labour Party to attach too much importance to the revolt and, pleased with a hand-written letter from Attlee, wrote back cheerfully to tell him not to worry.

"I realised it was chiefly the Welsh and I always anticipated that they and a few conscientious objectors would oppose. It does me good to see you are in such good fighting trim in the face of all your other difficulties—I am well."[3]

More serious was the publication at the beginning of May of the pamphlet *Keep Left*,[4] written by Richard Crossman, Michael Foot and Ian Mikardo, and signed by another twelve MPs as well, all members of a group which met regularly in the House of Commons. The pamphlet covered domestic as well as foreign and defence policy but its tone in discussing the latter was much sharper; this was the real target of the group's criticism. Their principal objection was that "Britain had been driven into a dangerous dependence on the U.S.A." Despite the confusion of British policy, there ran through it "one single and disturbing consistent note—a readiness to follow American strategic thinking". The authors recognized that Britain could not break suddenly with the USA and throw in her lot with Russia. She had to "regain her independence" but was not strong enough to do so by herself. Their

---

[1] *New Statesman*, April 1947.
[2] The Commons debate took place on 31 March and 1 April 1947.
[3] Bevin to Attlee, 5 April 1947. FO 800/493/PLT/47/5.
[4] The pamphlet was published by the *New Statesman*. Amongst the signatories were George Wigg, Stephen Swingler, Geoffrey Bing, and Woodrow Wyatt.

solution was to create a "Third Force" in the shape of a European Socialist alliance based on Britain and France: "working together, we are still strong enough to hold the balance of world power, to halt the division into a Western and Eastern bloc and so to make the United Nations a reality." They regretted the policy (which they attributed to Churchill and by implication to Bevin) of acting as America's junior partner in an alliance system of collective security against Communism: this was a counsel of despair which meant a third world war. A socialist Britain must try to heal the breach between the USA and the USSR. It should also withdraw completely from the Middle East, internationalize the Dardanelles and Suez and guarantee the integrity of Iran and the Arab states by a Great-Power treaty. The peaceful development of Africa rather than holding the Middle East by force was the way to defeat Communism.

The fact that within a few weeks of *Keep Left*'s publication, the economies of France, Britain and the rest of Western Europe were only saved from collapse by the promise of greatly increased American aid shows how unrealistic at that time was the proposal of a European Third Force, led by Britain and France, which would end Europe's dependence on the USA, hold the balance of world power and mediate between Russia and America. But it had a strong appeal to those in the Labour Movement who could not bring themselves to accept either a breach with the Soviet Union, a close relationship with capitalist America or a world governed by power politics.

Amongst Bevin's papers is a note from Gladwyn Jebb in which, identifying the author of this part of *Keep Left* as C(rossman) he makes the comment:

"Much of what C. says would have appeared sensible two years or even eighteen months ago. Indeed all our own papers were then based on the assumption that there should in no circumstances be any Anglo–U.S. line-up against the U.S.S.R. or indeed against Communism, until such time at any rate as the Soviets should have made it abundantly clear that they did not intend to co-operate with the West. It will be recalled with what passionate conviction the F.O. represented this thesis to the Chiefs of Staff and what care was taken to prevent even the smallest whisper getting round that we favoured the Americans rather than the Russians. . . . With the advent of the Labour Government (as C. admits) a fresh and determined effort was made to secure this vital co-operation."[1]

Keep Left had been published with a view to influencing the Labour Party conference at Margate, and Bevin had a meeting with the Party's Foreign Affairs Group to suggest that the Foreign Office might co-operate with Transport House in publishing a reply. To his surprise, and pleasure, he discovered that a pamphlet was already being written inside Transport House to be published under Labour Party auspices. The initiative had been taken by

[1] 5 May 1947. FO 800/493/PLT/47/8. Jebb's description of the FO attitude towards Russia in the later stages of the war is borne out by the wartime documents now available. See Victor Rothwell: *Britain & the Cold War 1941–47* (London 1982) cc. 2–3.

Morgan Phillips, (the Party Secretary), Hugh Dalton (as a member of the National Executive) and Denis Healey, at that time Secretary of the Labour Party's International Department. They put out in May a pamphlet, *Cards on the Table*, written by Healey, which vigorously supported Bevin's foreign policy.

"No Labour man blames Aneurin Bevan for the housing shortage but many seem to think that Ernest Bevin is personally responsible for the apparent deterioration in relations between the Big Three since 1945. . . . Even more seem to imagine that in 1945 the Labour Government could survey the world scene free from any immediate problems or commitments and choose . . . the precise policy best calculated to achieve a world socialist millenium."

For once Bevin had the case for his policy put for him by one of the ablest young men in the Labour Party, whose intellectual powers were fully equal to those of the *Keep Left* group and who wrote with a force and economy which Bevin could never achieve. The pamphlet is notable for a forthrightness of language which was a refreshing change in the Labour Party's discussion of foreign policy, hitherto dominated by the Left. Healey wrote of "a sustained and violent offensive against Britain by her Russian ally. . . . They thought they could see the British empire crumbling and that expansion to fill Britain's place in Europe and the Middle East would be easy".

"The attempt to destroy Britain's freedom of initiative," he continued, "was double-edged. On the one hand Russia opened a series of propaganda attacks through U.N. and the international Communist machine which aimed at isolating Britain morally as a decadent reactionary power. British policy in Greece, Syria, Indonesia, Spain and Palestine was a special target and though in every case submitted to the U.N. for judgment, Britain was wholly cleared of all accusations, much of the mud stuck. . . .
    On the other hand, there was an attempt to tip the scales against Britain in importance strategic areas, by diplomacy and direct action—in Trieste, Northern Persia and the Dardanelles, Greece, Turkey and Eastern Europe."[1]

Healey's second line of argument was to attack the suggestion that Britain was being dragged into conflict with the Soviet Union through Bevin's pursuit of a Churchillian policy of alliance with dollar imperialism. He pointed out that

"The idea that we should have extricated ourselves from the quarrel between Russia and the U.S.A. does not make sense; during the period under review, Britain was the main target of Russian hostility of which, until a few months ago, America was an undecided spectator."[2]

---

[1] *Cards on the Table* published by the Labour Party, London, May 1947, pp. 12–13.
[2] *Ibid.*, p. 18.

Britain's co-operation with the United States was based on pragmatic not ideological grounds:

"The aim of an Anglo–American understanding is to prevent war by proving to Russia that an aggressive anti-British policy is doomed to frustration. . . . Our hope is that sooner or later the Russians will realise that the policy they have pursued since 1945 is both impracticable and unnecessary."[1]

Finally, Healey dismissed the suggestion of *Keep Left* that Britain should have aimed at a policy completely independent of both Russia and the USA as the leader of a European bloc. However attractive at first sight, Europe and Britain were too weak to make such a policy practicable. Spelling out the extent to which both were dependent on American aid for their recovery, he concluded: "While we shall do everything possible to restore Europe as a vital and independent factor in world politics, we cannot base our policy on the assumption that this aim is already achieved."[2]

Cards on the Table, for all its simplifications and occasional lapses into casuistry, in many ways remains the best exposition of Bevin's views on the policy he had sought to pursue between 1945 and 1947. It was to be overtaken—as *Keep Left* was—by events between 1947 and 1949 when the split between East and West hardened, but in its statement of the hope that "sooner or later the Russians will realize that the policy they have pursued since 1945 is both impracticable and unnecessary" it represented an objective of which Bevin even at the height of the Cold War never lost sight. What pleased Bevin most was that someone else in the Labour Party had made the case for him. *Cards on the Table* in part reflected, in part stimulated, a shift in the mood of the Party. After the Spring of 1947, although Bevin's critics were never silenced, their numbers began to drop and, much more important (since their numbers had never been large), their influence on the rest of the Party dwindled. The tide began to flow in Bevin's favour and until his final year at the Foreign Office (1950–51), when the current changed again, he could feel, as he had never been able to in 1946, that he had first the growing support and eventually the solid backing of his Party. At the Labour Party Conference of 1949, even Crossman could declare, in a moment of enthusiasm: "We can be proud of four years of foreign policy."[3]

The Margate Conference held at the end of May 1947 came too early for this yet to show clearly, although the publication of *Cards on the Table* was very much a topic of discussion. A crop of resolutions renewed familiar criticisms on Greece, Germany, Palestine, relations with the Soviet Union, a Tory foreign policy and the class sympathies of the Diplomatic Service. Amongst the speakers were Zilliacus, Mikardo, Crossman, Millington and Tom Driberg;

[1] *Ibid.*, p. 16.
[2] *Ibid.*, p. 18.
[3] Labour Party Conference Report 1949, p. 193.

but they did not command the support they had the year before and Bevin in his reply to the debate was both more sure of himself and more relaxed.

One reason for this was that he dealt with specific issues raised from the floor and was able to give more satisfactory answers than his critics expected.[1] On Greece, for example, he could say that the USA had taken over British responsibilities, that British troops had been reduced to 5,000 and that these too were scheduled to come out in the near future. On the Dardanelles, he repeated his offer to consider revision of the Treaty of Montreux but remarked that this was a different matter from agreeing to the Russian demand for a base which would threaten Turkey's independence. On Egypt, he could say that he had done everything he could to negotiate a new treaty, and that it was the Egyptians who had broken off negotiations, on the issue of the Sudan, not bases. He accepted Egypt's right to take the dispute to the United Nations; was confident Britain could defend her case there and argued that no one was entitled to tear up a treaty which still had ten years to run just because they wanted to. On Palestine too he could say that the dispute was now before the United Nations and that Britain had taken it there—strong arguments with a Labour Party conference most of whose members still hankered after a foreign policy based on the United Nations.

And why not, Bevin asked. Britain's record in the UN was a good one. In the previous year, despite her financial difficulties, she had contributed nearly £8m (at 1946 values) to the organizations created by the UN. But there were practical difficulties and he cited the case of the Corfu Channel incident in which the Albanians had fired on British ships and killed 44 men. Instead of retaliating in the old style, he had taken the case to the Security Council where an overwhelming majority reached a decision in favour of Britain—and Russia vetoed it. Bevin made the telling point that it was one thing to use the veto where fundamental principles were involved or there was a question of war, "but where you are trying to keep tempers down and to use the arbitration machinery of the Security Council, I feel that this use of the veto was a grave abuse of what was intended."

He was told that it was thanks to his "unfortunate" policy that Britain had to maintain so many troops abroad. How many were there? 400,000 troops had been got out of the great wartime base in Egypt without the loss of a single soldier, and by the end of 1948 the number would be down to the 10,000 stipulated by the 1936 Treaty. In Indonesia there were no longer any British forces and the British Government had done everything in its power to bring about the settlement between the Dutch and Indonesia's Republican Government at Linggadjati. Within 90 days of the Italian peace treaty being ratified, 54,000 British troops were due to move out leaving only 5,000 until the new status of the Trieste territory was established and the Governor appointed.

[1] 29 May 1947. Labour Party Conference Report 1947: Debate, pp. 160–75; Bevin's reply, pp. 175–82.

The largest number of troops overseas was required for occupation duties: but in Germany the Allied Control Council was considering an American proposal to reduce all the occupying forces, and as for Austria, "Have I not travailed now for two years to get an Austrian treaty?" Bevin was able to announce agreement on the reorganization of the Bi-zone and point to the vindication of the original British figure for the level of German industry, now accepted by both the Americans and Russians as the right one. Finally he took a resolution calling on the Government to speed up trade with Russia. He had been trying to do so for eighteen months and at long last had got an answer. "We shall not delay. We are waiting on the doorstep."

There was more than a touch of the old Bevin restored in his final words:

"When I entered on this job two years ago, I said that if anybody expected me to produce great results within less than four or five years, they would be disillusioned. . . . That is why I have cultivated, for the first time in my life, as all my colleagues will agree, a quite remarkable patience. I must have been born again. . . . I am hoping—only hoping—that by next November we shall have said so much to one another that we shall be tired of talking and will be ready to agree instead."

2

At the end of March Dalton formally warned the Cabinet that they were racing through the US and Canadian dollar loans at an alarming and accelerating speed.

"This, I said, was a looming shadow of catastrophe, 'and I will not have it said hereafter that I have left my colleagues unwarned until the eleventh hour.' "[1]

Among the reasons which the Treasury gave were the rise in dollar prices (by 40% since the Loan had been negotiated) so that its value had correspondingly depreciated; the lag in restoring the production of food and raw materials in the rest of the world which meant expensive purchases in dollars from the USA; continued dollar expenditure on the British Zone of Germany; the energy crisis in the winter which had set back by nine months the rise in exports, and thus the increased ability to pay for imports; the failure to produce enough coal, so that Britain, once a major exporter of coal, now had to import it. On 12 May Dalton told the American Ambassador that the rate at which the UK was drawing on the loan meant that it would be exhausted by the beginning of 1948. This could only lead to the British defaulting on the terms of the loan, the obligation to make sterling convertible (due to take effect on 15 July 1947) and to dismantle the system of imperial preferences, with all the difficulties this would create in securing Congressional approval for any

[1] Dalton, p. 221; CM 33(47) 27 March.

further grant of aid. At the very least there would have to be severe cuts in imports, including food, and in overseas expenditure, including the British contribution to the Bi-zone and British forces stationed abroad.

This was a bleak prospect for Labour ministers who were reluctant to admit publicly how serious the situation was and to impose still heavier restrictions on the British people after the discomforts of the winer. In April, Dalton noted in his diary that Cripps

"Is very strong for bringing Bevin back to the Home Front. He wants him to take charge of planning and publicity. He said, quite truly, that Bevin is the one Minister among us who can really talk to the trade unions like an uncle . . . Cripps has pressed on Attlee the desirability of this change. I am in favour of it on balance, though not so hotly as Cripps. I so informed Attlee who was very cautious."[1]

The proposal came to nothing when it was discovered that Bevin had no wish to leave the Foreign Office, and nothing more was heard of changes at the top until later in the summer. But the problems remained and no one had any idea of how to avoid the crash that seemed inevitable once sterling became convertible and the dollar loan was exhausted.

Britain was not the only country in difficulty after the severe winter. Throughout Western Europe economic recovery had not only been set back in time but appeared to be in danger of breaking down in face of crippling shortages: shortage of food; shortage of coal; and shortage of dollars with which to purchase the other two from the only country which had an exportable surplus. Economic crisis was accompanied by political crisis. First of all in Belgium, then in Italy and France (5 May) the coalitions which had included the Communists in government broke up and the Communist parties went into opposition.

Nobody knew whether de Gasperi's Christian Democratic government in Italy or Ramadier's Socialist–MRP government in France would be able to survive without Communist support, the more so in France since de Gaulle had emerged from his tent and launched a new movement, the RPF, which was as hostile to the coalition of the Centre as to the Communists. Nor did anyone know whether the Communists, in opposition, would stay within the shaky framework of the constitution. It was only two years since the end of the European War, which had been a civil war as well in Italy and close to one in France. When the British and American troops were withdrawn from Italy, would the Communists then bring out the arms they had kept hidden and resume the role of the Partisans? If they did, would they have the support of the Yugoslavs? Similar questions were asked in France where the Communists had polled five million votes at the last election and dominated the trade unions' CGT.

[1] Dalton, pp. 236–8.

During the spring the UN Preparatory Committee for an International Conference on Trade and Employment (ITO) had been meeting in Geneva and Will Clayton, the Under-Secretary of State for Economic Affairs in the State Department had led an American team in trying to break down the resistance of the British and other governments to adopting a multilateral system of free trade on the original American model. During the course of the negotiations which lasted several weeks, Clayton reluctantly came to recognize that saving Europe from economic collapse would have to take precedence over any longer-term plans. Back in Washington, at the end of May, he summarized his impressions in a note for Acheson and Marshall:

"Europe (he wrote) is steadily deteriorating. The political position reflects the economic. . . . Millions of people in the cities are slowly starving. More consumer goods and restored confidence in the local currency are absolutely essential if the peasant is again to supply food in normal quantities to the cities. . . . The modern system of division of labour has almost broken down in Europe."

After calculating the current deficit in their balance of payments of the UK, France, Italy and the Bi-zone at five million dollars a year, Clayton added that this figure was based on an absolute minimum standard of living:

"If it should be lowered, there will be a revolution. *Only until the end of this year* can England and France meet the above deficits out of their fast dwindling reserves of gold and dollars. Italy can't go that long. . . . Without further prompt and substantial aid from the U.S.A., economic, social and political disintegration will overwhelm Europe."[1]

Clayton was not the only man in Washington thinking along these lines. On 5 March, a week before Truman's address to Congress, Acheson, as Acting Secretary of State in Marshall's absence, had written to the Secretaries of War and the Navy saying that the discussions of aid to Greece and Turkey had convinced him of the need for a study of "situations elsewhere in the world which may require analogous financial, technical and military aid on our part".[2] The others agreed and a joint committee was set to work with very wide terms of reference. Marshall himself, in the broadcast he made on his return from Moscow (28 April), spoke of European recovery being "far slower than had been expected. . . . I believe that action cannot await compromise through exhaustion." The Secretary of State followed these remarks by taking up another proposal of Acheson's and putting George Kennan in charge of a Policy Planning Staff with a brief to prepare a European recovery programme. On 19 May, Kennan told Acheson the PPS had prepared a tentative list of

[1] FRUS 1947 (3) pp. 230–32. Italics in the original. It is not certain when Clayton wrote his memorandum. The copy in FRUS is dated 27 May, but there is some evidence that he drafted it on the way back from Geneva, on 19 May, and that a copy was circulating in the State Department before 27 May.
[2] *Ibid.*, pp. 197–8.

principles for "a master plan for US assistance to Western Europe".[1] Four days later, on Acheson's prompting, Kennan came up with a short term project, "Coal for Europe", based on increasing coal production in the Ruhr, and argued that the long term programme would not only require several weeks to work out but was "the business of the Europeans. The formal initiative must come from Europe; the program must be evolved in Europe; and the Europeans must bear the basic responsibility for it."[2] On 8 May, in a speech at Cleveland, Mississippi,[3] which was a preview of Marshall's June speech at Harvard, Acheson fired the first shot in the most difficult part of the operation, the campaign which the Administration would have to undertake to convince a Congress with a Republican majority and American public opinion of the necessity of such a programme.

It has been forcibly argued[4] that these various activities in the State Department had not produced anything like a coherent plan, still less a programme, by the time Marshall delivered his speech at Harvard on 5 June. Kennan himself said as much and as late as 28 July one State Department official could write to another:

"The 'Marshall Plan' has been compared to a flying saucer—nobody knows what it looks like, how big it is, in what direction it is moving, or whether it really exists."[5]

The question whether German or French economic recovery was to be given priority in the crucial allocation of Ruhr coal was still unresolved and there were a host of other issues which had been neither recognized nor faced in the preliminary discussions before Marshall made his "offer". Ample proof of this is provided by the complex and difficult negotiations of the summer and autumn of 1947 in which the scope and content of the Marshall Plan were subsequently worked out.

Nonetheless, even if Marshall's Harvard speech marked the beginning not the end of the process which produced the European Recovery Programme, there is some danger that in demolishing the myths which have grown up around the Marshall Plan, revisionist historians may carry the work of demolition too far. The men most closely involved—Acheson, Kennan, Clayton, Marshall, Truman and their staffs—may not always have thought out or been in agreement about the implications or even the substance of what they were proposing, they may later have rationalized and embellished their immediate purposes, but they were clear that it was a new departure in American foreign policy, something more than a device to overcome the conflict between the State and War Departments over Germany (important though that was), an undertaking which would require exceptional efforts on their part to get Congress and the nation to accept. And if they left open to be

---

[1] *Ibid.*, pp. 220–3.
[2] Kennan to Acheson, 23 May, *ibid.*, pp. 223–30.
[3] Text in RIIA *Documents 1947–48*, pp. 17–23.
[4] By Professor John Gimbel in *The Origins of the Marshall Plan* (Stanford 1976).
[5] Moore to Wilcox, FRUS 1947 (3) pp. 239–41.

determined later, in discussion with the Europeans, the form which American aid was to take, they can just as well be praised for being realistic and for grasping the psychological importance of making a proposal in time as condemned for lack of preparation.

The decision to use Harvard's offer of an honorary degree to General Marshall as the occasion for launching the idea, even Marshall's decision to go to Harvard and receive the degree, were improvised. Acheson's speech at Cleveland had been fully reported abroad and endorsed by the President at a press conference as Administration policy. There were plenty of rumours that some new American initiative was being considered: on 15 May, for example, Raymond Aron wrote in *Combat* of "the more or less genuine news of a vast 'Lend-Lease for Peace' plan that America is about to produce". Nonetheless nothing was done to draw attention to Marshall's speech in advance. The American news agencies dismissed it with a few lines and it was not broadcast by the American networks.

It is easy to see why. Although Marshall said that any assistance which the US Government might give to help Europe's recovery "must not be on a piecemeal basis as crises develop" and spoke of American support for "a European program", he insisted that it was not for Americans "to draw up unilaterally a program designed to place Europe on its feet economically. The initiative, I think, must come from Europe. . . ."[1]

Yet Marshall had taken no steps to alert anyone in Europe to the importance of what he was going to say, considering the possibility of a message to Bevin and then deciding against for fear of offending Bidault. The British Embassy in Washington did not think it worth the cable charges to send an advance copy of the speech to London and, in face of the lack of interest shown by the American press, only three British correspondents thought it worth paying serious attention to it. The one that mattered was the despatch sent by the BBC's Washington correspondent Leonard Miall who had been tipped off in advance by Acheson.[2] For it was on a small wireless set by his bedside that Bevin first heard the report of Marshall's speech in the BBC's American commentary.

It is arguable that Bevin's action in the next few days was his most decisive personal contribution as Foreign Secretary to the history of his times. Without any advice from the British Embassy in Washington, and to the surprise of his officials, he came into the Foreign Office next morning and seized upon what was no more than a single sentence in Marshall's speech—"the initiative, I think, must come from Europe". Relying solely on his own intuitive judgement, he threw all his energy into conjuring up a European response of sufficient weight and urgency to give substance to Marshall's implied offer of American support.

---

[1] Text of the speech, June 5 1947, in RIIA *Documents 1947–48*, pp. 23–6.
[2] Leonard Miall's account, "How the Marshall Plan Started" is to be found in *The Listener* for 4 May 1961, pp. 779–81. He amplified it in a talk on Radio 3 on 29 October 1982.

"I assure you, gentlemen," he told the National Press Club in Washington later,[1] "it was like a life-line to sinking men. It seemed to bring hope where there was none. The generosity of it was beyond our belief. It expressed a mutual thing. It was 'Try and help yourselves and we will try to see what we can do. Try and do the thing collectively and we will see what we can put into the pool.' I think you understand why, therefore, we responded with such alacrity and why we grabbed the lifeline with both hands."

By the time Bevin said this, the historical importance of Marshall's Harvard speech had been accepted (perhaps too easily accepted) by everyone, but at the time it was Bevin's imagination in seeing what could be made of it and his boldness in taking the initiative which gave Marshall's remarks the resonance they needed to become effective.

3

Bevin's first move, after sending assurances to Washington that a response would be forthcoming, was to propose joint action to the French (9 June)[2] and a few days later to suggest that he should fly to Paris to see French ministers. Marshall, at a press conference on the 13th, made it clear that in referring to Europe, he included both Russia and the United Kingdom. Bidault, if only for domestic reasons, attached importance to letting the Russians know that they were planning to meet and discuss Marshall's speech, and Bevin followed suit with instructions to the British Ambassador in Moscow to tell Molotov that "the issue is an economic not a political one" and to ask for any observations the Russians might care to offer. "I am anxious," he added for the Ambassador, "to make this communication because it must be known whether the Soviet is likely to play."[3] At the same time Bevin sent messages to the Belgian and Dutch Governments to say that, as soon as he had explored the matter with the French, he proposed to bring them in.

On the 12th Bevin took one of his rare days off to receive the honorary degree of Doctor of Laws from Cambridge. Pierson Dixon, who accompanied him, expressed the pleasure of a former Cambridge don when he wrote in his diary:

"Cambridge was the most beautiful place in the world on a flawless June day. The academic ceremonial was grave and dignified, and Mr. B. got a tremendous ovation from the moment when the Public Orator addressed him as 'the best beloved scion (in Greek, ERNE) of his fatherland' and likened his efforts on behalf of his country to the labours of Hercules.

---

[1] 1 April 1949.
[2] Bevin to Duff Cooper in Paris, 9 June; and, with a timetable for following up Marshall's speech, 13 & 14 June, FO 800/465/FR/47/14–15.
[3] Bevin to Petersen, 16 June, in "European Reconstruction", a FO summary of developments between 5 June and 14 July, 1947.

"As a contrast we went after lunch to the Transport and General Workers' convalescent home at Littleport beyond Ely, where E.B. made a powerful speech to the men."

The day after, Bevin spoke to the Foreign Press Association, referring to "the most unselfish manner" in which the USA was acting and welcoming Marshall's removal of any misunderstanding by including Russia in the offer.

"We are more than ever linked with the destinies of Europe. We are in fact, whether we like it or not, a European nation and must act as such . . . [as] a link and bridge between Europe and the rest of the world."

With a reference to the cost of the two wars Britain had taken part in, he added,

"We have been the first in the ring and the last out on each occasion. Therefore it has been impossible to maintain our economic and financial position. But if anybody in the world has got it into his head that Britain is down and out, please get it out. We have our genius and science; we have our productivity, and although we have paid the price, I venture to prophesy that in a few years' time we shall have recovered our former prosperity."[1]

Before leaving for Paris, Bevin had a talk with the US Chargé in London, Gallman, and told him that he was thinking along the lines of an Anglo–French Monnet Plan (he had specially asked for Monnet to be available) and that the three important problems to be considered were food, coal and transport. In an expansive mood he told the Americans that the USA was in the same position as Britain at the end of the Napoleonic wars:

"When those wars ended, Britain held about 30% of the world's wealth. The U.S. today holds about 50%. Britain for eighteen years after Waterloo 'practically gave away her exports' but this resulted in stability and a hundred years of peace."[2]

On the 17th Bevin left for Paris taking with him a brief which throws light on the initial ideas he had thrashed out with his officials before talking with either the French or the Americans.

He was particularly anxious to avoid the initiative being taken by the Economic Commission for Europe which the United Nations had just set up and which he feared would be used by the Russians to block progress. Instead he wanted to set up an *ad hoc* steering committee before the end of June, as possible members of which he thought of Britain, France, two East European countries (Poland and Czechoslovakia), Belgium or Holland and Denmark. The USA would be free to decide whether it wished to be associated or not. All other European governments (except the Spanish) would be invited to provide information and join in the work of a series of functional committees dealing

---

[1] Speech at Foreign Press Association Lunch, 13 June 1947.
[2] Gallman to Marshall, 16 June 1947. FRUS 1947 (3) pp. 254–5.

with particular commodities such as coal and cereals. They must begin their work in time to report to the ECE meeting on 5 July and obtain its blessing by means of a covering resolution.

Bevin's intention was to make no mention of Germany unless the French raised it. He did not want to discuss a German contribution until he had got an agreed Anglo–American policy for the Bi-zone; but if the French offered to join the Bi-zone, that, of course, would be an advantage. He grasped the need to produce a report which would fire the imagination of the American people and Congress: it should give a vivid picture of the progress made towards European recovery and of Europe's plans to help itself. The British saw signs that the Americans might regard the Marshall offer as an incentive to European "integration" and were doubtful whether the US Government had realized the need to reconcile such a proposal with their other objective of multilateral trade, the basis of the US-sponsored International Trade Organization. Bevin was briefed to tell the French, if they raised the issue of European integration, that there was no time for more than a rough and ready calculation of European requirements and that it would be bad tactics to sell a plan to the USA on any basis which did not involve a return to multilateral trading as soon as possible.[1]

The American Ambassador in Paris reported that Bidault was put out by Bevin's visit, which he regarded as an attempt "to steal the show". "The truth is," the Ambassador added, "that Bidault wanted to steal the show and Bevin beat him by a day or two."[2] Dixon, however, believed that the British gesture in going to Paris was appreciated by the French and made agreement easier. The point on which French ministers insisted was the need to associate the USSR with the invitation to the other European nations. Bevin did not dissent. All he asked was a firm commitment from the French that, if the Russians used delaying or obstructive tactics, they would not tolerate them but would get on with the job of preparing a plan with the European governments which were ready to co-operate. He was also anxious that the Soviet Union should not be allowed to include political conditions unacceptable to the USA. "If they were willing to come in on the basis that there was a job to be done of a purely economic character, with the object of getting America to help to irrigate world trade, that was another question."[3]

Caffery, the US Ambassador, reported that

"The British feel that Russian participation would tend greatly to complicate things and that it might be best if Russians refused invitation."[4]

---

[1] For the brief dated 17 June 1947, see the FO summary "European Reconstruction". Refs. for this are given in footnotes 2 & 3 on p. 405.
[2] Caffery to Marshall, 16 June. FRUS 1947 (3) pp. 255–56.
[3] Bevin's talk with Bidault, 18 June, "European Reconstruction".
[4] Caffery to Marshall, 18 June, FRUS 1947 (3) p. 258.

Caffery believed the French ministers shared the same view, but thought it essential, in order to disarm domestic criticism, to issue a cordial invitation, without fixing a date so that no one could accuse them of holding a pistol to Molotov's head.

Bevin had to hurry back from Paris to take part in a Commons debate on foreign policy.[1] It was awkwardly timed and all he could say in answer to the questions put to him about Marshall's speech was that he regarded it as offering a great opportunity, had lost no time in getting things started and must now wait until he had a reply from the Russians.

When the view was expressed that Britain ought to have organized a plan for European recovery without waiting for Marshall's offer, Bevin asked:

"What did I have to organise it with? What could I offer? I had neither coal, goods nor credit. I was not in the same position as my predecessors at the end of the Napoleonic wars who devised the policy of spending our surplus exports to rehabilitate the world. . . . I have not had one ton of spare coal to ship to Western Europe to help in rehabilitation. I have had nothing with which to negotiate.

"When Mr Marshall came along and said he was willing to consider a European plan, I welcomed it. . . . I felt that it was the first chance that we had been given since the end of the war to look at the European economy as a whole. . . . I must confess to the House that I never asked him for particulars. . . . I said to myself at once—and the Cabinet agreed—'It is up to us to tell them what we want; it is up to us to produce the plan.' . . . The guiding principle that I shall follow in any talks on this matter will be speed. I spent six weeks in Moscow trying to get a settlement. I shall not be a party to holding up the economic recovery of Europe by the finesse of procedure or terms of reference. . . . There is too much involved."

When he was asked by the Communist MP, Piratin, whether there would be political conditions attached to the offer, he retorted that it had been the Soviet Union which had insisted on political conditions and created the division of Europe. Why? Who gained by it?

"When you strip all these things which produce political ideologies and get down to the masses, what do they want? They want to live. They want to be free, to have social justice; to have individual security; to be able to go home, turn the key in the lock and not be troubled by a secret police. . . . I find no difference in the hopes of the fathers or the love of the mothers for their children. . . . They have the same kind of dreams and aspirations. Why not let them live? Why set them at each other's throats? That is the basis of my approach to the problems of a war-scarred Europe and world."

The next day, Bevin fulfilled a promise he had made to the son of his Private Secretary, Pierson Dixon, and went down to address the Political Society at Eton. Dixon accompanied him and wrote in his diary:

"Sensing the seriousness of his audience, E.B. adapted himself in the astonishing way he has and delivered a first class, carefully balanced disquisition on the Empire, the

---

[1] HC, 19 June 1947.

new Britain and the place of youth in it. A fusillade of intelligent questions provoked witticisms in his best platform manner, such as the reply to the question: 'Do you expect the Russians to accept the invitation to join in the discussions about Marshall's offer?'—'The Tsar Alexander still hasn't answered Castlereagh's questions."[1]

After the talk Bevin went back to Pierson Dixon's home for a drink; he asked Dixon, according to his custom, if the two chauffeurs and the two detectives could join them, a fitting conclusion to his Eton visit.

He had not long, in fact, to wait for the Russian answer. On the 22nd, at 9 o'clock on a Sunday evening, the Soviet Ambassador came round with Molotov's reply: the Russians accepted the invitation and proposed a meeting in Paris on the 27th.[2] Bevin at once agreed.

4

Before he met Molotov and Bidault, Bevin had the opportunity for a thorough discussion with the Americans, the first real exchange between the two Governments since Marshall's speech nearly three weeks earlier. Will Clayton, the Under-Secretary of State in the State Department, accompanied by the newly appointed Ambassador Lew Douglas, arrived in London for three days of talks with ministers and officials (24–26 June).

Since he and Marshall had left Moscow two months before, a number of issues on which British and Americans were in disagreement had come to the surface. One was the plan for international control of atomic energy,[3] which the US was urging on the UN Atomic Energy Commission and which the Americans had hitherto believed the British supported. There was consternation in the US Delegation when Sir George Thomson, the Cambridge physicist, arrived to join the British delegation with the news that the British Government was considering a quite different plan which would drop the proposal for an international atomic agency "with positive functions of ownership and management" in favour of one which would rely principally upon inspection.

Marshall at once sent off a cable to Bevin expressing great concern, especially at the possibility that the British might act without consultation with the USA. Talks with Bevin and officials in London left the Americans with the impression that the British did not want to force the issue with the Russians by pressing either the American or their own plan, and that they were concerned with preserving their freedom of action in the development of

---

[1] Dixon's diary, 20 June 1947.
[2] Text of Molotov's reply in RIIA *Documents 1947–48*, p. 31.
[3] This was based on the Acheson–Lilienthal proposals modified by the Baruch plan. It was first put to the UN Atomic Energy Committee in June 1946 and supported by Britain and eight other members of the Committee.

atomic energy. Bevin told the Ambassador, Lew Douglas, that he had heard the American plan could deny the British the right to develop such energy for industrial and commercial purposes and that their anxieties on this score were coloured by their view that the US Government had gone back on the secret agreements which Churchill and Roosevelt had made for continuing the wartime sharing of atomic research and technical information.[1] When pressed by Douglas at a later meeting, Bevin replied that it was accepted in London that the Americans had devised their plan "with the thought in mind that it might be used to prevent the establishment of plants in countries other than the UK, [but] it could be applied similarly to the UK".[2]

While atomic matters were not raised in Clayton's talks with the British, both sides were aware of the lack of agreement, which continued to trouble the Americans and had not been resolved by the time Bevin left for his meeting with Molotov and Bidault at the end of June.

A second source of disagreement was also a legacy from wartime and America's plans to establish a multilateral system of world trade after the war, the latest version of which was the Geneva negotiations to set up an International Trade Organization. Throughout those negotiations, still incomplete, the British had led the resistance to American pressure for the rapid dismantling of protective barriers. Clayton had been in charge of the Geneva talks and on 16 June he received a troubled message from his deputy, Wilcox, drawing his attention to the contrast between Bevin's welcome for Marshall's offer of further US aid and a speech by Stafford Cripps (President of the Board of Trade) "bitterly criticizing US and disparaging importance trade negotiations and I.T.O."

Clayton's reply strongly denied any inconsistency between Bevin's and Cripps's speeches:

"Cripps is certainly right in saying that neither tariff negotiations nor I.T.O. could result in additional half-billion dollars monthly imports into U.S.A. in time to take care present European dollar shortage. Inference that aid program makes results Geneva negotiations unimportant entirely unjustified. It makes such negotiations more important than ever because without second permanent program of reciprocal multilateral trade, no temporary emergency program could possibly have any permanent worthwhile results."[3]

This was true enough, but in face of Europe's immediate needs there was no denying that the USA's long-term plans would at least have to be postponed and that the conditions which the American negotiators (including Clayton) had sought to impose on the British in return for the dollar loan would have to be abandoned. This, added to the long history of conflicting views and difficult

---

[1] Douglas to Marshall, 11 June, after conveying the latter's message to Bevin and discussing the matter with him. FRUS 1947 (1) p. 502.

[2] *Ibid.*, 29 June, pp. 539–40, and in general FRUS 1947 (1) pp. 489–540.

[3] Clayton to Wilcox, 17 June, *ibid.*, p. 955.

negotations between London and Washington on economic questions, could not fail to influence attitudes on both sides despite agreement that they had now to deal with an emergency situation.

The third issue sprang from Bevin's attempt at Moscow to force the pace over the reorganization of the Bi-zone. Clay's sceptical view that Marshall's agreement with Bevin would not survive the Secretary of State's return to Washington had proved well founded. Clayton before leaving for London (20 June) noted that in a talk he had with Marshall the Secretary of State had admitted "when he was in Moscow he was not sufficiently informed . . . to take the firm stand which he now takes. At that time the only advice and information which he had came from the occupation authorities. Since then he has had information and advice from other sources." The most important result of Marshall's change of mind was his acceptance of the State Department's view that the rehabilitation of Germany had to be placed in the wider context of rehabilitating Europe and that coal from the Ruhr had to be made available for other countries besides Germany.

In order to avoid an outburst from Clay, however, the Secretary preferred to gloss over this and instead concentrate attention on the shortcomings of the British. He asked Clayton "to make it quite clear to Mr Bevin that he regarded the British coal problem as pathetic" and later in his talk with the Under-Secretary repeated that he was "now convinced that the British have made an absolute failure in the Ruhr". He came out strongly in support of Clay's opposition to Bevin's plans for nationalizing the German coal industry, and told Clayton "that we could not sit by while the British tried out any ideas which they had of experimenting with socialization of coal mines; time does not permit of experimentation".[1] Socialization, however, was only part of the issue. If enough coal could be mined, the conflict of priorities between German rehabilitation and European recovery could be overcome. This was a programme on which the State Department and Clay could unite, and the complex of questions relating to the Ruhr coal mines—who was to own them, who was to manage them, how production was to be raised and how output was to be allocated—rapidly became the focus of American pressure on the British.

In the middle of May, Acheson had asked the US London Embassy for a full appraisal of the British situation which he described as "of critical importance" to the USA, including answers to the questions:

"Are we safe in assuming that Bevin is likely to remain in the F.O. for the remainder of the year? Is Bevin making any progress in lining up Labour back benchers in support of British foreign policy? Is his thinking still influenced by their critical attitude?"[2]

---

[1] Clayton's note of his conversation with Marshall, 20 June 1947. FRUS 1947 (1) p. 929.
[2] Acheson to the London Embassy, 17 May, *ibid.*, pp. 750–51. Referring to the newly-formed Policy Planning Staff in the State Department, Acheson wrote: "I should think it hard to begin thinking about American policy without considering what the British position is and where they think they are going." Fn. 1 on p. 750.

On 11 June the Ambassador sent a lengthy reply which began with a review of Britain's defence and foreign policy.[1] This was based, Douglas reported, on the assumption that another world war was improbable for 10–15 years, by which time it was hoped that either the UN would have become effective or Britain would have recovered sufficient authority to be able, with the USA, to keep the peace. The Soviet Union was seen as the only important potential enemy, the USA as at worst a benevolent neutral or at best an active ally in any war involving the Empire. British policy was equally concerned with the economic and military revival of Western Europe modelled on UK and US democratic principles.

The Embassy did not find that the independence of Burma and India had diminished the strategic importance of the Mediterranean in British eyes. The British position in the Mediterranean was weak and likely to get weaker before it grew stronger again; the assumption was that there was no risk of war for ten years and for the moment the one basic tenet was that no outside force other than the USA should be allowed to acquire a strategic position in the area. The British were particularly worried about Italy: If Italy went Communist, it would be hard for France to escape the same fate and the position of Greece and Turkey would be made even more precarious. With little hope of being able to retain troops in either Egypt or Palestine, the Chiefs of Staff looked to Cyrenaica as a base for the defence of the Mediterranean but could not be sure of their ability to use it as such until the future of the Italian colonies was settled. "Britain is reconciled to giving up Palestine as a base provided this does not leave a vacuum which any power other than the U.S. might fill." Repudiating any idea of a "Maginot line" of bases to defend the security of the Mediterranean area against the Soviet Union, they believed that the best defence would be achieved "by neutralising, if not eradicating, the virus of Communism in the area by improving the well-being of the people, and thus establishing their allegiance to Anglo–Saxon democracy". If that could be done, even without definite obligations, "what has been lost to them in Egypt and may be lost to them in Palestine, the British hope will be freely handed to them in time of crisis as a result of goodwill and respect".

The authors of the report were impressed by the seriousness with which the British were taking the policy of granting self-government to former colonies. They hoped by recognizing the force of nationalism to make it likely that a colony, on attaining independence, would choose to remain in the Common-wealth and thereby strengthen British influences. In short, those responsible for the United Kingdom's defence and foreign policy, "while seeking desper-ately to cut her cloth to fit her present stature", still saw Britain as the head of an Empire evolving into a self-governing Commonwealth and, as such, continuing to play an independent role.

The American observers confirmed that Bevin had returned from Moscow

---

[1] *Ibid.*, pp. 751–8.

in better health, in excellent spirits, "and in fighting mood against left-wingers". There was no indication of his leaving the Foreign Office, and the Margate Conference had strengthened his position in the Party. They concluded:

"Bevin will be sensitive to the critical attitude of back-benchers. This will not so much affect the fundamentals of his policy towards the U.S.S.R. as the manner in which it is outwardly implemented. We doubt that Bevin will play the part of broker, and we believe that as matters now stand Britain will be on our side in any serious issue."[1]

5

The American record of Clayton's and Douglas's talks in London at the end of June makes clear that this view was held not only by Bevin but by all the senior Labour ministers and permanent officials involved.

The talks opened at No. 10 on 24 June and went on for three days. Although the Prime Minister was present as well as Dalton and Cripps, Bevin was the principal spokesman on the British side and took the lead in trying to get the Americans to accept the thesis that Britain ought to be regarded as the partner of the USA in helping Europe through the Marshall Plan rather than "lumped in" with the other European countries. "Britain with an Empire," he asserted, "is on a different basis" and asked the USA to put the UK "in the position which we held in 1923–24 in economic reconstruction after the last war".

"I am worried about the loan and for practically all of my plans Mr. Dalton puts in a caveat as regards our resources. The rise in prices has thrown us a year out and the U.K. position compelled me at Moscow to draw in my horns. For that reason I could not support Secretary Marshall to the extent I desired and I think it would pay the U.S. and the world for the U.S. and the U.K. to establish a financial partnership."[2]

Clayton's reply was unambiguous. Referring to Bevin's opening remark

"That the U.K. wanted to be a partner in the European Plan and, if it could not be equipped financially to carry out such a partnership, its relations with the U.S. would become somewhat similar to relationship between the U.S.S.R. and Yugoslavia, Mr. Clayton could not see how the U.K. could find itself in a 'Yugoslav' position. He asked how the U.K. problem was different from other European countries. . . .

"Mr Clayton reiterated that he was unable to visualise the Administration going to Congress regarding new proposals for any one country and he felt that a European plan must be worked out. In this, Mr. Bevin's continued leadership would be welcomed."

---

[1] The quotation describing Bevin's position is not printed in FRUS, but has been taken from the full text of the report which is available in the National Archives, Washington.
[2] These and other quotations are taken from the record of the talks kept by the Americans and sent to the British on 1 July. FRUS 1947 (3) pp. 268–96.

413

Despite Clayton's warning shot, the British ministers did not easily give up their claim to a special position. Dalton broke in to say that one difference between the UK and other European countries was that the UK was helping in Germany; Cripps argued that another difference was Britain's trade with non-European countries, and Attlee pointed out that Britain's world responsibilities were shown by the decision she had taken to let Australian food supplies, which were badly needed in the UK, go to India instead. Bevin summed up by saying that

"If the U.K. was considered just another European country, this would fit in with Russian strategy, namely, that the U.S. would encounter a slump and would withdraw from Europe; the U.K. would be helpless and out of dollars, and as merely another European country, the Russians, in command of the Continent, could deal with Britain in due course."

Clayton was unmoved. He repeated that

"The U.K. as a partner in the Marshall program rather than as part of Europe, with special assistance to the U.K. partner, would violate the principle that no piecemeal approach to the European problem would be undertaken. He said that in the U.S. even a non-piecemeal approach would be hard to sell to the U.S. public and Congress and he frankly saw no possibility of interim arrangements for the U.K. as part of the European approach."

Clayton followed this up by pointing to the poor British record in raising the production of coal in the Ruhr and (another point on which he had been instructed by Marshall to speak bluntly) the unhelpful British attitude to measures proposed by the USA in Japan.

On the afternoon of the 24th it was the turn of the civil servants led by Sir Edward Bridges, the Secretary to the Cabinet, to try and get American recognition of Britain's special position "as a partner of the U.S. in world recovery". The Board of Trade representative, Sir John Henry Wood, developed the argument that, if Britain was forced into a pooling arrangement with the rest of Europe, she would find herself reduced to the lowest position so far as aid was concerned and, in view of her relative advantages in production over the rest of Europe, might well be better off outside the Plan, looking after her national interests by a series of bilateral deals. The officials, however, had no more success than ministers in getting the British case accepted, although they did secure an assurance from Clayton that dollar aid need not be tied to purchases of supplies in the USA but might be used, for example, to buy food for the UK from Canada and Latin America.

At the second meeting with ministers, on the 25th, Bevin tried again. He had already remarked on the previous day that he thought the Marshall Plan was "the quickest way to break down the iron curtain" and that Russia would not be able to hold its satellites against the attraction of help towards their economic revival. He now elaborated on ways in which he thought Britain could "get going on constructive political relationships" if she was not hobbled by her own shortages particularly of dollars. The Poles, for example, could provide food and were willing to do so, but naturally enough wanted payment in dollars in order to be able to buy American equipment. If Britain could not pay in dollars, he could not develop the closer relations with the Poles which he believed to be possible. Bevin's second example was Yugoslavia which "he was convinced would gradually come west". The Yugoslavs too needed equipment which Russia could not supply—for agriculture, railways, timber cutting —"but when he asked Cripps what he could give up for Yugoslavia, Cripps could offer little, primarily because of the steel shortage".

"Yet if the U.S. took the line that the U.K. was the same as any other European country, this would be unfortunate because the U.K. could contribute to economic revival. The U.K. held stocks of rubber and wool and 'we, as the British Empire' could assist materially. The British did not want to go into the program and not do anything—this would sacrifice the 'little bit of dignity we have left'."

The conflict between poverty and pride was obvious. The British were financially dependent on the Americans for their own economic survival, yet wanted to be treated as an equal partner in dispensing aid to the Europeans. Ministers complained vigorously of the terms imposed by the Americans at the time of the loan to Britain, particularly the clause directed against trade discrimination; yet even now Dalton and the Treasury team, although hinting at the difficulties ahead, were still not prepared to come out openly and admit that the UK would not be able to face the strain of making sterling convertible.

In the course of the discussion Clayton reassured the British that there was no idea of a "European pooling" which Bridges repeated, "would bring the U.K. down to the level of the lowest in Europe". It was his idea, Clayton explained, that there would be a series of bilateral agreements with individual countries taking into account their different needs. On the other hand, he laid stress on the need for a joint European programme and for "some proposals regarding a closer integration of the European economy", if Congress was to be convinced of the need for additional assistance. Ironically, in view of later developments, it was the British who complained that whenever they and other European countries tried to develop plans for integration they ran into the objection that they were infringing the American-sponsored principles of multilateral trade and non-discrimination enshrined in the ITO. The British note of Bevin's reply to Clayton reads:

"He found in Europe a desire to do what Mr. Clayton sought but also found Europe in effect committed by I.T.O. not to integrate. . . . Mr. Bevin said the British might obtain agreement in principle for a Customs Union and wondered if this would be enough to comply with I.T.O. rules. 'We have in I.T.O. [Bevin declared] an ideological plan which thwarts reconstruction', [adding that he] felt a five year plan for the first stages of integration would be necessary."

For three sessions Bevin and the rest of the British team had been frank in their criticisms of American policy and the proposals which Clayton had brought with him. There had been plain speaking on the American side, too, not least about the European and British performance in achieving recovery (e.g. in Germany) and about facile talk of the USA's need to find export markets for its surplus production. So outspoken an exchange could hardly have taken place between the representatives of any two other countries and it illustrates what Attlee meant by his cryptic remark when I once asked him, without notice, what was Bevin's greatest contribution as Foreign Secretary. His reply, without a moment's pause, was "standing up to the Americans".[1] But it was Bevin's strength that, while he never hesitated to "stand up to the Americans" in a way that no other political figure in Western Europe in these years ever did, he never lost sight of Europe's and Britain's need of the USA, never allowed himself to be misled by the illusion of a Third Force and combined his independence of comment with a readiness to co-operate in such a way as to ensure that the Americans in practice continued to treat the UK as their principal partner in carrying out the Marshall Plan and never as "merely another European country", still less as a satellite.

The British change of tactics on the second day of the London talks illustrates this very well. Having pressed their own point of view to the limit in the earlier discussions, the Foreign Office now produced the draft of a brief for Bevin to take to Paris which accepted, without further demur, Clayton's and Douglas's view of how the Marshall Plan should be visualized. They worked in the points to which the British attached most importance as comments within this framework and so provided a working paper on which, with a number of revisions, the Americans and British were able to agree within 24 hours.[2] When they met to consider it on the third day, all Bevin's energies were concentrated not on criticism of the Plan but on how to get it into operation and the points on which difficulty might arise.

Bevin summed up by saying that he now understood that

"The Marshall idea encompassed a relatively short term, say four years, and involved help to Europe in its purchases from the Western Hemisphere while Europe itself was getting underway. This would be of tremendous help."

It was agreed that the long-term needs of European reconstruction would have to be met by the International Bank: "We deal with the Congress on dire needs and on the long term must deal with the Bank." They went on to discuss what the Russians were likely to do, Clayton expressing the view that the Russians had a stronger case for long-term aid in the form of credits for capital equipment and development than short-term assistance. Bevin did not agree: if the Russians did not get in on the short-term programme, he did not think

---

[1] In conversation with the author.
[2] FRUS 1947 (3) pp. 283–8.

they would play at all. If so, he asked and got assurances from Clayton that the UK would be supported by the USA in going along with the others, whatever the Russians decided to do. The other point he made was to urge the Americans not to press too hard but to use cautious language in demanding balanced budgets, for example in France and Italy, except as a long-term measure. The fiscal measures which, he said, the French Government had courageously introduced were already producing "gripes", and he would not like the Americans or the British to appear as a source of deflationary pressure on the French people.

The immediate need, it was now agreed, was a statement to be prepared jointly by the European countries, the Western countries as a nucleus to start with, but with the scheme remaining open to others to join. This should set out why they still found themselves in serious economic and financial difficulties; what Europe needed to get back on her feet again; how much of what was needed could be found from inside Europe and how much would have to come from outside; the economic targets the Europeans themselves would agree to work to over the next few years, and the minimum amount of help they would need from the USA. Bevin's Paris plans, he told Clayton, were to try and get a small representative working party, perhaps from five countries (mentioning France, Czechoslovakia and Italy) to work up some proposals by early August for use in the US in September.

Clayton was frank in saying that most of his views came out of his own head as he had only had one talk with Marshall, principally about coal, and although the Planning Staff in the State Department was hard at work under George Kennan, he had no well-thought-out plan or scheme to lay out. Nonetheless, while avoiding any commitment, he and Douglas agreed that the brief Bevin was taking to Paris represented the US Administration's approach to Europe's economic problems, as far as this had yet gone—perhaps even further.

6

The day after reaching agreement with the Americans, Bevin flew to Paris for the conference with Molotov and Bidault. In retrospect, it has seemed to most historians that this meeting was a turning point in relations between the Soviet Union and the West and to some extent this was felt by those who took part in it at the time.

After two years' experience of dealing with the Russians, Bevin was certain that if they were to accept the invitation to join in working out a plan for European reconstruction, it would add immensely to the difficulties of the enterprise. From that point of view it would be a relief if they refused. But from another point of view Bevin saw quite as clearly that a Russian refusal would have serious consequences. Not only would it make it impossible to draw in the

417

countries of Eastern Europe like Poland and Czechoslovakia, thereby hardening the division of Europe, but it might well make it difficult for other
countries—for example, France with its large Communist Party, or Norway
which was very much exposed to Russian pressure—to take part in the
operation and so impair, even perhaps prevent, that European response which
Marshall had made the premise of American aid. This was quite enough to
make Bevin pause before accepting at all lightly the prospect of an open breach
with the Russians.

The question that troubled him was how the Soviet leaders could take part
in a project which must appear to them contrary to their interests. It was not in
the interests of the Soviet Union to see Europe recover, least of all with the aid
of the USA, but the exact opposite—to see its economic weakness perpetuated, thereby increasing the chances that the Communist parties in France
and Italy would be able to take power without serious resistance and the
people of Western Germany turn to the East in despair of any other future
except as part of a Communist Europe. This was no fantasy. Two years after
the end of the War it was clear that Europe would not recover on its own.
Britain was in no position to help and might well run into economic disaster
herself. Stalin did not need to have "a blue print for world revolution" or to
think in terms of another war, which the Soviet Union was in no condition to
wage. All the Russians had to do was wait, and the situation was bound to
develop to their advantage.

The one thing which could change it was American intervention which, if it
was successful, could not only restore confidence to Western Europe but might
undermine the Soviet hold on Eastern Europe. The Russians, then, on Bevin's
reckoning, could not be other than highly suspicious of and opposed to
Marshall's offer, yet for them too there were obvious difficulties in turning it
down out of hand. Leaving aside the use they themselves could make of
American aid (as they had of Lend-Lease)—if they could secure it on their
terms—they were also aware of a strong desire on the part of the Poles and the
Czechs (to mention only two cases for which there is evidence) to take
advantage of the American offer. Nor could the Soviet leaders take lightly the
risk of leaving the Western powers to go ahead without them, thus constituting
with American support the Western bloc to which the Soviet Union had
always been opposed. The Russians had gained a great deal from the
willingness of the Western powers to accept a Soviet veto rather than break up
the Council of Foreign Ministers. If the Soviet Government now made the
break itself, it would leave the other powers free to pursue their own policies in
Germany and Austria as well as the rest of Western Europe.

Bevin's anxiety was not so much that Molotov would break up the conference with a flat refusal of the American offer and the Anglo–French invitation,
as that he would try to impose conditions which might lead the Americans to
withdraw their offer or at least so delay action on the European side as to make
American aid arrive too late to prevent an economic collapse, in France and

Italy at least. Bevin, for the reasons already spelt out, was not eager to force a breach himself, but he was determined not to let Molotov manoeuvre the conference so as to delay a decision. His other anxiety was how firm Bidault could afford to be in standing up to Molotov in view of the strength of the French Communist Party. He told Lew Douglas, the US Ambassador, that he believed the unusually large party, of nearly a hundred, which Molotov brought with him had been selected because of their contacts with the French Communist organizations and did everything they could to bring pressure to bear on Bidault and Ramadier.

The conference opened at 4 o'clock on the afternoon of Friday 27 June at the Quai d'Orsay[1] and Dixon was relieved to note that, despite the almost tropical heat, Bevin was "in fighting form". He deliberately left Bidault however to take the lead in tabling the plan they had agreed on ten days before for a European programme of "self-help" to be presented to the USA by 1 September and for a directing committee composed of France, the USSR and the UK, with six specialized sub-committees involving other countries, to prepare it. Bevin was content to indicate his support and waited to see how Molotov would play his hand. Dixon, sitting at his side, admitted in his diary that he awaited the Russian's opening speech with more interest than ever before. It was made in a low key, with a cautious welcome for the proposal of a European plan but with a number of questions: What additional information had Bevin or Bidault got about the scope of the American proposals, and what had the two of them agreed to when they met on their own in Paris? After protestations of innocence from his two colleagues, Molotov then tabled his own proposals. Since none of them knew more than was contained in Marshall's speech, he suggested that they should ask the US Government exactly how much money they were prepared to advance in aid to Europe and whether they could be sure that Congress would vote such a credit.

Bevin at once replied that he could not agree to any such proposal. Marshall had not mentioned any specific sum but urged the European countries to get together and first formulate their own plan for recovery. No American or any other parliamentary government could commit Congress in advance, and it was not for borrowers to lay down conditions when seeking credit. He suggested that they should get down to business and work out a plan of their own which they could then put to the Americans. Until they had done that, he was strongly opposed to going to the US Government. Although rather more diplomatically, Bidault took the same line and Dixon noted that Molotov was obviously irritated with the "robust" way in which the French maintained their point of view.

Between the first and the second meeting at 5 p.m. on the 28th, Molotov had evidently consulted Moscow, for he now dropped his original proposal and

[1] British and French accounts of the meetings were given to the Americans (who were not represented) and are printed in FRUS 1947 (3) 296–307.

419

took a different line. The Russians took exception to the proposal to work out a joint European plan and only turn to the USA for what Europe could not provide by its own efforts. Each European country already had its own plan for recovery and the French proposal would represent an unjustifiable interference with national sovereignty. The job of the Conference was to put together a combined list of the needs which each country had of American aid and then discover how far the USA was prepared to go in meeting those needs. Molotov also raised the question of which countries should participate: in the first place it should be only those countries which had been occupied by the Germans and had contributed to the allied victory, not ex-enemy states. In particular, discussion of German problems must be reserved for the Council of Foreign Ministers and kept off the agenda of the present conference.

While it was obvious to the British and French delegations that there was a fundamental difference between the Russians' and their own conception of how to proceed, neither Bevin nor Bidault sought to force the issue at this stage. They assured Molotov there was no intention of interfering with national sovereignty: as Bevin said, no country would be forced to take a loan. They both made clear that they did not think Germany—or Italy—could be left out of account, but they were concerned to stress the common ground rather than the differences: Bevin's preliminary response to Molotov's statement was that they seemed to be nearer agreement than the day before.

Molotov, however, was not to be won over with fair words. Did they, he insisted, accept the Russian agenda or not, since there was a radical difference between that and the French agenda? (At this point a violent thunderstorm broke out overhead.) Bevin's reply was that they had better study each other's proposals over the weekend and see if they could reconcile the differences. With that they adjourned without much hope that they would do any better when they met again.

Over the weekend Bevin insisted, against the advice of his staff, in turning the Anglo–French agenda into a briefer statement of proposals, but this produced no effect. When they reassembled on Monday, 30 June, Molotov dismissed the British paper as a re-hash of the original French proposals with which the Soviet delegation disagreed: it was not an attempt to reconcile divergent views. He then went on to develop his objection to the idea of drawing up an overall European plan. It was both impracticable, since it could not possibly be prepared in a few weeks, and objectionable, since it would amount to the bigger powers telling the smaller countries what they had to produce, an open interference in their domestic affairs. This was something the Soviet Union would never countenance. They should concentrate on American aid, on establishing what each country needed and what the USA was prepared to give.

Both Bevin and Bidault were at pains to explain that they were not thinking of "planification" in the Soviet sense, but of a programme of voluntary co-operation in providing information about the contribution each country could make before they turned to the USA. The object of this proposal, as Bevin pointed out, was to increase, not reduce, the independence of Europe. It was certainly not in their minds to issue directions to countries telling them what they should or should not produce: every country would be free to decide for itself whether it wanted to co-operate or not. But this time neither Bevin nor—much more remarked—Bidault made any attempt to minimise the disagreement between the two sides. "In effect," Bevin said to Molotov, "what you are asking the U.S. Government to do is to give us a blank cheque. If I were to go to Moscow with a blank cheque and ask you to sign it, I wonder how far I would get." Bidault wound up the session with the remark that it was a fruitless discussion: they could wait until tomorrow but should then reach a conclusion.

At 10 p.m. that night, Bevin saw the US Ambassador, Caffery, and told him that "to all intents and purposes the conference had broken down", a breakdown which, he said, he had "anticipated and even wished for—given my certainty that Molotov had come to Paris to sabotage our efforts." He spoke particularly warmly of Bidault who had shown "great courage and had given the fullest, and even surprisingly solid and whole-hearted support, having in mind the present critical state of French internal politics." He added, according to Caffery: "I am glad that the cards have been laid on the table and that the responsibility will be laid at Moscow's door. They have tried to sabotage it in the conference room from the very beginning as I knew they would."[1]

The following morning, Tuesday, 1 July, Dixon reported rumours that the French were weakening. Nobody could find out what was happening since all the ministers were in Cabinet, and the officials in meetings. Duff Cooper was confident the French would stand firm and the British delegation filled in time by drafting a programme for continuing on an Anglo–French basis without the USSR. Half an hour before the conference re-assembled in the Salon des Perroquets in the middle of the afternoon, Hall Patch came back from seeing Bidault with reassuring news.[2]

Bidault was in the chair and introduced a new proposal which, as Couve de Murville admitted to the American Ambassador, was drawn up with a view to French internal politics. The wording had been modified but not the substance. The object, Couve explained, was to make one last effort to secure agreement which it was certain Molotov would refuse but which would disarm the French Communists and make it easier for the French Government to go ahead without the Russians.[3]

Molotov was not, of course, taken in by this manoeuvre, but used the new paper as a reason for proposing a further adjournment. In the meantime, he did his best to embarrass the French Government by asking if they had

[1] Caffery to Marshall, 1 July. FRUS (3) pp. 301–3.
[2] Dixon's diary, 1 July, 1947.
[3] FRUS 1947 (3) p. 305.

changed their view of reparations and now proposed to use German resources in order to meet the needs of those countries participating in a European plan rather than for reparations. Were the French also, he enquired, now in favour of raising the level of German industrial production?

Bevin saw no reason to waste another 24 hours before reaching a decision. The question was clear enough: did they accept the view that the European countries must first work out a programme of their own before approaching the USA or were they going to adopt the Russian proposal and merely send in lists of what they needed? Molotov, however, was not to be drawn before he had consulted Moscow once more, and Bevin finally agreed to wait provided they were promised an answer, Yes or No, the following day.

The fifth and final meeting of the Conference opened with a strong attack by Molotov on the British and French who, he declared, were using the Marshall offer (of which nothing was known definitely) to set up an organization under the direction of the larger states to which other countries would have to sacrifice their national independence in order to qualify for American aid. At this point, Bevin whispered to Dixon, "This really is the birth of the Western bloc". The Soviet Union, Molotov continued, must therefore reject the French plan, which not only threatened to infringe national sovereignty but, in addition, overlooked the Soviet Union's and others' claims to German reparations. He concluded with the formal statement that the Soviet Government considered it necessary to warn the British and French Governments against the consequences of such action which, if persisted in, would lead not to a united effort in the reconstruction of Europe but to very different results.

Bevin followed Bidault in repudiating the Soviet charges. After Molotov's warning, he had turned to Dixon and said that "This was pretty serious. Ought he not to get Cabinet sanction before he stated that we intended to go ahead alone with the French?" In fact, Dixon had taken the precaution of sending back to London at the weekend a paper giving Bevin's views on the action to be taken in the event of a breakdown. Duff Cooper, who took the paper, was instructed to get Attlee's agreement in case of need and this had been sent to Paris. So Dixon was able to reply: "Surely he was covered by the P.M.'s message of last night (which I had asked Duff to elicit for this very purpose) and we could safely go on."[1] Reassured, Bevin told Molotov he regretted the meeting should have ended with a threat. "We have faced consequences before and shall continue to carry out what we think our duty. . . . It will then be seen that there is no idea of domination. Perhaps by example we can win when by argument we can't."[2]

[1] Attlee to Bevin, 1 July, FO 800/465/FR/47/16 in reply to Bevin's report of the same date, FO 800/466/GER/47/32.
[2] From Dixon's unpublished notes in his diary which he wrote up at the end of each session. In addition to these, the principal sources are the texts of the speeches and documents published by the French Government at the time, (*Documents de la Conference à Paris 1947*). See also RIIA *Documents on International Affairs 1947–48*, pp. 18–58, and the reports of the American Ambassadors in Paris and London, FRUS 1947 (3) pp. 296–312.

The history of the thirty-five years since the Paris conference does not suggest that any other outcome was likely or that an accommodation could have been reached between two such different views of the future of Europe. In the six years since Hitler's attack had made the USSR an ally of Great Britain and the USA, the Soviet Union had secured a great expansion not only of its territory but of its power and influence. The basis of this, of course, was the leading part which the Russians had played in the defeat of Germany and the advance of their armies into Central Europe, but it was also the case that wherever the Western powers had been disturbed, or felt their interests might be affected by Soviet demands, they had in the majority of cases given way, originally for fear that the Soviet Government might make a separate peace with Germany, later, after the war, in order to avoid an open breach which would divide Europe into two hostile camps. In the course of 1947, all three of the leading Western governments—at different times, the French being the last—reached the conclusion that this process could not be continued indefinitely without the risk of its leading to a Communist Europe under a Soviet hegemony. Up to the Spring of 1947 there had always been sufficient room for manoeuvre to produce a compromise, such as the trade-off of the Italian for the Balkan treaties. By 1947, however, there was no more room for manoeuvre on the Western side. If something drastic was not done quickly, there would be an economic breakdown in Western Europe—in France, Italy, Germany, quite possibly Britain as well—before the end of the year. This time—for the first time—all three of the Western powers were convinced they had to take action even if it meant an open break with the USSR.

The American Ambassador in Paris, Caffery, reported how the situation appeared to two of the ablest Frenchmen of the post war generation, Hervé Alphand and Couve de Murville, the day after the conference broke up:

"The Russians the Frenchman said believe that the European nations will not be able to draw up an effective plan and more particularly that the U.S. will be unwilling to advance the credits necessary to make it work because the Soviets believe that the U.S. will undergo a profound depression within the next 18 months. The French believe that the Soviets are counting on this depression to put an end to the American aid for European reconstruction. This will mean that European economies will disintegrate and economic, social and political chaos will follow. When this catastrophe occurs the Soviets hope to take over the Western European countries with their well-organised Communist parties.

"In conclusion, Couve said that the French had for internal political and other reasons never wished to take the lead in establishing a European bloc. 'The Soviets, however, by their actions there have forced Europe to band together to save itself. They are the persons who have established the European bloc. It is now up to the European countries and to the U.S. to see that such a bloc succeeds.'"[1]

---

[1] Caffery to Marshall, 3 July 1947. FRUS 1947 (3) pp. 308–9.

Bevin gave his version to the American Ambassador in London, Lew Douglas, the same night. Before leaving Paris, he had agreed with Bidault the terms of a note to 22 European countries inviting them to send representatives to Paris by 12 July in order to set up an organization which would determine both the resources and the needs of Europe and start work on the 15th. Turkey and all the East European countries except Russia, were included in the invitation. Spain was excluded and Germany was to be represented by the occupying powers.[1] Bevin, however, was by no means certain of the response. He told Douglas that "he interpreted Molotov's warning to mean that they would use every subversive device to prevent other European nations from joining in the formulation of a program and would employ every method to create internal trouble".

Bevin repeated his admiration for the courage and firmness shown by Bidault and Ramadier in face of Soviet pressure.[2] He urged the US Government through Douglas, as he had through Caffery, to find

"Some method of giving France some immediate and temporary assistance [which] would have the effect of assuring French stability until such time as Congress might act. He was hopeful that we would be able to include the U.K. in this but he was more concerned during the interim period with France than with the U.K."

Bevin told Douglas that he was worried about the risks they had taken, but most of all about the USA.

"Would she provide in time the assistance which Europe desperately needed? . . . If, he said, no action is taken by the United States until late fall or winter, he thought that France, and with her most of Europe, would be lost."[3]

At least the first obstacle had been cleared: the Russians had not been allowed to hold up or block a European response to Marshall's offer. With the way to action clear, Bevin threw himself into the task of giving substance to that response and making sure that it was ready for submission to the Americans by the date agreed on, 1 September.

The Conference on European Reconstruction opened in Paris on Saturday 12 July. Of the 22 nations invited to send representatives, 14 accepted, 8 refused. The distinction between the two groups defined the Soviet sphere of influence. Several, if not all, of the eight who refused—the Poles, the Czechs and the Finns, for certain—would have sent representatives if it had not been for direct intervention by Stalin who left no doubt that the Soviet Union would regard acceptance of the invitation as an unfriendly act.[4] None the less Bevin

---

[1] Text in RIIA, *Documents 1947–48*, pp. 55–8.
[2] Bevin spoke in the same warm tones of the French leaders in his report to the Cabinet (CP (47) 197, 5 July), pointing out that Molotov's "concluding threats were directed particularly at France, and M. Bidault so interpreted them; but the French Government remained firm."
[3] Douglas to Marshall, 4 July, FRUS 1947 (3) pp. 310–12.
[4] A copy of Gottwald's telegram to Prague describing the Czechs' interview with Stalin was given secretly to the US Ambassador and is printed in FRUS 1947 (3) pp. 319–20.

was gratified that fear of Soviet disapproval had not extended further and that as many as 15 nations besides the British were represented. In recognition of the role which he had played, he was elected chairman and by the evening of the 12th a working committee (on which all the countries present were represented) had produced a substantial revision of the original Anglo–French plan. This was adopted unanimously at a plenary session on the 13th.

The next day, Sunday, was Quatorze Juillet and Bevin was in the mood to celebrate it appropriately. Leaving his staff to work he went off to see the traditional parade from the Champs Elysées, delivered a broadcast (in English) to the French people, enjoyed a lively dinner at the Embassy and then set off for an evening tour of Paris illuminated and *en fête*, with the Ambassador's wife as his chauffeur and Dixon and his detective, Ben Macey, in the back of the car. Dixon marvelled at the confidence with which the beautiful Lady Diana Cooper drove into the thickest crowds and persuaded the police to clear a way for her.

"We finally came to rest at a café in Montmartre, at a street corner packed with dancers and drinkers. The Secretary of State was spotted immediately, and called on to make a speech which he did amid immense enthusiasm."

It was 2 a.m. before they got back to the Embassy after a splendid night out.

Another day and a half was sufficient to bring the conference to an end. The conference then transformed itself into a Committee of Co-operation on which everyone had a seat with an Executive Committee of which the British, French, Italians, Dutch and Norwegians were members. Four sub-committees were established for Food and Agriculture, Energy and Power, Iron and Steel, and Transport. Membership of the Conference and its committees was entirely European, but in accordance with an agreed formula, the Co-operation Committee was to "seek the friendly assistance of the U.S.A. for the preparation of the report". The substance of the report was to be the production which each country hoped to achieve in the four years 1948–1951. Work was to begin at once and it was planned to hand over the report by 1 September.[1]

Even at the time this seemed an over-optimistic timetable. But Bevin was even more impressed with the need to act with urgency if American aid was to come in time; he preferred to give a hostage to fortune by naming a date rather than to play safe and risk losing the momentum he had created. The gamble came off. A report, though it did not satisfy the Americans, was produced before the end of September; American aid arrived in time to prevent the European economy from foundering, and the organization set up in Paris that

---

[1] The British records of the Paris meetings (CEEC) are to be found in (1) CAB 133/93, 133/67 and 133/42 (UK Delegation); (2) CAB 133/13 and 133/46 (Committee of Co-operation and Plenary Sessions); (3) CAB 133/48 (Executive Committee); (4) FO 371/62568–70 (Minutes of UK Delegation); (5) FO 371/62579–89 (Proceedings and Report of CEEC).

weekend in July 1947 proved sufficiently durable to last, as the OEEC, until 1960 when, with the addition of the USA and Japan it was succeeded by the OECD as the principal organ of economic co-operation between the industrialized nations of the non-Communist world.[1] As he returned to London, however, Bevin needed all the confidence and determination he could summon to believe—and to make others believe—that even the first stage of preparing an agreed programme was practicable within the time available.

Bevin had persuaded Oliver Franks, whose remarkable abilities had been revealed during the War, to return from Oxford and take the leading role as chairman of the Committee of Co-operation and its Executive in the negotiations that lay ahead. The job to be done would have been difficult at any time: to make a joint programme out of the plans—where there were plans—of sixteen nations differing as widely in their circumstances as Britain and Greece, Holland and Portugal, Sweden and Turkey. To do all this by agreement, without the power to insist, and to reconcile divergent interests without infringing national sovereignty or offending the *amour-propre* of governments which, in appearance at least, had all to be treated as equal and equally independent, truthful and efficient. All this represented an operation for which there were no precedents and for which procedures had to be improvised within a matter of weeks.

The intrinsic difficulty of the job was compounded by the political context within which it had to be done. Among the sixteen nations represented in the negotiations, there were no Germans; yet, as everyone recognized, the use to be made of German resources, beginning with coal from the Ruhr, then extending to the revival of German industry, was central to their success. Bevin and Marshall agreed in principle that this was a matter to be settled outside the Paris conference, but found it hard to reach agreement in practice. Even when they did—for example, on the level of German industry—the French protested so strongly at their exclusion that decisions had to be held up and negotiations re-opened.

As the target date of 1 September approached, the Americans who were following the Paris negotiations became increasingly critical of the report which was taking shape and increasingly pessimistic about the chances of Congress underwriting it. The British bore the brunt of American efforts to get the Conference to revise the report and meet their criticisms. Their role was complicated by the Labour Government's decision to suspend the convertibility of sterling and postpone any reduction of preferences, objectives which were high on the list of American priorities and which the British had accepted as conditions of the US loan. For it was the weakness of the British position that, at the same time that Bevin and the Labour Government were trying to give a lead to the European governments in agreeing on a four-year pro-

---

[1] OEEC: Organization for European Economic Co-operation; OECD: Organization for Economic Co-operation and Development.

gramme which would satisfy the Americans, they were having to struggle with a financial and economic crisis of their own which threatened to lead to disaster long before help could be expected under any Marshall Plan.

Finally, if the Russians were not present to hold up the proceedings at the Paris conference, this did not mean that they had ceased to make their influence or their hostility to the whole idea of the Marshall Plan felt. A major propaganda offensive against selling out Europe to American imperialism was launched by the Soviet and satellite governments in Eastern Europe and the Communist parties in Western Europe, and the Russians prepared to challenge the initiative taken by the Western Powers, and in particular the part to be played by Germany in their plans for European recovery, when the Council of Foreign Ministers met again in London in November.

CHAPTER 11

Coal, dollars and convertibility

I

The American administration itself was divided about Germany and the Marshall Plan, but this was no comfort to the British. For, however much Clay and the Army on the one hand and the State Department on the other might disagree over the priority to be given to Germany's own recovery and the use to be made of German coal, they agreed that the British were to blame for the failure to raise coal production in the Ruhr and that the proposal to nationalize the German mines would make matters worse and must be resisted.[1]

Both British and Americans believed that uncertainty about the future ownership of the Ruhr mines needed to be removed if production was to be raised. Clay's proposal was that ownership should be vested in German trustees until a German central government was established and the German people could vote on the issue of nationalization in more normal conditions, in five years time. Bevin looked on this as a device for delaying action: his own preference was still for ownership to be vested in the *Land Nordrhein-Westfalen*.

Clay objected that it was wrong to give one provincial state the control over major national resources and with it a dominant position in a future Germany. Murphy, Clay's Political Adviser, however, reported that the British had already gone too far in their talks with the *Nordrhein-Westfalen* government to back down and were taking the line that this was, in any case, a matter for Britain, not the USA, to decide.[2]

This was hardly a view the Americans were likely to accept in view of the fact that they were now partners in the Bi-zone and Marshall responded quickly with an invitation to an Anglo-American conference on the German coal problem to be held in Washington.[3] Clay's suspicions were at once aroused: he

---

[1] See FRUS 1947 (2) pp. 909–33.
[2] Murphy (Berlin) to Secretary of State, 24 June 1947, reporting on a talk with the British Political Adviser, Steele, *ibid.*, pp. 929–31.
[3] 27 June 1947, *ibid.*, pp. 932–3.

feared that a conference held under State Department auspices in Washington, not in Berlin, would result in German coal being allocated in a way that subordinated German to European (or, more precisely, French) interests. He cabled that he had already got General Robertson's agreement to his trusteeship plan, but he was unable to stop the proposal going forward.

Attlee, receiving the same proposal in the Foreign Secretary's absence in Paris, sent a note to Bevin strongly suggesting that they had better comply. It was already certain, he pointed out, that because of the deterioration in the UK's dollar position, they would have to ask the USA for revision of the Bi-zone financial arrangements and could only get increased food supplies for Germany (including the Ruhr miners) if the Americans found both the money and the food. If the British were to commit themselves to socialization of the Ruhr coal industry this might seriously prejudice the chances of additional American assistance for Germany. He suggested, tactfully, that Bevin would want to discuss the matter with other ministers as soon as he got back and that in the meantime consideration by the Cabinet of Bevin's socialization proposal should be postponed. [1]

Bevin did not give in so easily. Replying to Attlee's note from Paris, he said that the coal position in the Ruhr would need to be examined in the light of several factors: the probable failure of the talks with Molotov; the Bi-zone fusion agreement; the position of France and the need to step up coal production. He welcomed the US invitation, therefore, but asked Attlee to hold up any reply until he was back in London.[2] When he did get back he told Lew Douglas, the US Ambassador, that he was thinking of going to Washington himself to discuss the Ruhr and other questions. But he added that he must state firmly that socialization of the Ruhr industries was British policy and that they meant to put them under public ownership.

"His main political supporters were the trades unions which represented seven and a half million people. They were completely wedded to the idea of public ownership and were afraid that, if measures of socialization were not carried out quickly, there was a danger of the ownership of these industries with their dangerous war potential reverting to the large combines. If he showed any wavering on this point, he and his party would lose a great deal of public support. He wished Mr Marshall to be aware of this point."

Douglas's report to Marshall glossed over the evident firmness with which Bevin spoke.[3] A possible explanation may be the report which Attlee passed on to Bevin that, while dining with a group of MPs, Douglas had said that the Americans were not worrying about socialization of the Ruhr as they expected to take over the British zone in a few months' time when the UK went bankrupt. Whatever truth there was in this story—and Douglas said he could

[1] Attlee to Bevin 30 June 1947. FO 800/466/GER/47/31.
[2] Bevin to Attlee 1 July, *ibid.*, GER/47/32.
[3] Douglas to Secretary of State, 4 July. FRUS 1947 (3) p. 312.

not remember mentioning the Ruhr when Bevin taxed him with it—there was no doubt that Marshall and the State Department did not want Bevin to come to Washington and were not prepared to widen the talks, as Bevin wished, to include other German problems besides coal.[1] In Bevin's view coal was only part of the bigger problem of economic policy in the Bi-zone, including currency reform, food supplies and the division of the financial burden between Britain and the USA.[2] He wanted the question of ownership removed from the agenda altogether and, when told that the State Department would not agree to widening the agenda as he wished, replied that he would not feel justified in sending a party to Washington simply to discuss coal production. That could be done just as well in Berlin by the two Military Governors,[3] a view which Clay certainly shared. Bevin told Douglas bluntly that he was disturbed that the British would be "put on the mat for maladministration" and did not want to see them "placed in the position of defending what he thought, in view of the difficulties with France and with food, had not been too bad".[4]

Bevin finally agreed that a small delegation should go to Washington but won his point that the agenda should be widened. However, before the coal conference opened, on 12 August, the view that German questions—at least as far as the Bi-zone was concerned—were matters to be settled by the Americans and British and kept out of the discussions in Paris on European recovery, had been sharply challenged by the French who insisted that they could not be excluded from any decision about Germany. The exchanges which followed in July and August bring out the complexities lying beneath the surface of what appeared to be largely technical discussions.

The French were particularly incensed to hear that the British and American military governments had reached agreement on a new level of industry plan and were about to publish it in Berlin. The impetus for such a plan had come from Bevin and went back to his talks with Marshall in Moscow in April before any proposal of a plan for European recovery had taken shape. The framework in which Clay and Robertson had conducted their negotiations, however, was that of a self-sufficient Bi-zone, Bevin's original objective in April but one which now needed to be modified in the light of the wider objective, suggested by Marshall and enthusiastically taken up by Bevin, of a European recovery programme.

It was easy to argue in general terms that the recovery of Europe could not be brought about without a substantial expansion of German industrial output, but such a statement begged most of the important questions; how

---

[1] FO to Washington Embassy 11 July 1947. FO 800/466/GER/47/38.
[2] Douglas to Secretary of State, 12 July. FRUS 1947 (2) pp. 936–7. Further talks between Douglas and Bevin took place on the 17th & 25th July, *ibid.*, pp. 944–6.
[3] Secretary of State to Douglas, reporting the terms of the British *aide-mémoire* submitted on 17 July.
[4] Douglas to Lovett, 25 July 1947, *ibid.*, pp. 945–6.

much of the output was to be retained in Germany and how much exported, and who was to pay for the exports, whether (for example) they were to be supplied free as reparations, paid for at the going rate by Germany's neighbours or subsidized by the Americans. The French went further than asking questions: they objected fundamentally to the restoration of German industry to its old levels of production which they saw as a renewed threat to their own and Europe's security. They argued instead for the separation of the Rhineland and the Ruhr from Germany, or at least for the internationalization of the Ruhr, so that its coal resources could be used to build up the heavy industry of Germany's neighbours—in particular, French steel output—and so avoid re-creating Germany's former industrial preponderance. The French were in a desperately weak position but to be told that decisions had already been taken by the Americans and British without hearing the French objections or (as they believed) without weighing the long-term implications for Europe against the immediate need to cut occupation costs, was more than any French government could tolerate in silence.

On the eve of the meeting of 16 nations in Paris (11 July) Bidault told Clayton that the French Communists were saying: "To assemble a conference at Paris to examine the Marshall proposals amounts to the same thing as abandonment of reparations and modification of the French position as regards the Ruhr." Bidault agreed that it was necessary to improve the management of the Ruhr mines—with French participation—in order to increase production but he saw no reason at all to link this with raising the level of German steel capacity.

"He recalled that France was capable, if it receives sufficient coke from the Ruhr, of increasing its steel production very substantially and of meeting, with the help of Belgium and Luxembourg, all the requirements of Western Europe, including German needs."

When Clayton expressed the view that dismantling factories for reparations brought no gain to the recipients and that the question of the German level of industry must be settled quickly, Bidault became vehement:

"There must be no repetition of the error of Potsdam where German questions were settled without France. To begin the attempt to settle Europe's difficulties by abandoning reparations and by raising the level of German industry would have very serious consequences in Europe. No French Government could consent to it. The whole difficult task they had undertaken would be irremediably compromised. . . ."

Bidault said emphatically that if any public statement were made which could lead the French and Europe to believe that reparations had been abandoned and the raising of Germany's economic potential was contemplated, "the Conference [on the Marshall Plan] which is to meet Saturday would be doomed to failure and 'there would be no Europe' ".[1]

The force of Bidault's arguments, as both Bevin and the Americans recognized, derived from the political situation in France. The Communists, now in opposition, were bent on discrediting the Socialist-MRP attempt to govern without them. Germany and the Ruhr provided them with the best of all issues on which to arouse French opinion. If the Ramadier–Bidault government was forced out of office, or the French Communists forced their way back into the coalition, there was a real danger that France would not take further part in the Paris talks and that, without her, these might break down altogether.

A month of confusion followed, in which both Bevin and Marshall tried to meet the French objections but in different ways and on different conditions. In the middle of this tripartite misunderstanding the running fight between the US War Department and the State Department over German policy came to a showdown. Patterson, the US Secretary for War, resigned and Clay threatened to. Patterson's successor, Royall, negotiated an agreement between the two departments on the level of industry plan and the allocation of German coal supplies which looked remarkably like a treaty between sovereign states. Royall's mistake was to boast about it and tell a press conference in Berlin that "he feels free to boost German industrial production without consulting the French."[2]

This really put the fat in the fire. The Ambassador in Washington was instructed to tell Marshall that France would not accept a European recovery programme "built around an agreement with respect to German industry in which it had not participated".[3] On 8 August, the US Ambassador in Paris reported that "all work of technical committees of conference on European Economic Co-operation responsible for steel, coal and coke, has come to a stop because the French are reluctant to participate." The French representatives told the British that they would participate again "as soon as satisfactory arrangements have been made for level of industry discussions".[4]

The State Department was wholly on the French side. France was the key country in any European plan to match Marshall's proposals and her withdrawal would jeopardize their success. In a second trial of strength with the War Department—complete with further threats of resignation from Clay and of an appeal to the President—Marshall this time carried the day on offering Bidault a tripartite meeting with the British in London.[5]

---

[1] Caffery's report of the Clayton–Bidault conversation, 11 July. FRUS 1947 (2) pp. 983–6. The British Embassy succeeded in obtaining a copy of the record of the talk from a friend in the US Embassy and sending it to Bevin, 17 July. BP 16 (FO/B 64).
[2] Quoted in Lovett's dispatch to Marshall, 3 August. FRUS 1947 (2) pp. 1014–16.
[3] Memorandum of Marshall–Bonnet conversation, 5 August, *ibid.*, pp. 1021–2.
[4] Caffery to Marshall, 8 August, quoted in Gimbel, p. 241.
[5] Marshall to US Embassy in London, 8 August. FRUS 1947 (2) pp. 1024–6.

Bevin was relieved by the American volte face. He had accepted the earlier Marshall–Royall agreement, but had argued at the time that no procedural difficulties should be placed in the way of reaching an understanding with the French.[1] With Marshall over-riding Clay and the War Department's attempted veto, the obstacle to such discussions was removed, and so August 1947 saw Britain involved in a second set of talks on Germany, besides the so-called coal conference which opened in Washington on the 12th.

2

Bevin was in favour of tripartite talks as a gesture to help the French Government with its political difficulties but he was no more prepared than Marshall to reopen the negotiations on the level of German industry if he could possibly avoid it. The British could not continue to take part in the occupation of Germany, even as a partner in the Bi-zone, unless the country could be made self-supporting and the need for subsidies removed; the reconstruction of Europe could not take place without a major contribution from Germany, and the German workers would not put their backs into raising productivity until they had some certainty about their own industrial future, including the number of plants to be removed for reparations.

The clash of interests with the French was obvious. In an effort to narrow the gap, Clayton, Douglas and Caffery talked to Bidault and Monnet and finally whittled the French demands down to an international board for the allocation of Ruhr coal, coke and steel after but not during the occupation.[2] Washington refused to accept even this and Bidault, to his great discontent, was told that further discussion of the Ruhr would have to wait until after the London talks on the level of industry. Bevin was favourable to the idea of international control for the Ruhr, but linked this with some form of German public ownership, to which the French were indifferent and the Americans opposed. So far as the level of industry plan was concerned, the point on which he insisted was that the list of plants to be removed for reparations must be final, even if they reached agreement with the Russians on a quadripartite settlement at the November CFM.

The talks finally took place between 22 and 27 August, with Douglas in the chair and Hervé Alphand and Massigli representing France. The communiqué issued at the end did not disguise the extent of the disagreement which still remained. It recorded that the UK and US Delegations had stated the reasons why they could not postpone publication of the plan for revising the level of industry in the Bi-zone, and the French Delegation had given their reasons why they could not withdraw their objections pending a satisfactory outcome

[1] Douglas to Marshall, 11 August, *ibid.*, p. 1026, note 73.
[2] 12–13 August. FRUS 1947 (2) pp. 1023–9.

of discussions about the distribution of Ruhr coal and coke, "those resources being essential to European heavy industry". The most the British and Americans conceded was an assurance that the rehabilitation of Germany should not have priority over that of the democratic countries of Europe and a second that their plans for managing and controlling Ruhr coal production (which was under discussion in Washington) did not prejudge the mines' future status.[1] Nonetheless the talks had served their purpose. They had given Bidault the consultation which he said he needed to stay in office, while the British and Americans were now free to publish the revised level of industry plan and use it, without danger of a public protest by France, as the basis for Germany's contribution to the proposals for European recovery under discussion in Paris.

So, four months after taking the initiative in Moscow, Bevin had the satisfaction of seeing the obstacles overcome, the limits on annual German steel production raised—as Bevin had always wanted—from 5.8 million tons, under the March 1946 plan, to 10.7 million,[2] and the figures accepted for incorporation into the European Recovery Programme.

He had less cause for satisfaction over the second set of talks on Germany, the Coal Conference in Washington. The meetings lasted a month and a report prepared by the US co-ordinating secretary noted that "progress was very slow and there was throughout a note of stubbornness and withholding".[3] The disagreement which had held up the start of the talks remained unresolved; the British would have to give way in the end—and knew this—but they remained unconvinced and contested every point.

Nobody questioned that German coal production was too low and needed to be raised dramatically as the key to German and European recovery. The Americans believed that the solution was to return the mines to German management; give the USA an equal share—if possible with an American chairman—in the control group to which management was responsible and end the uncertainty about ownership by postponing any decision about nationalization for five years, during which it would be vested in one or more German trustees. The British believed that low production was not the result of poor British management but of the depressed state of the German economy: inadequate food and housing for the miners, no confidence in the currency, no consumer goods, no proper balance of imports in return for the export of coal, a rampant black market and complete uncertainty about the future of the mines.

There was only one way, Bevin argued, to end this uncertainty. The Ruhr industry was too important to be handed back to its former owners: there had

[1] Communiqué of 28 August 1947, reprinted in RIIA *Documents 1947–48*, pp. 625–6.
[2] The US Delegation had pressed for a ceiling of 12.5 million tons of which 1 million was to be for export. The British thought this too high and secured acceptance of their original figure. See McNeil's report to the Cabinet, 22 May. CM 49 (48). The final text of the revised plan is given in RIIA *Documents 1947–48*, pp. 626–32.
[3] FRUS 1947 (2) p. 964.

to be some form of public ownership. As an interim measure this could be vested in the *Land Nordrhein-Westfalen*. Coal production could not be raised as an isolated operation; what was needed was a new economic policy for the whole Bi-zone which would make it self-sufficient and end the dependency on American and British subsidies. Hence the importance Bevin attached to the new level of industry plan and his dislike of singling out the coal industry for separate discussion. The question the British and American governments needed to talk about was the financing of the Bi-zone, where the original division of the costs—as Bevin had foretold—had proved too much for the British with their rapidly dwindling stock of dollars and could no longer be borne.

After four weeks' hard-fought negotiations, Bevin finally agreed to delay the financial talks and accept the trusteeship proposal in principle. But he laid down a timetable for consultation with the other West European governments before final approval which exhausted the Americans' patience. Douglas was instructed that, if there was to be a "blow-up" over the reorganization of the coal administration, the State Department would "prefer to have it now rather than postpone it for the subsequent financial discussions". He was to tell Bevin that the USA planned to end the coal conference "tomorrow either with or without an agreement" and that under any circumstances it would "announce agreement in principle on the Management Plan and specific agreement on the US/UK Control Group being put into effect immediately at the close of the Conference tomorrow".[1] Bevin protested but accepted the American decision.

The joint communiqué issued at the end of the coal talks, on 10 September, transferred responsibility for coal production to German hands under the supervision of a joint US/UK control group. The question of ownership of the mines was left open, but when the two military governments published their Law No. 75 for the reorganization of both the German coal and steel industries, two months later, ownership, in both cases, was vested in German trustees pending a final decision by "a representative, freely-elected German government".[2] At least Bevin was able to secure a public commitment

"Not to allow the restoration of a pattern of ownership in these industries which would constitute excessive concentration of economic power and not to permit the return to positions of ownership and control of those persons who have been found, or may be found, to have furthered the aggressive designs of the National Socialist Party."

This promise was kept, but the legacy of the British occupation was not, as Bevin had hoped, the nationalization of the German coal and steel industries but the institution of *Mitbestimmung* (co-determination) between management and trade unions, a practice which, despite its success in Germany and the

[1] Memorandum of Stillwell-Douglas telephone conversation, 8 September, FRUS 1947 (2) pp. 957–9.
[2] Text of communiqué in RIIA *Documents 1947–48*, pp. 622–3 and of Law No. 75, pp. 637–45. Bevin's report to the Cabinet on the coal talks was circulated as CP (47) 261, 17 September 1947.

support of the Callaghan Government for the principles of the Bullock Report on industrial democracy, has still to be introduced in Britain itself.

The financial talks between the British and US Governments on the Bi-zone were eventually started in October and took two months to complete. Before they began, however, Bevin had already achieved one important relief. In July Clay and Robertson had agreed to raise the export price of Ruhr coal from 10 to 15 dollars a ton. This would substantially reduce the "hidden reparations" which benefited the French and other European countries at the cost of larger subsidies from the British and American taxpayer. The French were certain to protest (and did so, three times, in September) but after some hesitation in Washington the new price was confirmed. If the French were to be helped to pay for imports of coal from Germany it would have to be through the European Recovery Programme not at the expense of the occupation budget.

By the late summer of 1947, then, Bevin could see substantial progress on paper towards the programme which he had pressed on Marshall at Moscow of making the Bi-zone self-sufficient. Admittedly, against his wishes, he had had to accept American criticism of the British failure to raise German coal production and the postponement (in effect, the defeat) of his proposal to nationalize the Ruhr coal and steel industries. He had also still to reach agreement with the Americans on revising the division of bi-zonal costs, and still to see any of these agreements on paper produce tangible results. Nonetheless, comparing the prospect in Germany with what it had looked like after the breakdown of the Moscow talks in April, he could say that the Russian (and French) veto on restoring the German economy had been got rid of, thereby opening the way to European as well as German recovery; the Bi-zone had been reorganized and the burden of costs beyond the UK's capacity to pay would soon (he hoped) be ended. None of this could have been done without the United States' willingness and power to act, but it had been accomplished, despite the United Kingdom's weakness, without abandoning the British share in the occupation or in determining the future of Germany.

What had still to be done was to give substance to the idea of a European programme which Bevin had seized upon in June and to fit the bi-zonal programme into it. The American view was that the Europeans had to take the responsibility for producing this, but the reports out of Paris of what was being prepared by the committees meeting there under British chairmanship left the State Department very dissatisfied. Between 4 and 6 August, Clayton held a meeting with the US Ambassadors in London and Paris, General Clay's Political Adviser, Robert Murphy, and Paul Nitze, who had been sent over to Paris with the latest appreciation of the situation by the Department's Planning Board. Their recommendation was that the USA would have to intervene if it were to secure proposals which had any chance of being backed by Congress.[1] On the 14th the State Department responded by sending

---

[1] Report of the discussions by Wesley C. Haraldson, 8 August. FRUS 1947 (3), pp. 345–50.

guide-lines to Paris for use in "informal talks".[1] Among the criticisms Clayton made to the British and French negotiators were the failure to do more than put together sixteen shopping lists thereby producing an inflated total which it was out of the question to send to Congress, and leaving the European economy as fragmented and as far from self-sufficiency as ever. Instead of making immediate use of the largest under-utilized capacity in Europe, that of Germany, the French wanted to divert Ruhr coal and coke to the long-term plan of building up French in place of German heavy industry and in the meantime neglected to restore their agricultural production. The British refused to look at a customs union and failed to produce the 25 to 30 million tons of coal exports which could have transformed Europe's prospects. When Clayton and Caffery met Franks on 19 August they again criticized the absence of any programme for "the eventual elimination of trade and other barriers among the European group", and they quoted the State Department's advice that "an itemized bill summing up prospective deficits against a background of present policies and arrangements will definitely not be sufficient".[2]

The American representatives in Paris put their points as forcefully as they could, yet they were aware that there were limits to the pressure they could apply: both the British and the French governments, on whose leadership in Europe the State Department was relying, were in a precarious position and might well not be able to hold out until aid under the Marshall Plan could reach them. After reviewing the situation in Britain, France and Italy during their discussions of 4–6 August, Clayton and his group cabled to Washington recommending that without waiting for action to be taken on Marshall's proposals,

"All possibilities of rendering interim financial aid should be explored, even to the calling of a special session of Congress. Unless immediate aid were forthcoming, it was felt that the situation in these three countries might so deteriorate economically, politically and socially and in the field of foreign relations, that many of their [i.e. American] objectives in Western Europe and elsewhere might be unobtainable."[3]

At one stage of the discussion, the minutes record, Clayton suggested they should tell the State Department that "unless immediate steps were taken to extend aid to the UK and France, 'irreparable' damage would be done".[4]

If this was how the situation looked to the Americans, it bore even more sharply on the small number of men on the European side who knew how close their countries were to economic collapse and had to find a way out. In the

---

[1] Lovett to Clayton and Caffery, 14 August, *ibid.*, pp. 356–60.
[2] Clayton and Caffery to the Secretary of State, 20 August, *ibid.*, p. 364.
[3] *Ibid.*, pp. 345–6.
[4] *Ibid.*, p. 350. Murphy contested this but only because he wanted to make the point that the economic situation in Germany was even worse than in the rest of Western Europe. The effects, he said, remained to be seen "but the political direction in which 66 million Germans went might have a decisive effect on the European future".

summer of 1947 the question for the British was no longer whether the construction of a European recovery programme could be carried through to a successful conclusion, but whether Bevin could prevent the whole of his foreign policy being undercut and the Labour Government avoid being defeated by Britain's economic and financial problems.

3

The Government had not recovered its grip after the fuel crisis of February which Dalton estimated cost £200 million in lost exports (at 1947 values). Morrison, who had overall responsibility for economic policy, was away ill from January to April and did not give any impression that he was in command of the situation when he returned.[1] Although as Chancellor of the Exchequer Dalton had warned the Cabinet of the rising rate at which the US loan was being used up, he failed to do anything to check it. After a fairly steady gold and dollar deficit on the balance of payments of just over 50 million dollars a month for the first nine months of 1946, the rate had risen to 135 million a month in the last quarter of that year, then to over 200 million in February, and went on rising. Yet neither Dalton, his advisers in the Treasury nor the Bank of England made any move to secure the postponement of convertibility (which was due on 15 July under the Loan Agreement). The leading Labour Ministers (including Bevin) had always regarded this as a premature commitment and as Dalton later admitted, there was no rational ground in the trade figures for being less fearful of the consequences as the date approached.

"But there had gradually grown up (Dalton wrote afterwards), even in some most knowledgeable circles, a mood of optimism which we can now see to have been quite irrational.
    "I was gravely informed by some that 'convertibility has now been discounted' and 'when it comes it will make very little difference'. I am still surprised, looking back, by this profound error of practical judgment. It is quite clear now [1962] that we had no chance at all of holding this degree of convertibility in mid-1947."[2]

The Cabinet was not only slow to grasp the seriousness of the crisis into which they were slipping but even more reluctant to take action. Between the Budget on 15 April and convertibility on 15 July, Dalton wrote: "We debated much but decided little. In particular we were very slow in deciding on significant import cuts."[3] To bring their programme into a more realistic relationship with their resources could only mean jettisoning, or at least

---

[1] His opening speech in the Commons in the big economic debate on 8 July was regarded, even by his friends, as a failure. See B. Donoughue and G. W. Jones: *Herbert Morrison, Portrait of a Politician* (London 1973).
[2] Dalton, p. 257.
[3] *Ibid.*, p. 258.

postponing, a large part of it, a course of deflation accompanied by unemployment and a possible devaluation which inevitably recalled Labour's disastrous experience in 1931. Only really determined leadership could have brought the Cabinet and Parliamentary Party to face the sort of decisions needed in advance before these were forced upon them by events, and such leadership was not provided either by Attlee or the ministers most concerned, Morrison and Dalton.

Bevin's attention during June and July was concentrated on launching the plan for European recovery[1] in which he believed (justifiably, as it turned out) that he had found the only way of lifting Britain as well as the rest of Europe out of their economic difficulties. Like the rest of the Cabinet he accepted the official assurances that convertibility would not make a great deal of difference and until he talked to Lew Douglas, the American ambassador, on 25 July, ten days after sterling had been made convertible[2], there is no evidence that he realized how urgent was the threat that the run on sterling might bring about financial collapse before his plans for European self-help and American aid could begin to take effect.

What Bevin *had* realized was the need to secure the support of the unions for these plans in order to raise productivity and so increase the contribution Britain could make to their success. In a powerful memorandum which he sent to the Prime Minister on 4 July he set out possible items which might be included in the British contribution. At the head of the list and outweighing all the others in importance was coal, just as it was in the discussions on European recovery and the Bi-zone. He put the need at an annual British production of 240 million tons of deep-mined coal, of which the home market would take 200, leaving 30–40 million tons for export to Europe.[3] Attlee, in response, set up an official working-party in Whitehall, but as Attlee and Bevin both knew, the most effective appeal to the unions would come from Bevin himself, who, as still a member of the trade union "club", was looked on and listened to in quite a different way from other Labour politicians. So Bevin found the time not only to talk to Arthur Deakin and the other TUC leaders but to get out and talk to their members as well, first of all to his own Transport and General Workers (twice, in July and November), then the miners (twice again, in July) and finally to the TUC Annual Congress at Southport in September.

In each of these speeches Bevin tried to bridge the gap which prevented so many in the Labour Movement from seeing foreign policy as something which should concern or might affect ordinary people. The traditional way of doing this was to talk in highly abstract terms of support for pacifism, opposition to balance of power politics, international solidarity and the rest of the radical catechism. Bevin took exactly the opposite line, illustrating the way in which

---

[1] Bevin reported on his negotiations to four meetings of the Cabinet: 19 and 24 June; 8 and 29 July.
[2] See below, p. 451.
[3] Bevin to Attlee. FO 800/460/EUR/47/18.

foreign affairs affected the lives of working people by concrete examples within their own experience.

He told the Northumberland miners at their annual picnic in Morpeth[1] that previous peace settlements had been political; this time fundamental economic problems had to be solved as well. "Then it was 'hang the Kaiser' for some political crime. Now it is 'What are you going to do about the Ruhr?'"

He gave a whole series of examples to bring the "economic problems" home to his listeners.

"We have not been able to export coal to France. France has had to get coal from the U.S. The U.S. does not take fruit and vegetables from France, and we want them. If I could get coal from this country for France I could help to re-create the French national economy and we could get fruit and vegetables and other commodities and so end queues on this side. . . ."

A second example reflected the trouble he was taking in the summer of 1947 to persuade the Dutch not to resort to force in Indonesia but to continue talks with the nationalists.[2] This was the way he put it to the miners:

"I have been struggling for two years using my best offices to try and settle the Indonesian problem. . . . If it were settled now every woman in Northumberland would have her fat ration increased . . . This would release the simple little monkey nut which goes into margarine and oil. If I could get that shipped I could ship them things. . . .

"In Sweden they are burning wood because they cannot get coal. Bevan, who is speaking here today, cannot get on with houses in Northumberland because he cannot get wood. If you could get a normal exchange between wood and coal you would get your houses and they would get their machinery going. . . .

"All these things are dependent one on another. We want to make a crack somewhere in the vicious circle that has got the world tied up. One of the biggest cracks that could be made in the European economy and bring us eggs, bacon and other stuff to help Britain in her food supplies is coal for Europe."

To his own transport workers at Hastings Bevin appealed

"As an old leader of this Union, to send me back to London with a will behind it, as you have done before. I have met the dockers and all those in the war, when we were losing 700,000 tons a month. I asked them to give me four days off the turn-round of a ship. They put their backs into it and gave us six and that was one of the biggest contributions for defeating Hitler. My approach is the same now . . . One supreme effort over this year ahead, one hundred weight of coal more per man per day out of the pits, a quicker turn-round of a ship, a bit of overtime when you are asked for it . . . and you will look back on it, brothers and sisters, with pride because your children will bless you that you helped to make peace and not sow the seeds of another war."[2]

---

[1] Speech at Morpeth, 19 July 1947.
[2] Speech to the TGWU Conference, Hastings, 17 July 1947.

Before Bevin left for his second visit to the North East and the Durham Miners' Gala, he called Lew Douglas in to see him and told him that the convertibility of sterling had led to a drain on dollars which would rapidly exhaust the US loan. (The loss of dollars in July was, in fact, 500 million.) Bevin did not yet suggest suspending convertibility, but he made clear the effect which the crisis could have on British—and by implication on American —foreign policy.

A Commons debate had been fixed for 8 August: before then, he told Douglas, the Government would have to decide whether:

"a. To cut imports 'violently';
b. To cut multilateral trade;
c. To withdraw from Germany; and
d. Possibly to declare a state of emergency."

If Britain could be given some temporary relief, Bevin urged, they could go ahead; but without such relief they would not be able to play their part "and the consequences in France and Italy and elsewhere may be disastrous".

Douglas, reporting his conversation to Washington, added:

"I would not suggest temporary relief, if it is possible, to U.K. on straight economic grounds"—Douglas, like other Americans believed that Britain should not be allowed to avoid "grappling in earnest with her problems"—"but I think that if we are to be successful in Western Europe, we cannot afford to permit the British position so to deteriorate that her moral stature will be reduced to a low level."[1]

In such circumstances, it was inevitable that Attlee's leadership should be called in question.

On 25 July the parliamentary correspondent of the *Manchester Guardian* wrote: "Not since 1931 has Parliament broken up for a summer holiday with this sense of economic as distinct from foreign crisis threatening." The same ominous comparison with 1931 was made by others, but there is no evidence to show that Bevin, if he was ever approached, gave encouragement to any suggestion that he should play the role of a MacDonald and form a coalition.

More serious was the suggestion, reflecting much anxious discussion in the Parliamentary Labour Party, that Attlee should step down and let Bevin take his place as leader, not of a coalition but of a re-shuffled Labour Government. On 24 July Dalton wrote in his diary that George Brown, his PPS,

"Tells me that the boys all talked, during the all-night sitting this week on the Transport Bill, about the lack of leadership. Most were in favour of substituting Bevin for Attlee; they seemed to think that these two could just swap jobs."

On the way back from the Durham Miners' Gala, Dalton took the opportunity to sound Bevin out. There is only Dalton's account of their conversation,

[1] Douglas to Secretary of State, 25 July 1947. FRUS 1947 (3), pp. 43–4.

and he is not exactly a disinterested witness, but there is no doubt that Bevin, while critical of Attlee and most of his other colleagues, especially Morrison and Cripps, was not to be drawn on the question of taking Attlee's place. He agreed that Attlee was proving a weak leader; thought that Morrison was a sick man and "no more use now", and was shocked at a remark of Cripps, repeated by Roger Makins, that "we must be ready at any moment to switch over our friendship from the U.S. to Russia". But when Dalton mentioned George Brown's report "that a large number of our M.P.s wanted Bevin to become Prime Minister", the latter replied that his own PPS had told him the same thing "but that he didn't want to do anyone out of his job". Dalton told him that he had a gift for talking to the unions which made it natural, in such a crisis, for many in the Party to think of him "as our predestined leader".

"As the car turned up Downing Street, I urged him not to put out of his mind the possibility of becoming Prime Minister. He was unresponsive and so we parted."

Characteristically, Bevin saw the issue in terms of loyalty. He was as critical as Dalton of Attlee's leadership but he was indignant that Dalton should have tried to tempt him into "betraying Clem", and said so to a number of people who, of course, reported it back to both Attlee and Dalton.[1]

On the following Monday (28 July) Bob Dixon recorded in his diary:

"Conversations with Dalton and Morrison at Durham, Lew Douglas' indication on Friday that we (G.B.) could expect no help till March, and rumours that the U.S. and the Opposition have been intriguing to substitute a Coalition Government here with E.B. as P.M., have all brought matters to a head. Ministers (called the 'Nuclear' Ministers, i.e. Attlee, Bevin, Morrison, Dalton and Cripps) have been meeting on and off all day long. Personally, I feel E.B. will find it hard to resist the lure of the Premiership."

The same evening, however, George Brown told Dalton that "the movement to make Bevin Prime Minister had petered out"[2], and although it was to revive again later in the summer, it was not because of any encouragement from Bevin. In fact, although all the senior ministers were alive to the way in which their own political fortunes might be affected, they were confronted with the threat that none of them was likely to survive politically if the Labour Government failed to master the crisis.

There was still resistance in the Cabinet and Party to accepting the measures which were necessary.[3] It took nearly another three weeks to decide on suspending the convertibility of sterling. The delay was due not only to reluctance to admit that the warnings of the Opposition had been justified but

[1] Dalton, pp. 238–40.
[2] *Ibid.*, p. 240.
[3] Dalton's report on the balance of payments and the measures necessary to correct it was presented to the Cabinet in CP (47) 221, 30 July 1947.

to a powerful diversion of interest and long-drawn-out dispute within the Cabinet over the nationalization of steel.[1] A compromise sponsored by Morrison[2] was rejected by a majority in both the Cabinet and Parliamentary Party as abandoning the principle of nationalization, but not before much time had been spent and much suspicion and bitterness created which the Government could ill afford—least of all Morrison, the minister responsible for rallying support for the sort of programme the economic situation required. The culmination of the steel dispute, with Nye Bevan threatening to resign; with the Cabinet finally rejecting Morrison's scheme on 7 August, and the Parliamentary Party "in a very hysterical and steamed-up condition" (Dalton) holding a special meeting on the 11th, coincided with the climax of the economic crisis and at times appeared to take precedence over it in the minds of many Labour members and not a few ministers.

This was not a mistake Bevin made although he opposed Morrison's scheme and remained in favour of nationalization. Nonetheless, he was as much affected as other ministers by the feeling that the Government had lost its way. Both individually and collectively ministers were too tired to act with decision. Everyone criticized everyone else and all were critical of Attlee for failing to pull the Cabinet together. Late at night on 30 July, when the leaders met to decide between the options open to them, Dalton reported that Bevin "had obviously had a very good dinner and was at his worst", rambling on for an hour until Morrison walked out of the room, saying that he had "had enough of this drunken monologue", and Dalton complained that Attlee showed "no power of gripping and guiding the talk".

"The meeting broke up inconclusively, with Bevin lurching in his characteristic sailor's roll towards the door and inquiring 'Where do we sleep tonight —in 'ere?' "[3] At the Cabinet meeting the following morning when they ought to have settled the programme of import and other cuts, they spent their time arguing and repeating themselves about the nationalization of steel, with Bevan again threatening to resign if Morrison's plan was not thrown out, and Dalton if his economy measures were not approved.

If Bevin (according to Dalton) had been at his worst on the evening of the 30th, he had been at his best in the afternoon when he and other ministers had met the members of the National Coal Board and of the National Union of Mineworkers in No. 10. Having given the miners a five-day week, the Government was asking for an extra half-hour on the day to get more coal.

After Morrison had put the Government's case for raising output, Bevin related it directly to Britain's international position.

---

[1] C.M. 64–74 (47) covering 11 Cabinet meetings between 24 July and 25 August.
[2] Morrison's compromise was circulated as CP (47) 212: it provided for the Government to acquire control, but not ownership of the iron and steel industries. See also Morrison's and Wilmot's summary of the various options open to the Government in CP (47) 215, 28 July.
[3] Dalton's diaries, 30 July 1947.

"We cogitated a long time," he told the miners, "before we entered this loan business with the U.S.A. It was a leap in the dark. On the other hand, we could not see the reconstruction period being carried out unless we did it, and it was to give us a breathing space to enable the transference and demobilisation to be carried out, and to get the industry of the country going."

They thought they had bought time until 1948 and therefore acquiesced in the shorter week for coal, engineering and textiles. Now they found they had been caught short by the rise in prices. The result was to make it impossible to carry out the economic foreign policy on which he had set his heart, in particular producing goods to contribute to the reconstruction of Europe.

"You cannot carry out—as I want to do—a completely independent British policy dovetailed in with other people, until we can get out of this economic morass we are in. . . . I should hate to think that we are going to become a sort of financial colony of someone else, whoever it was, for one cannot have that without one begins to be told what to do."

He reminded them that they had been caught with the slump in 1931, and no one wanted to see that repeated. It was the Labour Movement's problem, not just the Labour Government's: "Labour is called upon to maintain the independence of this country." When Sam Watson spoke of a six-months campaign, Bevin told him it was not enough: they had to have two winters not one, and get to 1949 before they could relax. If the miners' leaders wanted them to, they would go and talk to the men. "We are Labour chaps like yourselves"—and didn't want to push too much on the union leaders; the problem was a national one. If only they could raise more coal, they could get fifteen or twenty industries going full blast and change the whole position of the country.[1]

Bevin was prepared to plead with the miners—and did so again at another meeting in Downing Street with the NUM on 21 August—but when Bob Dixon asked him

"Point-blank what we were going to do in October when the dollars ran out, he replied that the U.S. will see us through. I replied that none of us thought this. He said, leave it to me and Lew Douglas."[2]

In arguing to the miners that Britain's ability to produce more and so contribute to the reconstruction of Europe would enable her to play a more independent role in the world, Bevin was expressing his long-term view of foreign policy. But there was also a shorter-term view which in the circumstances of 1947 counted for just as much in his thinking, perhaps even more. Quite apart from playing any sort of role in the world, Britain had to get out of the "economic morass" in which she was floundering if she was to support and

[1] Verbatim record in FO 800/489/PLT/47/17.
[2] Dixon's diaries, 27 July, referring to a conversation "a few days ago".

feed her own people. Bevin had grasped far more realistically than any other member of the Cabinet that, however much they might appeal to the miners, the British were not going to manage this by their own efforts; they would have to get additional help from abroad, and that meant from the United States. The same argument that had led him—as he said, after much "cogitation" —to vote for the original American loan still applied. They had to go on buying time and find a way of filling the gap until 1949, the earliest date by which the British recovery would be sufficiently complete for them to stand on their own feet.

Bevin did not doubt that the programme of cuts on which Dalton was relying was necessary; but he did not believe, even if it was backed by the increased productivity for which he appealed, that it would turn the trick. This accounts for the overriding importance he attached to Marshall's offer. He saw this as a way of securing further American aid that did not compromise Britain's independence and could combine the short-term aim of getting help from abroad with the long-term objective of his foreign policy, enabling Britain to make her own contribution to European recovery and maintain her identity in working with the Americans, not be reduced to the role of a satellite. While agreeing, therefore, in principle that emergency measures had to be taken to stop the loss of dollars, Bevin wanted to know whether any which were proposed might impair American confidence in Britain as a reliable partner and so prejudice the co-operation with the United States on which he relied not only for achieving Britain's objectives abroad but her domestic recovery as well.

It was a difficult balance to strike. If Dalton thought that Bevin was over-cautious about the American reaction if the UK simply refused to pay its share of the joint expenses of the Bi-zone,[1] the Americans thought he showed far too little recognition of the extent to which Britain was dependent on US support. Bevin had to face both ways and consider the external as well as the domestic implications of the cuts for which Dalton was calling. If he needed a reminder of what was involved he got it in the form of a strong protest from Marshall at reports that Britain intended to withdraw her remaining troops from Greece and reduce those in Italy to the five thousand garrisoning Trieste. Abrupt action of this sort, the Secretary of State protested, made co-operation difficult. What were the implications of the British decision?[2] Bevin replied by asking Marshall what timetable he had in mind. He assured him that there was no change in Britain's general policy, and would not be without prior consultation. But there had to be a cut in Britain's overall foreign commitments.[3] Douglas saw Bevin again a week later, on 9 August, to reiterate the importance attached to no withdrawals being made from Greece or Italy

[1] Dalton, *Memoirs*, p. 269, referring to discussions on 18–19 October 1947.
[2] Marshall to Bevin, 2 August 1947. FO 800/451/DEF/47/9.
[3] Bevin's reply, *ibid*.

without further consultation.[1] It was the need to take this extra dimension into account, rather than (as Dalton believed) unwillingness "to face the plain facts of arithmetic", which made Bevin reluctant to admit to the world, even to her friends, how weak Britain's real position was.

4

In June 1947 when he seized on the suggestion thrown out by Marshall in his Harvard speech, Bevin had had a vision of how Britain could find a way out of both her external and domestic difficulties, and take the rest of Western Europe with her. At the Paris meetings in July he had faced and overcome the biggest obstacle (as he believed) in the shape of Russian opposition. After that the rest should have been plain sailing. It was not. In the first half of August, when the British dollar crisis came to a head, none of the negotiations necessary to create the new design had been completed. France and Italy were faced with even greater difficulties than Britain and when Bevin went away for a few days' holiday on 9 August, he had no idea whether the framework for co-operation between Western Europe and the USA which he had been trying to build up might not collapse.

If Bevin's hopes were to be realized, everything turned on being able to create a more stable and lasting relationship with the United States. Yet British differences with the Americans in the summer of 1947 were by no means confined to Germany and Western Europe. In Palestine, to take the most obvious example, 1947 and 1948 were years when the differences between the two countries were a constant threat to their partnership in Europe.

Following its decision in February, the British Government asked the UN Secretary General on 2 April 1947 to summon a special session of the General Assembly. This in turn would be asked to set up a special committee to study the Palestine question and report to the regular session of the Assembly.

When the special session was held Cadogan stated the British view that Britain "Should not have the sole responsibility for enforcing a solution which is not accepted by both parties and which we cannot reconcile with our conscience." This statement was not taken as seriously as the British intended it to be. However, the Assembly agreed to set up a Special Committee (known as UNSCOP) composed of representatives of eleven states on a regional basis, gave it the widest terms of reference and required it to report by 1 September 1947. The Committee spent some time in Palestine. The Arab Higher Committee, however, decided to boycott its proceedings, thereby allowing the Arab case to go by default. The Zionists on the other hand took every possible step to put their point of view to the Committee and its individual members.

By the time the Committee got to Palestine, relations between the Jews and

---

[1] Note of Bevin–Douglas talk. FO 800/468/GRE/47/32.

the British which had steadily deteriorated in the opening months of 1947, appeared to be approaching civil war. The pattern of events—and emotions—became sickeningly familiar: a Jewish attack on the Tel Aviv military head-quarters, followed by British troops beating up Jews brought in from a nearby district; a Jewish raid on the British officers' club in Jerusalem in which twenty British soldiers were killed, followed by the imposition of martial law; the execution of Dov Gruner and three other Jews in Acre fortress and the suicide of two others, followed by a Jewish bombing raid on the Cairo–Haifa train and a rescue raid on the Acre prison; the continual arrival of immigrant ships off the Palestine coast, to be intercepted by the Royal Navy, and their passengers transferred amid scenes of violence to internment camps in Cyprus.

The initiative in escalating the violence was taken by the Jewish under-ground organizations: their object was to wear down the British will to remain in Palestine. If it provoked the British forces to retaliation, as it did, so much the better from their point of view. For all their invective against the British as Nazis, they were confident that the British authorities would not allow the sort of measures the Germans had used in occupied Europe: shooting hostages, deliberate massacres, the elimination of the Warsaw Ghetto, the extermina-tion camps. Many Jews were disturbed at the terrorist tactics employed, but so wide was the gulf between the Jewish Agency and the Administration that Ben Gurion could suggest that the Palestine police made no serious efforts to root out the terrorist camps, declaring, "It is clear that the present regime derives concrete advantages from terrorism."

There was no longer any contact between the Zionist leaders and the British Government, and in the same speech (to the Jewish National Council) Ben Gurion declared that the intention of Britain was

"To liquidate the Jews as a people and to recognise only the existence of individual Jews who could serve as objects either of pogroms or pity. . . . The present British Government has no interest in reaching a settlement which would remove the differences between Jews and Arabs; it is more desirable for them . . . that such differences should persist."[1]

The illegal immigration was a different matter from terrorism, an issue about which the whole Jewish community felt passionately, and the efforts to stop which constantly led to bitter clashes with the British. This too was stepped up in a concerted effort to increase Jewish numbers before a decision was taken on the Zionist claim to Palestine.

Finally there was the weapon to which the British found no reply, the world wide publicity campaign financed—like the provision of arms and ships—by American Zionists and organized through Jewish connections with the press, radio and film worlds. The sufferings of the Jews during the War had produced widespread feelings of sympathy, indignation and guilt which were directed

---

[1] *Zionist Review*, 11 April 1947, p. 3.

against the British. The Arab cause and the British dilemma were ignored or swept aside, and the British were represented as faithful followers of Hitler in the persecution of the Jews. The figures are the best corrective to this picture of Palestine under British occupation as another concentration camp. In the two years between August 1945 and 17 September 1947, the number of those killed by violence totalled 347. Of these (reversing the experience of other colonial wars and wars of liberation) the highest proportion was 169 British killed by Jews. The Jewish deaths numbered 88, the Arab 85, and five were unidentified. The statistics however, even if they were printed, made little impression by comparison with photographs of the scenes of violence when British sailors boarded the refugee ships and transferred their passengers, when necessary by force, to internment camps in Cyprus.

Bevin was again pilloried by Zionist publicists as the author of the measures taken against the Jews in Palestine. But the British documents make clear, first, that his energies in the spring and summer of 1947 were concentrated on other matters—the future of Germany, the Marshall Plan and Britain's financial crisis—and second, that once he had announced the decision to refer the Palestine question to the UN, he was not involved in the civil and military administration of the country. On the two occasions[1] when the Cabinet discussed policy in regard to terrorism and martial law (on the second occasion, summoning the High Commissioner and the GOC to join them) Bevin was in Moscow and took no part in the discussion or decisions.

The episode in which he did become involved was the turning back of the immigrant ship *Exodus*. The *Exodus*, a converted ferry boat, the *President Warfield*, bought with American funds, embarked 4,500 Jews from Eastern Europe at Marseilles with the intention of landing them in Palestine while the UN Special Committee was in the country. The *Christian Science Monitor's* correspondent in Haifa reported: "The Jews here believe that one 'illegal' ship may be worth 10 million words in helping to convince the Committee". If they succeeded in getting it through despite the British naval patrols, this would be a convincing demonstration of Jewish determination to reach the Promised Land and a humiliating defeat for the British; if they were turned back, it would be a convincing demonstration of British brutality. The British did all they could to prevent the ship leaving France but she got away without clearance. This was the largest number of immigrants ever to run the blockade and the British believed that if they were to maintain limits on Jewish immigration except as part of an agreed settlement, they could not ignore the challenge. Bevin then told the French that they "intended to make an example of this ship by obliging her to return to a French port with all her passengers."[2] To this Bidault agreed. Bevin made the statement not because it was his personal decision (although he participated in it) but because as Foreign

[1] 20 and 27 March. CM 30 & 33 (47).
[2] Bevin's talk with Bidault, 12 July 1947. FO 371/61815.

Secretary he was responsible for approaching the French and happened to be in Paris at the time. And his remark, often misquoted, about making an example, referred to returning the passengers to France where they had embarked, not to Germany.

The Royal Navy boarded the boat off Palestine and a fight for its control (without use of guns) went on for hours, with a radio commentary by the immigrants and crew, which was widely reported. The captain believed he could beach his ship and get most of the immigrants ashore, but he was overruled by the representative of the organizers who told him that the first priority was the political effect of the operation on world public opinion. This could best be achieved by letting the British take her into port where the scenes after the fighting and the forced disembarkation of the immigrants into three British ships were witnessed by members of the UN Committee and by a large number of American and other journalists.[1]

The British ships carried the refugees back to France, where the French (as they had promised Bevin) offered them the opportunity to go ashore and settle in France or move on elsewhere. 130 took advantage of the offer but the rest refused to go anywhere but to Palestine. Provided they held firm, this was a battle of wills which the British could not win. French opinion was strongly on the refugees' side and their determination to defy the British won widespread publicity and admiration. What were the British to do? To take the Jews back to Palestine or even Cyprus would be to admit defeat openly. In reprisal for the execution of three terrorists, the Irgun had seized two young British sergeants and hanged them. The discovery of their bodies, which were booby-trapped and blown to pieces, produced a reaction among the British public of a quite different kind from anything that had gone before. British police carried out unauthorized reprisals of their own in a raid on Tel Aviv in which several Jews were killed and there were anti-Semitic riots, including the burning of a synagogue, in a number of towns in the UK.

It was in this highly charged atmosphere that the Cabinet had to decide what to do with the *Exodus* refugees. Bringing them to the UK was ruled out on the grounds that it would lead to more anti-Jewish demonstrations. No other country was willing to receive them, and Bevin told the Cabinet, on the day the sergeants' bodies were discovered (31 July), that if they were to find the accommodation needed to house and feed 4,000 it would have to be in territory under British control, either a colonial territory or possibly in the British or US zones of Germany.[2] When the choice was narrowed down to camps near Hamburg, the Jews claimed—and many who were not Jews accepted—that this was an act of unexampled cruelty, forcing them to return to the country in which millions of Jews had perished. The evidence does not support the claim that the decision was taken in order to "make an example". (That remark

[1] See the account in Bethell, pp. 320–43.
[2] CM 66 (47).

449

applied to their earlier return to France.) Or that it was seen as more than the best answer available to a practical problem which had to be solved. The fact that all the refugees were free to leave the ships and stay in France, and that the British would have liked nothing better than to see them do so, was ignored. But even viewed as a blunder rather than a crime, for experienced politicians like Attlee and Bevin and other senior ministers to make a mistake which played so completely into the hands of those whose purpose was to arouse world opinion against the British shows how far their judgement had been clouded by anger and frustration with the situation in which they found themselves placed in the summer of 1947.

The killing of the two sergeants and the uproar over turning back the *Exodus* were followed by a revulsion in British opinion against staying a day longer than was necessary in Palestine and in favour of withdrawal, whatever the strategic or political arguments to the contrary. It was a mood fully shared by Bevin and led him already on 2 August to warn the American Ambassador:

"We were disillusioned and disappointed by our thankless task as Mandatory and might be forced to give up the charge. The Palestine situation was poisoning relations between the U.S.A. and Great Britain."[1]

Unfortunately, while withdrawal might relieve the British and satisfy the Zionists who saw Britain as the enemy, it was to make even greater difficulties between the British and the US Governments.

Nothing else so much threatened Anglo–US relations as Palestine; but there were other clashes of view and interest as well. Thus the disagreement between the British and United States Governments over international control of atomic energy and disarmament was still no nearer to resolution. In mid-July of 1947 Bevin sent Attlee a memorandum on the UN and disarmament, which took as its starting point the dilemma of the Security Council. If the Great Powers were agreed, there was no danger of war; if they disagreed, the veto prevented action being taken. Bevin, however, had no more faith than in 1946 in plans to revise the Charter by limiting the use of the veto and requiring a permanent member of the Security Council to abstain from voting when accused of aggression. He thought that the Soviet Union would block this or any other scheme for getting round the power of veto. The right course, he argued, was not to force a show-down in the United Nations over the two draft conventions on atomic energy and conventional armaments, as the US Delegation wished to do, but to wait and see how the situation might be affected by developments on other issues. This would not mean any sacrifice of security, since there was little chance of getting this by pushing faster; on the other hand, if there was a general improvement in relations with the Russians,

---

[1] Report dated 4 August and Bevin's talk with Douglas on 2 August 1947. FO 800/487/PA/ 47/10.

this could improve the prospect of discussing an amendment to the Charter with some chance of success.[1]

As a result, a note was sent to the State Department (dated 12 August)[2] putting the view that, with no prospect of agreement on the proposals before the UN Atomic Energy Commission, it was undesirable and unnecessary to force atomic questions to an issue with the Soviets before the November meeting of the CFM. As the Note admitted, the Americans took the opposite view and there was a good chance of open disagreement between the two delegations when the Atomic Energy Commission met to consider its report at the end of August.

There was a third and immediate clash over another cherished objective of American policy, the establishment of an International Trade Organization and the elimination of Britain's imperial preferences which were still under negotiation in Geneva. On 25 July, Bevin had told Lew Douglas that the Americans were pressing

"Too hard and too fast . . . on the matter of non-discrimination which, although he agrees to it as a long-run policy, is not adapted or suitable to the present emergency conditions. By the year 1951 he thinks that they would be applicable but for the year 1948 he believes they are not."[3]

At a meeting in Paris on 31 July Cripps warned Clayton that Britain would run out of dollars in October and that this meant they would have to adopt any measures necessary to get the bare essentials they needed including any form of discrimination. "In such straits it was impossible for them to sign . . . any agreement which limited their freedom of action *in any way*."[4] In particular, while still supporting the Charter of the ITO and the General Agreement on Trade and Tariffs, they must insist on postponing the application of any rules against discrimination.

The American negotiators called for the strongest opposition to the British proposal and Wilcox, the vice-chairman of the US delegation to the Geneva talks, seeing the British demands as only one more proof of their unwillingness to abandon the system of empire preferences, urged that the British need for further aid from the USA put cards in the Americans' hands which they should not hesitate to play.

"If we cannot now obtain the liquidation of the Ottawa system, we shall never do so. What we must have is a front page headline that says 'Empire Preference System Broken at Geneva'. With this, the success of this whole series of negotiations is assured."[5]

---

[1] Bevin to Attlee, 16 July 1947. FO 800/451/DEF/47/7.

[2] FRUS 1947 (1) pp. 597–600.

[3] Douglas to Washington, 25 July, reporting on his talk with Bevin that day. FRUS 1947 (3) p. 43.

[4] Memorandum of Cripps–Clayton talks in Paris, 31 July. FRUS 1947 (1) pp. 969–70. See also the British *aide-mémoire* delivered in Washington on 29 July, *ibid.*, pp. 967–9.

[5] Wilcox to Clayton, the Chairman of the US Delegation, 6 August 1947, *ibid.*, p. 973.

Fortunately for the British, those in the State Department who knew most about the situation of the UK took a different view and Marshall telegraphed to the delegation in Geneva:

"Apparent Br. econ. and domestic political situation such that we must accede their demands for permission to discriminate."[1]

It was by no means clear, however, that the US Congress would not take Wilcox's rather than the State Department's view, see the British as defaulting on their earlier promises and regard this as a poor recommendation for Marshall aid or any other form of further assistance to a socialist government in difficulties. The risk of such a reaction was bound to be increased if the British took the step of suspending the convertibility of sterling.

5

It had not yet come to this when Bevin began his holiday on 9 August. On the 7th the Cabinet had at last rid itself of the diversionary issue of Morrison's compromise plan on steel and Bevin had turned out with the rest of the Cabinet for a House of Commons debate on the economic situation (6–8 August) which did nothing to increase anyone's confidence (including the Cabinet's) in the Government's ability to get on top of the crisis.

Part of the trouble was the near-exhaustion of ministers who had been in office without a break for seven years and had lost, at least temporarily, their powers of resilience. Bevin got away on the 9th but Morrison kept the House in session over the August bank holiday in order to pass the legislation needed to give the Government emergency powers. And hardly had the members of the Cabinet begun to recover from the strain of the last few months when they were summoned back to London.

Cuts were no longer enough. In the five days, 10–15 August, Britain suffered a drain on her dollar resources to the amount of $176 m; the Treasury thought it might rise to $300 m. a week, a rate which would exhaust the remaining $700 m. of the American loan in little more than two weeks.[2] The financial situation had got out of hand and Morrison, who had been left in charge while Attlee and other ministers took a holiday, brought as many as he could back for an emergency Cabinet on Sunday the 17th.

Bevin had only to come up from Swanage and went direct to the Foreign Office. While he was there, Dalton and Cripps came across from No 11 Downing Street to sound out the possibility of his taking over as Prime Minister. Once again, Bevin resisted the suggestion and nothing was said

---

[1] Secretary of State to Geneva, 2 August 1947, *ibid.*, p. 973.
[2] These were the figures Bevin gave to the US Ambassador, Lew Douglas, on 18 August 1947. FRUS 1947 (3) p. 60.

about any change when the Cabinet met at 5 o'clock and finally decided to suspend convertibility.

This proved to be more difficult than expected, at least if it was to be done with American agreement to let the British draw the remaining instalments of the loan. Bevin stayed on for a couple of days to help Dalton who wrote in his diary: "He has been a tower of good-humoured strength in these past days and handled many difficult interviews most skilfully".[1] Amongst these was breaking the news to the American ambassador for transmission to Washington.

After giving the facts about the run on sterling, Bevin told Douglas that if the issue had been purely a monetary one, he would oppose taking any steps. But more than this was at stake.

"A breach in sterling would necessarily lead to bilateral arrangements; shrinking of trade at the very time they were attempting to expand trade . . ., would have profound effects, adversely, on the attitude of both France and Italy with the possibility of political crises there . . . [and] would impair if not destroy all the efforts that had been made over the course of the last two years in the political field. . . . Certainly he felt that it would aggravate aggressive action throughout Europe and particularly in the danger spots by the Soviet."[2]

Although they were critical of Labour's inability to master Britain's economic problems, Douglas and those he reported to in Washington accepted Bevin's argument that the British Government had acted from necessity, and the suspension of convertibility did not disturb relations between London and Washington as much as would have appeared likely when the Loan Agreement was signed. Both sides had learned since then and were still learning.

Bevin at least was clear that however necessary it might be to stop the outflow of dollars and impose cuts, these were, at best, negative measures which would prevent Britain's position from getting worse but would do nothing to improve it. In the long run he had no doubt that such an improvement had to come from the nation's own increased efforts and this was the lesson he rubbed in when he spoke to the TUC Annual Congress on 3 September. His speech, lasting for eighty minutes, was described by the *Manchester Guardian* as "a tremendous oratorical triumph with which he overwhelmed the Congress".

He reminded his audience that in the past,

"When the balance of payments went wrong, the old system had one very simple method by which to deal with it. They restricted purchases abroad, they called in credit and they protected unemployment and I well remember on the Macmillan Committee in 1929 and 1930, saying to the then Governor of the Bank of England: 'Why do you say that in these difficulties it is better to keep people on the dole than to employ them?' His answer was: 'You see if you employ them, you import raw materials; if you employ

---

[1] Dalton, p. 264.
[2] Douglas to Washington, 18 August. FRUS 1947 (3) pp. 60–61.

them, they have a standard of consumption higher than we can afford, and therefore it is better to keep the people at the standard of living that the dole represents than to employ them.' "

That was the system the unions had fought against and which Labour in the Coalition government had broken with by the commitment to full employment after the war. This was what was now at stake in the Labour Government's appeal for increased production.

"I get accused of tying Great Britain up to America. My God! I am here this morning to appeal to you to fight for our independence in the workshop, in the mine, in the field. It is a very ignoble thing for any Foreign Secretary to have to deal with anybody upon whom you are dependent. Who wants that position? Who wants it with a trade union training such as I have had, who built a great union on purpose so that I could stand up equal to anyone in the world? . . . I want Britain to stand self-reliant and to come back, and I can only do that if you come forward. . . .

"Let me try and put it clearly. I have described the old method of starvation and you are familiar with it. We have now accepted the view that instead of starvation to save ourselves we will adopt production. That is the issue. If you do not give the production then this country will lose its position and back you will be forced, all of you, to the old 1926 position over again. Do not complain that you have not been warned, because that is the issue you have to fight."

This was Bevin on his own ground, speaking with a freedom and sureness of touch he rarely achieved in the House of Commons. He had put the same point in yet another meeting with the miners' leaders at Downing Street on 21 August:

"We are spending £600 million p.a. more than we are getting. There are two ways of solving the problem: one is to get the coal, make the goods, sell them and keep the standard of life up; the other is to restrict imports which will produce one and a half or two million unemployed in the country."

Bevin, however, was no sentimentalist when it came to industrial relations. He wanted the extra coal all right: as he told the TUC he was the first British Foreign Secretary for 400 years who had been able to offer nothing in the way of goods, money or coal. But he was not prepared to give the miners whatever they asked for. He told the miners' leaders at Downing Street that, without a guarantee that the men would do a full five days' work before being paid extra for Saturdays, he would advise the Cabinet not to accept any such offer. Otherwise the miners would simply be selling back to the country at two and a half times the leisure they had already been given.[1]

Bevin was not shocked by the miners' tactics, he thought they were the product of a long history of conflict in the mining industry under private

---

[1] Verbatim report in FO 800/493/PLT/47/20; and Bevin's advice to Attlee, 11 September 1947, *ibid.*, PLT/47/28.

ownership which was not going to be got rid of quickly. He told the TUC that in the end he believed the miners would respond to the nation's needs; but it would take time and the Government could not wait. It was for that reason that he had welcomed Marshall's proposal.

> The basis of that proposal is that Europe must determine what she can do for herself and if we are to maintain our independence as countries in Europe that is absolutely essential. If you go on merely borrowing money and living in a fool's paradise you will never get your own economy right. I was one of the reluctant people about the American loan for a long time. I joined in the end in supporting it, because on the calculations I thought it would give us till 1949, by which time I believed the re-conversion of this country would make it possible for us to stand on our own feet. Well, it has not worked out that way. . . . Our calculations were wrong . . . We are one move behind all the time; and we are a move behind because we have not got the production in our own resources to carry it out. Therefore we have asked the Paris Conference to put forward their proposals."[1]

The question still continued to be asked whether, in these circumstances, Bevin would not be better placed in No. 10 than in the Foreign Office. On 5 September Cripps came to see Dalton, who was just back from holiday, and argued that if they did not replace Attlee with Bevin, "the Government, the Party and the country were all sunk. There was no leadership, no grip, no decision." He proposed that the two of them together with Morrison should go and tell Attlee that he must resign in favour of Bevin. Dalton cautiously agreed, on condition that Morrison did too—"and I greatly doubted whether he would". Confident as ever, Cripps went off to see Morrison: Bevin was to be Prime Minister and Minister of Production, with Cripps as his chief of staff, Dalton at the Foreign Office, Attlee as Chancellor and Morrison as Deputy Prime Minister. Morrison fully agreed about Attlee, but not about Bevin: he thought that he himself should be Prime Minister and would not serve under Bevin. He told Dalton the next day that he did not trust Bevin not to knife him if he was No 2 and described him as "a strange mixture of genius and stupidity".

Undeterred by Morrison's resistance, Cripps went to see Attlee on 9 September and put his proposal on his own responsibility. Attlee took no offence but skilfully deflected Cripps' aim by asking "Why shouldn't *you* take on the job and become Minister of Production?" Although troubled at the effect this would have on Morrison's fortunes—since he would take over the latter's responsibility for economic planning—Cripps was captivated by the suggestion. And so, as Dalton commented, "The movement begun by Cripps, with my support, to put Bevin in Attlee's place, has now turned into a movement to put Cripps in Morrison's place, or at least in the most important part of it".[2]

The Cabinet reshuffle which followed was not settled until the end of

[1] Speech at TUC, Southport, 3 September 1947.
[2] Dalton, pp. 240–46.

September. It left Bevin where he wished to be, at the Foreign Office. On one point, at least, all the accounts agree, that he had never been prepared to lend support to any move to get rid of Attlee and make him Prime Minister instead. "Why should I do him out of a job?" he asked his Parliamentary Under-Secretary Christopher Mayhew. "What's Clem ever done to me?"[1] Francis Williams recalls that when he was approached, Bevin replied contemptuously, "Who do you think I am? Lloyd George?"

"Attlee," he added, "was the best Prime Minister any Labour Government could possibly have and anyone who wanted to get rid of him was a fool."[2]

So Attlee stayed at No. 10, showing by the way in which he handled the crisis the skill which justified his remaining Prime Minister. No one was more delighted than Bevin. "What a man", he said to Arthur Moyle, Attlee's Parliamentary Private Secretary. "He plucked victory from defeat. I love the little man. He is our Campbell-Bannerman."[3]

Cripps became, first, Minister for Economic Affairs, and then in November, Chancellor of the Exchequer when Dalton had to resign office as the result of a budget leak. This was an important change. For not only did Cripps take a firmer grip of the economic situation than either Morrison or Dalton, but he succeeded in removing the lingering suspicions with which Bevin had regarded him since the 1930s and establishing a partnership between Chancellor and Foreign Secretary which both strengthened the Government and benefited the country. Even before Cripps became Chancellor, Bevin was writing to him (16 October) suggesting ways in which the tax system could be altered to increase incentives,[4] and they rapidly established a degree of mutual

---

[1] Quoted by Donoughue and Jones, p. 414.

[2] Francis Williams, *Prime Minister*, p. 224.

[3] Quoted in Harris, p. 350.

[4] Bevin's views on incomes policy are always worth looking at. He wrote to Cripps on 16 October 1947 that the trouble was that industry relied on payment by results but that the higher paid man realized that if he worked harder and earned more, he put himself in a higher tax category. Bevin suggested that a taxable basis should be worked out with the unions for each grade of work, and that excess earnings which derived from premium bonuses, payment by results and straight piecework over and above this should be exempt. The result would be less pressure to push up standard wages and a preference for increased incentives which would be tax free. Per contra, when demand slackened and output fell off, the standard wage would be preserved. Bevin claimed that the wage position would become self-adjusting and, in addition, there would be an incentive to introduce new methods.

On the employers' side, Bevin proposed (a) that a percentage of profit should be free of tax if put back into the business; (b) that the tax should be lowered where there was no increase of price added to the final product as a result of increased wages or increased cost of materials and where the increase in profits was entirely due to increased output (measured against the previous year's production) and (c) that the tax should be raised where profits were achieved on lower production or without regard to wages or increased cost of materials. FO 800/493/PLT/47/28. Hugh Gaitskell who had just become Minister of Fuel and Power was impressed by Bevin's argument and wrote in his diary: "Truly remarkable for something thrown off by the Foreign Secretary in his spare time." (22 October, 1947, quoted by Philip Williams, *Hugh Gaitskell* (London 1979) p. 821.) It was eventually turned down as administratively unworkable.

understanding and confidence which had never existed between Bevin and Dalton, still less between Bevin and Morrison.

6

Meanwhile, in the last week of August the State Department had begun to bring pressure to bear on the participants in the Paris conference to produce a plan which would have a better chance of meeting American expectations of the European response to Marshall's offer.[1] The initial figures showed a grand deficit, *after* the Europeans' efforts to help themselves, of 28.2 billion dollars which the United States would be expected to meet. Even in 1951 Europe would still be nearly 6 billion dollars short of self-sufficiency. Clayton told Franks, the chairman of the Conference Executive Committee, that figures of this order were out of the question and that the European countries had not come to grips with their problems. Franks' view was that the Americans would have to impose conditions. This advice was accepted and seven such conditions were presented to the Executive Committee on 30 August. The Americans laid particular stress on the need to eliminate outside aid within a four-year period and on the need to produce a concerted inter-European approach instead of adding up unco-ordinated national requests. By way of illustration Clayton pointed to the fact that it was planned to operate all existing steel plants in the sixteen nations at full capacity from 1948 on, although there was nothing like enough coal or transport to make this possible.

In addition to a British lead in getting the Paris conference to revise its proposals, the Americans particularly wanted British concurrence in bringing into the Conference's reckoning their plans to raise the level of industry in the German Bi-zone and in making these part of the European Recovery Programme. The Bi-zone was the one area of Europe where the Americans (with British concurrence) were in control and the one part of Europe where there were large industrial resources which were standing idle and could be quickly brought into use. The Americans believed that putting these resources to work was essential to Europe's recovery and that the French must not be allowed to block this by insisting on priority for their rival Monnet Plan of long-term capital development which also depended on coal from the Ruhr. The American aim was to get the industrial rehabilitation of the Bi-zone made part of the Paris plan, thereby allowing the Americans, through their responsibility for the Bi-zone, to give a strong lead in producing "that element of material aid and subordination of separate national aims to co-operative approach [which] has been generally lacking".[2]

The Americans' recognition of the importance of the British role in the Paris

[1] This is documented in FRUS 1947 (3) pp. 356–435.
[2] The phrase is taken from Marshall's telegram of 8 September 1947 to Douglas in London, arguing the case for bringing the Bi-zone into the Paris discussions. FRUS 1947 (3) p. 418.

talks was not exaggerated. The French had able enough men to represent them in Hervé Alphand and Jean Monnet, but their political commitment to the success of the talks was weakened by their fundamental disagreement with the Americans over Germany and by their anxiety in face of determined opposition from the French Communist Party. Bevin stood out on the European scene as the one political leader with the determination as well as the personal commitment to drive the conference through to a successful conclusion.

It came as a shock to the Americans, therefore, to find Bevin refusing to fall in with their proposals and standing his ground when Marshall applied pressure. If the British prevented discussion of the Bi-zone, Marshall telegraphed to London, "we can hardly expect to be successful in opposing a French desire to protect Monnet Plan, Scandinavian tendency to withdraw from full participation and other centrifugal forces working against a co-ordinated area approach". The State Department saw the British opposition as another example of these same centrifugal forces and a reflection of British

"Reluctance to co-ordinate their recovery program with that of Western Europe. . . . It appears to the Department that British wish to benefit fully from a European program as suggested by Secretary of State while at the same time maintaining the position of not being wholly a European country".[1]

Marshall's telegram went on to suggest that the British feared, if the bi-zonal prgramme was made the subject of discussion in the Paris conference, that their own recovery programme would have to be submitted to a similar review by the other powers. Marshall explicitly denied that he wished to force Bevin's hand in this way, but he instructed Douglas to make the point that failure to include the Bi-zone could seriously prejudice the chances of achieving a European programme at all and to urge Bevin to consider the consequences of a continued British refusal.

When Douglas saw Bevin the next day, however, he had no success in changing his mind. With the support of his officials (Roger Makins and Hall-Patch were both present) Bevin maintained that they were already doing their best to incorporate the Americans' seven conditions in the Paris report and that any further intervention at this stage leading to a postponement of the final meeting might cause such dismay as to bring the work of the conference to naught. Franks had carried the participating countries as far towards a co-operative effort as was possible. "Any effort to press further would so impair national sovereignty that many countries would rebel". Bevin suggested that it would be sufficient if the report gave Franks authority to call the Committee on Economic Co-operation together for further discussion and additional work later.[2]

Clayton had had no more success with the Executive Committee of the

[1] Marshall to Douglas, 8 September. FRUS 1947 (3) p. 418.
[2] Douglas to Marshall, 9 September, *ibid.*, p. 420.

Conference. At a meeting on 10 September Franks and his colleagues told the Americans that "to meet entirely the U.S. conception of a programme would require a change in the terms of reference and this would mean a new conference". As a compromise, Franks took up the suggestion already made in London, that they should label the conference report as provisional and continue the work of reviewing the programme in Washington. To give both sides more time, the Executive proposed postponing the final meeting of the conference at which the Foreign Ministers would be present. The time gained would be used to revise the report with greater emphasis on mutual co-operation and to separate-out items of capital equipment which would have to be financed outside the programme. The Conference would then be recessed in order to allow work on the programme to continue and the participants would commit themselves to set up a multilateral organization with the power to review each country's performance.

While this compromise was being elaborated in Paris, Bevin as chairman of the Conference sent a message to Marshall expressing concern that

"The impression has been created that the work of the conference has been unsatisfactory and is now having to be done again under American pressure. This is, of course, not the case; but if the impression is allowed to persist it will do untold harm . . . [and] may prejudice the final outcome of the conference."[1]

One of the arguments Bevin used in his message to Marshall was that the harm which might be done by American pressure was out of proportion to any improvement in the report which it might secure. The same point had already been made by George Kennan, the head of the State Department's Policy Planning Staff. In a memorandum dated 4 September he argued that the USA

"Must not look to the people in Paris to accomplish the impossible. . . . No bold or original approach to Europe's problems will be forthcoming. . . . Worst of all: the report will not fulfill all of the essential requirements listed by Mr Clayton."

Kennan recommended that the US Government should accept this and "make efforts to have the report presented in such a way as to avoid any impression of finality.

"Let it come to us on the understanding that it will be used only as a basis of further discussion; try to whittle it down as much as possible by negotiation; then . . . decide unilaterally what we finally wish to present to Congress. This would mean that we would listen to all that the Europeans had to say, but in the end we would not *ask* them, we would just *tell* them what they would get."

According to Kennan "this was what some of the more far-sighted Europeans hope we will do."[2]

[1] Bevin's verbatim message sent by Douglas, 12 September. FRUS 1947 (3) pp. 428–9.
[2] *Ibid.*, pp. 397–405.

Between the 10th and 12th September the two Englishmen, Franks and Hall-Patch, persuaded the American team of Clayton, Douglas and Caffery to accept Bevin's suggestion and so leave the way open to the solution recommended by Kennan. The report was to be labelled "provisional" or "a first report" and it was to be revised to give greater emphasis to the principles or conditions to which the Americans attached so much importance, but no attempt would be made to re-cast it before the foreign ministers met to sign it. Instead, the Conference was to recess, leaving Franks with the authority, "after the report has been more carefully analysed by the U.S., to reconvene the conference for such further work as may be necessary".[1] In accepting this, the Americans also tacitly accepted Bevin's argument against pressing the inclusion of the Bi-zone at this stage and let it drop. The compromise met Bevin's anxiety that the work done in Paris should not be repudiated or the risk run of the Conference ending in failure, at the same time that it allowed the US Government the opportunity to carry through a thorough revision of the report's figures in the very different atmosphere of Washington. In reporting the compromise to Washington on 17 September and recommending its acceptance, Douglas confirmed that the procedure was now "entirely satisfactory" to Bevin.

Even when revised, however, the plan still showed a combined deficit with North America, for the four years 1948–51, of more than 22,000 million dollars. Some of this could be financed by loans from the International Bank and other credit operations, but this still left over 19,000M dollars to be found by the USA, a higher figure than the State Department believed Congress would ever agree to.

The revised text of the report was ready for the European foreign ministers to sign in Paris on 22 September.[2] The ceremony took place in the Quai d'Orsay and was presided over by Bevin. It was indeed thanks to Bevin that the Conference had met in the first place and that it had not broken down under American pressure but ended with sufficient appearance of success to keep hope alive.

The Americans were right in thinking that British resistance to being treated as simply one more European country played its part in Bevin's refusal to fall in with their proposals. But this was only part of the reason for his opposition. He had a better understanding than the Americans of the fragility of European confidence after the experience of the war, and the limits this placed on what could be asked at this stage (on what could be asked of the French, for example, in relation to Germany) and of the risks of trying to expand those limits too quickly by direct pressure. In all this Bevin spoke as the representative of Europe, not just of Britain, and did so the more effectively because he was the last person who could be suspected of dragging his feet in

[1] Douglas' summary report, 12 September, *ibid.*, pp. 429–30.
[2] It was circulated to the Cabinet on 17 September as CP (47) 260 and approved at its meeting on 20 September. CM 76 (47).

response to Marshall's offer. The State Department's initial impatience with Bevin gave way to recognition that he was serving the common interest as well as that of Britain by giving them honest if unpalatable advice instead of saying, as so many European politicians did, whatever he thought it would please them to hear. In agreeing to go along with the British view, the US Under-Secretary of State, Bob Lovett, conceded that the State Department "believes C.E.E.C. under Bevin's and Franks' leadership has made much progress in the short time it has been at work and taking into account limiting terms of reference."[1]

7

The Paris Conference on Economic Co-operation showed how little substance there was in the favourite idea of Crossman and the rest of the *Keep Left* group, of Western Europe as a Third Force independent of both the United States and the USSR. Even with the promise of American aid the sixteen nations meeting in Paris had found it virtually impossible to produce a practicable plan for mutual co-operation; and even if they had, it was now clearer than ever that they could not close the gap and avoid economic disaster by their own efforts without American aid. The Paris conference was necessary, psychologically in order to hold the Western European nations together and keep their hopes alive, politically in order to show Congress and American opinion that the Europeans had the will to help themselves. It is uncertain whether Bevin, in his own mind, had ever hoped for more from it. If he had, by the time the Conference ended he was satisfied to get a report which would allow further discussions to be moved to Washington where it was clear that the real decisions had to be made.

There was one other set of negotiations, however, still to be concluded in Europe the outcome of which could powerfully influence Congressional attitudes on Marshall aid. These were the negotiations in Geneva for a General Agreement on Trade and Tariffs, which threatened to founder in face of British insistence that the position in which they found themselves made it impossible to agree to the abolition or further reduction of imperial preferences on which the American negotiators had set their hearts.[2] A fresh attempt to persuade the British to make concessions came to the crunch just before Bevin left to sign the report of the Paris Conference. Cripps rebutted the American arguments with the counter argument that the offers of reciprocal tariff reductions had struck a balance and that any reduction or elimination of preferences by the UK would have to be compensated for by further reductions in US tariffs. The discussion became heated and reached a deadlock, Cripps saying that he would present

[1] Lovett to Douglas, 13 September, *ibid.*, pp. 430–31.
[2] The American case was persuasively set out by Wilcox, the Vice-Chairman of the US Delegation, in a statement reprinted in FRUS 1947 (1) pp. 986–93.

the latest American proposal to the Cabinet with a recommendation that it be not accepted.

Clayton and Douglas reported to Washington after the meeting that they felt "the whole situation was so serious and fraught with such grave danger that we should have a talk with Bevin." Bob Dixon recorded the subsequent meeting in his diary, just before leaving for Paris:

"A busy day in the Office, with Clayton and Douglas next door trying to blackmail E.B. and Cripps into dropping imperial preference under the threat of no help for Britain under the Marshall Plan."

Clayton and Douglas reported that the arguments on both sides were presented to Bevin, and that Clayton told him that, if the British were not prepared to make further concessions, he would have seriously to consider whether he should not recommend the Secretary of State that no agreement be concluded. He added:

"Whether an agreement was entered into on the basis of the British proposal or not, the whole matter would certainly come out in Congressional hearings on the Marshall Plan and would seriously prejudice public opinion and Congressional action with reference to British participation in that plan . . .

"[Douglas] pointed out that the matter had serious political as well as economic aspects which was the reason we had troubled Mr. Bevin with it."[1]

Bevin, however, was no more inclined than Cripps to give way. Both believed that the American negotiators could not afford to return home without an agreement. Cripps' reply after discussion in the Cabinet confirmed the line he had taken[2] and the Americans reluctantly but realistically accepted that "an open breach with the U.K. will hurt the Marshall plan more than their failure, under present circumstances, to give substantial elimination of preferences". At the same meeting of the Cabinet Bevin proposed a study group to examine the possibility of a customs union of the Commonwealth and Empire, and how this might be related to the proposal for a European Customs Union which had been put forward by the Committee of European Co-operation and which was being pressed by the US Government.[3]

Negotiations were therefore resumed at Geneva on a basis acceptable to the British. As a further concession an exchange of notes between the UK and Canada was arranged to coincide with the signature of the General Agreement in which the two countries undertook to release each other from their obligations under the Ottawa Agreements of 1932 to maintain existing margins of preference. The US negotiators described this undertaking by the UK and Canada as "the abrogation of the most important part of the Ottawa

[1] Report of discussions in London by Douglas and Clayton, 23 September, *ibid*. pp. 993–6.
[2] The British reply, dated 25 September, is printed in full in FRUS 1947 (1) pp. 998–1001.
[3] CM 77 (47), 25 September 1947

Agreements"[1] and were prepared, together with the British and 21 other countries, to sign the GATT on 30 October.[2]

Apart from its intrinsic importance in shaping the post-war development of international trade, the signature of GATT represented for both parties the successful turning of a second awkward corner in Anglo–American relations. As in the case of the convertibility of sterling, American insistence on breaking down the system of imperial preferences belonged to an earlier phase of US policy, the objectives of which, as the British pointed out, were in conflict not only with the economic facts of the post-war world but with the aims which US foreign policy had adopted with the Truman doctrine and the Marshall plan. This was harsh doctrine, however, for Congress to accept and the chances of securing congressional support for the objectives of the newer phase in US policy would have been seriously endangered if the earlier one of multilateral free trade had been abandoned, particularly as a result of British opposition. It was essential for Britain, in the economic circumstances of 1947, to secure release from both commitments, to the elimination of imperial preferences as well as to the convertibility of sterling; but it was no less essential to the British to secure such release in a way which, however reluctantly, the Americans could accept. The two agreements reached, in August, to suspend convertibility and in October to settle for a compromise on tariffs and preferences, represented effective diplomacy on both sides.

On both occasions, as in his refusal to fall in with US proposals for galvanizing the Paris conference, Bevin had shown that it was possible—and in his view essential—to combine a clear recognition of Britain's and Europe's dependence on American aid with the strength of character to face and hold out for an independent view of British—and indeed of American—interests, even in face of strong pressure from Washington. Bevin found himself having to stand up to criticism from opposite directions, in Britain (from both the Left-wing of the Labour Party and the Right-wing of the Conservatives) that he was surrendering British independence to American dictation; and in Washington not only from habitual critics of socialist Britain in Congress and the Press but also from friends of Britain who felt that he was making it more difficult for them to secure popular and congressional support for the Marshall Plan. Once again he succeeded in convincing the State Department that his great merit as a Foreign Secretary was his ability to combine reliability as an ally with the

---

[1] Winthrop Brown to Truman, 17 October, *ibid.*, pp. 1014–15.

[2] The meeting at Geneva was not the final stage in the long drawn out negotiations between the US and Britain on commercial policy which began at the same time as the negotiations for the Financial Agreement of 1945 and had an even earlier history during the War (see pp. 14–15 above). The Preparatory Committee which produced the Geneva draft for an International Trade Organization had then to secure the agreement of another 40 countries. This was done, with a number of modifications, at the Havana World Conference on Trade and Employment in March 1948. After receiving a report from Harold Wilson (CP (48) 84) the Cabinet approved signature of the Final Act and the General Agreement on Tariffs and Trade (GATT) at its meeting on 15 March 1948, CM 22 (48).

readiness to speak out when he thought the Americans were making a mistake.

While the negotiations on GATT were being concluded in Geneva and London, in the autumn of 1947 three very different sets of negotiations opened in Washington, in all of which Bevin, although remaining in London, was deeply involved.

In the first, Sir Oliver Franks led the Executive Committee of the recessed Conference on European Economic Co-operation in discussions on the Marshall Plan.

In the second, Sir William Strang led a British delegation in Anglo-American talks on the financing of the Bi-zone.

In the third, a British team of officials and staff officers held secret discussions on British and American policy in the Middle East, generally referred to as the Pentagon talks.

It was originally visualized, in adjourning the Paris conference, that it would be recalled after the talks in Washington and would then revise the initial production and import programmes, in order to take account of the participation of Western Germany and of what would be available in 1948. In view, however, of the rapid deterioration of the situation in France and Italy, this timetable had to be shortened and the idea of reconvening the Paris conference dropped. The Executive Committee stayed on in Washington working with the US officials concerned and reporting directly to the participating countries.[1] A Dutch staff member of the European group reports that the Americans used them as "part of a team charged with the difficult task of making the Paris Report as attractive as possible for the presentation to Congress" and that in the process "there was an inclination on the part of the Administration to change accounts, to colour presentations, to minimize some problems and over-emphasize others, to hide existing shortcomings and to applaud practically non-existing achievements in its efforts to win Congressional approval".[2]

The key Senate and House Committees (Foreign Relations and Appropriations) were recalled for 10 November and a special session of Congress summoned for the 17th. In order to keep France, Italy and Austria going until the main programme could be adopted, a bill for interim aid covering their needs up to April 1948 was introduced first asking for a total of $597 M. A vehement debate developed in which the State Department's past record and future plans were belaboured by critics from all sides, by those like Henry Wallace, who denounced the Marshall Plan as a provocation to the Soviet Union and likely to lead to war, as well as by those like Taft, who denounced it as economically unsound, tainted by socialism, incapable of altering the situation in Europe and mistaken in ignoring the greater danger in China.

---

[1] The British records of the Washington talks are in CAB 133/72, and in FO 371/62671–5; the US records are in FRUS 1947 (3) pp. 439–84.
[2] Ernst H. van der Beugel: *From Marshall Aid to Atlantic Partnership* (Amsterdam 1966) p. 93.

In step: Twenty-four hours after the formation of the new Labour Government, in July 1945, Attlee and Bevin leave Northolt aerodrome to take the place of Churchill and Eden at Potsdam.

The last of the Summit Conferences: Potsdam 1945. Stalin (standing), Truman, Byrnes (on Truman's right), Attlee, Bevin.

Bevin with one of his private
secretaries in the Secretary of
State's room at the Foreign Office.

Bevin ribs Vyshinsky after rebutting Soviet charges against Britain at the
UN Security Council, London, February, 1946.

The German problem: the ruins of Krupps' factory at Essen and an underfed German steel worker at Duisburg (*below*).

Bevin arriving for one of the sessions of the six-week long Council of Foreign Ministers held in Moscow, March–April 1947.

Bevin with the other Foreign Ministers, Marshall, Molotov and Bidault at the 1947 Moscow Council.

Sir Oliver Franks watches Bevin signing the agreement setting up the first OEEC as Europe's response to Marshall's offer, September 1947.

Bevin greets General Marshall, the US Secretary of State, at the UN session in Paris, September 1948.

The ruins of the King David Hotel, Jerusalem, blown up in July 1946.

The refugee ship *President Warfield* (renamed *Exodus*) brought into Haifa harbour by the Royal Navy, July 1947.

The British withdrawal from Palestine: General Cunningham takes the final salute,
May 1948.

Bevin and Molotov meet, divided only by an interpreter and a choice of neckties.

The Berlin airlift.

The Berliners demonstrate their determination to resist Russian/Communist
pressure in front of the ruined Reichstag, September 1948.

The British and American military governors during the Berlin crisis:
General Robertson and (*below*) General Clay, 1948.

Bevin with the two ambassadors (standing: Lewis Douglas, USA; Massigli, France) with whom he collaborated closely during the Berlin crisis. The fourth man is the Italian Ambassador.

Bevin speaking at an official dinner in London, attended by high-ranking US officers (Prime Minister Attlee on his right).

Bevin giving the thumbs up sign to Acheson at the conclusion of the devaluation talks in Washington, September 1949.

Bevin with Sir William Strang, the head of the Foreign Office, and his private secretary.

Bevin and the French Foreign Minister, Robert Schuman, talking together at the Foreign Office, January 1949.

Bevin aboard the *Queen Mary* on his final journey to the United States, September 1950. Seven months later he was dead.

After returning from a hearing by the Senate Appropriations Committee, Dean Acheson wrote to Marshall:

"Sessions devoted almost entirely to attacks on grain shortage, past relief abuses, German plant dismantling and reparation deliveries, and German currency system. While no direct attack was made on sin, I judge the Committee omitted that, feeling that the Department of State was an adequate substitute."[1]

The China Lobby worked hard to cut the European total and added at least $60 M. for aid to China, a manoeuvre which the President was only able to circumvent in March 1948 when he secured an additional $55 M. for the three European countries to cover their needs for the remainder of that month.

At one stage, Douglas reported to Washington that he had had secret talks with Bevin about the possibility of an interim aid programme for Britain by means of a loan of $700 M. from the US Export-Import Bank. Fortunately this proved not to be necessary and the British held out until the main Marshall aid programme came into effect.[2]

By 9 December the joint efforts of the American and European teams had produced the draft of such a plan in the form of an Economic Co-operation Bill which proposed to set up a European Recovery Programme (ERP) with an Economic Co-operation Administration (ECA) to run it. In view of the controversy over the bill for interim aid, however, it was judged best to get that through first before embarking on the main proposal which was not sent to Congress until 19 December and which asked for funds to be appropriated only for the first 15 months ($6,800 M.) instead of for the full period of four and a quarter years (a total which the Bill put at $17,000 M.).

Once the Bill was in draft form, there was not much that Bevin or Franks could do except wait for the result. It was a long wait. The Bill was not finally signed until 3 April which meant that the public debate lasted for five months. No argument was too extreme to be refused a hearing and even the best arguments were simplified in transmission to the point of crudity.

In the meantime, it was essential to the emerging pattern of Western co-operation, and particularly to the role the British might play in it, to get a new agreement with the Americans on the costs of the German Bi-zone. Bevin sensed the change in American opinion over Germany and the growing impatience, now that the Germans were seen more as potential allies than as ex-enemies, with setting limits to Germany's economic recovery, with de-nazification, dismantling and reparations. He continued to be worried that the pendulum was now swinging too far in the other direction, at least too fast for opinion in Europe to accept it. This made him all the keener to remain a partner in the occupation and retain a British voice in the development of policy towards Germany. But this was only possible if the British could reduce

[1] FRUS 1947 (3) p. 482.
[2] *Ibid.*, pp. 88–90, Douglas to Washington, 5 November 1947.

the burden of the occupation on their own economy.

Marshall had refused to discuss finance until the British had substantially agreed to the American proposals for the re-organization of the Ruhr's coal production including the postponement of socialization. This was a form of pressure which Bevin resented but had to accept. The coal talks finished on 10 September and the financial talks opened on 8 October with Strang again leading the British team.

Bevin's dilemma is reflected in his instructions to Strang. On the one hand, he must avoid putting the British in the position of finding troops while the USA found dollars: that would turn the British Army into mercenaries. On the other, he was to make it clear that the British could only maintain an occupying force in Germany (as the Americans wanted) if the US Government relieved them of the dollar burden, which in 1947 had amounted to £81 m. and in 1948, even when costs were to be shared equally with the USA, would still amount to £56 M. Finally, Strang was instructed that he must give no specific assurances beyond saying that they would do their best to fulfil their obligations unless their hands were forced by circumstances beyond their control such as the economic situation. Such were the shifts to which British diplomacy was reduced by penury.[1]

This was on 12 October. On the 24th, Bevin cabled Strang that, in return for a new agreement on the fusion of the two zones, he could go as far as to promise that British forces would not be withdrawn before 30 June 1948, although no public statement could be made to that effect since this might be taken to mean that they would be withdrawn after 30 June and that would affect the position at the CFM which was shortly to open in London.[2] Finally, in mid-November, Bevin got Attlee's agreement to an undertaking that, if a satisfactory division of costs could be reached, there was no question of the withdrawal of British forces from Germany nor would be before there had been consultation between the two governments on their policy towards Germany.[3]

It still took another month of difficult negotiation before a new financial agreement was completed on 17 December.[4] The British were relieved of any dollar payments for the last two months of 1947 and the whole of 1948, while their contribution in sterling to the total cost was reduced from a half to a quarter (excluding the cost of the occupation forces). In return the Americans were granted a controlling, instead of an equal, voice in the Joint Export-Import Agency and in the Joint Foreign Exchange Agency.

The drain on dollars represented by the continuing British commitment to share in the occupation of Germany had been one of Dalton's chief objections to Bevin's foreign policy. To get rid of this was not only an obvious economic advantage but strengthened Bevin's hand in meeting those critics at home who

[1] Bevin to Strang, 15 October 1947. FO 800/466/GER/47/42.
[2] Bevin to Strang, 24 October, *ibid.*, GER/47/43.
[3] Bevin to Attlee, 14 November 1947, *ibid.*, GER/47/44.
[4] Bevin reported it to the Cabinet the following day. CM 96 (47).

argued that, whether his foreign policy was good or bad, the country could not afford it. Like the coal conference and the new level of industry agreement, the financial agreement for the Bi-zone did not provide a solution to the German problem; at best they removed particular obstacles to a solution, but real progress on the ground as distinct from agreement on paper had to wait until the London meeting of the CFM showed whether it was to be on an agreed Four-Power pattern or rival Western and Russian models. The financial talks were completed (19 December) at precisely the moment when, with the breakdown of the London conference, far-reaching decisions on Germany could no longer be postponed.

CHAPTER 12

London, November–December 1947: "We cannot go on as we have been"

I

The Truman doctrine, promising that the USA would take over the burden of supporting Greece and Turkey, made no distinction between the two countries. But in practice there was a very importance difference. The threat to Turkey was external and was not actively renewed by the Russians. In the case of the Greeks, the threat was internal, of civil war with support from the Greeks' Communist neighbours, and this was certainly not ended by Truman's announcement. After the beginning of 1947 Bevin was little involved in Turkish affairs, but he remained very much involved in what was happening in Greece.

In the spring of 1947 the Committee of Investigation appointed by the Security Council had visited Greece, taken evidence in Athens and Salonika and toured the northern frontiers. In April 1947 it retired to Geneva to produce its report. This was not an easy document to draft with the Soviet and Polish representatives in opposition, but it gave substantial support to the Greek Government's claim that its northern neighbours, and particularly Yugoslavia, had been supporting guerilla warfare across the Greek frontiers. Apart from proposing to the Security Council that it should call on the states concerned to re-establish normal relations, the report recommended maintaining a continuing UN body on the spot. Its conclusions were supported by eight members of the Commission, with the Russian and Polish delegates refusing to sign and the French abstaining. In July and August a US resolution accepting the report and its recommendations was twice supported by 9 out of the 11 Security Council members and twice vetoed by the USSR. Blocked in the Council, the US took the matter to the General Assembly and finally on 21 October obtained a majority of 40–6 with 11 abstentions. A new UN Special Committee on the Balkans (UNSCOB) was then set up to observe the compliance of the four governments concerned (Yugoslavia, Albania, Bulgaria and Greece) with the recommendations adopted by the Assembly.

Long before the United Nations peace-keeping machinery had creaked into action, Greece had moved closer to civil war. At the French Communist Party's congress held in Strasbourg at the end of June, the Secretary-General of the Greek Communist Party, Zachariades, proclaimed their intention of establishing "a free democratic Government" in northern Greece and appealed for international support. On 9 July several thousand Communists were arrested in Athens and other parts of Greece on the grounds that a *coup* was being prepared; three days later a well-equipped guerilla force from Albania estimated at 2,500 attacked the town of Konitza. This followed a similar attack across the Yugoslav frontier which was investigated and confirmed by the UN team.

Bevin sent a message to Athens urging the Greek government to bring those arrested to trial as soon as possible, not to continue with indiscriminate arrests and not outlaw EAM. The Greek Prime Minister, Tsaldaris, asked him what reply he should give to the Communist terms (12 July) for calling off the civil war in return for the resignation of the government, the dissolution of parliament and a general amnesty under international guarantee. Bevin was reluctant to go as far as the Americans in condemning these outright but he left no doubt that he thought the offer a dangerous one to accept. Bevin, in fact, was increasingly anxious on financial grounds to get the remaining British troops out of Greece and reduce those in Italy and the 5,000 promised for Trieste. Nine thousand had been withdrawn from Greece between the end of March and July and on 30 July Bevin sent a message to Washington that they must withdraw the remaining 5,000.[1]

Marshall's personal reply left no doubt that the Americans were thoroughly put out by Bevin's announcement:

"I feel that the decision was made at a most harmful time and that such abrupt action makes co-operation unnecessarily difficult."[2]

Douglas was instructed to ask Bevin if this meant a change of policy on Britain's part, since "a large measure of US foreign policy has been predicated upon the British willingness to contribute what they can to the maintenance of stability in Europe."[3]

Bevin's reply to Marshall's reproaches was that this was part of a general reduction in overseas forces which implied no change at all in British policy. It was a contribution to the economic crisis regarded as necessary by the Cabinet and public opinion.[4] Marshall, however, continued to press for no action to be

[1] FRUS 1947 (5) p. 268.
[2] 1 August 1947. FRUS 1947 (5) pp. 273–4.
[3] *Ibid.*, 274–5.
[4] Bevin reported Marshall's protest to the Defence Committee at its meeting on 4 August 1947. DO (47) Minutes of 18th meeting.

taken in Greece and Italy, particularly before the Greek case and the report of UNSCOB had been considered by the UN.

The exchange between the two Secretaries of State continued until the end of the year. Marshall refused to accept Bevin's arguments and commented tartly to Lovett:

"It seems to me that our thorn-pulling operations on the British lion continue to be beset by her stubborn insistence on avoiding the garden path to wander in the thicket of purely local Labour Party misadventures. They are far too casual or free-handed in passing the buck of the international dilemma to U.S. with little or no consideration for the harmful results."[1]

Marshall maintained that the situation had got worse since the British originally announced their intention to withdraw and that Greece was now seriously menaced. Quoting the US Chiefs of Staff he told Douglas to put it to Bevin that:

"Although . . . British troops in Greece are not able and indeed are not intended to withstand armed attack in force, nevertheless their presence is regarded as symbolical of the determination of the Western democracies to ensure the continued independence of the Greek state. . . . Their withdrawal would be interpreted as an abandonment of the U.S.–U.K. joint responsibility at a very critical time."[2]

Bevin had to pay attention to Cabinet pressure for cuts and the unpopularity of the Greek commitment in the Labour Party, ("Suppose one soldier were killed," he said to Douglas, "and trouble between ourselves and the Soviet were precipitated—I would be in an untenable position"[3]), but he managed to postpone the withdrawal by stages.

On 23 December the long expected proclamation of a "Provisional Democratic Government of Free Greece" was made by the Communist leader, Markos. This at least brought the Communist challenge into the open and led to discussions in Washington whether the USA should send troops to support the Greeks. Bevin was away on holiday and sent a message to Attlee to say it was absolutely necessary that they should keep in step with the USA over Greece but not let themselves be pushed in front. As he understood very well, the reason why the Americans were so keen for the British forces to remain was the political difficulties, matching his own, which they foresaw in sending American troops into Greece—or Palestine.

As 1947 closed, the future of Greece appeared as uncertain as ever. But Bevin was able to extract real advantage from the exchanges with Marshall in another direction. This was in the Middle East.

In a strongly-worded memorandum (7 March 1947) the Chiefs of Staff had

---

[1] Marshall to Lovett, 25 August 1947. FRUS 1947 (5) p. 313.
[2] Marshall to Douglas, 8 September. FRUS 1947 (5) pp. 330–32.
[3] Douglas to Lovett reporting talk with Bevin, 1 September 1947, *ibid.*, p. 322.

protested at Britain's deteriorating position in the Middle East following the failure of the Egyptian negotiations; the reference of Palestine to the UN; the ending of British support to Greece; the failure to secure bases in Cyrenaica, and the decision to hand over power in India by June 1948. The first four of the six, they declared, represented decisions they had resisted; on the last they had not been consulted. They held to their belief that to retain a firm hold in the Middle East was essential.

"We lose the air bases vital for the action which alone can decrease the weight of attack on the U.K., and we lose the bases necessary for the security of our communications through the Mediterranean . . . We risk starting a war from the 'outer ring' of the North American Continent, South Africa, Australia and New Zealand, and except for the U.K. with no air bases from which to operate. Such a withdrawal to the 'outer ring' would entail long, arduous and costly operations before we could even start hitting back at the enemy; in fact the U.K. would begin the war by fighting in the last ditch, and it is open to serious doubt whether she could survive so long."[1]

Bevin had intervened from Moscow to prevent the Chiefs' of Staff paper being discussed while he was away[2], but he had been too pre-occupied with the situation in Europe and the sterling crisis to deal with their criticism when he got back. The Defence Committee met only three times in the summer, to discuss the size of the Forces in 1948 and the route to be taken by a new pipeline from the Persian Gulf to the Mediterranean.

A suggestion of Bevin's, however, in a discussion with Douglas on the withdrawal of British troops from Greece (1 Sept.) opened the way to a closer understanding with the USA in the Middle East to which Montgomery, Tedder and Admiral Cunningham attached more importance than anything else. Bevin remarked to Douglas that the trouble was that neither he nor the Cabinet knew what policy the USA was following in the Middle East. He suggested that what they needed was a joint review of the whole position. This was a personal idea of Bevin's for which he had not yet got Cabinet approval, but Marshall at once took it up, adding that in the meantime he hoped the British would postpone any steps to withdraw their troops from Greece. That was a price Bevin was very willing to contemplate if he could reach agreement with the USA on the much bigger question of the Middle East: it was a considerable diplomatic success on his part to divert the American reproaches over Greece—a topic on which the British were at a disadvantage—into discussions on the Middle East which could hardly fail to work out to Britain's advantage. The result was secret talks starting in the Pentagon on 16 October 1947 and continuing until 7 November between teams representing the Foreign Office, the State Department and the British and American Chiefs of Staff.

---

[1] DO (47) 23.
[2] Bevin to Attlee and Attlee's reply, 3 and 10 April 1947. FO 800/451/DEF/47/5–6.

At an early stage Bevin made his own views clear in a long conversation with Loy Henderson, Head of the State Department's Division of Near Eastern Affairs[1] while the proposal to hold such talks was still being discussed.

Bevin began with an emphatic statement of his inability to reverse the British decision to withdraw all troops from Greece even if he succeeded in deferring the date. As to the Near East, "I shall tell you frankly that, although I am often told that the American Government desires to co-operate with us, I find unfortunately that sometimes your Government adds to our difficulties." His first example was the obvious one of Palestine: terrorism and illegal immigration were supported and subsidized from the USA and "again and again" when he thought he was making progress towards a solution, the US Government had come out with a public statement which wrecked the negotiations.

From Palestine Bevin turned to Egypt. The Egyptians had turned down the concessions the British offered over the Sudan, and the offer of these would not be renewed. The British looked upon the Sudan as one of the most important British bases in the whole Middle East and Africa, and must have free use of it. Amongst these uses would be the power to prevent Egypt giving assistance to the enemy in any future world conflict. Bevin added that they were planning to review the Lake Tana project which would greatly increase the Sudan's agricultural resources.

If they were to leave Suez, then, Bevin declared, there must be a mutual defence treaty between Egypt and Great Britain. He hoped the US Government would take the opportunity to make a public statement in support of it as a contribution to world security. The British would have to have some base to withdraw to, and that meant Cyrenaica which they had fought to liberate and which they thought they were entitled to occupy if they were to remain as a force in the Near East. They had abandoned any idea of bases in Palestine, but would need to strengthen those which they maintained under treaty in Transjordan and would require access to them across Palestine.

Bevin reported that negotiations for the amendment of the Treaty with Iraq were going well: he hoped they would be concluded shortly and would allow the British to continue to make use of the Iraqi air bases at Habanniyah and Sha'aiba.[2] He also hoped that Iraq, with British—and American—help, could develop the Tigris and Euphrates valleys to the point where they could support two or three times their present populations and make Iraq one of the richest countries in the Middle East.

Bevin concluded with a glance at Iran, where he admitted that the British

---

[1] 9 September 1947. The note printed in FRUS 1947 (5) pp. 496–542 was made by Loy Henderson, who added "Although I am unable to record Mr. Bevin's exact words, I believe that the following represents with fair accuracy his ideas and his manner of expressing them. The first person is used as though Mr. Bevin were speaking." (p. 497). British record, FO 800/468/GRE/47/34.

[2] At a meeting of the Defence Committee on 24 September, Bevin strongly supported any Iraqi request for help in building up their forces. DO (47). Minutes of 21st meeting.

did not see eye to eye with the Americans and would be relieved to see the Iranians grant some kind of oil concessions to the Russians. Refusal to do so would be blamed on the Western powers and would "increase our tension with the Soviet Union and render my internal position here more difficult."

By the time the talks opened on 16 October, the British Chiefs of Staff and the Foreign Office had provided a set of briefs in amplification of Bevin's improvisation on 9 September.[1] The objective was "to get the U.S.A. to realise the importance of Britain's role in the Middle East to them as well as to us". Three main features of British Middle Eastern policy stand out from the papers. The first is the concern with strategy:

"The Middle East joins three continents and two oceans. Its fifty million or so inhabitants straddle the only possible communication routes between Europe, Asia, Africa and the Far East. The area has proved as vital for air and radio communication as for camel-caravans and steam-ships. . . . Unfortunately . . . not only is the area a vital prize for any Power interested in world influence or domination, but it is an area which cannot possibly defend itself against a Power with modern organisation and technical resources."[2]

In making his opening presentation, the Ambassador (Inverchapel) said that the British Chiefs of Staff advised the British Government that, in the event of a future war, "the Middle East will, as proved to be the case in both the last wars, be a strategic theatre second only in importance, or perhaps equal in importance, to the U.K.".[3] The reasons they gave for this were not just communications and oil, essential though it was to deny control of these to any hostile power, nor the importance of preventing such a power (for which read the Soviet Union) penetrating and dominating the Moslem world, but also the need to provide for the defence of the UK, by counter-attacks on the enemy direct. The Middle East was the one area with bases from which the RAF could hit at Russia and Eastern Europe in the event of war.

The second feature of British policy on which both the COS and the FO laid emphasis was the need to retain the co-operation of the Arab states, described in the COS brief as "the cardinal point in British policy" and by the FO as "the overriding consideration". The ultimate aim should be a strong Arab bloc pledged to mutual defence of Arab countries and looking to the UK and USA. In the meantime, they should avoid anything, such as a pro-Jewish solution to the Palestine policy, which would antagonize the Arabs.

The British admitted to no great hopes of reaching a settlement with Egypt, although they would try again. Since it was in Britain's interest that the Egyptian army and air force should be efficient, it would be better—if there was no hope of re-establishing the British position—to have a joint Anglo–US

---

[1] For the COS brief and the FO brief, see FO 800/476/ME/47/17–19. The note of the Ambassador's remarks on the opening day is to be found in FRUS 1947 (5) 565–8.
[2] Introductory paper submitted by UK representatives (undated), *ibid.*, (5) 569.
[3] *Ibid.*, p. 566.

military mission to train them, and in the last resort a US mission on its own. But the British were very anxious that the Americans should not respond to an Egyptian approach until they had made another attempt to negotiate the right of re-entry in the event of war.

In general what the British wanted from the Americans was to avoid anything which would undermine their position in the Middle East and to make clear (e.g. to the Egyptians) that they favoured the British retaining their position and not reducing their role. In particular, they argued that it was in both countries' interests to avoid association with rival Arab groups and the division of the area into spheres of influence.

One reason for taking this view becomes clear in the documents dealing with the third aspect of British policy, the economic. While the British continued to attach importance to promoting a rise in the living standards throughout the area, they recognized that they had not got the economic or financial resources to act on their own. It was inevitable that the USA should take the major share of responsibility for the development which was necessary to prevent social upheaval and a drift into chaos. The British sought to retain a part in this and to preserve their own commercial interests, especially in oil; they hoped, therefore, that it would be possible to make arrangements with the Americans that would keep competition within limits and work out joint plans for large-scale development projects.

The briefs prepared for the American team accepted the greater part of the British case.

"Given our heavy commitments elsewhere and Britain's already established position in the area, it is our strong feeling that the British should continue to maintain primary responsibility for military security in that area."

This meant that the British should retain bases in the Middle East and the Americans not take steps to acquire any. In return, the Americans were prepared to consider the British plea for help in carrying out development plans. One way of putting this was to propose a bargain:

"If, for political and strategic reasons, we [the Americans] want them [the British] to hold a position of strength in the Middle East, then they must have from us economic concessions with regard to the area which will make it worth their while to stay there."

The US Government was prepared to consider collaboration in a programme for development in which most of the funding would have to come from American sources. The provisos were that the projects should be put forward by Middle Eastern governments as their own; that there should be no demarcation into British and American spheres of influence and no insistence on a single organized Anglo–US channel for assistance such as the Wartime Middle East Supply Centre.

At the end of three weeks the two delegations were able to agree on parallel sets of recommendations to put before their Governments. The basis of these was recognition that the security of the East Mediterranean and the Middle East was vital to the security of both the USA and the UK.[1] The supporting documents make clear that the chief concern of both governments was to prevent the Soviet Union capturing control of Greece, Turkey or Iran (or indeed Italy) and so obtaining a foothold in the area. Neither Government could guarantee this on its own; they had to support each other and make sure their policies ran in parallel. The British role was to maintain the necessary bases; the Americans to provide economic and political backing. The general agreement was supported by an examination of British and American policies on 25 specific problems, ranging from French North Africa to Pakistan, with recommendations on how these could be brought more closely into agreement.[2]

Both sides were very careful to say that they had signed no treaty and agreed on no division into spheres of influence. But the National Security Council and the President on the American side, and the British Chiefs of Staff Committee with the Prime Minister in the chair and Bevin, Alexander and Cripps present (21 November 1947), approved the identical memorandum produced by the two groups and agreed to inform the other Government that they had done so.[3] In recommending endorsement, Bevin said that at the very least they should be able to avoid the clash of opposing policies between the USA and the UK which had given trouble in the recent past. The essential step on the British side was for HMG to assure the Americans that they were prepared to defend their position in the Middle East. If he could not give that assurance, then the Americans might well feel compelled to disinterest themselves in the area. Whether Bevin really believed this, it is impossible to say, but he went on to add that if he could give that assurance to Marshall then he thought it possible that US plans for assistance to Europe would be extended to the Eastern Mediterranean and the Middle East. The Ministers present and the COS accepted Bevin's arguments and he exchanged assurances with Marshall at an informal meeting on 4 December during the London CFM.[4]

2

It had only been possible to conduct the Pentagon talks on the understanding that Palestine was excluded from them. But Palestine was again at the centre of

---

[1] See the identical general statement made by the British and American groups to their governments. FRUS 1947 (5) 583.
[2] The US record of the Pentagon talks and the recommendations occupies pp. 488–626. The British record is in FO 800/476/ME/47/21. This includes (Sir) Michael Wright's over-all report to Bevin which Bevin forwarded to Attlee, together with the record of the proceedings, on 18 November 1947.
[3] *Ibid.*, ME/47/22.
[4] *Ibid.*, ME/47/28.

politics in the autumn of 1947. The UN Special Committee presented its report to the Secretary-General on 1 September and an *ad hoc* Committee of the General Assembly began discussion of it on the 26th of the same month. The Committee was unanimous in recommending that the British Mandate should end as soon as possible. A majority (7 out of the 11 members) recommended the partition of Palestine into a Jewish and an Arab state, with Jerusalem under direct UN administration. The two states were required to conclude a treaty of economic union and 150,000 Jewish immigrants were to be admitted in a transitional period of two years during which the British were to remain responsible for the Mandate. A minority including the Indian member favoured a bi-national federal state, but their recommendations received scant attention.

The country (hardly larger than Wales) was to be divided in such a way that each state should consist of three segments, joined by narrow corridors. Of all the plans for the partition of Palestine this was the most impracticable; but in Jewish (and American) eyes this was outweighed by the fact that the balance of advantage was in favour of the Jews. In order to include the most fertile parts in the Jewish state (including most of the citrus orchards, about half of which were Arab-owned) almost as many Arabs (450,000) as Jews (500,000) were placed under Jewish rule, but the size of the Jewish majority would be increased by the provisions for immigration.

When the British Cabinet met to discuss their attitude to the Report on 20 September, it had before it a paper from Bevin[1] in which he described the majority plan as "manifestly unjust to the Arabs" and recommended that Britain should decline responsibility for enforcing it on grounds both of conscience and expediency. Bevin's view was accepted without argument: the British must not allow themselves to be saddled with the responsibility for enforcing a plan which no minister was prepared to defend as either equitable or workable and which was certain to be rejected by the Arabs. Attlee in particular was influenced by what he described as

"A close parallel between the position in Palestine and the recent situation in India. He did not think it reasonable to ask the British administration in Palestine to continue in present conditions, and he hoped that salutary results would be produced by a clear announcement that HMG intended to relinquish the Mandate and, failing a peaceful settlement, to withdraw the British administration and British forces."[2]

Whatever the calculations of officials about voting in the General Assembly, there was no doubt that the politicians, including Zionist sympathizers such as Dalton and Nye Bevan, wanted only one thing, to be rid of a burden which they regarded as intolerable. In this they had the overwhelming support of public opinion.

[1] CP (47) 259 dated 18 September.
[2] CM 78 (47), 20 September 1947.

The calculations were in any case invalidated by the surprise Soviet decision to reverse its policy and join with the USA in supporting partition. But Creech-Jones' warning (26 September) that the British would not be responsible for any plan which was not acceptable to one or other of the parties and required force to implement it was not at first taken seriously. Only slowly was it realized that the British meant what they said—none more so than Bevin. On 16 October Creech-Jones put it to the UN *ad hoc* committee that before they voted they should ask themselves what measures would be needed to implement their decision and who would take them: the British would not be responsible either alone or as part of a UN force. When the leader of the US Delegation to the UN persisted in arguing that Britain as the Mandatory Power must see that the UN decision was carried out, the British delegation repeated that Britain would not and announced 1 August as the date for their withdrawal. For the final vote in the General Assembly, the US Government used all the means at its disposal—including direct intervention from the White House—to line up the necessary two-thirds majority for approval of the majority plan.[1] Bevin instructed the British delegate to abstain and not to vote against. But in his talks with Lew Douglas and Marshall (in London for the CFM) he made no attempt to conceal his anger at the part which he believed the United States, and in particular the White House, had played in encouraging Zionist claims and so making a compromise settlement impossible.[2]

In the meantime the Cabinet's Defence Committee, having approved the timetable for British withdrawal from India and Pakistan by 31 December 1947, turned to consider the arrangements for withdrawing from Palestine.[3] Bevin set out some of the problems which would arise in a preliminary note to the Prime Minister.[4] He suggested that the danger from the Arab armies had been much exaggerated and that the most likely action would be guerilla warfare with support from the Arab states in the form of money and arms for the Palestinian Arabs. It was not Bevin but the soldiers and officials who pressed for the arrival of the UN Commission to be deferred as late as possible on the grounds that the arrival of the UN Commission would provoke Arab disturbances and compromise the withdrawal plan.[5] The Cabinet accepted this view at its meeting on 4 December, laying down the principle that "while H.M.G. should do nothing to obstruct the carrying out of the U.N. decision,

---

[1] See Ganin, pp. 144–6, for the details.
[2] See the account of (1) Bevin's talk with Douglas on 28 October in Bevin's dispatch to Inverchapel, FO 371/61793. Douglas sent an edited version to Marshall, FRUS 1947 (5), pp. 1215–16; (2) Bevin's talk with Marshall on 24 November in FO 371/61796. Marshall gave his account in a letter to Lovett on the 25th, FRUS 1947 (5) pp. 1287–9; (3) Bevin's further talks with Marshall on 4 December in FO 371/61960, and 17 December in FO 800/487/PA/47/28. The American accounts are in FRUS 1947 (5) pp. 1298–9 and pp. 1312–13.
[3] DO (47). Minutes of 23rd meeting, 7 November; 25th meeting, 27 November; and 26th meeting, 11 December.
[4] Bevin to Attlee, 22 October 1947. FO 800/487/PA/47/19.
[5] 25th meeting of Defence Committee, 27 November.

British troops and the British Administration should in no circumstances become involved in enforcing it or in maintaining law and order while the UN Commission enforced it."[1] It was agreed that British civil administration should end on 15 May 1948, with the UN Commission arriving no more than a fortnight before that, and that the withdrawal be completed by 1 August.

The officials' committee on Palestine was equally opposed to the early evacuation of Tel Aviv which the UN Commission requested, whereas Bevin at a later meeting of the Defence Committee urged that they should try to help the Commission by leaving before 15 May, perhaps by 1 April. Bevin was also in favour of speeding up the rate of immigration to clear camps in Cyprus and Germany as quickly as possible. He thought this could be done by pushing up the quota by a few hundreds a month and by admitting groups of Jewish children outside the quota.[2]

In a two-day Commons debate on Palestine there was no disposition to criticize the decision to withdraw. In a speech which contained few polemical remarks, Bevin was careful not to criticize the UN plan, but made clear his belief that riding roughshod over the rights of either Jews or Arabs was no way to settle the problem, adding a phrase that still catches the eye today:

"I think that the Arab feeling in this question has been underestimated. It has got to be assessed at its correct value by everybody, or we shall not get a peaceful settlement. It is because I want it assessed at its proper value that I do not want the Arabs to be dismissed as if they were nobody."[3]

The other big issue besides Palestine which dominated the autumn session of the UN was the US proposal to by-pass use of the veto to block discussion in the Security Council by establishing an Interim Committee of the General Assembly where the veto would not apply. The British had originally feared that the US would press disagreement with the USSR over its plan for international control of atomic energy and make the second report of the Atomic Energy Commission in September the occasion for a show-down with the Russians. Bevin and the Foreign Office were opposed to this, partly because they thought it undesirable to force questions of atomic energy to an issue with the Soviets before the meeting of the CFM in November, and partly because there were still parts of the American proposals which they opposed.

Whether or not as a result of the British urging them to reconsider,[4] the Americans changed their plans and agreed not to make an issue of the AEC report in the General Assembly or the Security Council. Instead they decided to start talks with the British and the Canadians on the situation arising from

[1] CM 93 (47), 4 December, after discussing the joint paper from the Foreign and Colonial Offices, CP (47) 320, dated 3 December.
[2] Defence Committee, 11 December. DO (47) minutes of 26th meeting.
[3] HC debate, 11–12 December 1947; Bevin's speech on the 12th.
[4] The British anxieties were expressed in a note of 12 August. See pp. 409–10 above and FRUS 1947 (1), pp. 597–600 for the presentation and reception of the note in Washington.

the inability to reach agreement on international control[1] and to take up the issue of obstruction in the United Nations, in effect the Russian use or misuse of the veto.

The Americans did not consult the British in advance about their new initiative and the first Bevin heard of it was when Marshall introduced his proposal in a speech to the UN General Assembly on 17 September. The US Secretary of State did not mention the veto but his argument that the General Assembly had the right and the duty to consider situations and disputes threatening friendly relations between nations was obviously aimed at finding a way of by-passing the frequent deadlocks in the Security Council which the Soviet Union's use of the veto had produced. Marshall's proposal was that the General Assembly should set up an Interim Committee on Peace and Security on which every member of the UN would have a seat and which would have the power to report to the General Assembly and make its facilities continuously available during the next year.[2] Since it was only intended, in the first place, to operate for a limited time and to supplement not replace the existing machinery for peaceful settlement, the Committee could be set up *ad hoc* without requiring revision of the Charter.

The first British reaction was to ask the Americans whether they had considered that their proposal might result in Soviet withdrawal from the UN. The Americans said they thought this unlikely but agreed that the Russians and their satellites might boycott the new Committee; they did not consider that should deter them from going ahead with it.[3] The British were not opposed to the proposal in principle although they made a number of suggestions on procedure which they hoped would secure acceptance by the Russians. Discussions went on between the two delegations throughout September and October, but Russian opposition was unremitting. Vyshinsky denounced the proposal as an attempt to circumvent the Security Council and nullify the unanimity rule written into the UN Charter. When the vote was finally taken by the General Assembly's First Committee on 6 November, the British and 41 other delegations voted with the USA in favour of Marshall's proposal, the Russian bloc (6 votes) voted against and the Arab bloc (also 6 votes) abstained. Vyshinsky at once announced that the USSR would not take part in the work of the Interim Committee.

At the opening of the General Assembly Marshall had been followed by Vyshinsky who delivered a trenchant attack on the Truman doctrine, the Marshall Plan and the American plan for the control of atomic energy, all aimed (according to the Soviet spokesman) at the division and enslavement of

---

[1] This policy was recommended by Kennan's Policy Planning Staff in a paper circulated on 21 August 1947 (FRUS (1) pp. 602–14), endorsed by Osborn and the US Delegation to the UNAEC in late September (*ibid.*, pp. 671–3) and made known to the majority of the other delegations at an informal meeting on 3 October (pp. 671–5).

[2] Marshall's speech in RIIA *Documents 1947–48*, pp. 818–19.

[3] Conversation between G. Hayden Raynor, an advisor to the US Delegation and Gladwyn Jebb, 18 September 1947. FRUS 1947 (1) pp. 175–7.

Europe and the perpetuation of an American hegemony. In Bevin's absence, Vyshinsky was answered by his Minister of State at the Foreign Office, Hector McNeil, who won immediate acclaim for the vigorous way in which he met the Russian arguments.

Bevin was delighted. He had great faith in McNeil, whom he would have liked to see succeed him in due course at the Foreign Office, and he cabled his congratulations:

"It makes me very proud. Now be careful, sit back and take things quietly while looking for opportunities for constructive suggestions."[1]

A fortnight later McNeil sent Bevin a long letter giving his impressions of an Assembly which he confessed to finding bewildering:

"There are really two subjects worrying me. First of all, there is general pessimism about the ability of the U.N. to work. This seems primarily due to the apparent decision of the Soviets to block everything and to the rowdy and excessive language they use. Then secondly, and perhaps more alarmingly, there are more and more people admitting, however reluctantly, that they feel it is only a matter of time until we have war."[2]

When Bevin wrote back he told McNeil he should not be too pessimistic yet about the UN. "A lot of this business on the part of the Russians is a 'try out'." McNeil had been to see Beaverbrook and the Luces. Bevin was not impressed by their views:

"These wealthy people are always in a state of jitters. . . . That does not mean that Russia is not out for mischief, but it will not take the form of war unless America gets timid and withdraws. If she remains firm, resolute and determined to see her policy through, then Russia will not risk war for many many years to come. On the other hand if these delightful Congressmen and others do not remain firm in carrying out the Marshall Report but are niggardly in helping Western Europe, then Russia will push on and will succeed without war."

Bevin then proceeded to give his own version of Soviet history, as a background to the establishment of the Cominform:

"There never was a quarrel between Trotsky and Stalin over the thesis of the revolution. The dispute took place over tactics. Stalin believed that the Western Powers might attack Russia. He was determined to get through his five-year-plan to meet it. He was justified in that assumption so far as Germany was concerned. But now the war has been fought, my view is that Russia has gone back to the original Lenin idea. That is the situation which we have got to face."[3]

---

[1] Bevin to McNeil, 24 September 1947. FO 800/509/UN/47/8.
[2] McNeil to Bevin, 9 October 1947, *ibid.*, UN/47/11.
[3] Bevin to McNeil, 15 October 1947, *ibid.*, UN/47/13.

The British saw no point in forcing the issue of international control of atomic power in the UN. No one could seriously believe that the Russians and the Americans were likely to agree on a scheme and the only result would be a propaganda exchange leading to a hardening of positions. The possibility of reviving the wartime collaboration with the USA and Canada, however, was a different matter. Although Attlee and Bevin had now committed themselves —without telling the Americans or, for that matter, their own people—to Britain making its own atomic bomb and had no intention of giving this up, there were obvious advantages in pooling information and resources with the Americans. And with the two countries now rapidly re-establishing their partnership in other fields, it was natural to ask why this could not be extended to atomic matters as well. Natural, that is, for the British and even for the Americans in the State Department, such as General Marshall and George Kennan,[1] who were deeply involved in the developing relationship with the UK and aware that the British had grounds for feeling they had been unfairly treated. A Republican Congress, however, took a very different view, regularly admonishing the Administration not to give away the secrets of American "know-how" and requiring a literal interpretation of the restrictive provisions of the McMahon Act.

It came as a great surprise, therefore, when Sir John Cockcroft on a visit to the USA in November was told by the General Manager of the US Atomic Energy Commission that "the log-jam might break" within a week or so and was asked to run over the areas in which the British would be most interested to secure information.[2] This was welcome news indeed and it was only some months later that the British began to recognize that the reasons for the change of attitude were more complex and its scope much more restricted than they had at first realized.

The key lay in the Joint Congressional Committee on Atomic Energy of which Senator McMahon had been the first, and Senator Hickenlooper was the current chairman. The leading members of the JCCAE regarded it as the watchdog of America's national interest in preserving a monopoly of the A-bomb. What moved them was not a sudden conversion to the value of co-operation with the UK or any other foreign power but the discovery, for the first time in the Spring of 1947, that Roosevelt had signed two secret wartime agreements (the Quebec and the Hyde Park Agreements) which gave the British a veto over any decision to use the A-bomb, coupled with recognition that the allocation of uranium ore agreed by the Combined Development Trust provided the Americans with inadequate supplies to continue their atomic programme while leaving the British with a surplus. The Republican leaders insisted that the wartime agreements must be abrogated, any idea of a veto removed and Britain required to move all stocks of uranium ore to North

---

[1] See their remarks at the meeting of the American members of the Combined Policy Committee on Atomic Energy, 5 November 1947. FRUS 1947 (1) pp. 852–60.
[2] 13 November 1947. Gowing, p. 243.

America, where they should be "readily and securely" available to the US. In communicating these demands to Marshall, Hickenlooper, the chairman of the Congressional Committee, added:

"I shall oppose, as vigorously as I can, and publicly if necessary, any further aid or assistance to Britain unless these two matters are satisfactorily solved. . . . Their solution is a pre-requisite as far as I am concerned."[1]

The threat to make Congressional support for the Marshall Plan conditional on a new atomic agreement with the UK was taken seriously by the Administration. The State Department was able to deflect it with the proposal that negotiations should be opened at once with the British and Canadians on the future allocation of uranium supplies and the replacement of the wartime agreements with a new one, with provision for a more co-operative exchange of information in America's own national interests. This was finally agreed with the members of the Joint Congressional Committee and of the US Atomic Energy Commission at a meeting on 5 December and a cable sent off to Marshall in London on the 6th asking him to put the proposal for talks to Bevin and to stress their urgency in order "to avoid injection of the issues into the Congressional debate on European Recovery legislation".[2] Lovett put at the head of the agenda removing "misunderstandings on atomic energy matters which have grown up amongst the three countries" since the McMahon Act, but he asked Marshall, more realistically, to explain to Bevin that they had had to speed up the timetable "because of concern of some members of Congress over uranium in connection with ERP."

The British asked for "at least two days to consider issues which they [the Americans] have been milling over for two years", but there was no danger that anyone in London, least of all Ernie Bevin, would let slip a chance to restore the wartime partnership. A brief was prepared and approved by ministers in time for Cockcroft and Makins to fly to Washington and join Lovett and the American team for a meeting of the Combined Policy Committee on 10 December. Makins' initial report confirmed the hopes that had been raised of a breakthrough. The atmosphere in Washington, he cabled, was friendly and very different from that in which he had left the American capital ten months before. There was every sign that the Americans wanted to reach a fresh and fair understanding so that in future all three Governments "would play from the same score".[3] Working parties were at once set up to work out the details in the hope that agreement could be reached by Christmas. If it could, then this might well prove as substantial a success for British diplomacy as any concluded since the end of the war.

[1] 29 August 1947. FRUS 1947 (1) pp. 833–4.
[2] For the discussions leading up to the 5 December meeting, see FRUS 1947 (1) pp. 752–88 and for Lovett's telegram to Marshall on 6 December, 885–6.
[3] Gowing, p. 245.

Marshall's offer of economic aid and the European response were as much a watershed for Soviet as for British and American foreign policy. Up to the summer of 1947 developments in Europe had shown a net gain in favour of the USSR with good promise of this growing in the future. No doubt the same calculation, that Europe would not recover by itself, was made in the Kremlin as in the State Department, with the same conclusion that conditions would become increasingly favourable for the extension of Soviet influence through local Communist parties without any need for the Russians to do more than take advantage of the opportunities offered to them. The one thing that could spoil this prospect was American intervention to reverse the economic decline and restore the confidence of Europe. If this succeeded it would not only rule out any extension of Soviet control to the rest of Europe but in Russian eyes threaten to undermine their power over Eastern Europe. From the day, therefore, that Stalin made his choice to reject Marshall's offer, the Soviet Union started to tighten its hold on the countries already within its sphere of influence and to mount a campaign of political warfare with the combined resources of Soviet diplomacy and international Communism, in order to obstruct and defeat a European recovery based on American aid. This double riposte developed between Molotov's meeting with Bevin and Bidault in Paris in July and the breakdown of the London meeting of the CFM in December 1947 and represented a counterpart to the British and Americans' efforts to get things moving in the Bi-zone and to produce an agreed report which would secure Congressional support for a European Recovery Programme.

Given the character of the Stalinist regime in Russia at the time and the degree of control which the Russians have maintained over Eastern Europe since, it is hard to believe that moves to create a Communist monopoly of power would not have followed in any case once the peace treaties had been signed. Nonetheless, it was not until 1947 and particularly in the latter part of that year, that Communist control was unequivocally established. Other parties were still allowed to retain their existence in most East European countries at the beginning of 1947, although it was only in Czechoslovakia that the coalition government represented a real balance of political forces, and even the Czechs were no more able than other East European governments to ignore the Soviet directive against taking part in discussions on Marshall's offer.

Between the spring of 1947 and the summer of 1948 the Communists destroyed even the nominal independence of their other partners in the post-war national coalitions. The leadership of the peasant parties was ruthlessly eliminated and their organizations dissolved: examples are Bela Kovacs, Secretary General of the Hungarian Smallholders Party, arrested on 26 February 1947 and never seen again; Nikola Petkov, leader of the Bulgarian Agrarian Union arrested in June 1947, tried and executed on 23 September;

Juliu Maniu, leader of the Rumanian National Peasant Party, arrested in July 1947 and condemned (at the age of 74) to solitary confinement for life, and Stanislaw Mikolajczyk, leader of the Polish Peasant Party and a deputy prime minister in the coalition until January 1947, who fled from Poland in October after receiving information of his impending arrest, trial and execution. The Social Democratic Parties were destroyed by a different technique, by finding socialist allies within the party who were prepared (with Communist support) to force a split on the issue of working class unity, set up a United Workers Party with the Communists and carry out a purge of those who refused to join. This technique had already been tried in Germany where Otto Grotewohl had been prepared to split the SPD of which he was co-chairman in order to create the Socialist Unity Party (SED). The same role was played in Poland by Cyrankiewicz and in Hungary by Szakasits.

There is no need to go into the details of a passage of history which has often been recounted, but it is important to recognize the effect which these events had on Bevin and many others in the Labour Movement. Beginning with the Communist campaign preceding the Polish elections of 19 January, Bevin made a series of public protests at the unscrupulous and brutal methods which the Communists used to secure a monopoly of power and the propaganda with which they sought to disguise what they were doing. The protests had no more effect than those of the Americans, but the reports he received confirmed the views he held about Communism and brought home to the majority of the Labour Party and trade unions the gulf that separated them as social democrats from Communism as it was practised in the Soviet Union and Eastern Europe.

This was the more important since the Communists intensified and sharpened the propaganda campaign which they had maintained against the Western powers since 1945. The theoretical framework for this and the organization to co-ordinate it were established at the conference in Wiliza Gora which founded the Communist Information Bureau (Cominform) on 22–23 September 1947. In the declaration subsequently issued by the nine Communist parties represented (including the French and Italian as well as those from the Soviet Union, Yugoslavia, Czechoslovakia and other East European countries) the thesis of two camps was elaborated:

"The imperialist and anti-democratic camp having as its basic aim the establishment of the world domination of American imperialism and the smashing of democracy, and the anti-imperialist and democratic camp having as its basic aim the undermining of imperialism, the consolidation of democracy, and the eradication of the remnants of fascism."

The Cominform declaration continued:

"A special place in the imperialists' arsenal of tactical weapons is occupied by the utilisation of the treacherous policy of the right-wing Socialists like Blum in France,

Attlee and Bevin in Britain, Schumacher in Germany, Renner and Schärf in Austria, Saragat in Italy, who strive to cover up the true rapacious essence of imperialist policy under a mask of democracy and Socialist phraseology while actually being in all respects faithful accomplices of the imperialists, sowing dissension in the ranks of the working class and poisoning its mind."

Bevin was singled out by name for a special reference:

"It is not fortuitous that the foreign policy of British imperialism found its most consistent and zealous executor in Bevin."

A few lines later, Attlee and Bevin were accused, along with Blum and Ramadier, of "servility and sycophancy" in "helping American capital to achieve its aims, provoking it to resort to extortion and impelling their own countries on to the path of vassal-like dependence on the United States of America."

The Communist Parties were called upon "to take the lead in resisting the plans of imperialist expansion and aggression in all spheres—state, political, economic and ideological". The work of co-ordinating the activities of the various parties was to be carried out by the Cominform. That these were not just the views of a revived Communist International but of the Soviet Government was made clear by a major speech in which Stalin's leading henchman, A. A. Zhdanov, a member of the Soviet Politburo, endorsed them and attacked the USA and Britain. This was printed in the first number of the Cominform's new Journal, *For a Lasting Peace, for a People's Democracy*,[1] together with the communiqué announcing the foundation of the Cominform. It was followed up by other speeches from Malenkov, on the foreign policy of the Communist Party of the Soviet Union, (printed in the second number on 1 December), and by Molotov's address to the Moscow Soviet on the thirtieth anniversary of the Bolshevik Revolution (6 November 1947).[2]

What the tightening of Soviet control meant in countries where the Communists held the controlling power soon became clear and has already been described. Bevin hated what he saw happening, but although his protests were sincere enough never supposed that he could do anything to stop it. The question which concerned him more was how far the Communists would push their campaign in countries where they had not yet secured a controlling position.

"A special task," Zhdanov declared, "devolves on the fraternal Communist parties of France, Italy, Great Britain and other countries. . . . If, in their struggle against the attempts to economically and politically enthrall their countries, they are able to take the lead of all the forces prepared to uphold the national honour and independence, no plans for the enslavement of Europe can possibly succeed."

---

[1] 10 December 1947.
[2] Lengthy extracts from all three are printed together with the Cominform communiqué in RIIA *Documents 1947–48*, pp. 122–46, and are worth reading as the most authoritative statement of the Communist propaganda line.

What would this mean in practice? In Greece, the Greek Communist Party had gone over to open civil war and proclaimed a Provisional Democratic Government of Free Greece at Christmas 1947; in Czechoslovakia, in February 1948, the Communists overthrew the coalition government and seized power by a coup d'état. Would they be prepared to risk going as far as that in France and Italy, in both of which the Communists polled millions of votes, controlled the main trade union organizations and in Italy commanded local strongholds in the so-called "Red Zone" of Bologna, Parma, Modena and Reggio Emilia?

This is still a difficult question to answer and is not settled by the argument that, as the Communists did not succeed in capturing power in either country, they can never seriously have thought of making the attempt. It was surely considered and would have been made if the opportunity had offered.

To be wise after the event and dismiss such possibilities as fantasies is to show a lack of historical imagination and fail to understand the atmosphere of the time—just as it is to dismiss Soviet fears of the West. It was only two years since the War had ended: in the ten years since the beginning of 1938 all but four of the twenty nine countries of Europe[1] had experienced war, occupation, and liberation. This had been the most violent and frightening decade in European history; terrible experiences had taught people that the worst could happen. During the last three years the Communists, with the support of the Soviet Union, had acquired power over a hundred million people in Eastern and Central Europe. In the light of what men and women had seen takes place in their own towns and villages, there was a widespread fear, fanned certainly but not created by propaganda, that the Communists might well extend their power to other countries. This was well understood and exploited by the Communists themselves. Bevin never believed that the Soviet Government would risk starting another war; but he did believe in the summer and autumn of 1947 that, before Marshall aid could be made available, fear and want might combine to weaken resistance to the point where the Communists could secure power by a variety of devices which stayed well this side of war as traditionally understood.

In July 1947 the State Department had seen the main objective of the French Communist Party as making it impossible for the Ramadier ministry to govern without them and forcing their way back into the coalition. This would present a serious enough obstacle to carrying out what was then referred to as the Bevin–Bidault plan, and would be backed up by a propaganda campaign following on the priority given to German recovery and the betrayal of French national interests, and by a wave of strikes exploiting the discontent with low rations and wages and high prices and unemployment. More extreme mea-

---

[1] The count includes all the countries which were independent at the beginning of 1938, before the annexation of Austria, Estonia, Latvia and Lithuania, and when Spain was still suffering from civil war. It does not include Turkey. The four neutrals were Sweden, Switzerland, Eire and Portugal.

sures such as a general strike or civil strife were not precluded but were not considered likely.[1]

By October, however, it was reported from Paris that the Communist leadership recognized opinion in France had so far hardened against them as to make their return to the coalition highly unlikely. The Communists were now expected to adopt more openly disruptive measures, in order to sabotage economic recovery, and to foment strikes, demonstrations and public disorder to the point where the Ramadier Government would collapse. There was a possibility that this would bring in de Gaulle, whose RPF had won great gains in the October municipal elections; but the Communists were prepared to risk this, since they believed that the General's RPF was not yet well enough organized to stand up to a confrontation and the sooner that took place the better. This view of the Communists' objectives appeared to be confirmed by Thorez's speech on 29 October, castigating the French Communist Party for opportunism, indecision and vacillation, and proclaiming a switch from the tactics appropriate when the CP adopted the stance of a "governmental" party to the "mass tactics" of a sharpened struggle against American imperialism.

Great efforts were now made by the Communists through the CGT to step up the number of strikes and bring about a general strike. They succeeded in forcing the resignation of the Socialist prime minister Ramadier (19 November), but his place was taken not by de Gaulle but by another coalition headed by Robert Schuman (MRP). This held office from 24 November 1947 until July 1948 and with Jules Moch at the Ministry of the Interior showed that it had sufficient will to take the steps necessary to hold off any threat from the Communists. The strikes continued throughout November but failed to produce a decisive result and at the beginning of December Thorez returned from a hasty visit to Stalin with instructions (as the French Ministry of the Interior believed) to use anything short of armed force—including flying squads of Communist militants—to keep up the campaign, with which the workers were showing more and more impatience. These tactics were to be pursued at whatever cost to the Communist Party in France and preparations were reported for its cadres to go underground in the event of its being declared illegal. The Party, however, suffered a much more serious defeat than being banned, the collapse of the strike wave and a split in the CGT (dominated by the Communists since the Liberation) leading to the formation of a rival independent trade union group, *Force Ouvrière*, by Léon Jouhaux and five other trade union leaders (19 December).

Bevin followed with intense interest this contest for the support of the French working class. When he made his brief visit to Paris in September to sign the report of the Conference on European Economic Co-operation, he found time to call on Ramadier at the office of the *Président du Conseil* and, without any prompting, volunteered to examine the possibility of a closer

[1] See the memorandum on France by Matthews, Director of the Office of European Affairs, 11 July 1947, FRUS 1947 (3) pp. 717–22.

understanding and even union between the UK and France. With a combined population of 87 million people and their combined resources, including their colonies, they could be as powerful as the USA or the USSR.[1]

"As we came away," (the Ambassador, Duff Cooper, recorded), "Bevin said to me, 'We've made the union of England and France this morning'. He would certainly like to, and I believe if it were not for other government departments he might bring it off."[2]

Duff Cooper had no doubt that Bevin was in favour of a closer union between the two countries but equally that "certain departments and especially the Treasury and the Board of Trade, are opposed in principle to any closer collaboration between Great Britain and France".[3] No more than Churchill, at an earlier moment of even greater crisis, was Bevin able to develop such a proposal in a way that would influence events. In the long run he counted on the offer of American aid to restore French confidence, but until this began to appear in the New Year there was little he could do to help the French Government through the crisis. What delighted him was that, in these circumstances, with no effective intervention from outside and despite French distrust of American proposals for the revival of Germany, the French people and, most notable of all, a majority of the French working class repudiated the Communist line. It strengthened his conviction that wherever the mass of the people was free to express its opinions and not coerced, the majority would reject Communism and the Soviet Union.

Equally important was the question whether the Italian Communist Party (also represented at the founding conference of the Cominform) would be successful in carrying out the instructions from Moscow to do everything possible to defeat the Marshall Plan. Here too the elimination of the Communists from the post-war coalition (in May) had been followed by an intensification of the political struggle and much speculation on the advantages to the Soviet Union in the Mediterranean if Italy came under Communist control.

As in France, the Communists under Togliatti's leadership aimed to use strikes and the threat of public disorder on top of the exhaustion of Italy's economic resources to force the de Gasperi government out of office. They controlled the trade union confederation and were more successful than the French Communists in carrying the Socialists with them, splitting the Socialist Party and keeping the majority under Nenni as fellow-travellers. If they could not secure control of the government in Rome, another possibility, once the ratification of the Peace Treaty had been followed by the withdrawal of American and British troops, might be to set up a separate government of their own in Northern Italy. The partisans had virtually controlled the North at the end of the War and the Communists and Nenni Socialists still retained their

[1] Bevin–Ramadier talk, 22 September 1947. FO 800/465/FR/47/23.
[2] Duff Cooper, *Old Men Forget*, p. 377.
[3] *Ibid.*, p. 379.

hold over the municipal governments of Milan, Turin, Genoa and Bologna as well as other smaller cities. If they were successful, the common frontier with Yugoslavia opened up the possibility of recognition and assistance from Tito.

Memories of what had happened in the North in 1945 were vivid enough for such a move to be discussed seriously,[1] but the timing of the crisis in Italy was different from that in France. Although there were strikes and riots in Italy in November at the same time as in France, the last American and British troops did not leave until December 1947 and the elections which would provide a trial of strength between de Gasperi's Christian Democrats and the Communists were not due until April 1948. This gave more time for the Western powers to make their own bid for Italian support. The main burden of this fell on the Americans. The British were still cool towards their ex-enemies in the Mediterranean war and Bevin, although for different reasons, got on no better with Sforza, the Italian foreign minister, than Churchill had. He recognized the importance, however, of keeping Italy out of the Soviet sphere of influence and at the end of October 1947 invited Sforza to London, the first official visit by an Italian minister since the War. Of more immediate practical value was Bevin's promise to the Americans that the five thousand British troops holding the frontier between Italy and Yugoslavia would not be withdrawn.

It was against this background that the Council of Foreign Ministers assembled in London on 25 November 1947. While the situation in Italy was not to reach its crisis point for some months, the meeting coincided with the most critical weeks. Ramadier's government had fallen on the 19th; Blum had failed to get a majority in the Chamber and Schuman's cabinet had only taken office the day before in face of violent opposition from the Communists. What might happen in France was in the minds of everyone sitting at the conference table. The Soviet leaders had now openly adopted the thesis of the two camps and called for all-out resistance to the Marshall Plan, denouncing the Americans as engaged upon the enslavement of Europe with Bevin as their chief accomplice, surrendering Britain's national independence as well as betraying the interests of the European working classes. In a note to Attlee in October, Bevin minuted that negotiations for a revised Anglo-Soviet treaty had been in suspense since May and that the present trend of events in Europe made it difficult to believe they could be revived as anything more than a manoeuvre.[2] It remained to be seen whether, even at this late hour, sufficient common interest could be found to effect a compromise on the future of Germany or, if not, whether the deadlock would be prolonged, or one or other of the two camps provoked to a trial of strength.

---

[1] See for example the remarks of the Italian ambassador, Tarchiani, when he called at the State Department on 4 June 1947 (FRUS (3) p. 970) and the memorandum by the Policy Planning Staff dated 24 September 1947, *ibid.*, pp. 977–8.

[2] Bevin's note for Attlee before the HC debate on foreign affairs on 29 October. FO 800/502/SU/47/46.

4

Ever since his return from Moscow in the spring Bevin had spoken of this next meeting of the CFM as likely to prove of historic importance for the development of the post-war world. He had been equally consistent, however, in maintaining that until the London meeting took place, nothing irrevocable had been or would be decided. Nor was this said solely with an eye to its effect on a Labour Party still troubled by the prospect of an open quarrel with the Soviet Union: it also happened to be true. Bevin had made great efforts, beginning with his talks with Marshall in Moscow, to push forward the recovery of Western Germany and of Europe outside the Soviet sphere of influence and not to allow either to be held up any longer by the requirement of Soviet agreement or by fear of the consequences of going ahead without it. Yet the fact was that no effective steps had been taken to implment the agreements which had been reached (for example, on raising the level of German industry or fusing the British and US zones) and the most important agreement of all, the American undertaking to provide even interim aid to Western Europe, leave alone the full requirements of the Marshall Plan, was still in the balance.

This was an argument, however, which cut both ways. If the issue was still open, that meant that a settlement with the Russians was still possible; but it also meant that the Russians were still in a position to disrupt the Western Powers' plans.

The major campaign by the Communist parties and Communist propaganda to rouse opposition to these plans, represented as the "imperialist enslavement of Europe", suggested that the Russians took the same view and believed that it was still possible to mobilize sufficient opposition to discourage the Americans from implementing, and the French and other European peoples from accepting them.

Both possibilities were in Bevin's mind. Even after ten days of frustration and failure to reach agreement in the London conference, he was still prepared to say to Marshall that they should not entirely rule out the possibility of last-minute instructions from Moscow reversing the Russian line and opening the way to a settlement, as had happened over the Italian peace treaty in New York in December of the previous year.[1] But it was the other possibility which preoccupied Bevin, of the Soviet Government using the opportunity of the conference to hold up or even reverse the progress made with a Western initiative in default of four-power agreement. Such tactics would fit well with the propaganda and political warfare campaign which the Russians were already conducting.

Discussing the forthcoming conference at a meeting in Washington on 17 October, Strang said that Bevin was generally pessimistic about the outcome and thought that, while the Soviets would concentrate on attacking the fusion

1 Bevin–Marshall talk, 4 December 1947. FO 800/447/CONF/47/9.

of the British and American zones, they might also put forward proposals which the US and the UK would find it embarrassing to reject.

"These proposals might include the withdrawal of occupation forces, a seemingly reasonable settlement on reparations and economic principles, and possibly an offer of food-stuffs for Germany. Strang emphasised Soviet interest in obtaining a part in the Ruhr administration and thought they might be prepared to make concessions to this end with a view to confusing and hampering German reconstruction along Marshall Plan lines." [1]

What Bevin most feared was that, by reviving hopes of a four-power settlement on Germany without any real intention of making concessions, the Russians might draw the Western powers back from working out a three-power alternative and in effect secure an extension of the deadlock which worked to their advantage. It could be argued that this danger had to be balanced against the other, of missing a genuine opportunity for four-power agreement. But that no longer disturbed Bevin: he was convinced that firmness was the right policy in either case and that if the Soviet Government changed its line—as it had over the Italian peace treaty—it would be because the Western powers refused to give ground or be diverted by the Soviet tactics.

Bidault had taken advantage of his visit to the United Nations in September and October to try and start discussions with Marshall on the programme to be pursued if the London conference produced no agreement with the USSR. He had authority, he said, to discuss the whole German problem, obviously with the hope of getting the US Government to accept French views on the Ruhr, the Saar and opposition to a centralized German state. Marshall, however, was not to be drawn: they must not assume the London CFM would fail; the British too were involved and the French had not yet reached a decision to merge their zone with the other two. [2]

The French got a more positive response from the British. Shortly after Bidault's unsuccessful approach to Marshall, Chauvel, the Secretary-General at the Quai d'Orsay visited London and joined Massigli, the French Ambassador, in talks with Bevin and Foreign Office officials. Unlike Marshall, Bevin told the Frenchmen that he thought it was important to iron out their differences over Germany before the CFM met. Molotov, he said, would be anxious not to break off negotiations but this must not be allowed to hold up steps to organize the three Western zones as a unit. When Chauvel raised the possibility of the Russians proposing the withdrawal of all troops, Bevin was confident that British public opinion would not be taken in. He went on to declare that his long-term policy was a closer union between the UK and

[1] Memorandum of conversation between Strang, Murphy and Hickerson, 17 October 1947. FRUS 1947 (2) pp. 687–8.
[2] Discussions between Bidault and Marshall in New York, 18 September and 8 October. FRUS 1947 (2) pp. 680–85.

France, bringing in Italy and Benelux later and seeking to develop an area in Western Europe and Africa in which they could be self-supporting.

A two-part programme was drawn up for Anglo–French co-operation, the first of which covered discussion of the agenda for the London conference, the circumstances in which the meeting might be considered to have failed and the questions which would then have to be dealt with immediately, such as the fusion of the three zones, the Ruhr and the organization of West Germany. The second part listed longer-term objectives such as economic and financial relations, collaboration in colonial development, and after the CFM, plans for the permanent control of the Ruhr, a security system which would meet the needs of the two countries, as well as closer co-operation between the countries of Western Europe.[1]

From the talks which Strang held on 17 October with Murphy and Hickerson in Washington (the record of which was shown to the French), it appeared that at the official level, whatever Marshall might say to Bidault for the record, the Americans too were pessimistic about the London CFM and, if the discussions heralded no change in the Russian attitude, favoured a short meeting (two weeks at most) and indefinite adjournment. In the event of the CFM breaking down, Strang reported that the Americans thought it would be necessary to take certain steps at once. These included a new currency for Western Germany and the re-organization of the political structure of the Bi-zone. Although it would be premature to set up a German Government or Parliament, the provisional organization should have a clear political status and adequate executive authority, with the British and Americans confining themselves to minimum measures of supervision and security. It was no less important that British and US forces should remain in Berlin and the ACC continue to function.

Strang's report of the Washington talks represents Murphy and Hickerson as much more forthcoming on the consequences of failure to reach agreement in the CFM than the US official record, which focuses attention on what Strang said rather than on the American response.[2] As the date for the London meeting approached, Marshall showed increased anxiety to avoid any charge that the Western powers had made preparations in advance for what was to be done if the conference failed to produce agreement. When Strang asked (30 October) whether it would not be useful to start talks in advance on the organization of Western Germany, he was told (4 November) that any contact between the three Western deputies when they held their preliminary meetings in London must be purely informal and that there must be a clean break between the CFM discussions and any subsequent consultations for proceeding in Germany on a tripartite basis.

---

[1] British record of talks 19–22 October 1947. FO 800/465/FR/47.
[2] British record (Strang's report) FO 800/465/47/26; American record, FRUS 1947 (2) pp. 687–8 and also for further meetings on 24 October, pp. 689–91; on 30 October, pp. 692–5; and on 4 November pp. 697–8.

In the tenser atmosphere of London, such precautions looked highly unrealistic and Murphy, the US representative in the Deputies' meeting, cabled back to the State Department:

"I believe most intelligent Europeans would take it for granted that we had made our plans in view of lack of 4-power unity and the Soviet unilateral action. I believe their regard for us would be diminished if they felt that we had not made preparations."[1]

This was certainly the British and French view and although Bevin went through the required ritual of expressing hopes of four-power agreement in public, he was very clear that if the meetings produced no results, as he expected, the Western powers must know what they were going to do and must allow no delay in getting on with it.

The meetings of the Foreign Ministers' deputies fully confirmed the pessimistic view of the conference's prospects. After nine meetings, they could not reach agreement even on an agenda and then spent a further seven hours on 19 November without so much as being able to draft a joint report of their disagreement.[2]

On the evening before the conference proper opened, 24 November, Bevin saw both Molotov and Marshall separately. In view of the failure of the Deputies to settle anything, Bevin asked Molotov point-blank if he was prepared to make any progress or whether the Soviet view was that the other three had always got to agree with them. Molotov retorted that they had been threatened by the USA and complained of the aggressive attitude of the Western Press. Bevin answered that the British people were sick and tired of delays and obstructions and wanted a prompt settlement; but negotiations implied mutual concessions, not from one side only.[3]

The formal meetings of the 5th Council of Foreign Ministers opened in Lancaster House on 25 November and continued, over 17 sessions, until 15 December.[4] As a curtain-raiser to Molotov's performance in London, Marshal

---

[1] Murphy's reply, 20 November, *ibid.*, 725. Clay was even more emphatic. Cabling the War Department on 3 November he said: "We must have courage to proceed with the Government of West Germany quickly if CFM fails to produce an answer for all Germany. I doubt very much if this action would imperil the quadripartite machinery. We cannot continue successfully unless we establish a governmental machinery for West Germany. The resentment of the Germans against colonial administration is increasing daily. . . . Two and a half years without a government is much too long."
Clay, *Papers*, vol. 1, pp. 475–8.
[2] British records of the meetings of deputies Nov. 1947: FO 371/64636.
[3] Bevin's report of the interview to Marshall, FO 800/502/SU/47/47–8; Marshall's note, FRUS (2) pp. 730–31.
[4] The British records of the 5th session at the CFM are in FO 871/64629-30 (Briefs); 64637-8 (Items for discussion); 65341 (Agenda and minutes; 64645-6 (Proceedings). The US record of the London CFM and the subsequent 3-power talks in London is in FRUS 1947 (2) pp. 676–829. Bevin's forecast to the Cabinet on 25 November was not encouraging; he could see no evidence that the Russians would be more accommodating than they had been in London. "If the proceedings confirmed his fears, he would have to ask the Cabinet to consider a fresh approach to the main problems of our foreign policy." CM 90 (47).

Sokolovsky, the Russian representative on the Allied Control Council in Germany, had made a bitter attack on American and British policy in Germany at a meeting of the Council four days before, claiming that the Marshall Plan

"Aims at subjugating the economy of the American, British and French zones in Germany to American and British monopolies and at converting these regions of Germany, and primarily the Ruhr, into a war industry base of Anglo-American imperialism.[1]

In the CFM, after making a bold bid for German support by calling for the immediate creation of an all-German government, Molotov developed the same theme:

"There is evidently another plan for Germany, one designed to prevent her economic recovery, for fear that Germany might become a rival in the European and World Market. Hand in hand with this plan goes a policy of weakening Germany economically and destroying her as a united state. . . . In that event endeavours to utilize Germany will be made by those Powers which need one or other piece of German territory as a base for the development of a war industry, and Germany's reactionary forces as a support for a policy of dominating over the democratic countries of Europe and opposing the development of the democratic movement in the European countries liberated from fascism.[2]

Molotov's attack set the tone for most of the meetings which followed. Bevin did not allow himself, as on earlier occasions, to be provoked into losing his temper. His comment on Molotov's tirade was: "If we can treat the Soviet charges with the humour they deserve, we can promote peace". But neither he nor Marshall could continue to ignore, as they had so far, the Soviet campaign to represent the Western powers as the opponents of German unity and German recovery. Their reply was that the Russian call for an all-German government was a propaganda sleight-of-hand unless the four powers could agree on the conditions which were necessary to restore German unity and allow a German government to function—the abolition of zonal barriers, freedom of movement for people, ideas and goods, and the size of the economic burdens, such as reparations, the Germans would have to assume.[3] Each side in the set-piece exchanges manoeuvred in such a way as to show up the other as indifferent or hostile to the interests of the German people. Molotov continually attacked the Americans and British for dividing Germany, called for the dissolution of the Bi-zone and accused the British of planning to add the French zone and establish a government in Western Germany. Bevin replied that he was being criticized in Britain for showing too much patience in seeking four-power agreement. At the end of the nine days nothing had been settled

[1] Quoted in Herbert Feis: *From Trust to Terror* (London 1970) p. 277.
[2] Reprinted in V. M. Molotov: *Problems of Foreign Policy* (Moscow 1949) p. 507.
[3] See for example Marshall's reply on 5 December printed in RIIA *Documents 1947–48*, pp. 511–12.

and the conflict had been extended to the draft Austrian treaty, with the Russians still refusing either to give up or to define their claim to German assets.

Outside the formal sessions, there were private meetings in which each delegation tried to sound out the other's intentions. Molotov dined with Bevin and Cripps in the Foreign Secretary's flat at No. 1 Carlton Gardens and asked Bevin and Pakenham back to dinner at the Embassy, without any serious business being discussed.[1] In the course of the evening, Molotov probed his guests' knowledge of Karl Marx, recommending Bevin to study Marx in the commentary of Hilferding. Bevin was not to be outfaced. "You can tell Mr. Molotov", he said to the interpreter, "that I have read 'Ilferding and I found him tedious.' Molotov's smile suggested that the interpreter had mitigated the message in translation. To make sure, Bevin repeated in a louder voice: 'You can tell Mr. Molotov that I have read 'Ilferding and I found him tedious.' This time his meaning was clear and the subject of Marxism was abruptly dropped.[2]

More interesting were the two meetings which Bidault held with his Western colleagues. The first of these, with Marshall, Douglas and Dulles, took place on 28 November, and reflected the Americans' anxiety about the debates in Congress and the passage of the European Recovery Programme. Marshall described this as "of transcendental importance" and pressed Bidault, whatever his difficulties over Germany and such questions as the level of industry and the Ruhr, to balance very carefully the advantages of placating French public opinion against producing an adverse reaction in America.[3]

The following night (29 November) Bidault took Massigli and Couve to dinner with Bevin. He thought, as Bevin did, that Molotov wanted to keep the conference going if only to use "the opportunity for propaganda speeches, while the rest of them wasted time". They talked a good deal about Anglo–French co-operation, Bevin producing his favourite idea of combining to develop not only their own but their colonies' resources, which he claimed could make Western Europe independent of both the USA and the USSR. He also raised the question of military co-operation to which Bidault replied that they were anxious to start talks but had the impression the British were not sure they could be trusted. Bevin admitted there were doubts because of the position of the Communists in France. Bidault, however, assured him that he would send only men who were trustworthy and pressed for talks to start in the military as well as the economic field.[4]

A meeting between Bevin and Marshall followed at lunch in the Ambassador's house on 2 December.[5] Robertson and Clay were present as well as Lew

---

[1] 26 November 1947. FO 800/447/CONF/47/9.
[2] Pakenham, pp. 187–8.
[3] FRUS 1947 (2) pp. 737–9.
[4] FO 800/465/FR/47/28.
[5] The British record of the series of talks between Bevin and Marshall in London, 24 November–18 December 1947 is in FO 800/447/CONF/47/9.

Douglas and the US Ambassador in Moscow, Bedell Smith. The main topic of conversation was the Russian tactics in the CFM. Marshall confessed himself baffled by these: the Russians must know that American and British opinion was now in favour of taking action on their own if a breakdown occurred, yet Molotov appeared not only to be indifferent to this happening but actually to want it. Bevin's view was that after the breakdown of the Paris talks with Molotov in the summer, the Russians saw two choices open to them, to abandon their hold over the satellite countries or face a Western bloc. They had chosen the latter, being confident that they could split it.

France was the key and when Marshall asked what was the best way of steadying the French, Bevin replied: by putting the Interim Aid Bill into effect. If this could be done in a few days, it would make all the difference. Nodding in agreement, Marshall told Douglas to see that this point was put across to Republican members of the House Committee which was considering the Bill. Firm, as so often, in his support of the French, Bevin went on to say that he was confident they would pull through, particularly if they got interim aid. The real crisis, he suggested, would come in the spring when the snow melted on the Greek mountains and the Communists made a renewed effort to gain Greece.[1]

5

Speculation on the chances of agreement at the conference had now given way to discussion of the best way in which to end it. At a further meeting on 4 December held at Marshall's request, the American told Bevin that nothing would be more popular in the States than to break off and tell the Russians to go to the devil, but he suspected that this would be a temporary response and would be followed by a different one when the implications were fully understood. He wanted, therefore, to make sure that, if they had to break, it was on a point of substance which would carry conviction with American opinion and not on grounds chosen by the Russians.

Bevin took much the same view. He felt that public opinion in Britain was already prepared for a breakdown, and would expect them to act on their own. It was at this point that he remarked they should not entirely exclude the possibility of a Russian turn-around, as in the case of the Italian peace treaty. That might happen if Molotov, after probing for soft spots on the Western side, failed to find any. The important thing was to stand firm. They should give short answers: "no comment on nonsense". "If the Communist attempt to overthrow the Constitution in France failed", and if Congress passed the Interim Aid Bill, they would be in a much stronger position vis-à-vis the Russians. He added that Bidault had told him the French Government would have broken the Communist threat by next Sunday (7 December).[1]

[1] British record FO 800/447/CONF/47/9; US record FRUS 1947 (2) pp. 750–53.

When the Council at last turned to economics at its meeting on the 5th, Marshall proposed that they should drop generalities and find out what each delegation really had in mind for a settlement with Germany. The only response was another wide-ranging attack by Molotov on the Western powers.

The deadlock over procedure was finally resolved on the 8th and over the next three days, the conference made more progress than at any other time, actually settling a number of points including revision of the level of German industry, the break-up of cartels and greater Allied control through the Control Council of the distribution of German coal, steel and power. Any illusion of agreement, however, was dispelled on the 12th when the Council discussed a proposal for each occupying power to give an account of the reparations removed from its own zone up to the present. Molotov refused until they had reached a general settlement of reparations first and accused the Western Powers of exploiting and taking profits out of their own zones. A free-for-all followed with Molotov piling on one charge after another, Marshall retorting that his speech reflected on the dignity of the Soviet Government and Bevin adding that Molotov could at least have thanked his colleagues for listening to the end. Both the British and Americans later published detailed refutations of Molotov's charges but so far as any further discussions of their differences was concerned, it was obvious that the Foreign Ministers had reached an impasse.

After a weekend's pause for reflection, the Western Powers came to the meeting on 15 December determined to end the conference. Bevin was in the chair and expressed his doubts whether the CFM was a body which could ever reach a settlement of the German problem. It had been agreed that Marshall would reply to Molotov and that then, upon Bevin's motion, they would immediately adjourn the meeting. Bevin however failed to take his cue and, after some confusion, it was left to Marshall to move that the Council should adjourn on the grounds that Soviet obstruction made any real progress impossible. Molotov retorted that Marshall's proposal was intended to give the USA a free hand to act as it wished in Germany, but he did not oppose adjournment and Bidault thought it would be better to stop rather than further aggravate relations between the Four Powers. So after three weeks' public display of their disagreements, the Foreign Ministers broke up with nothing settled and no date fixed for their next meeting.[1]

All four proceeded to issue their account of the conference and justify the positions they had taken up. Bevin's was delivered to the House of Commons on 18 December. There was little if any disposition to disagree with his

---

[1] Marshall felt Bevin had let him down in the final session and took Bevin's slowness in picking up his cue as unreliability. According to Acheson this impression was based on a misunderstanding of the way in which Bevin's mind worked. "Bevin was no split-second operator. He moved slowly; he was often distracted. He could easily miss a cue and in the resulting confusion not know how to pick it up again. To a soldier, trained to precision in manoeuvre, what was really clumsiness appeared deliberate. This was a misjudgement. Ernest Bevin was as honourable and loyal a colleague as one could wish." (Acheson, *Sketches from Life*, p. 11).

conclusion that, while they should close no doors and maintain all the contacts they could, "We cannot go on as we have been". In a broadcast to the American people Marshall spelled out what this meant:

"We cannot look forward to a unified Germany at this time. We must do the best in the area where our influence can be felt."

But Germany, he added, was only part of the problem. The war had left a political vacuum in Europe.

"I fear there can be no settlement until the coming months demonstrate whether or not the civilisation of Western Europe will prove vigorous enough to rise above the destructive effects of the war and restore a healthy society. Officials of the Soviet Union and leaders of the Communist Parties openly predict that this restoration will not take place. We, on the other hand, are confident in the rehabilitation of Western European civilisation with all its freedoms.

"Until the result of this struggle becomes clearly apparent, there will continue to be a very real difficulty to resolve, even on paper, agreed terms for a treaty of peace. The situation must be stabilised."[1]

Marshall had always had his eye on the effect anything said in London might have on Congress and the legislation required to translate the Marshall Plan into action. This was the reason for his refusal to discuss in advance what was to be done if the CFM failed to reach agreement. Bevin had accepted this but as soon as the Council broke up he pressed Marshall not to leave London before they had put in hand the preparation of alternative plans for Germany and Europe.

At a meeting with Robertson and other British officials on 16 December, Bevin told them to go ahead with every means they could to raise industrial output in the Bi-zone, reach agreement if possible with the Americans about restoring political life on democratic lines, and work out possible concessions to the French on security to get them to bring in their zone with the other two.[2] But more was now needed than a plan for the rehabilitation of Germany.

When Marshall came round to the Foreign Office on the evening of the 17th, Bevin had a proposal ready and no sooner had Marshall sat down than he plunged straight in. As the *Manchester Guardian* was later to remark when Bevin's idea of a "Western Union" had become a commonplace: like the Greek historian Thucydides, "the more interesting Mr Bevin is, the more obscure and difficult he becomes."[3] This was evidently Marshall's reaction on the present occasion.

The gist of Bevin's idea was that they had to take a wider view of the situation they found themselves in than the dispute between the Western powers and the Soviet Union. In talking to Bidault earlier that day he had

[1] Marshall's broadcast, 19 December 1947. RIIA *Documents 1947–48*, pp. 536–7.
[2] FO 371/64250/16171.
[3] *Manchester Guardian*, 5 May 1948.

quoted with approval Douglas's remark: "The real issue is where power should rest in Germany and Europe".[1] But the issue would not be decided by material power alone. What was needed was a positive plan for an association of the Western democratic countries, comprising the Americans, the British, France, Italy, etc. and the Dominions.

"This would not be a formal alliance, but an understanding backed by power, money and resolute action. It would be a sort of spiritual federation of the West. He knew that formal constitutions existed in the U.S. and France. He, however, preferred, especially for this purpose, the British conception of unwritten and informal understandings. If such a powerful consolidation of the West could be achieved it would then be clear to the Soviet Union that having gone so far they could not advance any further."

There had been speculation of this sort in the Press but this was the first time that such a proposal was put forward by any of the leading men in office in the West. It was characteristically wide and vague and the phrase "a sort of spiritual federation" in particular, was an awkward way of saying what Bevin meant, in effect that those countries which shared certain common traditions and values, by virtue of which they described themselves as belonging to the West, should draw on these in organizing to act together and not leave the Communists with the initiative in the competition for men's loyalty to ideas. Nonetheless, coming immediately after the breakdown of the attempt to find a four-power framework, it offered an alternative which, although it was received non-committally by the American Secretary of State on this first occasion, was to prove as fruitful as Bevin's idea of what could be done with Marshall's offer of aid.

Bevin was not in favour of any public pronouncement for the moment. He wanted to put the planners to work first on the whole complex of problems involved in Germany. "We must always aim at an eventually united Germany. Then any German irredentist movement for unity would come from the West and not be a Russian-inspired movement coming from the East." They would also have to consider the problem of security which was of special concern to the French. There had been some idea of a three-power version of Byrnes' treaty. "He himself thought it might be better to have some treaty or understanding which also brought in Benelux and Italy." This was another suggestion with a future to it. "The essential task was to create confidence in Western Europe that further communist inroads would be stopped." Bevin was in confident form himself and he told Marshall that he had been "much fortified" by a decision of the TUC's General Council, which had approved his foreign policy with one dissenting voice, pledged TUC support for the Marshall Plan and "decided to oppose the communists resolutely if they attempted to start any trouble here."

Marshall's response was couched in practical terms. He had no criticism of

---

[1] Bevin's talk with Bidault on the morning of 17 December. FO 800/465/FR/47/31.

Bevin's general ideas, but they had to distinguish between the material and the spiritual aspects of the programme, and they needed an understanding between the two of them as soon as possible on their immediate objectives. "They must take events at the flood stream and produce a co-ordinated effect." Bevin thought they should begin with Germany and suggested that the two of them should meet the Military Governors, Clay and Robertson, the following day.[1]

One of the things Bidault had told Marshall was that he believed President Benes would be evicted by the Communists in Czechoslovakia. Bevin had received similar reports and feared they might prove accurate. He had already told his PPS, Bob Dixon, that he wanted him to go as Ambassador to Prague so that he could have someone he knew and could rely on in what might become the next crisis centre.[2]

Bevin was quite clear, however, that the Western Powers had to continue with the initiative they had taken with the Marshall Plan proposal, make their own plans for the future of Europe outside the Communist sphere and not wait to react to Soviet moves.

The following day, 18 December, he and Marshall met Clay and Robertson for lunch at 14 Princes Gate and heard their proposals for action to be taken in Germany. Clay was particularly keen to press ahead with currency reform at once, but thought it was worth while first to try and secure Soviet agreement in the Control Council. Robertson was prepared to go along with Clay, although less enthusiastic about making a further attempt to bring in the Russians, which he thought a waste of time. Clay then turned to the question of political organization. He and Robertson were agreed that they should stop short for the moment at expanding the German economic council in the Bi-zone but should add, slowly but surely, to its political responsibilities until it functioned as a government in all fields except those of external affairs and the export–import programme. There should be no formal constitution although, working on the basis of the paper the British had tabled in Moscow and again in London, they looked eventually to the creation of an elected German government at least in the British and American zones. Bevin insisted that their proposals must allow for an all-German government and thought there would need to be more consultation before they got Clay's proposals into the right shape.

Bevin had no intention of saying anything about future plans when he spoke in the House the next day, but Germany would have to be debated when the House reassembled in the late January and he asked for, and was promised, recommendations from the two C.-in-C.'s by 10 January. After a remark from

[1] The report of the Bevin–Marshall meeting printed in FRUS 1947 (2) pp. 815–22 was supplied by the British and is the same as that in the Bevin Papers, divided according to subject between FO 800/466/GER/47/5; 465/FR/47/29–31; 447/CONF/47/9.
[2] Dixon was replaced as Bevin's Principal Private Secretary by (Sir) Frank Roberts on 8 December 1947.

Marshall that they had leaned over backwards rather than do anything which would prevent agreement in the CFM—"We had been so honest that no one would believe us and we might well be criticized for being exceptionally naive"—Clay and Robertson each raised one further point. Clay's referred to Berlin. He warned the two Secretaries of State that the Russians were in a position to put pressure on the Western Powers and they should expect trouble. He and Robertson meant to hold out in the former capital as long as they could. If the going got too rough, they would have to report to their Governments but would not do so before they needed to.

Robertson raised the question of French participation. He emphasized the bad effect it would have on German opinion—and so on the German economy, particularly on coal and steel production—if it were known that the future of the Ruhr and especially the possible separation of the Ruhr from Germany were still under discussion. This was a pointed reference to the talks due to be held with the French in London in the New Year. Robertson urged that concessions should not be made to the French on the Ruhr as the price of getting them to join their zone to the other two. Although he did not say so in so many words, the British and Americans, having at last decided to go ahead in Germany without Russian concurrence, should not allow the French to hold them up.[1]

This was the third winter of the Occupation and every report from Germany, constantly made matter for reproach to Bevin in the House of Commons and in the Press, provided evidence that physical conditions were worse, rations lower, the Black Market more rampant and German belief in any improvement less than at any time since the War. Bevin's reply to his critics that they had to go to the limits in trying to get four-power agreement no longer satisfied anyone. Now at last—twelve months too late, the critics claimed—the British and Americans had decided to act on their own. But this was not the end of their difficulties, and the final statement made by the Military Governors pointed to the two major obstacles they had still to overcome, a confrontation mounted by the Russians, and a veto threatened by the French, before any visible results were likely to flow from their decision.

6

Before Marshall left London he received the news that Truman had at last been able to sign the Bill for Interim Aid to Europe. This followed a hard fought battle in Congress and cuts in the allocations to France and Italy. Truman immediately renewed the battle by sending the draft of the main Economic Cooperation Bill to Congress with a strong recommendation that

---

[1] Report of the meeting on 18 December in FO 800/466/GER/47/53 and 447/CONF/47/9. The British record is again printed in FRUS 1947 (2) pp. 822–7, and followed by the American record, pp. 827–9.

the United States should provide 17,000 million dollars for a four-year European Recovery Programme.

This was good news but it took another three and a half months for Congress to reach a decision and for the President to sign this second Bill on 3 April 1948. Until that was done there was no financial underpinning for everything Bevin had built his hopes on in the past nine months and his whole foreign policy could still collapse like a pack of cards. The result was not at all a foregone conclusion and Bevin simply had to live with the uncertainty knowing that far more than his own political future and that of the Labour Government—the independence of Western Europe and the recovery if not the independence of Great Britain as well—would be at stake if Congress (with a Republican majority) defeated Truman's and Marshall's proposal. For this reason, if for no other (and he still refused to exclude the possibility of a change of policy on the Russian side) Bevin did not draw a line across and say this was the end of the attempt to reach agreement with the Soviet Union. Indeed while the CFM was meeting in London and Molotov belabouring the British as lackeys of American imperialism, the Secretary for Overseas Trade, Harold Wilson, had gone off to Moscow (3 December) and reached agreement in principle on the long-drawn-out Anglo-Soviet trade talks. This agreement, signed on 27 December, provided for the exchange of 750,000 tons of Russian grain during 1948 in return for British machinery and equipment, and was intended to lead to a longer-term treaty after discussions to be held in the following May. Bevin's statement to the House—"We shall close no doors. We shall maintain all the contacts we can"—and his refusal to answer Molotov's attacks in kind (as he might have been tempted to a year before) was intended to play down rather than dramatize the failure of the London conference.

Subsequently, the year 1947 appears as the turning point in the recovery of Western Europe, in Britain's post-war foreign policy and in Bevin's career as Foreign Secretary. But at the time it was all a matter of faith; the justification by works had yet to come.

In March 1947 when the country had been on the edge of an economic breakdown and everything appeared to be running against the Labour Government, it would not have been difficult to find a majority in the Cabinet for the view which Dalton and at times even Attlee took that Britain could no longer afford a foreign policy. To the *Keep Left* group and the *New Statesman* Bevin's argument that Britain could not be indifferent to what filled the vacuum of power left by the War in Europe and the Middle East appeared an anachronism which had more in common with late Victorian imperialism than with the socialism of the new Britain of the mid-century. Bevin himself, when he left for Moscow at the beginning of 1947 had no certainty that the USA would take over British responsibilities in Greece and Turkey, and at the end of the year he had no idea at all what would take the place of the British administration in Palestine. Indeed, materially, at the end of 1947 it was hard to say that Britain or Western Europe were any better off than they had been in

March. The British, plunging into financial crisis, had had to swallow their pride and eventually devalue sterling. France and Italy could only get through the winter if they received interim aid from the USA and that was not certain until the day after the London CFM broke up. There had been much discussion of the Marshall Plan but not a dollar had yet been allocated to it; there had been much discussion of the re-organization of Western Germany but it is doubtful if it had yet led to a ton more coal being mined.

The two Secretaries of State had completed their discussions in a business-like way; but both were aware of the importance of the juncture they had now reached, with the Council of Foreign Ministers breaking up and no date fixed for a further meeting. It was unlikely that the Russians would accept the Western Powers' decision to throw over the rule of unanimity without putting their resolution to test; before that was settled Bevin saw little hope of improving or at least stabilizing relations with the USSR. The period ahead could be decisive in determining the future of Europe, but no one on the Western side—and perhaps on the Russian—could yet be sure how or where such a confrontation would take place.

All that Bevin had to set against these uncertainties was a series of understandings with the Americans, none of which had binding force or had yet been tested in practice and any of which could be repudiated by Congress. None the less there was no doubt about the much greater confidence with which he faced the future in December compared with March 1947. For this there were two main reasons. The first was his feeling that he now had much more support in the Labour Movement and the PLP, a very different situation from that of December 1946 when he was still suffering from the humiliation of a vote of no confidence moved by members of his own Party. The second was the conviction that he had not only found the right line for Britain to take in her foreign policy but that, with the change in American policy, the power would be provided to make it effective. He never doubted that the Americans would make good their promises and that the war-time partnership would be restored.

As if in confirmation of his confidence the year ended with a new agreement between the USA, Britain and Canada on atomic development.

The secret talks in Washington had by no means proved easy. The initial list of areas in which there could be exchange of information disappointed the British, being largely confined to matters of fundamental science, where the British were as likely to have something to give as to receive, and excluding the technological and military questions to which they most wanted answers. New topics might be added from time to time but there were no specific promises, and any extension of the list would have to be capable of justification to the Joint Congressional Committee in terms of the McMahon Act. In contrast to their lack of precision on the exchange of information, the Americans were both precise and pressing on their need for increased supplies of uranium ore, not only for a larger allocation in the future but for the immediate transfer of at least part of the stocks held in the UK. They were prepared to drop clause 4 of the Quebec Agreement restricting Britain's industrial exploitation of atomic energy and not to raise their former objections to the vulnerability of UK stocks and plants, but they also wished to eliminate clause 2, requiring mutual consent before the use of atomic weapons, and not even to include a requirement for consultation.

The stumbling block was the request to move existing stocks of uranium ore from the UK to the USA. In reporting to Bohlen in London on 17 December how the talks had gone, Kennan recognized that the difficulty stemmed not from the British representatives but "from Cabinet in London, where decision appears to be made, largely on emotional grounds, that none of supplies on hand in England are to be given up".

Makins had agreed to ask the Cabinet to reconsider their attitude and Kennan inquired whether there was any chance that Marshall could talk to Bevin before returning to Washington.

"We have been warned that Bevin is very sensitive about suggestions that materials should not be left in England because this would be 'insecure'. For this reason we have not introduced this argument here, but have stuck strictly to consideration of needs."[1]

But on the question of American needs, Kennan was in no doubt that the British position (which would mean that US stocks would be down to three weeks' supply at the end of 1949 while British stocks would be enough for five years' production) could not be defended to Congress and would have to be modified. At a discussion with Hickenlooper, on 20 December, the latter accepted that a transfer of part and not the whole of the stocks held in the UK was as much as it was practical to hope for, and Cockcroft and Makins flew back to put the case for such a concession two days before Christmas. The strongest argument was the frankness with which the Americans had treated the British representatives as partners in a common defence policy and their acceptance of a production programme in the UK which they were prepared to assist. They had made no attempt to use Marshall Aid as a bargaining counter, and their case was accepted by the Canadians as unanswerable. No one attached importance to the right of consultation on the use of the bomb, which the Chiefs of Staff considered of little practical value, and the ministers concerned (including Bevin) accepted the officials' view that they should agree to a package deal in which the revision of uranium allocations in favour of the USA was to be balanced by the exchange of technical information.[2]

In order to avoid anything in the form of an agreement which would have to be submitted to Congress or the UN, the *modus vivendi* as it became known, was embodied in similar declarations of intent made by the representatives of the

[1] Teletype conference between Kennan and Bohlen, 17 December 1947. FRUS (1) pp. 905–6.
[2] See Gowing pp. 248–54.

three countries at a meeting of the Combined Policy Committee on 7 January 1948.[1]

In practice the new arrangements did not represent a breakthrough or open the door, as the British had hoped, to the information which they wanted. The concessions proved to be almost entirely on the British side and the *modus vivendi* only the first step towards the resumption of the nuclear partnership which was not finally achieved until the 1950s, some years after Bevin's death.[2]

7

The British had decided to withdraw from Palestine, but only from Palestine. The prospect of a confrontation with Russia strengthened rather than weakened the arguments for holding on to their position in the rest of an area which both the Soviet and the Western High Commands regarded as of key importance strategically, whether the confrontation came to war or—as Bevin thought more likely—remained at the level of threat and counter-threat.

To British satisfaction, in the Pentagon talks the Americans had accepted that Britain should retain responsibility for organizing the defence of the Middle East. But how this was to be done was still a question to which after two years' search, Bevin had not found a satisfactory answer. The decision to withdraw from Palestine, which the COS had always regarded as the best alternative to Egypt, reduced the options, but to stay and impose partition would remove any hope of agreement with the Arab states. Looked at from that point of view, the decision to withdraw could be seen as keeping the other options open.

Bevin had not given up hope of reviving the negotiations with Egypt, now that the Egyptian approach to the UN had failed to produce any result. Twice, in December 1947 and in January 1948, he put up schemes to Attlee for a new approach which would by-pass the political difficulties that had led to breakdown a year before. Attlee was unimpressed.[3] On the second occasion he did not even need to say so: events elsewhere in the Middle East supplied sufficient answer.

For Bevin's real hopes in the winter of 1947–8 were focused not on Egypt but on Iraq. The Iraqi elections of March 1947 had produced a reforming Prime Minister of the younger generation in Salih Jabr, of whom the British hoped great things and with whom they believed they could do business. Salih Jabr staked his reputation on successful negotiations with the British to replace the

---

[1] Text in Gowing, App. 9, pp. 266–72.
[2] After the US Atomic Energy Act of 1954, the amendments to it of 1958 and the two agreements signed between the USA and the UK in July 1958 and May 1959. See Andrew J. Pierre: *Nuclear Politics* (London 1972) pp. 136–44.
[3] Bevin to Attlee, 15 December 1947, FO 800/457/EG/47/8 and Attlee's reply, 16th, *ibid.*, EG/47/9; minute from Bevin to Attlee 23 January 1948, *ibid.*, EG/48/1.

1930 Treaty and he could rely on the support of Nuri Said, whom the British had long regarded as their best friend and the outstanding politician in the Arab world. Bevin himself was determined to learn from his failure with the Egyptians. He insisted that to satisfy nationalist demands negotiations must be conducted from the beginning on the basis of an alliance between equals, in which all the facilities to be maintained by Iraq—in particular at the two air-bases—should be shared by the British and Iraqi forces and responsibility for planning Iraq's defence placed in the hands of a Joint Defence Board, with equal representation. In the event of war or the threat of war, Iraq would invite Britain to send the necessary forces into the country and would furnish all facilities and assistance.

Bevin regarded this treaty, signed at Portsmouth on board *HMS Victory* on 15 January, as a model for the sort of arrangements he would like to see made with other Arab governments, and there were grounds for thinking that these might be more solidly founded on mutual interests in the case of Iraq than in that of Egypt. Iraq was that much nearer to the Soviet Union for a threat from that direction to be more easily visualized than in Cairo, and in the oilfields and pipelines developed by the British-run Iraq Petroleum Company there were visible signs of the benefits of partnership. Oil royalties were increased after the War and an agreement on Iraq's sterling balances signed (on the day sterling's convertibility was suspended in August 1947) was more generous than Britain could really afford: *The Times* spoke of "almost quixotic generosity". Among other concessions the British relinquished their partial control of the State Railways and the port of Basra as well as withdrawing the Army formations stationed in the country since 1941 and handing back the two RAF bases provided by the Treaty of 1930.

The advantages from the British point of view were equally obvious. The two air-bases of Habbaniya and Shu'aiba would be returned to Iraqi sovereignty, but the RAF would continue to have access to them and British staff would maintain them in a state of operational efficiency. These provided the most advantageous position from which to defend, and in the last resort to destroy, the oil installations not only in Iraq but at Abadan and in the Persian Gulf. From Iraq they could bring help to Turkey or Persia and, if necessary, fly strikes into Southern Russia. The Royal Navy would be guaranteed free access to the Shatt-el-Arab; Iraq would continue to appoint British military instructors, send her officers to British training establishments, and ask Britain to provide experts to help with her economic and social development.

Bevin believed, and so did the Iraqis who signed the treaty, that there were advantages for both sides. What they failed to grasp was what the treaty looked like from outside to those who did not share their assumption of the necessity for the British to retain their position in the Middle East. A telling comment was made by the *Hindu* which remarked that, except for some concessions to nationalist sentiment, there was no difference between the old and the new treaties.

"We do not see what innovations there are in the new treaty to suggest that it is the model or the foundation stone for a Middle East defence system. Iraq's weaker status is evident not only in the defence arrangements but in the continuance of the foreign oil monopolies. A real regional system for the Middle East, working under the aegis of the United Nations, will only come when the economic independence of the Arab countries is assured."

Le Monde's judgement was the same: "The letter is changed, the spirit remains."[1]

The Iraqi reaction was in fact as violent as anything in Cairo. In face of continued rioting, the Regent felt obliged to repudiate the treaty (21 January) and after street battles with the police in which thirty were reported killed and 300 injured in a single day, the Government resigned. There was no doubt that the Prime Minister, Salih Jabr, had handled the negotiations too secretly, failing to make known the terms of the agreement or to prepare the ground for their acceptance; nor that the urban mob had a special grievance in bread shortages, and that most political leaders found it more profitable to exploit the violence for their own advancement than to support the Government. But when all these factors are taken into account the plain fact remained that the treaty which Bevin regarded as a model had led to a violent explosion of nationalist anger, and that it appeared nothing less than the severance of the British connection altogether would satisfy the national aspirations of the Iraqis any more than it would those of the Egyptians.

In face of such a setback a less persistent man than Bevin would have given up, or at least been led to accept that any hope of finding a new basis for Britain remaining in the Middle East would have to be deferred (he never abandoned it). However, so far as Iraq was concerned the violence with which the revised treaty had been rejected was not followed by a break with Britain. No attempt was made to renew negotiations by either side, and for the remainder of Bevin's period of office, there was a tacit agreement to leave things as they were. With Nuri back in power it even proved possible to embark on the sort of development to which Bevin attached so much importance, a major scheme for flood control and irrigation carried out with Western advice and assistance.

Even in Egypt the failure to work out a new relationship was followed by a continuation, however short-term, of the existing situation, including continued British occupation of the Suez base. And this was so even although the British refused to accept an Egyptian veto on their plans for the Sudan. On Bevin's initiative a joint Anglo–Egyptian committee was set up to assist constitutional reform in the Sudan and even reached agreement on what should be done. When this was rejected by the Egyptian Senate, the British Government, nonetheless, went ahead with Sudanese elections leading to the creation of a Legislative Assembly and the participation of Sudanese ministers in the government.

[1] Both quotations from George Kirk: *Survey of International Affairs, The Middle East 1945–50* (London 1954) p. 155.

But the most striking example of Bevin's persistence is his response, against the advice of his Permanent Under-Secretary, Slr Orme Sargent, to Transjordan's request for a new treaty.

For a quarter of a century the Hashemite ruler of Transjordan, Abdullah, had been Britain's most reliable ally in the Middle East. Disliked by his fellow Arabs, particularly Ibn Saud, and scorned as a creature of British imperialism, his impoverished and entirely artificial state nonetheless had considerable strategic value in British eyes because of its central position and the fact that it provided direct communication between the oil-producing areas of Iraq and Iran and the main British bases in Egypt and Palestine.

Until 1945 Transjordan had been administered in a loose association with Palestine as part of the British mandate. The termination of the Mandate at Abdullah's request in February 1946 (as a reward for his loyalty during the War) and the creation by treaty of an independent kingdom, although approved by the UN, had been bitterly denounced by both Zionists and Arabs. "Independence" was seen as a pretence to disguise the reality of continued dependence on British subsidies and British control, while robbing Palestine of an area which should naturally remain part of it. The British gave no encouragement to Abdullah's expansionist ambitions to create a "Greater Syria" with himself as King, but they provided a subsidy and helped to keep up the Arab Legion (then 8,000 strong) trained and commanded by British officers under Brigadier Glubb (Glubb Pasha as he was known).

Abdullah's proposal to revise the 1946 Treaty followed on the news of Bevin's negotiations for a new treaty with Iraq. "This craving for new treaties", Orme Sargent commented, "seems to be infectious in the Middle East". If the treaty with Iraq had not collapsed, a treaty with Jordan (which neither side saw as altering the existing relationship, only giving it more plausibility) could have been represented as part of the new regional arrangements which Bevin hoped to secure with the Arab states. But on its own it was a much more dubious proposition and faced Bevin with a dilemma. The fact that in Jordan there was no question of Britain giving up control could destroy whatever credibility Bevin's talk of a new model for Britain's relations with the Arabs still had. When Sir Alec Kirkbride, the British representative in Amman, sent reassurances that the appointment of a "tame" Arab officer would make sure that the proposed Joint Defence Board gave no trouble, Bevin minuted:

"This is bad. It is just the way that I do not want to treat the Arabs."[1]

There was also the risk that yet another treaty with an Arab state might be repudiated by nationalists and, more substantial, the certainty that it would be denounced by the other Arab states as justification for their suspicions of Bevin's proposals.

[1] Bevin's minute on Kirkbride's dispatch, 21 February 1948. FO 371/6889.

On the other hand, with British troops withdrawing from Palestine, the Chiefs of Staff saw enhanced value in the Arab Legion and great advantage in strengthening the British position in the Middle East. If Palestine was going to be partitioned there was an obvious case (which had always appealed to Bevin) for joining the rump Arab state, which had no prospect of viability on its own, to Transjordan – a better outcome (it could be argued) than seeing it annexed by the Jews. There was little doubt that Abdullah would be prepared to acquiesce in a Jewish State in Palestine if he got what was left over; this had long been one of the grounds for the distrust with which he was regarded by the other Arab states.

Sargent was still opposed, but after some hesitation Bevin came down in favour of going ahead even after the rebuff by the Iraqis. He was not however satisfied with the Foreign Office advice on how this would affect Palestine[1] and raised the question with Tawfiq Pasha, the Jordanian Prime Minister, when he came to London to sign the treaty. Glubb who acted as interpreter records that Tawfiq told Bevin that Abdullah had received many requests from Arabs on the West bank to provide protection when British troops withdrew. The Jordan Government (Tawfiq said)

"Accordingly proposed to send the Arab Legion across the Jordan when the British Mandate ended, and to occupy that part of Palestine awarded to the Arabs which was contiguous with the frontier of Transjordan."

Bevin repeated his reply twice: "It seems the obvious thing to do . . . It seems the obvious thing to do . . . but don't go and invade the areas allotted to the Jews."[2]

Bevin was satisfied with Tawfiq's assurances on this point and it was understood that Abdullah would come to an agreement with the Jews not to encroach on each other's territory.[3] Transjordan could thus provide an answer to the problem of partition and at the same time a substitute for the loss of Palestine as a strategic asset. In a note of 9 February 1948 Bevin is reported as speculating on the strategic advantages to Britain if a corridor could be maintained across the Negev providing direct communication from the Mediterranean at Gaza to Transjordan and the oilfields in Iraq and Iran[4]—an idea which strongly appealed to the Chiefs of Staff.

The Transjordan Treaty (signed on 15 March 1948) thus represented one more attempt on Bevin's part to find a firm basis for Britain's strategic position

---

[1] Bevin's minute "too indefinite" on a FO memorandum of 24 January 1948. FO 371/68817.
[2] Sir John Glubb: *A Soldier with the Arabs* (London 1957) pp. 63–6.
[3] Bevin to Kirkbride, 9 February 1948, reporting on his talks with Tawfiq. FO 371/68364 and 68366/E. 1916.
[4] FO 371/68368. Mr Ilan Pappe, to whom I owe these references, remarks that Bevin probably assumed that the Jews would occupy the whole coastal area unless the Arab Legion prevented it.

in the Middle East. Both the uses to which he proposed to put it, however, were to produce unforeseen complications, with the Arabs as well as the Jews, before the end of 1948.

PART IV

Test and Achievement, 1948–1949

CHAPTER 13

"The next 6 to 8 weeks will be decisive"

I

Over the New Year break Bevin put the finishing touches to a group of papers which he placed before the Cabinet at its meeting on 8 January. If 1948 was going to bring a showdown with the Russians then it was essential that he should make clear to his colleagues and get their support for the policy he intended to follow. As background he circulated a comprehensive review[1] of the hostile policy the Soviet Union had followed towards Britain and the West since the War. No doubt the Russians' first objective was to hasten their own reconstruction but they hoped to draw important advantages from the post-war confusion. Bevin repeated his familiar conclusion that the Russians were unlikely to be planning a war against the West, but were confident of getting what they wanted by other methods. Their policy was based on the assumption that the Marshall Plan would fail, the capitalist powers quarrel among themselves and their power disintegrate as a result of economic slumps. If that prediction was proved wrong, Soviet policy might change radically; but until then it was based on the idea of two worlds in conflict and on active opposition to reconstruction in the West on the only terms on which it appeared to be possible. Within their own sphere of influence, they had ruthlessly consolidated their position and could be expected to complete the process by action in Czechoslovakia in the next few months. In the rest of Europe they would continue to make use of local Communist parties to obstruct the Marshall Plan and could be expected to intensify this in the next few months, possibly attempting a *coup* in Italy.

Bevin was impressed by the need not to leave the Communists to enjoy the propaganda initiative. The West needed to put its own case positively.

"It is for us, as Europeans, and as a Social Democratic Government, and not the Americans, to give the lead in the spiritual, moral and political sphere to all the

---

[1] "Review of Soviet Policy". CP (48) 7, 4 January 1948.

democratic element in Western Europe which are anti-Communist and at the same time genuinely progressive and reformist, believing in freedom, planning and social justice—what one might call the 'Third Force'."

This was the subject of a second paper which Bevin concluded by calling for a more sustained effort to project the advantages of social democracy and meet the Communists on their own ground.[1]

It was the two other papers, however, which defined the objectives of British policy now that it was freed from the need to pay at least lip-service to four-power unanimity. The fact that Bevin was criticized for not expressing this freedom earlier did not disturb him; with a Labour Party always reluctant to listen to open criticism of the USSR it was better to be behind rather than ahead of the change in public opinion. Even now, however, he was not able to speak with anything like the same freedom in public that he was in private and so had to put up with a continuation of criticism in the press for failing to see the obvious and to act with sufficient sense of urgency.

The first of these two other papers discussed by the Cabinet did not mince words. It dealt with British policy in Germany, and defined its guiding principle as to prevent the gradual creation of "A Communist-controlled Germany on the pattern of . . . Eastern Europe." Three steps were proposed. For tactical reasons Bevin did not favour the setting up of a provisional German Government at Frankfurt immediately; by the end of the summer however he hoped to see, as Clay and Robertson had proposed, German bodies exercising in practice most of the functions of a Government and Parliament. He argued that the German economy would not recover until the Germans were given greater political responsibility and until a new currency was introduced. This second step would restore incentives for work and cut at the root of the black market. If the new currency could be accepted by all four Powers as a common currency for the whole of Germany, that would greatly relieve the effects of the split between East and West, and enough notes had been printed for this to be done; but if the Russians—or French—made difficulties, there should be no delay in introducing it in the Bi-zone. Finally, German industrial production should be raised, not only to improve the standard of living in Germany but to make the contribution to European recovery expected from Germany under the Marshall Plan. Bevin again underlined his belief that the way to achieve this was to give the Germans more political authority and responsibility.

Bevin was in favour of all possible steps to increase trade between the Bi-zone and Eastern Germany and the Soviet bloc, and was strongly opposed to American pressure to end dismantling and with it the payment of reparations, including reparations to the Soviet Union. "I shall offer the most stubborn opposition ever to this." He saw the continuing division of Germany

[1] "Future Foreign Publicity Policy". CP (48) 8, 4 January 1948.

as now unavoidable and likely to become sharper, but he believed that it would not last indefinitely. "The problem for us is to bring unity about as soon as possible but in such a way as to ensure that the forces of attraction operate from the West upon the East and not vice versa." Re-unification was a task primarily for the Germans but should be achieved with Western support, so that national unity could not be used as a slogan against the Western powers.

Bevin concluded that Britain would have a difficult role to play in mediating between the French who feared and resented German recovery and the Americans who became exasperated with French obstruction. He believed the key was the French need for security not only against Germany but against the USSR, and thought this might have to be met by a new three-power guarantee of the three Western zones against attack from any quarter.[1]

No disagreement was expressed in the Cabinet[2] with Bevin's statement of policy towards Germany; nor with his separate proposal to continue talks with the Russians on an Austrian treaty which, it appeared, might now be conducted independently of the breakdown of talks on Germany.[3] But French, German and Russian reaction to a statement made by Clay and Robertson showed how sensitive were the issues raised by the programme Bevin had outlined. The statement was made at a meeting with the Minister–Presidents of the Bi-zone Länder at Frankfurt on 7–8 January, before Bevin's paper had been approved by the Cabinet. In it Robertson spelt out the constitutional changes which it was proposed to make immediately. These included doubling the size of the German Economic Council and giving it the power to raise taxes; setting up a second House composed of representatives of the Länder reforming the Executive Committee into something more like a cabinet with an identifiable chairman elected by the Economic Council, and creating a bi-zonal high court and central bank. The publicity given to the meeting made it appear that the Military Governors' proposals represented a definite move towards the creation of a West German Government. This was certainly the objective now accepted by both Bevin and Marshall, but it was also the last thing they were going to admit in public. The Russians at once seized on the announcement as proof that the Western Powers were deliberately dividing Germany. There was much uneasiness amongst the Germans that this was bound to be the consequence of what was proposed, and the French protested vigorously that they had not been consulted and that the projected constitution would once again create a centralized German government.

Bevin told Massigli that he had been as surprised as anyone by the news from Frankfurt and the French Ambassador learned from other ministers that Bevin had expressed the same surprise at the Cabinet meeting on the 8th. Bevin, however, also told Massigli that as regards the reorganization of Western Germany, the British "would have to get on with matters and could

---

[1] "Policy in Germany". CP (48) 5, 5 January 1948.
[2] CM (2) 48 (including the confidential annex), 8 January 1948.
[3] See Bevin's memorandum on an Austrian Treaty, CP (48) 9.

not hold things up while the French ruminated on the other side of the fence." The French got the same reply, more diplomatically expressed, when they made a formal protest to Marshall.

Some gestures were made to the French, in particular acceptance of their claim to incorporate the Saar in the French economy. But no steps were taken by London or Washington to stop the Military Governors' plans for the Bi-zone going ahead and the new arrangements were promulgated on 9 February with only minor modifications and immediate effect.[1] Bevin and Marshall agreed that they had undertaken a commitment to the French to discuss the long-term future of Germany and a tripartite conference was called to meet in London on 23 February. But in a note for Marshall Bevin underlined his view that, while the interests of France and the Benelux countries could not be disregarded, the discussions in London must be designed to reach clear-cut conclusions. These could not be expected on all the topics to be discussed—for example on the two which most pre-occupied the French, control of the Ruhr or security against Germany—but there must be firm decisions on the development of political institutions in Western Germany—if possible, on a three-power; if not, on a two-power basis.

Marshall's view was expressed equally forcefully in Paris. The American Ambassador was instructed to tell Bidault that the French preoccupation with Germany was "outmoded and unrealistic". Germany might be a threat to French security in the distant future, but the immediate threat was "from another power" and in American opinion French security for many years to come would depend on the integration of Western Europe and the effective association of Western Germany with that development "during the coming year . . . first through economic arrangements and ultimately perhaps in some political way." If that were not done, "there is a real danger that the whole of Germany will be drawn into eastern orbit, with obvious dire consequences for all of us".[2]

The question of Western Europe to which Marshall referred was the subject of the final paper presented by Bevin to the Cabinet on 8 January. Its importance was indicated by its title: "The First Aim of British Foreign Policy".[3]

Bevin began by describing the situation which confronted the West:

"The Soviet Government has formed a solid political and economic block. There is no prospect in the immediate future that we shall be able to re-establish and maintain normal relations with European countries behind their line. . . . Indeed we shall be hard put to it to stem the further encroachment of the Soviet tide. . . . This in my view can only be done by creating some form of union in Western Europe, whether of a formal or informal character."

---

[1] For text, see von Oppen, pp. 268–79. The Bank Deutscher Länder was established on 14 February.
[2] Bevin's *aide mémoire* for Marshall 17 February 1948. FRUS 1948 (2) pp. 68–9; Marshall's instructions to US Ambassador in Paris, 19 February, pp. 70–71.
[3] CP (48) 6.

Arguing that it was not enough to promote economic recovery without a political and moral mobilization as well, Bevin continued:

"I believe therefore that we should seek to form with the backing of the Americas and the Dominions a Western democratic system comprising Scandinavia, the Low Countries, France, Italy, Greece and possibly Portugal. As soon as circumstances permit we should of course, wish also to include Spain and Germany without whom no Western system can be complete. Almost all the countries I have listed have been nurtured on civil liberties and on the fundamental human rights. Moreover, most Western European countries have such recent experience of Nazi rule that they can apprehend directly what is involved in their loss. All in a greater or lesser degree sense the imminence of the communist peril and are seeking some assurance of salvation. I believe, therefore, that the moment is ripe for a consolidation of Western Europe. This need not take the shape of a formal alliance, though we have an alliance with France and may conclude one with other countries. It does, however, mean close consultation with each of the Western European countries, beginning with economic questions."

In presenting his paper to the Cabinet, Bevin laid stress not only on "a greater measure of cooperation" among the countries of Western Europe, but on mobilizing the resources of Africa and the other British and European colonial territories. If these were included, the whole "would form a bloc which, both in population and production capacity, could stand on an equality with the Western hemisphere and Soviet blocs."[1] In the discussion Bevin was urged not to lay too much emphasis on the anti-Soviet aspects of his proposals —since this might satisfy the Right but would make it more difficult to rally the Socialists forces in Europe. There were also doubts about including Salazar's Portugal in a Western democratic system. But there was general support for his proposal, and Bevin was sufficiently encouraged to send a copy of his memorandum to Marshall.[2]

The State Department's reaction to Bevin's memorandum was warm, wary and inquiring. George Kennan wrote to Marshall that the prospect of a Western European Union was "one which we should welcome just as warmly as Mr. Bevin welcomed your Harvard speech. Only such a union holds out any hope of restoring the balance of power in Europe without permitting Germany to become again the dominant power."[3] However, like others in the State Department, Kennan had criticisms to make and a lot of questions to ask. Accordingly, while the Secretary of State sent off a message welcoming Bevin's initiative and describing his proposal as of "fundamental importance", Marshall avoided any commitment and the following day Hickerson and Reber, the director and deputy director of the State Department's Division of European Affairs had the Ambassador in to get down to practical questions.

Hickerson began by questioning whether Bevin was right to suggest extending the Treaty of Dunkirk to Benelux, since it was directed against Germany.

[1] CM 2 (48), 8 January 1948.
[2] It was presented by the British Ambassador on 13 January. FRUS 1948 (3) pp. 4–6.
[3] Kennan to Secretary of State, 20 January, *ibid.*, pp. 7–8.

He proposed instead that Bevin should look at the recent Rio Treaty for Inter-American Defence. This would allow, as Bevin himself saw was necessary, for the eventual entry of Germany into the arrangements.

Hickerson went on to ask whether Bevin was thinking of the USA taking a direct part in any European regional defence organizations. He himself, he said, envisaged the creation of a European third force "which was not merely the extension of US influence but a real European organization strong enough to say 'no' both to the Soviet Union and to the United States". If the Europeans, however, thought that no regional defence system would be complete without the USA, then he was sure the American Government would give such a proposal careful consideration, particularly if it could be brought under the charter of the United Nations. But the crucial factor would be the extent to which such a concept should be, and should be seen to be, "based principally on European initiative".[1]

This was as far as Bevin had got in his exchange with Washington when he was called on to open a two-day debate in the House of Commons on foreign affairs (22–23 January), and made his paper the central feature of his speech.

2

A month before, Herbert Morrison had warned Bevin that Churchill was preparing "a great speech" on the theme of the political organization of Western Europe, adding "I think we all have some sympathy with this idea but it would be a pity if the Leader of the Opposition got in first."[2]

Unhampered by the responsibilities of office and finding a release from the frustration of opposition in the European Movement, Churchill was in a position—and the mood—to outbid any attempt by Bevin to assume the leadership of Europe. Wisely, Bevin did not try to compete and told Morrison they would just have to take the risk of Churchill coming out first.[3]

Bevin was well aware, however, that after the breakdown of the London CFM, there was a great need to rally opinion and restore confidence in Britain and Western Europe as well as in the USA. No one else was in a position to do this: Bidault, because France was in too weak a position and he himself uncertain and depressed about the future; Churchill, because although able to stir the imagination, he lacked the power to act; Marshall or Truman because they dared not risk endangering the passage of the ERP legislation through Congress. Bevin was equally well aware of the dangers the other way. He knew that Bidault and many others held that the approaching Spring of 1948 was the danger period. Although there had been an open breach with the Russians, nothing had so far been done in practice to provide for either the recovery or

[1] Report of conversation by Hickerson, 21 January 1948, *ibid.*, pp. 9–12.
[2] Morrison to Bevin, 22 December 1947. FO 800/493/PLT/47/44.
[3] Bevin to Morrison, 24 December, *ibid.*, PLT/47/46.

the security of Western Europe. He himself might be pretty sure that the Russians would not risk war, but there were many millions of people in Western Europe—French, Italians, Germans—who were far from sure, who had no confidence in their governments' power to resist a combination of threats from outside and within, and whose fears, less than three years after they had just come through the experience of war and occupation, were highly vulnerable to Communist propaganda. Anything he might say which appeared to provoke the Russians could alarm them even more and weaken rather than rally European opinion. He had to be no less careful that anything he said—perhaps taken out of context—should not damage the prospect of getting the Marshall Plan accepted by Congress.

None the less, when Bevin rose to address a crowded House of Commons on 22 January, he did not disappoint the widespread feeling that this was a critical occasion calling for something more than an official brief written in the style of a communiqué. His speech for once bore the stamp of his own personality and struck (as *The Times* put it) "the dominant chord" of the debate.

His two main themes were Soviet policy since the War—by "every means in their power to get Communist control in Eastern Europe and, as it now appears, in the West as well"—and the means by which Western Europe could and should defend its independence. Speaking more plainly than ever before of Soviet tactics, he described the methods of the police state which they had used to eliminate opposition in Eastern Europe and the methods of political warfare they employed to intimidate weaker neighbours. He took Greece as an example:

"I know that I have been pursued in this country on this Grecian question as if it were a question between a Royalist and a Socialist or Liberal Government. It is nothing of the sort and never has been . . . It is a case of power politics. We have been trying to leave Greece an independent country and to get out of it; but we also want her northern neighbours and everybody else to leave her alone and get out of it."

What had brought matters to a head was the prospect of European recovery opened up by the Marshall Plan. The Russians prevented Eastern Europe from joining in a co-operative effort to take advantage of the American offer for the whole of Europe—including themselves—and they were using every means at their disposal, including political strikes (as in France) and threats to prevent Western Europe taking advantage of it to restore its economic vitality.

"But surely all these developments point to the conclusion that the free nations of Western Europe must now draw together. . . . I believe the time is ripe for consolidation. . . .

"I hope," he continued, "that treaties will be signed with our near neighbours, the Benelux countries, making with our treaty with France an important nucleus in Western Europe. We have then to go beyond the circle of our immediate neighbours. We shall have to consider the question of associating other historic members of European civilisation, including the new Italy, in this great conception. . . . We should do all we can to foster both the spirit and the machinery of co-operation. . . . Britain cannot stand outside Europe and regard her problems as quite separate from those of her European neighbours."

Western Union was the term he preferred to use but he emphasized that he was not thinking only of Europe as a geographical conception. "Europe has extended its influence throughout the world and we have to look further afield", in the first place to Africa and South-east Asia.

"That involves the closest possible collaboration with the Commonwealth and with overseas territories, not only with British but French, Dutch, Belgian and Portuguese.
    "These overseas territories are large primary producers . . . and their standard of life is capable of great development. They have raw materials, food and resources which can be turned to very great common advantage, both to the peoples of the territories themselves, to Europe and to the world as a whole. . . . There is no conflict between the social and economic development of those overseas territories to the advantage of their peoples and their development as a source of supplies for Western Europe."

He carefully avoided, however, any mention of the sort of relationship the United States might have with the new grouping. This necessary omission misrepresented his ideas which took the support of the USA in some form as essential to the whole enterprise. All he could do, and he did it with conviction, was to speak of what they already owed to the USA for the Marshall Plan and to pour scorn on those who claimed it was all done in America's own interest. Of course it was, "but it is everybody's interest as well; it is not exclusively American."

"The instinct is that it is much better to spend money now on rebuilding a healthy and self-reliant Europe than to wait for the devils of poverty and disease to create again conditions making for war and dictatorship. . . . If we are to look for hidden political motives, then I detect them much more clearly behind the attempt to sabotage the Paris Conference than behind the great Marshall offer."

Bevin deliberately did not attempt to define what he meant by Western Union. He could not because he himself did not yet see where the idea might lead. It would be very different however from the *fait accompli* imposed on Eastern Europe.
    His final words were delivered with emphasis:

"We shall not be diverted, by threats, propaganda or fifth column methods, from our aim of uniting by trade, social, cultural and all other contacts those nations of Europe and the world who are ready and able to co-operate. The speed of our recovery and the success of our achievements will be the answer to all attempts to divide the peoples of the world into hostile camps."[1]

A study of the debate which followed and of British press comment on Bevin's speech is illuminating. The two left-wing papers, the *New Statesman*

[1] Full text in RIIA *Documents 1947–48*, pp. 201–21.

and *Tribune* were sour and grudging, the latter declaring that indignant protests against Moscow's attitude did not

"Make a suitable alibi for the patent failures, the shocking mixture of sterile inactivity, of cynical wrong and dishonest self-righteousness which have distinguished British foreign policy in far too many fields."

When analysed it becomes clear that *Tribune* was concerned less with Europe than with Palestine and that what the *New Statesman* could not forgive was Churchill's claim that Bevin's statement "signalled the final conversion of the Labour Government to the principles of the Fulton Speech."[1] The *Manchester Guardian* spoke of "a new policy", but only to add a question-mark, and complained particularly that Bevin was "frankly inadequate" on Germany unaware that he had provided the Cabinet with a very clear programme which he was prevented from repeating in public because of French sensitivities.[2] In a later editorial, however, the *Guardian* (echoing *The Times*) spoke of the remarkable unanimity of public opinion reflected in the debate and conceded that, while Bevin and Churchill were equally imprecise about the meaning of "Western Union",

"That is no bad thing. There is a revolution in thinking and we must not expect clear-cut schemes and comprehensive diplomatic arguments until the idea has sunk in and men's minds have become used to it."[3]

The Times reported that Bevin's "dedication of British policy to the 'consolidation of Western Europe' has stirred Washington" and the *Sunday Times* that no pronouncement from Europe had roused Americans as much since Churchill's great war-time speeches.[4] No one in Britain, to judge from the British Press, was misled into supposing that Bevin was calling for a surrender of national sovereignty and the creation of a Europe federation. His emphasis was on co-operation, consultation and partnership, and he had specifically denied that he was proposing "a formal political union with France, as has sometimes been suggested". But the possibility of misunderstanding by nations whose constitutional traditions and practice were very different from the British was there from the beginning.

The Economist, giving its second thoughts ten days after the debate, took up Senator Vandenberg's description of Bevin's speech as "terrific":

"It was indeed terrific but precisely because of the prospect it presented of long and intricate negotiations, painstaking study and the unsensational discussion of committees. . . . Projects like this need a decade, and Western Europe will be busy with the execution of the Marshall Plan for the next five years."

---

[1] *Tribune*, 29 January 1948; *New Statesman and Nation*, 31 January.
[2] *Manchester Guardian*, 23 January.
[3] *Ibid.*, 24 January.
[4] *The Times*, 26 January; Washington Correspondent of the *Sunday Times*, 25 January.

But ten days' reflection, in *The Economist*'s view, had not removed "the first impression of boldness, hope and determination which was made by Mr Bevin's speech. He set the faltering pulse of Western Europe beating more strongly . . . [and] headed British foreign policy in a new direction."[1]

The Times gave a similar warning that those who looked in Bevin's speech for "the philosopher's stone with which to transform the present instability and uncertainty of Western Europe into the Utopian vision of another United States will be disappointed.

"There is no simple formula for Western Union. It will be the product of will and work. It will arrive, if at all, through countless acts of daily policy aimed by the instinct of community towards the same end. . . . What Mr. Bevin has done is to strike the dominant chord. Just as he was swift to seize the initiative offered by Mr. Marshall last June, so he has now been quick to offer an initiative himself."[2]

Bevin allowed a few days to pass for his speech to have its effect in Washington and then, on 26 January, tried again to get a commitment to the defence of Western Europe from the USA. The specific proposal which Inverchapel put to Lovett, the Under Secretary of State on the 27th, was for the USA and Britain to consider an agreement (Lovett called it a military alliance) between the two governments to reinforce the defence of Western Europe.[3]

Not surprisingly the answer was "No", certainly not before Bevin's European initiative had produced results. When the West European states had shown they meant business, then the USA would consider what part it could play in support of such a Western European Union, but with no commitment in advance.[4] Nothing could do more to prejudice the chances of getting the ERP accepted by Congress than to ask the USA for new and extensive military and political commitments. Nor had they any clear picture of what Bevin's proposals for a Western Union really amounted to. "You are in effect," Lovett said, "asking us to pour concrete before we see the blueprints."[5]

The weakness in Bevin's case was that he was not yet able to say what part the British themselves were prepared to play in the defence of Western Europe. Both governments were in the same difficulty, as the American Minister of Defence Forrestal's diaries make clear, of not having the armed forces with which to back up their foreign policy.

If it had not been for Bevin's stubborn resistance earlier, British demobilization would have gone further. The economic arguments for cuts became stronger with the crisis of 1947. The 1947 White Paper on Defence had estimated that there was a manpower shortage of half-a-million men which

---

[1] *The Economist*, 31 January 1948.
[2] *The Times*, 23 January 1948.
[3] Bevin to Inverchapel, 26 January 1948. FO 800/460/EUR/48/4.
[4] Lovett to Inverchapel, 2 February (after he had talked to Marshall) FRUS 1948 (3) pp. 17–18.
[5] Hickerson's note of the talk between Lovett and Inverchapel on 7 February, *ibid.*, pp. 21–3.

could only be relieved by releasing more men from the Forces, and the net cost in foreign exchange of British forces in 1946 had accounted for more than half the balance of payments deficit (£225 m.). With the convertibility crisis of August 1947, the services were under increased pressure to reduce their demands.

At meetings of the Defence Committee, the Minister of Defence, Alexander, had projected a cut in the total uniformed strength from 1,088,000 to 937,000 by 31 March 1948 and 713,000 by the same date a year later. This did not go far enough to satisfy either the Chancellor or the Prime Minister who was sharp in his criticism: the country's economic circumstances set limits which were being ignored. But Bevin came to Alexander's rescue, maintaining that if the UK was to have any influence on international affairs there must be an adequate backing of military power. Attlee refused to accept the figures without further examination, but when the Committee took up the question again, on 29 September, Bevin's view prevailed without further debate and it was agreed to recommend Alexander's projections to the Cabinet. When the report came to the Cabinet three days later it was again Bevin who spoke to it and carried it without discussion.[1]

Nonetheless, at the end of 1947, there were only 91 active infantry battalions, 50 fewer than at the outbreak of war in 1939. Conscription had been retained but the cut from 18 to 12 months' service, in face of a Labour back-bench revolt earlier in the year, had robbed it of much of its value. The War Office was warned in July 1948 that the strength of the army must be reduced to 305,000 (many of them twelve-month conscripts by 1950) and the last of the armoured divisions was threatened with disbandment. So short was the Home Fleet of trained men that only a handful of ships could be kept on active service and the autumn manoeuvres had been cancelled to save oil.

With his experience of wartime mobilization, Bevin himself was critical of the use the Services made of their manpower. He had expected conscription to provide a force of half a million in the UK with a back up of a further million trained reserves. He told Attlee he could see no justification for keeping 700,000 men in Britain[2] and engaged in a spirited correspondence with Montgomery, pressing for the provision of a small mobile and well-equipped striking force which, in an emergency, could be sent overseas at short notice to give confidence in British foreign policy. But he disagreed with Montgomery about the need to send a British Army as in 1914 and 1939 to fight on the continent. "We do not wany any more Dunkirks."

Bevin was echoing a widely held view which the other Chiefs of Staff and the Joint Planning Staff also shared. Undeterred by the fact that he was alone in his views, Monty, after further discussion with Bevin, produced his own staff

---

[1] Defence Committee DO (47) minutes of 18th meeting, 4 August; 20th, 18 September; 22nd, 29 September. CM 78 (47) 2 October 1947.
[2] Bevin to Attlee, 15 August 1947. FO 800/451/DEF/47/10. The same volume contains the correspondence between Bevin and Montgomery in the autumn of 1947.

paper and fought hard for it at a specially summoned meeting of the Chiefs of Staff Committee in No. 10 on 4 February.[1]

Tedder, the Chief of Air Staff and chairman of the COS opened by saying that it was economically and financially impossible to put an army on the Continent at the outbreak of war. The French would have to bear the brunt of any attack and British support would be limited to air and sea forces. He did not believe that Western Union would collapse without a specific promise from the British to fight on land.

Montgomery was strongly of the opposite opinion. He agreed that the main weapon in a war with Russia must be airpower, and that a land attack on the Soviet Union was out of the question. But to hold the line of the Rhine in the initial period before American support became effective would be of immense value and the British also needed air bases on the Continent. Anything which increased the depth of the UK's defences against air and rocket attack was worth having. Without a British contribution on land, Monty argued that a Western Union would never be achieved; the only way to make it effective was to plan to fight on the Rhine. Western Europe did not lack the manpower—the French alone could provide 30 divisions if the Americans could equip them —but the continental nations needed stiffening by leadership and that could be done with no more than two British divisions.

The Prime Minister took Tedder's side. At previous staff conferences it had been accepted that, in the event of war, the whole of Western Europe would be overrun and that any counter-offensive would be launched from the Middle East. Britain had not got the resources to carry that out and put land forces on to the European mainland; two divisions would make no difference. Attlee was no less disturbed by Montgomery's view that the French must be got to see that the Germans were too important to be left out of any Western Union and that the British must bring them in.

Bevin was also worried at the prospect of East and West vying for German support and building up German power to the point where it again became a menace. But he agreed with Montgomery that the Rhine was the right line and thought they were approaching the problem in the wrong way. To provide for the defence of Western Union national forces would have to be merged into a single force. Western Europe (he mentioned the UK, France, Benelux and possibly Italy) had the manpower, if they put their resources together. This was the assumption from which the COS should start and then see what forces could be provided and how they could be organized into a single force. After that they could decide how best to use them, while he worked to get the USA to face the necessity for them to be involved from the beginning.

It was finally agreed that, while the case for sending British troops to the Continent at the outbreak of war could not be accepted without further study (it was not finally accepted until May), Bevin's approach to the problem

[1] Record of the meeting in FO 800/452/DEF/48/7.

should be adopted. The COS were to examine ways of forming the Western European national forces into a single force, and to work out the extra cost of providing two British divisions. Before they could report, the news from Czechoslovakia brought a new urgency to the discussions.

3

When his former Private Secretary, Pierson Dixon, left in January 1948 to take over the British Embassy in Prague, Bevin wrote to wish him well and urge him to get Beneš's appreciation of the situation in his country:

"Dear Bob,
I do not want to take a false step with regard to Czechoslovakia. I have a great fear about the fate that is awaiting them. . . . Does he think he will be able to maintain the democratic position in his country? I wonder whether the Communists will get complete control? I want to be told by him frankly what we can do to assist in any way to maintain the freedom of her people."[1]

Dixon's reply, sent on 11 February, was not reassuring. He found Beneš in poor health and was far from convinced when the President repeated, several times, that the possibility of democracy collapsing was absolutely excluded. A fortnight later there was no more doubt.

In his report to Bevin Dixon emphasized the speed with which the Czech crisis had blow up. Discussions had been going on about elections which were expected in May 1948. There were, however, complaints from the non-Communist members of the coalition that the Communist Minister of the Interior had failed to carry out a decision of the Cabinet aimed at halting the packing of the police force with Communist nominees. When the ministers concerned could get no satisfaction from the Communist Prime Minister Gottwald, they resigned in protest. This proved to be a fatal mistake. The Communists at once declared that they had discovered a plot against the State and took emergency measures. Under Communist leadership, Action Committees were formed to take over public offices and the trade unions mobilized to take part in mass demonstrations. Communist control of the radio and press assured that only their version of what was happening was heard. Under pressure both the President and the Social Democratic Party capitulated, the former accepting the resignation of the non-Communist ministers and approving a new Government under the leadership of Gottwald in which the Communists held all the key ministries but representatives of the Social Democrats and other Parties agreed to serve. The speed with which the Communists put into operation what were evidently well prepared plans stunned their opponents and there was no resistance. Four days after the crisis

---

[1] Bevin to Dixon, 12 January 1948. FO 800/450/CZ/48/1. Dixon's reply, *ibid.*, CZ/48/5.

began with the resignation of the Ministers (21 February), the new Government had taken power and a full scale purge had started affecting all branches of Czechoslovak life. "The whole character of the State had been changed in less than a hundred hours."[1]

Douglas saw Bevin on the evening of the 25th and again on the 26th. He found him opposed to the US suggestion of referring the Communist coup to the UN. Technically it was a domestic matter and would only lead to prolonged and frustrating debate. Let them by all means protest as Bidault proposed, but what was really needed, Bevin said, was concerted action to stop the Russian drive and put new heart into France and Italy.

Dictating a record later of his conversation, Bevin went on:

"I explained that we were now in the critical period of 6–8 weeks which I had long foreseen would decide the future of Europe. . . . Such strong action might of course bear the risk of war. I hoped not and I was convinced that war was less likely if we acted firmly now than if we allowed matters to slide from crisis to crisis as had been done in the 1930s."

He pressed Douglas for consultation with the United States, bringing in France, Benelux and Italy. "We had to evolve a joint military and civil strategy." When Douglas asked for his precise ideas on what should be done, Bevin retorted that he could not give them, that was why he wanted the talks. They might have to be prepared to send troops as well as arms to help the Italian Government; more arms and equipment were needed for Greece and he could not exclude trouble in Germany in the next two months. The Western Powers must consider the whole European situation and what they ought to do.

"I had no fear of the future provided we got through the next six or eight weeks. But I was really anxious lest the period immediately before us should turn out to be the last chance for saving the West."[2]

When Douglas asked him if he had any information that the Russians were prepared to contemplate an early war, Bevin said "No". Douglas said he asked because Clay told him that for the first time he really thought the Russian Government wanted war soon. Bevin doubted it but added that Churchill, who had always shown a great flair for war, told him he regarded the next few weeks as vital to the future.[3]

When the Cabinet discussed the Czech coup on 5 March,[4] Bevin provided them with an account of what had happened and the lessons to be drawn from it, in particular the Communist technique for creating a coalition in which they

[1] Dixon to the FO, 27 February, reprinted as an annex to Bevin's report to the Cabinet. CP (48) 71, 3 March.
[2] Douglas's version is in FRUS 1948 (3) pp. 32–3.
[3] Another report of Bevin's talk with Douglas on the 26th. FO 800/502/SU/48/23.
[4] CM 19 (48).

held key posts such as the Ministry of the Interior controlling the police and the Ministry of Information, and used the other parties solely as a front.[1] He defined the fundamental issue with the Soviet Union as "a contradiction inherent in European politics at least since the foundation of the 3rd International.

"It is the contradiction between an imposed solution of social difficulties, which in the last analysis can only mean Dictatorship, and a voluntary, reasoned and human solution which is summed up in all we mean by the word 'Democracy'."

Nothing could be done about Czechoslovakia which was now absorbed into the Soviet orbit. To prevent any further extension of Soviet power, however, it was essential for the like-minded countries of the West to draw together, beginning as had already been agreed, with a treaty between Britain, France and the Benelux countries.[2] This was only a beginning, however. Making a note of the ideas which tumbled out while Bevin talked after the Cabinet meeting, his new PPS Frank Roberts wrote:

"His general conception is that, under the umbrella of the new five-power Treaty, we should work out a much wider scheme for the general co-ordination and defence of the whole world outside the Soviet orbit. What we should in fact be aiming at is a U.N.O. as it would have been had the Soviets co-operated."[3]

Among a long list of questions arising out of the Cabinet discussions which Roberts was told to look into were propaganda and re-creating the machinery of the wartime Political Warfare Executive; mobilizing the support of the major religions, beginning with the Christian churches but including the Buddhists and Islam as well; means to combat Communism and Fascism in the UK, and a new constitutional formula for independence within the Commonwealth which would make it possible to keep India, Pakistan and Ceylon as members now that they had become independent. In order to "grip and guide" an agenda which threatened to range over everything from strategy and diplomacy to trade and internal security, the Secretary of the Cabinet, Sir Norman Brook, suggested to Attlee that a committee of ministers should be set up with Bevin as a member and with the Prime Minister himself in the chair.

Fortunately, once he got down to what had to be done immediately, Bevin was much more practical than his proposed "agenda" might suggest. But he kept on repeating that what happened in the next six to eight weeks (roughly,

---

[1] CP (48) 71, 3 March.
[2] A second paper circulated by Bevin on 3 March, "The Threat to Western Civilisation", CP (48) 72, also discussed on 5 March.
[3] Roberts' notes of Bevin's ideas on how to push on with the policy accepted by the Cabinet, 5 March. FO 800/460/EUR/48/10.

up to the end of April) would be decisive for the future of Europe and that they could expect other shocks besides Prague. There were, for example, ominous reports from Berlin. Since the session on 21 January, the atmosphere in the regular meetings of the Allied Commandants had changed completely. Agreement had become impossible on even the most routine questions and the Soviet delegation seized on every item on the agenda to launch unrestrained propaganda attacks on the other three powers; the last five sessions had each lasted from nine to eleven and a half hours. The obvious question was whether all this was the prelude to a Soviet move to break up the four-power administration of Berlin. In Italy elections were due on 18 April, and the political battle in preparation attracted world-wide attention, with plenty of speculation—taken as seriously by governments as by journalists—whether the Communists would stage a Prague-style *coup d'état*.

Scandinavia was another area which Bevin had been watching with anxiety for some time. In the same week as the Prague coup, he was given confirmation of reports that the Finnish President, Paasikivi, was under strong pressure from the Russians to visit Moscow and had received a formal letter from Stalin proposing a pact of friendship and military alliance similar to those which the Soviet Union had signed with Hungary and Rumania. Stalin suggested that Paasikivi (who was 78 and in poor health) should go to Moscow or receive a Russian delegation in Helsinki for immediate negotiations. While the Finnish Cabinet was still debating what to do, on 8 March the Norwegian Foreign Minister sent for the British Ambassador and told him that, from three different sources, he had learned that Norway too might be faced with a Soviet demand to negotiate a pact as soon as or even before a Soviet–Finnish Pact had been concluded. The Finns and the Norwegians, like the Czechs, although few in number, were undeniably democratic and their absorption into the Soviet sphere of influence would be a serious defeat for the West; in the case of Norway it also involved the strategic threat of a possible extension of Soviet armed power to the Atlantic.

We do not know, and perhaps never shall, whether these different Soviet moves formed part of a concerted plan (probably not) or what were the Soviet objectives in making them and following them with the blockade of Berlin. But it was impossible for Bevin and the other men in office in Western Europe and the USA not to put the pieces together and act on the assumption that they were facing a calculated challenge by the Russians. All of them had seen what Hitler's tactics of one-at-a-time had secured in the 1930s and had seen Western appeasement fail to prevent a war in which all of them had been involved as recently as three years before. Bevin's own view was that, if the Russians found the Western Powers showing the will and unity to resist, they would not press beyond a point from which they could not retreat; but if the West showed itself irresolute, he saw a real danger that they might proceed to bring the rest of Europe under their control, piecemeal, by a combination of external and domestic threats adjusted to the circumstances of each country.

Bevin never had any doubt that the key lay in America's willingness to give military as well as economic support to Europe. Congress—powerfully influenced, like the Labour Party, by what happened in Prague—was now thought likely to back the European Recovery Programme, and as encouraging reports came in of the talks in Brussels on a European defence agreement, Marshall showed himself more forthcoming. On 11 March he asked the US Ambassador in Rome to discover de Gasperi's views on whether Italy should be included in Brussels treaty (the answer was, "No, not yet") and he responded promptly when Bevin the same day sent him a powerful message urging the need for the British and American Governments, without delay, to consult on the establishment of an Atlantic security system, the first mention of what was to become NATO.

The urgency in Bevin's message reflected his concern at the reports from Oslo of Soviet demands on Norway as well as Finland.

"Two serious threats may thus arise shortly; the strategic threat involved in the extension of the Russian sphere of influence to the Atlantic; and the political threat to destroy all efforts to build up a Western Union."

Bevin said that he had considered whether to invite the Scandinavian countries to join the defence system being negotiated in Brussels but concluded this would not work.

"He considers (the *aide-mémoire* continued) that the most effective steps would be to take very early steps, before Norway goes under, to conclude under Article 51 of the Charter of the U.N. a regional Atlantic Approaches Pact of Mutual Assistance, in which all the countries directly threatened by a Russian move to the Atlantic could participate, for example U.S., U.K., Canada, Eire, Iceland, Norway, Denmark, Portugal, France (and Spain, when it has a democratic regime.)"

They would then be working for three defence systems: one, involving the UK, France and Benelux with US backing; the second, "a scheme of Atlantic security with which the U.S. would be even more closely concerned"; and the third, a Mediterranean security system which would particularly affect Italy. They were making good progress with the first, but the threat to Norway made the second even more urgent. If such an Atlantic security system could be established, Bevin concluded:

"We could at once inspire the necessary confidence to consolidate the West against Soviet infiltration and at the same time inspire the Soviet Government with enough respect for the West to remove temptation from them and so ensure a long period of peace. The alternative is to repeat our experience with Hitler and to witness helplessly the slow deterioration of our position, until we are forced in much less favourable circumstances to resort to war in order to defend our lives and liberty. In Mr. Bevin's view, we can turn the whole world away from war if the rest of the nations outside the Soviet system become really organized, and in turn save Russia herself."[1]

---

[1] Text of the British Ambassador's *aide-mémoire* conveying Bevin's message 11 March 1948 in FRUS 1948 (3) pp. 46–8.

For the third time in nine months, Bevin had taken an initiative—one leading to the European Recovery Programme and OEEC, a second leading to the Brussels Treaty and Western European Union and now a third which was to lead to NATO. Without question, little if anything would have come of any of his proposals if the United States had not provided the resources and the will to turn them into reality. But as Marshall insisted every time, the initiative had to come from Europe and it was Bevin who made sure that it did.

On this last occasion, Marshall's response was immediate and unconditional. After consulting the President he wrote a letter marked "Top Secret" to the British Ambassador the very next day.

"Please inform Mr. Bevin that in accordance with your *aide-mémoire* of 11 March, we are prepared to proceed at once in the joint discussions on the establishment of an Atlantic security system. I suggest the prompt arrival of the British representatives early next week."[1]

Two days later Bevin confirmed that two British officials would reach Washington the following week and would be joined by Canadian representatives.[2] So by the time Bevin left London for Brussels via Paris on 15 March—no more than three weeks after the Prague coup—to sign the Treaty of Brussels, he had already put in train, with the all-important American agreement, arrangements to start on the next stage of his plan.

Nothing of what he hoped to secure could yet be communicated in more than the most general terms even to the Cabinet, but the reaction to the events of Czechoslovakia gave him increased confidence to go ahead on his own. For in the case of Czechoslovakia there were none of the doubts which there had been in the case of Greece about the monarchy and the character of the regime. The traditions established by Masaryk had not been destroyed by the German occupation. No one could say of the Czechs, as they could of other nations in the Soviet half of Europe, that they had never known what democracy meant. Nor could anyone accuse the Czechs of being anti-Russian or even anti-Stalin. Beneš and the coalition government (with a Communist Prime Minister) had made persistent efforts to pursue a policy acceptable to Moscow, including withdrawal from their original acceptance of Marshall's offer; and this policy had much wider support than in, for example, Poland or Hungary. This was still not enough: Moscow required total control in the hands of its nominees who proceeded to introduce the methods of the police state which Bevin had pointed to as the characteristic of Soviet-style Communism in practice. Whatever the *New Statesman* might say—including Richard Crossman in two highly misleading dispatches from Prague[3]—what happened in Czechoslova-

---

[1] Marshall to the British Ambassador, 12 March, *ibid.*, p. 48 and his memorandum to President Truman, also dated 12 March, *ibid.*, pp. 419–50.
[2] British Ambassador to Marshall, 14 March, *ibid.*, p. 52.
[3] The author was in Czechoslovakia immediately after the *coup* and in a position to judge how seriously Crossman misunderstood what was happening and misled the Czechs about British reaction.

kia (a country already sacrificed once, to no avail, to a policy of appeasement ten years before) effectively settled the argument about Soviet intentions and Bevin's foreign policy for the great majority in the Labour Party and the trade unions. After Prague Bevin was able to count upon the positive support of the Labour Movement for his foreign policy in a way very different from the attitudes of earlier years, 1945–7. A small number of fellow-travellers remained but they were isolated even from the broad Left and in a number of cases were expelled from the Party. This was not a permanent change. Foreign and defence policy was again to become a stumbling block to the Labour Party before Bevin died and to remain one; but for the next two years he could claim to speak for a nation united on foreign policy to a degree which no other European leader could do, and possibly not Truman either.

4

In the spring of 1948, as in the summer of the previous year, Bevin was involved with three sets of negotiations all going on at the same time and all requiring to be held in his mind and related to each other.

The first to begin, on 23 February, was the tripartite London conference concerned with the future of Germany, which Holland and Belgium subsequently joined. The conference went into recess on 6 March, while negotiations were transferred to Berlin; it reassembled in London on 20 April and finally reached agreement on 1 June.

The second, aimed at Europe's economic recovery, was the Conference on European Economic Co-operation recalled to meet in Paris on 15 March in order to create the counterpart organization (OEEC) to the American Economic Co-operation Administration (ECA) which President Truman set up under Paul Hoffmann as soon (3 April) as it had been authorized by Congress. This second conference of 16 European nations lasted from 15 March to 16 April.

The third, concerned with defence, began with the conclusion of the Treaty of Brussels on 17 March and continued on the one hand with creating an organization for the Western European Union (WEU) as a follow-up to the Brussels Treaty, and on the other in further negotiations with the Americans. These opened the way for the meetings held in great secrecy in Washington in the summer of 1948 which finally produced the draft of a North Atlantic Treaty.

In the first, the British and Americans met the French for twelve sessions (23 February–6 March) in the Old India Office, during most of which they were joined by representatives of the Benelux countries.[1] All three countries fielded strong teams including Douglas, Clay and Murphy for the USA; Strang (who

---

[1] FRUS 1948 (2) pp. 70–145.

acted as chairman of the conference), Robertson, Hall-Patch and Kirkpatrick for the UK; Massigli, Couve de Murville, Hervé Alphand and Koenig for France. Bevin was not present himself but took a close interest in the discussions and saw Strang or one of the other British representatives every day and often Douglas as well.

After the first round of talks, Bevin reported to the Cabinet that more progress had been made than he expected, narrowing the differences on international control of the Ruhr when the occupation came to an end, and the participation of the Bi-zone and the French zone of Germany in the European Recovery Programme.[1] But when the conference recessed they were still a long way from actual agreement on the political and economic organization of Western Germany and the fusion of the French zone with the other two.

On the last day of the meetings (6 March) Douglas, speaking unofficially, told Massigli and Strang that the US Government was willing to try and find a formula to provide for consultation between France, the UK and the USA in the event of a threat of aggression by Germany or a default on her part in regard to disarmament and demilitarization. This would take the form proposed under the original Byrnes' treaty and the Benelux countries would be welcome to participate. Douglas went on to say that the Americans were also considering setting up a military security board on a tripartite basis for the period of occupation, adding that in his view it would be a long time before American forces were withdrawn from Germany—not until the threat from the east had disappeared. Speaking equally unofficially, Massigli and Strang thought that if these ideas could be put into effect, they would do a lot to clear the way forward.[2]

Everyone taking part in the second set of negotiations, aimed at setting up a "continuing organization" for European economic co-operation, was acutely aware that a parallel debate in America on the role the United States should play in promoting European recovery had still not come to a conclusion. The debate cut across both parties, with Wallace in the Democratic Party and the isolationists in the Republican attacking the Marshall Plan for very different reasons. With 1948 an election year and the Republicans hopeful of winning, their willingness to go on treating foreign policy and the huge expenditures under the Economic Co-operation Bill on a bi-partisan basis was crucial to any hope of getting it through Congress. An extraordinary array of talent from both parties was mobilized in support of the Bill, including the US Ambassador in London, Lew Douglas, who acted as liaison between the State Department and Capitol Hill. The key figure was Senator Vandenberg, the Republican chairman of the Senate's Foreign Affairs Committee. His criticisms of the Bill and proposals for amending it were accepted, more or less without argument, by the Administration. In return, his conduct of the hearings by the

---

[1] CM 20 (48) 8 March. Bevin's report "Talks on Germany" was circulated as CP (48) 78, 7 March 1948.
[2] FRUS 1948 (2) pp. 138–9.

Senate Foreign Affairs Committee (which reported unanimously in favour of the Bill on 17 February after hearing more than 90 witnesses and receiving scores of written submissions); the powerful speech with which he introduced the Bill on the floor of the Senate on 1 March and his success in retaining the confidence of the Republican Party and the business community, were invaluable in securing the Bill's passage by conclusive majorities in both Houses in time for the President to sign it on 3 April.

Bevin wanted to recall the European Conference on Economic Co-operation in order to leave no doubt that the Europeans were pressing ahead with the programme of self help required by the Marshall Plan. But his suggestion alarmed the State Department which was anxious that nothing said in Europe should prejudice the chances of Congress passing the ECA Bill.[1] This had to be the overriding consideration, and it was not until 15 March—by which time the Americans were sure enough of the Bill getting through—that the recalled Conference met in Paris.

A lot more work in preparation for the meeting had been done by an interdepartmental committee (known as the London Committee) under the chairmanship of R. W. B. Clarke of the Treasury, and Bevin and Cripps, now in firm partnership, presented the London Committee's report, together with their own comments to the Cabinet on 8 March.[2] They regarded it as an open question whether, even with Marshall aid, Western Europe could recover to anything approaching the pre-war standard of living. It would certainly not unless the European nations made combined efforts of their own to match American aid. Commonwealth and Empire did not provide sufficient resources for the UK to contract out. The British had no option but to link themselves more closely with Europe, and the two ministers spelled out what this would mean.

"We are anxious that our colleagues should realise that the decision to involve ourselves in an economic organisation with other Western European countries and to play a leading role within it is a step of far-reaching consequences."

The process would be gradual but, once begun, difficult to reverse.

"Economically we shall have to make our plans in association with others. We shall not always be able to do as we would wish in our own interest. We shall be bound to take account of the collective interest. . . . Changes of a radical nature in our industrial and

---

[1] FRUS 1948 (3) pp. 352–66.
[2] A memorandum signed by Bevin and Cripps, CP (48) 75, was circulated to the Cabinet on 6 March with the London Committee's report attached. The Cabinet discussion took place on 8 March. CM 20 (48). An earlier paper by Bevin, "Machinery for Furthering the Project for a Western Union" was circulated as CP (48) 57, 18 February and discussed by the Cabinet on 23 February. CM 16 (48). On this occasion Bevin made a good deal of extending any closer union with Europe to include social as well as economic and defence measures. He asked for and secured the appointment of an inter-departmental committee to consider the possibility of securing a uniform standard of social services in the countries participating in Western Union.

agricultural structure may become necessary to secure the economic independence of the Western European countries as a whole and to use our collective resources to the best advantage."

Nor could this process be limited to the economic sphere: closer economic links would mean closer political links.

"This carries other risks. We shall be associating ourselves with partners in Western Europe whose political condition is unstable and whose actions may be embarrassing to us."

Having given their warning Bevin and Cripps were nonetheless wholehearted in urging that Britain had to take the lead in restoring "vigour and faith" to the peoples of Europe. They added a couple of sentences which, to American irritation, both men were fully to justify in the next two years:

"We shall of course have it in our power to moderate the process and to steer it with this in mind. Our influence in the European Organisation will be very great and should be decisive on major issues."

The report of the London Committee made clear what this meant. The Continuing Organization should work by securing inter-governmental agreements on specific proposals—thereby excluding discussion of "the various countries' hobby horses" such as French proposals for customs unions, Belgian schemes for transferability etc. "It is very important that the effective control should be in the hands of the national delegations . . . to prevent the secretariat (or an 'independent' chairman) from taking action on its own. . . . There should be no question of instructions being given by the Organization to individual members."

It was on this basis, after a discussion in which the Cabinet minute exceptionally records "All ministers expressed their views", that Bevin was authorized "to give a strong lead" to the reassembled Conference and to explain his policy in advance to the Dominion Governments.

American hopes of the Conference which met in Paris under Bevin's chairmanship went far beyond the British approach. To the many Americans who saw the root cause of Europe's weakness in the failure to follow their example and establish a United States of Europe, the European Recovery Programme appeared to offer a unique opportunity to break with the past and establish a new pattern. In a message to Robert Murphy on 6 March, Marshall wrote:

"Purpose and scope of E.R.P. and C.E.E.C. are far beyond trade relations. Economic co-operation sought under E.R.P., and of which C.E.E.C. is a vehicle, has as ultimate objective closer integration of Western Europe."[1]

---

[1] FRUS 1948 (3) p. 389.

Congress, if not restrained by the Administration, would have wished to make an explicit commitment to "integration" a condition of Marshall aid. The State Department, however, although no less convinced of the validity of the argument, knew that (as Marshall went on to say): "Full co-operation of the British is necessary if larger objectives are to be achieved." For this reason they believed it important to persuade rather than browbeat or impose conditions on the UK. They argued strongly for giving the Continuing Organization the independent authority which the British were determined to deny it. If this were not done, the Americans feared that

"The whole programme may degenerate into a series of bilateral deals between the U.S. and the individual countries and lip-service be paid to true economic co-operation by continuous discussions of customs unions and the like."[1]

They suspected the British of refusing to merge their identity into a European union, as the Americans understood the word, and of trying to retain their wartime "special relationship" with the USA.

"The special wartime position for Britain now", Lovett, the Under-Secretary of State declared, "would be inconsistent with concept of Western European integration and other objectives of E.R.P."[2]

Once Bevin had opened the Conference, a working party, co-chaired by Britain and France, took over the business of framing a constitution and deciding on the powers of the future OEEC. The British defended their position vigorously. Apart from objections in principle they argued on practical-grounds that more could be accomplished, even in such matters as statistics, by national representatives pooling information in sub-committees than by an international secretariat. They would have nothing to do with American ideas (indirectly but nonetheless forcefully conveyed) of building up the Organization through its Secretariat and giving it the power to review and criticize each participating country's economic programme, including production and investment. The reports from the Paris embassy made clear how disappointed the American team were with the British attitude.[3] What galled them was their recognition that, as Caffrey cabled on the 28th: "In the absence of British participation and leadership, it is unlikely that enough European countries can be brought together to create a unit of efficient economic dimensions."[4]

Bevin did not stay more than a couple of days in Paris after opening the Conference on European Economic Co-operation. But before moving on to

---

[1] Quoted from a State Department memorandum, 4 March 1948, *ibid.*, p. 387

[2] Lovett to US Embassies in London and Paris, 8 April 1948, *ibid.*, p. 417.

[3] See the dispatches from Caffery, US Ambassador to Paris, to Secretary of State, 20 March. FRUS 1948 (3) pp. 398–400 & 402. Marshall, while agreeing in general with Caffery's objectives (22 March pp. 400–401), remarked that they "seem a very large mouthful to bite off at once".

[4] *Ibid.*, p. 407.

Brussels to sign the Treaty which set up a Western European Union, he took advantage of meeting the other European leaders who had come to Paris to sound out their views, prepare them for the next stage in the consolidation of the West and infuse the faint-hearted among them with some of his own confidence that this was not only practicable but the best way both to limit further Soviet expansion and to avoid war.

The reaction of the three Scandinavian foreign ministers, when Bevin tried out his idea of an Atlantic security system, brought out their anxiety to avoid a choice between joining either an Eastern or a Western bloc. Tsaldaris came to plead for the inclusion of Greece in the Brussels Pact and more help against the guerillas, the Portuguese for the inclusion of Spain in OEEC and the European Recovery Programme. Neither got any encouragement. More interesting was Bevin's talk with the Italian Foreign Minister, Count Sforza. Bevin greeted him by holding out the hope of associating Italy with his plans for a 20-year development of Africa, but was evasive about returning any of her former colonies. Trieste was a different matter: Bevin told Sforza that he would be happy to return not just part but the whole territory to Italy tomorrow. Like everyone else he wanted to know what would happen in the Italian elections and explained to Sforza that he had sent Morgan Phillips and Denis Healey from Labour Party headquarters to press the Italian socialists to break with the Communists. Sforza was optimistic about winning the elections and even about dealing with a Communist attempt at a *coup*. Bevin urged that if there were an attempt, they must stand fast, until Britain and the USA could come to their aid. Sforza assured him that he, de Gasperi and Scelba (the Minister of the Interior) were resolute, believed the Carabinieri and the police were reliable and had created a stronghold in Rome in which they could hold out if the Communists tried a rising.

The most important talks were with the French. At an evening reception, Bevin informed Schuman (now Prime Minister) and Moch of the talks the British were to have with the Americans about an Atlantic security system and also about the security measures Attlee had announced in the House on the 15th against Communist or Fascist infiltration of the civil service. Both moves were well received by the Frenchmen.[1] Frank Roberts, however, reported that Bidault and Couve de Murville were both gloomy about the future and felt that Europe was nearer to war than ever. Bidault was sure that the Russians must see the West was preparing to organize itself but had not yet achieved anything and that this was the moment for them to strike.[2]

Ivone Kirkpatrick, the Foreign Office official who accompanied him to Brussels, wrote that Bevin was

---

[1] 16 March at the British Embassy in Paris. Records of this and of Bevin's talks in Paris referred to in the text are to be found in FO 800/460/EUR/48/16. See also FO 371/73089.

[2] Roberts' report of his own talk with Bidault and Couve de Murville on 16 March. FO 800/447/CONF/48/1.

"Painfully impressed by the low state of morale in the Allied camp. Our new Allies were all more or less borne down by the weight of Russian pressure. One of the Ministers said that the Russians would be in Paris by August, an opinion in which the French Chief of Staff concurred."[1]

The Treaty of Brussels, setting up Western European Union, was to last for fifty years and bound its five signatories to come to the aid of anyone of their number who was attacked. A permanent organization was established in London and provision was made for inviting other powers to join.[2]

After the treaty was signed, Bevin did his best to put some resolution into his partners. "He insisted", the US Ambassador in Brussels reported, "that Russia needs plain speaking and said his advices were to the effect she was not ready or willing to launch a war. He thought Stalin was a strong stabilizing influence against war."[3] While he regarded the WEU they had created as the first step towards a much bigger grouping, he also—unlike Bidault, who spoke only of immediate defence measures—pressed for it to develop other functions. He proposed regular meetings of the Consultative Council each month; closer economic and financial co-operation including clearing arrangements, so avoiding dollar and gold payments; the harmonization of social services, bringing in unions and employers as well as governments; and co-operation in security measures against Communist infiltration.

The meeting adjourned to hear Truman's address to Congress in which the President asked both Houses to agree to immediate legislation for selective service to keep the US Armed Forces up to strength. In a reference to the Brussels Treaty which had been signed the same day he declared it to be an act whose "significance goes far beyond the actual terms of the agreement itself" and one which "deserves our full support. . . . I am sure that the determination of the free countries of Europe to protect themselves will be matched by an equal determination on our part to help them do so."[4]

After they had heard Truman speak, the foreign ministers agreed on the approach now to be made to the USA—the real objective in Bevin's mind to which the Brussels Treaty was the necessary preliminary. Part of Bidault's bad mood was evidently due to pique that Bevin was taking the lead in dealing with the Americans. He was also very put out by Bevin's news that the US Government had prepared a draft declaration on Trieste and shown it to de Gasperi. This would spoil a similar declaration which he was preparing to make at Turin on the 19th and he insisted that nothing should be said by the Americans or the British until the 21st. In order to appease Bidault's wounded vanity, Bevin allowed him to inform the others about the contacts with Washington and to claim the credit for Marshall's reply that, once the Brussels

[1] Ivone Kirkpatrick, *The Inner Circle*, p. 205.
[2] The British records of the negotiations leading up to the signature of the Brussels Treaty are in FO 371/73045–66.
[3] FRUS 1948 (3) p. 57.
[4] Congressional Record, 17 March 1948, pp. 2996–8.

Treaty was signed, the USA would be ready to start talks. The Dutch and Belgians were sceptical whether an American President could be expected to make any commitment in an election year, but Bevin and Bidault insisted that they must put the question and a joint note was drafted to this effect.[1] Some of the other undercurrents of rivalry between the new allies came out when the Dutch Foreign Minister told Bevin privately that the French were jealous of the other powers and trying to keep control of European economic co-operation entirely in their hands. He asserted that the Benelux countries would never accept French leadership, considering themselves to be much more reliable than the French.[2]

Bevin had the imagination to see that underlying many of the difficulties with the French was the injured pride of an historic nation humiliated by its loss of power. He told the Norwegian Foreign Minister that he had agreed with Bidault to put the headquarters of the OEEC in Paris because "I wanted to give back to France her feeling of national confidence and self-respect".[3] For the same reason he took care to make the formal approach to Marshall jointly with the French, and when the talks between the USA, Britain and Canada on a defence pact opened in great secrecy at the Pentagon on 22 March, he instructed Gladwyn Jebb to raise immediately the question of inviting early French participation. The Americans, however, thought that the security risk of bringing in the French was too great and preferred to limit the exploration of possibilities to the British and Canadians. Although Jebb raised the matter again at the end of the first meeting, the American view was accepted, and the French were not invited.[4]

5

April 1948 saw the complex pattern of negotiations in which Bevin was involved move a stage nearer to definition. On the 3rd President Truman signed the Economic Co-operation Act giving legislative force to the Marshall Plan. Vandenberg laid particular stress on not leaving the execution of the Act's programme of expenditure in the hands of the State Department but securing an independent administrator with business experience. He found the man he wanted in Paul Hoffmann, President of the Studebaker Corporation and a member of the Republican Party. The day after he signed the Act, Truman appointed Hoffmann as Economic Co-operation Administrator. He was given Averell Harriman, Secretary of Commerce in the Democratic Administration, to assist him as a roving Ambassador in Europe.

[1] 17 March. Records of Bevin's talks in Brussels are in FO 800/460/EUR/48/17.
[2] Bevin and Baron van Botzelaer, 17 March, *ibid.*, and FO 800/447/CONF/48/1.
[3] Bevin and Lange in Paris, 15 March. FO 800/460/EUR/48/16.
[4] Record of the First Meeting, 22 March. FRUS 1948 (3) pp. 59–61. The complete US record of the meetings is in the same volume, pp. 58–75; Bevin's report to Attlee on the talks, 6 April, enclosing a report by Jebb dated 5 April, is in FO 800/452/DEF/48/17.

The passage of the ECA Bill into law did not finally settle the issue. In June the House of Representatives, on the motion of an economy-minded group of Republicans, ordered a cut of more than a quarter (over $2,000 M.) in the first year's appropriation and was only prevented from crippling the ECA programme by another powerful intervention from Vandenberg in the Senate. Even so it was not until the beginning of July 1948, more than a year after Marshall's Harvard speech of June 1947, that the ECA began to work and Western Europe began to feel the practical benefits of American support.

April also saw the establishment of the ECA's European counterpart in the OEEC. When the plenary body met under Bevin's chairmanship to approve the agreed draft it was clear that the British had won their month-long fight. The Organization was to be based in Paris; Spaak, the Belgian Prime Minister and the American choice for the office, was to be the chairman of its Council and the Secretary General was to be a Frenchman, Robert Marjolin. The Americans, however, would much have preferred Jean Monnet and they were disappointed with the powers assigned to the office which restricted the Secretary to carrying out the decisions of the Council and the Executive Committee. Spaak, an enthusiast for "integration", might be chairman of the Council, but the effective body was the seven-strong Executive Committee and the first chairman of this was to be British. The Americans would have liked the Executive to consist of the principal economic ministers of the countries involved, Cripps for instance in the case of the UK. The British representative, however, was not a minister, but a Treasury official seconded to the Foreign Office, Sir Edmund Hall-Patch, and directly responsible to Bevin. Nobody doubted his ability but nobody also failed to notice that Oliver Franks, widely regarded as the ablest man at Bevin's disposal, had been moved from Paris to become British Ambassador in Washington.

The American case was weakened by the fact that, under their own Economic Co-operation Act, separate bilateral agreements had to be signed with each of the participating countries and it was unavoidable that the negotiations should take place in Washington with the representatives of the national governments, not with the OEEC in Paris. They did not, however, accept their defeat over the OEEC constitution as final and the pressure which Hoffmann and Harriman exercised to try and push the UK in the direction of greater economic integration was to lead to constant friction between them and the British.

This disagreement should not be allowed to obscure what had been achieved in bringing the American Congress to turn the Marshall Plan into the Economic Co-operation Act and sixteen European nations to set up the OEEC, in face of every sort of doubt in the Western world and every device of opposition on the part of the Soviet bloc. The indispensable condition had been, as Marshall constantly insisted, a European initiative and this Bevin had done more than any other man to organize. It might not be in the form or with the commitment to federation which the Americans would have liked to see, but it was at least arguable that Bevin was a better judge than his critics of what was needed and what was practicable in the Europe of 1948 and certain that there was no one except the British capable of organizing a European response at all.

Bevin's second visit to Paris, however, promised little occasion for self-congratulation. It still remained to be seen how far in practice the combination of the ECA and the OEEC would bring about the recovery of Europe. The decisive confrontation which he believed necessary to convince the Russians that the West would not give way had yet to take place, whether in Italy, Berlin or somewhere else; and his conversations with the other European ministers in Paris showed how shaky was their resolution in face of fears of what might flow from standing up to the Russians.

Bevin had come to Paris with a double purpose: to inaugurate OEEC and to take the Brussels Pact a stage further. Aware of Benelux resentment against the French, he hoped that he would make progress in the WEU easier by stepping down from the chairmanship of the OEEC Council in favour of the Belgian Prime Minister, Spaak. Bevin had no wish to give WEU anything like a federal character, but he had a more positive view of its functions than the French. He proposed that the Brussels Powers' Chiefs of Staff should begin work at once on the contribution each country could make to the common defence and that the defence ministers should take part in the work of the military committee, not leaving it to the military experts. In addition, he proposed that the five Brussels powers should try to harmonize their economic and financial relations, mentioning a clearing system, eventually a Western Union Bank, and a free trade area, which he thought might provide a better framework than a customs union. He was no less eager to harmonize their social services and harness the trade unions. "The working men," he told Bidault, "must be given the impression that they had a share in Western Union and that their conditions of living would be improved as a result of it." Bidault was not impressed. Either, he said, these were steps towards confederation, which he opposed, or the creation of institutions was superfluous.[1]

An interview with President Vincent Auriol impressed on Bevin how much French opinion was dominated by the immediate fear of war. Auriol told Bevin that war with Russia would mean civil war as well in France and could easily lead to the destruction of the whole élite of the nation. The President insisted that the Western Powers were too weak to run risks and must not provoke the USSR or give them an excuse for precipitate action. Did Bevin not think that Clay's proposal for a provisional German Government might prove to be provocative? Could they not make a declaration in Moscow offering a basis for peace and co-operation?

Bevin was convinced that the real answer to French fears was not appeasement but firmness, particularly in Berlin, reports from which, as Bidault

[1] Bevin's talks in Paris, 16–17 April 1948. FO 800/460/EUR/48/20.

admitted, were making the French nervous. Bevin emphasized the misfortune it would be if the Western Powers were to leave Berlin under pressure, but it was clear that the one thing which would stiffen French resolution was to know what the US would do "if things went wrong". As Bevin had always believed, for all the talk of Europe as a Third Force and a United States of Europe, in practice the French were as eager as anyone—far more eager than he was himself—to look to the USA to save them. With Bevin it was the other way round. Sceptical of "integrationist" and Third Force rhetoric, in practice he attached more importance than Bidault or any other European leader to the European nations acting together to help themselves, but never believed that Western Europe was strong enough to provide for its own security or recovery without American help. He was as eager, therefore, as Bidault to get the Americans to commit themselves, and with the ECA passed by Congress and a European initiative given tangible form in OEEC and WEU he felt they were now in a position to press more strongly. Before leaving for London he sat down with Bidault and drafted a message to Marshall, reminding him that they had heard no more since Marshall had suggested joint defence talks on 25 March. The Brussels Powers, they reported, were going ahead with their own military talks, but they felt that an American initiative was now necessary if the impetus was not to be lost.[1]

As Bevin knew, but Bidault did not, the first part of their message was less than the truth. The Anglo–American talks from which the French had been excluded, had not produced a firm commitment on the part of the USA—that was impossible without the support of Congress—but they had been able to clear the ground on the assumption that US support would be forthcoming.

Six meetings in all were held between 22 March and 1 April under the chairmanship of the Ambassador in London, Lew Douglas, with Lester Pearson representing Canada, Oliver Franks, the British Ambassador, and Gladwyn Jebb the UK. General Gruenther and General Hollis (Chief Staff Officer to the British Minister of Defence) were amongst the military advisers present. The various alternatives for a defence pact suggested by Bevin —European, Atlantic, world-wide—were debated, with the Americans pointing to Italy, more even than Norway, as the country most directly threatened. A number of drafts were produced and discarded before the final version. Bevin was consulted by the British representatives, but Hickerson was at pains to impress on Gladwyn Jebb that all they had was a purely American position paper which "represents only a concept of what is desired at working level, and that British expectations should be based on nothing more than this."[2]

Nonetheless the recommendations of a document which, after a further year's discussions, was to become the North Atlantic Treaty, are worth looking at. There were five principal proposals.

[1] Bevin and Bidault to Marshall, 17 April. FRUS 1948 (3) p. 91.
[2] *Ibid.*, p. 72. Jebb's report to Bevin on the talks on 5 April 1948 is in FO 800/452/DEF/48/17. Bevin enclosed it with a memorandum which he sent to Attlee, 6 April, *ibid.*

The first was for the President to invite thirteen other countries to join the USA in a collective defence agreement for the North Atlantic, covering the continental territory in Europe or North America of any party to the Treaty and the islands in the North Atlantic as well. (Alaska, rather eccentrically, was included as one of these.) The thirteen countries were the five who had signed the Brussels Treaty, Canada, the three Scandinavian countries (not Finland), Iceland, Eire, Portugal and Italy.

Pending conclusion of this agreement, the President should issue a declaration that the USA would consider an armed attack against a signatory of the Brussels Treaty as an armed attack against herself and act accordingly.

The USA should be ready to extend similar support to any other European democracy which joined the Brussels Treaty. In the event that the Scandinavian states, Iceland and Italy did not wish to take such a step, the USA should consider the extension to them of some other assurance of immediate support in the event of an attack on them.

The fourth proposal was that, at the same time, the USA and the UK should announce that they were not prepared to countenance any attack on the political independence or territorial integrity of Greece, Turkey or Iran and would give full support to them in such an event.

Finally, when circumstances permitted, Germany (or the three Western zones) and Spain should be invited to adhere both to the Brussels five-power treaty and to the North Atlantic Defence Agreement. This objective, however, should not be publicly disclosed.[1]

The model, suitably adapted, was to be the Rio Treaty. Each party was to regard an armed attack on any other party to the treaty as an attack on itself, and the pact was to last for ten years with automatic renewal for further periods of five years unless denounced.

Bevin's reaction was wholehearted. After consulting Attlee and a few other colleagues, he cabled that they agreed the right course was for the USA to summon a conference to discuss the defence of the North Atlantic area and that this "would be the best guarantee of peace that could be imagined at the present time". They regarded the risk of provoking war as "very small" and argued that to proceed only with half measures which were purely economic and financial and not carry them to their logical conclusion, would lead the Soviet Government to the conclusion that this was all they were likely to do and could precipitate rather than avoid conflict.

The essential thing, Bevin reiterated, was to restore confidence; if that could be done, it would make the economic measures taken more effective and encourage resistance to infiltration. Solid backing for the Brussels Treaty, particularly if it referred to *any* aggressor, would give the French security in relation to Germany as well as Russia and might help to overcome the

---

[1] Final draft, undated. FRUS 1948 (3) pp. 72–5. It was presented to the final meeting on 1 April 1948. The NATO Treaty was signed in Washington on 4 April one year later.

long-standing trouble between France and Germany. A presidential declaration, Bevin added, without the backing of the Senate, would be inadequate and would leave people in doubt whether there was a real commitment. There was no substitute for a treaty, but if a North Atlantic defence system could be organized, it would be the first great step towards a world system of collective security.[1] There he had to leave the matter while the State Department began the delicate task of securing sufficient support in a Republican-dominated Congress to turn the paper scheme into a reality.[2]

6

The first thing Bevin did on his return from Paris was to ask for the news from Italy. The first general election since the 1946 vote for the Constituent Assembly took place on 18 April and was universally regarded as a political trial of strength between the American and the Soviet connections.

The earlier anxiety of the autumn of 1947 that the Italian Communists might attempt a *coup d'état* had given way to the fear that in an electoral alliance with the Italian Socialists (PSI) they might win sufficient votes to force their way back into the Government and eventually control it. Claiming to be the defenders of Italy's independence, the Communists attacked the Marshall Plan and the de Gasperi Government's support of it as intended to turn Italy and the rest of Europe into colonial dependencies of American imperialism and capitalism. Together, the Communists and Socialists had won just short of 40% of the popular vote in 1946 and beaten the Christian Democrats into second place. In 1947 the Italian Socialist Party had split on the issue of a common front with the Communists and a group led by Giuseppe Saragat, had seceded; but the majority of the PSI, led by Pietro Nenni, continued to support the alliance both in elections (in which they presented a common list) and in the trade union federation (LGIL) which was under Communist control. Many observers pointed to a possible parallel with Czechoslovakia where the Czech socialists had let themselves be persuaded to join a Communist-dominated Government. To Bevin's anger 37 Labour MPs signed a telegram of support to Nenni wishing him success (17 April).

The Left could win a substantial vote by hammering on economic grievances and social injustice which remained as great as ever in post-war Italy. They could also appeal to Italians' dislike of being forced to take sides in a divided Europe and their fear of war, appealing to the anti-clerical vote against the Church's intervention in politics, always on the conservative side. The Russians played a strong card by coming out (17 February) in favour of the

---

[1] Paraphrase of a telegram from Bevin delivered by Inverchapel, undated (around 6 April). FRUS 1948 (3) pp. 79–80.
[2] Cf., for example, Lovett's preliminary talk with Senator Vandenberg on 11 April, *ibid.*, pp. 82–4.

return of the former Italian colonies to Italy and although public opinion was shocked by the Prague coup, the Communists' boldness in seizing power, and the West's inability to prevent it, impressed many Italians with the fear that the Communist advance in Europe could not be stopped and that those who opposed it would be marked down for vengeance, as had happened in Czechoslovakia and the other East European states.

The Communists' weakest point was Italy's dependence on American aid and the Marshall Plan. To leave no doubt, the American State Department announced (15 March) that all economic aid would stop if the Communist–Socialist alliance won the elections, and Americans of Italian origin were urged to write to their relatives in Italy and drive home the point. In the middle of a campaign denouncing such aid the Communists were hardly in a position to protest, but at once did so. Marshall had already sent a message to Bevin at the beginning of March[1] urging him to join with the USA and France in demonstrating that the Italians were welcome as equal members of the Western group of nations. Bevin saw that a gesture over the ex-Italian colonies would help, and while unwilling to compromise British claims in Libya, was prepared to support an Italian trusteeship for Somalia and part of Eritrea.[2] Once the election was over he rapidly repented ("I have a little departed from a Policy to meet an election position", he minuted in April) and was anxious to get back "on the rails".[3] But Trieste was a different matter. He had already made his mind up that the scheme for a Free Territory in Trieste was unworkable and readily agreed to a joint announcement before the elections that the three Western Powers favoured its return to Italy. As the former Allies were quite unable to agree on a government; as the Yugoslavs had already in practice annexed the part of the Free Territory which they occupied; and as the majority in the Anglo–American zone preferred becoming part of Italy again to a precarious independence, the proposal was defensible on its merits. But its timing, in the middle of the election campaign, led to another storm of protest and it was turned down by the Russians, leaving the Anglo–American forces to continue their occupation, nominally on behalf of the UN.

In talking to Douglas Bevin spoke against wild talk of more forcible intervention in Italy. If there were an attempt at a *coup d'état*, de Gasperi should be told not to resign but to insist on remaining as the legitimate government, and then the question of military support could be considered. But he was receptive to the idea that the British Labour Party should do anything it could to strengthen the position of the Saragat group which had broken with Nenni.

The idea came from two different directions. Nye Bevan, worried about the

---

[1] 2 March, Marshall to London Embassy. FRUS 1948 (3) pp. 837–9.
[2] Minute by Bevin, 28 January 1948, FO 371/69328 and his paper for the Cabinet, CP (48) 43, 4 February.
[3] Minute by Bevin, 7 April 1948. FO 371/69331. See also Douglas's report of his talk with Bevin, 6 March 1948. FRUS (3) pp. 843–5.

Communists securing control of Italy, got Morgan Phillips, the secretary of the Labour Party, to ask Bevin what they were going to do about it. "I've just been lunching with Douglas" was Bevin's reply, "and he asked the same question. I told him 'Leave that to us.' Morgan, you're going to Italy tonight." Despite Phillips' protests, Bevin had him and Denis Healey on a plane by 6 p.m., finding an opportunity to intervene in a conference of Western socialist partners which the Labour Party had called in London to rally support for the European Recovery Programme. Morgan Phillips was to fly to Paris and clear his lines with the French Socialists, then go on to Rome to discuss who was going to London to represent Italy.[1]

Their first day in Rome was spent in persuading the different groups who had broken with the official Socialist Party (in particular Saragat's and Lombardo's) to sink their differences and create an executive committee of socialist unity which could be invited to the London meetings. On the second they met representatives of the PSI (without Nenni) and made a head-on attack on their "illusions" in continuing to co-operate with the Communists, scoffing at the idea that they could retain their independence as a party or maintain a position of neutrality between East and West. In particular they insisted that the PSI's tactics were isolating it from the rest of the West European socialist parties and that they could no longer count on the fraternal support of the British and French parties if they persisted in them, a point which went home with party workers in the North Italian industrial towns. In the end the PSI accepted an invitation to attend the London meetings, but took care not to send any of their leading figures.

It is impossible, of course, to say how much was due to this intervention, but it removed any doubt created by the Nenni telegram of where the Labour Party stood and may have helped to reduce the combined PCI/PSI vote from 39.7% of the 1946 poll to 31% in 1948. De Gasperi's Christian Democrats secured 48.5% of the popular vote and won an absolute majority of seats in the Chamber (305 out of 574).

The result was as great a fillip for confidence in the West as Prague had been a shock. Wisely, de Gasperi resisted pressure from the Vatican to form a one-party Catholic government and created a centre coalition, including representatives of what became a Social Democratic Party; this provided the basis of Italian governments for the next seven years.

Italy had been represented throughout the discussions leading up to the establishment of OEEC and Sforza had signed the treaty the day before the Italian election was held. The result of the election, therefore, was to confirm a policy of alignment with the West to which de Gasperi's government had already committed the country, rather than to re-align it, and since the PCI/PSI alliance fell far short of winning the election and the Communists made no attempt to seize power by extra-legal means, it can be argued that the

[1] This account was given to the author by Morgan Phillips.

fears expressed in the previous six months were greatly exaggerated.

This may be so: without access to Communist and Soviet records which may never become available, it is impossible to say what expectations or plans they entertained. But in the heavily-charged atmosphere following the Prague coup, it was impossible for men like Bevin, carrying the responsibility for acting in time—almost invariably on incomplete information—to dismiss the possibility that something similar might be attempted in the very different circumstances of Italy. In Czechoslovakia the Communist coup had been followed by every sort of assurance that it would make no difference to Czech relations with the West and that the Czech experience of Communism would be very different from what it had been in a backward country like Russia. No doubt the same things would have been said and even believed if Italy too had come under Communist rule; but no more than in the Czech case would they have proved to be true and the consequences in the Italian case would have extended throughout the Mediterranean. To state only the two obvious instances, the civil war in Greece might have had a different outcome, and the quarrel (still unrevealed in April 1948) between Tito and Stalin might have followed a very different course.

There was a widespread sense of relief felt not just by the politically involved but by the millions of ordinary unpolitical people throughout Western Europe, relief in particular at the blow which failure in Italy dealt to the most insidious of Communist arguments, that their advance was irresistible and the prudent had better come to terms with it. Bevin, who had never been as anxious about the result as the Americans, saw it as confirmation of his belief that, in anything like a free election, in any European country, the Communists would never win a majority, even in the favourable circumstances of an electoral pact with the Socialists, a powerful party machine and a well-organized campaign.

Bevin was no less pleased with the removal of another threat which, although much less widely known, had caused him great anxiety at the time. This was the Russians' demand that the Finns should send a delegation to Moscow to sign a pact of friendship and military alliance,[1] and reports that this might be followed by similar demands on Norway and Denmark. The Finns did not refuse outright: a delegation duly went to Moscow but did not give way in face of Molotov's demands and put up counter-proposals of its own. To the astonishment of the Western powers' representatives in Helsinki, the delegation returned after lengthy negotiations with a pact (signed on 6 April) which was more favourable than any obtained by Russia's Communist-controlled neighbours and which did not compromise Finnish independence. As in the case of Italy, it could be argued that the fears had been exaggerated, if not manufactured; and again, as in the case of Italy, it has to be said that no one knows for certain. To Bevin, however, the Finns' success provided

---

[1] Stalin's letter to President Paasikivi was delivered on 23 February 1948. RIIA *Documents 1947–48*, p. 315.

confirmation for another of his beliefs, not that the Russians' pressure had been exaggerated, but that the best way to deal with it was to stand up to them and refuse to be bluffed or frightened into capitulation.

Bevin, however, did not allow his relief over the news from Italy and Finland to persuade him that the danger was over. Finland, even Italy, were peripheral in importance by comparison with Germany. It was there that the real test had still to come and, if the Western powers failed to meet it, what they had achieved so far would be wiped out.

Working party discussions which had continued in Berlin while the London Conference on Germany was in recess had clarified the issues but not led to agreement between the Western Powers. The London Conference reconvened on 20 April with delegations from the three Benelux countries now taking part; but it was not until 1 June that they reached the point where they could draw up a communiqué setting out the results. By then the focus of interest had shifted to the Soviet blockade of Berlin.

The steps by which the blockade was imposed began in March 1948 and were not completed until August. This probably reflected similar hesitations on the Russian part to those on the Western side: how far they could increase pressure (or, in the Western case, resist it) without starting a war and what they could hope to gain by doing so. The occasion which the Russians chose for ending the meetings of the Four-Power Allied Control Council (20 March) was a protest against the action of the three Western powers in holding the London conference without Soviet representation. No doubt they hoped to re-impose on decisions about the future of Germany the veto which had led to the breakdown of discussions in the Council of Foreign Ministers. But there was also a chance, which Communist propaganda sought to exploit to the full, that the Western Powers would lose their nerve and pull out of Berlin, opening the way to something much bigger, the collapse of the Western position in Germany and ultimately—with an American withdrawal—in Western Europe as well.

From the end of March the Russians started to interfere on an ascending scale with the Western Allies' freedom of movement in and out of the city. General Clay was resolute: in a teletype conference with Washington on 10 April he told the American Chiefs of Staff:

"After Berlin will come Western Germany and our strength there relatively is no greater and our position no more tenable than Berlin. If we mean that we are to hold Europe against communism, we must not budge. . . ."[1]

But there were many, military as well as civilians (including the US Chiefs of Staff); Americans and Germans (including Berliners) as well as French and British, who doubted whether a western presence in an isolated Berlin could be

[1] Clay, *Papers*, vol. 2, p. 623.

sustained or defended against a Russian blockade and whether the Western Powers should run the risk of war to do so. As long as these divisions of opinion persisted—and they did so well into the summer—the Soviet leaders had every reason to tighten the blockade and see what increased pressure would produce.

CHAPTER 14

Berlin blockaded, Israel proclaimed

I

At the end of January 1948 the American Embassy in London sent back to Washington a full length review of the situation in Britain. Gallman, the Chargé d'Affaires, reported:

"Government has staged strong comeback since August/October when it appeared to be tottering and there was much public speculation Attlee would resign, government would not last more than a few months, there would be early general election or possibly a coalition government. This speculation has now completely died out."

Attlee had come through the crisis with enhanced reputation, and "virtually whole British Labour movement has, step by step, abandoned its sentimental attitude towards Soviet Union and ranged itself behind Bevin. . . .

"This remarkable change in its way almost as significant as the change in US from isolationism to internationalism."[1]

The change in Labour opinion was due not only to disillusionment with the Soviet Union, especially after Prague, but to a more positive view of the USA in the light of the Marshall Plan. The former spokesman of the *Keep Left* group, Dick Crossman, referring to the Marshall plan told the House of Commons in the January foreign policy debate:

"I will be frank. My own views about America have changed a great deal in the last six months. Many members have had a similar experience. I could not have believed six months ago that a plan of this sort would have been worked out in detail with as few political conditions."[2]

---

[1] FRUS 1948 (3) pp. 1069–77.
[2] HC, 23 January 1948.

A similar process of conversion can be traced in the two left-wing publications, *Tribune* and the *New Statesman*, and was carried further by Truman's victory in the 1948 elections and his Fair Deal programme, which led Jennie Lee, Nye Bevan's wife, to declare that the Americans "were catching up with our ideas of the welfare state."[1]

Bevin was as wary and scornful of the intellectual Left when it approved of his foreign policy as when it opposed him. He regarded it as one more proof of the instability of view which had been his chief objection to placing any reliance on them since the early 1930s,[2] and was only confirmed in this opinion when the high water-mark of left-wing approval of American foreign policy in 1950 was followed by as rapid a swing back to condemnation of the same Democratic Administration, well before the 1952 election. But, if Bevin was sceptical of the conversion of the Left, he was quick to take advantage of the greater freedom of action which it opened up to him.

The meeting of the socialist parties of all the countries participating in the ERP, called by the Labour Party, met at Selsdon Park on 21–22 March, and issued a strongly-worded declaration in support of the Marshall Plan.[3] Bevin was even keener to get the support of the international trade union than of the international socialist movement, but this took more doing. Communists and their allies were strongly entrenched in the World Federation of Trade Unions. Arthur Deakin had become President of the WFTU—against Bevin's advice —in September 1946 and had an American from the CIO as Vice-President, but the General Secretary, Louis Saillant, was a strong supporter of the Communist line, and the Executive Bureau, including the Russian Kuznetsov, was fairly evenly balanced between the two sides.

There was no doubt that the question of Marshall aid would split the Federation, but the way in which the split came about was important if trade union opinion was to be rallied to the Western side.

On Christmas Eve 1947 Bevin cabled to Franks (who had taken up his appointment as Ambassador in Washington) to explain the tactics on which he and the TUC had agreed. The TUC proposed to join with the American Congress of Industrial Organizations in calling for a meeting of the Executive Bureau in February 1948 at which the WFTU should decide its attitude to the Marshall Plan. If this proposal was turned down or blocked, there would probably, Bevin thought, be a break up, the blame for which would rest on the Communists, not on the TUC which would be seen to have tried to get an agreed declaration and which could then carry the British trade unions with it.[4] Events followed the pattern Bevin had forecast. Saillant met the TUC

[1] HC, 14 July 1949. See also her speech. HC. 27 January 1949.
[2] See Vol. I, index under Intellectuals and the Labour Movement.
[3] The memorandum and declaration are to be found in Appendix 1 of the LP Conference Report for 1948, pp. 222–32. It was to secure Italian participation in this conference that Morgan Phillips and Denis Healey visited Rome.
[4] Bevin to Franks, 24 December 1947. FO 800/493/PLT/47/45.

–CIO request with the reply that the earliest date on which the Executive Bureau could meet was 1 April. The TUC, determined to get a trade union expression of opinion before the Marshall plan legislation was passed into law by Congress, thereupon went ahead and called a conference of national trade union organizations to meet in London on 9–10 March. It was attended by 26 organizations from 14 countries and gave strong support to accepting the American offer of aid.

It was not, however, until January 1949 that the British and Americans withdrew from the WFTU and not before June 1949 that a preparatory conference was held in London to set up an alternative in the International Confederation of Free Trade Unions. There were good reasons for following a restrained approach with an eye to the situation not only in European countries like France and Italy where the Communists still dominated the trade union federations, but in Britain as well. Bevin and Deakin were well aware of the fact that, of the six major British unions, only two, the Miners and the General and Municipal Workers, could be counted on to support the General Council's line without a great deal of argument. Nine out of 48 of the T & GWU's Executive Committee between 1946 and 1948 were avowed Communists (and three of them members of the key Finance and General Purposes Committee) with a considerable body of support amongst the other members. Even the elections for the 1948–50 period still produced eight Communists out of 38 members of a reduced Executive. The National Union of Railwaymen hardly varied at all in its support of left-wing policies and it always required a hard fight to carry the engineers (AEU) and the shopworkers (USDAW) the other way. Outside the big six, there were several other left-wing unions, notably the Communist-controlled electricians (ETU). Martin Harrison's calculation is that, if the first ten years of the post-war period are looked at as a whole, the trade union block vote at Labour Part conferences was divided between 2.8m votes regularly cast in support of the National Executive, 1.8 m cast against and solidly left-wing, and 1 m which were unpredictable.[1]

These figures explain why, even in 1948, when the Communists and their remaining sympathizers in the trade union movement were very much on the defensive, the TUC leaders, with Bevin's agreement, never took their advantage to mean that they could give up campaigning and organizing in support of the Government's policies whether in foreign or economic affairs. In the Labour Party itself, however, in which membership was not open to Communists (despite great efforts to secure it after the War), it now became possible to take disciplinary measures against the handful of MPs who still actively opposed the Government's foreign policy. The numbers actually expelled were small—four in all before the 1950 election—but the fact that a party as tolerant of dissent as Labour could be brought to contemplate such a step showed how strongly the tide was now flowing against Bevin's critics.

---

[1] Martin Harrison, p. 214.

The change was precipitated by the Communist *coup* in Czechoslovakia. On 3 March the Labour Party's National Executive published a plain speaking statement which rubbed in the "warning" for democratic socialists:

"Communists cannot achieve their aims without support from a minority within the camp of democratic Socialism. As in Czechoslovakia so in Hungary, Rumania and Bulgaria, individual Socialists, by permitting or abetting Communist attacks on democracy, have connived at their own destruction.

"The issues before us no longer permit of any prevarication. Socialism is meaningless without democracy. . . . Any attempt to achieve Socialism by means which deny democracy and human rights, particularly by the operation of an all-powerful secret police, must lead inevitably to a dictatorship, indistinguishable in its impact on the common man from Fascism, as it existed in Italy and in Germany, as it still exists in Spain.

"Czechoslovakia is an acid test of sincerity. Those who seek to condone this crime show that they are false to the principles of Democratic Socialism for which the Labour Party stands."

Attlee announced in the House on 15 March that the Government had reached the conclusion that it was necessary "to ensure that no one, known to be a member of the Communist Party, was engaged on work the nature of which affected the security of the State". Forty-five Labour MPs signed a motion regretting Attlee's statement but only five voted against the Government in the division lobby, and the Party leaders, Attlee, Bevin and Morrison, were sure enough of their ground not to pull back. On the contrary they proceeded to apply the same principles to the Party itself. The occasion was the telegram which had been sent out by 37 Labour MPs wishing success to Pietro Nenni, the Italian Socialist leader who had followed precisely the course of entering into an electoral pact with the Communists which the NEC had denounced in the case of Czechoslovakia. Amongst the signatories were several who, two years before, had signed a telegram (also condemned by the NEC) to the Unity congress in Berlin called to register the fusion of the social democratic and communist parties of the Soviet zone in the Socialist Unity Party (SED).

The Nenni telegram was an open challenge to the Party leadership and was treated as such. The NEC sent a letter to each of the rebels, saying that it was "seriously disturbed by the activities over a long period of certain members which are considered to be subversive of Party policy" and warning them that unless assurances to desist from such conduct were received by 6 May, they would be expelled from the Party. All sent replies which, with one exception, the NEC felt able to accept. Some of them could hardly be called reassuring, but the only member whom the NEC at this time excluded from the Party was John Platts-Mills and this was expressly said to be in view of his "general political conduct", not just for signing the Nenni telegram.[1]

[1] Alfred Edwards, who had opposed the nationalization of steel, was expelled at the same time and on the same grounds of "his general political conduct".

At the Labour Party conference in May, Bevin had still to face a left-wing amendment in which Konni Zilliacus called on him "to close the long and uninterrupted chapter of failures" and face the fact that

"We must either co-operate with the working-class leadership of Europe, as it really exists in fact, or else be driven into the position of getting ready to fight the Socialist revolution in Europe."

But after Bevin had replied, the vote against Zilliacus's amendment and in favour of the Government's foreign policy was overwhelming: over four million to less than a quarter of a million.

The more commonly heard criticism in 1948 came not from the Left and those who blamed Bevin for the breach with the Soviet Union but from those who reproached the Labour Government for failing to take a more positive lead in uniting Europe outside the Soviet sphere. The movement in favour of some form of European unity—without any agreement on what form this was to take or how it was to be done—had gathered force in 1947–8 not only in Europe but also in the USA. In May an impressive Congress of Europe, representing all the unofficial bodies working for European unity (however divided in their views of it) was held at The Hague with more than twenty former Prime Ministers, including Churchill, and an even greater number of former Foreign Ministers amongst the gathering. Although nearly fifty Labour MPs accepted invitations, the Party's National Executive did everything it could to discourage them from going, issuing a statement which spoke in disparaging terms of European unity as "too important to be entrusted to exploitation by miscellaneous and unrepresentative interests", and succeeding in reducing the number who actually attended to twenty-six. The fact that Churchill was the commanding figure at the Congress undoubtedly coloured Labour views. It was not easy for Labour to accept Churchill's doubling of the role of world statesman and the wartime saviour of his country with that of the partisan leader of the Tory opposition denouncing the Government for sacrificing national interests to doctrinaire socialism. To the Left he was still the ogre of the Fulton speech, now summoning Europe to unite in an anti-Communist crusade led by the USA.

Bevin and Attlee did not share the general Labour antipathy to Churchill, and Bevin, as his letter to Morrison before his Western Union speech in January shows, had no intention of trying to compete with Churchill for the leadership of Europe—who could? But he and Attlee had good cause for feeling angered by the way in which Churchill, whom they rightly believed no more willing than they were to see Britain become part of a European federation, avoided awkward questions and rode off as a champion of Europe to universal applause.

Even if Churchill had not identified himself with the European Movement, however, the Labour Government would have had little sympathy with its activities. The last thing that could be said of Bevin with any truth was that he was not interested in or committed to Europe—more so than any other of Labour's leading ministers and indeed than many of his predecessors at the Foreign Office. But he was convinced that in the circumstances of the late 1940s neither European recovery nor European independence could be secured within a European, but only within an Atlantic framework, with the USA fully committed as a leading partner. This was combined with a pragmatic distrust for trying to draw up a constitution for a Europe whose future no one could yet foresee and with a determination which he shared with every other leading British politician not to compromise the British people's control over their own future.

If he had been free to speak out about his hopes for an Atlantic grouping of which Western Europe would form a part, this would have got rid of the damaging impression that he was simply opposed to, or at least lukewarm about, proposals for European unity without any proposal of his own to suggest. But he could not do this without seriously embarrassing the American administration in an election year when there was no certainty at all that Congress would ever accept the sort of regional security system Bevin had in mind. He was no more free to say, as he could have done with every justification, that talk of a united Europe was premature when it was American aid which alone gave any substance to hopes of securing either the recovery or the defence of Europe outside the Soviet sphere. This again would have been highly embarrassing to an American administration anxious to underplay the burdens it was assuming in Europe and to play up the ability of the Europeans to stand on their own feet. It would have been equally damaging to the fragile confidence of the Europeans in the face of Soviet pressure, and the last thing Bevin could afford to say if he wanted his plans for OEEC and the European Recovery Programme to succeed. All he could do was to stick to his formula of Western Union and refuse to let himself be drawn into saying what he meant by it, thereby laying himself open to criticism, still repeated, that he was either confused himself or deliberately confusing those who looked to Britain for a lead.

No one would have been able to see much of a coherent pattern in the dull and rambling speech he made in the House of Commons debate on foreign affairs on 4 May. While he was prepared to say flatly that he did not regard pooling sovereignty or creating a European federal state as a realistic way of establishing a Western Union, all he was able to point to as a starting point was the Treaty of Brussels and the OEEC. He made a vague reference to "wider conceptions" and a Canadian suggestion of regional defence arrangements, but no mention at all of the United States or an Atlantic Pact.

The one point which stands out clearly from the fog of words was the clear statement: "We are in Berlin as of right and it is our intention to stay there." He repeated this in a note to Attlee the following day. His advice was to avoid repeated public statements, to stay quiet and to take any chance of coming to terms with the Russians on disputed points.[1]

Behind the scenes he was active in securing the decision to fight a campaign in Western Europe, if necessary,[2] and on the same day pressed Lew Douglas strongly for an answer to the approach he and Bidault had made for joint talks with the Americans on defence. When Douglas said that there were difficulties about US support for the Brussels Treaty and doubts in the State Department, Bevin told him bluntly that it was no good blowing hot and cold; they must see the policy through.

When the time came to address the Labour Party Conference at Scarborough, he was still not free to speak with the urgency and directness he used in private. On this occasion, he began by quoting with approval a letter to *The Times* from one of his critics in which Seymour Cocks had said that "there could not be reconciliation between the Soviet theory of life and ours, and that therefore what we had to aim for was an attempt to live together, with both of us acknowledging that fact, and that is what I am trying to do." This was an early statement of the policy later to be known as co-existence. Bevin continued:

"We cannot change the communism of Russia, and I am not going to try. We cannot pursue, and we have no intention of pursuing, a policy in Eastern Europe of trying to change by force many of the things done in those states with which we do not agree. Those things will have to be worked out in the process of time. But equally we are not prepared to sit idly by and see a similar process of communization carried on over a weakened, distracted and disunited Europe."

To those who still had doubts about accepting Marshall aid, Bevin put the question, What would the Conference have had to say if the British Government had refused to go on when the Russians withdrew, and if the Executive had then come to ask for support for a policy of cutting rations and reducing the country's standard of living? The fact was that the UK could not see its way through its economic difficulties alone.

Characteristically, having carried the Conference so far with him, Bevin refused simply for the sake of unanimity to placate or ignore those who called for the withdrawal of British troops from Greece. Accepting that the Government side had done things in the civil war of which no one could approve and pledging himself to do all he could to stop the shooting of prisoners, he insisted that he could not ignore the fact that half-a-million people in Greece were homeless because of the "so-called rebellion" organized by the Communist Party, that children were being abducted and taken off to other countries and that Greece's neighbours were seeking to make another Czechoslovakia of her once Western support was withdrawn. In those circumstances he refused to be a party to deserting Greece.

[1] Bevin to Attlee, 5 May. FO 800/467/GER/48/17.
[2] See above, p. 524.

The size of the Conference vote in support of the Government's foreign policy was predictable. More striking was the fact that on the other major issue before the Conference, economic policy, a vote was not even called for. Although he took no part in the debate and was not even mentioned in the course of it, Bevin had played no less important a role behind the scenes than in foreign policy.

In the August debate of 1947 on the state of the nation, the Prime Minister had appealed to all workers not to press for increases in wages, and in the autumn, discussions took place between ministers and the General Council about the need to stabilize wages if inflation was to be kept under control. When the Government, however, published a White Paper on *Personal Incomes, Costs and Prices* on 4 February, the General Council complained that no proper consultation had taken place and that this made it difficult for those members who wished to co-operate with the Government to carry the unions with them. If the Government wanted the TUC's backing, this was not the way to go about getting it.

As usual, the General Council had recourse to Bevin and on 11 February a meeting was arranged at which he joined Attlee, Cripps, Morrison and Isaacs to talk over matters with the Economic Crisis Committee of the General Council led by Arthur Deakin. As a result the TUC for the first time accepted a policy of wage restraint which made heavy demands on the practices and traditions of the trade union movement. None the less, they got it endorsed at a special conference of Executive Committees in March by a majority of 5.4 million votes to 2 million and by the Labour Party Conference in May. In return the TUC asked for a number of assurances, including a capital levy and food subsidies, which Cripps embodied in his budget. This agreement with the trade unions lasted from the Spring of 1948 until the latter part of 1950 when the price increases due to the devaluation of September 1949 could no longer be contained. For the Government, even with Marshall aid, it was an indispensable part of any plan for mastering the country's economic difficulties.

Bevin secured agreement that regular quarterly meetings between ministers and the TUC should be resumed, and, assured of trade union support, Attlee raised the Economic Survey's target for production from 150 to 160% of the 1938 volume, a figure which was actually passed in 1949. For the unions it was a further step along the road of the social contract: the role of co-operation with Government in return for a voice in shaping policy to which Bevin and Citrine had worked to convert the trade union movement in the 1930s; which Bevin's entry into the wartime coalition had symbolized and which Bevin and Deakin now played a leading part in reviving. Although he made no claim to any credit, Bevin could, with justification, be considered as much the architect of the policy of a social contract between unions and government as of the Labour Government's foreign policy, both of which the 1948 Conference overwhelmingly endorsed.

2

On 17 April Lew Douglas wrote to Bob Lovett, the Acting Secretary of State in Washington about the latest of a series of talks he had had with Churchill. Douglas reported that the wartime leader was convinced that when the Russians developed an A-bomb, war was a certainty.

"He believes that now is the time, promptly, to tell the Soviet that if they do not retire from Berlin and abandon Eastern Germany, withdrawing to the Polish frontier, we will raze their cities. It is further his view that we cannot appease, conciliate or provoke the Soviets; that the only vocabulary they understand is the vocabulary of force; and that if, therefore, we took this position, they would yield."[1]

Bevin was frequently accused by the Left of following a Churchillian policy, but his advice in April 1948 was very different. In a message to Marshall, at the end of the month, he picked out two places where "we are face to face with Russian aggression and where we may expect them to be up to every devilment—Berlin and Vienna". There could be no question of letting themselves be forced out of either city but they would have to show a combination of firmness with "a determination not to be provoked into any ill-considered action which might result in an impossible position from which it would be difficult to retreat."

Bevin's information was that the Russians had ordered the Communists in France and Italy to drop direct action for fear of this involving them in war; the Bulgarian and Yugoslav governments were showing signs of hesitancy; "the Markos gang" was split and there were no signs of military preparations.

"All this goes to confirm Mr. Bevin's reading of present Russian policy, which is that they intend to do all they can to wreck E.R.P. and to cause us the greatest political embarrassment everywhere, but without pushing things to the extreme of war. The danger of course is that they may miscalculate and involve themselves in a situation from which they feel they cannot retreat. That is why Mr. Bevin thinks that H.M. Government and the U.S. Government are called upon to show particular prudence at the danger points."

If it was possible "to steer a safe course" for the next year or two, Bevin was hopeful that we "can if we so resolve call into being a sufficiently coherent and self-confident system in Western Europe to discourage the Russians from attempting adventures there. We may even see a change in Russian tactics." Success would depend on combining toughness and prudence in the meantime and in pushing ahead with the task they had set their hands to.

Bevin added that the most dangerous development would be if Russia suddenly became conciliatory, dividing the democracies and leading them "to

[1] Douglas to Lovett, 17 April. FRUS (3) pp. 90–91.

ease up on the creation of the solidarity" which was essential.[1] He can hardly have foreseen that the Americans themselves were about to offer the Russians the opportunity to do just this.

The original intention, deriving from a talk between Bob Lovett, the Acting Secretary of State, and President Truman, was to make clear privately to the Russians the USA's determination to insist on its rights in Berlin and resist "any further act of aggression" by the USSR against free states. At the same time the American Ambassador was to give assurances to the Russians that the USA had no expansionist plans, sought peace with the USSR and did not want war or disturbances which might lead to war.[2] However, in discussion between Washington and the Moscow Embassy the initial note of warning was changed to an insistence that the forthcoming elections would make no difference to American foreign policy. The state of American–Soviet relations was regretted, and the Russian Government assured that "as far as the U.S.A. is concerned, the door is always wide open for full discussion and the composing of our differences".

Bedell Smith, acting on Marshall's instructions, put these points in an "informal" talk with Molotov on 4 May.[3] Without asking the agreement of the US Government, however, the Russians published to the world an edited version of the Ambassador's statement together with Molotov's reply. This was hardly the way to open the door to diplomatic negotiations, but it represented a propaganda *coup* thanks to which as the US Chargé in Moscow ruefully reported to Washington the Russians were able to give the impression that the Americans had felt obliged to approach them with a proposal for talks in order to reduce the international tension and "to undercut US leadership of Western countries by sowing distrust among our friends not consulted in advance".[4]

There was no doubt about the latter point. Bevin sent at once for Lew Douglas and asked him what the hell was going on. Could he explain why, when their two countries were in close collaboration, the American Government had agreed to direct conversations with the Soviet Government without saying anything to the British in advance? Douglas could only reply that he was at a complete loss and knew nothing.[5] For 24 hours the American diplomatic service worked overtime to explain, from the full text of Smith's statement to Molotov, that no "proposal" of talks had been made and that the USA was not thinking of reversing its policy. Nothing could remove the impression, however, that, if nothing else, the Russians had got the better of

---

[1] *Aide mémoire* by Bevin, handed to the US Secretary of State on 30 April. FRUS 1948 (4) pp. 842–4.
[2] Footnote to Lovett's message to the Ambassador in Moscow, 24 April, *ibid.*, p. 834.
[3] The record of their transactions is in FRUS 1948 (4) pp. 834–57.
[4] Chargé in Moscow (Durbrow) to Washington, 11 May 1948, *ibid.*, pp. 858–9.
[5] Bevin–Douglas interview, 11 May 1948. FO 800/502/SU/48/21.

the Americans, and that the latter had let themselves be caught out talking to the Russians behind their allies' backs.

To add to the confusion, the Russian publication of Bedell Smith's statement was at once followed by the appearance in the *New York Times* (12 May) of an open letter to Stalin from Henry Wallace, who used the occasion to launch his campaign for the American Presidency. Brushing aside Marshall's denial, Wallace seized on "the exchange of notes" as "opening the door to negotiations" and called for an immediate meeting—"open and fully reported"—between representatives of the USA and the USSR. Wallace presented a six-point agenda for discussion and proceeded to give "my thoughts on the steps necessary to achieve the Century of Peace".

Stalin was happy to take advantage of the opportunity presented by Wallace with a reply (18 May) in which he described Wallace's letter as the most important amongst recent political documents, showing up the inadequacy of the Bedell Smith declaration of 4 May and even of the Soviet reply, by going beyond general declarations to a concrete programme for settling Soviet–American differences. Stalin went on to say that, while he did not know whether the US government approved of Wallace's programme, the Soviet Government certainly regarded it as opening the way to a peaceful settlement, which was "not only possible but absolutely necessary".[1] The State Department was now hopelessly on the defensive in face of a brilliantly executed propaganda offensive. The more it denied that Bedell Smith's statement had been a "proposal" and repudiated Wallace as representative of American opinion, the easier it was for the Russians to say that the American Government had first felt it necessary to try and get out of its present position by a unilateral offer of talks and now was rejecting a real chance to settle the differences between the two countries.

Whether the episode was taken to show the duplicity or the clumsiness of American diplomacy, it immediately revived European lack of confidence in American policy. This impression was more than confirmed by the erratic course of American policy over Palestine culminating in Truman's recognition of the state of Israel on 15 May.

In the winter of 1947–8 the Americans were confronted with the consequences of the policy of partition which they had taken the lead in getting the United Nations to adopt: either it would prove unworkable and would collapse in fighting between Jews and Arabs, or the United States would have to intervene to enforce it. The latter course was regarded by the President as well as by his critics as out of the question. While efforts continued to persuade the British to change their minds and accept a responsibility the Americans were unwilling to undertake themselves, a determined effort was made inside the Administration to reverse, modify or defer the policy to which the President had committed the USA. The fight was conducted by a combination not

---

[1] Wallace's letter and Stalin's reply in RIIA *Documents 1947–48*, pp. 160–64.

always agreed on its objectives. It included the State Department (Bob Lovett, Loy Henderson, and the Near Eastern Affairs office); the Defence Department (notably the Secretary for Defence, Jim Forrestal); the Policy Planning Staff of the National Security Council (under its Director, George Kennan) and the CIA. Their case was that the international interests of the USA in the Arab world were being sacrificed to Zionist pressures operating through domestic politics in an election year. Their opponents were the pro-Zionist lobby doing everything they could through their access to the White House to hold the President to his commitment to partition. The history, a classic of American political in-fighting, can be followed in the pages of the *Foreign Relations of the United States*, *The Forrestal Diaries* and from the published material drawn from the Truman and Clark Clifford papers.[1] The climax was a speech by Warren Austin, the US delegate to the UN Security Council on 19 March in which he declared that the American Government, in view of the deteriorating situation in Palestine, where there was daily news of clashes between Jews and Arabs, now believed that "a temporary trusteeship" should be established under the UN. This was taken by the Zionists and the rest of the world as an American abandonment of partition and a Jewish state in favour of a bi-national state, such as Bevin had proposed at the beginning of 1947.

Austin made his statement the day after Truman had yielded to his old friend Eddie Jacobson and seen Weizmann, reassuring the Jewish leader that there would be no change in American support for partition. The President's comment on the next day's proceedings in the Security Council was scribbled on his calendar:

"This morning I find that the State Dept. has reversed my Palestine policy. The first I know about it is what I see in the papers! Isn't that hell? I am now in the position of a liar and a double-crosser. I've never felt so in my life."[2]

The American change of policy faced Bevin with another dilemma. There had been much criticism at the UN of the British decision to withdraw from Palestine. Creech-Jones who had to bear the brunt of it wrote to Bevin that the common view—echoing Crossman in the *New Statesman*—was that British policy was pro-Arab and that his instructions were to thwart the UN on Palestine, creating a situation which would lead to revision of the partition plan and veto any attempt by the Security Council to provide for enforcement.[3]

Zionists saw it as part of a British plot to organize chaos from which they would then be called upon to rescue the country on their own terms. This was the last thing Bevin wanted, especially with the trouble he anticipated in Europe. He was never more sincere than when he told the House of Commons:

[1] FRUS 1948 (5); *The Forrestal Diaries* (London 1952); Ganin; John Snetsinger: *Truman, the Jewish Vote and the Creation of Israel* (Stanford 1974).
[2] Quoted in Margaret Truman: *Harry S. Truman* (London 1973) p. 388.
[3] Creech-Jones to Bevin, 21 February 1948. FO 800/487/PA/48/8.

"I do want to emphasise that we have to get into a position to enable us to get out of Palestine. That is the fundamental point of British policy."[1]

But that begged the question. For many who did not credit Bevin with Machiavellian motives still felt that for the British, who alone had armed forces in Palestine and knew the country better than anyone else, to walk out and leave it to be ravaged by civil war without lifting a finger was indefensible, and a betrayal of Britain's responsibility as a colonial power.

Now that the USA, after pushing so hard for partition, was backing away towards some form of compromise settlement, the pressure on the British to modify their refusal to co-operate was redoubled. Even before Austin's announcement, at a time when the Americans had gone no further than to talk of conciliation within the framework of partition, Creech-Jones had written to Bevin saying that he and Cadogan felt they could not maintain a negative attitude and refuse to co-operate, in view of Britain's obligations to the UN.[2]

Bevin was adamant. When the first signs of a change in the US attitude began to appear, he wrote to Creech-Jones that it was largely due to British firmness. The US Government had at last "been brought to face the facts and not unnaturally found them distasteful". He told Creech-Jones that he should not oppose any American initiative but must not give the impression that the British would remain in Palestine beyond 15 May simply because discussions were continuing. "To avoid this pitfall, we must continue to make it clear that we will not deviate from our announced policy of withdrawal." The only possible concession might be a longer overlap between the arrival of the UN Commission and the end of the mandate.[3]

The day after Warren Austin made the proposal of trusteeship, Loy Henderson saw the British Minister in Washington, Sir John Balfour, and pressed for Britain to join the USA in implementing the new plan (20 March). Bevin refused and at its meeting on 22 March secured Cabinet approval for his stand. The Cabinet minute records:

"There should be no change in the date fixed for the surrender of the Mandate; the British civil and military authorities in Palestine should make no effort to oppose the setting up of a Jewish state or a move into Palestine from Transjordan."[4]

Instead, the Chiefs of Staff should be asked to consider accelerating the rate of withdrawal.

Bevin's difficulty was that, with so much dependent—not just for Britain, but for the whole Western world—on the closest co-operation with the Americans in Europe, he could not say a word in public about the real reason

[1] HC, 23 March 1948.
[2] Creech-Jones to Bevin, 21 & 24 February 1948. FO 800/510/UN/48/3–4.
[3] Bevin to Creech-Jones, 13 February 1948. FO 371/68648.
[4] CM 48 (24).

for his refusal to fall in with their proposed change of policy in the Middle East. In Europe, although there were differences between them, he had found the Americans reliable allies; in the Middle East, he had not. Loy Henderson, one of those most anxious to secure British support, summed up Bevin's view in a note written at the end of March:

"The British are extremely bitter at what they consider to be lack of consideration for their difficulties in regard to Palestine in the past and because of their belief that internal political shifts in the U.S. will render the American Government an unreliable partner in the carrying out of any Palestine policy."[1]

The two parts of the sentence have to be taken together. His past experience had left Bevin not only bitter but unwilling to rely on any apparent change in American policy. With the Zionists already promised, and within sight of, the Jewish state, he believed there was less chance than ever of their accepting a compromise which fell short of it—and he had no confidence that the American Government, even if it now supported such a compromise, would not renege under Zionist pressure. In that case—and events were to show that it was a realistic, not a speculative hypothesis—the British could find themselves again involved in a situation from which they were only just extricating themselves—only once again to be thrown over by the Americans.

This is the key to Bevin's attitude in the weeks that followed. Great pressure was put on him by the Americans. Douglas was sent back repeatedly by Marshall to impress on Bevin the serious effect Britain's refusal to co-operate would have on Congress and American public opinion. Both sides used the argument that their disagreement would only benefit the Russians, and Douglas warned Bevin that if Britain would not co-operate in Palestine, then American co-operation in the rest of the Middle East, as agreed in the Pentagon talks, would become impossible.[2]

In the course of April Bevin had several talks with Morris Ernst, a Jew who was not a Zionist, and with him worked out a proposal which he put in a letter to Creech-Jones on 22 April. Partition would be dropped to satisfy the Arabs, but the ultimate creation of a Jewish state would be accepted. In the meantime, a quarter of a million Jews would be moved from Europe: 100,000 would be admitted to Palestine over eighteen months; the USA would be asked to take 100,000; Britain and France the rest. To deal with the existing situation in Palestine, the UN should appoint a Commissioner with a neutral C-in-C to whom both the Haganah and the Arab Legion would be responsible. A joint Jewish–Arab Council would be set up to govern and prepare a constitution; the Irgun and the Stern gang would be dealt with as terrorists. Bevin added

[1] Undated. FRUS 1948 (5 Pt.2) pp. 756–7.
[2] British records of talks with Douglas on 2nd, 19th, 21st, 23rd, 28th and 29th April, 4th May. FO 800/487/PA/48/2–31. For the US records over the same period, see FRUS (5) pp. 805–907.

that he did not contemplate putting British troops back into Palestine, but thought his scheme might offer the chance of a settlement.[1]

During April the fighting escalated, and the Jewish forces began to establish their superiority over the Arabs. In a message to Bevin on 2 May, Creech-Jones reported that there was not the slightest hope of a settlement emerging from the UN. The Zionists were counting absolutely on proclaiming a Jewish state on the 15th when the Mandate ended and American efforts were now concentrated on securing a truce. He was directing his own efforts to the same end, without much hope of getting more than a local ceasefire in Jerusalem. What he did not know—any more than Marshall or the rest of the US Administration—was that Truman had sent a second message to Weizmann on 23 April that he would do all in his power to recognize the Jewish state.

At a conference in the White House on 12 May, there was strong pressure from the President's pro-Zionist adviser Clark Clifford, to drop the truce plan and give immediate recognition to the State of Israel as soon as it was proclaimed. Lovett and Marshall strongly advised against such a move.

In a confrontation with Clifford, both declared that it would seriously diminish the office of President if, in a transparent attempt to win the Jewish vote, domestic political considerations were allowed to settle an international problem.

"I said bluntly," Marshall recorded, "that if the President were to follow Mr. Clifford's advice and if in the elections I were to vote, I would vote against the President."[2]

No decision was taken at the meeting on the 12th. But on the afternoon of the 14th the US delegation to the UN, having switched from partition to trusteeship and then to a truce, had just marshalled a majority of votes for the appointment of a UN mediator when it learned over the ticker-tape, along with the other delegates, that a State of Israel had been proclaimed and that the President had been the first to accord it recognition, 16 minutes later, without consulting or informing anyone.

It is important, if almost impossible, to keep the balance of judgement equal. If Truman's action made nonsense of the policy the State Department had been pressing on the British, it could be justified by the general support which his decision received in America and by the part it played in securing his re-election in November. If he had not been returned to the White House, the greatest losers would have been the British and the other Europeans, none more so than Bevin with his hopes of an Atlantic alliance.

Similarly with the creation of the State of Israel. This was justifiably hailed as a triumph against all the odds for Jewish courage and determination three

[1] Bevin to Creech-Jones, 22 April 1948. FO 800/487/PA/48/19. For a variant of Bevin's proposal on Palestine as a unified state with a central administration and the Haganah and the Arab Legion keeping order in their respective areas, see his letter to Creech-Jones of 1 May, *ibid.*, PA/48/29.
[2] FRUS (5) pp. 972–8.

years after an experience from which only a people of exceptional qualities and faith could have rescued anything. Only later was the price at which it was purchased to become clear in the humiliation of the Arabs, their alienation not only from Israel but from the West.

Bevin foresaw and warned against this, but he was not listened to, his views being ascribed to anti-Jewish bias. He still believed that events would justify his warning, but this did not alter the fact that the Zionist triumph, although he had for some time accepted it as the most likely outcome, represented a defeat and a damaging one. He had been proved wrong in the belief, on which he had staked his reputation, that it would be possible to find a compromise settlement, and if he could fairly claim that Truman's readiness to bend to Zionist pressure had made it impossible, there had also been errors of judgement and timing as well as faults of temper on his part. Rather than see Britain saddled with enforcing a division of Palestine which he believed inequitable and certain to be resisted by the Arabs, he had proposed the surrender of the Mandate and withdrawal, arguably the best way out of an impossible situation but one which incurred the criticism of abandoning to chaos and civil war a country for which Britain had accepted responsibility.

If it is unlikely that any other British foreign secretary would have succeeded in reconciling the conflict of interests he inherited, Bevin's masterful temperament made his failure more conspicuous. He could not even be sure in the summer of 1948 that the worst of all possible consequences, irreparable danger to the Anglo–US partnership, had been averted. For with the end of the Mandate, the Arab states openly intervened in the fighting and the British and American Governments came nearer to an open disagreement than at any other time in his period of office. On 17 May the US delegates to the Security Council submitted a resolution declaring a breach of the peace in Palestine. Under Article 39, which the resolution invoked, sanctions might be imposed on anyone named as aggressors, and there was no doubt that the Americans would name the Arab states. American anger was particularly directed against Britain's alliance with Transjordan, whose Arab Legion under British officers was attacking the Jewish parts of Jerusalem. The danger of Britain vetoing a resolution supported by the USA, France and the Soviet Union was only narrowly averted when the resolution received less than the necessary seven votes, the UK abstaining.[1] The Council resolved however to order a ceasefire within a time limit of 36 hours.

The same day Bevin, speaking with great seriousness to Douglas of the risk of their two countries drifting further apart, both in the Middle East and Europe, pointed to the danger of the USA lifting its embargo on arms for the Middle East in favour of the Jews, to be followed immediately by a demand

---

[1] For Bevin's instructions to use the veto, despite a plea from the British delegation, see the exchange of telegrams: UK delegation to Bevin, 20 May, FO 800/510/UN/48/18 and Bevin's reply, 21 May, FO 800/487/PA/48/38.

that Britain should fulfil its treaty obligations and resume arms deliveries to the Arabs.[1]

On 25 May Douglas met not only Bevin but Attlee, other senior ministers and the British Chiefs of Staff and after a sharp exchange on the question of sanctions, the outlines of an agreement emerged, with the British undertaking to put pressure on the Arab states if the Americans would restrain the Jews. Attlee and Bevin expressed the hope that the two countries might now work together to secure Arab acceptance of a Jewish state, and Douglas was later to describe this as a milestone in British thinking about Palestine. Bevin specified the two points on which he believed the Jews would have to make concessions:

"(i) The inclusion of Gaza and the Negeb in the Jewish state had been a mistake as there were no Jews there, and this must be righted.
"(ii) Jaffa and Acre which were purely Arab towns,[2] should be given back to the Arabs."

Douglas as well as Bevin thought these were reasonable demands which the Israelis could afford to concede in return for Arab acquiescence in the existence of Israel. Immediately the important thing was to maintain the two arms embargoes and avoid a situation which Tedder compared to "a repetition of the civil war in Spain during which both sides were supplied with arms by different sets of outside powers."[3]

On the 27th the British representatives in the Security Council proposed that the Council should call on both parties to stop fighting for a month during which there would be a general embargo on the supply of arms to Arabs and Jews alike. After concessions had been made to meet Jewish objections, the British resolution was carried on the 29th, and the UN mediator, Count Bernadotte, appointed on the US motion of 14 May, was given the task of applying its terms. The truce came into effect on 11 June, and lasted precariously until 7 July. This at least provided a breathing space during which the British and Americans could take steps to avoid the confrontation into which they had nearly been thrust before the crisis over Berlin came to a head.

3

The Communist coup in Prague and the Russian walk-out from the Allied Control Council in Germany had convinced the French Foreign Office that

---

[1] Bevin's talk with Douglas. FRUS 1948 (5) pp. 1031–6.
[2] These had been captured by the Israelis earlier in May.
[3] British record of the meeting on 25 May in FO 371/68650/E 7024; American in FRUS 1948 (5) pp. 1047–50.

France could no longer withhold agreement to the American and British plans to create a West German government. This change of attitude[1] opened the way to more rapid progress in the London Conference when it resumed on 20 April. At the end of a month's work, an agreed set of recommendations across the board was ready to be ratified by ministers.

At this point, however, French ministers drew back. One of the parties in the Coalition, the French Socialists, felt that after Stalin's letter to Wallace, another approach ought to be made to the Russians, while Bidault and the MRP were alarmed at the threat of a combined attack on the London agreement by de Gaulle as well as the Communists. This would make it difficult for them to remain in office and Bidault was looking for an excuse to withdraw or at least for additional concessions from France's partners with which to defend himself in the Assembly.

The view of the American negotiators was that they and the British should be prepared to go ahead with setting up a provisional government in the Bi-zone whether the French agreed or not. The question was whether Bevin would take the same view and it was with relief that Douglas reported that he was quite unmoved by the French change of front.[2] He responded to an urgent appeal from the British Ambassador in Paris, Oliver Harvey (1 June), for Labour Party help in stiffening the Socialists' resolution (not least that of the President of the Republic, Vincent Auriol), and asked Jim Griffiths, the Chairman of the National Executive as well as a minister, to go over to Paris with Will Henderson, Arthur Henderson's son, whom he had just appointed as his Parliamentary Under Secretary for Germany. He telegraphed to Morgan Phillips, the Party Secretary, to come back from Vienna to join them.[3]

The debate in the Assembly lasted for several days and was marked by furious opposition from the Gaullists and Communists. In the course of it Bidault sent Chauvel, the Secretary General of the Quai d'Orsay, over to London to see if he could not obtain some modification of the recommendations but Bevin made it absolutely clear that the British and Americans were not prepared, as had been freely reported in Paris, to re-open the negotiations. The vote was a close one, but in the event the Socialists as well as the MRP supported Bidault and, although loaded with reservations, an Order of the

---

[1] Communicated to General Clay by Couve de Murville, the Director-General for Political Affairs at the Quai d'Orsay, on 8 April 1948. FRUS 1948 (2) pp. 169–70.

[2] Douglas to Marshall, 24 May, reporting his conversation of that date with Bevin. FRUS 1948 (2) p. 273. Bevin reported the position and the recommendations of the London Conference to the Cabinet in CP (48) 134, 29 May 1948, which contains the French Note of 20 May. It was discussed at the Cabinet meeting on 31 May and Bevin's attitude approved. CM 34 (48). Bevin went back to the Cabinet on 14 June before the final vote was taken in the National Assembly and secured confirmation that, whatever the outcome of the debate, the British and Americans would go ahead with the recommendation of the London Conference, CM 39 (48).

[3] Harvey to Bevin, 1 June, FO 800/467/GER/48/2; Bevin to Harvey, 3 June, FO 800/494/PLT/48/20; Bevin to Morgan Phillips, 4 June, FO 800/465/FR/48/9; Bevin to Phillips, and to British Embassy in Paris, 8 June, *ibid.*, FR/48/10.

Day was passed by 300 votes to 286, agreeing to the recommendations already accepted by London and Washington.

What, after all this fuss, did the recommendations amount to?[1] The centre-piece was an agreed procedure and timetable for authorizing the Ministers President of the German Länder to convene a Constituent Assembly (by 1 September 1948) and draw up a constitution for a federal German state. With this went recommendations to the Military Governors on the broad principles such a constitution would have to meet before they could agree to it and on the powers to be reserved in an Occupation Statute which the occupying powers would publish prior to the formation of any German government. The recommendations were cast in such a form as to make possible the later adherence of the East German Länder and of the Soviet Union as the fourth occupying power, but no doubt was left that two at least of the three Western powers intended to go ahead without further attempts to secure this, even if that meant the continued division of Germany.

This political programme was flanked by two other agreements. The first, strongly opposed by Clay and the US Army, but included to satisfy the French and the Benelux countries, provided for an international authority for the Ruhr. The Ruhr would remain a part of Germany politically, but the International Authority, without owning or attempting to manage the Ruhr's coal, coke and steel industries, would exercise control over them by allocating their products between German consumption and export to other European countries, thereby guaranteeing to the French as well as the Germans access to the Ruhr's resources when the occupation ended. The second dealt with security against a revival of German military power by recommending that the three Western powers should pledge themselves to make no withdrawal of their occupying forces from Germany until the peace of Europe was secured or without prior consultation. A tripartite Military Security Board was to be set up to make sure that the disarmament and demilitarization of Germany were effective.

Every discussion of the future of Western Europe ran up against the problem of what was to become of Germany. By the end of 1947 Bevin had reached the conclusion that neither the Russians nor the Western powers would ever agree to Germany being united on terms which the other side would accept. In the London conference the Western powers had worked out a programme for the only practical alternative course if Germany was to remain divided—a West German state associated with the other non-Communist countries of Western Europe.

To reach agreement on this and to get it accepted, if only just accepted, by the French, the Belgians and the Dutch, was a considerable achievement on paper, but even more than with the Marshall Plan and the Brussels Treaty,

---

[1] The recommendations are printed in full in the annexes to CP (48) 138, circulated to the Cabinet on 4 June and noted at the meeting on 7 June. CM 36 (48). Substantial approval had been given by the Cabinet on 31 May, CM 34 (48) and was confirmed on 14 June, CM 39 (48).

many months of further unremitting effort lay ahead to translate the programme into action. Not only was there resentment amongst the Germans at the proposal that the Ruhr should continue under foreign control after the occupation ended and great reluctance to abandon hope of re-unifying the two halves of their country, but the French maintained a protracted resistance to implementing the Ruhr agreement without further modifications, as well as to the fusion of the French with the other two Western zones, and to every step in the process of handing over self-government to the Germans. A further tripartite conference on the Ruhr had to be called in November and a new draft agreement was only signed on 28 December. No agreement at all was reached in 1948 on the fusion of zones, the Basic Law for the administration of the future Federal Republic or the Occupation Statute, and it was not possible to promulgate any of these before the spring of 1949.

What was true of the German settlement was true, in greater or less degree, of the other elements—OEEC, ERP, Brussels Treaty—out of which Bevin hoped to see built up a future for Western Europe and Britain. In the summer of 1948 there was still only a set of plans and promises, the translation of which into reality over the next five years required the confidence that it could be done. After the overthrow of democracy in Czechoslovakia and in face of the threat to Berlin, that confidence was badly shaken. Bevin accepted that it would take years of effort to implement the proposals on which they had agreed since the breakdown of the London CFM; what made him far more anxious in the early summer of 1948 was the delay in providing the one thing which he believed could restore confidence in Europe and remove the fear of another war, an explicit commitment by the USA to act if the Soviet Union threatened to use force.

In the aftermath of the Prague coup, on 17 March, President Truman had called both houses of Congress together to hear him welcome the signature of the Brussels Treaty, and promise American support. In April and May, however, the impetus had been lost and on 4 June Bevin sent for Lew Douglas and asked him bluntly whether the USA was cooling off.[1]

The difficulty lay in American domestic politics. After great efforts an economy-minded Republican Congress had been persuaded to pass a Democratic Administration's Economic Co-operation Act, but to ask it to go further and undertake a military as well as a financial and economic commitment to Western Europe, had to be accepted as impossible in a Presidential election year. And no one believed that when the elections of November 1948 were over, Truman would still be President. In the Spring of 1948 his popularity, as registered by opinion polls, hit a low point of 32% compared with 70% at his succession to the Presidency.[2] The Democratic Party was split between supporters of Truman, Henry Wallace's Progressives and Southern Dixiecrats; and although bi-partisanship had produced a fair degree of co-operation

[1] FO 800/460/EUR/48/21.
[2] Truman, *Memoirs*, vol. 2, p. 188.

from the Republicans in foreign policy, the Administration's policies continued to come under attack from the Republicans' isolationist wing represented by such senators as Taft, Wherry and Hickenlooper.

In June, the House, led by John Taber and other advocates of economy, ordered a cut of 26% in the first year's appropriation for the European Recovery Programme and was only stopped by a dramatic appeal from Vandenberg to the Senate to override the House's action. The Administration was not strong enough to act on its own; it would have to have backing from Congress. That meant that, if anything at all was to be done to redeem Truman's promise, it would have to be at a pace and in a way acceptable to Vandenberg. As Republican chairman of the Senate's powerful Foreign Affairs Committee and president of the Senate *pro tempore*, he was the one man who could secure sufficient support on the eve of the election campaign from a Congress dominated by the Republican Party.

Vandenberg ruled out as impossible before a new President and Congress had been elected the procedure recommended by the secret Anglo–US talks in March. He proposed starting from the current interest in reforming the United Nations. This had produced a crop of proposals in Congress and Vandenberg proposed to use these as a springboard for a resolution nominally directed to that end but really intended to open the way to a North Atlantic Pact. In this way a formal expression by the Senate in favour of restricting the use of the Veto in the UN would be linked with a mechanism through which the USA could proceed to support such regional and collective security arrangements as the Brussels Treaty.[1] The draft of what became the Vandenberg Resolution was worked out between the Senator and the State Department, approved by the President on 7 May, by the Senate Foreign Affairs Committee, without dissent on the 19th.

Bevin was far from satisfied with what he heard was happening in Washington. A powerful message from him urging the start of negotiations on an Atlantic Pact was delivered to the State Department on 14 May and another on the 18th.[2] Marshall's reply (on 28 May) in effect invited him to read between the lines of the Vandenberg Resolution and accept that "the necessity for wide and whole-hearted public support in the United States required that [these matters] be approached with the greatest prudence and circumspection". Marshall added that, while there was no possibility of completing any negotiations before the next session of Congress in January 1949, the intervening time "can nevertheless well be utilized for the explorations and conversations which will in any case be necessary"[3] With that Bevin had to rest content.

The Vandenberg Resolution came before the full Senate on 11 June. In introducing it, Vandenberg laid stress on those clauses which reaffirmed the

---

[1] Vandenberg, p. 405.
[2] FRUS 1948 (3) pp. 122–3; 127–8.
[3] Marshall to Bevin, *ibid.*, pp. 132–4.

United States' commitment to the UN and called for voluntary agreement not to use the veto; for maximum efforts to get agreement to provide the UN with armed forces and reduce armaments; and, if necessary, a review of the Charter. Within this framework, however, were embedded three other clauses which picked up Article 51 of the UN Charter which Vandenberg had helped to draft at San Francisco and, in his own words, paraphrased the Rio Treaty for reciprocal assistance and defence between the American Republics which he had introduced in the Senate and which the Senate had approved by 72 votes to 1 in December 1947. The objectives which these three clauses committed the Senate to advise the President to pursue were the development of regional arrangements for collective self-defence under the UN Charter; association of the USA with such collective arrangements as affected its national security and assertion of the USA's determination to exercise the right of individual or collective self-defence under Article 51 should any armed attack occur affecting its national security. This was a formula which, Vandenberg claimed,

"Lives within the Charter but outside the veto. It permits congenial nations with common interests in peace and security to defend themselves 'until the Security Council has taken the measures necessary to maintain international peace and security'. The single word 'until' is the key to everything. 'Until' covers the whole time if, as and when the Security Council is deadlocked. Yet the Security Council can instantly resume jurisdiction whenever it is prepared to 'take the necessary measures'."[1]

While Vandenberg congratulated himself on his success in reconciling United Nations' righteousness with the claim to organize in self-defence, Bevin was impatient to know what would be the practical follow-up to the Resolution. The understanding was that, once the Resolution had been passed by the Senate (as it was by 64 votes to 6), the US Government would be free to undertake the talks with the Brussels powers for which Bevin continued to press.

All Bevin wanted to know was, When? At last on 23 June Marshall sent the message for which he had been waiting, that the US would be ready to start secret exploratory talks at the end of the month, although no Congressional action could be expected until the new President was installed in January 1949.[2] The French, in accepting the invitation, defined the problem which the Western powers had to face as "(1) an eventual threat, which is Germany; (2) an actual threat, which is the Soviet Union; (3) an immediate threat, which is Soviet action in Germany".[3] To keep the discussions as secret as possible, no special delegations were sent to Washington, each country being represented by its Ambassador: in the British case, to Bevin's satisfaction, this was Oliver Franks. Finally, on 6 July, the first meeting of the "Exploratory Talks on Security" took place in Washington and was followed before the end of the

[1] Vandenberg's letter to Harry M. Robbins, 9 December 1948. Vandenberg, p. 419.
[2] Marshall to Bevin, 23 June. FRUS (3) p. 139.
[3] Bidault's telegram to the French Ambassador in Washington 29 June, *ibid.*, pp. 142–3.

month by the attendance of US representatives at military talks held by the Brussels powers in London.

In the same first half of July the last of the sixteen bilateral economic agreements between the USA and the European countries participating in the European Recovery Programme was signed.[1] Agreement had not been reached easily, particularly between the USA and France and the USA and Britain. On 23 June Douglas reported from London that McNeil, Bevin's Minister of State, had told him that there were three breaking points on which the British Cabinet was prepared to risk disagreement rather than accept the American draft. Fortunately, Douglas was able to secure changes which removed most of the difficulties. On 25 June the Cabinet authorized signature of the agreement and progress towards realization of the European Recovery Progamme jolted forward another stage.[2]

4

The British and American governments expected the Russians to try and stop them from going ahead with the German settlement and to do this by putting pressure on them in Berlin. The city was divided (and still is) into four sectors, corresponding to the four zones into which Germany was divided. Each sector, like each zone, was under the control of one of the occupying powers which maintained a garrison and was responsible for the local German population. There was one important difference between the different sectors, however. Berlin was situated in the middle of the Soviet zone, and this allowed the Russians to draw directly on the resources of their zone to supply their sector with food, water and power, and to reinforce their garrison. The Western powers on the other hand, were cut off from their zones and could only supply their garrisons and a civilian population of nearly two and a half million Germans in the three western sectors if the Russians were willing to make local resources available from the Soviet zone and allow unimpeded access to Berlin from the Western zones (120 miles to the border crossing at Helmstedt) over Russian-controlled roads, railways and canals, or through Soviet air space.

The Russians did not need to stage an open challenge. The first steps to cut off Berlin from the West were taken in March 1948 but were described as temporary interruptions due to the need for repairs. The blockade of the Western sectors was not complete until August. Each step was followed by a pause to assess the danger of war which the Russians correctly concluded no one in the West wanted to risk any more than they themselves did. As the Russians well knew, whatever might be said in public about the Western

---

[1] The last was that between the USA and the US–UK Bi-zone signed in Berlin on 9 July.
[2] CM 42 and 43 (48), 24 and 25 June. The most serious objection was to the extension of MFN treatment to Japan and Korea in face of strenuous objections from Australia, New Zealand and the Lancashire textile trade. See Douglas's report to Washington 23 June, FRUS (3) pp. 1109–13 and CM 44 (48), 28 June.

Powers' right to remain in Berlin, there were many in Washington as well as Paris who began to ask privately whether it was worth risking a confrontation to stay there.

In June 1948 stocks in the Western sectors were sufficient to provide food for no more than 36 days and coal for the power stations for no more than 45. The idea that a city of two and a half million could be kept going by air-borne supplies alone seemed out of the question. Even Clay, who was a hard-liner, did not believe the combined air forces could lift more than 700 tons of supplies a day, compared with the 4,000 tons needed and the 8,000 actually achieved before the year end. The calculation on both sides was that, at best, the Western Powers could only hold their position in Berlin for a limited period of time, at the end of which they would have to choose between three options: using force to break the blockade, making a humiliating withdrawal under duress, or purchasing the right to stay by accepting the Russian terms. The last would include abandoning the London recommendations for the consolidation of the Western zones and returning to the four-power CFM with its built-in Soviet veto on any German settlement. By comparison the Russians ran no risk which they could not at once minimize by relaxing the blockade —with the possibility of always restoring it later. Not surprisingly the prudent course appeared to be to get out of Berlin before they were forced out, a course which General Bradley, the US Army's Chief of Staff, put to Clay in a teleconference as early as 10 April:

"Will not Russian restrictions be added one by one which eventually would make our position untenable unless we ourselves were prepared to threaten or actually start a war to remove these restrictions? Here we doubt whether our people are prepared to start a war in order to maintain our position in Berlin and Vienna.

". . . If you agree should we now [?not] be planning how to avoid this development and under what conditions, say, for example setting up Trizonia with capital at Frankfurt, we might ourselves announce withdrawal and minimise loss of prestige rather than being forced out by threat?"[1]

Clay's reply has already been quoted. He argued for staying until they were forced out, but he did so because, as he told Bradley, "I cannot believe that Soviets will apply force in Berlin unless they have determined war to be inevitable within a comparatively short period of time." And this, despite the most-overworked quotation in the literature of the Cold War,[2] Clay thought

---

[1] Report of Bradley–Clay teleconference in Clay, *Papers*, vol. 2, p. 622.

[2] This is Clay's report to Washington on 5 March that he could no longer say he thought war unlikely for at least ten years, but felt that it might come "with dramatic suddenness". However, Clay himself makes clear in his book (*Decision in Germany*, pp. 354–5), and the editor of his *Papers* (vol. 2, p. 568) confirms, that his purpose in sending the report was to support the US Army's efforts to get Congressional support for making good the deficiencies left by premature demobilization after the War. The report did not go through the normal command channels but was sent to General Chamberlin, Chief of Army Intelligence, after a visit he had paid to Berlin in late February and was intended for Chamberlin to use as he saw fit. Clay says that the change in attitude which he noticed on the part of the Russians turned out to be related to the decision to impose the blockade, not to preparations for war.

unlikely. Like Bevin, he believed the Russians were trying out the situation to see how far they could go with impunity, and argued that they were more likely to be encouraged by Western readiness to withdraw than provoked by Western determination to stay. Despite continued misgivings in the Western capitals, Clay's firmness prevailed and the combined Western force of 6,500 combat troops[1] was still in Berlin when the crisis blew up in the last ten days of June.

The occasion was the Western Powers' decision announced on 18 June to introduce a new currency in the three Western zones of Germany. Such a reform was indispensable to any economic recovery and had been under discussion for two years. When the Russians broke up the Allied Control Council in March 1948, that body was still considering a revised plan for a four-power scheme of currency reform to be applied throughout the whole of Germany, East as well as West. With the ACC no longer meeting and the Soviet veto removed, the way was open to go ahead in the Western zones, excluding Berlin in order to avoid a confrontation with the Russians. The latter, however, not only denounced the Western Powers for sacrificing the unity of Germany but matched them by introducing their own scheme of currency reform in the Soviet zone and (the decisive point) claiming to include the whole of Berlin in their zone. The difficulties which would be created by having two currencies circulating in Berlin were obvious and the three Western Powers offered to meet Soviet representatives in order to try and reach agreement on a single currency. It was even more important to resist the Russian claim that the three Western powers had no longer any rights in Berlin, a claim in preparation for which the Russians had already, on 16 June, walked out of the *Kommandatura*, the four-power body responsible for Berlin, as well as from the ACC.

While the meeting to discuss a single currency was still in progress, on the evening of 22 June, news was received that the Soviet Military Governor Sokolovsky had issued unilateral orders to the Berlin city authorities to recognize the new East Zone currency as alone valid throughout Berlin. Rejecting this, Clay and Robertson insisted that the four-power *Kommandatura* was the only agency authorized to deal with currency reform in the city, and that in view of the Russian refusal to let it act they would go ahead and introduce their own Western zone currency in Berlin.

In retrospect it is possible to see the next week as a turning point in the Cold War, at least in the sense that if the American and British governments had given way, it is difficult to believe that they could have carried through their plans to restore Western Germany and Western Europe and no longer allow the Russians to exercise a veto. The minimal basis of European confidence, already at a low point in France and Germany, would have been destroyed.

---

[1] The Russians were reported to have 18,000 troops in their sector and a further 300,000 in their zone, completely outnumbering the Western forces in both cases.

The handful of Berliners, who shared the responsibility for making the decisions in that week, including at least one woman, Luise Schroeder, the Acting Burgomaster of Berlin, were obliged to improvise. There was no contingency plan; they had to guess what the Russian intentions were and how great was the risk of war; they could not foresee what might be the consequences of their actions, only what they grasped intuitively would be the consequences of a failure to act.

On their side the Russians seem to have been confident that, if they made the blockade complete, as they virtually did on 24 June, they ran no real risk of war (despite the fact that the USA possessed the A-bomb and they did not). They believed that, if they kept up the pressure, the Western Powers would have to choose between abandoning the London recommendations as the price of staying in Berlin or abandoning Berlin as the price of sticking to the London recommendations.

Political—and military—opinion in the Western capitals was far from convinced that the three Allied powers either could or should attempt to maintain their presence in the city. If the men most involved in the decisions had weakened in their resolution, the Russian gamble might well have succeeded.

The first and bravest demonstration of resolution was made by the Berliners themselves. This was indispensable to firmness of decision in London and Washington. On 23 June in face of Communist intimidation, threats and mob violence, the Berlin City Assembly (meeting in the Soviet sector and denied police protection) voted in favour of the *Magistrat's*[1] recommendation that Marshall Sokolovsky's order in regard to currency should apply to the Soviet sector only and that the other three sectors would follow the orders of the Western Powers, thereby preserving the four-power status of the city. The Berlin leaders had no guarantee that the Western powers would not withdraw from Berlin, as Soviet propaganda hourly insisted they meant to. They had long had to bear the brunt of the Communists' war of nerves; to this was now added the threat of hunger for over 900,000 families and the prospect of reprisals if the whole city was taken over by their political enemies. Their refusal to be brow-beaten, confirmed by a mass meeting of 80,000 Berliners the next day, provided something Bevin and Marshall were always looking for, too often in vain, the readiness of Europeans to stand up and be counted, a readiness to help themselves without which, in the case of the Berliners, no efforts to help them from outside could have succeeded.

---

[1] This was the executive body of the City Government, a coalition of four parties including the Communist-dominated SED. Since the Communists' defeat at the Berlin elections of 1946, the Social Democrats had been by far the strongest party and supplied the Burgomaster. The Russians, however, refused to validate the election of the SPD leader Ernst Reuter to the office. His functions were discharged by the First and Second Deputies, Luise Schroeder and Ferdinand Friedensburg, both of whom showed courage in face of the Communists' war of nerves. Reuter, who finally became Burgomaster when the City Government split later in the year, remained throughout the unquestioned leader of Berlin's resistance to the Russians.

On the 24th Bevin warned the British Cabinet that a very serious situation might develop.[1] General Brownjohn the Deputy Military Governor was brought back to report direct to ministers on the 25th and was pessimistic about the chances of supplying Berlin by air or any other means. Bevin was not at all satisfied with Brownjohn's view and demanded, as a matter of urgency, technical advice on how the city could be supplied. At his request a small group of ministers (known as the Berlin Committee) was set up to keep the situation under review—in fact, to take decisions and report them to the Cabinet.[2]

The Russians had now cut the remaining road and rail links between Berlin and the West and ended the supply of electricity to the Western sectors of the city from the Soviet sector and the Eastern zone. It was at this juncture that the critical decisions had to be taken, and never was Bevin's capacity for action and the value of his relationship with Attlee more clearly displayed. The Committee on Germany represented the same concentration of power as Churchill's War Cabinet, of which three of its members, Attlee, Bevin and for a time Morrison as well had also been members. In addition to the Minister of Defence and Cripps as Chancellor of the Exchequer, the Chiefs of Staff were also present. It did not meet often—on two successive days in June and two in July, when crises threatened; four times more in 1948, twice in 1949. Attlee, however, unlike Churchill, was content to let the Foreign Secretary make the running. It was he, not the Prime Minister, who put proposals to the Committee and once he had its approval, spoke and acted in the Government's name.[3]

In the middle of June Bevin had gone for a holiday to Sandbanks. He had only been away a few days, however, when the Berlin crisis made it necessary to call him back and a torpedo boat was sent across the Solent to fetch him. When he met the US Ambassador on 26 June he already displayed a firm grasp of how to handle the situation, firmer at that stage, to judge from the American documents in both cases, than anyone in Washington.

Bevin presented Douglas with a five-point plan for handling the crisis.[4] With the recent muddle over American–Soviet talks in mind, Bevin laid a lot of stress on procedure. He asked for and got American agreement to his securing a complete exchange of information on Germany from whatever source and to making London "at least one place in which discussions of the issues that may arise out of the Berlin and general German situation may be held". He proposed to cut out the British Embassy in Washington and deal direct with Douglas, as he had throughout the London conference. With a government crisis in France, he hoped to bring in the French Ambassador, Massigli, as a

[1] CM 42 (48).
[2] CM 43 (48).
[3] The Committee's papers and minutes are to be found in CAB 130/88.
[4] Douglas sent a full account of Bevin's proposals to Washington at midnight on the 26th. FRUS 1948 (2) pp. 921–6.

link with Paris. Bevin also laid stress on involving the French as well as the British and American Chiefs of Staff in a joint appreciation of the military situation.

On the 26th the airlift had begun. The idea of supplying the civilian population of Berlin, not just the garrison, originated with an RAF officer, Air Commodore Waite. He succeeded in persuading General Robertson that it really was practicable and the two went together to put the figures to Clay.[1] Clay preferred the idea of sending an Army convoy up the autobahn, with orders to fight its way through to Berlin if necessary; but he knew that there was a group in Washington who wanted to pull out of Berlin altogether and he guessed that they would be willing to accept an airlift as a temporary measure which could always be dropped whereas they would refuse to agree to the convoy. This converted Clay and the airlift began on a small scale, with no great confidence that it could be sustained. Bevin, however, had seized at once on the possibility it offered of keeping the civilian population of Berlin supplied, and in his interview with Douglas he asked for it to be studied urgently by the Military Governors and Combined Chiefs of Staff, arguing that, apart from its practical value, it would be a powerful symbol of Western determination. He attached similar psychological value to bringing American strategic bombers to Europe (the B-29s capable of delivering A-bombs) as a way of impressing the Russians that they were in earnest—and pressed this too on the Americans. Finally, he began to probe the advantages and disadvantages of sending a Note to Moscow.

Bevin left no doubt in Douglas's mind that he attached great importance to firmness in face of the Russian challenge. "He believes" Douglas reported, "that the abandonment of Berlin would have serious, if not disastrous, consequences in Western Germany and throughout Western Europe. In this appraisal I concur." To counter reports to the contrary, Bevin issued a communiqué on the 26th saying "The statement that we intend to stay in Berlin holds good." The same day Bevin saw the Dominions High Commissioners and made sure that they understood the British intention not to give way.[2]

On the 27th Marshall responded to Bevin's five points, agreeing to his proposals about procedure and taking up his suggestion that American heavy bombers B-29s) might be moved to Europe. Was Bevin prepared to give clearance for some of them to be stationed in Britain as well as Germany?[3]

On the 28th Bevin reported to the Cabinet the statement he had already issued. His argument that there could be no question of yielding to Soviet pressure was not questioned and he was able to give some figures of what could be done to supply the city by air.[4] After the Cabinet meeting Douglas brought

---

[1] Interview with General Robertson.
[2] FO 800/468/GER/48/31.
[3] Marshall to Douglas, 27 June, FRUS (2) pp. 926–8; Douglas's interview with Bevin on the 28th, FO 800/467/GER/48/32.
[4] CM 44 (48).

General Draper, the Under Secretary for the Army, and General Wedemayer to see Bevin. When Draper said that, as its share of the operation, the US Air Force hoped to fly in 1500 tons a day, Bevin retorted that that was not enough, and that he was sure the USA could do better—a reply which made a very favourable impression on his visitors.[1]

Douglas told Bevin that the US Government had now decided to stand firm on Berlin. According to Forrestal, the Secretary for Defence, when Truman was faced with the question by his advisers, he replied, "We are going to stay. Period." When the Secretary for the Army, Royall, expressed concern that the problem had not been thought through, Truman answered that "we would have to deal with the situation as it developed", but that

"We were in Berlin by the terms of an agreement, and that the Russians had no right to get us out by either direct or indirect pressure."[2]

This was welcome news to Bevin but he pressed Douglas for a public statement of the US attitude. So far it had been left to the British to speak out and it was time the Americans made their position clear. He added that it would be a great help if Marshall could say something appreciative about the Berlin Social Democrats and their steadfastness.[3]

Bevin not only had Berlin to worry about but the worst dock strike of the decade in London, which occupied much of the Cabinet's time at five meetings between 22 and 29 June.[4] On the 28th Attlee sent over to the Foreign Office a handwritten note of what he proposed to say in a broadcast announcing the declaration of a state of emergency. Bevin had already agreed that troops should be used, if necessary, to clear food-stuffs which were in danger of rotting.[5]

Later the same day Bevin was able to give Douglas his answer about the bombers. The Cabinet (by which he meant the Berlin Committee and in effect Attlee and himself) agreed to three groups of B-29s landing (two going on to Germany and one staying) and eighty-two F.80 fighters also landing en route to Germany. He added that he thought it would be best to leave sending a note to Moscow until the moves for expanding the airlift and moving the US bomber force were more advanced.[6] In fact it was not until the middle of July that the first two groups of B-29s arrived, with a third following during August.[7]

[1] FO 800/467/GER/48/34, report dated 29 June.
[2] *Forrestal Diaries*, p. 427.
[3] Bevin–Douglas interview, 28 June. FO 800/468/GER/48/32.
[4] CM 41–45 (48).
[5] FO 800/494/PLT/48/24.
[6] Bevin's interview with Douglas, evening of 28 June. FO 800/468/GER/48/33.
[7] The Berlin Committee of the Cabinet agreed to the immediate dispatch of the two squadrons on 13 July, *ibid.*, GER/48/41. Bevin gave a short history of the B-29s and their transfer to Britain and Germany in a report to the Defence Committee on 13 September 1948. DO (48) 59.

Bevin went on later, in the course of a report to the House of Commons (on 30 June), to make the strongest statement yet from the Western side:

"If the intention is to make trouble for us in Berlin . . . H.M. Government cannot submit to that. We cannot abandon those stouthearted Berlin democrats who are refusing to bow to Soviet pressure."

After referring to the steps taken to institute the airlift, Bevin paused in order to give weight to his words, and then added:

"We recognise that as a result of these decisions a grave situation might arise. Should such a situation arise, we shall have to ask the House to face it. H.M. Government and our Western Allies can see no alternative between that and surrender—and none of us can accept surrender."[1]

In the evening, after his speech, he and Attlee met Douglas at No. 10. The Ambassador was able to tell them that Marshall was making an equally clear statement of the American attitude that day. But he added that the American Government wanted to send a note to Moscow immediately, making the point that once free access had been restored, the USA would be prepared to negotiate on the four-power administration of Berlin, either in the Council of Foreign Ministers or the United Nations.[2]

Bevin was opposed to this, preferring to hold up any approach to Moscow for 48 hours until the Russians had had time to digest what had been said and to realize the Western Powers' determination not to be frightened out of Berlin. He was certainly not influenced by an apparently conciliatory letter from Marshal Sokolovsky which, Douglas reported him as saying, "is characteristic of the sort of Soviet tactics which we may expect for the purpose of giving us a sense of false assurance as to the future, thus inducing us to relax our efforts."[3]

Bevin told Douglas that he was not opposed in principle to sending a note to Moscow, but felt that once it was delivered, they would have no further freedom of manoeuvre. For the same reason he was opposed to suggesting, as the American draft Note proposed, a meeting of the CFM or reference of the dispute to the United Nations,[4] arguing that the Russians would only take either as a sign of weakness. He thought it best to keep the note short and, instead of proposing resort to a body like the CFM or the UN, to restore the quadripartite machinery in Berlin which the Russians had broken up.

---

[1] HC 30 June 1948.

[2] Bevin and Attlee's meeting with Douglas, 30 June. FO 800/468/GER/48/36. Douglas's report in FRUS (2) pp. 936–8.

[3] FRUS (2) footnote 2 on p. 932. Sokolovsky's letter suggested conditions for restoring road and rail communications between the Western zones and Berlin without offering any guarantees that the restrictions would not be re-imposed whenever it suited the Soviet authorities.

[4] As was often the case—except over socialism—Clay agreed with Bevin. See his reply to Draper, 5 July, in *Papers*, vol. 2, p. 727.

Bevin's other suggestion was to let the Military Governors, Clay and Robertson, use Sokolovsky's letter to explore the situation with the Russian. The Americans, with some misgivings, accepted his view and agreed to defer the Note to Moscow until the 6th. Bevin still objected to any proposal to refer the issue to the UN, but agreed to say that, if the Military Governors could not settle the dispute, it should be sent to the CFM. In the meantime, he told Douglas, it would be wise to delay the arrival of the B-29s, not because of political difficulties, but in order to see what effect their Note had in Moscow.[1]

5

The interview between the other Military Governors and Sokolovsky produced no result other than to confirm, as Clay put it, "that the technical difficulties would continue until we had abandoned our plans for West German government".[2] Bevin was not surprised but the meeting had at least served to delay rushing to Stalin as the Americans had wanted, and to bring home to them that the Russians were using the situation in Berlin to try and re-open the entire German question.[3]

The joint Note to Moscow[4] finally delivered on 6 July, followed closely the line Bevin had suggested and did not propose anything more than a settlement of the local problem in Berlin. The last thing he wanted was to see the plans for the future of Western Germany, which had been put together with so much difficulty in the London conference brought into question again. On the other hand Bevin was alive to the danger—and the fear—of war, and was aware that the Western Powers could only face the prospect of war with the Soviet Union in the summer of 1948 as a last resort. It was true that the Americans possessed the A-bomb and the Russians did not, but consideration of the actual use of atomic weapons (as distinct from their deterrent effect) would be subject to every sort of political and psychological constraint without any guarantee of military success. On the other hand, when the Chiefs of Staff reported on their plans for an emergency which might lead to war, they left no doubt about the weakness of the forces on the ground in Germany. Nor was there any comfort to be had from the USA where Forrestal, the Secretary for Defence, noted in his diary that the Army's total reserves to meet an emergency anywhere in the world amounted to two and one-third divisions, or 30,000 men.[5] Everything therefore depended on the deterrent effect of the US Strategic Air Force, and in moving to Europe the B-29s,

---

[1] Bevin–Douglas meeting, 2 July. British report in FO 800/468/GER/48/39; Douglas's in FRUS (2) 942–6.
[2] Clay, *Decision in Germany*, p. 367.
[3] C. Marshall to Douglas, 3 July. FRUS 1948 (2) p. 947.
[4] Text in RIIA *Documents 1947–48*, pp. 586–8.
[5] *Forrestal Diaries*, p. 410; p. 431.

capable of delivering atomic bombs, the Americans were reinforcing General Clay with the only forces they had.

When Attlee and Bevin met the Chiefs of Staff again on 9 July they decided that, while it was premature to decide whether to hold Berlin even at the risk of war, the prudent course was to plan on the assumption of war and see what was required. General Robertson had been told that, in an emergency, he was to make a withdrawal to the Rhine and it was agreed to prepare two airfields in Holland for the RAF in Germany to use in covering such a withdrawal. But the Chiefs of Staff argued that the most urgent step was to set up a unified Western Union command. Ministers agreed but Bevin stressed the need to clear the proposal with the Americans who might otherwise think they were precipitating a crisis.[1]

In the meantime, without waiting any longer for the Russian reply to the Allied note, Bevin got the Cabinet's Berlin Committee on the 13th to agree to ask for the immediate dispatch of the B-29 bombers. The National Security Council in Washington authorized it on the 15th and a force of 60 planes reached the UK on the 17th.

There was no point in trying to plan the defence of Western Europe without the Americans. An invitation from the Western Union Permanent Commission, sent on the 15th, was accepted on the 16th, and an American team headed by General Lemnitzer flew to London to take part, as "non-members", in the discussions of how to meet a military emergency and how to increase the stock of military supplies.[2] A visit to Paris by Montgomery in July, however, showed how shaky a structure Western Union really was. Monty reported widespread defeatism and the fear that France would be left in the lurch and overrun by the Russians.[3] The French did not believe that the British would fight on the Rhine, and the other Chiefs of Staff, as well as Robertson, supported Monty's argument that a unified HQ had to be set up in the field with a Supreme Commander.

Bevin was worried that this might act as a provocation to the Russians to act swiftly. Although Montgomery pressed him hard, he continued to oppose appointing a Supreme Commander and to insist that, however firm a reply was given to the Russians, the door to negotiations must be left open.

Bevin was not altogether pessimistic: he was sure that the Russians also had their difficulties. Although it might have been a mistake for the West to get bottled up in Berlin, if the Western Powers now allowed themselves to be forced out, he was quite clear that would mean losing the diplomatic battle. But to avoid increasing the tension, he secured deferment of action on a Western European HQ and a Supreme Commander, at least until they heard from the Americans.

[1] Minutes of COS Committee, *ibid.*, DEF/48/36.
[2] FRUS 1948 (3) pp. 189–92.
[3] Montgomery's Reports 12 July, FO 800/453/DEF/48/43, and 14 July, FO 800/465/FR/48/11.

Later in July the argument was transferred to the Defence Committee. A review of the country's preparations for war revealed many gaps, and at a series of meetings in July and August the Committee discussed what needed to be done.[1]

At the meeting on 27 July Bevin was emphatic that the UK would not contemplate embarking single-handed on a war with the Soviet Union. If such a war become unavoidable it would have to be primarily an American undertaking. Britain's role would be subsidiary and the Americans would have to give assistance on the scale of the ERP if the British were to embark on a major rearmament programme. When the Committee next met on the 30th Attlee refused to be panicked, reminding the Committee that while the COS were right to sound the alarm, it was Ministers who had to decide, and that they must consider very carefully the timing of any measures in relation to what the USA was prepared to do and the negotiations in Moscow. Bevin thought the most important step to take was to halt the releases from the Forces under the National Service scheme which was costing them the loss of 8–9,000 trained men and women a week.

The Defence Committee's discussion resulted in a detailed programme for building up stocks of ammunition, overhauling communications, restoring the pipeline system, refitting vessels, etc.[2] But the essential step was to stop the rundown of the uniformed strength of the Forces which stood at 814,000 and was scheduled to fall to 743,000 by the end of March 1949. Bevin was not yet ready to contemplate recalling reservists which he thought would be taken as a move towards mobilization.[3] But he was ready to recommend the suspension of further releases. This came to the Cabinet on 26 August when Attlee was ill and Bevin in the chair. He criticized the scheme before them which provided for a block suspension of all releases between 1 September 1948 and 31 March 1949, condemning it as inequitable, and likely to lead to trouble. Instead each man should be asked to serve an additional three months beyond the date of his release. At the same time he asked the Cabinet to agree to the Ministry of Defence examining the working of conscription, with the sole reservation that the principle of national service was not to be questioned. Both proposals were adopted at the Cabinet's next meeting, the only opposition coming from Aneurin Bevan.[4] When the time came to put the suspension of releases to the Commons, ministers were very anxious to avoid stirring up Party opposition by any suggestion that they were proposing to lengthen the period of service.[5] Bevin was content to let events produce their own impression and before the

[1] The subject was first discussed on the 12th meeting of the Defence Committee on 21 July and subsequently on the 13th (27 July); 14th (30 July); 16th (18 August) and 17th (23 August).
[2] Contained in Alexander's report DO (48) 55 dated 19 August and discussed by the DC on 23 August.
[3] DC DO (48) minutes of 17th meeting, 23 August.
[4] CM 58 (48) 3 September 1948.
[5] CM 60 (48) 13 September.

end of November the Cabinet was prepared to go to the Parliamentary Labour Party and then to Parliament to secure an extension from 12 to 18 months.[1]

But the key in Bevin's mind was an Atlantic Pact and he pinned all his hopes on the talks which began with four days of meetings (6–9 July 1948) conducted by the Under Secretary of State, Bob Lovett. The five Brussels Powers were represented by their Ambassadors and Canada by Lester Pearson. Basing himself on the Vandenberg Resolution, Lovett had taken a tough line: the USA was not making any proposals, only exploring possibilities and ruled out in advance any idea of "military Lend-Lease", a United States unilateral guarantee or any form of automatic commitment to Western Europe. The objective was to strengthen the United States' own national security. Any association with Europe would have to provide for reciprocal guarantees and the Americans would first of all have to be satisfied, as in the case of the Marshall Plan, that the European powers were doing all they could to strengthen themselves. Even if they were, any proposals would have to be put to Congress, which meant that nothing could be settled before 1949.

Lovett's attitude of lofty disinterestedness, whether deliberately assumed or not, provoked the French Ambassador, Henri Bonnet, into saying that France was not interested in generalities or long-term plans but in knowing what measures the USA would take immediately to deal with the threat of war and to supply arms to France and her neighbours. Bonnet's protest, repeated by his deputy Bérard in the sessions of the working party that followed, only elicited a succession of snubs and embarrassed his colleagues. Whether they liked it or not, Franks, the Dutchman van Kleffens, and the Belgian Silvercruys understood that they had to work within the framework and the timetable set by the Americans, and that these were determined by the domestic situation in an election year with a President not expected to win and a Congress dominated by the opposing party. In effect, Lovett was serving notice that the United States had learned a lesson and was not going to repeat the procedure of the Marshall Plan by underwriting or guaranteeing the military as well as the economic recovery of Western Europe.

What emerged from the discussions was that membership of the Brussels Pact would do nothing for America's own security: the Pact was too narrow in its membership, too broad in its obligations. It was left to Franks, and particularly to Lester Pearson, to draw the conclusion that they had to take the idea of a North Atlantic Pact and develop it in such a way that it would meet the needs of both the Americans and the Europeans.[2] This was the job of a working party which held a series of fifteen meetings between July and September.

Thus Bevin found himself, as he had in the summer of 1947, at the centre of a web of interlocking negotiations—about Berlin, the implementation of the

---

[1] CM 75 (48) 22 November.

[2] The US record of the talks is to be found in FRUS 1948 (3) 148–82. The British record is in FO 800/453/DEF/48/30 and 35, together with a summary and commentary by the British Embassy.

London decisions on Western Germany, the European Recovery Programme, the Western Union military talks in London, and the NATO working party in Washington, not to mention Palestine and the Middle East. Together they composed the elements of Bevin's Grand Design or as he put it himself in a much more characteristic metaphor "the four legs of the table". These were: the European Recovery Programme and OEEC; the Brussels Treaty and Western Union; American military support for W. Europe (which, he added, would bring financial advantages even greater than ERP); and the organization of Western Germany.[1] In talking to Attlee, Bevin insisted that if one of the elements, or legs, was removed or weakened, the whole structure would collapse: the full picture had to be kept in mind in dealing with particular problems, and other ministers (he mentioned Cripps and Wilson) not allowed to endanger the design by ill-considered individual actions. Bevin knew to his cost that American foreign policy was constantly being confused by the unconsidered intervention of other departments besides the State Department —not to mention the White House itself—and he asked for assurance of Attlee's support in preventing anything similar developing in British foreign policy. Granted the difference between the British and American cabinet systems, the unique position Bevin held in the British Cabinet and the closeness of his relations with the Prime Minister, there was not much danger of this happening. Bevin's real problem was the lack of resources with which to match and implement his policy. Even so, looking in retrospect at the difference between the agenda of the two summers, it is possible to see the progress that had been made towards the realization of Bevin's design.

This was a comfort denied to Bevin himself. In the summer of 1947 he had gambled on avoiding the threat of economic collapse; in the summer of 1948 he had to gamble again, this time on avoiding the threat of war, knowing that the power to make the sort of miscalculation which could lead to war lay in American or Russian, not British hands. It was this combination of responsibility and dependence which frayed Bevin's nerves and at times his temper.

Ten years before, in 1938, Chamberlain (following another Czech crisis) had preferred appeasement to standing firm, and had only made war more certain. Bevin was determined not to repeat his mistake, but the soldiers, although they went along with the policy, left him in no doubt of the risks they were running. Everyone with a claim to expert knowledge agreed that the Russians were unlikely to start a war to force the Western Powers out of Berlin,[2] but the fact was that they continued to tighten the blockade and that if a war started as a result of miscalculation, there was little chance of stopping the Red Army from occupying Western Europe. Ordinary people could not make sophisticated calculations about Russian intentions but they remembered what occupation and war were like all too well: they saw what had

[1] Bevin's talk with Attlee, 19 June 1948. FO 800/460/EUR/48/26.
[2] See, for instance, the views expressed by Kennan and Bohlen in the Washington talks. FRUS 1948 (3) p. 157 and p. 177.

happened to the Czechs, what was now threatening in Berlin. A great many of them, in the summer of 1948, thought that war could begin again before the year's end (this time with atomic weapons) and that they would be in the front line. It was against this background of nervousness and fear that Bevin had to strike a balance. The French Government fell in mid-July and France was without a government for two months; Germany had no government; Bevin was the one political leader in office in Western Europe who had the stature to carry his own people with him and to represent European interests, if necessary against the Americans. Just how difficult this was comes out in the record of the Brussels Pact's Consultative Committee meeting at The Hague on 19 and 20 July.

The meeting opened with Bevin giving the other Foreign Ministers a résumé of the events leading up to the present situation in Berlin. He spoke confidently, asserting that the British and the Americans were determined not to be forced out of Berlin or let the Russians get control of the city in the next 3–4 weeks. He spoke of the airlift reaching a total of 4–5,000 tons a day and told them that the UK had agreed to provide bases for a force of B-29s, with more to follow. The object was not to start a war but to be in a strong position to negotiate, if and when the chance came.

Bidault (who lost his position as foreign minister when the French Government fell in the course of the meeting) answered by voicing the alarm which was widespread in Europe and pouring scorn on the American assurances of support. Precisely what were the Americans ready to do if war started? If it came to negotiations, what were they going to negotiate about? When Bevin asked him if the French wanted to get in touch with the USSR at all costs without any conditions, Bidault retorted that the French did not want the Western Powers to get into a hopeless position where the only ways out were war or a climb-down.

Bevin showed the division in his own mind when he said on the one hand that if the USA was not prepared to negotiate with the Russians, he would ask them how many divisions they were ready to put in the field; and then followed this up by declaring on the other hand that they could not go back on the London decisions about Germany, that they must try to keep the airlift going throughout the winter and that he had no intention of giving way.

On Berlin at least he received some support from Spaak who was relieved to find that Bevin thought it necessary both to stand firm and to regain the diplomatic initiative by starting talks. Bidault, however, went on to heap criticisms on the Washington talks. He was particularly put out that the Americans, as he put it, "had abandoned" the Brussels Pact. The Europeans had taken a great risk in signing the Brussels Treaty and had not been given credit for their initiative by the Americans. The USA was trying to get out of its obligations on the cheap by a general declaration involving no real obligations. The only guarantee would be the presence of American troops in Europe. The second day it was Spaak's turn to take up and develop Bidault's criticisms of an

Atlantic Pact. He saw it as no more than a paper scheme which the United States could not make militarily effective and which added nothing. What the Americans were proposing was another Rio Pact, cumbersome, lacking any automatic commitment and not corresponding to the actual military dangers.

Once again Bevin had to spell out the advantages of the Atlantic idea: it was easier to present to the American people and would be much more acceptable than the Brussels Pact to the Scandinavians. If trouble came, they would all be in it from the first day. They should press on with their own arrangements to show the Americans they were making progress and aim at getting a treaty stronger and more purposeful than the Rio Pact. Bidault's valedictory jeremiad reflected his anger at losing office. The Americans, he declared, had no consistent policy; the Atlantic Pact was a fabulous monster like the unicorn —no one knew what it amounted to. Treaties and alliances created risks and these ought to be compensated for by additional guarantees.[1]

The meeting broke up without any conclusions, leaving any follow-up to Bevin. While the other foreign ministers belly-ached and complained, he had kept his temper and not allowed his steadiness of judgement to be upset. Never was his value to the whole Western alliance more clearly demonstrated.

[1] FO 800/447/CONF/48/4.

CHAPTER 15

The West's resolution tested

I

His visit to the Hague made a deep impression on Bevin. He came back depressed at the weakness and lack of leadership, particularly among the French, and more convinced than ever that any purely European organization could not stand on its own feet unless linked with the United States. France's weakness, which impelled those Frenchmen who despaired of her recovery as a nation state to ideas of European Federation, had the opposite effect on Bevin, confirming his belief that Britain, however much she became, and must become, involved with Europe, must also—like the United States—retain her independence and look for her security in an Atlantic rather than European framework.

On the other hand, he was impressed with the strength of French and European fears that the United States policy-makers had too little grasp of how much was at stake for Europe in finding a peaceful solution to the Berlin crisis and their feeling of alarm at the well-founded reports that General Clay was proposing he should send an armed convoy up the autobahn and challenge the Russians to stop him restoring access to Berlin.

The Americans at once noticed a change in Bevin's attitude on his return from the Hague, suspected (wrongly) that he was "going soft" on Berlin and complained (rightly) that he was much more inclined to question their proposed tactics in dealing with the Russians. Bevin's foresight in getting London recognized as a clearing house for decisions in relation to Berlin now proved its value.

Douglas, the American Ambassador in London, enjoyed the confidence both of the State Department and Bevin, and was thoroughly experienced in European affairs after the Marshall Plan negotiations and then the London talks on Germany. He saw Bevin almost every day, sometimes more than once. With no French government for eight weeks, Massigli, the French Ambassador in London, was as well qualified as anyone to express a French point of view and was always able to get in touch with Paris. Through the third member of the group, Sir William Strang, the head of the FO's German Section, Bevin was able to keep in contact with Robertson, the British Military Governor, and through him with Clay, the outstanding personality on the Western side in Germany. Finally, when the negotiations moved to Moscow at the beginning of August, Bevin sent out his Principal Private Secretary, Dixon's successor, Frank Roberts, to act as British representative in place of the Ambassador who was away on sick leave.

In this way Bevin was at the centre of a network of communication reaching out to Washington and Paris on the one hand, to Berlin, Frankfurt and Moscow on the other. Unless the Americans were prepared to act on their own in dealing with the Russians—and although they discussed the possibility, they continued to attach greater importance to Western unity—they had to secure Bevin's concurrence, particularly as there was no one of comparable authority in Paris or anywhere else in Western Europe. If this frequently meant that Bevin was put under heavy pressure from Washington, it also placed him in a strong position. London was the place where the differences between points of view were thrashed out, where every proposal had to come in order to be agreed, modified or returned with a counter proposal. Douglas was not exaggerating more than was pardonable when he said that in the summer of 1948 Western policy was made in London in the constant exchange between Bevin, himself and Massigli.

Bevin had a high opinion of Massigli, who more than once refused to carry out instructions from the Quai d'Orsay when he thought them wrong and was not to be moved when Couve de Murville and Hervé Alphand came over to remonstrate with him. The difference of time between London and Washington meant that the frequent tele-type conferences between the Embassy and the State Department took place late at night and Massigli quite often slept on the couch in Douglas's room until the conference was over.

Bevin's relations with Douglas were not at all those conventional between a Foreign Secretary and an Ambassador. They were friends, seeing each other too often and too closely for either to conceal his hand from the other. "Ernie never tried to put me in a box," was Douglas's tribute. "He would blow his top, shout a bit and curse the Americans, but I did the same and neither of us ever walked out of the house." Bevin felt free to grumble about the US Government and the difficulties it made for him, and so did Douglas both about his own and the British Government. On occasion he found Bevin obstinate, especially when he was tired and became slow. Douglas, a banker by origin, who had proved as capable of managing Congress over the passage of the ERP bill as in negotiating with European governments, described Bevin as highly intelligent although inclined not to argue out the probable consequences of a policy but to reach the same conclusions by instinct.

While Bevin had been meeting the Brussels Pact ministers, there had been high-level conferences in Washington, attended by Clay as well as by the Republican shadow Secretary of State, Foster Dulles. These resulted in the decision, confirmed by the President, to stay in Berlin and to use any means that might be necessary. Precisely because the Americans had now decided "to carry this matter through to the end", they proposed that the three Powers should approach Stalin directly and impress on him the seriousness of the situation. Marshall added that they much preferred to do this in a personal interview and not by the dispatch of a formal note. They wanted to know at once what Bevin thought of the proposal.[1]

The short answer was, Not much.[2] "It would put Stalin in the position [reported Douglas] which Bevin is confident he would take, of agreeing to discussions, suggesting Moscow as the seat of them, and defining the agenda in accordance with his own desires."[3] Bevin was particularly opposed to the Western Powers communicating orally with Stalin thereby giving him the chance to twist what they said and use it against them. He would far rather send a note to Moscow and let the Ambassadors talk to Molotov.

The unexpected reaction from London was obviously not to the State Department's liking and the British draft of a reply to the Russians was described as "redolent with appeasement". Lovett said that he sensed "a definite weakening" in Bevin since his return from the Hague.[4]

Douglas defended him, saying:

"Bevin feels that he is doing his utmost to carry what he calls a fearful and a bankrupt France and that the pressure on him in the effort to maintain a united front among the Western European Powers is a very great burden."[5]

Two days later he reported:

"As to Bevin's intentions, purposes and determination, there can be no question whatsoever. They were reaffirmed this morning in strong language. Once again he said, 'the abandonment of Berlin would mean the loss of Western Europe' . . . I hope this will dispel any suspicions which you may entertain."[6]

At a meeting with Bevin Bohlen reported that he was "in a highly volatile and explosive condition". He kept coming back to the question, *What* was it proposed to say to Stalin, and complained that if he agreed it would only be

---

[1] Marshall to Douglas, 20 July. FRUS 1948 (2) pp. 971–3 including footnote on p. 971.
[2] Douglas's version of Bevin's views in *ibid.*, 978–9. Roberts' version in FO 800/502/SU/48/5.
[3] Douglas to Washington, 21 July. FRUS (2) p. 975, footnote 1.
[4] Marshall to Douglas, 21 July, *ibid.*, p. 975.
[5] Douglas to Washington, 22 July, *ibid.*, pp. 979–80.
[6] Douglas to Washington, 24 July, *ibid.*, pp. 982–3.

because the USA was pressing for it. After more grumbling, Bevin finally accepted a compromise which began with an approach to Molotov before going to Stalin and foresaw a strongly-worded note if they got nowhere, followed by a reference to the UN.[1]

Bohlen, recalling the meeting in his memoirs, thought Bevin's attitude reflected "the overriding fear of the British of being drawn into another war in circumstances in which they were not taking the lead" and criticized their attitude as playing into Moscow's hands.[2] But this was exactly what Bevin thought the Americans were doing by their approach to Stalin. He in turn criticized them for being in too much of a hurry to force the issue: either, like Clay, talking of fighting their way up the autobahn or insisting on going to the top and seeing Stalin, still without any clear idea of what they hoped to achieve.

The day after Bevin saw Bohlen he received another gloomy appreciation from Montgomery, who gave it as his personal view that it was now too late to get out of Berlin. The choice, therefore, was either to negotiate or to face the possibility of being forced to fight, with the certainty of losing Berlin at once.[3]

Despite this discouraging advice, however, a survey of the foreign situation which Bevin drew up for the Prime Minister on 28 July showed no inclination either to appease the Russians or to gloss over the difficulties ahead. He said categorically that it was impossible for the West to retreat from Berlin: it would be the greatest possible encouragement to the Communists and the greatest possible discouragement to our friends. On the other hand, it was not enough to stay in Berlin: that was only a means to an end. Bevin's conclusion would have surprised his American critics. He argued that it would be a mistake to buy a settlement in Berlin by concessions to Russia in West Germany, above all in the Ruhr. But the Russians would not make concessions themselves in Berlin for anything less. That meant the West must expect conditions in Berlin to get much worse during the winter, with the population hungry, industry at a standstill and the encouragement of unrest. Nonetheless the Western Powers would have to stick it out and make the Russians realize that they could only be put out by force—while keeping up contacts to see if negotiations were possible.

As many people believed that the Russians would follow the same tactics in relation to Vienna as to Berlin, it is interesting to find that Bevin did not. Certainly the Western Powers' communications were even more vulnerable in Austria than in Germany, but the difference was that Austria had a central government and this made the Russians see the only advantage worth the

---

[1] The US account of the meeting on 26 July is in FRUS 1948 (2) pp. 986–8; the British in FO 800/467/GER/48/42.
[2] Bohlen, *Witness to History*, pp. 279–80.
[3] Montgomery to Bevin, 27 July and Bevin's reply 3 August. FO 800/453/DEF/48/48 & 51.

trouble was in securing control of Austria as a whole. Their object was not to split Austria but to control the Austrian Government. Bevin concluded that the best course was to get a treaty signed and give the Austrian Government a chance. There was a risk of getting a Communist Austria but this was worth running if it secured Russian evacuation of the country and freed Austria from the burden of four-power occupation.[1]

2

When the meeting with Stalin finally took place on the night of 2–3 August, the results which flowed from it confirmed Bevin's scepticism. The first reports from Bedell Smith described Stalin as "in an extraordinarily amicable and co-operative mood", and Bohlen, at a council of war in Washington, said the outcome was "highly satisfactory".[2] This impression, however, was modified by later reports and completely reversed when the Western representatives got down to detailed negotiations with Molotov. The latter referred to "the insistent desire of Generalissimo Stalin for the postponement of the decisions of the London Conference" and re-opened all the questions dealt with in the earlier interview, following the old Soviet practice, as Bedell Smith put it, of "trying to sell the same horse twice".

This was on 6 August. At another three-hour meeting with Molotov on the 9th, the Russians dropped any mention of the London decisions and concentrated on Berlin, arguing that with the independent steps taken by the Western Powers in their zones, the quadripartite occupation of Germany had come to an end and the West had lost any right to be in Berlin. When Bevin saw Douglas on the 11th, he took a gloomy view and assumed that the talks in Moscow were likely to break down, but—contrary to the assumption Bohlen and other Americans were too ready to make about appeasement, lumping the British in with the French—he repeated that in no circumstances should they surrender Berlin and that he would rather hang on to the bitter end and be driven out than give way. The next two months, he added, were vital because they gave a chance to build up stocks in Berlin before the winter, and he pressed Douglas to get the rate of delivery by air lift raised to 7–8,000 tons a day.[3] Bevin saw the Berlin dispute as a trial of strength and thought it would be won by the side which had the stronger nerves and did not encourage the other side by pressing too hard to find a solution. The negotiations in fact did not break down and after a month of talks, endless drafting and re-drafting in

---

[1] Bevin to Attlee, 28 July 1948. FO 800/502/SU/48/8.
[2] *Forrestal Diaries*, pp. 440–41.
[3] Bevin's meeting with Douglas. FO 800/467/GER/48/49.

London, Washington and Moscow, and a further talk with Stalin, it was agreed to trade the lifting of the Berlin blockade against the withdrawal of the Western D-mark and acceptance of the Soviet zone's currency for all four sectors of the city. Instructions were sent to the four military governors to work out the details in Berlin with a time limit of 7 September.

While diplomatic and journalistic attention was focused on the talks about Berlin, time had not stood still in Western Germany. July was taken up with discussions between the three Military Governors and the 11 Minister Presidents of the Western Länder, at the end of which the Germans, with many misgivings about dividing their country, agreed to put the London recommendations into effect for Western Germany. In order to underline their hope that the exclusion of the Eastern Zone was only temporary, they pressed for and secured the omission of any mention of a Constitution, preferring the more ambiguous term, Basic Law. As long as they produced the framework for a Western German state, the British and Americans were indifferent what the arrangements were called. When the Parliamentary Council met in Bonn on 1 September, with 65 members selected by the 11 Länder, a draft of the Basic Law was ready and after electing Adenauer as President—a memorable choice—the Council set up a series of committees to examine it.

Implementation of the other parts of the London agreements was slower, principally because of the reluctance still felt by the French; but in August a start was made on the draft of the Occupation Statute and on negotiations to bring the external trade of the French Zone within the scope of the Anglo–American Joint Export–Import Agency. Despite the delays the process of carrying out the London recommendations was under way and with the establishment of the Parliamentary Council the decisive step towards creating the future Federal Republic had been taken.

This fact was fully appreciated in Moscow. At his first meeting with the Western Ambassadors Stalin had given the impression that his principal interest in the Berlin blockade was as a means of halting such a development.[1] In the course of August, however, as it became clear that the British and Americans were not to be diverted from the course to which they had committed themselves in the London recommendations, the Russians concentrated on the alternative objective, of sealing off the Eastern Zone, ending the four-power occupation of Berlin and making it the capital of a rival German government. The instrument of this policy was the German People's Congress for Unity and a Just Peace which had first assembled in Berlin at the time of the London Council of Foreign Ministers in December 1947. The original intention was to use the Congress to provide a representative base for all-German political institutions: delegates were invited from the Western as well as the

---

[1] See Bohlen's memorandum of 4 August analysing the report of the interview: "He makes it entirely clear that such suspension is the objective of the Soviet Government." FRUS 1948 (2) p. 1013.

Eastern zones and a plebiscite promoted for the whole country.[1] Few Germans, however, outside the Eastern zone, bothered to vote and the Russians fell back on the alternative of using the People's Congress to create a Communist state in the area they controlled. A draft constitution for the future Democratic Republic was considered at the third session of the Congress in August and a parallel course accepting the continued division of Germany put in hand on the eastern as well as the western side of the dividing line.

It was hard to see how the Russians could be persuaded to modify this policy in order to allow the continued anomaly, from their point of view, of the four-power occupation of Berlin in the middle of the Soviet Zone. At the end of August, when the talks were moved from Moscow to Berlin, the blockade had been in operation for ten weeks and, although the air lift had been built up, the Russians showed every confidence that if they kept up their pressure, winter would make it impossible to continue supplying a civilian population of 2.5 million by air and settle the issue in their favour. Why, then, should they take the negotiations in Berlin seriously unless they were to provide a way for the Western Powers to back down?

Once it was established that this was not the case, the Soviet negotiators threw over the basis for an agreement laboriously worked out in Moscow and put up the Soviet claims, Marshal Sokolovsky adding casually that Russian air manoeuvres would begin on 6 September and would involve Soviet use of the "corridors" on which the air lift depended.[2] To make this point unmistakably clear, the Soviet authorities and their SED allies stepped up the campaign of intimidation, threats and physical violence against the morale of the Berlin civilian population, and particularly against those city officials who remained loyal to the four-power arrangements for occupying the city which the Russians were bent on abolishing. Promises proved to be no more effective than threats in winning over the majority of Berliners. No less a body than the Council of Ministers of the USSR issued a decree on 19 July promising to meet the rations of every citizen from the Western sectors who was willing to register, but the highest number persuaded to do so never exceeded 4%. Soviet measures to keep control of the Berlin police force, the trade unions and the City Treasury only resulted in breakaway organizations, with the support of the Western military powers. This had finally extended to the City Assembly and *Magistrat*. On 26–27 August crowds organized by the SED made it impossible for the Assembly to hold its regular meetings and besieged the City Hall which was located in the Soviet sector. A further attempt to meet on 6 September led to rioting, molestation and the demonstrators' occupation of the Assembly Chamber.

The Communists' action (while the Military Governors were still meeting)

---

[1] May–June 1948. The Americans and French banned the plebiscite in their zones; the British disapproved but allowed voting to take place.
[2] For the US documentation of the Military Governors' talks in Berlin, 31 August–7 September, see FRUS 1948 (2) pp. 1099–142.

was followed by the biggest mass protest during the blockade; a crowd estimated at a quarter of a million jammed the Reichstag Square to hear Reuter and other speakers denounce the Communists' effort to impose their will on Berlin. After a young man had torn down the Soviet flag on the Brandenburg Gate, Russian troops fired into the crowd. A situation was being created in which there was a real risk of the occupying forces becoming involved to the point of open hostilities. When a *Magistrat* official asked the British liaison officer to intervene in order to protect a number of the men in his office, the British officer called up the British Military Governor, General Robertson, for authority to act, and the latter, to be certain of his ground, called the Foreign Office in London. Bevin personally authorized immediate intervention and the liaison officer had his answer within fifteen minutes. The majority of the City Assembly, without its SED members, transferred their activities and the administration along with them to the British sector. One of their first decisions was to call new elections for Berlin, in defiance of Soviet wishes, and set 14 November for the date.

As soon as it became clear that the Military Governors' talks would only lead to deadlock, arguments broke out again between the Americans and Bevin about what to do next.[1] Bevin was all for proceeding deliberately, not forcing a break but taking stock of the situation first. The State Department, on the other hand, was insistent that they must "face squarely up to the fundamental question of rights", and demand that the Soviet Government recognize the Western Powers were in Berlin by right. Even their own Ambassador in Moscow replied that "Molotov, or Stalin for that matter, will answer such a question with a categorical 'No' as both of them have done on repeated occasions during the past month."[2] The question to which Bevin could get no answer was what was to be done when the Americans had forced the issue, received a categorical "No" and appealed to the United Nations. What happened then? How was the blockade affected, one way or the other, by clarifying the "fundamental" issue—which in Bevin's view was a question of power not of juridical right? On 11 September he made it clear, with French support, that he would not accept the American proposal. Reluctantly, Marshall concluded that, whatever the dangers of the British approach, unity had to come first.[3]

The exchange of notes with the Russians which followed changed nothing, each side repeating the justification of its attitude; but by the time the Soviet reply was received (18 September) Marshall and Bevin were on the eve of setting out for Paris, where the next meeting of the UN General Assembly was to be held, and a new French Government had been formed, with Schuman in

[1] Douglas to State Department after talking to Strang who had been in touch with Bevin, 5 September, *ibid.*, pp. 1126–9.
[2] State Department to Moscow Embassy, 8 September, *ibid.*, pp. 1140–42; Bedell Smith's reply 9 September, *ibid.*, pp. 1142–4.
[3] Marshall to Douglas, 11 September 1948, *ibid.*, 1147–9.

place of Bidault at the Quai d'Orsay. This meant that it was possible for the three foreign ministers to sit down and thrash out face to face what was to be done next. More important in Bevin's view, the air lift on 18 September delivered a record 7,000 tons of supplies in a day, a better answer than anything else to Soviet pressure and prevarication.

3

Following the review of the gaps in Britain's defences already described, Bevin told the Defence Committee on 18 August that

"In his view a decisive struggle for power would take place in the next 6 to 9 months, and unless the Western Powers successfully withstood the pressure . . . the world would live in fear of war for many years."[1]

If it came to war with Russia, control of the Middle East would play a key role, and the Western Powers' chances of either avoiding war or winning one if it came to open fighting turned on the closest co-operation between Britain and the United States. Both were put at risk by continuation of the conflict in Palestine.

One of the charges repeatedly made against Bevin by the Zionists was that he encouraged the Arab states to attack Israel and that the British supplied them with arms. Bevin categorically denied the first charge[2] and no evidence has come to light to support it, other than his encouragement to Transjordan to occupy the areas allotted to the Arabs by the UN partition plan, "but do not go and invade the areas allotted to the Jews". It would indeed have been madness on his part to encourage hostilities in the Middle East when he was facing a confrontation with the Russians which carried the risk of war in both Europe and the Middle East. When fighting broke out, Britain took the lead in calling for a truce and pressing the Arabs to observe it. If both sides broke the truce it was almost invariably the much more efficient Israeli forces who gained by it and then refused to give up their territorial gains.

Transjordan's Arab Legion set a special problem for Bevin. It was subsidized by the British and commanded by an Englishman, Brigadier Glubb, with a number of other British officers. It numbered 14,000 in 1948 and was much the most effective force on the Arab side. But this like the other links with

---

[1] Defence Committee, DO (48), minutes of the 16th meeting.
[2] "It is absolutely untrue that H.M.G. encouraged the Arab Governments or forces to attack Israel. . . . It was suggested that I had . . . backed the wrong horse . . . and was surprised that they did not win. I did nothing of the kind. I uttered every warning I could to the Arab Governments not to indulge in this business." HC 26 January 1949.

the Arab forces was a long-standing feature of British defence policy in the Middle East, not directed against the newly created Jewish state. When the involvement of the Legion in fighting for Jerusalem went beyond the role Bevin had agreed to (the occupation of the Arab areas), he called for the withdrawal of British officers from the operations in Palestine and cut off further supplies of arms and ammunition, with serious consequences for the Legion's freedom of operation.

This arms embargo was one of the conditions of the UN truce and Bevin insisted on its observance by the UK despite the fact that the Egyptians and Iraqis whose armies had long been trained by the British, claimed that their right to military supplies under treaty was being set aside. Bevin maintained the ban despite Arab protests that the Israelis, using funds supplied by the American Zionists, were able to import large quantities of arms and equipment, particularly from Czechoslovakia, and thereby establish a superiority in *matériel* as well as moral superiority over the Arab forces.

The first truce in Palestine lasted less than a month (11 June–7 July 1948). During the interlude in the fighting, both sides bought arms wherever they could—the Jews with much greater success than the Arabs—and the UN Mediator, Count Bernadotte, produced new proposals for a settlement. The three most important of these were (1) setting up an economic union which would embrace Transjordan as well as Palestine and would make provision for both a Jewish and an Arab state with a central council to regulate their common interests; (2) an exchange of the Negev for Western Galilee, the first allocated to the Jews by the UN Resolution of November 1947 but now occupied by the Egyptians, the second originally allocated to the Arabs but now occupied by the Jews; and (3) the inclusion of Jerusalem in Arab territory with municipal autonomy for the Jewish community. Reporting Bernadotte's suggestions to the Cabinet, Bevin doubted that either side would accept them[1] but he put strong pressure on the Arabs to continue negotiations and agree to the extension of the truce which the British proposed at the UN.[2]

The Arab states, persuaded by Egypt and Syria, refused to listen and renewed the war, suffering further losses of territory to the Israelis in ten days' fighting before the Security Council imposed a second truce under threat of sanctions (18 July). This was even less effective than the first and unless a basis for a settlement could be found was virtually certain to end in further fighting.

Bevin told the Cabinet that he had no confidence in negotiations between Jews and Arabs producing any result. He believed the one solution was a settlement imposed by the Security Council which neither side might be willing to accept but in which both might acquiesce if it was backed by effective

[1] CM 48 (48), 8 July.
[2] In a letter sent to the Arab leaders, 5 July 1948. FO 371/68375/E 9168. See also a series of messages to Sir Alec Kirkbride, the British representative in Amman for use in speaking to King Abdullah, 6–12 July. FO 800/477/ME/48/16–22.

sanctions.[1] After sounding the Americans, Bevin decided to take the initiative in putting forward proposals both for a settlement and for a way of securing their adoption which he hoped the US Government and the UN Mediator would be willing to endorse. Unless the position could be stabilized on the basis of the *de facto* situation in Palestine, he believed that the Israelis would not only establish a Jewish state (which he accepted was there to stay), but would extend their rule over the greater part, even the whole of Palestine, thereby creating an Arab refugee problem and a lasting enmity between themselves and the Palestinian Arabs. He argued that to prevent this happening was not only in the British but in the general interest, including the long-run interest of the Jews.

Bevin put his ideas before the Cabinet on 26 August and secured their approval.[2] They were a revised version of Bernadotte's original scheme and were seen as proposals which the Mediator might recommend to the UN with British and American support. Palestine would be divided roughly along the lines held by the opposing forces. The Arabs would thus gain Southern Palestine and the Jews western and central Galilee as well as Jaffa. Bernadotte's idea of placing Jerusalem in Arab territory, which had been strongly resisted by the Jews, was dropped in favour of making it an autonomous city under a UN Governor with an international police force. The key proposal which Bevin hoped the Mediator would make was the incorporation of the Arab areas in Transjordan. That this was in British interests was obvious. It would strengthen the one reliable ally the British had in the Arab world, King Abdullah, and provide them with an all-important link across Southern Palestine from the Mediterranean and Egypt to Iraq and the other oil-producing states of the Persian Gulf. Abdullah was also the one Arab ruler realistic enough to come to terms with the Israelis, and union with Transjordan the only way, as Bevin had believed from the beginning, to provide a viable and secure future for the Arab parts of Palestine. If his plan could be given American support and put forward on the initiative of the UN Mediator, Bevin hoped that it would be seen to provide for the general interest of all parties in a settlement which would last, as well as for the special interest of the British in maintaining their position in the Middle East.

The next day Bevin gave Douglas a copy of his proposals. The Ambassador suggested that the prospect of American agreement would be improved if the British could say something about recognizing Israel. Bevin's reply was that if the scheme he had outlined was accepted he believed *de jure* and not just *de facto* recognition would follow without delay.[3] It was essential to the success of Bevin's plan that the initiative should come from the Mediator himself. He was

---

[1] CP (48) 207, 24 August 1948: see below.
[2] His paper CP (48) 207, dated 24 August was discussed by the Cabinet on the 26th. CM 57 (48).
[3] Bevin's talk with Douglas, 27 August 1948. FO 800/487/PA/48/68; FRUS 1948, (5 Pt 2) pp. 1352–9.

therefore relieved to learn that the US Government was willing to join in putting his proposals to Bernadotte and even more to hear that the Mediator was willing to adopt them, with few modifications, as his own.[1] Four days later, on 17 September, Bernadotte was assassinated by Jewish terrorists in Jerusalem, but he had signed a report embodying his recommendations to the UN the day before and on the 21st Marshall issued a statement accepting it on behalf of the USA as "a generally fair basis for a settlement".[2]

As Bevin had foreseen, neither side was willing to agree to the Bernadotte proposals. His reply to Arab protests was that they represented "the least disadvantageous solution"[3] and he refused, despite pressure from the Chiefs of Staff, to meet Arab requests for arms even when this meant handicapping Transjordan's Arab Legion.

Arab opposition (much of it directed against the aggrandisement of Transjordan) was as ineffectual as their resort to arms. Jewish opposition was a different matter. Israeli rejection of Bernadotte's report was total. Their spokesmen claimed the whole of Southern Palestine to the Gulf of Aqaba as well as the whole of Galilee and objected to the amalgamation of Arab Palestine with Transjordan. They enforced their opposition in two ways. The first was by military operations carried out without regard to the UN truce. An offensive launched against the Egyptians in mid-October made substantial gains in the south from which the Israelis refused all UN injunctions to withdraw. A second offensive in the north cleared Arab forces out of Galilee and left a number of Lebanese villages in Israeli hands. This effectively ruled out any hope of exchanging Galilee for the Negev.

The second way, in anticipation of the US presidential election on 4 November, was by stepping up Zionist pressure on the President to withdraw American support for the Bernadotte report.[4] Stiffer resistance by Marshall, Lovett and the State Department than on earlier occasions prevented an explicit disavowal of Marshall's statement of 21 September; but as the election

---

[1] Troutbeck of the Middle Eastern Office in Cairo was instructed to put the proposals to Bernadotte jointly with the American Robert McClintock. His brief was sent by the FO on 11 September. FO 800/487/PA/48/79–80. The meeting took place in Rhodes on 13 September. FRUS 1948 (5) pp. 1398–1400, prints the US report of the interview. Bevin met Marshall at the US Embassy in Paris on 20 September. FO 800/487/PA/48/86. Marshall's statement is in FRUS (5) pp. 1415–16.
[2] Bevin presented Bernadotte's Report to the Cabinet on 22 September as CP (48) 225. It was approved in its entirety, CM 61 (48).
[3] Bevin's talk with the Lebanese Foreign Minister 5 October. FO 800/510/UN/48/36. See also the records of his talks with the Egyptian Foreign Minister, 27 September and with the Iraqi, 29 September, (*ibid.*). When he heard that the Iraqis were pressing for an Arab attack to recover Jerusalem, he sent a stiff message of disapproval to the Regent, 2 October. FO 371/68376 E 11462.
[4] See the documents printed in FRUS 1948 (5 Pt 2) pp. 1430–1553. An example is the call which Clark Clifford made from the Presidential campaign train in Oklahoma to Lovett, saying "that the President had ordered him to send a telegram to the Secretary of State in Paris completely disavowing the statement made by the Secretary on 21 September in support of the Bernadotte Plan" (p. 1437).

campaign reached its height both the rival candidates, Dewey first, then Truman, re-endorsed the original UN partition plan of November 1947 which gave the Negev to Israel—adding that any modifications should only be made "if fully acceptable to Israel".[1] Nothing could be decided until the result of the election was known, but there appeared less and less prospect of the US Government being willing to give active support at the UN to a plan which they had originally joined the British in putting to the UN Mediator and in persuading him to adopt.

On the other side of the Mediterranean, in Greece, where another war was being fought, it was hard to believe in 1948 that Bevin's policy would prove any more successful than in Palestine.

He stuck to his belief that it was essential to deny the Communists control of Greece, more than ever now that Markos had set up a rebel government in the North. Alexander had forwarded to him in February 1948 an appreciation of Communist objectives approved by the Chiefs of Staff. This put their ultimate objective as the incorporation of a Communist Greece in the Balkan bloc and their immediate objective as control over Aegean ports and airfields, especially Salonika, which would threaten Anglo–US communications through the Mediterranean. Macedonia and Thrace would be absorbed by Yugoslavia and Bulgaria, which would help to create maximum chaos in Greece by their support for Markos in continuing the civil war.[2]

Bevin's difficulties with his critics were compounded by the fact that a year, even a year and a half or more after the Americans had agreed to take over responsibility for helping Greece, British troops although reduced to 3,000 had still not been replaced. In February 1948 Bevin asked Lew Douglas when the Americans were going to put in 10,000 marines,[3] and at the end of September he was still putting the same question to Marshall in Paris.[4] The Greek Army's summer campaign of 1948 drove Markos out of his stronghold of Grammos, but he was able to retreat into Albania and reappear in another part of Northern Greece a few weeks later. The UN Special Committee on the Balkans continued to report the provision of help to the rebels from across the northern frontiers and the abduction of Greek children. On the other side the Communists and their sympathizers denounced the Greek Government for the increasing number of arrests and executions which led up to the imposition of martial law at the end of October 1948.

The break for which Bevin had almost given up hoping came on the other side of Greece's northern frontiers, in the quarrel which Stalin forced on the Yugoslavs. The acrimonious correspondence between the Soviet and Yugoslav Communist Parties began in March 1948; the Red Army Mission was

---

[1] The President's statement published on 25 October is printed in FRUS 1948 (5 Pt 2) pp. 1512–14.
[2] Alexander to Bevin, 11 February 1948. FO 800/468/GRE/48/2.
[3] Bevin's meeting with Douglas, 15 February 1948, *ibid.*, GRE/48/3.
[4] 28 September, *ibid.*, GRE/48/8.

withdrawn and at the Cominform Conference held in Bucarest at the end of June, anathema was pronounced and Yugoslavia expelled for a heresy defined by Stalin later in the year when he wrote in the *Cominform Journal* that "the attitude towards the Soviet Union is now the test of devotion to the cause of proletarian internationalism".[1] This was the test which the Yugoslavs, proud of the fact that they were the only Communist Party in Eastern Europe which had not been put into power by the Russians, failed to pass in a sufficiently submissive form.

The first an astonished world knew of the quarrel was with the publication of the Cominform communiqué on 28 June. Bevin's first reaction was cautious. The Yugoslavs had been the most aggressive of the East European Governments in attacking British policy—over Trieste, Austria, Greece, Albania, the Balkan and Italian peace treaties. He had sat through too many anti-Western tirades by Djilas and others at the Paris Peace Conference and in the United Nations to be easily convinced that this was a real breach, a view which Tito himself was very reluctant to accept. In the survey of the foreign situation which he prepared for the Prime Minister at the end of July, Bevin wrote that it would be wrong to read too much into the Yugoslav–Russian exchanges. It was a family quarrel and did not mean that the Communist empire in Eastern Europe was crumbling.

Bevin was wrong, however. The breach was irreconcilable, certainly as long as Stalin lived, and it was to have far-reaching repercussions in Greece and throughout Eastern Europe, particularly when Soviet pressure failed to bring about either Tito's submission or his overthrow.

4

Marshall and Bevin had not met since the London meeting of the CFM in December 1947, and when they arrived in Paris in September 1948 there was much for them to discuss. During 1948 the Anglo–American partnership had grown closer but had also developed a number of frictions which bore heavily on Bevin. As the American documents make clear, he was the one man in office in Europe on whom the State Department felt they could rely. But Bevin was no "Yes-man". He was often critical of United States policy and he constantly aroused irritation and sometimes anger in Washington by his refusal, as an indispensable member of the cast, to play the role or speak the lines allotted to him in the American book.

In addition to Palestine and differences in the negotiations over the Berlin blockade, the Labour Government's refusal to take the lead in creating a United States of Europe was another constant subject of reproach by Americans. This reproach was not removed by the leading part Bevin played in

[1] Issue of 5 December 1948.

working for a North Atlantic Organization: on the contrary, a major reservation on the American side, clearly expressed by Kennan at the beginning of the Washington talks, was the anxiety that an Atlantic grouping should not close the door on "a real unification of Europe and the development of a European idea".[1]

OEEC was another source of friction. The British refusal to see it develop supra-national characteristics or turn itself into a customs union was constantly represented by Paul Hoffman (the ECA Administrator) and Averell Harriman (the US Special Representative in Europe) as "dragging their feet" and holding back Europe's recovery. A State Department dispatch to Douglas put very well the American dilemma in dealing with Bevin and the British. On the one hand, since his return from Paris,

"Hoffman has expressed grave concern over British attitude and feels they are not entering wholeheartedly into OEEC work." On the other, "He further believes that, unless they exercise real leadership to initiate and push forward effective measures for economic co-operation among OEEC nations, there is good chance ERP will fail."

Asking Douglas for concrete examples of "British failure to act or British unwillingness to co-operate fully towards integration of European economics", the State Department dispatch continues:

"The Secretary would have an opportunity to discuss this subject at Paris next month. It may be advisable, however, not to await Paris meeting. We suggest that you [i.e. Douglas] and Harriman discuss situation and if you agree call on Bevin jointly and forcefully call his attention to it."[2]

The fact that Britain was governed by a party with a socialist programme and that the US Congress had a Republican majority aggravated the permanent suspicion of the British in Washington. Bevin's determination to nationalize the Ruhr industries had been a great stumbling block in the Bi-zone negotiations in 1947, and now, in 1948, his refusal to abandon dismantling and reparations in the British zone showed every sign of becoming a major issue in Congress.

The danger of this happening had first appeared in the ECA debates in December 1947 and January 1948, when the demand had been heard (and resisted by Bevin) to stop reparation deliveries to the USSR. This had been extended to asking the question whether it was not in America's interest to restore Germany's economic capacity as the basis of European recovery rather than to reduce it by continuing with dismantling.[3] Even in January, the State Department reported "a tendency in Congress to resort to economic pressure on the UK and France to force them to act in accordance with US policy".[4]

[1] Kennan in the preliminary discussion on 9 July. FRUS 1948 (3) p. 177.
[2] State Department to Douglas, 20 August. FRUS 1948 (3) pp. 476–7.
[3] See the State Department memorandum 20 January 1948. FRUS (2) pp. 711–16.
[4] *Ibid.*, p. 715.

American opinion was responsive to the suggestion powerfully presented by German sources that the real motive behind the British opposition was fear of, and a desire to cripple, Germany as an industrial competitor, a view which fitted well with the belief that imperial preference and the sterling area were also artificial devices to provide protection for a British economy enfeebled by socialism against the natural superiority of American free enterprise.

A Technical Mission set up by the US Cabinet's *ad hoc* committee visited Europe in April and was politely received by the British. Their report, however, called for so drastic a revision of the dismantling programme that the State Department was convinced it would never be accepted by the British and French governments.[1] Bevin was astonished that a report on a matter as full of political implications for America's European partners as the restoration of Germany's industrial power should be framed in purely technical and economic terms. A similar report on the Ruhr steel industry had been prepared by George Wolf, of United States Steel, apparently in complete ignorance of what the Ruhr represented in recent European experience, namely Germany's capacity to wage war. Three years before, Bevin had been censured by the Americans, then bent on destroying Germany's industrial power, for setting too high a ceiling for German steel production; now he was censured for wanting to place any limit on it at all. American policy swung from one extreme to the other, despite the consistent advice of Clay (who knew more about the level of industry than any visiting experts) that the large number of plants now recommended for retention in Germany could not be put into operation and "would be idle for a number of years, and therefore contribute to recovery nowhere, and that this would result in an immediate and unbelievable loss of goodwill in Western Europe."[2]

Marshall was sufficiently impressed by British objections to get the US Cabinet to agree to a scaling down of the Technical Mission's report—only to learn (16 August) that Congress was showing so keen an interest in stopping dismantling that Hoffman, the Administrator of ECA, felt that he had to ask for yet another committee of industrialists to look into the matter.[3]

Both Clay and Douglas protested vigorously at what they regarded as the irresponsible handling of an inflammatory question, only to be told that the pressures of American politics were such that Hoffman felt he had no choice in the matter if the ERP were not to be harmed.[4] Bevin's reply was not received until 7 September. It took the form of a reasoned protest in which he argued that, if reparation deliveries were suspended as Hoffmann required until the new committee under the chairmanship of George Humphrey reported, there

[1] Memorandum by Saltzman, 1 July. FRUS (2) pp. 774–8.
[2] Clay to General Noce, Washington, 1 July 1948. Clay *Papers*, 2, pp. 712–13.
[3] Meeting between Hoffmann, Lovett and State Department officials, 16 August. FRUS 1948 (2) pp. 792–3.
[4] Exchanges between Washington and Douglas and Clay, 28 August–3 September, *ibid.*, pp. 796–803.

was a real chance that it would prove impossible to restore them, and the whole reparations programme would have to be abandoned. All that Marshall could reply was that it was in Britain's interest to co-operate, since members of the key congressional committees had made it clear to Hoffman that no future appropriations for the European Recovery Programme would be made until they could be satisfied that he had examined seriously the possibility of reducing American expenditures by retaining in Germany plants scheduled for reparations.[1]

Bevin did not question that the restoration of the German economy was essential to Europe's recovery. But he believed that it was unnecessary in pursuit of that objective to put an end to reparations and give an overriding priority to rebuilding the industrial strength of Germany as an ally against the Russians over the needs and fears of European nations such as the French and the Dutch who had suffered from German occupation. Britain's own claims were modest. In all the British took £29 M. in reparations, a sum dwarfed by the subsidies and imports of food the British provided for the Germans in their zone. Bevin was voicing a European and not only a British point of view when he said in a statement of the facts about dismantling published on 24 September that the British Government was committed to the disarmament of Germany "and the peace of mind of Germany's neighbours depends upon our honouring the undertaking."[2]

The disagreement between British and Americans over reparations was part of a more general friction arising from the changed relationship between the two countries. No American was in a better position to understand Bevin's difficulties than the Ambassador, Lew Douglas, and twice in August 1948 he sent back to Washington dispatches which put them more effectively than Bevin himself ever did. In the first of these, dated 11 August,[3] Douglas said that he was struck by the undercurrent of feeling against the USA both in and out of the government, and had tried to get to the bottom of it.

"Britain," he wrote, "accepts our assumption of world leadership in face of Russian aggression, . . . But Britain has never before been in a position where her national security and economic fate are so completely dependent on and at mercy of another country's decisions. . . .

"As British see it, given enough help from US and sufficient time, they will reverse adverse economic trends of inter-war years and repair economic damage of two world wars. While they do not expect to regain former relative supremacy, with help from US they are confident that in conjunction with British Commonwealth and Empire they will again become a power to be reckoned with, which, associated with the US, can maintain the balance of power in the world. . . .

"They feel we need them almost as much as they need us; the US can never again

---

[1] Bevin to Marshall, 7 September 1948. FRUS 1948 (2) pp. 804–7; Marshall's reply to Bevin, 16 September, *ibid.*, pp. 808–10.
[2] Oppen, pp. 331–4. This is the fullest statement of the British case.
[3] FRUS 1948 (3) pp. 1113–17.

retreat into isolationism; and that in all the world there is no more stable, predictable or reliable ally than British Commonwealth and Empire led by UK. . . .

"They regard as short-sighted and ill-considered any policy of ours which insists on treating UK on same basis as other Western European powers, or which weakens or fails to strengthen this bloc."

Douglas argued that it followed from their belief in their eventual recovery, that the British thought it essential not to make economic concessions while they were weak which would impede or interfere with this.

"The British have seen us modify our position. For example, they recall our opposition when they moved into Greece in December 1944 to stop Communism, and point to our subsequent acceptance of responsibility when they no longer had the power to hold Greece.

"In the economic field they recall our mistake in insisting, over their objection, on the premature restoration of sterling convertibility in the first American loan agreement."

Douglas went on to summarise the particular causes of anxiety about US policy which Bevin and the British had felt in recent months. At the top of the list was uncertainty about the course of action to be adopted over "the naked question of Berlin if it reaches the point where the issue may be war". Bevin, he added, would react strongly to an act of war committed by the Russians but felt that the Americans did not understand, in the same way as the British and the French, the magnitude of the stakes in the game. This accounted for the great stress he laid on the airlift.

Secondly, Douglas wrote:

"Our criticism that Britain is dragging her heels in re Western Union economic integration. UK feels we have too little awareness of the difficulties, and the length of time it will take to make concrete working arrangements or resolve complicated problem of UK's relationship to Commonwealth. They believe, rightly or wrongly, that nearly all of the constructive as distinct from platitudinous proposals have come from them."

The remaining issues causing the British anxiety all sprang from American failure to understand the seriousness of the UK's economic difficulties: the demand for economic concessions on a *quid pro quo* basis; indifference, often hostility, to the sterling area; insistence on the elimination of economic discrimination by a given date, without regard to circumstances; America's own failure to reduce tariffs or control inflation. Douglas said plainly that the Labour Government had added to its difficulties by the domestic politics it had pursued.

"But all things considered, . . . and compared with other European countries, Britain has done a reasonably respectable job. . . . It has faced its many difficulties, both at home and abroad, with a good deal of courage, determination and ingenuity. Labor and conservative thinking is remarkably alike here especially on foreign policy and foreign economic policy."

In a further dispatch at the end of August Douglas warned "against jumping to the conclusion that there is something wrong simply because the British disagree with us."

"Before taxing the British with obstructionism we must ask ourselves whether or not our own objectives in Europe have been worked out in clear and definite terms, framed realistically to take into account the economic and other complexities of the European picture. . . .

"Perhaps we can use the occasion of your visit to Paris (what a jolly time you will have!) to go into this whole problem.'[1]

The strain under which Bevin was working in 1948 was excessive, and at the beginning of September he was persuaded to take a week's break in Cornwall. Even then he was on the phone to Strang at least once and often more times a day about the negotiations in Berlin. In Bevin's case the anxiety which he shared with other ministers about the country's economic situation was compounded by the continuous pressure under which he found himself from the Americans to follow courses in which he had had no confidence (for example over negotiations with the Russians) or which he regarded as contrary to British interests.

5

The third General Assembly of the UN met in Paris on 21 September and remained in session until 12 November. It began with a series of set speeches from one after another of the leading delegates, with Vyshinsky renewing the two-year-old debate on disarmament. He proposed that each of the five permanent members of the Security Council should cut its armed forces by one-third; that the offensive use of atomic weapons should be banned by treaty and that an international body to supervise and control the implementation of these two proposals should be set up within the framework of the Security Council.

Whether rightly or not, the chances of the Russian proposals being taken at face value were nil: as the voting in the Assembly and its committees shows they consistently failed to attract any votes from outside their own satellite sphere of influence. The only variation was in the number of abstentions. Bevin's reply was given when he addressed the Assembly on 27 September. Characteristically he began with the work of the Economic and Social Council and the specialized agencies such as the ILO which appealed more strongly to him than the political side of the UN. Brushing aside the Soviet charges of American imperialism, he spoke warmly of what Europe owed to the USA: every European country would have come into the Marshall Plan if it had been

---

[1] Douglas to Marshall, 31 August 1948. FRUS (3) pp. 1118–20.

free to do so. Those who did not were forbidden to do so: that, and not any fear of seeing their national sovereignty infringed was the sole reason why they were outside. He criticized the Trusteeship Council for letting itself be used as a platform for political propaganda and, in words that ring oddly today but were spoken without trace of apology or self-consciousness, rejected as false and misguided "the idea that the possession of Colonies is bad in itself, and that colonial Powers cannot be trusted to guide backward peoples".

When he turned to the political record of the United Nations, Bevin described it as "black and depressing". It had been agreed from the beginning that international control of atomic energy was feasible—and only feasible—if the international control agency to be set up was given powers of international ownership, management and inspection. Why then was the Atomic Energy Commission saying that it could no longer continue with its work, why were they still unable to make any advance? The reason, in Bevin's view, was fundamentally simple, and clearly reflected his trade union experience.

"It is that, although they often put forward a point of view which cannot be disregarded and which should be intelligently discussed, the minority in these matters resolutely refuses to accommodate itself, even in the slightest degree, to the wishes and desires of the majority."

This was true not only of atomic energy and disarmament, but of practically all the political activities of the UN.

"This I must say with all the solemnity at my disposal. If the black fury, the incalculable disaster of atomic war, should fall upon us, one Power, by refusing its co-operation in the control and development of these great new powers for the good of humanity, will alone be responsible for the evils which may be visited upon mankind. This lack of co-operation has almost never been absent at any level of international political activity."

Bevin gave as an illustration of this last remark the use of the veto.

"So far as my Government is concerned we have consistently held the view that where the vital interests of countries were in question, the veto is not in itself an evil. It is the abuse of the veto which is the root of the trouble."

An example which could hardly be said to affect the vital interests of any Great Power, was the use of the veto to block the admission of states to the UN when they were acceptable to the majority of the Security Council: he cited Ceylon, Eire, Transjordan and Italy. Four of the five permanent members of the Security Council had already agreed to forgo their privilege in this connection but were unable to proceed because the fifth, the USSR, refused to do so.

It was not surprising, therefore, Bevin continued, if in the light of the Soviet attitude on security, atomic energy and the veto, they looked at Vyshinsky's proposals for disarmament with suspicion.

"We are invited to put our security in the pool with a nation which will not, and is determined not, to reveal to the world what it is doing. This looks to me, I must say, like a proposal to induce the rest of us to disarm while the USSR maintains absolute secrecy about its own military strength and activities."

Quoting from Stalin's *Problems of Leninism* to the effect that the peaceful co-existence of the Soviet Republic and the bourgeois states was impossible —"One or other must triumph in the end. And before that end supervenes a series of frightful collisions will be inevitable"—Bevin asked Vyshinsky how they could be expected to take his proposals at their face value, if no lasting agreement was possible with non-Communist states and everything the Soviet Government did had to be seen as tactics? This was not a question of objecting to the Soviet Union being a Communist state, any more than of objecting, as socialists, to the USA being a capitalist state. The question was whether the Russian Government still believed in Lenin's doctrine or was prepared to accept it as possible—as the British did—that states with different social and economic systems could live peacefully together.

It was important that the West's case should not go by default and none of the other leaders, Marshall, Schuman, Spaak, could speak with the authority and directness which came naturally to Bevin when he was at his best. Nonetheless the real job in Paris was to be done behind the scenes not on the stage and Bevin engaged in an intensive round of talks which lasted from 20 September to 5 October. In the course of these almost every problem in international relations was touched on, but the two most urgent matters were Berlin and Palestine.

When the three foreign ministers met at the Quai d'Orsay on the 20th, Bevin and Schuman were less concerned than Marshall about taking the Berlin dispute to the UN. They wanted to send a further note to the Soviet Government first, in order to put on record, after all the argument, a statement of the Western case and what the Western Powers were asking for in Berlin. Bevin also wanted to discuss what practical steps would need to be taken if they came to a break with the Russians—for example, in keeping the air-lift going and in handling the currency difficulties in Berlin. Marshall was prepared to fall in with their wishes, provided it was accepted that, if the Soviet reply was unsatisfactory, they would refer the issue at once to the UN. Both Bevin and Marshall felt much more confidence in Schuman than they had in Bidault and Bevin's own confidence was fortified by the news Clay brought of the air-lift's success[1].

He passed on the good news to the House of Commons on the 22nd, returning for a brief visit to London after he had reached agreement with the Americans and French on the text of the final note to the Russians. During the last three months, Bevin informed MPs, 200,000 tons of supplies had been

---

[1] British records of the meetings between the three foreign ministers, 20–21 September. FO 800/510/UN/48/36; US record, FRUS 1948 (2) pp. 1173–81.

delivered to Berlin, 60% by the Americans, 40% by the RAF. With the USA bringing in the bigger C54s, which could carry four times as large a load, Bevin announced that even on a pessimistic estimate of the weather, they were sure that they could see the winter through. In fact, although Bevin did not reveal this, Marshall had told him that the limiting factor was American anxiety lest too great a proportion of their air-transport fleet should be exposed to a sudden Russian attack: the limit set represented 30% of their total resources.

Bevin postponed any account of the exchanges with the Russians beyond making clear that the lifting of the blockade was an essential condition of any settlement. He turned to the remarkable impact on German recovery produced by the currency reform. With real money available, absenteeism had fallen and the black market was nearly crippled. Steel production had risen from 377,000 tons a month to 510,000 and coal was nearer to the level of 300,000 tons a day. The German people now saw a future before them and had begun to work with a will. Parallel with the economic recovery was the transfer of political responsibility to the Germans, and Bevin reported that following the recommendation of the London conference a West German government should be established early in the New Year.

The Soviet reply to the tripartite note changed nothing and on 26 September the Foreign Ministers confirmed that they would now place Berlin on the Security Council's agenda. Bevin repeated his old doubts about whether going to the UN would produce anything effective, but he agreed that it might, and that it was necessary for political and psychological reasons.[1] A Soviet proposal to call a meeting of the Council of Foreign Ministers instead and re-open the whole question of Germany "in accordance with the Potsdam Agreement" was rejected. Bevin was adamant in refusing to go back on what had been done in Western Germany; on the other hand, he and Marshall agreed that they would have to be prepared to hold a meeting of the CFM immediately provided the blockade was lifted in advance.[2]

When they met Schuman on the afternoon of the 4th, Bevin showed his firmness in face of French fears. He brought up the disarmament proposal which the Russians had moved in the General Assembly. Bevin declared that he was opposed to all such quantitative proposals, since it was never made clear what was the base-line from which they were calculated; but what really worried him was to hear that the French had an alternative proposal. He told Schuman flatly that he would not be a party to any resolution interfering with the West's resolve to build up their defences. They had gone far enough in disarming in 1946–7 and now had to reverse the process, whatever the fellow travellers might think.[3]

---

[1] British record FO 800/510/UN/48/36; US record FRUS 1948 (2), pp. 1184–6.
[2] Meeting of Bevin and Marshall, 4 October. FO 800/510/UN/48/36; FRUS 1948 (2) pp. 1211–12.
[3] FO 800/502/SU/48/44.

He was equally forthright in answering Schuman when the latter asked what would happen if the blockade were not lifted and bad weather interrupted the air-lift. Bevin was aware that Alexandre Parodi, for example, the French representative on the Security Council, looked on the reference to the UN as an opportunity to secure a settlement with the Russians, at whatever cost provided it removed the risk of war. With this in mind, Bevin was emphatic that they should not think of getting out of Berlin and above all should not allow the Russians to think that they were considering such a possibility. If the Russians believed that the West was contemplating giving way, they would put their price up and the result would be that a settlement would be further off than ever.

Bevin said that what worried him was having to play up to the Germans; but they could not continue to take Russian actions, for example in Czechoslovakia, lying down. He had recently re-read the history of the Yalta Agreement on Poland: they must not repeat the risks which had been taken then. Any sign of weakness would encourage the Russians.

Marshall as a former Chief of Staff added that, while he did not want to lay too much stress on A-bombs, it was their possession of them which enabled the West to discount any question of Soviet military action during the re-building of Western Europe. The Russians had previously thought that US public opinion would not permit A-weapons to be used; they had now changed their minds and were right to do so. He reported that the "Allies'" position was stronger than they realized.

Whether the French were convinced or not, they did not draw back from taking Berlin to the Security Council. The Soviet representative at once objected that the question did not fall within the competence of the Council and should be settled by direct negotiations between the governments concerned. The three Western powers rejected this argument and when the vote was taken on 5 October secured a vote of 9 to 2 in favour of the Security Council considering the matter. The Russian and the Ukrainian representatives thereupon announced that they would take no further part in the discussion of the question.

6

The meeting of the United Nations in Paris gave Bevin the opportunity to talk with a number of delegates from Middle Eastern and Asian countries. Inevitably Palestine dominated the discussions with the former, but the records of the talks show how much Bevin viewed the problems of the area, including Palestine, within the context of the need to contain Russia both in Europe and the Middle East. To the Turkish Foreign Minister he said that the US and the UK would support the Bernadotte Plan. The Arabs could not be expected to welcome it but he would press them strongly to acquiesce in it, and the Americans would look after the Jews. If they did not get agreement now, the Middle East would remain in turmoil and open to Russian penetration. He gave the Foreign Minister a report on the situation in Berlin and the position about the Italian colonies, and when Sadak asked how best Turkey could secure a direct American guarantee—the Turks showed little enthusiasm for a Mediterranean Pact with Greece and Italy—Bevin advised his visitor to wait until the American elections were over. The best starting point was the Brussels Treaty. When they had got US support for that, then they could go on to the Mediterranean and he thought it would be possible to get the USA to renew its guarantee to Turkey and Greece.[1]

Bevin's concern was the defence of the Middle East against attack or at least penetration by the Soviet Union. He explored with both the Egyptian Foreign Minister and the Head of the Iraqi delegation the difficulties which had led to the repudiation of the Sidqi Pasha agreement in one case and the Treaty of Portsmouth in the other. The Egyptian, Khashaba Pasha, told him frankly that it was necessary to reconcile Britain's defence needs (he did not admit they were Egypt's as well) with Egyptian *amour propre*, and to do this by some other means than British occupation. Bevin insisted that a British base in Egypt was essential, but said it was a joint problem to which the best approach was from the military-technical point of view before the politicians were brought in. The Iraqi assured him that the repudiation of the Portsmouth Treaty was due to the way it had been handled by the Iraqi politicians, and they agreed that the military clauses of the treaty could be looked at again to meet Iraqi objections. When his visitor went on, however, to express Arab disappointment at Bevin's support for the Bernadotte Plan, and press for a delay in its acceptance by the UN, Bevin told him roundly that this was the best solution the Arabs could hope for in the circumstances. If it had not been for the truce which he had done his best to promote, the Arabs would have been defeated. Marshall was under attack from the Jews for supporting the Bernadotte Plan and was, in fact, a good friend of the Arabs. Neither the British nor the Americans got much credit for it, but they had done their best for the Arabs.[2]

The tone in which Bevin talked to Arab representatives is well caught in a note which he dictated after seeing the Lebanese Foreign Minister:

"I explained that we had to consider the Middle East in the light of the general world situation and of the overriding problem of Soviet expansion. . . . We were collaborating closely with the U.S.A. and the only place where our policies tended to differ was Palestine. This was owing to the pressure put on the American administration by the Jewish population of the U.S.A. I had done my best to support the Arab countries before fighting had broken out and I had supported the cease fire because our information did not suggest that the Arabs were likely to meet with much success. I had

---

[1] Bevin's talk with Sadak, 27 September. FO 800/510/UN/48/36.
[2] Bevin's talk with Khashaba Pasha, 27 September, and with Sayid Najib ar Rawi, 29 September, *ibid.*

done all I could to prevent the White House lifting the arms embargo and offering loans to the Jews. Finally we had decided to support the Mediator's proposals as the least disadvantageous solution which would at least establish definite frontiers which could be maintained."[1]

When the Lebanese minister urged Bevin not to take the initiative in promoting the Bernadotte Plan in the UN, the latter told him that if they delayed, hostilities would be resumed and the Arabs would be worse off in face of American arms for the Jews. To the Iranian Foreign Minister, whom he saw on 1 October, Bevin said that he was no longer afraid that an incident in Berlin might lead to war between the Great Powers. Four or five weeks before, perhaps, but now that the Western Powers had shown they were determined and the question was before the UN, he did not think the Russians would let an incident occur or, if it did, would let it develop dangerously. There was more danger, he remarked, in the Russians following Leninist theory and adopting a calmer policy which would lull the rest of the world into a false sense of security. He urged the Iranians to recognize the importance of social and economic development. The greatest Soviet propaganda weapon was bad social conditions and the best defence against Communism lay in constant industrial and agricultural improvement to raise the standard of living.[2]

Bevin's attention as Foreign Minister was focused on Europe and the Middle East, but he took the links with the Commonwealth seriously and regarded these as the basis of the UK's claim to be regarded as a power with world-wide interests. It was at the height of the Berlin Blockade, for example, that Donald MacLachlan, then Foreign Editor of *The Economist*, recalled a group of journalists being summoned to meet Bevin and finding, to their surprise, that he wanted to talk, not about Berlin or the Middle East, but about Africa and its importance to the rest of the world. Bevin still saw Africa in colonial terms as a source of additional strength to the economies of Western Europe. African independence was the agenda of the next generation. But Asia was already in turmoil. The great question in the autumn of 1948 was, what would happen in China, where the final stage in the civil war was about to produce a Communist triumph. This final stage was played out without Western intervention, but in a paper which he circulated to the Cabinet[3] in December, Bevin set out some of the possible implications in the rest of Asia, including Hong Kong and Malaya. The Cabinet agreed that they could only wait and see what would emerge. Bevin added that the point he was constantly re-iterating to the Americans was that the West must avoid the Communist success in China being repeated in the Middle East.

In Southern Asia, Britain was still involved in what was happening. After Indian independence Bevin took part in continuing negotiations with the

---

[1] Bevin's talk with the Lebanese Foreign Minister, 5 October 1948, *ibid.*
[2] 1 October 1948. *ibid.*
[3] CP (48) 299, discussed by the Cabinet on 13 December. CM 80 (48).

Indians and Pakistanis about Kashmir. He was particularly anxious not to appear to favour one side rather than the other[1] and tried unsuccessfully to get the two new members of the Commonwealth to reach a settlement. Nehru and Zafrullah Khan, the Pakistan Foreign Minister, came to Europe for the UN session and the meeting of Commonwealth countries which (with India, Pakistan and Ceylon attending for the first time as independent members) opened in London on 11 October. Bevin had several meetings with both but, at the end of October, could only tell Marshall (with whom he took care to keep in touch) that he was doubtful if Nehru wanted to settle. At the same time he fended off a proposal from Attlee that the American Secretary of State should be asked to act as mediator, a suggestion Bevin was sure Marshall would reject, in view of his experience in China.[2]

The dispute between the Netherlands and the embryonic Indonesian Republic was another issue referred to the Security Council by two members of the Commonwealth, India and Australia, both of whom were strongly critical of the Dutch. American opinion, traditionally anti-colonial, went in the same direction. The Dutch, however, isolated and in an uncompromising mood, were fellow members of the Western European Union set up by the Brussels Pact and Bevin was placed in the awkward position of trying to mediate between some of Britain's closest associates with little thanks from any of them. This was another topic for discussion in Paris, where Bevin promised Dirk Stikker, the Dutch Foreign Minister, to do what he could to bring the Dutch and American positions closer together.[3]

It was always in Bevin's mind that, if the Russians and the Cominform found the expansion of Communism blocked in Europe and the Middle East, they would pay greater attention to the opportunities offered in Southern Asia and even Africa. In a note to Attlee, dated 13 May 1948, he mentioned the possibility of the Pakistanis looking to the Soviet Union out of resentment at British support for India and Kashmir.[4] In Indonesia, Sjarifuddin, head of the Republican Government until early in 1948, announced that he had been a secret member of the Communist Party since 1935 and in September joined an (unsuccessful) Communist *coup d'état* aimed at taking over the movement for independence. In Burma, separate insurrections by the rival Red Flag and White Flag Communist organizations contributed to the widespread disorder with which the Burmese Government was confronted in its first year of independence. The most striking case for the British was Malaya which was

---

[1] On 6 January 1948 Sir Orme Sargent wrote to Attlee to say that Bevin was worried lest the British should appear to be siding with India. With the difficult situation in Palestine, they must be on their guard against aligning Islam against them. FO 800/470/IND/48/1.
[2] Bevin's meeting with Marshall in Paris, 27 October 1948, *ibid.*, IND/48/33. On the same day, however, Bevin saw Nehru and noted his impression that the Indian leader was looking for a settlement more seriously than he had thought a week before. Most of their meeting was, in fact, taken up with the discussion of Indonesia. Bevin to Attlee 1 November 1948, *ibid.*, IND/48/36.
[3] Bevin's meeting with Stikker on 1 October. FO 800/510/UN/48/36.
[4] FO 800/470/IND/48/24.

still under British rule. The Malayan Communist Party's members were almost entirely Chinese and were stimulated to action by the approaching victory of the Communists in China. After being defeated in an attempt to use control of the trade unions as a way to capture power, they had taken to the jungle and launched a series of attacks against plantations and miners aimed (as in Greece as well as China) at subjecting enough territory to justify the proclamation of a Communist Republic. Their campaign had sufficient success to force the Malayan Government to declare a state of emergency in July 1948 and fly in additional forces including several hundred former members of the Palestine Police. Thanks to the support of the Malayan population, the British counter measures proved effective in defeating and eventually destroying the Communist threat. But this was not at all certain when Bevin spoke in the House of Commons on 15 September.

Bevin refused to agree that it was the grant of independence which had led to the disorders in Burma and expressed confidence that the Burmese Government would master its difficulties. But he endorsed the view that "throughout the whole of S.E. Asia there is a Cominform and Communist plan to eliminate from that territory every Western association of trade and of everything else. . . . Even if we suppress it in Malaya, as we shall, it may break out in Africa or somewhere else tomorrow". Bevin spoke of an attempt to use civil war as an instrument of policy, and was emphatic that they would meet it with determination in Malaya, but he pointed to the strain this put on the Armed Forces.

In fact the emergency in Malaya, on top of those in Germany and the Middle East, tipped the scale in convincing ministers that more resources would have to be devoted to defence, always an unpopular argument with the Labour Party but one which Morrison admitted would have to be accepted.[1] Bevin's support for the Chiefs of Staff was assured and he outraged the Opposition (with evident enjoyment) by suggesting that they, and Churchill in particular, were as much responsible as the Labour backbenchers for insisting on too rapid a demobilization of the Forces at the end of the War. At the meeting of the Defence Committee on 18 August, despite the inadequate forces in the Middle East (1 division and 1 brigade), the Committee decided to send an additional brigade to Malaya. But more men as well as more money had to be found. Conscription was always a sensitive subject for the Labour Party and Bevin, as the wartime Minister of National Service, played a crucial role in the decision to delay the release of conscripts by three months and extend the period of national service from 12 to 18 months.[2] By halting the rundown the overall strength of the Forces could be held at 790,000 instead of 716,000 on 31 March 1949 and expenditure on arms production in 1949 was

[1] Morrison in the House of Commons, 14 September 1948.
[2] See the minutes of the meetings of the Defence Committee in the second half of 1948, from the 12th on 21 July to the 23rd on 8 December.

raised by a third. Bevin could retort to those who criticized the British for dragging their feet that in 1948–9 they were spending 20 p.c. more on defence than the rest of the Brussels Powers put together and a greater share of their national income proportionately than the Americans.

CHAPTER 16

A Western plan emerges

I

Their visit to Paris in the autumn of 1948 brought home to both Bevin and Marshall the key position of the French in any European recovery and the demoralization produced by fear of war, fear of Germany, fear of Communism and the class war, fear of inflation and economic collapse. After many weeks without any government, the Queuille Government, in which Schuman was Foreign Minister, was widely regarded as the last chance for a coalition based on the parties of the political centre, the Socialists and MRP. If it fell, the general belief was that de Gaulle would come to power and that this would polarize the conflict with the Communists. The Communists, on the other hand, were set on proving that it was impossible to govern France without them and forcing their way back into the coalition. Vyshinsky, according to a French Ministry of the Interior report, approved this line of action in talks with the Communist leaders Duclos and Fajon on 25 September, promising Soviet financial support for the miners' strike on which the Communists pinned their hopes of bringing the country to a standstill. He told them that the Soviet Government regarded it as essential for the Communists to get back into the French government and prevent France being used as a base for the American domination of Europe and the preparation of war against the USSR.[1] On their side the Americans made it clear that, if the Communists did return to power, this would mean the end of US aid to France.[2] American policy remained one of supporting the centre coalition and giving no more encouragement to de Gaulle on the Right than to the Communists on the Left.

Bevin followed the same line, urging the Socialists to stay in the coalition. During his September visit he saw Ramadier, the Socialist Minister for

[1] The report was shown to the US Ambassador and sent to Washington on 20 October. FRUS 1948 (3) pp. 661–2.
[2] Caffery, the US Ambassador, reporting the statement made by the Counsellor of the Embassy, W. R. Tyler, to Devinat, Secretary of State to the Président du Conseil, 2 October, *ibid.*, p. 661.

Defence, as well as Schuman and argued that, while nothing could be arranged with the USA until after the elections, the French should get on with building up the military strength of Western Union. He told Ramadier they could do nothing as yet to align the responsibilities of the three Allied Commanders for the defence of Germany with the planning of the Brussels Pact organization, but he was pleased with the American decision to equip the three French divisions in Germany.[1]

The proposal which made the least appeal to him was the French initiative proposed by Schuman and Ramadier, and backed by Spaak (all of whom had been at The Hague meeting) in favour of a European Assembly.

Ramadier argued the case on the grounds of the need to appeal to the French public and especially parliamentary opinion, in face of incessant Communist propaganda. French opinion had seized avidly on the Marshall offer but had then flagged and needed reviving with another big objective. Sooner or later they would find that there were limits to what could be done practically without coming up against the barrier of national sovereignty: it was best for governments to take the lead and prepare public opinion in advance for breaking with such an out-of-date idea. Schuman argued that the French had to take some such initiative not only because public opinion in the USA and other countries besides France attached importance to the idea, but because it would make it easier to associate the Germans with such an assembly.[2]

Bevin argued, against this, that there were a lot of things which needed doing before they set up an Assembly and that they should concentrate on practical measures instead of getting caught up with European constitution making. "It was dangerous to launch big ideas and then to disappoint people."

In reporting back to Attlee on his talk with Ramadier, he reiterated his opposition to a European Assembly. For the sake of action with an immediate propaganda appeal, they would risk sharp disagreement on real questions of policy involving a surrender of sovereignty and hence would risk retarding the common cause. Although Bevin did not say so in so many words, he plainly thought that the French talked easily about abandoning national sovereignty because they had so little to lose.

On the other hand, Bevin wrote, he wanted to do something to help the French Socialists and to take the wind out of the sails of the critics at home and abroad who were always saying that the Labour Government was not going fast enough towards the unification of Europe. He suggested that each year, after the Assembly had met—say in January—the Western Union Prime Ministers accompanied by their leading colleagues should meet as a Council of Western Europe with the power to consider reports and take initiatives. This would provide a "Cabinet" for Western Europe with a permanent chairman serving for 2–3 years as President and a Secretary General. If it were to have a

---

[1] Bevin to FO, 3 and 4 October. FO 800/460/EUR/48/46.
[2] Bevin talked with Ramadier on 25 September, *ibid.*, EUR/48/35; with Spaak on the 29th, *ibid.*, EUR/48/10 and with Schuman on 2 October *ibid.*, EUR/48/42–3.

chance of succeeding, such a Council would need to have real problems submitted to it, and Bevin suggested as examples, the use of credit balances held by one country in another, migration, and a Customs Union. He admitted that what he was suggesting meant in effect a confederation but it would be better to avoid the name and call it a union of Western Europe. He asked for a discussion in Cabinet. Attlee accepted this, adding however: "While I agree on the need for a further advance to Western Union, I must confess that your proposal does not attract me very much."[1]

When he put his idea of a council of ministers to Spaak, Bevin told him that

"He wanted to build up in a traditional British way a sort of unwritten constitution in Western Europe in which Ministers could meet and then report back to Parliament; and in which public opinion could put forward to Governments resolutions and proposals. Proceeding in this way the people and Parliaments would be linked closer together."[2]

To Schuman he said British opinion would not accept a European Assembly which would not be responsible to anyone. A Council on the other hand made up of representatives of governments would. An Assembly could only pass general resolutions and do nothing; ministers could act. Schuman was not impressed. It was "really a Commonwealth of Western Union with an unwritten constitution", and very different from French ideas.[3]

The difference of views was not pressed by either side at this stage, but Bevin showed he was aware of the criticism of holding back European development when he told Spaak that he was very disappointed at the failure to produce a European Payments Union. As a result, the Marshall Plan was losing its effectiveness with public opinion. The British, he declared, were willing to do all they could provided they were not asked for fresh dollar or gold commitments. He showed the same concern in a cable about inter-European payments to Cripps, who was in Washington. "The whole thing has got into such a rut with finnicky decisions that the great spirit and purpose of Western Union is fading." He urged Cripps to do all he could to get the enterprise back on the right lines.[4]

Dewey, the Republican candidate in the presidential election, already vying with Truman for the Jewish vote, now came out in a speech at Salt Lake City threatening to hold up appropriations under the Marshall Plan if Europe did not federate quickly. Britain, as usual, was the villain of the piece, and when Bevin met Marshall on 4 October he burst out saying that the UK was not to be treated like a small country or accused of dragging her feet. It was the British who had taken the initiative in bringing Europe together. Marshall countered, with a touch of malice perhaps, with the remark that Churchill's

---

[1] Bevin to Attlee, 26 September; Attlee's reply 28 September. FO 800/460/EUR/48/36 & 38.
[2] Bevin's talk with Spaak, 29 September, *ibid.*, EUR/48/10.
[3] Bevin's talk with Schuman, 2 October, *ibid.*, EUR/48/42–3.
[4] Bevin to Cripps, 29 September 1948, *ibid.*, EUR/48/39.

influence in the USA was very great and that his Hague speech had made a big impact. Personally, he added, he was puzzled how Churchill could reconcile his call for European union with his insistence on the Commonwealth and on Britain's special relationship with the USA. Bevin declared that Churchill did not speak for Britain and had ignored the Brussels Treaty, the NATO discussions and the Commonwealth. "We were doing as much as British public opinion would stand for at the moment," and he referred to the trade unions which had to be carried with them. He outlined to Marshall his idea for a West European Cabinet, claiming once again that it was he who had first launched the idea of European union at the TUC in 1927. But he greatly objected to the suggestion that American appropriations should be used as a lever: this had really stung the British and was bad for US–British relations. Marshall's rejoinder was unanswerable: he did not write Dewey's speeches or control the American press.[1]

Bevin got little encouragement for his scheme of a Council of Ministers of Western Europe but he persisted, writing again to Attlee on 18 October and asking him to put it to the Dominions conference then meeting in London. He now added a proposal to bring in Western Germany and Italy and to set up a permanent secretariat. In a wordy sentence which nonetheless expressed his views clearly, he wrote:

"It would go a long way towards spiking the guns of those who wish to impose a constitution and who criticise H.M.G. for not going fast enough in the direction of Western Union; while at the same time preserving in effect the full sovereignty of the participating states and in reality basing the whole new system on the so-called 'empirical' approach rather than on the alternative basis of the adoption of some formal 'constitution'."[2]

Nothing he had seen or heard in Paris had changed Bevin's conviction that Europe was still a house of cards without the strength or the will to restore itself. He did not believe that rhetorical declarations about a United States of Europe would do anything to provide either. The key was to create a sense of security against the greatest fear of all, that of repeating the experience of war and occupation, and that could only come by bringing in the New World to restore the shattered balance of the Old through a North Atlantic, not purely European, defence pact. This had been his objective from the beginning, but, with the American elections in the balance, it was impossible for him either to say anything about the planning which had already taken place or to carry it further. To the world at large, therefore, he appeared to be putting obstacles in the way of the European Union which had been launched with such éclat at The Hague—without making any attempt to provide an alternative.

After the secret talks in Washington had produced the draft plan for NATO

[1] Bevin's talk with Marshall, 4 October, *ibid.*, EUR/460/48/48–9.
[2] Bevin to Attlee, 18 October, *ibid.*, EUR/48/50.

completed on 9 September, the best Bevin could produce in the way of a timetable was to propose that he should put it to the Defence Committee of the Cabinet (not the full Cabinet) on 8 October and thereafter to the Consultative Council of the Brussels Powers when this met on 26 October. Informal consultations with the Scandinavians and others could also take place but, as the State Department insisted, nothing more could be done to bring NATO into existence until the result of the November presidential election was known.[1]

The informal consultations showed up the weakness of Western Europe as anything more than a geographical expression. It was this weakness from which Schuman, Spaak and Monnet drew the conclusion that it was essential to merge national sovereignties into a European Community. Bevin drew the opposite conclusion that Western Europe, at least in the immediate future, had not the strength to do anything except as part of a larger grouping, and that what mattered was not to merge national sovereignties but to find a basis of power, which could only be in North America.

Talks with the Scandinavians had been going on throughout 1948. The root of the problem was Swedish insistence on sticking to their policy of neutrality. In June Bevin had seen the Swedish Ambassador and warned him against the Swedes pressing Norway and Denmark to adopt the same policy.[2] But the Norwegians and Danes were very reluctant to break with the Swedes (who were unique amongst the smaller European nations in the strength of their armed forces) and both Lange, the Norwegian Foreign Minister, and his Danish colleague, Rasmussen, came to see Bevin in late September to urge him to stop any approach being made by the USA at least for another three or four months. There was no doubt of Lange's conviction that the Scandinavian states ought to be part of any Atlantic system, but he pressed for more time to try and avoid a split with the Swedes, and Bevin promised to use his good offices with the Americans to postpone forcing the issue.[3]

In Southern Europe, the Portuguese Government was informed (7 October) that a proposal for an Atlantic security pact had been drawn up and that an approach would, in due course, be made to Portugal inviting her to join it.[4] The response was not encouraging. A press statement obviously inspired by Salazar (30 October) spoke of efforts to organize the defence of the West as very confused and advised scepticism about reports of Portugal's joining any such Pact. The American Ambassador reported that the Portuguese believed that, with Spain excluded and with France in its present state of weakness, plans for the defence of Western Europe could not be taken seriously.[4]

Any hint of including Spain remained an explosive issue in both Britain and

[1] 18 June 1948, *ibid.*, EUR/48/24.
[2] Bevin saw Rasmussen on 25 September 1948 and Lange on the 28th. FO 800/510/UN/48/36. Marshall saw the Swedish Foreign Minister, Unden, in Paris on 14 October but failed to shake his belief in a policy of neutrality. FRUS 1948 (3) pp. 264–6.
[3] US Ambassador's report from Lisbon, 8 October, *ibid.*, pp. 262–3.
[4] *Ibid.*, 8 November, pp. 1008–1111.

France. A House of Representatives amendment to the Economic Co-operation Act making Spain eligible to take part in the European Recovery Programme produced a strong protest from Bevin. The amendment was dropped in the final version of the Act and Marshall reassured Bevin that the view of the US Government remained that it was for the European countries setting up the OEEC to decide whether or not to include Spain.[1] Nonetheless, members of the Republican Party continued to express the opinion not only that Spain ought to be part of any ERP, but that with a strong army, well-placed airfields and a key position in relation to the defence of Western Europe and the Mediterranean—not to mention Franco's record of anti-Communism—the Spaniards ought obviously to be part of any Western defence pact. When Senator Gurney, chairman of the Senate's Armed Services Committee, flanked by liaison officers of the US Army, Navy and Air Force, paid a call on Franco and publicly recommended restoring diplomatic relations, there were sharp reactions in London and Paris. Bevin and Schuman agreed that the last thing they wanted was another UN debate on Spain which the Poles on the one hand and the Latin Americans on the other were eager to promote. This would only divide the Western Powers.[2] "It was low on the agenda," Bevin told Marshall, "and we should conspire to get it in the last position." There could be no solution without a change of regime and they should let sleeping dogs lie.[3]

Italy's former colonies were another divisive issue on which British views clashed with those of the French as well as the Italians. The differences were discussed in a series of inconclusive talks between Americans, British and French during the summer and with the Russians in the meetings of the Foreign Ministers' deputies.[4] The British were willing to agree that Somaliland should be placed under Italian trusteeship but not Eritrea (which they thought should be joined with Ethiopia) or Libya.[5] The latter was the important issue. Bevin had always wanted a British trusteeship for Cyrenaica. This was acceptable to the local population in preference to an Italian regime and would allow the British to build bases as an alternative if they had to withdraw from Egypt. The Americans and in the end the French too were prepared to accept the British claim, but there was no agreement about the other half of Libya, Tripolitania. The French wanted to see the Italians given trusteeships for all their former colonies, but particularly for Tripolitania where they feared that any move encouraging hopes of independence would have immediate repercussions in their own neighbouring colony of Tunisia.

---

[1] The amendment was moved by Rep. Alvin E. O'Konski, of Wisconsin. Bevin's protest was made on 1 April. For Marshall's reply, FRUS 1948 (3) p. 1036.
[2] Bevin's talk with Schuman, 2 October 1948. FO 800/460/EUR/48/42-3.
[3] Bevin's meeting with Marshall, 4 October 1948, *ibid.*, EUR/48/48-9. See also the report of Marshall's meeting with Bevin and Schuman, the same day, FRUS (3) pp. 1053-4.
[4] The most useful record of these talks is in FRUS (3) pp. 891–969, covering the whole year 1948.
[5] Discussion in the Defence Committee, 30 July, 14th meeting; 6 August, 15th meeting. Bevin put the British view to Douglas on 6 August. FRUS 1948 (3) pp. 936-9.

The British (with an ear to Arab opinion) were equally strongly opposed. The best that could be done was to agree to postpone any decision, at least until after the US elections, leaving the British to continue their *de facto* occupation.

It is arguable that no better solution was available but inevitably it led to resentment in Italy where the blame for Italy's failure to recover any of her colonies was laid on British hostility and American unwillingness to intervene. That in turn affected Italian attitudes towards joining any Western Union, particularly when the Italian Communist Party was campaigning strongly in favour of Italian neutrality. This did not worry Bevin unduly: in the long run he agreed with the Americans and the French in regarding the Italians as natural members of any Western grouping, but in the short run looked on them as more of a liability than an asset and was opposed to paying a price in treaty revision or the return of Italy's former colonies for their adhesion to either the Brussels Pact or NATO.

Marshall planned to visit Rome in order to encourage de Gasperi but before he could do so he found it necessary to fly back hurriedly from Paris to Washington. Press reports of a Truman plan to send Chief Justice Vinson to Moscow for an informal exchange of views with Stalin had caused an uproar. Truman, bent on trumping Wallace's electoral appeal to American Liberals as the friend of peace, had paid scant attention to the effect his move would have on opinion among America's allies. Bevin resigned himself to such alarms as part of the American democratic process, but only after Marshall had acted quickly to get Truman to abandon the idea.

The Vinson episode could be regarded as an aberration in American policy. More serious from Bevin's point of view was Hoffmann's demand that, until his latest committee had reported, all dismantling should be halted. Clay, Douglas and most of the American representatives in Europe as well as the State Department agreed with Bevin. Clay cabled from Berlin that nothing could do more to encourage resistance among the Germans to paying reparations at all, and Douglas from London that if the USA went back on its obligations to carry out the reparations programme this "might very seriously and adversely affect our ability to establish and maintain a united and solid front among the Western Powers".[1] However, Bevin's meeting with Marshall in Paris (28 September), his repetition of his arguments in another letter to Marshall (1 October) and in a lengthy discussion with Hoffmann and Harriman in London on 13 October, failed to shake Hoffmann's contention that, if Congress and the American public realized that dismantling was still going on in the British zone, "the entire E.C.A. appropriation would be placed in jeopardy".

"They did not wish to appear to be pointing a pistol at Mr Bevin's head; they were interested in one thing only and that was European recovery which was precisely the

---

[1] Clay to Draper, 28 August. FRUS 1948 (2) pp. 798–800; Douglas to Marshall, 1 September, *ibid.*, 800–1.

same thing Mr Bevin was interested in . . . If dismantling could not be stopped, Mr Hoffmann and Ambassador Douglas could not answer for the consequences."

Bevin's reply that US policy had swung round by 180 degrees, while he had consistently argued for an annual German steel production of 10.7 million tons, made no impression. "It is a squalling kid you have left in my lap", he complained. "It is a very difficult political situation." It might be, but Bevin knew he had to find a way out of it. At the end of the day, a face-saving formula was produced which substituted the removal of key parts for dismantling plants by taking them to pieces. This Bevin finally undertook to put to the British Cabinet and to the French Government. Three days later he wrote to Douglas to say that he had secured agreement and that no more dismantling, in particular no more dismantling of blast furnaces, would take place until the Humphrey Committee had finished its investigation.[1]

2

The third meeting of the Brussels Powers' foreign ministers took place in Paris on 25 and 26 October. Schuman presided and showed himself a much more confident and less prickly chairman than Bidault.[2]

The first item on the agenda was the report of the Committee of Ambassadors on the Washington talks and Bevin at once posed the question, on the answer to which his whole concept of British foreign policy turned, were they now prepared to conclude some form of Atlantic Pact? Answering his own question, Bevin argued that a guarantee of the Brussels Pact by the USA or a presidential declaration of support was not enough. Great Britain could no longer play the role she had played in 1914 and 1940: in any future war everybody would have to be in from the beginning.

Spaak admitted that there had been initial hesitations in Belgium but reported that public opinion was now ready for what was seen as the logical next step after the Brussels Pact and OEEC. Stikker and Bech agreed, and Schuman capped the argument by saying that the French saw the Brussels and Atlantic Pacts not as alternatives, but as supplementary.

Again taking the lead, Bevin argued against bringing in any other power at this stage. If the Italians were invited, the Greeks and Turks would press to be asked, and there would be a similar delay if they approached the Scandin-

---

[1] The British documentation of these transactions is to be found in (1) three reports by Bevin to the Cabinet, CP (48) 203, 15 August 1948; CP (48) 234, 14 October; CP (48) 259, 8 November; and (2) the Cabinet minutes for 16 August, CM 56 (48); 15 October, CM 63 (48); and 18 November, CM 74 (48). A report of Bevin's meeting with Marshall on 28 September is in FO 800/510/UN/48/36, and a letter from Bevin to Robertson reporting on his meeting with Hoffmann, 13 October in FO 800/467/GER/48/75. The American documentation is to be found in FRUS 1948 (2) pp. 796–852.
[2] British records of the Third Consultative Council divided by topic in FO 800/487/PA/48/90; 460/EUR/48/52–4; 447/CONF/48/4–7; 455/DEF/48/59–60.

avians. They should take no final decision on who would eventually join, but press ahead now with the Brussels group of five, the USA and Canada. This too met with general assent and Spaak proposed that the existing committee of ambassadors should get on with drawing up a treaty on the basis of the Washington draft of 9 September.

The contentious ground was reached on the second day when Schuman, supported by Spaak, argued that the task of creating European unity could not be left to private organizations but must be taken up by Governments. A gesture was called for and he proposed a preparatory conference, the members of which would be nominated by national Parliaments.

Preparatory for what? was Bevin's immediate question. He had still had no answer to his repeated inquiry what a European Assembly was supposed to do. Was it a constituent assembly which would settle down to draft a constitution for Europe or a sort of European UN? British policy, he repeated, was to bring nations together into a closer association by the pursuit of common policies. With their Commonwealth experience, they thought it unwise to try to formalize through a constitution the links which already existed. If what was at the back of people's minds was such a Constitution, it would be better to say so plainly. A merging of sovereignty might weaken rather than strengthen Western Europe.

Once an Assembly was set up, it would become a pressure group for a United Europe, would aggravate political divisions and cause a lot of problems for Governments which would be bound to take notice of its recommendations. Bevin declared himself unimpressed by the argument that the Americans wanted such a development: he was used to American pressure and they should not be too much influenced by it. They had, in fact, achieved much since he had launched the idea of Western Union in January and it would be irresponsible to place their fate in the hands of parliamentarians who had hitherto distinguished themselves by impracticable proposals.

His own proposal, as they knew, was for a European Council of Ministers. He would be willing to see Germany associated with it, as well as Italy and Austria. It could meet quickly, in the New Year if they so wished, and would have the great virtue of keeping developments in the hands of governments. He suggested they should set up a small preparatory commission of eighteen appointed by governments which would take both suggestions into account, his own for a Council of Europe and Schuman's for an Assembly, meet in private and report to governments.

The rest of the meeting was taken up with the sort of consultation between governments which Bevin thought worth any amount of parliamentary debate and constitution-making. He and Schuman reported to the others on the position in Berlin, Bevin arguing that they could not afford to make concessions, divorcing it from other and larger issues and supposing that if they compromised over Berlin this would not affect the balance between East and West as a whole.

From Berlin they turned to the future of the Italian colonies. Bevin made no bones about the British wanting the trusteeship of Cyrenaica and not being willing to agree to postpone a settlement much longer—except in the case of Tripolitania, which it would be disastrous to return to the Italians. This was precisely what Schuman feared. They must either settle all the Italian colonies or postpone a decision for all of them: they could not exclude Tripolitania, which the French thought should be returned to the Italians.

Bevin admitted, when they turned to Palestine, that he was by no means sure that the US government would continue to support the Bernadotte Plan under pressure of the rivalry between Dewey and Truman for the Jewish vote in the elections. Spaak and Schuman were sympathetic but had little faith that the Bernadotte Plan would be accepted or could be enforced.

Reading the records now, it is hard to avoid the impression that Bevin could easily have gone along with the others in agreeing to call a European Assembly, taking it, in Schuman's words, as a "gesture" and calculating that it was unlikely to do more than provide a sounding board. It is very doubtful if any of the others expected it to do more. No doubt, concern at the use Churchill made of it to embarrass the Labour Government coloured Bevin's view; but the main reason was the conviction, which he made no attempt to conceal, that this was a wrong turning not only for the UK but for the rest of Europe, the pursuit of an illusion which would distract them from the real tasks to be undertaken. This was the argument he used again with Ramadier, the French Minister of War, in a talk the same evening.[1] The propaganda effect would soon be lost and any attempt to draft a constitution would produce disunity. Europe had to be built on a solid basis of economics and defence. The Frenchman argued that ordinary people needed illusions. "If you spoke only of armaments, they did not like them, and if only of economics, they did not understand them." But Bevin was unimpressed: a European Assembly would raise false hopes only to disappoint them when it proved ineffectual. Bevin made a full report to the Cabinet on 4 November on the discussions and secured approval for the conclusion of a North Atlantic Treaty on the lines of the September draft and for pursuing further his proposal of a Council of Ministers of Western Europe.[2]

Although the French had agreed to go on with the NATO talks, it was clear from Ramadier's remarks that they regarded any Atlantic Pact as a matter for the future which did nothing to provide security in a situation where 35 Soviet divisions (with a similar number in reserve) greatly outnumbered the handful of divisions of which the Western Powers disposed. Ramadier insisted that what mattered was what the Americans were prepared to do now; the British and French might need to press them for an answer at once and should do it

---

[1] Bevin's talk with Ramadier, 26 October. FO 800/465/FR/48/17.
[2] Bevin's report to the Cabinet, CP (48) 249, 2 November 1948; and the Cabinet discussion on 4 November, CM 68 (48).

together, not singly. Bevin tried to reassure him by pointing out that the American elections would soon be over and it would then be possible to move quickly on the Atlantic Pact. Canada had already come in and he expressed satisfaction with the Commonwealth conference which had given strong support on questions of defence. He agreed that they had a formidable task and little time in which to achieve it, but repeated his belief that, if the Western Powers showed energy and foresight in organizing themselves, there would be no war.

Ramadier wanted to bring in the Italians, but Bevin turned a favourite French argument against him: it was better to build on the Brussels Powers and equip their forces than to spread limited resources too thinly over the whole of Europe. Faced with a prospect of reducing the amount of American equipment available for the French Army, Ramadier dropped the Italians and agreed that the essential problem was the defence of the Rhine.

There was no doubt that this was the view of Montgomery, who had been appointed C.-in-C. of the Brussels Pact forces at the end of September. In a memorandum drawn up on the same day as Bevin saw Ramadier, Montgomery defined the strategy for the defence of Western Europe as (a) to hold the Rhine from Holland to the Alps until US aid made it possible for the Allies to fight back and recover lost territory, and (b) to hold the land-bridge between Asia and Africa in the Middle East and keep the Russians out of Africa.

If there was any question of withdrawal from the Rhine, it would have to be towards the South West. Montgomery said bluntly that Italy did not belong to Western Union and there were no plans to fight on Italian soil. Instead, they would seek to hold the gap between the Alps and the sea on the Franco–Italian border.[1]

The joker in the pack in planning the defence of the southern flank was Yugoslavia. The publication of the correspondence between the Russian and Yugoslav Communist Parties confirmed Western beliefs about the heavy-handed way in which the Soviet Government treated its East European satellites, but gave no clue to the way in which the quarrel would develop. At the end of July 1948 an international conference to settle the control of navigation on the Danube met in Belgrade. The Soviet delegation was led by Vyshinsky and the Yugoslavs took their place among the six East European delegations which voted as a bloc under Russian leadership. For once the Russians had the majority and used it to reject by 7 votes to 3 all 28 of the amendments proposed by the British, American and French delegations. The result was to guarantee Soviet control of the river at least as far upstream as the Austrian frontier, with no overt sign of Yugoslav misgivings. Tito remained in office despite the Soviet anathema and there was no indication of any attempt to come to terms with Moscow. But there was no indication either, apart from one or two soundings, of any wish to come to terms with the West, and Bevin

---

[1] 26 October 1948. FO 800/454/DEF/48/61.

and Marshall agreed that for the present the wise course was to let the situation develop without any attempt to exploit it.

The obvious place in which to look for the effect of the Soviet–Yugoslav quarrel to appear was Greece. In one of the first contacts after the split "a high-ranking Yugoslav official" had told a member of the American Embassy staff that the Yugoslavs were

"Extremely anxious to liquidate the Greek situation as soon as possible since Greek refugees placed intolerable burden on Yugoslav economy. He added that he felt quite certain U.S.S.R. was not now particularly interested in Greece. When our Chargé remarked that Greek situation could easily be liquidated if Yugoslav aid were discontinued, official insisted that there would be no aid."[1]

In the course of the next twelve months this was to prove an accurate forecast but when Marshall gave a report to Bevin on a visit he had paid to Athens in October, he drew a depressing picture of continuing divisions at the top, poor morale and disappointment at the failure of the Grammos offensive to destroy the rebels.

When Bevin asked him if he regarded the situation as hopeless, Marshall replied that he did not, provided the necessary measures were taken in time.[2] Amongst these was a recommendation that the United States should find the money to finance an increase of 15,000 in the Greek Army and the replacement, proposed by the Greeks themselves, of the Army's Commander-in-Chief. But it took time for the "necessary measures" to produce their effect. Despite the divisions in their own leadership, the rebels scored minor successes in Thessaly and Macedonia as late as the end of 1948 and shelled Salonika on Christmas Day. In the meantime the findings of UNSCOB that substantial support had been given to the rebels from across the frontiers were contested by the Soviet bloc at every step in the General Assembly's Political Committee, and the Assembly's decision to continue its Special Committee and its efforts to mediate between the Greeks and their neighbours had no effect at all.

The day before he met Marshall Bevin saw Amr Pasha, the Egyptian Ambassador in London, for the second time in three days and gave him a frank appraisal of Egypt's position which would have surprised those who saw Bevin urging on the Egyptians to attack Israel. When Amr said that he was despondent, Bevin agreed that Egypt was in a precarious position. The country had fallen behind in economic and social progress and the troops in the Negeb might be in for a disaster. The Egyptian Government had misled the people about the true state of affairs: the traditional game of attacking the British was played out and they had now to face the facts. What was needed

[1] A report from the US Chargé in Belgrade circulated by the State Department to US embassies in Europe on 6 July 1948. FRUS (4) pp. 1084–5.
[2] Marshall's reports on his visit, 20 and 21 October 1948, *ibid.*, pp. 162–6. His talk with Bevin took place on 27 October. See footnote on p. 165, and for the British report, FO 800/468/GRE/48/10.

was a national government representative of all parties which was strong enough to tackle their real problems.

Bevin would not give the British assurances of support for which Amr asked, telling him that he wanted to see an end to the British protection of Egypt and the creation instead of a Middle East defence system in which Egypt would occupy a key position, the sort of pooling of resources which was being built up in Western Europe with American help. When Amr asked why they could not have an Anglo–Egyptian treaty on the same lines as that between Britain and Turkey, Bevin pointed out that the latter depended on Britain having a base in Egypt. If the Egyptians wanted to show their goodwill to the UK, they should support the proposal for a UK trusteeship in Cyrenaica.

He was no more forthcoming when Amr asked whether there was a possibility of an Anglo–US–Egyptian treaty replacing that between Egypt and the UK: it would encounter Russian opposition and also be opposed by the Zionists in the USA. The interview ended with Bevin turning down a request for arms from the stocks held in the Canal Zone. The Egyptians were not short of arms, he told the Ambassador; the real trouble was that their soldiers would not fight because they disliked the present regime in Egypt.[1]

3

Bevin's meeting with Marshall at the end of October, before the Secretary returned to America, ran over all the issues now before the United Nations: not only Greece, but Berlin, Austria, Palestine, Kashmir and Indonesia.

At the Security Council's meeting on 22 October, Bramuglia, the Argentine President, had introduced the so-called "neutral powers" resolution on Berlin,[2] calling for an immediate end of the blockade followed by a meeting of the four military governors to arrange for a single currency in the city on the basis of the Soviet Zone mark. The three Western Powers accepted the resolution; the Russians rejected it on the grounds that it did not provide for the introduction of the East mark simultaneously with the lifting of the blockade. When Bevin met Marshall on the 27th he was firm in refusing to take the issue from the Security Council to the General Assembly, the president of which, the Australian Foreign Minister, Dr Evatt, was ambitious to get into the act. Bevin argued that they should stand pat on the Security Council resolution, should handle proposals from the neutrals tactfully, but take no initiative, keep a solid front and wait and see.[3] He took the same line when the two of them met Schuman later in the day and found him anxious about French public opinion and its eagerness to see something being done. Bevin

---

[1] 23 and 26 October 1948. FO 800/457/EG/48/13.
[2] It was sponsored by Argentina, Belgium, Canada, China, Colombia and Syria.
[3] Bevin's talk with Marshall, 27 October. FO 800/467/GER/48/77; FRUS 1948 (5 Pt. 2) pp. 1520–22.

declared he was against doing anything. The Russians were also in a difficult position and they should not run after them. If the three powers were known to be meeting, the Russians would take this to mean that they were trying to find a way out and would be encouraged to make no concessions. This was accepted, the Western Powers agreeing to keep in touch but not make any overt move.[1]

Palestine was more difficult. Bevin complained to Marshall that, while the UK had maintained the arms embargo despite strong pressure from the Arabs and an appeal to treaty obligations,[2] the Jews had been able to buy arms where they liked, in particular from the Czechs. The British could not be expected to sit by and allow the Arab Legion to be defeated because it was short of arms and ammunition. The Arabs were bitter because the Jews were breaking the truce and getting away with it. If they would play the game and observe the truce, he would not raise a finger; but the British could not leave Transjordan unsupported if, after defeating Egypt, the Jewish forces swung round and attacked Abdullah. They were bound by treaty to come to the help of Transjordan and must support the Arab Legion, the one force capable of enforcing any partition plan.

Marshall recognized Bevin's dilemma and assured him that he had been making great efforts to control the supply of arms to the Jews. Bevin was anxious about the effect the situation might have on Anglo–US relations and he urged Marshall to give American support in the Security Council when the British moved for the UN to re-appoint an international commission to keep the peace under threat of applying economic sanctions.[3]

Back in London the same evening Bevin saw the Transjordan Minister and refused to be drawn. He told him they were trying to secure the withdrawal of Jewish forces through the Security Council. If that failed, there would be a new situation which would have to be examined. The Arabs' troubles, he added, sprang from their lack of cohesion and refusal to take British advice until it was too late.[4]

Bevin, however, kept up his pressure on Marshall. Meeting him in Princes Gate on the 30th, he told him that the Jordanians had only four days' ammunition left unless the British sent in supplies. Marshall replied that it would be very difficult for the USA if they did. Who had broken the truce? Bevin demanded. They had agreed to apply sanctions if the truce were broken, and nothing was being done. He promised Marshall, however, that he would take no action unless there was a Jewish attack and repeated the need for their two countries to co-ordinate their policies.[5]

---

[1] Bevin's meeting with Marshall and Schuman, 27 October, *ibid.*
[2] On 12 July Bevin had cabled to the British minister in Amman at the start of the nine days' war: "I will do my utmost to help King Abdullah, but I cannot, repeat not, do this by the supply of ammunition." FO 371/68572.
[3] Bevin's talk with Marshall, 27 October.
[4] Bevin's talk with the Transjordan Minister, 27 October. FO 800/487/PA/48/92.
[5] Bevin's talk with Marshall and Douglas, 30 October, *ibid.*, PA/48/93.

Austria was different again. The Moscow conference had produced no more progress than on Germany. (The Austrian delegation invited to attend estimated that it spent 716 out of its 720 hours in Moscow in its hotel rooms.) Nor did the special Austrian Treaty Commission, which met 84 times between May and October 1947. The breaking off of negotiations over Germany, however, at the London meeting of the Council of Foreign Ministers, did not extend to Austria. On the contrary, when the Foreign Ministers' Deputies for an Austrian Peace Treaty met in London in January 1948, the Soviet Union took up a proposal made by the French which accepted the fact that no agreement could be reached on the definition of German assets and suggested that the Russians should give up their claims in return for a lump sum in compensation. The figure which the Russians asked in compensation was too high, but at least it provided a basis for negotiation and this in turn suggested that Soviet policy in regard to Austria might be changing, perhaps opening the way to the early conclusion of a treaty.

At this point, however, the Communist *coup* in Austria's neighbour, Czechoslovakia, raised the question whether it was in the interests of either the Western Powers or an independent Austria to conclude a treaty which would mean the withdrawal of the occupation forces. If that took place, the Western Powers would no longer hold an unbroken front running from Italy to the North Sea, and Austria would be left without protection against a Czech-style *coup*, whether or not in combination with the re-entry of Soviet forces. As the Russians blew hot and appeared ready to make further concessions in order to get the treaty signed, the Western Powers blew cold, their suspicions of Russian intentions revived by what had happened in Czechoslovakia and by the opening moves in the blockade of Berlin.

Bevin was very reluctant to give up the attempt to get a treaty as soon as possible. The growing tension over Berlin, however, and fears that the same tactics might be applied to Vienna[1] led the Western Powers to look for an issue which would postpone negotiations on the treaty without breaking them off and without allowing the Russians to put the blame on the West. The British found the answer by raising the question of Yugoslav territorial claims on Austria (nearly a thousand square miles of Carinthia) and Yugoslav reparation claims, which the Austrians were united in rejecting and the Russians could hardly do other than support. By the middle of May resumption of the talks (after 110 meetings of the Deputies) was postponed indefinitely.

The breach between the Russians and the Yugoslavs naturally led to speculation whether the Russians would continue to support the latter's claims against Austria. Hints that they would were reported by Norbert

---

[1] These fears were at their height in April. Travel restrictions were imposed by the Russians and particularly directed at the British. In May, however, the restrictions were abandoned and, although anxiety continued that access to Vienna might be cut off in the same way as to Berlin, this faded in the course of the summer and was discounted by the autumn.

Bischoff, Austria's Political Representative in the USSR, at the beginning of October and Gruber told Bevin that he had been approached by the Russians with the suggestion that talks should be resumed. Reporting this to Schuman, Bevin speculated in turn whether this was a bargaining counter to Berlin or an anti-Tito move. While he thought it would be a good thing to get an Austrian treaty, he was not prepared to pay a further price for it and wondered whether the Russians were taking a tactical step backwards in accordance with Leninist theory.[1] When the two of them met Marshall the following day (3 October) and Bevin asked whether they should not resume negotiations, the reply he got was discouraging. Since the signature of a treaty would be followed by the withdrawal of troops, Marshall thought it better to leave things as they were.[2].

With an eye to Austrian opinion, which could not easily accept an indefinite continuation of the occupation, it was finally agreed that the Austrian Government should formally request the resumption of the treaty negotiations. All four Powers agreed and a date was fixed for the Deputies to re-assemble in London in February 1949. But 1948 ended, to Bevin's as well as Austrian disappointment, as another lost year in the attempt to re-establish the independence Austria had lost ten years before.

The Soviet Union not only supported Yugoslav claims against Austria but Yugoslav charges against the British and Americans in Trieste. These were laid before the Security Council in August and were met with the counter charge that the Yugoslavs had virtually incorporated their zone of the Free Territory into Yugoslavia and turned it into a police state. This exchange of incivilities, renewed in November, did not affect the situation in Trieste but was no doubt intended to show that Tito had no intention of compromising Yugoslavia's claims because of the breach with the Cominform and to force the Russians into giving the Yugoslavs public support.

Behind the scenes there were already signs that Stalin's demand for compliance which had led to the excommunication of Tito was going to be extended throughout the Soviet bloc. Rajk was summoned from Budapest to Moscow in July and demoted from the Ministry of the Interior to that of Foreign Affairs; Gomulka, absent from the Cominform meeting which had condemned Tito, was dismissed as Secretary General of the Polish Communist Party on the last day of August and denounced by *Pravda* as a Titoist nine days later; the Albanian leader, Xoxe, incurred the same charge and was dismissed on 3 October. This was the prelude to the treason trials of 1949. If Tito remained in power, unscathed, it was not because there had been any change in Stalin's determination to be as much master of the satellite empire as he had made himself of the Soviet Union—and by the same means.

But in public—for example in the bitter debates on the reports of the UN

---

[1] Bevin's talk with Schuman in Paris, 2 October 1948. FO 800/510/UN/48/36.
[2] FO note of meeting between Bevin, Schuman and Marshall, in Paris on 3 October, *ibid*.

Special Committee on the Balkans investigating the help given by Greece's northern neighbours to the Greek rebels[1]—the Communist states still voted as a bloc and rejected unanimously the UN's call to the Greeks and their neighbours to settle their differences.

Subsequently it has become clear that the repercussions of the Stalin–Tito quarrel were already being felt throughout the Balkans; that the Yugoslavs were giving less help to the Greek rebels than they had, that the Albanians and the Bulgarians were separating themselves from the Yugoslavs, that the Macedonian Communist organization (NOF) and the Greek rebel movement itself were split between Titoists and Stalinists. But the effect of these shifts was not seen until 1949: in the last three months of 1948 morale in Greece fell to its lowest point, after the rebel forces captured Vitsi in September and some Government units panicked and fled. In desperation, the Sofoulis Government declared martial law and (with a prime minister well over eighty) would have resigned if anybody could have been found to replace it. The American Administration debated cutting its losses and at the end of December even Bevin, who had endured more obloquy than anyone for support of the Greeks, telegraphed to Washington that he felt so discouraged that he too wondered whether they should not get out of Greece entirely, if there was not a rapid improvement.[2]

It is unlikely that either the Americans or Bevin seriously supposed they could withdraw from Greece, but the fact that they were prepared to discuss the possibility amongst themselves, and not just threaten the Greeks with it, shows how despondent they felt about the situation—and how exasperated with the Greeks—nearly two years after Truman had made his declaration of support.

In Greece, as in Austria, Trieste and every other focus of conflict in Europe, the issue was bound to be affected by the outcome of the major confrontation between Russia and the West over Germany and particularly over Berlin. Until that was settled, one way or the other, nothing else could be.

Outside Europe, Bevin did not make much more progress during 1948 with either of the two disputes in which he tried to bring the parties together. In December he sent a message to Marshall to say that he was more optimistic than he had been about Kashmir. Both sides had agreed to a plebiscite and everything turned on finding the right man to administer it. When his suggestion of Eisenhower was turned down, he came up with other names and finally, in the New Year, got Admiral Nimitz to take on the job.[3] While sceptical whether Nehru really wanted a settlement in Kashmir, Bevin relied heavily on the Indian Prime Minister to persuade the Indonesians to come to

---

[1] Three reports were published in June, September and October 1948 and debated in the General Assembly in the autumn.
[2] 29 December 1948. FRUS (4) p. 221.
[3] Bevin to British Embassy for Marshall, 6 December 1948. FO 800/470/IND/48/39–40, and Bevin to Attlee, 18 December, *ibid.*, IND/48/43.

terms with the Dutch. On 17 December he showed Attlee a draft in which he urged Nehru to understand the difficulties in The Hague, where Stikker was making every effort to get a liberal settlement. If the Dutch Prime Minister and Foreign Minister were to resign it would mean the breakdown of negotiations.[1] He told Nehru that, if he could get Hatta to clarify his position, he (Bevin) would try to get the Dutch to issue a statement which would reassure the Indonesians.[2] When Nehru called a conference on Indonesia, in New Delhi in January, Bevin told him that he had no hard feelings at the British not being invited and wished him success.[3] Despite the difficulties over Kashmir, links with Delhi remained strong and Bevin and Attlee continued to consult Nehru freely on Asian questions, including China.

Foreign Office efforts, however, to organize the containment of Communist activities in South East Asia elicited little response in the winter of 1948–9. The French and Dutch were interested since they were already confronted with the problem. The Commonwealth countries, however, not only India and Pakistan, but Australia and New Zealand as well, were unwilling to do anything to support the colonial powers in Indo-China and Indonesia; and US State Department officials, preoccupied with the Communist successes in China, showed reluctance to see the United States become involved further south.[4] The conclusion was that little could be done until Bevin had the chance to talk to the newly appointed Secretary of State, Dean Acheson, and see if he could change the Americans' minds.

4

Where in the midst of all this diplomatic activity was the man? Ernie Bevin was after all a personality not easily overlooked and even less easily contained within an official role. The answer is, nonetheless, that he was so deeply absorbed in his job as Foreign Secretary that he had neither time nor energy to spare for anything else. As anyone can see who looks at his engagement book he had an exceptionally crowded timetable with little opportunity to look at the flow of telegrams and papers until he got to the end of his day. Apart from official functions, appearing at a reception or speaking at a dinner, meetings at a time of crisis like the initial stages of the Berlin blockade were as likely to take place in the evening as any other time, especially if it was necessary to call America where the day started five or six hours later. If there was nothing else to do, there were always his boxes. He read nothing apart from official papers

---

[1] Bevin's report to the Cabinet, 13 December 1948. CM 80 (48)
[2] Bevin to Attlee, sending him the draft reply to Nehru on Indonesia, 17 December. FO 800/470/IND/48/42.
[3] Meeting between Bevin, Menon and Gordon-Walker, 11 January 1949, *ibid.*, IND/49/2.
[4] See Ritchie Ovendale's article in *International Affairs*, vol. 58, no. 3, summer 1982: "Britain, the U.S. and the Cold War in South East Asia 1949–50" which makes use of the unpublished evidence in the FO papers and of FRUS.

and his one relaxation, particularly when in an hotel abroad, was to reminisce about his earlier years in the Movement, his triumphs and feuds, with a glass of whisky in his hand and one or two of his staff who bore up stoically under the burden of enforced attendance, frequently late at night.

None of this was surprising. He had never found it easy to make personal friends and had never made much real effort to do so. His private life, especially since he had become a minister eight years before, had been meagre. He had always lived for his job and, whether as General Secretary, Minister of Labour or Foreign Secretary, had been reluctant to leave his office at the end of the day. He believed, not without reason, that he held the post of Foreign Secretary at a time of great importance and great difficulty for the nation he felt himself to represent, a time when the pattern of international relations and Britain's and Europe's place in it were being decided for at least a generation and when he had fewer resources than any of his predecessors to shape them. He did not think he was powerless or unable to influence decisions; on the contrary, he saw himself, and again not without reason, as the only man in office on this side of the Atlantic in the late 1940s who had the strength to take the lead in Europe outside the Soviet bloc, to hold the confidence of the Americans and yet retain sufficient independence to oppose them when he thought their policy wrong. But to do this made exceptional demands on his confidence and on his powers of concentration. He met the first without difficulty, not over-awed by the responsibility and trusting his own judgement as he had done all his life, no more impressed by the fact that opinion in the Labour Party had now swung round to his view than he had been when it was opposed to him. But the need to concentrate his attention so that he did not miss a move or a shift in the complicated pattern of international politics which he carried in his head required all the remaining energy of a man now in his late sixties and far from well. Without further ambition, except to carry through the task he had set himself of safeguarding the recovery of the UK and Western Europe, he lived wholly absorbed in what he was doing, amazed, as he more than once remarked, at the patience he had learned.

What sustained Bevin's confidence was the conviction, by no means common at the time, that if the Western Powers could get through the immediate future without suffering a collapse of nerve, history would prove to be on their side and not the Russians'. And this in turn derived from his belief that in the USA there was available the basis of power necessary to restore sufficient sense of security to release the European peoples' own talents and energies.

Western Europe (he believed) would in the end save itself by its own exertions, or not at all, but it needed a catalyst, which Bevin had first sought in the Marshall Plan for Europe's economic recovery but which he now believed required in addition the association of the United States with Europe's security, not in the form of a guarantee which would fail to carry conviction but in a joint enterprise, the embryonic North Atlantic Treaty Organization. It was with this in view that he had moved Oliver Franks, after the part he had played in Paris in setting up the OEEC and the Marshall Plan, to Washington to play a similar role in setting up NATO. Americans and Europeans alike protested that he had weakened OEEC by removing the natural leader of the British delegation. Bevin was not impressed: in his view the job Franks now had to do in Washington was more important and indeed the key to the success of the European Recovery Programme. In a message to Franks, which he sent at the end of November, he asked Kirkpatrick to say that he relied on him to push through NATO as he had done the ERP: it was the best possible way of securing peace.

While, therefore, the greater part of Bevin's time for the rest of 1948 continued to be taken up with Berlin, Palestine, Greece and other issues before the United Nations, the real focus of his attention was the NATO discussions in Washington. The most important outcome of the many meetings he held in Paris in the autumn of 1948 was the secret communication delivered to the State Department after the meetings of the Consultative Council to say that the Brussels Powers had now agreed to negotiate a North Atlantic Pact with the USA and Canada.[1] Truman's electoral victory of 4 November transformed the situation in Washington. Immediately afterwards he took the September 9 report with him to study during a brief vacation at Key West. The Brussels Powers had already proposed this as the basis for the next stage of the discussions and on 6 November the President, now armed with an authority he had never enjoyed before and a clear run of four years ahead, approved the general principles of the report and the next steps to be taken. Hickerson's note passing this on to Chip Bohlen in Paris added that Lovett, the acting Secretary of State "has touched base with Vandenberg and hopes to do shortly with Connally", the two key figures in Congress.[2]

While the negotiations to which he attached overriding importance were going on secretly in Washington, Bevin could not afford to pay less attention to the public performances which continued at the UN meetings in Paris until the middle of December. If he had little faith in the United Nations as an agency for producing a settlement, he understood very well that, if it could provide nothing else, it offered a stage on which, through the reports of speakers, resolutions, manoeuvres, negotiations behind the scenes and rumours transmitted by the press, radio and newsreels, each Party in the various disputes could (and must) appeal to public opinion, in a bid to arouse sympathy or indignation, to raise or depress confidence and so on across the whole range of political warfare.

No dispute brought out more clearly than Berlin the conflicting pressures between which Bevin had to try and steer a consistent course. On the one hand was the fear of war and occupation, the more serious since, in the event of war,

---

[1] Text of the joint note, delivered on 29 October. FRUS 1948 (3) p. 270.
[2] Hickerson's cable to Bohlen in Paris, 9 November, *ibid.*, p. 271.

Berlin could not be held and the best the Western Powers could hope for was to fall back and make a stand on the Rhine. Bevin was equally clear that, if they were to stay in Berlin, as he thought essential in view of the encouragement they had given to the city's population to resist Soviet pressure, they could not rely indefinitely on the air-lift and would have to reach a settlement with the Russians at some stage. Anything which gave the impression that the Western Powers, particularly the Americans, were pursuing a "tough" policy and refusing the chance to negotiate spread alarm among America's European allies, particularly the French. On the other hand, these anxieties made it all the more essential—while not discouraging any initiative, particularly from the neutral members of the Security Council or the UN Secretariat—to make sure that this did not draw the Western Powers into purchasing a settlement at the price of concessions they had so far refused to make. That was the risk they had taken in bringing the dispute to the United Nations, but it was a risk which they could not avoid running if they were to continue to carry public opinion with them in the USA and Britain as well as in Western Europe. The only way to limit it was to combine readiness to listen to any proposal which might be made with vigilance in grasping its implications in practice.

The real issues were to be discovered not by arguing over principles and rights but by paying attention to procedure and timing; the small print of schedules for lifting the blockade and controlling the issue of currency. This was the direction in which Bevin sought to steer the UN peace efforts in examining the currency and trade aspects of the Berlin situation. On the initiative of the Secretary General a committee of experts from the six neutral members of the Security Council tried to work out a settlement of the currency question on the basis of introducing the East mark as the sole Berlin currency.[1] The committee continued to meet after the UN session ended but failed to secure agreement of all the four Powers to its proposals and finally, in February 1949, reported that there was no point in going on.

Bevin had gone along with the UN initiative, accepting the committee of experts' draft plan as a basis for discussion (it was turned down by the Americans). He did so not because he thought that it would produce a settlement but because he was satisfied to see the UN's attempt to find a way out of the impasse—which he could not repudiate but regarded with little enthusiasm and considerable anxiety—diverted from political to technical issues.

The fact that the committee of experts took more than two months to produce no result did not worry Bevin. Between the French desire to find a compromise and the intermittent American impulse to sharpen the issue and bring it to a head, Bevin throughout the Berlin dispute laid most stress on the importance of time, of not being rushed into anything, in the belief that the

---

[1] Gunnar Myrdal was appointed by the Secretary General as his representative and Nicholas Kaldor as the Committee's secretary.

more time the West had to organize itself, the more the balance of advantage would swing to its side. In the summer of 1948 this appeared a bold gamble as far as Berlin was concerned; but at the turn of the year, with the air-lift still in operation despite the weather—6,000 tons on a clear day, Bevin told the House of Commons on 9 December—and with the resistance of the Berliners hardening not weakening, it no longer seemed unrealistic to argue that the best course was to stand pat and leave it to the Russians to find a way out of a trap which had failed to work.

The passage of time also worked to change the local situation in Berlin itself. If it no longer seemed likely that the Russians would achieve their objective of ending the four-power occupation and forcing the Western Powers out, the original Western objective of restoring the joint quadripartite occupation of the whole city was becoming daily more unrealistic. A bitter struggle fought for control of the city government between the SED, backed by the Russians, and the other parties, backed by the Western Powers, led to the establishment of rival *Magistrates*, one situated in the Soviet sector, the other in the British.

Elections for the City Assembly were already overdue and the SED and the Russians did everything in their power, including spreading rumours of a Soviet take-over by force, to prevent them from being held.[1] But the Berliners refused to be intimidated and on 5 December 83.9% of the 1,500,000 eligible voters cast their votes for one or other of the three democratic parties.[2] The result was to make clear beyond any doubt on which side the majority of Berliners stood. Indeed a major anxiety of the democratic coalition's leaders was that the Western Powers might show less resolution than the people of Berlin and reach a compromise with the Russians which would sacrifice Berlin for the sake of a general settlement.

This was a groundless suspicion as far as Bevin was concerned. Not only did he take seriously the commitment to those who had stood up to be counted in Berlin, but he was firmly opposed to any resumption of negotiations which might re-open the future of Germany. Bevin was convinced that the Russians' primary purpose in starting the Berlin blockade had been, not to gain a local advantage, but to pressure the Western Powers into abandoning the programme laid down in London for the future of the Western zones of Germany. Until sufficient progress had been achieved to make that programme irreversible, he wanted no general settlement and was certainly not prepared to sacrifice Berlin in order to get one. The German negotiations in which Bevin was interested in the autumn of 1948 were not with the Russians over Berlin, but with the French over the implementation of the London Agreements.

Since the currency reform the economic recovery of Germany had made

[1] Bevin reported on the situation to the Cabinet on 11 November and secured agreement to the elections being held in the Western sectors. CP (48) 260 and CM 70 (48).
[2] The figure for abstentions was 13.7%. This included those who listened to the SED advice not to vote. 2.4% represented invalid votes. For details see Davison, p. 229 and sources cited there.

great strides, alarming the French and stiffening their resistance to a programme they had only accepted with reluctance. At a meeting of the Military
Governors on 4 November, Clay reported the Frenchman, General Koenig, as
saying that

"The 'climate' in Germany was becoming such that he had grave doubts as to whether
he would be able to approve a constitution and the subsequent formation of a Western
German Government. . . . Germany, and particularly the Ruhr, was being allowed to
come back too rapidly."[1]

Clay's forecast that the French would place every sort of obstacle in the way
of implementing the London programme proved correct. By the middle of
December the German Parliamentary Council could not complete its work on
the draft constitution because the Military Governors could not agree on the
draft of the Occupation Statutes; no progress had been made on the proposed
Military Security Board or the merger of the French zone with the Bi-zone, and
agreement at the six-power talks on the Ruhr, which had begun in London five
weeks before, was held up by French efforts to re-open the whole question of
the future of the Ruhr.

The Ruhr was the symbol which focused all French fears of a revival of
German power and, until the London talks could be brought to a conclusion,
there was no hope of making progress with the other questions. The talks
started badly, with what Lew Douglas described as a "stink bomb". The day
before they opened, the British and American Military Governments published Law No. 75 on the re-organization of the German iron, coal and steel
industries. The preamble re-stated the compromise reached by the Labour
Government and the US Administration on the issue of nationalization:

"Whereas Military Government has decided that the question of the eventual ownership of the Coal and Iron and Steel Industries should be left to the determination of a
representative, freely-elected German government . . ."

This was a compromise, however, which the French had never accepted,
arguing that ownership should be international. When the Law was published, there was a great outcry in France, in which Gaullists and Communists
combined, that the French had been confronted with a *fait accompli*. This was
true. Bevin was determined to keep open the option of nationalization, and the
Americans, although they felt no enthusiasm for that, wanted to re-assure the
Germans that ownership of the Ruhr industries would remain in German
hands and so overcome German reluctance to contribute to the European
Recovery Programme until this was settled. The French Government had
never been left in any doubt of the British and American positions and, if the
timing of the announcement was maladroit, there was good reason to remove

---

[1] Clay's report to Washington, 5 November. FRUS 1948 (3) pp. 438–40.

any doubts about ownership before the discussions started on the powers of the future international authority.

In reporting to the House of Commons, Bevin said that he had given a lot of thought to international ownership of the Ruhr industries when he first took office but had eventually rejected it because

"It would lead to endless friction, it would depress production and would make German co-operation in the great work of European reconstruction difficult, if not impossible."

The solution, he concluded, was to separate the question of security from that of recovery:

"What we have to do is to make sure of complete security (for France and all other neighbours of Germany) in a way which will permit and encourage Germany, without loss of self-respect, to play a proper part in the economic reconstruction of Europe."[1]

This was the American view too, well expressed by Lovett in a telegram to Marshall on 13 November:

"The only real solution of the German problem is, so far as France's security is concerned, within the framework of a stronger economic and political organisation of Western Europe in which Germany must play an important role. . . . International ownership and management (of the Ruhr industries) do not increase the safeguards France is seeking but would, in fact, have the opposite effect either in creating such resentment on the part of Germany that they could not be maintained or in so reducing production that the Ruhr could not contribute to the existing needs of European recovery."[2]

Both Lovett and Bevin saw the guarantee of French security as being provided by continued German disarmament (to be supervised by the Military Security Board, which, as Bevin told the House, had not been given the attention it deserved) plus a North Atlantic security system. There would be an international authority for the Ruhr but its job would be to settle the allocation of the products of the Ruhr industries—coal, coke, steel—between the needs of Germany and those of Germany's neighbours, between the domestic market and exports.

The French, however, were not content with allocation and if they could not secure the separation of the Ruhr from Germany (their initial demand) or the international ownership of its industries, sought to expand the powers of the international Authority to give it rights of supervision and control over the management of the Ruhr's mines and steelworks. It was this issue which proved the stumbling block in London and led to six weeks of discussions before agreement was reached.

[1] Bevin in HC, 9 December 1948.
[2] Lovett, Acting Secretary of State, to Marshall in Paris, 13 November. FRUS (2) pp. 492–4.

Bevin did not take part personally in the talks but again took the closest possible interest in them and in the settlement which was eventually put together. He had always attached importance to a Military Security Board provided with the necessary powers of inspection and enforcement to prevent German rearmament, including industrial rearmament. Agreement on this, including provision for co-operation with the Ruhr Authority, was one of the essential elements of the settlement and a directive from the Military Governors of the three Western Zones setting up the Board was published on 17 January.[1] A second, without waiting for fusion of the French Zone with the other two (a fusion which never, in fact, took place) was to include French representatives in the US–UK Coal and Steel Control Groups which were to supervise the German managements (e.g. in regard to production and investment) during the period of occupation. The key question, how far these powers when the occupation ended, should be transferred to the Ruhr Authority, the Military Security Board or some other international body, was left open to be settled in the light of the experience gained with the control groups. In the meantime it was agreed that Germany as well as the six powers should be represented on the Ruhr Authority, her vote being cast by the Occupation Authorities to begin with.

The Ruhr Authority never came into existence, being replaced, on French initiative, by the European Coal and Steel Community; but the negotiations and agreement played their part in helping the French to make the transition to a much more positive view of how the Ruhr's resources were to be employed in the interests of Europe (including Germany), not of Germany alone. In the short-term by going some way to meet French objections they opened the way in the New Year of 1949 to agreement on the Occupation Statutes and the constitution of a West German state.

So by the end of 1948 Bevin could claim that Soviet pressure on the Western Powers through the blockade had failed either to force them out of Berlin or to prevent them from carrying out the programme for Western Germany on which agreement had been reached with much difficulty in the London conference concluded at the beginning of June seven months before. If not yet irreversible, sufficient progress had been made towards implementing it for him to feel confident that whatever settlement of the Berlin confrontation was finally found, it would not be at the expense of abandoning the framework in which the economic recovery of Western Germany (and with it Germany's contribution to European recovery) was taking place.

Satisfaction was tempered by the fact that the revision of the dismantling and reparations programme was still unsettled. In Germany and the USA the question had been blown up into an issue out of proportion to the economic facts. Bevin sympathized with the French and the other European nations' indignation at the loss of reparations on which they had counted and their

[1] Text in Oppen, 350–55.

anxiety at seeing the industrial power of Germany restored. But more than anything else he wanted to get the issue removed from the agenda: as long as it remained unsettled it was the British who had to bear the brunt of German resentment and American criticism.

In another strongly argued memorandum handed to the State Department on 4 December, Bevin pointed out that eight months had passed since he had agreed to co-operate with the Americans in reviewing the reparations programme in the British Zone, and the effect of continued uncertainty was to put a heavy strain on relations with the Germans. Before a German Government was created, it was surely imperative to reach agreement, if only to give the Allied Military Security Board a firm basis on which to work. Bevin therefore pressed the US Government, as a matter of urgency, to restate its policy on the demilitarization of Germany and to confirm its continued acceptance of the agreed level of 10.7 m. tons for Germany's annual steel production.[1]

The State Department could only reply that it had to await the report of the Humphrey Committee, whose chairman continued to repeat that his committee was not qualified to evaluate political and security factors. In December the Committee ended its visits to Europe with a week of talks in London (6–14 December), which, once again, as it had throughout 1948, provided the place in which differences over the future of Germany were thrashed out between the British, French and Americans, with Hoffmann, Harriman and Douglas taking part as well as members of the Humphrey Committee, and with Bevin as a powerful presence off-stage pressing the case for reparations and the need for a decision.[2] Disagreement on the list of plants to be recommended for retention in Germany was at least reduced, but the year ended with the Committee's report still unpublished and the issue still unresolved.[3] In the Cabinet Nye Bevan came out strongly for building up the Germans as a barrier against Communism; Dalton, supported by Addison, was strongly opposed; Cripps thought they ought to make up their minds whether they regarded Germany as still a danger or an ally. Bevin could only say he was trying to steer a middle course.[4]

5

By the autumn of 1948 American economic aid to Europe under the ERP was arriving on a substantial scale. While officials of the Economic Co-operation Administration continued to be critical of the British for their refusal to take the lead in implementing American ideas on the closer integration of Europe

[1] FRUS 1948 (3) pp. 838–41.
[2] Documentation of the talks in London, *ibid.*, 841–51.
[3] See Bevin's report to the Cabinet on the Humphrey Committee's proposals. CP (48) 303. A further report, CP (48) 306 dealt with British policy towards Germany and the present state of progress towards its double objective of creating a strong and democratic Western Germany linked to the other countries of Western Europe. This was discussed on 22 December. CM 82 (48).
[4] Dalton's diary, vol. 36, "end of 1948".

economically, a joint ECA–State Department committee in Washington reported in mid-October that France presented the most serious problem in European recovery. Although the French were receiving from the USA, the UK and other countries in OEEC aid "far in excess" of what could be justified on economic considerations, the trend of improvement apparent in the Spring of 1948 had been reversed and there was no confidence that the Queuille–Schuman Government, or any other based on the political centre, could master the country's problems in face of Gaullist as well as Communist opposition.[1]

The report produced a sharp reaction from Harriman, Caffery and Bruce who saw the situation in Paris at close quarters and no action was taken either to put pressure on the French Government or to cut the allocation of aid to France. Bevin's advice, which Marshall as well as Harriman thought it essential to seek first, was to be patient, and it was soon justified by events. Acting, as everyone in France assumed, on instructions and with financial support from the Cominform,[2] the Communists used their control of the CGT to call for a further series of strikes—railwaymen, miners, dockers—as a way of halting the ERP and as a trial of strength with the Queuille Government. The strikes started at the beginning of October but failed to secure the degree of support for which the Communists hoped. The country was not brought to a standstill and the Government not only survived but defeated the challenge. Meeting Marshall three days after the Communists had failed to enforce a 24-hour general strike in Paris, Queuille told him confidently that the back of the strike movement was broken and that the Government was resolved to carry out a purge of Communists from positions of responsibility in the Administration and the nationalized industries.

Bevin's anxiety was that the Government might push repressive measures too far when the strikes collapsed and the men went back. He sent a message to the British Ambassador in Paris recalling the mistake made in alienating Labour by the Trade Union Act passed after the 1926 General Strike and by the Taft–Hartley legislation in the States. He urged the French to tackle the situation in and through the unions, and to set up better arrangements for conciliation and arbitration, adding that he did not want Harvey to make representations but would be glad for his views to be known.[3]

---

[1] See the memoranda by Hickerson (12 October), and Labouisse and Moore (16 October). FRUS 1948 (3) pp. 666–70. The former, who was Director of the State Department's Office of European Affairs, described the French as "temperamentally selfish, individualistic, and reluctant to co-operate with anyone, French or otherwise. . . . Since the First World War the French have been devitalised, since the Second World War they have been demoralised and exhausted, and for the last year they have been in a state of acute jitters."

[2] The French Ministry of the Interior secured a report of the French Politburo meeting on 30 September at which, after meetings Duclos and Fajon had held with Vyshinsky and the Soviet Ambassador, Bogomolov, it was decided to launch the strike campaign. The report was forwarded to Washington by the US Ambassador. FRUS 1948 (3) pp. 661–2.

[3] Frank Roberts to Harvey, 5 November 1948. FO 800/465/FR/48/19.

There could be no better news for Bevin, however, than evidence of a stronger and more confident government in Paris, and at the end of December he wrote personally to Schuman, urging the French Foreign Minister to come over to London as early as possible so that they could get to know each other better and examine a whole range of questions on which he was anxious to reach agreement with the French.[1]

The issue on which the British continued to differ fundamentally with the French (and for that matter with the Americans as well), was on anything which might suggest a federal organization for Europe. On 26 November 1948 the committee set up by the Brussels Powers a month before met to consider proposals for furthering European unity. Attlee and Bevin rejected Churchill's suggestion that the British delegation should represent all parties and instead announced five names, only one of which, that of Hugh Dalton, was at all well known to the world. Dalton's position as a Cabinet minister was offset by his known lack of enthusiasm for the "European idea" unless it was in the form of a united socialist Europe.

The main proposal before the Committee, supported by the French and Belgian delegations, was for a European consultative assembly, to consist of 300–400 members drawn from the sixteen states belonging to the OEEC and Western Germany. They were to meet not more than three times a year, beginning in 1949, and by implication were to function neither as a constituent assembly nor as a federal elected Parliament. The brief given to the British delegation instructed it to oppose such an assembly and work instead for Bevin's counter-proposal of a European ministerial council responsible to governments. On 3 December, Hector McNeil, Bevin's Minister of State, who was in Paris on UN business, wrote to warn him that Dalton was apparently moving towards a compromise which would combine the French plan for an Assembly with Bevin's council of ministers. McNeil shared Bevin's dislike of an assembly at this stage of Europe's post-war development, remarking that if it was elected by proportional representation, 30% of its members would be Communists and forecasting (with an eye to Churchill) that Opposition would vie with Government members and use it as a platform for pre-election propaganda.[2]

Bevin needed no urging. On the 6th he took the matter to the Cabinet and secured authority to reiterate to Dalton that the Government was opposed to an Assembly.[3] In his letter he gave three objections: that such a scheme would not fit in with the Commonwealth; that it would not be possible to include Germany, whereas it would be possible to associate the Germans with a council; and that it was too early to commit the peoples of Western Europe to a federal solution, a customs union or a European parliament before the

[1] Bevin to Schuman, 29 December, FO 800/460/EUR/48/68. For the talks, which took place on 13–14 January 1949, see below pp. 656–8.
[2] McNeil to Bevin 3 December 1948, *ibid.*, EUR/48/63.
[3] CM 78 (48).

European governments had had more experience of working together and gaining understanding of each others' problems.[1]

When he opened the foreign affairs debate in the House three days later,[2] Bevin argued that the British Government during 1948 had done more than anyone "to promote European collaboration and effort in the economic field, and greater understanding in the political". He refused, however, "to be stampeded into unpractical if attractive expedients" or to disappoint the people of Western Europe by setting up "a mere facade". Still avoiding any definition of what he meant by Western Union he repeated that it was "not concerned with a geographical conception of Europe alone". He had always believed that they had to look further afield, to the Commonwealth and the overseas territories of the European Powers, as well as to "the USA and the countries of Latin America (which) are clearly as much a part of our common Western civilisation". Knowing that the three months' pause in the NATO negotiations was about to end the next day, Bevin was guarded in what he said, but his speech made clear enough that the key to an effective Western Union, in his view, remained a North Atlantic system of collective security. This alone, by bringing in the power and resources of the American continent, would give confidence to Western Europe and by doing so afford a chance of ending the age-long struggle between Germany and France.

When the US Minister of Defence, Forrestal, visiting London, asked A. V. Alexander and the British Chiefs of Staff if some form of Lend-Lease might not serve as an alternative to an Atlantic Pact, he got the answer that this would be better than nothing, as a stopgap, but still "totally inadequate".[3] Bevin was not present at the meeting but sent a minute to the Prime Minister after reading the record of it:

"I agree with Mr Alexander. I do not think Lend-Lease is a substitute. This leaves out of account France's fears that she may be left in the lurch regarding Germany. That country is still an uncertain quantity. If France is not given the absolute assurance of a Treaty, we shall not be able to deal with the German problem and bring Germany towards the West. If France is left open, Germany might well feel she can turn East with impunity. Because of our difficulty with Russia now we must not let that blind us to the greater danger of Germany *and* Russia. . . . Lend-Lease by itself will cause the fabric of Western Europe to fall."[4]

It was not, however, until 10 December that the so-called Ambassadors Committee—the Ambassadors of the five Brussels Powers, the Canadian Under-Secretary of State for External Affairs, Hume Wrong, and Bob Lovett, the US Under-Secretary of State—resumed their meeting at the point where

---

[1] Bevin to Dalton 6 December 1948. FO 800/460/EUR/48/64.
[2] HC, 9 December 1948.
[3] Forrestal's version of the meeting, which took place on 13 November, is in *The Forrestal Diaries*, pp. 489–90; the British version is in FO 800/454/DEF/48/62.
[4] Bevin's minute, dated 18 November, *ibid.*, DEF/48/64.

they left off after producing the September 10th document. In the intervening three months the Governments of the Brussels Powers had considered the report, and at the end of October announced their agreement on the desirability of a North Atlantic Treaty and the next steps to be taken. With the American elections over and the Truman Administration confirmed in office, the Brussels Powers Permanent Commission met in London, with Bevin there to urge them on, and turned agreement in principle into the 13 articles of a draft treaty complete with a commentary on the points of disagreement. This became known as the November 20th document and was, in fact, very close to the final draft.

Forwarding both documents to the Prime Minister for the Defence Committee, Bevin minuted that he did not want a situation in which the UK would be an outpost still left in doubt about American action. For that reason the language of the treaty had to be definite. He added a sentence which shows how far he saw NATO as the necessary framework of power without which talk of the future of Europe was rhetoric:

"We shall never fix the German–French problem unless it is (definite). The finding of words that may leave ambiguity will be disastrous."

Bevin wrote that he preferred to leave any comment on the other nations to be invited to join the Pact until there had been discussions with the Americans, but at present he was against inviting the Italians if only because he did not see how they could be included and the Greeks and Turks left out.[1]

It was a few days after this, while he was resting at Eastbourne, that he got Kirkpatrick to send Oliver Franks the message urging him to push through NATO as he had pushed through the ERP. He repeated his doubts about being in a hurry to bring in the Italians and warned him to be careful, in any approach to Eire, that the question of partition was not raised, with the effect this could have on the Irish vote in the USA.[2]

Franks understood very well the overriding importance Bevin attached to getting a North Atlantic security pact. However, Press reports that the Brussels Powers were presenting the USA with a text of the treaty on a take-it-or-leave-it basis put up departmental as well as congressional backs in Washington[3] and when the Ambassadors met Lovett on 10 December they were uncertain how the Americans wanted to proceed.[4]

Fortunately what was clear was that they did want to proceed. At their next meeting on the 13th at which the Canadian Hume Wrong gave a powerful lead, Lovett spoke of concluding the Treaty by 1 February and Franks found

[1] Bevin to Attlee, 22 November. FO 800/483/NA/48/3.
[2] Kirkpatrick to Franks, 29 November. FO 800/454/DEF/48/65.
[3] See, for example, the reception Hoyer Millar, the Minister at the British Embassy, received in the State Department on 27 November. FRUS 1948 (3) p. 297.
[4] British minutes of the 8th meeting of the Washington exploratory talks on security. FO 800/454/DEF/48/68. The US minutes are printed in FRUS (3) pp. 310–14.

the way out of the procedural difficulties by proposing that they should hand the various documents over to a working party and tell them to produce a report which might be sent to Governments before Christmas.[1]

The American representative on the working party was George Kennan, head of the State Department's Policy Planning Staff, and no one gave a better analysis of the situation NATO was designed to meet than he had produced in a staff paper dated 23 November. This was accepted by Marshall and the State Department, with "no disagreement anywhere". Kennan wrote that there was "a valid long-term justification for a formalisation, by international agreement, of the national defence relationship among the countries of the North Atlantic community . . .", but it was important to understand that "the conclusion of such a pact is not the main answer to the present Soviet effort to dominate the European continent and will not appreciably modify the nature or danger of Soviet policies". A military danger, Kennan continued, existed and was probably increasing rather than otherwise. But the basic Russian strategy was the conquest of Western Europe by political means and "in this program, military force plays a major role only as a means of intimidation.

"If a war comes in the foreseeable future, it will probably be one which Moscow did not desire but did not know how to avoid. The political war, on the other hand, is now in progress; and if there should not be a shooting war, it is this political war which will be decisive."

A NATO Pact would affect the political war only insofar as it increased the self-confidence of Western Europe in face of Soviet pressure. Such a stiffening was needed and desirable.

"But it goes hand in hand with the danger of a general pre-occupation with military affairs, to the detriment of economic recovery and of the necessity for seeking a peaceful solution to Europe's difficulties."

This pre-occupation, already widespread both in Europe and the USA, was regrettable because it addressed itself to what was not the main danger:

"The need for military alliances and rearmament on the part of the Western Europeans is primarily a *subjective* one, arising in their own minds as a result of their failure to understand correctly their own position. Their best . . . course of action if they are to save themselves from communist pressures, remains the struggle for economic recovery and for internal political stability."

Kennan's conclusion was in favour of pressing ahead with the NATO Pact as quickly as possible, but of never losing sight of its primary purpose, to increase European confidence and to build up armaments only insofar as it

[1] British minutes of the 9th meeting, 10 December, *ibid.*, DEF/48/69; US minutes, *ibid.*, pp. 315–21.

was necessary to recreate such confidence and not for their own sake.[1]

Kennan's paper puts the real purpose of NATO better than the formal preamble of the treaty and in terms which Bevin would have endorsed. If it was to carry conviction, however, especially for the sceptical French, it had to deal with security in military terms and to be cast, as Bevin said, in unambiguous language. The draft produced by the working party made good use of the work done in London. The heart of the matter was contained in articles 4 and 5.

Article 4, Consultation, which it was agreed covered attacks against overseas as well as metropolitan territories, read:

"The Parties will consult together whenever in the opinion of any of them,
(a) the territorial integrity, political independence or security of any of the Parties is threatened; or
(b) there exists any situation which constitutes a threat to or breach of the peace".

Article 5, Mutual Assistance, went further than consultation:

"The Parties agree that an armed attack against one or more of them occurring within the area defined below shall be considered an attack against them all; and consequently that, if such an armed attack occurs, each of them, in exercise of the right of individual or collective self-defence recognised by Article 51 of the U.N. Charter, will assist the party or parties so attacked by taking forthwith such military or other action, individually and in concert with the other parties, as may be necessary to restore and assure the security of the North Atlantic area."

I have quoted these two articles in full, for to get the United States to sign them, in full reversal of the historical traditions of her foreign policy, was the peak of Bevin's achievement as Foreign Secretary, one which every one of his predecessors from Canning onwards would have recognized and one which, for over 30 years, has provided the security and confidence which Bevin sought for Western Europe.

There was still disagreement on the area to which the undertaking of mutual assistance was to apply. The French argued strongly for the inclusion of North-west Africa and the Western Mediterranean. When it came to the other states to be invited to sign the Pact, the French this time argued for the inclusion of Italy as well as Iceland, Norway, Denmark, Ireland and Portugal. It was agreed, however, that Greece and Turkey should not be invited and that the assurances to be given to them instead should also be given to Italy if she were not invited.[2]

The report of the working party, with the draft treaty, was approved by the Ambassadors' Committee at its meeting with Wrong and Lovett on 24

---

[1] Policy Planning Staff Paper, PPS 43: "Considerations affecting the conclusion of a North Atlantic Security Pact". FRUS 1948 (3) pp. 283-8. The quotations are taken from pp. 284-5.
[2] The full text of the report including the draft treaty is in FO 800/483/NA/48/4 and in FRUS (3) pp. 333-43.

December. Writing personally to Bevin after Christmas, Franks said that they had made better progress than he had hoped for and that this was largely due to the changed attitude of the Americans. In the summer they had been wary, vague and reluctant to move fast or be accused of committing Congress. Now, with the elections over and public opinion in favour, they were anxious to get on and have something to show Congressional leaders early in the New Year; they were also prepared for definite commitments in place of ill-defined obligations. Franks, who had been instructed to support the French on the inclusion of N.W. Africa, reported that no-one else was in favour and the Americans were opposed. On the other hand, Franks reported that the Americans favoured including the Italians and, in the absence of a unanimous European view, he thought they would put on pressure to secure this.[1]

Throughout the negotiations, Attlee and Bevin had used the Defence Committee to settle the instructions to be sent to Franks.[2] Asking for the Committee to be called in time for Franks to be briefed for the next meeting with Lovett, Bevin told Attlee that he thought the draft was generally satisfactory. He believed they should stick on Italy, getting her into the Council of Europe first. To include Italy and leave out Greece and Turkey would cause resentment, and he suggested that the USA might be prepared to agree to a longer duration for the Pact if it was truly Atlantic and not extended to the Mediterranean. This would mean excluding any part of Africa, but Bevin felt this had to follow if Italy was excluded. As to the duration of the treaty, he proposed that Franks should be instructed to go for a period of 20 to 40 years.

Bevin wrote his comments for Attlee on the last day of 1948.[3] The NATO treaty was not yet signed, still less ratified by the Senate, but Bevin was within sight of his goal and there could not have been a more satisfactory way for him to end a year which had tested his resolution and ability as Foreign Secretary to the full.

6

Whatever hopes Bevin had entertained in the summer of 1948 of agreement with the United States on a settlement in Palestine were dissipated in the autumn. Bevin's final attempt to find a solution collapsed for the same reason as the earlier ones, the unwillingness of the President—whatever advice he might receive from the State Department—to support a settlement unacceptable to the Zionists.

---

[1] Franks to Bevin, 29 December 1948. FO 800/454/DEF/48/72.
[2] The most important discussion was on 7 October. At this Bevin presented a report (DO (48) 64, 20 September) on the Washington Talks and the draft treaty which they had produced. For the discussion see the minutes of the Defence Committee's 20th Meeting 1948.
[3] Bevin to Attlee, 31 December 1948. FO 800/487/PA/48/95.

The documents published in the *Foreign Relations of the United States* make clear the steps by which co-operation between the two Governments over Palestine broke down, from their disagreement over imposing sanctions on Israel for its refusal to withdraw from the territories it had occupied in breach of the UN truce, to the American attempts to water down the Bernadotte proposals when these came to be debated by the General Assembly's Political Committee.[1] In the absence of the support from the Americans on which Bevin had counted, the British had little chance of carrying the proposals on their own, and after a vote on 3 December in which the Arab states combined with the Soviet bloc to defeat the key recommendation on the combination of Arab Palestine with Transjordan, the initiative Bevin had taken in the summer was dead. The Israelis remained in occupation of their territorial gains and the United Nations' face was saved by the appointment of a Conciliation Committee to take over the late Mediator's functions and produce a "final" settlement.

What was to be done now? However exasperated Bevin might feel with the Americans, too much was at stake in Europe—and in the Middle East—to let differences over Palestine weaken the alliance. On 14 December he asked Douglas to come and see him, and proposed a "Palestine lunch" at which Douglas could meet the Chiefs of Staff and hear other British views besides his own before returning to the USA. Bevin's remarks at the preliminary meeting made clear the way his mind was now working. He had abandoned the idea of making partition between Transjordan and Israel the basis for a Palestine settlement, and had no other proposal to take its place. His attention was focused not on Palestine but on the Middle East as a whole, and particularly on how the British were to maintain their strategic position there—on which, as he reminded Douglas, the Americans as well as the British were relying. Transjordan might not be acceptable as the key to an overall Palestine settlement but Abdullah was still Britain's only reliable ally in the Arab world and Transjordan a major strategic asset provided that access to it from the Mediterranean and Egypt could be maintained. Bevin's interest in Palestine was now narrowed down to the question: was it possible to agree on a southern frontier for Israel which would allow Transjordan and Egypt to establish a common frontier in the Negev?[2]

When Douglas met Bevin, Alexander and McNeil as well as the soldiers at Bevin's lunch on the 20th, the background to their anxieties became clear. Bevin repeated a remark that had puzzled Douglas at their earlier encounter, saying they must avoid a China situation developing in the Middle East. When questioned, it turned out that the British feared Arab frustrations and their disillusionment with the West would provide a fertile ground for Communist

---

[1] Douglas showed some sympathy with Bevin's complaint that the vacillations of American policy made them impossible to work with over Palestine. See his dispatch to Washington on 26 October 1948 in FRUS 1948 (5 Pt. 2) pp. 1516–20, and his talks with President Truman on 6 November, *ibid.*, 1570–72.
[2] FO 800/487/PA/48/95.

penetration. The Arabs believed the British had always sacrificed their interests to reaching agreement with the USA, and Stalin could exploit their discontent by switching Soviet support to the Arabs instead of the Israelis. Bevin frequently expressed the view that Israel itself might become a Communist state in view of the influx of immigrants from the Soviet bloc countries.[1]

Douglas summed up by saying that what the British wanted was a defence scheme which would provide protection for the Suez base and their access to Middle Eastern oil while also providing a foothold from which to attack Russia. While Tedder, chairman of the COS added that this was essential to the defence of Western Europe as well as the Middle East, Douglas went on to ask why they assumed that Israel would be hostile or even neutral. The Israelis, as the British did not dispute, had shown themselves to have the best army in the Middle East. Surely the problem was how to associate them with the West. Why not a regional pact for all the Middle East, including Israel? Bevin's reply was that this was his objective, but how could they get the other states (for example, Pakistan) to join if the Jews had alienated the whole Moslem world? When Douglas and McNeil agreed that it was important to reach agreement with moderate Israeli leaders, mentioning Ben Gurion and Moshe Shertok, Bevin's comment was that no Jews were moderate where Israel's interests were at stake. But he suggested two conciliatory gestures, sending a Consul General to Tel Aviv and releasing the 11,000 Jews still held in Cyprus; nor would he delay full recognition of Israel once her frontiers were settled. But they must also do something for the Arabs and the need to reinforce the RAF in Amman was mentioned as a way of retaining Arab confidence in Britain as an ally.

The upshot was that the British wanted to reach previous agreement with the Americans on Israel's southern frontier and then get the Americans to use their man on the new Conciliation Committee to secure its endorsement and Arab–Israeli acquiescence in the line agreed.[2] The answer, as Douglas must have foreseen, was that—like so many other British plans for US support on Palestine—this was not a course the State Department was free to follow even if it had wanted to.[3] Long before that was made clear, however, the Israelis had supplied their own conclusive answer.

On 22 December, Israeli forces on their southern front attacked an Egyptian brigade which had been encircled at al-Falluja since October, and bombed

---

[1] Bevin had several times drawn the Americans' attention to intelligence reports that among the Jewish immigrants from Eastern Europe were a number of Communists trained in the techniques of underground work. The unexpected Soviet switch to support of partition in the UN; the readiness of Czechoslovakia to supply large quantities of arms and equipment to Israel; and the contacts believed to exist between the Israeli terrorists and the Soviets led the State Department as well as the US Joint Chiefs of Staff to take the possibility of Soviet infiltration seriously. See the State Department memorandum of late August 1948. FRUS (5 Pt. 2), pp. 1360–63.

[2] The account given here is a combination of the British and American records: FO 800/487/PA/48/96 and FRUS (5 Pt. 2) p. 1670 and pp. 1680–85, covering both meetings.

[3] See note 4 on *ibid.*, p. 1685 in which this conclusion is recorded after a meeting between Douglas and officials of the State Department on his return to Washington.

Gaza and neighbouring villages. Each side vigorously proclaimed that the other had broken the truce first. When the British on 29 December moved a resolution in the Security Council for a ceasefire and withdrawal to the positions occupied before the October fighting, they carried it with the necessary two thirds majority; but the USA joined the Soviet Union and the Ukraine in abstaining. The resolution had no more effect than its predecessors. The Israelis rolled up the Egyptian right flank, pinning their forces in the Gaza strip and opening the way to drive into Egyptian territory in Sinai.

The British reacted strongly. Franks was instructed to deliver a note to the Americans in which the British declared that if the Jews did not withdraw from Egyptian territory they would take action against them under the 1936 Treaty with Egypt. Considering that the Egyptians had been doing all in their power to repudiate the treaty, the British were hardly on strong ground but they appear to have been impressed by reports from Amman that the Israelis had simultaneously put pressure on King Abdullah to make peace at once under threat of war. The British read the situation as a danger to the lines of communication between Egypt and Transjordan which they regarded as vital to their strategic position. They proceeded to move equipment into Transjordan and threatened to supply arms to the other Arab countries, if the Americans were unable to persuade the Jews to withdraw from Egyptian territory.[1]

The President's intervention was prompt and unequivocal. In a note which Ben Gurion described as so severe it "might have been written by Bevin himself", Truman called for an immediate withdrawal as the minimum requirement to give proof of the Israelis' peaceful intentions.[2] The Israelis complied but in their reply protested that they had no thought of invading Egypt and had made no threats to Abdullah. It was they who were the victims of aggression for which they blamed the British Government's encouragement to Egypt and the Arab states to invade Palestine in the first place.

The Egyptian defeat had caused an outburst of anger against the Government in Cairo and led to the Prime Minister's assassination by a member of the Moslem Brotherhood. The new Prime Minister had no wish to see the 1936 Treaty invoked by the British and offered to negotiate an armistice with the Israelis. But the situation was still tense and on 3 January the Defence Committee authorized sending a British force to hold the port of Aqaba against any attempt by the Israelis to capture it.[3] Israeli forces were reported to have re-entered Egyptian territory and local fighting to be still continuing, when on 7 January four RAF Spitfires, and later a fifth, which had been sent up on reconnaissance, were shot down by Israeli fighters.

---

[1] Text of the British note verbatim and records of Franks' interview with Lovett, 30 December 1948 in FRUS (5 Pt. 2) pp. 1701–3. Sir Alec Kirkbride's report from Amman which was made available to the Americans is printed on pp. 1699–1700.

[2] 30 December. Text in FRUS (5 Pt. 2) p. 1704.

[3] DO (49) Minutes of 1st meeting, 3 January 1949.

This time the United States used its influence in both London and Tel Aviv to calm tempers and prevent the incident escalating into war. But the shock of recognition that it might have done so led to a renewed outburst of criticism of the Government's policy. Crossman, both in the press and Parliament,[1] put the blame for the shooting down of the Spitfires on Bevin personally, implying that he would not have been sorry for an excuse to involve Britain in a war with Israel. Among Bevin's papers is a note to Attlee dated 28 December warning the Prime Minister that if further RAF flights continued to be made over Palestine, Britain would be accused of violating the UN truce. Bevin agreed that political considerations should not be allowed to override operational needs, but there is no evidence that the decision to continue the operation was made on his instructions or on anyone's orders other than those of the AOC in the Canal Zone.

The last thing Bevin wanted, with the Berlin situation still unresolved and the possibility of war in Europe not to be ruled out, was to see a war start in the Middle East. The strong British note to Washington was directed to preventing this happening, and was made use of by the Americans, who shared Bevin's anxiety, to put pressure on the Israelis and secure their withdrawal from Sinai. It was easier for Ben Gurion to present this as due to a British "ultimatum" than to American intervention.

Bevin defended his Palestine policy at a Cabinet meeting on 16 January.[2] The key sentences of his explanation read:

"We have not opposed the creation of a Jewish state and by supporting the Bernadotte proposals we recognised that the existence of such a state was an accomplished fact. . . . We have sought a settlement including the existence of a Jewish state in which the Arabs could reasonably acquiesce and which they would not bend all their energies to undo."[3]

Nye Bevan attacked the Government's policy by questioning, not the strategic importance of the Middle East, but the assumption that this could be safeguarded by supporting unstable and reactionary governments in the Arab states. The Jewish successes against them had exposed the experts' over-estimate of their strength. "We should have done better" he argued, "to base our position in the Middle East on the friendship of the Jews who would have been glad to give us all the facilities needed to establish strong military bases in Palestine." Bevan poured scorn on the idea that Egypt might invoke the 1936 Treaty, demanded to know what authority had been given to send up the RAF planes or move forces to Aqaba, and declared it might be difficult to prevent a split in the Party, particularly if there was further delay in recognizing Israel.

Bevan's case for looking to the Jews rather than the Arabs for Britain's

[1] "I Accuse Bevin", article in the *Sunday Pictorial* 16 January and speech in the House of Commons 26 January 1949.
[2] CM 3 (49).
[3] CP (49) 10, to which a lengthy historical memorandum was annexed.

strategic needs was countered by the argument that this ignored the importance of the Commonwealth's connection with the Moslem world. But his
warning about a split in the Party was heeded: there was agreement that the
time had come for extending *de facto* recognition to Israel and for releasing
the remaining Jews held in Cyprus. The following day Bevin came back
with the suggestion that he should ask the USA to recognize the Kingdom of
Transjordan at the same time as the UK recognized Israel, but he made no
attempt to reverse the main decision.

When Bevin repeated his defence of his policy in the House of Commons on
26 January, he failed to convince his critics that his object had been to strike a
balance between the conflicting claims of Arabs and Jews. He was careful to
avoid polemics but his acceptance of recognition was grudging; he found
nothing to say in appreciation of the Jewish achievement in creating Israel,
and his reminder (however justified) that the Arabs, with more than half a
million refugees driven from their homes, felt as strongly as the Israelis that
right was on their side, grated on the ears of those who were convinced that he
was actuated by a deep prejudice against the Jews. Although the Government's majority was not in question, it was reduced from 177 to 100 with
seventy members of the Parliamentary Labour Party abstaining.

The decisive factor had been American support for Israel. Bevin and Attlee
sent Franks to see the President on 13 January (before the Cabinet meeting on
the 16th) with instructions to argue forcefully for retaining Arab control of the
southern Negev so as to provide an overland route from Egypt to Transjordan
and Iraq. Truman was friendly but firm: "He was not prepared to make a
point of the Negev. It was a small area and not worth disagreeing over."[1]
American opinion supported him. The Israeli victories which aroused fears
amongst British officials that the new state would follow an expansionist policy
only increased American admiration for the Jews' refusal to let anything stand
in their way. This was now true of many in the State Department and the
Pentagon as well as the White House. After talking to Lovett and other officials
Franks reported a noticeable hardening in their attitude. The British had
backed the wrong horse: the main goal should now be not to contain the
Israelis but "to win them over into the Anglo–American camp and not to
alienate them permanently."

"It was clear," Lovett added, "as indeed had been proved by recent events, that the
State of Israel would be the most dynamic, efficient and vigorous Government in the
Near East in the future."[2]

Bevin never found it easy to admit defeat but Hector McNeil, his Minister of
State, whose opinion he valued highly, undertook to get him to face the facts,
however unpalatable, in particular the fact that the British no longer had the

---

[1] Franks to Bevin, 13 January 1949. FO 371/75337/E 1932.
[2] Franks to Bevin, 13 January 1949. FO 371/65334/E 613 and E 614.

means of the military resources to act unilaterally. "It is essential even when the Jews are most wicked and the Americans most exasperating not to lose sight of this point." No doubt the President had double-crossed the British, but that was no consolation. It did not alter the fact, as McNeil put it, that "As long as America is a major power and as long as she is free of major war, anyone taking on the Jews will indirectly be taking on America." British policy thus led to a dead end, from which there could only be retreat.[1]

Bevin did not come round easily. In a draft letter to Franks of 3 February, he wrote that the American attitude appeared to be not only "to let there be an Israel and to hell with the consequences," but "peace at any price and Jewish expansion whatever the consequences." But there were cooler judgements to persuade him he was exaggerating. Sir John Troutbeck, the head of the British Middle East Office in Cairo and no friend of the Zionists, cabled to him on 4 January that he believed the Israelis were telling the truth when they denied any intention of seizing Egyptian territory or threatening Transjordan, at least for the present.[2] Similarly the retiring Permanent Under Secretary, Sir Orme Sargent, wrote in mid January:

"The worst that we need consider is that the Jews should seize the whole of Palestine up to the Jordan including Jerusalem, for I agree with the Minister of State that the Jews are not going to invade Egypt or Transjordan in order to annex any territory belonging to these countries.[3]

It was these more realistic assessments which prevailed. In fact, relations between Britain and Israel began to improve, however slowly, from this point onwards.

There were several reasons for this. One was the ending of the Arab–Israeli war and the resumption of contacts between the two governments following recognition. During the war the estrangement between them had been complete. Seeing themselves as a small embattled people, the survivors of the Holocaust, ringed with enemies and once again fighting desperately for survival, the Israelis had come to regard the British, and Bevin in particular, as their arch enemies, bent upon their destruction and urging on the Arabs to carry it out. Bevin, on the other hand, seeing himself engaged in a fight for the survival of the Western world in face of the threat of economic collapse and Soviet expansion, had come to regard the Israelis as the principal source of instability in the key area of the Middle East, where their aggressive attitude in defiance of the United Nations was alienating the Arabs from the West and putting a heavy strain on the all-important Anglo–American alliance. Bevin's anxieties crowded out recognition of the Jewish epic achievement in turning

[1] Minute by McNeil, 14 January 1949. FO 371/65337/E 1881.
[2] Troutbeck to Bevin, 4 January 1949. FO 371/65334/E 156/G.
[3] Sargent's minute, 17 January 1949. FO 371/75336/E 1273.

the disaster of the extermination camps into the triumph of Zionism, just as the Israelis' anxieties left no room for recognizing the load Bevin was carrying in trying to organize the recovery and security of Europe; or his warnings to the Arabs and his efforts to damp down hostilities in the Middle East (e.g. by refusing to supply arms to Britain's allies); or his desire to get a settlement in Palestine which would not leave the Arabs committed to its overthrow.

With the opening of contacts between the governments in Tel Aviv and London, there was a better chance of these distortions and misunderstandings being removed. Once he had accepted recognition, Bevin took pains to make sure that the first British representative to be appointed, Knox Helm, serving at the time in Budapest, should understand that his job was to persuade the Israelis "to forget the past and to handle the future". Bevin, who briefed him personally on the line he was to take, added that the Jews would have nothing good to say about him ("they hate me") but that Helm's job was not to justify the past[1].

The conclusion of armistices between Israel and the five Arab states (the first in February 1949, the last in July) reduced tension and raised hopes of a peace settlement. 1949, in fact, was a much more peaceful year in the Middle East than 1948 had been.

Bevin still hoped that Transjordan would acquire what was left of Arab Palestine, but he dropped the idea of a strategic link across the Negev of which he and the generals had made so much at the December meeting with Douglas. When the Israelis pushed south to the Gulf of Aqaba, the British contented themselves with strengthening their garrison in Aqaba itself (in Jordan) but let the Israeli occupation of the Negev pass without protest. In a personal message to Kirkbride in Amman Bevin wrote that he might feel they had not reacted strongly enough. Nothing, however, but British intervention in force inside Palestine would have stopped the Israelis securing access to the Red Sea through the Gulf of Aqaba and so by-passing the Suez Canal, and they could not have carried the USA with them in such a move.[2]

With the presidential election over, Bevin found the Americans prepared to take a firmer line with their Israeli protégés: examples are the President's letter at the time their troops crossed into Egypt and US intervention on a number of occasions when there were hitches in the armistice negotiations.[3] This removed one of Bevin's major grievances and made Anglo–American co-operation easier. In April Bevin was beginning to talk enthusiastically to

---

[1] Author's interview with Sir Knox Helm.
[2] Bevin to Kirkbride, 10 March 1949. FO 800/477/ME/49/9.
[3] In March 1949 when the Israelis threatened to attack the Arab Legion which was taking over an Arab area in Samaria from Iraqi troops, Acheson secured assurances from Shertok which enabled Bevin to defer issuing supplies of ammunition to the Legion. Bevin to Attlee, 17 March 1949. FO 800/488/PA/49/18 and Washington Embassy to FO 23 March, *ibid.*, PA/49/19.

Acheson about schemes for raising the standard of living in the Middle East.[3] Finally, one should mention his relief at seeing the NATO Pact signed and the prospect of the Berlin blockade being called off.

[4] See Chapter 17, Section 4, p. 672.

The plan realized; the North Atlantic Treaty signed

I

The eleven months between the imposition of the Berlin blockade in June 1948 and its removal in May 1949 were the decisive period of the Cold War, finally settling the map of Europe and the balance of power as it has lasted down to the present. The centrepiece of the confrontation was the blockade itself and its counterpart, the air-lift. If the latter had failed in face of winter (and on the last day of November 1948, fog reduced the number of aircraft able to land in Berlin to ten) or if the Berliners' resistance had weakened in face of the siege conditions under which they were obliged to live, not just the future of Berlin, but the future of Europe, would have been decided differently.

The reverse, however, was not necessarily true. It did not follow, even if the Americans and British were able to maintain their position in Berlin by means of the air-lift, that this would lead to a local settlement accepted by both sides, still less certainly that that in turn would open the way to a post-war settlement of Germany and Europe which would be accepted *de facto* by all parties and actually provide an important element of stability in the second half of the 20th century. To secure such a result called not only for a change of policy on the part of the Russians but for skill and an unusual degree of unity on the part of the Western Powers in taking advantage of the opportunity which this presented to them.

The part Bevin played in these transactions, now to be described, represented the culmination of the policy he had pursued at least since 1947, when British power had reached its lowest point ever, and the peak of his achievement as Foreign Secretary—an office in which, with Molotov's replacement by Vyshinsky (March 1949) he had out-lasted all his post-war contemporaries, Byrnes, Marshall, Bidault and Molotov. In the summer of 1949, it was difficult to recognize how considerable an achievement it was, partly because it represented so much less than had been hoped for, especially by Bevin's own party, at the end of the War, partly because no one could foresee whether it would provide a lasting settlement. In the earlier months of 1949, indeed, it was still an open question whether anything could be achieved at all and much hard negotiating lay ahead, with Britain's allies even more than with the Russians.

The year began well enough with a visit by Robert Schuman which appears, in retrospect, to mark a high point in mutual confidence between Paris and London. Many Frenchmen, including a number in the Quai d'Orsay and General Koenig, the Military Governor of the French Zone, had not yet brought themselves to accept the necessity of a changed attitude towards the Germans. Bidault's successor had the advantage of having grown up and been educated in Alsace-Lorraine under German rule, of having served in the German Army in World War I and of being widely read in German as well as French. The Schuman Plan was still more than a year away and the new foreign minister had to take care to guard his flanks and watch his communications with Paris. Nonetheless, French opposition on every issue connected with Germany had made it so difficult to reach agreement amongst the Western Powers on a common policy for the future of Europe that great importance was attached in London and Washington to the signs of Schuman's more open-minded approach.

Ernie Bevin as British Foreign Minister was a surprise for which nothing in the centuries of diplomatic intercourse between the two nations had prepared Schuman. Dean Acheson, the American Secretary of State who became a firm friend of both men, delighted in the contrast between them, describing Schuman "as slender, stooped, bald with long nose, surprised and shy eyes and smile, (who) might have been a painter, musician or scholar . . . rather than a former President of France who had put the Communists out of the Government"; while Bevin "short and stout with broad nose and thick lips, looked more suited for the roles he had played earlier in life than for diplomacy". Schuman's humour "was quiet, gentle and ironic—Bevin's broad and hearty", and the latter's idiosyncratic use of English, his West country speech and tempestuous changes of mood frequently baffled the Frenchman.[1] Unlike Blum, another French intellectual politician with whom Bevin got on well, Schuman belonged to the Christian Democratic MRP, not to the French Socialist Party. But he had enough experience of men and politics to allow him to appreciate Bevin's strengths as well as his weaknesses, and he was particularly struck by the fact that, although Bevin had fewer pretensions to an appreciation of the place of France in European history and civilization than most of his predecessors, none of them had shown himself a stauncher friend of France.

At the end of their two days of talks (13–14 January 1949), Schuman remarked on the confidence in each other which had allowed them to talk

---

[1] Acheson, *Present at the Creation*, pp. 270–71.

openly and frankly about their differences. This is borne out by the record. They began, on the 13th, with the Italian colonies, Bevin voicing British opposition to the Italians returning to Eritrea (with the memories this stirred of the Abyssinian war) and his doubts about their returning to Tripolitania. He was equally opposed to bringing Italy into the Brussels Pact or NATO at this stage, arguing that what mattered was to get the latter set up quickly and accepted by the US Senate, leaving questions of membership and other details until later. Schuman largely agreed, but when Bevin asked him if it was essential to include Algeria, Schuman replied: "Absolutely". There was no chance of getting NATO accepted in France if it was not. Yes, Bevin said, he saw the difficulty. What worried him was anxiety lest they should repeat the mistake of 1918 when the chance of getting the USA right into the affairs of Europe had been lost. Could the French find a formula for Algeria?

In the afternoon they turned to Germany. Bevin told Schuman that he would like to finish with reparations as soon as possible but looked on the UK as a trustee for the other European nations which had been promised a share in them. One of the reasons why he wanted to see a German government set up as soon as possible was to transfer such burdens to the Germans themselves. Schuman expressed particular thanks to Bevin for his understanding of the French position on the Ruhr, promising that he would stand by the decisions of the London conference despite criticism of them in France. He added that he would like to see the Allies' administration in Germany civilianized. Bevin agreed, but argued that the Berlin crisis had made this impossible. If the Allies had not stayed in Berlin, but had let themselves be put out, he believed that the Russians by now would have been on the Rhine. He was evidently testing out Schuman's reaction, for the latter replied that, although French opinion was not happy about making Berlin a symbol of resistance to the Russians, France was firm in support of Western policy.

At the end of the first day, Bevin accepted that there would have to be a wider European body in addition to the proposed Council of Ministers but argued in favour of keeping it under the control of ministers.[1] Schuman countered by saying that if ministers were to fix the Assembly's agenda, this would surely give them sufficient control. The French, he told Bevin, attached great importance to the idea and he believed it would make it much easier to settle such questions as Germany and the Ruhr if these could be put in a European context.

The following day Schuman returned to the subject. He was afraid, he said, that the British attitude would cause great surprise and disappointment in France, especially Bevin's insistence that delegations should not be representative of Parliaments but appointed by governments (in the UK they would represent the majority party) and should vote en bloc, not according to the

[1] Bevin had discussed the constitution of the Council of Europe at the Cabinet meeting on 12 January 1949. CM 2 (49).

views of individual members. Bevin replied that they were trying to meet continental opinion. The British had originally been opposed to any idea of a conference; they had now come round to this, but thought it could not become an irresponsible assembly saying and voting whatever people liked. With a show of feeling that impressed all his listeners, he went on to say that he had strained every nerve to save Western Europe, declaring:

"We must direct our economy and policy and our defence measures in such a way that we should have France back in her old position. All his actions, whether wise or unwise, had been actuated by the desire to get Western Europe united."

Schuman was moved and said so: he had known before of Mr Bevin's act of faith in France and now he had had personal experience of it.

Nonetheless the division between them was still there and worried both men. At dinner at the French Embassy the same evening, Bevin assured Schuman that he was in no way opposed to closer European unity, but it must be solidly built, and they had to learn to walk before they could run. He hoped the French would not insist on building the whole fabric from the outset. Perhaps, he suggested, it was better that there should be two proposals, a French and a British one, for the other European powers to choose between. He added that he was in favour of Strasbourg as the seat of whatever European organization it was decided to set up.[1]

The value of the confidence established in their London meeting was shown in the next three months when both men came under heavy pressure from the Americans in negotiations about Germany. Even when Bevin thought the French were being unduly difficult, he told Douglas that Schuman had been so helpful in other matters that he did not feel able to press him.

The difficulty over the Council of Europe remained. The discussions in Paris which had been broken off in December were resumed in January 1949, but produced no agreement. The British representatives were embarrassed by the instructions they had received from Bevin, particularly the insistence that delegations should represent governments not parliaments and should cast a block vote. Dalton, who led the delegation and had little sympathy himself with the European idea, reported that he had only held the British representatives together with difficulty in face of the Europeans' arguments. The issue had now grown into one of confidence between the British and their continental allies, publicly debated, with more than one suggestion that the Europeans should go ahead without them.

When the Consultative Council of the Brussels Powers met in London on 27 January, Bevin was left in no doubt of British isolation.[2] This did not deter him from defending his position vigorously. If they were starting from scratch, he

---

[1] British record of the talks, 13–14 January 1949. FO 800/465/FR/49/4. See also FO 371/79072–4.
[2] British record in FO 800/460/EUR/49/4.

said, it would be easy. But they had already done a lot for economic recovery, defence et cetera, and set up institutions for these purposes. If the Assembly were free to discuss economic questions, there was a possibility of conflict with the OEEC. Spaak, Schuman, Stikker, all thought Bevin exaggerated the dangers, and told him so. No one proposed that the Assembly should be other than consultative or have the power to commit governments: why should they worry about differences of opinion? Bevin, while still protesting against being pressed to make a decision, used the break at lunch to consult Attlee and, after lunch, gave way to the extent of handing the matter over to the Permanent Commission. Fortunately the Commission was able to come up with a compromise which he was able to accept without too much loss of face.

Bevin's change of front at the January Consultative Council avoided a crisis at a time when it was essential, with negotiations over NATO and Germany coming to a head, to maintain as much unity as possible among the European states and not to provoke more American criticism of the British holding back. But it was a change of front, forced on Bevin by tactical considerations, rather than a change of mind still less a change of heart. He was as unconvinced as ever of the value of the Council of Europe and unwilling to put his weight behind it.[1] In one of his most famous remarks he prophesied: "If you open that Pandora's Box you never know what Trojen 'orses will jump out."

For the moment, however, there was general relief that a way out of the impasse had been found, and this was strengthened by a parallel change in the British attitude towards proposals for the reform of OEEC. This was a matter on which the Americans—particularly Harriman and Hoffman in the ECA —had been pressing Bevin and Cripps for months past. The Inter-European Payments Scheme which the British had been largely responsible for devising in 1948 was a step towards co-operation, but in American eyes did not go nearly far enough. What OEEC needed was greater political authority. After arguing that the members of the Executive Committee ought to be cabinet ministers, not civil servants, Harriman came round to the view—encouraged by Spaak, the chairman of the OEEC Council—that a leading political figure should be appointed as Director General of OEEC in order to give it greater drive and effectiveness. Harriman's—and Spaak's—candidate for the job was Spaak himself; Bevin and Cripps, however, resisted this proposal, whoever it was to be, as firmly as they had the earlier one.

Nonetheless, there was obvious force in the argument that OEEC required stronger political direction and in January Bevin and Cripps came up with a plan of their own. This was for a consultative group of ministers from the leading countries which the Chairman, Spaak, could call together in order to push on business between meetings. Bevin put this to Harriman at a meeting on 12 January at which they also discussed a new factor which was bound to

---

[1] The Cabinet discussed the Council of Europe and its relation to the Committee of Ministers on 28 January (CM 8), 24 February (CM 15), 28 April (CM 30) and 2 May (CM 31). Bevin's attitude was shared by Attlee and the great majority of Labour ministers.

affect the operations of OEEC: this was the need, which was already foreseen, for the USA to provide support for rearming the European countries included in a North Atlantic Treaty and the relationship between a programme for military aid and ERP. Bevin was strongly in favour of keeping the two separate.[1] This was Hoffman's view too but as he had already pointed out to Harriman,[2] given the limited resources available in European countries, any increase in their military budgets must retard their economic recovery. This was another argument for strengthening OEEC.

When the Consultative Council of the Brussels Powers met in London at the end of January, Spaak was scathing in his criticism of their lack of progress in producing a common defence programme. After ten months, nothing had been done: no country knew what was needed of it, there was no timetable, and no plans. Bevin argued that the Brussels Powers had to make their own plans for rearmament. At the same time he put forward the British proposal for strengthening the leadership of OEEC.[3] This was well received and adopted by the OEEC Council in the middle of February.

On 1 March, Harriman and Douglas came to see Bevin and outlined to him the US proposals for military assistance under the North Atlantic Treaty before they put them to the other European countries. This was a subject on which there was no disagreement between Bevin and the Americans, and he responded by laying stress on the need to establish the principle of *mutual* aid and reciprocity.[4] Douglas pressed for an early decision. Washington needed to have a list of the Brussels Powers' requirements by the end of March. Bevin and Cripps had no difficulty in agreeing that the American proposals provided a good basis on which to work and Bevin undertook to call a special meeting of the Brussels Pact Consultative Council in London on 14 March.

Before the Brussels Consultative Council met, the other Consultative Council set up for OEEC held its first session in Paris, with Cripps representing the UK as the Americans had always wanted him to. The contrast between the course of the two meetings brings out well the complexity of the relationship in which Bevin and Cripps were involved with the Europeans on the one hand, the Americans on the other.

Harriman reported back to Washington that in Paris Cripps had gone a long way to persuade the other European ministers to adopt a programme calling for a drastic reduction of dollar imports from the USA and the development of new sources of supply for Europe outside the dollar area. Harriman said bluntly that such a programme, discriminating against US exports to Europe, would have a disastrous effect on American public opinion and the chances of continuing Marshall aid. The USA would not accept a solution for Europe's

---

[1] Note of Harriman's meeting with Bevin and Cripps at the FO, 12 January FO 800/460/EUR/49/1.
[2] Hoffman to Harriman, 8 January. FRUS 1949 (4) pp. 367–8.
[3] British record FO 800/460/EUR/49/4.
[4] FRUS 1949 (4), pp. 136–9.

economic problem which was autarchic in character and he turned the meeting round to drop Cripps' plan and look for an alternative.[1] This was the revival of an old dispute between the Americans and the British which was to become much more serious during the course of the year. What is interesting is that in the OEEC Consultative Council, which the British had taken the lead in setting up in order to meet American criticisms, it was they who were once again seen as the chief obstacle to US policy.

In the Brussels Consultative Council, however, the roles were reversed. Bevin presented a draft of the formal request for military assistance on a basis of mutual help which the US Administration wanted in order to present to Congress, and it was Spaak (who had criticized the British to Harriman for their inability to see beyond their own national interests) who now made the greatest difficulty, objecting to the share of the burden which it was proposed to allot to Belgium. Without a common plan, he declared, and clear proof that others were being asked to do as much, he could not defend the proposal in parliament. It was only after much argument, in which Bevin showed patience as well as skill, that he was able to shepherd his continental colleagues into accepting the result which he had undertaken to produce for Harriman and Douglas [2]

While there were no longer negotiations with the Russians, the difficulty of reaching agreement with his allies was hardly less demanding in the early months of 1949, an impression which is greatly strengthened by the record of negotiations over Germany.

2

At the beginning of 1949 only two parts of the framework within which the development of a West German state was to take place had been blocked in. One was the draft Ruhr Agreement setting up an International Authority for the Ruhr, published on 28 December 1948 but still to be approved by the Allied governments; the other was the Military Security Board, charged with maintaining demilitarization and disarmament in the Western Zones, the directive on which had been promulgated on 17 January but which had yet to be set up. Still remaining to be decided were the Basic Law or constitution of the new state; the Occupation Statute reserving the rights of the Occupying Powers; the future of reparations and dismantling; the prohibition and restriction of German industries, particularly in view of the European Recovery Programme and plans for re-arming Western Europe; the fusion of the French zone with the Anglo–American Bi-zone, and the relationship of the

---

[1] Harriman's report to Hoffman and Acheson, 12 March. FRUS (4) pp. 374–7.
[2] British record of the Brussels Treaty Consultative Council meeting, 14–15 March. FO 800/448/CONF/49/1. Records of the meetings of the Council during 1949 are to be found in FO 371/79242–4 and 79246–51.

latter with OEEC and the ERP. On all these there was disagreement, by no means always dividing the parties concerned along the same lines but always strongly felt. All were the subject of negotiations in the first three months of 1949, always difficult and sometimes acrimonious, involving at one time or another the three Occupying Powers, the three Military Governors (not always in agreement with their home governments), the Benelux powers, the German Parliamentary Council and the rival German parties. Bevin took part, either personally or at one remove in all of them and, at the end, had to go to Washington to try and reach agreement with Acheson and Schuman on the issues which negotiation had been unable to settle.

In drafting the Occupation Statute and the agreement on the fusion of the three Western zones, Bevin acted as a conciliator to bring the American and French positions closer together. Thus, in February, he sent Sir Ivone Kirkpatrick, his principal adviser on German affairs, to Paris with a personal message to Schuman urging him to intervene so that further delays in settling the occupation statute should not hold up the establishment of a West German government.[1] Leaning the other way, he got the Americans to accept limits which both the British and French thought necessary to the predominant voice claimed for the US Military Governor in virtue of the American share of occupation costs.[2] On the other hand, when the Germans put forward the draft of the Basic Law, Bevin was more prepared to accept the proposed division of powers between the Federal Government and the Länder than either the Americans or the French, who agreed in thinking it gave too much power to the centre.[3]

The issue which really roused Bevin, however, was the continued American pressure on both British and French to abandon reparations, stop dismantling and scrap all but a minimum of restrictions on the re-creation of Germany's industrial power. The issue was brought to a head in the middle of January 1949 by the Humphrey Committee's Report, recommending that 167 industrial plants should be removed from the reparations list, and by the Military Governors' report that they could not agree on the limits to be placed on industrial development in Germany. When Bevin asked that the two questions should be discussed together, Acheson refused, believing that this would open the way to a trade-off and that, in view of Congressional opinion, the Administration ought to stand firm both on the Humphrey Report and on the question of prohibitions and restrictions.[4]

Bevin (whom Douglas reported as appearing "listless and tired") maintained that he did not have a free hand in the matter and that the Cabinet

---

[1] FRUS 1949 (3) pp. 29–31: Holmes' report on 7 February of his talk with Kirkpatrick, on the latter's visit to Paris, 4 February.
[2] *Ibid.*, pp. 55–62.
[3] The draft of the Basic Law and the electoral law was reported to the British Cabinet by Bevin (CP (49) 50 and 53) and approved on 10 March, the same meeting at which the Cabinet approved the NATO Treaty. CM 19 (49).
[4] FRUS (3) pp. 546–55.

insisted on taking the two questions together, as did the French. If this could be accepted, he promised to go as far as possible to meet the Americans on the Humphreys Report and to get the French to do the same.[1] Acheson's reply was that the British had better realize that, if they were not careful, Congress would pass legislation going far beyond the Humphrey Report and leading to a cut in American funds for countries receiving reparations and equipment. When Douglas passed this on, Bevin said that he wondered whether it would not be better for the UK to take the risk of a reduction in its appropriation under Marshall aid rather than agree.[2]

Acheson was finally persuaded to concede that restrictions should be discussed at the same time as dismantling provided that the negotiations did not last longer than 4–5 days. He was at once faced with an angry message from General Clay saying that the British were moved by fear of economic competition rather than security and that to accept restrictions on German industry would be a price out of all proportion to the value of the industrial plants they might be able to save from dismantling.[3]

Douglas was given instructions which reflected Clay's views and left him little room for manoeuvre. Bevin's argument that the USA was ignoring the danger of re-creating German military power, including the risk of German industry coming under Soviet control, was brushed aside.[4]

Douglas, who had borne the brunt of the often angry arguments with Bevin, felt that the USA was pushing its two principal allies too far and failing to understand the strength of their case. In cables to Murphy (who had been Clay's Political Adviser and was now acting director of the German office in the State Department), he wrote that of course there were economic interests involved—Labour's concern about unemployment on Clydeside and in the shipbuilding areas—but broad national economic factors could not be excluded. "For example, in resisting British and French, we are often advocates of German economic interests and even of our own." He was convinced that the British and French attitude was "not dictated exclusively or predominantly by political and commercial considerations". There really was a case on security grounds which was not being given proper weight.[5]

Acheson was sympathetic but maintained the pressure. Douglas was instructed to tell Bevin that if the British could not agree to four irreducible conditions, negotiations would be suspended, discussion of the Humphrey Report would be separated from the question of restricted industries, all offers

---

[1] *Ibid.*, pp. 555–9.
[2] Acheson's message, 4 March and Bevin's reply, 7 March, *ibid.*, pp. 559–60.
[3] Clay's message to Voorhees, Under-Secretary of the Army, 14 March, *ibid.*, pp. 564–5.
[4] Bevin presented a full report to the Cabinet (CP (49) 23) on 8 February 1949 and after a long discussion was given the authority he requested to make concessions, if necessary, on the list of plants to be dismantled. The minutes specifically record agreement that "no aspect of reparations policy should be influenced by considerations of protecting British industry against fair competition by the Germans". CM 10 (49).
[5] Douglas to Murphy, 18 March. FRUS (3) pp. 575–7, and 19 March, *ibid.*, pp. 577–81.

of concessions would be withdrawn and any new discussions would have to start from scratch. When Bevin, in a rush to catch the boat to the USA, said that he would have to see what he could do in Washington, Douglas told him flatly that, "after discussions with Washington, I thought he could do no better and might have greater difficulty". The ultimatum, though politely worded, was clear enough. Douglas's report continues:

"He (Bevin) then reviewed disagreed and reserved items; indicated a desire to reach agreement now; asked me to go over the problems with Kirkpatrick, to whom, in my presence, he gave instructions to do his best to get settlement."[1]

Douglas did not conceal his distaste for the instructions he had been given but carried them out. After a week's further negotiation with Kirkpatrick he was able to report on 31 March that they had reached agreement on both questions. In his final report to the Cabinet Bevin foretold that nobody would be pleased with the settlement, the Germans would protest at the restrictions which remained and the French at the concessions. Nonetheless it would remove reparations from debate in Congress where it threatened to compromise the ERP appropriations; it was a gesture towards the Germans at a time when it was all-important to win their confidence and it removed a source of controversy on the eve of signing the Atlantic Pact.[2]

Many American officials thought it was ridiculous for the USA to be paying out a billion dollars a year for the support of Germany and allowing the British and French (whose occupation of Germany, leave alone their own economic recovery, was dependent on American financial aid) "to wreck our plans for Germany by their foot-dragging tactics". This was the phrase used by Kenneth Royall, Secretary of the Army, at a National Security Council meeting in the White House at the end of January. The US Government, he argued, should reach a decision on its overall policy towards Germany, then get the British and French to accept it by "using all forms of pressure open to us e.g. withholding E.C.A. aid, refusal to come into the Atlantic Pact, refusal to approve the Ruhr Agreement".[3]

Neither Harriman nor Acheson was prepared to accept this rough and ready way of dealing with the British and French, but the idea of an over-all package instead of the piecemeal settlement of separate German issues made a strong appeal—always provided (as Acheson insisted) that the Americans, before dealing with the British and French, could first of all agree what their own long range policy towards Germany should be. It was decided, therefore, to set up a sub-committee of the NSC, with the Secretaries of Defence and the Army and the Administrator of ECA as members and the Secretary of State in the chair.

[1] Douglas to Murphy, 24 March *ibid.*, pp. 588–91.
[2] Bevin's report to the Cabinet on the negotiations. FO 800/467/GER/49/17.
[3] The meeting took place on 28 January 1949 and the report was made by George Kennan. FRUS (3) pp. 87–9.

A steering group, under the chairmanship of George Kennan, was given the actual job of defining such a policy.

For all his ability, Kennan was not the man for the job he had been given. In November of the previous year he had produced a powerfully argued "Program for Germany"[1] in which he had urged the US Government not to commit itself to the creation of a West German state which would mean a divided Germany and a divided Europe. Kennan produced a modified version of this argument on 8 March[2] only to tell Acheson the next day that he did not feel able to defend it against those who had the responsibility for operations in Germany. The task of providing a statement of policy towards Germany on which all could agree was handed over to Murphy.

By the time Murphy was ready to send a revised draft to Acheson[3] (on 23 March), opinion was beginning to crystallize in favour of a new and simpler approach to the relationship between the three occupying Powers and a future West German government. The initiative came from Schuman who, instead of writing more and more reservations into the Occupation Statute and the agreement on fusion of the three Zones, with the effect of making them unworkable, had turned French policy round. Francois-Ponçet, the former French Ambassador to Germany in Hitler's time, told Kennan in Frankfurt:

"The occupation statute one was laboriously grinding out in London was over-complicated, impractical and deadening. M. Schuman, who knew Germany from the old days, had no enthusiasm for continuing on this line. He felt that the time had come for a sweeping and forward-looking solution to these problems which would give not only hope and inspiration to German political life but also respite to the Allies from their own wearisome internal differences. . . . The differences which had arisen among the Allies over the handling of the German problem were absurd, tragic and unnecessary. . . . We should seize the occasion to place the whole German question on a new and higher plane."[4]

Kennan was sure that Francois-Ponçet was speaking under instructions, and this was confirmed when Schuman invited Clay to Paris and held a frank exchange with him lasting three-and-a-half hours which the American Pro-Consul described as the most satisfactory he had ever had with any French official.[5]

3

With this change of attitude on the part of the French, there was at last a real possibility of removing the differences which had so far prevented the three

---

[1] 12 November 1948. FRUS 1948 (2) pp. 1325–38.
[2] FRUS 1949 (3) pp. 96–102. The conversation between Kennan and Acheson follows on pp. 102–105.
[3] FRUS (3) pp. 118–37.
[4] Kennan's report, 21 March, *ibid.*, pp. 113–14.
[5] Report of Schuman–Clay interview on 20 March, *ibid.*, pp. 115–18.

governments reaching agreement on Germany. By the time Bevin and Schuman arrived in Washington, ostensibly for the signing of the NATO Treaty, Murphy and the NSC Steering Group had produced a paper on US policy towards Germany and a tentative approach to the two visiting foreign ministers for which Acheson secured the President's approval on 31 March[1]. At Acheson's preliminary meeting with Bevin later the same day, however, the first item to be raised was something quite different, Stalin's willingness to discuss raising the blockade, of which Bevin had been informed in great secrecy before leaving London and which gave the forthcoming discussion of Germany a new urgency.[2]

On 2 February, Stalin had replied to four questions submitted by an American journalist, one of which dealt with the conditions on which the Soviet Union would be prepared to lift the blockade of Berlin. It was noted with interest that in answering this, Stalin limited himself to pointing to the postponement of a separate West German state as a necessary condition and said nothing of a settlement of the currency question in Berlin on which, ostensibly, negotiations had broken down in 1948.[3] Following this, Bevin had a discussion with the Cabinet Committee on Germany and on 9 February had sent a message to Washington that the British were convinced there was no hope of a solution to the currency problem or of the blockade being lifted in the foreseeable future, and therefore were in favour of consolidating the Western position in Germany, introducing the Western Mark as the sole currency in West Berlin by 10 March and facing up to an indefinite continuation of the air-lift with an increased British share.[4] Instructions were also sent to the British Ambassador in Paris and to the British Military Governor to co-operate with the Americans in overcoming French reluctance to agree. The French finally accepted a target date and the Western mark was made the sole legal currency in West Berlin on 20 March.

The following day Philip Jessup, US Ambassador-at-Large, told the British and French that he had made an informal inquiry of Malik, the Soviet representative to the UN, whether there was any special significance in Stalin's omission of any mention of the currency question in his recent answers to questions.[5] Malik promised to find out, and a month later, on 15 March, Jessup met him by invitation in New York. The answer from Moscow was that the omission was "not accidental" and the two men then went on to discuss the possibility of lifting the blockade and proceeding to a meeting of the Council of

[1] FRUS 1949 (3) pp. 140–56.
[2] The British record of Bevin's talks in Washington, FO 800/448/CONF/49/3 and 483/NA/49/10. Additional telegrams between Bevin and Attlee and the Cabinet are to be found in 467/GER/49/22–6. US record of the Washington talks on Germany is in FRUS 1949 (3) pp. 156–84.
[3] Text of questions and answers in RIIA *Documents 1947–48* p. 614. Acheson's comments are printed in RIIA *Documents 1949–50*, pp. 149–53.
[4] Kirkpatrick's message to the US Counselor, Holmes, 9 February. FRUS 1949 (3) p. 671.
[5] The fullest documentation on the diplomacy of the Berlin crisis in 1949 is in *ibid.*, pp. 643–855.

Foreign Ministers.[1] At a further meeting on the 21st, Malik passed on a message from Vyshinsky (who had recently succeeded Molotov as Soviet foreign minister) that if a date could be fixed for the CFM to meet, "there can be a reciprocal lifting of the restrictions on transportation and trade in Berlin".[2]

This was the position, still known only to a handful, when Bevin and Franks arrived for the first of their meetings with Acheson, Murphy and Jessup on the afternoon of 31 March and from the morning of the 1st with Schuman and Couve de Murville as well. Acheson had taken Marshall's place as Secretary of State in January. He had spent two years, between the summer of 1945 and that of 1947, as Under-Secretary to Byrnes and Marshall, was well-versed in the complexities of American foreign policy making and had played a leading part in launching and later recruiting support for the Marshall Plan. Surprisingly, however, he had never met either Bevin or Schuman before. Within a week he had shown he could get on well with both. But no one could have foreseen the real friendship which developed between Acheson, the most articulate and polished of Americans, quick in thought, with a wicked turn of phrase and great intellectual as well as social confidence which could easily be taken for arrogance or at least impatience with fools, and a man as different and unpredictable in his likes and dislikes as Ernie Bevin who had never trusted Byrnes and had never succeeded in penetrating Marshall's reserve.

The meetings did not begin easily. Bevin was full of doubts and suspicions about the Jessup–Malik contacts. The proposed step might imperil many things.

"We are not ready with Western Germany; the N.A.T.O. Pact has not been ratified; the European Council has not been set up. The Soviets might drive a wedge between the countries of Western Europe. They may put up counter proposals frustrating further action. They might upset E.R.P., Ruhr control and the other arrangements. Recently we have gone a long way in Western Europe. It was not clear that Malik had acted officially."[3]

No doubt the difficulties Bevin made reflected temperament as well as calculation: he was still feeling resentment at the pressure to which he had been subjected by the Americans over reparations and restrictions on German industry, but by showing reluctance he also placed himself in a stronger position to exact concessions. He did not seriously suggest that they should not follow up the chance of ending the blockade; but with more experience than the other foreign ministers of negotiating with the Russians, he was genuinely worried at the prospect of seeing the progress they had made so painfully since the last CFM put at risk, at least until he had examined with great care

[1] Jessup's account, *ibid.*, pp. 695–8.
[2] *Ibid.*, pp. 701–4.
[3] American record of the first meeting of the three foreign ministers, 1 April. FRUS (3) pp. 709–12.

what was being offered. It was eventually agreed that Franks and Couve should join Jessup in producing a draft of the statement he might read to Malik at their next meeting.

The real question for Bevin was how far they were going to be able to reach agreement amongst themselves on Germany on which they had been labouring, still without success, for two years. Acheson's reply was that, if they succeeded with "the new approach" on Germany to which he pinned his hopes, many of the difficulties would disappear. Bevin did not dispute this. He thought the French would be strongly influenced by the signature of the NATO Pact, adding: "Schuman has an entirely different point of view toward the Germans and is trying to bury past enmities." Nor was his own mind closed to new possibilities. He told Acheson that he had been wondering whether, with the Pact signed, they should not see if the Russians were fed up with their experience in Europe and would be glad to negotiate a settlement which would allow them to get out of Europe and go home.

"Maybe we should tell them we are ready to discuss in a CFM all European questions, such as Austria, Trieste, our rights under the Balkan Treaties. . . ."[1]

But that was for the future: the important thing now was to learn Schuman's reaction to the idea of a new approach to a German settlement, and on that the news was more encouraging than anything Bevin and Acheson could have hoped for. The long drawn out resistance on the part of France to going ahead with a three power settlement of Western Germany was reversed: "It was essential", Schuman said, "to perfect 3-power agreement on Germany, particularly if we become engaged in 4-power discussions."[2] This opened a prospect of getting something done which had been lacking from all earlier meetings on Germany, whether four-power or three-power.

Bevin asked to see the new American proposals before making any comment, but when the discussions were resumed on 6 and 8 April, after the signing of the NATO Treaty, he showed himself as ready as the other two to scrap the cumbersome Occupation Statute with its 28 clauses and approve an arrangement much closer to the Austrian model. The Western Powers would no longer attempt to govern Germany, but would leave the Germans free to go ahead and govern themselves, as well as run their own economy, subject to certain specified areas in which the Western Powers would retain reserved powers. Military Government would be dismantled and the functions of the Allied authorities divided, military functions being exercised by a C.-in-C., all other functions by civilian High Commissioners with very much reduced staffs. When it came to the Basic Law, Bevin urged his colleagues, and the French in particular, to take a liberal attitude towards the work of the Parliamentary Council and not press objections to the point where the

---

[1] Bevin's meeting with Acheson, 31 March. FO 800/448/CONF/49/3; FRUS (3) pp. 156–8.
[2] Bevin–Acheson–Schuman meeting, 1 April. FO 800/448/CONF/49/10; FRUS (3) 158–60.

compromise which had been agreed with difficulty between the Christian Democrats and the Socialists would be broken up and the latter refuse to accept the new constitution. He succeeded in getting a letter of guidance sent to the Military Governor, excluding Berlin from the initial organization of the Federal Republic (as the French insisted), but otherwise saying that they "would give sympathetic consideration" to proposals which met particular points, such as that raised by Bevin on the division of powers between the Federal Government and the Länder and not attempting to dictate what they required.[1]

The real difficulty for Schuman was the fusion of the French with the other two zones and the French fear that they would be constantly outvoted by the other two members of the joint Allied High Commission. The circumstances in which a High Commissioner could appeal to the governments took up a large part of four meetings.

These difficulties, however, did not prevent the three Foreign Ministers achieving "prodigies of agreement", as Acheson described them. At the end of a week's discussions they settled the Occupation Statute and the Trizonal Agreement; drafted communications to the Bonn Parliamentary Council and the Military Governors; decided their attitude towards the German draft of a Basic Law; accepted the agreements reached in London on dismantling plants, and on prohibited and restricted industries and finally confirmed the earlier agreement on the International Ruhr Authority—all between the 6th and 8th April.

Moreover, Schuman's reversal of policy was sufficient to open the way not only to agreement on Germany but to exploiting the Jessup–Malik opening to an agreement with the Russians on lifting the blockade. The two were related. Bevin was still concerned to make sure beyond any doubt that if a West German Government (as was likely) had not actually been set up by the time a meeting of the Council of Foreign Ministers took place, this would not be construed as an undertaking to suspend the preparations for such a government. In any communication to the Russians, Jessup was to state: "These preparations will continue."[2] With that safeguarded, however, and the agreements for creating a German government at last signed, Bevin was ready for Jessup to continue his meetings with Malik.

---

[1] Bevin cabled and telephoned to London to secure Cabinet approval for the "new approach" to the German settlement. The main features of the American proposals were put before the Cabinet by Attlee on 7 April with a strong recommendation by Bevin not to miss the opportunity they offered. He was given authority to proceed as he thought best. CM 26 (49).

[2] Meetings with Acheson and Jessup on 31 March and with the same plus Schuman on 1 April. FO 800/448/CONF/49/10; FRUS (3) pp. 709–12. The statement that it was finally agreed Jessup should make to Malik on 5 April is on p. 716.

4

Bevin's primary purpose in going to Washington at the end of March had been to sign the North Atlantic Treaty, and this was still, in his mind, more important than anything else, the foundation of security on which the economic recovery of Europe, and the prime condition of that, Europe's recovery of confidence, depended.

The NATO talks in Washington had begun again on 14 January 1949. Seven more meetings were necessary before, at the 18th session on 15 March, there was at last an agreed text of the draft treaty.[1] The new Secretary of State, Dean Acheson, now took over the chairmanship himself; Sir Oliver Franks continued to represent the UK and, with Hume Wrong, the Canadian Ambassador, contributed most to help Acheson produce a positive result. The opposition came from the French Ambassador, Henri Bonnet, who as late as 1 March (14th Meeting), said that France would have to reconsider its participation in the Pact, if her government was asked to sign a treaty which included Norway but not Italy and which did not satisfy her on the inclusion of Algeria. At this point, Franks suggested that it did not really help to lay down conditions:

"Although it might be a defect of national temperament on his part, it made it more difficult for Sir Oliver to reach an agreed solution if a pistol was put at his head. His natural instinct was to react against it and he did not wish to be put in that position.

"M. Bonnet said that his natural reaction was the same, when he was engaged in a negotiation and had the impression of talking to a wall."

Bonnet, however, withdrew any suggestion of conditions and the situation was eased when Acheson remarked that the USA could now agree to the inclusion of France's Algerian departments. In fact the French got their way on Italy as well as Algeria, despite the reluctance of all the other parties to include the Italians at this stage. In return, the French dropped the objection, which they had made for the purposes of bargaining, to the inclusion of Norway. Norway, Iceland, Greenland (and therefore Denmark) were of importance to the Americans and Canadians for their own northern defences, but quite apart from the tactical opposition of the French (who were more interested in the Mediterranean than the North Atlantic), the Scandinavians themselves were divided about the wisdom of abandoning their traditional neutrality. Many meetings between them and the Americans were necessary before Norwegians and Danes—but not the Swedes—accepted the invitation to join, after the collapse of the latter's efforts to set up a Scandinavian neutrality pact.

The Irish tried to make the ending of partition a condition of joining, but got

---

[1] The British record of the negotiations is in FO 800/455/DEF/49/3 and FO 371/79218–41. US record in FRUS 1949 (4) pp. 1–293.

no response and were left out.[1] The Portuguese were troubled about the exclusion of Spain but finally accepted in time to be one of the original signatories. Although Italy's inclusion extended the Pact to the Mediterranean, no one was in favour at this stage of bringing in Greece and Turkey, still less Iran, or of creating a Mediterranean or Middle East Pact.[2]

More important than the question of who should be included was the question of the obligations to be assumed, particularly by the USA, and of how these would be viewed by Congress. Acheson had the Vandenberg Resolution to rely on, but the translation of its generalities into the wording of a treaty raised constitutional difficulties about any automatic involvement of the United States in collective action. In the middle of February an unscheduled debate in the Senate led to accusations that the country was being committed in advance. At this point the State Department backed off and considered omitting any mention of military action. Before doing so, however, Acheson sought Oliver Franks' advice on the effect this would have on the other parties to the Treaty.[3] In the light of Franks' reply it was decided to go for the phrase eventually included in Article 5. An armed attack against one was to be considered as an attack against all, and in the event of sudden attack

"Each of them will assist the Party or Parties so attacked by taking forthwith, individually and collectively and in concert with the other Parties, such action as it deems necessary, including the use of armed force, to restore and maintain the security of the North Atlantic area."[4]

The relationship of the Treaty to the UN Charter, and which articles of the Charter it was to be brought under, was another reef that had to be circumnavigated. Duration was fixed at twenty years and agreement recorded on a number of points of interpretation before the text was released to the press on 18 March. The same evening, after laying the Treaty before the House of Commons, Bevin made one of his rare broadcasts. Starting with the failure of the UN to fulfil its purpose of guaranteeing the prevention of war, and tracing the development of Western co-operation from the Treaty of Dunkirk through the Marshall Plan and Brussels Pact, he described the Pact "as an endeavour to express on paper the underlying determination to preserve our way of life—freedom of the press, freedom of religion, and the rights and liberty of the individual".

Although the Pact could never have come into existence if it had not been for

---

[1] Acheson–McBride talk, 11 April, *ibid.*, 292–3.
[2] Bevin's message delivered on 14 March, *ibid.*, pp. 209–10 and p. 233.
[3] For the row in the Senate, see Acheson pp. 281–2, and for the consultation with Franks and Truman, FRUS (4) pp. 113–17.
[4] Bevin reported to the Cabinet on the negotiations and secured agreement to this re-phrasing (which he thought an improvement) at the meeting on 22 February. CM 14 (49). The text of the Treaty was approved by the Cabinet, which recorded its congratulations to Bevin, on 10 March. CM 19 (49).

American strength and the willingness of the Truman Administration to assume unprecedented obligations in time of peace, and although it was driven through in the final negotiations by Acheson's skill and determination, it was Bevin who right through 1948 had argued persistently against American doubts and French scepticism, in season and out, that such a pact was both possible and necessary as the only way to recreate European confidence. He himself always laid emphasis on the part played by Canada, particularly Lester Pearson, the Canadian Secretary of State, and for a man who in earlier days had been accused of "hogging the credit", he made little attempt to claim a special role. Nonetheless, it was with pride that he said, on 4 April, when his turn came to sign with the eleven other foreign ministers:

"I am doing so on behalf of a free and ancient parliamentary nation and I am satisfied that the step we are taking has the almost unanimous approval of the British people. . . .

"Our peoples do not want and do not glorify war, but they will not shrink from it if aggression is threatened."

This was not only the climax of his career as Foreign Minister but—with a German settlement at last secured and the prospect of the Berlin blockade being lifted—the greatest ten days of his life. Even the creation of the TGWU could not compare with the events in which he was now a principal actor.

He had still time while he was in Washington to talk about other parts of the world besides Europe and the North Atlantic. One was the Italian colonies on which he had five separate meetings with Acheson and Dulles, with Sforza and with Schuman without getting any nearer to agreement. Britain, Bevin said, meant to keep Cyrenaica; favoured a union of Eritrea with Ethiopia; was ready for Italian Somaliland to go back to Italy and, while not prepared to propose the return of Tripolitania as well to Italy, was no longer opposed to it. The point on which he was adamant was his refusal to use British troops to put the Italians back: he did not want another Palestine.[1]

Bevin expounded his general ideas on the Middle East in a talk with Acheson on 2 April. He was no longer anxious for any declaration about Turkey or Iran, or for a military pact: his interest had reverted to economic development. He mentioned schemes for developing the resources of the Nile, Lake Tana and the Euphrates and spoke of plans for resettling the 800,000 Arab refugees from Palestine. The best way of fighting Communism was by raising the standards of living of the 100 million people who lived in the area between Turkey and Pakistan. It was also a way of developing new markets for British and European exports. Acheson was interested, seeing a connection with Truman's Point IV, to which he was trying to give some sort of substance, and with America's wish to see Western Europe find another outlet for trade in place of Eastern Europe.[2]

[1] FO 800/483/NA/49/10; FRUS 1949 (6) 897–8.
[2] 800/448/CONF/49/3. For Truman's Point IV, see below, p. 681.

The Foreign Office attached importance to Bevin persuading Acheson that the USA should take greater interest in what was happening in South East Asia. The British Commissioner General for the area, Malcolm MacDonald, had written to Bevin just before he met Acheson, urging the need to look at South East Asia as a whole, as the Communists did, not simply country by country, and to recognize that if the West did not react firmly it would quickly lose Burma and Indonesia to begin with, and a large part of the rest of a highly important part of the world to follow.[1] Bevin left with Acheson a memorandum written by Osler Dening, his principal adviser on Far Eastern affairs, which expressed British anxiety that, as security increased in Europe and the Middle East, Russian pressure in that part of Asia might grow. This was an area they could not afford to neglect. The conditions there were favourable to the growth of Communism and offered the Russians the chance of a big success without war. Any initiative to resist Communism in Asia would have to come from the Asian powers themselves, particularly India and Pakistan, acting in their own self-interest. But Britain and the USA might hope to prompt the initiative and help it with technical assistance, capital goods and the provision of arms on a small scale.[2]

In talking to Acheson Bevin did not spend time on the detail but gave a graphic account of how South East Asia and the Middle East fitted into his picture of the world. In the latter there were 100 million Moslems, potentially a force not to be ignored in the world balance of power. Britain provided the "best window" on this area and Bevin thought that rather than trying to create a joint military pact, the British and Americans should adopt a common line in developing the resources, particularly oil, needed for its defence. He then went on to develop the same theme in South East Asia, where 60% of the population were also Moslems. Russia had an obvious opening. Britain could exercise influence through Pakistan but would need American help. He proposed to set up a conference standing for South East Asia in which Britain, the USA, Australia and New Zealand could co-operate for economic and political purposes as distinct from a military pact as MacDonald had suggested. A common front from Afghanistan to Indo-China would make it possible to contain the Russians, rehabilitate and stabilize the area and provide communications across the world. He ended by underlining Britain's intention to stay in Hong Kong, and if necessary make it "a Berlin of the East".[3]

The most important thing to be done immediately, however, was to give substance to the North Atlantic Treaty they had signed, Article 3 of which committed "the Parties, separately and jointly, by means of continuous and effective self-help and mutual aid, [to] maintain and develop their individual and collective capacity to resist armed attack". The Foreign Ministers had agreed that it would be necessary to constitute a NATO Council and a Defence

[1] MacDonald to Bevin, 23 March 1949, received 28 March. FO 371/76033/F 4545/1073/61G.
[2] FO 371/76023/F 4486/1023/61G, and F 5743; FRUS 1949 (7) pp. 1135–7.
[3] FO 800/448/CONF/49/3.

Committee, leaving it to a working party to hammer out the details of the Organization. But it was essential to take steps immediately to set up a programme of military aid if this was to secure the assent of Congress.

Bevin's stand in favour of leaving the Brussels Powers to draw up their own request for military aid had been accepted by the Americans.[1] Douglas reported that Bevin told him, if Washington had changes to suggest, it would be best to do so by interpreting the language of the request and clarifying any points "according to our own lights. . . . Bevin said it would be impossible to re-assemble the Consultative Council and have them make the changes we had in mind".[2] In fact, the request came close enough to meeting Washington's needs, and Bevin's advice was accepted.

There was one issue, however, on which Bevin again stood up to the Americans, this time in support of the Dutch. American opinion had sharply condemned the Dutch for breaking off negotiations and using force in Indonesia. The US representative on the Security Council sponsored a resolution calling on the Dutch in uncompromising terms to release the Republican leaders, facilitate their return to Jogjakarta and form a federal government by 15 March. This was resisted by the Dutch who maintained that they were still committed to independence for Indonesia and that outside interference was more likely to delay than expedite a settlement. Nonetheless, the Security Council passed the American resolution on 28 January and on 4 March Acheson cabled Douglas and Harriman that, if the Dutch continued to ignore it, the USA might find it necessary to refuse assistance to them under any military aid programme.[3]

Bevin was as eager as anyone to see the Dutch reach agreement with the Indonesians: their failure to do so put a heavy strain on relations between the West and Asian leaders like Nehru. But he urged the Americans not to drive Stikker into a corner when he was trying to get a settlement. Their insistence on the UN resolution was making that more difficult, if only by encouraging the Republican leaders to put up their terms. In the meantime he persuaded Stikker to take part in the Brussels Pact Consultative Council with the casuistical argument that Acheson's message was not intended to apply pressure but only to state the facts.[4]

In an annexe to their request for aid, the Brussels Powers, at Bevin's suggestion, had stated the principle that there must be "solidarity among and equality of treatment for" the five of them. No one should be singled out for special action and WEU should "deal with US on a basis of oneness". In this

---

[1] At a discussion in London, 25 March, Harriman agreed with Douglas when the latter said: "If we ask WEU (Western European Union), to re-write their request we really are coercing. We tell them we want them to be spontaneous, but we won't let them be. . . . If they are in fact spontaneous, we are not barred from stating an opinion." FRUS 1949 (4) p. 247. Western European Union (WEU) not the organisation *set* up by the Brussel's Treaty.
[2] *Ibid.*, p. 245.
[3] *Ibid.*, p. 163 and p. 165.
[4] Douglas to Acheson, 7 March, *ibid.*, pp. 165–6.

way, as Bevin explained to Douglas, they hoped to protect the Dutch against discrimination by the USA and, if need be, the French in Indo-China and the British in Malaysia. In consequence, it should be left to WEU to make the allocations of American military aid amongst its members.[1] The issue was still not settled however when the Foreign Ministers assembled in Washington.

At dinner on Bevin's arrival in Washington, Acheson had told him that he had just spent two-and-a-half hours with Stikker leaving him in no doubt that Congress was profoundly convinced the Dutch were in the wrong and, if they did not liquidate their dispute with the Indonesians, would refuse to vote money for arms in their case. Acheson, in fact, had said that it might well lead to the defeat of the whole Military Assistance Programme. Stikker had been very upset and had said the Netherlands might not sign the Atlantic Pact. If so, Acheson asked Bevin, what would the UK do?[2]

Bevin did not equivocate: the British would sign whatever the Dutch did. But he got hold of Stikker as soon as he could and persuaded him to drop the phrase about "equality of treatment" from the WEU request for aid. Instead he got him to accept the inclusion of a clause in the US reply saying that the allocation of US aid should be by common agreement between the Brussels Powers and the USA, thereby avoiding any mention of equality of treatment on the one hand or of the USA's right to discriminate between the members of WEU on the other.[3] Fortunately, by the time Bevin discussed the matter with Acheson again on 2 April, both Dutch and Indonesians had agreed to resume talks, and Bevin, while admitting the Dutch had been foolish, urged Acheson now to put pressure on the Indonesians and not to ignore the danger, if the Dutch withdrew, of a complete breakdown in Indonesia which would let in Communism.[4] Finally, when he saw Stikker off after they had both signed the NATO Pact, he told him that this was the big chance for Holland and urged him to take it by following his own as well as Acheson's advice in getting Van Royen, the Dutch representative at the UN, whom both thought well of, out to Batavia as quickly as possible.[5]

This episode is worth recalling because it illustrates well the role Bevin played—and which the Americans accepted, and indeed expected him to play—in mediating between Britain's European allies and the USA. The Military Aid Programme was not approved by Congress nor the Dutch–Indonesian negotiations concluded without a lot more time and trouble, but at least the dangerous connection between the two had been broken and prevented from holding up the exchange of letters on the Programme immediately after the NATO Treaty had been signed.

[1] *Ibid.*, p. 230 and p. 246. Douglas and Harriman supported Bevin. Douglas to Acheson, 27 March, pp. 251–3.
[2] 31 March, FO 800/483/NA/49/10; FRUS (4) pp. 258–61 for Acheson–Stikker meeting.
[3] The final text of the WEU request and the US reply in FRUS (4) pp. 285–8.
[4] Bevin's talk with Acheson, 2 April. FO 800/448/CONF/49/3.
[5] Bevin's talk with Stikker, 4 April, *ibid.*, 483/NA/49/10.

While Bevin was in the USA, the UN General Assembly resumed its third session (1 April–18 May) in New York, where the Security Council had its seat and was in more or less permanent session. Bevin kept away from both. Now that secret talks had begun about the Berlin Blockade he was particularly anxious for the UN not to be brought into the act again. Once the parties concerned had to conduct their exchanges in public, freedom of action was lost and diplomacy gave way to manoeuvring for propaganda effect.

The fact that the Australian Foreign Minister, Herbert Evatt, was chairman of the General Assembly made Bevin more, not less, uneasy. He regarded Evatt as an ambitious politician eager to show his independence of the UK and to make a reputation at the UN by taking up problems which the Great Powers were unable to solve. On his way to New York, he sent a message back to Attlee asking him to make it clear to Evatt when he passed through London that his various initiatives in the Assembly—attempts at mediation over Berlin and Greece, and his belief that by careful handling he could induce the Russians to take a less unfriendly line—were certainly not helpful and were not regarded as such in London. Bevin felt that the Russians could be expected to launch a new campaign full of specious promises—including an offer to call off the Berlin blockade—in order to try and hold up developments in Western Germany. He was anxious the Western Powers should not fall into the trap, and that the President of the Assembly should not play the Russian game by setting up as a mediator and so weaken the West's determination to hold its ground in Germany.[1]

In fact, Foreign Ministers of the leading Powers only appeared at the General Assembly on special occasions: normally, Britain was represented at the General Assembly, not by the Secretary of State but by one of the Ministers of State—Hector McNeil and later Kenneth Younger—and on the Security Council by the Permanent Representative, Sir Alexander Cadogan. Bevin, however, was constantly consulted on the line to be taken in committees as well as the main bodies. Amongst Bevin's papers is a letter from Christopher Mayhew, his Parliamentary Under Secretary, in which he apologizes for a remark he had made during a debate in the UN Economic and Social Council to the effect that the UK was close to an over-all balance of trade. This had led to an outcry in the USA, reported in turn by British papers and the subject of questions in the Commons. Mayhew was accused of making it more difficult for Marshall aid to be given to Britain when (as he wrote to Bevin) he had only been trying to defend the achievement of the Labour Government against attacks. On such occasions Bevin was at his best. Thanking Mayhew for his explanation he wrote back:

[1] Bevin's message to the Prime Minister relayed by Strang, 28 March 1949. FO 800/511/UN/49/20 and Bevin to Strang, 31 March, *ibid.*, UN/49/51.

"No harm was done except in the peroration. The thing to do in future is to avoid perorations. Do not worry too much: when you get into a tangle like this, we old ones have to get you young ones out of trouble. Anyway I understand the circumstances and do not let it daunt you. But I repeat what I said on Saturday, do not make any further comment. Good wishes."[1]

Although Bevin did not attend any UN meetings while he was in America he was closely involved with the issues which figured prominently on the UN agenda. Both sprang from the break up of European empires: the Dutch in South-East Asia, the Italian in Africa. The Dutch were already under fire at the Security Council when Nehru's Delhi conference, attended by nineteen states (including Australia, New Zealand and Pakistan but not Britain), powerfully reinforced the condemnation of the so-called Second Police Action. The American resolution followed, setting a deadline by which the Dutch had to conform to the Security Council's demands. It was the Dutch insistence on ignoring the timetable dictated to them and going about the transfer of power in their own way which led to the pressure from the State Department. Apart from his intervention to make sure that the Dutch were not denied a place in the American military aid programme, Bevin sought to avoid a confrontation between the Dutch and the UN by joining with the Canadians in persuading the Security Council (on 23 March) not to insist on the letter of their resolution but to instruct the UN Commission to help the Dutch and the Republicans reach agreement on a round table conference. It was the agreement at least to preliminary negotiations which enabled Bevin to find a way out for Stikker in Washington.

India and Australia, however, were dissatisfied with what they regarded as evasion of the original Security Council resolution and, with the agreement of Evatt, got the Indonesian question put on the agenda of the General Assembly. A further meeting in Delhi attended by representatives of India, Australia and nine other states organized support for their opposition. They failed to get a majority, however, on 10 May when a vote at the General Assembly postponed discussion until the next session. By that time the Dutch had brought off their Round Table conference with the Indonesians at The Hague and reached agreement on the transfer of sovereignty to the United States of Indonesia on 2 November 1949, a resolution of the dispute which was welcomed by the General Assembly and would have been by the Security Council as well if the USSR had not interposed its veto.

Bevin was well aware—Nehru made sure of that—of the damaging effect of this long drawn out dispute on the credibility of the Western Powers, but unlike the Americans, who were openly critical of the Dutch, Bevin acted as far as possible behind the scenes giving unobtrusive support to Stikker against his

---

[1] Letters of 25 and 28 February 1949. FO 800/495/PLT/49/2 & 6. Also in Bevin's papers is a copy of a letter from A. D. K. Owen (Assistant Secretary General of the UN) to Cripps saying that Mayhew had given one of the most effective speeches on behalf of the UK for a long time.

critics at home as well as abroad and steadily encouraging him to come to terms with the Indonesians. No one was more relieved to see the dispute resolved in the autumn of 1949 without a breach between the Dutch and their allies. For that Stikker gave the principal credit to Bevin and years after the latter's death still spoke with enthusiasm of the debt he owed to Labour's Foreign Secretary and described him as a great friend of the Dutch people.[1]

In his Washington talks with Acheson, Bevin came closer to reaching agreement on a solution for the intractable problem of the Italian colonies, particularly Tripolitania, where the British were still responsible for the administration.[2] Bevin believed the best solution was an American trusteeship for Tripolitania, but had to accept that it was not practical politics. He hoped, however, that with Italy accepted as a member of NATO it might be easier to find a way out of the impasse and after a fruitless discussion in the UN he had sufficient success with Sforza, when the Italian Foreign Minister visited London early in May, to produce a formula known as the Bevin-Sforza Agreement.

This postulated independence for Libya in ten years. During that period the British would act as trustees for Cyrenaica and the French for the Fezzan. Tripolitania would be administered for two years by the British and then by the Italians for the remaining eight. Italian Somaliland was to be put under Italian trusteeship at once; Eritrea was to be divided between Abyssinia and the Sudan, with certain rights reserved for Italy in the towns of Asmara and Massawa. Despite hostile demonstrations in Tripolitania and Soviet opposition, this plan was approved by the Political Committee of the General Assembly in May, but failed by one vote to secure the necessary two-thirds majority in the Assembly itself.

This defeat, unexpectedly, led to a solution of the problem. The Italian government, abandoning all hope of regaining a place for Italy in Libya or Eritrea, came out in favour of the immediate independence of both territories, and the British decided, since the UN could not agree on anything, to push ahead with self-government for the Senussi in the Cyrenaican half of Libya as well. This gave great satisfaction to Bevin who at last saw a way of securing British bases in Cyrenaica and keeping Britain's pledge to the Senussi at the same time, and the way was opened to a settlement finally accepted by the United Nations in the autumn of 1949.

In addition to Indonesia, Greece and Spain were two other issues which the Soviet Union had used to attack Bevin's foreign policy as long ago as the first session of the United Nations in London in January 1946, and on many occasions since. Both were still capable of rousing suspicion and doubt in the Labour Party about the Government's policies, although much less so than in earlier years, and both figured again on the UN agenda in 1949.

[1] In conversation with the author.
[2] See the exchanges between the USA and the UK in March before the Foreign Secretary's visit to Washington. FRUS 1949 (4) pp. 528–42.

Spain was the more easily and quickly dealt with. There was a growing body of Republican opinion in the USA in favour of making Spain a member of NATO. This was turned down by Acheson and three separate statements rejecting the idea were made at Westminster. An attempt by Franco to secure a loan from the US Export-Import Bank was also refused by Acheson on the grounds that Spain was not a good credit risk. Nonetheless four Latin American countries got a majority in the Political Committee of the UN General Assembly (7 May) for a resolution leaving member states free to resume diplomatic relations with Spain if they wished. When the proposal came before the General Assembly itself (16 May) Hector McNeil put the British position in a double-edged speech which delighted Bevin, declaring that they found:

"Authoritarian governments, prohibition of assembly and association, censorship of the press, denial of fair trial, improper restraint of criticism and political opposition and the maintenance of a police state repugnant, whether these existed in Spain, Bulgaria or anywhere else."[1]

The Latin American resolution was put to the vote but failed to get the two-thirds majority needed.

The other "Fascist" regime which Bevin had been continually reproached for supporting was that in Athens. Bevin had no opinion of Greek politicians whether in power or in opposition, but for more than four years he had held to the view, however unpopular, that the Communists should not be allowed to turn Greece into another Balkan satellite. While the Greek civil war entered its last phase, Greece reappeared on the UN agenda with Evatt, as President of the General Assembly, and the UN Secretary General renewing their efforts to mediate between the Greek Government and their northern neighbours. An earlier attempt had broken down in January 1949, but Evatt, to Bevin's anger, refused to give up and tried again in April. On 19 May, the day after the third session of the General Assembly closed, he issued a statement announcing that the conciliators proposed to add one more to the long series of commissions which had studied the Greco-Albanian frontier since 1913.

Although 1949 had begun badly for the Greeks, with morale still further depressed by rebel successes in January, the appointment of General Papagos as C.-in-C. and of a coalition including all but one of the leading politicians, raised hopes that the war could at last be ended not by negotiation in which no Greek had any faith, but in the field. The rebels were in even worse shape than the Government. The need to choose between Tito and Stalin had split the leadership which was already divided by a disagreement on tactics between Markos, its nominal head, and Zakhariades, the Moscow-trained Secretary General of the Party. The conflict between the two leaders ended in Markos' removal as a defeatist. Zakhariades persuaded a majority of the Greek

---

[1] Quoted in RIIA *Survey of International Affairs 1949–50* (London 1953) pp. 297–8.

Communist leadership to back the Cominform against Tito. But support for the Stalinist line brought little profit for the Greek Communists. If Djilas is to be believed, Stalin had already written off their rising,[1] although no doubt he would have taken advantage of a Communist victory. On the other hand, the Yugoslavs, who had given far more support than the Russians, began to reduce their aid from November 1948 and had no reason to go on at all when the Greek Communist leadership lined up with the rest of the Cominform against them. The breach between Tito and his former allies, the Bulgarians and the Albanians, altered the whole pattern of politics in the Balkans. Instead of uniting to support the Greek Communists, they became absorbed in fighting each other over Macedonia.

The Greek Communist leadership was divided not only over Titoism but over their own struggle, whether to continue the civil war or to aim at a compromise short of victory. They had to rely on pressed service to keep up their numbers, while seeing more and more deserters giving themselves up. When fighting was renewed in April 1949 the National Army gained the upper hand. The rebel government appealed to the UN, in the person of Evatt, but the Greek Government, with the backing of Washington and London, refused to treat. Although unknown at the time, Gromyko too approached the British and Americans about mediation in Greece as well as the lifting of the Berlin blockade.[2] Before the UN met again, the National Army won a decisive victory on Mt. Grammos in August and settled the matter.

The other perennial item on the General Assembly's agenda—disarmament—highlighted the frustrations of the United Nations. Both the Commission on Conventional Armaments and the Commission on Atomic Energy (AEC) met throughout the first half of 1949. The first produced a plan (French in origin) for the collection and verification of information about armaments which ran into immediate opposition from the Russians when discussed by the Security Council. In face of the Soviet veto all that could be achieved by the end of the year was to send the plan to the General Assembly. The AEC pursued a different course and achieved even less. It finally resolved in the summer of 1949 to report that it was pointless to go on with its work until the six permanent members of the Commission could find a basis for agreement among themselves. With no prospect of such agreement on either conventional or atomic armaments, both the Russians and the Western Powers spent their time in tactical manoeuvres designed to put the onus of failure on the other side and exploit this in their propaganda campaigns. In the meantime, the real decisions were either made by national governments

---

[1] Milovan Djilas, *Conversations with Stalin* (London 1962) p. 164, reporting an exchange between Stalin, Dimitrov, himself and Kardelj in Moscow, February 1948.
[2] Gromyko's approach was reported by Bevin to the Cabinet on 19 May. If it gave an opportunity for a general settlement of Balkan problems (set out in CP (49) 113), Bevin thought it worth pursuing and would not exclude a settlement on Greece alone if a wider agreement proved difficult. His proposal to discuss a response on these lines with Acheson was approved and the discussion took place in Paris on 26 and 31 May 1949. FO 800/448/CONF/49/5 & 7.

unilaterally (the Soviet A-bomb and the American H-bomb), or by negotiation between allies (the secret talks on atomic energy between the British and Americans, and NATO's military aid programme).

Bevin himself had always shown a personal interest in the work of the UN Economic and Social Council and the specialized agencies, including his old friends in the ILO. In the three years after the War these had made considerable efforts to provide technical assistance to under-developed countries and in December 1948 the General Assembly adopted a statement of policy bringing together the different initiatives in a unified programme, but with no indication of where funds were to come from. However, when President Truman came to deliver his Inaugural Address at the beginning of his second term of office, he came out for

"A bold new program for making the benefits of our scientific advances and industrial progress available for the improvement and growth of underdeveloped areas."

Truman invited other countries as well as the USA to pool their technological resources and establish a co-operative enterprise.

Truman's Point IV at once aroused Bevin's enthusiasm. Earlier discussions, he told a Foreign Press Association lunch (25 January), had centred on leading backward peoples to self-government:

"But I have always taken the view that if this were to be successful, their organised and planned economic development must coincide with it."

He recalled an interest in such matters going back to his membership of the Colonial Development Committee set up by the 2nd Labour Government. When he became Foreign Secretary, he had been struck by the failure of the powers with overseas territories to raise the standard of living of the mass of the people.

"I want all these people to be able to say that, because of their association with Western civilisation, disease has been eliminated, people are healthier, people are better, they feel freer. . . . The President's programme offers a foretaste of what I call collective benefit, of scientific advice, industrial progress and co-operation in all these fields."

The UN Economic and Social Council set up a Technical Assistance Board to co-ordinate a 20 million dollar programme, of which the USA contributed 60% and the UK (the next largest) 10%. Eventually the USA launched its own programme as well, and so did the British Commonwealth in the Colombo Plan for South East Asia drawn up with strong support from Bevin at the Conference of Commonwealth Foreign Ministers held under his chairmanship in Ceylon in January 1950.[1] An unexpected benefit for Bevin was the

---

[1] See below pp. 745–7.

effect which Truman's advocacy of Point IV had in reconciling to Bevin's policy of alliance with the USA those in the Labour Party who were still troubled by association with capitalist America.

The Soviet Union and its satellites refused to have any part in the UN's technical assistance programme, another illustration of how, even in its social and economic work and in the work of the specialized agencies, the UN suffered from the quarrel between the Soviet and the Western blocs. But it was, of course, in the Security Council, where the Soviet Union was able to utilize a veto, that the consequences of the quarrel were both most obvious and most serious.

In November 1947 in an effort to get round the block, the General Assembly had accepted an American proposal to set up an Interim Committee on Peace and Security which would remain in continuous session, available in an emergency and, unlike the Security Council, not hampered by any require- ment of unanimity. The life of the Interim Committee was prolonged at the end of 1948—again in face of opposition from the Soviet Union which refused to recognize or take part in the meetings—and on 2 April 1949 the General Assembly adopted four recommendations from it on the settlement of disputes by conciliation. But, while useful, the Interim Committee was no substitute for an effective Security Council functioning as it had been intended to when the UN Charter was drawn up. This was Bevin's justification for the creation of NATO. Presenting the Treaty to the House of Commons for its approval on 12 May, he declared:

"No such arrangement as N.A.T.O. would have been found necessary at all if the effectiveness of the Security Council as an instrument for ensuring the immediate defence of any member against aggression had not been undermined by the Soviet use of the veto and by other actions of the Soviet government. . . . That is why we have signed this treaty; because we have learned by bitter experience that we cannot get it at present through the Security Council."

PART V

Controversy Revived

CHAPTER 18

The Berlin blockade lifted; another sterling crisis

I

Bevin's speech in the House of Commons in May 1949 was an answer to the massive political campaign on which the Soviet Union and its Communist supporters in all countries concentrated their energies, denouncing the NATO Pact as an aggressive treaty aimed at the USSR and in violation of the UN Charter.[1] The principal vehicle for this campaign was the Partisans of Peace, an organization whose origin went back to a conference of intellectuals held at Wroclaw in August 1948. Besides party members a considerable number of people accepted invitations to this who were by no means Communists but thought they could serve the cause of peace by meeting Communists and engaging in debate with them. An International Committee of Intellectuals for Peace was set up which planned a series of meetings in the major cities of the world, beginning with the World Congress of Partisans of Peace in Paris in April 1949 which, in turn, set up a World Committee for Peace and started to issue its own magazine *In Defence of Peace* in the summer.

Following the familiar "Front technique", the Communist organizers managed to combine a prominent role for eminent non-Communists with controlling the activities of the organization and directing these exclusively against "the American Warmongers" and their allies. Every device of publicity was employed to capture the cause of peace, appeal to the widespread fear of another war and impress on the great number of people everywhere who distrusted politics but were deeply worried by the international situation, the belief that the way to work for peace was by joining the millions who looked to Moscow to secure it for them. Among the organizations which were recruited for the campaign with the object of mobilizing non-Communist opinion was

---

[1] See the Soviet statement published on 31 March 1949. RIIA *Documents 1949–50*, pp. 38–42.

the World Federation of Trade Unions, the World Federation of Democratic Youth (both of which held widely publicized world congresses in 1949) and the Women's International Democratic Federation. The World Peace Movement became a major instrument of Soviet foreign policy comparable with the Popular Front Movement of the 1930s, capable, for example, of securing the signatures of millions without any Communist affiliations for the Stockholm Peace Appeal of 1950 and raising doubts and sowing confusion in the minds of many more. Appealing over the heads of "reactionary" governments to the peoples of the non-Communist world, and taking full advantage of the freedom of expression available in Western Europe and the USA, this presented a formidable challenge which democratic governments, certainly the Labour Government, with far less experience of manipulating public opinion and a dislike of such practices found it hard to counter.

The essentials of Bevin's own reply in the Commons could be reduced to three.

First, the Western Powers had tried for more than two years to collaborate with the Soviet Union, only to find themselves faced with a choice between accepting Soviet demands or being blocked by Soviet use of the veto and the unanimity rule—not just in the Security Council but in the CFM, over the Marshall Plan and European economic recovery as well as the German peace settlement. This had worked solely to the disadvantage of the West and to the advantage of the USSR. For while the Western Powers let themselves be inhibited from acting to deal with the consequences of the War in Germany and Western Europe, the Russians had proceeded unilaterally and often ruthlessly to impose political and economic control over the half of Europe they occupied, without taking any notice of either their allies or the wishes of the peoples who lived there.

The Western Powers had therefore to choose between acting on their own or allowing the situation in Western Europe to get to the point where, without any risk of war, a Communist take-over—in Western Germany, perhaps, or France or Italy, leave alone Greece—was a real possibility. The choice had been deferred from one meeting of the CFM to the next, in the hope that some possibility of four-power agreement would emerge. After two years the Western Powers had decided to go ahead on their own, first of all in the European Recovery Programme, after Russia had refused to take part or allow the East European countries to benefit from it; then in the organization of Western Germany, the Brussels Pact and finally NATO.

To those who argued that the action of the Western Powers increased the risk of war, Bevin replied, on 12 May (and this was his second point):

"The policy that has been followed by the Soviet Union seems to be to talk of peace and accuse others of being war-mongers, but at the same time to carry on a policy of promoting unsettlement all round. . . . We were driven to consider in the light of these facts how like-minded neighbourly peoples whose institutions had been marked down for destruction could get together not for the purpose of attack but in self-defence.

"The accusation has been made that the Atlantic Pact is an aggressive thing and that it will bring war. My answer is that the absence of the Atlantic Pact did not stop war in 1914 and 1939, and I suggest that if a pact like this had existed and the potential aggressor had known what he would have to face, those wars might have been avoided. . . .

"The real purpose of this pact is to act as a deterrent. Its object is to make aggression appear too risky to those who are making their calculations."

Bevin went on to rebut the argument that the Treaty was inconsistent with the UN Charter, by pointing to Article 51 which foresaw the inherent right of a group of nations to make common arrangements for self-defence and secure themselves against attack until such time as the Security Council was able to act.

Finally, there was one further question which Bevin mentioned but did not answer in his Commons speech: whether the circumstances were such as to make any measures of self-defence necessary. He pointed to what had happened in Eastern Europe, in particular Czechoslovakia and the Berlin blockade, as sufficient evidence for the House to judge for itself. But it was not evidence of an "armed attack" of the kind for which the Treaty provided. The real answer in Bevin's mind is clear enough from frequent remarks in private. He saw the NATO pact as necessary not in order to stop a Russian armed attack, which he did not anticipate, but to reassure the peoples of Western Europe. Without a guarantee they could believe, their experience of war and occupation and their fears of a repetition would continue to inhibit their recovery of confidence. Only an association which included the USA could provide such a guarantee, and the provision of arms was needed to afford visible proof that it was more than a paper promise. Bevin did not disagree with the argument often heard in the Labour Party that the way to fight Communism was by improving people's economic and social conditions. But he believed the argument too often ignored the fact that such improvement, dependent as it was on Western Europe's economic recovery, could not be achieved until people had sufficient security to give them confidence to work for the future.

Bevin also believed that Communist propaganda, ostensibly devoted to peace was in fact aimed at playing on and exploiting the European peoples' fear of war and thereby forcing the Western Powers to seek four-power agreement on the old terms of unanimity or nothing. Bevin's purpose was to reduce that fear, and thereby retain the Western powers' freedom to act on their own. NATO had to take the form of an alliance to be effective, but its *purpose* was less military than political and psychological, concerned with under-pinning Western Europe's will to resist pressure and the exploitation of its fears. This was certainly true in the initial years when the forces at NATO's disposal were only capable of fighting a delaying action and if war had broken out with the Soviet Union it could only have been won by the United States' use of atomic weapons.

Bevin could have spelled this out in the House; it would undoubtedly have helped him with his own Party, a substantial part of which found it hard to swallow a military alliance in peacetime and one joining "socialist" Britain with capitalist America against the Soviet Union. For obvious reasons, however, he was not free to do this. The effectiveness of NATO in restoring confidence on the European mainland depended on taking it at its face value, as a guarantee against armed attack.

The strongest argument on Bevin's side was Russian actions in Europe since the War: as the Russians' own proverb says, "What you are doing speaks so loud that I cannot hear what you are saying". This might not provide evidence of an "armed attack". But the rancorous hostility towards the West with which the Communist leaders accompanied their appeals for peace and collaboration; the nature of Communist power as illustrated by the regimes the Soviet Union had imposed on Eastern Europe and illuminated by the excommunication of Tito; the purges and treason trials in the satellites; the *coup* in Czechoslovakia; the blockade of Berlin and the civil war in Greece; the large forces stationed in Eastern Europe; the loyalty which the large French and Italian Communist parties showed in following the Moscow line and working to sabotage European recovery—all these combined to create for the majority, as for Bevin himself, the strong impression of a menace, psychologically if not politically comparable with that which ten years before had led to war despite all the efforts at appeasement. When Bevin drew the comparison with 1939 and said that this time they had learned their lesson and not waited for war to break out before drawing together in self-defence, and when he added that this time they had secured the support of the USA in advance, not as in 1917 or 1941 years after the war began, his argument chimed with their experience.

But not for everyone. Only six votes were cast against the House of Commons approving the NATO Pact, with both the Conservative and Liberal parties giving it their full support. In offering the congratulations of the Cabinet on what had been achieved during the past few weeks—the signature of NATO, the settlement with Germany and the lifting of the Berlin blockade —Attee described it as "the successful termination of many months of skillful and patient negotiation by the Foreign Secretary". It was as considerable an achievement as any British Foreign Secretary had been able to report to Parliament, the restoration of a balance of power in Europe after the most destructive war in history, something on which his own Party as well as the Cabinet might have been expected to congratulate him. But despite a threeline Whip, there were 112 abstentions, the great majority on the Labour side of the House. Some must have been due to illness or absence abroad, but the number was comparable with the 124 who had abstained in November 1946 and 59 members of the Labour Party were identified as abstaining on both occasions.

The scale of this protest vote provides evidence of the hold which the socialist–radical tradition in foreign policy—for example the repudiation of considerations of power in international relations, the attraction of peace as a slogan and the residual image of Soviet Russia as a socialist country—still exercised in the Parliamentary Labour Party, particularly among its middle-class, professional, university-educated members. Few of those who abstained came from the working class, trade union, elementary school-educated side of the Party, and Professor Berrington concludes from an investigation of the abstainers' background that "the foreign policy dissidents conformed striking-ly to the popular stereotype of the socialist intellectual."[1] By comparison with the autumn of 1946 criticism of Bevin's foreign policy in May 1949 was muted: the debate was over. Apart from the strength of the arguments on Bevin's side, there was no alternative policy on which even the critics could agree, leave alone win support from the majority of the Party. Nonetheless, among a number generally estimated between 75 and 100 members, perhaps a quarter of the Parliamentary Labour Party, the feeling that a Labour government ought to follow a foreign policy in accordance with socialist principles persisted and the debate was to be revived.

2

The situation of Germany mirrored that of Europe, with the added complica-tion that the appeal for peace and the fear of war could be backed by the appeal of a united Germany and the fear of being held responsible for the perpetuation of the division. The Communist leaders in East Germany launched a parallel campaign for Unity and a Just Peace, a German version of the Stockholm Peace Appeal and the Partisans for Peace, which combined the same double appeal to neutralism and nationalism. On 9 May 1949 Otto Grotewohl urated a National Front to fight for the future of Germany on a non-party basis, with support from both East and West Germany. Great efforts were made to involve neutralist groups in West Germany (such as the Nauheim Circle) and to bring together East and West German politicians.[2] The proposals in cir-culation (the precise status of which was never made clear) included the with-drawal of all occupying troops, establishment of a central government for all Germany in Berlin and the issue of a single currency for the whole country.

These were attractive propositions to most Germans and with the long delay in reaching agreement on the Occupation Statute and the Basic Law for a West German state, there was alarm in the American as well as the British Military Government that there would be much more response to the idea of a rapprochement with the East than would have seemed imaginable a few

1 Hugh Berrington: *Backbench Opinion in the House of Commons 1945–55* (Oxford 1973) p. 63 and Appendix 2.
2 For example, the meeting which Rudolph Nadolny, a former German ambassador to Moscow and an emissary of the Soviet military administration in East Germany, held with leading figures in West Germany at Bad Godesberg on 13 March 1949. Report in FRUS 1949 (3) pp. 224–5.

months before. Concluding a pessimistic report to Acheson on 2 April, Clay's Political Adviser, James Riddleberger, wrote:

"Confusion, doubt and dissatisfaction are mounting in Western Germany. . . . If the present differences over the Bonn constitution, . . . and the other stumbling blocks to creation of a viable West German state are not speedily resolved, we may be faced with a very different political and psychological situation . . . (in which) the Soviet 'Unity and Rapallo' line might assume force and meaning."[1]

Bevin was equally worried. The German Social Democrats felt they had gone to the limit in compromising their views on the division of powers between the federal government and the Länder. When Clay declared that he and the French Military Governor were still not satisfied with the draft Basic Law, the SPD drew back and was divided on the question whether it should not withdraw its support and go into opposition, a line which made a strong appeal to its intransigent chairman, Kurt Schumacher. Alarmed at the prospect of the German Social Democrats becoming the equivalent of the Nenni Socialists in Italy, Bevin sent a message to Washington to urge that no further pressure be put on them and the draft of the Basic Law be accepted rather than imperil the West's German programme.[2]

The break-through on a German settlement achieved in Washington in early April appeared to remove these dangers, and Bevin was successful in getting agreement from Acheson and Schuman to a compromise on the federal government's powers which the Military Governors were instructed to suggest before opinion in the German Parliamentary Council crystallized.

Clay, however, who had little use for the German Socialists, their programme of nationalization and a strong central government, or their links with the British Labour Party, was determined to get the Germans to make the changes on which he had originally insisted and to put the SPD down. Koenig agreed wholeheartedly. Together they overrode Robertson, withheld the message sent by the Foreign Ministers and said nothing about the compromise it had recommended. However, Clay had reckoned without Bevin who insisted that the US Government should curb its high-handed representative. When Clay still refused, Bevin made it an issue of confidence:

"Mr Bevin finds it difficult to believe that after the three Foreign Ministers have met and agreed in Washington, . . . the U.S. Government will continue to allow their Military Governor to maintain his present attitude."

Acheson faced it out with the Department of the Army, accepted the challenge that the State Department should assume full responsibility for the negotiations with the Germans, arranged for Murphy to fly at once from Washington

---

[1] *Ibid.*, pp. 233–5.
[2] *Aide-mémoire* handed to Douglas on 23 March, *ibid.*, pp. 229–30.

to take these over and invoked the President's authority. This time even Clay recognized he had gone too far and, after a talk with Murphy, was persuaded to continue the negotiations himself on the basis of the Foreign Ministers' compromise. This he did with a final virtuoso display of his diplomatic ability, carried the Germans (the SPD included) through to agreement on the amended text of the constitution and, before he gave up office as Military Governor, had the satisfaction of seeing it passed by the Parliamentary Council (8 May) and approved by the Military Governors on 13 May.[1] For all his disagreements with Bevin and Robertson on detail, Clay—unlike Koenig —was as firmly committed as either to the creation of the German Federal Republic and, like them, among its principal architects.

Bevin had been very uneasy about the effect the Jessup–Malik talks and the prospect of renewed four-power talks on Germany might have on the negotiations in Bonn. In a message sent on 20 April he repeated: "The Bonn talks are crucial", and would not agree to any further move with the Russians until the Military Governors had delivered the Foreign Ministers' message to the Germans and got agreement on the Basic Law.[2] When that difficulty was removed he was still unwilling to go as fast and far as the Americans and French wanted, although by now the newspapers were full of reports of talks and of Evatt taking a hand. Douglas, talking to Bevin on the evening of 25 April, found him "depressed and discouraged" particularly by the news of the Chinese Communists shelling British warships. "China is lost and we have to face the Yangtse matter in Parliament tomorrow. What a day to make approaches to the Russians." He was critical of Jessup's eagerness and "almost violent", Douglas reported, "in his comment on 'Evatt's meddling'". What Bevin was afraid of was a Soviet trap.

"He said that if we were not extremely cautious we ran the risk of losing Germany and that he would like to see Bonn in his pocket before talking to the Russians. . . . He believed that the principal object of the Soviets was to produce a detente in the hope of preventing ratification of the Atlantic Pact by continental countries."[3]

The next day a Tass communiqué was published to the effect that, if a date could be agreed for the CFM to meet, the Berlin blockade could be lifted. This made the negotiations public and Bevin accepted that there was now no turning back. He sent a personal message to Acheson, saying that the Americans could count on him to do his utmost to carry them through to success, but added that he was "disquieted and uneasy" about the course they were embarked on.

---

[1] The crisis and its resolution can be followed in FRUS (3) pp. 237–62. Bevin's two *démarches* are printed on pp. 244–5 (20 April) and pp. 247–8 (21 April).
[2] Sir Alexander Cadogan's summary of Bevin's telegram to Jessup and Chauvel, 20 April, *ibid.*, pp. 725–6.
[3] Douglas to Acheson, 25 April, *ibid.*, pp. 730–31.

"It is when negotiations begin on a 4-power basis that our difficulties really arise. . . . Their ideas and objects are exactly opposed to ours . . . thinking in terms of a heavily centralised totalitarian state, controlled by the Communists . . . geared to the economy of the E. European states and the Soviet Union and bitterly hostile to Western Europe and America. I am not saying that they are likely to achieve this, but that is what they are aiming at. . . .

"It is almost certainly the Russian intention that the meeting of the CFM will be used to foster opposition in the public mind, especially in France, to the ratification of the Atlantic Pact. My hope had been that the Pact would be safely in force before we opened up with the Russians again."[1]

Bevin's conclusion was a plea to Acheson to join in preventing the spread of an easy optimism that "merely because the Russians have shown some readiness to raise the blockade, the rest will be plain-sailing". Three days later, agreement was reached to hold the CFM on 23 May in Paris and raise all restrictions on communications with Berlin and between the Western and Eastern zones in advance, on the 12th.

Before the blockade was lifted, Bevin paid a visit to Berlin. The airlift had supplied two and a half million people for eleven months and inflicted a major defeat on the Russians. The greater part of the ground organization, a quarter of the tonnage of supplies and a third of the flights had been contributed by the British in a remarkable and sustained example of Anglo–US collaboration. Apart from thanking those involved and meeting Clay and Reuter, on the way back Bevin saw Adenauer and Schumacher separately as well as the Minister President of *Nordrhein-Westfalen*, Karl Arnold, at Ostenwalde. It was his first visit to the country which occupied so much of his time and thoughts since he had attended the Potsdam conference. He reported to Acheson that the three German politicians were agreed in expecting little from the meeting with the Russians; and that they were united in believing there could be no compromise with the SED regime in the East Zone. Their concern was that the West might agree to a withdrawal which would leave them at the mercy of the East Zone *Volkspolizei* and the Communist Party before they had got a democratic state properly organized.[2]

At least the constitution had been agreed before the Foreign Ministers met and after ratification by the *Landtäge*, was promulgated as the Basic Law of the Federal Republic of Germany on the day the CFM opened in Paris, 23 May. Writing to the King before leaving for Paris, Bevin was prepared to agree that there had been a great advance on Germany in the past year. The Russians, however, would not take this lying down and having failed to dislodge the Allies from Berlin would now try a change of tactics with the same object of delaying the consolidation of Western Europe including Western Germany. Bevin told the King that he thought that they might propose the

[1] Bevin to Acheson, delivered by Franks on 2 May, *ibid.*, pp. 748–50.
[2] Bevin's letter to Acheson, 10 May. FO 800/467/GER/49/31; Report of Bevin's and Robertson's interviews with Schumacher and Arnold, 9 May, *ibid.*, GER/49/21 & 30.

so-called Warsaw programme[1]—the withdrawal of troops, a peace treaty and an all-German government—hoping to set up a buffer state without close links with either side, and relying on the effectiveness of Communist penetration to take over the whole of Germany. As a last resort, they might offer the extension of the Basic Law and Occupation Statute to the whole of Germany. There could be dangers for the West in such a proposal, particularly the fact that the Eastern zone, unlike Western Germany, had a highly centralized government. Still the risks would be worth running if the opportunity offered, provided the Allies got two safeguards: the extension of ERP to all Germany and the participation of a united country in the Council of Europe.[2]

3

Elaborate steps were taken by the three Western powers to work out an agreed position before the members of the Council of Foreign Ministers assembled for their sixth (and as it turned out, final) meeting. Kennan, seeing his original programme of November 1948 discarded piece by piece, complained to Acheson that by the time the French and British had finished writing in safeguards he could only conclude that "we do not really want to see Germany unified at this time and that there are no conditions on which we would really find such a solution satisfactory".[3] Bevin would not have disagreed. It remained his opinion that the meeting of the CFM had come too soon, before the alternative policy they had worked out since the London meeting at the end of 1947 had had time to establish itself. He was far more concerned to prevent this being undermined than he was to explore the possibilities of re-unifying Germany. Acheson, aware that he had still to secure Congress's ratification of the NATO Pact and get its agreement to a military aid programme, was also inclined to ask what price they were prepared to pay for four-power agreement on Germany, particularly if it was likely to remain no more than a paper agreement. Much thought was therefore given to possible lines of approach which the Soviet delegation might adopt and how these could best be dealt with. More realistically, a fall-back plan was prepared for a *modus vivendi* based on the continued division of the country and the lifting of the Berlin blockade, although Bevin urged the Americans not to dismantle the air-lift in case the Russians re-imposed it.

The Council met in the Palais de Marbre Rose, a florid *fin-de-siècle* mansion built by Count Boni de Castellane for his American bride in the centre of Paris.

---

[1] Declaration at the Warsaw Conference by the Soviet Union to her allies in answer to the London conference on Germany, 24 June 1948. RIIA *Documents, 1947–48*, pp. 573–4.
[2] Bevin to King George VI, 19 May. FO 800/467/GER/49/32. An earlier report of Bevin's to the King, 24 March, provides a good summary of British policy before the Washington talks, *ibid.*, GER/49/16.
[3] Kennan to Acheson, 20 May. FRUS 1949 (3) pp. 888–90.

Bevin, reluctantly setting out for another protracted session, reflected that as the one survivor he had spent 28 weeks already in the Council of Foreign Ministers in pursuit of four-power agreement—not to mention the Paris Peace Conference and the UN—with meagre results. This time at least there were fresh faces, Acheson and Schuman, with both of whom he felt at ease, and Vyshinsky in place of Molotov. Acheson, expecting the Polish-born lawyer to be a dangerous and adroit antagonist, was disappointed to find him instead a long-winded and boring speaker.[1] Bevin, who had a particular dislike of Molotov, did not regard Vyshinsky as much of an improvement, seeing in him the infamous prosecutor who had hounded the defendants in the Soviet state trials of the 1930s. Bevin's staff noticed with relief, however, that he did not have Molotov's capacity for needling and provoking their chief.

The seating plan round the green baize table put the British to the left of the French, then the Russians and to their left the Americans. Speaking followed the same order and to take advantage of this, it was agreed that Schuman would open the session, Bevin goad Vyshinsky into showing his hand and Acheson give the West's reply. As each speech was followed by two translations, there would be plenty of time to agree on what to say next.[2]

It did not take long, however, to make clear that the Russians were even less inclined than the Western Powers to open up a wide-ranging discussion. Their proposal was simple: "Go back to Potsdam", whatever that might mean; re-establish the Allied Control Council (from which they had walked out), restore the unanimity rule and resume where they had broken off. The Western foreign ministers required no briefing to say, each in his own way, that a great deal had happened in Germany since the London CFM, even more since the Potsdam conference four years before; that it was useless to think of turning back the clock and that they had to start from the stage they had now reached.

On 28 May Bevin presented the proposals of the three Western powers: the incorporation of the Eastern Zone into the framework of the Basic Law and Occupation Statute, extending the Bonn constitution to the whole country with one currency and the abolition of zonal barriers to trade and communications. Reparations would end and with them the Soviet-controlled industrial enterprises in Eastern Germany. Free elections would follow throughout Germany for a national government on the federal model and military government would be replaced by a four-power High Commission with powers of supervision exercised by majority vote. To nobody's surprise Vyshinsky rejected the Western plan and ten days went by with the two sides vying to show the indifference of the other to the interests of the German

---

[1] Acheson's personal account of the conference is in *Present at the Creation*, c. 33.

[2] The British record of the meetings of the three Western Ministers outside the formal sessions and of Bevin's conversations while in Paris is to be found in FO 800/448/CONF/49/5 & 7 and in FO 371/76775–83. The US record of the CFM sessions is in FRUS (3) 856–1065. This has the advantage of giving many remarks in the Conference verbatim.

people, the recovery of Europe, the peace of the world, the principles of the UN, the obligations entered into at Potsdam etc.

Reporting to the King that he had had to listen to interminable Russian speeches invoking Potsdam as "the Soviet bible and infallible panacea for all Europe's ills", Bevin remarked that "the circumstance that the Soviet Government have not adhered to the Potsdam Agreement except when it suits them does not seem to deter them". He added:

"It was noteworthy that Mr Vyshinsky, M Schuman and Mr Acheson are all lawyers by profession. They consequently tended to embark with zest on long legalistic arguments which Mr Bevin was alone in finding tiresome".[1]

A private talk between Acheson and Vyshinsky moved the discussion on to Berlin but with no more result than when they discussed Germany. Vyshinsky called for a return to the former situation with the four-power *Kommandatura* acting as before on the basis of unanimity. His proposal ignored the fact that the city was now divided, with rival administrations, and that, as in the case of Germany, it was impossible simply to start again where they had broken off. Acheson's counter-proposals called for new city-wide elections and a new city assembly to draft a permanent constitution for the whole of Berlin. Everything the Berliners might want to do except die, Acheson reported to the President, required unanimous four-power permission.

Bevin was fed up and said so. When he suggested meeting twice a day to speed up progress, Vyshinsky refused to agree to morning meetings. Bevin said that the length of Vyshinsky's speeches would put him to sleep in the evening, to which Vyshinsky retorted that something was already putting Bevin to sleep in the afternoon. Quite right, said Bevin, he recommended the practice; it was restful and helped one through the meetings.[2]

Bevin went off to Blackpool for the annual conference of the Labour Party, where he spoke on 8 June. When he resumed his place, he found his colleagues still elaborating their disagreement on Berlin. There were difficulties over restoring communications with the city and these renewed suspicions that the Russians meant to re-impose the blockade. On the 9th, Acheson proposed that the Council should direct the four commanders in Berlin to complete their negotiations by the 13th. Vyshinsky rejected the proposal but when Acheson, as chairman, moved to end the meetings, suddenly announced that he had received new instructions and could agree. Bevin, however, remained suspicious and in a note to Acheson urged that by 31 October they should build up 4–5 months' stocks in Berlin. If they did, it would prove of great negotiating value at the next CFM.[3]

On the 10th, the foreign ministers, at Vyshinsky's insistence, took up the

[1] Bevin to King George VI, 6 July 1949. FO 800/460/EUR/49/19.
[2] Acheson, p. 298.
[3] Bevin to Acheson, 13 June. FRUS 1949 (3) p. 832.

question of a German peace treaty. Having reached no agreement on a common plan for the future of either Germany or Berlin, it seemed nonsensical to Bevin and the others to discuss a peace treaty, but Vyshinsky insisted on saying his piece at great length for the record. Bevin had had enough. In what the American report describes as "a strong final statement" he protested at the "over-abundance of ego and virtue demonstrated by Vyshinsky in his effort to prove that the USSR alone sought a peace treaty for Germany". He challenged him to read the record of the Moscow and London CFM meetings and reach any conclusion other than that the USSR had always been a stumbling block in the Allies' efforts to reach a German settlement. He was perfectly willing to consider proposals, continue negotiations and exchange views through diplomatic channels, but he was not willing to go on sitting through the same timeless arguments day after day.[1]

One reason for Vyshinsky's insistence on playing up a German peace treaty when, in Acheson's phrase, they were "light-years apart" on the substance of it, was given in another report to the President. Acheson cabled back on the 11th that the big change revealed by the meetings was the defensive attitude of the Russians, who were now far more concerned to retain their hold over the Eastern zone than, as in the past, to use it as a springboard from which to extend their influence into the West. At the Moscow and London meetings of the CFM they had bid strongly for German support, but were now not prepared to risk their control of Eastern Germany for the sake of any propaganda effect. "Return to Potsdam and the degree of control demanded over Berlin are hardly positions which would be attractive to any Germans," a conclusion borne out by a consultation Murphy had with German politicians from both the CDU and SPD in Frankfurt on the 8th. It was natural therefore, Acheson concluded, that Vyshinsky should want to make the most for German ears and for the Soviet peace offensive of a German peace treaty, a completely theoretical subject which involved no risk to Soviet policy and could be treated almost exclusively from a propaganda point of view.[2]

In the meantime, on a more practical plane, informal indications had come from the Soviet delegation that they had no more hopes than the Western powers of being able to bridge the differences on either Germany or Berlin but very much wanted to reach an "accommodation". This led Acheson to put to Vyshinsky privately an agenda of "small matters" taken from the *modus vivendi* paper which had been prepared with such an outcome in mind. Vyshinsky was not only amenable but added the Austrian treaty as another item which he thought could be settled quickly.[3]

Before the conference ended and he left Paris, Bevin was anxious to pay a visit to Léon Blum, for whom he had a warm regard. He took time off on the afternoon of 12 June and found the Frenchman looking frail (he died the

[1] US Report to President of 17th meeting on 10 June, *ibid.*, pp. 972–4.
[2] Acheson to President Truman, 11 June, *ibid.*, pp. 977–9.
[3] Acheson's meeting with Vyshinsky, 11 June *ibid.*, pp. 980–83.

following spring) but full of life and delighted at the visit. They agreed that the situation in France two years before, in the summer of 1947, had been very dangerous. It was much better now, and Blum spoke of France's future with confidence. The same evening, the 12th, after a parade of disagreement in the plenary session, the four principals met privately to see, as Bevin, the day's chairman, put it, "if between us we cannot mend some of the broken strands.

"The audience is gone, the curtain is down. We are now in the dressing room behind the stage. It is our hope that we could look into a few detailed matters and see if we cannot try to fix things up. We will dispense with polemics."[1]

Between the 12 and 20 June, a series of restricted meetings, with much hard fought argument over the small print, produced a modest agreement approved by all four exactly a month after the conference had opened. The earlier agreement to lift the blockade and resume trade between the zones was confirmed; if the CFM meeting was the price which had to be paid for that, it was worth it. The surprising part was agreement on the terms of an Austrian Treaty made possible by Russia abandoning Yugoslavia's frontier and reparation claims and accepting 150 million dollars in return for her own claim to German assets in Austria. This, unfortunately, proved to be an illusion: the detailed questions turned over to the deputies provided the Soviet Union with an excuse—however bare-faced—to postpone completion of the Treaty for another six years. But for the moment it counted as a success in the search for any sign of agreement between East and West.

On the final evening, after the communiqué had been signed, champagne had been drunk and the participants had dispersed, Vyshinsky sent out a message calling for the Council to reconvene. He had, it was learned privately, received instructions in the roughest terms from Moscow to get a change made in the Austrian agreement. So back they had to come. Arriving after a very good dinner at the same time as Acheson, Bevin seized the American's arm as they stepped out of the creaking lift and (according to one of Acheson's favourite stories) asked him:

"Do you know The Red Flag? The tune's the same as 'Maryland, my Maryland'. Let's sing 'em together as a sign of solidarity, as we Labour blokes say.

"And so we did, robustly, arm-in-arm, walking through the sedate Second Empire anterooms, with the final bars at the very entrance of the meeting-room."

When Vyshinsky made his request, Bevin

"Congratulated him on a new record. Soviet agreements were fragile things, but today's was the frailest yet. It had not even survived the day."[2]

---

[1] US record of 19th meeting, 12 June, *ibid.*, pp. 985–92.
[2] Acheson, p. 301.

He saw no reason, however, to reconsider their adjournment or to change the words of the agreement. Schuman and Acheson briefly agreed and even Vyshinsky could see that there was no more to be said.

4

The Palais Rose Conference confirmed the refusal of the Western powers to abandon their plans for Western Germany and the failure of the Russians to force them to do so by blockading Berlin. This was a decisive defeat for whatever plans the Russians had for extending their influence into Western Germany, either (on the earlier model) through reliable Communists acquiring key positions in an all-German government from which they could hope to take it over on the familiar East European pattern, or (on the later model) through creating a unified Germany freed from occupation and neutralized between the two blocs.

The remaining option was to turn the Eastern Zone into a separate German state under Communist rule. Steps to this end had already been taken: in March 1949 the East German *Volksrat* approved a draft constitution prepared as long ago as October 1948 and agreed that elections should be held for a new *Volkskongress*. The Russians, however, were reluctant to admit failure and accept a second-best. The East German leaders insisted that in casting their votes the electorate would be supporting the Campaign for Unity and a Just Peace with its object of a united Germany under a single government. Polling took place on 15–16 May, a week before the CFM and produced a much higher negative vote than anyone had anticipated, one-third (42% in East Berlin) of a 95% turn out.

The *Volkskongress* assembled in Berlin at the end of May, approved the draft constitution and at the same time sought, unsuccessfully, to have a delegation received by the CFM to support the Russian programme for a united Germany. After the end of the Paris Conference there was a pause to see what would happen in West Germany: the campaign for unity and peace was maintained but with increasing evidence that it had failed. It was not until 3 October that the Russians called in the East German party leaders and told them to go ahead with the creation of a German Democratic Republic. The *Volksrat* thereupon set up a provisional government, appointed Grotewohl as Prime Minister and fixed elections for October 1950, in a year's time.

There was no comparable hesitation on the part of the Western powers. Bevin saw a West German government as the logical culmination of the policy he had followed ever since he had made up his mind that four-power agreement to create a unified Germany was unobtainable on any terms that were acceptable to the West. Its establishment was as important for Western policy in Europe as in Germany, a key to the economic recovery of non-Communist Europe, to its integration (however defined), and to its continued independence.

Bonn had been chosen as the provisional capital and the three members of the Allied High Commission were appointed before the CFM met, with John McCloy replacing General Clay and André François-Poncet, who was a supporter of Schuman's new approach to Germany, replacing General Koenig, who was most emphatically not. Sir Brian Robertson alone of the four Military Governors, at Bevin's request, continued to hold office as High Commissioner.[1] Elections were held on 14 August and the Bundestag elected Adenauer as the first Chancellor of the Federal Republic on 15 September. The Federal Republic claimed to be acting "on behalf of those Germans to whom participation was denied", a claim repeated by the DDR the following month, leaving two rival regimes each denying the other's legality and neither prepared to admit that it represented anything less than the undivided German people.

The consolidation of two Germanies was matched by measures to consolidate the two Europes. In Eastern Europe this took the form of a tightening of Russian control. In the first stage the Peasant Parties and their leaders had been eliminated. In the second, Social Democratic parties were split: those unwilling to join forces with the Communists were forced out of existence, those who were willing were given a share of office on sufferance.

The possibility remained, however, of opposition, or at least unreliability, within Communist parties which had been enlarged by the absorption of other parties, particularly the social democrats, and by the admission of new members, a proportion of them at least opportunists rather than converts. Tito's successful defiance of his excommunication and Moscow's failure either to tame or replace him was an example which Stalin had no more intention of forgetting than of forgiving, and greatly increased suspicion and fear throughout the Soviet empire. In Europe, the tide had turned against the Soviet Union: the Marshall Plan, NATO, the failure of the Berlin blockade and the creation of a West German government were all defeats for the Russians, and seen as such in Eastern Europe. Stalin and his lieutenants needed no prompting to make sure of what they held.

Throughout the satellites, a series of purges of the governing parties was carried out during 1949. 200,000 out of a million members of the Hungarian United Workers' Party were expelled or put on probation; about a quarter of 2,300,000 members of the Communist Party in Czechosolovakia. More striking was the purge of ministers and leading party officers. Amongst the best known were Gomulka, former Secretary-General of the Polish United Workers' Party; in Hungary Laszlo Rajk, formerly Minister of the Interior and

---

[1] With Clay's disappearance from the German scene, the split in authority which had caused so much trouble between the State and War Departments came to an end. As US High Commissioner, McCloy was responsible directly to the Secretary of State and was also the representative of ECA in Germany. Until the formal establishment of the High Commission in September, McCloy also served as US Military Governor, thereafter handing over command of the US Army of Occupation to an American General who had no political or economic responsibilities.

Foreign Minister, tried and executed as an "imperialist agent" along with Matthias Rakosi, President of the People's Independent Front. In Bulgaria, Traicho Kostov, a veteran Secretary General of the Communist Party and a Deputy Prime Minister was tried for treason and hanged before the end of 1949; in Albania, Xoxe, deputy Prime Minister was tried for Titoism and sentenced to death in June. Arrests were widespread: in Czechoslovakia they were reported to number thousands. No one could feel safe, any more than in Russia in the 1930s. This was precisely the effect intended.

At the same time, Yugoslavia was isolated from the Eastern bloc; subjected to a complete economic blockade by the satellites as well as the Soviet Union; excluded from the Council for Mutual Economic Assistance (COMECON) set up in January 1949, and accused of every sort of crime, charges which were then used to justify severing diplomatic relations, the arrest or expulsion of Yugoslav missions. Part of the war of nerves waged against Tito by his former allies was the withdrawal of Soviet support on the question of Trieste and on Yugoslav claims against Austria, accompanied by border incidents and the angry exchange of protests.

Consolidation in non-Communist Europe followed a very different pattern. Its aim was not to curb local initiatives and enterprise, but to create the conditions in which these could revive as the mainspring of Europe's recovery. In Bevin's opinion, even after the NATO Treaty had been signed and the Berlin blockade lifted, the most important of those conditions was still security. Talking with Acheson and Chip Bohlen on one of the last days of the Paris CFM, he said he had been reading the papers for the meeting of the Western European Union Consultative Council at Luxembourg. "The picture they gave of our present situation showed that the cupboard was pretty bare and that we were depending to a large extent on bluff." What you mean, Acheson replied, is that you would like to see the Arms Bill go through Congress as quickly as possible. Bevin agreed: he would be much happier if it could be got through by the autumn.[1]

But, as Acheson found when he got back from Paris, getting Congress to agree was easier said than done. The bi-partisan approach to foreign policy was breaking down. The reasons for this were complex: the bitterness of the Republicans at their failure to win the 1948 election; the replacement of General Marshall, a national figure, by the younger Dean Acheson who was soon to become the target of violent partisan criticism; the anger of the powerful China lobby at the triumph of the Chinese Communists which they laid at the door of the Democratic Administration and its preoccupation with Europe; a revulsion against the apparently endless demands being made on the USA—by the same Europeans—in her new and still unaccustomed role of super power. Within hours of signing the North Atlantic Treaty on 25 July, President Truman presented Congress with a request for the authorization of

[1] British minute of conversation, 16 June 1949. FO 800/460/EUR/49/16.

military aid up to 1,400 M. dollars. It had been well understood that such a request would follow as a logical sequel to the NATO Pact, but the amount and the wide discretionary powers which the President asked for in its use led to a congressional revolt in which Vandenberg as well as Taft, and Democratic as well as Republican senators, took part. It was only after the Bill had been re-written, the President's discretion hedged around and the amount for NATO cut by 10% and spaced over two years that the Bill was finally passed on 22 September.

July 1949 was a bad month for the Administration and particularly for its Secretary of State. An attempt to recruit bi-partisan support for a revived atomic partnership with the UK led to another political storm and had to be hastily replaced by a proposal for exploratory talks with the British and Canadians.[1] The situation was not made easier by reports, which proved to be all too true, that the British were running into another financial crisis comparable with that which had led to the suspension of convertibility two years before.[2] The state of mind of at least some members of the Administration was shown by the outburst of the Secretary of Defence, Louis Johnson, at a private lunch on 12 August, when he declared:

"The U.K. was finished, there was no sense in trying to bolster it up through the E.C.A., M.A.P., N.A.P.[3] or assistance in the field of atomic energy. Even the Canadians . . . were disturbed with the prospect that we might give atomic secrets to the British. . . . As the Empire disintegrated we should write off the U.K. and continue co-operation with those parts of the Empire that remained useful to us."[4]

Finally, at the end of July, Acheson put out a thousand page White Paper on China which, although interpreted today as a fair and even scholarly presentation of American policy towards China, "evoked bellows of pain and rage from the China bloc in Congress",[5] leading to further attacks on the Administration's neglect of China and cossetting of unreliable Europeans.

Despite the increased opposition, neither the President nor the Secretary of State reneged on their undertakings to Europe even when Senator McCarthy took up the running in Congress. American funds for European recovery continued to flow and were supplemented by funds and supplies for European rearmament. In Europe economic recovery began to take effect and a start was made on the job of re-building Western Europe's defences. Where differences began to appear in the latter half of 1949 it was in the relations between the UK and her European allies, particularly the French, which Bevin had been at such pains to foster in the earlier half of the year. These differences were

---

[1] See below, pp. 725–7.
[2] See below, pp. 704–15.
[3] ECA, Economic Co-operation Administration, the Marshall Plan; MAP, Military Assistance Programme; NAP, North Atlantic Pact.
[4] Report by the Under Secretary of State, Webb. FRUS 1949 (1) p. 514.
[5] Acheson, p. 307.

reflected in attitudes to the Council of Europe, which was brought into existence in the summer.

Bevin had signed the Statute and agreed to a European Assembly; but he continued to insist that it should not be free to discuss defence, the function of NATO and Western European Union, or economics, the function of OEEC. When Harold Macmillan, speaking in the House of Commons debate on 21 July spoke of a "European parliament in embryo", Bevin was quick to express his concern.

His fears were confirmed when the Assembly met for the first time on 10 August 1949 and remained in session for a month. Protests were at once made at the attempt of the Committee of Ministers to limit its agenda and a fortnight's debates followed on such items as the political unification of Europe, a Human Rights convention, economic and social policy. Six committees were created and presented reports for further discussion in the final week. Before adjourning, the Assembly set up a Standing Committee to give it a form of continuing existence, and requested revision of the Statute to get rid of the Committee of Ministers' control over its agenda, and to give the Assembly not the Committee the power to admit new members and double its size.[1]

Although Bevin was loth to admit it, more was involved than arguments about constitutions and procedure, and more than could be explained by the wartime experience of the French and other European peoples producing a disillusionment with the nation state and the search for an alternative to fill the void which was wholly foreign (the word is used advisedly) to British sentiment. The NATO–OEEC model had one great disadvantage in French eyes, it was based upon a revival of that wartime partnership between the two English-speaking powers, that "special relationship", from which the French had been and were still excluded. The relations between Washington and London were different from those between either and any European government; both the difference and the exclusion were resented. As French confidence revived, so France naturally sought to assert its former leadership in Europe as a counter-balance, admitting without any doubt Europe's need of the United States and the UK as allies, but not of an exclusive Anglo–American hegemony.

Insofar as the French gave a lead in the direction of closer European integration, they made a strong appeal to American opinion, particularly when, with Schuman's "new approach", they came forward with the view that a firm Franco–German relationship must be the basis of such an integration, and vice versa, that integration of both nations into a European community was the only solution to the problem of Franco–German relations.

At a meeting on 13 September 1949 to discuss US relations with the UK and Canada in atomic matters, George Kennan was called upon by the Under-

---

[1] Council of Europe: Reports of the Consultative Assembly, 1st session 10 August–8 September 1949.

Secretary of State, Webb, to expound the State Department's current thinking about the UK and Europe, and did so in these terms:

"The UK tended to exert a retarding influence on Western European plans for closer political and economic integration. The UK was most chary of entering into any arrangements which might tend to derogate from her sovereignty and she was continuously preoccupied with her Empire commitments. The net result was that UK participation tended to place a ceiling on Western European attainments towards unification."[1]

As Kennan went on to say, apart from anything else, "in trying to play a role of leadership on the Continent, the UK was continuously finding itself entering into commitments on which it could not deliver." The development of the financial crisis and the impact of devaluation on Britain's relations with her allies—not only the Americans but also the French—opened a new chapter of difficulties for the Labour Government.

5

The Government was now long past its meridian and within sight of a general election widely expected either before the end of 1949 or early the following year. Although it had shown great energy in its first two years, by 1949 the hopes of 1945, inflated by the ending of the War and an unassailable majority, had faded. The burst of legislative activity and the series of nationalization measures had failed to produce the re-making of British society. The extension of the Welfare State and the creation of the National Health Service were felt to remove past injustices rather than to open the way to a more just society in the future. Many complained that life in post-war Britain was frustrating, depressing, and colourless. This was especially true of the middle-class floating voters whose discontents might be over-represented in the media but whose support was essential if Labour was to hold its majority.

The Opposition, which had been slow to recover from its defeat in 1945, was revived by the evidence of disillusion with Labour's domestic policies and by the energy generated in working out new policies of its own and reconstructing its party organization. The Labour Government, by contrast, gave the impression that it had not only run out of steam but of ideas. Its most skilful electioneer and party manager, Herbert Morrison, sensitive to the need to recapture the middle ground of politics, came out in favour of "consolidation", an approach turned into a programme entitled *Labour Believes in Britain*. This was approved by the Party leadership at a conference in Shanklin on the Isle of Wight (February 1949), and endorsed by the Party conference at Blackpool in June. Setbacks in the local elections in May, including the loss of control of

[1] FRUS 1949 (1) p. 521.

Morrison's own London County Council for the first time for fifteen years, showed the swing away from Labour with which the Party was confronted. The militants were sure it could not be reversed by Morrison's formula of consolidation. They secured the inclusion of additional if unexciting proposals for nationalization in the programme, without however, changing its character. There is no reason to believe that Labour would have done better if they had. Whether or not there was a radical alternative, the fact is that Labour in 1949–50 had surrendered the initiative and stood on the defensive. Churchill and the Conservatives, scenting the possibility of reversing 1945 and returning to power, were not slow to move on to the offensive.

Foreign policy played little part in Labour's discussion of its programme; no more did Labour's Foreign Secretary. Always awkward and difficult in Party (as distinct from trade union) gatherings, Bevin was a notable—and noted—absentee from the Shanklin Conference. He continued to see his role in national, not party, terms, and the Opposition's concentration of its attack on the Government's socialist record in home affairs made this easier. But his position was bound to be affected by the renewal of partisan politics in 1949–50, and before 1949 ended, the quarrel was extended to Britain's attitude towards a Council of Europe.

The immediate problem, however, which involved Bevin was alarm over an adverse balance of payments. 1948 had been a good year for the British economy, and although Cripps still held to a policy of austerity in his budget in April 1949, 1948–9 saw a bonfire of the controls and an easing of the rationing which people found so irksome now that three years had passed since the end of the war.[1] It could no longer be made a reproach to Bevin that the costs of foreign policy were threatening economic recovery; on the contrary, it was the pay-off of foreign policy in the form of Marshall aid which provided the basis of the recovery. At the same time the measures taken to increase output for export began to produce results. The key was trade union co-operation which Bevin had powerfully helped to secure. Attlee's figure of 150% of the 1938 volume as the target for 1948 was raised to 160%; and the figure of 135% actually achieved in 1948 was followed by 151% in 1949. The precariousness of the recovery however was shown by yet another sterling crisis which threatened to be as serious in its effects as that of 1947.

If its causes were a matter for argument, there was no doubt about its symptoms. For ten years since the beginning of the War in 1939, the UK had acted as banker for the foreign exchange transactions of the Sterling Area. In 1949 this consisted of the British Commonwealth and Empire (except Canada), Eire, Burma, Iraq, Jordan and Iceland. The crucial balance was with the USA, which in the post-war period had more of the supplies everyone wanted

---

[1] Potatoes ceased to be rationed in the spring of 1949; bread in July. All clothes, textiles and shoes were freed in March 1949; the petrol ration was doubled for the summer months. Meat, on the other hand, continued to be short, and the carcass meat ration at the end of March 1949 was the lowest ever.

than anywhere else in the world. As a result, not only the UK itself, but the Sterling Area as a whole, imported more from the USA than it was able to pay for by exports. This "dollar deficit" was adequately covered by Marshall aid to Britain up to the end of the first quarter of 1949, but in the second quarter Sterling Area exports to the USA started to show a big drop in quantity and prices. As a result the gap between what the Sterling Area bought from the USA, and paid for in dollars, and the dollars it was able to earn by exports rapidly increased, leading in turn to a fall in the UK's monetary reserves, which had to do duty for the whole of the Sterling Area.

Ever since the end of the War there had been speculation in the Soviet Union, as much as in Western Europe, about the consequences of an American slump for a world as dependent as that of the late 1940s on the continued strength of the US economy. In fact, the recession of 1949 proved to be nothing like the slump of 1929 which marked the onset of the Great Depression. After the abolition of wartime controls in the USA in late 1946, the pent-up demands for goods and services had created a seller's market. By the end of 1948 this excessive demand had spent itself: as a result sales, prices, production and employment in the American market all fell off in the first half of 1949, and this was reflected in the drop in imports. Given time, however, economic activity in the USA was likely to revive and there were clear signs of this—with a corresponding revival of demand for imports—in the first half of 1950 even before the outbreak of the Korean War in June gave a new stimulus to it.[1]

It was a measure of the vulnerability of the British balance of payments that, even with the dollars provided by Marshall aid, there was insufficient margin to wait a few months and see if this would happen. The economy was overloaded by all the things the Labour Government was trying to do at the same time—increasing expenditure on the Welfare State, maintaining forces and bases overseas, starting a rearmament programme, paying its share of the Berlin airlift and acting as banker to the Sterling Area. The figures, when completed for the three months April to June 1949, showed a rise in the British dollar deficit from $330 m. to $632 m. American aid covered little more than half of this, and British reserves of gold and dollars fell from $1,912 m. on 31 March to $1,651 m. on 30 June.

At a meeting of the Cabinet's Economic Policy Committee on 15 June —while Bevin was still in Paris—Cripps faced his colleagues with the possibility of "a complete collapse of sterling" and the exhaustion of the country's reserves within 12 months.[2] He was given authority to postpone for three months all new purchases to be paid for in gold or dollars. This was first aid—"absolutely essential", Cripps told the House of Commons later, but "no solution for our difficulties".[3] The question was, What could provide such

---

[1] The volume of American industrial production, which fell from 192 in 1948 to 176 in 1949, recovered to 189 in the first half of 1950 and to 211 in the second half.
[2] Dalton's diaries, 15 June 1949.
[3] Cripps in the House of Commons, 6 July 1949.

a solution? Cripps spoke of the need for an early election and Dalton reported in his diary: "As we go out, C.R.A[Attlee] says '1931 over again'"—the economic crisis which had turned into a political crisis as well, bringing down the second Labour Government, splitting the movement and sending them into the wilderness for the rest of the 1930s. Dalton, recalling the convertibility crisis of 1947 (in which he had had to withstand the pressures now on Cripps), added the heartfelt question in his journal: "Shall we never get free?".

Reporting the latest figures supplied by Cripps, Lew Douglas warned the State Department that the UK was in a financial position as dangerous as that which had followed convertibility two years before. Picking up the comparison with 1931, he said he doubted if Labour ministers would let themselves drift into a similar disaster, preferring to meet a crisis head on. He believed, however, that the Labour movement would resist the devaluation of sterling, which was already widely discussed abroad.[1]

As soon as he got back from Paris and talked to Attlee and Cripps, Bevin sent off a personal message to Acheson saying that he had not realized, when talking to him on 20 June, how serious the situation had become. He asked for the earliest possible talks with the US Secretary of the Treasury, John W. Snyder, already due to visit Europe; the Canadians were also being asked to send a minister.[2]

At the end of June, with both Bevin and Morrison back, the line to be followed was discussed by the full Cabinet. Bevin refused to be rushed into panic measures. Dalton reported with approval on 30 June:

"E.B. says in Cabinet that all may be easier after July. That will be the difficult month. But 'others', i.e. Americans, 'don't want to be blown up', and he thinks they will see how much, for them, turns on backing us. All this in one of his hopeful asides, with a pretty confident smile."[3]

The next day, 1 July, nearly all the Cabinet was present for a meeting of the Economic Policy Committee, which continued into the afternoon. *The Banker* reported an almost universal belief in the City that devaluation was inevitable, a view which had long been held in the USA.[4] Cripps, however, remained adamant in opposing such a move and was supported by Dalton who was also strongly opposed to the programme of cuts in domestic expenditure (e.g. £100 M. off food subsidies) and other orthodox steps, again reminiscent of 1931, such as raising the bank rate "in order to increase confidence abroad". Whose confidence, Dalton asked, arguing that the UK's budgetary position, with a large surplus in prospect, was sounder than that of most other countries, and that they should not give in to pressure from the City. Bevin, as well as Morrison, Nye Bevan and Attlee, all spoke against cutting food subsidies.

[1] Douglas to Webb, 16 June. FRUS 1949 (4) pp. 784–6.
[2] *Ibid.*, pp. 790–91.
[3] Dalton, 30 June 1949.
[4] *The Banker*, June 1949, p. 71.

Morrison thought devaluation might be the least of evils and Attlee was inclined to agree with him. Bevin, however, came down on the other side, Dalton recording in his Journal, again with approval:

"E.B. says neither devaluation nor cutting subsidies will lead you anywhere in this situation. Only immediate action should be taken to stop purchasing. Tell workers they can't have increased wages now, but we aim to stabilise. In W. Europe we can't afford to run the risk of unemployment. If we do, all the Atlantic Pacts in the world won't save us. Americans are playing with fire. This can't be settled on financial level. Must be taken on highest level. Try for temporary tide-over with Snyder."[1]

Bevin was already feeling his way towards more far-reaching talks with the Americans at which they would get away from technical arguments about the measures needed to deal with the immediate crisis and bring out the interests which the Americans and British had in common. This was also the theme of Douglas's dispatches from London:

"What we are facing," he cabled to Acheson, "is more than a British dollar crisis—it is an Anglo–American problem, the implications of which go far beyond the question of the exchange rate of sterling and British dollar reserves.

"The failure of our two governments to cooperate closely in the immediate future, in full appreciation that a problem of mutual concern is before us, might very well prejudice the Marshall program, the many aspects of our foreign economic and political policy which depend upon its success and might give comfort and support to Communist and Soviet designs."[2]

Douglas's argument found a ready hearing from Acheson for whom, as for Bevin, the Anglo–American relationship was central to their joint efforts to organize the Western world. There were others, however, in the ECA, in other Washington offices than the State Department—in the Treasury, for example —and in Congress, who saw the issue in terms of the conflict of economic philosophies (and interests) which had put a strain on Anglo–American relations from the wartime discussions on Bretton Woods and Lend–Lease through the negotiation of the post-war Loan and the convertibility crisis. On the one side was the American belief in the restoration of a multilateral competitive system of world trade with the removal of all restrictions (which many in Britain saw as the reflection of the Americans' own interests as the strongest economic power); on the other, British insistence that restrictions and special arrangements of a discriminatory character were necessary to give their own and the other European economies time to recover from the disruption of war. Many in America saw this as special pleading by a socialist government more interested in creating a protected economy in which the operation of "natural" economic laws would be frustrated for the sake of indefensible political objectives.

[1] "A sound meeting!", was Dalton's comment. Diaries, 1 July 1949.
[2] Douglas to Acheson, 22 June 1949. FRUS (4) pp. 787–90.

For Americans, recognition of the British as an indispensable partner in organizing the West—and therefore of the need to help her recover economic viability—was in conflict with exasperation at finding the UK as the most determined opponent of plans for pushing ahead with the liberalization of trade, and the principal obstacle to the closer integration of Western Europe, economically, financially and politically. The British, for their part, had to strike a balance between fear of being pushed, in the name of liberalization, into a repetition of the convertibility crisis of 1947 and their determination not to compromise their control of their own economy in the name of integration, and on the other hand their overriding need of American support, not only for economic but for reasons of foreign policy and defence as well.

OEEC illustrates the contradictions of the situation. The British had taken the initiative in setting up OEEC but opposed any move to give it greater authority *vis-à-vis* national governments, without which the ECA chiefs, Hoffman and Harriman, argued that it would remain ineffectual. The Labour Government persisted throughout the remainder of 1949 in refusing to agree to the appointment of Spaak—or, for that matter, of Oliver Franks or anyone else—to strengthen the organization or to allow it to embark on the integration (whatever, as Bevin remarked, that might mean) of Western Europe's national economies.

Similarly they had taken the initiative in producing the 1948 Agreement on Intra-European Payments which removed some of the financial obstacles to mutual trade. But when the ECA supported a Belgian proposal for a new payments scheme which would give greater freedom of trade on a multilateral basis, the British opposed it.[1] After much argument, a compromise was found which satisfied the ECA officers,[2] but the suspicion remained that the opposition of the UK—and particularly of Cripps, the British Minister on the OEEC Council and the embodiment, in American eyes, of doctrinaire socialism—was the product not only of the financial difficulties in which the British found themselves but of a more deep-seated reluctance to see a competititve multilateral system of free trade restored.

To begin with, at least, Bevin took trouble to keep the French as well as the Americans informed of the financial crisis with which the British were threatened. On 29 June, while the argument about a new European payments scheme was still going on, Bevin sent a message to the British Ambassador in Paris, Oliver Harvey, to let Schuman know that he was very anxious to keep in step with the French, not let the difficulties over the payments scheme weaken European unity and, if possible, reach agreement about finance before either of them talked to the US Secretary of the Treasury, Snyder, when he visited Europe.[3]

[1] See Harriman's circular letter to ECA missions in Europe following the meeting of the Consultative Group of OEEC ministers on 3–4 June. FRUS (4) pp. 403–5; and the report by Spaak transmitted by the US Chargé in Brussels, 2 June, *ibid.*, pp. 399–400.
[2] See Harriman's circular letter of 1 July, *ibid.*, pp. 405–7.
[3] FO 800/460/EUR/49/17.

Schuman responded at once, offering to come over to London for talks on 4 July, returning to Paris the same evening. Cripps as well as Bevin was present when he arrived at the Foreign Office, but it was Bevin who did most of the talking, insisting that they could not continue to deal with financial difficulties without discussing their political implications. There was a major disequilibrium between the dollar and sterling areas. Temporary expedients would be discussed with Snyder but they had to find a more permanent solution if they were not to run into the danger of a world divided into a dollar area, an area of Russian autarchy and a sterling area forced to pursue autarchic measures itself. This would upset relations with Europe as well as with the USA. In passing he mentioned devaluation but thought it offered no lasting solution. He was particularly anxious, he stressed, not to make a settlement with the USA which excluded Europe.

Unfortunately, Schuman had no advice to offer. Bevin said the British did not want to ask the Americans for more money. The US could help by stockpiling and fixing a floor for sterling area raw materials, but these were temporary expedients. He wanted to propose high-level talks in Washington in September and in the meantime exchange views with the French: the objective was a unified economy for the non-Communist world and an end to conflict between the dollar and sterling. It was agreed that Cripps' visit to Washington for the International Monetary Fund meeting in September would provide a good opportunity for talks and in the meantime Bevin proposed that he and Schuman should talk again when they met for the Council of Europe in Strasbourg.[1]

6

In fact there were no further discussions with the French before the announcement of devaluation more than two months later. The truth was that it was only in talks with the Americans that the British could hope to find any solution to the dollar-sterling problem. Britain was no longer the great trading nation she had once been, but Britain's and half the world's trade in 1949 was still in sterling. The relation between sterling and the dollar, therefore, was crucial to the economy of the whole of the non-Communist world. The way it was settled was bound to affect Britain's European partners, but none of them was in a position to help and might well impede or delay a solution if the problem was dealt with by discussion in the OEEC.

One of the fears recurrent in American discussion at the time was that the British would decide to go it alone, creating a protected and autarchic trading area, centred on London, using sterling as its basic currency and seeking to include as much as possible of Europe. Reporting this as one of the possibilities

[1] British record of the Bevin–Schuman meeting. FO 800/465/FR/49/13.

likely to be considered by the Labour Government, Douglas said he believed the creation of such an insulated sterling area would take too long and cut across too many national interests to provide an answer to the present problem. But suspicion that the British might make the attempt and extend it to Western Europe persisted. Harriman, ECA's Special Representative in Europe, who was to accompany Snyder to London for the talks with the British, cabled Acheson on 25 June:

"I cannot avoid the thought that Cripps may hope to high-pressure us into acceptance of his ideas of a closed discriminatory sterling area expanded to include the continental countries as far as possible. Needless to say, I would view such a course as disastrous."[1]

The proposal to divide the world into three areas, the sterling area plus Western Europe; the dollar area, and the Russian, came up in the Commons debate of 18 July and Bevin told the House:

"I confess that I have been tempted in that direction. When one feels baffled by one's problems one has to examine every possible solution. I have examined that one on more than one occasion, but I could not fail to see all the political repercussions that could flow from it. . . .
"The best contribution which we can make to the world is to reduce the number at least to two, because if we try to develop the three I can see one of the most terrible conflicts arising."

Bevin did not go back on this view. Both he and Cripps had told Schuman that their aim was to create a unified system for the non-Communist world. Only if they failed to find a solution along these lines was he prepared to consider the alternative of an autarchic sterling area. He was too experienced a negotiator, however, not to recognize that the possibility, as a last resort, was a card in his hand when it came to convincing the Americans that they could not stand aside and had to help find a solution.

The first attempt was not encouraging. The day before Snyder and Harriman left Paris for London, Cripps made a statement in the House (6 July), giving the figures for the dollar deficit in the June quarter and announcing the standstill on further dollar purchases. He announced that the Commonwealth Finance Ministers would meet in London a week later, and it did not need much foresight to guess that they would be asked to agree to similar cuts in dollar imports—in fact, as it turned out, a reduction of 25% in dollar imports into the sterling area on the figure for 1948 ($1,200 instead of $1,600 m.). Snyder, clutching a fundamental faith in free enterprise, gave the impression of an outraged matron in a bawdy house, interpreting Cripps' invitation to discuss the sterling-dollar problem as a euphemism for more aid, and in Acheson's words "got out of the country as fast as possible".[1] He left the

[1] Harriman to Acheson 25 June. FRUS 1949 (4) pp. 792-3.
[2] Acheson, p. 322.

impression of a man who was unable, or at least unwilling, to focus on a set of problems so remote from his own experience of economics. The differences, he cabled Acheson, were fundamental.[1] The most they could agree on was that technical discussions should go on through the summer as groundwork for the decisions to be taken in Washington when ministers met there in September 1949 for sessions of the IMF and the International Bank.

Cripps reported to the House of Commons on 14 July but, exhausted and unwell, left immediately afterwards for five weeks of complete rest in a Swiss clinic. While he was away the debate on what other steps should be taken continued between the parties, in the Press and between ministers and their advisers. With an election due at any time within the next 12 months, the Opposition parties, with strong support from the Press and British as well as American Business, claimed that the weak position of Britain was due to Socialist mismanagement of the economy, particularly increased government expenditure on the Welfare State, and called for a return to economic orthodoxy beginning with cuts in social expenditure. Strong pressure to the same effect came from senior civil servants. Dalton's diary is full of references to "all the old stuff about the need to restore confidence and hence to make large reductions including changes of policy in public expenditure".[2] Before leaving for Switzerland, Dalton reports, Cripps cleared the room of all but ministers at a meeting of the Economic Policy Committee and said that he did not trust his own officials and advisers. Douglas Jay told Dalton that the officials "were half expecting us to be beaten at the election and are beginning to think in terms of a Tory Government and a Tory policy".[3]

In any discussion of deflation there was no doubt where Bevin stood as a result of his experiences as a trade union leader. In a debate in the House on 18 July he replied to Opposition arguments that the policies they urged had been tried between the Wars:

"We lost 250 million working days in strikes and lock-outs. . . . We had an average of 1,700,000 unemployed. . . . We paid £1,290 million in unemployment pay.[4] . . . That was an experiment in trying to deal with the problem without control, by mere manipulation, by endeavouring to get this balance of exchanges working. . . .

"The automatic operation of unemployment and deflation was dealt its death blow when Mr Lloyd George and the present Leader of the Opposition (Churchill) introduced the social services in 1910, 1911 and 1912. The system advocated by the last speaker can only work if starvation operates quickly, if unemployment and other things operate quickly. Immediately the social services were introduced into the world, resistance became stronger, the system would not operate and has never worked since."

---

[1] Snyder to Acheson, 9 July. FRUS (4) pp. 799–800.
[2] A criticism of the original brief prepared for the Washington talks which Gaitskell succeeded in getting re-written: see the entry under 12 September on Dalton's return from the Council of Europe Consultative Assembly. The divisions in the Cabinet and Whitehall over devaluation are well described in Philip Williams, pp. 196–203.
[3] Dalton, 19 July 1949.
[4] The period Bevin was referring to was between 1922 and 1938, when the population of the UK rose from just under 43 million to 46.5 million.

It was in this speech that Bevin made the remark that the USA "is as much a welfare state as we are, only in a different form". As illustration he referred to the fact that part of the trouble the UK was having with its balance of payments was due to the American welfare policy of fixing basic prices for its agriculture.

Instead of getting into a panic and cutting the standard of living of the British people, Bevin argued that they should sit down with the Americans and Canadians and find a solution to the dollar problem of the sterling area which would take political as well as economic considerations into account. They had already met to do this with the Commonwealth countries, trying to find the right kind of mechanism to deal with the dollar problem of the sterling area. Besides the population of 600 million in the sterling area, another 200 million were affected by its operation. Of course they had to put forward a short-term programme, but Bevin went on to suggest that if they could hit on a way to achieve it, something much bigger was possible:

"In fact, if we could bring the dollar area and the sterling area together and produce the right co-operation, then we could make Truman's fourth point a living reality in helping to lift up the standard of life throughout the whole of that great area."

The next day, 19 July, the senior Labour ministers held a council of war on the date of the next election. Cripps sent a message urging that they ought to hold one as soon as possible in order to give Bevin and himself a fresh mandate for their Washington talks in September. This could only mean an August election and was not taken seriously by Cripps' colleagues. Nye Bevan, however, was strongly in favour of an election before the end of the year, arguing that the next Budget would be unpopular and Parliament become demoralized with nothing to do in the last session. Bevin disagreed. He wanted no election while the talks with the Americans were on and thought these might last to Christmas, although he was optimistic about their outcome, believing that the American Administration and the military did not want the present Government to fall. ("Foreign Secretaries", Dalton noted, recalling Arthur Henderson, "never want elections, for these disturb the next international negotiations!") Dalton favoured an election early in 1950, not later than February and this was Attlee's preference too. Nothing was decided but, with Nye Bevan still dissenting, there was a convergence of views towards a date in February.[1]

In the middle of the discussions Bevin held a conference on the Middle East to which he had summoned the same group of British representatives with whom he had met four years before at the beginning of Labour's period of office. Opening the meeting on 21 July, Bevin remarked that the Russians had not been as active in the Middle East as he had expected, but if they set to work seriously could cause the British great difficulties.

[1] Dalton's diaries, 19 July.

"Because the old regimes, which we were forced to support, would not stand up to revolutionary conditions and would be swept away. These regimes were greedy and selfish and had not allowed any of the wealth which they have made out of war and out of the oil to benefit the poorer classes."

With the Palestine issue out of the way he regarded this as a favourable moment for putting into effect a great plan which would appeal to the imagination and raise the standards of living of the masses (including the refugees) throughout the area from Pakistan to Turkey.

For the first time there was a British representative, the Minister in Tel Aviv, Knox Helm, who could put the Israeli point of view and Bevin agreed with him that Israel had a part to play in the framework he had outlined.[1]

In preparation for the conference, Bevin had asked the Israeli Ambassador, Dr Eliash, to come and see him (19 July). According to the Ambassador's account, Bevin began the conversation by saying that he had difficulty in dealing with Israel because he did not know what its policy was. Britain was less involved and more detached from Palestinian affairs since the creation of the UN Conciliation Committee. As for the past, he admitted that he had failed. However, it was better that things had happened in the way they did: negotiations on a settlement "might have taken generations". Bevin said he was willing to serve as a mediator on the questions in dispute if both sides wished him to do so. He surprised the Ambassador by saying that he was opposed to the repatriation of Arab refugees to Israel, preferring to see them re-settled in the Arab states. He was also prepared to accept the partition of Jerusalem under some form of international control. The Ambassador ended his dispatch to Tel Aviv with the conclusion that Bevin was not after all "a sworn enemy" and appeared to want to add to his historical portrait the features of a man who had finally contributed to Israel's establishment.[2]

At the conference Bevin still spoke with bitterness of the way in which he had been maligned by the Zionists. He visualized the Negev as "a No Man's Land" with free communication between Egypt and Jordan as well as between Israel and the Red Sea; he brought up the idea of Haifa being managed by a joint Israeli–Arab Board, and still adhered to the view that the Arab part of Palestine should be annexed to the Kingdom of Jordan.

The report which Bevin made to the Cabinet after the conference made clear the balance he thought British policy had to strike. On the one hand

"HM Government accept Israel as an established fact and intend to grant her *de iure* recognition at the earliest suitable moment. They regard it as a matter of high importance that she should be orientated towards the West and play her part in the

---

[1] Author's interview with Sir Knox Helm.

[2] Israeli State Archives, FO files 36/14. Eliash–Bevin, 19 July 1949. Bevin kept no record of the interview but when it was leaked to the press, he told his officials he did not want to dispute the Ambassador's account. FO/37/75207 E/2043 28 October 1949. I owe my account of the interview and its subsequent history entirely to Mr Ilan Pappe.

defence of the Middle East against Communist penetration and Soviet aggression. For this purpose they will use their best endeavours to have friendly and mutually profitable relations with her."

On the other hand, the British

"Were bound to have regard to their existing friendships and alliances with the Arab States . . . It would be too high a price to pay for the friendship of Israel to jeopardize, by estranging the Arabs, either the base in Egypt or Middle Eastern oil.
"Subject always to these interests being safeguarded, HMG are anxious to promote not merely peace but friendly relations between Israel and the Arab States . . ."[1]

The difficulty of keeping the balance even is illustrated by the division of opinion among the British representatives at the July conference over an agreement between Israel and Jordan to see the Arab West Bank incorporated in the latter's territory. When the Ministers in Tel Aviv and Amman (Knox Helm and Kirkbride) urged that Britain should encourage a settlement, they were met with the argument that it was more important for Britain to reach agreement with the Egyptians on the defence of Suez, and not to risk losing that by accepting a settlement between Jordan and Israel which would only arouse Egyptian and Arab resentment,[2] Bevin wanted both but felt he had to give priority to Egypt as the key to the defence of the Middle East.

With Britain out of Palestine and a Jewish State established, the Cabinet showed no disposition to debate British policy and accepted Bevin's memorandum without dissent. The question they could not put off, however, was the future of sterling. During Cripps' absence, the other Treasury ministers, Gaitskell and Jay, had come round to devaluing sterling before the Washington talks in order to boost the reserves and create a new and more hopeful situation. Dalton, too, after talking to them, changed his mind and at a three-day discussion in Cabinet at the end of July, opinion appeared to be moving in this direction.[3] No decision was taken until Cripps got back from his sanatorium, but there was no recovery during the summer either in the dollar deficit or of confidence in sterling. When he returned, on 19 August, Cripps was persuaded by what had become the majority opinion in the Cabinet and agreed to a devaluation of as much as 30%, a figure criticized as excessive but

---

[1] Bevin's report to the Cabinet on Middle East policy. CP (49) 183, 25 August. Minutes of the Conference of HM representatives in the Middle East, 21 July 1949 (FO 371/75012). It has been claimed that these documents provide evidence for the charge that the British did everything in their power deliberately to prevent the establishment of peaceful relations between Israel and its Arab neighbours (report from Jerusalem by Cox News Service of New York in *The Times*, 24 January 1983). However, if the sentences quoted in *The Times* reprint are restored to their context, and the minutes and Bevin's report read together as a whole, it will be clear that they do not at all support this interpretation.
[2] Minutes of the Middle East Conference, July 1949. FO 371/75012. It was not until 24 April 1950 that Abdullah annexed the West Bank, with British and US acquiescence. See below, p. 775.
[3] 27–29 July. In Cripps' absence, Attlee took over the Chancellor's responsibilities. CM 49, 50, 51 (49).

justified at the time by the need to make British exports in North American markets competitive and to convince everyone that this was not a tentative first step but the limit. The decision was taken before Bevin and Cripps left for the USA but was kept secret.[1] The precise extent of the devaluation was left to Bevin and Cripps to discuss with the Americans, and no announcement was to be made until after their visit had been completed.

[1] The decision was taken in principle at the first of two Cabinet meetings on 29 August. CM 53 (49).

CHAPTER 19

Washington, September 1949 (sterling devalued); Paris, November 1949 (the Petersburg Agreement)

I

Once again, on 31 August, Bevin set out across the Atlantic, his second trip in six months. The Cunarder RMS *Mauretania* docked at New York on 6 September and a crowd of journalists swarmed on board to ask if he and Cripps had come in search of yet more dollars to bail the British out. Refreshed by the voyage, Bevin was in good form, said emphatically that that was not what they had come for and set the coming meetings in a context of achievement rather than crisis. He reminded his questioners of what had been done in the past 18 months: the Brussels Pact, OEEC and the ERP, the remodelling of the British Commonwealth with independence for India, Pakistan and Ceylon; the Atlantic Pact; the Council of Europe ("a very tentative beginning —but it has begun"), the establishment of a democratic government in Western Germany.

"I doubt whether so many impressive and far-reaching political advances have been made in any other eighteen months of the world's history. . . . We live so near to it, we don't always see it. . . .

"The worry we now have is: We are afraid that this will all be frustrated if we cannot settle the economic maladjustment. . . . We cannot have one democratic world politically, if it is to be based upon two worlds economically. We must harmonise our economic affairs."

The talks began in Washington the next day.[1] Each delegation had brought a train of advisers who crowded into the conference room, and according to

---

[1] The British record of the Washington meetings and Bevin's conversations outside the Conference room is in FO 800/448/CONF/49/10; the US record is in FRUS 1949 (4) pp. 803–41. Acheson's personal account is in *Creation*, c. 36.

716

Acheson, the first few days were everything a conference should not be, with rising exasperation among those taking part. The Americans had leaned over backwards from the beginning of the crisis not to tell the British what they ought to do; they still did not know whether the British had decided on devaluation, and the British ministers gave no hint. As a result the discussion had to be conducted in general terms and became increasingly unreal.

The only episode that brought the proceedings to life was an unscheduled performance by Bevin. Hoffman, speaking with evangelical fervour, delivered a homily to the British in which he exhorted them to forgo the easy markets of the sterling area, cut their costs—obviously including wages and the benefits of the welfare state—and earn dollars by exporting to the American market. This, after all, was what the British had been trying to do, with considerable success until the American recession, and Hoffman's self-righteous tone roused Bevin's wrath. With a sovereign indifference to protocol and the agitation of the rest of the British delegation, he proceeded "to 'ave a go" and read Hoffman a lesson in return.

Bevin said he had been interested for many years in British industry and had frequently heard free traders urge British workers to make the sacrifices necessary to compete in the great American market. Every time, as soon as they made a little progress, Congress set up a howl about cheap foreign labour and raised the tariff to new heights. Would Mr Hoffman guarantee that, if Europe sought to balance its payments by exports to the USA, Congress would let them come in?

It was clear to the British, however, that there was no point in going on with the talks unless they told the Americans what had been decided on devaluation. So, after consultation with London, the six ministers and Hoffman met by themselves. The decision in favour of devaluation, and even more the size of the cut proposed, convinced the Americans that the British were prepared to take stringent measures to get themselves out of their difficulties and not just ask for help. No one could now say that the British were not trying to make their exports competitive, nor that the Labour Government lacked courage with an election close at hand, in presenting a programme of higher prices at home, which would make wage restraint more difficult for the ministry, and further cuts in government expenditure.

Once the British had demonstrated that they took their predicament seriously, they did not lack friends who were prepared to accept that it was an Anglo–American and not just a British problem to which they had to find solutions. Chief amongst these was Dean Acheson who goes on in his memoirs to describe the relationship which he established with Sir Oliver Franks, the British Ambassador:

"Not long after becoming Secretary of State, I made him an unorthodox proposal. On an experimental basis, I suggested that we talk regularly, and in complete personal confidence, about any international problems we saw arising. Neither would report or quote the other unless he got the other's consent. . . . The dangers and difficulties of such a relationship were obvious, but its usefulness proved to be so great that we continued it for four years. We met alone . . . at the end of the day before or after dinner. No one was informed even of the fact of the meeting. . . .

"Later, comparing the relations between our governments during our time with those under our successors, we concluded that, whereas we had thought of these relations and their management as a part of domestic affairs, they had reported them as foreign affairs."

The relationship between Lew Douglas and Bevin was not comparable with that between Franks and Acheson; but it was certainly closer and their exchanges franker than those between Bevin and any other ambassador, and exceptional at any time. Finally, the friendship of Bevin and Acheson, perhaps closer than that of any other Foreign Secretary and Secretary of State, was founded on the belief that there was a greater degree of identity than of conflict between the interests of the two countries and that much depended for the Western world upon acting on that belief. It can be argued that in 1949, with Bevin and Acheson in office, the "special relationship" between the USA and Britain counted for more in the policies of the two countries than at any other time apart from the Second World War.

The talks in Washington which concluded on 12 September illustrate what this meant in practice. The communiqué did not mention devaluation which was not announced publicly until the 18th. Accepting the sterling area's reduction of dollar imports as unpleasant but necessary, at least temporarily, the ministers set up working groups to look at the ways in which the sterling area could increase its dollar exports so as to be able to pay its way when Marshall Aid ended. Amongst these were increased American investment in the sterling areas; stockpiling of rubber and tin; a thorough revision of American and Canadian customs procedures; the negotiation of further reductions in US tariffs, and agreement by the Americans and Canadians to waive the conditions of the 1945 Loan and allow the UK to discriminate in favour of imports from non-dollar areas. The most important innovation was not just for the three governments to discuss jointly questions any one of which was capable of raising a political storm, but to set up a permanent Economic Council of the three countries to continue the discussion.

The talks established that it was possible to reach "a satisfactory equilibrium between the sterling and dollar areas by the time exceptional dollar aid comes to an end". The concealed assumption, of course, was the devaluation of sterling. Even so, it is worth adding at this point that the UK (alone of the European members of OEEC) was able to achieve a balance and dispense with Marshall Aid by the end of 1950 instead of 1952 when it was due to end. In September 1949 such an outcome was still uncertain, but the success of their talks took a load off Bevin's and Cripps's minds.

It is important to keep clear the sequence of the discussions in Washington. Bevin's and Cripps's talks with the Americans lasted from the 7th to the 12th September, but the communiqué issued at their end made no mention of the devaluation of sterling which was not announced until 18 September. During the interval Bevin and Acheson, leaving further discussion of economic and financial problems to the experts, moved on to a series of talks with Schuman about their joint problems, but said nothing at all to their French allies about the decision to devalue sterling. As we shall see in the next section, this omission was to have important consequences.

This second round of talks in which the French took part lasted from 13 to 17 September. They took the form not of negotiations but of a stock taking, in which the three foreign ministers discussed informally their difficulties in agreeing on common policies and the limits to their freedom of action set by public opinion in each of their countries. Sometimes all three were present together, but there were occasions when Bevin and Acheson talked separately with Schuman or met on their own.

A working party had produced plans for the North Atlantic Treaty Organization which Bevin and Acheson quickly agreed on. The key was a Standing Group representing the Chiefs of Staff of the USA, the UK and France. Bevin was disappointed that the Americans were not ready to join the British as full members of the three European, as well as the North American and North Atlantic, regional groups which were to do the detailed planning. He told Acheson: "We regard our own partnership with the USA as the really vital thing", but was reassured when the Secretary of State replied that American representatives would play an active part in the work of the three groups, without being members, and that in any case these arrangements would not in any way limit "the ultra-secret global planning arrangements" which now existed between their two countries. (This phrase appears in the British but not in the American record of the conversation.)[1]

Before he left Britain Bevin had told Douglas that he thought they had reached a new stage of the German problem. He had already made up his mind that dismantling would have to stop soon. Nonetheless the decision went against the grain. He grumbled to Acheson that it was all right for the Americans; they had been lucky and finished their dismantling quickly. He was caught between a public opinion at home and a public opinion in Germany whose demands were in conflict. Neither Bevin nor Schuman was yet ready to take a decision. But it was agreed that the three of them would meet again before the end of the year, settle dismantling then and make a thorough review of their policies towards Germany.[2]

There were some subjects on which it was easy for the three foreign ministers to agree. Spain, for example—"let sleeping dogs lie"—and Yugoslavia, where the Americans were cautiously responding to equally cautious inquiries about aid and a dollar loan. "Tito may be a scoundrel," Bevin remarked, "but he's

---

[1] British account, 14 September, FO 800/483/NA/49/15; US account, FRUS (4) pp. 325–8.
[2] Tripartite meeting on 15 September. British record FO 800/448/CONF/49/10; US record in FRUS (3) pp. 599–603. See Acheson, p. 326. A further meeting between the three was held on 29 September, *ibid.*

our scoundrel." They did not at all agree, however, about the ex-Italian colonies on which the French were still unreconciled to the view reached by the British and Americans, that the only practicable course was to let the Libyans become independent without any intervening period of trusteeship.[1]

While the foreign ministers were meeting in Washington, delegates were beginning to assemble in Peking for a Chinese People's Consultative Conference which, before the end of the month, approved the constitution and programme of the Chinese People's Republic, the final act in the triumph of Mao Tse Tung. The question of recognition was already troubling the Foreign Office. The State Department's view was that there was nothing to be gained by hasty action. Bevin told Acheson that he too was not in a hurry to offer recognition, but the British had big commercial interests in China, were instructing their consuls to stay on in order to keep a foot in the door and intended to remain in Hong Kong.[2] He thought American and British interests in China were divergent, even if both sides should try to reconcile their policies as far as possible. He also thought that by being too obdurate the Americans, instead of separating them, would drive the Chinese into the Russians' arms: on which Acheson commented that they were already there, and there was no reason for thinking recognition would have any effect. All that could be done was to promise to stay in touch with each other.[3] Bevin still found the Americans unresponsive on the importance of South East Asia and if anything was to be done there the British would have to take the initiative on their own.[4]

2

The tripartite talks ended on 17 September with mutual expressions of satisfaction. But the atmosphere of confidence which had been established between the three partners was shattered by the revelation that the British had spent a week in confidential talks with the French without mentioning that they had decided on the devaluation of sterling—and had told the Americans in advance.

The first the French heard of it was the evening of 17 September before the public announcement. To add insult to injury, the communication was made not by Bevin or Cripps, but by Roger Makins, at that time an Under Secretary at the Foreign Office, who passed on the information to the French Finance

[1] 15 September, 1949.
[2] Attlee told the Cabinet on 26 May that the common front against communism would crumble in Asia unless those who lived there were convinced of British determination to hold Hong Kong. CM 38 (49).
[3] Bevin's talk with Acheson, 13 September. FO 800/448/CONF/49/10; FRUS (9) pp. 81–5; Bevin's talk with Acheson and Schuman, 17 September. CONF/49/10; FRUS (9) pp. 88–91; Acting Secretary of State to US Ambassador in Australia, 21 September, p. 91.
[4] See the references in Ritchie Ovendale's third article (cited on p. 869), p. 455.

Minister, Petsche, at the British Embassy. Makins reported that the French expressed consternation. Petsche described it as "une décision brutale" and Alphand, according to Makins, became "somewhat hysterical".[1] A formal *démarche* was at once made through the British Ambassador in Paris.

The British were clearly surprised by the sharpness of the French reaction. The Foreign Office proposed to reply that in view of the need for secrecy, they could not give the French any greater advance notice and had in fact informed them at the same time as the members of the Commonwealth. In view of the talk about devaluation, the French should not have been taken by surprise. But the repercussions of the decision to devalue sterling were not as easily dismissed as that. Bevin had gone out of his way at an earlier stage in 1949 to try and improve relations with France, and at the beginning of the sterling crisis had got Schuman to come to London for talks in which he insisted on the need to remain in close contact with the French. But what had happened after that?

The answer, from a French point of view, was clearly put by Henri Queuille the French Prime Minister, when he summoned the US Ambassador, Bruce, to see him on 22 September. In July, the British had raised their bid to OEEC for Marshall aid from $940 m. to $1,114 m. As a result the allocation of Marshall aid had to be altered (the British eventually got $962 m.) and Great Britain in place of France (as Queuille put it) "became the most favoured nation and, as a result, the French felt that the interests of France, as well as those of other continental countries, had been sacrificed to some extent to British claims".[2]

In the view of the other members of OEEC and of the American ECA the sterling–dollar problem was something which Richard Bissell, one of Hoffman's deputies, cabled to Harriman, "cannot be left exclusively to British–Canadian–American discussions in Washington, since all members of O.E.E.C. are vitally concerned".[3] Nonetheless, the discussions had taken place in Washington, not in Paris, and the joint communiqué reporting them spoke of continuing consultation between the UK, Canada and the US to facilitate

"The solution of problems which today adversely affect the working of the entire O.E.E.C. group and yet are not susceptible of solution within that group."[4]

This was before the announcement of the devaluation of sterling which was bound to force a general devaluation of European currencies. The scale of the British devaluation was much greater than anything the French had expected and was followed by a devaluation of the German mark by 25%—again far more than the French had expected and without any provision to establish a

---

[1] Makins' report to Cripps, 17 September. FO 800/465/FR/49/14.
[2] Bruce's report to Acheson, 22 September. FRUS 1949 (4) p. 661.
[3] Bissell to Harriman, 5 August, *ibid.*, p. 416.
[4] Para. 15 of the joint communiqué issued on 12 September. RIIA *Documents 1949–50*, pp. 224–9.

single price for German coal for domestic use and export. Queuille described this as the final straw which would break his Government's back and spoke bitterly of the thanks the French got for stifling their doubts about Anglo–American policy in Germany only to see the Germans given economic advantages over France and America's and Britain's other European allies.[1]

The clearest explanation of the assumptions behind the State Department's policy at this time is to be found in a report which George Kennan gave to the American members of the Combined Anglo–US Policy Committee on atomic energy on 13 September, the day after the tripartite talks ended. Those talks, Kennan said, confirmed the State Department's conclusion "that it would be better if the UK were not too closely tied politically and economically to Western Europe, but rather that it should be aligned with the U.S.A. and Canada". He gave several reasons for this conclusion. The UK was wary of any surrender of national sovereignty and preoccupied with her Commonwealth commitments. She tended, as a result, to hold back European plans for closer political and economic integration. The future strength of Western Europe would have to rest on a firm Franco–German relationship: it might be possible to work this out with the French, but not with the British if it meant their becoming involved in a programme of Western European unification. Finally, in trying to play a role of leadership on the Continent, the UK was continually taking on commitments it could not fulfil.

The State Department had decided, therefore, that

"An attempt should be made to link the U.K. more closely to the U.S.A. and Canada and to get the U.K. to disengage itself as much as possible from Continental European problems. It should assume more nearly the role of adviser to Western Europe and its problems, and less the role of active participant. It was hoped that the U.K. could be persuaded to disengage itself quietly from the Council of Europe."[2]

Such a policy, far from reducing, could only increase the French objections to the prospect of a continuing economic partnership between the Americans, the British and the Canadians from which they were to be excluded. They took this to mean that the Americans were giving priority to this "Atlantic" relationship over the "European" OEEC. They now learned that the State Department was actively encouraging the British to withdraw from their European commitment. The Americans saw this as opening the way to more rapid European integration, but in French eyes it meant that the British would be able to enjoy the advantages of a special relationship with the USA while leaving France and the other continental nations to work out on their own, without British participation, how they were to come to terms with the reviving power of Germany.

For their part the British were delighted to see the special relationship with

[1] Bruce's report of his interview with Queuille on 22 September. FRUS (4) p. 662.
[2] Minutes of the meeting of the US members of the CPC, 13 September. FRUS 1949 (1) pp. 520–26.

the USA extended from defence to economics. They were equally relieved at American recognition of the impossibility for the UK, with its world wide commitments, of integrating fully in some form of a European union. But they were soon to show that they did not accept—any more than the French did, though for very different reasons—that the logical conclusion was for the UK to withdraw from Europe and leave the continental nations to form a union without them.

In the event, neither the sterling–dollar crisis which so much preoccupied the British and Americans during the summer of 1949 nor the devaluation proved to have such serious economic consequences as had been feared. By the Spring of 1950 the American economic recession had ended, British exports had recovered and the UK's gold and dollar reserves were rising. The political consequences, however, of the way in which the British and Americans had acted to solve the crisis proved more serious and more lasting than either had foreseen.

3

Like every other Foreign Minister, Bevin had to take part in the general debate with which the UN General Assembly opened its new session in New York, an exercise which Acheson described as an "utter futility".

When his turn came to speak Bevin asked why it was that they were unable to reach compromise solutions with the Soviet group. His answer was to point not to the ideological differences but to the Communist conviction that the non-Communist area of the world was bound to fall victim to its own contradictions. Bevin declared his own belief that the assumption would be proved false: the course of events, including a recurrence of the great slump of 1929, was not inevitable. Refusing to be frustrated by the failure to achieve universality, for which he blamed Soviet intransigence, the nations willing to co-operate had learned to go ahead on their own, with "better results than merely waiting for world collapse".

But such co-operative action had had to be taken outside the framework of the UN. Inside the framework the division between the two worlds continued to block effective action. Israel was admitted as a new member in March 1949, but fifteen other states failed to secure the necessary support across the line drawn by the Cold War, among them Austria, Finland, Eire, Italy and Ceylon, and on the other side Bulgaria, Hungary and Rumania.

In his speech Bevin referred to three issues of concern to the United Nations: the future of the former Italian colonies, the Greek civil war and the dispute between the Soviet Union and Yugoslavia. On the first of these, the possibility of a settlement had been opened by the changes of attitude which followed the defeat of the Bevin–Sforza proposals in May. The question was taken up by the General Assembly's First Committee on 30 September and argued to and fro for six weeks. Finally on 21 November, a resolution was adopted by the General Assembly by 48 votes to 1 (Ethiopia) with 9 abstentions. A united Libya was to become independent not later than 1 January 1952, with a UN Commissioner and an advisory council to help bring this about. Italy was given a ten-year trusteeship of Somaliland, to be followed by independence, and a UN Commission was appointed to visit Eritrea and consult the wishes of the inhabitants before coming up with new proposals in 1950. On the Italian colonies, therefore, the UN could claim credit for producing a compromise acceptable in some degree to all the principal parties, except the French, and solving a problem which had defeated the CFM.

Greece, like the Italian colonies, remained on the UN Agenda, and the General Assembly in November renewed the mandate of UNSCOB to keep watch on the help given across the frontiers to guerilla groups. But the war was over and on 16 October even the Greek Communist Party was constrained to announce that it had decided to "discontinue the armed struggle for the time being, leaving only small guerilla detachments as a means of exerting pressure". On 27 October Bevin reported to the Cabinet that the remaining British troops in Greece were finally being withdrawn.[1] The cost of the civil war to a small and impoverished nation had been appalling: well over 100,000 dead, including more than 5,000 executed by one side or the other, the majority by the Communists; three-quarters of a million homeless and 28,000 children taken abroad. The physical and psychological damage was greater than that suffered under the German occupation and, even with external aid, it was not until 1952 that recovery began to gather momentum.

In his speech admitting defeat to the Sixth Plenum of the Greek Communist Party, Zakhariades, its Moscow-trained Secretary-General since 1921, identified only one specific cause of failure, the treachery of Tito.[2] The threatening tone of the charges with which the Russians and their satellites continued to assail the outcast Yugoslavs aroused, and was intended to arouse, fears that violence might be used to overthrow Tito. Bevin, speaking at the UN, quoted from a Russian note which spoke of the Soviet Government being

"Forced to use other more effectual methods to defend the rights and interests of Soviet citizens in Yugoslavia and to call to order the Fascist violators who have gone too far."

What were these "other, more effectual methods"? Bevin asked. The Russian action in blockading Berlin had been "designed to persuade the world that the Soviet Union was prepared to risk war rather than be denied their objective". What was happening in regard to Yugoslavia reminded him of the warnings the Western Powers had received the year before, that they would be forced out of Berlin unless they submitted to Soviet pressure. Bevin warned

[1] CM 62 (49).
[2] Woodhouse, p. 285.

Vyshinsky: "This is a matter that does not solely affect the two countries; when things start, you do not know where they are going to end."

He went on to describe the steps the Russians had taken to impose their will on Eastern Europe as "an imperialistic policy under a new disguise". Part of it was the systematic perversion of language:

"Peace is only peace when it produces results approved by the Politburo. If we have any opinions ourselves and dare to express them, we are labelled warmongers. . . . Yugoslavia was also peace-loving as long as she found favour, but has become a warmonger overnight. . . . Czechoslovakia (on the other hand) became peace-loving overnight in February 1948."

The most sensational news of September 1949 was Truman's announcement that the Russians had succeeded in making and exploding an atomic bomb. The Russians said nothing. Whether or not Truman's announcement was deliberately timed with this in view, it certainly helped the Administration to end the two-month-long battle which it had been fighting with Congress over the Military Assistance Programme. On 6 October the President was able to sign the bill into law. The original figure the Administration asked for, $1,450 m., had been cut to $1,314 m. $1,000 m. of this was designed for the members of NATO. $211 m. of the rest went to Greece and Turkey, with $75 m. to be spent "in the general area of China" as a sop to the China lobby. The figure of $1,000 m. has to be seen in relation to a separate appropriation for the costs of US foreign policy which, even after cuts in Congress, provided $5,810 m. for the fifteen months April 1949–June 1950. Of this total more than 82% ($4,852 m. dollars) was allotted to the European Recovery Programme. These were staggering figures, if compared with anything which would have seemed conceivable at the end of the War and are an index of the revolution which had taken place in US foreign policy.

In September 1949 the President agreed that talks dealing with atomic energy should be resumed on the same tripartite pattern as the recent economic and financial talks (US–UK–Canada); and the Combined Policy Committee, with Britain strongly represented by Franks, Makins, Hoyer-Millar and Cockcroft, held a number of meetings in Washington between the 20th and 30th of that month.[1] The American aim was to secure the greatest possible concentration of materials, research, production and the storage of atomic weapons in the USA or Canada and the least possible in the UK. In return for accepting such a joint programme, the UK would be supplied with atomic weapons by the USA. Franks and Makins said flatly that such a proposal was out of the question. The British Government had decided that the UK should have its own atomic energy programme and it was not negotiable. The British representatives were equally resolute in refusing to

[1] US records of the meetings in FRUS 1949 (1) pp. 520–662; British records used by Gowing, c.9.

agree to the storage of all atomic weapons in North America: they insisted that the UK must have a store of bombs under its own immediate control in the UK. It was finally agreed that the Combined Policy Committee should approve a brief report and then adjourn while the three Governments considered the next step.

The report which Makins made on his return to London was discussed at length by the officials involved, the Chiefs of Staff and the "atomic" Ministers during October. Makins emphasized the difficulty even sympathetic Americans had in accepting the existence of a British atomic programme. Among the reasons advanced were Britain's strategic vulnerability, the need for the fullest rationalization and efficiency, and the burden on an over-strained economy; but these did not wholly explain the American position. "There is", Makins suggested, "perhaps an ill-defined and almost unconscious feeling that atomic energy is and should remain an American monopoly, both for military and industrial purposes, and this feeling is rationalised in different ways." He might well have gone on to say that there was an equally "ill-defined and almost unconscious feeling" on the British side, also "rationalised in different ways", that the UK at whatever cost, must continue to have its own atomic programme. This came out clearly as the group in London discussed how far Britain could afford to go in seeking an integrated programme with the Americans. At a meeting of Ministers on 1 November, Bevin said he had

"Great fear of our placing ourselves too much in the power of the Americans on the industrial side of atomic energy no less than in atomic weapons production."

He argued that further industrial use of atomic energy might become possible more quickly than seemed likely at the moment, and it would be false economy to make any sacrifice which would impair Britain's ability to deal with the US on equal terms. Bevin recalled that in 1946 the Americans had wished to prevent Britain from having any programme at all and doubted whether at heart they had ever departed from that attitude.[1]

Bevin's misgivings appeared justified when talks were resumed in Washington at the end of November. The British found that the Americans had reverted to their original proposals, which made the UK's role in developing atomic energy and weapons completely subordinate to that of the USA. What is clear from the American records and from the difficulty Franks had in finding a date for the resumed talks is that in the course of November American attention became absorbed in the debate on whether or not to go ahead with the much more powerful H-bomb. The benefits to be derived from a joint programme with the British and Canadians no longer appeared important.

When new British proposals were submitted on 29 December, Acheson

---

[1] Quoted in Gowing, p. 292.

found them "difficult" and it appeared that Louis Johnson, the Minister of Defence, had thrown out any idea of an agreement with the British. Exchanges continued in desultory fashion for a little longer but were abruptly ended when Klaus Fuchs, a naturalized British scientist who had worked in Los Alamos and later at Harwell, was arrested on a charge of spying for the Russians. That and the opening of McCarthy's witchhunt put an end to any further discussion of a joint Anglo–US atomic programme for the rest of Bevin's, and of Acheson's, period of office.

4

Bevin had been far from well during his American visit. On his second evening after moving from Washington to New York, the Achesons took him and the Jessups to the musical of the day, *South Pacific*. Word got round that Bevin was in the theatre and the whole cast played to him. "He enjoyed himself so obviously and so expansively", Acheson wrote, "that actors and audience caught his gaiety.

"After a tumultuous final curtain with many calls, and much waving by and to him, we started to follow the departing audience up the aisle. The sudden demand on his heart brought on an attack. Inspector Macey took command in an instant. Ernie was stretched in the aisle with sweat pouring down his face. A towel soaked in ice-water was brought to cool his face, nitro-glycerine administered. The police emptied the theatre."

The crowd waited outside to see him leave, and they were not disappointed. Once the pain passed, Bevin rejoined the Achesons with apologies for frightening everyone, and waved his hand as the crowd cheered. Acheson's account continues:

" 'Where are we goin' now?' Bevin asked when the cars moved off.
    " 'We're going back to the hotel to see that you go to bed,' I told him.
    " '*Then* what are you goin' to do?' he persisted.
    " 'Probably take the Jessups up to our apartment for a nightcap before we turn in.'
    " 'I thought so,' he said triumphantly. 'And I'm comin' too. I need a drink more than any of you.'
    " 'It isn't good for him, is it?' I appealed to Inspector Macey. 'He'd much better go to bed. Isn't that right, Inspector?'
    " 'Well, sir,' said "Big Ben" from the front seat. 'I don't rightly know what's best for him. But I've a fair idea of what he's going to do.'
    "And so he did."[1]

These attacks of angina became more frequent in the remaining eighteen months of Bevin's life. They were liable to occur at any time, including conferences. Lord Franks recalls several times having to adjourn a meeting to

---

[1] Acheson, *Sketches from Life*, pp. 27–8.

give Bevin time to recover, taking him into another room and finding a sofa on which he could lie down until the pain passed. Lord Franks adds that until the last few months before Bevin's death, his powers did not appear to be seriously affected. However sharp the attack, Bevin always insisted on resuming and showed an astonishing ability to pick up where he had broken off.

By the end of September 1949, however, he had been away from the UK for more than a month, and, apart from his health, was showing the usual signs of unease at being cut off from his base for any length of time. Before he could return, however, he had first to pay a visit to Canada at the beginning of October, a promise given in appreciation of the support which the Canadian Government and Lester Pearson in particular had given over NATO and devaluation. He made two speeches, in Ottawa and Montreal, arguing that if Britain was in economic difficulties that was not because her people had lost their vigour or their spirit. It was because during the War they had poured out everything they had to defeat Hitler and after the War when the world was in an unparalleled mess, had undertaken burdens beyond their resources in the effort to organize recovery.

"When people tell me that a country who could achieve what we have in four and a half years is decadent, then I say, Come and see us sometime and you will be surprised."[1]

If anyone said, on the other hand, that Britain could easily solve its problems by resorting to the methods adopted in the past, he asked, What were those methods?

"They were restriction of credit, the holding up of raw materials, the creation of unemployment, the forcing down of wage incomes and the readjustment of prices. . . . If you adopt that method again you will do more to introduce communism throughout the world than anything anyone can suggest. . . . If an adjustment is necessary in our economic system, I suggest it is morally wrong to select one section of the community to bear the whole burden. . . . We must share alike in carrying out that adjustment."

As he reminded his audience in Montreal, Bevin had held office for more than nine tumultuous years since he entered Churchill's Government in 1940. He was a representative of Britain outside normal Canadian experience, and the directness with which he spoke won a reception which surprised and delighted him.

Bevin travelled back through New York. On the way he learned of the Russian response to yet another attempt to get a peace treaty signed with Austria. The hopes raised at the Palais Rose meeting of the Council of Foreign Ministers in Paris had soon been dashed: no Russian signature was forthcoming. During their meetings in New York earlier in September the three foreign ministers had decided to take up the matter again with Vyshinsky who was in

[1] Speech at Canadian Club in Ottawa, 4 October 1949.

New York for the UN meetings. Four meetings with him at the end of September failed to remove the block, although one of them, on the 28th,[1] had lasted from 10 p.m. to 3 a.m. in an atmosphere which Bevin described to Attlee as "not good". Finally on 6 October the Russian made it clear that he had instructions not to yield an inch on any matter of substance.[2] This put an end to Bevin's efforts to help the Austrians and it was not until four years after his death, in 1955, that the Russians suddenly reversed their position and signed the treaty as part of their campaign to deter the German Federal Republic from joining NATO.

Bevin was disappointed but not surprised at the Russian response. More than anything else he wanted to put behind him the six demanding weeks he had spent in North America and get on board the *Queen Elizabeth*, bound for home.

It was seven weeks after leaving Liverpool that he reached London, to find politics dominated by the prospect of an election and a possible change of Government.

The Cabinet was divided not only about the best date for the election but also about the scale of the cuts necessary to curb demand and avoid inflation now that devaluation was stimulating exports. With Bevin back, a decision could at least be taken whether to rule out an election before the end of the year. Only Cripps and Nye Bevan in the end opposed this and an announcement was made on 13 October. Reports that in anticipation of a Labour defeat the City was marking down government securities incensed Bevin. Dalton reported "E.B. was hot against the money-lenders . . . and says 'Couldn't we start an alternative to the Stock Exchange, something like the Public Trustee's Office?' "[3] It took another week of meetings before the Cabinet could agree on a programme of cuts in capital investment and Government expenditure.[4] When presented to Parliament on 24 October these were greeted with derision by the Opposition and described by the Press as inadequate and an anti-climax after the expectations that had been built up. Although the first part of this judgement was later shown to be wrong, the second was what counted immediately. Even the friendly *News Chronicle* wrote: "Ministers are beginning to wear the air of beaten men . . . Mr Attlee and his colleagues are so far behind the public mood that they are almost out of sight".[5]

Bevin had his own particular problem in Britain's relations with Europe which had been compromised, as both the Europeans and HM Opposition

---

[1] British record, FO 800/448/CONF/49/10.

[2] *Ibid.*, the US records of the Washington talks on Austria are printed in FRUS 1949 (3) pp. 1146–76.

[3] Dalton's diaries, 13 October 1949.

[4] The Economic Policy Committee considered the programme first and their recommendations were presented to the Cabinet by the Prime Minister in CP (49) 205, 20 October 1949. The Cabinet discussed the economic situation on 18 and 20 October (CM 59 and 60) and approved the EPC paper on 21 October (CM 61) in preparation for the HC debate on 26–27 October.

[5] *News Chronicle*, 27 October.

claimed, by the way in which devaluation had been handled and by the Labour Government's attitude towards the Council of Europe. In August the Assembly of the Council had met for the first time at Strasbourg and confirmed both Bevin's predictions, that it would be used as a platform for the European Movement in its campaign for a Federal Europe and for politicians out of power to attack those who had the responsibility of office. Relations between the Tory and Labour leaders of the British delegation were bad, Morrison and Churchill quarrelling publicly in front of a crowd of astonished foreigners. Inevitably Morrison came off worst. Churchill outshone everyone else present and enjoyed to the full his reputation as the protagonist of "United Europe" whose return to power was impatiently awaited by the majority of the "Europeans" in the Assembly.

The Americans hoped that the meetings in Paris at the end of October would produce some real progress towards European economic integration,[1] and as a first step wanted to see Spaak made Director General of OEEC.[2] While taking care not to use the word "integration" Acheson sent a personal message to Bevin on 14 October urging him to take the lead in securing Spaak's appointment: nothing would do more to impress opinion in the USA. Bevin, however, told Douglas flatly that the Labour Government would not accept the appointment of Spaak or anyone else to a position which would give OEEC political powers.[3] Equally discouraging news for the Americans came from Paris where the Queuille Government which had shown resolution in tackling France's economic problems, fell on 6 October, as Queuille himself had said it would, and France was again left without a government for three weeks.

To re-appraise American policy towards Western Europe, a two day meeting was held in Paris (21–22 October) bringing together a group of the most experienced American representatives abroad. Four Ambassadors, Douglas (London), David Bruce (Paris), Dunn (Rome), Kirk (Moscow), were joined by Harriman and Hoffman representing ECA; John McCloy, the US High Commissioner for Germany; Chip Bohlen and George Perkins, the Assistant Secretary of State for European Affairs.

The general opinion of the group was expressed by Douglas when he said that continental, and especially French, opinion was in a state of great uneasiness, as a result of the wide gulf which had opened up between the UK and the Continent in the last six months.[4] A major factor in creating that gulf had been the devaluation of the pound and reports to the effect that the US was encouraging British "desolidarisation" from the Continent.

---

[1] Acheson's conversation with Schuman, 15 September, and with van Zeeland, 16 September—both before the announcement of devaluation. FRUS 1949 (4) pp. 421–4.
[2] Jessup's note for Acheson, 5 October, with Harriman's definition of the role he saw Spaak playing, *ibid.*, pp. 425–6.
[3] Douglas's report to Acheson on conversation with Bevin, 18 October, *ibid.*, pp. 430–31.
[4] Record of meeting of US Ambassadors, Paris, 21–22 October. FRUS 1949 (4) pp. 472–96.

The memorandum Acheson had sent for the meeting however endorsed such a policy. Its tenor can be summed up in four propositions:

European integration is essential if the revival of German power is to be contained and harnessed.

"France and France alone can take the decisive leadership in integrating Western Germany into Western Europe".

"We recognise there are good reasons why the U.K. feels it would have to stop short of steps involving merger of sovereignty at this time".

While developing co-operative actions by the U.S., British Commonwealth and Europe, a second line of policy for the U.S.A. should be to encourage the development of new institutional arrangements by some countries within the larger group. "The needs of the continental countries," Acheson added, "are in some respects more urgent and more compelling, and seem to me to require such action, even if the UK finds that its participation must be less than complete." [1]

Acheson went on to say that he meant by "progress towards integration . . . the earliest possible decision by the Europeans . . . for the creation of supra-national institutions operating on less than a unanimity basis for dealing with specific economic, social and perhaps other problems". Such institutions "would fall short of the needs of the time if they did not involve some merger of sovereignty"; but the UK would only be expected to participate "to the extent that it is willing and able to"—on the same basis as the USA and Canada.

This last assumption was disputed by virtually all the participants in the Ambassadors' conference which Bohlen summed up by saying that:

"The central event of the meeting was the complete agreement that European integration without the U.K. was impossible. This must be forcefully brought to the Department's attention, since it was clear that the Department had not entirely accepted the idea." [2]

The discussion, even in summary form, makes fascinating reading because of the insight it affords into Britain's situation as it appeared to men who were among the best informed and most sympathetic Americans. McCloy, for instance, asked whether they had not given too much emphasis to the increase of Russian power and too little thought to the collapse of the British Empire, which might be more important than the problem of Russia. Douglas was doubtful if any British Government could master the long-term factors in the country's economic decline: mounting costs at home and the growth of nationalism abroad leading to the disintegration of the sterling area. In spite of gifts (not loans) of 7,000 m. dollars from the USA and Canada, Britain was in the worst financial condition since the Napoleonic wars. Their ties with the Commonwealth made the British naturally prudent in accepting com-mitments in Europe and this was powerfully reinforced by the Socialists'

[1] Acheson to Perkins, 19 October, *ibid.*, pp. 469–72.
[2] *Ibid.*, p. 493.

determination to allow nothing to interfere with their power to control domestic economic activity. This was the fundamental contradiction between the Labour Government's attitude and the economic and political integration of Western Europe, and it made the present regime a very poor prospect in bringing that about. Harriman was equally pessimistic about the chances of getting the British to co-operate in European integration or even in carrying out what they had agreed to do in signing the OEEC Charter. Their opposition to Spaak's appointment showed how unwilling they were to reinforce the authority of OEEC.

But there was also a contradiction in American policy since one after another of those present confirmed Bruce's view that "no integration of Western Europe was conceivable without the full participation of the UK". Echoing what Dunn had said about the Italians, Bruce reported:

"No Frenchman, however much of an Anglophobe he may be or however embittered . . ., can conceive of a viable Western European world from which the U.K. would be absent. . . . The French know that such dissociation would be fatal to the cause of European integration."

The need to integrate Germany into Europe and the fear of her power reviving and of the Germans perhaps choosing Russia rather than the West in the event of another war, reinforced this argument. The State Department was unrealistic in thinking that France by herself could take the lead in bringing about the integration of Germany into Western Europe: as Douglas put it, Britain could not be left in the back-yard if the unification of Western Europe was to take place.

This unanimous view was put forcibly to the Department at the end of the conference,[1] but despite much insistence that the British "must" be made to change their attitude (Bruce: "We have been too tender with the British since the War"; Harriman: "Our biggest post-war difficulty was that we seemed unable to say 'No' to Britain to the same degree as we have to other European countries"), no one had any convincing suggestion of how to overcome the conflict that the British saw between their own interests and becoming part of an integrated Europe. Perkins, the Assistant Secretary of State who acted as chairman, reminded the group that there were other considerations than purely European in Americans' own thinking about the UK.

"This was consistently true of the Pentagon . . . when military questions were under consideration. There was the whole Commonwealth to think about; Britain's world position. All these things must be taken into consideration when studying the problem of how far to press Britain in the matter of European integration."
"There followed," the report adds, "a general discussion around the relative dangers of abandoning European integration because of England's unwillingness and placing so much pressure on England that we might lose her support in addition to abandoning integration."

---

[1] Perkins to Acheson, 22 October. FRUS 1949 (4) pp. 432–4.

Douglas pinned his hopes on the elections ("There are elements who are acutely aware of the necessity for further British co-operation with the Continent") and Harriman argued that NATO offered the best framework, and security rather than economic or political integration the best starting point, for American policy towards Europe. But the sum total of this conference's advice, as Acheson pointed out, was that there was no magic way forward and that they had to go on trying to square the circle and get the British to go as far as possible in their commitment to Europe and not allow them to block progress towards integration.

So once again Douglas went back to Bevin, armed with quotations suggested by Acheson from Bevin's "Western Union" speech of January 1948 and flattering references to "the speed and effectiveness" of his response to Marshall's offer, the courage he had displayed in standing up to Molotov in Paris, "the extraordinary job that had been done by Franks in the OEEC, under his, Mr Bevin's, wise counsel and direction."[1] Bevin's vanity was oversize, but he knew it and was too old a bird to be caught that way, especially when Douglas finally got round to the appointment of a prominent personality to give new life to OEEC. Bevin's reply was a masterpiece of evasion. That was quite a different matter, he said, from proposing the appointment of Spaak, for whom he had the highest esteem but who could not be spared from Belgium. He would certainly talk to Cripps and perhaps they might set up a small working party to examine the question.[2] This return to the old impasse was underlined by a message from Spaak that "until what he termed the 'mystery' of British policy was revealed, European union was impossible on either the economic or the political plane". What puzzled Spaak, he told the US Chargé in Brussels, was how the British leaders could fail to see where the real interests of the UK lay.[3] But who was to say what those were? As Spaak admitted, it was not the personal view of Bevin or Cripps which they had to contend with, but the collective view of the Cabinet. If there was any doubt about this, it was removed at the Cabinet meeting on 27 October at which Bevin presented two papers, one dealing with the British policy towards the Council of Europe, the other (a joint production of the Foreign Office and Treasury, signed by both Bevin and Cripps) considering proposals for the economic unification of Europe.[4]

The first of the two papers was unequivocal in arguing that Britain must continue to support the Council of Europe. It was an important element in the structure of confidence and unity which the British had been seeking to build in Europe.

---

[1] Acheson to Douglas, 24 October. FRUS (4) p. 433.
[2] Douglas's report to Acheson, 26 October, *ibid.*, pp. 435–7.
[3] Millard's report to Acheson from Brussels, 27 October, *ibid.*, pp. 437–8.
[4] The first, CP (49) 204, is dated 24 October; the second, CP (49) 203, is dated 25 October. The Cabinet discussion is recorded in CM 62 (49).

"Whatever may be our opinion as to the ultimate relationship between this country and the Continent, or between the continental nations, we should do nothing now to undermine the general hopes of solidarity and co-operation which the Council has aroused in Europe."

But it was equally clear that there were limits beyond which Britain could not go. These had been laid down by the Economic Policy Committee in January 1949[1] in terms which were repeated in the October paper:

"Though we may make considerable sacrifices for the sake of European economic co-operation, we should not run risks which would jeopardise our own chances of survival if the attempt to restore Western Europe should fail, and we should not involve ourselves in the economic affairs of Europe beyond the point at which we could, if we wished, disengage ourselves."

In arguing for the re-affirmation of this principle, the October memorandum specifically mentions among "the wider interest which H.M.G. are always obliged to keep in mind" not only the relationship with the Commonwealth, but "almost equally important, our new relationship with the United States". Together these ensured that

"We must remain, as we have always been in the past, different in character from other European nations and fundamentally incapable of wholehearted integration with them."[2]

The same principles applied to OEEC and the second document again referred to "a new relationship with the USA" which together with the Commonwealth links must take priority over economic relations with Europe. Both papers were approved by the Cabinet without dissent and Bevin's conclusion accepted that "we should treat with strict reserve any scheme for pooling of sovereignty or for the establishment of European supra-national machinery."[3]

5

Whatever hopes the Americans had of progress towards European integration received little encouragement from the talks in Paris at the beginning of November. On 31 October Hoffman addressed the Council of OEEC and urged them to adopt a programme that would take Europe "well along the road to economic integration". The Council applauded and agreed unanimously to embark "wholeheartedly" on measures to implement Hoffman's proposals. Eventually this produced the European Payments Union but only

[1] EPC (49) 6, 25 January 1949.
[2] CP (49) 204.
[3] CM 62 (49).

after months of difficult negotiations with the British. It was only when British policy changed in May 1950 and Hugh Gaitskell replaced Cripps for the final negotiations in June that agreement was reached. OEEC was given the means to make it "probably the most successful international organisation to date", as J. F. C. Dow described it in 1964.[1] But it was far more on the basis of co-operation, which Bevin thought the only realistic one, than of integration.

Talking to Bevin and Cripps on 2 November, after the OEEC meeting, Harriman and Hoffman believed that they had won over the former at least to the appointment of Spaak, only to discover to their anger that Bevin had arranged a meeting of the OEEC ministers without telling them and virtually killed the proposal.[2] Bevin's opposition was founded not upon personal dislike of Spaak, but on the belief that neither Spaak nor the Americans had thought through what a political figure at the head of OEEC was going to do and, more important, on the conviction that OEEC would never succeed as an instrument of European integration but only if it was based on more effective co-operation between governments.

Bevin was equally discouraging in the Committee of Ministers when it met to discuss the role of the Council of Europe and its Assembly, the other hope of the integrationists. He was practical about membership of the Council, getting agreement in principle to associating Germany with the Council but urging that they should proceed discreetly in making Germany a member and not stir up controversy. He also got agreement not to press an invitation to Austria which could only be embarrassing to her. But he opposed enlarging the role of the Assembly and, in face of Schuman's doubts, got the Assembly's economic recommendations referred to OEEC.[3]

There was still one more meeting to be held in Paris, on Germany, and the contrast between its success and the failure to find common ground on European integration is instructive. One explanation might be that Acheson now joined the other two foreign ministers and that on Germany the USA was in a position to give a lead which it carefully refrained from taking over "European" questions. But Acheson had been present when the three discussed Germany in Washington in September and on that occasion despite American unwillingness to see further delay, no decisions had been taken. As late as 25 October Acheson cabled McCloy that, after reviewing the crucial question of dismantling, the State Department still took the view that "nothing must be done which could give rise to inference U.S. is seeking to impose solution on French or British".[4] The decisive difference between the talks on Germany in September and those in November was the change in the British attitude. This opened the way for a new relationship between the Western Powers and Germany which Americans had wanted to see for some time. But

[1] J. F. C. Dow: *The Management of the British Economy, 1945–60* (Cambridge 1964), p. 52.
[2] Harriman to Acheson. FRUS 1949 (4) p. 44.
[3] 2nd Session of the Committee of Ministers, 3–5 November 1949. FO 800/460/EUR/49/33.
[4] Acheson to McCloy, 25 October. FRUS 1949 (3) pp. 614–18.

no comparable change took place in the British attitude towards Europe: as a consequence, the way remained blocked. So far was it still true at the end of 1949, as the conference of US Ambassadors in Paris had recognized, that the condition of effective action in Europe was the willingness of the British to co-operate with the Americans, a willingness now shown in the one case, that of Germany, but still withheld in the other, that of European integration. This view is supported both by the origin of the November meeting in Paris and by its postscript.

On Bevin's way back from Canada, he had spent a few hours on 6 October in New York with Acheson who had taken advantage of the meeting for a further discussion on Germany.[1] Since they had talked in mid-September, the Russians had gone ahead with setting up an East German state, the DDR, with a Communist-controlled government which it was widely believed would make Berlin its capital. Now that the air-lift was over and the new West German state had chosen Bonn for its capital, morale had fallen abruptly in the Western sectors of Berlin. The Berliners felt forgotten and isolated; the Russians and the East sector Communists put every difficulty they could in the way of implementing the agreement on restoring communications; unemployment was high, the budget deficit alarming and confidence in the future low. To counter the anticipated move to make Berlin the capital of the DDR, Acheson told Bevin the State Department wanted to make the Western sectors into the 12th Land of the Federal Republic. Bevin thought this an ill-considered proposal. Something had clearly got to be done to deal with the critical economic situation in West Berlin but this was a different matter from making a precipitate decision, the consequences of which could not be foreseen. With strong support from Couve de Murville, Bevin persuaded Acheson that they should ask the High Commissioners to examine the position of Berlin and wait for their recommendations.

Apart from French opposition, the Germans themselves (particularly Adenauer) were doubtful about the value or wisdom of making Berlin juridically part of the Federal Republic. Other and less provocative forms were found for strengthening the association of the city with West Germany and of giving it economic aid, and the matter was settled and out of the way before the end of October.[2]

The other question Acheson raised with Bevin was the timetable of the postponed talks on dismantling. Bevin suggested the High Commissioners should produce a report by the end of the year. But after he got back to London, he became more and more uneasy at the mounting German campaign against dismantling, overwhelmingly directed against the British, and a vehicle for pent-up German resentment of the Occupation. No one was any longer prepared to defend a policy which had become unpopular on both sides

[1] FO 800/448/CONF/49/10.
[2] See the documents in FRUS 1949 (3) pp. 399–435, and Kirkpatrick's notes to Attlee (as acting Foreign Minister), dated 7 and 11 October, FO 800/467/GER/49/48–9.

of the House of Commons, and Bevin now became convinced it was dangerous to delay any longer. On 28 October, he wrote urgently to Acheson and Schuman, suggesting that, while they still retained some bargaining power, they should aim at a comprehensive settlement with the new German government, and secure concessions in return for abandoning the dismantling of anything other than war plants. Amongst the measures Bevin had in mind was German agreement to serve on the International Authority for the Ruhr; and to accept the Military Security Board.

Despite the short notice, Acheson at once agreed to Bevin's proposal of a meeting. This might be the break-through he had been hoping for and he sent off a personal message to Schuman with a copy for Bevin. In this long and eloquent letter, which he had been drafting when Bevin's message arrived, he argued that circumstances presented the French with a chance that might not recur to take the lead in integrating the Federal Republic "promptly and decisively" into Western Europe. With the division of Germany and the establishment of rival German states, the moment was psychologically and politically ripe to turn Western Germany at least towards the West. No nation had a greater stake in bringing this about than the French and no one else could do it.

"I believe," Acheson wrote, "that our policy in Germany and the development of a German Government which can take its place in Western Europe, depends on the assumption by your country of leadership in Europe on these problems."[1]

There was no comment from Bevin on the prospect Acheson opened up, which was to be proved more than visionary when Schuman produced his famous Plan six months later. But having taken the initiative in calling for a meeting on Germany Bevin did his best to suppress his own feelings about the Germans and turn a retreat on dismantling into laying the foundation for the more positive relationship with Germany which was the object of American policy.

The meeting actually began badly. McCloy had told the Press that they had come to Paris to cut down the programme of dismantling, to the embarrassment of Schuman and the anger of Bevin. The latter laid about him furiously but, when he ran out of breath, was disarmed by Acheson's apt quotation from the Book of Common Prayer: "The remembrance of our sins is grievous unto us; the burden of them is intolerable."[2]

Bevin's proposal of combining concessions from the Occupying Powers on dismantling with commitments from the German Government formed the basis of the discussion, which ranged widely from broad questions of policy to the detailed production figures for specific plants. The real problem was

---

[1] Acheson to Schuman, 30 October. FRUS 1949 (3) pp. 622–5.
[2] Acheson, pp. 337–8.

whether Schuman could carry the French Cabinet with him, and this would not be known until it met on the evening of the second day. As Bevin pointed out, the figures being bandied about had far more psychological than economic significance. Their exaggeration by the Germans, however, meant that the concessions made by the Occupying Powers appeared to have much greater value than was, in fact, the case, and enabled them to secure solid commitments from the Germans in return. Finally, after two days of discussion, Schuman went off to put the case to the French Cabinet and came back, at 11 o'clock at night, with the news that he had got approval, provided there was no increase in the permitted figure for German steel production of 11.1 million tons a year, another of the symbolic figures which gave the controversy its emotive force.[1]

6

What in the end emerged from the November meetings? The High Commissioners were given a new directive for negotiations with Adenauer which covered three sets of issues linked together in the Petersberg Agreement finally signed on 22 November.

The primary objective was stated to be the incorporation of the Federal Republic in the European community. The Federal Republic was to be admitted as an associate member of the Council of Europe; to take part in the International Monetary Fund and Bank, WHO, FAO, ILO, IRO, GATT and other international organizations; and to begin the appointment of consular and commercial representatives with a Bureau to supervise its representation abroad.

The second group of decisions committed the Federal Government to apply for membership of the International Authority for the Ruhr and to co-operate with the High Commission in the work of the Military Security Board, thereby publicly accepting the need for both bodies.

The third group consisted of the concessions made by the Occupying Powers: the removal from the dismantling list of over 400 synthetic oil and rubber plants; of all factories in Berlin and of seven steel plants including the August Thyssen Works at Hamborn. The only major steel plants not removed from the list were the Hermann Goering Werke at Salzgitter and Krupps at Essen. Bevin and Acheson had been ready to include the former but in view of Schuman's plea that it would cost him his political life, it was agreed to omit it. The tripartite agreement on prohibited and restricted industries, however, remained in force, in particular the limit of 11.1 million tons p.a. on steel production.

---

[1] British record of the discussions in Paris. FO 800/448/CONF/49/19 and 467/GER/49/52. Acheson's reports to Washington, FRUS 1949 (3) pp. 305–8; 632–8.

Finally it was agreed to examine the question of terminating the state of war with Germany, with no great hope of finding a solution to the legal complexities, but more immediately to avoid recognition of the DDR.[1]

There were a number of questions the Petersberg Agreement did not settle. The most important was whether, with the end of dismantling, Western Germany was to be re-armed. On 7 November Moscow announced that the Polish-born Russian, Marshal Rokossovsky, had been appointed as Minister of Defence in Warsaw, a move which highlighted Soviet measures to re-organize the satellite armed forces variously estimated (without counting Eastern Germany) as providing the Russians with half-a-million to a million additional trained men. Inevitably people asked whether either side in the Cold War would leave unarmed the nation which had provided the most formidable fighting force in the world only a few years before. Rumour reported that the Americans had pressed the British and French to agree to some form of German rearmament at the Paris meeting. This was untrue, but the denials suggested that if German rearmament, possibly in the form of a German contribution to a West European Army, had not yet been discussed by the Foreign Ministers, it soon would be.

This was a subject on which British and French found it easy to agree. The French National Assembly, after hearing Schuman's report on the Petersberg Agreement, passed a resolution expressing total opposition to German rearmament or the accession of Germany to the North Atlantic Pact. When the French Ambassador called to present a copy of the resolution, Attlee assured him that Bevin and he were equally strongly opposed and wished to associate themselves with the views of the French Government.

Bevin's suspicions of the Germans were not at all removed by the Petersberg Agreement. Dalton noted in his Journal:

"In Cabinet Ernie, expounding recent talks with Acheson, Schuman and three Allied High Commissioners, said: 'Stalin's policy is just stupid, but the Germans are really dangerous.'"[2]

On the other hand, Bevin left no doubt that he was in favour of the Agreement, accepted that a new basis had to be found for relations with the German government which had now come into existence, had taken the initiative in calling the conference and was pleased with the results.

There was a postscript to the discussion of German problems at the Paris meeting. At the end, Acheson raised the question of European integration, arguing that unless Germany could become part of Western Europe there was no possibility of her developing on other than nationalistic lines. Bevin's reply

---

[1] Text of the Directive to the High Commissioners, 11 November. FRUS 1949 (3) pp. 306–8. Text of the Petersburg Agreement, 22 November, *ibid.*, pp. 343–8.
[2] Dalton's diaries, 20 November 1949. Bevin's report was circulated as CP (49) 237 and taken at the Cabinet on 17 November. CM 67 (49).

was that a lot had been accomplished since he had first spoken of Western Union in January 1948, but he had to warn them that the UK could never become an entirely European country because of its overseas connections. American criticism of the UK's policy on Europe was over-simplified and it caused much resentment. He would do his best to keep foreign policy out of party politics and would refrain from criticism of other countries: unity between the three of them was vital. Bevin spoke emotionally and Schuman assured him that "Europe" was inconceivable without Great Britain. Acheson said nothing, but it was evident that on European integration, unlike Germany, the deadlock remained and the British were not prepared to move.[1]

When the House of Commons debated foreign affairs on 17 November, Bevin spoke in the same terms. There had been a lot of misunderstanding, he said, and propaganda on the Continent and elsewhere about the attitude of HMG. Their chief aim since the breakdown of four-power collaboration had been

"To consolidate and revive Europe, maintain liberty, try to restore morale and mutual confidence and arrest the spread of communism amongst us. . . . We want to bring about a sound relationship between Europe, the Commonwealth and the USA. We do not want a wedge to be driven between any of them, if we can help it."

Party politics were already affecting foreign policy as became evident from the exchanges between the parties on the Council of Europe. Bevin stuck to his view that the important thing was the Committee of Ministers. The Opposition, championing the rights of the Assembly, was not at all prepared to be lectured on how the Council of Europe should work. Churchill, assuming (rightly, as it turned out) that this was the last foreign affairs debate of an expiring Parliament, spoke of Bevin's swan-song as Foreign Secretary, and pronounced his verdict on his performance. Bevin, he declared, had substantial victories to his credit, but he had no integral scheme of thought, and he was swayed, even dominated, by his personal likes and dislikes.

The Opposition was equally critical of the Government's German policy, in particular the failure to finish with dismantling four years after the War had ended. In an earlier debate (21 July) Churchill had become incensed with Bevin for putting the blame for the problem they found in Germany on the policy of "unconditional surrender" which, Bevin claimed, Churchill accepted without consulting the War Cabinet. This led to an angry exchange in the House and further correspondence afterwards. Now Bevin had to sit and listen to Churchill and the Tories attacking him for his failure to develop a new approach to Germany when this was precisely what he had tried to do in Paris, but was not yet in a position to describe. The negotiation of the Petersberg Agreement was not completed until 22 November and it was essential not to create difficulties for Schuman by a premature disclosure—with the result, as

[1] 10 November 1949. FO 800/448/CONF/49/19.

Bevin said rather wrily in a message to Acheson, that he only created difficulties for himself.

Parliamentary proceedings had in fact lost their interest until an election could decide whether Labour was to continue in office or the Tories to replace them, a decision which would affect not only the nationalization of steel (the legislation for which had been passed but could not be implemented until after the election) but, as many abroad hoped, British policy towards Europe as well. The results of devaluation were beginning to show in rising exports and production and an increase in gold and dollar reserves.[1] With this encouragement, a meeting of senior ministers on 7 December finally decided to fix the date for the election as 23 February, with a public announcement on 17 January.

Bevin might not be much of a party politician but he had a special interest in the links between the trade union movement and the Labour Party, and had been very concerned at the gap which he found had opened up between them as a result of devaluation. He set himself to improve relations and in particular to get a renewed commitment from the TUC to wage restraint. During 1949 the rise in prices moved ahead of rises in wages and there was growing resentment amongst skilled workers at a wages policy which narrowed the differential between skilled and unskilled work. Once again Bevin's ties with the trade union movement proved their value to the Labour Government. He persuaded the Cabinet to drop the idea of exempting the lower paid workers from the wage standstill which was proposed and went with Cripps to meet the TUC's Economic Committee—a committee which he had persuaded the TUC to set up in the 1930s.[2] As a result, on 23 November the TUC General Council approved a statement recommending that the policy of wage restraint should be continued until 1 January 1951 provided that the index of retail prices remained between limits fixed in advance. These recommendations, which Bevin's successor, Arthur Deakin, played a leading part in securing, went beyond anything the TUC had been prepared to do to assist the Government of the day even in wartime, and were only accepted by a much reduced majority at a Special Conference of Executive Committees held in January. But they *were* accepted and that, just before an election, was worth a lot to the Labour Government.

Equally pleasing for Bevin was the news that, while he had been in the USA, the Trades Union Congress had endorsed Deakin's report on the TUC's withdrawal from the World Federation of Trade Unions by six million to one million votes. Preparatory steps to form a new International Confederation of Free Trade Unions free from Communist attempts to dominate it had already been taken and were ratified by a constituent congress representing 43 million workers in London in December. Bevin had never liked the WFTU. He had

---

[1] Cripps first reported this at the Cabinet meeting on 10 November. CM 65 (49).
[2] CM 66 (49), 14 November.

strongly advised Deakin against getting involved with it, and now that all links with it were broken he was delighted.

Bevin was far from well and on the day the Cabinet decided the date of the election was trying to recuperate in Eastbourne. While he was away the differences which had held up the Anglo–US agreement under the Mutual Defence Assistance Act became acute. The Americans had settled with the other European members of NATO but until all the bilateral agreements were completed the President was not empowered to sign the executive order which would give effect to the Act.

On 14 December Franks informed the State Department that the British Cabinet was deeply concerned about the terms of the agreement, in particular the amount it was expected to contribute as mutual aid and the much smaller amount than anticipated (in materials) which it was to receive.[1] An urgent enquiry from Acheson to the London Embassy brought the reply that, in Bevin's absence, the Cabinet had got its back up about continuing pressure from the USA, particularly on European integration, and had reacted against demands for extra defence expenditure. Franks' report of his conversation with Acheson, however, changed the atmosphere, and with Bevin taking a hand, instructions were got back to Franks which made it possible for him to complete negotiations on the agreement after Christmas and so allow the President on 27 January to release the funds for military assistance under the Act.

---

[1] Franks' statement to Acheson and the subsequent exchange of messages between Acheson and the US Chargé in London, Holmes, 15 & 19 December. FRUS 1949 (4) pp. 360–65.

CHAPTER 20

Colombo, January 1950; General Election, February 1950

I

As long ago as February 1949,[1] Bevin had urged on Attlee that a meeting of Commonwealth Ministers should be held in Ceylon. His persistence finally produced a date in January 1950.

The reason why Bevin wanted this particular meeting place is soon explained. Twice in the course of 1949, he had sought to persuade the Americans that the West's successes in Europe were being offset by an adverse shift in the balance of power in South East Asia. The force of his argument was increased by the triumph of the Chinese Communists which was followed by the signature of a Sino–Soviet Treaty giving the Russians their first major ally. The impact on Asia of a Communist China, aggressively hostile to the West, was immense, and Nehru warned the Western powers that the whole of South East Asia as well as China might be closed to them if they continued to concentrate on Europe and neglect the new world emerging between the Indian Ocean and the Pacific.

If the United States would not act, then the British must. This was the conclusion of the Permanent Under-Secretary's Committee set up by Sir William Strang on succeeding as head of the Foreign Office in 1949 to act as a counterpart to Kennan's Policy Planning Committee in the State Department.[2] It was advice which Bevin was very willing to accept.[3]

If action was aimed in the first place at promoting economic co-operation it appeared to be within Britain's power and was endorsed, with some misgivings on Cripps' part, by the Cabinet on 27 October.[4] The Commonwealth,

[1] Bevin to Secretary of State for Commonwealth Relations, 19 February 1949. FO 800/445/COM/49/6.
[2] FO 371/76386/W 5572/3/500 G PUSC (32), "The U.K. in S.E. Asia and the Far East".
[3] *Ibid.* Strang to Bevin, 16 October 1949 and Bevin's minute, undated.
[4] CM 62 (49).

revitalized by the decision of India, Pakistan and Ceylon to stay in, was the obvious framework, the more so as it now represented a group of nations the majority of which belonged to the Eastern and Southern hemispheres.

A related question was whether or not to recognize the Communist government in China. Bevin had more of a free hand than either Acheson or Schuman. In Britain there was nothing like the emotional resistance in America to recognizing the fact that Mao had won, and that Chiang Kai-Shek was finished. It was true that the attack on HMS *Amethyst* when she went up the Yangtze in support of the British Embassy at Nanking gave no grounds for believing that China's new rulers regarded the British with any more favour than the Americans or other "Western imperialists". However, insofar as there was a China lobby in Britain, the business interests which composed it favoured recognition as soon as possible in the hope that this would enable them to continue trading there.

On 1 November Bevin sent a message to Acheson, saying that he was disposed to go ahead, on the grounds that the Communists were now undeniably in control of three-quarters of China and that the best way to protect British trading interests was by keeping a foot in the door. The real question was one of timing. When they met in Paris in mid-November, Acheson was still opposed to recognition, while Schuman was anxious to delay until after ratification of the agreements the French had reached with Bao Dai. The Indians were in favour of early recognition and likely to go ahead by the end of the year; this weighed with the British Government, who were anxious to keep the Indians in step with the rest of the Commonwealth.

Bevin put the question to the Cabinet on 15 December, recommending recognition with the date left to his discretion.[1] Writing personally to Acheson, he expressed his regret that they had not been able to agree:

"We want to keep in close association with you, but we have to be careful not to lose our grip of the situation in Asia and to take into account the views of our Asian friends. . .

"We feel that the only counter to Russian influence is that Communist China should have contacts with the West, and that the sooner these contacts are established, the better."[2]

If they could not agree on how to come to terms with the Communist capture of power in China, the three Western Powers did not find it much easier to agree on what to do to prevent something similar happening in other Asian states. In South East Asia, guerilla warfare in which Communist forces were actively engaged was widespread in Burma, Malaya and Indo–China and was a possible threat to the newly established Indonesian Republic. One suggestion was a Pacific Pact similar to the North Atlantic Treaty and this found

---

[1] Bevin circulated a paper on 15 December, CP (49) 248; this was taken at the Cabinet meeting on the 17th. CM 72 (49).
[2] Bevin to Acheson, 16 December. FRUS 1949 (9), pp. 224–6.

support in such diverse quarters as Australia, Siam, the Philippines, South Korea, Japan and Formosa[1] (where Chiang Kai-Shek and the Chinese Nationalists had retreated) and was endorsed by Eden and Churchill.[2] Nationalism, however, and the desire to get rid of Western colonial rule and Western intervention made it likely that any Pact proposed by the West would be rejected as really directed to the restoration of Western power. Strong opposition to such a Pact was expressed by Nehru and endorsed by Acheson. Bevin agreed: the conditions for a Pacific or South East Asian Pact on NATO lines simply did not exist, there were too many internal conflicts in the area. But he wrote to Attlee that an economic approach might be more fruitful; "there is a good deal here which the West has to offer the East and a solid basis for co-operation".[3] It was with this more than anything else in mind that Bevin kept on pressing for a meeting of Commonwealth ministers in Asia.

In taking the Marshall Plan rather than NATO as a model, Bevin was acting on his belief that the best way to oppose Communism was to attack the living conditions which gave force to its appeal in parts of the world plagued with such poverty as Asia. Frustrated by the lack of resources and adverse political circumstances which denied him the chance to put his ideas into practice in the Middle East, he was determined to attend the Colombo Conference in person in the hope that it might be possible, before he gave up office, to start a scheme with a better chance of success in South East Asia. Bevin did not think such a scheme should be limited to members of the Commonwealth and he had Truman's Point IV very much in mind. But the backing of the Commonwealth countries in the area, not only Australia, but particularly of newly independent Asian nations like India, Pakistan and Ceylon, gave him the element which was missing in the Middle East.

In the political sphere, Bevin hoped that he could secure the agreement of the other members of the Commonwealth to go along with the British decision to recognize the new regime in China and, less hopefully, to join with Britain, France and the USA in recognizing Bao Dai in Indo-China. Finally, although he had for reasons of health to decline an invitation to visit Karachi, he planned to talk to Ghulam Mohammed, the Pakistan Finance Minister, as well as Nehru about relations between their two states, particularly the continuing dispute about Kashmir.

This was the background to the Colombo Conference.

---

[1] When Chiang Kai-Shek took refuge in Formosa the island again became known by its traditional Chinese name of Taiwan. During the discussions of 1950–51 however, it continued to be referred to in the West as Formosa, the name by which it had been known during its annexation and occupation by the Japanese, 1895–1945.
[2] The former during a tour of Australia and New Zealand in February 1949; the latter in a speech in New York on 25 March 1949.
[3] Bevin to Attlee, 21 April 1949. FO 800/445/COM/49/19.

As the time for making the journey drew nearer, the question arose whether Bevin was fit enough to go. He finally agreed to an examination at the Manor House Hospital in Golders Green, for which he had secured union support before the war. His own doctor, Sir Alec McCall, and the head of the hospital, Lord Uvedale, called in a heart specialist as well. All three agreed that he was unfit to travel and told him so. Bevin was unimpressed. If it came off as he hoped, he said with a characteristic touch of exaggeration, it could mean peace for a hundred years; but if he wasn't there he was afraid nothing much would be decided. "I'm going and I don't care if I come back in my box."[1]

So the day after Boxing Day 1949 he took the train from Victoria and set off for the East. He was in a poor state and according to McCall who travelled with him, they very nearly lost him on the first leg of the journey on the night train between Paris and Rome. The pilot of the plane which took him on to Suez was told to fly low over the Mediterranean and by the time he went on board HMS *Kenya* he looked so ashen that several of the officers wondered if he would survive the voyage. But the rest, the sun and the sea air worked wonders and by the time he reached the Indian Ocean he looked a different man as a photograph of him addressing the ship's company shows. It was on that occasion, while talking about the world situation that he suddenly interjected that he was worried about the position in Korea, a remark that surprised his listeners at the time but was to be remembered when six months later HMS *Kenya* was involved in hostilities off Korea.[2]

The climax of the voyage was a dinner on the final night. By mistake a bottle of brandy was placed in front of the Secretary of State which he proceeded to down glass by glass. He captivated the company by a stream of anecdotes and stories, but paid for it by arriving in Colombo in very poor shape.

The Conference opened the day after Bevin arrived—9 January—and lasted six days.[3] He was lodged in the Prime Minister's residence, with its gardens full of tropical flowers, and at the opening session—to the delight of the Press—was borne up the stairs to the first floor conference room in a gorgeous palanquin so that he should put no strain on his heart. This did not at all suit the former General Secretary of the TGWU, and thereafter he insisted on walking up, whatever the cost in effort. The Ceylonese Prime Minister, Senanayake, presided at the meetings at which the leading figures besides Bevin were Nehru and Lester Pearson, the Canadian Minister for External Affairs. When McCall asked Senanayake how his unruly charge was managing in the discussions, the Ceylonese replied: "I am amazed by his sharpness.

[1] Interview with Lord Uvedale.
[2] Barclay, 67–9.
[3] British records in CAB 133/78 & 79.

He sits there apparently half-asleep but pounces on any point which is important."[1]

Although there were still advocates of a Pacific Pact, including the Australians,[2] it was not discussed at the Colombo Conference. Bevin's argument however that like-minded countries with interests in the East should act together to resist Communism by improving the standard of life of the peoples of South East Asia was readily accepted. To his great satisfaction the Australians agreed to take the initiative in proposing a joint programme with the offer of an Australian contribution as a start.[3] A Commonwealth Economic Consultative Committee was created, and the headquarters of a Commonwealth Technical Assistance Committee was set up in Colombo. This was the origin of the Colombo Plan in the establishment of which Bevin played as decisive a role as in that of the Marshall Plan. Before he gave up office he was to see six-year development plans prepared by the Governments of India, Pakistan, Ceylon, Malaya, Singapore and North Borneo envisaging a total expenditure of £1,868 m. of which £1,084 m. was to be provided from external sources, principally the UK and the older Dominions.

The scale of the aid was modest in relation to the needs of the huge population of the area, but the promises given were fulfilled and the plans carried out. No less important, in Bevin's eyes, was the example the Colombo Plan provided of successful co-operation between newly independent Asian nations and established ones of European stock, not only the UK but Australia, Canada and New Zealand. This was the concept of a Commonwealth translated into action, on the basis which Bevin had always believed right for Europe as well, that of co-operation, not integration, with national governments responsible for the assessment of needs and capacities and the role of the Consultative Committee confined to co-ordination, criticism and advice. In the long run American participation was essential, and as Bevin had hoped, the British initiative was followed by an American economic mission to develop a parallel programme of economic aid to South-East Asia. Its recommendations were accepted and acted on[4] only to be overtaken by the transformation of American and Asian attitudes towards each other as a result of the Korean war.

Bevin had far less success at Colombo in getting agreement on political issues. Britain's recognition of the Communist Government in China had been announced while Bevin was on his way to the East (6 January 1950). It pleased the Asian members of the Conference and had undoubtedly been influenced by Indian assessments of the situation in China; but it failed to convince the four

---

[1] Interview with McCall.
[2] See the statement by P. C. Spender, the Australian Foreign Minister on 20 February 1950 (after the Colombo conference) that Australia would join a Pacific Pact if other powerful nations would.
[3] Report of the UK Delegation to London on the meetings of 10–12 January. FO 800/445/COM/50/1–4.
[4] FRUS 1950 (6) pp. 87–94, 11 May 1950.

older members of the Commonwealth—Canada, Australia, New Zealand and South Africa—who took the same view as the USA and withheld recognition.

On Indo–China it was the other way round. He had promised Schuman to do his best to get Commonwealth agreement to wider recognition for the Bao Dai regime and when Britain and the USA granted recognition on 7 February, their lead was followed by Australia, New Zealand and South Africa. Nehru, however, spoke equally strongly on the other side and condemned Bao Dai as a puppet of the French. Amongst Asian governments only Siam and South Korea recognized Bao Dai's regime during 1950.

A third issue, discussed as long ago as the 1947 Commonwealth Conference in Canberra, was a peace treaty with Japan. The Australian and New Zealand Governments, riled by their continued exclusion from any influence on American occupation policy in Japan, were vigorous in claiming a voice in the peace settlement. In November 1949, Bevin had asked Acheson what the Americans were going to propose so that he could be briefed for the discussion which was certain to take place at Colombo.[1] Acheson promised to inform him in time, but to his embarrassment had to send a message in December to say that he could tell Bevin nothing.[2] Franks reported that the real trouble was the Americans' own inability to agree on what was the best course to follow.[3] The deadlock in Washington had not been resolved by the time Bevin left for Colombo, and Bevin had to do the best he could to play for time and prevent Commonwealth views from hardening before the Americans were ready to make proposals.

Outside the formal sessions Bevin took the chance to talk to the Indians and the Pakistanis about the bad relations between their two countries. Once again, economic issues proved easier to deal with than political. At a meeting with Nehru and Ghulam Mohammed, on 11 January, Bevin tried to find a way to end their mutual blockade and succeeded in getting the latter to offer to release supplies of jute in the hope that India would supply coal in return.[4] Kashmir, however, was a different matter. Nehru was a great critic of British and American policy, but on Kashmir he was adamant in refusing to consider any procedure which would not secure India's claim *in toto*. In September 1949 he had flatly rejected the UN Commission's proposal of arbitration, leading Bevin to write to Attlee that he regretted they had ever agreed to support India's candidacy for a place on the Security Council.[5] The Pakistan High Commissioner complained that the Labour Government attached so much importance to Indian views that they overlooked the interests of Pakistan, which were not treated on their merits—to which Bevin retorted that he got

---

[1] Bevin's talk with Acheson, 12 November. FO 800/462/FE/49/34.
[2] Bevin to Franks, 8 December, *ibid.*, FE/49/37.
[3] Franks to Bevin, 9 December, *ibid.*, FE/49/38.
[4] Bevin's report on his talk with Nehru and Ghulam Mohammed, 11 January 1950. FO 800/470/IND/50/51.
[5] Bevin to Attlee, 17 September 1949, *ibid.*, IND/49/10.

exactly the same complaints from the Indians.[1] Both Ali Khan and Nehru pressed Bevin to visit their countries while he was in the East and it was only when Attlee overruled him on grounds of health that Bevin finally refused.[2]

On balance, however, Bevin regarded the Colombo Conference as a success. He had made the long journey in the hope that he would be able to secure some practical results in economic co-operation and he attached more importance to success in this direction than to his failure to resolve political differences. The fact that the leaders of the newly independent Asian states and representatives of the older Commonwealth countries, including the former imperial Power, were able to meet on a footing of equality and discuss difficult political and economic questions frankly, was a considerable political achievement in itself. No one contributed more to this than Bevin himself. Although in poor health and liable to fall asleep in the hot conference sessions, his belief in the value of the Commonwealth connection, his common sense and practicality, the natural authority which his long experience of foreign affairs now gave him and the friendly relations he established with every one of the other delegates, gave him a key role which even that other prima donna, Nehru, was prepared to accept.[3]

At the end of a strenuous week of meetings Bevin and the British party paid a visit to Kandy. Among the sights were a herd of elephants bathing in a river and as Bevin stood surveying them, his private secretary, R. E. Barclay, reflected on the resemblance between them: "The same plodding step and rolling gait, as well as a sense of humour and a very long memory."[4] In the Foreign Secretary's honour, the Ceylonese opened the shrine of the Temple of the Tooth supposed to house one of Buddha's teeth. Despite the disapproval of his doctor, Alec McCall, who was sure the effort would kill him, Bevin removed his shoes (revealing a large hole in the heel of one of his socks) and slowly made his way up several flights of stairs to the inner sanctum where the Tooth was revealed in a nest of jewel-studded caskets. He showed the same capacity to enjoy himself as a tourist when he arrived in Egypt and made the traditional sight-seeing visit to the Pyramids. The loquacity of the guide amused him and when the Egyptian ended his piece with an eloquent passage about the thousands of years the Sphinx had lain silent in the desert, Bevin remarked: "And now you're trying to make up for lost time on his behalf."[5]

The journey from Ceylon to Egypt on board another cruiser, HMS *Birmingham*, did Bevin good. He wrote in a letter to Ivy Saunders from Aden:

[1] Bevin's talk with the Pakistan High Commissioner, 28 October, *ibid.*, IND/49/17.
[2] Bevin to Liaquet Ali Khan 13 December 1949, *ibid.*, IND/49/28.
[3] See the letter from General Freyberg VC, the Governor General of New Zealand, reporting the impression Bevin had made on the New Zealand Minister for External Affairs and the "intense admiration" which Doidge felt for "the wonderful job Bevin has done for Britain". 15 May 1950. FO 800/449/CONF/50/22.
[4] Barclay, p. 70.
[5] *Ibid.*, p. 72.

749

"I am afraid the note I sent from Colombo was curt but I could not write I was so exhausted. . . . I worked very hard and had great trouble with Pains and Breathing. I tried to walk the stairs but had to use the chair. I went to Kandy. They made a great fuss of me, did all they could, including the Tooth.

"The rest in the Boat has been good. I was in bed four days but then I began to mend yesterday. Sunday was the best day I had had for ages. The sea was calm. We cruised about 14 knots. I gave Sunday talk to the officers and men, spent the day on deck and ended up with a good wild west film."[1]

3

After his visit to Southern Asia, where the British could claim to have adapted themselves to the new post-war world with considerable success, Bevin's visit to the Middle East was a painful reminder of the frustrations and failures which British policy had experienced in that part of the world since 1945. The British had successfully defended the Middle East against both the Italians and the Germans while failing to prevent the Japanese from overrunning the greater part of South East Asia. Since the War the record had been reversed: the British had had a degree of success in coming to terms with nationalism in Asia which eluded them in the Middle East.

As Kennan put it in talking to Hector McNeil, the power to take offensive air action from the Middle East was an essential part of the defence of Western Europe.[2] So far the line represented by the Northern tier of states, from Greece and Turkey through Iraq and Iran to Pakistan, had been held. South of it the British had lost Palestine (unnecessarily, in the view of Bevin's critics); failed to replace the existing treaties with Egypt and Iraq; and made two gains, the revised treaty with Jordan and the treaty with Libya (the latter still to be concluded when Bevin was in Cairo). The whole area remained unstable and vulnerable to Soviet tactics of penetration.

During 1949 the single-mindedness of the Israelis; continued support from the Zionist organizations abroad, especially in the USA; divisions among the Arabs and the weakness of the UN had enabled Israel to consolidate most of the advantages it had won in the fighting. But Bevin's forecast that the war would not be followed by a lasting settlement was to prove all too true: there were four more outbreaks of fighting by 1983 and still no resolution to the conflict.

With the armistice concluded, the arms embargo had been lifted in August 1949 and Britain resumed the supply of arms to Egypt and Iraq as well as Jordan. Bevin had some sympathy with the Arab desire to overcome their disunity, but when he was informed of secret moves towards a union of Syria and Iraq in the summer of 1949, felt it necessary to warn both parties that they were likely to encounter strong opposition from the French and probably the

[1] Letter dated Aden, 23 January 1950.
[2] In a conversation reported by McNeil on 11 August 1949. FO 800/477/ME/49/16.

Turks as well.[1] He kept in touch with Nuri in Iraq and wrote to Acheson in November that he was worried by the French refusal to countenance any change in the *status quo* in the Middle East. In talking with Schuman, he said, he had warned him of the danger of putting obstacles in the way of Arab unity and so offering the Russians the opportunity to take the lead in promoting it. But Bevin admitted that he had no proposals of his own to make and got no response from Acheson.[2]

Bevin was concerned that, with the Americans taking an increasing interest in Asia and the Pacific as well as the North Atlantic and Europe, they were less likely to accept responsibilities in the Middle East. He told Spender and Doidge, the Australian and New Zealand Ministers for External Affairs, when they were talking in Colombo, that the Americans showed a disposition to draw back, not to go beyond the Elbe-Po-Western Mediterranean line and not to station any forces in the Suez Canal Zone. He used this as grounds for asking if Commonwealth countries ought not to take a greater share of the responsibility for defending the area which linked them together.[3] The crux of the matter, however, as he well knew, was Britain's own ability to reach a joint defence agreement with the Egyptians in place of the 1936 Treaty.

Both the new CIGS, Sir William Slim, and the new head of the Foreign Office, Sir William Strang, had repeated the arguments in favour of such a pact during visits to Cairo in the course of 1949, and discussions between the two countries at the technical level—started at the Egyptian request[4]—had produced a comprehensive scheme for the air defence of Egypt. But while the British representatives saw this as a combined operation, the Egyptian Government—according to the record of the talks—"lacked sufficient support to commit themselves". Their spokesmen argued that the RAF should be withdrawn from Egypt during peacetime and the Egyptian air force equipped by the British to take its place.

When the talks began in the summer of 1949, Bevin had urged the Ministry of Defence to do all they could to meet the Egyptian requirements in equipment.[5] He was less forthcoming, however, when he received a private proposal from King Farouk for a secret agreement between the King and the British. In a personal message delivered in great secrecy through the two Ambassadors, the King said he would be much happier to have the British troops remain where they were but could not fly in face of the popular demand for their evacuation. If a joint defence agreement could be something reached between HMG and himself, Farouk suggested he would be able to put it into

[1] See the correspondence between Bevin and the British representatives in Damascus, 30 August & 2 Sept. 1949, FO 800/477/ME/17 & 19; and Baghdad, 31 August & 6 Sept., *ibid.*, ME/477/18 & 21.
[2] Bevin to Acheson, 12 November 1949, *ibid.*, ME/49/26.
[3] Bevin's talk with Spender and Doidge at Temple Trees, Colombo, 13 January 1950, *ibid.*, ME/50/1.
[4] Bevin to Attlee, 4 February 1949. FO 800/457/EG/49/5.
[5] Letter of 22 July 1949, *ibid.*, EG/49/10.

751

effect in an emergency on his own initiative and, once the forthcoming elections were over, it could be translated into an open agreement. Bevin's reply was that while the UK would certainly intervene in the case of an external attack on Egypt, such an arrangement as the King proposed was out of the question, if only on constitutional grounds.[1]

By the time Bevin reached Cairo, elections had taken place and the Wafd, which led the campaign for the expulsion of the British while in opposition, had been returned to power. This was hardly a propitious moment to arrive and Bevin had to content himself with talking in general terms to Nahas Pasha, the new Prime Minister, about the desirability of a new agreement between their two countries. In conversation with the Foreign Minister, he pointed to the American use of bases in the UK as part of the NATO defence plan, arguing that, with NATO looking after the defence of Western Europe and with the USA taking an increased interest in the Far East, there was a gap in the Middle East. Saleh el Din agreed about the gap but would not accept that Americans using facilities in the UK were in the same position as the British in Egypt: the difference was that the USA and the UK treated each other on a basis of equality. This was the heart of the matter as far as the Egyptians were concerned: even without raising the question of the Sudan, they were unwilling to consider any defence agreement without the prior evacuation of the Canal Zone, a condition which the British, including Bevin, equally stubbornly refused to consider. All Bevin could do was to say that he hoped once the new government had taken stock, it would be willing to resume talks; but there was not the slightest ground for supposing that these might lead, as Bevin tried to suggest, to the same sort of result as those which had preceded NATO.

The King was more pliable, seeing the continued presence of the British as the best guarantee of retaining his throne; his complaint was that he was still under a cloud, regarded by the British as a wartime accomplice of the Germans and Italians and therefore not invited to pay a state visit to London. Bevin's reply could hardly be regarded as diplomatic. He told the King that he was more concerned with the future than the past and that when President Auriol came on the state visit to London for the following March, no one would refer to the French surrender in 1940, but would look ahead to the common undertakings between France and Britain for the defence of Western Europe. If they could establish a similar basis for agreement between Britain and Egypt on the defence of the Middle East, then he would certainly speak to the Prime Minister about a possible visit by Farouk.[2]

Bevin surprised the Egyptian leaders he met by talking, not (as they expected) about the Treaty and defence, but about the need to raise the standard of living of the mass of the population and create a more equitable

---

[1] Bevin to Campbell in Cairo, 19 October 1949, *ibid.*, EG/49/13 and Bevin's talk with Amr, 23 November, *ibid.*, EG/49/17.
[2] Bevin's talks in Cairo, 28 January 1950. FO 800/457/EG/50/3–5.

society if they were to avoid revolution. It was disinterested but unpalatable advice.

Bevin broke his journey home from Cairo with brief stops in Rome and Paris. This time it was the turn of his staff to be surprised, knowing his prejudice against priests, when he asked for a visit to the Pope to be included in his programme. His talks with Sforza and de Gasperi were largely taken up with arrangements for carrying out the UN decision on the Italian colonies. In the course of the conversation, he made a remark, the far-sightedness of which attracts more attention thirty years later than it did at the time. Talking about the future of the Horn of Africa (Ethiopia, Eritrea, Somaliland) he said:

"The Russians had their headquarters in Addis Ababa and there were great possibilities for them to stir up trouble in view of the racial difficulties, particularly in the Union
of South Africa. He was apprehensive lest they might get control of a Nationalist
movement among the coloured peoples." [1]

The French ministers he saw wanted to hear what had been said at Colombo about Indo–China which had become an issue of confrontation between the French Government and the Communist Party. Aware of French (and Italian) criticism of Britain's attitude to Europe, Bevin said he had been thinking what the next move should be and would like to hold a tripartite meeting in London with Acheson and Schuman as soon as possible after the British election, with the next year in Europe as the main item on the agenda. In the meantime, he hoped the French would not find it necessary to make a decision about Finebel, a proposal for a customs union between France and the Low Countries. The French made the stock reply that they did not want to proceed without British agreement; but added that there was strong pressure on the Government to draw up plans for Europe. The plan which Schuman produced at the meeting in London in May was to show that this was not an empty statement.

4

Bevin arrived back in England on the day the election campaign began, 4 February. The possibility that Labour might be turned out and Churchill regain office attracted more attention from the world press and radio than any earlier British election. If they were puzzled by the lack of excitement in the campaign—which Churchill himself described as sedate—the overseas commentators were impressed by the turn-out, on a February day which ended in heavy rain, of 84 per cent of the electorate, the highest percentage ever recorded up to that time.

As Foreign Secretary Bevin had had less opportunity than any minister to cultivate his constituency, and Wandsworth Central, which he had

[1] Bevin–Sforza–de Gasperi, 1 February 1950. FO 800/449/CONF/50/2.

represented since 1940, was no longer regarded as a safe seat for Labour. In 1950 he was nominated for East Woolwich, another London borough, where even with four opponents he had an over-all majority of 10,000 in a total vote of 43,000.[1] Palme Dutt, a leading Communist candidate among the hundred who stood in the 1950 election, was put up against Bevin; in common with ninety-six others out of the hundred (all of whom were defeated) he lost his deposit, polling 601 votes in a working class constituency. Bevin was not well enough to take much part in the campaign or undertake an election tour. He spoke no more than a dozen times in his constituency, on one occasion (reported with satisfaction by Tass, the Soviet news agency) to a gathering of no more than 75 women, 6 men and 8 children. He made even fewer appearances outside his constituency: rather surprisingly one was at Lewisham, Morrison's constituency in South London. "I'll come for you, Mabel," he told Morrison's agent, Mrs Raisin, "but not for that so-and-so candidate of yours."[2] The Lewisham meeting was a success, but upset Bevin's heart, and he had to be given treatment before he was able to go home.

None of Bevin's speeches won more than a few lines in the Press, but this did not affect his value to the Party as the Labour leader whose personality still commanded more confidence among the electorate at large than any other Minister.

Whatever led the 28 million voters to vote the way they did, the issues on which the 1950 campaign was fought were domestic. Speaking at Diss, Bevin recounted an anecdote—his natural way of expressing his views—which makes clear the achievement of the Labour Government to which he attached most importance. He told his audience that during the sittings of the Macmillan Committee in 1929 he had asked a well known banker:

"Why do you persist in using all your power in the City to keep 1½ to 2 million unemployed rather than provide employment and work?" The banker's reply was: "The system depends upon it. If you give these men work and wages, they will buy so many clothes and will eat so much food, they will demand such houses that the system cannot work and therefore it is cheaper and better for the State to keep people on the dole than to provide employment." Bevin's comment was that "Labour has wiped out the necessity for our industrial system to use unemployment and low wages as a means of adjustment".[3]

His remark brings out the priority he attached to full employment and the way in which his view of Labour's programme continued to be shaped by his trade union experiences. It also brings out an issue which lay at the root of much of the disagreement between the Labour Government and its critics abroad. As *The Economist* put it: "The disadvantages of a policy that tolerates inflation and seeks to mitigate its effects by physical controls can be very

---

[1] Bevin polled 26,604 and the runner up, the Conservative candidate, 14,234.
[2] Donoughue and Jones, p. 452.
[3] *The Times*, 7 February 1950.

clearly seen from outside, while the benefit of such a policy—that it leaves full employment undisturbed—accrues at home."[1] *The Economist* went on to say that while there were no differences between the parties on the non-economic side of foreign affairs, there was a strong hope among Britain's allies on both sides of the Atlantic that a Conservative government would be more ready to promote European integration and make sterling convertible. *The Economist* thought these hopes might prove to be short-lived even if the Tories replaced Labour, but there was no doubt that there was much speculation abroad on the prospect of a change in Britain's European policy at least if Churchill was returned to power. In the UK itself, however, there was little or no discussion of foreign affairs.

Churchill himself provided the one exception to this, in an unexpected direction, with his Edinburgh speech of 14 February. A fortnight before, President Truman had published instructions to continue work on the development of the hydrogen or so-called "super" bomb. The news came as a shock and not surprisingly led to the revival of proposals for a direct personal approach by Western leaders to Stalin to avoid an atomic armaments race. Churchill saw his opportunity and took it. After criticizing the Labour Government for the failure to produce a British atomic bomb, he went on to say:

"I cannot help coming back to this idea of another talk with Soviet Russia upon the highest level. The idea appeals to me of a supreme effort to bridge the gulf between the two worlds. . . . It is not easy to see how things could be worsened by a parley at the summit if such a thing were possible."

For this to be said by Churchill who had more experience of negotiating with Stalin and even of reaching agreement with him than anyone else in the West was news which went round the world immediately, and there were many prepared to believe (as Churchill may have done himself) that he possessed qualifications which would enable him to meet Stalin on terms unattainable by anyone else. On the other hand, even as old a friend of Churchill's as Smuts took the view that any overtures to the Russians at this time would be taken as a sign of weakness and that Churchill had taken the contrary position for electoral reasons. In his broadcast the following evening Bevin went no further than the comment: "This is not a problem which can be solved by any stunt proposals." Morrison referred to Churchill's soap-box diplomacy; to launch such a proposal in the heat and excitement of a general election was irresponsible.

Churchill was unimpressed by these rebukes:

"Why should it be wrong for the British nation to think about these supreme questions of life and death, perhaps for the whole world, at a time when there is a General Election . . . the only time when the people really have a chance to influence . . . events?"[2]

---

[1] *The Economist*, 11 February 1950, p. 301.
[2] Churchill's broadcast on 17 February.

Bevin's use of the "scornful word, stunt", he declared, "only showed how far his mind dwells below the true level of events".

On his final tour of the campaign Churchill returned to the attack, and poured scorn in his turn on those socialists who took so poor a view of democracy as to believe that such questions were above the heads of the working classes, and could only be mentioned as a stunt. His words, he claimed:

"Have not only dominated the election, they have rolled around the world and may have created a new situation. . . . It is clear to most people that more vision than Mr Bevin possesses is required in the handling of our foreign affairs."[1]

This was rousing stuff from a master of electioneering. But, far from creating a new situation, it met with a cool reception from both the American and Russian governments. Nor, despite the attention it attracted in the Press, is there evidence that the Edinburgh speech had any influence on the result of the election. The view of most observers was that, however regrettable it might be, the majority of electors made up their minds on grounds that had little to do with foreign policy.

The poll was taken on 23 February. The final result cut Labour's lead over all parties from the 146 of 1945 to six or eight, if one excludes the two Irish nationalists. The Cabinet met that evening. Dalton thought it was the worst possible situation. He would have preferred to see the Tories in office with a bare majority rather than Labour, and forecast that there would have to be another election in a few months. Bevin was not so pessimistic. He thought they should stay in office and "consolidate".[2] That was the general view. It meant dropping any idea of controversial legislation and of carrying through the nationalization of steel, but Labour would remain in office. Since Bevin was less interested in new legislation or parliamentary politics than in keeping control of foreign policy, this was what mattered from his point of view.

Nor was he much involved in the two questions which consumed the interest of the PLP in the next few months: how to avoid defeat in the House and what conclusions to draw from the failure to win a convincing majority. He made only two speeches in the House in the first ten months of 1950, thereby inevitably raising the question whether he was fit to continue in office. When he was well enough and sometimes when he was not, he turned up to vote with the rest of the Party and so helped to see it through to the end of July without disaster, despite the vigour with which the Opposition kept up the parliamentary battle and pressed snap divisions. But in this he was only one of the rank and file and the parliamentary leadership of the Party was in the hands of Herbert Morrison, whose skill as a Leader of the House no one—not even Ernie Bevin—could deny.

[1] Churchill's speech at Manchester, 20 February.
[2] Dalton's diaries, 25 February 1950.

The 1950 election turned out to be a political anti-climax. Churchill and the Tories were disappointed in their hopes of regaining office after five long years in opposition; Labour, on the other hand, had run out of steam and could not recover its impetus without a period in opposition to settle its differences and give a new generation of leaders the chance to come to the top. In this situation Attlee had little incentive or much scope for making many changes in his ministerial team, and the key posts remained in the hands of the four men, Attlee, Bevin, Morrison and Cripps, who had held them in the last government.

Both Bevin and Cripps were sick men. Cripps finally gave up in October, and Bevin in March 1951, dying five weeks later. Between 1 March and 31 July 1950, months which saw the proposal of the Schuman Plan and the outbreak of the Korean War, Ernie Bevin was away from the Foreign Office, either in hospital (he had two operations) or convalescent, for 85 out of 153 days; between November 1949 and November 1950 he spoke only twice in House of Commons' debates and gave only two major speeches outside, at the UN in September and the Labour Party Conference in October. There was much sympathy with the courage Bevin and Cripps showed in face of persistent pain and ill-health, but inevitably the question began to be asked whether the two highest political offices apart from the head of government should continue to be held by men who were in such poor condition physically. An effective understudy, Hugh Gaitskell, was at least available for Cripps and he replaced him as Chancellor in the autumn, but Bevin lost his Minister of State, Hector McNeil, when the latter was promoted to be Secretary of State for Scotland.

All of which makes it necessary to ask, whether it would not have been better if Bevin had given up the Foreign Office and Attlee appointed someone else as Foreign Secretary in his second administration. Bevin had already completed his main work in shaping British policy after the War in carrying through the Marshall Plan and in creating the Atlantic alliance. The course for the next Labour government had been set, and if he had gone in the spring of 1950 he would have been spared the difficult choices presented by the Schuman Plan and German rearmament. Why then did Attlee not bring himself to do in the spring or summer of 1950 what he had eventually to do at the beginning of 1951, and persuade Bevin to move to some other, less demanding, office?

The question was one about which Attlee consulted Bevin's doctor several times during the course of the year. The answer McCall gave was that, while Bevin's mobility was affected so that he could no longer travel except with difficulty, his mind and judgement were not. In fact he recovered sufficiently to travel to New York in September and speak at the UN. Bevin himself was determined to stay at the Foreign Office, whatever the cost in effort or pain, believing that there were still problems to be overcome, for example, in regard to Germany and the defence of Western Europe, which no one else in the

Labour Party had the experience or authority to handle. It was a view which Attlee shared, maintaining in later discussion that as long as he received the medical advice he did, Bevin's continued presence at the Foreign Office, even when no more than half as effective as he had been, was worth more to the Labour Government, both at home and abroad, than anyone who could have taken his place.

Attlee's difficulty was to know who could take his place. When he was willing to think about it, Bevin's own choice was Hector McNeil or Jim Griffiths. The first, however, was thought to be lacking in experience and the second was unwilling. Attlee at one time thought of bringing Sam Watson, the leader of the Durham miners, into Parliament as an eventual replacement. Watson was not only one of the trade union leaders of whom Bevin had a high opinion but a man with a lifelong interest in foreign affairs, and he had frequently discussed them with him. Like Griffiths, however, Watson was unwilling. "Sam never wanted to travel south of Durham," Attlee told Kenneth Harris. "Would have been a drawback in a Foreign Secretary."[1] Aneurin Bevan had the stature but Attlee, who admired his gifts, had never regarded him as politically stable and had kept him away from foreign affairs and defence. His appointment would be taken to foreshadow the abandonment of Bevin's policies and a swing to the Left. Morrison, who wanted the job and had more experience of office than anyone else in the Cabinet, failed miserably when he got it in 1951. At a time when the Western alliance was suffering from more internal strains than usual, Bevin as one of its architects remained, even in failing health, a guarantee to the world that Britain under a Labour government could be relied on not to go back on the commitments undertaken for her. In a year which saw war break out in the Far East and the fear of war mount sharply in Europe, such reassurance was worth a lot. Attlee's partnership with Bevin had played an important part in the success of the Labour Government. Bevin's was still a name to conjure with in securing the continued support of the TUC for a government with a reduced majority.

Putting these considerations together, it is not difficult to see why Attlee preferred not to take risks, either abroad or at home, but to keep Bevin at the Foreign Office as long as possible and deputize as Foreign Secretary himself when Bevin was too unwell to act. In any case, on the issue where Bevin came under most criticism, his policy towards Europe, there is no reason to suppose that Attlee (who shared his views) would have appointed anyone as Foreign Secretary, or indeed could have found anyone amongst possible Labour candidates for the post, who would have followed a different policy. Attlee himself, Morrison, Dalton, Cripps, Gaitskell, Bevan, had none of them as much feeling for or understanding of Europe as the man who had made commitment to Western Europe's recovery and independence the foundation of his policy.

[1] Harris, p. 450.

So Bevin stayed for another year, suffering a lot of pain but still a powerful voice behind the scenes even when he had to conduct business from his bed. Writing to Francis Williams from Manor House Hospital in the spring of 1950 he described the symptoms of his heart condition: pains from angina pectoris; "fibillations or something of that kind which seems to take the breath out of me"; swelling of the legs and ankles which forced him to lie up and rest. But, he continued, "I am nearly out of the wood . . . I am giving close attention to the papers for the Acheson visit. I want to turn that into a success if I can . . . I believe I am going to make a good recovery."[1]

When he got back, Kenneth Younger, McNeil's successor as Minister of State who felt that a man as unfit as Bevin ought not to continue as Foreign Secretary, wrote in his diary:

"I have to admit that when he pulls himself together he usually does pretty well for short periods. In Cabinet he appears to be asleep, but then suddenly weighs in with comments which show that he knows exactly what has been said. One can't help admiring his guts and nervous energy . . . for there is no doubt that he is in considerable pain and only a shadow of his real self."[2]

Three days before Hugh Gaitskell had written in his diary that Bevin was "remarkably resilient . . . one day hardly capable of coherent speech, the next . . . shrewd, sensible, imaginative—all his old best qualities."[3] ,

Perhaps the greatest drawback was Bevin's need to conserve his energies for Foreign Office business and negotiations, and his inability to expound and defend British policy at a time when it came in for increased criticism both abroad and at home. Thus he missed the big debates on the Schuman Plan and the Korean War and made no statement in Parliament on British policy towards Europe between 28 March and 13 November, all subjects on which there was no one who could take his place adequately.

If 1950 had been a year of consolidation, as Bevin hoped, with the framework of foreign and defence policy now established, this would not have mattered so much. But 1950 turned out to be a year of turmoil; even before the invasion of South Korea in June, there were sharper divisions of policy and opinion than usual within the Western alliance.

There were seveal reasons for this. One, without any doubt, was the shock of learning that the Russians now possessed atomic weapons, and a revival of the fear of war. The growth of confidence which Bevin had hoped to see created by the signature of the NATO Treaty was held back by the delay in producing adequate forces on the ground and the conclusion that the alliance could do nothing to prevent Western Europe from being overrun by the Russians. This encouraged a revival of anti-American feeling, especially in France, and

---

[1] Francis Williams: *Nothing So Strange, An Autobiography* (London 1970) p. 281.
[2] Younger's diary, 29 May.
[3] Quoted in Philip Williams, *Gaitskell*, p. 215.

cynical comments about the Continent not being able to survive a second liberation by the Anglo–Saxons.

Newspaper and radio reports from the United States presented an equally disquieting picture. In his memoirs Dean Acheson says that "the bi-partisan foreign policy of the 1947–49 period gave way, from 1950 to 1952, to partisan in-fighting as bloody as any in our history". No longer looking forward to a return to power, the Republicans were suffering under the bitter frustration of their fifth failure to win the Presidency. The Communists' success in China; the loss of America's monopoly of the A-bomb; the fears of subversion aroused by the Hiss case and the arrest of Klaus Fuchs, were combined with dislike of the Administration's "profligate" policy abroad and a witch-hunt for Communists and fellow-travellers at home. At the same time the announcement that the United States was working on a much more powerful hydrogen-bomb produced an anguished reaction in more liberal quarters and urgent appeals from Democratic leaders, as well as the Secretary General of the UN, for renewed efforts to avert war.

In Europe, Truman's directive to proceed with the development of the H-bomb and the firmness with which he and Acheson turned down proposals for a new approach to the Russians, shocked many who were already uneasy about seeing Western Europe allied with the USA, a reaction which was only strengthened by the virulence of Republican attacks on Acheson and the Administration for being "soft on Communism". In Paris, for example, the influential *Le Monde* criticized French membership of NATO for committing France to anti-Communism without providing any effective guarantee of French security. It was impossible, *Le Monde* argued, to create a European force which, if war broke out, could hold up the Russians for the time necessary for the Americans to arrive: the right course for Europe, on political no less than military grounds, was to constitute a neutral third force between American capitalism and Stalinist Russia.

French opinion was particularly disturbed by the prospect of rearming Germany as the obvious way in which to strengthen Western Europe's defences and a course on which it was believed, despite many denials, the Americans had already decided. German rearmament was no less explosive an issue in Germany itself where it was inevitably bound up with the other major issue which troubled most Germans, the question of re-unification. The National Front organized by the East German regime bracketed both in its campaign for peace and German unity.

The divisions in Western opinion, which grew more marked in the six months between the autumn of 1949 and the spring of 1950 on such matters as the Bomb and fears of a Third World War, neutralism and German rearmament, the continued division of Germany and Europe, encouraged the Communist-inspired Partisans for Peace to redouble their efforts. The third meeting of the World Committee for Peace opened in Stockholm on 15 March 1950 and produced an Appeal which was addressed to "people of good will all over the world" and by concentrating solely on the prohibition of atomic weapons, secured the signature of many millions, not less—according to its organizers—than one-eighth of the human race, if one included the entire population of the USSR. The World Peace Committee held two further meetings in the summer of 1950 and made preparations for a second World Congress to meet in Britain in the autumn.

The success of the Stockholm peace campaign, and the divisions and anxieties in the West to which it was able to appeal, reflected a crisis of confidence in the alliance. There was thus more need than ever for Western governments to rally opinion and restate the common interests which the North Atlantic powers had in maintaining their association. It was more than a month, however, after the formation of the second Attlee government before Bevin made any move to break a silence which had continued since November. *The Economist* was reflecting a common view in London when it wrote that the Western alliance was suffering from Bevin's failure to give the sort of lead which he had provided in the past and that the Foreign Secretary needed to do something to dispel the impression, on both sides of the Atlantic, that the Labour Government's policy towards Europe was the expression of a "petulant isolationism".[1]

6

Just before Bevin's return from the Far East at the beginning of February, the Council of the OEEC approved the second annual report with which Hoffman, the head of ECA, was to approach Congress for a further appropriation of Marshall aid. Neither the report nor Hoffman made much of the success —"almost fantastic" *The Economist* called it—which the Marshall Plan had already achieved at only the half-way mark. Western Europe, which had been on the edge of economic collapse in 1947, had surpassed by 15% the pre-war levels of production in industry and all but reached them in agriculture. Investment in capital goods was running at a higher level than in 1938—in engineering by as much as 20%—and seven billion dollars of this had been earmarked for overseas dependencies. If inflation had largely been avoided and prices held stable, the opposite danger of deflation and severe unemployment, except in one or two cases, had also been averted. This was success beyond the expectation of anyone in 1947–8. But as the first, overriding aim to stave off the complete economic collapse of Europe and make good the dislocation of war began to be secured, two other objectives had come to assume greater importance, particularly for Americans: one was to get back to a world of freely convertible currencies and multilateral trade; the other to see repeated in Europe "the miracle wrought by the Founding Fathers" and use

[1] *The Economist*, 25 March 1950.

the Marshall Plan to bring about the political and economic integration of Europe.

Bevin had thrown himself with enthusiasm into the original purpose of the Marshall Plan at a time when there was no confidence in France or anywhere else in Europe that it could be translated into effective action. But he regarded both the other objectives with which Hoffman and the ECA now sought to identify the OEEC in quite a different light. This was to revive the old disagreement between the British and the Americans about the post-war economic settlement. The British, responsible for the second biggest trading area in the world, the sterling area, looked upon the Marshall Plan and OEEC as inadequate instruments for solving the general imbalance in world trade, and refused to let American pressure push them into a commitment to European integration which they believed no one, least of all the Americans, had thought out.

It was not European integration, however, but a proposal starting with the ECA staff in Paris to create a more effective system of inter-European payments and so increase multilateral trade between the OEEC countries which provoked a new clash between the British and their allies. The existing system was widely criticized as complicated, arbitrary, and inefficient, and the much simpler proposals put forward for a European Payments Union found general acceptance amongst the majority of OEEC members. The negotiations, however, were brought to an abrupt halt in February 1950 when Cripps presented a memorandum flatly rejecting the concept of a multilateral clearing system on which the proposals were based.

Once the election was over and Gaitskell was given charge of the negotiations, a new set of proposals was put forward by the British which brought in not only the UK but the whole sterling area.[1] This was agreed with the other OEEC countries early in July 1950 and the document signed in September. The European Payments Union was one of the major successes of post-war European co-operation. It did more than anything else to make a success of OEEC and by the time it was wound up with the return to world-wide convertibility in 1954 it had made a notable contribution to a period of economic growth which compared favourably with, and may well have exceeded, the rate achieved in any earlier period of European history. But in the meantime the British again presented themselves in an unfavourable light to both their European and American allies, and the Congressional hearings in Washington on the appropriations needed for the next year of Marshall Aid revived criticism of "British sabotage of European integration", as if Britain were the only obstacle in the way of "accomplishing in 25 months" as Hoffman admitted, "what might under less compelling circumstances easily require 25 years".

The Truman administration, under siege from McCarthy and the "political

[1] See FO 371/87100–133 and Philip Williams, *Gaitskell*, pp. 219–224.

primitives" who ran with him (Acheson's phrase this time), was in no position to come to the support of its British allies. In face of Republican spite and Democratic cowardice, the President had to intervene in support of Acheson who had made himself a political untouchable by his testimony on behalf of Alger Hiss and his plain speaking on American policy in Asia. Bevin thought it best not to answer Britain's American critics and to keep publicity on the differences between the allies to a minimum to avoid encouraging the Russians.[1] He believed the best answer was to arrange a meeting with Acheson and America's NATO allies in London as soon as possible, preceded by another frank discussion of their differences between Acheson, Schuman and himself. He was able to announce this in the House of Commons on 20 March and say that it had been agreed to meet early in May.

Bevin made the announcement at the end of the only Commons debate on Europe (28 March 1950) in which he was able to take part between 17 November 1949 and 13 November 1950. The favourable response to his speech underlines how much his absence and silence were felt—and criticized—in the ensuing six months. Although nobody had expected it, *The Economist* said,[2] the debate turned into a great occasion. The principal credit for this was given to Churchill whose speech recalled his finest during the War by its power to bring back great themes to Parliament. But the Foreign Secretary also earned the paper's approval:

"Nor did Mr Bevin—though he was naturally more cautious—fail to rise to the challenge. . . .
  "In a peroration made moving by its combination of massive commonsense and wide vision, he revealed his preference for closer unity based not so much on Europe as on the Western world as a whole."

Taking a different line from Churchill who had spoken of the need to unite Europe, Bevin declared:

"What we have done is to attempt not only the unity of Western Europe, but the unity of the Western world. . . . I am sure that, while there is talk of integration in Western Europe, Western Europe will not be strong enough in itself; it is the integration of the Western World that will give the strength and power necessary to defend ourselves."

One of the risks for Bevin of not confining himself to his official brief was the danger that in an unguarded moment he would let out what was in his mind at the moment without sufficient regard for its diplomatic repercussions or what he himself might say in calmer mood. This had already cost him dear in the case of the Zionists and was now to do the same in Germany.

In fact from the time of the London CFM at the end of 1947 Bevin had been a prime mover in the policy of creating a Western German state and bringing it

---

[1] Bevin to Franks, 20 March 1950. FO 800/460/EUR/50/9.
[2] *The Economist*, 1 April 1950.

into the community of Western nations on terms of equality. He had played an important role in mediating between the Americans on the one hand and the French and various European governments on the other; in return he had had to bear the brunt of what he regarded as a largely fictitious campaign against the British, manufactured in Germany, over dismantling as an operation designed to cripple a future commercial rival. This had not diverted him from his policy but it had not encouraged him to alter his view of the Germans which was confirmed by the outcry raised in Germany over the invitation to the Federal Republic to join the Council of Europe at the same time as the Saar.

Bevin told the House of Commons that he did not think it was right under the Occupation Statute for Germany to start bargaining about the terms on which she would join the Council of Europe. If they came in wholeheartedly "we on our part will accept them as an act of faith and not delay too long in getting to the next stage". By that he meant handing back the conduct of foreign policy to the Federal Republic, only after which could she act as an equal in the Committee of Ministers. Given the feeling in both France and Britain revived by Adenauer's attempt to lay down conditions for Germany's acceptance of the invitation, this was a strong but not unreasonable statement. The trouble came over Bevin's reference to the League of Nations' experience with Germany in the 1920s: there had been a lot of courting of the Germans to get them in, only to find later that they treated the League with contempt.

When Churchill interrupted to say that the Hitler revolution had taken place in between, Bevin retorted: "The Hitler revolution did not change the German character very much. It expressed it." When Churchill again said "No", Bevin insisted:

"That is what it did. It was latent there right from Bismarckian days. I had to deal with them as well as the right hon. gentlemen. I had to deal with them as employers, and in shipping, and in many other things where I got into close contact with these gentlemen."

Bevin refused to accept that the overriding purpose of British policy should be winning Germany for the West. That raised the question of rearming Germany. It did not matter, he told Churchill, whether they set up a German army or, as Churchill had proposed, Germans serving in a European army, it was still giving the Germans arms and that would not only set the clock back a long way in relations with Russia but would be fatal to any hopes of bringing France and Germany together. He was, therefore, strongly opposed to talking about arming the Germans in any form.

No German politician at this stage was going to call for rearmament, but Bevin's remarks gave great offence, and led to protests from both Adenauer and Schumacher. Bevin remained unrepentant, convinced as a matter of policy that it was necessary to make the Federal Republic a partner in the Western alliance, but still regarding Germans with an ineradicable distrust and refusing to follow the Americans in running after them.

Bevin's readiness to speak out on Germany did him no harm with his European colleagues when the Committee of Ministers met at Strasbourg at the end of March, and this time he was able to make a proposal which did something to meet the criticism that his attitude to the Council of Europe was entirely negative.[1] Rejecting a proposal to give the Assembly full control over its own agenda, he headed off another confrontation with an alternative, to set up a joint consultative committee of five representatives of the Committee of Ministers and seven from the Assembly's General Council Affairs Committee which would act as liaison between the two bodies. With the help of a good dinner, to which he invited the members of both Committees, he won general assent and got his proposal adopted.

At this point, however, when he was beginning to get a grip on European affairs again, the deterioration in Bevin's physical state caught up with him. After getting back from Colombo he had had to go to the Manor House Hospital for injections to relieve the condition of his heart and had spent a weekend in hospital between 10 and 14 March. He had only been back from Paris a week when he had to go into hospital again, this time for an operation for haemorrhoids and stayed there recovering and resting from 11 April to 4 May. When the Consultative Council of the Brussels Powers met in mid-April, Kenneth Younger deputised for Bevin and Hugh Gaitskell for Stafford Cripps, neither of whom was well enough to attend. A good piece of news for Bevin was that the NATO "strategic concept" had been turned into a working plan and accepted by the NATO Military Committee of Chiefs. The speed with which this had been done surprised everybody but the forces with which to carry out the agreed plan did not exist, a fact to which Bevin thought European politicians should devote more attention than to making speeches in the Council of Europe Assembly and devising constitutions for a European Union. Bevin, however, was under strict orders from his doctors to stay away and keep out of controversy, in the hope that by resting he could recruit his strength for the important meetings with Acheson and Schuman in May.

[1] This had been cleared in advance with the Cabinet in a paper CP (50) 49 circulated on 20 March and approved on the 27th. CM 15 (50).

CHAPTER 21

London, May 1950 (the Schuman Plan); Korea invaded

I

One piece of good news for the Labour Government was a recovery in Britain's overseas trade and balance of payments following the devaluation of the pound. The deficit on trading account which had been $539 m. in the third quarter of 1949 had been turned into a surplus of $40 m. in the first quarter of 1950 and $180 m. in the second. The gold and dollar reserves showed an increase of 20%. Presenting his final budget on 18 April, Cripps was able to give a cheerful account of the country's commercial situation with a sharp increase in exports. Points rationing was abolished in May and the abolition or relaxation of controls continued. Cripps refused, however, to abandon his policy of austerity, cutting food subsidies and increasing the tax on petrol. In fact the Government did better in its first six months than anyone had expected and the local elections in May showed no sign of any further swing to the Opposition.

The better news of the country's economic position helped to make the British more flexible in discussing the European payments scheme. But the difficulties over this, although a powerful irritant in relations between Britain and her allies, and contributing to the crisis of confidence which afflicted the Western alliance, were not at its heart. The root of the trouble was Europe's fear of war, which found expression in a variety of ways from the success of the Stockholm peace campaign and the growth of Third Force neutralism to a revival of anti-Americanism. Acheson believed the answer was a much greater combined effort to translate the paper plans of NATO into visible military strength. He came to London for the 4th NATO Council meeting to convince America's allies that they had got to commit themselves to making the effort, and that this would call for the creation of combined and not larger national forces.

So far as NATO was concerned, the London meetings were "make-or-break". This presented no problem for Bevin, who continued to see the Atlantic Treaty as the centrepiece of British policy without which neither the Commonwealth nor Western Europe could stand alone. British difficulties with the USA were not over foreign and defence policy, but over American pressure on economic and financial policy: pressure for the liberalization of trade, an inter-European payments scheme and economic integration with Europe.[1] Bevin told the Cabinet that he hoped they would be able to reach closer understanding with the Americans on the Far East, especially China, and most of all on Western Europe and how the 40 million Germans of the Federal Republic were to be brought into it in a way acceptable to France. Ironically, in view of the plan the French themselves were about to produce, the Cabinet discussion underlined the need to persuade the French to adopt a "more realistic view of the future place of Western Germany in Western Europe". They might begin by bringing the Germans into the Council of Europe and OEEC; but Bevin insisted that the only satisfactory solution in the long run was to make Germany part of NATO. He added that one of the reasons for substituting NATO for the original conception of Western Union was that the French and Italians could feel greater security against the revival of German power and accept some measure of German rearmament if these took place within an Atlantic not a European framework.[2]

This was a matter for the Foreign Ministers and High Commissioners of the three occupying powers who were to meet in advance of the NATO Council. Before the French joined them, Acheson had agreed to Bevin's request that the Americans should spend a couple of days with the British alone in continuation of the regular consultation established at the Washington meetings the previous September. There were, therefore, three sets of talks, to follow on one after the other, and the seriousness with which the British as well as the Americans took the occasion is shown by the thoroughness of the preparations. Teams of officials worked together in London for a fortnight before the principals met, preparing a series of joint papers. The main Anglo–American committee met seven times and its sub-committees on another fifteen occasions. A parallel series of talks was carried on with the French, with six meetings of the full tripartite committee and no less than eighteen of its sub-committes including eight on German economic problems. By the time Bevin came out of hospital and Acheson arrived from Paris, a great deal of work had been put into defining areas of agreement and disagreement.

Acheson, however, arriving with the conviction that something had to be done, complained that his initial talks with the British alone "got nowhere". He was taken aback by the deterioration in Bevin's physical condition:

[1] CP (50) 92, approved by the Cabinet on 8 May, printed as a statement of the British objectives in the meetings.
[2] CP (50) 80 also approved by the Cabinet on 8 May, sets out British policy on Germany and Europe.

"I found Ernest Bevin in distressing shape when we met. . . . He had recently undergone a painful operation and was taking sedative drugs that made him doze off quite soundly during the discussion. His staff seemed accustomed to it, though I found it disconcerting."[1]

Kenneth Younger shared Acheson's impression, writing in his diary:

"At the talks themselves he has been in far from his best form. He said himself that he is only half alive. The doctors give him so many drugs that he often has difficulty in staying awake and in taking a proper grip of the meeting of which he has been chairman. At other times he has been quite all right, and in fact very good."

After describing the talks as "largely futile" and blaming the Prime Minister for allowing Bevin to continue in office, Younger went on:

"Things might have been saved if Dean Acheson had come over with any clear idea of what he wanted to say, but in the event he failed to take any lead at all. I attended three out of the four meetings and have seldom felt more embarrassed. Ernie was too ill to speak at two of them and could barely read out the agenda, let alone take charge. Acheson, when the ball was thrown to him, said a few banalities and stepped down before one thought he had begun. Ernie then said 'What's the next item?' and on we went. This happened on numerous occasions, and once Makins had to butt in from the second row to prevent the whole meeting collapsing."[2]

Kenneth Younger believed that the reason for "the fiasco" apart from Bevin's health, was Acheson's loss of nerve under "the vicious campaign against him in the USA so that he dare not put forward a constructive policy". In his own memoirs Acheson speaks of his impatience with British reluctance to accept the role in Europe which seemed obvious to the Americans but presented all the familiar difficulties to the British. His impatience was sharpened by advance knowledge of the Schuman plan for combining France's and Germany's coal and steel resources as the basis for a European economic union.

Schuman gave Acheson the outline of the plan while the American was in Paris on his way to London. This was done under pledge of secrecy before it had been presented to the French or German Cabinets, and on the understanding that Acheson would say nothing about it to Bevin. The plan had been conceived by Jean Monnet, the head of the French Planning Commission, in searching for some means by which to open the way to a united Europe. The greatest obstacle in the way, he writes in his Memoirs, was French fear of German industrial domination.

"All successive attempts to keep Germany in check, however, mainly at French instigation, had come to nothing, because they had been based on the rights of conquest

---

[1] Acheson, p. 384.
[2] Younger's diary, 14 May 1950.

and temporary superiority. . . . But if the problem of sovereignty were approached with no desire to dominate or take revenge—if on the contrary the victors and the vanquished agreed to exercise joint sovereignty over part of their joint resources—then a solid link would be forged between them, the way would be wide open for further collective action, and a great example would be given to the other nations of Europe."

Monnet's idea, as bold and imaginative as any in European history, was for the French Government to propose that the whole of French as well as German coal and steel production should be placed under an international Authority open to the participation of the other countries of Europe. It was aimed, at a single blow, to replace Franco–German enmity with a partnership in the very area on which national power depended, coal and steel, and to provide the basis for a European union, at first economic, in the long run political as well, which had so far eluded everyone.

Having conceived the idea, Monnet took only three weeks in the course of April 1950 to turn it into a plan of no more than 104 lines of text. His object was to provide Schuman with a proposal which would enable France to take the initiative in regard to both Europe and Germany at the May talks in London. It was essential to the success of the operation to act quickly and in complete secrecy. Acheson's presence in Paris was a coincidence which Schuman and Monnet turned to their advantage, and so little did the American Secretary of State grasp the significance of what was proposed when Schuman explained it to him through an interpreter that Monnet had to be sent for to calm his fears that it was some sort of huge coal and steel cartel.

There was only one other person whom Schuman and Monnet took care to alert, and that was Adenauer. On the morning of 9 May, the day on which the plan was to be put to the French Cabinet, a private emissary of Schuman's, a friend from Lorraine, delivered an urgent personal message from the French Foreign Minister to the Federal Chancellor, while he was in a Cabinet meeting. Whether Adenauer had been forewarned or not, it took him a very short time to send back a reply agreeing to Schuman's proposal. It was only after he received this that Schuman, when the French Cabinet meeting was already breaking up, put his proposal to his colleagues. According to Monnet, Schuman's remarks were "even more elliptical and less audible than usual" and most members of the Cabinet only learned exactly what they had agreed to from the next day's papers. But they agreed, that was what mattered.

Acheson was later to conclude that it had been a mistake for the French not to say anything to Bevin in advance—and not to allow him to say anything —about a move which, if it succeeded, would transform the whole pattern of European relations. He could not be sure that it would have made any difference to the British reaction, but it would at least have avoided prejudicing its reception by the manner in which it was sprung on Bevin.[1] On the other hand, it is easy to see why Schuman and Monnet were against informing

---

[1] Acheson, p. 385.

London in advance. With many years' experience of the British, Monnet believed that in the long run they would be willing to join the scheme, but thought it probable that this would only be after its success had proved that it was not in their interests to stay out. Of course an attempt must be made to persuade them to take part from the beginning, but he was opposed to giving them any opening—such as consultation—which would enable them to block, water down, or at least delay what was proposed, thereby robbing the plan of the all-important element of shock. If there was a risk in not telling the British, it could be argued that their consistent opposition to anything which smacked of European integration, made it a greater risk to give them any chance to forestall the psychological coup which Monnet and Schuman planned. The fact that the British had treated the French with scant courtesy and a complete disregard of French interests over devaluation, made it the easier to justify such a course; and there was satisfaction for a proud nation, after so long following the lead of "the Anglo–Saxons", to see France, without asking anyone's leave, take an initiative which both re-asserted her independence and re-established her claim to be the natural leader of Europe.

Once Acheson had grasped the implications of the Schuman–Monnet plan, nothing could have given him more encouragement: here at last was what the United States had been looking for, a move from inside Europe towards closer European integration. But he was under no illusions about the problem it would present to the British. As he sat down to his first session of talks with Bevin he was in the awkward position of having been told something which could introduce an entirely new element into the situation they were discussing but which he was under promise not to reveal to his—and Schuman's—colleague. His embarrassment grew when, at lunch with Bevin and Attlee, a mysterious message was received asking for an appointment in the afternoon at which the French Ambassador would deliver an important message. Acheson had to sit and listen while his hosts speculated on what this could be. Bevin and Attlee only heard of the plan when the Ambassador informed them of the announcement Schuman had made in the Chamber of Deputies, about which it soon became clear that Acheson knew more than the Ambassador himself. His suspicions aroused, Bevin rounded on the American Secretary of State and accused him of going to Paris to put the finishing touches to a scheme which was to be kept from the British until it could be presented to them as a *fait accompli*. As Acheson admits, the circumstantial evidence in support of this suspicion was strong. He believed that he eventually succeeded in persuading Bevin that his decision to travel to London via Paris had been made for quite different reasons and with no knowledge of what he would hear from Schuman. Nonetheless the way in which the news reached Bevin, a sick and naturally suspicious man, did not augur well for a favourable reception.

Before the announcement of Schuman's Plan cast its shadow over the discussions, Acheson and Bevin had agreed upon the urgency of building up the defence of Western Europe. A paper accepted by both sides, argued that the next 3–4 years were critical, that the West was falling behind the Soviet Union in military preparedness, and that if the gap became too wide the Russians might be tempted into taking risks. Acheson's conclusion was that they must strengthen the defences of Western Europe immediately and that this meant strengthening the West European economies. It was essential to integrate Germany into the Western camp. A "continuing group" in NATO was necessary to make sure that the build-up was effective, and Acheson said that—apart from the consideration of further military aid to other NATO nations—the USA would clearly have to continue to take an economic interest in Europe after Marshall aid ended in 1952.[1]

When they resumed in the afternoon, Bevin had been told of Schuman's initiative. No mention was made of it in the discussions, and outside the formal sessions Acheson laboured to moderate Bevin's anger over the failure to take him into his confidence. He succeeded so far that the British statement put out on the following day was non-committal and not so hostile as it had threatened to be. In retrospect, however, it is clear that the discussion of the all too familiar differences between the British and the Americans led nowhere and was out of date once Schuman's proposal offered an alternative way forward and no longer depended on British agreement.

The fact that the round of meetings in London was to begin with two days of discussions between the British and Americans, followed by two more days of tripartite talks to which Schuman was then admitted and finally by a full meeting of the NATO Council had not gone unnoticed by the French. Such a sequence conformed to Bevin's view of the way in which the Atlantic alliance should work: first of all, the British and Americans, as the two world powers and wartime allies, should meet and reach agreement by themselves; then the French, their partners in the occupation of Germany, should be brought into the discussions, and finally the remaining NATO powers. It was a pattern which corresponded with the British view of their own position as closer to that of the USA than to that of the other European powers; it was also one which, it could be argued, corresponded to post-war realities, since if it came to a show down with the Russians the only nation on the European side of the Atlantic which could still be relied on to stand firm was the British. Its continuation would obviously suit the UK which held on to and hoped to recover its standing as a world power—and for the same reason resisted becoming part of an integrated Europe. On the other hand it was not a pattern which the other European nations, especially the French and Germans, would continue to accept, as their confidence and power recovered; nor, insofar as the Americans wanted to see such a recovery in Western Europe as well as the UK, was it one within which they could be content to see their own role confined.

---

[1] The British record of the Anglo–US and the tripartite talks in May 1950 is in FO 800/449/CONF/50/24–6. The US record is in FRUS 1950 (3) pp. 828–1107. Acheson's personal account is in *Present at the Creation*, c. 42 and c. 43.

The pressures to which Acheson and the State Department were exposed were reflected in his reaction to a paper which underlined the need for continued consultation and the "special relationship" between the USA and the UK. Acheson expressed his "immediate and intense displeasure" with the document. "Of course a unique relation existed between Britain and America —our common language and history insured that. But unique did not mean affectionate." He would be prepared, he said, to say openly that the USA must have the closest possible relations with the UK, but it was equally plain that it was impossible to allow it to be known that any such paper had been agreed to or even drawn up. All copies of the paper were accordingly collected and burned. In justification Acheson pointed to the use his political enemies in the USA could make of such ammunition. But, with the first initiative to come from the French fresh in his mind, he also had in mind the trouble it could create among the other members of NATO and the undesirability of allowing the USA's future relationship towards Europe to be pre-empted by the UK's claim to a special relationship.[1]

2

On 11 May Schuman arrived in London to join the other two foreign ministers. Before the full meeting Bevin asked his two colleagues to meet him privately and, speaking slowly and forcefully, protested at the position in which he had been placed by leaving him in ignorance of the Schuman Plan despite the fact that all three countries were involved in the administration of Germany and the principle of consultation was well established. Was this a new precedent and, if so, what deductions were to be drawn?

Before Schuman replied, Acheson seized the chance to intervene. Bevin's anger, he said, was understandable, but he was exaggerating the significance of what had happened. They all understood their duty to one another as allies. But sometimes domestic circumstances made it necessary for each of them to follow a line of his own without consultation. He understood that, on this occasion only, Schuman had thought secrecy more important than consultation.

"Similarly, last autumn . . . the British Government found it advisable to devalue the pound. That was a serious problem in which secrecy was also important. It affected France. M Schuman and Maurice Petsche, the French Finance Minister, were in Washington. The impending devaluation had been discussed with the Secretary of the Treasury and me but not with M Schuman and M Petsche. They had not complained since they understood the need for secrecy."[2]

---

[1] Acheson, pp. 287–8.
[2] Acheson, p. 386. Acheson's statement that the French had not complained was dramatically effective but historically inaccurate. See pp. 720–22 above.

Schuman took a different line. The French were concerned at the deadlock in Europe and felt obliged to precipitate matters. They had wanted to produce a psychological shock on both the European and the German plane, and they had not been able to wait because of the danger of a leak to the press which would have destroyed its effect. It was not a Franco–German matter only, but European, an attempt to create a European economic organization. There was no question of a decision, only of a proposal. To this Bevin replied formally that he would give the explanations offered to his Government. Schuman added, however, that having made his statement, he offered his personal regrets to the other two for causing them embarrassment.

Acheson's account concludes:

"Bevin had had enough. 'Let's join the others,' he said, getting up. As we left the room, Schuman took my arm. 'You have a large deposit in my bank,' he said."[1]

The arrival of the French team brought a distinctively European point of view into the discussions. The initial paper[2] had analysed the international situation in terms of the balance of power. While he agreed with the analysis and the need to build up Western defences, Schuman said, it was necessary to take into account the state of mind on the Continent in deciding how to present the ideas and arguments in the document. He mentioned in particular the success of the Communist peace campaign; the fear that splitting the world into two blocs made war inevitable; anti-American feeling and hurt national pride, and the argument that the safe policy was one of neutrality between the two blocs.

Acheson agreed that analysis of the situation was one thing, its presentation quite another. But with some asperity he insisted that they had got to take quick action to build up the West's defences and provide the necessary economic backing. Something other than more talks had to follow from their discussions. This pointed to the use of Germany's economic potential which must not be allowed to fall into Russian hands.

Younger was inclined to be impatient with proceedings in which he had only just become involved and to hanker after new initiatives—without being able to say what these should be. But he felt that the tripartite meetings went better than the Anglo–American:

"Ernie was pretty sick at the morning meetings but quite lively each afternoon. At least the meetings went forward competently from one item to the next, and there was usually some exchange of views and clarification of positions."[3]

Two of the five meetings were taken up with German affairs. In discussing his new plan, Schuman said that he thought it could only have been put

[1] Acheson, p. 387.
[2] It was given the reference number Tri/P/1 and is to be compared with UK–US/P/3.
[3] Younger's diary, 14 May 1950.

forward by France. Such a proposal from any other Government would scarcely have been accepted by the French and would not have produced the requisite change in the psychological atmosphere. A lot of work would still have to be done on the technical and political difficulties of the plan, but the French offer was "neither a *fait accompli* nor a bright idea thrown out at random".

Attlee had already made a statement in the Commons to the effect that, while the Schuman plan had implications which would require careful study, the British Government regarded it as "a notable contribution" towards the solution of a major European problem and welcomed the French initiative. Bevin took the opportunity to say across the conference table that "he had always considered that the divisions caused by national frontiers made it impossible for European heavy industry to function economically, and he therefore wished to give the French proposal not only a welcome but a helping hand."[1] What that meant remained to be seen. Adenauer on the other hand had been quick to grasp the advantage of the Schuman Plan to Germany. In place of the Ruhr Authority, the Military Security Board and all the cumbersome machinery of the Occupation, it opened up to the Germans quite unexpected economic prospects plus the status of a founder member on equal terms with France, in the creation of the future European Community. Germany's economic recovery was about to take off: she could not be treated for very much longer as a defeated nation. The brilliance of Monnet's conception was to offer an alternative to the revival of German nationalism as an outlet for reviving German energies. Instead of being treated as a threat, these were to be harnessed to strengthening the security of Germany's neighbours and providing a basis of power for the unification of Europe. Adenauer's response was not only to send an immediate message of agreement to Schuman but to accept the invitation to join the Council of Europe as an associate member. Although it took until mid-June to carry this through the *Bundestag*, against the votes of the SPD, this was a well-timed gesture.

Acheson rubbed in the point at the London meetings that the duration of the Occupation and the life of the High Commission could not last beyond a couple of years more: this was the length of time they had to work out a new relationship with the Germans. From the record of the London discussions it is evident that the French themselves had not yet grasped the implications of their own Coal and Steel Plan. They still argued about the future ownership of the Ruhr industries, the Ruhr Authority and the level of German steel production in terms that reflected the thinking of an earlier period before the Plan had been conceived. A working party was finally set up to review the Occupation Statute, the termination of the state of war and the necessary German co-operation which would justify relinquishing controls. This was a first step towards the agreements signed in Bonn almost exactly two years later

[1] British record of the 3rd meeting, 12 May.

(26 May 1952) and ratified in October 1954, bringing the Occupation regime to an end. In the meantime the Foreign Ministers authorized the High Commissioners to reassure the Germans that

"The Federal Republic does not lie alone and unprotected in Europe. Under Articles 5 and 6 of the N.A.T.O. Treaty, an armed attack upon the occupation forces of the Western Allies in Germany will be considered as an armed attack against all the parties to the Treaty. . . . So long, therefore, as the Western occupation forces remain in Germany the Federal Republic enjoys protection under the North Atlantic Treaty."[1]

In their final session, the Foreign Ministers turned away from Europe and heard a strong plea from Schuman for Allied support in Indo–China. In addition to the economic aid and military equipment which Acheson had already promised, Schuman wanted a joint declaration of Allied solidarity. This was more than Bevin felt able to make in view of the unfavourable response he had received from the Asian governments. The communiqué eventually spoke of the three Powers' intention to give support to the independent nations which had emerged in S.E. Asia, without specifying whether Indo–China was, or was not, included in that category.[2]

The Middle East was another area in which there was need to harmonize their policies. When the negotiations between Abdullah and the Israelis failed to produce agreement, the British decided to raise no further objection to Abdullah going ahead with the incorporation of the rump of Arab Palestine in Jordan. This was announced—to protests from Israel and the Arab League—on 24 April. The British argument to the Americans was that it was better to settle the future of the Palestinian Arabs on the West Bank than leave the situation to deteriorate to the point where it could lead to renewed conflict. The State Department did not dissent but declined to give public approval to Abdullah's action.[3] The British were still providing a subsidy of £3.5 m. to pay for the Arab Legion and Bevin secured Cabinet approval for extending the Anglo–Jordanian Treaty to Abdullah's newly acquired Palestinian territories. This brought further protests, although the British issued a statement to make clear that they had no intention of establishing bases on the West Bank in peacetime and at the same time extended *de jure* recognition to Israel.[4]

With that question settled, the way was now open for a further step which the British and Americans had been discussing, a joint declaration aimed at preventing the alteration of the armistice lines by force. There were divided opinions about including France, but Bevin favoured a tripartite declaration

---

[1] 22 May 1950. FRUS 1950 (3) pp. 1085–6. The statement on Germany issued by the three foreign ministers immediately after their conference on 14 May, is to be found in RIIA *Documents 1949–50*, pp. 319–21.
[2] Communiqué, 13 May 1950. RIIA *Documents 1949–50*, pp. 318–19.
[3] See FRUS 1950 (5) pp. 868–76.
[4] Bevin secured the Cabinet's approval on 25 April 1950, CM 25 (50), on the basis of his paper, CP (50) 78.

and Acheson agreed on the grounds that the French were supplying arms to Syria and this loophole needed to be stopped.[1] As a result of discussions begun in London Bevin agreed to join the other two ministers in issuing the tripartite statement of 25 May 1950 which declared the three powers' opposition to an arms race developing between the Arab states and Israel, and their "unalterable opposition" to the use of or threat of force to violate frontiers or armistice lines, with an undertaking to act immediately to prevent such a violation. The Arab states, angered by what they saw as recognition of the territorial gains the Israelis had obtained by force, took this as one more example of the West's capitulation to Zionist pressure.

But the main concern of all three delegations was with East–West relations and the framework of Western co-operation. Kenneth Younger summed up his impressions of the talks under these two heads.

"(1) The Americans are under a compulsion to 'hot up the cold war' in every way on account of the state of American opinion, while the French, for a similar domestic reason, are above all anxious not to seem to close the door against agreement with the Russians. The difference is only one of emphasis but it is important.

"(2) We and the Americans want to start building up an Atlantic Community which includes and transcends Western Europe, while the French still hanker after a European solution in which the only American function is to produce military and other aid. This difference is important because it stems from two quite different conceptions. Ernie has no faith in the solidity or efficiency of France or Belgium and believes Western Europe will be a broken reed, and will not even attract the loyalty of Europeans or impress the Russians, unless it is very solidly linked to North America. I think this is realistic though depressing."[2]

After a weekend's pause, the fourth session of the NATO Council opened at Lancaster House on 15 May. More than a year had passed since the NATO Treaty had been signed; yet the increase in military strength on the ground or in the air was negligible. At first sight the 4th session could hardly be said to have produced much more in the way of real decisions. Yet Acheson, who had been impatient with the results of the previous week's meetings wrote later that it was the first meeting at which they advanced beyond the point of adopting resolutions and faced up to the problems which underlay the reassuring phrases, in particular the lack of military power and the inadequacy of the economic resources to provide it. "The strategic concept," Acheson said, "was seen to be little more than a division of functions which, beyond what could be done by our (US) strategic bombing and naval capabilities, had little prospect of being performed." Refusing to gloss over the incompatibility between "a balanced collective force" and the wish of individual nations to increase their own national forces, Acheson insisted that the first was the only course open to

---

[1] Bevin's minute ("I prefer tripartite"), c.6 May 1950. FO 371/81910/E 1023; Acheson to State Department, 11 May, FRUS 1950 (5) pp. 158–62 and US record of meeting on the same date, *ibid.*, (3) pp. 1027–31.
[2] Younger's diary, 14 May.

them within their limited resources, even with American aid. At the end of three days' debate, his argument was accepted, and a body of Deputies, to remain in continuous session in London, was set up to turn the concept into an organization disposing of men, money and material.

Younger regarded this second week of meetings as "not exciting but quite efficient . . . Ernie Bevin seemed a bit better and got through successfully to the end. It would be untrue to say that he did as well as he would have done if fit . . . However he did as well as was necessary."[1] Acheson too, if he felt that Bevin in the previous week's talks had often been a passenger carried by his staff, appreciated the effort Bevin made to give a lead in meetings and to find ways of getting round difficulties in drafting the guidelines for the Deputies. He not only seconded Acheson's efforts to bring some sense of urgency into the discussions but also succeeded in bringing home to the Americans the anxieties felt by the Europeans. In a personal letter which Schuman sent to Bevin after the conference, the French Foreign Minister referred to

"The long and remarkable speech you made on the 17th. . . . This speech certainly made a great impression on the American Delegation and was largely responsible for the agreement and the directions which we drafted for the Deputies and which are of such importance for all the European nations."

What Bevin said in his speech was that the traditional way of fighting in Europe, with certain countries left to hold the line until they were exhausted and then others came in, was no longer possible. It was not enough to build up the strength for ultimate victory or to instruct the planners to work on the grand concept of "balanced collective forces":

"They have at the same time to see what will be on the ground if attack comes. It would be a terrible blow to Europe to say: 'Well, we shall liberate you again, but you have got to go under first and we have not organised sufficient strength to remain on the Continent'. . . . The best insurance against war is if the aggressor knows that we shall give a good account of ourselves in the opening stages as well as later on."[2]

When Bevin said that he wanted the points he had made put into the directive to the planners, he carried the whole meeting with him.

In the past twelve months, with the accumulating difficulties over Britain's relations with Europe—in the Council of Europe and OEEC, over devaluation and the European payments scheme—culminating in the problem posed by Schuman's coal and steel plan, Bevin had lost the role of leader in European affairs which he had held from 1947 to 1949. But he was still accepted as the leader of America's European allies in NATO and in that capacity still retained, as Schuman's letter shows, the confidence of the Europeans as well as the Americans.

[1] Younger's diary, 20 May.
[2] British record of the 4th NATO Council meeting in FO 800/483/NA/50/7; US record in FRUS 1950 (3) pp. 94–125; communiqué in RIIA *Documents 1949–50*, pp. 287–9.

On his return to Washington Acheson spoke of the "great perhaps revolutionary significance" of the recommendations of the NATO Council. But it was the Schuman plan which captured the headlines, achieving everything in the way of impact which Monnet and Schuman had hoped for, while the NATO communiqué passed almost unnoticed.

The question to which Bevin wanted an answer was, what procedure the French proposed to follow. Schuman promised an answer, but only after he had returned to Paris. In the meantime, Jean Monnet had spent six days in London (14–19 May) meeting Sir Edwin Plowden and other officials in an effort to explain the details of the Plan and remove their doubts. Monnet had not given up hope of carrying the British with him, but his original wariness about making any concessions which would weaken the basis of the plan was strengthened by his belief that the impact already achieved by "the Schuman bombshell" meant that

"The essential prize had been won, irrevocably. Europe was on the move. Whatever the British decided would be their own affair."

His contacts with his English friends left him in little doubt that it would be a hard battle to convince the British. Putting his finger on the real difference between them and their European allies, he wrote in his Memoirs:

"Britain had not been conquered or invaded: she felt no need to exorcise history."

He told Schuman and Massigli:

"The British will not find their future role by themselves. Only outside pressure will induce them to accept change."

And to Cripps, who asked him whether France would go ahead with Germany and without the UK, he replied:

"I hope with all my heart that you will join in this from the start. But if you don't, we shall go ahead without you. And I'm sure that, because you are realists, you will adjust to the facts when you see that we have succeeded."[1]

When Schuman showed a disposition to offer the British special conditions, Monnet prepared his own counter-coup. He went immediately from his talks in London to see Adenauer in Bonn and secured on the spot a joint communiqué announcing agreement between the two Governments to accept the principles of the French plan. This was meant to cut the ground from under the

[1] Jean Monnet: *Memoirs* (tr. by R. Mayne London 1978) pp. 306–8.

British feet, and to leave no doubt Monnet quotes with satisfaction Attlee's subsequent statement in the House:

"This fact (i.e. the Franco–German agreement) naturally determined the course of the subsequent exchange of views between the two Governments and made difficult the achievement of H.M.G.'s desire to play an active part in the discussion of the French proposal, but without commitment to the acceptance of its principles in advance."

This was the issue which Bevin had been probing when he asked, what procedure the French proposed to follow. But the question was one of substance not simply of procedure. The British objected to entering into negotiations in which they were committed to accept in advance the principle "of pooling resources under an international authority possessing certain sovereign powers". Monnet's answer was unequivocal: no commitment, no negotiation. "On this point I remained firm from beginning to end."[1]

On 23 May Bevin sent a message to the British Ambassador in Paris asking him to follow up Schuman's promise to send him a reply about procedure. The same day, however, the Foreign Office announced that Bevin was going back into hospital for further treatment—in fact for a second operation, this time for a fistula—and although it is virtually certain that it would have made no different to the result, in the exchange which followed between the Foreign Office and the Quai d'Orsay, Bevin was in no condition to take more than a nominal part.

Before entering the London Clinic, Bevin managed to take part in one more Commons debate, this time on the Far East. It was a depressing occasion: Bevin was plainly a sick man and although Eden expressed the House's good wishes for his recovery, many who saw him shared Younger's doubts whether he would ever be fit again to continue in so exacting an office. This was his last public appearance for more than two months. Before going into hospital he sent off a message to Schuman suggesting that the important thing was to get talks on the coal and steel plan started as soon as possible and not wait for a full-dress conference.

"In my view the most desirable step would be the earliest institution of direct conversations between France and Germany. H.M.G. would like to participate in these from the outset, with the hope that by obtaining a clearer picture of how these proposals would operate in detail, they would be able to join the scheme."[2]

This was the sort of opening Monnet and his collaborators were determined not to allow the British. Bevin's message to Paris crossed with a memorandum from Paris which repeated the conditions on which the French insisted in advance: agreement by the participants to pool their coal and steel resources and to accept the decisions of the new High Authority as binding.

[1] Monnet, pp. 311–12.
[2] White Paper on Anglo–French Discussions, May–June 1950. Cmd. 7970 Document 6.

It took, in all, ten days, eleven notes and 4,000 words before each side accepted that the other would not give way. Left to himself Schuman might have adopted a compromise, but Monnet, as he says, "was resolved not to consider it". He sent a note to the French Government in which he argued:

"To accept British participation on those terms—i.e. in a special capacity—would be to resign oneself to advance to the replacement of the French proposal by something that would merely travesty it . . . there would be no common rules and no independent High Authority, but only some kind of O.E.E.C."[1]

To make an end of it, Monnet persuaded the French Government to send a draft communiqué to the seven governments they had approached asking for their concurrence by 8.00 p.m. on 2 June. Bevin had already gone into hospital for his operation; and both Attlee and Cripps were away from London on holiday. Kenneth Younger, confronted with the French message, hunted out Edwin Plowden, and together they set off to look for Herbert Morrison, the acting Prime Minister. They tracked him down in the Ivy Restaurant after an evening in the theatre and called him out to talk in a corridor. Morrison shook his head: "It's no good," he said, "we can't do it, the Durham miners won't wear it."[2] After consulting Bevin, who declared he would not be dictated to, Morrison held a thinly-attended Cabinet to give formal approval. The question to which the French required an answer by 8 p.m. was whether the British Government in common with the others invited to take part in the discussions would make a declaration that "they set themselves as an immediate aim the pooling of their coal and steel production and the institution of a new High Authority", whose decisions were to be binding. The view of the ministers and officials present was that there was a real difference of opinion which it was better to face straight away. No British Government could accept such a commitment without the opportunity to assess the consequences for the country's key industries, export trade and level of employment.[3] No minister dissented then or later, and on 3 June a joint communiqué was published in Paris on behalf of six European governments who accepted the French conditions but without any British signature.

Bevin's operation took place on the same day. Leaving aside for the moment the question whether, if he had been fit, there would have been a different outcome to the exchanges with the French, there is no doubt that the Government suffered from the fact that Bevin was not available to put its case. A two-day debate on the Schuman Plan was promised for the last week of June, but Attlee announced that Bevin would not take part in it: he and Cripps would be the principal speakers for the Government.

[1] Monnet, p. 313.
[2] Donoughue and Jones, p. 481, reporting a conversation with Younger.
[3] The Ministers present were: Morrison (chair), Addison, Shinwell, Tomlinson, Alexander, Isaacs, McNeil, Gordon-Walker, Jay and Younger. The officials present were Bridges (who had prepared the paper for the meeting CP (50) 120); Norman Brook; Plowden and Strang.

In the interval before the debate took place, the Government's reputation suffered further damage, this time self-inflicted, from the publication by the Labour Party's National Executive Committee of the 12-page statement on "European Unity". This had been planned months before the Schuman Plan was announced. According to Dalton, Chairman of the Party's International Committee, Bevin had several times asked him for a reasoned statement of Labour's policy towards Europe and, as in the case of "Cards on the Table", a draft had been written by Denis Healey. Its publication, however, in the Press on 13 June, demonstrated what *The Economist* called the Labour Party's "almost phenomenal gift for bad timing". For 13 June was the day on which Attlee had promised a White Paper giving the text of the notes exchanged with the French and a statement of the Government's attitude. The documents printed in the White Paper gave the impression that the British Government had not turned down the Schuman proposals out of hand, but had shown an understandable desire not to accept commitments in advance of knowing what they were, and would still seek means of joining at a later date.[1]

This impression, however, was wiped out by the publication of the Executive's statement "European Unity" the day before. Its presentation by Dalton, the most "anti-European" of Labour ministers, at a press conference at Transport House, laid particular stress on the Labour Party's rejection of any idea of union with countries which had not adopted its own socialist policies of full employment, public ownership and a planned economy.

It was not only the timing but the tone of the statement that was ill-conceived. It reads as if it were aimed at Labour Party activists and designed to re-assure them that Labour's foreign policy was still governed by socialist principles. Its critical attitude towards the majority of Britain's European allies was unconcealed.

"The Labour Party believes that its policy of full employment and fair shares is vital to British recovery, and that if the whole of Europe followed the same policy many of its problems would disappear. The price of economic liberalism today is class war and social unrest."[2]

The pamphlet declared that Socialists would welcome a European economic union if it was based on international planning for full employment, social justice and stability; but that was only possible on a basis of national planning for the same ends and this was not the case in any Western European country outside of Scandinavia and Britain.

It could not be said that "European Unity" was isolationist, as Hoffman described it in a Senate hearing, since it insisted that Europe could not solve any of its problems by itself and that the real task was to create a greater degree

[1] Cmd. 7970. See reference at top of p. 860.
[2] *European Unity*, a statement published by the NEC of the British Labour Party, May 1950, p. 8.

of unity in the non-Communist world, not just in one part of it. It was equally outspoken in repudiating any notion of Third Force neutralism between America and Russia, which attracted a great deal of support in Europe in 1950. Nonetheless it presented a distorted picture of the policy which Bevin and the Labour Government had actually followed towards Europe, virtually ignoring the years of effort devoted to the political and economic recovery of Western Europe and the creation of the Atlantic alliance as a guarantee of its independence. Its mention of the Schuman Plan was cursory, added without any reference to the conditions the French had imposed, and had obviously been included at the last moment to a draft prepared with something quite different in mind, the proposals for political federation to be discussed by the Council of Europe in August.[1] Even in putting the Labour Government's case against European integration, a misleading impression was left. It highlighted the argument from socialist principle, and played down the practical arguments such as Western Europe's dependence on American support; the importance to Britain of her position as a world trading power, and as the centre of the Commonwealth. It was these which carried more weight with Bevin and Attlee and which united the Labour Party with that large number of Englishmen who had no use for socialism but were nonetheless opposed to Britain becoming part of a European federation.

The damage was done, however, providing all the evidence that was needed for those in the United States who had always claimed that the trouble with Britain was its socialist government and for those in Europe who were confirmed in their belief that the British would never see themselves as Europeans and that "Europe" would have to be made without, even perhaps against, the United Kingdom.[2]

The debate in the House occupied two days in the last week of June. The Opposition made the most of the embarrassment caused to the Government by "European Unity"—which Attlee could not deny having seen, whether he had read it or not—and avoided the issue of handing over powers to a supranational body by concentrating on a motion urging the Government to participate in the Paris talks with the same reservation as the Dutch, i.e. the right to withdraw if the proposals proved unworkable.

The attack on the Government was led by Churchill and Eden who argued that Franco–German rapprochement was so important and the absence of the UK from the talks so pleasing to the Russians that the French initiative could not be allowed either to fail or to succeed without British participation. They

---

[1] This is said explicitly in the second paragraph on p. 1.

[2] One passage in "European Unity" was much quoted on the Continent: "In every respect except distance we in Britain are closer to our kinsmen in Australia and New Zealand on the far side of the world than we are to Europe. We are closer in language and in origins, in social habits and institutions, in political outlook and in economic interest. The economies of the Commonwealth countries are complementary to that of Britain to a degree which those of Western Europe could never equal." (p. 4).

agreed that the abrupt manner in which the French had made their proposal, and their refusal to make concessions on the preliminary declaration were deplorable, but thought they were easily explained in view of the Labour Government's record of obstructing the European Movement. The Opposition maintained that the risks of staying out of the conference were greater than those of going in; that the Dutch reservation provided adequate protection, and that the French could have been influenced to make greater concessions. Cripps' reply was that much more was at stake for Britain than for a country like Holland. The British produced one-half of the coal and one-third of the steel of the interested countries, and depended on these for their position as a manufacturing nation. How could they agree to hand over control of these industries without knowing more about what was proposed, for example whether the High Authority would have the power to close coalfields and steel works? Rejecting the objective of a European federation, Cripps argued that this was incompatible with the UK's position in the Commonwealth, and as an Atlantic and world power.

As in the case of the Council of Europe, it is hard to see why the Labour Government could not have gone along with the same reservation as the Dutch. One reason was because there was widespread scepticism about the practicability of the Schuman Plan and French ability to bring it off. Another was suspicion of the political complexion of the French and German Governments and their links with heavy industry—"the Catholic 'black international'", Younger wrote, "which I have always thought to be a big driving force behind the Council of Europe". However much Kenneth Younger and the other MPs of his generation felt that a new initiative was called for in foreign policy, it was not in this direction. On the morning of the second day while ministers were assembling for a Cabinet meeting, the Lord Chancellor, Jowitt, remarked to Dalton: "If we go down on this, I can't think of any better issue to go to the country on."[1] In fact the Labour vote in the House was solid and in both the divisions called for the Government had a clear majority, 309 to 296 on one, 309 to 289 on the other.

4

Looking back from the vantage point of 1969, Dean Acheson wrote of Britain's refusal to join in negotiating the Schuman Plan as "the great mistake of the post-war period . . . from the bitter fruits" of which "both Britain and Europe are still suffering . . .

"Some decisions are critical. This was one. It was not the last clear chance for Britain to enter Europe, but it was the first wrong choice . . ."[2]

---

[1] Dalton's diaries, 27 June 1950.
[2] Acheson, pp. 385 and 387.

The assumption that Britain's only future lay in entering Europe is not one that all British politicians or voters would endorse even in the 1980s. Even for those like the author who came to believe in the course of the 1950s (but not in 1950) that Britain ought to join the EEC, this is not a judgement to be accepted without closer examination.

Suppose for the sake of argument that Acheson and the Americans were right in saying that failure to bring about a closer association between Britain and Western Europe was "the great mistake", it is not the case (as Acheson recognized) that this was the last chance to bring it about. Although the European Coal and Steel Community came into operation without the British, the next stage in the development foreseen by Monnet was held up by the eruption of the question of German participation in Europe's defence, the long-drawn-out uncertainty over French ratification of the Pleven Plan and its final rejection, throwing the whole future of European integration into doubt. Only in 1955 were the negotiations for a European Community resumed, leading to the Treaty of Rome in 1956. By then the arguments which had counted most in 1950 no longer carried the same conviction. The Conservative Party, which had criticized the Labour Party's attitude in 1950, was then in power and, thanks to the setback over the Pleven Plan, the ground lost by the initial refusal of 1950 was not so great that it could not have been made up by a reversal of British policy. It was Britain's refusal to take part in these, and the establishment of a rival in the European Free Trade Association which was both more damaging and less defensible than the refusal to participate in the Schuman Plan negotiations.

It has often been argued that if the British had taken part in the 1950 discussions they could have secured better terms for their entry into the EEC. But, if this argument has any force, it applies to the negotiation of the Treaty of Rome in 1955–6 not to the 1950 negotiations. In 1950, although Monnet already had a European Economic Community in mind as the long-term objective, he was immediately concerned with the more specific problem of reconciling the French to the revival of German industrial power. He believed that this had to be done quickly and that it could only be done at all by creating a supranational framework to contain Germany's reviving economic strength. He feared that the participation of the British might be fatal to both, by dragging out the negotiations and by tipping the scale against acceptance of the supranational principle to which there was considerable resistance in the other countries involved as well as in Britain. The price of the UK taking part in the 1950 discussions might well have been not to modify but to defeat the plan. By 1955–6 the Coal and Steel Community was established and British participation in the negotiations for the EEC might have secured a result more acceptable to them without endangering Monnet's achievement in laying the economic foundations for the reconciliation of France and Germany after the war.

Reading between the lines of Monnet's memoirs strongly suggests that in

1950 he preferred to see Britain join the Six after the structure of the new Community had been established and that it was for this reason that no attempt was made to consult the British beforehand. In any case, Labour's parliamentary majority was slender and an election was generally thought to be likely, perhaps within a matter of months: Conservative criticisms of Labour's attitude and Churchill's role as a leader of the European Movement might well mean that, if they won a majority, the decision to stay out would be reversed. Even under a Labour Government co-operation between Britain and her European allies in other fields than the economic, for example, in defence, increased; and even in the economic, the decision not to take part in the Schuman Plan was followed within a few days by the resolution of the difficulties in OEEC and the acceptance of a European Payments Union by Britain and her European partners which has been described as the most successful example in practice of international economic co-operation in the post-war period.

Nonetheless, without prejudging the question whether it was "the great mistake of the post-war period", there is no doubt that the British rejection of the French invitation strengthened the irritation and distrust between British and other European politicians and journalists already evident in the Council of Europe and the OEEC. As *The Economist* pointed out, the conditions the French attached to their invitation were coloured by suspicion of the good faith of the Labour Government in anything directed towards closer European economic unity. This was confirmed by the Government's reply which disappointed all those in Europe and the USA who looked to Britain to play a leading role in Europe and obscured how much leadership Britain had already provided in 1947–49.

"One can regret", *The Economist* wrote in a leading article, " that the issue was brought up by such unworthy tactics. One can regret that so mighty a principle as the pooling of sovereignty was invoked, and such high hopes of permanent pacification aroused, in support of a proposal which only those versed in its formidable technicalities can really understand—and whose actual practical accomplishments may yet turn out to be small. One can be deeply distrustful of the French and American leaning to the dangerous and difficult principle of federalism, and disappointed at the failure to realise how much sovereignty has already been pooled in defence matters by much less spectacular and more workmanlike methods, in which the British have been the reverse of backward.

"But when all these things have been said, the fact remains that at the bar of world opinion, the Schuman proposal has become a test. And the British Government have failed it."[1]

As the Opposition urged in the parliamentary debate, all they had to do was to agree to participate in the Paris talks with the same reservation as that made by the Dutch—that they would withdraw if the proposals put forward proved

---

[1] *The Economist*, 10 June 1950.

demonstrably to be unworkable. But they preferred to say "No" and stay away.

Bevin was a sick man at the time, and resentment at the way in which the proposals were sprung on him may have clouded his initial judgement; but this was confirmed by the rest of the Labour Cabinet as well as by their civil service advisers and in the event not revoked by the Conservatives when they came into office.

A good deal was made at the time, and has been since, of the Labour Party's hostility, on ideological grounds, to a Europe which had rejected the British "path to democratic socialism". The NEC statement on "European Unity" lends colour to this view which undoubtedly represented, and has continued to repesent, the attitude of an important section of the Party. But this was hardly characteristic of Bevin, who had been criticized by the Left from the beginning for his refusal to apply socialist principles to foreign policy and for his advocacy of a close alliance with "capitalist America".

Bevin shared with other Labour ministers a determination not to allow a supranational European Authority, any more than the US Government, to interfere with the achievements of which they were most proud: full employment, the welfare state, the nationalized industries, and the right of a Labour government to follow its own pattern of socialist planning. But there is a simple test which suggests that, in Bevin's case at least, resistance to any threat of outside intervention was based far more on an attachment to retaining Britain's national sovereignty than to socialist principle. The test is to ask, whether his attitude would have been different if the other European governments with which Britain was called upon to integrate had been socialist in character. The answer is almost certainly that it would not. He was certainly quite unmoved by the appeals of French socialists like Guy Mollet.

The arguments which carried more weight with Bevin than any on ideological grounds are familiar enough: first, his view of Britain as a power with worldwide interests in a way which was not true of any other European nation, and second, his belief that Western Europe after the War—including the UK—was incapable of achieving either recovery or security by itself without the participation of the USA.

There followed naturally from these premises, from Britain's world role and the insufficiency of any purely European concept, the conclusion that Britain's relationship with Europe, while close and of great importance to her, could not be exclusive. She could not, in Bevin's eyes, be confined within a European framework, merge with other European powers to form an embryonic United States of Europe or abandon her special relationships with the USA and the countries of the Commonwealth.

Monnet believed that in their attitude to the sort of European integration he had in mind there was little difference between Englishmen of any party. Churchill's imagination was genuinely stirred by the European idea which he stated so clearly and with such eloquence in the great speech he made at

Zurich in September 1946. But in the debate on the Schuman Plan Churchill used words which could easily have come from Bevin:

"I cannot conceive that Britain would be an ordinary member of a Federal Union limited to Europe in any period which can at present be foreseen."[1]

Whatever the commitment of some of those closest to him, such as Duncan Sandys, the return of the Conservative Party to office in 1951 was not followed by a reversal of Labour's policy, but by a refusal to participate in the Pleven Plan for a European Army, a project which Churchill himself had taken the lead in proposing to the Council of Europe while in opposition.[2]

On this occasion Churchill circulated a memorandum to the Cabinet (29 November 1951) in which he said explicitly that he had "never contemplated" the UK joining the Schuman Plan on the same terms as the continental partners.

"We should have joined in all the discussions, and, had we done so, not only a better plan would probably have emerged, but our own interests would have been watched at every stage.

"Our attitude towards further economic developments on the Schuman lines resembles that which we adopt about the European Army. We help, we dedicate, we play a part, but we are not merged and do not forfeit our insular or Commonwealth-wide character.

"I should resist any American pressure to treat Britain as on the same footing as the European states, none of whom have the advantages of the Channel and who were consequently conquered."

So much for the argument that if Churchill had been in office in 1950 the result of Schuman's initiative, so far as Britain was concerned, would have been any different. When there was no longer political advantage to be gained from using "Europe" as a stick with which to beat the Labour Government, Churchill's views were very close to Bevin's. In the same paper he declared:

"I am not opposed to a European Federation including (eventually) the countries behind the Iron Curtain, provided that this comes about naturally and gradually. But I never thought that Britain or the British Commonwealth should either individually or collectively become an integral part of a European federation and have never given the slightest support to the idea. . . .

"Our first object is the unity and consolidation of the British Commonwealth and what is left of the former British Empire. Our second, the 'fraternal association' of the English-speaking world; and third, United Europe, to which we are a separate, closely—and specially—related ally and friend."[3]

---

[1] Churchill in the House of Commons, 27 June 1950.
[2] The refusal (on Eisenhower's advice) was announced by Eden at a press conference in Rome on 28 November 1951.
[3] C (51) 32, CAB 129/48.

Churchill's remark about the European states being conquered points to one of the most important factors in keeping alive in the years immediately after the War Britain's historic feeling of separateness from Europe. Exactly ten years before Schuman's proposal, Jean Monnet had devised the striking formula of common Anglo–French citizenship accepted by a British Cabinet of which Churchill had just invited Bevin to become a member. But the decision which counted was the refusal to commit the full strength of the RAF to a Battle of France already lost, thereby preserving the fighter force which, after France's defeat, won the Battle of Britain. In the summer of 1950, similar thoughts recurred.

After citing the usual reasons given for Britain's reluctance to commit herself to the Schuman Plan, Monnet says in his *Memoirs* that he sensed something else, a deeper and less articulate worry, and he quotes some notes he made at the time, in 1950:

"Britain (he wrote) has no confidence that France and the other countries of Europe have the ability or even the will to resist a possible Russian invasion. . . .

"Britain believes that in this conflict continental Europe will be occupied, but that she herself with America, will be able to resist and finally conquer.

"She therefore does not wish to let her domestic life or the development of her resources be influenced by any views other than her own, and certainly not by continental views."

Repeating these notes in his *Memoirs* (published in 1976), Monnet added the comment:

"If this, as I suspected, was what the British felt in their heart of hearts, we had no hope of convincing them for a long time to come."[1]

Bevin was right about one thing, and that the most important, that Western Europe could not provide for its own defence by itself, even with a German contribution. Pushing NATO through, however, had drained his energies and his anxiety lest anything should weaken or divert attention from the task of building it up led him to regard the search for a distinctive European identity and community as incompatible with the Atlantic pattern of Western Union. To the Americans as well as the Europeans the two were complementary and mutually supporting, and the co-existence of NATO and the EEC for a quarter of a century supports their belief.

The Labour Movement, parochial in its origins and orientated towards domestic problems, had little natural sympathy with the European Movement and even less when its leadership was captured by Churchill. The price of Churchill's and the Conservatives' successful use of the Council of Europe to attack the Government, in compensation for their frustration at Westminster, was to complete the alienation of Labour.

[1] Pp. 316–17.

The fact that "Europe" became identified with moves towards federation and the surrender of national sovereignty was a major stumbling block. So far as the immediate tasks were concerned, Bevin believed that this was so much rhetoric, a form of political escapism which offered no real alternative to the hard grind of securing co-operation by agreement between national governments who alone had the power to get things done. This did not exclude pooling resources and accepting collective decisions in specific areas—for example, in defence. But he saw these as the product of voluntary agreement between governments—as in the European Payments Union—not of a permanent surrender of powers to a supranational authority such as Monnet proposed in the Coal and Steel Community.

There were few people in Britain in 1950, whether Socialists or not, who really believed that Britain should hand over to a supranational authority control of the two industries on which her industrial power had been built. The French and Germans had powerful motives to take so radical a step: in the French case, the fear of Germany's recovery; in the German case, the chance to escape from the alternative of permanent restrictions on production and allocation. Monnet's stroke of genius lay in seeing how these two could be made to reinforce each other, if France, the weaker partner but temporarily in a position of greater advantage, could use this to leap ahead of events and create a common interest before Germany's revival had reached the point where there was no longer an incentive to accept the French proposal. There was no comparable motive on the British part and the way in which the French presented the plan to the British—insisting on prior acceptance of the proposals in principle—suggested that they were not anxious to have the British accept.

But the French attitude, as *The Economist* pointed out, was coloured by suspicion of the good faith of the British Government in anything directed towards closer European economic unity. The weakness of the Government's case was its refusal to explore the possibilities of the most arresting and original idea anyone had produced in a Europe which was desperately in need of regaining its confidence in its own capacity for action.

Everything that had ever been said, however unfairly, by their critics on both sides of the Atlantic about the British dragging their feet, failing to give constructive leadership, being unprepared to think of anything beyond their own limited interests, now appeared confirmed. Critics at home were angered by the woodenness of the Government's reaction, by its inability to respond with at least a gesture to a proposal designed to put an end to the historic enmity between France and Germany and by the gift for bad timing which instead produced the NEC report on "European Unity" at precisely this moment. Britain's international reputation, it was said, had reached its lowest point since the War. Much of this was exaggerated. The scheme finally arrived at for a European Payments Union and the success of OEEC; the efforts to give a lead to Europe in making something of the Brussels Pact and NATO; the reliance which, even when they were most exasperated with the British, the Americans knew they could put on the British as on no other of their European allies: these were proof that when Bevin and the British, sceptical of "integration", "federation" and "supranationality" as fashionable catchwords, stuck to the tried methods of co-operation between governments, it was because they wanted results and thought little of gestures.

Nor was the divergence between Britain and the Six yet irreparable. The Europeans might have lost faith in Britain, but they had not much faith yet in themselves. Progress on the lines laid down by Monnet was fitful, the failure of the Pleven Plan a bad setback, and the French commitment to supranationality far from final.

But the sense of a lost opportunity remains. There were two men in British politics after the War, Bevin and Churchill, who had the imagination to grasp and the resolution to push through a scheme which offered possibilities comparable to Bevin's response to Marshall's offer. It is a sad fact that Bevin, although in office, no longer had the strength or resilience to add to what he had achieved in 1947–9; and that Churchill, although he could see the possibilities, was out of office, and by the time he returned, no longer had the inspiration or the driving force to retrieve the opportunity that had been missed.

It might not have worked. The pull of Britain's interests outside Europe, the difficulty of matching her very different traditions with those of France and Germany might still have proved too great, but the irony is that the feature which Bevin most disliked, the surrender of sovereignty to a supranational authority, has proved to be far less substantial a threat than he feared. Although a European Economic Community has now been in existence for a quarter of a century, decisive power still rests in the hands of the national governments not of the supranational authority—a pattern somewhere between, but still arguably closer to Bevin's pragmatic view than Monnet's vision of the future, a pattern which may continue to evolve but, if so, at a pace which would have alarmed Bevin less than it would have disappointed Monnet.

5

The debate on the Schuman Plan was overshadowed by the news of the North Koreans' invasion of South Korea received in London on the evening of 24 June.[1] Acting with resolution Acheson and Truman called immediately for the UN Security Council to meet, which it did 24 hours after the attack had begun. The Soviet representative was not present and by a vote of 9–0 (Yugoslavia

---

[1] Korean local time is nine hours ahead of GMT, fourteen hours ahead of Washington's Eastern Standard Time. Thus the attack took place in the early hours of 25 June by Korean time, but on the 24th by London and Washington time.

abstaining) the Council declared a breach of the peace, calling for an immediate cease-fire and withdrawal.

That was on the evening of the 25th. Next day—the first day of the Schuman Plan debate in the Commons—Attlee and Younger went to see Bevin in hospital. All three agreed that the UK must give full support to the USA in calling for action by the UN. No Soviet forces were directly involved, but it was hard to believe that the North Koreans, whose forces were not guerillas but well-equipped regulars trained by Soviet military advisers, had acted without Russian agreement. The attack was directed against a government which could make a direct claim on American protection, and this was available close at hand from the USA's major base in Japan. It was, therefore, more favourable ground on which to repel an act of aggression than in Indo–China, particularly as the absence of the Soviet representative from the Security Council made it possible to do this under the auspices of the United Nations.

On the morning of the 27th, before the debate on the Schuman Plan was renewed, the British Cabinet had before it the draft of a statement by the President, announcing American air and sea cover for the South Korean forces, the dispatch of the 7th Fleet to patrol the strait between Formosa and the Chinese mainland and increased military assistance to the Philippines and Indo–China. The President's statement spoke of the resort to armed aggression and war by "centrally directed Communist Imperialism". According to Dalton the Cabinet thought this particular phrase "ham-fisted" and it was agreed to urge the Americans to drop it. Bevin when consulted had said he did not think it would be possible to isolate Korea and did not want to discourage the USA from helping the British to fight Communism in Malaya or the French in Indo–China. But the majority of the Cabinet, alarmed by American action to protect (and thereby involve) Formosa, were against any reference to Communist encroachment in other parts of Asia and Bevin was ready to accept that the UN resolution should be strictly confined to Korea.

It was finally agreed that Britain should support the American representative in the Security Council in calling on members of the UN to come to the aid of the South Koreans and Dalton summed up the Cabinet discussion as: "Anyhow, it is felt they (i.e. the Americans) are our friends, they are calling the Russian bluff now and we must keep in line with them." The only doubts were expressed by Nye Bevan who was "rather excited about lack of consultation".[1]

The resolution, which gave UN authority to the US operations, was carried by 7 votes to 1, in the continued absence of the Russian representative but with the Yugoslavs opposing and with India as well as Egypt abstaining. The sight of the United Nations acting to stop aggression aroused widespread approval in Britain and indeed throughout the non-Communist world.

There were problems, however, and they were soon to impose heavy strains on the Western alliance. Although the British and other nations eventually

[1] CM 39 (50) 27 June; Dalton's diaries, 27 June 1950.

sent troops to Korea, the brunt of the fighting from first to last was borne by the Americans, who felt that they were being left to carry the burden of a war which it was to everyone's interest to see won. The fact that they were doing the fighting meant that the decisions about the conduct and scope of the war were taken by Americans, with little regard for the views of anyone else, and in the case of the C.-in-C., General MacArthur, with little regard for the views of the US Government. No less important, the Korean War, although fought under the UN flag, was inevitably linked with earlier American policy and experiences in Asia, in particular the anger of the China Lobby and the Republican Party at the triumph of the Chinese Communists and the possibility of using the Korean War and the Nationalists' retention of Formosa as a springboard from which to reverse Chiang's defeat. American policy in Korea thus further inflamed the already bitter domestic controversy in which an irreconcilable section of the Republican Party was prepared to go to any lengths, including impeachment, in order to vent its rancour against the Democratic Administration.

This partisan attack drew support and further aroused a public opinion which, now that American forces were involved in fighting "the Commies", swung sharply towards seeing the issue in black and white terms. You were either on one side or the other, and allies who wanted to introduce qualifications, distinguish between Chinese and Russian Communists or question the wisdom of MacArthur's decisions, were lumped together with "cryptos", appeasers, fellow-travellers, and other secret enemies. The temper of the McCarthy years was already in the making. Alger Hiss, denounced as a Soviet agent, became the symbol of "the enemy within" and in the summer of 1950 General Marshall and Dean Acheson had to listen to themselves being attacked in the Senate as traitors and criminals who had sold America down the river. The demand was for military not diplomatic solutions and the freedom of manoeuvre of the Democratic Administration and the State Department in particular was greatly reduced.

The rising tide of hysterical anti-Communism in the States alarmed and threatened to alienate the British and America's other allies. They feared that the Korean War would become a crusade against Communism and extend to mainland China with the possibility it would turn from a local into a third world war. The disaster in which General MacArthur involved the USA later in the year by his refusal to stop short of the Yalu River, so bringing China directly into the war—a disaster which Truman, Marshall and Acheson were unable to prevent—appeared to show that there was good reason for their fears.

There was a danger that the divergence between British and American policy in Asia, first made explicit by the difference over recognizing the Chinese People's Republic, might now become a rift. Both Governments could see the danger but each was under strong pressure from public opinion pulling in opposite directions. Alarm that Britain might be dragged into war sharpened anti-Americanism, always latent in the Labour Party, and as a study of the Press shows, soon began to undermine confidence in American leadership. While supporting American moves in the UN Security Council, the British Government thought it wise to find out if there were second thoughts in Moscow now that the USA had committed itself to fight, and instructed its Ambassador to take soundings. The Indians, convinced that if only the Communist Government in Peking were given the Chinese seat in the Security Council and the Russian representative returned, the way would be open to a cease-fire, urged such a course on all concerned which, not surprisingly, the Russians favoured and the Americans rejected.

America's European allies were affected by an additional fear, not only that the war would spread, but that the Americans would become so heavily involved in "the wrong war", against the Chinese, as to leave the Russians a free hand in Europe. The Germans, in particular, living in the Western half of another artificially divided country were alarmed at their vulnerability to the same tactics. The news of the Korean invasion produced something close to panic in a disarmed West Germany, where it was at once coupled with the build-up by the Russians during 1949–50 of the 60,000 strong East German *Volkspolizei*, part of which was equipped and trained as a military force under the command of Wilhelm Zaisser, better known during the Spanish Civil War as the Communist General Gomez. A Soviet army, put at 27 divisions, was also stationed in East Germany, more than a match for NATO's 12 poorly equipped and unco-ordinated divisions with little air support. On 3 July Adenauer formally requested the High Commission to make increased provision for the defence of Germany.

In France the outbreak of war in Korea—at once seen as war by proxy between the two super powers—reinforced the neutralist thesis that the only safe course was to contract out of the contest altogether. What chance was there now, it was asked, of American armaments with which to re-equip a French Army? Worse still was the prospect opened for the French by the US High Commissioner, John McCloy's remark that, while the USA remained opposed to re-creating a German army, it was "very difficult to deny the Germans the right and the means to defend their soil".[1] It was easy to guess that if Europeans pressed the USA to make better provision for their defence after Korea, the Americans would reply by pointing to the untapped reserve of German manpower, a reserve the Russians would certainly not hesitate to use.

In the Berlin crisis two years before, Bevin had been able to inspire confidence that the crisis would not get out of hand as long as he was at the centre of things. In the summer of 1950 it could not escape comment that the Foreign Secretary was confined to bed in the London Clinic and that, as anxiety grew, there was no one to give the reassurance which he had provided in 1948. By 29 June, however, he was well enough to go out for a drive and in

---

[1] McCloy's remark was made on 22 July 1950.

the first week of July, he began to resume the direction of Foreign Office business from his hospital room.

The first thing he did was to brief Franks for talks with Acheson, writing that if the Russians really were ready to co-operate in re-establishing the *status quo* in Korea, they would almost certainly raise the question of Formosa and Chinese representation in the UN. While the USA had whole-hearted backing from world opinion in the action it had taken in Korea, Truman's order to the US 7th Fleet to prevent any attack on Formosa was a different matter.

"I do not believe they could rely on the same support for their declared policy in connexion with Formosa."

Bevin, therefore, urged the Americans in any public statements to concentrate on the Korean issue and play down other matters such as Formosa.

Acheson, in no mood for appeasement and determined to scotch any such thoughts on the part of the British, sent a return message which more than met Bevin's invitation to speak frankly. The message he instructed Douglas to deliver gives the impression of being directed more at the Indian proposals to seat the Chinese Communists at the Security Council and secure the return of the Russians, than at anything Bevin himself had said in his letter to Franks, but Acheson left him in no doubt that there would be no retreat from the statement the President had made about Formosa or Peking's representation in the Security Council. Acheson assured Bevin that the American objective was to neutralize Formosa not to take possession of it, but they were not prepared to see hostile forces seize it and use it as a base against them. "We are not willing to see it go involuntarily to Peiping in the present state of affairs in Asia."[1]

Douglas reported that when he delivered Acheson's message to Bevin in hospital, the latter "seemed somewhat surprised and a little taken aback at the vigour of your response". Acheson had told Douglas to ask Bevin what advantage he could see in trying to get China into the Security Council and Russia back to it when this would be used "solely to sow confusion and doubt and delay or hinder the primary objective of both of us—namely, to show that armed aggression does not pay".

Acheson concluded his instructions to Douglas:

"I want to leave him (Bevin) in no doubt of seriousness with which I view implications of his message and their possible effect on our whole future relationship."[2]

It was this sting in the tail which disturbed Bevin. He stuck to his guns, however, saying that the UK position in Korea was not to be taken as a commitment that they would go along with the Americans on Formosa, and

[1] Acheson's message to Bevin, 10 July. FRUS 1950 (7) pp. 347–51.
[2] Acheson's personal message to Douglas, 10 July, *ibid.*, pp. 351–2.

that great care must be taken not to weaken Britain's relations with the Commonwealth, especially with India and Pakistan. However, as a result of further efforts on both sides, the gap was narrowed. Bevin made it clear that the British were not in favour of raising the question of Chinese representation in the UN, and that they regretted the Indian attempt at mediation which they had done their best to persuade Nehru not to pursue. He spoke appreciatively of "the stand which the U.S. Government have taken in Korea on behalf of us all", and assured Acheson that he was not in favour of a deal with aggressors. His anxiety about Formosa sprang from the desire not to give the Russians a chance to divide Asia from the West on the Asian problem.[1] In return the President clarified the US position in his message of 19 July to Congress, declaring that the military neutralization of Formosa was without prejudice to the political questions affecting it, which remained to be "settled by peaceful means as envisaged in the Charter of the UN."[2]

The restoration of confidence was no doubt made easier by the failure of both the Indian and the British efforts to find a peaceful solution. The Indian attempt at mediation collapsed when the Russian representative returned to the Security Council, without waiting any longer for the Chinese Communists to secure admission—and showed himself as obstructive as ever. The British approach to Moscow proved equally fruitless, with the Russians issuing a version of the exchanges which Attlee at once had to correct in public. Talks were duly held in Washington between 20 and 24 July, with Franks and Tedder representing the UK and at least served to clarify the American view of the situation. What came as a surprise to the British was the length of time the Americans expected the fighting in Korea to last—some months—and the forces they thought would be needed to push back the North Koreans. The British had hitherto thought that any troops they might be able to contribute would not reach Korea in time, but they now decided to offer ground forces.[3] These never amounted to more than a brigade of The Gloucesters—in addition to naval forces—but they fought with distinction and their presence, as well as that of ground troops from eight other countries by the end of 1950, helped to answer the Soviet argument that the Korean affair was solely a US venture.

By the time the talks in Washington took place, Bevin was out of hospital —he left on 14 July—and convalescing in Eastbourne. Before he went, Churchill had asked for a Commons debate on the state of Europe's defences, preferably in secret session. Attlee was clear that there would have to be a debate, but wanted Bevin's advice, before the Cabinet met, on whether it

---

[1] Bevin's reply to Acheson, 15 July. FRUS (7) pp. 395–9. See also Douglas's account of two talks with Younger, Strang and other Foreign Office officials, on 14 and 15 July, *ibid.*, pp. 380–85 and 390.
[2] The quotation from Truman's message and Oliver Franks' response to Acheson, 19 July, are on pp. 430–32 of FRUS 1950 (7).
[3] US record of the Washington talks, 20–24 July, FRUS (7) pp. 462–5; the British offer was approved by the Cabinet on 25 July, CM 50 (50).

should be open or in secret.[1] Bevin's reply, sent by return, still shows something of the quality of judgement which, when it was not clouded by prejudice—or in this case ill-health—had drawn so many people to turn to him for advice.

He wrote back to Attlee that, if it was necessary to have a debate, it would be better to have it in public, for what was said would certainly not remain secret and Congress, in voting appropriations for the arms bill, would demand to know the conclusions. As for Russia, "with the leaky condition of France, the Russians probably already have all the information they want". The French presented a difficulty. They had now got a government under Pleven which was most helpful to the UK, "the Government I have been personally hoping to see in France for a long time with Moch in the position where we have always hoped to see him" (i.e. as Minister of Defence). Criticism of the French in the House would increase Pleven's difficulties, but this would not be avoided by holding the session in secret. Finally, the strongest reason of all, the British public would expect, in peacetime and with conscription in operation, to know what Parliament was doing.

Bevin concuded by saying that everyone knew that there would have to be a reorganization of Western Europe's defences. As a result of economic difficulties in Europe, the position was not up to war pitch or anything like it. Progress could only be "as fast as our colleagues would allow", but the smaller allies would look to Britain for a lead. So he suggested that Attlee should see Churchill and put the situation to him.

"If he insists, then he must have his debate, but I should offer any information he requires. I would, therefore, say let us risk a public session. Winston may have a sense of responsibility. I do not know. If he has not, neither will he have it in a private session."[2]

It was not until August that the Government was ready to announce its plans to strengthen the country's defences but in the meantime an offer from the USA to move two more bomber groups and a fighter group to UK airfields was accepted without publicity by the Cabinet on 10 July.[3]

6

Bevin returned to the Foreign Office after his holiday at Eastbourne on 27 July and put in an appearance at the House for the defence debate the same day, voting but not speaking. Churchill only failed by one vote to get the secret session he had pressed for, but he spared the Government nothing in an impressive demonstration of the weakness of Western defences. He claimed

[1] Attlee to Bevin, 12 July 1950, FO 800/483/DEF/50/2.
[2] Bevin to Attlee, 13 July 1950, *ibid.*, DEF/50/5.
[3] CM 44 (50).

that, even without calling on the satellites' forces, the Russians might have 80 divisions (25 to 30 of them armoured) for immediate use against Western Europe's 12 (two of them armoured). The force of 180 US heavy bombers stationed in East Anglia was the one real weapon the West possessed and should be protected at all costs; yet the Government had sold 100 jet fighters to Argentina and over 100 to Egypt.

When Shinwell gave figures to show that a quarter of Government expenditure and 7.6% of the national income was going on defence, Churchill denounced the measures proposed as puny. Thwarted in Westminster, he went off to make more trouble for what he regarded as incompetent leaders at the Council of Europe in Strasbourg.

The day that Bevin got back, Lew Douglas had called to see how he was after his rest and to bring a message from Acheson suggesting that it would be a good thing if British and American policies on Formosa could be reconciled. Bevin was unresponsive. He told the Ambassador that he could not deal with Formosa at the moment. It was part of the general problem of China and could not be settled in isolation from other questions such as Hong Kong and Malaya. He thought it best to take up the whole Far Eastern situation at the meetings which it had been arranged for him and Schuman to have with Acheson in Washington in the first half of September.[1]

Bevin's instinct was sound. General MacArthur was about to pay a visit to Formosa, the aftermath of which opened up the possibility of war between the USA and China and raised the question who was making American policy in the Far East, MacArthur or Truman and Acheson.

For the moment Bevin's concern was with the impact of the Korean War on Europe, and he travelled to The Hague and Strasbourg for meetings with his European opposite numbers immediately before the second session of the Council of Europe Assembly opened. This was the first meeting to be attended by a delegation of eighteen Germans. True to form the Assembly opened with an expression of its disapproval of the attitude of the Committee of Ministers. Bevin, who had now become the whipping boy for all the Assembly's frustrations, was directly criticized by name, having given particular offence on this occasion by not waiting for the ceremony at which the newly-built *Maison de l'Europe* in Strasbourg was handed over to the Council for its use. Instead, not feeling well, he had left for London by road accompanied by his doctor.

Churchill again made use of the Assembly as a platform, stealing the show by calling for "the immediate creation of a unified European Army . . . and the creation of a European Minister of Defence". How this was to be effected, who was to recruit and organize such an army and appoint a European Defence Minister remained obscure, but Churchill's gesture caught the headlines and was passed by 89 votes to 5, with most of the Labour Party delegates among the

[1] Bevin's talk with Douglas, 29 July. FO 800/462/FE/50/29.

27 abstentions. The proposal was then sent to a sub-Committee of the General Affairs Committee, where the running was made by Duncan Sandys, Churchill's son-in-law and a zealot in the European cause. On 15 August Bevin sent Dalton, the leader of the British delegation, a cable saying that the question of defending Europe was under discussion with European governments and the USA and was not within the competence of the Council of Europe. The Assembly's resolution appeared "to be designed to discredit Governments and to usurp their responsibilities".

The Labour Government's point of view on the Schuman Plan was put to the Assembly by a Durham miner, Billy Blyton, the only man present at Strasbourg (Dalton claimed) who had ever worked in any of the industries affected by the Plan. Bevin had talked beforehand to Schuman at The Hague and had assured him that he would take no initiative which would upset progress between the six powers who were now engaged in discussions of how the Plan was to work.[1] Monnet, in fact, was less worried by the attitude of the Labour Government than by the counter-proposals put forward at Strasbourg by Macmillan as Deputy Leader of the Tory group. These would have turned the High Authority into no more than a committee of representatives from the coal and steel industries. Monnet wrote to Schuman that the resolution, if carried, would "endanger the success of all our efforts. The British are waging a skilful campaign to sabotage our plan."[2] On the Labour side, the next generation of leaders present at Strasbourg—Callaghan, Healey and Crosland—showed themselves as firmly opposed as Bevin, Attlee, Cripps and Morrison.

Bevin saw as clearly as Churchill that drastic steps needed to be taken to strengthen Europe's defences, and with five years' experience of mobilizing Britain's manpower in wartime he had a very good idea of what was required. But he regarded the Council of Europe as a useless instrument for such a purpose. Nothing effective could be done without the USA. No European Minister of Defence needed to be appointed or new machinery created: it already existed in the Brussels Pact and NATO. All that was needed was the will to take decisions.

Expenditure on defence had always been a problem for the Labour Party. Precisely for that reason, Attlee and Bevin recognized that nothing would make a bigger impression on their European allies—or the rest of the world—than for the British to take the lead in increasing their contribution to NATO. In the previous December (1949) the Cabinet had accepted a figure of £780 m. for the year 1950–51 and agreed that there would have to be an increase. But the effort by the Defence Committee—spread over four meetings in October and November 1949—to frame a three year programme, had ended inconclusively, with the Defence Chiefs arguing for a minimum expenditure of £810 m. a year and the Chancellor declaring that it was impossible to

---

[1] Bevin's report of his talk with Schuman, 1 August 1950. FO 800/462/FR/50/29.
[2] Monnet, pp. 334–5. The letter to Schuman was written on 15 August. Cf. p. 315: "Neither Party wanted any High Authority."

find such a sum without cutting the social services.[1] The election supervened and nothing was done to renew the discussion until the outbreak of fighting in Korea had made it urgent.

It was not so much the war in Korea as the need to reinforce the defences of Western Europe and the UK which forced the issue. As an emergency measure, on 25 July, the day before the defence debate, Cripps proposed a supplementary defence estimate of £100 m., and a week later (1 August) presented the Cabinet with a four-year plan (1951–54) with priority for a total expenditure of £3,400 plus an additional £800 m. for the supply departments. This was on the assumption that the UK would supply £2850 m. of the total £3,400 m. for the defence budget and the USA the balance of £550 m.[2]

Nye Bevan expressed his opposition to a change of policy—abandoning "social and political defence against Communist encroachment in favour of rearmament"—on which he was to resign the following April. Bevin was not present to answer, but Nye received little support. Cripps' proposals were approved and at the next meeting of the Cabinet on 11 August, with Bevin back in his seat, Alexander went on to propose an extension of the length of National Service from 18 months to 2 years and substantial increases (£56 m. a year) in the Services' pay.[3] It was agreed to recall Parliament to discuss defence and subsequently to pass the amendment to the National Service Act through all its stages on 14 September.[4]

Bevin sent advance news of the announcement about National Service to the other Brussels powers urging them to take similar steps, which would increase confidence in Europe and impress both the Americans and the Russians. The Ambassadors were instructed to say that:

"Mr Bevin does not believe that the Russians will venture on aggression against Europe if the European Powers show their determination to fight. The Russian tradition is to push in when they calculate that they can obtain gains without encountering serious opposition. Moreover, their main objective would be to secure European resources *intact*."[5]

Bevin showed something of his old grasp and energy when he sent two memoranda to the Prime Minister urging him to keep an eye on coal exports while he was away in America. This was no time to break contracts with Britain's allies in Europe, as the Coal Board was proposing to do, and he had summoned representatives of the Ministry of Fuel and Board of Trade to a

---

[1] CM 72 (49); Minutes 19th, 20th, 21st, 22nd meetings of the Defence Committee, 19 October; 15 November; 21 November and 25 November 1949.
[2] CM 52 (50).
[3] CM 53 (50).
[4] CM 55 (50) 4 September.
[5] Bevin to British embassies in Brussels Pact countries, 22 August. He sent a copy to Alexander for his visit the following week to Paris, where Bevin wanted him to press the French to take a similar step.

meeting. He was not satisfied with their answers, proposed to raise the question in Cabinet and wanted "Clem" to see that they did not prejudice Britain's good name abroad for the sake of half a million tons out of an annual production of 200 million.[1] He also began to take an interest in German steel scrap exports to the UK, sending a message to say that if he could have assurances from the Federal Government that these exports would continue, it would help him to take a liberal line over lifting restrictions on German industry.[2]

His main concern, however, was to re-establish good relations with the French before he and Schuman met Acheson in Washington. Throughout the summer French opinion had been in a very anti-British mood culminating in the debates at Strasbourg. Talking to Massigli, the French Ambassador after the Council of Europe Assembly had adjourned, Bevin said they must not allow what had been said to damage relations between the two countries, putting much of the blame on Churchill, Reynaud and Spaak, three former prime ministers out of office, all of whom had been playing party politics.

In an effort to restore confidence, Bevin re-stated to Massigli the British position on the two main issues of the Schuman Plan and defence. When the French were ready, the British would meet them and try to conclude an industrial agreement; he was opposed to the Tory resolution Macmillan had moved at Strasbourg and would not take it up. He was quite sure that, if the British did put up a new plan, they would be accused of sabotage: the French could be sure that they would do nothing to make agreement between the Six more difficult. Bevin pointed to the extension of military service as proof that the British were determined to build up a strong defence system for Western Europe and expressed the hope that France would follow suit. They would not, however, let themselves be side-tracked by discussions of a European army or any other novelty which could hold up developments.[3]

The question that worried the French most, however—and Bevin not much less—was whether Europe could be defended without German participation, and if so what form this should take. Bevin had now resumed attendance at the Cabinet and at the meeting on 4 September he reported that the Americans, in pressing for an integrated defence force for Europe, were prepared to contribute increased forces of their own but were also pressing for the integrated force to include a German contingent. At the Defence Committee Bevin had argued that the political—and military—implications of creating a German army before Western Europe was stronger were too far-reaching to be accepted. They were not yet in a position to deal with an attack from East Germany, leave alone Russia. The most he felt it safe to do was to create some form of gendarmerie under the control of the Federal Government for which

[1] Bevin to Attlee, 30 August, FO 800/500/APP/SC/50/1 and 5 September, FO 800/470/APP/IND/50/4.
[2] Kirkpatrick to Steel, 9 September 1950. FO 800/467/GER/50/11.
[3] Bevin's talk with Massigli, 31 August. FO 800/465/FR/50/12.

there was a precedent in the *Bereitschaften* of the East German *Volkspolizei*. This was a suggestion of Adenauer's and Bevin was ready to agree to a force of 100,000 which was believed to be the number in the DDR. But beyond that he was not prepared to go. The Defence Committee also agreed to station in Germany one of the two new armoured divisions which was to become available in March 1951, bringing the British Army of the Rhine up to a strength of two armoured and one infantry division.

Bevin explained his proposals to the Cabinet and was given authority to discuss with them with an open mind when he got to Washington. But when he saw Massigli at a second meeting just before leaving for New York, the Frenchman was pessimistic. His Government was very doubtful about a federal gendarmerie, and even more disturbed about American talk of German units, asking whether this was not too high a price to pay for American willingness to become involved in Europe.[1]

The impression left on the reader of the documents, as it must have been on Bevin at the time, is that despite "the new approach" represented by the Schuman Plan, French distrust of the Germans was still strong and might well become dominant if the need for Germans to be rearmed was pressed too hard. This was the last question Schuman and Monnet wanted to see raised.

In the meantime, MacArthur's visit to Formosa at the end of July had been followed by a communiqué in which Chiang Kai-Shek (as Acheson put it) "crowed" that the foundations had been laid for the joint defence of Formosa and the renewal of military co-operation with the Americans in the fight against Communism. "We are convinced that our struggle against the Communist aggressors will end in final victory."[2] MacArthur followed this up on 26 August by sending a cable to the convention of American Veterans of Foreign Affairs in which he spoke of "a leadership characterized by timidity or vacillation" and declared:

"Nothing could be more fallacious than the threadbare argument by those who advocate appeasement and defeatism in the Pacific that if we defend Formosa we alienate continental Asia."

With some difficulty[3] the President succeeded in getting an order sent to MacArthur directing him to withdraw his message to the Veterans. MacArthur complied, but not before his statement had been published in full and read into the *Congressional Record* on a Republican motion. In a broadcast on 1 September Truman declared that the USA wanted neither Formosa nor any

---

[1] Defence Committee, 1 September 1950. DO (50) 66 and minutes of 17th meeting; CM 55 and 56 (50) 4 and 6 September 1950; Bevin's report on a talk with Massigli at the FO 5 September. FO 800/467/GER/50/10.
[2] Chiang's communiqué, 1 August, in RIIA *Documents 1949–50* pp. 657–8.
[3] According to Acheson, Louis Johnson, the Secretary of Defence, asked him "whether we dare send" such a message. Acheson p. 424.

other part of Asia, and that the 7th Fleet would leave the Formosan Straits at the end of the Korean War. But the belief remained strong that the USA, whatever its President and Secretary of State might say, was on a course which would lead to war with China, a belief which was turned into fact before the year-end.

CHAPTER 22

Washington, September 1950 (German rearmament); Bevin's resignation and death

I

Bevin left London on 7 September for the eighth and, as it turned out, last of his diplomatic Marathons in the USA. Nothing could restore his health, but a quiet if anxious summer following the long rest in hospital enabled him to face the round of meetings that lay ahead. Hugh Dalton, calling at the Foreign Office shortly before he set off, in order to report on the proceedings at Strasbourg, wrote in his Journal:

"I saw E.B. this morning. He is very quiet and has lost some weight, but has his wits about him. 'Neither I nor Churchill can last much longer,' he says. He has been working hard on our relations with China, not believing at all that China is a Russian satellite. He has been in touch with Nehru and using his ambassador in Peking as well as our own to assure them that he doesn't want to attack them or to deny them Formosa when the Korean trouble is over."

Bevin told Dalton that he had sent Franks to urge Acheson to repudiate MacArthur's message to the Veterans, if he could not prevent its delivery. His frankness in speaking to Acheson had at first produced a rude response, but he had stuck to his argument that it would be fatal for the future to antagonize the new China or ignore the feelings of the new India; he had told Franks to go and have not one but a series of talks at the State Department on these lines and he believed this was having some effect.

"Ernie doesn't trust Lew Douglas any more," Dalton added. "He thinks he sees too much of Churchill and tells him too much."[1]

In anticipation of his visit Bevin secured the Cabinet's decision[2] to let him get US agreement, if he could, to a resolution in the UN General Assembly that

---

[1] Dalton's diaries, 2 September 1950.
[2] CM 55 (50) 4 September.

Formosa should revert to China once the pacification of the Far East had taken place. He had also, with Cabinet approval, told Acheson that he would feel bound to vote for the Peking Government taking China's seat on the Security Council if this came up independently of the Korean conflict. However, once the three foreign ministers met in New York the agenda was almost entirely taken up with the repercussions of the Korean war on Europe. The situation in Asia was only touched on directly in a single session on 14 September.

One reason for this was General MacArthur's counter-offensive, which started with a seaborne landing at Inchon on 15 September, and which it was hoped would open a new phase of the war and reverse the disasters with which it had started. A second was the President's announcement, on 9 September, after Bevin and Schuman had left for New York, that he had approved "substantial increases" in the strength of the American forces stationed in Western Europe. During the course of the meeting, Acheson repeated several times that the argument used by Bevin and Schuman in May (that Europe must be defended not liberated, and that the USA must be prepared to fight in any war from the first day) had made a great impression on him and that the President's announcement was a response to this.

In his first talk with Bevin, on 12 September, Acheson went further. The US Government, he told him, favoured the creation of an integrated staff, on the lines of the wartime Supreme Headquarters under Eisenhower which had directed the invasion of Europe. They would, in due course, be prepared to provide an American as C-in-C and in the meantime proposed a Chief of Staff working under the NATO Standing Group. They also considered that the NATO Military Production and Supply Board should be turned into a full-time body. All this Bevin was delighted to hear: taken with the British lead in getting the Europeans to increase their period of military service, it promised action at last to turn NATO into a military organization on the ground and not just on paper.[1]

The stumbling block was the Pentagon's insistence that none of these proposals should be put into effect unless the Europeans on their side agreed, as part of the package, to the inclusion of armed German units in the defence force. Acheson himself, although he did not say so, thought the timing of this requirement a mistake. In his memoirs he writes:

"I agreed with their [the Pentagon's] strategic purpose and objective, but thought their tactics murderous. Once we established the united command and had a planning center, the inevitable logic of mathematics would convince everyone that any plan without Germany was untenable. To insist on requiring the inclusion of Germany at the outset would delay and complicate the whole enterprise."[2]

---

[1] The British record of the Washington talks 12–26 September and Bevin's reports to London are in FO 800/449/CONF/50/27; the US in FRUS 1950 (3) pp. 1108–1301; pp. 207–354. Acheson's personal account is in *Present at the Creation*, pp. 435–45.

[2] *Ibid.*, p. 438.

Acheson, however, was almost alone amongst American leaders in thinking this. The general view was put by McCloy, the US High Commissioner, when he said on the steps of the White House after seeing the President, "In some manner, in some form, the Germans would be enabled, if they want to, to defend their own country". The day Bevin landed in New York, McCloy went on to speak of ten German divisions under German officers. With the Americans being asked to send more troops to Europe themselves, provide money and equipment for the other European forces and take the responsibility for setting up a unified command—all at the same time that they were bearing the burden of the fighting in Korea—it was hard to deny the force of the argument for a German contribution. Suppressing his doubts about the timing, Acheson's job in the tripartite talks was to get his colleagues' agreement.

Bevin's first response was to try and head the Americans off by pressing Adenauer's proposal for a gendarmerie in answer to the East German *Bereitschaften*. "You've got the right idea, me lad," Acheson reports him saying, "but you're going about it the hard way."[1] Schuman, in turn, warned Acheson that if he were asked to accept the need for German units, even in principle, at this stage, the French Assembly would reject what he agreed to. "Everything might go wrong" including the hopes they had built on the Schuman Plan as a new approach to Franco–German relations. He insisted that the French Government would be willing to discuss the formation of German units only when France and the other NATO powers had been re-armed.

Despite the skill which Acheson admired in Schuman's conduct of "a kind of filibuster", the American Secretary of State was not to be put off. At the end of the second day of talks, Bevin cabled back to Attlee:

"At today's meeting Dean Acheson made it quite clear that the President's undertaking to station troops in Europe is dependent on the assembling of a sufficient force to make the whole enterprise successful. . . . In the U.S. view this could not be achieved without some German participation in the defence of Europe."

Bevin believed that if the British and the French were prepared in principle to accept the incorporation of German units in a Western force, then the question of timing and method could be left over for further discussion.

"Consequently, in view of the stakes involved, I propose to give general concurrence."[2]

This was a reversal of Bevin's earlier attitude and the Cabinet, when it heard his report, was not convinced. He was told that he should continue to explore but not at this stage agree in principle to any form of German rearmament which went beyond the discussion of 6 September. Repeating back to him his

---

[1] Acheson, p. 442.
[2] Bevin to Attlee, 13 September. FO 800/449/CONF/50/27.

own argument on that occasion, the Cabinet's response was that it was very important to keep in mind the Russian reaction to proposals for German rearmament while Western defences were still so weak.[1]

When the discussion in New York continued on the 14th, Bevin said little until he heard from London, but it was clear to him that he would have to take a firm line, one way or the other, when the NATO Council met the following day. When the other NATO ministers were confronted with the division between the Americans and the French, they would look to the British to give a lead.

After all he had said against giving arms to the Germans, to turn around and support the Americans was hard for him to swallow and was to be made the subject of reproaches from Dalton, Bevan and other Labour ministers when he got back. Three arguments, however, weighed heavily with him.

The first and most important was that the USA was now prepared to undertake a direct commitment to the defence of Western Europe in advance of the outbreak of war, so that its forces would be involved in any fighting from the first day. This was an unprecedented step for any American government to take. It represented a commitment which Bevin had pursued steadily over several years and without which he believed any plan to defend Europe was impracticable. The outbreak of fighting in the Far East and the fear which this had revived of a Russian attack in Europe made such a commitment more important than ever, and if the price to be paid for it was German rearmament, in Bevin's view "the stakes involved" were so great that it would have to be accepted.

The second argument followed on from this. They were no longer talking —as Churchill had been in the Council of Europe—of German units serving in a European army. Bevin had consistently held that the defence of Europe on a purely European basis was impracticable; hence his efforts to set up an Atlantic alliance and the preference which he had expressed at the London meetings in May for bringing Western Germany into NATO rather than for the sort of European arrangement favoured by the French and represented by the Schuman Plan. In the New York discussions he repeated that

"I thought it was a mistake to lay too much emphasis on the word 'Europe' and to speak in terms of a European army. The United States and Canada, together with other members of the British Commonwealth, would all be involved and the issue at stake would be the defence of the whole free world."[2]

In this context—in effect, the original Western Union of his January 1948 speech—German armed forces would be more acceptable and less dangerous than in a purely European defence force which they might well come to dominate.

---

[1] CM 58 (50) 14 September.
[2] Bevin's report of the tripartite discussion on 12 September. FO 800/449/CONF/50/27

Finally, Bevin was influenced by the argument that a plan for the defence of Western Europe based on the Rhine was politically unacceptable. Dirk Stikker, the Dutch Foreign Minister, told the NATO Council when it met, that such a plan, involving the evacuation or abandonment of three and a half million inhabitants in the north-eastern provinces of Holland, appeared to Dutchmen as "raving lunacy". Bevin agreed with him. They must fight as far to the East as possible and hold any enemy forces outside Western Europe, not leave it to be liberated later. But the problem, as Bevin went on to say, was how to reconcile these political requirements with the forces available: if the military planners were to be asked to draw up a different plan, they would need to be told where the additional forces were to come from.[1]

Summarizing these arguments in three more cables to Attlee which the Prime Minister read out to a hastily summoned Cabinet on the 15th, Bevin pressed for a Cabinet decision by 10.30 New York time, the same day.

"Our country is a leading Power and I cannot take part in discussions without giving some opinion. We must either reject the US thesis or accept it and co-operate with them. Otherwise Great Britain will look weak and indecisive."

Bevin ended by repeating his recommendation that he should give general support in principle to the American proposal, leaving timing and methods to be worked out later.

The Cabinet was in a difficult position but was impressed with the argument that American financial assistance for the UK's new defence programme would be linked with its attitude on German participation. It finally agreed, grudgingly, to let Bevin say that "it was in general agreement to an acceptance in principle of German participation in Western defence", adding that it attached importance to French concurrence and that the first step should be the expansion of the gendarmerie.[2]

When the NATO Council met on the 15th, with news still coming in of the US landing at Inchon and the opening of MacArthur's counter-offensive, the difference between Schuman and Acheson was plainly stated. Bevin held back until the end of the general debate and then sought to reduce the area of disagreement. His starting point was the need to avoid treating the question of Germany in isolation: a bald resolution about German troops would be inviting disaster. They should explain to the public what they were trying to do—to create an integrated force for the defence of the West and not to wait, as in 1914 and 1939, until after the blow had fallen. It should be made clear that the plan embraced providing the necessary equipment and paying for it, as well as setting up a unified command and organizing training. This would deter any aggressor as well as encourage their own people.

[1] Stikker and Bevin in the first session of the NATO Council, 15 September. The British record of the NATO Council meetings, 15–26 September, FO 800/449/CONF/58/27; the American in FRUS 1950 (3) pp. 207–354.
[2] CM 59 (50), 15 September.

This was the essential first step; the question of German participation came second and it should be left to the Occupying Powers to decide how and when an approach should be made to them. In the meantime they needed to press ahead at once with a strong gendarmerie, a question which was separate from that of Germany taking part in a unified defence force and which required an answer at once.

On the 16th, the fifth consecutive day on which the three Foreign Ministers had been engaged, either by themselves or in the NATO Council, in thrashing out how Europe was to be defended, the Americans circulated a paper setting out their proposals, including the appointment of a Supreme Commander. The Council listened to an unprovocative but unambiguous statement by Schuman of the reasons why the French could not agree. Acheson fell back on Bevin's formula, to establish a unified defence force first and then approach German participation. At the afternoon meeting, however, he accepted that there was no point in continuing to discuss the substance of the question for the present and turned to the question of what could be said to the public. Several ministers were in favour of another meeting of the Council in the near future, but Acheson said he did not think it was worthwhile to fix a date.

"Impression left on me by Mr. Acheson's statements", Bevin said in his report to London after the meeting on the 16th, "was that there was a danger of the Council adjourning tonight for good. I therefore intervened to say that I was not at all happy about Mr. Acheson's proposal. . . .

"We must not give the impression that we were throwing in our hand. We had been asked to solve in two days a problem of centuries. We were at an historic moment. What we were trying to do was to build not merely a European army but a world force for peace. We could not afford to throw away that idea. . . ."

Bevin argued that the difference between the American and French points of view was not as great as appeared.

"If it was, then Governments must face the fact and say so. But we should reflect long and deeply before doing that. We should take more time. We could not afford to be driven by our timetable into wrong decisions."[1]

Pearson supported Bevin, and Acheson finally agreed to hold another meeting of the Council after the weekend. It was also agreed to bring over the French and British ministers of defence (Jules Moch, a notable opponent of any form of German rearmament, and Shinwell) to reinforce the tripartite discussions in which, to everyone's relief, General Marshall would appear in place of Louis Johnson as US Secretary of Defence.

---

[1] FO 800/449/CONF/50/27.

The resumed meeting of the Council after the weekend did not reach any conclusion either. A majority was prepared to accept the American proposals for a unified force including German units, but was clearly reluctant to press the French too hard. The same majority accepted Bevin's view that, while agreeing to German participation in principle, they should recognize it would take a considerable time to work out the details and safeguards. From a private talk with Acheson on the 15th, Bevin knew that this was close enough to a realistic timetable to give the Americans what they needed to go ahead with the rest of the package, including the unified force. It remained to secure French assent even to this.

When the three foreign ministers met on their own (18–19 September) to discuss other matters in relation to Germany, they were surprised at how much they were able to agree on, amounting to a programme for removing the Federal Republic from the position of a defeated and occupied enemy to that of an ally. Their communiqué, published on the 19th,[1] contained provisions for setting up "mobile police formations" which, while organized on a Land basis (to satisfy the French), would be at the disposal of the Federal Government, and for handing over to a Ministry of Foreign Affairs responsibility for Germany's relations with other countries. But when the three Defence Ministers, Moch, Marshall and Shinwell joined the three foreign ministers to see if they could get any nearer to agreement on the main issue, German units taking part in a European defence force, they failed to overcome their differences.

With Shinwell bringing reassurance of Cabinet backing, Bevin sharpened up his support for the American proposals. They should go ahead at once with building up an integrated force until it was strong enough to warrant the appointment of a Supreme Commander and Staff, "and it should be agreed now that at that moment German units should be organized.

"We understood French doubts, but considered that when we, like the USA were committing ourselves to station forces permanently on the continent, we were entitled to be clear that all the decisions necessary to the creation of an effective force had been taken. . . . We must not be obliged to argue the question of German participation again at a later stage, after our joint enterprise was under way. The question must be settled now."[2]

Was there not agreement that, while German units should not be created at present, they would be essential at some stage, and could a formula not be found to cover this? The answer was, No. Schuman said they could not agree that ultimately German units would be needed and would not be ready to discuss the question for, say, another nine months. To which Acheson replied

---

[1] Text in RIIA *Documents 1949–50*, pp. 333–6.
[2] Bevin's report on the joint meeting of foreign and defence ministers, 22 September. FO 800/449/CONF/50/27.

that the American proposals to provide troops, equipment and finance for Europe's defence could not be carried out, so long as the German problem remained unsettled.

The one hope appeared to be that time would make agreement easier. This had been Bevin's advice all along and Hervé Alphand, Schuman's assistant, said to Acheson, "Don't press so hard; we will find a solution". Through Joseph Bech, the Foreign Minister of Luxembourg, Acheson learned privately —before Schuman did—that Monnet and Pleven were working on what became the Pleven Plan for a European Defence Community.[1] So it was agreed to put off the meeting of the NATO Defence Committee from 12 to 28 October, in the hope that this would allow some relaxation of positions, and to publish a communiqué outlining the scheme for an integrated NATO force to defend Western Europe under a Supreme Commander.

In terms of any attack which might take place in 1950 or 1951 the discussion was academic. Even if it was decided in October to include German armed units, none would be equipped, trained and ready to go into action before 1952 (actually it turned out to be 1954). It was the psychological impact of the American scheme which was important immediately, in keeping up the morale of the Europeans and convincing both them and the Russians that something serious was being done to provide for Europe's defence. What worried Bevin, as he reported back to London, was the possibility, if no more progress was made in October and the deadlock continued, that the Americans would lose heart. His advice was not to put more pressure on the French—"we should be beating against a brick wall"—but to persuade the Americans to go ahead with the rest of the package, without a commitment in advance on German participation, recognizing that the more they did to build up the American forces stationed on the Continent and to equip the French, the more difficult the French would find it to maintain their opposition.[2]

As in the May meetings in London, Bevin finished more strongly than he began. His Personal Private Secretary, Roderick Barclay, writing to Roger Makins on the 22nd said that in the first week he had been in a jumpy state, alternating between excessive optimism and excessive pessimism.

"He was also, as the Ambassador put it, seeing ghosts everywhere and the first telegram informing him that the Cabinet had not given him the green light to go ahead . . . caused somewhat exaggerated alarm and despondency. The feeling that he had not perhaps got full support from his colleagues at home, combined with a tendency to suspicion . . . of some of the other Foreign Ministers (not always excluding the Americans) was leading him to be so extremely cautious in his utterance at the conference table that there was a good deal of uncertainty as to what his position really was. Even when he had received full authority from the Cabinet, Bob and I had the greatest difficulty in persuading him to make a clear and positive statement."

---

[1] Acheson, p. 444.
[2] Bevin's report of 23 September. FO 800/449/CONF/50/27.

But the atmosphere now, Barclay continued, was much better. Bevin and Acheson were going along together on most questions and combined "today ... in expressing their great indignation at the tiresomeness of the French about Germany". He concluded that the Secretary of State had stood up to the programme surprisingly well and had been in better shape physically and mentally than at any other conference during the past year or so. After a tiring day he was taking off a party of Americans, including the Achesons, to see the Sadlers Wells Ballet perform at the Metropolitan.[1]

All these discussions had taken place to the accompaniment of bulletins from the battle front in Korea where a real and not a hypothetical war was taking place. The first two months of the war had gone badly for the West, MacArthur being forced to give ground continually until only the south-east corner of the peninsula was still held by the UN forces. The success of MacArthur's counter-attack, however, which by the day Bevin left, 29 September, had led to the recapture of Seoul and the headlong retreat of the North Koreans was a great fillip to Bevin and the others who had been labouring to create a means of collective security, in face of the scepticism of those who thought it unnecessary and the faint-heartedness of those who believed it would never work.

Before he left he had the chance to express this to the UN General Assembly. Writing to Miss Saunders on the day he had to go out to Lake Success, 25 September, he sounded very weary:

"I am feeling in a bad way today, my breath is bad. I went to Hyde Park yesterday. The weather was fine but it was very cold. I think this has upset me.

"I am speaking at the Assembly this afternoon. Then I shall not have to go down there again, Younger takes over. . . . We leave here on Friday and I am longing to be home."

Nonetheless, in his final appearance in a body in which he had fought some of his earliest battles with the Russians in 1946, the encouragement he felt triumphed over his physical condition. Admitting that the year before he had been pessimistic about the future of the United Nations, he declared his satisfaction that the UN Organization

"Has proved itself capable of doing what many doubted whether it could do—it has displayed the unity and determination required to take prompt and effective action against aggression."

When the UN General Assembly met on 20 September, Acheson put forward a set of proposals (known as the "Uniting for Peace" resolution) for strengthening the capacity of the United Nations to take the sort of collective action which had saved Korea even if the Security Council was paralysed by the veto. In his reply, Vyshinsky put the whole blame for the danger to peace

[1] Barclay to Makins. FO 800/511/US/50/46.

and the conflict in Korea on the North Atlantic Powers who were engaged in fomenting war while the USSR was devoted to "peaceful, productive and creative work". In order to avert war he called on the Assembly to prohibit the use of A-weapons, promote a pact between the five major Powers and call for a reduction of armed forces by one-third in 1950.

It fell to Bevin to answer Vyshinsky, and he did so with conviction. Ever since 1945, he said, the major Powers had been trying to settle Europe, but it became clear that nothing would satisfy the Russians which did not place Eastern Europe under regimes subservient to Moscow. They had encountered the same difficulty in Germany, where the Russians had no use for a unified Germany that was free to choose its own form of government. He spoke of the threat of another act of aggression, Korea style, taking place in Germany and argued that the Western powers had no option but to build up their military forces to resist the threat from Russia. He came out strongly in favour of Acheson's proposals and argued that resolutions in the UN, as proposed by Vyshinsky, could never achieve disarmament. That would only come with confidence, and confidence could never grow in the atmosphere produced by Russia's use of the Communist Fifth Column to create every sort of difficulty for other states "on the assumption that if enough chaos is created, it is possible to seize power".

"Then there is the Soviet proposal for a one-third reduction in armaments.

"Well, really. Look at the facts. The Soviet army is larger than the armies of all Europe and their armaments are greater than all of ours put together.

"This makes it look as though talk of peace petitions and peace campaigns is really a kind of propaganda barrage to weaken the victim before launching the attack."

If the Soviet Union was serious about reaching agreement with the other major powers, Bevin declared, it could use the opportunity afforded by the case of Austria to prove its sincerity. A year ago they had been on the verge of agreement, only to encounter a deadlock deliberately engineered by the Russians.

"If the Soviet Delegate was prepared to act in accordance with his proclaimed willingness to reach agreement, we could have a treaty tomorrow.

"In the meanwhile, no amount of calling us warmongers or hurling insults at us will divert us. . . . We are determined, if necessary, to fight to the end for the liberty for which we have struggled so hard and which we are resolved to defend."[1]

After some modification in committee, Acheson's proposals were accepted on 3 November by 52 votes to 5, with two abstentions, more than a month after Bevin had left for home.

By then the course of the Korean War had plunged the UN into a new crisis, the origins of which went back to the time he was still in New York. Once the

[1] Bevin's speech to the General Assembly, 25 September 1950.

UN counter-offensive was launched and carried the fighting back towards the North, the question which opened up was the future of Korea and whether MacArthur's forces should cross the 38th Parallel which had been the entirely artificial boundary between the rival Korean states since the US and Russian withdrawal in 1949. If the UN forces carried the war into North Korea, what would be the reaction of the Russians and more particularly of the Chinese, whose territory marched with the northern frontier of Korea across the Yalu River? Would either intervene?

During August the Chinese, with Russian support, had started up a diplomatic offensive against the Americans, accusing them of aggression against the new China, not only by preventing the liberation of Formosa and fomenting war in Korea but by air attacks on Chinese territory across the Yalu. Nehru, claiming to represent Asian opinion and to know what the Chinese were thinking through the Indian Ambassador in Peking, was emphatic that any move across the 38th Parallel would be taken by the Chinese as direct provocation and would lead to an extension of the war. Opinion in the American administration and among America's allies was divided.

Simply to return to the *status quo* before the attack, seemed to many, including Bevin, an inconclusive way of carrying out the Security Council's original recommendation of 25 June—to repel the armed attack and to restore international peace and security in the area.

While the Americans were still weighing the balance of risks, Bevin agreed to the British taking the lead in sponsoring a resolution in the Assembly recommending that "all appropriate steps be taken to ensure conditions of stability *throughout Korea*", and that elections be held under the auspices of the UN "for the establishment of a unified, independent and democratic government in the sovereign state of Korea".

To his disappointment Bevin was unable to get the support of Nehru who held to the view that the Chinese were not bluffing and that, if UN forces crossed the 38th Parallel, they would intervene. However, the resolution was adopted in the General Assembly on 7 October by 47 votes to 5, with 8 abstentions. It implied the crossing of the 38th Parallel without saying so, and any doubt was removed when, the day after it was adopted (on 7 October), MacArthur pushed his troops across into North Korean territory. What the resolution had failed to make clear was *how* its objective of "a unified, independent and democratic government" was to be achieved, only that "all appropriate steps be taken". It was left to General MacArthur to strip away its ambiguities and to announce, on 9 October, that unless the North Koreans surrendered at once, "I shall proceed to take such military action as may be necessary to enforce the decrees of the United Nations". This was certainly not what the sponsors of the resolution of 7 October had meant; nor can the resolution by itself be regarded as leading inevitably to Chinese intervention; but it contributed to that extraordinary muddle of misunderstanding and misjudgement out of which burst the near disasters of November and December.

3

On his return from UNO, Bevin went straight from the boat to the Labour Party conference which had opened at Margate on 2 October 1950. Many of those present were taken aback by his appearance and thought it likely that they were seeing him at Conference for the last time.

But if Bevin was physically reduced, he still had the instinct to square up to those who disagreed with him. His first appearance at a Party Conference had been in 1917 when as a brash but even then supremely confident young trade union delegate he had attacked Labour's decision to join the Lloyd George coalition. He had never gone out of his way to win over Conference. Before the War, with the Transport Workers' block vote in his pocket, he had rarely needed to and did not care who took offence when he reminded delegates of their dependence on the trade unions. In the ten years since he had become a minister, he had gained much in authority, but more often than not had intervened to bring the discussion down to earth and remind delegates of things many of them would have preferred not to hear. Even if they disagreed with him or disliked his manner, however, most delegates were impressed by the consistency of his views in office and the bluntness with which he expressed them. Some harsh things had been said about Ernie Bevin in Labour Party Conferences but never that he was a trimmer, courted popularity or quit in face of opposition. It was hard to think of a Labour Government without him—and harder still to think who could take his place as Foreign Secretary.

This time Shinwell moved acceptance of the Executive's report on the international situation which claimed that the UN action in Korea was a shining example of collective security. He placed the responsibility for the deterioration in international relations on the Soviet Union and put the argument for the Labour Government's decision to raise defence expenditure to 10% of the national income and extend conscription from 18 months to two years on the grounds that the way to avert war was to provide an adequate deterrent against aggression. The Executive Report and Shinwell's speech were a vindication of the stand Bevin had made in insisting that Labour in office could not contract out of the conflicts which divided the post-war world, but must act in common with other nations willing to organize and defend the non-Communist world.

It was left to Bevin to wind up the debate and to answer those who were still not convinced and had moved a counter-resolution calling for renewed efforts to create friendly relations with the Soviet Union, outlaw the bomb and limit armaments. He deliberately drew attention to the fact that it was the second time he had argued the case for collective security in a Labour Party

814

conference in Margate, a characteristic reference to the occasion which had earned him more criticism in the party than anything else, his attack on George Lansbury for failing to give a lead in resistance to Mussolini's attack on Abyssinia. They had failed to halt aggression then and war had followed in 1939. "It should have been stopped in 1935." This time they were not going to make the same mistake.

So by way of the Berlin blockade, he came to Korea and asked his audience what any of them would have done if they had been in the Government and been faced with what happened in Korea, "a deliberate organization of aggression".

"Because the tanks the North Koreans used were not made in North Korea, they were sent there. It was intended to wipe out South Korea and then present the United Nations with a *fait accompli*."

The Security Council did the only thing they could do and said the time had come to resist. But to be able to resist meant building up a combined force with other like-minded peoples in advance.

"Do you think we like it? Do you think, after all the years of fighting we have done in the Labour Movement in the hope of getting a peaceful world, that we like having to do it? Is there any Minister who likes going down to the House of Commons to ask for £3,600 million for war? The man who would do that for fun would go to hell for pleasure. . . .

"Is there any delegate in this Conference who would go back to his constituents and say we are doing wrong in paying the proper insurance premium now for our security? We blamed the Conservatives for knowing Hitler was on the move and not making adequate preparation . . . because they would not go in for collective security. . . . We are in office now and shall we refuse to do what we called upon others to do which would have prevented the 1939 war if they had only done it?"

He was not going to allow those who opposed the Executive's report to claim a monopoly of the love of peace. Everyone wanted peace: the question was how to get it.

"Can you lay down your arms and be safe? China had no arms and Japan walked in, Abyssinia had no arms and Mussolini walked in . . . Czechoslovakia had no arms and a *coup d'état* was carried out one evening and their liberty was gone. Inside that iron curtain now stretching from the Baltic to the Black Sea, there is no freedom. Do you want that to be extended? Would you sit down and let it be extended? I could not. I could not be a member of a party that decided that was their policy, and I do not believe you could either."[1]

It was not a great speech; but it had the unmistakable ring of sincerity if only because Bevin no longer had the force to do more than say, without artifice, what he believed and had argued passionately to convince the Party of for

---

[1] Labour Party Conference Report 1950, pp. 146–50, 5 October 1950.

more than five years. There was no standing ovation or vote of thanks; and the argument about the character of a Labour Government's foreign policy was to be renewed, but the card vote showed more convincingly than anything else could—by 4.8 million votes to 800,000—that in his generation he had won it.

In fact most of October passed without undue alarm over the situation in Korea. Bevin was far more concerned with the problems surrounding Germany's part in the defence of the West and the new development of the Pleven Plan than with the Far East. So great was the secrecy surrounding the Plan's launch that Acheson was warned to say nothing to the French Minister of Defence, Jules Moch, or the French Minister of Finance, who were in Washington for talks with the Americans and neither of whom had been told of it. Nothing was said to the British either, before Pleven's announcement in the National Assembly on 24 October. Like the Schuman Plan, Pleven's was seen in both countries as a further French move to capture the initiative taken by the British in promoting the Atlantic concept with a French version of the organization of Western Europe. This would not reject the North Atlantic Pact but establish a separate continental group within it under French leadership and without British participation.

The plan called for the appointment of a European Minister of Defence responsible either to the Council of Europe or some other new elected body, with a European Defence Council of ministerial rank and a single European defence budget. The states taking part in the scheme would contribute units from their national armies to form a European army. These units would merge at the lowest possible level, perhaps that of the battalion; Germany would be allowed to contribute such units but there would be no German national army or defence minister. The French government also wished to make agreement on the Schuman Plan a prior condition of carrying out these new proposals. The Assembly accepted them by a 3–2 majority and, by 402 votes to 168, endorsed the Government's determination not to permit the re-creation of a German army.

Bevin had not liked Churchill's idea of a European Army or a European Minister of Defence, believing that the only solid basis on which to proceed was the Atlantic Pact. He liked it no better when taken up by the French. He described the Pleven Plan as unrealistic[1], a view shared by the Americans. Acheson recorded that it caused "consternation and dismay" in Washington and General Marshall regarded it as "hopeless".[2] Apart from the impracticability of the proposals—a European Defence Minister and budget before a European Government or federation had been formed—there was the obvious objection of the delays which they would create. Franks told Acheson he thought Schuman and Monnet were sincere in their belief in the plan, but was

---

[1] Bevin's talk with Van Zeeland, chairman of the NATO Council 25 October 1950, FO 800/483/NA/50/11.
[2] Acheson, pp. 458–9.

not sure about the motives of other members of the French Government.[1] Moch had certainly left a strong impression on General Marshall that he was looking for any means to put off a decision on German participation and might well think he had found it in the new proposals, which would take months of negotiation to work out and afford endless opportunities for further delay.[2]

Two further factors complicated the situation. One was the German reaction to the Pleven Plan, which was highly critical. Politicians and press protested at the contrast between the requirement that Germans should share in the defence of Europe and the refusal to treat German units in a European army on equal terms with those of other nations. If German participation was essential to Europe's defence, so the argument ran, then the occupation regime should be ended and German sovereignty fully restored as a condition of German willingness to rearm.

The second factor was the opening of a new Communist campaign in favour of the demilitarization of Germany, launched on 20 October at a meeting of the Eastern bloc in Prague. This was followed by a Soviet note to the Western Powers (3 November) proposing a quadripartite conference with this as its agenda. Elections had taken place in East Germany on 15 October, producing official figures of 98.539% voting and 99.719% of the vote going to the single list of candidates. The constant theme of the election campaign and of the new Government led by Otto Grotewohl was reunification linked with demilitarization, only prevented by the determination of the West not to listen. The impact of the Soviet invitation to talk was most immediately evident in France, where those eager to delay German rearmament joined the Communists and others eager to restore relations with the East in arguing that the prospect of Germans in arms again had so alarmed the Russians that they were willing to compromise with the West or, if the West refused to talk, to resort to war.[3]

When the NATO Defence Ministers met in Washington at the end of October, Jules Moch presented the Pleven Plan and did so with such intransigence as to unite all but the Belgian and Luxembourg ministers in rejecting it. Acheson instructed the US Ambassador in Paris to inquire urgently of Pleven and Schuman if "Moch's quasi-dictatorial intransigence" reflected the French Government's real views and to make clear that, if it did, there was little hope of agreeing on a plan for the defence of Western Europe. Bevin felt that the French were so hostile towards the British it would be far better for him to say nothing and leave it to the Americans to bring the French round to a more reasonable frame of mind. At the Defence Committee on 8 November, Alexander reported the frustration of the NATO Defence

[1] Conversation between Franks, Acheson and George Perkins, 25 October. FRUS 1950 (3) pp. 404–6.
[2] Marshall's talk with Moch, 16 October, *ibid.*, p. 384.
[3] Bevin reported to the British Ambassador in Paris that the French Ambassador had been to see him to urge that the Soviet proposals could not be ignored. The Western Powers must make some response, 23 October, FO 800/465/FR/50/19.

Committee, with the French refusing to consider the inclusion of German units in NATO forces and the Americans refusing to go ahead with the rest of the package, including a US Commander, until they did. In a moment of exasperation Attlee demanded why they should not ask the French outright whether they intended to fight or had already made up their minds to give in. Reversing their normal roles, Bevin told him: "Not yet." They should wait and see what results American pressure would produce.[1]

The Americans hoped Bevin could influence the French Socialists, but a talk he had with Guy Mollet, regarded as the rising man in the Socialist Party, ended with anger on both sides. Mollet was very critical of the Socialists' MRP partners, whose plans for European federation (he said) were based on three states with Christian Democratic governments hostile to socialism, Italy, France and West Germany. Irritated by Mollet's partisan spleen, Bevin told him he had done his best to maintain good relations with Bidault and Schuman, and that he had to work with any French Foreign Secretary, whatever his party. If there was a third world war, he believed it would be due to the Western Powers' indecision and lack of preparedness, for which the French were responsible. Mollet was not impressed, and when Bevin angrily asked him if he did not believe in the reality of the Soviet threat and the danger of war, retorted "No, he did not".

"You and your friends" Bevin declared, "are as bad as the Chamberlain Government." "He is no friend of ours", he told his Private Secretary when Mollet left, and he would have no more to do with him.[2]

At least the British need not hold up their efforts while the French prevaricated. During October the Ministry of Defence put up a revised version of the rearmament plans; cutting the time from four to three years and increasing the amount from £3,440 m to £3,800 m. Bevin combined with the Chancellor to say this was too much, at least without a promise of increased aid from the USA, but finally agreed to £3,600 m. spent over the years 1951–54. The Cabinet accepted this in November as the British contribution when the NATO Defence Ministers met. The Chiefs' of Staff aim was to produce a British Army of ten regular and twelve Territorial divisions; re-equip the RAF with 2,450 modern aircraft by 1954 and provide the Navy with nine or ten new aircraft carriers.[3]

Bevin had originally planned to visit Germany in November. On his 1949 visit he had said he wanted to come back and speak to the Ruhr miners. Adenauer responded with an invitation to address the *Bundestag*, the first visitor to be asked to do so. Bevin was then seized with doubts: what could he say except platitudes and what would the French and the Dutch think when the first foreign parliament he addressed was the German? The visit was in fact

---

[1] Defence Committee, Minutes of 21st meeting, 8 November 1950.
[2] Note of talk between Bevin and Mollet, 31 October 1950. FO 800/465/FR/50/20.
[3] Defence Committee minutes, 19th and 20th meetings, 16 and 25 October; CM 72 (50), 9 November; CM 74 (50) 16 November. Bevin was present at all four meetings.

beyond Bevin's physical capacity and he finally cancelled it, as he had earlier his attendance at the Rome meeting of the Committee of Ministers of the Council of Europe.[1]

In the middle of November the Council of Europe was discussed in all the principal parliaments of Western Europe, in London, Paris, Rome and Bonn.

When he came to wind up the debate in the Commons, Bevin put the blame for the failure of the Council of Europe on the European Movement, which had insisted on forcing the pace of integration before Europe was strong enough to stand on its own, and on ministers out of office who had used the Assembly as a platform to attack their Governments. After Churchill and Bevin had finished calling each other saboteurs, the latter came back to the view which had guided his policy throughout: "Ever since we have been in office we have striven to bring together not only Europe, but North America as well." The Atlantic Pact was what mattered, more than anything else, and they could not now be diverted to a European Army: "The less must be absorbed in the greater."

The French debate, which followed the next day, brought strong criticism of the British, with at least one ex-Premier, Paul Reynaud, urging that Europe should go ahead and unite without Britain, and on 19 November the Standing Committee of the Council of Europe Assembly voted by 11 votes to 10 in favour of such action. The margin was too narrow, however, and a debate in the Assembly itself on 22–23 November registered the defeat of the federalists by the functionalists.

Bevin was irritated but not impressed by the French attacks. In practice the one chance of making any provision for the defence of Europe in the critical period of the next one or two years was by finding a formula which would enable the French plan for a European Army to be by-passed and serious efforts concentrated in the NATO framework. He told Stikker, the Dutch Foreign Minister, that his preference for NATO was "not because I was anti-European but because I did not believe Europe alone could ever be strong enough to defend itself." It was a practical, not a sentimental question. "If it would please the French, I had no objection to recognizing the special ties which bound the European countries together; but the organization itself must, I was convinced, be Atlantic."[2]

Bevin had already proposed a meeting with the French and Americans at official level to decide on a reply to the Soviet note. But he told Attlee he thought they should not be in a hurry. It was essential that before they met the Russians they should have reached agreement on the defence of Western Europe, which in effect meant on how the Germans were to take part in it.

---

[1] The correspondence is in FO 800/467/GER/50/14–17.

[2] Bevin's talk with Stikker at the FO, 23 November. FO 800/483/NA/50/12. Bevin had made the same point at the Cabinet meeting on 30 October. If the French could persuade the other continental powers to set up a European Army, the British should not oppose it; but they should not join it or promote it, CM 69 (50), views again endorsed by the Defence Committee on 27 November (minutes of 22nd meeting).

Unless they had settled that first they would be in a very weak negotiating position.[1] His own hopes rested on the NATO deputies producing a plan along the lines suggested by Acheson, the French agreeing to negotiations starting on arming German units while discussion of the Pleven Plan continued.[2] By the end of November the Deputies had produced the compromise Bevin was looking for, the Spofford Plan[3]—when the Americans ran into disaster in Korea.

4

At the end of October, Chinese troops had appeared in force on the Korean side of the Yalu River (the boundary between the two countries) and had thrown back American and South Korean troops. General MacArthur, however, refused to read the signs and the US Chiefs of Staff and Government in Washington failed to impose restraints on him. Instead of seeking by diplomatic means, as Bevin urged, a cease-fire and a demilitarized zone along the Korean–Chinese border, or a withdrawal to the 40th parallel which the British COS favoured,[4] MacArthur was still bent upon the conquest of North Korea by force of arms, ignoring the danger of a full-scale intervention by the Chinese of which there had been plenty of warning from Peking.

On 26 November, well-equipped regular troops of the Chinese Army in overwhelming numbers launched a major attack on MacArthur's forces and drove them back in what soon turned into a headlong retreat. The General was a master of publicity and poured out from his Tokyo HQ a stream of messages exculpating himself from all blame, placing the responsibility on those who had interfered with his freedom of action and calling for immediate reinforcements. The uproar to which this led in the USA, the climax of the long and bitter quarrel between the parties over US policy towards China, added to the alarm caused by the news from Korea. Outside the USA the alarm was less over the defeat inflicted on American troops than over the prospect of the much feared and talked about third world war. A more sophisticated version was that the USA was in danger of getting into a war with the wrong adversary in the wrong place, leaving Europe undefended against the Russians.

President Truman added greatly to these fears at a press conference on 30 November when he said that he would take whatever steps were necessary to meet the military situation, and in face of the question, "Does that include the A-bomb?", added that it included "every weapon that we have". Had there

---

[1] Bevin to Attlee, 22 November. FO 800/503/SU/50/4.
[2] See the talk between Spofford and Hoyer–Millar of the Foreign Office, 8 November. FRUS 1950 (3) pp. 435–6.
[3] The draft of the Spofford Plan (30 November 1950) is to be found in FRUS 1950 (3) pp. 501–5.
[4] These views were endorsed by the Cabinet on 13 November. CM 73 (50).

been "active consideration of its use?" "There has always been active consideration of its use." Other questions, unconnected with the bomb, again produced the correct answer that the question, what weapons to use in relation to particular targets, was one for the theatre commander to settle. Within a few minutes a summary of Truman's replies sent round the world a garbled version that the President was considering using the A-bomb and that the decision would be left to the discretion of MacArthur.

At the time, the House of Commons was engaged in a two-day debate on the international situation which Bevin opened on 29 November. He had no answer, however, to the questions which everyone was asking, what the Chinese intended to do and whether the USA was going to let itself be drawn into a full-scale war with them. The House was restless and not at all satisfied with his assurance that he had been in touch with Washington: MacArthur appeared to have gone his own way with scant regard either for Washington or the UN.

Concern turned to outcry when the summary version of Truman's press conference was received on the second day of the debate. There had been a growing loss of confidence in American leadership and its ability to control MacArthur, and this now reached crisis point with the report that the use of the A-bomb was being considered. There was a strong demand, particularly amongst Labour back-benchers, that the Prime Minister should fly at once to Washington.

Attlee's decision to do so, taken at an emergency Cabinet meeting, and Truman's prompt acceptance, were received with relief throughout the non-Communist world. No one was more pleased than Nehru who had continued to urge on Bevin the importance of bringing the Chinese into the UN and the danger of their intervention in Korea, despite the shock to Indian opinion of the Chinese invasion of Tibet.[1] Even more striking was the suggestion from the French, with whom relations had been considerably strained, that Pleven and Schuman should come to London for a talk with Attlee before he left for Washington. It was evident that he was going as more than the spokesman of the UK and even the USA's allies in NATO—that it was hoped he would represent to America the fears and doubts of all the states which had supported the original decision by the UN to resist the North Korean attack.

The possibility that Bevin might accompany Attlee was ruled out by his inability to face the long journey by air. But he took part in the discussion with the French on 2 December.[2] Apart from the fear of the A-bomb being used, Pleven expressed anxiety at reports that the USA intended to get the UN to declare China an aggressor and use this as authority to bomb targets in Manchuria. He was also very worried about China's support for Ho Chi Minh in Indo–China and was under strong pressure from French public opinion to

---

[1] Cf. Bevin's talk with the Deputy Indian Foreign Minister on 15 November and the message which Krishna Menon brought Bevin on 21 November. FO 800/462/FE/50/41 & 42.
[2] The British record is in FO 800/465/FR/50/23 & 24.

engage in talks with the Chinese. For his part, Attlee was struck by the success of the Russians—without moving a man—in embroiling the West deeply in the Far East. He insisted that the trap into which they must not fall was that of committing the bulk of the West's available forces against China and paying too little regard to what might happen elsewhere.

After lunch, Attlee brought the discussion round to Europe as the crucial area, and the differences over German rearmament and a European Army which had driven the French and British still further apart. The compromise worked out by the NATO Deputies—the Spofford Plan[1]—appeared to offer a way forward. It would allow the process of raising German units to start, perhaps on the basis of brigade groups rather than divisions, without waiting for the outcome of the discussions on a European Army which the French would be free to invite other European governments to take part in. Were the French prepared to accept such a compromise?

The most Schuman could say was that they might accept the Spofford Plan in principle, but hold up its implementation, at least until they had explored the Russian suggestion of a four-power meeting. Attlee asked, with a touch of asperity, how the creation of a European Army would make a difference: why should the Russians not make *this* a pretext for abandoning the proposed talks? Or, Bevin added, the appointment of a Supreme Commander which the French were so anxious to see made? Another hour of talk brought the French no nearer to convincing the British that their arguments—including those for a European Army—were more than pretexts for postponing any sort of decision.

Attlee finally reached Washington on 4 December. In two long cables sent the day before, the US Embassy in London briefed the President and Secretary of State on the mood in Britain. The features they selected are illuminating: the fear that events were out-pacing British control and that the USA might reach a point of no return beyond which diplomacy would give way to war; the desire, shared by Conservatives (including Churchill and Eden) as well as by Labour, to explore every chance of a settlement with Russia; concern over the impact on the economy of the increased arms programme; a great desire to end the UK's dependence on the USA; "a yearning in all quarters 'to get the U.K. out of the queue with Denmark and Luxembourg'"; misgivings over the swing to the Right in the recent American mid-term elections and the threat this might pose to the steadiness of US policy; anxiety about the divergence between US and UK policy towards China; doubts as to the wisdom of rearming Germany and a feeling that America had been precipitate in pushing this so hard and arousing French resistance.[1]

Truman and Acheson showed themselves very willing to discuss the situation with Attlee. Six meetings were held between the principals, and a number of others, for example on economic matters, between other members

---

[1] FRUS (3) pp. 1698–1706.

of the two teams.[1] The Labour Party appears to have convinced itself that Attlee's visit to Washington was crucial in preventing the use of the A-bomb. This is a myth. The misunderstanding over Truman's remarks in his press conference had been cleared up before Attlee went and not much remained to be done to satisfy the British that the Americans were not seriously considering the use of atomic weapons. These figured very little in the discussions. Apart from learning what was going on in Korea, the most important objective for the British was to persuade the USA that it should be prepared to negotiate with the Communist Government in Peking, to consider admitting it as a member of the United Nations, and to include the future of Formosa as well as Korea on the agenda to be discussed with Peking. The Americans saw such a programme as starting on the slippery slope of appeasement; declared it to be politically impossible to put to Congress or the American people, and insisted, as Acheson put it, that no Administration could hope to persuade Americans to follow a vigorous policy of resistance to aggression on one ocean front, in Europe, while accepting the success of aggression and a policy of withdrawal on the other, in Asia.

Acheson said that there would not be many Americans who would advise the President to embark on an all-out war against China, but they were pessimistic about the possibilities of negotiation. He called it the worst moment to negotiate with the Communists since 1917. Nor were the Americans, whatever their private thoughts about MacArthur, prepared to accept their Allies' wish to have a greater say in the conduct of the Korean campaign. A war could not be run by a committee and as long as they were supplying the men and the means to carry it on, they would listen to the views of their allies, but would make their own decisions.

If all this was disappointing to the British, the Americans in their turn were irritated by the disposition of their allies to be more concerned with the possible consequences than with the fact of the defeat suffered by the US forces and the United Nations in Korea, and to write it off as a loss lest the USA should be diverted from the more important task of securing Western Europe against the Russians. On the other hand, when the Americans turned to Europe, they found the British unresponsive to their suggestions that the UK should increase its rearmament programme and inclined to make a great deal of the difficulties America's own rearmament and stockpiling were creating for them. Acheson, missing Bevin, described Attlee as a Job's comforter and his thought "as a long withdrawing, melancholy sigh".

Nonetheless at the end of four days of discussion, it was the general opinion—shared by Acheson—that the British and American positions were substantially closer than at the beginning. Speaking at the National Press Club, Attlee promised that the British would remain in Korea as long as the

[1] Attlee's brief for the talks, 2 December 1950 is in FO 800/481/MIS/50/9. The British record of the talks is in FO 800/445/COM/50/14; the US record in FRUS (3) pp. 1706–88. Acheson's personal account is on pp. 480–85 of *Present at the Creation*.

Americans and had no intention of following a policy of appeasement. At their fourth meeting Acheson assured Attlee, with the President nodding agreement, that "the UK was the only real ally on whom they could rely."

In a private report to Bevin, Attlee said that more was forthcoming over the table (for example, on the A-bomb) than appeared in the communiqué. The reason for reticence was domestic politics and heavy attacks on Acheson personally. This ruled out specific agreements in writing and meant a strong emphasis on a tough line towards China. Feeling was too strong to allow the British to press for the admission of China to the UN but he believed he had at least shaken the American Chiefs of Staff on the risks of war with China, even a limited war. On other matters he was well content with the result. As soon as the Spofford Plan could be put through NATO, the Americans would appoint Eisenhower (for the second time) as Supreme Commander in Europe and hoped this would break the deadlock. Attlee concluded that the Americans accepted the UK as their principal ally with whom, in the last resort, they would be prepared to continue the struggle together and alone. They had made progress on economic matters too. "The U.K. was lifted out of the European queue and we were treated as partners, unequal no doubt in power but still equal in counsel."[1]

The House of Commons would have liked a more specific commitment to consult on the use of the A-bomb. But Attlee was satisfied and in a broadcast to the nation said "there was no ground whatever for any apprehension that this weapon would be used lightly or wantonly".[2] The announcement, immediately after Attlee's return, that the UK—alone of the sixteen OEEC countries —had reached a position in which it required no more Marshall aid[3] was an added fillip for those who longed to see the UK more of an equal partner and less a dependant of the USA.

It was left to Bevin, remembering how desperate the situation had looked when Marshall's offer was made three years before, to send the former Secretary of State a personal message.

"I sat in the House of Commons yesterday and heard the Chancellor announce the suspension of Marshall aid, and had you been there I should have wanted to go and say to you with a full heart 'thank you'."[4]

5

The two governments had regained confidence in each other and for the moment the crisis was overcome. But its underlying causes remained: the war

---

[1] Attlee to Bevin 10 December. FO 800/517/US/50/57.
[2] *The Times*, 18 December 1950.
[3] This did not of course apply to American aid under MAP in carrying out the British re-armament programme.
[4] Bevin to Marshall, 14 December 1950. FO 800/517/US/50/58.

in Asia and the fear of war in Europe. As soon as the Americans suffered another setback at Chinese hands, in January, the crisis was renewed. For the rest of the time Bevin remained Foreign Secretary, the Atlantic alliance with which he was identified came under increasing strain. The Cabinet was divided—and individual ministers divided in their own minds, as Kenneth Younger's and Hugh Dalton's diaries show—between the desire to stop the war in Korea turning into a war with China and, if need be, to dissociate Britain from American measures threatening to do that, and the desire to avoid disrupting the alliance on which so much depended. This would have been a difficult situation for any Foreign Secretary to handle; it was doubly so for a man as ill and physically handicapped as Bevin.

So far the combined efforts of the Prime Minister and his staff at the Foreign Office had helped Bevin get through what was officially seen as a bad patch, preserving appearances and not admitting how ill he was. This was made easier by the fact that he still had good days as well as bad and that on the good days he still showed something of his former grasp of affairs with which he had been familiar for so long, and could still make an effective speech in the UN or the Party Conference, even if it was no longer delivered with the old vigour and assertiveness. But after the December crisis nothing could be the same again. The House's impatience with Bevin's explanations and the demands for action to prevent the situation getting out of hand, stripped away appearances. If the Foreign Secretary was not fit enough to make the journey, then he must step down and the Prime Minister must take his place.

The fact that for more than five years Attlee had left Bevin virtually a free hand and not interfered in foreign policy made it all the more striking when he did feel it necessary to step in. This was underlined when Attlee, without Bevin, proved able to cope with the crisis sufficiently well to restore confidence between the allies and allay the immediate anxieties. Bevin was no longer felt, and—a sad blow to his confidence—could no longer feel himself to be indispensable as Foreign Secretary, and with that the main reason was removed for trying to prolong a situation which was increasingly seen as unsatisfactory.

The change was not abrupt. For one thing Attlee had no better idea who could succeed Bevin than after the election. Bevin still continued to take part in Cabinet discussions, to send instructions to Franks and exchange messages with Acheson. Attlee went out of his way to send him a personal report on his December talks in Washington[1] before reporting to the Cabinet, and he wound up the foreign affairs debate which Attlee had opened on his return.

The debate was a sad occasion.[2] The House listened with a mixture of sympathy and restiveness as Bevin repeated, in a voice that could only be heard with difficulty, his belief that, although they were living in grim times,

[1] 10 December, 1950. See footnote 1, p. 824.
[2] 14 December 1950.

these need not necessarily lead to war. He felt sufficiently confident in the state of Anglo–American relations to talk about some of the differences between the two countries, over recognition of the Communist Government in Peking and the admission of China to the UN.

"I could not bring myself to believe it was the right policy to adopt a line such as we adopted with Russia in 1917–18. . . . We acted for too long in a way which made Russia feel she was a nation at bay. We did not take advantage of the opportunity of establishing relations when the change took place and the New Economic Policy had to be introduced."

The Government had tried to learn that lesson and not repeat the same mistake in the case of China, resolving

"Not to become obsessed with the Communist conception of China but rather to bear in mind that the mass of Chinese scarcely understand what Communism means, and try if we could to bring them along and keep them in association with the other nations of the world."

This turned out to be Bevin's last speech in the House. When the next crisis over China blew up with the USA at the beginning of January, Attlee kept the exchanges with Washington in his own hands, resuming with the President where he had left off in December.[1]

Attlee asked Bevin's advice but found it at odds with the growing criticism of the USA in the Cabinet and the Party. Bevin did not want an all-out war with China any more than the critics but he thought they exaggerated the risk of America starting a major war with China and underestimated the consequences of the USA retiring into isolation if her allies opposed her too strongly.[2] His last words to Attlee on the subject were:

"We have to imagine what it would be like to live in a world with a hostile Communist bloc, and unco-operative America, a Commonwealth pulled in two directions and a disillusioned Europe deprived of American support."

Kenneth Younger, the Minister of State at the Foreign Office, expressed himself bitterly in his diary against Bevin's unwillingness to stand up to the Americans and lobby against them in the UN, only to write in the next paragraph: "Actually I do not myself know yet just how far *I* am prepared to go." With Bevin no longer able to give the strong lead he had in the past, the Cabinet did not exactly distinguish itself. On Thursday, 25 January, in Bevin's absence, Younger carried a majority of the Cabinet in favour of voting against the USA in the Security Council—"against what everyone thought Ernie

---

[1] See Attlee's letter of 8 January 1951; Truman's reply of 9 January; and Attlee's response of the 13th. FO 800/462/FE/51/3; 6 & 10.

[2] Attlee consulted Bevin on 10 January and Bevin sent him a memorandum on the 12th drawn up after discussion between Strang, Makins, Dixon and himself. FO 800/517/US/51/6 & 7.

would have done".[1] Gaitskell, now Chancellor of the Exchequer, was so troubled by the anti-Americanism displayed ("with Strachey it was pathological"[2]) that he told Attlee he might have to resign if the Cabinet's decision was adhered to. The next day the Cabinet reversed its vote, "wobbling about" in Dalton's scornful phrase. By then Bevin was in hospital with pneumonia (he was taken ill on the 22nd) and out of the argument for good.

In his last six weeks before falling ill Bevin had been more active on the other major issue which troubled the Government, that of rearming the Germans. Dalton who was fanatical on the subject, believed there was even stronger feeling in the Party on this than on the United States or China. "Nye and I encourage this. Strachey also."[3] Younger, for whom Bevin could do nothing right, blamed him for this too:

"He has wavered from one view to another on German rearmament, first trying to delay it, then joining the Americans in bullying the French . . . then having cold feet about it and vainly thinking of going back."[4]

Dalton, however, who was much less critical of Bevin, thinking him "Quite good and cautious over China and the U.N.", saw Bevin as sharing and understanding the Party's anxieties about Germany.[5]

There is no doubt that Bevin changed his mind after his reluctant agreement in Washington. He sent two cables to catch up with Attlee on the Prime Minister's December visit to the States saying that he had had second thoughts about the Spofford Plan and arguing that the circumstances were now entirely different from those in which he had originally accepted it.[6] In particular, the American promise to send substantial reinforcements to England at an early date could no longer hold good in view of the disaster which had overtaken their forces in Korea.[7] He appears to have been equally impressed by reports from the British Ambassador in Moscow that the Soviet note proposing a meeting of the Council of Foreign Ministers was meant to make clear that the Russians regarded steps to re-create German armed forces as quite different from measures by the Western Powers to build up their own strength. "It might be no less dangerous to ignore this warning in our present condition of weakness than it was to ignore the warnings of the Chinese in regard to an approach to the Manchurian border by UN forces." Bevin admitted that the Chiefs of Staff—and Morrison—disagreed and thought that to back-pedal at this late hour could have the most serious consequences. But he held to his own

---

[1] Younger's diary, entries for 7, 21, 28 January 1951.
[2] Dalton's diaries, 9 February 1951 and 6 pages written in mid-February in amplification of his diary.
[3] Dalton, mid-February.
[4] Younger, 4 February 1951.
[5] Dalton, 18 January 1951 and 20 December 1950.
[6] Bevin to Attlee, 6 December 1950. FO 800/456/DEF/50/21.
[7] Bevin said Marshall had told him that five and a half additional US divisions would be sent to Europe in 1951.

view that while there could be no question of going back on British agreement to the principle of rearming the Germans, they should consider the timing of its application, in particular the time between publicizing the NATO decision to rearm the Germans and the build-up of sufficient Allied forces to deter the Russians from preventive action.

Whatever Attlee thought of Bevin's cable he made no serious attempt in his meetings with the President to question the Spofford Plan. Acheson was unwilling to reconsider what had been agreed to: they had to press on with the Spofford plan and carry the French with them.

"We were so near the edge of the precipice that secondary points must be sacrificed."

The Prime Minister had no option but to concur; nor had Bevin.[1]

6

Even before Attlee got back from Washington, Acheson was pressing Bevin for a meeting of the NATO Council in Brussels as soon as possible.[2] This was to be Bevin's last international conference and he took the precaution of putting down in advance what he wanted to achieve, four points in all. While (a) approving the Spofford plan in principle, he would argue for (b) no official approach to the Germans at present. Instead, the High Commissioners should approach Adenauer privately and ask him how Germany could best play its part in the defence of Western Europe. This would take time, which Bevin wanted to see used (c) for the immediate appointment of Eisenhower as Supreme Commander and (d) for the proposed four-power talks with the Russians.[3]

The result of the Brussels meeting was better than Bevin had anticipated. The key was the Americans' willingness for Eisenhower's appointment to be announced as Supreme Commander of an integrated NATO force made up of national contingents under a single international command corresponding to SHAEF, the Supreme HQ Allied Expeditionary Force from which Eisenhower had directed the invasion of Europe in 1944. At the same time Acheson informed his colleagues of a big increase in US military strength and called for increased efforts on the part of NATO's European members. This was already under discussion in London and although Bevin could give no figures, he made sure that the fact that Britain was alone among the other powers in taking steps to accelerate its defence preparations was not overlooked.[4] The Spofford

[1] British record of the meetings. FO 800/445/COM/50/17.
[2] Bevin to Attlee, then in Ottawa, 10 December. FO 800/456/DEF/50/25.
[3] Minute by Kirkpatrick, FO 800/483/NA/50/15 and memorandum from Shuckburgh to Dixon, dated 13 December, *ibid.*, NA/50.
[4] See Bevin's talk with Acheson on 18 December and Brook's urgent communication from the Cabinet not to mention a specific figure in FO 800/456/DEF/50/26 & 27.

Plan was approved and the communiqué spoke of "unanimous agreement on the part Germany might assume in the common defence"; but Bevin's view was accepted that the High Commissioners should explore this with Adenauer, and let the Germans make proposals, not confront them with a cut-and-dried scheme.

Bevin's object was not only to avoid making hasty decisions from which there could be no retreat but to relate proposals for a German contribution to talks with the Russians. Attlee told Dalton that "Ernie thought of this [i.e. German rearmament] as a card to play in Four-Power Talks."[1] This was not a view Acheson would have accepted and Bevin wisely kept his own counsel; but he did press for a positive reply to the Russian proposal of talks, maintaining that Ministers should talk to the Russians and not leave it to officials as they had in 1939. After Acheson had cleared the room of their staffs, so that he could speak frankly, the three foreign ministers finally agreed on a draft reply which proposed that "representatives of the four Governments" should try to find "a mutually acceptable basis for a meeting of the foreign ministers . . . and recommend a suitable agenda." The last point was important since it was common ground that the Western Powers should not agree to discuss demilitarization by itself, as the Russians proposed ("The only German military force which exists at present is that which for many months in the Soviet zone has been on military lines with artillery and tanks"), but must widen the agenda of any meeting to look at the underlying reasons why it had proved impossible for the four powers to reach agreement.[2]

Summing up in his report to the Cabinet, Bevin claimed that they had got what they wanted, Eisenhower's appointment and recognition of the need to increase the NATO defence effort, while avoiding any action on German rearmament which would tempt the Russians into aggressive action and leaving open an area of negotiation with the USSR.[3] It is unlikely that Bevin believed either that German rearmament could be avoided or that talks with the Russians would lead to agreement; his object was to play for time and avoid over-hasty decisions, and this he had achieved.

Timing was still, in Bevin's view, the all-important consideration in the consolidation of Western Europe. When Morrison remarked in the Cabinet that he thought Britain had gained little from membership of the Council of Europe and would be well out of it, Bevin sent him a note which represents his last word on a very sore subject. He told Morrison he was not at all sure he was

[1] Dalton's record of his talk with Attlee (Diaries, 20 December 1950), following his protest to the Prime Minister against rearming the Germans. "I said I knew that Ernie shared my apprehensions about West German rearmament and that I had confidence he would be prudent."
[2] British record of the Tripartite discussion on 19 December, FO 800/449/CONF/50; US record in FRUS 1950 (3) 531–606; text of the identical notes sent by the three Western Governments to the Russians, 22 December 1950, RIIA *Documents 1949–50*, pp. 176–8.
[3] Bevin's report to the Cabinet, 1 January 1951. FO 800/449/CONF/51/1. The same volume contains the record of the tripartite talks in Brussels, 18–20 December and of the meeting of the Brussels Treaty Consultative Council, 20 December.

not right but he had always been loth to do anything that might lead to the Council's collapse, for two reasons. The first was the shakiness of European morale and "the danger of knocking away an institution to which many continental people who have lost confidence in their own countries and in themselves pin hopes". The second was the value of the Council as the only international arena in which the Germans could play a part.

A more opportune moment for "standing up to the pretensions of Strasbourg" would be after Eisenhower had instilled more confidence by establishing more effective defence forces; after the problem of relations between NATO and OEEC had been solved ("so that we do not look as if we were sabotaging two European institutions at the same time") and after Germany had become associated with or a member of NATO. He added that perhaps another twelve months might see all these three things accomplished.

Another piece of evidence that Bevin, when not called upon to speak in public, had not lost his grasp of affairs is provided by a personal note he wrote to Oliver Franks on 13 January. He had seen a letter from the Ambassador to William Strang advising that it would not be wise for the Prime Minister to intervene with the President on the Americans' plans for using their strategic air force. Bevin agreed that a message from the Prime Minister was a last resort but he did not think they could let the present state of affairs continue. "This is a position which it would be impossible to justify to Parliament or to public opinion if anything went wrong." He suggested that while the Chief of Air Staff, Sir John Slessor, was in Washington for talks with the American COS he should raise the matter with them, and he enclosed a message for Acheson proposing this:

"We have agreed," he wrote, "to the pressure of U.S. bomber aircraft in this country . . . I should however say it was implicit in the many talks which I had with Ambassador Douglas . . . that we should be consulted about any plans for the use of these aircraft. In fact that understanding has been the basis of our agreement to their presence here. . . .
"As I conducted many of the negotiations with Douglas, I feel a personal responsibility for making sure that no misunderstanding exists in the use to which the U.S. air forces in the U.K. might be put. I cannot feel that I have discharged that responsibility while the British Government has no information as to the strategic plan in support of which these aircraft might be used at very short notice nor how far its plan accords with our own."[1]

Acheson agreed and although Bevin himself played no further part, the question was discussed between Slessor and the American COS leading on to further talks between the two Governments after Bevin had given up office.

There is irony in the fact that the only other recommendation he made in these final weeks related to an issue which had defeated him from the

---

[1] Bevin to Franks (enclosing message for Acheson) 13 January 1951; Acheson's reply, saying the discussion had taken place, 26 January; Makins' note to the PM on the need for further talks, 14 February. FO 800/456/DEF/51/1–2; 5–6.

beginning, a new treaty with Egypt. One Middle Eastern question at least, on which he had spent a great deal of time, was removed from the agenda, the future of the former Italian colonies. He was particularly pleased with Libya's independence, recalling wartime pledges to the Senussi of self-government which had now been honoured.

The same day that a Libyan state was proclaimed, 2 December, uniting Cyrenaica, Tripolitania and the Fezzan, the UN Assembly approved the proposals to which Bevin had finally got agreement for Eritrea and Somaliland. But an agreement with Egypt which would have rounded off the post-war settlement in North-East Africa was as remote as ever. The British view, reiterated in strategic talks with the Americans at the end of October, was that "whoever controls the Middle East controls the access to three continents. Whether or not this area is held will determine whether or not we have a 'big free world' or a 'little free world'."[1]

The latest of many meetings, this time between Bevin and the Egyptian Foreign Minister Saleh el Din in New York in September, had left the two sides as far apart as ever. But the outbreak of war in the Far East reinforced the argument for the Western Powers' retaining strategic control of the Middle East, which the Americans still regarded as a British responsibility, and while Attlee went off to North America in December, Bevin tried again, holding several further meetings with Saleh el Din in London.[2] Although no agreement was reached, Bevin showed himself still a resourceful negotiator and told Acheson in Brussels that he thought one was possible. He even talked about sounding Israel on a separate defence agreement if the negotiations with Egypt proved successful.[3]

In May 1950 the British Chiefs of Staff had defined "the ideal military arrangement in the Middle East" as "a regional pact consisting of the UK, the Arab League States, Israel, Turkey, Persia and possibly Greece, in which *Egypt as a willing partner* would provide the base facilities required."[4] The stumbling block was still the words I have italicized. The terms Bevin had tried to get would have allowed for the transfer to Egypt of the responsibility for the key Canal Zone Base. This was more than the COS were prepared to agree to and Bevin thought their counter-proposals—a British lease of the base—stood less chance of being accepted. His last memorandum to Attlee on the Middle East, reviewing the negotiations (20 February 1951), concluded by reiterating the need to make a settlement with Egypt which could come into operation before the 1936 Treaty expired. It took three more years before an agreement was finally reached in 1954, the terms of which were not so far from those for which Bevin had argued: evacuation of British troops from the Zone

---

[1] Sir Oliver Franks at the meeting of the British and American Chiefs of Staff, Washington, 26 October 1950. FRUS 1950 (3) p. 1693.
[2] On 4, 7 and 9 December 1950. FO 800/457/EG/50/18–20.
[3] Bevin's talk with Acheson, in Brussels, 19 December, *ibid.*, EG/50/22.
[4] At the Defence Committee meeting on 19 May, Minutes DO (50) 40.

over a period of twenty months; maintenance of the base by civilian labour and its reactivation should Egypt be attacked. Whether this would have succeeded in reconciling the West's strategic requirements with Egyptian nationalism will never be known: the Treaty was swept away in the Suez fiasco.

7

With Bevin's removal to hospital suffering from pneumonia (22 January) public comment on his position could no longer be restrained. To his indignation it was widely assumed that he would now resign, and discussion turned to possible successors. Dalton canvassed names with Hugh Gaitskell without finding any that carried conviction.[1] The one name that might have done, that of Nye Bevan, was ruled out for Attlee and the majority of the Cabinet by the belief that his appointment would mean, or be taken to mean, a radical departure in foreign and defence policy, a belief confirmed by his reaction to the increased defence programme (raised to £4,700 m. over two years) and his subsequent resignation. Dalton's suggestion was that if Bevin could not go on, Attlee should combine the Foreign Office with the Premiership until the election.[2] Dalton himself was no longer a candidate:

"I don't want soiled bedclothes," he told Gaitskell. "If I'd had it in 1945 I might have made something of it. But now? With only a few months to go before an electoral defeat or war? Oh no. But we both thought Ernie would go on."

So did Bevin. He had been too much of a fighter all his life to be reconciled, even now, to the idea of resignation. He recovered from the attack of pneumonia sufficiently to go to Eastbourne in February to convalesce. He still refused to accept that he was no longer fit to carry on, and unhappy and depressed, convinced himself that every word of the Press comment on the need for a new Foreign Secretary was inspired by one or other of his colleagues. At the beginning of March he returned to the Foreign Office and tried to resume his duties.

Attlee had put off taking action for as long as he could, not only because he had real affection for the man who had been his closest ally and adviser throughout his administration and knew how badly Bevin would be hit by having to give up the Foreign Office; but for political as well as personal reasons. The first was the great regard he had for Bevin's experience and judgement in international relations; he could still see no one to fill his place adequately. The second was the change it would bring in the balance of the Cabinet. With Bevin as well as Cripps removed, the Government would have lost its two outstanding figures; and, with Bevin, its strongest link with the

---

[1] Dalton's diaries, 9 February 1951.
[2] *Ibid.*, 28 January.

trade unions. He could bring in Gaitskell to replace Cripps; but he could neither appoint Nye Bevan, the other obvious leader in the next generation, to succeed Ernie Bevin without tilting the balance to the Left, nor deny him an office equivalent to Gaitskell's without risking his resignation and a split in the Party. Either way there was a danger of sharpening the divisions within the Party. The longer Attlee could delay the departure of Bevin, the longer he could put off the troubles that lay ahead.

But the advice he received from the doctors no longer left him any option. Neither Sir Alex McCall nor Lord Uvedale believed that Bevin's mind or judgement were impaired by his illness. "He was still all right" the latter said "as far down as his neck." But his physical disabilities, his difficulty in breathing and movement, his inability any longer to play the public role of a Foreign Secretary, and take part in debates and conferences and to travel were now such that, in their view, he ought not to continue. McCall repeated his view to Bevin, who (he says) knew very well that it had to come but still found it hard to reconcile himself to it. On 19 February Dalton noted in his diary that he had heard from Attlee for the first time that Bevin was going.

For both the personal and political reasons I have mentioned, Attlee wanted to keep him in the Cabinet, and proposed the office of Lord Privy Seal with no departmental responsibilities, and some ill-defined functions on the domestic side. Bevin could not refuse, but giving up an office with which he had become so closely identified for more than five years broke his spirit. "As I saw him off for the last time from the Park Door," the last of his Private Secretaries wrote, "he looked old and frail and miserable. There was nothing I could say which could offer much comfort. Anyhow I was feeling a bit emotional myself."[1]

Two things added bitterness to Bevin's departure. 9 March was his 70th birthday and a special effort had been made by the Foreign Office to celebrate it as a mark of the esteem and affection in which he was held by his staff. The sum of sixpence each had been contributed by all the members of the Foreign Service from Permanent Under Secretary and Ambassadors to messengers and typists; a large cake was prepared, and a desk and dinner service presented. It was a happy occasion and with justifiable pride Bevin said afterwards that nothing like this had ever been seen before—in an institution, he might have added, notorious for its socially exclusive and aloof attitudes. Unfortunately while the party was in full swing, the Prime Minister, unaware of what was taking place on the other side of Downing Street, rang up to speak to Bevin. When he had been brought to the phone, Attlee said he must now go ahead with the Cabinet reshuffle and announce Bevin's resignation as Foreign Secretary. All Bevin could say to his wife when he got back was, "I've got the sack." Everyone present felt the pathos of seeing a man once as strong and confident as Ernie Bevin so stricken. "I think," Pat Kinna said, "he is the only person I have seen with a broken heart."

---

[1] Barclay, p. 51.

What made it harder for Bevin to bear was that, of all people, Herbert Morrison should take his place. Visiting him two days later Francis Williams found him still brooding on what had happened. "There was no need for Clem to turn me into an elder statesman." His dislike and scorn for Morrison were as strong as ever. "He's enjoying himself now but let him wait a month or two. It'll be different then." He would have preferred Jim Griffiths, and when Francis Williams expressed surprise, replied "Well, Nye then. I'd sooner have had Nye than 'Erbert. He might have turned out quite good."

Bevin still managed to attend Cabinet meetings, but spent much of his time dozing. Dalton's comment in his diary, though brutal, proved to be accurate: "EB at Cabinet today seemed quite finished. Out of harness, he'll soon drop."[1] Even so, eight days after Dalton made that entry, Bevin still had the strength to look for, and the skill to find, a compromise between Gaitskell and Bevan over the health charges which all the members of the Cabinet, apart from Bevan and Wilson, accepted.[2]

Attlee intervened to see that he was not disturbed in the Foreign Secretary's official residence at Carlton Gardens, and he retained his room in the House of Commons. It was there that Francis Williams brought a group to see him a month after the conversation reported above. He found him shrunken in appearance and thought he could not last much longer: he was to die three days later. But Bevin made an excuse to keep Williams back and talk about old trade union days.[3] It was forty years since he had first become a full time official of the Dockers' Union in Bristol. He recalled a pensions scheme he had negotiated for the milling industry.

"It made all the difference in the world to those chaps. We didn't think the other side would agree, but they did. It was a nice afternoon. I think they must have been wanting to go to the races."

A lifetime of experience was summed up in his advice on negotiating:

"Always remember, Francis. The first thing to decide before you walk into any negotiation is what you'll do if the other chap says 'No'."[4]

He still hoped the Russians would not go on saying "No" for ever.

"I'd have liked to stay until there was a chance of agreement, bringing them and the Americans nearer. I'd set my heart on it."

He was at last reconciled to the fact that that was over and hoped to leave soon for a long holiday in the Canaries. "I'll be all right if I get away to the sun."

[1] Dalton's diaries, 12 March 1951.
[2] Philip Williams, *Gaitskell*, p. 250 and p. 266.
[3] Francis Williams, *Ernest Bevin* (London 1952) p. 272.
[4] Another remark recorded by Sir Roderick Barclay was drawn from the same experience: "Patience in negotiation is very essential. Somebody has to get worn out anyway." p. 88.

The next day he was much worse with severe chest pains, but recovered enough during the following day to urge his wife to go to the international football match at Wembley. It was too cold for him to take the risk but he told her not to be a martyr and stay at home because of him. Later that afternoon, 14 April, while he was reading official papers in bed, he had another attack and before a doctor could reach him, he was dead, the key to his red box still clutched in his hand.

Bevin's death attracted great attention in the Press and many tributes poured in, both from Britain and abroad. Behind the conventional phrases two things clearly emerged. The first was agreement that his qualities as a man—courage, loyalty, simplicity, sincerity—combined to produce a character which was as much out of the ordinary as that of a Churchill or in the next generation a de Gaulle. *The Times* summed up the general opinion when it wrote: "He had his weaknesses . . . he made his mistakes, some serious. But there was no question of his greatness." The other was the extent to which Bevin had captured the popular imagination by his rise from farm boy to first a national, then an international figure—much less common for a man born in 1881 than it has become since—without any advantages to start with and without courting anyone's favour.

When a memorial service was held later in the month, a congregation of two thousand filled Westminster Abbey, representing the whole range of national life from the Monarchy to the trade unions. The Cabinet was led by Attlee who left hospital to attend; the Opposition by Churchill. The Lord Chancellor, and the Speaker of the House were followed by representatives of the Armed Services, of the Cabinet Office, the Ministry of Labour and the Foreign Office; of the employers, the nationalized industries and the TUC; Ambassadors of foreign powers; the Lord Mayors of London and Bristol; Commonwealth High Commissioners, representatives of the UN, the ILO, NATO, and other international organizations. And when all these were seated a crowd of men and women who had come representing no one but themselves, many of them trade unionists, pressed in to fill every available space. No voice was raised in question when later that summer a casket containing his ashes was placed in Westminster Abbey and Attlee declared in his address that it was "Altogether fitting that the mortal remains of our friend Ernest Bevin should find their last resting place in this ancient shrine of our nation." The inscription on the stone marking the place read:

Ernest Bevin

1881–1951

Statesman

PART VI

Epilogue

CHAPTER 23

Bevin's place in British history

I

In the last talk he had with Ernie Bevin, a short time before his death, Francis Williams asked him what he thought had been his greatest achievement as foreign secretary. Bevin would not give him an answer. All he would say was: "Tell them to ask the question in twenty years' time." It was a reply which reflected Bevin's sense of historical perspective, "his apprehension" (as Acheson described it[1]) "that he was acting in the main stream of history."

How is the question to be answered, now that more than thirty years have elapsed since his death and much has become known that was unknown at the time?

In the first eighteen months after the War, by the beginning of 1947, it became clear that none of the schemes considered during the War for conducting foreign policy after it was viable. This was true of the war-time alliance of the Council of Foreign Ministers, of Western Union and of the United Nations. It was this lack of a framework for international relations which frustrated Bevin and led to the criticism that he was producing no more than a series of improvisations to deal with specific problems, that he had no clear concept of the role Britain might play—in short, no policy.

If in the winter of 1946–7, when he was ill and depressed, Bevin had followed Attlee's advice to withdraw from the Middle East and Mediterranean, and had yielded to Treasury pressure to slash overseas expenditure, he would have restored his popularity with his own Party. He had to give ground so far as to accept cutting support for Greece and Turkey, but he refused to consider withdrawal as a general policy or to give up the search for a way in which Britain could still continue to play a major role in world affairs. He stuck to his belief that Britain could not retreat into herself; that the standard of living her people expected and her economic recovery depended on rebuilding

---

[1] Acheson, p. 35.

her trade with the world; and that Britain's position in the Middle East (including access to its oil) was an asset she could not afford to abandon.

What gave Bevin the chance to vindicate his stand and to follow a more positive policy was obviously the change in attitude of the US Government which, at the end of the War, had been quick to disengage itself from the special relationship with Britain and reluctant to accept a continuing commitment to Europe. Without this change on the part of the Americans, Bevin could have accomplished little. But it was an essential condition of success for the United States to find a European partner. No other nation in Europe at that time was in a position to fill such a role other than the British, neither the French, the Italians nor the Germans. This was Bevin's opportunity; he recognized and seized it decisively.

The use he made of that opportunity has already been described: his role in taking up Marshall's offer and creating the OEEC; his steadfastness in the trial of strength over Berlin; his grasp of the logic which made Europe's recovery dependent on Germany's and the latter on the conversion of the occupation regime into partnership with a West German State.

Bevin never thought it likely that the Russians would risk a war. He saw the real danger in the use they could make of Western fears and indecisions. He was convinced however that confidence would not be restored by anything the Europeans could do by themselves. Hence the persistence with which he urged on the US Government from early in 1948 that, besides supplying economic aid, the Americans would have to join in setting up an organization for the collective defence of Western Europe if sufficient self-confidence was to be restored among the Europeans to release the energies needed to fuel Europe's economic and political recovery.

Bevin's part in creating the Atlantic alliance crowned his achievement, as the necessary counterpart in his mind to the Marshall Plan and the rehabilitation of Germany. Of course it was not a single-handed achievement, but without Bevin's determination to push through his policies and his sense of timing, his Foreign Office officials could only have produced plans and recommendations. There was no other member of the Attlee Cabinet who had the authority (and the political courage) to commit a Labour Government to such an undertaking. But Bevin did more than supply the political will. Lord Franks, who was more deeply involved than any other official in the negotiations over the Marshall Plan, OEEC and NATO, believes that during his first two years at the Foreign Office (which at the time appeared lacking in positive achievement) Bevin had developed an overall picture of the changes taking place in the world, and had evolved two or three lines of policy which he then had the time to lay down and impress on the FO as the basis of British foreign policy.[1]

---

[1] Author's interview with Lord Franks.

The US documents bring out another facet of Bevin's achievement: the American recognition that there was no one else in Western Europe in 1947–9 capable of mastering the obstacles presented by European fears and scepticism, by Communist opposition, and by the tough conditions they themselves felt it necessary to impose. What is remarkable is that, in carrying out a policy which throughout depended on American resources and willingness to accept the British as partners, Bevin managed to combine an independence that frequently exasperated the Americans to the point of angry protest, with retaining their confidence as the man on whom they could most rely amongst their allies. There is no period, except during the Second World War, when the special relationship between the two countries has been stronger than in 1947–49.

2

NATO provided a framework for Britain's East–West relations; the Commonwealth for her changing relations with her former Empire. Bevin's hopes of creating a third framework in which to develop a new relationship with the countries of the Middle East came to nothing.

The most difficult single problem in the Middle East, the future of Palestine, involved the British not only in conflict with Zionists and Arabs but with the United States as well. The highly charged emotions surrounding the fate of the Jews and the Zionist dream of a Jewish state have obscured the line of policy Bevin was trying to pursue.

There were two fixed points by which he tried to steer his course. One was the belief that there could only be a stable settlement in Palestine if account were taken of Arab as well as Jewish claims. The other was the importance which he attached to the United States as the key factor in finding a solution.

The first of these two points—the Arab factor—accounts for the Zionists' anger with Bevin, the second—the American factor—for the Arabs'. His inability to reconcile the two accounts for his failure.

In 1945–6 Bevin believed that he could strike a balance between Jewish and Arab claims provided he could secure American support. His experience in those first eighteen months forced him to recognize that such support could never be relied on to promote a settlement which failed to satisfy the Zionists. But he was still determined not to abandon his first point and let Britain be saddled with the responsibility for imposing on the Arabs by force a settlement which was weighted against them.

He saw only one way out—for Britain to resign the mandate and withdraw. Another foreign secretary might have handled the matter with less show of personal feeling and a better sense of timing, but he might also have lacked the courage which Bevin showed in sticking to withdrawal in face of the pressures and criticism to which he was subjected. Better that, he believed, than to let

Britain become more deeply embroiled in a conflict which she could not resolve, and which might lead to an open quarrel with the Americans.

Both governments had recognized that they must not allow the angry exchanges between them over Palestine to affect their co-operation in Europe. The fact that this was extended to the Middle East as well shows how far both Americans and British saw that part of the world in terms of its relationship to Europe and the conflict with the USSR.

Bevin's difficulty in creating a regional defence agreement was neither with the Americans—nor even with the Russians—but with the Arabs. The Jewish victory in Palestine added to the obstacles already presented by Arab nationalism and the revolt against imperialism. The Arabs were as critical of British policy as the Jews, blaming the British for abandoning the 1939 White Paper, and for the Arabs' defeat in the Arab–Israeli war. What was the point of a regional agreement which would exclude action against Israel, a much more visible enemy to the Arabs than Russia?

There is an obvious contrast between the success of Bevin's policy in Europe and his lack of success in the Middle East. But it is a matter of debate how far this was because he had a better grasp of the situation, and was more sure of his judgement in dealing with Europe; or because there was nothing solid to build on in the Middle East comparable with Europe.

To raise such a question is to highlight the course Attlee urged on Bevin in 1946–7, to consider withdrawal from the whole area. How much would have been lost if Bevin had followed Attlee's advice? How much was gained by staying?

It is noticeable that the pressure for withdrawal which had led to the debates in the Cabinet's Defence Committee and between Bevin and Attlee died away as relations with the Soviet Union worsened. Once the conflict could no longer be disguised, neither British nor Americans doubted that the Middle East had to be held and denied to the Russians.

If Bevin failed in his object of putting Britain's position in the Middle East on a more acceptable basis, British forces remained under the existing treaties occupying bases from Libya in the West to the Persian Gulf in the East. They retained the use of the airfields in Iraq and Egypt, the wartime base in Suez, control of the Canal and the equally important network of communications to India, the Pacific and the Far East.

With hindsight we know that all this was to be swept away in the aftermath of Suez. But there is a case for arguing that the minimum Bevin succeeded in maintaining for the ten years after the War was worth the effort by providing Western control of the Middle East and access to its oil during the most dangerous years of the Cold War when the division between Eastern and Western spheres of influence was not yet stabilized. By the time Britain's power in the Middle East was ended, the Americans were willing to take their place.

Bevin's policy in the Middle East as well as Europe was based upon assumptions about relations between Russia and the West which are still a matter of controversy. The later history of those relations, however, as well as what is now known about the wartime alliance and the character of Stalin's regime does not seem to me to encourage the belief that there was any real opportunity, when Hitler was defeated, of avoiding the suspicions and settled hostility of the Cold War.

If there was such an opportunity, it was not within Bevin's power to make anything of it. For the Russians realized where the balance of power now lay between the USA and Britain. A deal with the Americans was something for which the Russians might have been willing to offer concessions in return. If the Americans were ready to make such a deal, then the British would have to accept it, whatever their misgivings. (This was the possibility that Bevin feared at the time of the Moscow meeting with Byrnes in December 1945.) But a deal with the British alone was not something for which Stalin was willing to pay a price. If Stalin miscalculated in throwing away the goodwill which Russia had accumulated in the West, there is nothing to show that anything Bevin or any other Englishman could have said would have persuaded him to act differently. The commonest criticism of Bevin in 1945–7, that he was responsible for the deterioration of Anglo–Russian relations, seems to me to have lost most of its substance with the passage of time.

The criticism which, some would argue, has been substantiated by time is over his attitude, not so much to Europe (for no British foreign secretary ever attached more importance than Bevin to Europe's continued independence and economic recovery) as to anything that smacked of European federation.

The pros and cons of this argument have already been discussed in connection with the Schuman Plan. The debate about Bevin's attitude to European integration, however, raises a more fundamental question. Like Attlee's argument for withdrawal from the Middle East in 1946–7—and even in part the search for a socialist foreign policy—it is a specific example of the more general criticism that, for all his achievement, Bevin failed to recognize the permanence of the change in Britain's international position at the end of the War and, in a vain attempt to maintain a world role, set the country off on the wrong course.

3

This criticism of Bevin's policy may well seem to be substantiated by the subsequent course of British history and the painful experience of scaling down the country's commitments—and pretensions—to match her much reduced resources. That this had to be done eventually is incontestable but the force of the argument, so far as Bevin is concerned, rests upon a concealed assumption which needs to be looked at more closely. That assumption is that the sooner this process could have been put in hand after the end of hostilities, the better, and that Bevin is to blame for not having acted accordingly.

But is the assumption correct? I suggest that it can be shown to be ill-founded on several grounds.

The first is that it leaves unanswered the question, what part the British were going to play in the peace settlement.

If the British had been defeated in 1945, that question would have been answered for them, as it was for the Germans. But they had not been. However misguided it may appear now, they thought they had won. Unlike General de Gaulle, Attlee and Bevin found vacant seats waiting for them at Potsdam. Britain was one of the victor states occupying the territory of her former enemies; a Permanent Member of the Security Council with the power of veto; still head of a large empire with widespread possessions; well ahead of any other state except the two Superpowers in military, industrial and technological resources. Her interests and responsibilities were world wide, at least as wide as those of either Russia or America. For her to abandon these, or even seriously reduce them, at short notice was out of the question. Apart from its effect abroad, it would have been a blow to national morale that no newly elected government could be expected to strike after a war from which Britain had emerged victorious.

If Britain was not to take her part in what happened after the War, why had she fought—unlike her allies, without being attacked first? Neither Bevin nor Attlee felt so much confidence in the goodwill or wisdom of the Russian and American governments as to be willing to leave them to make the post-war settlement by themselves. With Germany, Japan and Italy defeated, with France (excluded from Potsdam) and China only nominally represented, Britain alone had the prestige and, despite her economic difficulties, the political experience and military power to make an independent voice heard. But if she meant to do that, then she had to accept her share of the obligations of victory, maintaining armies of occupation, contributing to the costs of relief and reconstruction and making available her resources in shipping and communications.

The British, then, expected to play a part in the peace settlement corresponding to the part they had played in the War. But the last thing they wanted to do was to become involved unnecessarily in additional commitments or to embark on an aggressive foreign policy. If any nation was weary of war it was the British, who had been at war (as Bevin reminded the UN) for one day in three between 1914 and 1945, the only one of the wartime allies to take part in both wars from the first day to the last, for twice as long as the Americans.[1] The most important factor in the criticisms of Bevin between 1945 and 1947 was the

[1] The UK was at war for 52 months in 1914–18, the USA for 20; the UK was at war for 71 months in 1939–45, the USA. for 44. The USSR was at war for 49 months between 1941 and 1945, but of course suffered much greater losses than either of her allies.

reluctance of the British to contemplate the possibility of renewed international-
al conflict now that the war was over.

This makes it all the more impressive that the strong lead which Bevin gave
in foreign affairs in 1947 steadily gathered support to the point, in 1947–9,
when it came as near consensus as any British foreign secretary has been able
to count on in time of peace. This change could never have taken place if
British public opinion had not come independently to the same conclusion
Bevin had already reached, that there was a real danger of the Soviet Union
and other Communists taking advantage of the weakness of Western Europe to
extend their power. We know now that this did not follow, but nobody knew it
at the time. This was a generation for whom war and occupation were not
remote hypotheses but recent and terrible experiences. The fear of another
war, the fear of a Russian occupation, haunted Europe in those years and were
constantly revived—by the Communist coup in Czechoslovakia, by the Berlin
blockade, and by the outbreak of war in Korea in 1950 which produced
near-panic in France and Germany. It is unhistorical to dismiss these fears as
groundless because the war and occupation did not occur.

If the British were persuaded that Bevin was right to join the United States
in organizing Western Europe's recovery and security, it was not because they
wanted to see their country playing a major role in the world but because they
were convinced that there was no alternative. This, they believed, was the
lesson to be learned from the 1930s when nothing had been done to stop Hitler
and Mussolini until it was too late to do so without war. The analogy may have
been faulty (I think it was) but it is by no means clear that the conclusion was
wrong, however arrived at.

Just as it is easy, but misleading, to assume now that the Russians had no
aggressive intentions, so it is easy to assume that—even if they had—once the
USA had decided to resist any further expansion by the Soviet Union,
Marshall Aid, the revival of Germany and the extension of American military
protection to Europe would follow automatically.

Neither the American documents, however, nor the British support so
simplistic a view. On the contrary they strongly suggest that without Britain to
give a lead in mobilizing a European response (the condition of Marshall Aid);
to act as a mediator between the United States and European opinion
(particularly French) on the rehabilitation of Germany, and to overcome the
obstacles represented by the fears, scepticism and lack of confidence which
were rife in Europe, the history of these years might have been very different.

The argument on economic grounds does not seem to be different from the
political. Later, the attempt to play a world role economically and in particular
to maintain sterling as an international currency was seen as imposing a heavy
handicap on the management of the domestic economy.[1] But there was a great
difference between the years 1945–50 and the later 1950s and 1960s. At the

---

[1] See, for example, Susan Strange: *Sterling & British Policy* (London 1971).

time when he was Foreign Secretary Bevin saw the sterling area, with the position it gave Britain as the centre of the world's second largest trading area, as an asset, like the links with the Commonwealth and her access to Middle Eastern oil—assets which Britain, as a country more dependent on overseas trade for her recovery than any other, could not afford to give up.

No foreign secretary was more alive to economic arguments, but he saw an active foreign policy and the international role which this involved, both politically and economically as a way of overcoming, rather than increasing, Britain's economic problems. The record shows that this was more than rhetoric. It was Marshall and the Military Assistance Programme—two of the four "legs" of Bevin's foreign policy—which enabled Britain and the rest of Western Europe to stage the remarkable economic recovery of the 1950s. By the end of 1950 Britain was able to dispense with Marshall aid, two years ahead of schedule.

Later, of course, her performance began to fall seriously behind that of the other West European countries but it would be hard to put the blame for that on Bevin's foreign policy. In the late 1940s and early 1950s this materially helped the British reach an economic position in which long-term decisions could be taken on other grounds than the emergencies which had marked the earlier years—the end of Lend Lease; the US loan agreement; the convertibility crisis; devaluation.

If on no other grounds, then, Bevin's policy in regard to the Atlantic alliance and the East–West balance he helped to establish can be justified by the protection and stimulus to recovery it provided, to Britain and to Western Europe in the dangerous and unstable period after the War. If Britain had withdrawn into herself at that time and shed her commitments, who can say what might not have happened?

But Bevin's policy looked further ahead than that. For however much he talked of Britain continuing to play a world role, in practice he grasped and acted on the fact that the British no longer had the resources to conduct a foreign policy (political, economic, defence) on their own.

What Bevin saw was necessary and aimed at was *not* continuity, but a decisive break with the most important tradition in British foreign policy—a permanent alliance with North America and Western Europe, the sort of commitment which British Governments had always refused to consider in the past. Recognizing that such an alliance and such a commitment were not viable if they amounted to no more than Western Europe plus Britain, Bevin went on to give his proposal of Western Union substance, not by an American guarantee to come to the rescue of Europe, but by securing the direct involvement of the USA in Europe's defence, an equally drastic break with American traditions.

Our familiarity with the Western alliance and its shortcomings can result in our all too easily taking for granted what it has provided, namely a basis for collective action and security, the lack of which had so much frustrated Bevin in his first two years, and the need for which he saw extending beyond the transitional period into the post-war world which was emerging from it.

The other fact all too often overlooked by those who criticize Bevin for his attitude to European integration is that the North Atlantic alliance was not secured at the expense of Britain's neighbours. On the contrary, it provided for Europe what was dangerously lacking after the War, the stabilization of the balance of power between East and West along a line which has not varied for nearly forty years. This is an achievement which few people in Europe would have believed possible in 1945–50, and was the essential condition, as no one foresaw more clearly than Bevin, of Western Europe's recovery of its confidence, of the unequalled period of prosperity which followed—and of its attempts at closer association in the EEC.

To sum up, I believe that the argument I have developed points to two conclusions. The first is that there were substantial reasons, accepted by a Labour Government which had already begun on the process of withdrawal in Asia and the Commonwealth, for not pushing it further until the dangerous instability of the situation after the war had been replaced by a new balance of power. The second is that the part Britain undertook to play in helping to create that balance was not incompatible with a subsequent reduction in her commitments.

Far from agreeing therefore that Bevin saddled Britain with a world role she could not sustain, I suggest that what he did was to provide his successors with the indispensable basis of security in the Western Alliance on which they could then proceed to make whatever adjustments were necessary and to develop such options as entry into Europe and withdrawal from the Middle East and from east of Suez.

Bevin himself was too close to what he had helped to achieve, too conscious of the dangers that could destroy it, to explore such options. But this seems much less important than the achievement itself and the opportunities which it created for those who came after. Whether they made the best use of them is another matter. To take only one example: in failing to take Britain into Europe in 1955–6 when the opportunity was renewed, I am sure they did not.

The same argument applies to nuclear weapons. After sharing with the Americans in the development of the A-bomb Bevin and Attlee were faced with having to accept their exclusion from further co-operation and under American pressure having to abandon the idea of producing one of their own. The decision will always remain a controversial one. But what Bevin was doing when he backed the proposal to continue was to prevent an option being closed off which, once abandoned, could never be re-opened. What his successors would do when the bomb was produced was again another matter. It did not necessarily commit Britain to the attempt to maintain an independent nuclear deterrent; but it gave those who followed him a choice, which otherwise would have been denied them. It was the same line of thought that led his one-time critic Nye Bevan in 1957 to refuse to accept for a Labour

Foreign Secretary a unilateral commitment to give up nuclear weapons in advance. "Do not disarm him diplomatically, intellectually and in every other way before he has a chance to turn round."[1]

Throughout its history, the alliance by which we have lived since the Second World War has undergone a number of metamorphoses. It may be that the time is ripe for another. But we should not fail to recognize that the Western Union of which Bevin first spoke in January 1948 has provided—with all its imperfections and limitations—a framework in which Britain and Western Europe have been able to enjoy an independence, a prosperity and security, never of course immune from crises or guaranteed to continue, but in practice lasting already for thirty five years, a period longer than that which separates the Vienna Settlement after the Napoleonic Wars from the Revolutions of 1848, and twice as long as that which followed the Treaty of Versailles. This is a future which would have seemed far beyond the dreams of most people in Europe in the troubled years of 1945–50, and the part Bevin played in securing it, at a time when the whole pattern of international relations was in flux and for the first time the British found their power to influence it much reduced, was an achievement comparable with that of any of his predecessors.

4

Bevin's period of office as Foreign Secretary, although the climax of his career, occupied only the last five-and-a-half years of a seventy-year life, which had begun as inauspiciously as that of any man who has played a comparable part in British history.[2]

He was born in April 1881 in a remote Somerset village on the edge of Exmoor. Illegitimate, and brought up in real poverty, he lost his mother when he was eight, and left school when he was eleven. At thirteen he went to Bristol and had a succession of blind alley jobs until he settled down to work as a carter. He completed his education by taking part in the Baptist Chapel, and the Adult Sunday School Movement before moving on from nonconformity to Socialism.

The turning point in his career was the summer of 1910, at the age of 29, when a strike in the Avonmouth and Bristol docks involved the carters. Bevin was persuaded to bring them together and form a carmen's branch of the Dockers' Union with such success that, within a year, it numbered 2,050 members, a third of the Union's members in Bristol. It was characteristic of Bevin that having organized the men, he went on to organize the employers as well, persuading them to come together for the first time, to recognize the union, set up a joint Arbitration Board and conclude the first comprehensive agreement covering their employees' hours, wages and conditions of work. In

[1] Foot, *Bevan*, vol. 2, p. 575.
[2] A fuller version of Bevin's career up to 1945, summarised here, is given in the two preceding volumes of this biography.

the spring of 1911, he was appointed a full-time union official at a salary of £2 a week.

Bevin started his trade union career at a time when labour unrest had broken out on a scale not seen in Britain since the 1840s. It was a rough apprenticeship in which he learnt to turn a hostile meeting round, shout down the opposition, and fight off not only strike breakers but rival unions. But Bevin did more than survive; by March 1914 he had become one of the union's three national organizers.

The war interrupted the industrial conflict, but the three years after the Armistice saw it renewed on an even bigger scale, corresponding to the wave of revolutionary violence which swept across Europe after the Russian Revolution and the defeat of the Central Powers. The Triple Alliance of miners, railwaymen and transport workers was renewed and turned to syndicalist ideas of Direct Action. What impressed Bevin most was less the rhetoric of overthrowing the capitalist system than the need, if pressure on Government and employers was to be exercised effectively, to devise an instrument which would mobilize the potential strength of a working class movement. The search for this is the key to his activities between 1918 and 1926.

The search took many forms, in all of which he played a leading role. They include the National Transport Workers' Federation; the Triple Alliance; the Council of Action which Bevin got established in 1920 to halt the supply of arms to the Poles in their counter-invasion of the Soviet Union; the Industrial Alliance; the General Council of the TUC and his greatest achievement as an organizer, the amalgamation of 22 unions into the TGWU which with Bevin as its general secretary and a membership of 650,000 on the eve of the Second World War became the largest trade union in the world.[1]

He had other successes besides the creation of the TGWU and the Council of Action. One was the Shaw inquiry into dock labour in 1920, in which Bevin represented the NTWF as well as the Dockers' Union and won national acclaim as "The Dockers' K.C." For the first time the public saw the intellectual mastery by virtue of which this uneducated man was capable of presenting the dockers' case for a minimum wage in a speech which lasted in all for 11 hours without ever losing the thread of the argument in the detail. He followed this up by a further 17 days' cross examination of expert witnesses and argument with a leading KC, Sir Lyndon Macassey, winning a majority verdict as well as the congratulations of the court and finally creating joint machinery with the employers to implement it.

His most sensational success was the Industrial Alliance, the plan which he drafted in 1925 for the transport workers and railwaymen to support the miners against the owners' insistence on reducing wages and lengthening hours. Under the threat of a national strike, on 31 July 1925 (Red Friday) the Prime Minister, Baldwin, reversed government policy and intervened to provide a subsidy for nine months and a new inquiry into the coal industry.

[1] In the year of Bevin's death it had grown to 1,285,000.

The Government used the nine months to prepare for next time; the trade unions did not. If they had been thinking seriously in terms of overthrowing the Government or the capitalist system, they might have done. But they were not: they refused to see the implications of their own actions. When the nine months ran out and the deadlock between miners and mineowners was repeated, the unions renewed their promise to support the miners. But when the TUC failed to secure a settlement which the miners would accept they found that this time the Government was prepared to accept the challenge of a general strike.

After fifteen years of talk about Direct Action no plans of any sort existed. They had to be improvised by a Strike Organization Committee dominated by Bevin. His improvisation was masterly and the response to the strike orders surprised everyone. Bevin had at last got what he had been working for, close on three million workers acting as if they were members of one union. The question to which neither he nor anyone else on the union side had an answer, or had foreseen, was what happened if the Government refused to capitulate and they had to take on the organized powers of the State? The union leaders were not prepared for this and called off the strike amid much bitterness and recrimination.

The lesson Bevin drew from the failure of the General Strike was the limits to what could be done with union power, even when it proved possible to mobilize it. He was not content, however, to say "Never again". There must be some way, he felt, to give expression to that power and get the views and needs of organized labour listened to without involving the unions in a challenge to the State.

He had first of all to pull his own union together and reverse the fall in membership and funds which followed the General Strike. Characteristically, he refused to give up his plan to complete the building of Transport House in which, within a few hundred yards of Parliament, he brought together under a single roof the headquarters of the TGWU, the TUC, and the Labour Party. This reflected his determination not to abandon the claim for trade union views to be heard in all major decisions, national as well as industrial. The principal instrument to which he looked to achieve this after 1926 was the TUC, its General Council and its annual conference.

One line of approach which Bevin was ready to explore was meeting representatives of the employers to discuss the changes he saw coming in industry—"rationalization", in the jargon of the day. This led to the Mond–Turner talks held between the TUC and a group of employers led by Sir Alfred Mond in 1928–29.

A second line of approach was the lead he gave in urging the TUC to express trade union views on economic policy. He persuaded the General Council for the first time to set up an Economic Committee, served by a small research staff. He himself accepted an invitation to serve as the only trade unionist on the important Macmillan Committee on Finance and Industry (1930–31) where he impressed John Maynard Keynes as the member who understood his unorthodox ideas better than any of the others. A total of 49 days spent in listening to 57 expert witnesses, and another 19 days of discussion, including in all 9 hours' exposition by Keynes, was not a bad education in economics.

Bevin as well as Citrine was a member of the Economic Advisory Council set up by MacDonald in January 1930, and he joined Keynes, Tawney and Cole in proposing a plan to increase purchasing power and launch big schemes of capital development. (Bevin was a Keynesian by the light of nature.) The Council, like the Mond–Turner talks, ended in disappointment and a breakdown of communications in 1931 when the TUC refused to back MacDonald's National Government. But the efforts which Bevin and Citrine had made to establish a new role for the TUC were not wasted: they laid the ground for the change of attitude in the later 1930s when both employers and Government showed increasing willingness to consult the unions.

As a socialist, Bevin continued to believe that only the socialization of the basic industries such as coal and public transport would meet the needs of those who worked in them and of the community. But pending such changes —which could only be achieved with a Labour Government in power—a trade union leader could not confine himself to opposition.

When he first joined the trade union movement in 1910 it was still struggling for recognition, even of the right to collective bargaining. By the time he became Chairman of the TUC in 1936 its right to be consulted on legislation or represented on any inquiry dealing with social and industrial matters was increasingly taken for granted. Bevin's attitude to the Labour Party, however, was equivocal. He was punctilious in seeing that his union paid the political levy and supported official union candidates: he was equally ready to help the Party out in a financial emergency. In *The Herald* he had provided the Movement with its own paper, and largely by his own efforts raised its circulation, first to one, then to two million.

On the other hand he never concealed the distrust and often the scorn, with which he regarded politicians and insisted on the autonomy of the trade unions. Perhaps if he had been elected to parliament in 1918 while he was still in his thirties, and become, as he certainly would, a leader of the Parliamentary Party, he would have understood its difficulties better. As it was, he was too inclined to treat the Party as an inferior partner (lacking in virtue) of the trade union movement, which constantly (in the person of Ernest Bevin) needed to chastise and correct it. The tension to which this led between him and the Party is one of the recurrent themes in his career.

It would be a mistake, however, to under-rate the role which Bevin played in the Labour Party in the 1930s.

In the crisis of 1931, it was the opposition of the General Council, led by Bevin and Citrine, which stiffened the resolve of Arthur Henderson and other Labour ministers to resign rather than join MacDonald in setting up a National Government. In the split that followed and which threatened to be as disastrous for the Labour Party as the General Strike had been for the trade unions, Bevin did everything in his power to rally support for the Party, both in the unions and in the country, including standing for election and being defeated at Gateshead.

The other political issue on which Bevin had a decisive influence was Labour's foreign policy, ten years before he became Foreign Secretary. He took a great interest in developing international relations with the European trade union movements, and played as big a role in the International Transport Workers' Federation as in the TUC. He matched this with the part he took as the leading trade union figure at ILO conferences where, among other successes, he secured for the seamen's unions the international charter (1936) on conditions of work for which they had campaigned for 16 years. There were few years when he did not attend an international conference in Europe, and he built up a network of contacts in Central and Western Europe which alerted him much earlier than most people in Britain to what was happening. For Bevin Czechoslovakia was not a far-off country, and he was particularly impressed by the destruction of the trade unions by Hitler, and by Dollfuss in Vienna in February 1934. The Labour Party, however, as distinct from the trade unions, found it hard to recognize the danger from the dictators, pinned its hopes on the League and identified support for the League with disarmament and the renunciation of war.

Bevin forced the issue at the 1935 Party Conference when, with the news expected hourly of the Italian invasion of Abyssinia, he insisted that Lansbury had to choose between his pacifist views and continuing as leader of the Labour Party. His attack on Lansbury was never forgiven him, but he turned the conference round to accept that support for the League must include support for sanctions. He went on, with Dalton, to persuade the Parliamentary Party to abandon its opposition to rearmament and in the autumn of 1937 carried both the TUC and Labour Party Conferences in favour of rearming the country to defend itself.

5

Bevin regarded his Presidency of the TUC in 1936–7 as the peak of his career and prepared to retire when he was 60. Instead, he found himself drawn into office in 1940 as a leading member first of the Coalition, then of the Labour Cabinets and so placed at the centre of events in the ten years which stand out uniquely in British 20th-century history as the decade of decisions.

Many people in the Labour Movement were surprised when he accepted Churchill's invitation to go to the Ministry of Labour. Why, Arthur Deakin asked, did he not hold out for something like LG's Ministry of Munitions in World War I? Bevin, however, understood very well what he was about. His object, he said later, was to give the Ministry of Labour the same importance in wartime as the Treasury in peacetime. What he foresaw was the replacement of finance by manpower, and the manpower budget, as the basis of the wartime planning of the country's resources and the ultimate limit on its mobilization. But to achieve his aim he had to concentrate control over the supply of manpower, whether to the Forces or to industry, in his own hands and extend it to include responsibility for the use which industry made of it. Having secured this position, he defended it successfully against all comers. Five months after taking office, Churchill brought him into the inner War Cabinet over the heads of other ministers with far greater experience: once there, there was no question of his leaving it. Only four other men, Churchill, Attlee (as leader of the Labour Party and Deputy Prime Minister) Eden and Anderson equalled this record of uninterrupted membership from the end of 1940 to May 1945. Bevin and Anderson were the key figures in the Lord President's Committee which acted, in effect, as the War Cabinet for Home Affairs.

Altogether this was a powerful position, but only if Bevin was equal to it. The risk he took was enormous. In order to mobilize the nation for total war—a job which had hardly been started when he took office—he had to disturb every established practice and vested interest in the country, and tell other ministries (Supply, Aircraft Production, the Admiralty) as well as management and unions that they had to double their output with half the numbers, ignore traditional demarcations and accept women workers on an unprecedented scale. At the same time, he had to involve himself in all the most sensitive issues in a highly conservative industrial society—wages, hours, conditions, differentials, the dilution of skilled work, training, joint consultation and strikes.

Bevin deliberately doubled the odds against himself by refusing, in face of the experts and outraged middle class opinion, to use the compulsory powers he was given to impose industrial conscription, or the direction of labour. Bevin's case was that in 1940 and 1941 there was as yet no general shortage of manpower as distinct from particular shortages, and that when it came, compulsion and direction would be accepted by working-class opinion if voluntary methods of recruitment for industry had been exhausted first. He was determined to carry the trade unions with him step by step. But it was easy to say—and *was* said freely—that Bevin was putting the unions' interests before the needs of the nation.

Churchill did not leave Bevin to defend himself. Rounding on the critics in the Commons in July (29th) 1941, the Prime Minister declared:

"It is the fashion nowadays to abuse the Minister of Labour. He is taunted with being an unskilled labourer representing an unskilled union. I daresay he gives offence in some quarters; he has his own methods of speech and action . . . But if you tell me that the results he produces do not compare with those of totalitarian systems of government, I reply by saying, 'We shall know more about that when we get to the end of the story.'"

Churchill's confidence was justified: long before the end of the story, the results were very clear. By the time Britain reached the peak of its wartime mobilization, in September 1943, twenty-two-and-three-quarter-million men and women out of a population of thirty-three million between the ages of 14 and 64, were serving in the Forces, Civil Defence, or were employed in industry. This was a level of mobilization never achieved by Hitler's dictatorship in Germany. And it included the conscription and direction of women—one of the boldest acts of policy ever carried out by a democratic government—a measure from which even Churchill had drawn back and which had been accepted by a hesitant Cabinet solely on Bevin's insistence.

All this had been achieved on a basis of consent, with the minimum of coercion. There were no special courts, and only a negligible number of prosecutions. Bevin himself described it as "the voluntary submission of a free people to discipline". Another way to put it is, an example of what can be achieved by democracy when combined with resolute leadership, a feat of organization for which the only parallel in modern British history is Lloyd George's organization of the munitions industry in the First World War.

In addition to mobilization, Bevin bore the chief responsibility for wartime labour policy, and succeeded in keeping industrial troubles to under half the level of strikes in the first war. He refused to abandon the framework of collective bargaining in favour of the Government fixing wage rates, and introduced the practice of joint consultation between management and unions throughout industry. At the same time he not only consulted the TUC on policy, but used the unions to help find the labour needed for the war factories and emergencies, and in the process established a new relation between Government and the trade union movement.[1]

After the War Bevin was no longer concerned directly with industrial policy, but he continued to play a unique role in relations between the Attlee Government and the trade union movement. Britain ended the war with a rundown industry; immense debts; the loss of her overseas assets; and continuing shortages, including the rationing of bread which had not been introduced in wartime. To restore her economic viability, Britain had to push her exports up to 175% of the level for 1938. This was achieved within 1% of target in 1951, without a runway inflation, at a time of full employment and

---

[1] In his book *Modern British Politics*, Professor Samuel Beer of Harvard, writes:

"The changes in the pattern of policy caused by the war, particularly the urgent extension of economic mobilization and control in 1940, provided the basis on which the new power of the organized working class was founded. After the war this new position was sustained by the continuation of economic planning and the process of bargaining from which the policy of wage restraint emerged in 1948 illustrates how it enabled the unions to shape and influence Government programs. Nor did their power vanish when the Conservatives took office for, although less favourable to planning than Labour, they too were obliged to manage the economy. . . . The system of direct communication which was established by Ernest Bevin in 1940 remained basically unaltered. . . . The critical moment in the forging of this new 'social contract' was not 1945 but 1940. The major readjustment resulted not from a shift in the electoral balance of power, but from a shift in the balance of economic power. . . . (pp. 214–15).

with a union membership rising to 8 million at the end of the period. It was in fact largely due to the Government's practice of consultation and the unions' willingness to co-operate with its policy of wage-and-profit restraint to a degree which went beyond anything asked for in either of the wars.

I draw no conclusions from this for the more recent period; but historically I think it is fair to say that during his lifetime Bevin's conception of the role of the trade unions did not prove incompatible with the national interest, had in fact proved indispensable to it both during the War and in meeting the economic crisis of 1947–49.

The degree of mobilization which had been achieved made Bevin all the more determined that the débâcle of demobilization in 1918 should be avoided. He insisted on taking the entire responsibility into his own hands; produced a scheme of great simplicity, and went to immense trouble to get it explained to everyone. "There will be no wangling" he promised—and was believed. The orderly way in which demobilization was carried out by comparison with 1918 was a major contribution in itself, and one reason for this was Bevin's interpretation of his responsibility for demobilization to mean not simply releasing men and women from the Forces or war industry, but finding them jobs, or offering them further education and training.

Political differences over post-war planning put a strain on the coalition, and Bevin's refusal to force the issue while the war had still to be won brought him under criticism from Labour MPs. But it was he who took the lead in getting a public commitment from all parties (in the form of White Papers which he presented to Parliament) to a policy of Full Employment (which *The Economist* rightly described as a revolutionary change in state policy) and the implementation in full of the Beveridge Report, whoever should win the election. With his own Wages Councils Act he hoped that he had made permanent the advances in industrial relations which he had initiated during the War.

More important than any legislation was the change his tenure of the Ministry of Labour produced in humanizing social administration. Of a hundred examples which might be given, perhaps the best is the persistence with which he pressed for the State to undertake the cost of rehabilitating the injured and disabled, "an investment in human skill", as he described it, a conception finally embodied in the 1944 Act.

Bevin ended the War with a reputation second only to Churchill's for getting things done. When Labour won the 1945 election, he wanted to go to the Treasury, and one may well speculate on what he might have achieved if his energies and imagination had been applied to the Country's domestic problems, to industry, taxation, trade, housing. One may also speculate on the difference it would have made to the Labour Party's subsequent attitude towards a man whose achievements it has been reluctant to recognize, if he had not, at Attlee's request, gone to the Foreign Office, and been brought again into conflict with traditional Party views on foreign and defence policy. What, despite that, he made of his years as Foreign Secretary, this study has attempted to show.

6

When Attlee's biographer came to sum up his life, he began: "Attlee was a Victorian."[1] This was not a description anyone would have thought of applying to Ernie Bevin. When he died, *The Times* wrote in a leading article:

"Like Mr Churchill, he seemed a visitor from the 18th century; he was of the company of Chatham and Samuel Johnson. His place, one felt, was among big men, men of strong hearts and strong opinions."

Bevin's character alone would secure him a place in British history—"the embodiment (as Francis Williams says of him) of all natural and unlettered men drawing upon wells of experience unknown to the more literate", or as Bevin himself more characteristically put it, "a turn-up in a million".

A man of fierce and often difficult temperament, of formidable confidence and resourcefulness which he needed to rise to the top by his own efforts, Bevin was one of that small number of men in each generation about whom anecdotes collect. The anecdotes are important. They point to the fact that in his later years Bevin's bluntness of language and occasional lapses from discretion—like Churchill's idiosyncratic pronunciation of French—endeared him to the nation as a "character" who was seen as embodying some of the historic characteristics which Englishmen (in this, no different from other nations) like to recognize in themselves. In Bevin's case, the impression was strengthened by the fact that he was unashamedly himself on all occasions, entirely without class-consciousness (that special English vice), refused all honours and was indifferent to wealth or the trappings, as distinct from the substance, of power.

But the anecdotes can also be misleading, for two reasons. The first is because they suggest—in Churchill's case as well as Bevin's—a psychological simplicity which ignores the depth of feeling, the inner conflicts and wide swings of mood which went along with—and contributed to—their strength of character. Francis Williams, who knew him well, remarks in his biography that he was conscious of mysterious reaches in Bevin to which no one had access.

The second reason why the anecdotes can mislead is because they divert attention from the seriousness with which Bevin devoted himself to the tasks he undertook and obscure the scope of his achievements. It is with those achievements that this study has been concerned.

Bevin was a controversial figure in his lifetime and many of the controversies

[1] Harris, p. 565.

in which he was involved are still alive. There are those who regard his build-up of union power and the claims which he established for the unions to be consulted as a major factor in Britain's decline. There are others who blame him for the failure to establish a Jewish state in Palestine under British auspices; for failing to break with the past and follow a socialist foreign policy; for taking the side of the Americans against the Russians; and by pursuing the illusion of a world role for Britain after the War, for losing her the chance to take a lead in creating a United Europe. But history is by its nature a continuing debate and even the figures who bulk largest in it are frequently those about whom there is the greatest difference of opinion, from Cromwell to Gladstone.

Ernest Bevin seems to me to belong to that small group of men who can be said to have had a decisive impact on the history of their own times. I say this in virtue of three achievements, the importances of which can hardly be denied even by his critics.

The first is the contribution he made to building up the strength and securing acceptance of the role of the British trade union movement. The second is the unique part he played in mobilizing the country's manpower and industrial strength to win the war against Hitler, a part which can justly be regarded as second only to Churchill's.

Unlike Churchill, however, Bevin did not go into opposition in 1945, but stayed in office as the strongest figure in the Government which established the Welfare State and mixed economy of modern Britain. It was as Foreign Secretary in this that he secured the American support which enabled Britain and Western Europe to achieve economic recovery by virtue of the Marshall Plan operation, and preserve their independence by virtue of NATO. After altering the balance of power in his own society he went on to restore the balance of power in Europe.

To Bevin there was a clear link between the three. His aim had been to bring the working class within the national community on equal terms. It was this which provided the continuity between his trade union career in opposition and the national responsibilities he accepted as a minister. He sought not to raise himself but the class from which he came.

At the time of his death the *News Chronicle* summed up the dominant impression in all that was written and said about him:

"Ernest Bevin was not a working man who became a statesman. He remained a working man with all the attributes that this implies—and to these he added statesmanship. In this he was the first of his kind.

"He was a great Englishman. His life symbolises the rise of the British working people, not only to power, but to political responsibility."[1]

There are no words which better sum up his career or would have given him greater satisfaction.

[1] *News Chronicle*, 16 April 1951.

Sources and Bibliography

1   Unpublished sources

The most important of these are:

(A)   The Bevin Papers, the Foreign Secretary's working files kept by his Principal Private Secretary in Bevin's Private Office. These are now available in the Public Record Office at Kew as class number FO 800. The volumes (or pieces) are divided according to country or subject indicated by the abbreviations, EUR (Europe), SU (Soviet Union), MAN (Manpower), DEF (Defence), PLT (Politics), etc., with the year and the number of the folio added. Thus a characteristic reference will read, FO 800 [class number]/512 [piece no.]/US/47/25 [country/year/folio number].

(B)   The central collection of British Cabinet records:

(i) CAB 128, vols. 1–28: Cabinet minutes, conclusions and confidential annexes of the Labour Government of 1945–51. For these I have employed the abbreviation CM 34 (46) i.e., Cabinet minutes for the 34th meeting in the year 1946.

(ii) CAB 129, vols. 1–45: Cabinet papers circulated to ministers and marked CP (46) 34, i.e., the thirty-fourth in the series for the year 1946.

(iii) International Conference records, CAB 133 e.g. CAB 133/15, records of the Council of Foreign Ministers meeting in London, September–October 1945; CAB 133/78, records of the Colombo conference, Jan. 1950.

(iv) Minutes of papers of Cabinet committees, of which Bevin was chairman or a member: the Overseas Reconstruction Committee (CAB 134/594–601); the Manpower Ministerial Committee (CAB 134/509–10); the Committee of Ministers on Germany (sometimes referred to as the Berlin Committee) 1948–9 (CAB 130/88).

(v) Minutes and papers of the Cabinet's Defence Committee 1945–51: DO (46), giving the year, CAB 131/1–131/11.

(vi) Minutes and papers of the Chiefs of Staff Committee: (a) for 1945–46: CAB 79/37–54 (minutes); CAB 80/96–103 (memoranda). (b) for 1947–51: DEFE 4/41 (minutes); DEFE 5/1–29 (memoranda); DEFE 6/1–16 (Reports of the Joint Planning Staff).

(vii) Prime Ministers's Office: PREM/8 (Attlee).

(C)   The general political files of the Foreign Office, FO 371, a huge and undifferentiated collection of documents for which there is no adequate guide or catalogue. In cases where copies of a document appear both in the Bevin papers and in FO 371, I have preferred to give a reference to the former.

(D)   Bevin wrote few private letters. I have been able to see and make use of a number of them written while he was abroad to Arthur Deakin and to Miss Saunders.

(E)   Private papers and diaries:

1. Lord Attlee's papers in the Bodleian Library, Oxford.

2. Hugh Dalton's diaries and papers in the British Library of Economics and Political Science, London School of Economics.

3. Sir Pierson Dixon's diaries, used in part by his son, Piers Dixon, MP., in his life of his father, *Double Diploma* (1968).

4. Arthur Creech-Jones' papers in Rhodes House, Oxford.

5. Crossman, Cunningham and Monroe papers, Middle East Centre, St. Antony's College, Oxford.

6. Sir Kenneth Younger's diaries.

7. Extracts from their diaries made available to me by the Rt. Hon. Chuter Ede (Home Secretary in the Attlee Government), and Sir Alan Lascelles (Private Secretary to King George VI).

(F)   Minutes of meetings of the Parliamentary Labour Party for 1945–51.

(G)   Thanks to the cooperation of Israeli colleagues (see Preface), I have been able to use a number of documents from

(1) The Zionist archives in New York (ZANY);

(2) Archives of the American Jewish Committee (AJC);

(3) The Central Zionist Archives, Jerusalem (CZA). The latter include minutes and papers of:

The Jewish Agency Executive Committee;

S25, the Political Department of the Jewish Agency;

Z5, the Jewish Agency Offices in the USA.

2   Published Sources

(A)   By far the most important collection is the:

Foreign Relations of the United States: The Conference of Berlin (The Potsdam Conference) 1945. 2 vols. (Washington 1960).

Foreign Relations of the United States 1945 9 vols. (Washington 1967–69).

Foreign Relations of the United States 1946 11 vols. (Washington 1969–72).

Foreign Relations of the United States 1947 8 vols. (Washington 1971–73).

Foreign Relations of the United States 1948 9 vols. (Washington 1972–75).

Foreign Relations of the United States 1949 9 vols. (Washington 1974–77).

Foreign Relations of the United States 1950 7 vols. (Washington 1976–80).

Foreign Relations of the United States 1951 vols. 1–3 & 6 (parts 1 and 2) (Washington 1977–80).

(B)   *The Papers of General Lucius D. Clay, Germany 1945–49* 2 v. ed. J. E. Smith (Bloomington, Ind., 1974).

(C)   *Anglo French Discussions regarding French proposals for the Western European Coal, Iron and Steel Industries, May–June 1950.* Cmd. 7970 (London 1950).

(D)   Council of Europe, Consultative Assembly, Reports and Documents 1949 and 1950.

(E)   United Nations   (1) General Assembly, *Proceedings 1946–51.*
　　　　　　　　　　　(2) General Assembly, *Official Records, 1946–51.* (including as Supplement 2, *Reports of the Security Council to the General Assembly*).
　　　　　　　　　　　(3) Security Council, *Official Records 1946–51.*

(F)   Labour Party Annual Conference Reports, 1945–50.

(G)   TUC Annual Congress Reports 1945–50.

(H)   Royal Institute of International Affairs: *Documents on International Affairs, 1947–48* (ed.) Margaret Carlyle (1952).
Royal Institute of International Affairs: *Documents on International Affairs, 1949–50* (ed.) Margaret Carlyle (1953).
Royal Institute of International Affairs: *Documents on Germany under Occupation, 1945–54* (ed.) B. Ruhm von Oppen (1955).

3   Pamphlets

(A)   Labour Party publications: "The Old War and the New Society" (1942).
"The International Post War Settlement" (1944).
"From a People's War to a People's Peace" (1944).
"Cards on the Table" (1947).
"European Unity" (1950).

(B)   Fabian Society Publications
Leonard Woolf: "Foreign Policy, The Labour Party's Dilemma" (1947)
R. H. S. Crossman and Kenneth Younger: "Socialist Foreign Policy" (1951).

(C)   New Statesman Publications: "Keep Left" (1947)
"Keeping Left" (1950).

4 Speeches

I have been able to make use of the complete collection of Bevin's speeches printed (in full) for government use by the Foreign Office. These are in separate parts for each year of his period of office as Foreign Secretary, 1945–50. Parts 1 and 2 bear the title: *Speeches by the Rt. Hon. Ernest Bevin M.P.* Parts 3–6, beginning in 1947, are enlarged under the title *Public Statements respecting Foreign and General Affairs*: in addition to all Bevin's speeches, these include a number of statements by other government spokesmen. It is hoped that a copy of this collection will be placed in the PRO.

Hansard, Parliamentary Debates, 1945–51.

5 Oral Evidence

BRITISH
Lord Alexander of Hillsborough (A. V. Alexander)
Lord Attlee
Lord Avon (Anthony Eden)
Sir Roderick Barclay
Lord Beaverbrook
Sir Harold Beeley
Dame Florence Bevin
Lord Bridges
Lord Butler
Lord Citrine
Arthur Creech-Jones
Richard Crossman
Lord Dalton
Miss Alison David
Arthur Deakin
Sir Maurice Dean
Chuter Ede
W. N. Ewer
Lord Franks
Vic Feather
Hugh Gaitskell
Lord Gladwyn (Gladwyn Jebb)
Archie Gordon
Sir Knox Helm
Lord Henderson
Sir John Henniker-Major
Albert Hourani
Sir Ian Jacob
A. P. Kinna
Sir Ivone Kirkpatrick
Sir Alan Lascelles
Sir Frederick Leggett
Lord Longford (Frank Pakenham)
Lord Mayhew
Elizabeth Monroe
Lord Montgomery
Lord Morrison of Lambeth (Herbert Morrison)
Lord Normanbrook
Morgan Phillips
Sir Edward Playfair
Sir Frank Roberts
Sir Brian Robertson
Sir Orme Sargent
Miss Ivy Saunders

Sir Ben Smith
Lord Strang
J. J. Taylor
Lord Uvedale
Sam Watson
Lord Waverley (John Anderson)
Percy Wells
Sir Tom Williamson
George Woodcock

AMERICAN
Dean Acheson
Benjamin Cohen
Lewis Douglas
Dave Dubinsky
George Kennan
George Marshall
J. J. McCloy
George Meany
Matt Wall

Ernst Reuter
Jean Monnet
Dirk Stikker
David Ben Gurion
Eliahu Elath

6   *Newspapers and Periodicals*

*The Times, Manchester Guardian, Daily Telegraph, Financial Times, The
Observer, Sunday Times, Daily Express, Daily Mail, Daily Herald, News
Chronicle, Evening Standard.
New York Times, Christian Science Monitor, Herald Tribune, Le Monde.
The Economist, Spectator, New Statesman and Nation, The Listener,
Cornhill Magazine.
Foreign Affairs, International Affairs.*

7   *Memoirs and Biographies*

(Unless otherwise stated, the place of publication is in all cases London. This
applies to books by American authors where I have used the British edition.)

A.   MEMOIRS
Acheson, Dean, *Sketches from Life* (1961)
—— *Present at the Creation* (1970).
Adenauer, Konrad, *Memoirs 1945–53* (Eng. tr. 1966).
Barclay, Sir Roderick, *Ernest Bevin and the Foreign Office 1932–69* (1975).

Bedell-Smith, W., *Moscow Mission 1946–49* (1950).

Blum, J. M. (ed.), *The Price of Vision, The Diary of Henry A. Wallace 1942–46* (Boston 1973).

Bohlen, Charles E., *Witness to History 1929–69* (1973).

Byrnes, James F., *Speaking Frankly* (NY 1947).

—— *All In One Lifetime* (NY 1958).

Churchill, Winston S., *Triumph and Tragedy* (vol. VI of *The Second World War*) (1954).

Clay, Lucius D., *Decision in Germany* (1950).

Cooper, Duff, *Old Men Forget* (1953).

Dalton, Hugh, *High Tide and After, Memoirs 1945–60* (1962).

de Gaulle, Charles, *The Complete War Memoirs* (NY 1964).

Djilas, Milovan, *Conversations with Stalin* (tr. from the Serbo-Croat, 1962)

Dilks, David (ed.), *The Diaries of Sir Alexander Cadogan 1938–45* (1971).

Eden, Anthony, Earl of Avon *The Eden Memoirs: The Reckoning* (1965).

George Brown, Lord, *In My Way, Political Memoirs* (1971).

Gladwyn, Lord, *The Memoirs of Lord Gladwyn* (1972).

Harriman, W. Averell and Abel, Elie, *Special Envoy to Churchill and Stalin 1941–1946* (NY 1975).

Hillman, William (ed.), *Mr President: Personal Diaries, Papers &c. of Harry S. Truman* (NY 1952).

Ismay, Lord, *The Memoirs of Lord Ismay* (1960).

Kennan, George, *Memoirs 1925–50* (NY 1969).

Kilmuir, Earl of, *Political Adventure* (1964).

Kirkpatrick, Sir Ivone, *The Inner Circle* (1959).

Krushchev, Nikita, *Krushchev Remembers* (Boston 1974).

Leonhard, Wolfgang, *Child of the Revolution* (1957).

Mallaby, George, *Each in his Office* (1972).

Martin, Kingsley, *Editor* (1968).

Millis, Walter (ed.), *The Forrestal Diaries* (NY 1951).

Montgomery, Viscount, *The Memoirs of Field Marshal Montgomery* (1958).

Morrison, Herbert, *An Autobiography* (1960).

Murphy, Robert, *Diplomat Among Warriors* (NY 1964).

Pakenham, Frank, *Born to Believe* (1953).

Pearson, Lester B., *Memoirs 1948–57. The International Years* (1974).

Spaak, Paul-Henri, *The Continuing Battle, Memoirs of a European* (Eng. tr. 1971).

Stikker, Dirk, *Men of Responsibility* (NY 1966).

Stimson, Henry L. and Bundy, McGeorge, *On Active Service in Peace and War* (NY 1947).

Strang, Lord, *Home and Abroad* (1956).

Sulzberger, C. L., *A Long Row of Candles* (NY 1969).

Truman, Harry S., *Memoirs*: vol. 1., *Year of Decisions 1945* (1955), vol. 2, *Years of Trial and Hope 1946–53* (1956).

Vandenberg, Arthur H. (ed)., *The Private Papers of Senator Vandenberg* (Boston 1952).

Williams, Francis, *A Prime Minister Remembers* (1961).

—— *Nothing so Strange* (1970).

B. Biographies

Cooke, Colin, *The Life of Richard Stafford Cripps* (1957).
Dixon, Piers, *Double Diploma, The Life of Sir Pierson Dixon* (1968).
Donoughue, Bernard and Jones., G. W., *Herbert Morrison. Portrait of a Politician* (1973).
Foot, Michael, *Aneurin Bevan*, vol. 2, *1945–60* (1973).
Harris, Kenneth, *Attlee* (1982).
Martin, Kingsley, *Harold Laski* (1953).
Thomas, Hugh, *John Strachey* (1973).
Williams, Francis, *Ernest Bevin* (1952).
Williams, Philip, *Hugh Gaitskell* (1979).

8   Historical and Political Studies

A.   British Post-war Politics

Allen, V. L., *Trade-Union Leadership, A Study of Arthur Deakin* (1957).
Attlee, C. R., *The Labour Party in Perspective* (1937).
Beer, Samuel H., *Modern British Politics* (1969).
Berrington, Hugh, *Backbench Opinion in the House of Commons 1945–55* (Oxford 1973).
Bryant, Sir Arthur, *Triumph in the West, Based on the diaries of Field Marshal Alanbrooke* (1959).
Goldsworthy, David, *Colonial Issues in British Politics 1945–61* (Oxford 1971).
Gordon Walker, Patrick, *The Cabinet* (1972).
Gowing, Margaret M., *Britain and Atomic Energy, 1939–45* (1964).
—— *Independence and Deterrence, Britain and Atomic Energy 1945–52*, vol. 1, *Policy Making* (1974).
Guttsmann, W. A., *The British Political Elite* (1964).
Harrison, Martin, *Trade Unions and the Labour Party since 1945* (1960).
Haseler, Stephen, *The Gaitskellites* (1969).
Havighurst, Alfred F., *Twentieth-Century Britain* (NY 1962).
Hoffman, J. D., *The Conservative Party in Opposition 1945–51* (1964).
Hopkins, Harry, *The New Look, A Social History of the Forties and Fifties in Britain* (1963).
Jackson, Robert, J., *Rebels and Whips* (1968).
McKenzie, Robert, *British Political Parties* (1955).
Medlicott, W. N., *Contemporary England 1914–64* (1967).
Meehan, Eugene, Jr., *The British Left-wing and Foreign Policy* (New Brunswick 1960).
Milliband, Ralph, *Parliamentary Socialism* (1961).
Pelling, H.M., *A Short History of the Labour Party* (1961).
Seaman, L. C. B., *Post-Victorian Britain 1901–1951* (1966).

B.   British Foreign Policy

Barker, Elizabeth, *Britain in Divided Europe* (1971).

Bartlett, *The Long Retreat* (1972).

Beloff, Max, *New Dimensions in Foreign Policy* (1961).

Epstein, Leon D., *Britain, Uneasy Ally* (Chicago 1954).

Fitzsimons, M. A., *The Foreign Policy of the British Labour Government* (Notre Dame 1953).

Frankel, Joseph, *British Foreign Policy 1945–73* (1975).

Gordon, Michael R., *Conflict and Consensus in Labour's Foreign Policy 1914–65* (1965).

Henderson, Sir Nicholas, *The Birth of NATO* (1982).

Manderson-Jones, R. B., *The Special Relationship. Anglo–US Relations and Western European Unity 1947–56* (1972).

Nicholas, H. G., *Britain and the United States* (1963).

Northedge, F. S., *Descent from Power, British Foreign Policy 1945–73* (1974).

Pierre, Andrew J., *Nuclear Politics* (1972).

Rothwell, Victor, *Britain and the Cold War 1941–47* (1982).

Strange, Susan, *Sterling and British Policy* (1971).

Vital, David, *The Making of British Foreign Policy* (1968).

Watt, D. C., *Personalities and Policies* (1965).

Windrich, Elaine, *British Labour's Foreign Policy* (Stanford 1952).

Woodhouse, C. M., *British Foreign Policy since the Second World War* (1961).

Woodward, Sir Llewellyn, *British Foreign Policy in the 2nd World War* (1962).

C.   International Affairs 1945–51

Bell, Coral, *Negotiation from Strength* (1962).

Calvocoressi, Peter, *Survey of International Affairs 1947–48* (1952).

—— *Survey of International Affairs 1949–50* (1953).

—— *Survey of International Affairs 1951* (1953).

Clemens, Diane Shaver, *Yalta* (NY 1970).

Feis, Herbert, *Between War and Peace, the Potsdam Conference* (Princeton 1960).

Hudson, G. F., *The Hard and Bitter Peace* (1966).

Knapp, W. F., *A History of War and Peace 1939–65* (1967).

McNeill, W. H., *America, Britain and Russia, Their Cooperation and Conflict 1941–46* (1953).

Mee, Charles L. Jr., *Meeting at Potsdam* (1975).

Seton-Watson, Hugh, *Neither War nor Peace, The Struggle for Power in the Post-War World* (NY 1950).

Toynbee, Arnold J. and Toynbee Veronica M. (ed.), *The Re-alignment of Europe* (1955).

Wheeler-Bennett, J. W., and Nicholas, Anthony, *Semblance of Peace* (1972).

D. US Foreign Policy

The principal works by revisionist historians are marked with an asterisk. For criticism of their views, see the books by R. J. Maddox, R. W. Tucker and Raymond Aron, and the articles by C. S. Maier and J. L. Richardson cited in section 9 below. Anthologies of the opposing views are provided in the books edited by Thomas G. Paterson and J. V. Compton.

* Alperowitz, Gar, *Atomic Diplomacy, Hiroshima and Potsdam* (NY 1965).

Aron, Raymond, *The Imperial Republic* (Eng. tr. from the French 1975).

Beugel, E. H. van der, *From Marshall Aid to Atlantic Partnership* (Amsterdam 1966).

* Compton, James V. (ed.), *America and the Origins of the Cold War* (Boston 1972).

Dallek, Robert, *Franklin D. Roosevelt and American Foreign Policy, 1932–45* (NY 1979).

Ferrell, R. H. (ed.), *The American Secretaries of State* vol. XIV, Richard L. Walker, *E. R. Stettinius*; George Curry, *James F. Byrnes* (NY 1965). Vol. XV, Robert H. Ferrell, *George C. Marshall* (NY 1965). Vol XVI, Gaddis Smith, *Dean Acheson* (NY 1972).

* Fleming, D. F., *The Cold War and Its Origins* (1961).

Gaddis, J. L., *The U.S.A. and the Origins of the Cold War* (NY 1972).

* Gardner, Lloyd C., *Architects of Illusion, Men and Ideas in American Foreign Policy 1941–1949* (Chicago 1972).

Gardner, Lloyd C., Schlesinger, Arthur and Morgenthau, Hans J., *The Origins of the Cold War* (Lexington 1970).

Gardner, Richard N., *Sterling-Dollar Diplomacy* (rev. edn. NY 1969).

Gimbel, John, *The Origins of the Marshall Plan* (Stanford 1976).

Hoffmann, Stanley, *Gulliver's Troubles or the Setting of American Foreign Policy* (NY 1968).

* Horowitz, David, *The Free World Colossus: A Critique of American Foreign Policy in the Cold War* (rev. edn. NY 1971).

Jones, J. M. *The Fifteen Weeks* (NY 1956).

* Kolko, Gabriel, *The Politics of War 1943–45* (NY 1968).

* Kolko, Gabriel and Kolko, Joyce, *The Limits of Power, The World and U.S. Foreign Policy 1945–54* (NY 1972).

Kuklick, Bruce, *American Policy and the Division of Germany* (Ithaca 1972).

Lafeber, Walter, *America, Russia and the Cold War 1945–66* (NY 1967).

Lippmann, Walter, *The Cold War* (NY 1947).

Maddox, R. J., *The New Left and the Origins of the Cold War* (Princeton 1973).

Paterson, Thomas G. (ed.), *Cold War Critics* (Chicago 1971).

Paterson, Thomas G., *Soviet–American Confrontation, Post War Reconstruction and the Origins of the Cold War* (Baltimore 1973).

Price, Harry Bayard, *The Marshall Plan and its Meaning* (Ithaca 1955).

Rostow, W. W., *The United States in the World Arena* (NY 1960).

Spanier, John W., *American Foreign Policy since World War II* (NY 1971).

Tucker, R. W., *The Radical Left and American Foreign Policy* (Baltimore 1971).

* Williams, W. A., *The Tragedy of American Diplomacy* (Cleveland 1959).

Yergin, Daniel, *Shattered Peace* (Boston 1977).

E.   THE COLD WAR, SOVIET FOREIGN POLICY, AND EASTERN EUROPE

Bethell, Nicholas, *The Last Secret* (1974).

Brzezinski, Z. K., *The Soviet Bloc* (Cambridge, Mass. 1967).

Feis, Herbert, *From Trust to Terror, The Onset of the Cold War 1945–50* (1970).

Fontaine, André, *A History of the Cold War* (Eng. tr. from the French, 1968).

Hall, Louis J., *The Cold War as History* (1967).

Hammond, Thomas (ed.), *The Anatomy of Communist Takeovers* (New Haven 1975).

Healey, Denis, *The Curtain Falls* (1951).

Herz, M. F., *The Beginnings of the Cold War* (Bloomington, 1966).

Hingley, Ronald, *Joseph Stalin, Man and Legend* (1974).

Ionescu, Ghita, *The Break-up of the Soviet Empire in Eastern Europe* (1965)

Korbel, Josef, *The Communist Subversion of Czechoslovakia 1938–48* (Princeton 1959)

Löwenthal, Richard, *World Communism* (NY 1966).

Luard, Evan (ed.), *The Cold War* (1964).

Lukacs, John, *A History of the Cold War* (NY rev. edn. 1966).

Mackintosh, J. M., *Strategy and Tactics of Soviet Foreign Policy* (1962).

Mastny, Vojtek, *Russia's Road to the Cold War* (NY 1979).

Mosely, Philip, *The Kremlin and World Politics* (NY 1960).

de Porte, A. W., *Europe between the Super-Powers* (New Haven 1979).

Seabury, Paul, *The Rise and Decline of the Cold War* (NY 1967).

Seton-Watson, Hugh, *The East European Revolution* (1950).

—— *The Pattern of Communist Revolution* (1953).

Shulman, Marshall, *Stalin's Foreign Policy Re-appraised* (Cambridge, Mass. 1963).

Tolstoy, Count Nikolai, *Victims of Yalta* (rev. edn. 1979).

Ulam, Adam B., *Expansion and Co-existence, Soviet Foreign Policy 1917–67* (NY 1968).

—— *The Rivals, America and Russia since World War II* (NY 1971).

—— *Stalin: The Man and his Era* (NY 1973).

Wolfe, Thomas W., *Soviet Power and Europe 1945–70* (Baltimore 1970).

F.   WESTERN EUROPE AND GERMANY

Bader, William B., *Austria between East and West 1945–48* (Stanford 1966).

Balfour, Michael and Mair, John, *Four Power Control in Germany and Austria 1945–46* (1956).

Davison, W. Phillips, *The Berlin Blockade* (Princeton 1958).

Diebold, William, *The Schuman Plan* (NY 1959).

Freymond, Jacques, *Western Europe since the War* (NY 1964).

Gimbel, John, *The American Occupation of Germany* (Stanford 1968).

Grossner, Alfred, *West Germany From Defeat to Rearmament* (Eng. tr. from the French 1955).

McGeehan, Robert, *The German Re-armament Question* (Urbana, Ill. 1971).

Merkl, Peter H., *The Origin of the West German Republic* (NY 1963).

Morgan, Roger, *The United States and West Germany 1945–73* (1974).

Nolte, Ernst, *Deutschland und der Kalte Krieg* (Munich 1974).

de Porte, A. W., *De Gaulle's Foreign Policy 1944–46* (Cambridge, Mass. 1968).

Postan, M. M., *An Economic History of Western Europe 1945–64* (1967).

Richardson, J. L., *Germany and the Atlantic Alliance* (Cambridge, Mass. 1966).

Triffin, Robert, *Europe and the Money Muddle 1947–56* (New Haven 1957).

Williams, Philip, *Politics in Post-War France* (1954).

Willis, F. Roy, *France, Germany and the New Europe 1945–67* (rev. edn. Stanford 1968).

—— *Italy Chooses Europe* (NY 1971).

Windsor, Philip, *City on Leave, A History of Berlin 1945–62* (1963).

G. THE MIDDLE EAST (INCLUDING ZIONIST POLITICS IN THE U.S.A. AND GREECE) AND THE FAR EAST

Bauer, Y., *Flight and Rescue, Brichah* (NY 1969).

Bethell, Nicholas, *The Palestine Triangle* (1979).

Cohen, Michael J., *Palestine, Retreat from the Mandate* (NY 1978).

—— *Palestine and the Great Powers 1945–1948* (Princeton, 1982).

Crossman, R. H. S., *Palestine Mission* (1946).

Fitzsimons, M. A., *Empire by Treaty* (Notre Dame 1964).

Ganin, Zvi, *Truman, American Jewry and Israel 1945–8* (NY 1979).

Goldmann, Nahum, *Sixty Years of Jewish Life* (NY 1970).

Hurewitz, J. C., *The Struggle for Palestine* (NY 1950).

Kimche, Jon and Kimche, David, *A Clash of Destinies, The Arab–Jewish War and the Founding of the State of Israel* (1960).

Kirk, George, *The Middle East in the War* (rev. edn. 1953).

—— *The Middle East 1945–50* (1954).

Kuniholm, Bruce R., *The Origins of the Cold War in the Near East: Great Power Conflict and Diplomacy in Iran, Turkey and Greece* (Princeton 1980).

Lenczowski, George, *Russia and the West in Iran, 1918–48* (Ithaca 1949).

Longrigg, S. H., *Oil in the Middle East* (1968).

Miller, A. D., *Search for Security: Saudi-Arabian Oil and American Foreign Policy 1939–49* (Chapel Hill 1980).

Monroe, Elizabeth, *Britain's Moment in the Middle East 1914–58* (1963).

Nachmani, Amikam, *British Policy in Palestine after WW2, the Anglo American Committee of Inquiry, 1945–46.* Unpublished D. Phil. thesis, University of Oxford, 1980.

Persson, Sune O., *Mediation and Assassination, Count Bernadotte's Mission to Palestine* (1979).

Snetsinger, John, *Truman, the Jewish Vote and the Creation of Israel* (Stanford 1974).

Stein, Leonard, *Weizmann and England* (1964).

Sykes, Christopher, *Cross Roads to Israel* (1965).

Vatikiotis, P. J., *Politics and the Military in Jordan, A Study of the Arab Legion 1921–57* (1967).

Wasserstein, Bernard, *Britain and the Jews of Europe* (1979).

Greece

Alexander, G. M., *The Prelude to the Truman Doctrine: British Policy in Greece 1944–1947* (Oxford 1982).

Clogg, Richard, *A Short History of Modern Greece* (1979).

Iatrides, John, *Revolt in Athens, The Greek Communist "Second Round" 1944–45* (Princeton 1972).

Kousoulas, George, *Revolution and Defeat, the Story of the Greek Communist Party* (1965).

O'Ballance, Edgar, *The Greek Civil War 1944–49* (NY 1966).

Wittner, Lawrence, S., *American Intervention in Greece 1943–49* (NY 1982).

Woodhouse, C. M., *The Struggle for Greece 1941–49* (1976).

Xydis, Stephen, *Greece and the Great Powers 1944–47* (Salonika 1963).

Far East
Darby, Philip, *British Defence Policy East of Suez 1947–48* (1973).
Jones, F. C., Borton, Hugh, and Pearn, B. R., *The Far East 1942–46* (1955).
Mansergh, Nicholas, *Survey of British Commonwealth Affairs, Problems of Wartime cooperation and Post-War Changes 1939–52* (1958).
Nagai, Y. and Iriye, A. (eds.), *Origins of the Cold War in Asia* (NY 1977).
Porter, Brian, *Britain and the Rise of Communist China 1945–54* (1967)
Thorne, Christopher, *Allies of a Kind* (1978).

9   *Articles*

Heller, Joseph, "Failure of a Mission: Bernadotte and Palestine, 1948", *Journal of Contemporary History*, 14 (1979).
Lawford, Valentine, "Three Ministers", *Cornhill Magazine* No. 1010, Winter 1956–7.
'X' (George F. Kennan), "The Sources of Soviet Conduct", *Foreign Affairs* XXV, July 1947.
Maier, Charles S., "Revisionism and the Interpretation of Cold War Origins", *Perspectives in American History* IV (1970).
McFarland, Stephen L., "A Peripheral View of the Origins of the Cold War: The Crisis in Iran, 1941–47", *Diplomatic History*, 4,4 (1980).
Monroe, Elizabeth, "Mr Bevin's 'Arab Policy'", *St Antony's Papers* No. 11, (1961).
Ovendale, Ritchie, "The Palestine Policy of the British Labour Government 1945–46", *International Affairs*, July 1979, vol. 54, No. 3
—— "The Palestine Policy of the British Labour Government 1947: The Decision to Withdraw", *International Affairs*, January 1980, vol. 56, No. 1.
—— "Britain, the US and the Cold War in South East Asia, 1949–50", *International Affairs*, Summer 1982, Vol. 58, No. 3.
Richardson, J. L., "Cold War Revisionism: A Critique", *World Politics*, xxiv (1972).
Schlesinger, Jr., Arthur, "The Origins of the Cold War", *Foreign Affairs* XLVI October 1967.
Slonim, Shlomo, "The 1948 American Embargo on Arms to Palestine", *Political Science Quarterly*, 94, 3 (1979).
Thorne, Christopher, "Britain, Australia and the N.E.I., 1941–45", *International Spectator* (The Hague, August 1945).
Wiener Library Bulletin 1977, vol. XXX New Series Nos. 41/42. Ilan, Amitzur, "Messianism and Diplomacy 1945–48, the Struggle for a Jewish State".
Wiener Library Bulletin 1978, vol. XXXI, New series Nos. 45/46. Special Number on 30th anniversary of the State of Israel. This includes:
Cohen, Michael J., "Why Britain Left: The End of the Mandate".
Heller, Joseph, "Anglo Zionist Relations 1939–47".
Nevo, Joseph, "Abdallah and the Arabs of Palestine".
Schoenbaum, David, "The USA and the Birth of Israel".

Index

873